T0191622

Communications in Computer and Information Science 643

Commenced Publication in 2007
Founding and Former Series Editors:
Alfredo Cuzzocrea, Dominik Ślęzak, and Xiaokang Yang

More information about this series at http://www.springer.com/series/7899

Lin Zhang · Xiao Song
Yunjie Wu (Eds.)

Theory, Methodology, Tools and Applications for Modeling and Simulation of Complex Systems

16th Asia Simulation Conference
and SCS Autumn Simulation Multi-Conference
AsiaSim/SCS AutumnSim 2016
Beijing, China, October 8–11, 2016
Proceedings, Part I

Editors
Lin Zhang
Beihang University
Beijing
China

Yunjie Wu
Beihang University
Beijing
China

Xiao Song
Beihang University
Beijing
China

ISSN 1865-0929 ISSN 1865-0937 (electronic)
Communications in Computer and Information Science
ISBN 978-981-10-2662-1 ISBN 978-981-10-2663-8 (eBook)
DOI 10.1007/978-981-10-2663-8

Library of Congress Control Number: 2016946015

Printed on acid-free paper

This Springer imprint is published by Springer Nature
The registered company is Springer Science+Business Media Singapore Pte Ltd.

Preface

AsiaSim/SCS AutumnSim 2016 (the 2016 International Simulation Multi-Conference) was a joint conference of the 16th Asia Simulation Conference and the 2016 Autumn Simulation Multi-Conference. The Asia Simulation Conference (AsiaSim) is an annual international conference started in 1999. In 2011, the Federation of Asian Simulation Societies (ASIASIM) was set up and the AsiaSim became an annual conference of ASIASIM. The SCS Autumn Simulation Multi-Conference (SCS AutumnSim) is one of the premier conferences of the Society for Modeling and Simulation International (SCS), which provides a unique opportunity to learn about emerging M&S applications in many thriving fields. AsiaSim/SCS AutumnSim 2016 was the first conference jointly sponsored by ASIASIM and SCS and organized by the China Simulation Federation (CSF), Science and Technology on Special System Simulation Laboratory (STSSSL), and Beihang University (BUAA). It was also co-sponsored by the China Simulation Federation (CSF), the Japanese Society for Simulation Technology (JSST), the Korea Society for Simulation (KSS), the Society for Simulation and Gaming of Singapore (SSAGSG), the International Association for Mathematics and Computers in Simulation (IMACS), the Chinese Association for Artificial Intelligence (CAAI), China Computer Federation (CCF), the China Electrotechnical Society (CES), the China Graphics Society (CGS), and the China Ordnance Society (COS).

This conference is a big event that provides a unique opportunity to learn about emerging M&S research achievements and applications in many thriving fields, focusing on the theory, methodology, tools and applications for M&S of complex systems; it provides a forum for the latest R&D results in academia and industry.

The papers contained in these proceedings address challenging issues in M&S theory and methodology, model engineering for system of systems, high-performance computing and simulation, M&S for smart city, robot simulations, M&S for intelligent manufacturing, military simulation, as well as cloud technologies in simulation applications.

This year, AsiaSim/SCS AutumnSim received 639 submissions. Submissions came from around 15 countries and regions. After a thorough reviewing process, 267 papers were selected for presentation as full papers, with an acceptance rate of 41.8 %. These papers are published in the proceedings in the four volumes, 643–646. Volume 643 mainly addresses the issues of basics of M&S theory and methodology. Volume 644 discusses M&S for intelligent manufacturing and military simulation methods. In Vol. 645, cloud technologies in simulation applications, simulation and big data techniques are covered. And Vol. 646 presents M&S applications and simulation software.

The high-quality program would not have been possible without the authors who chose AsiaSim/SCS AutumnSim 2016 as a venue for their publications. Also, we would like to take this opportunity to thank the ASIASIM Federation for allowing us to host AsiaSim 2016 in Beijing.

We also thank the members of the Program Committee for their valuable effort in the review of the submitted papers. Finally, we would also like to thank our technical co-sponsors and sponsors. Your contributions and support have helped to make AsiaSim/SCS AutumnSim 2016 a memorable and successful event.

We hope that you enjoy reading and benefit from the proceedings of AsiaSim/SCS AutumnSim 2016.

October 2016

Lin Zhang
Xiao Song
Yunjie Wu

Organization

Sponsors

Federation of Asian Simulation Societies (ASIASIM)
The Society for Modeling & Simulation International (SCS)

Co-Sponsors

China Simulation Federation (CSF)
Japanese Society for Simulation Technology (JSST)
Korea Society for Simulation (KSS)
Society for Simulation and Gaming of Singapore (SSAGSG)
International Association for Mathematics and Computers in Simulation (IMACS)
Chinese Association for Artificial Intelligence (CAAI)
China Computer Federation (CCF)
China Electrotechnical Society (CES)
China Graphics Society (CGS)
China Ordnance Society (COS)

Organizers

China Simulation Federation (CSF)
Science and Technology on Special System Simulation Laboratory (STSSSL)
Beihang University (BUAA)

Honorary Chairs

Chuanyuan Wen, China
Robert M. Howe, USA
Yukio Kagawa, Japan
Sadao Takaba, Japan
Sung-Joo Park, Korea
Tianyuan Xiao(†), China

General Chairs

Bo Hu Li, China
Qinping Zhao, China

Deputy General Chair

Agostino Bruzzone, Italy

General Co-chairs

Satoshi Tanaka, Japan
Jonghyun Kim, Korea
Axel Lehmann, Germany
Zicai Wang, China
Xianxiang Huang, China

Program Committee Chair

Lin Zhang, China

Program Committee Co-chairs

Bernard Zeigler, USA
Tuncer Ören, Canada
Ralph C. Huntsinger, USA
Xiaofeng Hu, China
Soo-Hyun Park, Korea
H.J. Halin, Switzerland
Kaj Juslin, Finland
Roy E. Crosbie, USA
Ming Yang, China
Xiaogang Qiu, China
Satoshi Tanaka, Japan
Jin Liu, China
Min Zhao, China
Shiwei Ma, China
Francesco Longo, Italy
Agostino Bruzzone, Italy

Program Committee

Anxiang Huang, China
Yoonbae Kim, Korea
Yu Yao, China
Fei Xie, USA
Toshiharu Kagawa, Japan
Giuseppe Iazeolla, Italy
Mhamed Itmi, France
Haixiang Lin, Netherlands
Henri Pierreval, France
Hugh HT Liu, Canada
Wolfgang Borutzky, Germany
Jong Sik Lee, Korea
Xiaolin Hu, USA
Yifa Tang, China
Wenhui Fan, China
Bernard Zeigler, USA
Mingduan Tang, China
Long Wang, China
ChaoWang, China
Doo-Kwon Baik, Korea
Shinsuke Tamura, Japan
Pierre Borne, France
Ratan Guha, USA
Reinhold Meisinger, Germany
Richard Fujimoto, USA
Ge Li, China
Jinhai Sun, China
Xinping Xiong, China

Changjian Bi, China
Jianguo Cao, China
Yue Dai, China
Minrui Fei, China
Chen Guo, China
Fengju Kang, China
Guoxiong Li, China
Jin Liu, China
Shiwei Ma, China
Jipeng Wang, China
Zhongjie Wang, China
Hongjun Zhang, China
Qinping Zhao, China
Guomin Zhou, China
Gary S.H. Tan, Singapore
Francesco Longo, Italy
Hong Zhou, China
Shin'ichi Oishi, Japan
Zhenhao Zhou, China
Beike Zhang, China
Alain Cardon, France
Xukun Shen, China
Yangsheng Wang, China
Marzuki Khalid, Malaysia
Sergio Junco, Argentina
Tieqiao Wen, China
Xingsheng Gu, China
Zhijian Song, China
Yue Yang, China
Yongsheng Ding, China
Huimin Fan, China
Ming Chen, China
Javor, Andras, Hungary
Nabendu Chaki, India
Koji Koyamada, Japan
Osamu Ono, Japan
Yunjie Wu, China
Beiwei Guo, China
Ni Li, China
Shixuan Liu, China
Linxuan Zhang, China
Fei Tao, China
Lei Ren, China
Xiao Song, China
Xudong Chai, China
Zonghai Chen, China
Yuhao Cong, China
Guanghong Gong, China
Zhicheng Ji, China
Weidong Jin, China
Bo Hu Li, China
Ma Ping, China
Shaojie Mao, China
Zhong Su, China
Jianping Wu, China
Min Zhao, China
Huizhou Zheng, China

Organization Committee Chair

Yunjie Wu, China

Organization Committee Co-chairs

Shixuan Liu, China
Zaijun Shi, China
Linxuan Zhang, China
Ni Li, China
Fei Tao, China
Beiwei Guo, China
Xiao Song, China
Weijing Wang, China
Lei Ren, China

General Secretaries

Shixuan Liu, China
Xiao Song, China

Special Session Chairs

Ni Li, China
Linxuan Zhang, China

Publication Chairs

Shiwei Ma, China
Xiao Song, China

Publicity Chairs

Fei Tao, China
Baiwei Guo, China

Awards Committee Chairs

Lin Zhang, China
Axel Lehmann, Germany

Awards Committee Co-chair

Yifa Tang, China

Awards Committee Members

Sung-Yong Jang, Korea
Wenhui Fan, China
Xiao Song, China

Contents – Part I

M&S Theory and Methodology

High Performance Computing and Simulation

M&S for Smart City

Contents – Part II

HMI & Robot Simulations

M&S for Intelligent Manufacturing

Visualization and Virtual Reality

Contents – Part III

Cloud Technologies in Simulation Applications

Fractional Calculus with Applications and Simulations

M&S for Energy, Environment and Climate

SBA Virtual Prototyping Engineering Technology

Contents – Part IV

M&S Applications

Simulation Software

Social Simulations

Verification, Validation and Accreditation (VV&A) of M&S

M&S Theory and Methodology

A Self-adaptive Shuffled Frog Leaping Algorithm for Multivariable PID Controller's Optimal Tuning

Yingying Xiao[1,2(✉)], Bo Hu Li[1,2,3], Tingyu Lin[1,2], Baocun Hou[1,2,3], Guoqiang Shi[1,2], and Yan Li[4]

[1] Beijing Complex Product Advanced Manufacturing Engineering Research Center, Beijing Simulation Center, Beijing 100854, China
[2] State Key Laboratory of Intelligent Manufacturing System Technology, Beijing Institute of Electronic System Engineering, Beijing 100854, China
[3] Science and Technology on Space System Simulation Laboratory, Beijing Simulation Center, Beijing 100854, China
[4] Beijing Simulation Center, Beijing 100854, China

Abstract. To insure the multi-input multi-output (MIMO) system has good system response and anti-jamming capability under no decoupling, this paper proposed a self-adaptive shuffled frog leaping algorithm to solve the multivariable PID controller's optimal tuning problem. First, the mathematical description of optimal tuning problem of multivariable PID controller is given. Second, a modified SFL with a parameter adaptive adjustment strategy in the basis of convergence analysis is proposed to enhance SFL's global searching ability and to improve its searching efficiency. Finally, a classical simulation example proposed by Wood and Berry is used to compare the performance of our modified SFL with SFL proposed by Thai and wPSO proposed by Shi, and the optimal results of PI/PID controller demonstrate the effectiveness of our algorithm.

Keywords: Multi-input multi-output (MIMO) system · Optimal tuning · Proportional-integral-derivative (PID) controller · Shuffled frog leaping algorithm (SFL) · Parameter adaptive adjustment

1 Introduction

The PID controllers are widely used in industry, and the optimal tuning of its three gains is the key [1] to the design of a suitable controller which can get satisfactory response for the target system.

In the past few decades, many intelligent technologies have also been proposed [2, 3]. But in industry, many processes are multi-input-multi-output (MIMO) systems [4] with features of high nonlinear, time invariant, pure time delay and variable parameters, which need multivariable controllers. Because those methods used successfully in SISO system cannot be directly applied to MIMO system [5], the design of multivariable PID controllers has aroused wide interest in academia and industry.

Recently, intelligent computing technique develops rapidly and has been applied to many optimization problems, including optimal tuning problem of PID controller.

L. Zhang et al. (Eds.): AsiaSim 2016/SCS AutumnSim 2016, Part I, CCIS 643, pp. 3–16, 2016.
DOI: 10.1007/978-981-10-2663-8_1

Intelligent optimal tuning method for multivariable PID controller can get nice response and good stability without decoupling the MIMO system to weaken the coupling influence. Therefore, using intelligent algorithms to this optimal tuning problem has become a hotspot in recent decades, and some efforts have been made [6–12].

Shuffled frog leaping algorithm (SFL) is a kind of intelligent algorithm proposed by Muzaffar M. Eusuff & Kevin E. Lansey [13]. Comparing the performances of five algorithms including GA, memetic algorithm (MA), PSO, ACO and SFL, Elbeltagi et al. has found out that the performance of SFL is similar to that of PSO, and it has higher success rate, better solution quality but quicker solution speed than GA [14]. However, the basic SFL has the problems of low efficiency and local optimum like GA and PSO. As far as we know, Thai-Hoang Huynh [5] firstly proposed a modified method (named ThaiMSFL) for optimal tuning of multivariable PID controller, while neither benchmark testing nor comparison with PSO-based algorithms have been done. Meanwhile, this paper just presents the optimal tuning problems of decentralized PI and centralized PID controllers, the other important one of decentralized PID controller is not considered.

Consequently, this paper mainly focus on the convergence analysis and improvement strategy of SFL, and its application to the optimal tuning problems of multivariable PI and PID controllers. Detailed comparisons with many proposed methods are also presented in our paper.

2 Optimal Tuning of Multivariable PID Controllers

The structure of multivariable PID control system [6] is shown as Fig. 1, where $G(s)$ is a linear MIMO processor and $C(s)$ is a multi-variable PID controller. Y_d is the desired outputs, Y is the actual outputs, E is the error vector and U is the control input vector.

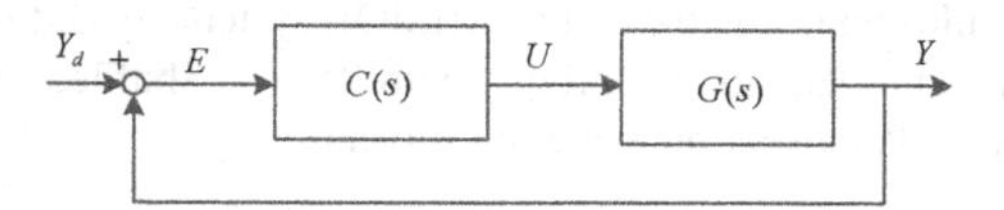

Fig. 1. The structure of multivariable PID control system

The transfer function matrices describing $G(s)$ and $C(s)$ are denoted as follows.

$$G(s) = \begin{bmatrix} g_{11}(s) & \cdots\cdots & g_{1n}(s) \\ \vdots & \ddots & \vdots \\ g_{n1}(s) & \cdots\cdots & g_{nn}(s) \end{bmatrix} \quad C(s) = \begin{bmatrix} c_{11}(s) & \cdots\cdots & c_{1n}(s) \\ \vdots & \ddots & \vdots \\ c_{n1}(s) & \cdots\cdots & c_{nn}(s) \end{bmatrix} \tag{1}$$

$$\text{Where} \quad c_{i,j}(s) = K_{p_{i,j}}(1 + 1/T_{i_{i,j}}s + T_{d_{i,j}}s) \tag{2}$$

Which is also can be rewritten as

$$c_{i,j}(s) = K_{p_{i,j}} + K_{i_{i,j}}/s + K_{d_{i,j}}s \tag{3}$$

Where $K_i = K_p/T_i$ is the integral gain, while $K_d = K_pT_d$ is the derivative gain.

Assuming processor $G(s)$ can get stable under PID controller $C(s)$, and then the controller design can be simplified to a variable tuning problem, whose variable vector can be defined as $\theta_{i,j} = [K_{p_{i,j}}, K_{i_{i,j}}, K_{d_{i,j}}]$. Thus, solution can be coded to a real number vector, noted as $\Theta = [\theta_{1,1}, \theta_{1,2} \cdot \ldots \cdot \theta_{n,n}]$. For a decoupled PID controller, $C(s)$ becomes

$$C(s) = \begin{bmatrix} c_{11}(s) & \ldots\ldots & 0 \\ \vdots & \ddots & \vdots \\ 0 & \ldots\ldots & c_{nn}(s) \end{bmatrix} \tag{4}$$

and Θ becomes $\Theta = [\theta_{1,1}, \theta_{2,2} \cdot \ldots \cdot \theta_{n,n}]$.

Fitness of solution is usually evaluated by integrated squared error (ISE) and integrated absolute error (IAE), which can be seen below.

$$J_{IAE} = \int_0^{T_f} \sum_{i=1}^{n} \rho_i |e_i(t)| dt \tag{5}$$

$$J_{ISE} = \int_0^{T_f} \sum_{i=1}^{n} \rho_i |e_i^2(t)| dt \tag{6}$$

Where ρ_i is the weighted coefficient of each component e_i, and T_f illustrates the evaluation period. Then, the optimal problem can be stated as to solve the optimization problem showing in (7).

$$\min_{\Theta} J(\Theta) \tag{7}$$

Where J is ISE or IAE.

3 Modified Shuffled Frog Leaping Algorithm

3.1 Basic SFL

The basic SFL algorithm is derived from the behaviors of frogs seeking food in a pond [14]. Firstly, a population with N frogs is randomly generated, sorted by the fitness value, and divided into M groups. Then, a local search step is running for n times in each group. In each step, the worst frog X_w is updated according to the local optimum or global optimal frog. After all groups have finished local search step, all frogs will be mixed together, resort and regrouped into M groups, and then repeat the local search process until the termination condition is satisfied. The update strategy of local search can be described as:

$$D^k = r(X_b^k - X_w^k) \tag{8}$$

or

$$D^k = r(X_g^k - X_w^k) \tag{9}$$

$$X_w' = X_w^k + D^k \tag{10}$$

where D^k is the displacement of the worst frog in the k-th iteration, r is usually a random number (0,1), X_b^k and X_g^k is the local best frog and the global best frog in the whole population. A new frog is firstly calculated according to X_b^k. And if the new frog X_w' is better than the old one, then $X_w^{k+1} = X_w'$ is acceptable. Otherwise, the new frog according to X_g^k will be calculated, and if this frog is better than the old one, $X_w^{k+1} = X_w'$ will be acceptable, or a new random frog will be selected.

In a word, it is intuitively understood that the efficiency of SFL algorithm is influenced by the update strategy in local search step. In order to ensure the convergence precision and convergence speed in finite iterations, the update strategy should be modified. More theoretical analysis can be seen in the following sections.

3.2 Convergence Analysis

Our last paper analyzes the convergence feature of SFL based on the theory of geometrical sequence [15], and to be described easily, the worst frog's update strategy (formula 10) can be extended as formula 11.

$$X_w' = \alpha X_w^k + \beta D^k \tag{11}$$

The paper reveals that "From the worst frog's rearranged sequence of $\Delta X_w^{k+1}/\Delta X_w^k = \alpha + \beta(\Delta X_b^k/\Delta X_w^k - 1)$, whose proportional coefficient is $l = \Delta X_b^k/\Delta X_w^k - 1$, it can be seen that the convergence speed and accuracy of SFL are related to two coefficients noted as α and β. Under reasonable adjustment of them, SFL will converge to Pareto optimal solution in probability and have faster convergence speed, to balance the performance of global and local search." A proportional coefficient based self-adaptive adjustment method is also described in the paper, which gives a simple variable scope of α and β in three different cases of l ($l > 0$ $l = 0$ and $l < 0$). But this method is just based on the intuitionistic analysis, and has no more detailed theories about how to dynamic change the variable scope of α and β during every local search iteration.

Motivated by system stability analysis method in digital signal process theory, this paper tries to present the relationship between the search performance and the variable scope of α and β to get the suitable parameters adaptive adjustment method. Note the update strategy in k-th and (k-1)-th iteration to be formula 12 and 13,

$$X_w(k) = aX_w(k-1) + b(X_b(k-1) - X_w(k-1)) \tag{12}$$

$$X_w(k-1) = \alpha X_w(k-2) + \beta(X_b(k-2) - X_w(k-2)) \tag{13}$$

thus, (12) – (13) to get (14) as below.

$$\begin{aligned} X_w(k) - X_w(k-1) = (\alpha - \beta)(X_w(k-1) - X_w(k-2)) \\ + \beta(X_b(k-1) - X_b(k-2)) \end{aligned} \tag{14}$$

Formula 14 is a difference equation and describes the time variant characteristics of X_w. Thus, using the Z transform method, the system transfer function can be presented as formula 15 and 16.

$$\begin{aligned} X_w(z) - z^{-1}X_w(z) = (\alpha - \beta)(z^{-1}X_w(z) - z^{-2}X_w(z)) \\ + \beta\,(z^{-1}X_b(z) - z^{-2}X_b(z)) \end{aligned} \tag{15}$$

$$\begin{aligned} G(z) = X_w(z)/X_b(z) &= (z^{-1} - z^{-2})/(1 - z^{-1} - (\alpha - \beta)(z^{-1} - z^{-2})) \\ &= (z-1)/(z^2 + (\beta - 1 - \alpha)z + (\alpha - \beta)) \end{aligned} \tag{16}$$

The system transfer function described in formula 16 can be considered as a discrete-time system whose input is $X_b(z)$ and output is $X_w(z)$. Therefore, the stability theory of Discrete-time System in Digital Signal Process can be used to analyze the convergence features.

It is obvious that the system's 'zeroes' are (0, 1), and the 'poles' are $\left(1 + \alpha - \beta \pm \sqrt{(1 + \alpha - \beta)^2 - 4(\alpha - \beta)}\right)/2$. To ensure the system convergence, the first principle that all poles are located in the unit circle of z-plane, which means $\left|\left(1 + \alpha - \beta \pm \sqrt{(1 + \alpha - \beta)^2 - 4(\alpha - \beta)}\right)/2\right| < 1$, should be firstly satisfied. Meanwhile, to avoid being trapped in local optimum, the second principle of keeping the randomness in the iteration is also important. Those two principles will be consistently throughout the analysis below.

As is mentioned in our last paper, the variable scope of α and β can be divided into three different cases according to l, and this paper continues to use this analytical framework.

(1) $l > 0$. In this case, $\Delta X_b^k / \Delta X_w^k > 1$, which means the update distance of local optimal variable X_b is bigger than the update distance of local worst variable X_w, implying X_b is changing rapidly, and unlikely to be trapped into the local optimum. So, it is reasonable to move the worst frog rapidly to the best one. We can set $\beta = 1$, and the 'poles' are simplified into $\left(\alpha \pm \sqrt{\alpha^2 - 4\alpha + 4}\right)/2 = [1, \alpha - 1]$. Therefore, the first principle should be satisfied as

$$|\alpha - 1| < 1 \Rightarrow \alpha \in (0, 2) \tag{17}$$

Formula 17 illustrates that α should be in the range of (0, 2) when $\beta = 1$ to insure X_w would converge to X_b after a few iterations, and when α is closer to 0 or 2, the convergence speed will be slower. If we denote α as $\alpha \in (1 - \Delta, 1 + \Delta)$, than $\Delta \in (0, 1)$. Thus, the smaller Δ is, the faster convergent speed the worst frog has. Meanwhile, to satisfy the second principle, β can be expanded to $(0.95, 1.05)$ to enhance the global search ability. In a word, α and β can be generated randomly using formula 18 when $l > 0$.

$$\begin{cases} \alpha = 1 - \Delta + rand \times 2\Delta \\ \beta = 0.95 + rand \times 0.1 \end{cases} \tag{18}$$

(2) $l = 0$. In this case, $\Delta X_b^k / \Delta X_w^k = 1$, which means the update distance of local optimal variable X_b is equal to the update distance of local worst variable X_w, implying X_b and X_w are both changing in this iteration, and it is hard to figure out which one is closer to the global optimum. Consequently, the influence of those two frogs should be considered simultaneously when we get a new frog, and α can be set to 1. Under such case, the 'poles' are simplified into $(2 - \beta \pm \beta)/2 = [1, 1 - \beta]$. Therefore, the first principle should be satisfied as

$$|1 - \beta| < 1 \Rightarrow 0 < \beta < 2 \tag{19}$$

Formula 19 illustrates that β should be in the range of (0, 2) when $\alpha = 1$ to insure X_w would converge to X_b after a few iterations, and when β is closer to 0 or 2, the convergence speed will be slower. If we denote $\beta \in (1 - \Delta, 1 + \Delta)$, then $\Delta \in (0, 1)$. Thus, the smaller Δ is, the faster convergent speed the worst frog has. Meanwhile, to follow the second principle, α can be expanded to the range of $(0.95, 1.05)$ to enhance the global search ability. In a word, α and β can be generated randomly using formula 20 when $l = 0$.

$$\begin{cases} \alpha = 0.95 + rand \times 0.1 \\ \beta = 1 - \Delta + rand \times 2\Delta \end{cases} \tag{20}$$

(3) $l < 0$. In this case, $\Delta X_b^k / \Delta X_w^k < 1$, which means the update distance of local optimal variable X_b is smaller than the update distance of local worst variable X_w. That implies X_b may be easily trapped into the local optimum. So the randomness of the iteration is important to promote the global search ability. In this situation, to follow the second principle, α can be set to be a random value ranged in $\alpha \in (1 - \Delta, 1 + \Delta)$ and $\Delta \in (0, 1)$. The 'poles' are transformed to be (21). Thus, the first principle of ensuring poles locate in the unit circle of Z-plane should be satisfied as

$$\left| \left(2 \pm \Delta - \beta \pm \sqrt{(2 \pm \Delta - \beta)^2 - 4(1 \pm \Delta - \beta)} \right) \middle/ 2 \right| < 1 \tag{21}$$

To solve the inequality in formula 21, we can find out that the variable range of β should change and be dependent on Δ. If we set $\beta \in (\Delta, 2-\Delta)$, the plots will always locate in the unit circle under different Δ to keep convergence. In a word, α and β can be generated randomly using formula 22 when $l<0$

$$\begin{cases} \alpha = 1 - \Delta + rand \times 2\Delta \\ \beta = \Delta + rand \times (2 - 2\Delta) \end{cases} \tag{22}$$

Then, the changeable range of the new frog should be in a quadrangle whose shape is related to Δ. The smaller Δ is, the more slender this quadrangle is, which is around the line of $D = (X_b - X_w)$ or $D = (X_g - X_w)$. Otherwise, the bigger Δ is, the quadrangle is to be a slender one around the best frog. Thus,using fomula 22 with randomly generated Δ can get entirely different changeable range of new frog to satisfy both two of our principles.

According to the analyses above, it comes to the conclusions, that

1. Different methods to generate α and β can make the worst frogs have different evolution features, which affect the whole population's behavior that is to be more random for the global search capability or to accelerate the convergent speed.
2. Based on the value of l, two coefficients of α and β can be randomly generated under the control of Δ using formula (18, 20, 22), and adaptively adjusting the range of Δ can balance algorithm's global random search capacity and local fast convergence capacity.

3.3 Improvement Strategy

The basic improvement strategy proposed in this paper is to self-adaptively choose different coefficients formulas to update the worst frog in every-iteration, which can be concluded as

$$X'_w = \alpha X_w^k + \beta D^k, D^k = (X_b - X_w), \text{ or } D^k = (X_g - X_w) \tag{23}$$

Where

$$\begin{cases} \alpha = 1 - \Delta + rand \times 2\Delta, & \beta = 0.95 + rand \times 0.1 & (l > 0) \\ \alpha = 0.95 + rand \times 0.1, & \beta = 1 - \Delta + rand \times 2\Delta & (l = 0) \\ \alpha = 1 - \Delta + rand \times 2\Delta, & \beta = \Delta + rand \times (2 - 2\Delta) & (l<0) \end{cases} \tag{24}$$

Meanwhile, in order to accelerate the search efficiency, Δ should be adaptively adjusted to control the convergence speed. One of the important features of directing the adjustment of convergent speed is the standard deviation (Std.) of the global optimal sequence $X_g(k)$ within a certain time window. It is a statistical variable to reflect the dispersion degree of $X_g(k)$, and can illustrate the updating frequency of the global optimal frog in the iteration process. When X_g changes slowly, the randomness should be enhanced to make sure new frog has the ability to jump far away from the current best frog for better solution, otherwise, keeping suitable randomness and following the best frog is acceptable. In this paper, this can be denoted as

$$stdJ_i = \begin{cases} std([J_i, J_{i-1}, J_{i-2}]), & i<4 \\ 0, & others \end{cases} \tag{25}$$

Where J_i is the fitness of global optimal frog in $i-th$ iteration. It's easy to figure out that when $stdJ_i$ is small, the global optimal solution will change slowly, and it can be easily trapped in the local optimal location. On the other hand, acceptable global search ability can be got in the latest three iterations. Therefore, in this paper, Δ is self-adaptive adjustment according to the following formula.

$$\Delta_i = \begin{cases} 0.01 + 0.99 \times rand, & 0 \le stdJ_i < 0.01 \\ 0.01 + 0.09 \times rand, & 0.01 \le stdJ_i < 0.1 \\ 0.001 + 0.009 \times rand, & 0.1 \le stdJ_i < 1 \\ 0.0001 + 0.0009 \times rand, & stdJ_i \ge 1 \end{cases} \tag{26}$$

In summary, the modified method proposed in this paper can be concluded into a coefficient self-adaptive adjustment technique based on proportional coefficient l and Std. of X_g. More details can be seen in Table 1.

Table 1. Self-adaptive coefficients adjustment

$stdJ \in$	$l > 0$	$l = 0$	$l<0$
$(0, 0.01)$	$\alpha = 1 - \Delta + rand \times 2\Delta$, $\beta = 0.95 + rand \times 0.1$ $s.t. \Delta \in (0.01, 1)$	$\alpha = 0.95 + rand \times 0.1$, $\beta = 1 - \Delta + rand \times 2\Delta$ $s.t. \Delta \in (0.01, 1)$	$\alpha = \alpha = 1 - \Delta + rand \times 2\Delta$, $\beta = \Delta + rand \times (2 - 2\Delta)$ $s.t. \Delta \in (0.01, 1)$
$(0.01, 0.1)$	$\alpha = 1 - \Delta + rand \times 2\Delta$, $\beta = 0.95 + rand \times 0.1$ $s.t. \Delta \in (0.01, 0.1)$	$\alpha = 0.95 + rand \times 0.1$, $\beta = 1 - \Delta + rand \times 2\Delta$ $s.t. \Delta \in (0.01, 0.1)$	$\alpha = \alpha = 1 - \Delta + rand \times 2\Delta$, $\beta = \Delta + rand \times (2 - 2\Delta)$ $s.t. \Delta \in (0.01, 0.1)$
$(0.1, 1)$	$\alpha = 1 - \Delta + rand \times 2\Delta$, $\beta = 0.95 + rand \times 0.1$ $s.t. \Delta \in (0.001, 0.01)$	$\alpha = 0.95 + rand \times 0.1$, $\beta = 1 - \Delta + rand \times 2\Delta$ $s.t. \Delta \in (0.001, 0.01)$	$\alpha = \alpha = 1 - \Delta + rand \times 2\Delta$, $\beta = \Delta + rand \times (2 - 2\Delta)$ $s.t. \Delta \in (0.001, 0.01)$
≥ 1	$\alpha = 1 - \Delta + rand \times 2\Delta$, $\beta = 0.95 + rand \times 0.1$ $s.t. \Delta \in (0.0001, 0.001)$	$\alpha = 0.95 + rand \times 0.1$, $\beta = 1 - \Delta + rand \times 2\Delta$ $s.t. \Delta \in (0.0001, 0.001)$	$\alpha = \alpha = 1 - \Delta + rand \times 2\Delta$, $\beta = \Delta + rand \times (2 - 2\Delta)$ $s.t. \Delta \in (0.0001, 0.001)$

Table 1 shows how to choose suitable formula and Δ to generate α and β to decide the new frog's location for updating the worst frog X_w, according to $stdJ_i$ and l. Intuitively, in each row, the random changeable range of new frog in $l<0$ is bigger than that in $l > 0$, which implies that it is appropriate to reduce the randomness to ensure faster convergence when the best frog is still updating faster than the worst frog. Moreover, in each column, the smaller $stdJ_i$ is, the bigger the changeable range of Δ is, which implies that it is more appropriate to enhance the randomness to help new frog with better solution when X_g is updating more slowly.

In conclusion, $stdJ_i$ and l are two important parameters, which can respectively reflect the global search ability and the search efficiency. Our improvement method is a dynamic equilibrium strategy to balance new frog's changeable scope and convergence speed, which means increasing the randomness are suitable when the population may easily fall into local optimum, while searching space should center on the surrounding ranges of local optimal solution to avoid unnecessary iteration attempts, which will improve the searching efficiency.

4 MSFL Based Tuning of PID

In this section, a classical simulation example of a binary distillation column plant described by Wood and Berry [3] is considered to illustrate the effectiveness of the proposed MSFL. The transfer function is given as

$$G(s) = \begin{bmatrix} \dfrac{12.8e^{-s}}{1+16.7s} & \dfrac{-18.9e^{-3s}}{1+21s} \\ \dfrac{6.6e^{-7s}}{1+10.9s} & \dfrac{-19.4e^{-3s}}{1+14.4s} \end{bmatrix} \tag{27}$$

This well-known system has strong interaction between inputs and outputs. In this paper, decentralized PI and PID controller, as well as centralized PID controller are considered, and J_{IAE} is chosen to be the performance indicator with the weight constants $\rho_1 = \rho_2 = 1$ and $T_f = 150(s)$. The following simulations all run in MATLAB 2009b using its Control System Toolbox, and for results that have been presented, J_{IAE} is recalculated under the given Θ to eliminate errors caused by different computing environment.

For decentralized PID controller, the proportional integral and derivative gains are diagonal matrices, and derivative gains are equal to zero when using decentralized PI controller. So, the vectors of solution for decentralized PI and PID controller are represented respectively as follows, and the parameter ranges are all set to be in [−1,1].

$$\begin{aligned} \Theta_{PI} &= \begin{bmatrix} K_{p_{1,1}} & 0 & K_{i_{1,1}} & 0 & 0 & 0 \\ 0 & K_{p_{2,2}} & 0 & K_{i_{2,2}} & 0 & 0 \end{bmatrix} \\ &= \begin{bmatrix} K_{p_{1,1}}, & K_{i_{1,1}}, & K_{p_{2,2}} & K_{i_{2,2}} \end{bmatrix} \end{aligned} \tag{28}$$

$$\begin{aligned} \Theta_{PID} &= \begin{bmatrix} K_{p_{1,1}} & 0 & K_{i_{1,1}} & 0 & K_{d_{1,1}} & 0 \\ 0 & K_{p_{2,2}} & 0 & K_{i_{2,2}} & 0 & K_{d_{2,2}} \end{bmatrix} \\ &= \begin{bmatrix} K_{p_{1,1}}, & K_{i_{1,1}}, & K_{d_{1,1}}, & K_{p_{2,2}}, & K_{i_{2,2}} & K_{d_{2,2}} \end{bmatrix} \end{aligned} \tag{29}$$

Where

$$-1 \le K_p \le 1, -1 \le K_i \le 1, -1 \le K_d \le 1 \quad (30)$$

4.1 PI Controller

Firstly, many optimal tuning methods of decentralized PI controller have been presented in many articles (Qing-Guo Wang, 1997 [2]; Thai-Hoang Huynh, 2008 [5]; Wei-Der Chang, 2007 [6]; M. Willhuice Iruthayarajan, 2009 [7]; Muhammad Ilyas Menhas, 2012 [10]), and the results can be seen in Table 2. Four other algorithms are executed 10 times for comparison, including wPSO, Basic SFL, MSFL proposed by Thai (ThaiMSFL) [5] and MSFL. Because authors did not give the value of $D_{\max}$ in ThaiMSFL, this paper assumes $D_{\max} = \|0.5 \times (Upper - Lower)\|$. The maximum iteration number is set to 1000, and parameters of wPSO, Basic SFL, MSFL are the same as those mentioned above. The results are shown in Tables 2, 3 and Fig. 2.

Table 2. Optimal tuning results of decentralized PI controller

Proposed	$K_{p_{1,1}}$	$K_{i_{1,1}}$	$K_{p_{2,2}}$	$K_{i_{2,2}}$	J_{IAE}
BLT[a]	0.3750	0.0452	−0.0750	−0.0032	23.3939
TraditionalGA[b]	0.5511	0.0018	−0.0182	−0.0067	11.5482
Multi-crossover GA[b]	0.9971	0.0031	−0.0141	−0.0071	10.4350
CMAES[c]	0.8485	0.0026	−0.0132	−0.0069	10.3816
PBPSO[d]	0.8261	0.0027	−0.0117	−0.0068	10.4071
DBPSO[d]	0.8198	0.0019	−0.0327	−0.0085	11.1981
MBPSO[d]	0.8429	0.0024	−0.0237	−0.0079	10.7771
Executed	$K_{p_{1,1}}$	$K_{i_{1,1}}$	$K_{p_{2,2}}$	$K_{i_{2,2}}$	J_{IAE}
wPSO	0.897756	0.002657	-0.01333	-0.007	10.3223
Basic SFL	0.563401	0.119609	0.009599	-0.00644	14.3778
ThaiMSFL	0.8902	0.002765	-0.01274	-0.00697	10.3312
Proposed MSFL	0.8949	0.002619	-0.01327	-0.007	10.32518

[a]Data taken from Qing-Guo Wang (1997) [2]; [b]Data taken from Wei-Der Chang (2007) [6]; [c]Data taken from M. Willhuice Iruthayarajan (2009) [7]; [d]Data taken from Muhammad Ilyas Menhas (2012) [10]

Table 3. Statistical performance of different algorithms for decentralized PI controller

Executed	FWorst	FBest	FMean	Suc. (f < 10.34)	Time
wPSO	10.3244	10.3223	10.3233	100 %	2837.554
Basic SFL	22.6433	14.3778	18.0002	0	3318.436
ThaiMSFL	10.3768	10.3312	10.3448	50 %	6494.697
MSFL	10.32824	10.32518	10.3271	100 %	4508.794

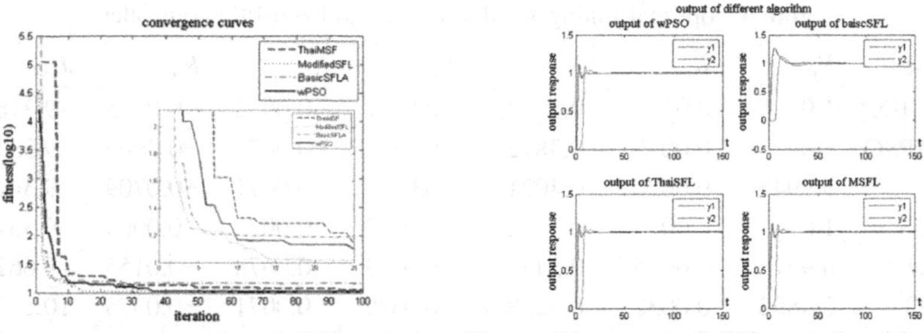

(a) convergence curves of different algorithms (b) output of different algorithms

Fig. 2. Results of different algorithms for decentralized PI controller

From Table 2, we can see that the best J_{IAE} is 10.3816 for CMAES in all seven proposed methods. For four methods executed in this paper, only Basic SFL cannot get solution around 10.3. Meanwhile, in Table 3, only wPSO and proposed MSFL can keep every J_{IAE} around 10.3 in 10 times. More details can be seen in Fig. 2, which shows convergence curves and outputs in step input of different algorithms.

Figure 2(a) and its magnified part clearly illustrate that the convergence speed of MSFL is faster than that of any other three algorithms, and it also has excellent global search ability to get better convergence accuracy as wPSO. Meanwhile, ThaiSFL has global search ability which can direct the algorithm to find the optimal solution, but its convergence speed is slower.

4.2 PID Controller

A couple of articles (M. Willhuice Iruthayarajan, 2009 [7]; Muhammad Ilyas Menhas, 2012 [10]) have given the simulation results for optimal tuning of multivariable decentralized PID controller (as shown in Table 4 of methods have been proposed). Four methods mentioned above are executed 10 times in this paper. Maximum local search number of SFL-based algorithms is reset to 8, including basicSFL ThaiMSFL and MSFL, and the maximum iteration number is reduced to 200. Other parameters are the same as before. The results are shown in Tables 4, 5 and Fig. 3.

Table 4 shows that the best J_{IAE} of eight proposed methods is 9.3347 for PID-MPSO and CMAES. For four methods executed in this paper, three algorithms of wPSO ThaiMSFL and MSFL can get solutions better than 9.3347, while only the solution of Basic SFL is worse than 9.3347 but still close to 10. Furthermore, MSFL has capacity to get the smallest fitness of 7.732789, which implies MSFL has better global search ability than the other threes. Meanwhile, regarding to Suc. ($f < 8.5$) in Table 5, which illustrates the successful rate of obtained solutions is less than 8.5, we can see that MSFL has more stable search efficiency (the Suc. ($f < 8.5$) is 70 %) than wPSO and ThaiMSFL. More details can be seen in Fig. 3, which shows convergence curves and outputs in step input of different algorithms.

Figure 3(a) and its magnified part clearly illustrate that the convergence speed of MSFL is faster than any other three algorithms, and it also has excellent global search

Table 4. optimal tuning results of decentralized PID controller

Proposed	$K_{p_{1,1}}$	$K_{i_{1,1}}$	$K_{d_{1,1}}$	$K_{p_{2,2}}$	$K_{i_{2,2}}$	$K_{d_{2,2}}$	J_{IAE}
RGA-SBX[a]	1.0	0.0025	0.3892	−0.0317	−0.0072	−0.0885	9.3786
PID-MPSO[a]	1.0	0.0025	0.3872	−0.0332	−0.0073	−0.0909	9.3347
DE[a]	0.9945	0.0026	0.4021	−0.0289	−0.0071	−0.0709	9.3421
CMAES[a]	1.0	0.0025	0.3872	−0.0332	−0.0073	−0.0909	9.3347
PBPSO[b]	0.9976	0.0025	0.345	−0.0313	−0.0078	−0.0155	9.6621
DBPSO[b]	0.9892	0.0032	0.3238	−0.0389	−0.0071	−0.0375	10.1136
MBPSO[b]	0.8508	0.0040	0.4061	−0.0979	−0.0157	−0.0439	12.3954
Executed	$K_{p_{1,1}}$	$K_{i_{1,1}}$	$K_{d_{1,1}}$	$K_{p_{2,2}}$	$K_{i_{2,2}}$	$K_{d_{2,2}}$	J_{IAE}
wPSO	0.999507	0.00324	0.55944	−0.03879	−0.00883	−0.12376	8.39939
Basic SFL	0.310249	0.008954	0.334643	−0.13871	−0.01378	−0.3191	9.900721
ThaiMSFL	0.738852	0.002171	0.501704	−0.04908	−0.00926	−0.18766	8.546229
MSFL	0.538034	0.008532	0.135454	−0.21295	−0.009	−0.33966	7.732789

[a]Data taken from [7] [b]Data taken from [10]

Table 5. Statistical performance of different algorithms for decentralized PID controller

Executed	FWorst	FBest	FMean	Suc. (f < 8.5)	Time
wPSO	8.557066	8.39939	8.50975	20 %	688.3342
Basic SFL	184.4461	9.900721	33.20823	0	1101.441
ThaiMSFL	9.362223	8.546229	8.953228	0	2017.462
MSFL	8.572521	7.732789	8.41131	70 %	1556.375

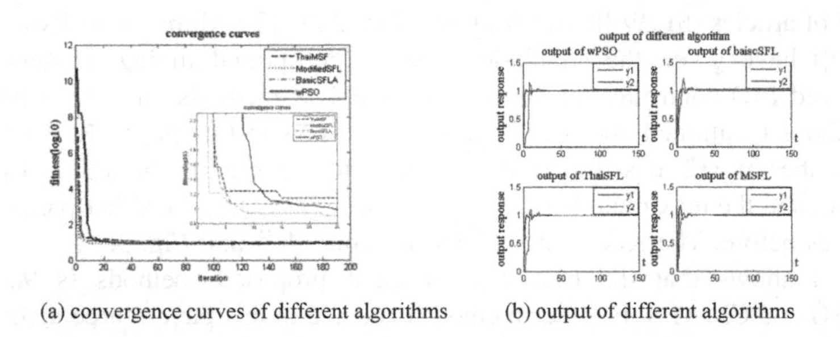

(a) convergence curves of different algorithms (b) output of different algorithms

Fig. 3. Results of different algorithms for decentralized PID controller

ability to get better convergence accuracy. Meanwhile, wPSO and ThaiSFL have global search ability which can direct the algorithm to find the optimal solution, but its convergence speed is slower than MSFL and Basic SFL.

In one word, MSFL is effective to solve the problems of optimal tuning for multivariable PID controller.

5 Conclusions

This paper has analyzed the convergence features of shuffled frog leaping algorithm (SFL) based on system stability analysis method in digital signal process theory. Meanwhile, an Improvement Strategy has been proposed to balance the global and local search ability. It uses two evaluated parameters (proportional coefficient l and Std. of X_g) to randomly generate different update coefficients (α and β) in every iteration.

This paper also presents an actual problem for optimal tuning of multi-variable PID controller to illustrate the performance of MSFL, which has been proved to be an NP-hard problem. Simulation analyses to design PI/PID controllers for the Wood-Berry distillation column have demonstrated the effectiveness of our algorithm.

Acknowledgements. This work is supported by the Foundation item of Project supported by the National High-Tech R&D Program, China (No. 2015AA042101).

References

1. Wang, W., Zhang, J., Chai, T.: A survey of advanced PID parameter tuning methods. ACTA AUTOMATICA SINICA **26**(3), 347–355 (2000)
2. Wang, Q.-G., Zou, B., Lee, T.-H., Bi, Q.: Auto-tuning of multivariable PID controllers from decentralized relay feedback. Automatica **33**(3), 319–330 (1997)
3. Luyben, W.L.: A simple method for tuning SISO controllers in a multivariable system. Ind. Eng. Chem. Product Res. Dev. **25**, 654–660 (1986)
4. Chen, D., Seborg, D.E.: Design of decentralized PI control systems based on Nyquist stability analysis. J. Process Control **13**(1), 27–39 (2003)
5. Huynh, T.-H.: A modified shuffled frog leaping algorithm for optimal tuning of multivariable PID controllers. In: IEEE International Conference on Industrial Technology, (ICIT 2008), pp. 1–6 (2008)
6. Chang, W.-D.: A multi-crossover genetic approach to multivariable PID controllers tuning. Expert Syst. Appl. **33**(3), 620–626 (2007)
7. Willhuice Iruthayarajan, M., Baskar, S.: Evolutionary algorithms based design of multivariable PID controller. Expert Syst. Appl. **36**(5), 9159–9167 (2009)
8. Han, K., Zhao, J., Xu, Z.-H., Qian, J.-X.: A closed-loop particle swarm optimizer for multivariable process controller design. J. Zhejiang Univ. SCIENCE A **9**(8), 1050–1060 (2009)
9. Wang, J., Gao, X.: Design of multivariable PID controller of electroslag remelting process based on improved shuffled frog leaping algorithm. Control Decis. **26**(11), 1731–1734 (2011)
10. Menhas, M.I., Wang, L., Fei, M., Pan, H.: Comparative performance analysis of various binary coded PSO algorithms in multivariable PID controller design. Expert Syst. Appl. **39** (4), 4390–4401 (2012)
11. Willjuice Iruthayarajan, M., Baskar, S.: Covariance matrix adaptation evolution strategy based design of centralized PID controller. Expert Syst. Appl. **37**(8), 5775–5781 (2010)
12. Reynoso-Meza, G., Sanchis, J., Blasco, X., Herrero, J.M.: Multiobjective evolutionary algorithms for multivariable PI controller design. Expert Syst. Appl. **39**(9), 7895–7907 (2012)

13. Eusuff, M.M., Lansey, K.E.: Optimization of water distribution network design using the shuffled frog leaping algorithm. J. Water Resour. Plan. Manage. **129**(3), 210–225 (2003)
14. Elbeltagi, E., Hegazy, T., Grierson, D.: Comparison among five evolutionary-based optimization algorithms. Adv. Eng. Inform. **19**(1), 43–53 (2005)
15. Xiao, Y., Li, B.-H., Chai, X., Wang, Q.: Convergence Analysis of shuffled frog leaping algorithm and its modified algorithm. J. Huazhong Univ. Sci. Technol. (Nat. Sci. Ed.) **40**(7), 15–18 (2012)

An Accurate Global Time Synchronization Method in Wireless Sensor Networks

Bilal Ahmad(✉), Ma Shiwei, Fu Qi, Wang Meixi, and Rui Ling

Shanghai Key Laboratory of Power Station Automation Technology,
School of Mechatronics Engineering and Automation,
Shanghai University, No. 149, Yanchang Road, Shanghai 200072, China
{abilali,masw}@shu.edu.cn,
{18818218275,meixifly,ruiling0812}@163.com

Abstract. Time synchronization is a hot research topic for data fusion, localization, duty cycle scheduling, and topology management. Global time synchronization is preferred to bring all sensor nodes of a wireless sensor network (WSN) on a common notion of time in the applications (surveillance and target tracking) where coordinated actuation and cooperative communication is desired for the meaningful coordination and data consistency. In this study we proposed an accurate global time synchronization method in WSNs based on a single reference node. We have checked its performance in terms of accuracy and simulation results prove it accurate as end to end latency and jitter decrease as the number of observations increase.

Keywords: Time synchronization · Wireless sensor networks · Accuracy · End to end latency

1 Introduction

1.1 Basics of Wireless Sensor Networks

Sensor is a tiny device with a small hardware and very limited memory. It runs on a minute battery. It changes a physical phenomenon into a signal for its meaningful processing. Sensor nodes being smaller and cheaper, and because of their various usages are rapidly making their place in the present day scientific technology like MEMS (Micro Electro Mechanical System). We can monitor the condition at any location with the help of these small sized devices. Architecture of a wireless sensor node is represented in Fig. 1.

A sensor network is composed of sensor nodes, sink, sensor field and controller. Nodes operate by gathering and routing the information before transferring it to the sink. A simple WSN architecture is shown in Fig. 2. The information is transferred in very few messages leading to reduced energy consumption. WSNs have both advantages as well as disadvantages. Among the advantage, their implementation cost is less, the network may be deployed anywhere and they can be monitored through a global monitoring system. The disadvantages include inadequate security, difficulty in configuration and reduced speed as compared to a wired network. Sensor nodes which are densely

L. Zhang et al. (Eds.): AsiaSim 2016/SCS AutumnSim 2016, Part I, CCIS 643, pp. 17–24, 2016.
DOI: 10.1007/978-981-10-2663-8_2

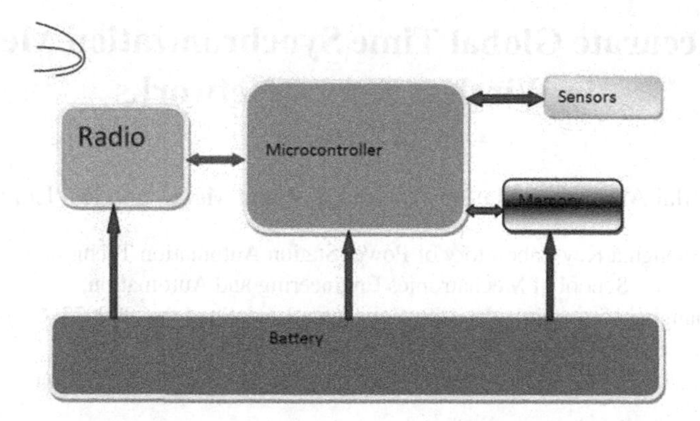

Fig. 1. Architecture of a wireless sensor node

deployed, deployment may be random or deterministic, for deterministic deployment routs are predefined while for premier case it's really very challenging. Few of them are control nodes also referred as base stations. These nodes are connected with each other wirelessly and base station connects them with some other network.

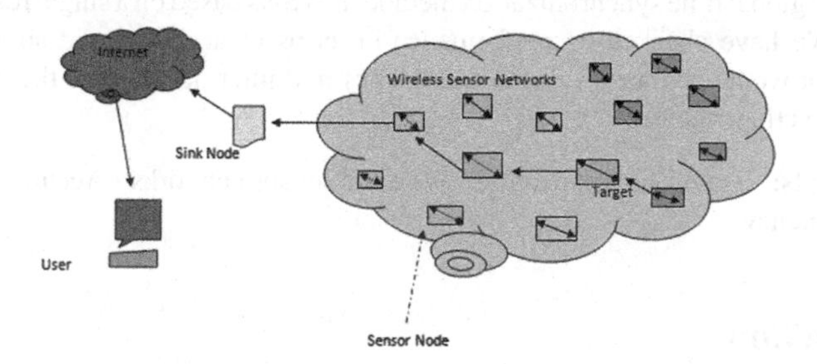

Fig. 2. Architecture of a wireless sensor network

1.2 Time Synchronization and Its Pre-requisites

Time synchronization is the backbone for almost all wireless sensor network applications. Because if the ordering of event is not correct, there is delay in transmission or nodes are not synchronized with each other, then information packet will be lost. For low duty cycle applications and time related events nodes must keep precise time synchronization for significant information processing. They should sleep and awake together so that periodic messages exchange can hold successfully, otherwise duty cycle will be high and more energy will be consumed as number of timing messages increase. Time synchronization protocols should more or less fulfill the following characteristics:

Scalability: Some WSNs applications require hundreds and thousands of nodes. Time synchronization protocols should be scalable to be implemented on larger networks.

Robustness: Time synchronization protocols should be robust, as robustness also increases quality of service.

Energy efficiency: Energy is a big concern for sensor nodes as they have small batteries. For their long life operations energy efficient time synchronization protocols are required to be designed.

Accuracy: Law enforcement applications (object tracking and battlefield surveillance) need accurate time synchronization protocols. Because basic demand of such applications is reduced end to end latency and reduced jitter.

Flexibility: The wide ranges of applications require flexible and adaptive time synchronization mechanism. Each application demands a different behavior so time synchronization protocol must be flexible to cope with each application for meaningful processing of data.

Security: Wireless nodes are prone to faults and data fetched by them is easily accessible by attackers so time synchronization protocols should be secure. Researchers these days are paying attention on it with high level encryption and decryption keys. Due to the failure of sensor nodes the network topology may change, so time synchronization algorithms must be dynamic so that network operation is not affected.

Our proposed method adopts centralized synchronization mechanism. Because it is easy to control centralized synchronization schemes to achieve maximum benefits and the centralized synchronization methods are not topology sensitive. Root/reference node broadcasts timing message to the other node residing in its communication range, which compares its clock value and adjusts its clock with the root node's local clock value. Then it sends ACK message to the root node. To reduce the round trip time; second node shares root node's timing information and computed offset value to the next hop and other nodes set their local clock upon global time initiated by the root node. By means of similar approach whole network get synchronized through periodic messages exchange.

The rest of the paper is organized as: Related work is discussed in Sect. 2, measurement model and simulations are represented in Sect. 3, and finally research work is concluded in the Sect. 4.

2 Literature Review

Time synchronization is essential for TDMA based applications like, duty cycling, data fusion and object tracking. This is an operation in which it is ensured that all physical distributed processors are functioning at a common notion of time. This function is useful for security and fault tolerance. The data of all nodes is collected in order to arrange a meaningful result. That is why clocks are synchronized at a common time. Two basic features must be taken into account for stable/useful time synchronization i.e. clock offset and clock skew. Figure 3 represents the time synchronization phenomenon.

Clock of a sensor node is shown in Fig. 4. Frequency is measured instead of time in time keeping scenarios. In ideal cases time intervals between the events are constant but in practical situations different clocks exhibit different time due to their internal properties of the local oscillator and manufacturing. Due to the defects in crystal oscillator, local clocks of the sensor nodes drift from each other and clock offset increases linearly between the nodes. For accurate fetching of information data sensed by a sensor node

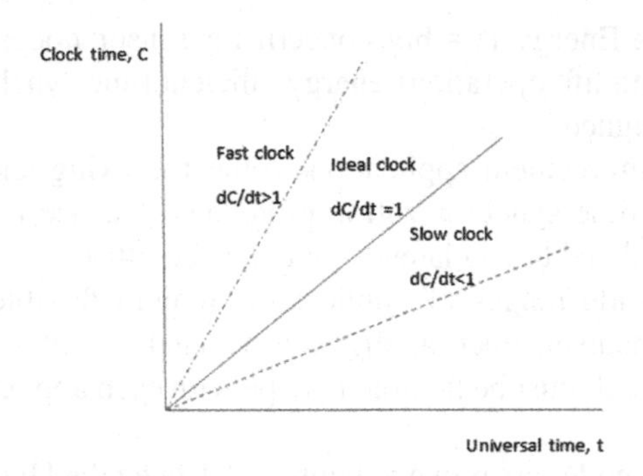

Fig. 3. Time synchronization

is required to be time stamped. This time stamping is either performed at the time of information collection or at the time of collected data processing.

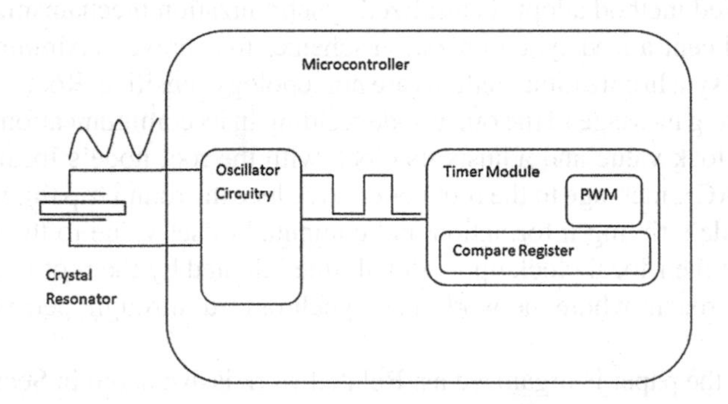

Fig. 4. Clock structure of a sensor node

Time synchronization is the fundamental problem of the WSNs due to the resource constraints WSNs (smaller hardware and limited energy at the end sensor node). Local clocks of the sensor nodes must be synchronized not only because of specific application requirements but for the channel access also [1]. Nodes use crystals to count the frequencies and various factors (e.g. aging, temperature, environmental factors) affect it as a result local clocks of the nodes run at different rate so there is natural difference in the clock of two nodes [2].

There are three basic ways to synchronize the clocks of the sensor nodes (a) via an intermediate node [4], (b) through pairwise synchronization assuming that clock drift and clock offset are linear as mentioned in [3] and (c) through a leader and all other nodes synchronize their clocks upon it [5].

Getting accurate time synchronization in the presence of non-deterministic delays is very difficult. The delays are categorized as send time, access time, transmission time, propagation time and reception time [3, 4] and these uncertainties are minimized by MAC layer time stamping [3, 5]. Accurate time synchronization protocols are under research these days due to their verity of application for the efficient completion of their operations [6–8]. Higher accuracy is achieved in [9] through lower communication overhead and topology is maintained stable through resynchroniztion mechanism. In [10] authors conducted a brief survey to represent the secure time synchronization in hostile environment where compromised/malicious nodes may exist.

3 Performance Evaluation

In this section we present the system model for time synchronization to achieve high accuracy through a new messages exchange mechanism, which has low messages complexity. Moreover we will discuss the simulation results and discuss the reduced end to end latency with the passage of number of rounds of messages exchange.

3.1 Synchronization Framework

Node A is the reference node and is responsible for the mutual time consensus in the sensor network. It broadcasts timing information to the node B which compares and adjusts its clock value as per the received timing information and sends acknowledgment back to the root node. Meanwhile to reduce burden on the root node, node B shares the computed values to the next hop and node C also adjusts its time on the global time. Synchronization procedure is represented in Fig. 5.

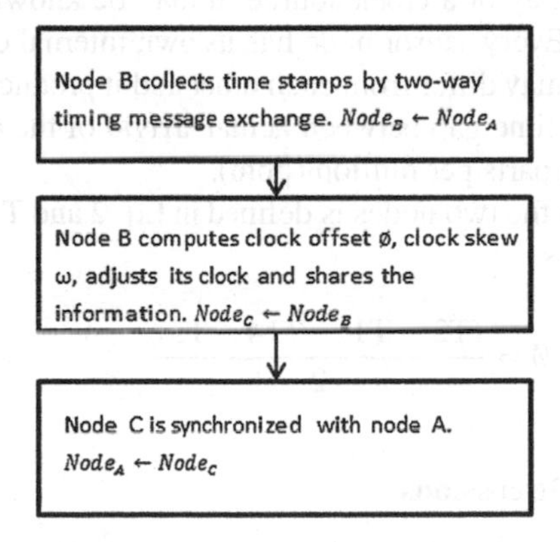

Fig. 5. Flowchart representation of the proposed scheme

Messages exchange mechanism for the communicating nodes is described in Fig. 6 below.

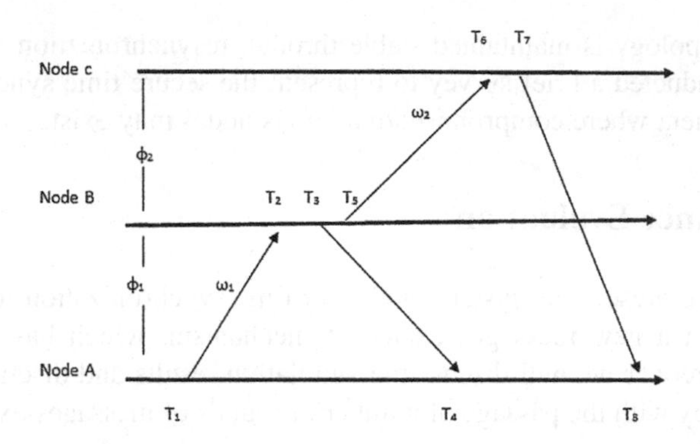

Fig. 6. Timing messages exchange mechanism

Where Ø1 is the phase/clock offset between node A and node B whereas Ø2 is the clock offset between node B and node C. Similarly ω1 represents the clock skew between node A and node B while ω2 is the clock skew between node B and node C. The general clock equation is shown below:

$$T(t) = \text{Ø} + \omega t \tag{1}$$

Clock offset is the delay of a clock source. It may be known or unknown and it is measured in time units. Every sensor node has its own internal clock and due to manufacturing defects clocks may differ from each other and it produces clock skew. In other words clock skew is the time gap between actual arrival of the clock and the expected arrival. It is measured in parts per million (ppm).

Clock offset between the two nodes is defined in Eq. 2 and T represents local (send/receive) time at the nodes.

$$\text{Ø} = \frac{(T2 - T1) - (T4 - T3)}{2}. \tag{2}$$

3.2 Simulations and Discussions

Simulations are carried out through MATLAB for the set of communicating sensor nodes shown in Fig. 6. The parameters set up for the simulations are shown in Table 1.

Table 1. Simulation parameters

Parameter	Symbol	Values
Number of observations	N	25
Fixed propagation delay	d	0.2–0.6
Clock offset	$Ø_1$ and $Ø_2$	1.5–3
Clock skew	ω_1 and ω_2	0.9–1.1

As mean square error (MSE) is the better performance index to judge the performance of any proposed estimator. Figure 7 illustrates the MSE of the estimated clock offset Ø1 and Ø2 versus the number of rounds of messages exchange. Curves in both plots for the values (0.9, 1.0, and 1.10) of ω1 and ω2 clearly show that the MSE of the estimated clock offset have decreasing pattern and converges as long as the number of rounds of messages exchange increase and it establishes the effectiveness of proposed method. It is also obvious the simulation results prove the fact that the MSE of the clock offset is directly related to the clock skew values i.e. higher is the clock skew value, higher will be the MSE of the estimated clock offset and vice versa. MSE of the clock offset is lowest without clock skew error (ideal case: for $\omega = 1$).

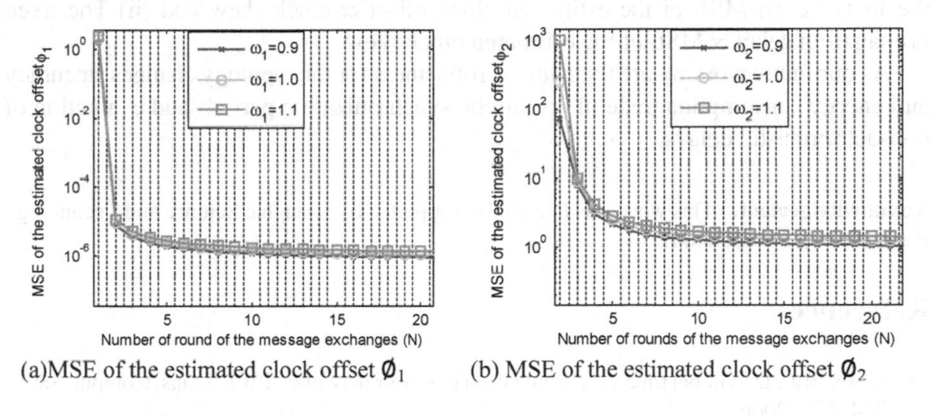

(a)MSE of the estimated clock offset $\emptyset_1$ (b) MSE of the estimated clock offset $\emptyset_2$

Fig. 7. MSE of the estimated clock offset

The MSE of the estimated clock skew ω1 and ω2 versus the number of rounds of messages exchange is shown in the Fig. 8. The fixed propagation delay *d* is set to 0.2 ms, 0.4 ms and 0.6 ms. We can see from both the figures that MSE of the clock skew converges with the passage of timing rounds. From the MSE of the estimate clock skew another fact is also validated that the distance between the nodes is directly concerned with the fixed propagation delay. Larger is the distance between sensor nodes higher will be the fixed propagation delay and higher is the MSE of the estimated clock skew.

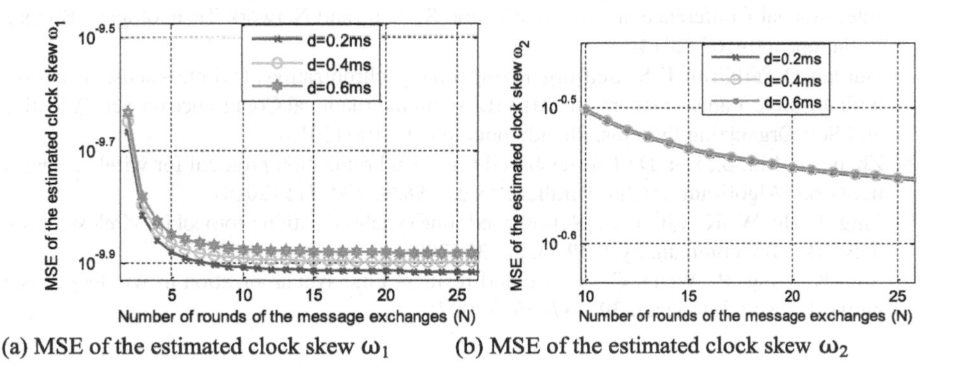

(a) MSE of the estimated clock skew ω_1 (b) MSE of the estimated clock skew ω_2

Fig. 8. MSE of the estimated clock skew

4 Conclusions and Future Work

This paper presents the performance of our proposed method during round trip synchronization. The proposed method is computationally simple, includes skew compensation even for the higher values of the clock skew like 1.10, accurate and easy to implement. It is obvious from the simulations that it reduces end to end latency and convergence pattern of the MSEs, reflects that our method deals the jitter in an efficient way. Message complexity is low and as a result accuracy is high. Simulation results clearly validate the facts i.e. (i) MSE of the estimated clock offset $\propto$ clock skew and (ii) The fixed propagation delay $\propto$ MSE of the estimated clock skew.

As our future work we are focusing on robustness for the topology changes, accuracy and energy consumption tradeoff during the synchronization periods and evaluation of non-deterministic delays.

Acknowledgement. This work was financially supported by Shanghai Science and Technology Foundation (13510500400).

References

1. Li, Q., Rus, D.: Global time synchronization in sensor networks. IEEE Trans. Comput. **55**(2), 214–226 (2006)
2. Wu, Y.C., Chaudhari, Q., Serpedin, E.: Time synchronization of wireless sensor networks. IEEE Signal Process. Mag. **28**(1), 124–138 (2011)
3. Ganeriwal, S., Kumar, R., Sirivastava, M.B.: Timing-sync protocol for sensor networks. In: Proceedings of the 1st International Conference on Embedded Networked Sensor Systems, pp. 138–149 (2003)
4. Elson, J., Girod, L., Estrin, D.: Fine-grained network time synchronization using reference broadcasts. ACM SIGOPS Oper. Syst. Rev. **36**(SI), 147–163 (2002)
5. Maroti, M., Kusy, B., Simon, G., Ledeczi, A.: The flooding time synchronization protocol. In: Proceedings of Sensor System, pp. 39–49 (2004)
6. Bhende, M., Wagh, S.J., Utpat, A.: A quick survey on wireless sensor networks. In: 4th International Conference on Communication Systems and Network Technologies, Bhopal, India, pp. 160–167 (2014)
7. Gurcan, O., Yildirim, K.S.: Self-organizing time synchronization of wireless sensor networks with adaptive Value Trackers. In: 2013 IEEE 7th International Conference on Self-Adaptive and Self-Organizing Systems, Philadelphia, pp. 91–100 (2013)
8. Zhang, J., Lin, S., Liu, D.: Cluster-based time synchronization protocol for wireless sensor networks. Algorithms Archit. Parallel Process. **8630**, 700–711 (2014)
9. Ping, J., Hu, W.-K., Lin, J.-C.: Ratio-based time synchronization protocol in wireless sensor networks. Telecommun. Syst. **39**(1), 25–35 (2008)
10. Sun, K., Ning, P., Wang, C.: Secure and resilient time synchronization in wireless sensor networks. Adv. Inf. Secur. **30**, 347–367 (2007)

A Novel Adaptive Cooperative Artificial Bee Colony Algorithm for Solving Numerical Function Optimization

Bin Liu(✉), Wei-min Li, and Shuai Pan

Air and Missile Defense College of AFEU, Xi'an, China
{liubin19870101,lwm168}@126.com, 18392548322@163.com

Abstract. Considering the disadvantages of the traditional Artificial Bee Colony (ABC) Algorithm, a Novel Adaptive Cooperative Artificial Bee Colony (ACABC) Algorithm is proposed in this paper. Some ideas including dividing bee swarm into two parts: main-bee swarm and vice-bee swarm, bringing a judge principle for local optimum points and narrowing bee swarm search interval adaptively are introduced and consequently served as the core of novel Adaptive Cooperative Artificial Bee Colony Algorithm. The performance of PSO, DE, ABC and ACABC algorithms are compared using 10 kinds benchmark testing functions. Simulation results show ACABC owns better optimizing precision and speed and preferable anti-jamming ability, which can be applied for solving other complicated optimization problems.

Keywords: Artificial Bee Colony Algorithm · Adaptively narrow search interval · Swarm cooperation · Escaping from local optimum points · Numerical function optimization

1 Introduction

Karaboga (2005) developed the Artificial Bee Colony (ABC) algorithm, which is inspired by nectar source optimizing mechanism of honey bees, is a novel heuristic swarm intelligence algorithm. *Karaboga and Basturk* (2008) shows that ABC has superior performance compared with many other existing swarm intelligence algorithms. *Karaboga and Basturk* (2007) and *Karaboga and Ozturk* (2011) and *Karaboga et al.* (2014) show that Artificial Bee Colony algorithm owns several merits such as simplicity in concept, few variables in control and easiness in application, which is widely used in discrete optimization, numerical optimization, multi-objective optimization, PID controller, design of IIR filters, machine learning, software testing and so on.

After the ABC was created, some scholars put forward many improvement measures focusing on its defaults such as blind search, slow optimizing speed and easily being trapped in the local optimum points. *Ayan and Kılıç* (2012) investigate a self-adaptive mutation for improving search precision; *Lee and Cai* (2011) advance interval distinguishment strategy and bee swarms cooperation mechanism for improving search precision; *El-Abd* (2010) introduces Diversity Strategy for polishing up global search ability; *Bao and Zeng* (2010) and *Ding and Feng* (2009) study

L. Zhang et al. (Eds.): AsiaSim 2016/SCS AutumnSim 2016, Part I, CCIS 643, pp. 25–36, 2016.
DOI: 10.1007/978-981-10-2663-8_3

selection strategy for enhancing global search ability; *Zhu and Kwong* (2010) and *Bi and Wang* (2011) study G-best strategy and elitist strategy for increasing optimization result; however, to the best of the author's knowledge, the problem of escaping from local optimum points has not been well discussed. Hence, we propose some improvement strategies as follows for A Novel Adaptive Cooperative Artificial Bee Colony Algorithm.

Firstly, to enhance search purpose for honey bee swarm, we divide bee swarm into core-bee swarm and vice-bee swarm and introduce adaptive narrow bee swarm search interval mechanism. Secondly, we meliorate search strategy of employed bees and onlookers and introduce fine scouts to increase convergence speed. Thirdly, a "pheromone-weak-proportion" selection strategy is given to improve bee swarm global search ability. Finally, in order to enhance the ability to escape from local optimum points, we propose a judge and escape principle when trapped in such situation.

The rest of this paper is organized as follows. In Sect. 2, we describe the standard ABC algorithm with flow chart at first, and then analyzes its disadvantages, followed by some particular improving measures of ACABC algorithm in Sect. 3. In Sect. 4, we provide details of 10 benchmark problems and parameter settings of ACABC and contrast algorithms. In Sect. 5, we give simulation results and analysis for comparing the performance of the above algorithms. In Sect. 6, we conclude the work of this paper and then brings forward some deeper directions for further study. In section (Acknowledgement), we give acknowledgments of this paper. At last, we provide references in section (References).

2 Artificial Bee Colony (ABC) Algorithm

2.1 Background of ABC

The ABC algorithm is a heuristic swarm intelligence algorithm, which abstracts nectar source optimizing mechanism from honey bees to solve optimization problems. The ABC algorithm divides honey bee swarm into employed bees, onlookers and scouts. In the process of solving optimization problems, ABC algorithms abstract solution and value of optimization problems to position and quality of nectar sources. Detailed introduction of optimization process about ABC algorithm is given as follows.

Each employed bee notes one nectar source and the number of onlookers is equal to that of employed bees. Employed bees exploit nectar sources and carry relative information to onlookers. Onlookers select good nectar sources through the information carried by employed bees via selection mechanism. Then all the employed bees and onlookers find new nectar sources through a neighborhood search from noted nectar source under a given probability. And then both employed bees and onlookers note better nectar source. If a nectar source noted by employed bees or onlookers is not improved through a given number called limit, the employed bee or onlooker is abandoned and replaced by a scout. Scouts search the global space to find new nectar source randomly. The steps mentioned above are repeated until the optimum is found. The flow chart of ABC algorithm is shown in Fig. 1.

2.2 The Drawbacks of ABC Algorithm

Researchers have reported that ABC algorithm has excellent representation in most of benchmark problems, while the ABC algorithm presents some probability when encountering a few complex optimization problems, which proved that the ABC algorithm is still left for improvement. Based on systematic analysis of the traditional ABC, its disadvantages can be listed as follows.

(1) Blindness in search, slowness in convergence speed. Both employed bees and onlookers present some randomness on the direction and range of search. Although such randomness strategy can improve global search capability of the algorithm to some extent, it makes some vain search attempts and slows down the convergence speed of the algorithm.

(2) Being easily trapped in local optimum points. Selection strategy of standard ABC algorithm adopts gambling selection, which is in fact a greedy selection mechanism and easily trapped in local optimum points. Though the following improving strategies start rectifying selection mechanism, the result is just decreasing the probability of being trapped in local optimum rather than avoiding that.

(3) It is difficult to escape when trapped in local optimum. The standard ABC algorithm adopts limit parameter to control abandoning fixed nectar sources. Only when the random nectar is better than the fixed one can the standard ABC algorithm escape from local optimum. Considering randomness presents in executing limit and selecting better nectar source after executing limit, the standard ABC algorithm presents some randomness when encountered with some complex multimodal optimization problems.

This paper focuses on the problems of the ABC algorithm mentioned above, and introduces the strategy of ACABC to develop reasonable rectifying.

3 Adaptive Cooperation Artificial Bee Colony (ACABC) Algorithm

In order to improve optimizing ability of ABC algorithm, we put forward several meliorating strategies aiming at the flaws mentioned in Sect. 2 as follows.

In order to improve optimizing ability of ABC algorithm, we did some exploration focus on reorganization and cooperation among whole honey bee swarm and search interval adaptive optimizing. Several Main meliorating strategies aiming at the flaws mentioned in Sect. 2 as follows.

(1) Reorganizing honey bee swarm

Firstly, we rearranged the whole honey bee swarm form better to worse based on nectars compare. Then, we divide the whole honey bee swarm into two parts from a certain honey bee, selected the better swarm as core-bee swarm and the worse swarm as vice-bee swarm inspired from *Van den Bergh and Engelbrecht* (2004).

Core-bee swarm is responsible of noting and rectifying superior global nectar sources, while vice-bee swarm is responsible of noting and rectifying inferior local nectar sources. In order to balance search speed and global search precision of ACABC algorithm, the number of core-bee swarm is 3-to-4 times of that of vice-bee swarm.

In other words, the whole honey bee can divided into advanced part and inferior part, the core-bee swarm is the advanced part of the whole honey bee, and the vice-bee swarm is the inferior part of the whole honey bee. Both core-bee swarm and vice-bee swarm can divided into employed bees and onlooker bees and scouts.

(2) pheromone-weak proportion selection strategy

To restrain the drawbacks of gambling selection results in trapping in local optimum easily, we put forward pheromone-weak proportion selection strategy. Firstly, we linearly translate nectar into "Pheromone". Then, we use non-linear logarithms decreasing the increase velocity to weak the proportion or influence of advanced pheromones. All in all, "pheromone-weak proportion" selection strategy depends on resets proportion to restrain the greedy of gambling selection to some extent. This selection strategy can be defined as (1).

$$\begin{cases} f(i) = \begin{cases} \dfrac{fit(i) - fit_{\min}}{fit_{\max} - fit_{\min}}, if \quad fit_{\max} \neq fit_{\min} \\ 1, \quad else \end{cases} \\ p(i) = \dfrac{\ln(1 + f(i))}{\sum\limits_{n=1}^{N} \ln(1 + f(n))} \end{cases} \tag{1}$$

(3) Upgrade strategy for employed bees

Upgrade strategy is the key element of overcoming blindness in search and increasing convergence speed. Core-bee swarm is the superior swarm noted advanced nectars, which selects nectars source among whole bee swarm randomly for upgrading to avoid trapping in local optimum triggered by self-cross as (2). Vice-bee swarm is the inferior swarm noted inferior nectars, which selects nectars source among superior nectars (e.g. the first quartered of the sequenced whole bee swarm) randomly for upgrading to guarantee search pertinence and convergence speed as (3).

$$V_{ij} = x_{ij} + (2 \times \text{rand} - 1) \times (x_{ij} - x_{kj}) \quad k = round(rand * popsize) \tag{2}$$

$$V'_{ij} = x'_{ij} + (2 \times \text{rand} - 1) \times (x'_{ij} - x_{k'j}) \quad k' = round(rand * popsize/4) \tag{3}$$

(4) Upgrade strategy for onlookers

Onlookers are an important means to discover superior nectars. In order to avoid trapping in local optimum triggered by employ bees' self-cross, we introduce another nectar produced randomly for upgrading to increase the ability of global searching show as (4). By the way, we consider decreasing the proportion of random nectar to guarantee convergence speed.

$$V_{ij} = x_{ij} + \frac{1}{2} \times (2 \times \text{rand} - 1) \times (x_{ij} - x_{kj}) + \tfrac{1}{2} \times (2 \times \text{rand} - 1) \times (x_{ij} - x'_{vj}) \quad k = round(popsize/4 + 0.5) \tag{4}$$

(5) Mutation strategy for scouts

The standard ABC algorithm use limit control scouts to find new nectar sources, which is very similar with mutation strategy of GA (genetic algorithm) algorithm. Given that the parameter testing of limit is very complicated, we choose mutation strategy to control scouts instead of limit. In order to find better nectar sources to replace abandoned ones, we select the best one from N random nectars as the new scout nectar as (5).

$$\begin{array}{l} \textit{for} \quad i = 1 : \textit{popsize} \\ \textit{if} \quad \textit{rand} < \textit{mr} \\ \text{Randomly generate N nectar soures} \\ \text{Selecting the best nectar source for scout} \\ \textit{end} \\ \textit{end} \end{array} \tag{5}$$

(6) Adaptive optimizing search interval

To improve search pertinence of vice-bee swarm and find high quality new nectar sources to escape from local minimum in the search later stage, we produced adaptive optimizing search interval mechanism as shown in (6).

Detailed steps as follows: firstly, we should find the center “a” of the whole bee swarm and regard it as geometry center of the new search interval. And then, we gradually narrow search span through exponential function to shrink search interval. Lastly, we should rectify the new interval and guarantee it within the initial interval.

$$\begin{cases} a = \dfrac{1}{N}\sum_{i=1}^{N} popsize(i) \quad (N < popsize) \\ lb' = a - \dfrac{e^{-count/stopnum} * (ub - lb)}{n} \\ ub' = a + \dfrac{e^{-count/stopnum} * (ub - lb)}{n} \\ lb'' = \begin{cases} lb' & lb' > lb \\ lb & lb' < lb \end{cases} \\ ub'' = \begin{cases} ub' & ub' < ub \\ ub & ub' > ub \end{cases} \end{cases} \tag{6}$$

(7) Breaking out local optimum

Given that the optimizing value would remain unchanged when trapped in local optimum, we introduce a counter to count the loops since the optimizing value keeps still. When the counter number exceeds given number noted by certain parameter, we reckon that the ACABC algorithm is trapped in local optimum. Abandon the inferior nectars (e.g. 3/4 to 4/5 inferior bees of the whole bee swarm) instead of random nectars produced in local interval as (6).

(8) Replacing invalid nectar source

It is inevitable for employed bees and onlookers to replace invalid nectar source which is created in the process of upgrading strategies. To ensure global optimizing capability of ACABC algorithm, core-bee randomly select nectar source in the global interval. To improve convergence speed of ACABC algorithm, vice-bee randomly select nectar source in the local interval as (6).

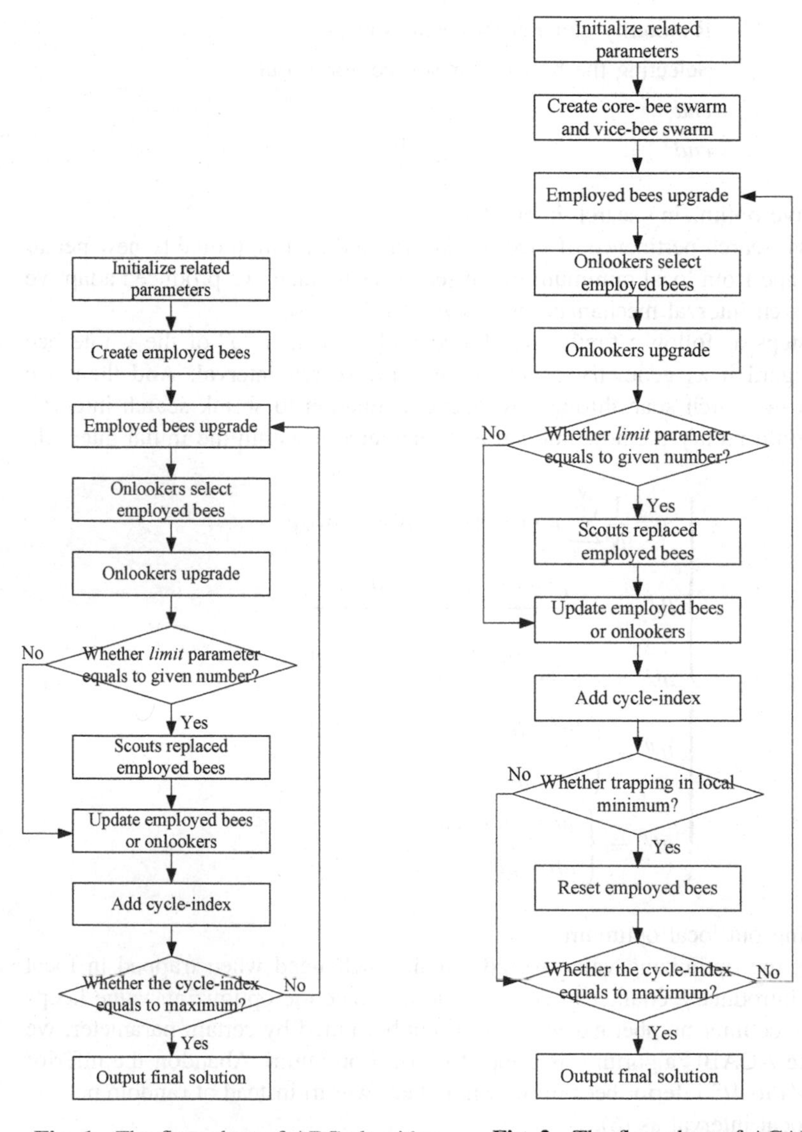

Fig. 1. The flow chart of ABC algorithm

Fig. 2. The flow chart of ACABC algorithm

The steps mentioned above are repeated until reach the termination criterion. The flow chart of ACABC algorithm is given in Fig. 2.

4 Benchmark Functions and Experiment Setting

(1) Benchmark functions

We Select 10 benchmark testing functions widely used in the realm of numerical function optimization. Table 1 shows the define definitions, ranges and optimizing solutions. Functions 1-to-4 are unimodal functions used to test optimizing precisions of different algorithms. Function 5 is a noise function that is difficult to find the optimal solution, which is used to test robustness of different algorithms. Functions 6-to-10 are multimodal functions which have several local optimal solutions and they are used to test the capability of searching global optimum and escaping from local optimums.

Table 1. Benchmark functions

Test function		Optimum solution	
Function expression	Interval	Solution	Minimum
$f_1(x) = \sum_{i=1}^{D} x_i^2$	$[-100, 100]^D$	$x_i = 0, i = 1, 2, \cdots$	0
$f_2(x) = \sum_{i=1}^{D} \lvert x_i \rvert + \prod_{i=1}^{D} \lvert x_i \rvert$	$[-100, 100]^D$	$x_i = 0, i = 1, 2, \cdots$	0
$f_3(x) = \sum_{i=1}^{D-1} 100(x_{i+1} - x_i^2)^2 + (x_i - 1)^2$	$[-100, 100]^D$	$x_i = 1, i = 1, 2, \cdots$	0
$f_4(x) = \sum_{i=1}^{D} (x_i - i)^2$	$[-100, 100]^D$	$x_i = i, i = 1, 2, \cdots$	0
$f_5(x) = \sum_{i=1}^{D} ix_i^4 + rand(0, 1)$	$[-100, 100]^D$	$x_i = 0, i = 1, 2, \cdots$	0
$f_6(x) = 0.5 + \frac{(sin\sqrt{x^2+y^2}) - 0.5}{[1 + 2(x^2+y^2)]^2}$	$[-100, 100]^D$	$x_i = 0, i = 1, 2, \cdots$	0
$f_7(x) = \sum_{i=1}^{D} x_i^2 - 10\cos 2\pi x_i + 10$	$[-100, 100]^D$	$x_i = 0, i = 1, 2, \cdots$	0
$f_8(x) = 20 + e - 20e^{-0.2\sqrt{\frac{\sum_{i=1}^{D} x_i^2}{D}}} - e^{\frac{\sum_{i=1}^{D} \cos 2\pi x_i}{D}}$	$[-100, 100]^D$	$x_i = 0, i = 1, 2, \cdots$	0
$f_9(x) = \frac{\sum_{i=1}^{D} x_i^2}{4000} - \prod_{i=1}^{D} \cos(\frac{x_i}{\sqrt{i}}) + 1$	$[-100, 100]^D$	$x_i = 0, i = 1, 2, \cdots$	0
$f_{10}(x) = \sum_{i=1}^{D} (-x_i) \cdot \sin(\sqrt{\lvert x_i \rvert})$	$[-500, 500]^D$	$x_i = 420.9687,$ $i = 1, 2, \cdots$	-420.9687*D

Table 2. Results for all algorithms to different benchmark problems

		PSO	DE	ABC	CABC
$f_1(x)$	Best	6.7701e−087	2.3557e−086	6.9376e−112	6.7107e−157
	Mean	3.3251e−084	3.6909e−085	9.6409e−095	1.4041e−114
	Worst	2.7265e−083	1.1476e−084	3.7424e−094	1.4032e−113
	Std.Dev	8.0265e−084	3.5695e−085	1.9040e−094	4.2093e−114
$f_2(x)$	Best	6.6629e−042	4.8843e−045	6.7231e−055	9.4819e−078
	Mean	1.8602e−040	9.0939e−045	6.2331e−049	4.4725e−053
	Worst	1.1855e−039	1.9836e−044	1.5819e−048	4.3813e−052
	Std.Dev	3.4314e−040	4.0995e-045	1.3710e−048	1.3116e−052
$f_3(x)$	Best	0	0.0041	0	0
	Mean	0	2.7714	0.3931	0
	Worst	0	11.0229	3.9308	0
	Std.Dev	0	4.0417	1.1792	0
$f_4(x)$	Best	0	0	0	0
	Mean	0	0	0	0
	Worst	0	0	0	0
	Std.Dev	0	0	0	0
$f_5(x)$	Best	0.1431	5.2971e−004	2.2202e-005	3.9646e−005
	Mean	0.5788	0.0052	1.4473e-004	3.3340e−004
	Worst	0.9757	0.0249	3.3334e-004	6.9024e−004
	Std.Dev	0.2991	0.0074	1.0357e-004	2.1779e−004
$f_6(x)$	Best	0	1.6532e−007	0	0
	Mean	0.1453	0.0485	0	0
	Worst	0.4844	0.4844	0	0
	Std.Dev	0.2220	0.1453	0	0
$f_7(x)$	Best	1.9899	0	0	0
	Mean	6.0692	0	1.2935	0
	Worst	10.9445	0	1.9899	0
	Std.Dev	3.2225	0	0.7771	0
$f_8(x)$	Best	8.8818e−016	8.8818e−016	8.8818e-016	8.8818e−016
	Mean	1.2434e−015	8.8818e−016	9.3291e-016	8.8818e−016
	Worst	2.6645e−015	8.8818e−016	2.6645e-015	8.8818e−016
	Std.Dev	1.7405e−015	0	1.0658e-015	0
$f_9(x)$	Best	0.0099	0	0.0074	0
	Mean	0.0389	0.0022	0.0179	0
	Worst	0.0813	0.0148	0.0435	0
	Std.Dev	0.0236	0.0047	0.0111	0
$f_{10}(x)$	Best	−2.0949e+003	−2.0949e+003	−2.0949e+003	−2.0949e+003
	Mean	−2.0357e+003	−2.0949e+003	−1.9370e+003	−2.0949e+003
	Worst	−1.9765e+003	−2.0949e+003	−1.7988e+003	−2.0949e+003
	Std.Dev	59.2000	0	82.3526	0

(2) Experiment setting

We choose PSO algorithm (*Yiqing et al.* (2007)), DE algorithm (*Storn* (2008)) and standard ABC algorithm (*Karaboga and Basturk* (2008)) as the comparison algorithms for ACABC algorithm. Maximum cycle number (*MCR*) is set to 1000, swarm size (*SS*) is set to 100. The rest parameters of PSO algorithm: $\omega = 0.7298$, $c_1 = c_2 = 1.4962$. The rest parameters of DE algorithm: $F = 0.5$, $CR = 0.1$. The rest parameters of ABC algorithm: $MR = 0.6$, $limit = 30$. The rest parameters of ACABC algorithm: $MR = 0.6$, mutation probability $mr = 0.05$, core-bee number is 80, vice-bee number is 20, *bearing-threshold* is 30. In the process of experiment, take the dimensionality of benchmark functions to 5, each algorithm to each problem implements 20 runs independently.

5 Experiment Results and Analysis

PSO, DE, ABC, ACABC algorithms are tested to optimize the 10 benchmark problems using the settings mentioned above. Table 2 lists the comparison results including the best values, the mean values, the worst values and standard deviations. Figures 3, 4, 5, 6, 7, 8, 9, 10, 11 and 12 show the convergence graphs of 10 benchmark problems.

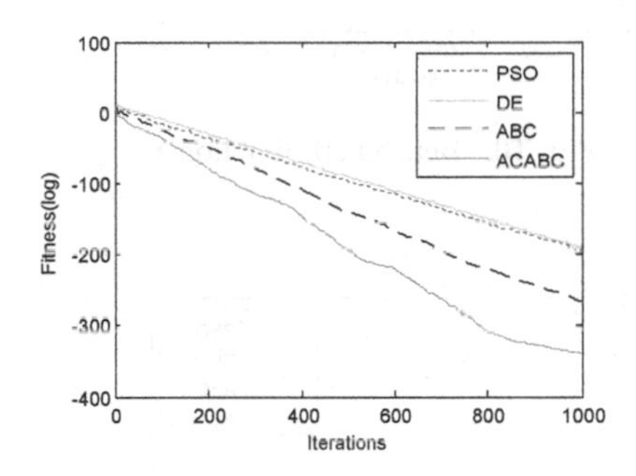

Fig. 3. Benchmark function 1

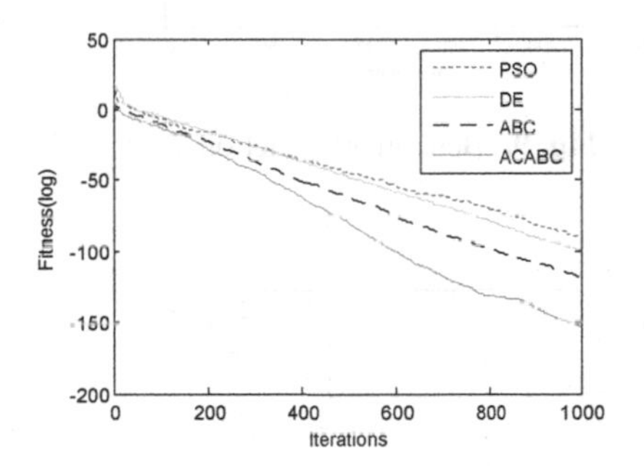

Fig. 4. Benchmark function 2

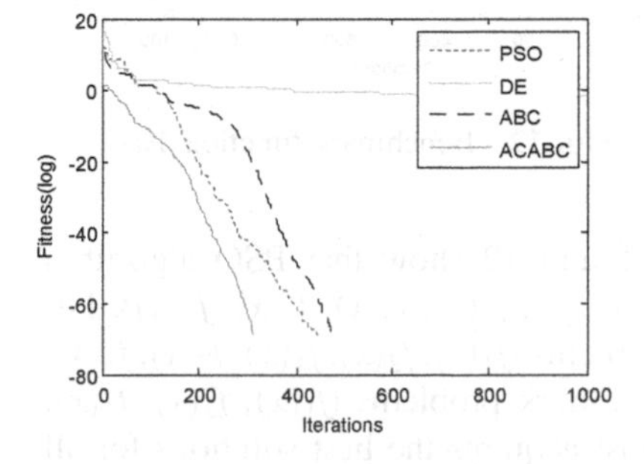

Fig. 5. Benchmark function 3

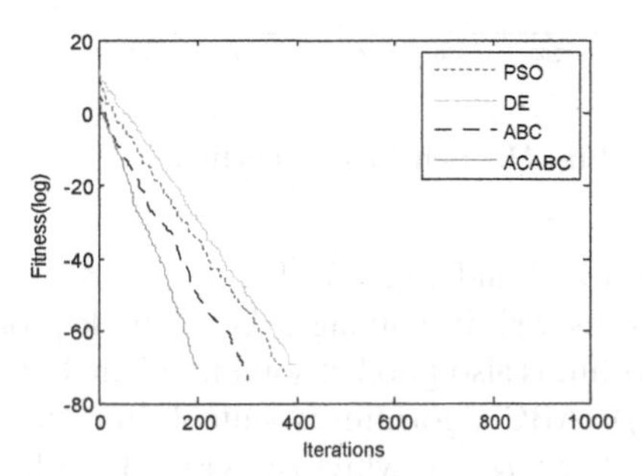

Fig. 6. Benchmark function 4

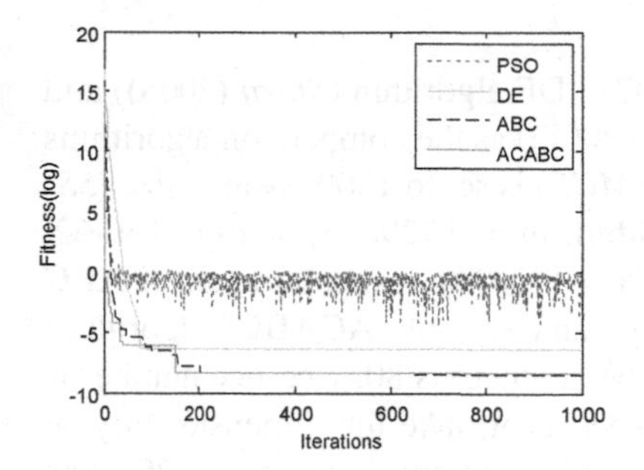

Fig. 7. Benchmark function 5

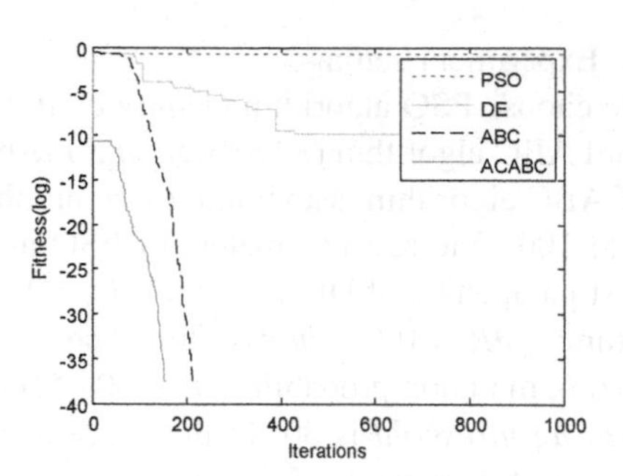

Fig. 8. Benchmark function 6

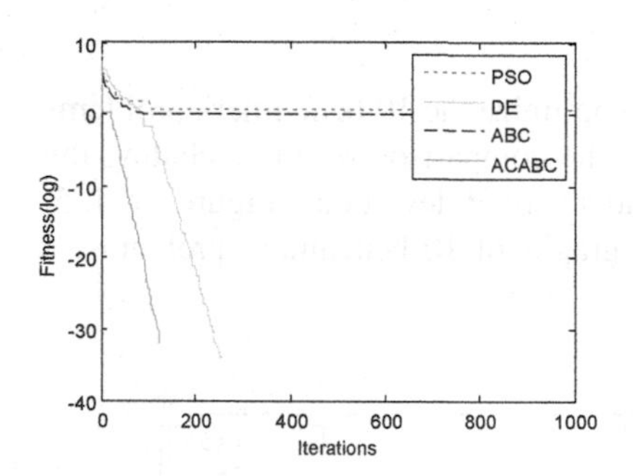

Fig. 9. Benchmark function 7

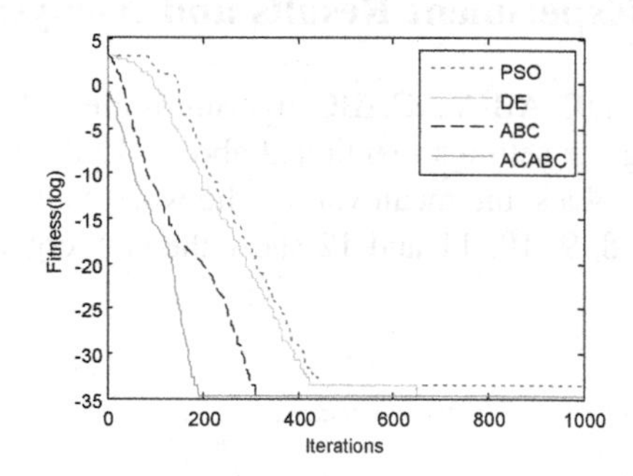

Fig. 10. Benchmark function 8

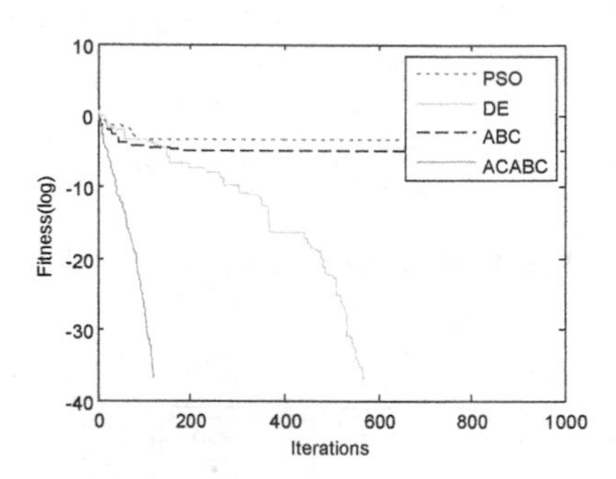

Fig. 11. Benchmark function 9

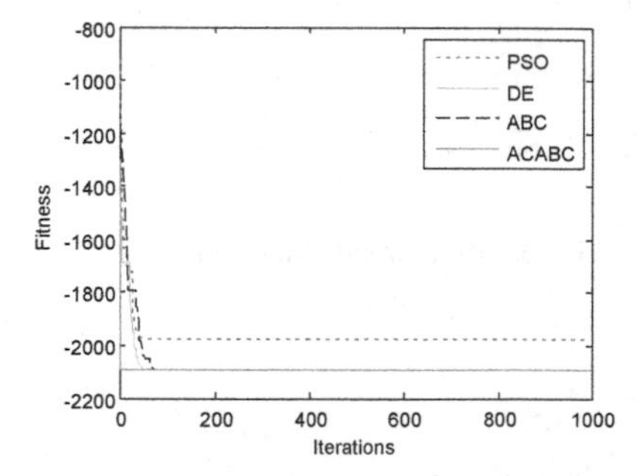

Fig. 12. Benchmark function 10

Table 2 and Figs. 3, 4, 5, 6, 7, 8, 9, 10, 11 and 12 show that PSO algorithm performs well in solving 5 benchmark problems ($f_1(x)$, $f_2(x)$, $f_3(x)$, $f_4(x)$, $f_8(x)$), DE algorithm is also good at solving 6 benchmark problems ($f_1(x), f_2(x), f_4(x), f_7(x), f_8(x)$, $f_{10}(x)$), ABC algorithm is suitable for the 6 benchmark problems ($f_1(x)$, $f_2(x)$, $f_4(x)$, $f_5(x)$, $f_6(x)$, $f_8(x)$), while ACABC algorithm almost acquires the best solutions for all benchmark problems. From the comparison above we can draw a conclusion that PSO algorithm, DE algorithm, ABC algorithm have some pertinence when encountered with different benchmark problems while ACABC algorithm has superior universality in solving that 10 benchmark problems.

There are 4 groups of benchmark problems on which all algorithm acquire ideal results ($f_1(x), f_2(x), f_4(x), f_8(x)$). As to problem 1 and 2 ($f_1(x), f_2(x)$), ACABC algorithm and ABC algorithm acquire better results than PSO algorithm and DE algorithm. As to problem 8 ($f_8(x)$), ACABC algorithm and DE algorithm acquire better results than PSO algorithm and ABC algorithm. As for problem 4 ($f_4(x)$), four algorithms acquire ideal results. Comparing both quantity and quality of the 5 benchmark problems, we can draw the following conclusion, both ABC algorithm and its modified algorithm have better performance than the other two algorithms.

ABC algorithm can't search or stably search the optimizing solutions on benchmark problems 3, 7, 8, 9, 10 ($f_3(x), f_7(x), f_8(x), f_9(x), f_{10}(x)$), which indicates that ABC algorithm is trapped in local optimum points and can't escape from them. While ACABC algorithm acquires optimizing solution on the same 5 benchmark problems, manifesting that ACABC has better ability in global search and local optimum escape.

The ACABC algorithm acquires sub optimums on benchmark problem 5 (very near to the best results) while receives best solutions in the rest of benchmark problems which means ACABC algorithm is more suitable than the other 3 algorithms in solving complex numerical optimizing problems.

In short, improved algorithm ACABC owns better precision, faster speed in convergence, better robustness in anti-interference, which has potential in solving more complex optimizing problems.

6 Conclusion and Further Works

Considering the disadvantages of the standard ABC algorithm, we introduce an ACABC algorithm based on ideas of bee-swarm distinguishing, local optimum judging principle and adaptive optimizing search interval. Using 10 kinds of test functions and simulation of comparing 4 different algorithms, it is shown that ACABC algorithm is better than other algorithms in solving complex optimizing problems within lower dimensions. The main innovation ideas mentioned at this paper about distinguishing swarm, judging local optimum and adjusting search interval can also be used to improve other swarm intelligence optimizing algorithms. In the future work, we will gradually raise the dimension of benchmark functions, make further research and improve ACABC algorithm to extend its ability of solving different dimension numerical optimizing problems.

Acknowledgements. The authors would like to acknowledge the constructive comments and suggestions of editors and referees.

References

Karaboga, D.: An idea based on honey bee swarm for numerical optimization, vol. 200. Technical report-tr06, Erciyes university, engineering faculty, computer engineering department (2005)

Karaboga, D., Basturk, B.: On the performance of artificial bee colony (ABC) algorithm. Applied Soft Comput. **8**(1), 687–697 (2008)

Karaboga, D., Ozturk, C.: A novel clustering approach: artificial bee colony (ABC) algorithm. Appl. Soft Comput. **11**(1), 652–657 (2011)

Karaboga, D., Basturk, B.: Artificial bee colony (ABC) optimization algorithm for solving constrained optimization problems. In: Melin, P., Castillo, O., Aguilar, L.T., Kacprzyk, J., Pedrycz, W. (eds.) IFSA 2007. LNCS (LNAI), vol. 4529, pp. 789–798. Springer, Heidelberg (2007)

Karaboga, D., Gorkemli, B., Ozturk, C., Karaboga, N.: A comprehensive survey: artificial bee colony (ABC) algorithm and applications. Artif. Intell. Rev. **42**(1), 21–57 (2014)

Ayan, K., Kılıç, U.: Artificial bee colony algorithm solution for optimal reactive power flow. Appl. Soft Comput. **12**(5), 1477–1482 (2012)

Lee, W.P., Cai, W.T.: A novel artificial bee colony algorithm with diversity strategy. In: 2011 Seventh International Conference on Natural Computation (ICNC), vol. 3, pp. 1441–1444. IEEE (2011)

El-Abd, M.: A cooperative approach to the artificial bee colony algorithm. In: 2010 IEEE Congress on Evolutionary Computation (CEC), pp. 1–5. IEEE (2010)

Bao, L., Zeng, J.H.: Self-adapting search space chaosartificial bee colony algorithm. Appl. Res. Comput. **27**(4), 1330–1334 (2010)

Ding, H., Feng, Q.: Artificial bee colony algorithm based on Boltzmann selection policy. Comput. Eng. Appl. **45**(31), 53–55 (2009)

Zhu, G., Kwong, S.: Gbest-guided artificial bee colony algorithm for numerical function optimization. Appl. Math. Comput. **217**(7), 3166–3173 (2010)

Bi, X.J., Wang, Y.J.: Artificial bee colony algorithm with fast convergence. Syst. Eng. Electron. **33**(12), 2755–2761 (2011)

Yiqing, L., Xigang, Y., Yongjian, L.: An improved PSO algorithm for solving non-convex NLP/MINLP problems with equality constraints. Comput. Chem. engineering **31**(3), 153–162 (2007)

Storn, R.: Differential evolution research–trends and open questions. In: Chakraborty, U.K. (ed.) Advances in Differential Evolution, pp. 1–31. Springer, Heidelberg (2008)

Van den Bergh, F., Engelbrecht, A.P.: A cooperative approach to particle swarm optimization. IEEE Trans. Evol. Comput. **8**(3), 225–239 (2004)

An Event-Thinking Development Framework for Reusable Model of Parallel and Discrete Event Simulation

Haibo Ma(✉), Yiping Yao, and Wenjie Tang

College of Information System and Management,
National University of Defense Technology, Changsha, China
mahaibo168@126.com, {ypyao,tangwenjie}@nudt.edu.cn

Abstract. Parallel and Discrete Event Simulation (PDES) is an important way to dispose problems of analysis simulation for large-scale complex simulation system. How to apace develop reusable model is a key issue to be solved in development of those reusable component model-based PDES applications. However, developing these models usually involves combined knowledge of both very specific domain and PDES, and models built by different domain instead of simulation experts usually have different structures, diversiform interfaces and bind with simulation platforms closely. As a result, they are difficult to be programed efficiently meeting new application requirements while reducing the development costs. To address the problem, this paper first proposed an event-thinking Framework for Developing Reusable component Model of PDES supporting model reuse as well as model calculation parallelization, which contains two parts: (1) four-type basic event structure; (2) object-oriented schedule mechanism. Based on this framework, then our three-phase development approach is elaborated helping domain experts program PDES reusable models fleetly. The case implementation of a naval vessel model indicates that the model using the framework has good reusability and is easy to be developed in PDES applications.

Keywords: Event-thinking framework · Model reuse · Simulation model development · Model calculation parallelization

1 Introduction

The continuous evolution of complex systems such as social system, ecosystem and war system has greatly influenced people's daily life and society. Modeling and simulation of complex system has become an important way to study the characteristics of these systems, which is regarded as "the third ways of understanding and transforming the world after theoretical research and experimental research" [1]. Complex simulation systems are usually composed of a large number of elements, in which there exists many objects, and the interactions between objects is complex [2]. Therefore, it is a motivated task to solve the problem of how to describe and model behavior and relationship of individuals.

Military simulation applications, especially those model-oriented component applications are representative simulation problems in Parallel and Discrete Event Simulation

L. Zhang et al. (Eds.): AsiaSim 2016/SCS AutumnSim 2016, Part I, CCIS 643, pp. 37–46, 2016.
DOI: 10.1007/978-981-10-2663-8_4

(PDES) [3], which contains many simulation models such as warship, plane, submariner and radar. Building application from existing reusable simulation models rather than from scratch is considered as a promising approach to improve the development efficiency, as well as to minimize engineering efforts and resource costs [4, 5]. Reuse-oriented models are developed to be reused across simulation platforms with little or even no modification. Consequently, one of the major concerns is how to develop PDES reusable component models. However, there are some challenges to implement such beneficial models. On the one hand, military simulation systems are usually completed by cooperation development of many research organizations, and the models are delivered as packaged executable code considering the security and protection of intellectual property rights. On the other hand, developing these domain models usually involves combination of both specific domain and PDES knowledge, and component models built by different domain experts instead of simulation experts usually have different structures, diversiform interfaces and bind with simulation platforms closely. As a result, they are difficult to be programed efficiently. Our laboratory research team had previously proposed "Sample, Entity and Model" Three-Level-Parallelization Support Framework for parallel acceleration of large-scale analytic simulation, in which providing "model calculation parallelization" mechanism to fully exploit the parallelism of the analytic simulation [6]. However, there is still non approach for developing reusable supporting "model calculation parallelization". Therefore, there is urgent need of appropriate approach for non-simulation domain experts to fleetly develop reusable component model supporting PDES as well as "model calculation parallelization".

Motivated to solve the mentioned issues, we firstly proposed an event-thinking framework for developing reusable component model of PDES supporting model reuse as well as model calculation parallelization, which contains two parts: (1) four-type basic event structure; (2) object-oriented schedule mechanism. Based on this framework, then our three-phase development approach is elaborated helping domain experts program PDES models fleetly. Section 2 introduces some related work. Section 3 presents our event-thinking model development framework and three-phase approach is elaborated in detail. Section 4 describes a case of naval vessel simulation model application. Finally, our conclusion will be made with an indication of the future work.

2 Related Work

2.1 Characteristics of PDES

Simulation models and events are the basic component of PDES modeling. The simulation entity constitutes the state of the whole simulation system. Each event is assigned a logical time stamp, which indicates that the discrete simulation time point for the event occurs. The simulation entity can schedule any future events in the event, and the simulation time is processed by the event. However, it also brings difficulties to the construction of the simulation model. In practical projects, simulation models are developed by different domain institutions independently, then the models are delivered to assemble the application by PDES developer. However, due to lack of PDES knowledge, the models developed cannot support parallel simulation well accelerating in the simulation platform. It is unrealistic for domain experts to learn to become a PDES expert and proficiency different simulation platform interfaces.

To deal with the above challenges, this paper designs a four-type event simulation model framework to specify simulation entities; also we design the interaction mechanism based on simulation object scheduling. Complex computation are executed in black box of simulation model while event schedule logic is organized by simulation object. The model provides service with interfaces for scheduling by the other models and achieving loose coupling. The simulation model framework and interaction mechanism reasonable make complex simulation models easy to be developed as a passive model that supports platform independent and has excellent reusability. Moreover, we considered about model calculation parallelization to further exploit the parallelism efficiency of model layer in the framework.

2.2 Existing Model Development Approaches

Various reusable model development approaches have been developed before. (1) Based on a specific modeling language in which people designs special simulation function module as primitive and control module as simulator, different models created with the same modeling language can be reused for the corresponding simulator. However, most of simulation modeling languages are usually related to domain knowledge closely and each research field involves some specific platforms, so that there is congenitally deficiency for them to create models that can be reused across multi-domain platforms, such as continue system simulation language ACSL [7], discrete event system simulation language GPSS [8], and multi-field physical simulation language MODELICA [8]. (2) Using a modeling specification which defines uniform internal structure, behavior constraint, and external interfaces for models, models will have good reusability if they do not bind with any platforms. However unfortunately, existing modeling specifications do not emphasize that model development should be independent with other simulation platforms. For example, ESA proposed a reusable simulation model description specification SMP (Simulation Model Portability Standards) [9]. It is not supported well to reuse the models on other runtime platforms, because the execution of a SMP model depends on services provided by the SMP simulation platform. The University of Arizona gives a thorough discussion of parallel discrete event system specification DEVS [10], which mostly focuses on the hierarchical structure of components. (3) Some models are based on simulation environment which provides runtime supporting platform for model running. The reusability of them is also limited. Taking HLA [11] for instance, each federate provides some interfaces which compiles with the HLA interface specification, and federates developed by different developers can communicate with each other via the runtime infrastructure using these interfaces. But these federates are hard to use in other simulation platforms, such as SUPE [12], POSE [13], and Charm++ [14], because these platforms cannot "identify" any HLA service interfaces. Fortunately, an efficient reusable simulation model development specification (RUM Specification) was previously proposed by our doctoral researcher to avoid the above problems for reusable models without binding with simulation platforms [15, 16], however, it does not provide any consideration for model calculation parallelization in Three-Level-Parallelization Support Framework.

As far as the authors know, there is not adapted approach to guide users to develop models to achieve such passive component models that reuse across platforms. Also, none of them have considered about "model calculation parallelization". To solving the issues, we propose the event-thinking model development framework.

3 The Event-Thinking Model Development Framework

As discussed in above sections, there is urgent need of appropriate approach for non-simulation domain experts to fleetly develop reusable component equipment model supporting PDES simulation applications as well as "model calculation parallelization". To address the problem, this paper proposed an event-thinking framework for developing reusable component model of PDES, supporting model reuse as well as model calculation parallelization. The framework first designs a model based on the four event types simulation model framework to specify discrete event modeling of simulation entities; on the other hand, it designs the interaction mechanism based on simulation object scheduling, in which event processing logic is encapsulated by simulation object. The simulation model framework and interaction mechanism make complex simulation models easy to be developed into a passive model that supports component-based extension, platform independent and has excellent reusability. Based on this framework, then our three-phase development approach is elaborated helping domain experts program PDES reusable models fleetly.

3.1 Four-Type Basic Event Structure

Event conception is the foundation of parallel and discrete modeling, which is defined to describe the system's behaviors when state transforms in the running time. It is a complicated work to organize the complex PDES system very articulately at the system design stage because event is the dynamic conception in the system. So in this paper, we extend the event from system layer to model layer, and use event to describe models' static computation module. When developing the simulation system, each event of model will be scheduled as a reasonable system event in dynamic running time, which is efficient to assemble the system. In the event-thinking Framework, a complex model are divided into independent function computation modules as model event, and they are classified to four type basic event.

1. Initial event (IE): initialize model initial data set when the model is created. The data set is parsed from scenario file. In the life circle of the model, the initial event is only scheduled once, and it has only input port without output port (Fig. 1a).

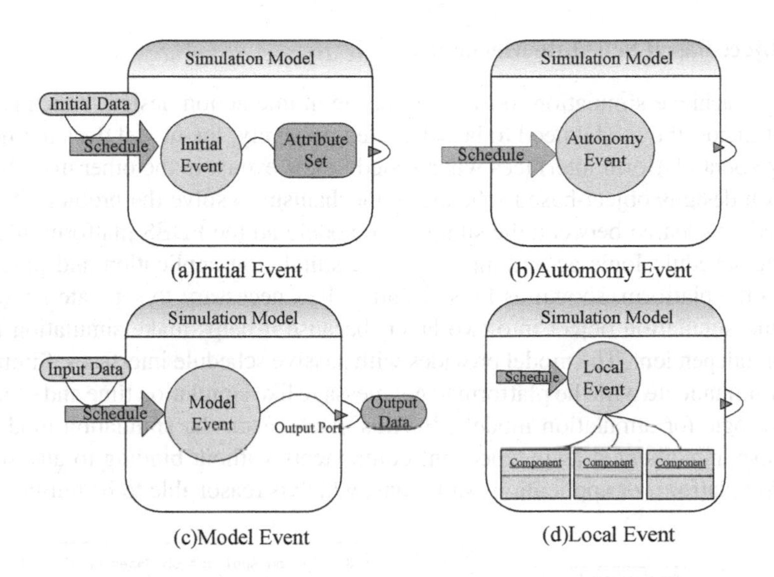

(a)Initial Event (b)Automomy Event

(c)Model Event (d)Local Event

Fig. 1. Four type basic event structure

2. Autonomy event (AE): change model inner state parameters. This kind of event has neither input port nor output port (Fig. 1b). Autonomy event is scheduled to change some state variables or control switch of the other computation modules, for example the events to turn on/off the detection radar.
3. Model event (ME): execute typical business computing logic usually with input data and output data port (Fig. 1c). Model event is similar with a simple atomistic module. The implement of the computation module mains a black box to the dispatcher, and the model event is only responsible for executing input data and return the output result. The model event should not directly schedule the other event inner the model. Whether the downstream event is triggered, depends on what the output data the dispatcher receives. The dispatcher will judgment condition statement and decide what event to be scheduled next. This design is very important, because which guarantee that the model is a passive scheduled and reasonable a reusable model.
   Model events consist of the main components of a complex simulation model, each one is independent and loose coupling. On the one hand, a single model event encapsulates an independent function model; on the other hand, a number of model events consist of the simulation model's complete function set, and more model events can be extensible flexibly according to new requirement. At the same time, if some special computation modules logic contain huge computing cost, it should be implemented with multi-thread way, and the model event will be identified to supporting model calculation parallelization for parallel acceleration.
4. Local event (LE): encapsulate some auxiliary computing functions like mathematic functions (Fig. 1d).

The framework completely satisfy demand of PDES model development, helping domain experts to develop PDES models without any PDES knowledge.

3.2 Object-Based Schedule Mechanism

The key to achieve simulation loose coupling lie in interaction design, which has two essential factor: the model need to be scheduled passively; the model does not need to consider about platform interfaces when schedule the events in the other models. This subsection designs object-based scheduling mechanism to solve the problem. Simulation object is situated between the simulation model and the PDES platform, it encapsulate the schedule logic according to specific simulation application and plugin the model to the platform, shown as Figs. 2 and 3. It is necessary to separate simulation model and simulation object into two layer, because it helps make simulation model platform independent. The model provides with passive schedule interfaces. Simulation object communicate with the platform to get message like simulation time and organizes schedule logic for simulation models. By this mechanism, the simulation models are completely implemented as independent components without binding to any specific simulation platform or applications situations, which is reasonable to be reused.

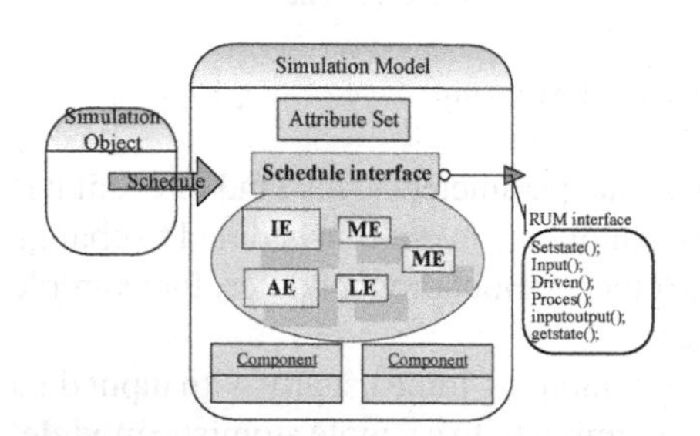

Fig. 2. Object-based schedule mechanism

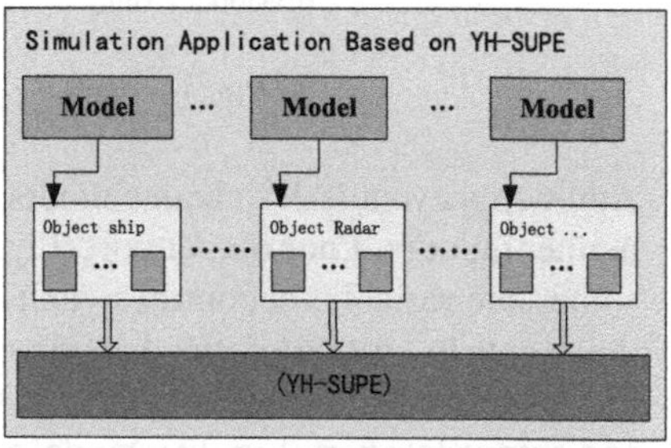

Fig. 3. Simulation model-object hierarchy

Object-based Schedule Mechanism also stipulates that model event in the same simulation model should not communicate directly with each other but through the simulation object. With organic synthesis of four type basic event structure, domain experts can easily develop the PDES model.

3.3 Three-Phase Model Developing Approach

The event-thinking framework strike to provide experts with domain a convenient way to develop reusable PDES models when cooperate develop reusable component model-based military PDES applications. The three-Phase development approach will be present as follows to guide domain expert using the framework.

- Phase1: quickly design the simulation model development framework. Domain experts classify computation modules of the simulation model according to the four type basic event. All functional modules should be designed into the following function form: initialEvent_XXX(), selfEvent_XXX(), modelEvent_XXX(), localEvent_XXX(). For modules that contains complex computing algorithm, specially, the designer should identify as supporting model calculation parallelization.

- Phase2: Implement each type event functions. This usually involves domain knowledge. Unit test should be fully carried, which is very important to control the quality of the model. Also, the modules identified as supporting model calculation parallelization should be implemented through multi-threaded as much as possible.
- Phase3: Implement the models via RUM Specification. RUM Specification provides with six standard service interfaces to achieve their independence and improve their reusability. The six interfaces is shown in Fig. 4.

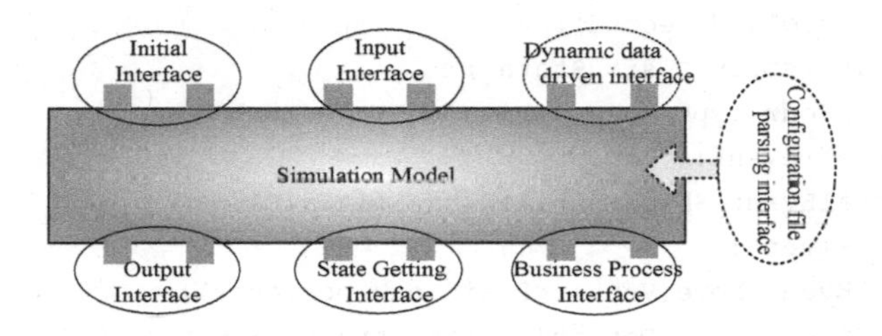

Fig. 4. RUM Specification interface structure

4 Application

Naval vessel models are very common in military simulation application. We take the warship model to test and verify the event-thinking framework and its reusable model development approach.

4.1 Warship Reusable Model Implementation

We analyzed naval vessel through a CMPA (Capacity, Mission, Process, and Action) description method to describe its functional modules implemented as "model event". These computational modules are classified into four type events: initial event, autonomy event, model-event and local-event (Table 1).

- Step1: build the four-type event model framework
- Step2: Implement the above event computational modules, for example, Fig. 5 shows the example of the modelEvent_RadarDetect (TargetStruct target).
- Step3: Encapsulate the warship model via RUM Specification with six standard service interfaces, supporting to assemble different simulation applications.

4.2 Application in SUPE

Air-defense and antimissile of naval vessel is a typical scene. It usually contains three kinds of simulation entities: naval vessel, battle plane and missile. In this case, we developed these three reusable model by the event-thinking framework, and built a case application running on SUPE platform. The procedure of air-defense and antimissile of

Table 1. Reusable naval vessel model code structure

```
Class CShipModel{
public: //RUM Specification Interface
int setstate(string& simuState);
int input(TargetStruct& target);
int driven(JammerStruct& jammer);
int process(double dSimuTime);
int output(bool& detected);
int getstate(string& simuState);
private: //Four Type Event-thinking Framework
//(1)initial-event:
void initialEvent_Ship(InitialData initialData);
//(2)model-event:
void modelEvent_Move(Vector<Position> positons);
void modelEvent_RadarDetect( TargetStruct target);
void modelEvent_MissileFire( AttackTarget target);
void modelEvent_ArtilleryFire(Vector<Target>tags);
void modelEvent_WeaponAssign(Vector<TargetTyep>);
void modelEvent_ElectronicJam(Vector<Weapontype>);
//(3)self-event:
void selfEvent_ChangeStateParams();
void selfEvent_TurnOn_OffRadar();
//(4)Local-event:
void localEvent_GeographicTransform(GeodataType);}
```

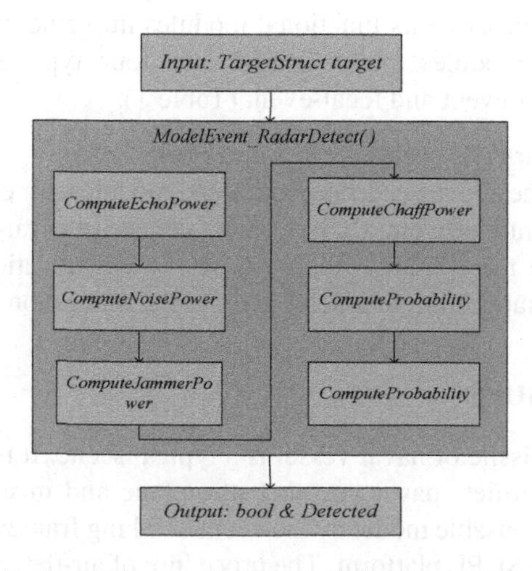

Fig. 5. Radar computation module execution flow

naval vessel is that, firstly, the battle plane opens its radar to search targets. Once it finds an enemy naval vessel, the battle plane will launch a guided missile to attack it; secondly, the guided missile flies to the enemy naval vessel under the control, and in the end of flight, it will opens its radar to locate the target by itself; finally, the naval vessel detects the guided missile using its radar and then uses jammer and interceptor missile for anti-missile and air defense. Each simulation model maps an object which maintains simulation time, model states and schedule the modules events in its model by service interfaces. The events will be executed according to logical time stamp in the system event table. As shown in Fig. 6, simulation models are reusable model resources. They are passively scheduled independently without bind with simulation platforms interfaces. Furthermore, SUPE platform provides model calculation parallelization mechanism, thus those complex computation modules identified as supporting calculation parallelization will be detected and accelerated by multi-core parallel.

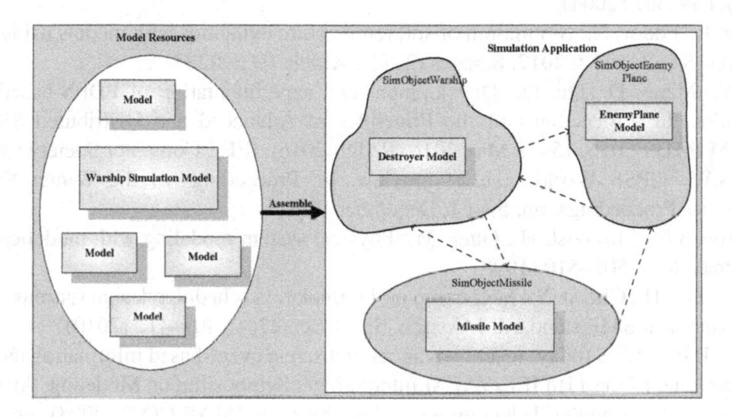

Fig. 6. Air-defense and antimissile of naval vessel

5 Conclusion

Model reusability is important for PDES, not only for minimizing engineering efforts and resource costs, but also for improving the reliability. Current model development methods face several obstacles developing these reusable models, such as diversiform interfaces, coupled tightly, bound together with simulation platforms and without consideration about supporting model computation parallelization. With main contribution, this paper proposed the event-thinking reusable model development framework that supports model reuse as well as model calculation parallelization to solve the above obstacles. Based on the framework, the three-phase development approach is elaborated helping domain expert program PDES reusable models fleetly. The case implementation of a naval vessel indicates that the model using the framework has good reusability and is easy to be developed. As for our future work, we plan to implement more reusable models for PDES applications as library resource.

Acknowledgments. We appreciate the support from Research Fund for Doctoral Program of High Education of China (No.20124307110017) and Research Project of State Key Laboratory of High Performance Computing of National University of Defense Technology (No. 201303-05).

References

1. Li, B.H., Chai, X.D., Li, T.: Research on high performance simulation technology of complex system. J. China Acad. Electron. Inf. Technol. **7**(3), 221–229 (2012)
2. Tang, W., Yao, Y., Zhu, F.: A GPU-based discrete event simulation kernel. Simul. Trans. Soc. Model. Simul. Int. **89**(11), 1335–1354 (2013)
3. Fujimoto, R.M.: Parallel and Distributed Simulation Systems. Wiley Inc., New York (2000)
4. Hofmann, D.M.A.: Challenges of model interoperation in military simulations. Simulation **80**(12), 659–667 (2004)
5. Sandor, R., Fodor, N.: Simulation of soil temperature dynamics with models using different concepts. Sci. World J. **2012**, 8 pages (2012). Article ID 590287
6. Yao, Y., Meng, D., Qu, Q.: Development and experimentation of PDES-based analytic simulation. In: Proceedings of the Principles of Advanced and Distributed Simulation, SIGSIM-PADS 2016, 15–18 May 2016 (PADS-2016). IEEE Computer Society (2016)
7. Cox, S.W.: GPSS World: a brief preview. In: Proceedings of the Winter Simulation Conference Proceedings, pp. 59–61, December 1991
8. Mattsson, S.E., Elmqvist, H., Otter, M.: Physical system modeling with modelica. Control Eng. Pract. **6**(4), 501–510 (1998)
9. Koo, C., Lee, H., Cheon, Y.: SMI compatible simulation scheduler design for reuse of model complying with SMP standard. J. Astron. Space Sci. **27**(4), 407–412 (2010)
10. Zeigler, B.P.: DEVS today: recent advances in discrete event-based information technology. In: Processing of the 11th IEEE/ACM International Symposium on Modeling, Analysis and Simulation of Computer Telecommunications Systems (MAS-COTS 2003), pp. 148–161 (2003)
11. SISC: IEEE Standard for Modeling and Simulation High Level Architecture (HLA)-Framework and Rules (2000)
12. Yao, Y.P., Zhang, Y.X.: Solution for analytic simulation based on parallel processing. J. Syst. Simul. **20**(24), 6617–6621 (2008)
13. Wilimarth, T.L., Kalé, L.V.: POSE: getting over grainsize in parallel discrete event simulation. In: Proceedings of the International Conference on Parallel Processing (ICPP 2004), pp. 12–19, August 2004
14. Bisset, K.R., Aji, A.M., Bohm, E., et al.: Simulating the spread of infectious disease over large realistic social networks using charm++. In: Proceedings of the IEEE 26th International Parallel and Distributed Processing Symposium WorkShop, pp. 507–518 (2012)
15. Zhu, F., Yao, Y.P., Chen, H.L., Yao, F.: Reusable component model development approach for parallel and distributed simulation. Sci. World J. (2014)
16. Zhu, F., Yao, Y.P., Tang, W.J., Chen, D.: A high performance framework for modeling and simulation of large-scale complex system. Future Gener. Comput. Syst. **2015**(51), 132–141 (2015)

A Kind of Attitude Algorithm for High Dynamic IMU

Lianpeng Li(✉) and Zhong Su

Beijing Key Laboratory of High Dynamic Navigation Technology, University of Beijing Information Science and Technology, Beijing, China
1543280889@qq.com, sz@bistu.edu.cn

Abstract. High dynamic inertial measurement unit (IMU) can measure the attitude information of the high dynamic environment. At the most severe working condition of IMU, affecting by the cone effect, the general attitude algorithm is difficult to accurately calculate the carrier's attitude information, which is named Coning motion. In order to realize the resolving of attitude coning motion vector in high dynamic environment fastly, improving the accuracy of resolving IMU, the design of high dynamic IMU resolving method is particularly important. Combining with the traditional attitude algorithm, on account of the characteristics of the object movement under high dynamic environment, presents a high dynamic IMU attitude resolving method. On the basis of the conventional algorithm, improving coning motion resolving method, all of them consist a combination of dynamic rotation vector method. The simulation results show that compared with the conventional method of rotating vector, the proposed high dynamic IMU can get more accurate result.

Keywords: IMU · High dynamic environment · Rotation vector method · Slewing method

1 Introduction

With the rapid development of high dynamic navigation technology, more and more attention has been paid to the research and application of IMU and high dynamic attitude solution algorithm. IMU has been widely used in aviation, aerospace, navigation, land navigation and geodetic surveying, drilling and open tunnel, geological exploration, robotics, vehicles, medical equipment and many other fields [1, 2]. On the basis of that, the demand of people for IMU in high dynamic environment and solving the attitude of the carrier is increasing day by day.

The high dynamic environment, especially for the bullet, means high speed, high rotation, high overload and so on. High spin carrier must have angular vibration and linear vibration, which will cause attitude solution of coning error, sculling error,

Fund Project: National Natural Science Foundation (61261160497); Beijing city science and technology project (Z131100005323009); the quality of graduate education in Engineering (5111524102).

L. Zhang et al. (Eds.): AsiaSim 2016/SCS AutumnSim 2016, Part I, CCIS 643, pp. 47–56, 2016.
DOI: 10.1007/978-981-10-2663-8_5

scrolling error and many errors. As for high dynamic IMU calculating the attitude angle, coning motion is the most severe environmental conditions and can will induce serious drift about the math platform. That is to say, if we can accurately calculate the attitude of carrier under the cone motion condition, we will be able to accurately calculate the attitude of the rest environments. At present, the accuracy of the conventional attitude algorithm is not high, it is difficult to meet the requirements of the application environment for precision, which limits the application of high spin carrier in national defense, industry and civil fields. So, based on the conventional attitude algorithm, it's very important and necessary to propose a method that improving the attitude calculation accuracy of the high dynamic IMU.

For this, predecessors have made unremitting efforts (Fig. 1).

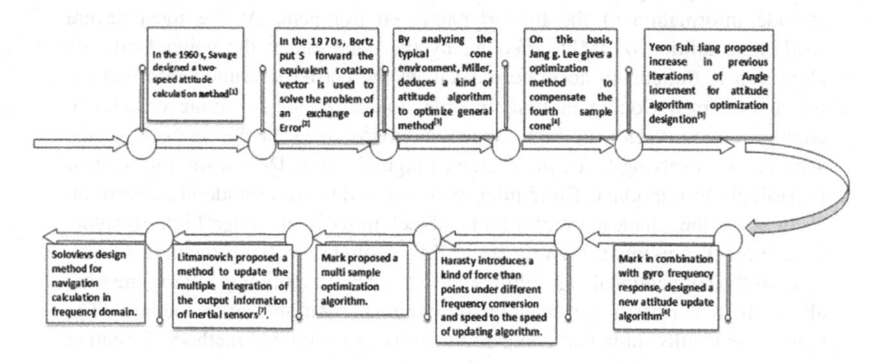

Fig. 1. Development of attitude solving method for high dynamic moving carrie

Based on the previous work [8], this paper improves the rotation vector method, the four element method and the Slewing method. Furthermore puts forward a kind of combined dynamic rotation vector method. The algorithm introduces the integral of rolling angle from slewing method, and derives the improved the slewing method with rotation vector method solution for counting yaw angle and pitching angle. The simulation results show that the proposed algorithm can significantly reduce the error of the cone motion attitude calculation and improve the accuracy of the cone motion calculation attitude.

2 The Research of Algorithm

2.1 Coning Motion

Coning motion is a complex angular motion method, which can be expressed by the rate of cone angle and cone angle. Carrier with high-speed rotation under high dynamic environment must exist coning motion [9]. Conical coordinates system and body coordinate system can be determined by three angles, precession angle δ_1, nutation angle δ_2, rotation angle δ_3. The three angles called cone attitude.

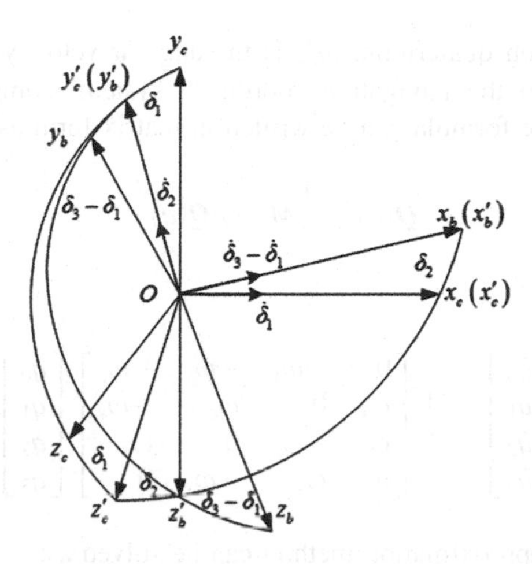

Fig. 2. Coning motion introduction

Due to the existence of the cone effect, the high dynamic IMU must take the error caused by the cone effect into account in the calculation of the carrier's high rotation.

2.2 Conventional Methods

The rotation vector method is a geometric method of describing harmonic vibration [10]. By using angular increment to calculate the equivalent rotation vector, the optimal algorithm of the cone motion environment can be obtained, which is particularly suitable for use in high dynamic environments.

The quaternion [11] is a mathematical concept which was established in 1843, but only in the last forty years, it has been applied in the rigid body kinematics. The quaternion is made up of 1 real unit 1 and 3 imaginary units $\vec{i}, \vec{j}, \vec{k}$, making up 4 solid elements contain super complex. If the $\vec{i}, \vec{j}, \vec{k}$ are regarded as the base vectors, then the quaternion can be divided into two parts: scalar and vector. It is expressed as:

$$Q = q_0 + q_1\vec{i} + q_2\vec{j} + q_3\vec{k} = q_0 + \vec{q} \tag{1}$$

And q_0 is a scalar, $\vec{q}$ is a vector.

Vector can be regarded as a special case of quaternion when $q_0 = 0$. For the determination of the base, $q_r(r = 1, 2, 3)$ is the projection of the vector $\vec{q}$. Then the quaternion Q can also defined as a set of four scalar and scalar array $Q^{(0)}$ is expressed as:

$$Q^{(0)} = (q_0\ q_1\ q_2\ q_3)^T \tag{2}$$

The form of the quaternion differential equation is:

$$\dot{Q}(t) = \frac{1}{2} Q(t).\omega_{nb}^{bq} \tag{3}$$

And $Q(t)$ is rotation quaternion. ω_{nb}^{bq} is the angular velocity of bullet coordinate system that relative to the navigation coordinate system' component in the bullet coordinate system. The formula can be written in matrix form as:

$$\dot{Q}(q) = \frac{1}{2} M^{*}(\omega) Q(q) \tag{4}$$

or:

$$\begin{bmatrix} \dot{q}_0 \\ \dot{q}_1 \\ \dot{q}_2 \\ \dot{q}_3 \end{bmatrix} = \frac{1}{2} \begin{bmatrix} 0 & -\omega_x & -\omega_y & -\omega_z \\ \omega_x & 0 & \omega_z & -\omega_y \\ \omega_y & -\omega_z & 0 & \omega_x \\ \omega_z & \omega_y & -\omega_x & 0 \end{bmatrix} \begin{bmatrix} q_0 \\ q_1 \\ q_2 \\ q_3 \end{bmatrix} \tag{5}$$

Using the Picard approximation method can be solved as:

$$Q(t) = e^{\frac{1}{2}\int M^{*}(\omega)dt} Q(t_o) \tag{6}$$

The rotation vector method is also based on the idea of the vector rotation of the rigid body. What different from the quaternion is that in the attitude update cycle, the quaternion method calculates the attitude four elements, and the rotation vector method calculates the attitude change four elements, then calculates the attitude four elements. Equivalent rotation vector method is divided into two steps: ① Calculating rotation vector. The rotation vector describes the change of the carrier's attitude.② Updating the quaternion. Quaternion describes the carrier's real-time position vector relative to the reference frame. For algorithm essentially, attitude algorithm method of quaternion pirkanmaa algorithm is a essentially list sample rotation vector method.

2.3 Combined Dynamic Rotation Vector Method

Classical Cone Motion Model. As shown in the figure below, a vector do slightly angular vibration around its equilibrium position which namely coning motion [12] (Fig. 3).

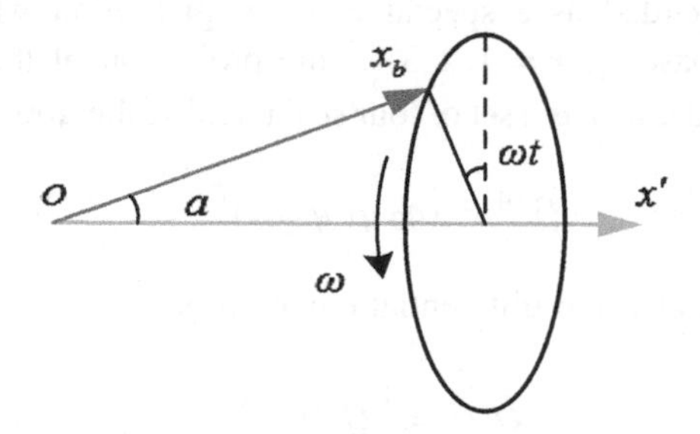

Fig. 3. Coning motion

Then there are the following mathematical formula:

$$\phi = \begin{bmatrix} 0 \\ a\cos\omega t \\ a\sin\omega t \end{bmatrix}, \dot{\phi} = \begin{bmatrix} 0 \\ -a\omega\sin\omega t \\ a\omega\cos\omega t \end{bmatrix} \tag{7}$$

$$\omega = \dot{\phi} - \frac{1-\cos|\phi|}{|\phi|^2}\phi \times \dot{\phi} + \frac{1}{|\phi|^2}\left(1 - \frac{\sin|\phi|}{|\phi|}\right)\phi \times (\phi \times \dot{\phi}) \tag{8}$$

In the case of the cone motion shown in Fig. 2, referring to the coordinate system, the angular velocity of the vector is:

$$\omega = \begin{bmatrix} (\cos a - 1)\omega \\ -\omega\sin a\sin\omega t \\ \omega\sin a\cos\omega t \end{bmatrix} \tag{9}$$

ϕ is the angle increment, a is half cone angle, ω represents cone motion frequency. In the classical theory of cone motion model, most people generally believe that the cycle of cone motion attitude drift is caused by swing process, not rotation [13].

Combined Dynamic Rotation Vector Method. Based on the Slewing method and the rotation vector method, the combined dynamic rotation vector method is designed and optimized. First, based on the rotation vector method, the information of angular velocity is calculated by the slewing method [], getting the roll Angle integral [15]. Put it into the angular velocity from gyroscope, then we obtain the accurate pitch angle and yaw angle. And then we get accurate carrier attitude. The flow chart is as follows (Fig. 4):

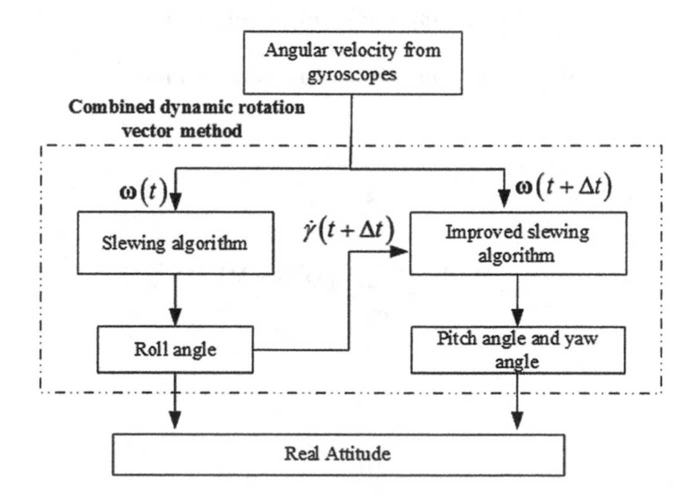

Fig. 4. Combined dynamic rotation vector method

3 Conical Attitude Algorithm

3.1 Slewing Algorithm

Assume that the angular velocity condition of the body coordinate system, from the time t to $t + \Delta t$ moment, can be expressed as:

$$\boldsymbol{\omega}^b(t + \Delta t) = \boldsymbol{C}(\boldsymbol{\alpha} \cdot \Delta t)\boldsymbol{\omega}^b(t) \tag{10}$$

In the formula, the α is the directional rotation speed, which is equivalent to the cone motion frequency ω (Fig. 5).

From the above relations, a rotating coordinate system can be established:

$$\boldsymbol{X}^s = \mathbf{C}(-\boldsymbol{\alpha} \cdot \Delta t)\boldsymbol{X}^b \tag{11}$$

The angular velocity of a rotating system relative to the inertial system:

$$\boldsymbol{\omega}_s = \boldsymbol{\omega}(t) + \boldsymbol{\alpha} \tag{12}$$

The conversion formula of the rotation system to the inertial system is:

$$\boldsymbol{X}^e = \boldsymbol{C}(\boldsymbol{\omega}_s \Delta t)\boldsymbol{X}^s \tag{13}$$

The conversion matrix of the machine system to the inertial system is:

$$\boldsymbol{C}_{\mathrm{b}}^{\mathrm{e}} = \boldsymbol{C}(\boldsymbol{\omega}(t) + \boldsymbol{\alpha} \cdot \Delta t)\boldsymbol{C}(-\boldsymbol{\alpha} \cdot \Delta t) \tag{14}$$

Define three successive angular velocity: ω_1, ω_2, ω_3 (Fig. 6).

$$\boldsymbol{W}_1 = [\omega_1 \quad \omega_1 \times \omega_2 \quad \omega_1 \times (\omega_1 \times \omega_2)] \tag{15}$$

$$\boldsymbol{W}_2 = [\omega_2 \quad \omega_2 \times \omega_3 \quad \omega_2 \times (\omega_2 \times \omega_3)] \tag{16}$$

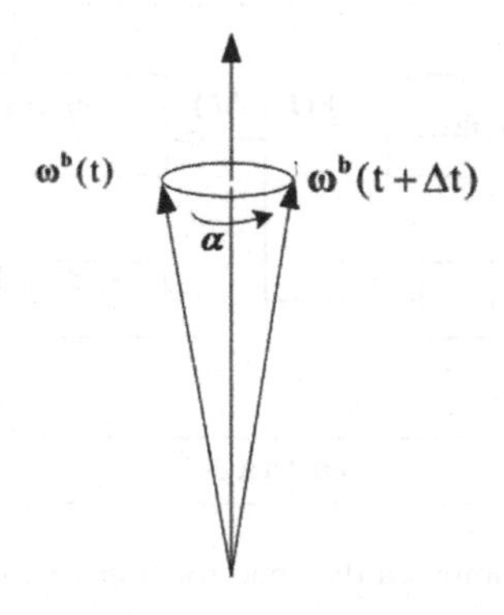

Fig. 5. Rotating coordinate system

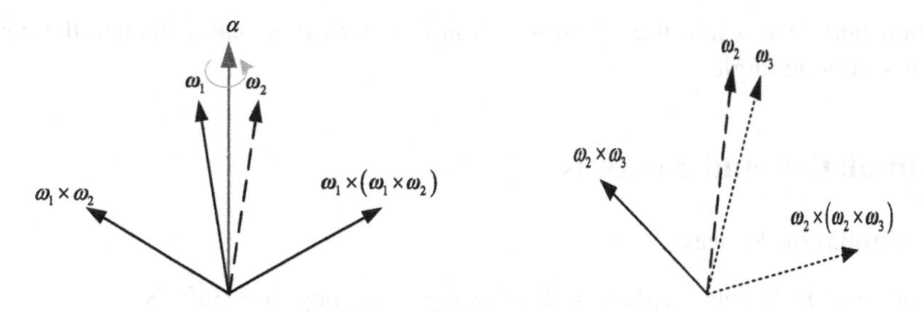

Fig. 6. Vector relation diagram

For $\boldsymbol{C}(\boldsymbol{\alpha}\cdot\Delta t)=\boldsymbol{W}_2\boldsymbol{W}_1^{-1}$, then the α is available:

$$\alpha=\frac{\arcsin \boldsymbol{C}(2,1)}{\Delta t} \tag{17}$$

Carrier's attitude information is:

$$\vartheta=\arcsin \boldsymbol{C}_{\mathbf{b}}^{\mathbf{e}}(2,1),\ \ \psi=-\arctan\frac{\boldsymbol{C}_{\mathbf{b}}^{\mathbf{e}}(3,1)}{\boldsymbol{C}_{\mathbf{b}}^{\mathbf{e}}(1,1)},\ \ \gamma=-\arctan\frac{\boldsymbol{C}_{\mathbf{b}}^{\mathbf{e}}(2,3)}{\boldsymbol{C}_{\mathbf{b}}^{\mathbf{e}}(2,2)} \tag{18}$$

3.2 Composite Cone Motion Calculating Method

Considering the rotation, introduce the rotating system's angular velocity that relative to the inertial system. It's:

$$\boldsymbol{\omega}=\boldsymbol{C}(\dot{\gamma}\cdot t)^{\mathbf{b}}\boldsymbol{\omega}(t)+\boldsymbol{\alpha}-\boldsymbol{\gamma} \tag{19}$$

The conversion matrix of the body system to the inertial system is:

$$\boldsymbol{C}_{\mathbf{b}}^{\mathbf{e}}=\boldsymbol{C}\big(\boldsymbol{C}(\dot{\gamma}\cdot t)^{\mathbf{b}}\boldsymbol{\omega}(t)\cdot\Delta t+(\boldsymbol{\alpha}-\boldsymbol{\gamma})\cdot\Delta t\big)\boldsymbol{C}(-\boldsymbol{\alpha}\cdot\Delta t) \tag{20}$$

In an update cycle:

$$\dot{\gamma}=\frac{\gamma(t)-\gamma(t-\Delta t)}{\Delta t} \tag{21}$$

$$C(\rho)=W_2W_1^{-1},\ C(\boldsymbol{\alpha}\cdot\Delta t)=W_2W_1^{-1} \tag{22}$$

The attitude angle of the carrier can be obtained by calculating the α.

$$\rho=\arcsin\left[\frac{\boldsymbol{C}(2,1)+\boldsymbol{C}(1,2)}{2}\right],\ \ \rho=(\alpha-\dot{\gamma})\Delta t,\alpha=\frac{\rho}{\Delta t}+\dot{\gamma} \tag{23}$$

Then introduce α into the C_b^e substitution matrix formula can calculate the coning motion's attitude angle.

4 Simulation and Analysis

4.1 Simulation Process

Simulation 1: Half cone angle $\alpha = 2°$; Coning frequency $\omega = 360°/s$.

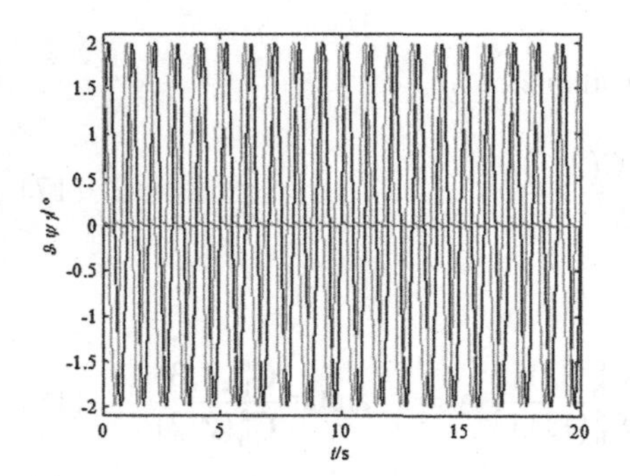

Fig. 7. The results of the Picard algorithm (Color figure online)

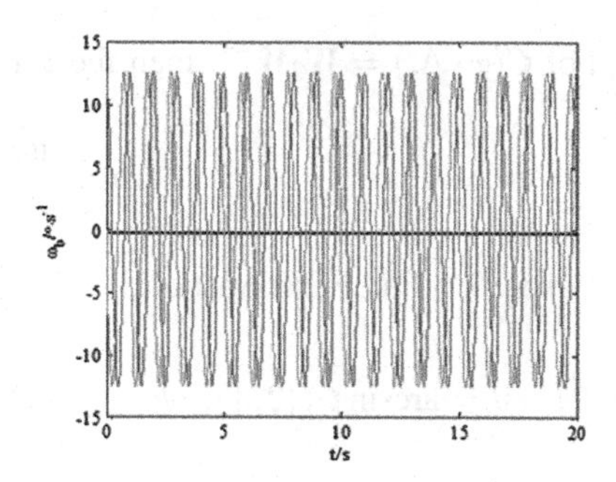

Fig. 8. Slewing algorithm (Color figure online)

In Fig. 7, green line is the roll angle. The red and blue line are pitching angle and yaw angle respectively; In Fig. 8 blue line is the roll angle. The red and green line are pitching angle and yaw angle respectively.

Simulation 2: Half cone angle $\alpha = 2°$; Coning frequency $\omega = 360°/s$; rotation 180°/s.

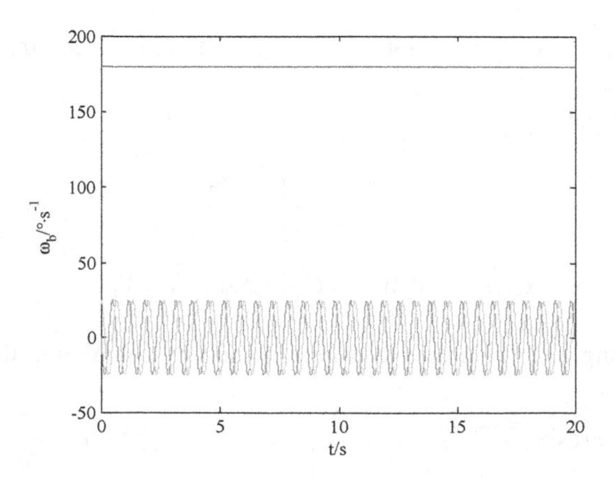

Fig. 9. Slewing algorithm

The blue line is the roll angle. The red and green line are pitching angle and yaw angle respectively (Fig. 10).

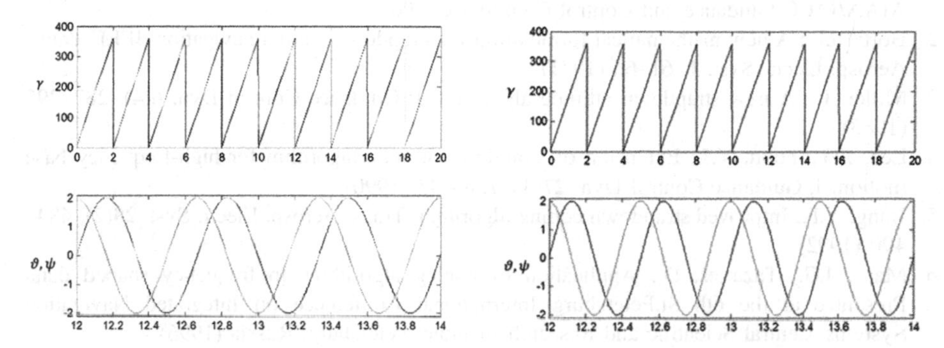

Fig. 10. Slewing algorithm (Color figure online)

Fig. 11. Improved Slewing algorithm (Color figure online)

4.2 Simulation Analysis

From Figs. 7 and 8, the roll Angle γ was calculated by pirkanmaa method, which can eliminate the error of the rotation Angle through the Slewing method. In Fig. 9, with the addition of the self rotation angle, the pitch angle ψ and the yaw angle ϑ calculated by the Slewing method exist errors. From Figs. 10 and 11 the rolling angle γ of the combined dynamic rotation vector method is derived from the Slewing method, which can obtain the rolling angle γ accurately. The improved Slewing method can obtain the calibration pitch angle ψ and yaw angle ϑ. They together constitute the combination of dynamic rotation vector method.

5 Conclusion

In this paper, a method for calculating the attitude angle of the carrier in the cone motion environment by high dynamic IMU is proposed. On the basis of improving the rotation vector method, the four element method and the Slewing method, we get a new combined dynamic rotation vector method.

The simulation results show that compared with the traditional rotation vector method, the combination of the dynamic rotation vector method can not only get the roll angle accurately, but also can obtain the pitch angle and yaw angle accurately. But it still does not solve the attitude's calculation in high rotation speed environment and the error model is not established, which is the author for further study.

References

1. Savage, P.G.: A new second-order solution for strapped-down attitude computation. In: AIAA/JACC Guidance and Control Conference (1966)
2. Bortz, J.E.: A new mathematical formulation for strapdown inertial navigation. IEEE Trans. Aerosp. Electr. Syst. **1**, 61–66 (1971)
3. Miller, R.: A new strapdown attitude algorithm. J. Guidance Control Dyn. **6**(4), 287–291 (1983)
4. Lee, J.G., Yoon, Y.J.: Extension of strapdown attitude algorithm for high-frequency base motion. J. Guidance Control Dyn. **27**(4), 738–743 (1990)
5. Jiang, Y.F.: Improved strapdown coning algorithm. Trans. Aerosp. Electr. Syst. **28**(2), 484–490 (1992)
6. Mark, J.G., Tazartes, D.: Application of coning algorithms to frequency shaped data. Presented at the 6th St.Petersburg International Conference on Integrated Navigation Systems, Central Scientific and Research Institute, Petersburg, Russia (1996)
7. Gusinsky, V.Z., Lesyuchevsky, V.M., Litmanovich, Y.A., Musoff, H., Schmidt, G.T.: New procedure for deriving optimized strapdown attitude algorithm. Control Dyn. **20**(4), 673–680 (1997)
8. Savage, P.G.: Strapdown inertial navigation integration algorithm design, part: 2: velocity and position algorithms. J. Guidance Control Dyn. **21**(2), 208–221 (1998)
9. Lai, J., Lv, P., Liu, J., et al.: Analysis of coning motion caused by turntable's vibration in rotation inertial navigation system. In: 2012 IEEE/ION Position Location and Navigation Symposium (PLANS), pp. 869–876. IEEE (2012)
10. Ahn, H.S., Won, C.H.: Fast alignment using rotation vector and adaptive Kalman filter. IEEE Trans. Aerosp. Electron. Syst. **42**(1), 70–83 (2006)
11. Wie, B., Barba, P.M.: Quaternion feedback for spacecraft large angle maneuvers. J. Guidance Control Dyn. **8**(3), 360–365 (1985)
12. Mao, X.R., Yang, S.X., Xu, Y.: Coning motion stability of wrap around fin rockets. Sci. China Ser. E: Technol. Sci. **50**(3), 343–350 (2007)
13. Hao, Y., Xiong, Z., Gao, W., et al.: Study of strapdown inertial navigation integration algorithms. In: Proceedings of 2004 International Conference on Intelligent Mechatronics and Automation, pp. 751–754. IEEE (2004)
14. Patera, R.P.: Attitude propagation for a slewing angular rate vector. J. Guidance Control Dyn. (2010)
15. Patera, R.P.: Attitude propagation for a slewing angular rate vector with time varying slew rate. In: Proceedings of the AAS/AIAA Astrodynamics Specialist Conference (ASTRODYNAMICS 2011), pp. 2529–2546 (2011)

Controller Design for the Electrical Load Simulator Based on H∞ Control Theory

Ma Jie, Liu Xinyue(✉), and Zhang Shuqi

Control and Simulation Center,
Harbin Institute of Technology, Harbin 150001, China
xinyue1993.hu@163.com

Abstract. This paper took the electrical load simulator system as research object, applying H∞ control theory to the controller design for the system. After building the system model, the generalized plant was derived and the standard H∞ problem was proposed. The selecting basis of weighting function was illustrated in detail and by virtue of the Matlab robust toolbox and LMI method, the H∞ controller was synthesized. According to the simulation results, the feasibility on torque servo and surplus force suppression was verified. Finally, the advantages of H∞ control theory on improving the load simulator system performance were analyzed by comparison with classical control theory.

Keywords: Electrical load simulator · Controller design · H∞ control theory · LMI

1 Introduction

Electrical load simulator is a key half hardware-in-loop simulation equipment of aircraft flying control system, which calculates the actual load on missile rudder in the flight according to the movement of it during the experiment and applies it to the rudder-surface, making the rudder work in the same stress state as it does in the flight [1].

When referring to the control problems, whether it can track the input signal accurately is an important standard to evaluate the performance of the system. Meanwhile, the electrical load simulator does passive movement with the rudder, thus the angle position output of the rudder causes interference on it in the form of surplus torque [2]. So, special attention is given to the problem of surplus torque suppression for a long time.

The classical control theory studies feedback system according to the concept of amplitude margin and phase margin for the SISO case, satisfying the desired performance specification [3]. However, when taking the influence of the movement of the rudder on the load simulator into account, it can be regarded as a MIMO system. A single controller can't realize both accurate tracking and effective surplus torque suppression at the same

This research work is partially supported by Specialized Research Fund for the Doctoral Program of Higher Education (20122302110017) and the National Natural Science Foundation of China (Grant No. 61333001, 61427809)

L. Zhang et al. (Eds.): AsiaSim 2016/SCS AutumnSim 2016, Part I, CCIS 643, pp. 57–66, 2016.
DOI: 10.1007/978-981-10-2663-8_6

time. Thus, a feed-forward unit is often set to compensate the surplus torque and the outer-loop controller to track the input signal accurately.

On the other hand, H∞ control is a kind of theory which yields the controller through optimization of the infinite norm of certain performance index [4]. H∞ control theory provides an effective method of frequency domain controller design for MIMO systems [5]. Since many problems can be transferred to H∞ standard control problem, it is generally applied to practical engineering. This paper applied H∞ control theory to the electrical load simulator system. By analyzing the desired performance specification, the weighting function was determined in the process of generalized plant setting and the optimized controller was synthesized by virtue of matlab robust toolbox based on LMI. Finally, the system performance was analyzed by simulation and the advantages of H∞ control on torque servo and surplus torque suppression were derived by comparing with the controller based on the classical theory.

2 System Composition

Electrical load simulator is such an equipment which utilizes servo motor as the transition element and converts electric energy to mechanical energy of the motor rotator. It loads on the rudder angle position servo system, accomplishing the simulation of load torque by controlling the loading motor [6].

The system composition of load simulator system is showed in Fig. 1. It is composed of loading system, load-bearing system, torque sensor and coupling equipment [7]. The load-bearing system is the rudder angle position servo system, which is the handling unit of missile flying controlling. The loading system is the load simulator, which is a torque servo system, simulating the load on the aircraft in the process of flying. The two sections are connected by the torque sensor and the coupling equipment. During the dynamic loading experiments, the rudder does active movement, while the load simulator does passive movement with the rudder and does torque loading at the same time [8].

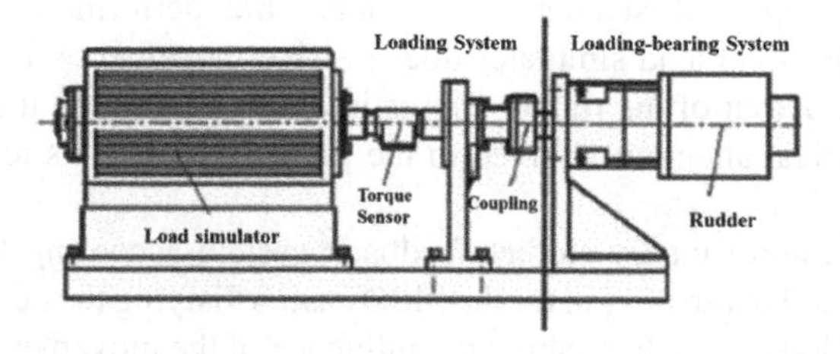

Fig. 1. System composition of electrical load simulator

3 Mathematical Model of the Electrical Load Simulator

Choosing permanent magnet synchronous motor (PMSM) as loading motor and torque sensor as the output measuring element, utilizing current of vector control strategy and taking the effect of the reaction torque on the loading system into account, the integrated mathematical model of the electrical load simulator system is showed in Fig. 2.

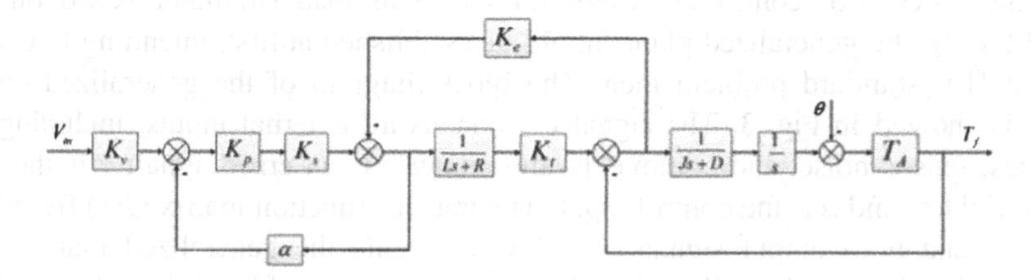

Fig. 2. Mathematical model of the electrical load simulator

Where R is the stator resistance, L is the inductance of d-axis and q-axis, V_{in} is the input voltage instruction, J is the load rotating inertia converted to the motor shaft, D is the friction coefficient, K_t is the torque coefficient, K_e is the back emf coefficient, K_p is the current control gain, K_s is the inverter-fed circuit equivalent gain, α is the current feedback coefficient, K_v is the proportion coefficient from the given input to i_q, T_A is the system connecting stiffness, θ is the rudder angle position output, T_f is the output torque.

Let $R' = R + K_pK_s\alpha$, the open-loop transfer function of the system is:

$$\begin{aligned} T_f = & \frac{T_AK_tK_pK_sK_v}{JLs^3 + (JR' + LD)s^2 + (R'D + K_eK_t + T_AL)s + T_AR'} V_{in} \\ & - \frac{\left[JLs^3 + \left(JR' + LD\right)s^2 + \left(R'D + K_eK_t\right)s\right]T_A}{JLs^3 + (JR' + LD)s^2 + (R'D + K_eK_t + T_AL)s + T_AR'} \theta \end{aligned} \tag{1}$$

Let

$$P(s) = \frac{T_AK_tK_pK_sK_v}{JLs^3 + (JR' + LD)s^2 + (R'D + K_eK_t + T_AL)s + T_AR'} \tag{2}$$

$$L(s) = \frac{\left[JLs^3 + \left(JR' + LD\right)s^2 + \left(R'D + K_eK_t\right)s\right]T_A}{JLs^3 + (JR' + LD)s^2 + (R'D + K_eK_t + T_AL)s + T_AR'} \tag{3}$$

Thus, the transfer function can be denoted by:

$$T_f = P(s)V_{in} - L(s)\theta. \tag{4}$$

4 H∞ Standard Problem of Electrical Load Simulator

Note that H∞ control theory receives more and more attention from the researchers in recent years. This kind of controller design method can describe the desired performance specification of the control systems in frequency domain range and achieve the requirements of frequency integer through filtering of the sensitive frequency band, ensuring the realization of the controlling purpose [9].

In the process of controller design for electrical load simulator based on H∞ control theory, the generalized plant should be established at first, intending to convert it into a H∞ standard problem then. The block diagram of the generalized control system is showed in Fig. 3. The signal ω contains all external inputs, including disturbances, sensor noise, and commands; the output z is an error signal; y is the measured variables; and u is the control input. The transfer function matrix $G(s)$ from input signals ω and u to output signals z and y represents the generalized plant, which contains what is usually called the plant in a control problem plus all weighting functions, and $K(s)$ is the controller.

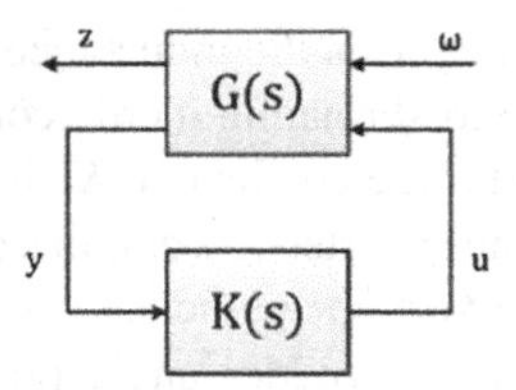

Fig. 3. Block diagram of generalized control system

The equation of relationship between input and output is described as:

$$\begin{bmatrix} z \\ y \end{bmatrix} = G(s)\begin{bmatrix} \omega \\ u \end{bmatrix} \tag{5}$$

Suppose that the state space realization of the generalized control system is:

$$G(s) = \left[\begin{array}{c|c} A & B \\ \hline C & D \end{array}\right] = \left[\begin{array}{c|cc} A & B_1 & B_2 \\ \hline C_1 & D_{11} & D_{12} \\ C_2 & D_{21} & D_{22} \end{array}\right] \tag{6}$$

$$u = K(s)y \tag{7}$$

The closed-loop transfer function from ω to z is denoted by:

$$T_{z\omega}(s) = G_{11} + G_{12}K(I - G_{22}K)^{-1}G_{21} \tag{8}$$

The aim of standard H∞ control problem is to design a controller $K(s)$, letting the closed-loop system as showed in Fig. 3 internal stable, and minimizing the H∞ form of the transfer function $T_{z\omega}(s)$ from ω to z [10].

It is hoped that accurate tracking of referred input signal as well as the surplus torque suppression caused by the movement of the redder can be achieved. According to the former analysis, the control structure of the closed-loop system is showed in Fig. 4.

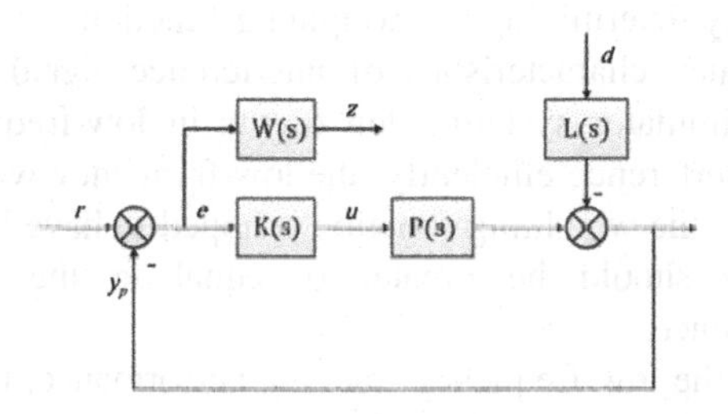

Fig. 4. Control structure of closed-loop system

Regard the referred input signal *r* and the interference signal *d* as the outer input signal ω of the generalized plant; system tracking error *e* as the measuring output signal y; design the weighting function $W(s)$ which represent the performance index and then regard the output of it as control output signal z; input signal of H∞ controller as $u = K(s)y$, leading to output feedback of H∞ control. It can be concluded that at this time the electrical load simulator system can be expressed in the form of standard H ∞ problem.

Analyze the above control structure of the load simulator, the relationship among each system signal can be denoted as follows:

$$\begin{aligned} z &= W(s)e = W(s)(r + L(s)d - P(s)u) \\ y &= e = r + L(s)d - P(s)u \end{aligned} \tag{9}$$

The equation of relationship between input and output is described as:

$$\begin{bmatrix} z \\ y \end{bmatrix} = \begin{bmatrix} W(s) & L(s)W(s) & -W(s)P(s) \\ 1 & L(s) & -P(s) \end{bmatrix} \begin{bmatrix} \begin{pmatrix} r \\ d \end{pmatrix} \\ u \end{bmatrix} \tag{10}$$

$$u = K(s)y \tag{11}$$

Thus, after settling the detailed expression of the weighting function, the state space realization of the generalized plant can be finally derived by programming with Matlab.

5 Selection of Weighting Function

Whether the effect of H∞ controller is good or bad depends on the selection of weighting function in a great degree. Different weighting functions should be designed to meet different control requirements [11].

Focus on the electrical load simulator generalized plant established before, in order to realize accurate tracking of referred input and surplus torque suppression, the frequency characteristics of both referred input signal and interference signal should be considered when finally determining the weighting function.

Firstly, the frequency characteristics of interference signal are considered. The interference of load simulator system often occurs in low-frequency range [12]. In order to inhabit the interference efficiently, the low-frequency weighting value should be as large as it can. So the weighting function is hoped to have low pass property and its turning frequency should be greater or equal to the frequency width of low-frequency interference.

When considering the low-frequency tracking performance, under ideal condition, $W(j\omega) \to \infty$ is supposed when $\omega = 0$ to obtain higher static precision [13]. In general case, enough small tracking error just needs to be guaranteed within certain frequency range. Thus, $W(j\omega)$ is designed to be flat within this range; Moreover, since there is only requirements of stability but no tracking performance within high-frequency range, when the frequency is larger than certain value, $W(j\omega)$ can also be flat and the ratio of numerator and denominator of $W(j\omega)$ should be less than 1.

At the same time, when taking the order of the H∞ controller into consideration, since it is supposed to be the same as the order of the generalized plant, when the weighting function is optimized, the order of it should be as low as possible [14].

Comprehensive considering the requirement on static loading precision, double ten bandwidth index and interference elimination rate, the expression of weighting function is denoted as follows:

$$W(s) = \frac{0.88s + 628}{s + 1.26}. \quad (12)$$

6 Design of H∞ Controller Based on LMI Method

The common methods of yielding a H∞ controller are the solution based on Ricatti equation and the solution based on LMI. In order to compute the Ricatti equation, some assumptions are proposed. However, the assumptions are usually not tenable in actual designing problems, this can be solved by some means but the design index may change at the same time [15].

The main idea of the solution based on LMI is to transfer the H∞ norm index into matrix inequality according to bounded real lemma and obtain the condition of existing of solution by the LMI method and solve it [16]. Only the stabilizability and measurability of closed-loop system needed to be internal stability should be guaranteed. The relationship between the number of controlling inputs and evaluation outputs as well as that between the number of interferences and measuring outputs are arbitrary [17]. So the solution based on LMI is employed in this paper according to above analysis. After obtaining the state space realization of load simulator generalized plant, derive the expression of the H∞ controller by virtue of related statements in matlab robust toolbox.

7 Simulation Results and Analysis

7.1 Synthesis of the H∞ Controller

Firstly, derive the state space realization of generalized plant by means of matlab under the situation that system parameters and weighting function are already known, the result is as follows:

$$\begin{gathered} A = \begin{bmatrix} -697 & -419 & -709 & 166 \\ -173 & 193 & 482 & -88 \\ 456 & -1451 & -218 & 283 \\ -58 & 144 & -35 & -23 \end{bmatrix} \\ B_1 = \begin{bmatrix} -0.06 & -0.06 \\ -0.80 & -0.80 \\ -0.51 & -0.51 \\ 4.42 & 4.42 \end{bmatrix} \quad B_2 = \begin{bmatrix} -52.8 \\ -49.2 \\ -108.2 \\ 22.0 \end{bmatrix} \\ C_1 = \begin{bmatrix} 4.5 & -17.8 & -21.8 & -136.2 \end{bmatrix} \\ C_2 = \begin{bmatrix} 3.7 & 4.1 & -3.8 & -0.4 \end{bmatrix} \\ D_{11} = \begin{bmatrix} 0.88 & 0.88 \end{bmatrix} \quad D_{12} = 0 \\ D_{21} = \begin{bmatrix} 1 & 1 \end{bmatrix} \quad D_{22} = 0 \end{gathered} \tag{13}$$

Then, by virtue of matlab robust toolbox, utilize the 'hinflmi' statement and then synthesize the H∞ controller based on LMI, the result is as follows:

$$K(s) = \frac{4.8 \times 10^8 s^3 + 3.6 \times 10^{11} s^2 + 4.7 \times 10^{14} s + 3.2 \times 10^{17}}{s^4 + 8.6 \times 10^5 s^3 + 3.4 \times 10^2 s^2 + 6.5 \times 10^{14} s + 7.6 \times 10^{14}}. \tag{14}$$

7.2 Analysis of System Performance

Apply the H∞ controller to electrical load simulator system and analyze the closed-loop system performance:

(1) When the interference signal is 0, referred input signal is unit-step signal, the step response result is showed in Fig. 5. It can be concluded that the static loading precision is 0.078%, and overshoot is 0.

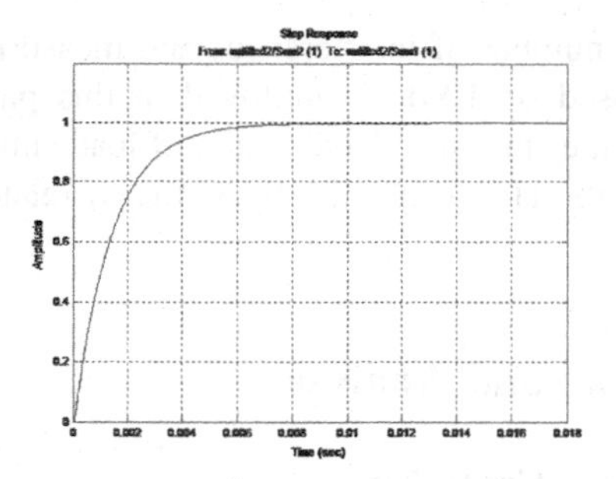

Fig. 5. Unit step response

(2) When the referred input signal is 0, the amplitude of the interference signal is 15° and the frequencies of the interference are 2, 5, 8, 10 Hz separately, surplus torque suppression result is showed in Table 1.

Table 1. Surplus torque suppression results

Frequency (Hz)	Surplus torque without the controller (N/m)	Surplus torque with the controller (N/m)
2	0.95	0.01
5	2.95	0.12
8	5.74	0.43
10	8.57	0.78

It can be concluded that in different frequencies of the interference, the rates of interference elimination are all above 90 %, the effect on surplus torque suppression is obvious.

(3) Closed-loop frequency characteristic is showed in Fig. 6.

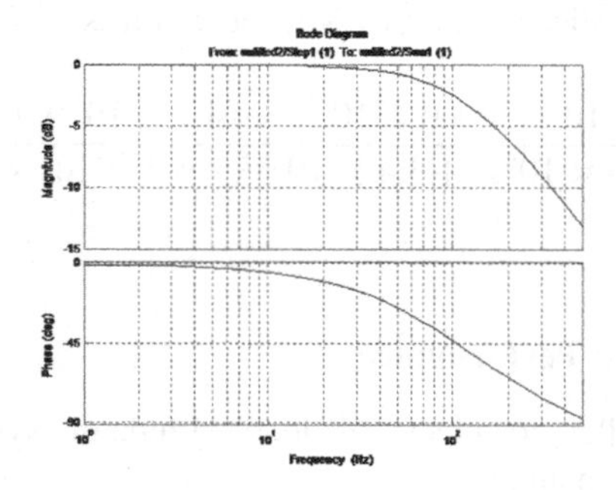

Fig. 6. Closed-loop frequency characteristics

When the frequency is 10 Hz, the change in amplitude is 0.049 dB and the change in phase angle is 5.29°, perfectly meeting the requirement of double ten index.

7.3 Comparison with Classical Control Theory

When applying classical control theory to the control of electrical load simulator, considering that the requirements mainly focus on the torque servo performance in frequency domain, cascade lead-lag compensation is employed to derive outer-loop controller. Meanwhile, feed-forward compensation controller is employed to solve the problem of surplus torque. Analyze and compare these two kinds of control systems, we can draw the conclusion that the controller based on H∞ control theory has following advantages:

(1) The synthesis of H∞ controller reduces the accounts of system controllers, that is, realizing the optimization of system performance using a single controller, which simplifies the structure of the closed-loop system.
(2) When applying the outer-loop controller by means of cascade lead-lag compensation into the system, the step response always has great overshoot, while there is almost no overshoot when H∞ controller is employed to the system, which leads to a better result.
(3) In term of surplus torque suppression, both feed-forward compensation controller and H∞ controller has a significant effect in eliminating the surplus torque. Since the expression of feed-forward compensation controller is derived according to system parameters, the form of it is relatively fixed, which leads to the restriction of the effect of compensation in some degree. By contrast, when designing the H∞ controller, weighting function can be selected flexibly in order to realize the further optimization of the effect of surplus torque suppression.

8 Conclusion

Focusing on electrical load simulator system and being based on H∞ control theory, this paper established the generalized plant, chose the suitable weighting function according to the requirements of system performance and finally synthesized the H∞ controller utilizing the LMI method. In order to investigate the effect of the H∞ controller, the performance of this system was compared with the closed-loop system applying the classical control theory. Then the advantages in accurately tracking input signal and efficient surplus torque suppression of the system designed in this paper were demonstrated in the end.

References

1. Ju, T., Dahai, P., Hefa, Y.: Analysis of coupling between operating system load simulator and aircraft stable loop. J. Chin. Civ. Aviat. Flying Sch. **20**(4), 29–31 (2009)
2. Chenggong, L., Hongtao, J., Zongxia, J.: Generation mechanism and suppression of electrical load simulator surplus torque. J. Beijing Aeronaut. Astronaut. Univ. **32**(2), 204–208 (2006)
3. Zeren, M., Ozbay, H.: On stable H∞ controller design. In: Proceedings of the American Control Conference, pp. 1302–1306 (1997)

4. Xingjian, F., Chaonan, T., Yikang, S., Kaixiang, P.: Development and research status of H∞ control theory. Comput. Sci. Autom. **23**(1), 25–29 (2004)
5. Jian, Z.: H∞ Robust Control Theory and its Application in Double Inverted Pendulum. Academic Dissertation of Dalian Maritime University (2003)
6. Nam, Y., Lee, J., Hong, S.K.: Force control system design for aerodynamic load simulator. In: Proceedings of the American Control Conference, Chicago, Illinois, pp. 3043–3047 (2000)
7. Jinbo, W., Shaoan, L., Weijia, L., Zhouping, Y.: Controller of the new-type electrical load simulator. Process Autom. Instrum. **31**(3), 1–4 (2010)
8. Fan, J., Zheng, Z., Lv, M.: Optimal sliding mode variable structure control for load simulator. In: Systems and Control in Aerospace and Astronautics Conference, pp. 1–4 (2008)
9. Pingli, R., Gongyu, P., Bin, L.: Modeling and H∞ control of vehicle electronic control air suspension. Mech. Des. Manuf. **8**(8), 101–103 (2009)
10. Yuexuan, W., Junjie, C., Yuping, H., Zhongzhe, Z., Yue, Z., Guoping, Z.: Study on electrical loading technique of new-type rudder load simulator system. Aerosp. Control **32** (2), 78–81 (2014)
11. Chaohao, C., Qi, W.: Electrical power system stabilizer based on H∞ control theory. Power Grid Tech. **24**(10), 11–14 (2000)
12. Mingyan, W., Ben, G., Yudong, G., Hao, Z.: Design of electric dynamic load simulator based on recurrent neural networks. In: Electric Machines and Drives Conference, pp. 207–210 (2003)
13. Qiang, F.: Research on Design Method for Passive Torque Servo Control System and its Application. Academic Dissertation of Harbin Institute of Technology (2006)
14. Xianyong, H., Jie, W., Jinming, Y., Jie, S.: Constant power H∞ robust control of wind powered motor with above rated wind speed. Control Theory Appl. **25**(2), 321–325 (2008). H∞ Robust Control. Control Theory and Application
15. Ming, Q., Jiajun, Y., Zhao, L., Geng, Y.: Study on electrical power-assisted steering system based on H∞ robust control thoery. J. Huazhong Univ. Sci. Tech. **30**(12), 71–73 (2002)
16. Guojun, L., Xiang, L., Xianhong, S.: H∞ control of generated system based on LMI method. Inf. Commun. **11**(2), 37–39 (2013)
17. Fangshe, G., Yunfeng, Y., Yudi, G.: Superb robust control and simulation based on LMI. Comput. Simul. **26**(2), 65–68 (2009)

Markov Based Dynamic Slot Allocation Algorithm

Rongrong Liu, Xiaofeng Rong(✉), Shujuan Huang, and Lianjong Zhong

College of Computer Science and Engineering, Xian Technological University, Xi'an, China
xiaofengrong@126.com

Abstract. It is a vital method that slot allocation can improve the performance of Ad Hoc network. The time slot is divided into two parts in this paper, that is fixed slot time and dynamic slot time. ON/OFF model is used to describe data packet sending translation mode for each node based on fixed time slot allocation. It is realized by Markov one step transfer matrix. This paper also proposed a time division multiple access algorithm based on Markov ergodicity (MTDMA) simulated under OPNET platform. The experiment results show that MTDMA algorithm has better performance for the node owning different traffic than fixed TDMA under OPNET platform.

Keywords: TDMA · Ergodic · Time slot allocation algorithm · Simulation modeling

1 Introduction

Ad Hoc network is a distributed, self-organized wireless network. In the absence of fixed communications infrastructure, the radio communication terminals in a certain area can be deployed in real-time communication, so it has important application value in military communication, disaster relief and other specific scenarios. At present, the existing TDMA algorithm can be divided into three categories: fixed time slot allocation, contention time slot allocation and dynamic time slot allocation assignment algorithm.

In practical applications, however, each nodes have its own traffic characteristics and a reasonable allocation algorithm determines the performance of the over all network. Therefore, how to effectively combine the limited time slot resource with the actual demand of time slot in each node of the network is particularly important in the TDMA algorithm [1]. [2] derived a collision-avoid dynamic slots assignment algorithm based on fixed TDMA, and the algorithm divides different priorities for each node by judging the priority of each nodes. Combined with fixed time slot allocation and

Supported by Industrial Science and Technology Research Project of Shaanxi Province of China (NO. 2015GY031).

L. Zhang et al. (Eds.): AsiaSim 2016/SCS AutumnSim 2016, Part I, CCIS 643, pp. 67–76, 2016.
DOI: 10.1007/978-981-10-2663-8_7

dynamic slot allocation it can improve the utilization of time slot. However, this algorithm for node traffic has very high requirements when the node traffic has great discrepancy lower priority node will accumulate large number of packets, lead to reduce the overall network throughput. In [3] the source is divided into equal length time slots, and uses binary tree block divided method to uniform distribution of resources. There has some small time slot blocks when the time slot is divided into several times by using the method of binary tree block divided method. If there is no good method to use them it will cause a large waste of time slot resources. Although these methods improve the performance of delay, throughput and other performance, there still have shortcomings such as large delay etc. under the different requirements of QoS (Quality of Service) [4].

Different time slot assignments have different influence to the whole network parameters performance [5], want to improve the performance of the MANET as much as possible need according to the different impact of the parameter's needs to obtain better improve the overall system quality of service [6]. This paper uses ON/OFF model to describe node's traffic, and Markov based TDMA algorithm (MTDMA) is proposed according to each node ON state Markov ergodic.

2 Markov Model

2.1 Markov Process

Markov is the random process without aftereffect. According to parameter set T and state space E Markov process $\{X(t), t \in T\}$ can be divided into three categories: discrete time and discrete state Markov process, continuous time and discrete state Markov process, continuous time and continuous state Markov process. This paper adopts discrete time and discrete state Markov process.

2.2 The Transfer Probability of Markov Chain

Definition 1. Assume the state space of random sequence $\{X(n), n = 0, 1, 2...\}$ is E. If any m non negative integer $n_1, n_2, \ldots .n_m (0 \leq n_1 < n_2 < \ldots < n_m)$, any natural k number and any $i_1, i_2, \ldots i_m, j \in E$ satisfy:

$$P\{X(n_m + k) = j | X(n_1) = i_1, X(n_2) = i_2, \ldots, X(n_m) = i_m\}$$
$$= P\{X(n_m + k) = j | X(n_m) = i_m\} \quad (1)$$

Then $\{X(n), n = 0, 1, 2...\}$ is called a Markov chain. The right side of the formula 1 is called the k step transition probability of Markov at the time n's referred as $P_{ij}(k)$

$$P_{ij}(k) = P_{ij}(n, n+k) = P\{X(n+k) = j|X(n) = i\}, k \geq 1 \quad (2)$$

When $k = 1$, P_{ij} called one step transition probability. One step transition probability can written into matrix form, as shown in formula 3 is finite state space, when $N \to \infty$ it is infinite state space, and this paper uses finite state space one step transition probability.

$$P = \begin{pmatrix} p_{11} & p_{12} & \cdots & p_{1N} \\ p_{21} & p_{22} & \cdots & p_{2N} \\ \vdots & \vdots & & \vdots \\ p_{N1} & P_{N2} & \cdots & P_{NN} \end{pmatrix}. \quad (3)$$

2.3 Ergodic of Markov Chain

Defination 2. For a finite Markov chain, if there is a positive integer satisfy:

$$P_{ij}(k) > 0, i, j = 1, 2, \ldots N$$

It's a ergodic chain, that is $\lim_{n \to \infty} P_{ij}(n) = P_j$, and limit distribution $\{P_j, j = 1, 2, \ldots n\}$ is the only solution of equations $P_j = \sum_{i=1}^{n} P_i P_{ij}, j = 1, 2, \ldots n$ which meet conditions of $P_j > 0 (j = 1, 2, \ldots, n), \sum_{j=1}^{n} P_j = 1$.

3 Model Design

The model mainly consists of three parts including network topology, terminal node model and process model. Terminal node model constitute the entire network topology, terminal node model consists of different process model and each process model consists of corresponding finite state machine through C code to achieve specific functions.

3.1 Topology Design of a Network

8 nodes is set up in the whole network randomly distributed in the logical area. The nodes distribution is shown in Fig. 1. 8 nodes in the network are TDMA nodes, all of these nodes have active contract issuing function.

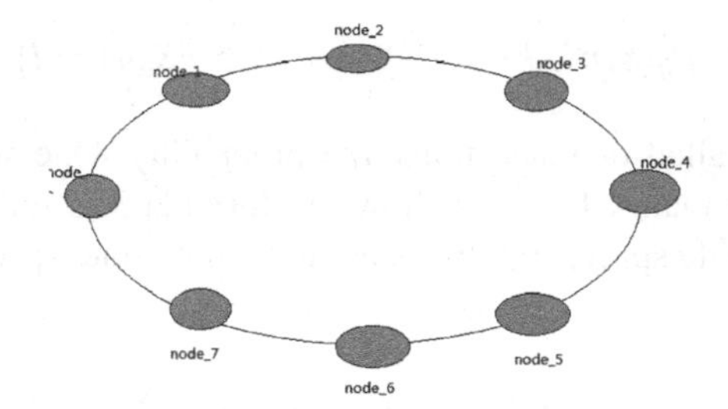

Fig. 1. Network model

3.2 Design of Terminal Node Model

Each node in the network has same internal model, and consists six processing modules. Each module completes specific function as shown in Fig. 2.

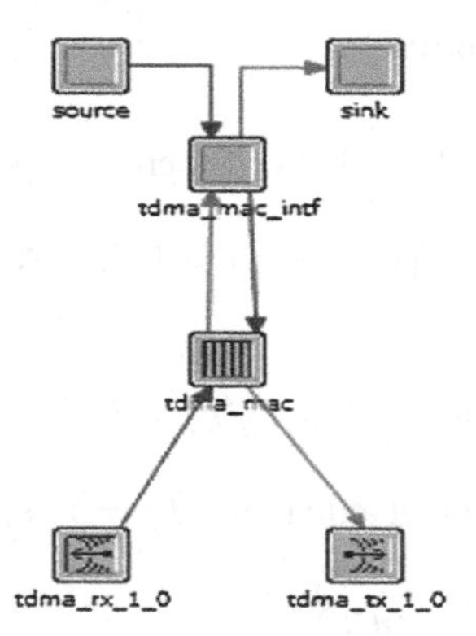

Fig. 2. Node model

- Data source module: The module is responsible for generating the data packets, using the ON/OFF state transition model with certain interval. The packet is sent to the next layer immediately once it is generated.
- The sink module (sink): According to the data packets received by the node to calculate and collecte each performance parameters.
- tdma_mac_intf module: Judge the type of packets, if a packet is received by this node send to the upper lawyer; if the packet is generated by its own then obtain the source, destination address and other information etc., it will be sent to the lower layer on the packaging.
- tdma_mac module: According to the ergodicity of the Markov chain, each node is divided the dynamic part of the time slot at the same time judge the type of data packet, aimed at the different types of data package to make corresponding processing.
- Receiver (tdma_rx_1_0): Responsible for receiving data packets and sending it to tdma_mac_intf module.
- Transmitter (tdma_tx_1_0): Responsible for sending the data packets generated by the node to the channel.

3.3 Design of Process

In the network, each terminal node model can realize corresponding functions through specific process model, This paper mainly uses the data source module to generates data packets, and uses tdma_mac module to distinguish data packet type and complete the relevant operation. Each process model is composed of several different finite state machine, and process model can choose corresponding finite state machine to realize specific function according to actual demand.

At present, commonly used data packet generation model includes wavelet transform model, ARIMA model, ON/OFF model, etc. ON/OFF model is simple and practical, it can reflect the good ergodicity of the Markov chain. Therefore, this paper uses this model to generate data in accordance with the ergodicity of Markov chain as shown in Fig. 3. Each node of the source alternates between ON state and OFF state. When the source is in the ON state, the nodes generate packets at a constant interval, and when in the OFF state, it does not generate packets. ON/OFF state of each node according to the series manner, which means each node's ON/OFF state conduct one by one. If a node doesn't on its ON/OFF state, it does not generate packets. Superposition of the n node's ON/OFF state can be formed with the ergodicity of Markov chain state transition matrix.

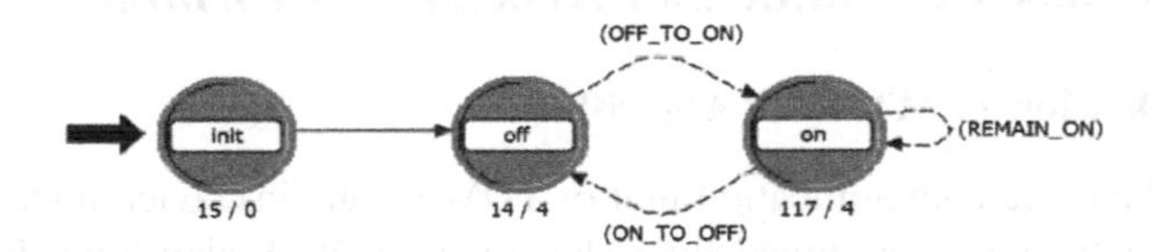

Fig. 3. Process model of ON/OFF

tdma_mac module process model is shown in Fig. 4. The tdma_mac module mainly determines the data packet type and divides the dynamic time slot. The tdma_mac module judges the method of processing the data packet through the received data packet type. There are two major types of data packets received in this model, for the node itself generate data packets and the node received data packets. The data packets received by the node are divided into the destination is this node and destination node isn't this node. When tdma_mac module received a packet firstly to judge the data packet's type, if the packet is generated for its own node then trigger finite state machine from_HL this packet will put into a buffer when arrived at the node time slot it will process it by trigger finite state xmit; if the node receive a data packet it will triggered finite state machine from_NTWK, first of all to judge whether the destination address of the packet is this node, if it is transmit this data packet upper layer, if not destroy it.

In the aspect of slot allocation, tdma_mac module through the finite state machine xmit completes the data packet transmission and dynamic time slot division. This module first to judge whether the current time is in this node time slot. If in the node time slot, according to the periodicity of ON state, ximt calculates the length of

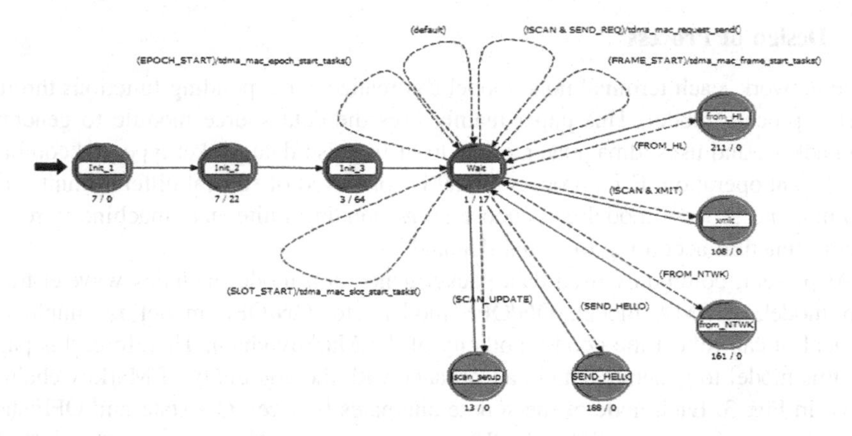

Fig. 4. Process model of tdma_mac

dynamic time slot. As then it check whether there is any packet in the buffer queue, if the buffer has packet then use FIFO (First In First Out) to take the data packets out and send it to the low layer.

4 Markov Based Dynamic Slot Allocation Algorithm

4.1 Time Division of MTDMA Algorithm

Time slot is the basic communication unit of TDMA data link. Each node can send or receive data in their own assigned time slot. Fixed TDMA algorithm divides frame period into equal length time slots and assigns to each node, while in practice there are some difference in the traffic of each node. In the practice, the node's real demand of time slot changes with their traffic, thereby increasing the difficulty of time slot allocation. Based on the problem above, in order to ensure the stability of the packet transmission, MTDMA algorithm based on the actual demand divides frame period into two part: fixed time slot and dynamic time slot as shown in Fig. 5. The fixed time slot guarantees the minimum delay of the whole system, while dynamic time slot according to the ergodicity of Markov chain guarantees sending data packet stable. This time slot allocation algorithm improves several parameters such as end-to-end delay, and the slot allocation will described in Sect. 4.3 in details.

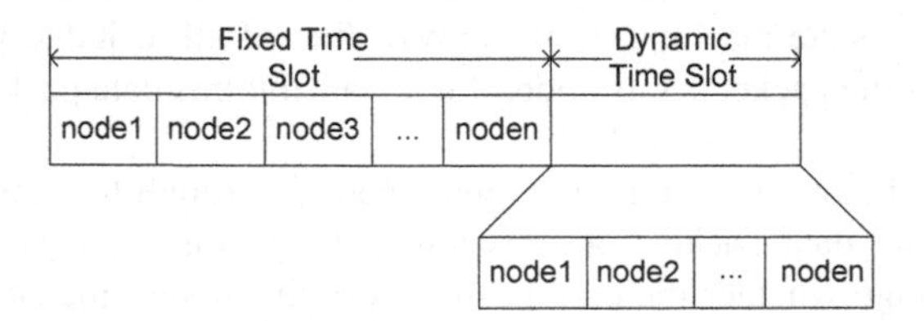

Fig. 5. MTDMA frame structure

4.2 Time Slot Allocation Mathematical Model of MTDMA Algorithm

Nodes ON/OFF model has two states, ON state and the OFF state. From Definition 1 knows the paper uses finite state space Markov chain, and N = 2, substitute it into formula (2) can get the following expression.

$$P_{12}(1) = \{X(n+1) = OFF|X(n) = ON\} \tag{4}$$

$$P_{21}(1) = \{X(n+1) = ON|X(n) = OFF\} \tag{5}$$

According to formula (3) can achieve:

$$P = \begin{pmatrix} P_{11} & P_{12} \\ P_{21} & P_{22} \end{pmatrix} \tag{6}$$

In this paper, nodes generate data packets in a serial way, adjacent packets generation interval is Δt, therefore, to collect the stats of each nodes with equal interval Δt. Set *Ni* is ON state duration time and *Fi* is OFF state duration time of the node i. T is the sum of the ON state and the OFF state for all nodes, P_{12} and P_{21} is two parameters in (4) and (5):

$$P12(1) = 1/(N_i/\Delta t)$$

$$P_{21}(1) = 1/\{(T - N_i)/\Delta t\}$$

Substitution $P12$ and $P21$ into (6) can achieve node i's Markov one step state transition matrix. Since there is a integer k satisfy $P_{ij}(k) > 0, i, j = 1, 2, \ldots N$, so this is a ergodicity chain. According to the ergodicity of Markov chain can obtained, for node i its absolute probability is:

$$P_{21}/(P_{21} + P_{12}) = N_i/T \tag{7}$$

$$P_{12}/(P_{21} + P_{12}) = (T - N_i)/T \tag{8}$$

4.3 Implication of Slot Allocation of MTDMA Algorithm

In time slot allocation MTDMA algorithm calculates fixed time slot and dynamic time separately. The fixed time slot is a preset value, while dynamic slot part is combined with the absolute of each node. This section mainly introduces the calculating process of dynamic slot part.

4.3.1 Calculate Dynamic Slot Part

This paper uses ON/OFF model to generate data packet, since ON/OFF model generates data packet with fixed interval Δt, so different ON state duration can describe different traffic. The ON state has three kinds of different duration, and each node's

Table 1. ON/OFF Sustained time

ON (sec)	OFF (sec)	Node number
3.2	0.8	node1, node5
1.6	0.8	node2, node6
0.8	0.8	node3, node4, node7, node8

ON/OFF state last time is shown in Table 1. Experimental results shows that the generated data packet accord with the Markov process, and has the ergodicity. To ensures that each node in the ON state began to generate a packet, that is, each node generates at least one packet in each ON state, at the same time to ensure that the node have different traffic the value of Δt is 0.8 s.

Combination formula 8 and the formula (9) can obtain the absolute probability of each node:

$$P_1 = N_i/(3.2 \times 2 + 1.6 \times 2 + 0.8 \times 4 + 0.8 \times 8) = N_i/19.2$$

$$\begin{aligned} P_2 &= (3.2 \times 4 + 1.6 \times 2 + 0.8 \times 4 + 0.8 \times 8 - N_i)/(3.2 \times 2 + 1.6 \times 2 + 0.8 \times 4 + 0.8 \\ &\quad \times 8) \\ &= (19.2 - N_i)/19.2 \end{aligned}$$

ON/OFF model generates packet in series, so superposition each node ON state absolute probability, computing each node ON state accounts for the whole network ON state. Each node's ON state of the entire network ON state probability is represented by Ri, the probability expression is:

$$\mathrm{R_i} = (N_i/19.2)/\sum_{i=1}^{n}(N_i/19.2) = N_i/\sum_{i=1}^{n}N_i.$$

4.3.2 Slot Allocation

Assume that frame period is L, each frame period have 8 fixed time slot part S1, S2,..., S8 and a dynamic slot part D. From Sect. 4.3.1 knows that Markov one step transfer probability is Ri. Therefore, the formula to calculating the length of time slot assigned to each node during the running process is:

$$\mathrm{Zi} = \mathrm{Si} + \mathrm{D} \times \mathrm{Ri}.$$

5 Simulation Realization

5.1 Preference Set

Dynamic slot allocation algorithm based on Markov chain is tested under the OPNET Modeler 14.5 environment. In the simulation process, 8 nodes randomly distributes in the logical scenario. The fixed time slot length of each node is 0.44 s, the whole network dynamic time slot length is 0.48 s, which means one frame period is 4 s. The maximum capacity of a member node to send a packet is 500 bytes, when packets size larger than 500 bytes need to sending subcontractor. In this paper packet size increases from 100 bytes to 1000 bytes, the simulation time is 30 min.

5.2 Result Analysis

First of all, simulation process use ON/OFF model to simulate node generating data packets which are accordance with Markov process. During the simulation process according to different Markov ergodic of each node to calculate and distribute dynamic time slot, at same time collect all the parameters until the end of simulation. End-to-end delay describes a period of a data packet generated until it arrives its destination node used time. Throughput describes the total amount of data packets received by a node per unit time. Thus, the smaller end-to-end delay, and the bigger throughput results the good performance of the overall network. The simulation results are mainly concerned with two performance parameters: end-to-end delay and throughput. Finally, two performance parameters are compared with simulation result of fixed TDMA algorithm.

End to end delay of the simulation results is shown in Fig. 6. The horizontal coordinates is the simulation time, and the longitudinal coordinates is the delay time. It can be seen that with the increase of the data packet MTDMA it has a greater improvement on the end to end delay than the fixed TDMA algorithm. This is due to the maximum capacity limited. When data packet is bigger than 500 bytes it need to send packets. Subcontract leads to nodes traffic increasing while fixed TDMA to each node's time slot length is fixed, so with the increasing of the node traffic the number of packets that cannot be sent increased at the same time, and which increases the end-to-end delay. While MTDMA algorithm combined with the advantages of fixed and dynamic time slot, which not only guarantees the minimum delay of the system but also can dynamically allocates time slot length according to the node traffic, reduces the time that the data packets waiting in the queue, and reduces the end-to-end delay. With the increasing of packet size the end-to-end delay is lower. So as shown in Fig. 6, when a packet size is less than 500 bytes it doesn't need to subcontracting, compared with fixed TDMA algorithm, when packet size less than 500bytes in end-to-end delay MTDMA algorithm improved by about 15 %. While when packet size is bigger than 500bytes MTDMA algorithm improved by about 30 %.

The throughputs of the two algorithms are shown in Table 2. According to the data in the table can see that in terms of throughput MTDMA algorithm is improved by about 6 %. During the simulation process each node generates a size fixed data packet, however, throughput size directly proportional to with the data packet size. Therefore in throughput respects MTDMA algorithm improves in small.

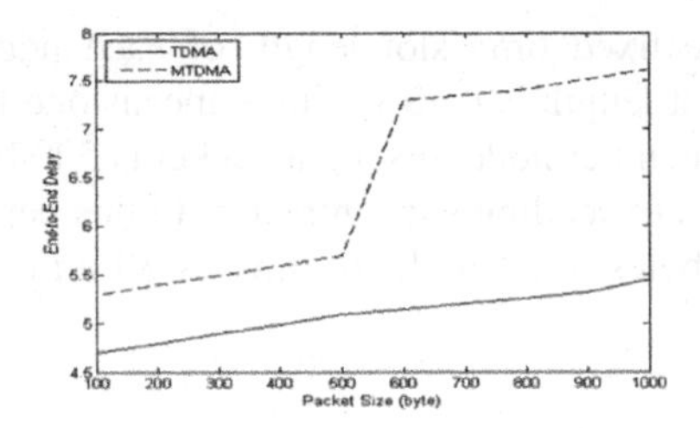

Fig. 6. Network average ETE delay

Table 2. Average network throughput comparison

Packet size (bytes)	100	200	400	600	800	1000
Fixed TDMA	4843	9687	19375	28924	38543	48156
MTDMA	4854	9706	19404	29093	38774	48444

6 Conclusion

This paper aims at solving the problem of dynamic slot allocation algorithm, and proposes dynamic slot allocation based on Markov chain. Testing results show that the algorithm has both low end-to-end delay and stable throughput, and improves TDMA data link network performance effectively.

References

1. Rui, D., Long, Z., Yu-wen, W., Fan-ji, M.: Modeling of TDMA-based dynamic slot assignment algorithm for data link. Commun. Technol. **44**(02), 105–107 (2011)
2. Ge-xin, P., Sheng-li, X., Cai-yun, C.: A collision-avoid dynamic slots assignment algorithm based on fixed TDMA. Acad. Res. **2**(11), 115–200 (2005)
3. Jian-xun, L., Xiao-guang, F., Zhe, Z., Ming, W.: TDMA dynamic slot allocation algorithm based on priority. Comput. Eng. **37**(14), 288–290 (2011)
4. Wilson J.W., Stein, J., Munjal, S., et al.: Capacity planning to meet QOS requirements of joint battle management and command and control application. In: Proceedings of IEEE Military Communications Conference, pp. 983–989 (2005)
5. Yong, Q., Jun, Z., Tao, Z.: Effect of TDMA timeslot assignment on traffic delay. Chin. J. Electron. **37**(10), 2277–2283 (2009)
6. Liu, J., Sheng, M., Xu, Y., et al.: End-to-end delay modeling in buffer-limited MANETs: a general theoretical framework. IEEE Trans. Wireless Commun. **15**(1), 498–511 (2015)

Simulation for POD-Driven Ship Course ADRC Steering

Zaiji Piao and Chen Guo(✉)

Information Science and Technology College,
Dalian Maritime University, Dalian, China
874885171@qq.com, dmuguoc@126.com

Abstract. To the problem of podded propulsion ship course control, through the establishment of MMG(mathematical model group) ship motion mathematical model, and the model of wind and flow interference, the design method of each part of ADRC(active disturbance rejection control) has been analyzed delicately. And course controller based on the ADRC theory has been designed. In semi-submersible vessel "Taiankou" case, the designed controller is simulated in MATLAB for POD-driven ship course control.

Keywords: Podded propulsor · MMG model · Course control · ADRC

1 Introduction

Appeared in the 1990s, POD propulsion mode has a considerable advantage as a new way of electric propulsion in maneuverability, economy, installation, maintenance and many aspects. Using generators to transform other forms of energy into electric energy, then using motor to transform electric energy into mechanical energy, podded propeller realized the non-mechanical mode transfer of energy. POD propulsion ship does not have the traditional ship steering gear, and itself can rotate 360 degrees, which cause the better maneuverability [1]. Ship is a multiple input and multiple output dynamic system in uncertain environment. During the course of the motion of the ship, the movement of the ship will have a lot of inertia due to the great quality, and marine equipment has certain delay to the directives. Ships sailing in the sea will be affected by the factors of flow field and the sea environment such as wind, flow and so on, and the ship motion has the characteristics such as nonlinearity and uncertainty [2, 3]. For pod propulsion ship, course automatic control system is an important and indispensable part. With the emphasis on navigation safety and operation requirements, the requirements of course control is higher and higher. Ship course control is usually implemented by the autopilot, and the basic principle of autopilot is through the control method to adjust the pod turning angle so as to eliminate the heading error.

At present, most of autopilot used traditional PID control method. However, with the increasing of control requirements, some shortcomings of PID method gradually exposed, for example, adaptive performance is very poor, and the parameter setting needs to depends on manual experience to judge [4]. Aiming to its disadvantages, professor Jingqing Han first puts forward the active disturbance rejection control

L. Zhang et al. (Eds.): AsiaSim 2016/SCS AutumnSim 2016, Part I, CCIS 643, pp. 77–85, 2016.
DOI: 10.1007/978-981-10-2663-8_8

(ADRC), which can achieve good control effect on many occasions. The ADRC technology organically inherited and enriched the PID control reasonably, and apply more effective nonlinear control to compensate system's external and internal interference [5]. However, because design controller needs to adjust too many parameters, it is not conducive to the design of the controller, professor Zhiqiang Gao [6] put forward linear Active Disturbance Rejection Control(LADRC), and the controller without reducing control quality, greatly reduces the need to adjust the number of parameters, so as to simplify the design process and enhance the system's rapid response ability.

MMG ship motion mathematical model of a ship equipped with two SSP POD propellers named "Taian Kou" has been built in this paper and the course automatic control with ADRC controller is simulated in MATLAB.

2 Manoeuvring Model for Podded Propulsion Ship

2.1 Coordinate System

This article studies the ship that moves on the ocean with three degrees of freedom, generally by using two coordinate systems: inertial coordinate system and attach coordinate system (Fig. 1). Inertial coordinate system is fixed in the earth's surface, as a benchmark reference system, x_0 axis pointing to the north, y_0 axis pointing to the east; Attach coordinate system is fixed in the ship, the x axis pointing in the direction of the bow, y axis point to starboard, u is for shipping longitudinal velocity; v is for shipping transverse speed; r is for turn bow angular velocity; Ψ is for course Angle; δ is for the turning angle.

2.2 Modeling Method of MMG Model

At the end of the 1970s, the Japanese ship manoeuvring mathematical model group, proposed a set of ship motion mathematical model, often referred to as MMG model,

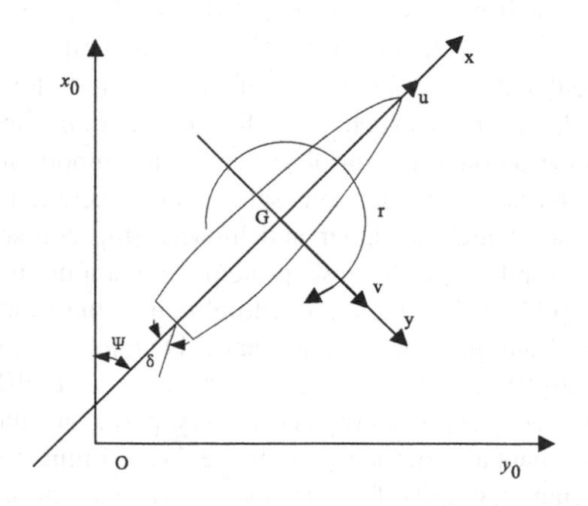

Fig. 1. Coordinate system

also known as separate type model. Its main feature is the role in ship hydrodynamic forces and moments according to the physical significance, decompose for the role in the bare hull, propeller and rudder hydrodynamic forces and moments, and between them interfere with each other hydrodynamic forces and moments. For the podded ship without a rudder, tail, so the overall force is divided into the hydrodynamic forces and moments of bare hull and pod. According to the modeling mechanism of MMG equations of POD-driven ship is:

$$\begin{cases} (m+m_x)\dot{u} - (m+m_y)vr = X_H + X_P + X_{current} + X_{wind} \\ (m+m_y)\dot{v} + (m+m_x)ur = Y_H + Y_P + Y_{current} + Y_{wind} \\ (I_{zz}+J_{zz})\dot{r} = N_H + N_P + N_{current} + N_{wind} \\ \dot{\psi} = r \\ \dot{x}_0 = u\cos\psi - \text{v}\,\sin\psi \\ \dot{y}_0 = v\cos\psi + \text{u}\,\sin\psi \end{cases} \quad (1)$$

There are two kinds of viscous fluid dynamic model can be used for approximate estimate, one is a kind of "jingshang" model, another is kind is "guidao" model, this paper adopts the latter. "guidao" model is as follows:

$$\begin{cases} X_H = X(u) + X_{vv}v^2 + X_{vr}vr + X_{rr}r^2 \\ Y_H = Y_v v + Y_r r + Y_{|v|v}|v|v + Y_{|r|r}|r|r + \\ \qquad Y_{vvr}v^2 r + Y_{vrr}vr^2 \\ N_H = N_v v + N_r r + N_{|v|v}|v|v + N_{|r|r}|r|r + \\ \qquad N_{vvr}v^2 r + N_{vrr}vr^2 \end{cases} \quad (2)$$

The calculation method of the hydrodynamic derivatives please reference [7].

The ship equipped with a pair of SSP pod propulsion is the object in this paper, which is the stern has two pods, each pod has two propellers, it provide force and moment of ship motion and it should be divided into two parts, one part is produced by the propeller thrust T, the other part is the pod hull itself generated transverse force N [8], computation formula is as follows:

$$\begin{cases} X_P = 2(1-t_p)(T_P+T_s)\cos\delta - 2(1-t_R)N\sin\delta \\ Y_P = 2(1-t_p)(T_P+T_s)\sin\delta + 2(1+a_H)N\cos\delta \\ N_P = 2(1-t_p)(T_P-T_s)\cos\delta 0.5L_{PS} - Y_P L_{OP} \end{cases} \quad (3)$$

δ is steering Angle for pods; L_{PS} is the lateral distance between the two propeller; L_{OP} is the distance from the center of the ship to the pods [9]; T_P and T_S respectively represent left and right pod propeller thrust; t_P is the thrust deduction coefficient; t_R is the steering resistance deduction coefficient.

$$T_P = \rho n_P^2 D^4 K_T(J_P) \quad (4)$$

$$K_T = 0.7 + 0.3589 J_P + 0.1875 J_P^2 \quad (5)$$

In formula (7) ρ is for the density of sea water; n_P is the left screw rotational speed; D is the propeller diameter; $J_P = U_P/(n_P D)$ is the speed ratio; K_T is based on pod propeller open water performance of the map which was used curve fitting and interpolation methods find out the thrust coefficient [10], the specific formula see (8).T_S calculate in the same way as T_P.

$$N = \frac{1}{2}\rho f_a A_P U_P^2 \sin(a_P) \tag{6}$$

$$U_P = (1-w)\left[u^2 + (v + x_P r)^2\right]^{1/2} \tag{7}$$

In the formula (9), A_P is the effective area for the pod. Pod's area, though not as big as a rudder, but its transverse force on the numerical can't be ignored. $a_P = \beta_P - \delta$ is the angle of attack, $\beta_P = \arctan[-(v + x_P r)/u]$. In the formula (10), U_P is the effective flow velocity; w is the company flow coefficient.

Ship in the process of sailing, the water movement under the influence of the hull, said the company flow or flow. It makes propeller thrust is different from usual open-water case. When the ship longitudinal motion, this paper used double screw ship company flow coefficient's calculate formula:

$$w_0 = 0.55C_b + 0.20 \tag{8}$$

When Marine horizontal and rotary motion, using a practical model:

$$w = w_0 \exp(-4v_p^{'2}) \tag{9}$$

v_p' is for the propeller cross-flow velocity, calculation formula is:

$$v_p' = v' + l_p' r' \tag{10}$$

l_p' is the propeller position of dimensionless x coordinates, people often make it 0.5 L.

Propeller is working at the back of the ship; its suction effect makes the water flow speed in front of the propeller faster. According to Bernoulli's theorem, the pressure there must decreases. The frontal thrust reduction coefficient used this formula:

$$t_p = 0.5C_p - 0.18 \tag{11}$$

C_P is for ship diamond coefficient [11].

2.3 Basic Structure of ADRC

The Active Disturbance Rejection Control (ADRC) is not very strict with the mathematical model of controlled object, and under the influence of interference, can through the special structure of nonlinear feedback compensate the external and internal error of

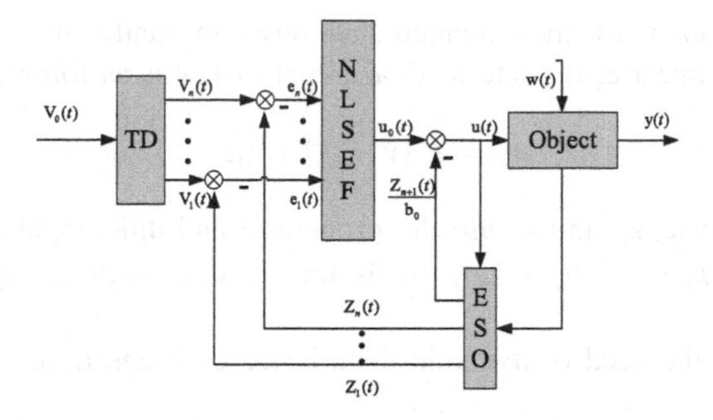

Fig. 2. The structure of ADRC

the system in time [12]. ADRC is a typical advanced control technology which has excellent control effect and the requirements are not very high. ADRC is mainly composed of tracking differentiator (TD), extended state observer (ESO) and nonlinear state error feedback control law (NLSEF) three parts [13], the structure is shown in Fig. 2.

2.4 Linear Active Disturbance Rejection Control Principle

Because ADRC has many parameters and some parameters' physical meaning is not clear, there are no accurate formulas of various parameters, some parameters can only be achieved by experience, parameter setting has been a difficult problem [14]. The Cleveland state university professor Zhiqiang Gao make extended state observer linearization and combined with integral differential control designed linear ADRC [15].

By making $fal(e, 1, 0, \delta) = e$, you can get the state equations of linear extended state observer:

$$\begin{cases} e = z_1 - y \\ \dot{z}_2 = z_2 - \beta_{01} e \\ \dot{z}_2 = z_3 - \beta_{02} e + bu \\ \dot{z}_2 = -\beta_{03} e \end{cases} \tag{12}$$

Whose character expression:

$$\lambda(s) = s^3 + \beta_{01} s^2 + \beta_{02} s + \beta_{03} \tag{13}$$

Usually, the stability of characteristic equation form as $\lambda(s) = (s + \omega)^3$ is better and have better transition process, so β_{01}, β_{02}, β_{03} expressed as the following form:

$$\begin{cases} \beta_{01} = 3\omega_0 \\ \beta_{02} = 3\omega_0^2 \\ \beta_{03} = \omega_0^3 \end{cases} \tag{14}$$

Among them, ω_0 is for the extended state observer bandwidth.

Expression of linear error state feedback control law is as follows:

$$u_0 = k_p(v - z_1) + k_d z_2 \tag{15}$$

v is the target course, k_p and k_d are the proportion and differential coefficient of the error of heading. $k_p = \omega_c^2, k_d = 2\omega_c$. ω_c is for the state feedback system bandwidth [16].

As a result of the need of dynamic disturbance compensation, control quantity u said as follows:

$$u = \frac{u_0 - z_3}{b_0} \tag{16}$$

3 Simulation and Discussion

POD electric propulsion system is mainly composed of ship power system, podded propeller, speed control system and rotation control system four parts. The ship mainly through the control of speed control system and rotation control system to integrated control the ship's course. Control block diagram is as follows (Fig. 3):

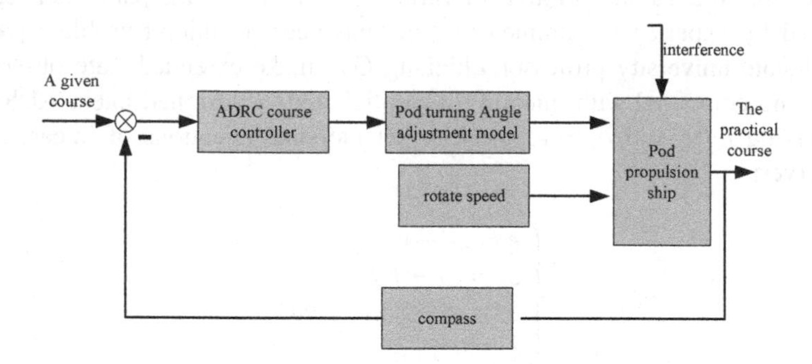

Fig. 3. Control block diagram

Taking "taian kou" as an example for simulation, the ship adopts two sets of SSP - 5 power drive system. LADRC controller's parameters: $b_0 = 1.0, \omega_o = 1.5, \omega_c = 1.0$. The given course is 20˚, initial speed is 15.3 kn, the ship's main engine rate is 140 r/min, flow rate of 0.5 kn, direction of flow is 30˚, wind speed is 10 kn, wind direction Angle is 30˚. The ship course control simulation model in MATLAB is as follows (Fig. 4):

The simulation of the course angle curve and the lateral velocity curve and the curve of the turning angle is as follows (Fig. 5, 6 and 7):

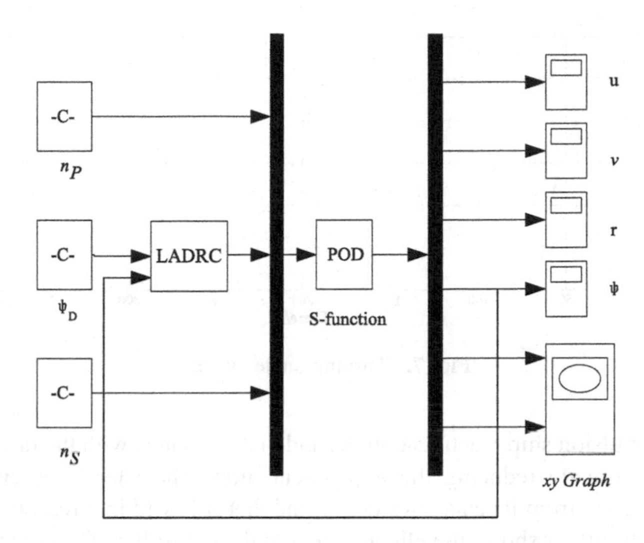

Fig. 4. The simulation diagram

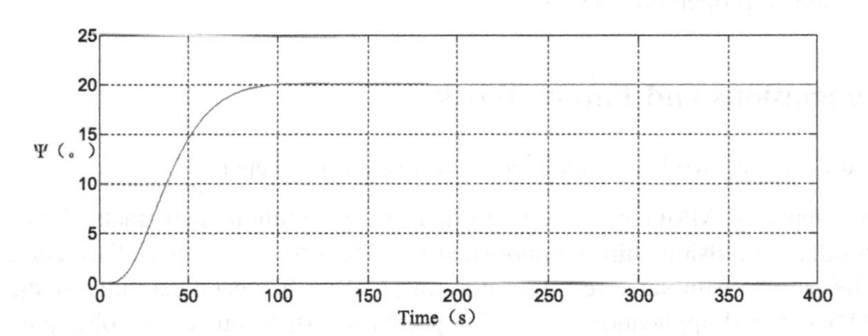

Fig. 5. Course angle curve

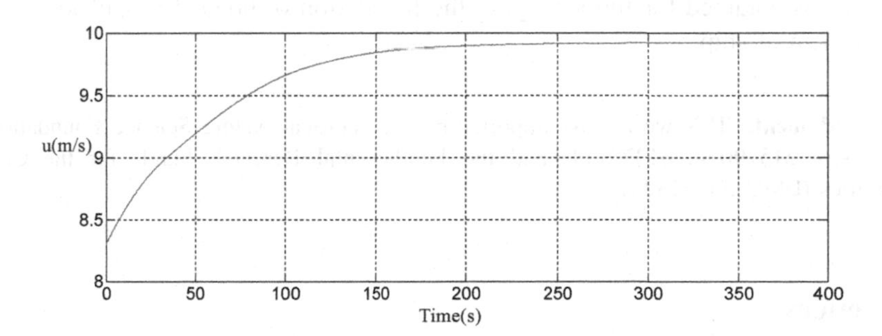

Fig. 6. Lateral velocity curve

The simulation results show that the course angle curve quickly reaches the expected value without overshoot, and the LADRC course controller has good control effect. The controller can meet the control requirements in certain interference conditions, rapidly

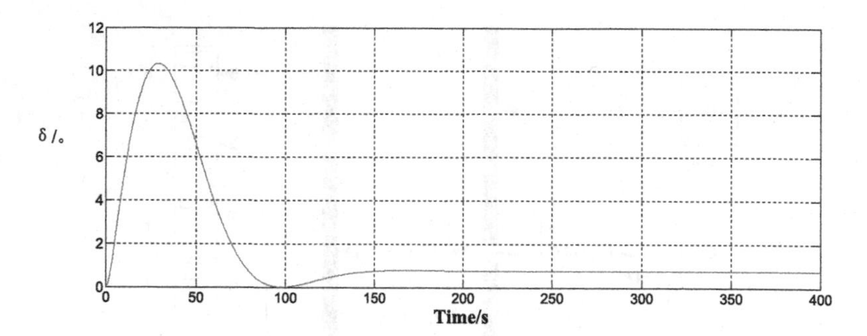

Fig. 7. Turning angle curve

made POD propulsion ship reach its course, and in accordance with the desired heading stable running, greatly reducing the adjustment time. The lateral velocity is a very important indicator, from its curve we could find that it is within a reasonable range of variation, which further shows the effectiveness of the controller. The controller made a desired turning angle which could reduce the work intensity of POD, and save energy and increase ship operating economy.

4 Conclusions and Future Work

The main research work is completed as follows in the paper.

(1) By applying MMG modeling mechanism, the motion mathematical model of podded propulsion ship is established according to its the special structure.
(2) The active disturbance rejection control (ADRC) has been carefully studied and ADRC based application on podded propulsion ship course control is presented.
(3) A linear active disturbance rejection controller(LADRC) has been designed, which was applied to simulation of podded propulsion ship, and the ideal control result is obtained for further laying the foundation of podded propulsion control problem of ship.

Acknowledgment. This work was supported by the National Nature Science Foundation of China (Nos. 51579024, 61374114) and the Fundamental Research Funds for the Central Universities (DMU no. 3132016311).

References

1. Xian, Y., Nie, W.-T.: Present situation and prospects of podded rotary electric propulsion systems. Jiangsu Ship **24**(6), 28–29 (2008)
2. Lei, Z.-L.: Active Disturbance Rejection Control on Ship Dynamic Positioning System. Dalian maritime University, Dalian (2014)

3. Zhang, X.-K., Jing, Y.-C.: The control system modeling and numerical simulation. Dalian maritime University Press, Dalian (2004)
4. Chen, X.-L., Cheng, Q.-M.: The development of ship autopilot control technology. J. Nanjing Chem. Ind. Univ. Nat. Sci. Ed. **23**(4), 101–105 (2004)
5. Fossen, T.I.: Guidance and Control of Ocean Vehicles. Wiley, Chichester (1994)
6. Gao, Z.-Q.: Scaling and bandwidth-parameterization based control tuning. In: Proceedings of American Control Conference, pp. 4989–4996 (2003)
7. Jia, X.-L., Yang, Y.-S.: Mathematical Model of Ship Motion: the Mechanism Modeling and Ferreting Modeling. Dalian Maritime University Press, Dalian (1999)
8. Liang, X.-L.: Modeling and Simulation of POD-ship's Motion. Dalian Maritime University, Dalian (2008)
9. Bao, Y.: The HMI development of simulation and real time controlfor POD propulsion system. Dalian Maritime University, Dalian (2006)
10. Gou, T.-T.: The Research of Control System of Podded Electric Propulsion. Jiangsu University of Science and Technology, Zhenjiang (2012)
11. Hui, Z.-G.: Semi-submerged Ship Maneuvering Motion Simulation. Dalian Maritime University, Dalian (2009)
12. Pan, J.-X.: Research on Intelligent Control for Large Ship Course. Dalian Maritime University, Dalian (2014)
13. Xi, Q.-C.: Research on Ship course control Based on the ADRC. Dalian Maritime University, Dalian (2014)
14. Lei, Z.-L.: Research on Intelligent Control and Simulation of Dynamic Positioning for a Rescue Ship. Dalian Maritime University, Dalian (2011)
15. Gao, Z.: From liner to nonlinear control means: a practical progression. ISA Trans. **24**(41), 177–189 (2002)
16. Yuan, D., et al.: Research on frequency-band characteristics and parameters configuration of linear active disturbance rejection control for second-order systems. Control Theory Appl. **12**(12), 1630–1640 (2013)

Enhanced Null Message Algorithm for PDES with Diverse Event Density

Bin Wang[1], Yanlong Zhai[1(✉)], Han Zhang[2], and Duzheng Qing[2]

[1] School of Computer Science, Beijing Institute of Technology, Beijing, China
ylzhai@bit.edu.cn

[2] Science and Technology on Special System Simulation Laboratory, Beijing Simulation Center, Beijing, China

Abstract. Parallel discrete event simulation technology has become an important means for the study of complex systems, and with the human research system getting more and larger, the scale of complex system simulation is more and more big. Time synchronization algorithm is the core of parallel discrete event simulation, which determines the effect of parallel acceleration. Traditional conservative time synchronization algorithm, such as CMB null message algorithm, is to use the null message to avoid deadlock, and then propel the logical process step by step; but when the difference between the time step of model is large, the CMB algorithm will send a lot of useless null messages, resulting in the low efficiency of parallel. To solve the problem of large difference between lookahead of the LP, based on null message algorithm, we present a null message optimization algorithm based on time step and event in parallel discrete event simulation, which greatly accelerates the speed of the parallel simulation and improves the efficiency of the parallel simulation.

Keywords: Conservative time synchronization algorithm · Parallel simulation · Null message algorithm

1 Introduction

1.1 Parallel Discrete Event Simulation

Simulation is a system that represents or simulates the behavior of another system during a period of time. In the computer simulation, the system to simulate is a computer program and the system to be simulated is called physical system. We can consider the physical system as a system that composed of interactive physical processes in some way [1, 9]. In Parallel Discrete Event Simulation (PDES), every physical process is modeled as a logical process (LP), the interaction between the physical processes is modeled as a message with a timestamp between the corresponding LPs, also called event. LP will process the received events, and the results of the processing may modify the state variables or schedule new events for themselves or other LP.

In parallel environment, different LP are allocated to different processors. Every LP moves forward in an event driven manner, and the message with the timestamp is exchanged when required. Every LP must deal with all its events in the order of the time stamp (including the ones that are generated by itself and the other LP). If you do not

L. Zhang et al. (Eds.): AsiaSim 2016/SCS AutumnSim 2016, Part I, CCIS 643, pp. 86–95, 2016.
DOI: 10.1007/978-981-10-2663-8_9

process the events in the order of the timestamp, it may result in inconsistent with the simulation results of the serial operation. In serial environment, it can be done by the centralized list to complete the event processing in the order of timestamp. But in parallel environment, the situation is not so simple. The error caused by the process of event handling in the reverse order is called the causality error. The problem that ensures that the event is processed in the order of timestamp is the synchronization problem.

There are two classic algorithms to solve the synchronization problem: conservative synchronization algorithm and optimistic synchronization algorithm. In the conservative synchronization algorithm, every LP is strictly in accordance with the order of the timestamp to process events. In the optimistic synchronization algorithm, it is not as strict as the conservative synchronization algorithm to avoid the occurrence of errors, but when the error is detected in the process of using some mechanisms to recover from the error.

1.2 Conservative Time Synchronization Algorithm

1.2.1 Null Message Algorithm

The first synchronization method in history is based on the conservative mechanism. The fundamental problem to be solved in the conservative mechanism is to determine when the LP can handle the event "safely" [2].

Algorithm 1 shows the procedure for each LP to process incoming messages in accordance with the timestamp order. The conservative mechanism can fully guarantee that events which LP is processing do not result in violations of local causality constraints. So, LP that contains no "safe" events must be blocked. But if appropriate precautions are not taken, it will lead to deadlock [4–6].

```
While (parallel simulation is not over)
    Wait until each FIFO contain at least one message
    Remove smallest time stamped message M from its FIFO
    Local time = time stamp of M
    Process M
```

Algorithm 1. A centralized event processing loop for the original version

1.2.2 Improved Null Message Algorithms

Although traditional CMB algorithm solves the problem of synchronization between processes, because each process sends an empty message to its downstream process, this will produce a large number of null messages, resulting in a particularly large communication load, a waste of system hardware resources, low efficiency [3]. An improved null message algorithm is a demand-driven approach. For example, when in the LP1 the queue receives LP2 is an empty queue, it will lead to LP1 cannot determine whether the event is processed safely, and then LP1 will be blocked. Then LP1 will send a null message request to LP2. When LP2 receives this null message request, a null message with a timestamp value of T will be sent back, T = LP2 local time + lookahead. So LP1 can break the block, continue to move forward safely.

LP change to create and send empty messages, send messages to reduce the useless empty and the cost of resources and time, compared with the initial null message algorithm has significant performance improvement. The approach changes the time of creating and sending the null message, reduces the resource and time of the transmission of the useless null message, and has obvious performance improvement compared with the original null message algorithm [7, 8]. If the difference between lookahead of the LP is small, the efficiency of the demand-driven approach is also relatively fast; but when the difference between lookahead of the LP is relatively large, the efficiency of the algorithm is greatly reduced. Therefore, the performance of a null message greatly depends on the lookahead, small lookahead often reduces the performance of the null message algorithm [10–12].

2 Enhanced Null Message Algorithm

In this section, we present a null message optimization algorithm based on time step and event in parallel discrete event simulation, compared to the traditional null message algorithm, it makes some improvement. Figure 1 is the schematic diagram of the model of the algorithm present. When the difference between lookahead of the LP is relatively large, it greatly reduces the transmission of invalid port messages and empty messages, saves the simulation time, and improves the simulation efficiency.

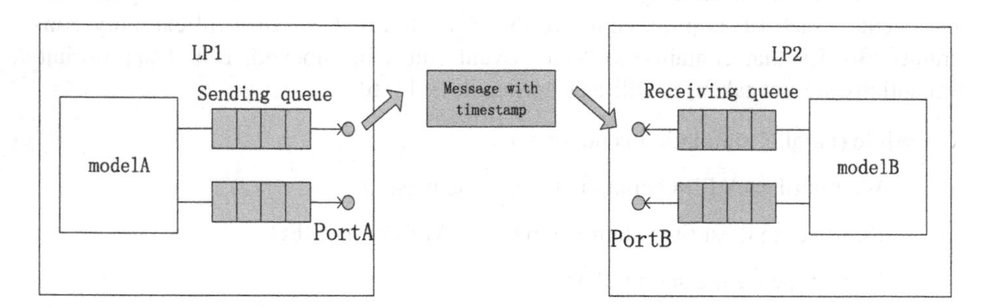

Fig. 1. Model of transmission among LPs.

2.1 Avoid Busy-Waiting by Using Synchronized Messaging

In the traditional null message algorithm, the outermost layer is an infinite loop, only when the end of the simulation engine loop is over. In the multi process parallel synchronization algorithm, 4 steps are performed in the loop: checking the receiving queue and sending queue, sending the null message request, sending the null message and receiving message. It is not difficult to see that this logic In the execution will generate a problem: if LP1 has the empty receiving queue, it will send an null message request to the upstream LP2 and LP2 send an null message, and when LP1 receives a message by the non-blocking way, that is, return immediately if there is no message arrival, then parallel synchronous logic will performs a next loop. Because there is no message received, the status of the LP1's receive queue will not change, the original empty receiving queue is still empty, and null message requests will not be sent repeatedly. LP1 do not need to send a null message request, there is no null message can be sent. And then LP1 receives messages in the way of non-blocking, if it have not received any message to return, then the entire parallel synchronization will be meaningless looped once. In other words, when at least a receive queue is empty and no message arrival, engine will have been executing loop that has not the actual operation, which is a waste of computing resources (CPU and memory).

To solve this problem, we adopt the method of combining blocking and non-blocking to optimize the way of the receiving message. In the current parallel synchronous loop, if in the stage of checking sending and receiving queue, we find there is empty receive queue, create an null message request and the request flag bit is set to 1, this represents we create and send the request, are waiting to receive the message. Then in the stage of receiving message, receive the message in the way of blocking, that is, the program has been blocking until the arrival of a new message, and then continues to loop, thus this avoids continuous loop.

2.2 Communication Strategies to Optimize Performance

2.2.1 Simulation Messages Optimization

In the simulation application, the time step of the model depends on the actual situation and the time step of some model is relatively large. For example, for the model of cruiser, it maybe update its state information every a few seconds or tens of seconds, while for the model of airplane, it maybe update its state information every 0.01 s because the requirement for accuracy is highly strict. So when the difference on the time step among models is relatively large, lots of useless messages maybe be transmitted among models.

In the parallel discrete event simulation, the model can get the latest information of the port, and then send to the downstream model when the parallel simulation engine is pushed forward. When the time step of upstream model is far less than that of the downstream model, such as, port of the upstream model may be updated every 1000 times, while the downstream model will take out the state information from the corresponding input port, and execute, obviously the port data that upstream model send to downstream model 999 times before has an effect on the downstream model, that is, the useless port message. The passing of port message requires cost of resources and time, and useless port messages cost the simulation time and hardware resources, but no sense, it should be avoided to send. So when the difference between time steps of the models are relatively large, this part of logic is needed to optimize to eliminate the transmission of the useless port message.

To solve this problem, we use the current time and time step of the downstream model to optimize this port of logic. Figure 2 is the schematic diagram of the mechanism of sending port messages. Suppose modelA is in LPA and modelB is in LPB, the output port PortA of the modelA is connected with the input port PortB of modelB. When the engine propels, according to the connecting relationship, it need to send current port data of PortA to modelB, used to update information of the model B. At

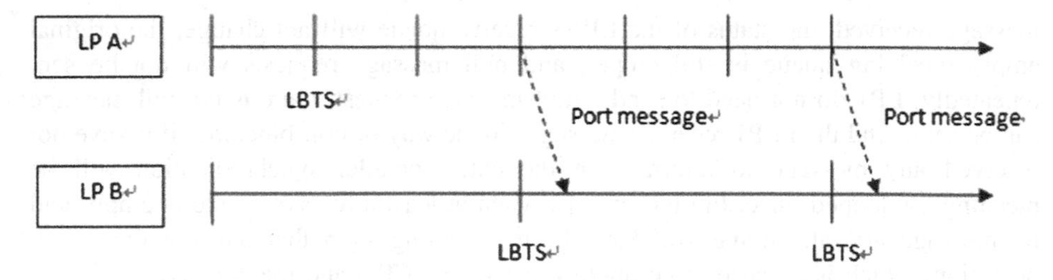

Fig. 2. Mechanism of sending messages.

this point we need to determine whether the data PortA sends is useful to modelB, according to the condition:

$$\text{TAcur} \leq \text{Ticur} + \text{Tiperiod AND TAcur} + \text{TAperiod} > Ticur + Tiperiod \quad (1)$$

In the condition, TAcur represents the timestamp of PortA, that is, the current simulation time of the modelA, while TAperiod represents the time step of the modelA; Ticur represents the current simulation time of the modelB, while Tiperiod represents the time step of the model B. If the above conditions are met, port data of the PortA is useful for the model B and need be sent to the downstream model B, or do not have to be sent. When the difference between time steps of the model is relatively large, by the above conditions to filter the port data, the transmission of useless port messages can be greatly reduced.

2.2.2 Synchronization Messages Optimization

When the receiving queue of LP2 downstream modelB is located on is empty, LP2 will send a null message request to LP1 the upstream modelA is located on, requesting LP1 to send a null message with timestamp (local time + lookahead), and LP2 can continue to move forward.

For example, the time step of the upstream modelA is 0.001, while the time step of the downstream model B is 1. In order to explain the problem, the time step of model is set to the lookahead of LP, that is, the lookahead of LP1 is 0.001, and the lookahead of LP2 is 1; In LP2, corresponding LP1's receiving queue is empty, LP2 will send a null message to LP1; Local time of LP1 is 0. LP1 will return a null message with timestamp value of 0.001 (local time + lookahead) to LP2. Now the time LP2 can propel to safely is 0.001, but 0.001 is far less than the lookahead of LP2, that is 1, shows that is the time downstream LP2 can propel to is far less than one of its next frame, so even though engine propels, executive operation won't be conducted, and the engine propulsion is called Invalid propulsion. In the above example, since the time of the first 999 null messages that LP1 sends to Lp2 are less than the time of the next frame of LP2, the first 999 propulsions of the downstream LP2 is invalid. And the most effective way to reduce or even eliminate this is to avoid the transmission of null message from the upstream engine.

To solve the above problem, we can use the timestamp in the null message request sent by the downstream LP2 and the timestamp in the null message created by the upstream LP1 to optimize. Figure 3 is the schematic diagram of the mechanism of sending null messages. When the downstream LP2 sends a null message request to upstream LP1, we will set the null message's timestamp to the time of LP2's next frame. When receives LP2's null message request, LP1 will create a null message whose timestamp will not be set simply to the time of LP1's next frame but using the following way:

If T2next > T1next, null message time Tnull is set to T2next (the timestamp of null message request);

If T2next $\leq$ T1next, null message time Tnull is set to T1next(the timestamp of LP1's next frame);

After null messages is created, it is not sent directly, but is inserted to a sending queue of LP1. The null message will be sent only if the condition is met: T1next $\geq$ Tnull.

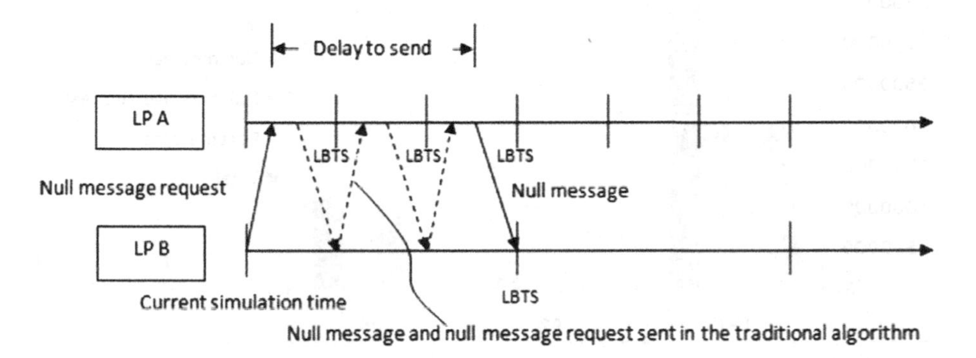

Fig. 3. Mechanism of sending null messages.

This null message transmission mechanism can avoid that the upstream engine whose time step is small send invalid null messages to the downstream engine whose time step is large, this reduces the burden of communication, saves the hardware resource, improves the efficiency of the simulation.

3 Experiment

In parallel simulation, there may be many models. It is assume that the parallel simulation engine has a model. A simulation engine is abstracted a logical process, and the lookahead of LP is set to the time step of the model. The parallel simulation based on the time step and event is different from the other simulation, and its advance of time is not continuous, but is fitxed time point. Such as, the time step of a model is set to 1, and its local time is set to 10. Then, the next advance time of the corresponding LP is 11, that is, the next time step of the model. The LP won't randomly advance to 10.5. Even if a message LP receives makes the LP advance to 10.5, because of the time step of model, LP will not advance to 10.5. The message is the useless message, and the advance the message leads to is the invalid advance.

In the traditional CMB null message algorithm, when a LP propels to a time step, the LP will send a null message (localtime + lookahead) to downstream LP, the null message can tell the downstream LP the time of advance safely. In order to test the performance of the enhanced algorithm when the difference in time step among models is relatively large, we use MPI communication technology to implement the communication of the three LPs which represent three engines of parallel simulation. According to connection among 3 LPs, the safe advance of LP need next time step time of the other two LPs. The local time of three LPs are initialized to 0, the lookahead of LP1 to 0.001, the lookahead of LP2 to 0.002, the lookahead of LP3 to 1, the maximum

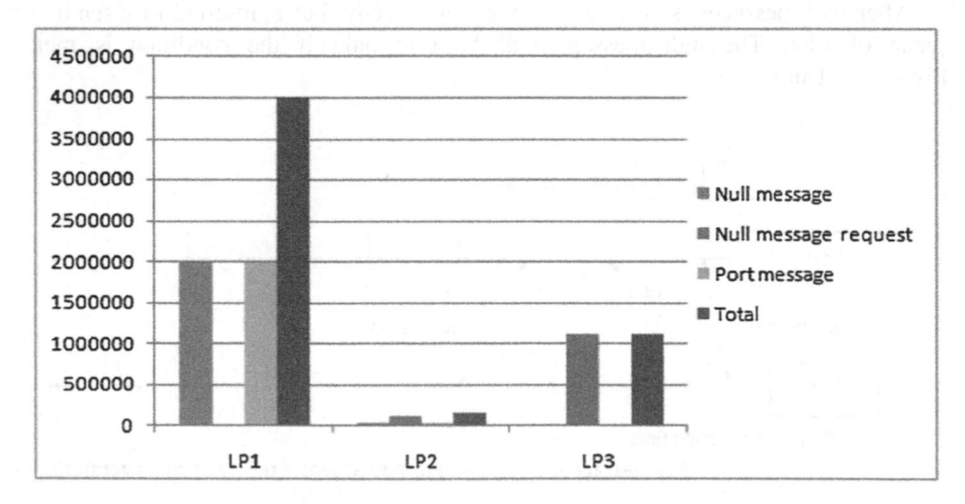

Fig. 4. The number of messages in the traditional CMB algorithm

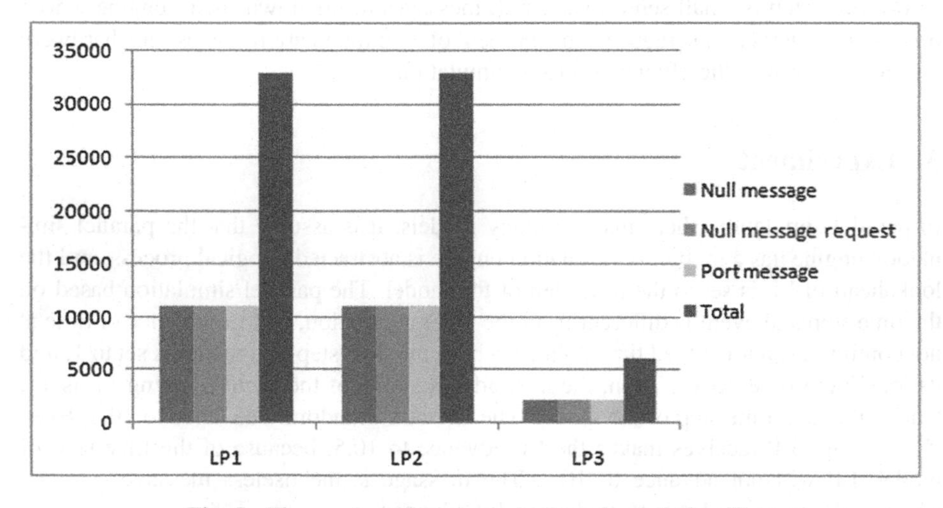

Fig. 5. The number of messages in the enhanced algorithm

simulation time to 1000. And count the number of null messages sent by each LP, the number of null message requests and the port messages. The experiment results are as shown in Figs. 4 and 5.

4 Evaluation

In parallel discrete event simulation, when the difference between time steps of the model is relatively large, under the premise of ensuring the correctness of the simulation results, the new algorithm greatly reduces the number of messages sent. Statistical results are as follows:

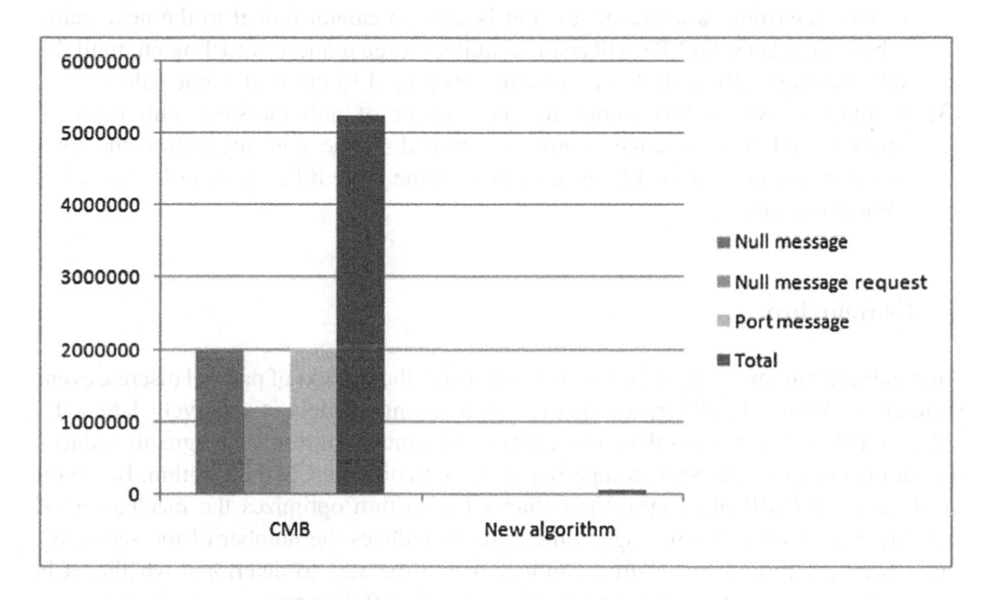

Fig. 6. No. of messages in two algorithm.

Table 1. No. of messages in two algorithm

	Null message	Null message request	Port message	Total
CMB	2022000	1200003	2022000	5244003
New algorithm	24000	24000	24000	72000

Based on the above experimental data, we can draw the following conclusions:

(1) In the traditional CMB algorithm, when the difference between time steps of the model is relatively large, LP with the minimum lookahead will send a large number of null messages, and most of them are useless messages, which do nothing to safely advance of the downstream process. For each propulsion, LP will send port messages to the downstream LP, so that the downstream LP updates

state information, but only a very small number of port messages are really needed by downstream LP, most of the port message is no sense. The transmission of a large number of useless port messages and null messages is a waste of hardware resources, which reduces the efficiency of simulation (Fig. 6 and Table 1).

(2) In the traditional CMB algorithm, LP3 with large lookahead (large time step of model), we can find that LP3 has sent a large number of null messages request. This is because when the receiving queue of LP3 with large lookahead is empty, it will send a null message request to the upstream LP, requesting them to return the null message; After LP1 with small lookahead receives the request, it immediately sends an null message (timestamp = local time + lookahead). But when the timestamp t1 of LP1's null message is less than the timestamp t3 of LP3's next frame, although LP3 receives LP1's null message reply, because t1 < t3, LP3 cannot determine whether next event is safe, so cannot propel to the next frame whose time is t3; So LP3 will send an null message request to LP1 again, until the null message LP1 reply to can ensure LP3 propel to the next frame safely.

(3) Comparing with CMB algorithm, the number of null message, null message request, and port message is greatly reduced in the new algorithm; the total number of messages sent between LPs with the large differences in lookahead is almost the same.

5 Conclusion

An enhanced null message algorithm is presented in the context of parallel discrete event simulation. When the difference in time step among models is relatively large, the enhanced algorithm ensures the correctness of the simulation results and greatly reduces the number of messages sent, comparing with the traditional CMB algorithm. Based on the traditional CMB algorithm, the enhanced algorithm optimizes the mechanism of creating and sending the message, which greatly reduces the number of messages; By calculating the time of downstream models next time step to determine whether it is necessary to send port messages to the downstream LP, this greatly reduces the transmission of useless port messages, saves hardware resources and improves the simulation efficiency. In the implementation of the algorithm, using the method of combining blocking receiving with non-blocking receiving to solve the problem of infinite loop in the process of execution. Then in the process of sending port message, when the model needs to send multiple port messages with the same timestamp at a time, it will cause that the simulation becomes slow. In order to speed up the efficiency, we group the port messages need to be sent according to LP, and then they are sent by group. This reduces the number of repeated packing and repeated transmission, and reduces the number of loop of the execution in parallel, improves the efficiency of simulation. In addition, tests show the enhanced is effective comparing with the traditional CMB algorithm when the difference in time step among models is relatively large.

References

1. Misra, J.: Distributed discrete-event simulation. ACM Comput. Surv. **18**(1), 39–65 (1986)
2. Bain, W., Scott, D.: An algorithm for time synchronization in distributed discrete event simulation. In: Proceedings of the Second Joint International Conference on Vector and Parallel Processing: Parallel Processing, vol. 5, p. 5. Springer-Verlag (1992)
3. Su, W., Seitz, C.L.: Variants of the Chandy-Misra-Bryant distributed discrete-event simulation algorithm. In: Proceedings of the SCS Multiconference on Distributed Simulation (1988)
4. Fujimoto, R.M., Weatherly, R.M.: Time management in the DoD high level architecture. ACM Sigsim Simul. Dig. **26**(1), 60–67 (1999)
5. Brown, R.: Calendar queues: a fast O(1) priority queue implementation for the simulation event set problem. Commun. Acm Cacm Homepage **31**(10), 1220–1227 (1988)
6. Vanmechelen, K., Munck, S.D., Broeckhove, J.: Conservative distributed discrete-event simulation on the Amazon EC2 cloud: An evaluation of time synchronization protocol performance and cost efficiency. Simul. Model. Pract. Theor. **34**(9), 126–143 (2013)
7. Fowler, M., et al.: Parallel discrete event simulation. In: Simulation Conference, pp. 30–53 (1997)
8. Simmonds, R., Unger, B., Bradford, R.: Applying parallel discrete event simulation to network emulation. In: Proceedings of Fourteenth Workshop on Parallel and Distributed Simulation, PADS 2000, pp. 15–22. IEEE (2000)
9. Fujimoto, R.M.: Parallel simulation of discrete event systems. IEEE Trans. Parallel Distrib. Syst. **23**(5), 1 (2012)
10. Ferscha, A., Tripathi, S.K.: Parallel and distributed simulation of discrete event systems. In: Handbook of Parallel and Distributed Computing, pp. 1003–1041. McGraw-Hill (2001)
11. Peterson, G.D., Chamberlain, R.D.: Exploiting lookahead in synchronous parallel simulation. In: Winter Simulation Conference Proceedings, pp. 706–712. IEEE (1993)
12. Page, E.H., Nance, R.E.: Parallel discrete event simulation: a modeling methodological perspective. ACM SIGSIM Simul. Dig. **24**(1), 88–93 (1994)

An Overview of Conceptual Model for Simulation

Yang Zou, Yiping Yao(✉), Zhiwen Jiang, and Wenjie Tang

Computer College, National University of Defense Technology, Changsha, China
nudt_zouyang@163.com

Abstract. Conceptual model is the first abstraction of the real system and plays a role of bridge between domain expert and developer. This paper discusses the research on conceptual model. It begins with an introduction to conceptual model, and addresses the definitions of conceptual model and some conceptual modeling methods, and then discusses the conceptual model validation techniques and the applications. Finally some conclusions are concluded.

Keywords: Conceptual model · Definition · Validation · Conceptual modeling

1 Introduction

Conceptual model is the consistent description of the real system. It is normally described and expressed by language, semantic, graph and son on which is independent of platform and simulation code. Conceptual model is the first abstraction of real system and it can narrow the discrepancies between problem domain and solution domain, which is convenient for developer and user to understand and can help them achieve the agreement on the research problem [1, 2].

During the period of abstracting real system into simulation conceptual model, conceptual model has the following meanings:

(1) An effective communication tool. Through the conceptual model communication between domain expert and developer is convenient. Expert can illustrate the concepts and rules about the real system clearly and developer can grasp the requirements in order to have a proper understanding of the real system.
(2) A good problem solving model. That develops the conceptual model from real system and then develops simulation model from conceptual model is easier than that develops simulation model from the system. This model reduces the difficulty of problem solution.
(3) An effective method for problem solution. There are various entities involved in the simulation and modeling, the relation is so complex. Within reasonable assumptions the complexity of the real system is cut down and developer can hold the core content which is relative to the character of system and is concerned by the user.
(4) A method for ameliorating simulation resource. Abstraction result is dropped while the simulation model has implemented. After that the same phenomenon needs to be abstracted again which leads to poor use ratio. The construction of conceptual model can help raise the reusability [3, 4].

L. Zhang et al. (Eds.): AsiaSim 2016/SCS AutumnSim 2016, Part I, CCIS 643, pp. 96–100, 2016.
DOI: 10.1007/978-981-10-2663-8_10

2 Definitions

Dr. Robert Sargent proposed an opinion that conceptual model can be implied into simulation VV&A and defines the conceptual model as "a mathematical, logical or linguistic expression for specific research" [5]. In this opinion, Sargent emphasizes that conceptual model is relative to application. Dr. Dale Pace defines conceptual model as "translating modeling requirements into detailed simulation specifications (and associated simulation design) which fully satisfy requirements" [6]. Robinson defines conceptual model as "a non-software specific description of the simulation model that is to be developed, describing objectives, inputs, outputs, content, assumptions and simplification of the model" [7, 8]. Glossary of M&S terms which created by US DoD defines conceptual model as "the agreement between simulation developer and the user about what the simulation will do" [9]. FEDEP defines conceptual model as "the abstraction of real world that serves as a frame of reference for federation development by documenting simulation-neutral views of important entities and their key actions and interaction" [10].

To sum up, conceptual model should have the following proprieties [7]:

(1) Conceptual model is a simplified representation of the real system.
(2) Conceptual model has no relative with platform or software.
(3) Conceptual model plays a role of bridge between developer and user.

3 Modeling Method

So far, there have been various modeling methods for conceptual model. Some are platform common used while the others are relied on particular application. Here we introduce several methods which are wildly used.

The function-oriented modeling method has been dominated before 1990s which is represented by structured analysis and design method IDEF, function model is the core established by conceptual modeling. There are two problems existing in this method: (1) unable to express the timing process and support the procedure description, hard to describe the constraint on the time sequence between the various activities (2) the volatility of the function itself reduces the versatility of practical applications. These problems lead the function description of military conceptual model hard to solve and can't describe the relation between functions with poor logic.

The procedure-oriented modeling method defines the procedure as partially ordered sets composed by activities. There is a clear sequence between activities which result in the execution by the triggering events. Procedure can contain sub-procedure and sub-procedure can also contain sub-procedure. This modeling method has a representation of workflow, GANTT, IDEF3 and Petri net, etc. It has an emphasis on dynamic modeling features such as status, activities and so on, but it has poor description ability on static characteristics. Attributes and structure of model can be hard to describe with applying this method.

The object-oriented modeling method models by the view of structural model. Object system is decomposed into the relationship between the entities in the analysis phase while how to solve the implementation of the entities and their relationship is done in the modeling phase. Based on some object-oriented technologies and concepts, there has been proposed a variety of modeling methods where UML modeling has been widely recognized and used. There is a commercial tools support for this method with strong performance but it has a poor reusability and hard to master communication between experts and developers is also difficult.

The ontology-oriented modeling method is similar to the object-oriented modeling method. Nowadays the most popular view of ontology is posed by Gruber in the 1994: Ontology is a formal and explicit specification of the conceptual model. In layman's terms, the modeling result of this method is to abstract a certain area of the real world into a group of concepts (such as entities, attributes, process and so on) and the relationship between the concepts. Information processing in this area will be extremely convenient with the construction of ontology. There is an obvious problem with this approach that developers must be familiar with the field knowledge, otherwise, it will be difficult to grasp the characteristics and behaviors of system and hard to meet the needs.

Though a lot of methods are proposed, there still isn't a common method that can do conceptual modeling for all simulation application. Further study needs to be conducted.

4 Validation Techniques

As mentioned above, conceptual model is the abstraction from the real system to the simulation model and plays an important role in the development and validation of simulation model. Whether the conceptual model is precise needs to be validated. Conceptual model validation is performed while a simulation has not been tested by direct comparison of simulation results with an appropriate Ref. [7]. Conceptual model validation is primarily concerned with determining whether or not the simulation can support the intended uses.

In the 1996, DMSO drew up the conceptual model verification, validation and accreditation RPG. It defined conceptual model verification and validation as "determining that the theories and assumptions underlying the conceptual model are correct and the representation of the validated requirements is reasonable and at the correct level of abstraction".

The description of conceptual model can be divided into two kinds: template and formal. Nowadays conceptual model validation is mainly focused on the qualitative and subjective investigation by the domain experts on the basis of conceptual model description. We called this method Expert Verification Method.

DMSO concludes 76 methods for model Verification, Validation and Accreditation. These methods are divides into 4 kinds: informal method, static method, dynamic method and formal method [7]. In these methods there are 24 methods are suitable for conceptual model. Informal method means getting the assortment result of conceptual model by experts or the experience of experts. Static method means getting the assortment result by figure, table and so on which includes cause-and-effect diagram, state transition analysis data flow analysis, model interaction analysis and result analysis. Dynamic method means getting the assortment result by the execution of model. Because of the characteristic of not running there are only two methods: comparison test and standard test. Formal method means getting assortment result by using strict math language for inference.

Due to the not running of conceptual model, few dynamic methods are suitable for conceptual model validation while formal methods are listed a lot and are the most effective. DMSO pointed that it is the trend that using formal method for conceptual model validation though it hasn't reached the anticipation.

In addition, Robert G. Sargent, Jennifer Chew, Cindy Sullivan and Don Caughlim have a talk about conceptual model verification and validation. They indicate that mathematical analysis and statistical method can be used to test the correctness of conceptual model theory and assumption.

5 Applications

Conceptual model is wildly used in modeling and simulation [11, 12, 13]. Here we take the CMMS as an example.

CMMS is conducted by DMSO to describe a set of methodologies and tools to develop mission space conceptual models [14]. In the DoD M&S Master plan there is a part of the plan that providing a common technical framework for M&S. It includes three sub-objectives: "establishing a common HLA, developing CMMS and establishing data standards". Conceptual model of M&S (CMMS) are "simulation implementation-dependent functional descriptions of the real system processes, entities and environment associated with a particular set of mission". DMSO designs CMMS as "serve as a first abstraction of the real system and as a frame of reference for simulation development" [15, 16].

6 Conclusions

This paper has an overview of conceptual model. To sum up, it is observed that it is difficult to describe conceptual model because we don't know what the conceptual model should contain. There still doesn't exist a general conceptual modeling method due to the same problem mentioned above. About conceptual model validation, though a lot of methods are concluded they still focus on the static validation, there is a long way for formal validation to be maturely used.

Acknowledgement. We appreciate the support from State Key Laboratory of High Performance Computing, National University of Defense Technology (No. 201303-05) and Research Found for the Doctoral Program of Higher Education of China (No. 20124307110017).

References

1. Broah, J.J.: Conceptual modeling – the missing link of simulation development. Spring Simul. Interoperability Workshop (2002)
2. Pace, D.K.: Ideas about simulation conceptual model development. Johns Hopkins APL Technical Digest (2000)
3. Balci, O., Arthur, J.D., Ormsby, W.F.: Achieving reusability and composability with a simulation conceptual model. J. Simul. **5**(3), 157–165 (2011)
4. Pace, D.K.: Development and documentation of a simulation conceptual model. In: Proceeding of Fall Simulation Interoperablity Workshop (1999)
5. Sargent, R.G.: An overview of verification and validation of simulation models. In: Processing of 1987 Winter Simulation Conference (1987)
6. Pace, D.K.: Conceptual model description. In: Proceedings of 1999 Spring Simulation Interoperability Workshop (1999)
7. Robinson, S.: Tutorial: choosing what to model-conceptual modeling for simulation. In: Proceeding of 2012 Winter Simulation Conference (2012)
8. Robinson, S.: Conceptual modeling for simulation: issues and research requirements. In: Proceedings of the 2006 Winter Simulation Conference (2006)
9. U.S. Defense modeling and simulation office (DMSO). Conceptual models of the mission space (CMMS) (1997)
10. U.S. Defense modeling and simulation office (DMSO). Verification, validation and accreditation recommended practice guides (2004)
11. Pace, D.K.: Conceptual model development for C4ISR simulation. In: Proceeding of 5th International Command and Control Research and Technology Symposium (2000)
12. Yilmaz, L.: A conceptual model for reusable simulation within a model-simulator-context framework. In: Proceedings of CMS 2004 Conference on Conceptual Modeling and Simulation (2004)
13. D North Atlantic treaty organisation. conceptual modeling (CM) for Military modeling and simulation (M&S). North Atlantic Treaty Organisation (2012)
14. U.S. Office of the under secretary of defense (Acquisition and Technology). Modeling and Simulation (M&S) Master Plan (1995)
15. Sheehan, J., Prosser, T., Conley, H.: Conceptual model of the mission space (CMMS): basic concepts, advanced techniques, and pragmatic examples. In: Proceeding of Spring Simulation Interoperability Workshop (1998)
16. Liu, J., Yu, Y., Zhang, L., Nie, C.: An overview of conceptual model for simulation and its validation. Procedia Eng. **24**, 152–158 (2011)

A Clustering-Based Artificial Bee Colony Algorithm

Ming Zhang(✉), Na Tian, Zhicheng Ji, and Yan Wang

Engineering Research Center of Internet of Things Technology Applications
Ministry of Education, Jiangnan University, Wuxi 214122, China
zmjiangnan@126.com

Abstract. An advanced Artificial Bee Colony (ABC) algorithm based on fuzzy C-means (FCM) clustering method is presented in this paper, aiming to make a balance between the exploitation and exploration. Firstly, FCM method is employed to divide the population into subpopulations, so that individuals only interact with those in the same subpopulation. Furthermore, the idea of overlapping area has been introduced to the clustering partition, in order to promote the information sharing among different subpopulations. Inspired from the fact that elitist can accelerate convergence, two modified search mechanism has been proposed. The results of experiments based on a set of benchmark functions indicate that our approach is efficient and effective when comparing with some state-of-the-art ABCs.

Keywords: Artificial bee colony algorithm · Fuzzy C-means clustering · Overlapping area · Modified search mechanism

1 Introduction

Artificial Bee Colony (ABC) algorithm is proposed by Karaboga in 2005 [1]. ABC algorithm has been validated to have comparable performance to other algorithms [2]. Nevertheless, ABC algorithm is confronted with some challenging problems. When solving unimodal problems, the convergence rate of ABC seems to be slower than other algorithms, e.g., Particle Swarm Optimization (PSO). Besides, it is much easy for ABC algorithm to get stuck in local optimal points when dealing with complicated multimodal problems. The reason may be attributed to the search strategy which performs well in exploration but badly in exploitation.

Researchers have proposed many improved variants of ABC from several aspects. In order to accelerate convergence rate, global best solution, as an effective method for improving exploitation, has been frequently employed by researchers [3, 4]. Another way to improve the solution equation is to introduce controlling parameters to ABC algorithm, such as inertia weight and acceleration coefficients in [5]. Besides, ABCs incorporating other operations have been widely studied. For example, Basturk and Karaboga [6] utilized the ratio of variance operation and the frequency of perturbation. A modified ABC algorithm with information learning method (termed as ILABC), was presented by Gao et al. [7]. However, the utilization of multi-population strategies in ABC has a limited development, more work is needed in this field.

L. Zhang et al. (Eds.): AsiaSim 2016/SCS AutumnSim 2016, Part I, CCIS 643, pp. 101–109, 2016.
DOI: 10.1007/978-981-10-2663-8_11

This paper focuses on the hybridization of fuzzy C-means clustering (FCM) with ABC algorithm [8]. The motivation lies in that individuals only interact with those in the same subpopulation after dividing the whole population into subareas by FCM. Besides, FCM is improved by using partial overlapping areas to promote the information sharing among different subpopulations in ABC (termed as OCABC). In order to deeply enhance the performance of ABC, the information of local and global best solutions, acting as guiding factors, is applied to the employed and onlooker phase, respectively. The experimental results show that the proposed approaches can improve both the exploration and exploitation performance of OCABC. This paper is structured as follows. The contexts of theories, i.e., original ABC algorithm, FCM method as well as ABC with FCM, are introduced in Sect. 2. The experiments and conclusion are presented in Sects. 3 and 4, respectively.

2 The Clustering-Based Artificial Bee Colony Algorithm

2.1 The Original ABC Algorithm

ABC algorithm is composed of two kinds of bees, termed as employed bees and onlooker bees, and both of them account for half of the whole population. Each candidate solution represents the position of a bee, and its corresponding fitness value denotes the nectar amount of food source. Assuming that initial population, consisting of *SN* solutions with *D*-dimensional vector $X_i = (x_{i,1}, x_{i,2}, \ldots, x_{i,D})$, is randomly generated by (1).

$$x_{i,j} = x_{\min,j} + rand(0, 1)(x_{\max,j} - x_{\min,j}) \tag{1}$$

where $i = 1, 2, \ldots, SN, j = 1, 2, \ldots, D, x_{\min}$ and $x_{\max}$ represent the lower and upper bounds of the search space, respectively. After initialization, each employed bee randomly chosen a solution and update it by the following equation:

$$v_{i,j} = x_{i,j} + \phi_{i,j}(x_{i,j} - x_{k,j}) \tag{2}$$

where i, $k \in \{1, 2, \ldots, SN\}$ and k is different from i; $j = 1, 2, \ldots, D$, $\phi_{i,j}$ is randomly chosen in $[-1, 1]$. Then, each onlooker bee purposefully select a solution to generate a candidate one according to the probabilities based on greedy selection mechanism. And the update process is similar to that in the employed bee phase. Probability p_i is calculated as follows:

$$p_i = fit(X_i) / \sum_{i=1}^{SN} fit(X_i) \tag{3}$$

where $fit(X_i)$ denotes the fitness of X_i. A solution would be abandoned if it had not been improved in a predetermined cycles (termed as *limit*) and the employed bee associated with it would be converted into scout bee to produce a new solution by (2).

2.2 Fuzzy C-Means Clustering

Dunn developed FCM method [8] and it can divide data sets into several subgroups or clusters using fuzzy memberships which means that it is an indirect clustering method. The search space is denoted by $X = \{x_1, x_2, \ldots, x_n\}$, and n data points will be divided into C clusters. The essential purpose of FCM is to minimize the specific objective function as follows:

$$J_m = \sum_{i-1}^{n} \sum_{k=1}^{c} u_{ik}^m \|x_i - v_k\|^2 \tag{4}$$

with constraints as follows:

$$\begin{cases} \sum_{i=1}^{c} u_{ik} = 1, & for\ 1 \le k \le n \\ 0 \le u_{ik} \le 1, & for\ 1 \le k \le n\ and\ 1 \le i \le c \end{cases} \tag{5}$$

where m is the fuzzy value (1 for hard clustering and increasing value for fuzzy clustering); v_k represents the center of the kth cluster; u_{ik} denotes the fuzzy membership of the ith point to the kth cluster; $\|x_i - v_k\|$ means the Euclidean distance between x_i and v_k. Fuzzy partition is carried out with fuzzy membership $U = [u_{ik}]$ and cluster centroids $V = [v_k]$, updated by (6) and (7):

$$u_{ik} = \frac{(\|x_i - v_k\|)^{-2/(m-1)}}{\sum_{j=1}^{c} (\|x_i - v_k\|)^{-2/(m-1)}} \tag{6}$$

$$v_k = \frac{\sum_{i=1}^{n} u_{ik}^m x_i}{\sum_{i=1}^{n} u_{ik}^m} \tag{7}$$

The stop condition of iteration is $\max_{ik}\{\|u_{ik}^{t+1} - u_{ik}^t\|\} < \varepsilon$, where ε denotes a predetermined termination value in [0,1] and t means the step of iteration. J_m can converge to a local minima by this iterative procedure. After calculating the fuzzy membership $U = [u_{ik}]$, each individual chooses a cluster with biggest u_{ik} is the.

2.3 Artificial Bee Colony Algorithm with FCM and Its Improvement

Artificial Bee Colony Algorithm with Improved FCM. Aiming to increase the convergence rate and make a balance between the exploitation and exploration of ABC, FCM is integrated with the idea of overlapping (OFCM), which enables clusters to communicate with each other. The process is as follows:

1. Initialize $U^0 = [u_{ik}]$;
2. At t-iteration: calculate the cluster centroids $V^t = [v_k]$ with U^t by (7);
3. Update U^{t+1} by (6);
4. If $\|U^{t+1} - U^t\| < \varepsilon$ then go to step 5; otherwise, go to step 2;
5. For each centroid: select the top M solutions from the population by descendingly sorting the fuzzy membership $U = [u_{ik}]$ to form the corresponding cluster. M, the size of each cluster, is set as $M = \lceil n/c \rceil + 1$.

The difference between OFCM and FCM on the calculation of U is the selection of partition method. Each individual in FCM belongs to the cluster that has the largest u_{ik}, so that clusters have different numbers of individuals, while each cluster centroid n OFCM attracts the same number of individuals by sorting the fuzzy membership descendingly. One of the advantages of OFCM is that controlling the size of each cluster can prevent some clusters being too small to exchange information with others. Besides, it is inevitable that some individuals may belongs to more than one clusters, i.e. overlapping area, shown in Fig. 1. The overlapping areas play the role of communication between different clusters that contributes to acceleration of the convergence rate. Meanwhile, a few individuals may be excluded from the clusters because of lower fuzzy membership to any clusters, who would not update until entering clusters.

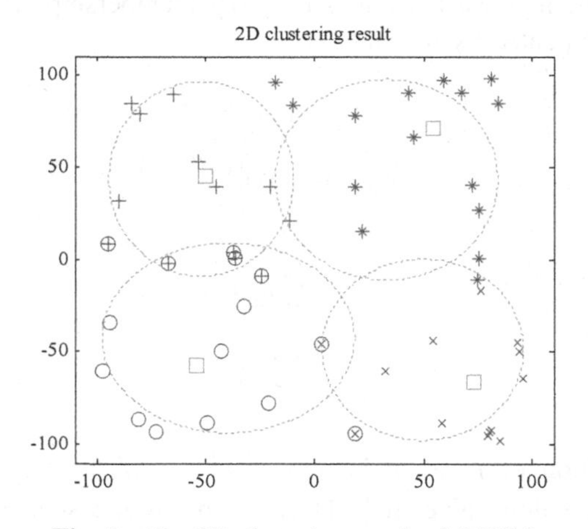

Fig. 1. The 2D clustering result of OFCM

Clustering Period. Clustering process is periodically performed in our approach to efficiently improve the exploitation ability. Although OFCM can benefit the algorithm, frequent utilization might cause a confusing partition of clusters. Therefore, periodic clustering is necessary to enable the population to generate steady clusters. Thus, an additional parameter termed as Q is employed to control the clustering period.

The Improvement of OCABC. As mentioned above, overlapping areas in OFCM contribute to exploit the search space, while the influence of best solution in each neighborhood is diffused slowly by the overlapping neighbors. It is worth noting local best solution and global best solution, which are better individuals, play a critical role in guiding the exploration toward promising direction [3, 4], inspired from which, two novel search strategies are proposed:

$$v_{ij} = x_{lbest,j} + \phi_{ij}(x_{lbest,j} - x_{p,j}) \quad (8)$$

$$v_{ij} = x_{gbest,j} + \phi_{ij}(x_{gbest,j} - x_{p,j}) \quad (9)$$

where ϕ_{ij} and j are the same as in (2); p is a randomly selected integer in [1, Q] and $p \neq i$. *lbest* and *gbest* represents the indexes of the best individuals in the corresponding subpopulations and the whole population, respectively. Equations (8) and (9) serves as the search equations of the employed and onlooker bees, respectively, which obviously play the guided role among the neighborhood in OCABC, denoted as OCABC-guided.

3 Experiments and Analysis

3.1 Experimental Settings

The proposed OCABC-guided is evaluated on 20 widely used benchmark functions f_1–f_{20} in [7]. f_1–f_6 are continuous unimodal functions; f_7 and f_9 are discontinuous step function and noisy quartic function, respectively; f_{11}–f_{20} are multimodal functions. The population size of all algorithms is 100, and *limit* is 200. The dimension *D* is 30, and *FEs* is 100000. Each algorithm is performed 50 independent runs for each objective function.

Table 1. Performance comparisons among ABC, OCABC, ABC-guided and OCABC-guided

Algorithms		f_1	f_2	f_3	f_4	f_5
OCABC-guided	Mean	**6.30e-50**	**2.67e-46**	**9.25e-51**	**1.88e-107**	**2.00e-26**
	SD	**8.55e-99**	**3.04e-91**	**1.91e-100**	**3.54e-103**	**9.82e-52**
ABC-guided	Mean	4.18e-38	7.97e-38	1.61e-38	1.02e-98	9.13e-21
	SD	2.20e-75	8.33e-75	2.40e-76	3.87e-196	1.59e-41
OCABC	Mean	1.33e-13	1.06e-09	1.01e-14	5.93e-28	3.30e-08
	SD	1.18e-25	3.05e-18	5.55e-28	3.30e-54	1.79e-15
ABC	Mean	1.58e-10	3.74e-05	1.59e-12	2.95e-23	4.65e-07
	SD	4.97e-20	2.83e-09	6.22e-24	2.55e-45	7.14e-14
Algorithms		f_9	f_{10}	f_{11}	f_{12}	f_{13}
OCABC-guided	Mean	**5.70e-03**	**1.83e-01**	**0**	**0**	**0**
	SD	**6.60e-06**	**5.90e-02**	**0**	**0**	**0**
ABC-guided	Mean	3.16e-02	2.29e + 01	**0**	**0**	**0**
	SD	1.10e-04	1.24e + 03	**0**	**0**	**0**
OCABC	Mean	1.34e-01	1.98e-01	2.36e-12	5.32e-10	2.86e-07
	SD	1.40e-02	2.04e-02	4.77e-23	9.47e-19	8.14e-13
ABC	Mean	3.54e-02	2.41e-01	5.71e-09	4.89e-08	7.85e-04
	SD	6.52e-05	7.13e-02	1.91e-16	3.86e-15	5.34e-06

Table 2. Performance comparisons of ABCs on 30-dimentional functions

Algorithms		ICABC-guided	ILABC	COABC	ABCbest1	ABCbest2	ABC
f_1	Mean	**4.59e-43**	7.54e-43	6.28e-21	3.50e-30	6.34e-22	5.16e-10
	SD	**1.73e-84**	5.11e-43	1.72e-40	9.75e-60	1.02e-43	4.23e-19
f_2	Mean	**1.97e-40**	8.61e-39	8.35e-09	7.44e-27	3.29e-15	2.89e-05
	SD	**1.02e-79**	1.59e-38	2.94e-16	6.43e-53	8.80e-30	8.29e-10
f_3	Mean	**3.08e-44**	1.72e-43	1.59e-23	5.82e-31	4.71e-23	3.78e-11
	SD	**6.49e-88**	6.66e-44	1.16e-45	1.10e-61	6.10e-46	5.58e-22
f_4	Mean	**2.21e-106**	1.36e-92	5.74e-42	1.27e-66	4.39e-37	3.93e-22
	SD	**2.59e-211**	3.05e-92	1.34e-82	7.75e-132	1.66e-72	2.07e-42
f_5	Mean	**1.10e-23**	6.02e-23	7.58e-11	1.31e-16	4.77e-12	1.78e-06
	SD	**5.14e-47**	5.76e-23	3.57e-21	9.91e-34	1.82e-24	3.60e-13
f_6	Mean	**2.55e + 00**	2.96e-00	2.02e + 01	7.80e + 00	1.09e + 01	1.97e + 01
	SD	3.84e-01	**2.60e-01**	1.01e + 01	9.26e-01	1.50e + 00	1.86e + 01
f_7	Mean	0	**0**	**0**	**0**	**0**	**0**
	SD	0	**0**	**0**	**0**	**0**	**0**
f_8	Mean	**8.50e-01**	8.40e-01	1.26e + 00	9.10e-01	9.24e-01	1.74e + 00
	SD	9.50e-03	0.0204	1.25e-02	7.70e-03	**5.30e-03**	5.58e-02
f_9	Mean	**2.10e-02**	2.20e-02	5.91e-02	2.89e-02	3.30e-02	1.32e-01
	SD	**3.09e-05**	1.05e-02	3.94e-05	7.07e-05	7.16e-05	9.04e-04
f_{10}	Mean	5.21e-01	**1.01e-01**	1.60e + 00	1.24e + 01	1.39e + 01	2.39e-01
	SD	5.03e-01	**1.50e-01**	1.22e + 00	5.48e + 02	5.01e + 02	6.29e-02
f_{11}	Mean	**0**	**0**	1.31e-13	**0**	**0**	5.00e-02
	SD	**0**	**0**	5.15e-26	**0**	**0**	5.00e-02
f_{12}	Mean	**0**	**0**	1.60e-03	**0**	**0**	4.50e-01
	SD	**0**	**0**	2.71e-05	**0**	**0**	2.605e-01

(*Continued*)

Table 2. *(Continued)*

Algorithms		ICABC-guided	ILABC	COABC	ABCbest1	ABCbest2	ABC
f_{13}	Mean	**0**	3.64e-13	7.66e-11	8.22e-16	1.78e-06	5.89e-04
	SD	**0**	5.01e-14	5.81e-20	6.55e-30	1.07e-11	6.93e-06
f_{14}	Mean	**3.17e-15**	7.27e-13	11.9231	8.57e-06	4.17e-06	132.5631
	SD	**2.36e-15**	9.96e-13	1.40e + 03	0	3.31e-25	1.49e + 04
f_{15}	Mean	**2.70e-14**	2.77e-14	5.89e-09	5.81e-14	5.76e-11	9.94e-06
	SD	**1.81e-29**	1.58e-15	1.26e-17	1.41e-28	5.03e-22	3.15e-11
f_{16}	Mean	**1.57e-32**	**1.57e-32**	3.06e-20	2.58e-32	6.51e-24	1.76e-11
	SD	8.32e-96	**0**	2.44e-39	2.62e-65	2.17e-47	3.35e-22
f_{17}	Mean	**1.50e-33**	1.34e-32	2.63e-18	2.69e-31	4.80e-22	1.29e-09
	SD	**0**	0	4.84e-35	5.21e-62	1.97e-43	1.10e-18
f_{18}	Mean	1.20e-15	**6.25e-23**	2.83e-05	1.80e-15	1.43e-07	2.26e-04
	SD	**2.03e-30**	**4.83e-23**	2.95e-10	2.17e-30	5.74e-14	9.03e-08
f_{19}	Mean	1.35e-31	**1.34e-31**	4.91e-20	5.63e-30	1.54e-19	5.00e-09
	SD	**0**	**0**	6.30e-39	3.91e-59	1.42e-37	2.79e-17
f_{20}	Mean	**0**	**0**	**0**	**0**	**0**	**0**
	SD	**0**	**0**	**0**	**0**	**0**	**0**

3.2 Comparison Among ABC, OCABC, ABC-Guided, OCABC-Guided

In this section, different variants of ABC (ABC, OCABC, ABC-guided, OCABC-guided) are compared, where ABC-guided denotes the original ABC with guided information of global best solution. Table 1 contains the mean best value and standard deviations of 10 objective functions. Q and C in OCABC-guided and OCABC is set to 20 and 3, respectively.

The results show that OCABC-guided outperforms others on all functions, followed by ABC-guided, however, the gap between them is small, which indicates that the guiding effect of local best solution and global best solution plays an important role on the exploitation ability. In general, OCABC performs better than ABC, although superiority on some functions, such as f_9–f_{11} is slight, which indicates that integrating OFCM in ABC has a positive effect on the performance.

3.3 Comparison with Other ABC Hybrids

With C setting to 4, Table 2 presents the comparison of six algorithms, including ILABC [7], COABC [4], ABCbest1 [3], ABCbest2 [3] and ABC [1], involving mean best values and standard deviation. Generally, OCABC-guided performs significantly better than other algorithms, especially for f_1, f_2, f_3, f_4, and f_{13}. For the remaining functions, OCABC-guided has comparable performance with others, except for f_{18} and f_{19}, on which ILABC wins. Apparently, OCABC-guided is more robust than others, because of lower standard deviation on most cases.

4 Conclusion

To balance the exploitation and exploration in ABC, a novel ABC based on overlapping fuzzy C-mean clustering (OCABC) was presented, so that different subpopulations concentrate on different sub-regions and information exchange among different subpopulations are encouraged. Further, OCABC-guided was proposed based on local best individual and global best individual. The efficiency of overlapping FCM and guiding effect was verified, and the experimental results indicated that OCABC-guided performs competitively in terms of the solution accuracy.

In the future work, the scalability of OCABC-guided and the influence of parameters, such as the number of centroids and clustering period, will be investigated.

Acknowledgement. This project is supported by National Hi-tech Research and Development Program of China (863 Program, Grant No. 2014AA041505), the National Science Foundation of China (61572238), the Provincial Outstanding Youth Foundation of Jiangsu Province (BK20160001).

References

1. Karaboga, D.: An idea based on honey bee swarm for numerical optimization. Dept. Comput. Sci., Erciyes University, Kayseri, Turkey, Technical report-TR06, October 2005
2. Karaboga, D., Basturk, B.: A powerful and efficient algorithm for numerical function optimization: artificial bee colony (ABC) algorithm. J. Global Optim. **39**(3), 459–471 (2007)
3. Gao, W.F., Liu, S.Y., Huang, L.L.: A global best artificial bee colony algorithm for global optimization. J. Comput. Appl. Math. **236**(11), 2741–2753 (2012)
4. Luo, J., Wang, Q., Xiao, X.H.: A modified artificial bee colony algorithm based on converge-onlookers approach for global optimization. Appl. Math. Comput. **219**(20), 10253–10262 (2013)
5. Li, G.Q., Niu, P.F., Xiao, X.J.: Development and investigation of efficient artificial bee colony algorithm for numerical function optimization. Appl. Soft Comput. **12**(1), 320–332 (2012)
6. Basturk, B., Karaboga, D.: A modified artificial bee colony algorithm for real-parameter optimization. Inf. Sci. **192**(1), 120–142 (2012)
7. Gao, W.F., Huang, L.L., Liu, S.Y., Dai, C.: Artificial bee colony algorithm based on information learning. IEEE Trans. Cybern. **45**(12), 2827–2839 (2015)
8. Bezdek, J.C., Ehrlich, R., Full, W.: FCM: the fuzzy c-means clustering algorithm. Comput. Geosci. **10**(2–3), 191–203 (1984)

The Multi-innovation Based RLS Method for Hammerstein Systems

Zhenwei Shi[1,2], Zhicheng Ji[1(✉)], and Yan Wang[1]

[1] Engineering Research Center of Internet of Things Technology Applications Ministry of Education, Jiangnan University, Wuxi 214122, P.R. China
zcji@jiangnan.edu.cn
[2] Wuxi Electrical and Higher Vocational Schools, Wuxi 214000, P.R. China

Abstract. In the study, a multi-innovation RLS with a forgetting factor (FF-MRLS) method is put forward to identify the parameters of a class of Hammerstein model. Two simulation experiments verify the proposed method is superior to the conventional FF-RLS method in terms of convergence rate and tracking performance.

Keywords: RLS · Hammerstein model · Backlash · Multi-innovation

1 Introduction

Hammerstein model with backlash can be found in many applications fields, such as servo motion control fields, sensor detection fields, gear transmission mechanism etc. [1]. The nonlinearity with backlash often leads to the deterioration of system performance, even cause the system unstable [2]. Therefore, in order to obtain better control performance, some compensation for the backlash measures must be taken. One way to compensate for the backlash is to identify the backlash and perform the backlash inverse [2]. System identification with backlash has attracted the interest of many researchers [3, 4] for several decades.

Since famous scholar Ding introduced the idea of multi-innovation into system identification, the multi-innovation identification method has been researched and applied widely [5, 6]. Multi-innovation methods, including the multi-innovation LS and gradient methods, can improve the precision of system parameters identification. Owing to the multi-innovation method apply not only some new data, at the same time, use the past data in every recursion, the accuracy of parameter identification is improved. About the parameter identification of time-varying systems, it is most widely used identification method that the RLS with forgetting factor method [7].

In this study, based on the ideas of the multi-innovation [5, 6] and the RLS with forgetting factor, we derive a multi-innovation RLS with forgetting factor method, which can track time-varying parameters.

The rest of the organizations of this study are as follows. Section 2 derives the identification model of the Hammerstein with backslash systems. Section 3 provides the FF-MRLS method for Hammerstein with backslash systems. Section 4 verifies that the FF-MRLS method is feasible. In Sect. 5 some conclude is given.

L. Zhang et al. (Eds.): AsiaSim 2016/SCS AutumnSim 2016, Part I, CCIS 643, pp. 110–119, 2016.
DOI: 10.1007/978-981-10-2663-8_12

2 The Hammerstein Model Description

2.1 Hammerstein Model

We consider the same class of systems as in [4]. For completeness, the Hammerstein model is shown as follows

$$y(t) = \frac{B(z)}{A(z)}\tilde{u}(t) + \frac{1}{A(z)}v(t), \tag{1}$$

$$\tilde{u}(t) = BC(u(t)), \tag{2}$$

where $y(t)$ and $u(t)$ are the system output and input, $\tilde{u}(t)$ is the output of the backlash block, $v(t)$ is a zero mean and variance σ^2 of the random white noise, z^{-1} represents a post shift operator: $[z^{-1}v(t) = v(t-1)]$, $B(z)$ and $A(z)$ are scalar polynomials in the unit delay operator, and they are as follows

$$A(z) = 1 + a_1 z^{-1} + a_2 z^{-2} + \ldots + a_{n_a} z^{-n_a}, \tag{3}$$

$$B(z) = b_0 + b_1 z^{-1} + b_2 z^{-2} + \ldots + b_{n_b} z^{-n_b}. \tag{4}$$

Assumed the order of the system is known, $u(t) = v(t) = y(t) = 0$ when $t \le 0$.

2.2 Backslash Characteristic

The backslash characteristic $BC(\cdot)$ can be represented as [1, 8]

$$\tilde{u}(t) = BC(u(t)) = \begin{cases} k_L[u(t) + d_L], & u(t) \le c_L \\ k_R[u(t) - d_R], & u(t) \ge c_R \\ \tilde{u}(t-1), & c_L \le c_R \end{cases}, \tag{5}$$

where $k_L > 0$, $k_R > 0$, $d_L > 0$ and $d_R > 0$ are constant parameters characterizing the backlash and

$$c_L = \frac{-d_L k_L + \tilde{u}(t-1)}{k_L}, \tag{6}$$

$$c_R = \frac{d_R k_R + \tilde{u}(t-1)}{k_R}. \tag{7}$$

The backslash characteristic can be expressed by

$$\begin{aligned} \tilde{u}(t) = \{\{k_L(u(t) - d_L) + k_R(u(t) - d_R) - k_R(u(t) - d_R)\}f[u(t)]\}F[u(t)] \\ + \tilde{u}(t-1)(1 - F[u(t)]). \end{aligned} \tag{8}$$

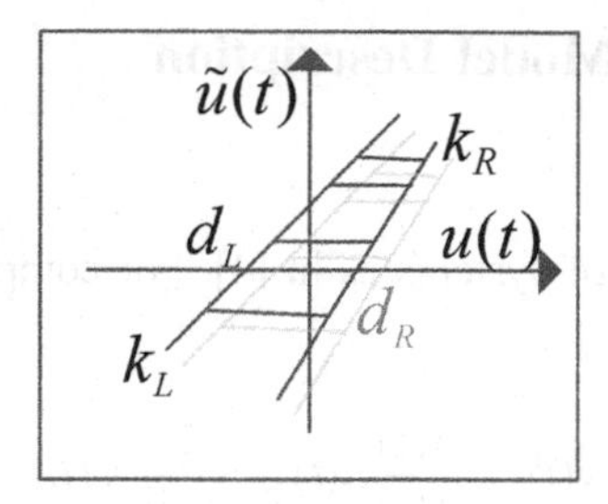

Fig. 1. The backlash characteristic

Such a backslash is shown in Fig. 1. In this note, we introduce two switching functions [9]

$$f[u(t)] = \begin{cases} 0, & u(t) \geq c_R \\ 1, & u(t) \leq c_L \end{cases}, \quad F[u(t)] = \begin{cases} 0, & c_L < u(t) < c_R \\ 1, & others \end{cases}. \tag{9}$$

Equation (8) can be equivalently rewritten as

$$\begin{aligned} \tilde{u}(t) = {} & u(t)F[u(t)]f[u(t)]k_L + u(t)F[u(t)](1 - f[u(t)])k_R + F[u(t)](f[u(t)] - 1)k_R d_R \\ & + F[u(t)]f[u(t)]k_L d_L + \tilde{u}(t-1)(1 - F[u(t)]). \end{aligned} \tag{10}$$

2.3 The Linear Regression Model for Hammerstein Model

In order to obtain unique parameter identification, let $b_0 = 1$ [10]. Then, (1) is modified into [11]

$$y(t) = \tilde{u}(t) + \sum_{l=1}^{n_b} b_l \tilde{u}(t-l) - \sum_{l=1}^{n_a} a_l y(t-l) + v(t), \tag{11}$$

and (11) is substituted for the separated $\tilde{u}(t)$ leading to the following equation

$$\begin{aligned} y(t) = {} & u(t)F[u(t)]f[u(t)]k_L + u(t)F[u(t)](1 - f[u(t)])k_R + F[u(t)](f[u(t)] - 1)k_R d_R \\ & + F[u(t)]f[u(t)]k_L d_L + \tilde{u}(t-1)(1 - F[u(t)]) + \sum_{l=1}^{n_b} b_l \tilde{u}(t-l) - \sum_{l=1}^{n_a} a_l y(t-l) + v(t). \end{aligned} \tag{12}$$

To estimates parameter of the system, we parameterize the (12) as

$$\begin{aligned} y(t) &= \boldsymbol{\varphi}_v^{\mathrm{T}}(t)\boldsymbol{\theta}_v + \boldsymbol{\varphi}_u^{\mathrm{T}}(t)\boldsymbol{\theta}_u + \tilde{u}(t-1)(1 - F[u(t)]) + v(t), \\ &= \boldsymbol{\varphi}^{\mathrm{T}}(t)\boldsymbol{\theta} + \tilde{u}(t-1)(1 - F[u(t)]) + v(t). \end{aligned} \tag{13}$$

where $\boldsymbol{\theta}_u := [b_1, b_2, \ldots, b_{n_b}, a_1, a_2, \ldots, a_{n_a}]^{\mathrm{T}} \in R^{n_b + n_a}$, $\boldsymbol{\theta}_v := [k_L, k_R, k_R d_R, k_L d_L]^{\mathrm{T}} \in R^4$,

$$\boldsymbol{\varphi}_v(t) = [u(t)F[u(t)]f[u(t)], u(t)F[u(t)](1-f[u(t)]), F[u(t)](f[u(t)]-1), \\ F[u(t)]f[u(t)]]^{\mathrm{T}} \in R^4,$$

$$\boldsymbol{\varphi}_u(t) = [\tilde{u}(t-1), \tilde{u}(t-2), \ldots, \tilde{u}(t-n_b), -y(t-1), -y(t-2), \ldots, -y(t-n_a)]^{\mathrm{T}} \in R^{n_b+n_a}.$$

Thus the Hammerstein model with backlash is described by (13). While it is almost difficulty to identify the parameter $\boldsymbol{\theta}$, on the basis of this form of structural style, the output (13) contains internal variables $\tilde{u}(t-1)$ that cannot be measured. Referring to [8, 12], set a internal output $y_c(t)$

$$y_c(t) = y(t) - \tilde{u}(t-1)(1-F[u(t)]), \tag{14}$$

the output (13) is expressed as follows

$$y_c(t) = \boldsymbol{\varphi}^{\mathrm{T}}(t)\boldsymbol{\theta} + v(t). \tag{15}$$

3 The Multi-innovation RLS with a Forgetting Factor Method

Some symbol definitions are given. $\|\mathbf{X}\|^2 = tr[\mathbf{X}^{\mathrm{T}}\mathbf{X}]$ expresses the matrix $\mathbf{X}$ norm; $\mathbf{I}$ stands for an appropriate unit matrix and $\mathbf{1}_n$ represents as a unit column vector of n-dimensions.

Set the following weighting output vector $\mathbf{Y}_c(q,t)$ and weighting information matrix $\boldsymbol{\Phi}^{\mathrm{T}}(q,t)$

$$\mathbf{Y}_c(q,t) = \begin{bmatrix} y_c(t) \\ y_c(t-1) \\ \vdots \\ y_c(t-q+1) \end{bmatrix} \in R^q, \mathbf{V}(q,t) = \begin{bmatrix} v(t) \\ v(t-1) \\ \vdots \\ v(t-q+1) \end{bmatrix} \in R^q, \tag{16}$$

$$\boldsymbol{\Phi}^{\mathrm{T}}(q,t) = \begin{bmatrix} \boldsymbol{\varphi}^{\mathrm{T}}(t) \\ \hat{\boldsymbol{\Phi}}^{\mathrm{T}}(t-1) \\ \vdots \\ \boldsymbol{\varphi}^{\mathrm{T}}(t-q+1) \end{bmatrix} \in R^{q\times(4+n_b+n_a)}, \boldsymbol{\varphi}(t) = \begin{bmatrix} \boldsymbol{\varphi}_v(t) \\ \boldsymbol{\varphi}_u(t) \end{bmatrix} \in R^{4+n_b+n_a}, \tag{17}$$

where the positive integer q is expressed as a number of innovative, so (15) is re expressed as the matrix equation of the following form

$$\mathbf{Y}_c(q,t) = \boldsymbol{\Phi}^{\mathrm{T}}(q,t)\boldsymbol{\theta} + \mathbf{V}(q,t). \tag{18}$$

Define and implement the minimum of the quadratic criterion [5, 13]

$$J_1(\boldsymbol{\theta}) := \sum_{l=1}^{t} \left\| \mathbf{Y}_c(q,l) - \boldsymbol{\Phi}^{\mathrm{T}}(q,l)\boldsymbol{\theta} \right\|^2. \tag{19}$$

In order to be able to identify the parameters of time variation, a forgetting factor μ is leaded into (18) and (19) is rewritten as [14]

$$J_2(\boldsymbol{\theta}) := \sum_{l=1}^{t} \mu^{t-l} \left\| \mathbf{Y}_c(q,l) - \boldsymbol{\Phi}^{\mathrm{T}}(q,l)\boldsymbol{\theta} \right\|^2. \tag{20}$$

Define the matrix as

$$\mathbf{W}_t = \begin{bmatrix} \mathbf{Y}_c(q,t) \\ \mu^{1/2}\mathbf{Y}_c(q,t-1) \\ \vdots \\ \mu^{t-2/2}\mathbf{Y}_c(q,2) \\ \mu^{t-1/2}\mathbf{Y}_c(q,1) \end{bmatrix} \in R^{qt}, \tag{21}$$

$$\mathbf{H}_t = \begin{bmatrix} \boldsymbol{\Phi}^{\mathrm{T}}(q,t) \\ \mu^{1/2}\boldsymbol{\Phi}^{\mathrm{T}}(q,t-1) \\ \vdots \\ \mu^{t-2/2}\boldsymbol{\Phi}^{\mathrm{T}}(q,2) \\ \mu^{t-1/2}\boldsymbol{\Phi}^{\mathrm{T}}(q,1) \end{bmatrix} \in R^{(qt)\times n}. \tag{22}$$

From the (20)–(22), we can get

$$\hat{\theta}(t) = (\mathbf{H}_t^{\mathrm{T}}\mathbf{H}_t)^{-1}\mathbf{H}_t^{\mathrm{T}}\mathbf{W}_t = \left[\sum_{l=1}^{t} \mu^{t-l}\boldsymbol{\Phi}(q,l)\boldsymbol{\Phi}^{\mathrm{T}}(q,l)\right]^{-1}\left[\sum_{l=1}^{t} \mu^{t-l}\boldsymbol{\Phi}(q,l)\mathbf{Y}^{\mathrm{T}}(q,l)\right]. \tag{23}$$

From the (21) and (22), we can have

$$\mathbf{H}_t = \begin{bmatrix} \boldsymbol{\Phi}^{\mathrm{T}}(q,t) \\ \mu^{1/2}\mathbf{H}_{t-1} \end{bmatrix}, \quad \mathbf{W}_t = \begin{bmatrix} \mathbf{Y}_c(q,t) \\ \mu^{1/2}\mathbf{W}_{t-1} \end{bmatrix}. \tag{24}$$

Define the matrix $\mathbf{Q}(t) \in R^{n\times n}$ and reference (23), $\mathbf{Q}(t)$ is represented as a recursive form

$$\mathbf{Q}^{-1}(t) = \mathbf{H}_t^{\mathrm{T}}\mathbf{H}_t = \mu\mathbf{Q}^{-1}(t-1) + \boldsymbol{\Phi}(q,t)\boldsymbol{\Phi}^{\mathrm{T}}(q,t). \tag{25}$$

According to (23)–(25), we can derive

$$\hat{\boldsymbol{\theta}}(t) = \hat{\boldsymbol{\theta}}(t-1) + \mathbf{Q}(t)\boldsymbol{\Phi}(q,t)[\mathbf{Y}_c(q,t) - \boldsymbol{\Phi}^{\mathrm{T}}(q,t)\hat{\boldsymbol{\theta}}(t-1)]. \tag{26}$$

Reference the matrix theorem

$$(A+CB)^{-1} = A^{-1} - A^{-1}C(I+BA^{-1}C)^{-1}BA^{-1}, \tag{27}$$

based on (25), we derive

$$\mathbf{Q}(t) = \frac{1}{\mu}\left[\mathbf{Q}(t-1) - \mathbf{Q}(t-1)\boldsymbol{\Phi}(q,t)[\mu\mathbf{I}_q + \boldsymbol{\Phi}^T(q,t)\mathbf{Q}(t-1)\boldsymbol{\Phi}(q,t)]^{-1}\boldsymbol{\Phi}^{\mathrm{T}}(q,t)\mathbf{Q}(t-1)\right], \tag{28}$$

where $\mathbf{I}_q$ expresses as a q dimensional unit matrix

A gain matrix $\mathbf{L}(t)$ is defined as follows

$$\mathbf{L}(t) = \mathbf{Q}(t-1)\boldsymbol{\Phi}(q,t)[\mu\mathbf{I}_q + \boldsymbol{\Phi}^{\mathrm{T}}(q,t)\mathbf{Q}(t-1)\boldsymbol{\Phi}(q,t)]^{-1} \in R^{n\times q}. \tag{29}$$

Thus, (28) can be rewritten as

$$\mathbf{Q}(t) = \frac{1}{\mu}\left[\mathbf{Q}(t-1) - \mathbf{L}(t)\boldsymbol{\Phi}^{\mathrm{T}}(q,t)\mathbf{Q}(t-1)\right]. \tag{30}$$

Combining (16), (17), (29), (30) and (31), the FF-MRLS method is expressed.

But, some identification difficulties comes from the inability to estimate the intrinsic variables $\tilde{u}(t-l)$, the unknown parameters c_L and c_R, and the unknown output correction $y_c(t)$, so the proposed FF-MRLS method is not used to estimate $\boldsymbol{\theta} = \left[\boldsymbol{\theta}_v^{\mathrm{T}}, \boldsymbol{\theta}_u^{\mathrm{T}}\right]^{\mathrm{T}}$. A solution is on the basis of the auxiliary model identification method [15] and interactive identification strategy: $\hat{\boldsymbol{\theta}}(t) = \left[\hat{\boldsymbol{\theta}}_v^{\mathrm{T}}(t), \hat{\boldsymbol{\theta}}_u^{\mathrm{T}}(t)\right]^{\mathrm{T}}$ expresses as the identification of $\boldsymbol{\theta} = \left[\boldsymbol{\theta}_v^{\mathrm{T}}, \boldsymbol{\theta}_u^{\mathrm{T}}\right]^{\mathrm{T}}$; the output of the auxiliary model $\hat{\tilde{u}}(t)$ replaced the variable $\tilde{u}(t)$ and the unknown output correction $y_c(t)$ and the parameters c_R and c_L are displaced by their identification value $\hat{y}_c(t)$, $\hat{c}_R$ and $\hat{c}_L$. When $\tilde{u}(t-1)$ is displaced by the identification value $\hat{\tilde{u}}(t-1)$, the $y_c(t)$ is computed by

$$\hat{y}_c(t) = y(t) - \hat{\tilde{u}}(t-1)(1-\hat{F}[u(t)]). \tag{31}$$

Replacing $\tilde{u}(t-1)$ and $\boldsymbol{\theta}_v(t) = [k_L, k_R, k_R d_R, k_L d_L]^{\mathrm{T}}$ with the identification value $\hat{\tilde{u}}(t-1)$ and $\hat{\boldsymbol{\theta}}_v(t) = [\hat{k}_L, \hat{k}_R, \hat{k}_R\hat{d}_R, \hat{k}_L\hat{d}_L]^{\mathrm{T}}$ in (6), (7), the identification value of c_L and c_R is computed by

$$\hat{d}_R = \frac{\hat{k}_R\hat{d}_R}{\hat{k}_R},\ \hat{d}_L = \frac{\hat{k}_L\hat{d}_L}{\hat{k}_L},\ \hat{c}_L = \frac{-\hat{d}_L\hat{k}_L + \hat{\tilde{u}}(t-1)}{\hat{k}_L},\ \hat{c}_R = \frac{\hat{d}_R\hat{k}_R + \hat{\tilde{u}}(t-1)}{\hat{k}_R}. \tag{32}$$

$\hat{c}_R$, $\hat{c}_L$ replace c_R, c_L in above functions and (9) is rewritten into

$$\hat{f}[u(t)] = \begin{cases} 0, & u(t) \geq \hat{c}_R \\ 1, & u(t) \leq \hat{c}_L \end{cases}, \quad \hat{F}[u(t)] = \begin{cases} 0, & \hat{c}_L < u(t) < \hat{c}_R \\ 1, & others \end{cases}. \tag{33}$$

Combining (26) and (29)–(33), we get the following FF-MRLS method for the Hammerstein model with backlash:

$$\hat{\boldsymbol{\theta}}(t) = \hat{\boldsymbol{\theta}}(t-1) + \mathbf{Q}(t)\hat{\boldsymbol{\Phi}}(q,t)[\hat{\mathbf{Y}}_c(q,t) - \hat{\boldsymbol{\Phi}}^{\mathrm{T}}(q,t)\hat{\boldsymbol{\theta}}(t-1)], \tag{34}$$

$$\mathbf{Q}(t) = \frac{1}{\mu}\left[\mathbf{Q}(t-1) - \mathbf{L}(t)\hat{\boldsymbol{\Phi}}^{\mathrm{T}}(q,t)\mathbf{Q}(t-1)\right], \tag{35}$$

$$\mathbf{L}(t) = \mathbf{Q}(t-1)\hat{\boldsymbol{\Phi}}(q,t)[\mu\mathbf{I}_q + \hat{\boldsymbol{\Phi}}^{\mathrm{T}}(q,t)\mathbf{Q}(t-1)\hat{\boldsymbol{\Phi}}(q,t)]^{-1} \in R^{n\times q}, \; 0<\mu\leq 1, \tag{36}$$

$$\begin{aligned}\hat{\boldsymbol{\varphi}}_u(t) = {} & [\hat{\bar{u}}(t-1), \hat{\bar{u}}(t-2), \ldots, \hat{\bar{u}}(t-n_b), -y(t-1), -y(t-2), \ldots, -y(t-n_a)]^{\mathrm{T}} \\ & \in R^{n_b+n_a},\end{aligned} \tag{37}$$

$$\begin{aligned}\hat{\boldsymbol{\varphi}}_v(t) = {} & [u(t)\hat{F}[u(t)]\hat{f}[u(t)], u(t)\hat{F}[u(t)](1-\hat{f}[u(t)]), (\hat{f}[u(t)]-1) \\ & \hat{F}[u(t)], \hat{F}[u(t)]\hat{f}[u(t)]]^{\mathrm{T}} \in R^4,\end{aligned} \tag{38}$$

$$\hat{\boldsymbol{\varphi}}(t) = \begin{bmatrix} \hat{\boldsymbol{\varphi}}_v(t) \\ \hat{\boldsymbol{\varphi}}_u(t) \end{bmatrix} \in R^{4+n_b+n_a}, \quad \hat{\boldsymbol{\Phi}}^{\mathrm{T}}(q,t) = \begin{bmatrix} \hat{\boldsymbol{\varphi}}^{\mathrm{T}}(t) \\ \hat{\boldsymbol{\varphi}}^{\mathrm{T}}(t-1) \\ \vdots \\ \hat{\boldsymbol{\varphi}}^{\mathrm{T}}(t-q+1) \end{bmatrix} \in R^{q\times(4+n_b+n_a)}, \tag{39}$$

$$\hat{y}_c(t) = y(t) - \hat{\bar{u}}(t-1)(1-\hat{F}[u(t)]), \tag{40}$$

$$\hat{\mathbf{Y}}_c(q,t) = [\hat{y}_c(t)\; \hat{y}_c(t-1) \cdots \hat{y}_c(t-q+1)]^{\mathrm{T}} \in R^q, \; q \leq t, \tag{41}$$

$$\begin{aligned}\hat{\boldsymbol{\theta}}(t) = {} & \begin{bmatrix} \hat{\boldsymbol{\theta}}_v(t) \\ \hat{\boldsymbol{\theta}}_u(t) \end{bmatrix} \in R^{4+n_b+n_a}, \; \hat{\boldsymbol{\theta}}_v(t) = [\hat{k}_L, \hat{k}_R, \hat{k}_R\hat{d}_R, \hat{k}_L\hat{d}_L]^{\mathrm{T}} \in R^4, \\ \hat{\boldsymbol{\theta}}_u(t) = {} & [\hat{b}_1, \hat{b}_2, \ldots, \hat{b}_{n_b}, \hat{a}_1, \hat{a}_2, \ldots, \hat{a}_{n_a}]^{\mathrm{T}} \in R^{n_b+n_a},\end{aligned} \tag{42}$$

$$\hat{d}_R = \frac{\hat{k}_R\hat{d}_R}{\hat{k}_R}, \; \hat{d}_L = \frac{\hat{k}_L\hat{d}_L}{\hat{k}_L}, \; \hat{c}_L = \frac{-\hat{d}_L\hat{k}_L + \hat{\bar{u}}(t-1)}{\hat{k}_L}, \; \hat{c}_R = \frac{\hat{d}_R\hat{k}_R + \hat{\bar{u}}(t-1)}{\hat{k}_R}, \tag{43}$$

$$\hat{f}[u(t)] = \begin{cases} 0, & u(t) \geq \hat{c}_R \\ 1, & u(t) \leq \hat{c}_L \end{cases}, \quad \hat{F}[u(t)] = \begin{cases} 0, & \hat{c}_L < u(t) < \hat{c}_R \\ 1, & others \end{cases}, \tag{44}$$

$$\begin{aligned}\hat{\bar{u}}(t) = {} & u(t)\hat{F}[u(t)]\hat{f}[u(t)]\hat{k}_L + u(t)\hat{F}[u(t)](1-\hat{f}[u(t)])\hat{k}_R + \hat{F}[u(t)](\hat{f}[u(t)]-1)\hat{k}_R\hat{d}_R \\ & + \hat{F}[u(t)]\hat{f}[u(t)]\hat{k}_L\hat{d}_L + \hat{\bar{u}}(t-1)(1-\hat{F}[u(t)]).\end{aligned} \tag{45}$$

The FF-MRLS method steps are as follows:

Step 1: Set up q and μ initialize: let $\hat{\boldsymbol{\theta}}_v(t-1) = \mathbf{1}_4/p_0$, $t = q$, $\hat{\boldsymbol{\theta}}_u(t-1) = \mathbf{1}_{n_b+n_c}/p_0$, $\mathbf{Q}(t-1) = p_0\mathbf{I}_{4+n_a+n_b}$, $\hat{\bar{u}}(t-l) = 1/p_0$, $\hat{y}_c(t-l) = 0$, $l = 0, 1, 2, \ldots,$ $\max(n_b, q-1)$, $p_0 = 10^6$;

Step 2: Gather the data $\{y(t-l), l = 1, 2, \ldots, n_a\}$ and the identification data $\{\hat{\bar{u}}(t-l),$ $l = 1, 2, \ldots, n_b\}$ form $\hat{\boldsymbol{\varphi}}_u(t)$;

Step 3: Gather the inner data $\hat{\bar{u}}(t-1)$ and the data $u(t)$,

Step 4: Calculate the $\hat{\boldsymbol{\varphi}}_v(t)$, $\hat{\bar{u}}(t)$ and $\hat{y}_c(t)$ by (38), (40), (43) and (44);

Step 5: Structure $\hat{\mathbf{Y}}_c(q,t)$ by (41) and $\hat{\boldsymbol{\Phi}}^{\mathrm{T}}(q,t)$ by (39);

Step 6: Calculate $\mathbf{Q}(t)$ by (35) and $\mathbf{L}(t)$ by (36),;

Step 7: Renew the identification value $\hat{\boldsymbol{\theta}}(t)$ by (34);

Step 8: $t = t+1$ and go to Step 2.

4 Example Simulation

Example 1: Study the Hammerstein time-invariant model with backlash:

$$y(t) = \sum_{l=1}^{1} b_l \bar{u}(t-l) - \sum_{l=1}^{2} a_l y(t-l) + u(t)F[u(t)]f[u(t)]k_L + u(t)F[u(t)](1 - f[u(t)])k_R$$
$$+ F[u(t)]f[u(t)]k_L d_L + F[u(t)](f[u(t)] - 1)k_R d_R + \bar{u}(t-1)(1 - F[u(t)]) + v(t),$$

where the backlash characteristics are depicted in Fig. 1.

The linear parameter values are $b_1 = 0.135$, $a_1 = -0.2$ and $a_2 = 0.35$, and the backlash parameter values are $k_R = 1.5$, $k_L = 1.2$, $d_R = 0.7$ and $d_L = 0.6$. $\{u(t)\}$ is an uncorrelated persistent excitation signal sequence with zero mean and unit variance $\sigma_u^2 = 1.0^2$, and $\{v(t)\}$ is a white noise with zero mean and variance $\sigma_v^2 = 0.5^2$. The FF-MRLS in (34)–(45) and FF-RLS methods are applied to identify the Hammerstein system parameters, respectively and the parameter identification errors δ are depicted in Fig. 2, $\delta = \left\|\hat{\boldsymbol{\theta}}(t) - \boldsymbol{\theta}\right\| / \|\boldsymbol{\theta}\|$ and $\mu = 1$.

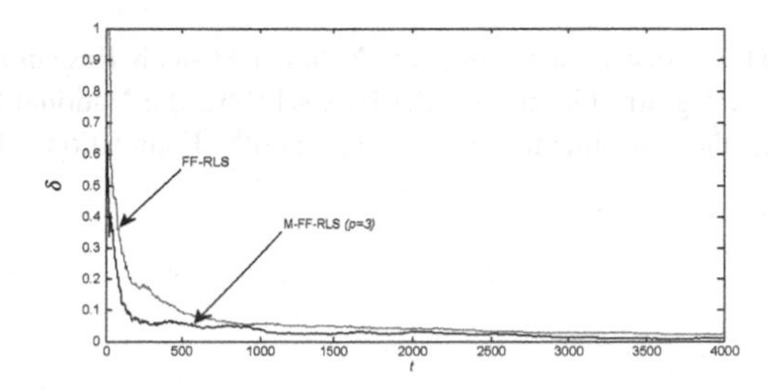

Fig. 2. The parameter identification errors δ versus t.

Example 2: Study the Hammerstein time-varying model with backlash:

$$y(t) = \sum_{l=1}^{1} b_l \tilde{u}(t-l) - \sum_{l=1}^{2} a_l y(t-l) + u(t)F[u(t)]f[u(t)]k_L + u(t)F[u(t)](1-f[u(t)])k_R$$
$$+F[u(t)]f[u(t)]k_L d_L + F[u(t)](f[u(t)]-1)k_R d_R + \bar{u}(t-1)(1-F[u(t)]) + v(t)$$

$$\mathbf{\theta}_u = [b_1, a_1, a_2]^{\mathrm{T}} = [0.135, -0.2, 0.35]^{\mathrm{T}}, \mathbf{\theta}_v(t) = [k_L(t), k_R(t), k_R(t)d_R(t), k_L(t)d_L(t)]^{\mathrm{T}},$$

where the parameters of backlash are described in [8].

In the simulation example, the noise variance is $\sigma_v^2 = 0.2^2$. Using the FF-RLS and FF-MRLS ($q = 3$) methods with $\mu = 0.994$, respectively, to identify the time-varying system. Parameter identification lines are depicted in Fig. 3.

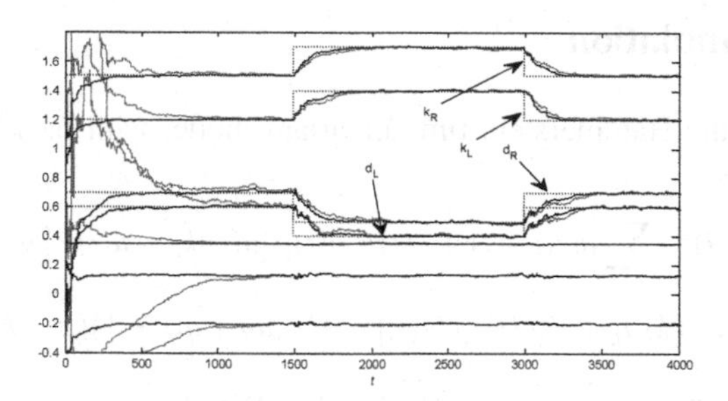

Fig. 3. Figure 3. The parameter identification lines versus t. Red lines: the FF-RLS method; Back lines: the FF-MRLS method. (Color figure online)

5 Conclusions

A FF-MRLS method is derived for Hammerstein model with backlash. The simulation examples prove that the proposed method gives the higher convergence speed and promotes the parameter identification accuracy compared to traditional FF-RLS method.

Acknowledgments. This work is supported by National Hi-tech Research and Development Program of China (863 Program, Grant No. 2014AA041505), the National Science Foundation of China (61572238), the Provincial Outstanding Youth Foundation of Jiangsu Province (BK20160001).

References

1. Dong, R., Tan, Q., Tan, Y.: Recursive identification algorithm for dynamic systems with output backlash and its convergence. Int. J. Appl. Math. Comput. Sci. **19**(4), 631–638 (2009)
2. Barreiro, A., Baños, A.: Input–output stability of systems with backlash. Automatica **42**(6), 1017–1024 (2006)
3. Vörös, J.: Parametric identification of systems with general backlash. Informatica **23**(2), 283–298 (2012)
4. Vörös, J.: Modeling and identification of systems with backlash. Automatica **46**(2), 369–374 (2010)
5. Ding, F., Chen, T.: Performance analysis of multi-innovation gradient type identification methods. Automatica **43**(1), 1–14 (2007)
6. Ding, F.: Several multi-innovation identification methods. Digit. Signal Process. **20**(4), 1027–1039 (2010)
7. Toplis, B., Pasupathy, S.: Tracking improvements in fast RLS algorithms using a variable forgetting factor. IEEE Trans. Acoust. Speech Signal Process. **36**(2), 206–227 (1988)
8. Vörös, J.: Identification of nonlinear cascade systems with time-varying backlash. J. Electr. Eng. **62**(2), 87–92 (2011)
9. Wang, D., Chu, Y., Yang, G., Ding, F.: Auxiliary model based recursive generalized least squares parameter estimation for Hammerstein OEAR systems. Math. Comput. Model. **52** (1), 309–317 (2010)
10. Wang, D., Chu, Y., Ding, F.: Auxiliary model-based RELS and MI-ELS algorithm for Hammerstein OEMA systems. Comput. Math Appl. **59**(9), 3092–3098 (2010)
11. Ljung, L., Söderström, T.: Theory and practice of recursive identification (1983)
12. Janczak, A.: Identification of nonlinear systems using neural networks and polynomial models: a block-oriented approach. Springer Science & Business Media, Berlin (2004)
13. Ding, F., Liu, P.X., Liu, G.: Multi-innovation least-squares identification for system modeling. IEEE Trans. Syst. Man Cybern. B Cybern. **40**(3), 767–778 (2010)
14. Bittanti, S., Bolzern, P., Campi, M.: Convergence and exponential convergence of identification algorithms with directional forgetting factor. Automatica **26**(5), 929–932 (1990)
15. Ding, F., Liu, G., Liu, X.P.: Parameter estimation with scarce measurements. Automatica **47** (8), 1646–1655 (2011)

Control Strategies for Network Systems Based on a Novel Event-Trigger Mechanism

Ke Zhang[1(✉)], Min Zheng[1,2(✉)], and Yijie Zhang[1]

[1] College of Mechatronic Engineering and Automation, Shanghai University, Shanghai 200072, China
{zhangke306shdx, zhengmin203}@163.com, leo_dragon@126.com

[2] Shanghai Key Laboratory of Power Station Automation Technology, Shanghai 200072, China

Abstract. In this paper, a kind of data retransmission mechanism for network control system based on event trigger is introduced, to reduce the influence caused by packet loss in the process of network communication. At first, this paper presents an event trigger mechanism, to be applied to judge whether the signal of the sensor to be sent to the controller through the network, the network control system model combining with the data retransmission mechanism is constructed, then analyzing the stability of this system and constructing feedback gain for this model accordingly. Finally through the simulation experiment proves the effectiveness of the method.

Keywords: Event-trigger · Data retransmission · H_∞ control · NCS

1 Introduction

With the wide use of network technologies, the control systems become more and more intelligent and distributed. Signals of each node in the networked control systems transmit and exchange through the internet, which brings some new problems such as time delay and communication channel bandwidth limitations. Meanwhile, these challenges put forward new opportunities and catch much more concern [1–8]. The existence of network deduced delay will degrade the performance of the system and even lead to instability. It is hard for the traditional control methods to be applied to the networked control systems directly. On the other hand, the limited communication capacity may lead to challenges in real-time control requirements. At present, most of the networked control systems are based on the time triggered communication mechanism; however, this kind of mechanism will cause the waste of the network resources. In order to reduce the unnecessary waste of resources of network communication, some event triggering control methods were proposed in [9–12]. Event trigger control only takes effects under guaranteeing certain performance for the closed-loop systems. Once the predefined event trigger condition was set up, control tasks executed immediately. Compared with the traditional time trigger control, event trigger control can reduce the network resource utilization while keeping the control performance. In addition to delay and communication bandwidth limitations, there is packet loss problem in

L. Zhang et al. (Eds.): AsiaSim 2016/SCS AutumnSim 2016, Part I, CCIS 643, pp. 120–126, 2016.
DOI: 10.1007/978-981-10-2663-8_13

networked control systems, which will deteriorate performance and even make the system unstable with the increase of packet loss rate. Therefore, how to solve this problem is still need further research.

In view of the above discussion, the main purpose of this paper is to promote the event trigger mechanism on the premise of improving the utilization ratio of network resources and reducing the impacts of packet loss. This paper mainly includes the following contents: in Sect. 2, the model of networked control system with data retransmission mechanism is constructed. Then, the condition of asymptotically stable with H_∞ performance is given in Sect. 3. Simulations and experimental results are presented and discussed in Sect. 4. Finally, the conclusion is presented in Sect. 5.

2 System Descriptions with New Event Generator

Consider the system described by

$$\begin{cases} \dot{x}(t) = Ax(t) + Bu(t) + B_\omega\omega(t) \\ z(t) = Cx(t) + Du(t) \end{cases} \tag{1}$$

where $x(t) \in R^n$, $u(t) \in R^m$, $\omega(t) \in L_2[0, \infty)$ and $z(t) \in R^p$ are the system state vector, the control input, external disturbance and the objective vector; A, B, B_ω, C and D are the parameter matrices with appropriate dimensions; the initial state of system (1) is $x(t_0) = x_0$. As depicted in Fig. 1, the sensor collects information of the object with a fixed cycle h, the event trigger generator filters the received sampling data according to the predetermined trigger conditions. If the triggering conditions are satisfied, the sampled signal is sent to the controller twice, otherwise don't send it.

The following triggering algorithm will be used in this paper:

$$t_{k+1}h = t_k h + \min_l\{lh|e^T(i_k h)\emptyset e(i_k h) \geq \delta x^T(t_k h)\emptyset x(t_k h)\} \tag{2}$$

where $\delta \geq 0$; $\emptyset$ is a symmetric positive definite matrix; $e(i_k h)$ is the difference between the current state of sampling time and the last sent state, that is $e(i_k h) = x(i_k h) - x(t_k h)$, $i_k h = t_k h + lh$, $l \in N$; h is sampling period of sensor; $t_k h$ denotes the release time from sensor.

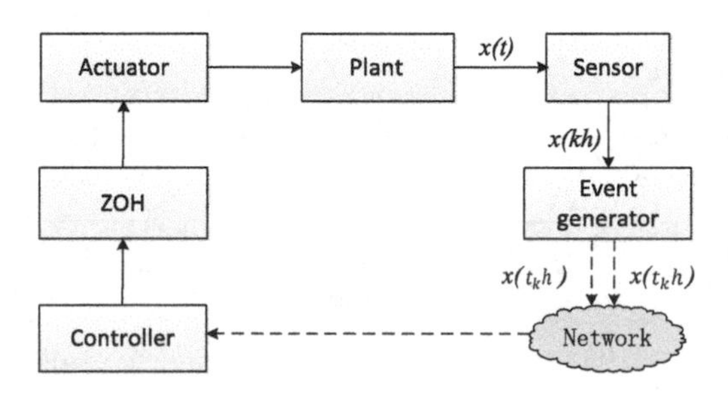

Fig. 1. Structure of an event-triggered networked control system

Remark 1: The sensors are time-triggered with constant sampling period h. The sampling sequence is described by the set $S_1 = \{0, h, 2h, \ldots, kh\}$. The controllers and the actuators are event-triggered; the successfully transmitted sampled sequence at the sensors is described by the set $S_2 = \{0, t_1h, t_2h, \ldots, t_kh\}$.

The control input at the actuator is generated by a zero-order-holder (ZOH), and the NCS can be described by

$$\begin{cases} \dot{x}(t) = Ax(t) + Bu(t) + B_{\omega}\omega(t) \\ z(t) = Cx(t) + Du(t) \\ u(t) = Kx(t_kh), t \in [t_kh + \tau_{t_k}, t_{k+1}h + \tau_{t_{k+1}}) \end{cases} \tag{3}$$

where K is the state feedback control gain; τ_{t_k} is the transmission delay.

As shown in Fig. 2, the sensor end will send two times the data that satisfy event triggering conditions, and the delays are $\tau_{1_{t_k}}$ and $\tau_{2_{t_k}}$ respectively. The signals will hold in interval $[t_kh + \tau_{t_k}, t_{k+1}h + \tau_{t_{k+1}}]$, where $\tau_{t_k} = \min\left(\tau_{1_{t_k}}, \tau_{2_{t_k}}\right)$, $\tau_{t_{k+1}} = \min\left(\tau_{1_{t_{k+1}}}, \tau_{2_{t_{k+1}}}\right)$. The time interval Ω of ZOH is divided into subsets $\Omega_l = [i_kh + \tau_{i_k}, i_kh + h + \tau_{i_{k+1}}]$, i.e. $\Omega = \cup \Omega_l$, where $i_kh = t_kh + lh$, $l = 0, \ldots, t_{k+1} - t_k - 1$. If l is $t_{k+1} - t_k - 1$, *then* $\tau_{i_{k+1}} = \tau_{t_{k+1}}$, otherwise $\tau_{i_k} = \tau_{t_k}$. Let $\eta(t) \triangleq t - i_kh$, $t \in \Omega_l$. Obviously $\eta(t)$ satisfies $0 < \eta_1 \le \eta(t) \le h + \bar{\tau} = \eta_3, t \in \Omega_l$, where $\eta_1 = \inf_l\{\tau_{i_k}\}$, $\eta_3 = h + \sup_l\{\tau_{i_{k+1}}\} = h + \bar{\tau}$; h and $\bar{\tau}$ are the sampling period and maximum allowable time delay respectively. The controller of (3) is:

$$u(t) = \mathrm{K}(x(t - \eta(t)) - e(i_kh)), t \in \Omega_l \tag{4}$$

Then the closed loop networked control system is

$$\begin{cases} \dot{x}(t) = Ax(t) + BK(x(t - \eta(t)) - e(i_kh)) + B_{\omega}\omega(t) \\ z(t) = Cx(t) + DK(x(t - \eta(t)) - e(i_kh)), \ t \in \Omega_l \end{cases} \tag{5}$$

where the initial condition $x(t) = \varphi(t), t \in [t_0 - \eta_3, t_0]$, $\varphi(t_0) = x_0$, $\varphi(t)$ is continuous function in $[t_0 - \eta_3, t_0]$.

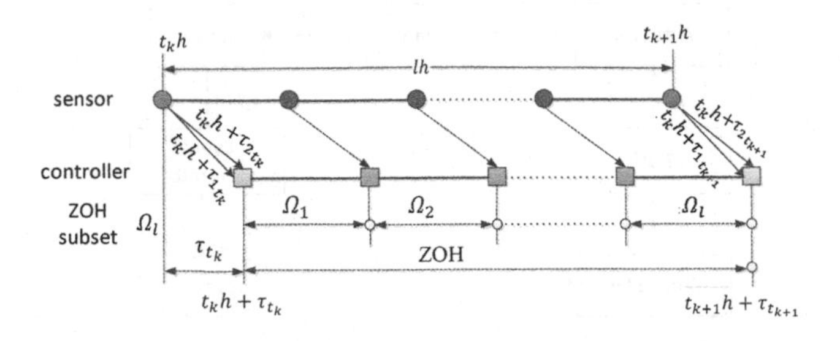

Fig. 2. Subsets partition of ZOH

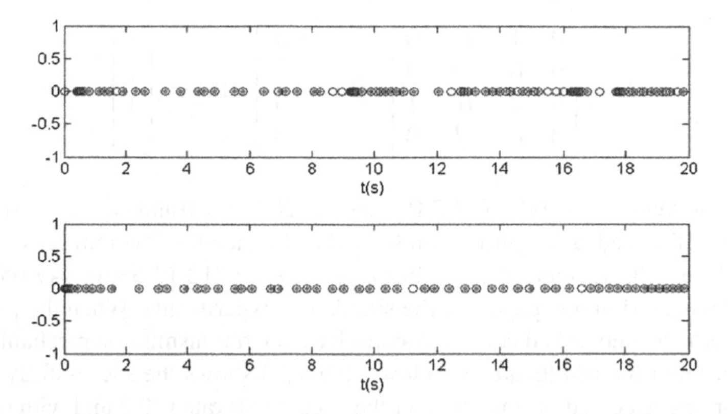

Fig. 3. Data receiving rate of mechanisms without or with retransmission

3 H_∞ Stability Analysis

The stability conditions and H_∞ analysis for system (5) are stated as the following theorems.

For the given positive constants η_1, η_3, γ, δ and a matrix K, under the event triggered communication mechanism (2), if there are positive matrices $P > 0, \emptyset > 0, S_i > 0 (i = 1, 2), R_j > 0 (j = 1, 2, 3, 4), \begin{bmatrix} Q_1 & * \\ Q_3 & Q_2 \end{bmatrix} > 0$ with appropriate dimensions, such that (6) holds, then the system (5) is asymptotically stable.

$$\begin{bmatrix} \Pi_{11} & * \\ * & \Pi_{22} \end{bmatrix} < 0, \tag{6}$$

where $\Pi_{11} = [(1,1) = S_2 - S_1,\ (2,2) = Q_1 - S_2,\ (3,2) = Q_3,\ (3,3) = Q_2 - Q_1,\ (4,3) = -Q_3,\ (4,4) = -Q_2]$ $\Pi_{22} = [(1,1) = S_1 + \delta\emptyset,\ (3,3) = -\emptyset,\ (4,4) = -\gamma^2 I] + l_1^T l_2 [I, I, I, I]^T l_1 + col\{2Pl_1 - C^T l_3,\ (DK)^T l_3,\ -(DK)^T l_3, 0\}$, $l_1 = [A, BK, -BK, B_\omega]$, $l_2 = [(\frac{\eta_1}{2})^2 R_1,\ (\frac{\eta_1}{2})^2 R_2,\ (\eta_2 - \eta_1)^2 R_3,\ (\eta_3 - \eta_2)^2 R_4$, $l_3 = [C, DK, -DK, 0]$.

Remark 2: The proofs of Theorems 1 and 2 are similar as [13], so we omit the proofs here for briefness. For the predetermined $\tilde{\emptyset}$ and K, the parameter δ can be selected according to Theorems 1 and 2. We also can co-design the feedback gain K and triggering parameter δ.

4 Simulation Experiments

Consider a networked control system with the following parameters

$$\mathrm{A} = \begin{bmatrix} 0 & 1 & 0 & 0 \\ 0 & 0 & -1 & 0 \\ 0 & 0 & 0 & 1 \\ 0 & 0 & \frac{10}{3} & 0 \end{bmatrix}, \mathrm{B} = \begin{bmatrix} 0 \\ \frac{1}{10} \\ 0 \\ \frac{-1}{30} \end{bmatrix}, \mathrm{B}_{\omega} = \begin{bmatrix} 1 \\ 1 \\ 1 \\ 1 \end{bmatrix} \tag{7}$$

The initial states $x_0 = [0.98\ 0\ 0.2\ 0]^T$, let $\gamma = 200$, $\bar{\tau} = 0$ and $\omega(t) = 0.01\sin(2\pi t)$, for different δ, the feedback control gain K can be obtained by Theorem 2. For example, let $\delta = 0.1$, $h = 0.01$, then the feedback gain $\mathrm{K} = [12.12\ 33.68\ 447.65\ 254.83]$. Truetime 2.0 is used in this paper for the simulation experiments. When the packet loss rate is not zero, the networked control systems have the retransmission mechanism or not are simulated and the results are as follows. Figure 3 shows the successfully sent data from sensors are accepted or not when let the packet loss rate is 0.2 and with or without using data retransmission mechanism.

In Fig. 3, the graphic symbol ∘ denotes instants of the un-received data, and the symbol ⊚ denotes instants of the accepted data. It can be seen that the control system

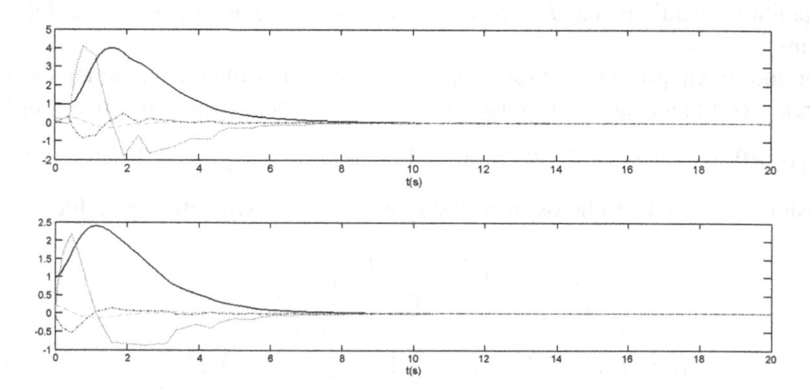

Fig. 4. State responses for the packet loss rate is 0.2

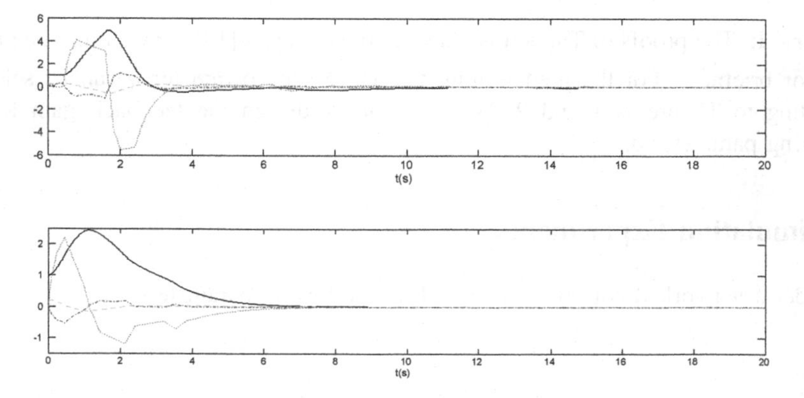

Fig. 5. State responses for the packet loss rate is 0.3

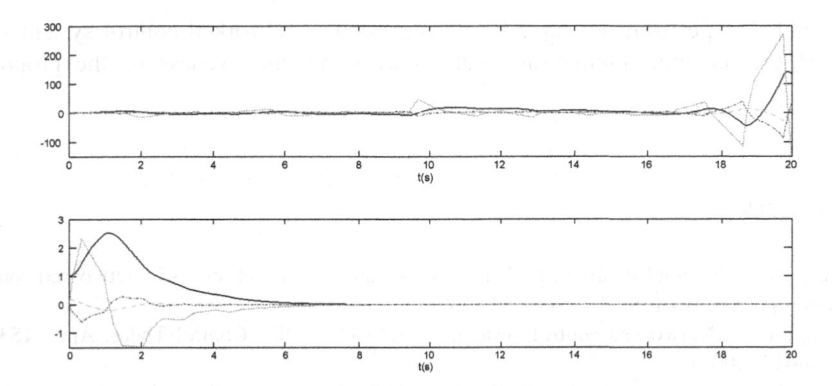

Fig. 6. State responses for the packet loss rate is 0.5

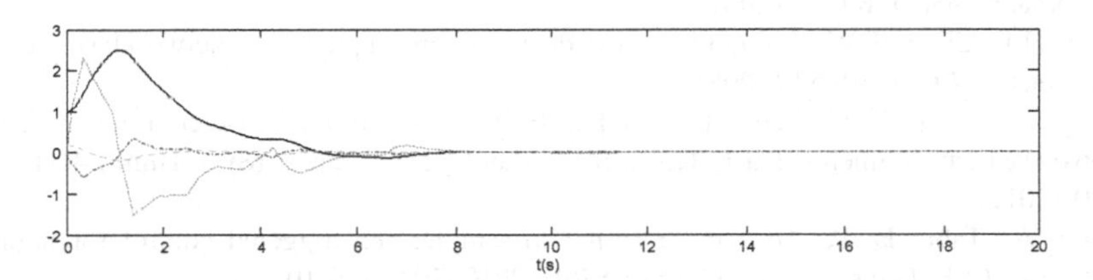

Fig. 7. State responses for the packet loss rate is 0.6

with data retransmission mechanism will still be able to improve the utilization of network resource. The comparison results are shown in Fig. 4 for with or without data retransmission scheme. The receiving rate of useful signals is improved for the retransmission method.

For further comparison, simulation results with different packet loss rates are shown in Figs. 5, 6 and 7, where the packet loss rates are 0.3, 0.5, and 0.6 respectively. It can be seen that the results based on our retransmission mechanism are better than the mechanism without using retransmission. Figure 5 shows that the settling time is shorter by our approach. When increasing the packet loss rate to 0.5, as shown in Fig. 6, our approach can keep the system stable, whereas the other approach cannot guarantee system stability. Figure 7 shows that the networked control system can still keep stable even when the packet loss rate reaches 0.6. According to the above discussions, the data retransmission mechanism proposed in this paper can reduce the effects from the networked packet loss.

5 Conclusions

A new event-trigger scheme with data retransmission mechanism has been investigated in this paper. This method not only can reduce the network traffic load and improve the utilization rate of network resources, but also can improve the robust stability under networked circumstances with high packet loss rates. The conditions of asymptotically stable with H_∞ performance have been given for the networked control system with event-trigger scheme. Simulation results shown the effectiveness of the proposed method.

References

1. Hespanha, J.P., Naghshtabrizi, P., Xu, Y.G.: A survey of recent results in networked control systems. Proc. IEEE **95**(1), 138–162 (2007)
2. Yang, T.-C.: Networked control system: a brief survey. IET Control Theor. Appl. **153**(4), 403–412 (2006)
3. Kim, D.S., Lee, Y.S., Kwon, W.H., Park, H.S.: Maximum allowable delay bounds of networked control systems. Control Eng. Pract. **11**(11), 1301–1313 (2003)
4. Xiong, J., Lam, J.: Stabilization of linear systems over networks with bounded packet loss. Automatica **43**(1), 80–87 (2007)
5. Gao, H.J., Chen, T.W., Lam, J.: A new delay system approach to networkbased control. Automatica **44**(1), 39–52 (2008)
6. Peng, C., Tian, Y.-C., Yue, D.: Output feedback control of discrete-time systems in networked environments. IEEE Trans. Syst. Man Cybern. Part A (Syst. Hum.) **41**(1), 185–190 (2011)
7. Anta, A., Tabuada, P.: To sample or not to sample: self-triggered control for nonlinear systems. IEEE Trans. Autom. Control **55**(9), 2030–2042 (2010)
8. Camacho, A., Martí, P., Velasco, M., Lozoya, C., Villà, R., Fuertes, J.M. et al.: Self-triggered networked control systems: an experimental case study. In: IEEE International Conference on Industrial Technology, pp. 123–128 (2010)
9. Heemels, W.P.M.H., Gorter, R.J.A., van Zijl, A., Van den Bosch, P.P.J., Weiland, S., Hendrix, W.H.A., et al.: Asynchronous measurement and control: a case study on motor synchronization. Control Eng. Pract. **7**(12), 1467–1482 (1999)
10. Donkers, M.C.F., Heemels, W.P.M.H.: Output-based event-triggered control with guaranteed L∞ gain and improved and decentralised eventtriggering. IEEE Trans. Autom. Control **57**(6), 1362–1376 (2012)
11. Tabuada, P.: Event-triggered real-time scheduling of stabilizing control tasks. IEEE Trans. Autom. Control **52**(9), 1680–1685 (2007)
12. Wang, X., Lemmon, M.D.: Event-triggering in distributed networked control systems. IEEE Trans. Autom. Control **56**(3), 586–601 (2011)
13. Peng, C., Yang, T.C.: Event-triggered communication and H_∞ control co-design for networked control systems. Automatica **49**(2013), 1326–1332 (2013)

An Integrated Model Predictive Iterative Learning Control Strategy for Batch Processes

Chao Han and Li Jia(✉)

Department of Automation, College of Mechatronics Engineering and Automation, Shanghai University, Shanghai, China
jiali@staff.shu.edu.cn

Abstract. A novel integrated model predictive iterative learning control (MPILC) strategy is proposed in this paper. It systematically integrates batch-axis information and time-axis information into one uniform frame, namely the iterative learning controller (ILC) in the domain of batch-axis, while a model predictive controller (MPC) with time-varying prediction horizon in the domain of time-axis. As a result, the operation policy of batch process can be regulated during one batch, which leads to superior tracking performance and better robustness against disturbance and uncertainty. The convergence and tracking performance of the proposed learning control system are firstly given rigorous description and proof. Lastly, the effectiveness of the proposed method is verified by examples.

Keywords: Batch process · Integrated learning control · Iterative learning control (ILC) · Model predictive control (MPC) · Model identification · Dynamic R-parameter

1 Introduction

Batch processes have been used increasingly in the production of low volume and high value added products, such as special chemicals, pharmaceuticals, and heat treatment processes for metallic or ceramic products [2]. However, with strong nonlinearity and dynamic characteristics, optimal control of batch processes is more challenging than that of continuous processes and thus it needs new non-traditional techniques.

Batch processes have the characteristic of repetition, and thus iterative learning control (ILC) can be used in the optimization control of batch processes [3]. But for ILC, only the batch-to-batch performance is taken for consideration but not the performance of real-time feedback. As a result, it is difficult to guarantee the performance of the batch process when real-time uncertainties and disturbances exist. Therefore, an integrated optimization control system is required to derive the maximum benefit from batch processes, in which the performance of time-axis and batch-axis are both analyzed synchronously. However, most reported two-dimension control results [1, 4] assume that the batch processes are linear or can be locally linearized for the feasibility of proof and analysis. How to extend 2D controller design method to more general nonlinear processes is challenging.

L. Zhang et al. (Eds.): AsiaSim 2016/SCS AutumnSim 2016, Part I, CCIS 643, pp. 127–135, 2016.
DOI: 10.1007/978-981-10-2663-8_14

To solve this problem, inspired by MPC with time-varying prediction horizon, a novel integrated iterative learning control (MPILC) strategy with model identification and dynamic R-parameter for batch processes is proposed in this paper, which not only combined feedback controller in time-axis with iterative learning optimization control in batch-axis, but also improved the accuracy of the model through online identification. Moreover, we made the first attempt to give rigorous description and proof of the convergence and tracking performance of the proposed integrated learning control system to verify that a perfect tracking performance can be obtained despite the existence of model-plant-mismatch. Lastly, an example illustrates the performance and applicability of the proposed integrated optimization control. Simulation results demonstrate that the proposed integrated control strategy has better tracking performance and robustness.

2 Design of Integrated MPILC Strategy with Model Identification and Dynamic R-parameter

In this paper, the control signals of both ILC and MPC are designed as an integrated control system as shown in Fig. 1. The ILC part guarantees the convergence while the MPC part keeps the robustness and stability.

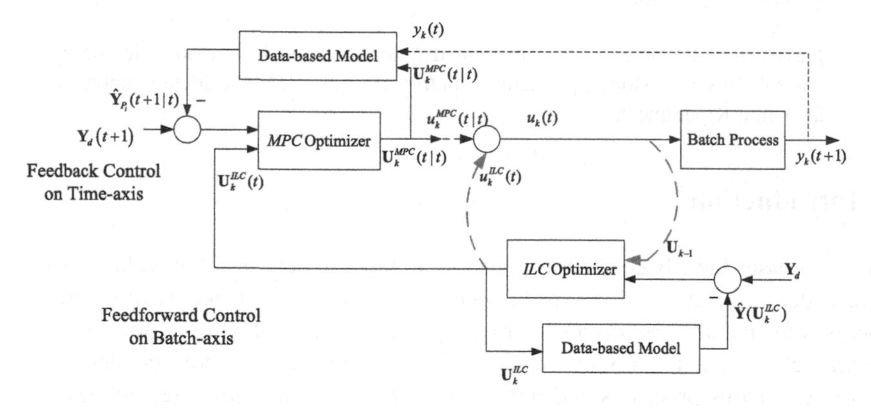

Fig. 1. Integrated model predictive iterative learning control system

2.1 Integrated MPILC System with Dynamic R-parameter

As discussed above, the objective of ILC is to design a learning algorithm which implements the control trajectory $\mathbf{U}_k^{ILC}$ such that the product quality asymptotically converges to the desired product qualities along the batch axis. The quadratic cost function of ILC along batch axis can be formulated as:

$$\min J_1(\mathbf{U}_{k+1}^{ILC}, k+1) = \left\|\mathbf{Y}_d - \hat{\mathbf{Y}}(\mathbf{U}_{k+1}^{ILC})\right\|_{\mathbf{Q}}^2 + \left\|\Delta\mathbf{U}_{k+1}^{ILC}\right\|_{\mathbf{R}_{k+1}}^2 \quad (1)$$

subject to

$$\Delta\mathbf{U}_{k+1}^{ILC} = \mathbf{U}_{k+1}^{ILC} - \mathbf{U}_k \tag{2}$$

$$\mathbf{U}^{low} \le \mathbf{U}_k^{ILC} \le \mathbf{U}^{up}, \mathbf{Y}^{low} \le \mathbf{Y}_k \le \mathbf{Y}^{up} \tag{3}$$

where

$$\mathbf{Y}_d = \begin{bmatrix} y_d(2) \\ y_d(3) \\ \vdots \\ y_d(L+1) \end{bmatrix}_{(L+1)\times 1}, \mathbf{U}_{k+1}^{ILC} = \begin{bmatrix} u_{k+1}^{ILC}(1) \\ u_{k+1}^{ILC}(2) \\ \vdots \\ u_{k+1}^{ILC}(L) \end{bmatrix}_{L\times 1}, \mathbf{U}_K = \begin{bmatrix} u_k(1) \\ u_k(2) \\ \vdots \\ u_k(L) \end{bmatrix}_{L\times 1},$$

$\mathbf{U}^{low}$ and $\mathbf{U}^{up}$ are the lower and upper bounds of the input sequence, $\mathbf{Y}^{low}$ and $\mathbf{Y}^{up}$ are the lower and upper bounds of the output sequence. $\mathbf{Q}$ and $\mathbf{R}_{k+1}$ are both weighting matrices defined as $\mathbf{Q} = q \times \mathbf{I}_L$ and $\mathbf{R}_{k+1} = r_{k+1} \times \mathbf{I}_L$, where r_{k+1} and q are both positive real numbers.

On the other hand, the MPC strategy is applied along time axis to obtain the superior tracking performance and better robustness against disturbance and uncertainty. For the k-th batch, the MPC strategy with time-varying prediction horizon can be given by the following quadratic cost function:

$$\min . J_2(\mathbf{U}_k^{MPC}(t|t), k) = \left\|\mathbf{Y}_d(t) - \hat{\mathbf{Y}}_{P_t}(t+1|t)\right\|_{\mathbf{Q}}^2 + \left\|\Delta\mathbf{U}_k^{MPC}(t|t)\right\|_{\bar{\mathbf{R}}}^2 \tag{4}$$

subject to

$$\mathbf{U}^{low} \le \mathbf{U}_k^{MPC}(t|t) + \mathbf{U}_k^{ILC}(t) \le \mathbf{U}^{up}, \mathbf{Y}^{low} < \mathbf{Y}_k < \mathbf{Y}^{up} \tag{5}$$

$$\hat{\mathbf{Y}}_{P_t}(t+1|t) = \hat{\mathbf{Y}}_{P_t}(\mathbf{U}_k^{MPC}(t|t) + \mathbf{U}_k^{ILC}(t)) \tag{6}$$

Where

$$P_t = L+1-t,\ t = 1, 2, \cdots, L,\ \mathbf{Y}_d(t+1) = \begin{bmatrix} y_d(t+1) \\ y_d(t+2) \\ \vdots \\ y_d(L+1) \end{bmatrix}_{P_t\times 1}, \hat{\mathbf{Y}}_{P_t}(t+1|t)$$

$$= \begin{bmatrix} \hat{y}(t+1|t) \\ \hat{y}(t+2|t) \\ \vdots \\ \hat{y}(L+1|t) \end{bmatrix}_{P_t\times 1},$$

$$\mathbf{U}_k^{MPC}(t|t) = \begin{bmatrix} u_k^{MPC}(t|t) \\ u_k^{MPC}(t+1|t) \\ \vdots \\ u_k^{MPC}(L|t) \end{bmatrix}_{P_t\times 1}, \mathbf{U}_k^{ILC}(t) = \begin{bmatrix} u_k^{ILC}(t) \\ u_k^{ILC}(t+1) \\ \vdots \\ u_k^{ILC}(L) \end{bmatrix}_{P_t\times 1},$$

$$\Delta\mathbf{U}_k^{MPC}(t|t) = \begin{bmatrix} u_k^{MPC}(t|t)-u_k^{MPC}(t-1|t-1) \\ u_k^{MPC}(t+1|t)-u_k^{MPC}(t|t) \\ \vdots \\ u_k^{MPC}(L|t)-u_k^{MPC}(L-1|t) \end{bmatrix}_{P_t\times 1},$$

$$u_k(t) = u_k^{MPC}(t|t) + u_k^{ILC}(t) \tag{7}$$

$u_k(t)$ is the actual integrated control input at instant t of the k-th batch, which is the sum of ILC control signals $u_k^{ILC}(t)$ and MPC control signals $u_k^{MPC}(t|t)$. $\bar{\mathbf{R}} = \bar{r} \times \mathbf{I}_L$, where $\bar{r}$ is a positive constant.

It should be noted that above MPC prediction horizon P_t is time-varying which ranges from current instant t to the final instant of a batch and the control horizon is the same length as prediction horizon.

2.2 Model Identification with Batch-to-Batch Updated Algorithm

In this work, Neuro-fuzzy model (NFM) [6] is employed to identify the proposed batch process. The NFM is described by the function $\hat{\mathbf{Y}}_k = \mathbf{\Phi}(\mathbf{U}_k)\mathbf{W}_k$, where $\mathbf{W}_k = [w_1(k), w_2(k), \cdots w_N(k)]^T$ are model adjustable parameters, and $\mathbf{\Phi}(\mathbf{U}_k)$ is a matrix decided by $\mathbf{U}_k$. It is evident that $\mathbf{U}_k$ is the variable of function $\mathbf{\Phi}(\cdot)$. More specificity, $\hat{\mathbf{Y}}_k = \mathbf{\Phi}(\mathbf{U}_k)\mathbf{W}_k$ can be written as

$$\hat{\mathbf{Y}}_k = \sum_{i=1}^{N} \hat{\alpha}_i \cdot f_i(\mathbf{U}_k) = (f_1(\mathbf{U}_k), f_2(\mathbf{U}_k), \ldots, f_N(\mathbf{U}_k)) \cdot (\hat{\alpha}_1, \hat{\alpha}_2, \ldots, \hat{\alpha}_N)^T = \mathbf{\Phi}(\mathbf{U}_k) \cdot \mathbf{W}_k$$

And the function $\mathbf{\Phi}(\mathbf{U}_k)$ is

$$\mathbf{\Phi}(\mathbf{U}_k) = \frac{[\mu_1(V(\mathbf{U}_k)), \mu_2(V(\mathbf{U}_k)), \cdots, \mu_N(V(\mathbf{U}_k))]}{\sum_{j=1}^{N} \mu_j(V(\mathbf{U}_k))}$$

where $V(\mathbf{U}_k) = [\mathbf{Y}_k, \mathbf{U}_k] = [v_1, v_2, \cdots, v_M]$, v_i is the i-th input variable of the NFM $(i = 1, 2, \cdots M)$,$\mu_j(V(\mathbf{U}_k))$ denotes Gaussian membership function $\mu_j(V(\mathbf{U}_k)) = \exp\left(-\sum_{i=1}^{M} \frac{(v_i - c_{ji})^2}{\sigma_j^2}\right)$, and c_{ji} and σ_j are center and width, respectively.

Owing to the model-plant mismatch, the process output may not be same as the one predicted by the model. The offset between the measured output and the model prediction is termed as model prediction error defined by

$$\hat{e}_k(t) = y_k(t) - \hat{y}_k(t) \tag{8}$$

And the tracking error is defined as

$$e_k(t) = y_d(t) - y_k(t) \tag{9}$$

Since batch processes are repetitive in nature, the parameters of the model can be modified along the batch direction to eliminate model-plant mismatch. Based on our previous work [6], assuming that the matrixes $\mathbf{W}_k$ and $\mathbf{\Phi}(\mathbf{U}_k)$ are both bounded, the following parameter updated strategy is convergent.

$$\mathbf{W}_k = \left(p_1 \cdot \mathbf{\Phi}^T(\bar{\mathbf{U}}_k)\mathbf{\Phi}(\bar{\mathbf{U}}_k) + p_2 \cdot \mathbf{I}_N\right)^{-1} \cdot \left(p_1 \cdot \mathbf{\Phi}^T(\bar{\mathbf{U}}_k)\bar{\mathbf{Y}}_k + p_2 \cdot \mathbf{W}_{k-1}\right) \tag{10}$$

Where

$$\bar{\mathbf{Y}}_k = \begin{pmatrix} \mathbf{Y}_{k-winnum+1}^T & \mathbf{Y}_{k-winnum+2}^T & \cdots & \mathbf{Y}_k^T \end{pmatrix}^T, \ \bar{\mathbf{U}}_k = \begin{pmatrix} \mathbf{U}_{k-winnum+1}^T & \mathbf{U}_{k-winnum+2}^T & \cdots & \mathbf{U}_k^T \end{pmatrix}^T$$
$$\mathbf{P}_1 = p_1 \cdot \mathbf{I}_{\min\{k,winnum\}\cdot T}, \ \mathbf{P}_2 = p_2 \cdot \mathbf{I}_{\min\{k,winnum\}\cdot T}$$

where *winnum* represents the size of sliding window. In this work, $p_2 = \beta k^2$, p_1 and β are both positive real numbers.

Although the parameters of the model are convergent, there always exist uncertainties/disturbances that vary from batch to batch. Thus, without loss of generality, we assume that the prediction errors of the model converge to a very small region along batch axes, namely $\hat{e}_k(t) \in \Theta_{\hat{e}}$ as $k \to \infty$. Above mentioned region is denoted by $\Theta_{\hat{e}} = \left\{\hat{\mathbf{E}}_k \middle| \|\hat{\mathbf{E}}_k\|_{\mathbf{Q}} \le M_{\hat{e}}\right\}$, where $\hat{\mathbf{E}}_k = [\hat{e}_k(2), \hat{e}_k(3), \cdots, \hat{e}_k(L+1)]'$. It should be noted that the model-plant mismatch is eliminated by the proposed batch-to-batch updated algorithm.

In summary, the following steps describe the algorithm of MPILC strategy.

Algorithm 1.

Step1 Identify data-based model based on historical batch operation date points. Let $k=1$ and initialize $\mathbf{U}_k$, $\mathbf{Q}$ and $\mathbf{R}_k$.

Step2 Update the parameters $\mathbf{W}_k$ of data-based model according to Eq. (10). Solve the optimization problem Eq. (1) to achieve $\mathbf{U}_k^{ILC}$. Set $t=1$.

Step3 At the t-th instant of the k-th batch, compute $u_k^{MPC}(t|t)$ and $u_k(t)$ according to Eq. (4). And then measure the corresponding output $y_k(t)$.

Step4 If $t \le L$, set $t=t+1$ and go back to Step 3, else set $k=k+1$ and go to Step 2.

3 Performance Analysis

Theorem 1. Consider a batch process controlled by MPILC Algorithm 1. With the strategy of model identification according to Eq. (10) and dynamic R-parameter in Eq. (1), the control sequence $\mathbf{U}_k$ of MPILC policy will converge to a constant sequence along batch cycle, whose increment corresponds to zero, namely $\Delta\mathbf{U}_k^{ILC} = \mathbf{U}_{k+1}^{ILC} - \mathbf{U}_k \to \mathbf{0}$ as $k \to \infty$.

Motivated by our previous work [7], the definitions of bounded tracking and zero tracking are extended to the integrated learning control system.

Definition 1 Bounded-tracking. If there exists a $\delta = \delta(\varepsilon) > 0$ for every $\varepsilon > 0$ and $\mathbf{U}_k = \mathbf{U}_k^{MPC*} + \mathbf{U}_k^{ILC}$ such that the inequality $\left| \|\mathbf{E}(\mathbf{U}_k)\|_{\mathbf{Q}}^2 - M^* \right| < \varepsilon$ holds when $r_{k_0+1} < \delta$ for every $k > k_0$, where M^* is positive.

Definition 2 Zero-tracking. If it is bounded-tracking and there exists $\delta > 0$ and $\mathbf{U}_k = \mathbf{U}_k^{MPC*} + \mathbf{U}_k^{ILC}$ such that the equality $\lim_{k\to\infty} \left| \|\mathbf{E}(\mathbf{U}_{k+1})\|_{\mathbf{Q}}^2 - M^* \right| = 0$ holds when $r_{k_0+1} < \delta$, where M^* is positive.

Theorem 2. Considering the condition of perfect model, if function $g(\cdot) = \|\mathbf{E}(\cdot)\|_{\mathbf{Q}}^2$ is derivable and the optimal solution are not in the boundary, namely in the local extreme points, then for any $\mathbf{U}_{k_0}$ in time k_0, system based on the proposed integrated optimization problem described by Eq. (1) is zero-tracking. Moreover, on the condition of model-plant mismatch, the tracking error $\mathbf{E}(\mathbf{U}_k)$ of the optimization problem described by Eq. (1) can be bounded in a small region with respect to the batch index k, namely $\mathbf{E}(\mathbf{U}_k) \in \Theta_e$ as $k \to \infty$, where $\Theta_e = \left\{ \mathbf{E}(\mathbf{U}_k) \middle| \|\mathbf{E}(\mathbf{U}_k)\|_{\mathbf{Q}} \le M_{\hat{e}} + \sqrt{\varepsilon} \right\}$.

4 Example

To demonstrate the effectiveness of the proposed algorithm, we implement the proposed method to a classical batch process proposed by Kwon and Evans [5]. The mechanism model of the batch process describing polymerization process is as follow:

$$
\begin{aligned}
\frac{dx_1}{dt} = f_1 = \frac{\rho_0^2\rho}{M_m}(1-x_1)^2\exp(2x_1+2\chi x_1^2)A_m\exp\left(-\frac{E_m}{uT_{ref}}\right) \\
\frac{dx_2}{dt} = f_2 = \frac{f_1x_2}{1+x_1}\left[1-\frac{1400x_2}{A_w\exp(B/uT_{ref})}\right] \\
\frac{dx_3}{dt} = f_3 = \frac{f_1}{1+x_1}\left[\frac{A_w\exp(B/uT_{ref})}{1500}-x_3\right]
\end{aligned} \tag{11}
$$

with

$$
\rho = \frac{1-x_1}{r_1+r_2T_c}+\frac{x_1}{r_3+r_4T_c}, \rho_0 = r_1+r_2T_c, T_c = uT_{ref}-273.15 \tag{12}
$$

where x_1 is the conversion, $x_2 = x_n/x_{nf}$ and $x_3 = x_w/x_{wf}$ are dimensionless number average and weight average chain lengths (NACL and WACL), respectively, $u = T/T_{ref}$ is the control variable which is bounded in the interval $[0.93486, 1.18539]$. The final time, t_f was fixed to be 313 min, the initial value of the states used were $x_1(0) = 0$, $x_2(0) = 1$, $x_3(0) = 1$, and the desire value is $y_d = (0.8 \quad 1 \quad 1)$.

In the simulation, we choose NFM model as the prediction model, and three different NFM models are firstly constructed to represent the mapping relationship of $u \to x_1$, $u \to x_2$, $u \to x_3$, respectively. The control object is to drive system output $\mathbf{y} = (x_1 \quad x_2 \quad x_3)$ approximating to $\mathbf{y}_d^f = (0.8 \quad 1 \quad 1)$,

R is considered to be dynamic parameter as follow:

$$
\mathbf{R} = r\cdot\mathbf{I}_L,\ r = \tau_1\left(1-\exp\left(-\tau_2\sum_{i=1}^{3}\left|\bar{\hat{e}}_{k,i}(t_f)\right|\right)\right) \tag{13}
$$

Eq. (13) indicates that r would be decreasing while $\sum_{i=1}^{3}\left|\bar{\hat{e}}_{k,i}(t_f)\right|$ decreasing. Thus if the sufficient small error between model and plant can be achieved, then the output in current batch would close to desire output sufficiently. Parameters in the simulation are chosen as $\tau_1 = 1\times 10^3$, $\tau_2 = 0.1$, $q_1 = 0.1$, $q_2 = q_3 = 1\times 10^4$, $\bar{r} = 100$, $winnum = 15$.

The control performance of the proposed two-dimension integrated control strategy is compared with the one-dimension iterative optimization control method [6]. To test the robustness of the proposed integrated learning algorithm against disturbance, the output of WACL x_3 is corrupted by $5\% \times 1$ disturbance at instant $t = 4$ of the 5-th batch in this case. As seen from Fig. 2, the proposed integrated control strategy has faster convergence rate and can maintain good performance despite the existence of noise.

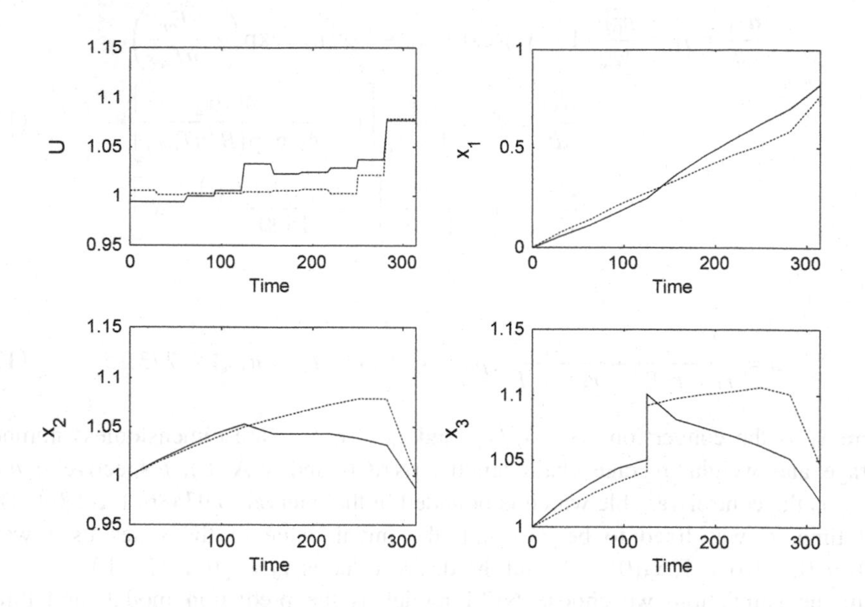

(a) 5-th batch output and input trajectories based on two controller systems

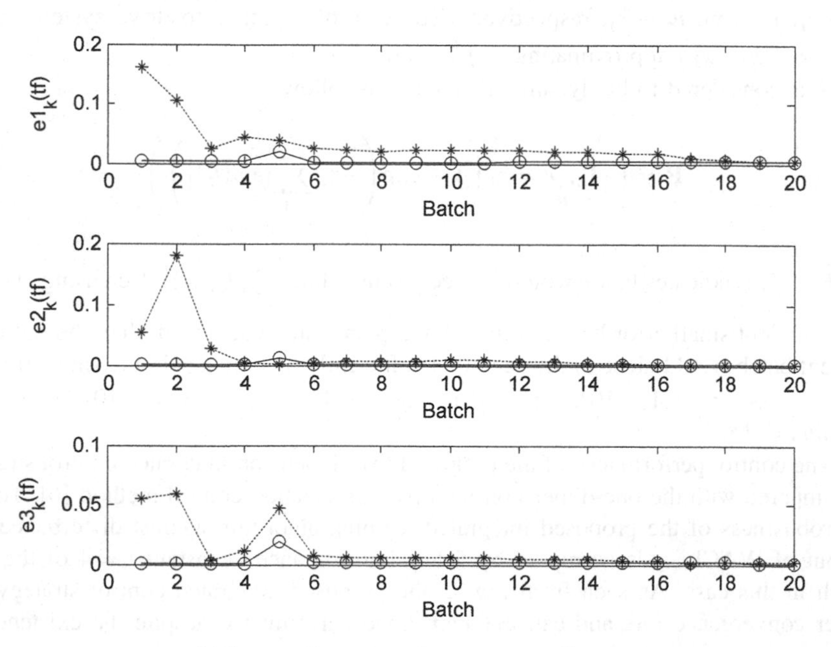

(b)Curves of error based on two controller systems

Fig. 2. 5-th batch trajectories and curves of error based on two controller systems under disturbance (solid line: integrated control strategy; dotted line: ILC)

5 Conclusion

In this paper, a novel integrated model predictive iterative learning control (MPILC) strategy with model identification and dynamic R-parameter was proposed, which not only combined feedback controller in time-axis with iterative learning optimization control in batch-axis, but also improved the accuracy of the model through online identification. Moreover, we made the first attempt to give rigorous description and proof of the convergence and tracking performance of the proposed integrated learning control system to verify that a perfect tracking performance can be obtained despite the existence of model-plant-mismatch. Lastly, an example illustrated the performance and applicability of the proposed integrated optimization control. Simulation results demonstrate that the proposed integrated control strategy has better tracking performance and robustness.

References

1. Chen, C., Xiong, Z.-H., Zhong, Y.: Design and analysis of integrated predictive iterative learning control for batch process based on two-dimensional system theory. Chin. J. Chem. Eng. **22**, 762–768 (2014)
2. Bonvin, D.: Optimal operation of batch reactors: a personal view. J. Process Contr **8**, 355–368 (1998)
3. Lee, J.H.. Lee.F K.S., Iterative learning control applied to batch processes: an overview. Control Eng. Pract **15**(10), 1306–1318 (2007)
4. Rogers, E., Owens, D.H.: Stability Analysis for Linear Repetitive Processes. Springer, Berlin, Heidelberg (1992)
5. Kwon, Y.D., Evans, L.B.: A coordinate transformation methord for the numerical solution of nonlinear minimum-time control problems. AIChE J. **21**, 1158–1164 (1975)
6. Jia, L., Shi, J.P., Chiu, M.-S.: Integrated neuro-fuzzy model and dynamic R-parameter based quadratic criterion-iterative learning control for batch process control technique. Neurocomputing **98**, 24–33 (2012)
7. Jia, L., Yang, T., Chiu, M.-S.: An integrated iterative learning control strategy with model. J. Process Control **23**, 1332–1341 (2013)

Research on Nonlinear H∞/Adaptive Backstepping Control Method for a Hex-Rotor Unmanned Aerial Vehicle

Zhuo Zhang[1(✉)], Zhenghua Liu[1,2], and Nuan Wen[1]

[1] School of Automation Science and Electrical Engineering, Beihang University, Beijing, China
zhangzhuo608@163.com

[2] Science and Technology on Aircraft Control Laboratory, Beihang University, Beijing, China

Abstract. This paper concentrates on attitude control and tracking control about the hex-rotor Unmanned Aerial Vehicle (UAV). This kind of aircraft is a nonlinear, coupled MIMO system. Considering the model uncertainties and the external disturbances, good robustness is one of the key factors for the UAV. Based on the characteristics of the hex-rotor UAV model, nonlinear H∞ controller and adaptive backstepping sliding mode controller are designed to realize the attitude and position control respectively. And the control strategies are verified by the simulation. It's proved that the control system has strong robustness to both the disturbance and the parametric variation.

Keywords: The hex-rotor UAV · Nonlinear H∞ control · Adaptive backstepping control · Robustness

1 Introduction

Similar to the quadrotor, the hex-rotor is a nonlinear, strong coupling and underactuated MIMO system, so it's necessary to adopt a kind of nonlinear control strategy. The main control algorithms are sliding-mode algorithm [1], backstepping [1], adaptive neural network [2], $H\infty$ [3–7], nonlinear dynamic inversion [8], ADRC [9] and ESO [10]. Among them, nonlinear $H\infty$ algorithm is suitable for MIMO system, and takes in account of the nonlinear characteristic of the system. The nonlinear $H\infty$ attitude controller is designed in this paper. Ling Jinfu [11] adds adaptive algorithm on the base of backstepping to improves the robustness of the system. Sliding mode algorithm has less need to the model precision. In this paper, sliding mode algorithm is introduced into adaptive backstepping control. At last, the simulation results verify the strategies proposed in this paper have better robustness and effectiveness.

L. Zhang et al. (Eds.): AsiaSim 2016/SCS AutumnSim 2016, Part I, CCIS 643, pp. 136–145, 2016.
DOI: 10.1007/978-981-10-2663-8_15

2 Simulation Models

Number the six rotors $r1 \sim r6$. The structure of the hex-rotor studied in this paper is shown in Fig. 1.

2.1 Dynamical Model

The motion of the hex-rotor UAV is discussed respectively from line movement and angular motion.

(a) Line Movement

The hex-rotor UAV position equations can be expressed by the Newton-Euler formalism. Ignore the air resistance effects when the hex-rotor UAV hovers and flies slowly. The equations of line movement in the inertial frame are as follows:

$$\begin{pmatrix} \ddot{x} \\ \ddot{y} \\ \ddot{z} \end{pmatrix} = \begin{pmatrix} -\left(c_\phi s_\theta c_\psi + s_\phi s_\psi\right)F/m \\ -\left(c_\phi s_\theta s_\psi - s_\phi c_\psi\right)F/m \\ -c_\phi c_\theta F/m + g \end{pmatrix} \tag{1}$$

Where x, y, z represent the position of the UAV in the inertial frame, F is the sum of lift. θ, ϕ, ψ represent the Euler angles.

(b) Angular Motion

Ignore the gyroscopic effect, because the rotor mass and the size of the hex-rotor UAV are small. The angular motion equation is established in body fixed frame as:

$$\tau = \begin{bmatrix} L \\ M \\ N \end{bmatrix} = \begin{bmatrix} \dot{p}I_x + qr(I_z - I_y) \\ \dot{q}I_y + pr(I_x - I_z) \\ \dot{r}I_z + pq(I_y - I_x) \end{bmatrix} \tag{2}$$

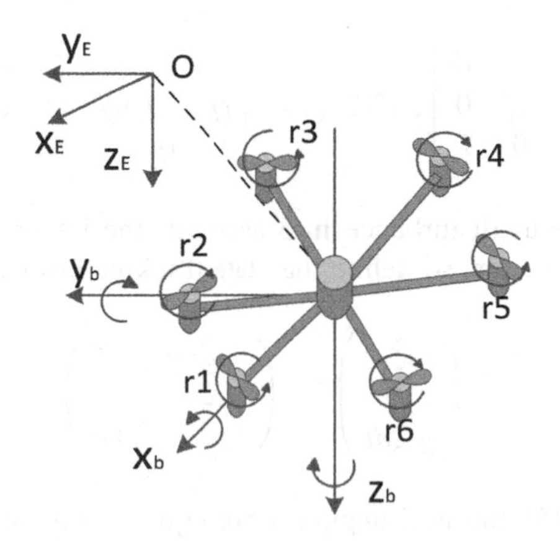

Fig. 1. The hex-rotor UAV structure diagram

where, τ is the torque applied by six rotors, L, M, N are the components of τ in each axis, and I_x, I_y, I_z are rotational inertias correspond to each axis respectively. θ and ϕ are assumed to be very small when hex-rotor UAV is flying, so the relationship between $(p \quad q \quad r)$ and $(\dot{\theta} \quad \dot{\phi} \quad \dot{\psi})$ is come down to:

$$(\dot{\phi} \quad \dot{\theta} \quad \dot{\psi})=(p \quad q \quad r) \tag{3}$$

So (2) can be expressed in the inertial frame as:

$$\begin{cases} \ddot{\phi} = \left(L + \dot{\theta}\dot{\psi}(I_y - I_z)\right)/I_x \\ \ddot{\theta} = \left(M + \dot{\phi}\dot{\psi}(I_z - I_x)\right)/I_y \\ \ddot{\psi} = \left(N + \dot{\phi}\dot{\theta}(I_x - I_y)\right)/I_z \end{cases} \tag{4}$$

3 Controller Design

According to (1) and (4), design the dual-loop control structure: the inner attitude loop and the outer position loop.

3.1 Nonlinear H∞ Attitude Controller Design

Considering the external disturbance and the effects of unmodeled nonlinearity, the angular motion equation in (4) can be rewritten as the following form:

$$M(\xi)\ddot{\xi} + C(\xi, \dot{\xi})\dot{\xi} = \tau + \omega \tag{5}$$

where, $\xi = [\phi \quad \theta \quad \psi]^T$, ω is the combined disturbance of external disturbance and unmodeled uncertainty. From (4), $M(\xi)$ and $C(\xi, \dot{\xi})$ are expressed as:

$$M(\xi) = \begin{bmatrix} I_x & 0 & 0 \\ 0 & I_y & 0 \\ 0 & 0 & I_z \end{bmatrix}, \quad C(\xi, \dot{\xi}) = \begin{bmatrix} 0 & (I_x - I_y)\dot{\psi} & 0 \\ (I_z - I_x)\dot{\psi} & 0 & 0 \\ 0 & (I_x - I_y)\dot{\phi} & 0 \end{bmatrix}$$

Taking the continuous disturbance into account, the integral of tracking error is introduced in the state vector, so define the state tracking error as:

$$x = \begin{pmatrix} \dot{\tilde{\xi}} \\ \tilde{\xi} \\ \int \tilde{\xi} dt \end{pmatrix} = \begin{pmatrix} \dot{\xi} - \dot{\xi}_r \\ \xi - \xi_r \\ \int (\xi - \xi_r) dt \end{pmatrix} \tag{6}$$

Substitute (6) into (5), the new angular error equations are established as:

$$\dot{x} = Ax + B_0 + BM^{-1}(\xi)(\tau + \omega) \tag{7}$$

with

$$A = \begin{pmatrix} -M^{-1}(\xi)C(\xi,\dot{\xi}) & O & O \\ I_{3\times3} & O & O \\ O & I_{3\times3} & O \end{pmatrix} \quad B_0 = \begin{pmatrix} -\ddot{\xi}_r - M^{-1}(\xi)C(\xi,\dot{\xi})\dot{\xi}_r \\ O \\ O \end{pmatrix} \quad B = \begin{pmatrix} I_{3\times3} \\ O \\ O \end{pmatrix}$$

To minimize the necessary torques, defined the control variable in the more general form [6]:

$$u = M^{-1}(\xi)T_1\dot{x} + C(\xi,\dot{\xi})T_1 x \tag{8}$$

with $T_1 = (T_{11} \quad T_{12} \quad T_{13}), T_{11} = \rho I_{3\times3}, \rho > 0$

Substitute (8) into (7), the control law is obtained as follow:

$$\begin{aligned}\tau &= M(\xi)\ddot{\xi}_r + C(\xi,\dot{\xi})\dot{\xi}_r + T_{11}^{-1}u \\ &- T_{11}^{-1}(M(\xi)T_{12}\dot{\tilde{\xi}} + (M(\xi)T_{13} + C(\xi,\dot{\xi})T_{12})\tilde{\xi} + C(\xi,\dot{\xi})T_{13}\int \tilde{\xi}dt)\end{aligned} \tag{9}$$

Define the new disturbance:

$$d = M(\xi)T_{11}M^{-1}(\xi)\omega \tag{10}$$

The angular motion equation can be rewritten in the affine system form as:

$$\dot{x} = f(x,t)x + g(x,t)u + k(x,t)d \tag{11}$$

where

$$f(x,t) = T_0^{-1}\begin{pmatrix} -M^{-1}(\xi)C(\xi,\dot{\xi}) & O & O \\ T_{11}^{-1} & I_{3\times3} - T_{11}^{-1}T_{12} & T_{11}^{-1}(T_{12} - T_{13}) - I_{3\times3} \\ 0 & I_{3\times3} & -I_{3\times3} \end{pmatrix} T_0$$

$$g(x,t) = k(x,t) = T_0^{-1}\begin{pmatrix} M^{-1}(\xi) & 0 & 0 \end{pmatrix}^T, \; T_0 = \begin{bmatrix} T_{11} & T_{12} & T_{13} \\ O & I_{3\times3} & I_{3\times3} \\ O & O & I_{3\times3} \end{bmatrix}.$$

Define the output signal as:

$$z = Q^{1/2}x + R^{1/2}u \tag{12}$$

with $Q = \begin{bmatrix} \omega_1^2 I_{3\times3} & O & O \\ O & \omega_2^2 I_{3\times3} & O \\ O & O & \omega_3^2 I_{3\times3} \end{bmatrix}$, $R = \omega_u^2 I_{3\times3}$ $(\omega_1,\ \omega_2,\ \omega_3,\ \omega_u > 0)$.

The optimal control u^* is obtained as:

$$u^*(\mathrm{x}) = -R^{-1}g^T(\mathrm{x},t)\left(\frac{\partial V^*(x)}{\partial x}\right)^T \tag{13}$$

where, $V^*(x)$ is the Lyapunov function of the system and the positive solution of the following equations:

$$\begin{aligned} &\frac{\partial V^*(x)}{\partial x} f(x)x + \frac{\gamma^2}{2}\frac{\partial V^*(x)}{\partial x} k(x)k^T(x)(\frac{\partial V^*(x)}{\partial x})^T \\ &-\frac{\gamma^2}{2}\frac{\partial V^*(x)}{\partial x} g(x)R^{-1}g^T(x)(\frac{\partial V^*(x)}{\partial x})^T + \frac{1}{2}h(x)h^T(x) = 0 \\ &V^*(0) = 0 \end{aligned} \tag{14}$$

Introduce Riccati algebraic equation to compute $V^*(x)$. The nonlinear Riccati algebraic equation is proposed as follow:

$$\begin{aligned} &\dot{P}(x,t) + P(x,t)f(x,t) + f^T(x,t)P(x,t) \\ &\quad - P(x,t)\left(g(x,t)R^{-1}g^T(x,t) - \frac{1}{\gamma^2}k(x,t)k^T(x,t)\right)P(x,t) + Q = 0 \end{aligned} \tag{15}$$

Without loss of generality, suggest P^* to be in a more explicit form [4] and [6]:

$$P^* = T_0^T \begin{pmatrix} M(\xi) & O & O \\ O & Y & X-Y \\ O & X-Y & Z+Y \end{pmatrix} T_0 \tag{16}$$

with X, Y and $Z \in R^{3\times3}$ are constant, symmetric and positive definite matrices. $V^*(x)$ can be obtained as:

$$V^*(\mathrm{x}) = \frac{1}{2}\mathrm{x}^T P^*(\mathrm{x},t)\mathrm{x} \tag{17}$$

So $u^*(x)$ can be rewritten as:

$$u^*(x) = -R^{-1}g^T(x,t)P^*(x,t)x = -R^{-1}T_1x \tag{18}$$

Take (19) into (9), the torque input is obtained as:

$$\tau = M(\xi)\ddot{\xi}_r + C(\xi,\dot{\xi})\dot{\xi}_r - T_{11}^{-1}(M(\xi)T_{12} + R^{-1}T_{11})\dot{\tilde{\xi}} \\ - T_{11}^{-1}(M(\xi)T_{13} + C(\xi,\dot{\xi})T_{12} + R^{-1}T_{12})\tilde{\xi} - T_{11}^{-1}(C(\xi,\dot{\xi})T_{13} + R^{-1}T_{13})\int \tilde{\xi}dt \tag{19}$$

Take P^* into Riccati algebraic Eq. (14), T_1 is obtained as:

$$\rho = \omega_1/\sqrt{\omega_u^2 - \gamma^2},\ T_{12} = \left(\rho\sqrt{2\omega_3\omega_1 + \omega_2^2}/\omega_1\right)I,\ T_{13} = (\rho\omega_3/\omega_1)I$$

Substitute (11), (13) into (14), after some manipulation, it's proved that the derivation of Lyapunov function $\dot{V}^*(x) < 0$, and the system is stable.

3.2 Adaptive Backstepping Sliding Mode Position Controllers Design

Taking the height channel for example, adopt adaptive backstepping sliding mode control strategy to derive the control input F. The math model of height channel is:

$$\begin{cases} \dot{x}_1 = x_2 \\ \dot{x}_2 = g - (\cos\phi\cos\theta)F/m + d_z \end{cases} \tag{20}$$

where $x_1 = z, x_2 = \dot{z}$, d_z is external disturbances. The reference height $z_d = x_{1d}$. The height error e_1 and the velocity error e_2 are as follows:

$$e_1 = x_1 - x_{1d} \tag{21}$$

$$e_2 = x_2 - \alpha_{\dot{z}} \tag{22}$$

here, $\alpha_{\dot{z}} = \dot{x}_{1d} - c_1 e_1$, is the estimated value of x_2. $c_1 > 0$, and is adjustable.

Chose Lyapunov function as:

$$V_1 = 0.5e_1^2 \tag{23}$$

The derivative of V_1 to time is:

$$\dot{V}_1 = e_1 e_2 - c_1 e_1^2 \tag{24}$$

Define the switching function as:

$$s_z = k_z e_1 + e_2, k_z > 0 \tag{25}$$

The derivative of the switching function is:

$$\dot{s}_z = k_z(e_2 - c_1e_1) + (g - (cos\theta cos\phi)F + d_z) - \dot{\alpha}_z \tag{26}$$

Select the exponential reaching law as:

$$\dot{s}_z = -\varepsilon_z \cdot \mathrm{sgn}(s_z) - h_z s_z\, \varepsilon_z > 0, h_z > 0 \tag{27}$$

Design the control law as:

$$\begin{aligned} F =& \mathrm{m}(-h_z s_z - \varepsilon_z \mathrm{sgn}(s_z) - k_z(e_2 - c_1 e_1) \\ & - \mathrm{g} + \dot{\alpha}_z - \hat{d}_z/m)/\cos\theta\cos\phi \end{aligned} \tag{28}$$

$\hat{d}_z$ is the estimate of d_z. Select the adaptive law as:

$$\dot{\hat{d}}_z/m = \gamma_z s_z, \quad \gamma_z > 0 \tag{29}$$

Select the proper value of h_z, c_1 and k_z, which can ensure $\dot{V}_2 \leq 0$, namely the system is stable.

The virtual controllers of channel x, y are designed in the same way.

4 Simulation and Discussion

In this section, take the prototype in [12] as the research object to verify the control system above from two cases: spot hover and robustness. Besides that, compare the effect with adaptive backstepping strategy.

4.1 Spot Hover Verification

Set the initial states to zero. Without any distraction, enter the target location: $x, y, z = (5, 5, -5), \psi_d = 30°$. The simulation results of adaptive backstepping (hereafter referred to as AB) controller and nonlinear $H\infty$/adaptive backstepping sliding mode (hereafter referred to as H/ABS) controller are shown in the Fig. 2. At 15 s, change the target location to $x, y, z = (5, 5, -6), \psi_d = 20°$, the response of height and yaw angle is showed in the Fig. 3.

It can be seen from Fig. 2 that the two kinds of control strategies guarantee the hex-rotor UAV arrive at the target location and keep hovering steadily. But the H/ABS controller can ensure the UAV response progress faster with less fluctuation than the AB controller.

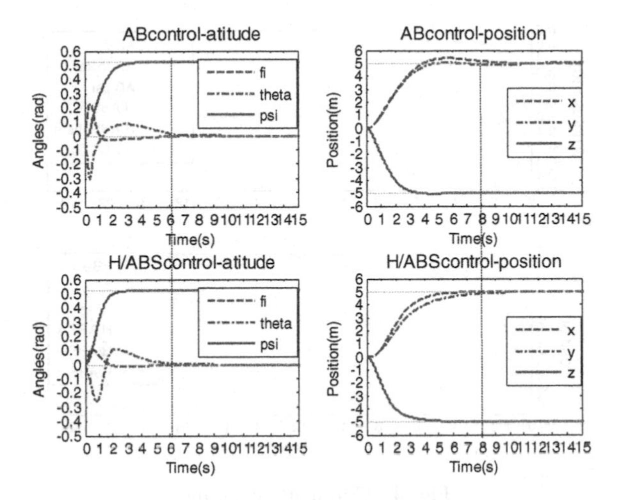

Fig. 2. Spot hovering

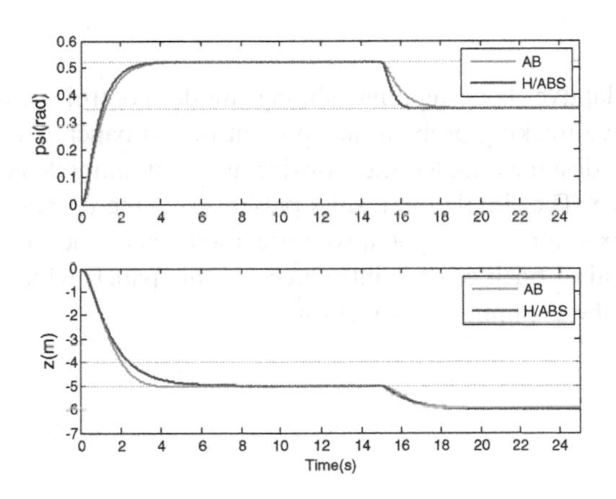

Fig. 3. Command tracking

4.2 Robustness Verification

Considering the parameter uncertainty and the continuous external distraction, an uncertainty of 30 % in the rotational inertias has been considered in the simulation. From 5 s to 20 s, add Gaussian white noise with mean 0 and variance 0.5 N · m to L, M, N and with mean 0 and variance 10 N to F. The effects of the two control strategies are shown in Fig. 4.

In Fig. 4, comparing the fluctuation of height and attitude angles, the H/ABS controller has better effect on restraining the continuous disturbance.

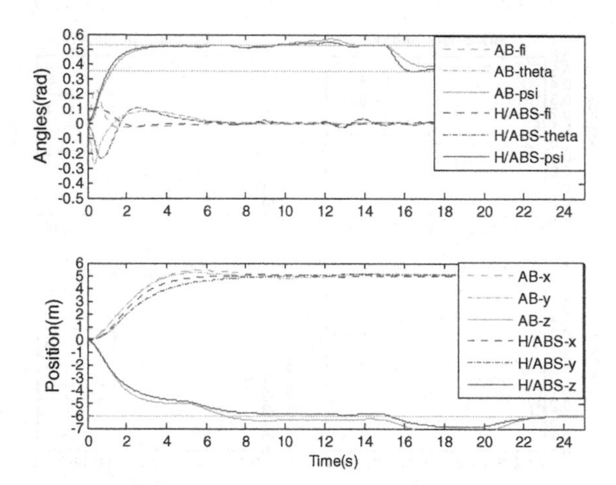

Fig. 4. Command tracking

5 Conclusion

Nonlinear $H\infty$/adaptive backstepping sliding mode control strategy to improve robustness and solve tracking problem has present in this paper. The proposed control strategy has been designed under the consideration of unmodeled uncertainty and external disturbance. The simulation results presents that the proposed control strategy can ensure the hex-rotor UAV spot hover accurately and track commands quickly. Besides, the integral of track error is introduced in this paper, which has the desirable effect of reducing the continuous distraction.

References

1. Bouabdallah, S., Siegwart, R.: Backstepping and sliding-mode techniques applied to an indoor micro quadrotor. In: Proceedings of the 2005 IEEE International Conference on Robotics and Automation, ICRA 2005, pp. 2247–2252. IEEE (2005)
2. Suresh, K.K., Kahn, A.D., Yavrucuk I.: GTMARS - flight controls and computer architecture. Georgia Institute of Technology, Atlanta (2000)
3. Chen, M., Huzmezan, M.A.: Simulation model and H∞ loop shaping control of a quad rotor unmanned air vehicle. In: Modelling, Simulation, & Optimization, pp. 320–325 (2003)
4. Ortega, M.G., Vargas, M., Vivas, C., et al.: Robustness improvement of a nonlinear H ∞ controller for robot manipulators via saturation functions. J. Robot. Syst. **22**(8), 421–437 (2005)
5. Chen, B., Lee, T., Feng, J.: A nonlinear H∞ control design in robotic systems under parameter perturbation and external disturbance. Int. J. Control **59**(2), 439–461 (1994)
6. Johansson, R.: Quadratic optimization of motion coordination and control. In: Proceedings of 1990 IEEE International Conference on Robotics and Automation, vol. 2, pp. 1204–1209. IEEE (1990)
7. Wang, C.: Optimal Control Theory. Science Press, Beijing (2003)

8. Xie, K.: Research on Three Dimensional Route Planning and Trajectory Control for Quad-rotor UAV. Beihang University (2015)
9. Xia, G.: Research on Quadrotor unmanned helicopter robust control Based on ADRC. Beihang University (2014)
10. Song, S.: Research on the Modeling and Control for the Tiltrotor Aircraft. Beihang University (2015)
11. Ling, J.: Study of Flight Control Algorithm for Quad-rotor Aircraft. Nanchang University (2013)
12. Zhao, C.: Fault Analysis of Execution Units and Flight Control for Hex-Rotor Unmanned Aerial Vehicle. University of Chinese Academy of Sciences (2015)

A Hybrid Model of AR and PNN Method for Building Thermal Load Forecasting

Tingzhang Liu[1,2(✉)], Kai Liu[1,2], Ping Fang[1,2], and Jianfei Zhao[1,2]

[1] Shanghai Key Laboratory of Power Station Automation Technology, Shanghai, China
Liutzhcom@163.com

[2] School of Mechanical Engineering and Automation, Shanghai University, Shanghai, China
jzshilk@126.com

Abstract. A hybrid method which combines time series model and artificial intelligence method is proposed in this paper to improve the prediction accuracy of building thermal load. Firstly, a simple auto regressive (AR) model is utilized to predict present load using previous loads, the order and the parameters of AR model are identified by the data produced by DeST. Then, a 3-layer back-propagation neural network optimized by particle swarm optimization (PSO) neural network (PNN) is set up to predict the error which is derived by comparing the precious AR predicting load. The error and its corresponding meteorological data generate the training sample data. At last, the hybrid model, named autoregressive and particle swarm neural network (APNN), is obtained. It uses historical load information and real-time meteorological data as input to predict a refined real-time load by adding error to preparative load. To evaluate the prediction accuracy, this hybrid model APNN is compared with several common methods via different statistical indicators, the result show the APNN hybrid method has higher accuracy in thermal load forecasting.

Keywords: Hybrid model · Thermal load forecasting · AR · PSO · APNN

1 Introduction

Building load forecasting has attracted more attention to both academic researcher and government with the rapid urbanization progress in the world especially developing countries, for example China. Building thermal load prediction plays an important role in energy saving during architectural design period because accurate load prediction will offer optimal grid power distribution as reference. Various techniques of load forecasting had been reported for past decades. In summary, they can be classified as traditional methods based on mathematical models [1, 2] and artificial intelligent techniques [3–5]. Hybrid of the referred methods [6–9] has also achieved good performances. However, the stochastics and nonlinearity influence the load forecasting accuracy strongly.

Auto-Regressive (AR) method is a widely used model for stationary time series modeling. It is a sequence of data collected in regular intervals, such as an hour, a day, a month or a year. Time series can be also used as a resource of knowledge acquisition

L. Zhang et al. (Eds.): AsiaSim 2016/SCS AutumnSim 2016, Part I, CCIS 643, pp. 146–155, 2016.
DOI: 10.1007/978-981-10-2663-8_16

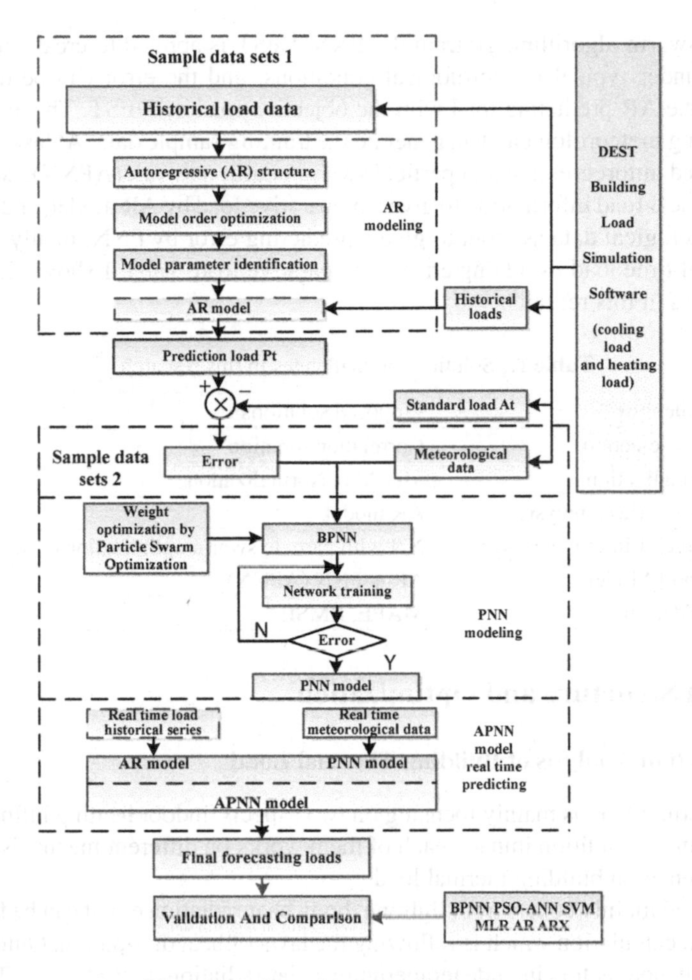

Fig. 1. Design schematic of hybrid model

and a method for forecasting the future values [10, 11]. Artificial neural networks (ANN) have been widely used in load forecasting due to their strong capability to model non-linear mapping relations between inputs and outputs (I/O) [3]. But their drawback is the lack of incorporating uncertainties associated with inputs, parameters of network and I/O relation so as to obstruct their further applications.

In this paper, a hybrid method which combines time series model and ANN is proposed to improve the prediction accuracy of building thermal load, which is shown in Fig. 1. A simple auto regressive (AR) model is utilized to predict present load using previous loads, the order and the parameters of AR model are identified by the data produced by DeST (a building simulation software). Obviously, the AR model has good real-time property but has poor forecasting accuracy for load because it considers the previous loads only. Therefore, a particle swarm neural network (PNN) is set up to predict the error of the load forecasted by AR model. The PNN has the 3-layer back-propagation neural network (BPNN) structure, and the weights of BPNN are optimized by particle swarm algorithm. To train the PNN, DeST is applied to create numbers of loads data under typical meteorological conditions, and the error can be derived by comparing the AR predicting load with the objective load by DEST. The error and its corresponding meteorological data generate the training sample data. At last, the hybrid model, named autoregressive and particle swarm neural network (APNN), is obtained. It uses historical load information to give a preparative load by AR model, and uses real-time meteorological data as input to give a predicting error by PNN, finally it predicts a refined real-time load by adding error to preparative load. Table 1 shows the solution for challenges in this research.

Table 1. Solution for challenges in this research

Challenges	Proposed solutions
Input selection	Correlation function
Normalization	Mix-Max Normalization
Time Series Analysis	AR model
Artificial Intelligence system	NN with particle swarm optimization (PNN)
Hybrid Model	AR + PNN (APNN)
Validation	MAPE, RMSE

2 Model Structure and Optimization

2.1 Formation Analysis of Building Thermal Load

Building thermal load is mainly focusing on two aspects, indoor heating influences and outdoor weather condition impact, each of them works on different mechanism but has a great influence on building thermal load.

Indoor load mainly comes from lighting, body heat radiation etc. It can be forecasted by simplified calculation which is following the laws of heat dissipation. Outdoor environment influence factors include temperature, solar radiation, humidity etc. The whole building load is generated under the combined action of indoor and outdoor influence. In our previous research, different models from indoor/outdoor information mentioned are built, such as auto regressive model with exogenous inputs (ARX) combining the

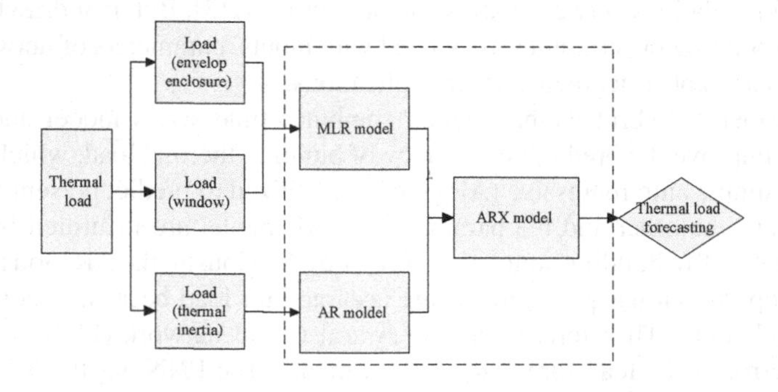

Fig. 2. Structure of three kinds of thermal load prediction models

multiple linear regressive (MLR) with meteorological data input and auto regressive (AR) with historical data input. The structure of three kinds of thermal load prediction models is shown in Fig. 2.

2.2 Time Series Model

Taking into account the thermal storage of building space, the historical thermal energy will be stored in a certain form of building materials because of thermal inertia. Naturally, thermal inertia will impact the thermal load at current moment. In the hourly forecasting model, the key to the AR model is to find out the optimal order ensuring prediction accuracy. The formulation of AR model is:

$$load_t = W_1 load_{t-1} + W_2 load_{t-2} + W_3 load_{t-3} + \cdots + W_i load_{t-i} + e \tag{1}$$

Where load is the prediction result, w_{t-i} is i-th order of auto-regressive parameters, $load_{t-i}$ is i-th load prediction result, e is the white noise.

According to function (1), continuous study i-th order of AR model (i = 1…7) to gain the minimum error value based on data of July. The absolute error compared with simulation data is shown in Fig. 3 and Table 2.

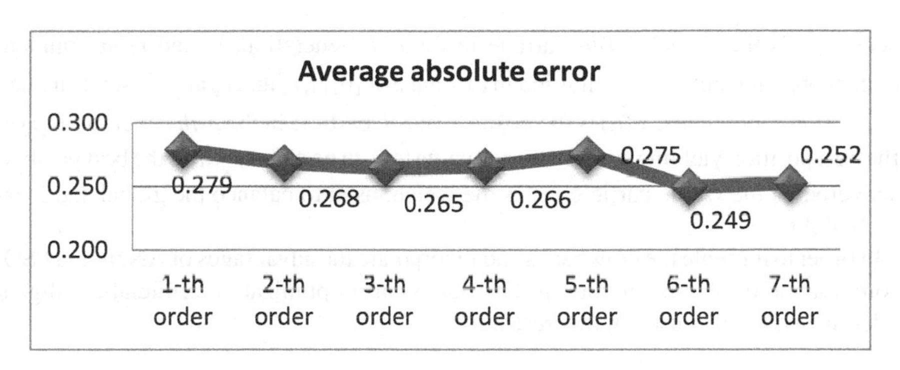

Fig. 3. Forecasted load of different order for i = 1…7 absolute error

Table 2. Forecasted load of different order for i = 1…7 absolute error

Model order	i = 1	i = 2	i = 3	i = 4	i = 5	i = 6	i = 7
Absolute error	−0.107	−0.084	0.008	0.004	0.095	0.208	0.208
	−0.046	−0.040	−0.027	−0.065	−0.094	−0.226	−0.280
	−0.064	−0.067	−0.064	−0.069	−0.391	−0.341	−0.280
	…	…	…	…	…	…	…
	−0.222	−0.281	−0.316	−0.328	−0.306	−0.056	−0.076
	0.031	0.110	0.072	0.087	−0.023	−0.022	−0.107
Average	0.279	0.268	0.265	0.266	0.275	0.249	0.252

It can be seen clearly, the absolute error is the minimum value when AR model is built by six order (i = 6).

2.3 Artificial Intelligent Model

Artificial Neural Network (ANN), has been verified that it is a universal intelligent method widely applied in engineering in past literatures.

Particle Swarm Optimization (PSO) algorithm is proved to be efficient with non-linear functions in optimization problems. PSO algorithm is introduced by Kennedy and Eberhart, emulating flocking behavior of birds to solve the optimization problems. Each solution is regarded as a particle in the study. All particles have positions and velocities.

The particles fly through the D dimensional problem space by learning from the historical information of all the particles. Therefore, the particles have the tendency to fly towards better search area over the course of search process. Each particle's velocity and position is formulated by:

$$v_j(n+1) = \omega \cdot v_j(n) + c_1 r_1 \left(p_j(n) - x_j(n)\right) + c_2 r_2 \left(p_g(n) - x_j(n)\right) \quad (2)$$

$$x_j(n+1) = v_j(n+1) + x_j(n) \quad (3)$$

where $v_j(n)$ is the speed of *j-th* particle in the *n-th* generation, r_1 and r_2 are random numbers obeying uniform distribution in the range of [0,1], c_1 and c_2 are constants named acceleration coefficients, $x_j(n)$ is the position of *j-th* particle in the *n-th* generation, $p_j(n)$ is the best position yielding the best fitness value for *j-th* particle, $p_g(n)$ is the best position discovered by the whole particles, w is the weight used to balance the global and local search abilities.

In order to mitigate the drawbacks and incorporate the advantages of ANNs and PSO, a combination of neural network and particle swarm optimization artificial intelligent model named PNN is used in this research.

3 Experiment Design and Data Acquisition

3.1 Data Acquisition

There are many building simulation software like Energy plus, TRNSYS and so on. Integrated building simulation software named DEST was exploited which is widely used in civil and commercial building. DEST building simulation software is the integration of the building environment and its air conditioner control system. DEST can be used as a building environment and its control system simulation platform because its advantages of flexibility and the calculation module have good openness and scalability.

A medium-sized office-building in an academic institution which located in Shanghai is being experimented. The simulation target room is in the middle of second floor of the building. The internal structure is shown in Fig. 4. The sample data of simulation

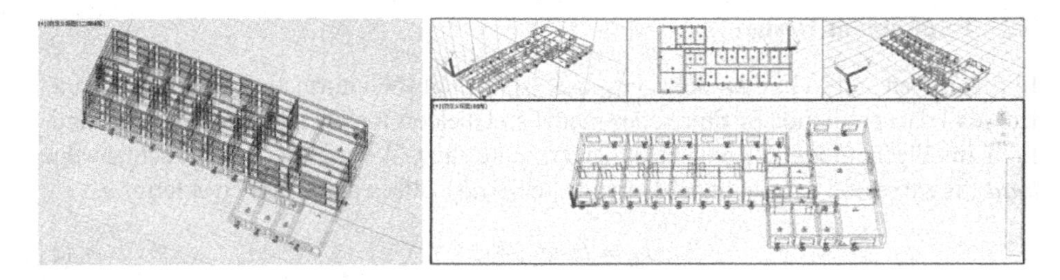

Fig. 4. Architecture internal structure

results is shown in Table 3. The whole sample year meteorological data trend is shown in Fig. 5.

Table 3. Simulation result data sample

Date	Temperature °C	Solar radiation $W/(m^2 \cdot K)$	Humidity $W/(m^2 \cdot K)$	Heating/Cooling load (KW)
1.1-0	6.47	0.00	0.00	1.62
1.1-1	5.71	0.00	0.00	1.72
…	…	…	…	…
7.31-22	30.50	0.00	24.21	3.59
7.31-23	30.64	0.00	24.03	3.43
…	…	…	…	…
8.1-8	26.90	54.44	19.53	2.05
8.1-9	26.23	75.30	19.00	2.01
…	…	…	…	…
12.31-23	7.14	0.00	6.42	1.40

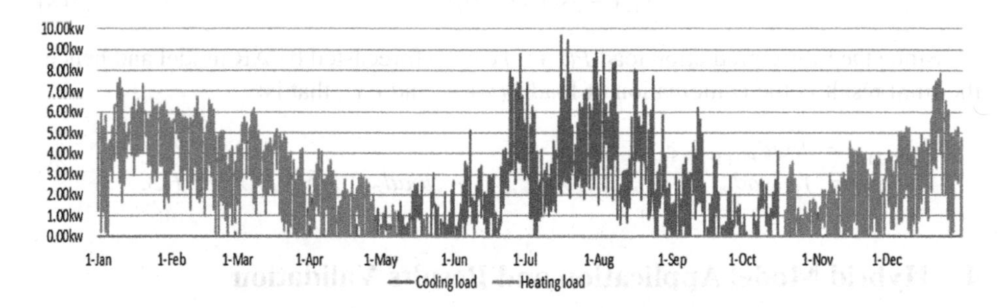

Fig. 5. The whole sample year load data trend

It can be seen clearly from the whole load trend curve that the maximum heating load is January, and the maximum cooling load is July. For this reason, this paper select two months (January, July) data as the proposed hybrid model input.

3.2 Experiment Design

In this research, a hybrid model is proposed so that all the information, including historical load data prediction by time series model and meteorological information used in artificial intelligent model can both be utilized for modeling. We consider that the actual value $load_{At}$ is expressed as a set of predictive values $load_{Pt}$ plus a prediction error terms e_{Pt}.

$$load_{At} = load_{Pt} + e_t \quad (4)$$

First of all, the historical information is exploring the historical information load $p_{(t\text{-}i)}$.

$$load_{Pt} = f_1(load_{P(t-1)}, load_{P(t-2)}, load_{P(t-3)}, \cdots, load_{P(t-i)}) \quad (5)$$

Once load P_t is available, the error terms actually are the difference between the actual values and predictions, that is:

$$e_t = load_{At} - load_{Pt} \quad (6)$$

Here, this research assume that the prediction error term e_t is caused by the past conditions of factors and by employing the APNN model to describe the relationship between them, the error term can be defined as:

$$e_t = f_2(T_{t-1}, R_{t-1}, H_{t-1}) \quad (7)$$

Where f is a nonlinear function determined by PNN and $T_{t\text{-}1}$, $R_{t\text{-}1}$ and $H_{t\text{-}1}$ are the meteorological information at time $t\text{-}1$ as temperature, solar radiation and humidity. After sufficient training and learning, the trained PNN can be used to forecast the future prediction error which is e_{t+1}:

$$e_{t+1} = f_2(T_t, R_t, H_t) \quad (8)$$

Since the future prediction load $P(t + 1)$ can be forecasted by AR model and hence, the final result is the combination of load $P(t + 1)$ and e_{t+1}, that is:

$$\begin{aligned} load_{A(t+1)} &= load_{P(t+1)} + e_{t+1} \\ &= f_1(load_{P(t)}, load_{P(t-1)}, load_{P(t-2)}, \cdots, load_{P(t-i+1)}) + f_2(T_t, R_t, H_t). \end{aligned} \quad (9)$$

4 Hybrid Model Application and Results Validation

Simply referring to previous discussion, the proposed Hybrid model is introduced and concluded as the best fit model for forecasting the building load value of Shanghai city. In order to reinforce this conclusion, several popular prediction methods are examined for comparison.

In this experiment, the Mean Average Percentage (MAPE) and the Root Mean Error (RMSE) statistical index were introduced to regard as performance comparison.

$$MAPE = \frac{1}{N}\sum_{t=1}^{N}(\frac{|a_i - p_i|}{a_i}) \times 100\% \tag{10}$$

$$RMSE = \sqrt{\frac{1}{N}\sum_{t=1}^{N}|a_i - p_i|^2} \tag{11}$$

Where *ai* and *pi* are the actual value and prediction value of building load (cooling or heating) of *i* hour, *N* is the number of testing hours. The data of July and January were used for predicting cooling and heating load separately. The experiments results are show Figs. 6, 7 and Table 4.

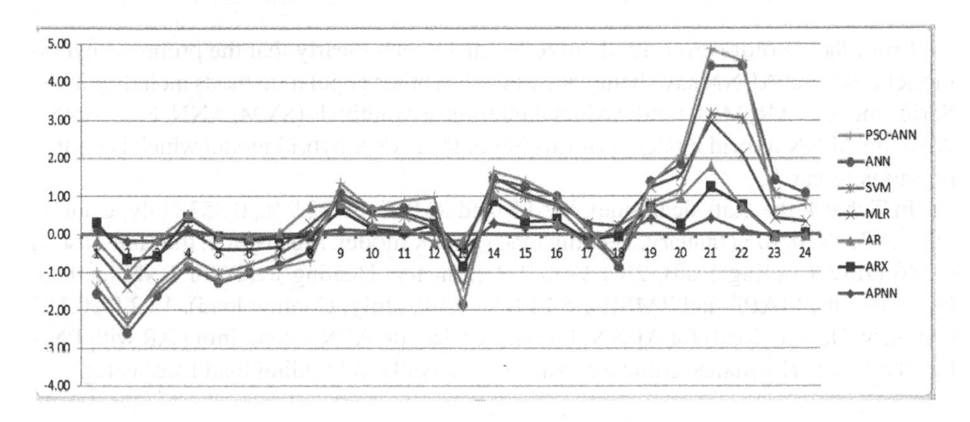

Fig. 6. Forecasting error trend of cooling load in July by different methods

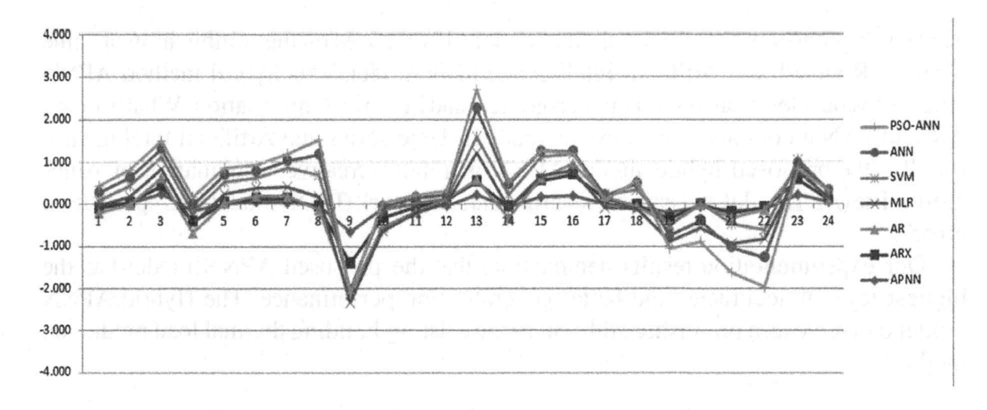

Fig. 7. Forecasting error trend of heating load in January by different methods

Table 4. Performance examination for different prediction methods

	July (CL)		January (HL)	
Methods	MAPE (%)	RMSE (kw)	MAPE (%)	RMSE (kw)
PNN	21.4	0.286	20.1	0.271
BPNN	37.9	0.491	21.9	0.290
SVM	45.3	0.559	33.0	0.354
MLR	46.5	0.546	24.3	0.308
AR	25.9	0.353	13.1	0.205
ARX	24.4	0.332	16.2	0.240
APNN	**14.0**	**0.186**	**12.2**	**0.183**
Average	30.8	0.393	20.1	0.264

From the absolute error trend curve, it can be seen clearly that the proposed hybrid model ARX and APNN have better accuracy than other popular methods including Time Series models (AR, MLR) and Artificial Intelligence methods (SVM, ANN, PSO-ANN). Also the APNN hybrid model performs better than ARX hybrid model which is built in previous research.

In Table 4, the statistical index MAPE and RMSE are 25.9 %, 0.353 (July, Cooling load), 13.1 %, 0.205 (January, Heating load) for AR model. Meanwhile, they are 21.4 %, 0.286 (July, Cooling load), 20.1 %, 0.271 (January, Heating load) for PNN method. However, the MAPE and RMSE are 14.0 %, 0.186 (July, Cooling load), 12.2 %, 0.183 (January, Heating load) for APNN. It is shown that the APNN combining AR with PNN has the best performance compare to all other models in building load forecasting.

5 Conclusion

This study proposed a hybrid prediction model APNN based on the combination of Time Series AR model and Artificial Intelligence PNN model. This hybrid method APNN takes into consideration of both meteorological and historical information. What's more, AR and PNN model also have best accuracy in Time series and Artificial Intelligence. Finally, the proposed hybrid model APNN is a more creative combination of Auto-regressive (AR) model and particle swarm neural network (PNN) model into "prediction error".

Our experimentation results demonstrate that the proposed APNN model has the highest level of accuracies and better generalization performance. The Hybrid APNN model can serve as a promising addition to the existing building thermal load prediction methods.

Acknowledgment. Thanks to the supports by National Natural Science Foundation (NNSF) of China under Grant 61273190 and Shanghai Natural Science Foundation under Grant 13ZR1417000.

References

1. Haida, T., Muto, S.: Regression based peak load forecasting using a transformation technique. IEEE Trans. Power Syst. **9**(4), 1788–1794 (1994)
2. Huang, S.J., Shih, K.R.: Short-term load forecasting via ARMA model identification including non-Gaussian process considerations. IEEE Trans. Power Syst. **18**(2), 673–679 (2003)
3. Kandil, N., Wamkeue, R., Saad, M., Georges, S.: An efficient approach for short term load forecasting using artificial neural networks. IEEE Trans. Power Syst. **28**, 525–530 (2006)
4. Mori, H., Kobayashi, H.: Optimal fuzzy inference for short-term load forecasting. IEEE Trans. Power Syst. **11**(1), 390–396 (1996)
5. Al-Kandari, A.M., Soliman, S.A., El-Hawary, M.E.: Fuzzy short-term electric load forecasting. IEEE Trans. Power Syst. **26**, 111–122 (2004)
6. Alamaniotis, M., Ikonomopoulos, A., Tsoukalas, L.H.: Evolutionary multi-objective optimization of kernel-based very-short-term load forecasting. IEEE Trans. Power Syst. **27**(3), 1477–1484 (2012)
7. Elattar, E.E., Goulermas, J.Y.: Generalized locally weighted GMDH for short-term load forecasting. IEEE Trans. Syst. Man Cybern. C Appl. Rev. **42**(3), 345–346 (2012)
8. Chen, T., Wang, Y.C.: Long-term load forecasting by a collaborative fuzzy-neural approach. IEEE Trans. Power Syst. **43**, 454–464 (2012)
9. Akdemir, B., Cetinkaya, N.: Long-term load forecasting based on adaptive neural fuzzy inference system using real energy data. Energy Process **14**, 794–799 (2012)
10. Jin, M., Zhou, X., Zhang, Z.M., Tentzeris, M.M.: Short-term power load forecasting using grey correlation contest modeling. Expert Syst. Appl. **39**, 773–779 (2012)
11. Masataro, O., Hiroyuki, M.: A Gaussian processes technique for short-term load forecasting with consideration of uncertainty. IEEE Trans. Power Energy **126**(2), 202–208 (2006)

A MKL-MKB Image Classification Algorithm Based on Multi-kernel Boosting Method

Ni Li(✉), Wenqing Huai, and Guanghong Gong

School of Automation Science and Electrical Engineering, Beihang University, Beijing, China
lini@buaa.edu.cn, huaiwenqing1992@163.com,
buaacorresponding@163.com

Abstract. Aiming at the low accuracy and poor applicability of traditional SVM classifiers, this paper proposes an image classification system based on MKL-MKB (multi kernel learning-multi kernel boosting). This approach firstly integrates existing feature extraction methods to extract features like wavelet, Gabor, GLCM and so on. A weak classifier is constructed by using a synthetic kernel in kernel space. We use Nystrom approximation algorithm to calculate weights of kernel matrixes of multi-kernel model. Then we make a decision level fusion of weak classifiers under Adaboost framework to impair weights of weak kernels. Finally, experiments are carried out to verify the validity and applicability of the proposed algorithm by testing on terrain remote sensing images and several UCI data sets.

Keywords: Image classification · SVM · Multi-kernel · Adaboost

1 Introduction

Image classifications are significant in image processing which has a wide range of applications in many fields including terrain detection in the field of national defense, face recognitions in the field of security, image retrievals in the field of the Internet applications as well as cancer diagnosis in the medical field. Most image supervised classification algorithms are based on statistical models. Users need to manually label a large number of image samples and then obtain a model from labeled training samples. However, in practice, it's difficult to label so many samples. To solve the problem, active learning has become a hot research topic in the field of kernel pattern recognition. The research mainly includes three aspects: feature extraction, similarity/distance calculation and classification algorithm model.

In recent years, more and more research show that those classification methods using single feature can only be effective to specific target recognitions instead of common ones. A large number of researchers use combinations of different features to build classifier models. These researches extract local and global information from images and then get classifiers in the framework of a boosting algorithm. Their effects are usually better than single classifiers. Viola [1] in 2004 first used Adaboost in the field of human face recognition to learn Haar features and used a cascade classifier to improve the recognition speed and accuracy greatly and expand the field of image classification

L. Zhang et al. (Eds.): AsiaSim 2016/SCS AutumnSim 2016, Part I, CCIS 643, pp. 156–164, 2016.
DOI: 10.1007/978-981-10-2663-8_17

development space. Shunmugapriya [2] in 2011 proposed an alternative approach for Classifier Ensembles by using Boosting method which obtained satisfying results on three UCI data sets. Next, Shen [3] from Australia expanded binary boosting classification into multi-class boosting. He proposed a novel classification criterion for multi class problems and an optimal method for training multi-class boosting. Ban [4] introduced the Adaboost algorithm to deal with the problem of digital detection making the accuracy greatly improved. Akbari [5] put forward a Gentle Boost and used many experiments to verify that the algorithm is better than traditional boosting algorithms.

Thanks to Support Vector Machine (SVM) [6, 7] theories, kernel methods are paid much attention to. Since 1992 when Boser proposed SVM methods, SVM has succeeded in promoting the rapid popularization and development of nuclear methods and gradually penetrated into many areas of machine learning. But these methods are based on single kernels. Because of differences in characteristic of distinct kernels, performance of kernel functions diverse a lot in different situations. In view of these problems, in recent years, there have been a lot of researches on the combination Kernel methods, that is, multi kernel learning methods.

Multi-kernel models [8, 9] are a kind of more flexible kernel learning model. Recent theories and applications have proved that replacing single kernels with multiple kernels can enhance interpretabilities of decision functions. Lanckriet [10] in 2004 proposed Multi-kernel Learning, which combines several kernel functions and remedies the deficiency of SVM. He laid a solid foundation for the practical application of MKL. A scene classification algorithm based on multi kernel fusion was proposed by Chen [11] which enables the test set of samples to remain independent. In the same year, Zhou [12] used multi-kernel SVM model to solve multi-modal tasks, providing a reference for multi feature classifications. In 2016, Q.Wang [13] proposed a discriminative multiple kernel learning (DMKL) method for spectral image classification.

In this paper, we propose an image classification algorithm for terrain remote sensing images. In feature selection, we integrate the existing algorithms using wavelet, Gabor and GLCM and other features to characterize images. At the same time, we introduce the idea of multi-kernel learning. Linear classifiers in kernel space are used to construct a weak classifier set with a number of features. In this way, discriminant information contained in kernel functions is transferred to a set of weak classifiers. Then we use a Boosting algorithm to make decision level fusion and get a strong classifier combination. The effectiveness of the proposed algorithm and the generality of the framework are proved by the identification of several standard classification samples from UCI data sets.

2 An Image Classification System Based on MKL-MKB (Multi Kernel Learning - Multi Kernel Boosting)

According to characteristics of terrain images, with extractions of features [14] such as wavelet, Gabor and GLCM, now we propose an image classification system based on MKL-MKB in this paper. The schematic diagram is as follows:

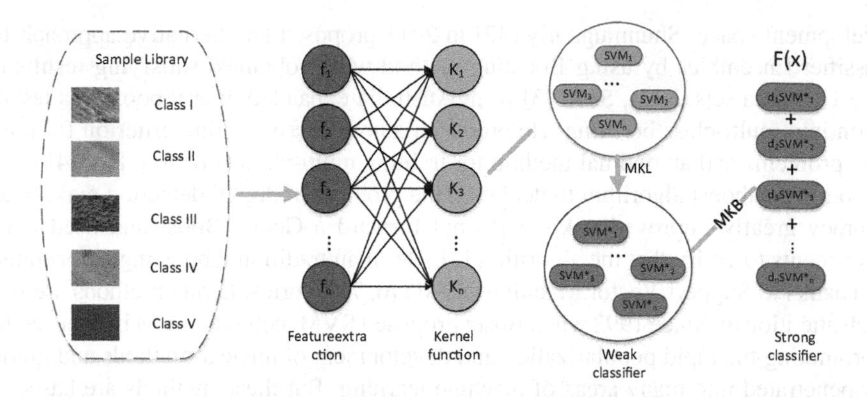

Fig. 1. Schematic diagram of MKL-MKB system

As shown in Fig. 1, firstly, we set up a series of sample libraries according to the samples to be classified. Samples are classified into several classes such as lake, grass, bareland, greenland and so on. Each class is given a label and divided into a test set and training set and then extracted their features. For each feature, we select one kernel function to make a SVM classifier, and then obtain results. Next, a new set of classifiers SVM* are obtained by multi kernel processing of each SVM classifier. This process will be introduced in next section. Finally, we apply these new classifiers to the decision layer fusion. By reassigning weights of each classifier we can get a strong classifier and complete the classification of images (Fig. 2).

The algorithm flowchart is as follows:

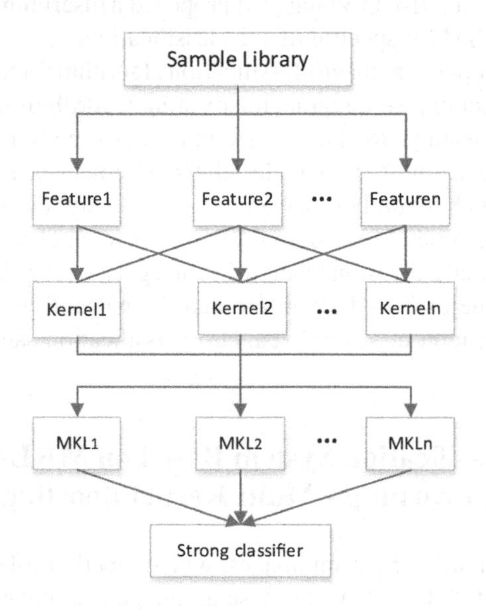

Fig. 2. Algorithm flowchart

Specific algorithm processes are as follows:

(a) Select a sample library;
(b) Extract several features from the library integrating existed sample extraction methods;
(c) Obtain a series of MKL weak classifiers with several features by training samples with our multi-kernel model;
(d) Initialize the weights of all the training examples into 1/N, in which N is the number of samples;
(e) for m = 1 ,……, M:
   i. Train the weak classifier ym(),minimize weighted error function:

$$\varepsilon_m = \sum_{n=1}^{N} \omega_n^{(m)} I(y_m(x_n) \neq t_n) \tag{1}$$

   ii. Calculate the discourse power α of the weak classifier:

$$\alpha_m = \ln\left\{\frac{1-\varepsilon_m}{\varepsilon_m}\right\} \tag{2}$$

   iii. Update the weights:

$$\omega_{m+1,i} = \frac{\omega_{\text{mi}}}{Z_m} \exp(-\alpha_m t_i y_m(x_i)), i = 1, 2, \ldots N \tag{3}$$

   Zm is a normalized factor which makes the sum of all ω is 1.

$$Z_m = \sum_{i=1}^{N} \omega_{\text{mi}} \exp(-\alpha_m t_i y_m(x_i)) \tag{4}$$

   iv. Get the final classifier:

$$Y_M(x) = sign(\sum_{m=1}^{M} \alpha_m y_m(x)). \tag{5}$$

3 A Multi-kernel Method for Terrain Image Classifications

SVM is a general learning algorithm based on Structure Risk Minimization (SRM) whose basic idea is to construct an optimal hyper plane in the sample input space or the feature space. It makes the distance between the hyper plane and the two kinds of samples to reach the maximum so that the best generalization ability is obtained. Its solution is globally optimal and it involves on artificial design of network architecture. For nonlinear problems, SVM tries to transform them into a linear problem in another space by nonlinear transformations (kernel function). In this transformation space, the optimal linear hyper plane can be solved. This nonlinear transformation can be realized by the inner product function which is kernel function.

Kernel functions map features from a low dimension space to a high dimension space. But at present, the SVMs we use are single kernels. When we use them, we need to choose a kernel function according to experience or experiments and specify its parameters, which is very inconvenient. On the other hand, in practice, features are often no single but heterogeneous. For image classification systems, we may use color, texture or spatial related features. Their best kernel function may not be the same. If we let them share the same kernel function, there is a great chance that we may not be able to get a best mapping. Considering these questions, we introduce a multi kernel function learning method.

Now we define the following as the synthesis of kernels:

$$M = d_1 k_1 + d_2 k_2 + \cdots + d_n k_n \tag{6}$$

M is the multi-kernel after the synthesis; k_n is a single kernel, d_n is their weight.

We give some basic kernel functions, such as linear, polynomial, RBF and sigmoid kernel. For each kernel, we can specify multiple sets of parameters. And then we use a linear combination of them as the final kernel function. By training, the weight (d) of each kernel in this linear combination can be obtained. Due to the fusion of various kernel functions, we can take care of the heterogeneous characteristics. Since the process of learning weights is automatic, we don't need to consider which kernel and which parameter to use. We just combine possible kernels and parameters. As mentioned before, this paper uses wavelet, Gabor and GLCM to express characteristics (Fig. 3).

The following figure is a schematic diagram of the process of synthesis:

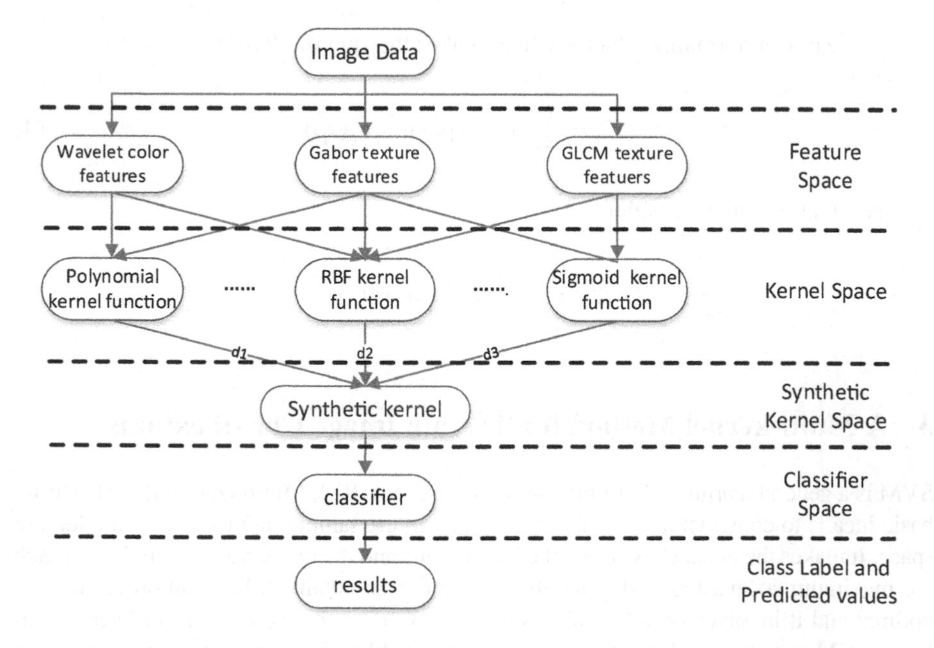

Fig. 3. Process of synthetic kernel

Expressions of the kernel functions in the above figure:
Polynomial kernel function:

$$K(x,z) = \left[x^{T}z + 1\right]^{q} \tag{7}$$

RBF kernel function:

$$K(x,z) = \exp\left(-\frac{|x - z|^{2}}{\sigma^{2}}\right) \tag{8}$$

Sigmoid kernel function:

$$K(x,z) = \tanh\left(v\left(x^{T}z\right) + c\right) \tag{9}$$

x, z are training data; σ, q are constant; v is a norm of measurement; c is a displacement parameter.

Next, we describe our synthetic kernel with a linear combination of the above kernels. Suppose k(x, z) is a known kernel function, $\hat{k}(x, z)$ is its normalized form.

$$\hat{k}(x, z) = \sqrt{k(x, x)k(z, z)} \tag{10}$$

Weighted synthetic kernel:

$$k(x,z) = \sum_{j=1}^{M} \beta_j \hat{k}_j(x,z), \beta_j \geq 0, \sum_{j=1}^{M} \beta_j = 1 \tag{11}$$

Multi kernel learning models need to calculate the weights of the linear combination of multiple kernel matrices. But the traditional multi kernel learning classifier transforms this problem and corresponding classification algorithms into an optimization problem. But the process of transformation requires a lot of complex derivations. In addition, the process of determining the kernel combination coefficients is integrated into the final optimization problem. Multiple kernel matrices need to be stored in memory, from beginning to end. To a certain extent, this creates a waste of space.

To improve efficiency of existing multi-kernel classifiers, we try to introduce the Nystrom approximation algorithm [15] into the fusion of multiple kernel functions. The core of this idea is to separate calculating kernel combination coefficients from the classifier's algorithm framework. The kernel combination coefficients are determined by the Nystrom approximation algorithm firstly and then the final kernel matrix is involved in the classifier framework after the combination. In this way, the waste of space is effectively reduced. The unique nature of the Nystrom approximation algorithm also greatly reduces the computational complexity of the final algorithm.

4 Experiment and Discussion

The sample set used in this paper contains 4435 training samples and 2000 test samples. It is divided into six classes and feature dimension is 36. Experimental results are as follows:

Table 1. Experimental results

Classifier	SVM_1	SVM_2	SVM_3	SVM_4	MKL	MKL-MKB
Kernel	Linear	Polynomial	RBF	Sigmoid	Above	–
Acc/%	80.65 %	81 %	84.55 %	32.05 %	87.1018 %	91.2199 %
Time/s	447.62	450.55	447.63	451.37	481.36	512.74

As can be seen from the experimental results, the MKL-MKB algorithm proposed in this paper has a great improvement on image classification accuracy compared with other methods. Classification accuracy has been obviously enhanced (Fig. 4) and Tables 1, 2 and 3.

To prove the algorithm's universal applicability, this paper uses five UCI data sets to test the performance of image classification algorithms. The data set information is shown in the following table:

Table 2. UCI dataset information

No.	Name	Feature no.	Class no.	Sample no.
1	Iris_new	4	3	150
2	Ionosphere	34	2	351
3	LIBRAS movement	90	15	360
4	Wine	12	3	178
5	Yeast	8	10	112

We assigned sample data as 1:4. In order to avoid contingency, each data set was carried out 10 times. The results are as follows:

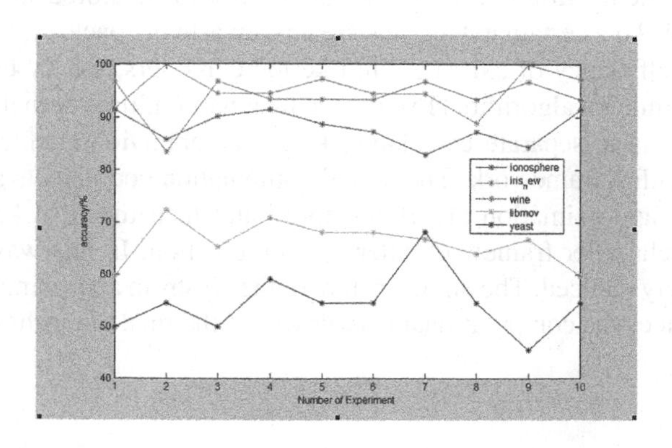

Fig. 4. Results of test data

Experimental results on UCI data are as follows:

Table 3. Experimental results on UCI datasets

Sample \ Acc	Based on MKL-MKB/%	Based on standard SVM/%	Based on MKL/%
Iris_new	96.6667	83.3333	93.6667
Ionosphere	91.4286	82.8571	88.0000
LIBRAS Movement	72.2222	59.7222	66.1111
Wine	100	88.8889	95.2778
yeast	68.1818	45.4545	54.5455

We can see that this algorithm in most samples has also achieved good results, confirming the applicability of the proposed algorithm.

5 Conclusion and Future Work

In this paper, firstly, we propose an image classification system based on MKL-MKB (multi kernel learning- multi kernel boosting), which processes samples through a multi-kernel model. Then we use existing features to form a completely new synthetic nuclear space. Nystrom algorithm is introduced to separate the calculation process of kernel combination coefficients from the algorithm frame of the classifier. From terrain images to several UCI data sets, the validity and applicability of the algorithm are verified. This algorithm not only can be used in classifying topographic images but also medical and Internet areas.

References

1. Viola, P., Jones, M.J.: Robust real-time face detection. Int. J. Comput. Vis. (IJCV) **57**(2), 137–154 (2004)
2. Shunmugapriya, P., Kanmani S., Prasath, B.S., et al.: Classifier ensembles using boosting with mixed learner models (BMLM). In: 2011 International Conference on Recent Trends in Information Technology (ICRTIT). IEEE, pp. 151–155 (2011)
3. Shen, C., Hao, Z.: A direct formulation for totally-corrective multi-class boosting. In: IEEE Conference on Computer Vision and Pattern Recognition. IEEE Computer Society, pp. 2585–2592 (2011)
4. Ban, K.D., Yoon, Y., Yoon, H.S., et al.: Number detection in natural image with boosting classifier. In: International Conference on Ubiquitous Robots and Ambient Intelligence, pp. 525–526 (2012)
5. Akbari, F., Sajedi, H.: SMS spam detection using selected text features and boosting classifiers. In: Information and Knowledge Technology. IEEE (2015)

6. Shahid, N., Naqvi, I.H., Qaisar, S.B.: Quarter-sphere SVM: attribute and spatio-temporal correlations based outlier & event detection in wireless sensor networks. In: IEEE Wireless Communications & Networking Conference. IEEE, pp. 2048–2053 (2012)
7. Sahri, Z., Yusof, R.: Fault diagnosis of power transformer using optimally selected DGA features and SVM. In: Control Conference. IEEE (2015)
8. Niranjan, S., Shin, Y.C.: Sparse multiple kernel learning for signal processing applications. IEEE Trans. Pattern Anal. Mach. Intell. **32**(5), 788–798 (2010)
9. Close, R., Wilson, J., Gader, P.: A Bayesian approach to localized multi-kernel learning using the relevance vector machine. In: IEEE International Geoscience and Remote Sensing Symposium (IGARSS), pp. 1103–1106 (2011)
10. Lanckriet, G.R.G., Tijl, D.B., Nello, C., et al.: A statistical framework for genomic data fusion. Bioinformatics **20**(16), 2626–2635 (2004)
11. Chen, T.T., Liu, C.J., Zou, H.L., et al.: A multi-instance multi-label scene classification method based on multi-kernel fusion. In: Sai Intelligent Systems Conference. IEEE (2015)
12. Zhou, Y., Cui, X., Hu, Q., et al.: Improved multi-kernel SVM for multi-modal and imbalanced dialogue act classification. In: International Joint Conference on Neural Networks. IEEE (2015)
13. Wang, Q., Gu, Y., Tuia, D.: Discriminative multiple Kernel learning for hyperspectral image classification. IEEE Trans. Pattern Anal. Mach. Intell. (PAMI) (2016). doi:10.1109/TGRS.2016.2530807
14. Bi, X., Pun, C.M., Yuan, X.C.: Multi-level dense descriptor and hierarchical feature matching for copy-move forgery detection. Inf. Sci. **345**, 226–242 (2016)
15. Damoulas, T., Girolami, M.A.: Pattern recognition with a Bayesian kernel combination machine. Pattern Recogn. Lett. **30**(1), 46–54 (2009)
16. Lee, K.M.: Locality-sensitive hashing techniques for nearest neighbor search. Int. J. Fuzzy Logic Intell. Syst. **12**(4), 300–307 (2012)

Optimization for Accelerating Large Scale Agent Based Simulation

Zhen Li(✉), Gang Guo, Bin Chen, Liang Ma, Yuyu Luo, and Xiaogang Qiu

College of Information System and Management, National University of Defense Technology, Changsha, China
lizhen08@nudt.edu.cn

Abstract. Parallel agent based simulation is popular used in artificial society. However, it brings great challenges to the execution efficiency when facing large scale artificial society where the number of agents in the simulation is up to millions. A simulation kernel with conservative synchronization strategy and multi-thread scheduling paradigm for large scale parallel agent based simulation is introduced. Based on the simulation kernel, the paper proposes two optimization strategies: a container based agent management scheme and an event based load balance strategy. The paper then design several experiments to evaluate the optimization performance, it shows that the optimization strategies can obtain up to 5x speedup compared to the basic simulation kernel.

Keywords: Agent based simulation · Parallel discrete event simulation · Synchronization strategy · Load balance

1 Introduction

Agent-based modeling and simulation is becoming more and more important and popular way to model the complex system composed of interacting and autonomous 'agent' [1]. Especially in social simulation, it offers a quantitative approach to study the laws of human activity. While in social simulation, more and more grandiose plans were proposed, they want to construct a city or country even world wide-scale artificial society to supervise and study the real world [2]. Thus million event billion scale agents will bring a huge challenge to the execution of simulation.

Parallel Agent Based Simulation (PABS) method extends from the Parallel Discrete Event Simulation (PDES) [3], it utilizes different computational units to execute a portion of agents separately, which can bring a considerable performance promotion.

Traditional PABS method was designed in distributed computing platform, such as Repast HPC, ROSS, etc. While the communication costs between models in different computer nodes is still a fatal disadvantage in distributed computer based PABS. Many researches dedicate to the problem [4–6], regretfully as the scale of agent number raise rapidly and the degree of coupling between agents, the high communication overhead and latency limit the performance of PABS.

The immergence of multi-core platforms solves the communication latency fundamentally. In multi-core platforms, parallel computational units are the cores

L. Zhang et al. (Eds.): AsiaSim 2016/SCS AutumnSim 2016, Part I, CCIS 643, pp. 165–175, 2016.
DOI: 10.1007/978-981-10-2663-8_18

integrated in one chip, and all the cores share the common RAM memory. Thus, the communication between agents can even be replaced by the changes of memory points from C++ language perspective. As a consequence, the cost of communication can even be limited to a constant. In the meantime, as the development of computer technology, the performance of a single computer can be comparable with the TOP1 supercomputers from 10 years ago, which means we can build large scale simulation applications in a single computer. So more and more researches turn to concentrate on the multi-thread based parallel computing methods, and some multi-thread based simulation kernels are proposed, such as ROSS-MT [7], and HPSK [8]. However the multi-thread based optimization work above mainly focus on the PDES (Parallel Discrete Event Simulation), there is seldom optimization strategy for PABS (Parallel Agent Based Simulation), especially for large scale agent based simulation.

In the paper, we design a multi-threaded parallel agent based simulation kernel. The simulation kernel is mainly focus on the optimization for synchronization and scheduling of large number of agents in the simulation. To solve the problem, main contribution of the paper is list as follow:

(a) Propose a container based agent management scheme to optimization of time synchronization cost between agents.
(b) Propose an event based load balance strategy to filter the inactive agents when scheduling.

The rest of paper is organized as follow: Sect. 2 illustrates some related work. The basic introduction of multi-thread based simulator OneModel is given in Sect. 3. In Sect. 4, the paper illustrates the Optimization methods and we design three experiments to evaluate the performance of the proposed methods in Sect. 5.

2 Related Work

Parallel agent based simulation is designed based on the PDES method. The whole agent models are executed by several Logical Processes (LPs). The LPs are usually assigned to different physical processing units. Due to the interaction of agents, there are usually data exchange and agent migration between LPs. Hence, there should be a synchronization operation to avoid the causal errors. And load balance strategy is also widely researched to keep the load in different LP balance.

For the time synchronization problem, there are two basic time synchronization algorithm, which are conservative and optimistic strategy. Conservative strategy prohibits any causality error from occurring, whereas optimistic strategy uses detection and recover approach: causality errors are detected, and a rollback mechanism is invoked to recover.

SASSY is a typical optimistic strategy simulator based on time warp algorithm. And in order to reduce the rollback overheads, many methods are proposed [9]. But in large scale agent based simulation, a rollback operation may cause even hundred and thousand more rollback through the social network among agents which lead poor execution efficiency. So the paper thinks that the conservative synchronization strategy is more suitable for large scale agent based simulation. SPADES [10] is a typical conservative strategy simulator which uses a global event queue to process the simulation time. But SPADES is mainly used in artificial intelligence area with small number of agent. Another conservative simulator is RePast, and in order to support large scale agent simulation, it is extended to RepasteHPC [11] to realize distributed simulation. RepasteHPC introduce DR method to reduce the communication cost. But when the number of agents increases, the communication and DR cost is still relative high.

Load balance strategy is to balance the computational task and reduce the communication cost among LPs. Much work has emerged to predict the communication between LPs and design load migration algorithm. However, these works are based on the multi-process paradigm which LPs are executing on the different process. Recently, some work has emerged to design a multi-thread oriented simulation kernel in multi-core platform. In multi-thread paradigm, LPs are executed on different threads, and the whole states of agents are shared between LPs which lead a relative low communication cost and reduce the migration cost. Ryan James Miller [12] proposes a threaded version of WARPED. ThreadWarped employ a master-worker pattern, in which defines a collection of threads, one for Time Warp housekeeping functions (called the manager thread) and one or more other threads for scheduling and processing simulation events (called worker threads). However, ThreadWarped gains speedup only by process events in parallel. Wenjie Tang designs a HPSK model [8], which gains speedup by both scheduling LPs and processing event in parallel. Furthermore, some work turn to exploit the computational power from GPU thread in heterogeneous platform.

3 OneModel: A General Multi-threaded Parallel Agent Simulation Kernel

In this section, we introduce a general conservative parallel agent based modeling and simulation environment which is the main modeling tool of the large scale artificial society in our research.

3.1 A Modified DEVS Component Model

For large scale complex systems, a common and effective way of modeling is to break down them into components and construct system model through composition. With standard component models, simulation engines can be separated from model relatively.

As a formal method, DEVS is well suitable for rigorous specification of models. However, as to agent based simulation, agent is a basic and independent component, and coupled component is not needed. To make it simpler and easier to understand, a modified DEVS is proposed as the formalism of standard component models:

$$
\begin{aligned}
&M_c \triangleq <T, I, E, S, \tau, f, g> \\
&f : S_t \times I_t \times E_t \rightarrow S_{t'}; g : S_t \times I_t \times E_t \rightarrow E_{t'} \\
&E \triangleq \{e = <t, receiver, type, sender, content>\} \\
&t, t' \in T, t' = \tau(t) \geq t
\end{aligned}
$$

The event list E is explicitly described and each event e contains information including time, receiver, type, sender, and content. External and internal events are not distinguished for they are treated almost the same way in simulation. Through input I, a model can get information from other components. Output is implicitly included in state S because others can learn all about the component through its state. The time advance function τ is used to compute the next time of possible event or state update. The state transition function f transfers the model to a new state until the next update. The event generate function g is used to generate new events during the state transition.

The advantage of the modification is that it is easy to understand modeling process and natural to represent dynamic behavior. However, it is complicated for parallel simulation because component models are managed and scheduled by different LPs. Input from other components and events output to other components must be state consistent and temporal correct. It is just the causal order of messages between LPs that leads to various complicated parallel simulation algorithms.

3.2 Parallel Simulation Through Two-Phase Synchronization

The idea of parallel simulation of modified DEVS models is based on two-phase synchronization as show in Fig. 1. During the first phase, all component models are locked read-only and read input from each other. Synchronization is put at the end of the phase to guarantee all components get what they need and states each gets are consistent. During the second phase, all components are updated according to the minimum event time. Synchronization is also put at the end of the phase to guarantee

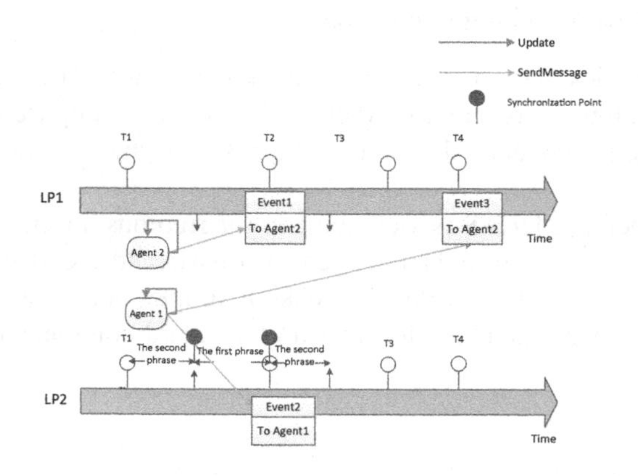

Fig. 1. Two phase synchronization process

completion of update and message delivery. If the executing order of concurrent events does not matter, parallel simulation will produce same result as sequential simulation.

The performance of parallel algorithm is mainly affected by load balance of component models, communication of messages and synchronization between LPs. It is also a fact that the number of component models is usually many times the number of processors in large scale agent simulations. As a result, if large scale component models can be evenly distributed in LPs, high performance can be expected.

3.3 Multi-threaded Design

Traditional PDES method is designed on the distributed computers with MPI. However, as the simulation applications get larger and more complex, the communication cost between processes becomes the bottleneck. On the other hand, as the development of multi-core platform, a single computer can easily reach the performance of computer clusters 10 years ago. Many works have showed that the multi-threaded parallel simulation kernel can perform a better performance. Therefore, multi-threaded design of simulation kernel is proposed to solve the communication problem.

Figure 2 shows the general scheduling architecture of multi-threaded parallel agent simulation kernel. In the architecture, in order to gain a better load balance, the management of agents is separated from the threads, and each agent maintains its own event queues. Communications between agents are realized through the delivery of events. In the multi-threaded architecture, as the threads share the same address space, events are sent by creating its copy and insert the memory point to the target event queue. An event queue router which is designed as a map from the agent names to its event queue is needed for searching the target event queues.

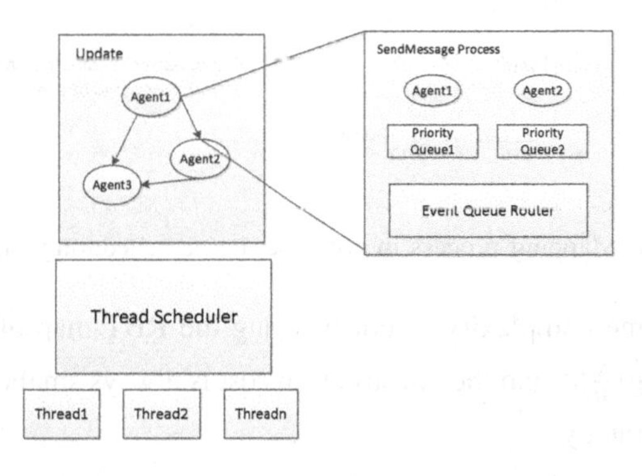

Fig. 2. Multi-threaded scheduling architecture

4 Optimization Strategy

The general purpose OneModel simulator just uses one priority queue to maintain the whole events generated by the whole agents. When the number of agents reach to million, the operation of event queue will cause relative high overheads.

The main destination of the proposed optimized simulation kernel is to support large scale agents running. In this section, the paper analysis the characteristic of the scheduling algorithm, and propose two optimization strategies.

4.1 Container-Based Agent Management

In large scale agent simulation, the number of N can reach up to millions or billion. To construct a RBT map of N node need the time complexity of o(N log N), which will cost tremendous amount of time when N is large enough.

In order to speed up the construction of the RBT map, the key point is to reduce the number of node in the map. So, use the hierarchical management thought for reference, we divided the whole agents into M containers, and then the agents and events are managed through two layers. The first layer is a map between containers and their event queue (denoted as CTQ), and each container maintains the second layer, which is a map between the agents in one container and their names (denoted as NTA). The mapping process is shown as Fig. 3.

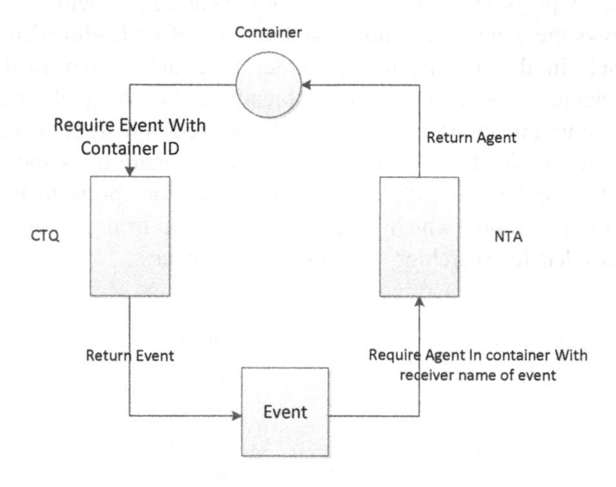

Fig. 3. Mapping process in container-based scheduling strategy

Theorem 1. The time complexity of constructing the RBT map of CTQ and NTA is $o(\mathrm{MlogM} + \left(\frac{\mathrm{N}}{\mathrm{M}}\right)\log\left(\frac{N}{M}\right))$, and the construction cost is always smaller than that in agent based scheduling strategy.

Proof. The time complexity of construction process of CTQ and NTA is o(MlogM) and $o(\frac{N}{M}\log\frac{N}{M})$, ignoring the impact of other factors, the time complexity of constructing the RBT map of CTQ and NTA is $o(\mathrm{MlogM} + (\frac{\mathrm{N}}{\mathrm{M}})\log(\frac{N}{M})$. Defining the function f as $\mathrm{f} = \mathrm{MlogM} + \left(\frac{\mathrm{N}}{\mathrm{M}}\right)\log\left(\frac{N}{M}\right) - \mathrm{N}\log N$, then take a second derivate of f, we have $f'' = \frac{1}{M} + \frac{3n}{M^2} + \frac{2nlog\frac{N}{M}}{M^2}$, obviously $f'' > 0$ always true where $1 < M < N$, so f is convex function, the maximum of f is obtained when M = 1or N and its value is zero.

So we can draw the conclusion that the construction cost is always smaller than that in agent based scheduling strategy when $1 < M < N$.

4.2 Event-Based Load Balance Strategy

In agent-based load balance strategy, since the agents which have events needed to be scheduled at the moment simulation time are not known, so lots of agents are scheduled with nothing to do, and waste most of the computational resources. Thus based on our container-based scheduling strategy, the paper proposes an event-based load balanced strategy.

In container-based scheduling strategy, through CTQ and NTA, we can obtain the specific target agent component from arbitrary event as Fig. 5 shows. And the events with specific time stamp in each container can be easily gets from the event queue. So in event-based load balanced strategy, we separate the scheduling process into two phases. In the first phase called Executable Events Collecting, we collect all the events to be scheduled at the simulation time in each container into a vector. In the second phase called Parallel Execution, we distribute the events in the vector to the parallel threads averagely, and then in each working threads, the specific target agent component is obtained with the events and agent execute the Update() function with the event. Algorithm 2 presents the pseudo code.

Algorithm 2 event-based scheduling process

Executable Events Collecting:
1: For each thread t_i parallel do
2: For each container C_{t_ij} do
3: EventSet ← CTQ(C_{t_ij})
4: Get parallel events NEs at current time in EventSet
5: Push NEs into an event vector ParallelEvents
6: End for
7: End for

Parallel Execution:

Update()
8: For each thread t_i parallel do
9: For each event e in ParallelEvents do
10: ContainerID c ← container index of e
11: Agent A ← $NTA_c(recevier\ name\ of\ e)$
12: Execute update function of A with e
13: End for
14: End for
SendMessage()
15: ContainerID c ← container index of e
16: EventSet ← CTQ(c)
17: Push e into Eventset

Suppose the number of working thread is limited and is denoted as T. Denote the number of agent which have event to be scheduled as S.

Theorem 2. The time complexity of the event-based scheduling algorithm is $o(\frac{S+M}{T}\log M + \frac{S+M}{T}\log\frac{N}{M})$, and is always better than that of agent-based scheduling algorithm.

Proof. As shown in Algorithm 2, the event-based scheduling process can be separate into two parts. In Executable Events Collecting phase, each thread maintains $\frac{M}{T}$ containers. Line 3 searches the RBT of M nodes, the time complexity of it is $o(\log M)$, and line 4 searches the EventSet which is also a RBT structure. Suppose each agent in container has an event in EventSet, thus the number of nodes in EventSet is $\frac{N}{M}$ and the search operation have the time complexity of $o(\log\frac{N}{M})$. So, the time complexity of Executable Events Collecting phase is $o(\frac{M}{T}(\log M + \log\frac{N}{M}))$. In the Parallel Execution phase, each thread maintains $\frac{S}{T}$ events. Line 11 searches the RBT map of $\frac{N}{M}$ nodes, and line 16 searches the RBT map of M nodes. So the time complexity of Parallel Execution phase is $o(\frac{S}{T}(\log M + \log\frac{N}{M}))$. Accumulating the two parts, the time complexity of the event-based scheduling algorithm is $o(\frac{S+M}{T}\log M + \frac{S+M}{T}\log\frac{N}{M})$.

Let $f = \frac{S+M}{T}\log M + \frac{S+M}{T}\log\frac{N}{M} - \frac{N}{T}\log N - S\log N$, take a first derivate of f, we have $f' = \frac{\log\frac{N}{M} + \log M}{T}$. Since $f' > 0$, f reach the maximum value $f = \left(\frac{S}{T} - S\right)\log N$ when $M = N$. Since $T > 1$, so $f < 0$ is always true which means the time complexity of the event-based scheduling algorithm is always better than that of agent-based scheduling algorithm.

5 Experiment

In this section, the paper designs a simple but large scale agent-based simulation experiment to make a comparison of different scheduling algorithm. The agent number of the simulation is 1 million, and in order to model the unbalance load between agents, we set a parameter denoted as P to control the percentage of updating agents in an execution cycle. The hardware environment is a 12-core Xeon c2050 CPU with 64 GB memory. The Modeling and simulation support is based on OneModel.

In order to illustrate the performance difference, the paper designs three experiments.

Firstly, the paper design an experiment to make an comparison of the performance between optimized and basic simulation kernel. The experiment executes on different number of threads, and records the average execution time among time step in simulation. The result is shown on Fig. 4.

As we can see that, the optimized simulation kernel can get up to 5x speedup compared with the basic one when the thread number is 12. It shows that the proposed container-based agent management and event-based load balance method is effective. They optimize the performance of simulator from the synchronization and execution phrase respectively.

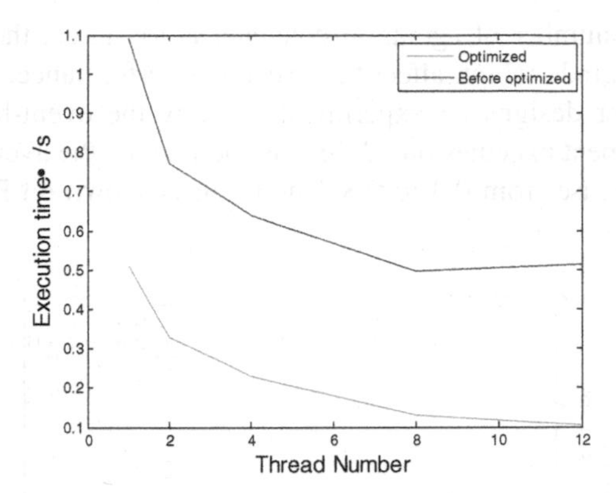

Fig. 4. The execution time comparison between optimized and basic simulation kernel

Secondly, the paper designs an experiment to test performance in different setting of container. For the experiment, as the number of container increase from 1 to 1 million, we record the whole execution the between time steps including the synchronization time and update time. Different number of container mainly affects the performance of synchronization between the whole agents. The result is shown on Fig. 5, and the x-axis is set as logarithmic coordinate.

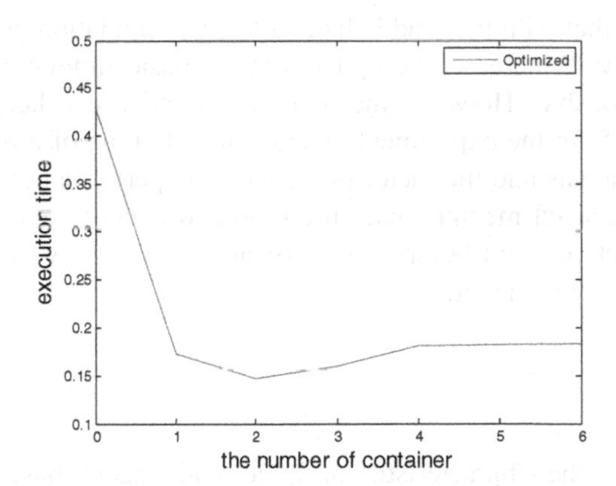

Fig. 5. Execution time under different container

From Fig. 5, we can obtain that more container can get better performance among a specific threshold. However, once exceed, the performance will degrade then. The threshold in the experiment is around 100 containers namely each container hold 10 thousand agents. The reason is that the container based agent management method divide the synchronization into two phrases which is synchronization in container and between containers. In container, the event queue is a RBT structure. When a new event comes, it can be organized by time increased order. So the synchronization in container can be completed during execution to accelerate the synchronization process.

However, when the number of agents in container is too large, the sort efficiency of RBT will greatly degrade which affect the execution performance.

Finally, the paper designs an experiment to show the event-based load balance strategy. The experiment executes on 12 threads and records the average update time of a time step as P increase from 0.3 to 0.8. The result is shown on Fig. 6.

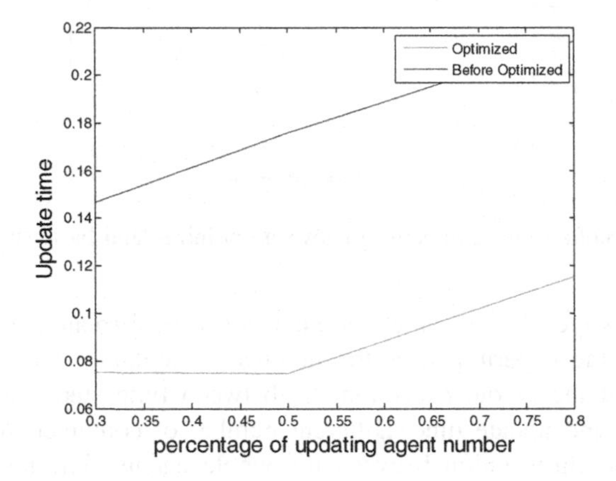

Fig. 6. The update time comparison

Figure 6 shows that with the load balance strategy, simulation performance can get up to 2x speedup. As P increase, the update time of basic simulator also increase and obey a linear relationship. However the optimized method can keep a steady performance when $P < 0.5$. In the experiment, average update time of a time step is used to execute the whole agents and the factor that affects the performance is mainly the load in threads. The optimized methods uses the proposed event-based load balance strategy, it filter the inactive agent before execution and reduce the wasted time caused by the scheduling of inactive agent.

6 Conclusion

The paper analyzes the characteristic of large scale agent based simulation, and introduces a conservative parallel simulation kernel OneModel. It uses multi-thread scheduling paradigm to reduce the load unbalance overheads and the communication cost between agents. Based on OneModel, the paper then proposed two optimization strategies which design from two aspects. From the first aspect, the paper design a container based agent management scheme to optimization of time synchronization cost between agents. It uses a hierarchical management method to reduce the scheduling overheads of the large number of agents and the events scheduled. From the second aspect, the paper design an event based load balance strategy. It design based on the multi-thread paradigm, and divide the events instead of agents to the threads equally. With the two optimization strategies, the OneModel simulation kernel can get up to 5x speedup.

Acknowledgment. This work was supported by the Natural Science Foundation of China (Grant No. 9102403071303252, 61403402, 41201544 and 71343282) and the HPC project (13010502) funded by NUDT.

References

1. Macal, C.M., North, M.J.: Tutorial on agent-based modeling and simulation. J. Simul. **4**, 151–162 (2010)
2. Stroud,P.: Spatial dynamics of pandemic influenza in a massive artificial society. JASSS **10** (49) 2007
3. Fujimoto, R.M.: Parallel and Distributed Simulation Systems. Wiley, New York (2000)
4. Scheutz, M., Schermerhorn, P.: Adaptive algorithms for the dynamic distribution and parallel execution of agent-based models. J. Parallel Distrib. Comput. **66**(8), 1037–1051 (2006)
5. Wang, Y., Lees, M., Cai, W., Zhou, S., Low, M.Y.H.: Cluster based partitioning for agent-based crowd simulations. In: Proceedings of the 2009 Winter Simulation Conference, pp. 1047–1058. IEEE Press, Austin (2009)
6. Ho, D.P., Bui, T.D., Do, N.L.: Dividing agents on the grid for large scale simulation. In: Bui, T.D., Ho, T.V., Ha, Q.T. (eds.) PRIMA 2008. LNCS (LNAI), vol. 5357, pp. 222–230. Springer, Heidelberg (2008)
7. Carothers, C.D., Bauer, D., Pearce, S.: Ross a high-performance, low memory, modular time warp system. J. Parallel Distributed Computing 53–60 (2000)
8. Wenjie, T., Yiping, Y., Feng, Z.: A hierarchical parallel discrete event simulation kernel for multicore platform. Cluster Comput. **16**, 379–387 (2013)
9. Vulov, G., He, T., Hybinette, M.: Quantitative assessment of an agent-based simulation on a time warp executive. In: Proceedings of the 2008 Winter Simulation Conference, pp. 1068–1076. IEEE Press, Florida (2008)
10. Riley, P.F., Riley, G.F.: SPADES—a distributed agent simulation environment with software-in-the-loop execution. In: Proceedings of the 2003 Winter Simulation Conference. IEEE Press, New Orleans, pp. 817–825 (2003)
11. Collier, N.: Repast HPC Manual. Argonne National Laboratory, Argonne (2010)
12. Miller, R.J.: Optimistic parallel discrete event simulation on a beowulf cluster of multi-core machines. In: Master dissertation, Cincinnati University, July 2010

A Sequential Latin Hypercube Sampling Method for Metamodeling

Zhizhao Liu, Ming Yang, and Wei Li(✉)

Control and Simulation Center, Harbin Institute of Technology, Harbin, China
{liuzhizhao2007,fleehit}@163.com, myang@hit.edu.cn

Abstract. For utilizing the original sampling points and improving budget allocation efficiency, we propose a sequential Latin Hypercube Sampling (LHS) method for metamodeling. The sequential method starts with an original LHS of size n and constructs a new LHS of size kn that has the original points as more as possible. The sampling points of LHS are described by some matrixes and it is proved that there is no need to delete original points for the new LHS. A subtraction rule is applied for adding new sampling points. The original and addition sampling points are proved to be a strict LHS. The method is applied for metamodeling to demonstrate the effectiveness.

Keywords: Latin hypercube sampling · Sequential method · Metamodel

1 Introduction

Simulation is an important way to acquaint real system for human, including queuing system, manufacturing system, aerospace, finance, corporate decision-making and so on. With the development of simulation technology, the simulation systems usually have a high reliability [1]. As the real system is complicated, simulation analysis of complex systems has become a focus of scientific research. One of the problems is the time consuming. A metamodel is a simplified mathematical model of a simulation system that has a similar input-output relationship in the form of a function. Analysis based on metamodel is an effective solution to reduce time consuming. So some analysis methods can be applied on the metamodel, including uncertainty analysis [2], sensitivity analysis [3] and optimization [4].

During metamodeling, it is a problem to determine the sampling number. Little sampling points will lead to a bad metamodel, inaccurate results and even wrong conclusions. Too much sampling points will lead to unnecessary running times, which should be avoided for the time consuming simulation system. Sequential experiment design is an effective method to solve the problem, which utilizes the original sampling points and gets the suitable sampling size by adding a special amount of sampling points in an iteration [5, 6]. Chen and Zhou [7] gave a variety of design criteria to evaluate the need of allocating more simulation budget at simulated versus unsimulated points and proposed a sequential experimental design framework for stochastic kriging. Chen and Li [8] added one new sampling point in every iteration and gave a greedy algorithm to favor the new design point.

L. Zhang et al. (Eds.): AsiaSim 2016/SCS AutumnSim 2016, Part I, CCIS 643, pp. 176–185, 2016.
DOI: 10.1007/978-981-10-2663-8_19

In this study, we discuss a sequential Latin Hypercube Sampling (LHS) method for metamodeling. LHS is a popular stratified sampling method and have a good character of space filling. In the recent years, there are two classes of sequential LHS method. One is the general sequential LHS, which starts with a LHS of size n and gets a new LHS of size $n+m$ which obtains the original points. The most well-known methods are proposed by Wang [9] and Wei [10], but the methods only can give a similar LHS finally. We proposed some methods in this case [11, 12], which obtain a strict LHS. But the time consuming of generate LHS is an outstanding shortcoming. As the general sequential LHS method is difficult, some sequential LHS methods that satisfy $n+m = k \times n$ are illustrated by Ding, Wang and Li [13] and Tong [14]. In this paper, we discuss why it is easy to achieve a strict LHS in this case and propose a sequential LHS (SLHS) method for metamodeling.

In Sect. 2, we review the sequential strategy for metamodel and the classical LHS procedure. In Sect. 3, a mathematical description of sequential problem is given. And then, a sequential LHS method is proposed and some necessary proves are given. In Sect. 4, numerical examples are performed to test the proposed method. Finally, the conclusion and some thoughts for the future research are given.

2 Theoretical Background

In Sect. 2.1, the sequential strategy for metamodeling is introduced. A popular experiment design, LHS, is discussed in Sect. 2.2, including the summary and the procedure.

2.1 Sequential Strategy for Metamodel

The flow diagram of sequential metamodel is shown in Fig. 1. First of all, the initial training sampling size is determined. Then, the training sampling and predicting sampling are designed. The next step is constructing a metamodel based on the training sampling. The validation of metamodel is implemented to determine whether the metamodel is adequate. The training sampling and predicting sampling are used to evaluate the fitting and forecast abilities of metamodel. Multiple Correlation Coefficient (R^2) is an evaluation index, which is shown in Eq. (1). Under ideal condition, R^2 equals to 1. If R^2 is less than threshold value, addition sampling is nedded and a new metamodel is built. The procedure ends if the metamodel is adequate.

$$R^2 = 1 - \sum_{i=1}^{n} (y_i - \hat{y}_i)^2 \Big/ \sum_{i=1}^{n} (y_i - \bar{y})^2 \quad (1)$$

where y_i is the i th output value. $\hat{y}_i$ is the i th predictive value, $i = 1, 2, \cdots, n$. $\bar{y}$ is the mean of outputs.

In this paper, we focus on the design of addition sampling. As LHS has a special structure, the main problem is how to generate the addition sampling so that the original sampling and the addition sampling construct a new LHS strictly.

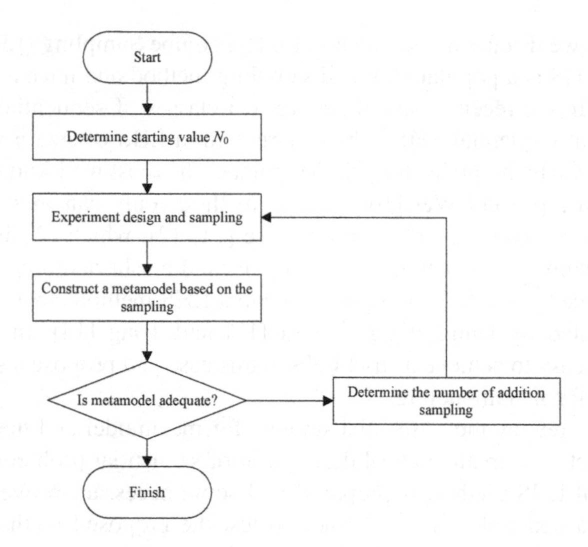

Fig. 1. Strategy for metamodeling

2.2 A Procedure of Latin Hypercube Sampling

LHS is a stratified sampling algorithm, which can ensures that each input variable has all portions among its range, copes with many input variables and is computationally cheap to generate. In practice, LHS can be obtained as follows. Suppose that the input variables are $x_1, x_2, \ldots, x_r$ and the range of x_i is $u_i = [a_i\, b_i]$, $i = 1, 2, \ldots, r$. Then, LHS can be obtained as follows.

a. divide the range u_i into n equiprobable intervals $u_{i1}, u_{i2}, \ldots, u_{in}$, $i = 1, 2, \ldots, r$. So the intervals satisfy $u_{i1} \cup u_{i2} \ldots \cup u_{in} = u_i$, $u_{ij} \cap u_{ik} = \emptyset$ and $P(x \in u_{ij}) = 1/n$, where $j, k = 1, 2, \ldots, n$.
b. for the j th interval of variable x_i, the cumulative probability can be obtained as:

$$Prob_{ji} = (j - 1)/n + r_{ji}/n \tag{2}$$

where r_{ji} is a uniform random number ranging from 0 to 1. So all the probability values can be noted as $Prob = (Prob_{ji})_{n \times r}$.
c. transform the probability into the sample value x_{ji} by the inverse of the distribution function $F(\cdot)$:

$$x_{ji} = F_i^{-1}(Prob_{ji}) \tag{3}$$

Then, the sample matrix is

$$X = \begin{bmatrix} x_{11} & x_{12} & \cdots & x_{1r} \\ x_{21} & x_{22} & \cdots & x_{2r} \\ \vdots & \vdots & \ddots & \vdots \\ x_{n1} & x_{n2} & \cdots & x_{nr} \end{bmatrix}$$

d. the n values of each variables are paired randomly or in some prescribed order with the n values of the other variables. Then the sample matrix of LHS can be written as:

$$X' = \begin{bmatrix} x'_{11} & x'_{12} & \cdots & x'_{1r} \\ x'_{21} & x'_{22} & \cdots & x'_{2r} \\ \vdots & \vdots & \ddots & \vdots \\ x'_{n1} & x'_{n2} & \cdots & x'_{nr} \end{bmatrix}$$

where each row is a sample point.

Figure 2 shows an example of LHS in size of 5, where each interval of each input variable has one sample point.

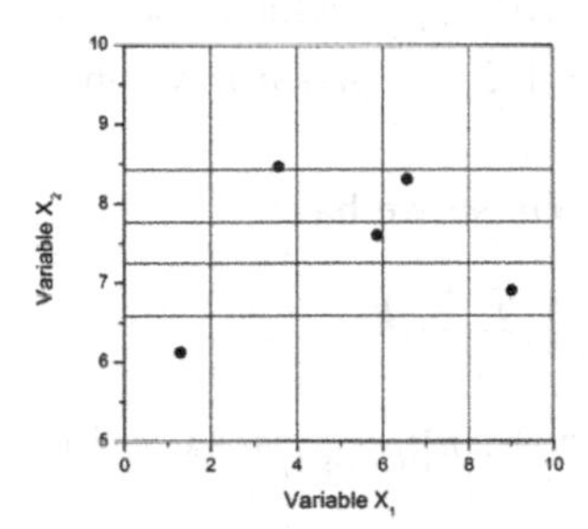

Fig. 2. An example of LHS

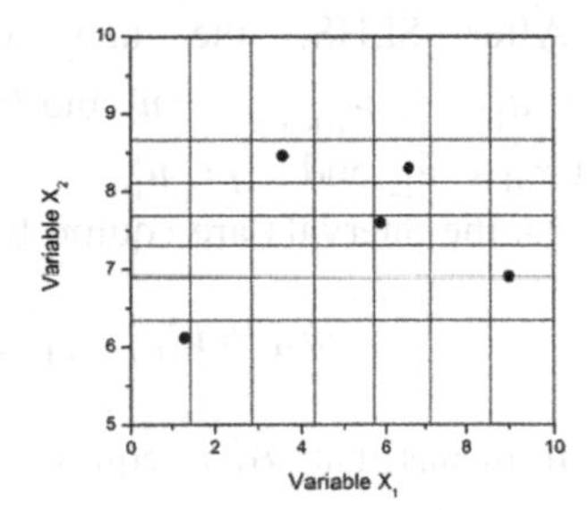

Fig. 3. Original samplings in extension LHS

3 Sequential Latin Hypercube Sample Method

The Sequential LHS method of has two purposes. One is to construct a strict LHS with a larger size than original LHS. The other is to reserve the original sample points as more as possible in the new LHS. In this study, the sequential method is an integral multiple extension method of LHS. Assume that there is an original LHS noted as $A = \{X_1, X_2, \ldots, X_n\}$, where X_i is a sampling point, $i = 1, 2, \ldots, n$. The objective of extension is to get a new LHS of size kn noted as $B = \{X_1, X_2, \ldots, X_{kn}\}$, where $k \geq 2$ and k is an integer. B satisfies the constraint condition as shown in Eq. (4).

$$\max \text{card}\ (A \cap B) \tag{4}$$

where card$(\cdot)$ denotes the number of elements in set. For general extension of LHS, the original sampling points may be not accord with the structure of extension LHS, which is shown in Fig. 3. So we need to discuss how many original samplings need to be reserved for the SLHS.

3.1 Analysis of the Problem

A related result is given as the following theorem.

Theorem A: Supposed that there are r input variables, the LHS set is $A = \{X_1, X_2, \ldots, X_n\}$ and the SLHS set is $B = \{X_1, X_2, \ldots, X_{n+m}\}$, where $n + m = kn$, $k \geq 2$ and $k \in Z$. Then, max card $(A \cap B) = n$.

Proof: Pick two sample points $X_p = [x_{p1} \quad x_{p2} \quad \cdots \quad x_{pr}]$ and $X_q = [x_{q1} \quad x_{q2} \quad \cdots \quad x_{qr}]$, $1 \leq p, q \leq n, p \neq q$.

For the first variable x_1, $u_1 = u_{11} \cup u_{12} \ldots \cup u_{1n}$ and $P(x \in u_{1i}) = 1/n$, $i = 1, 2, \ldots, n$. Assume that $x_{p1} \in u_{1s}$ and $x_{p2} \in u_{1t}$. By the definition of LHS,

$$u_{1s} \cap u_{1t} = \emptyset \tag{5}$$

After SLHS, the new intervals are $u^*_{11}, u^*_{12}, \ldots, u^*_{1(n+m)}$ which satisfy $u^*_{11} \cup u^*_{12} \ldots \cup u^*_{1(n+m)} = u_1$ and $P(x \in u^*_{1i}) = 1/(n+m), i = 1, 2, \ldots, (n+m)$. Assume that $x_{p1} \in u^*_{1u}$ and $x_{p2} \in u^*_{1w}$.

As the intervals are equiprobably divided and $n + m = kn$, so we have

$$u_{1i} = u^*_{1(ki-i+1)} \cup u^*_{1(ki-i+2)} \cdots \cup u^*_{1(ki)}, \; i = 1, 2, \ldots, k$$

It means that u_{1i} is equiprobably divided into k intervals, $u^*_{1(ki-i+1)}, u_1(ki - i + 2)^*, \ldots, u^*_{1(ki)}$.

Then

$$u^*_{1u} \subseteq u_{1s}, \; u^*_{1w} \subseteq u_{1t} \tag{6}$$

By Eqs. (5) and (6) and properties of sets, we obtain

$$u^*_{1u} \cap u^*_{1w} = \emptyset$$

So x_{p1} and x_{q1} are not in one interval among the new intervals.

Similarly, every variable of X_p and X_q are not in one interval of each new intervals.

As p and q are selected randomly, the set A satisfied the new structure of extension LHS. Then there is no need to delete any sample point of the original LHS, which completes the proof. □

3.2 Procedures of SLHS

From Theorem A, it is concluded that all the original sampling points can be reserved in the SLHS. A SLHS method is proposed based on the theorem and a two-time extension algorithm [13]. Supposed that there is a LHS of size n, the sample matrix is $X^{(old)}_{n\times r}$, the order matrix is $L^{(old)}_{n\times r}$ (Every element of $L^{(old)}_{n\times r}$ is the interval number of the corresponding element of $X_{n\times r}^{(old)}$), the cumulative probability matrix is $U_{n\times r}^{(old)}$ (Every element of $U_{n\times r}^{(old)}$ is the cumulative probability of the corresponding element of $X_{n\times r}^{(old)}$, that is the $Prob_{ji}$ in Eq. (2)) and the random matrix is $R_{n\times r}^{(old)}$ (Every element of $R_{n\times r}^{(old)}$ is the random value of the corresponding element of $X_{n\times r}^{(old)}$, that is the r_{ji} in Eq. (2)). $(k-1)n$ new sample points, $X_{(k-1)n\times r}^{(2)}$, is needed to create to get SLHS of size kn noted as $X_{kn\times r}^{(new)} = \begin{bmatrix} X_{n\times r}^{(old)} \\ X_{(k-1)n\times r}^{(2)} \end{bmatrix}$. The detail steps of SLHS are as follows:

Step 1. Compute the distribution of original sample points in the new sample structure.

a. Transform $L_{n\times r}^{(old)}$ into the new sample structure and get the order matrix $L_{n\times r}^{(1)}$ as shown in Eq. (7).

$$l_{i,j}^{(1)} = kl_{i,j}^{(old)} - (k - m) \tag{7}$$

where $kr_{i,j}^{(old)} \le m < kr_{i,j}^{(old)} + 1,\ m \in Z,\ i = 1, 2, \cdots, n,\ j = 1, 2, \cdots, r$

b. Transform $R_{n\times r}^{(1)}$ into the new sample structure and get the random matrix $R_{n\times r}^{(1)}$ as shown in Eq. (8).

$$r_{i,j}^{(1)} = k[r_{i,j}^{(old)} - (\mathrm{m} - 1) \cdot 1/k] \tag{8}$$

where $kr_{i,j}^{(old)} \le m < kr_{i,j}^{(old)} + 1$, $m \in Z$, $i = 1, 2, \cdots, n$, $j = 1, 2, \cdots, r$ 。

Step 2. Generate the new sample matrix $X_{(k-1)n\times r}^{(2)}$.

a. Generate a new order matrix $L'_{kn\times r}$ of size $kn \times r$ and every column of $L'_{kn\times r}$ is a random rank of the integer number from 1 to kn.
b. For every column, delete the element that is the same as the corresponding column in $L_{n\times r}^{(1)}$ and get the matrix $L_{(k-1)n\times r}^{(2)}$.
c. Generate a random matrix $R_{(k-1)n\times r}^{(2)}$ where r_{ij} is a uniform random number ranging from 0 to 1.
d. Compute the cumulative probability matrix $U_{(k-1)n\times r}^{(2)}$ as shown in Eq. (9).

$$u_{i,j}^{(2)} = (l_{i,j}^{(2)} - 1 + r_{i,j}^{(2)}) \big/ kn \tag{9}$$

e. Compute the sample matrix $X_{(k-1)n\times r}^{(2)}$ as shown in Eq. (3).

Step 3. Get the order matrix $L_{kn\times r}^{(new)}$, the random matrix $R_{kn\times r}^{(new)}$, the cumulative probability matrix $U_{kn\times r}^{(new)}$ and the sample matrix $X_{kn\times r}^{(new)}$ of SLHS.

$$L_{kn\times r}^{(new)} = \begin{bmatrix} L_{n\times r}^{(1)} \\ L_{(k-1)n\times r}^{(2)} \end{bmatrix}, \; R_{kn\times r}^{(new)}$$
$$= \begin{bmatrix} R_{n\times r}^{(1)} \\ R_{(k-1)n\times r}^{(2)} \end{bmatrix}, \; U_{kn\times r}^{(new)} = \begin{bmatrix} U_{n\times r}^{(old)} \\ U_{(k-1)n\times r}^{(2)} \end{bmatrix}, \; X_{kn\times r}^{(new)} = \begin{bmatrix} X_{n\times r}^{(old)} \\ X_{(k-1)n\times r}^{(2)} \end{bmatrix}$$

From the *step* 2-b, it can be seen that every column of $L_{kn\times r}^{(new)}$ is a random matrix of the integer number from 1 to kn. If $L_{kn\times r}^{(new)}$, $U_{n\times r}^{(new)}$, $R_{kn\times r}^{(new)}$ and $X_{kn\times r}^{(new)}$ satisfy the Eqs. (2) and (3), it can be proved that $X_{kn\times r}^{(new)}$ is a LHS of size kn. The proof is as follows:

Proof: Take Eqs. (6) and (7) into Eq. (2) and we have

$$\begin{aligned} u_{i,j}^{(1)} &= \left(l_{i,j}^{(1)} - 1 + r_{i,j}^{(1)}\right)\Big/kn \\ &= \left(kl_{i,j}^{(old)} - (k-m) - 1 + k[r_{i,j}^{(old)} - (\mathrm{m}-1)\cdot 1/k]\right)\Big/kn \\ &= k\left(l_{i,j}^{(old)} - 1 + r_{i,j}^{(old)}\right)\Big/kn \\ &= \left(l_{i,j}^{(old)} - 1 + r_{i,j}^{(old)}\right)\Big/n = u_{i,j}^{(old)} \end{aligned}$$

That is

$$U_{n\times r}^{(1)} = U_{n\times r}^{(old)}$$

Then

$$x_{i,j}^{(1)} = F^{-1}(u_{i,j}^{(1)}) = F^{-1}(u_{i,j}^{(old)}) = x_{i,j}^{(old)}$$

That is

$$X_{n\times r}^{(1)} = X_{n\times r}^{(old)}$$

So $L_{n\times r}^{(1)}$, $R_{n\times r}^{(1)}$, $U_{n\times r}^{(old)}$ and $X_{n\times r}^{(old)}$ satisfy the Eqs. (2) and (3).

From the *step* 2-d and *step* 2-e, we have that $L_{(k-1)n\times r}^{(2)}$, $R_{(k-1)n\times r}^{(2)}$, $U_{(k-1)n\times r}^{(2)}$ and $X_{(k-1)n\times r}^{(2)}$ satisfy the Eqs. (2) and (3), which completes the proof. □

4 Numerical Examples for Metamodeling

We pick up six test functions, which are widely used and suitable for validating the effectiveness of proposed method. The functions are shown from Eqs. (10) to (15).

Table 1. TCLHSG and SSPs of CLHS and SLHS

Test Function	Method	TCLHSG/s	SSPs
f_1	CLHS	4.73	155
	SLHS	4.65	80
f_2	CLHS	5.44	155
	SLHS	5.26	80
f_3	CLHS	8.72	315
	SLHS	8.57	160
f_4	CLHS	4.60	155
	SLHS	4.76	80
f_5	CLHS	53.22	635
	SLHS	52.28	320
f_6	CLHS	3.45	155
	SLHS	3.13	80

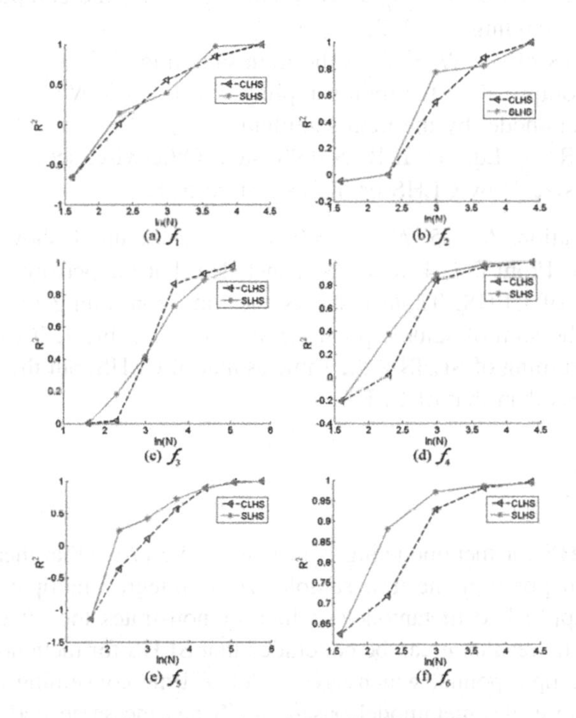

Fig. 4. Results of CLHS and SLHS

$$f_1(x) = \mathrm{e}^{-4\ln 2\times(x-0.0667)^2/0.64}\sin^6(5.1\pi x+0.5), x\in[01] \tag{10}$$

$$f_2(x) = x(x+1)\sin[(2x-0.5)^2\pi-1], x\in[-1.5,1] \tag{11}$$

$$f_3(x,y) = 200 - (x^2 + y - 11) - (x + y^2 - 7)^2, x, y \in [-6, 6] \tag{12}$$

$$f_4(x,y) = 10e^{(-0.03(x-3)^2 - 0.03(y-3)^2)} + 8e^{(-0.08(x+5)^2 - 0.08(y+5)^2)} + 7e^{(-0.08(x-4)^2 - 0.04(y+7)^2)}, -10 \leq x, y \leq 10 \tag{13}$$

$$f_5(x) = \sin(x_1)e^{[(1-\cos(x_2))^2]} + \cos(x_2)e^{[(1-\sin(x_2))^2]} + (x_1 - x_2)^2, \ -5 \leq x_i \leq 5, i = 1,2 \tag{14}$$

$$f_6(x) = (x_1 + 2x_2 - 7)^2 + (2x_1 + x_2 - 5)^2, \ -10 \leq x_i \leq 10, \ i = 1,2 \tag{15}$$

Classical LHS (CLHS) and SLHS were applied for the LHS generation. Set the initial sample size noted as N_0 and sample size of the predict sampling noted as N_p. The steps are as follows:

a. Generate a LHS of size $N = N_p$ as the predict sampling and compute the output Y_i of the predict sampling, $i = 1, 2, \cdots, N_p$.
b. Generate a LHS of size $N = N_0$ as the train sampling.
c. Compute the output Y_i of the train sampling, $i = 1, 2, \cdots, N$.
d. Generate a metamodel by the train sampling.
e. Compute the R^2 by Eq. (1). If $R^2 > 0.98$, stop. Otherwise, set $N = N \times n_{step}$ generate LHS of size N by CLHS or SLHS and go to b.

In this application, $N = 5$, $N_p = 1000$, $n_{step} = 2$. Figure 4 shows the results of CLHS and SLHS. From Fig. 4, it can be concluded that the performance of SLHS is the same as that of CLHS. Table 1 shows the time consuming of LHS generation (TCLHSG) and the sum of sample points (SSPs). From Table 1, it can be concluded that the time consuming of SLHS is the same as that of CLHS, but the number of LHS points is much less than that of CLHS.

5 Conclusion

In this paper, SLHS for metamodeling is proposed. We prove that there is no need to delete the original points if the new sample size is integral multiple for the original LHS. SLHS is applied to metamodels, which demonstrates the effectiveness of the algorithm. From the results, it can be concluded that SLHS for metamodeling preserve all the original sample points, which saves a lot of time consuming to take the new sample. Furthermore, the metamodel based SLHS has the same performance as that based on CLHS.

SLHS we proposed is a special case of general extension of LHS (GELHS). However, GELHS is difficult to apply in practice because of the time consuming problem. SLHS can reserve all the original sampling points and generate a strict LHS at last, which cost much less time than GELHS. As general extension is common in practice, a fast GELHS is the further work.

Acknowledgements. This research is supported by the National Natural Science Foundation of China (Grant No. 61403097).

References

1. Yang, M., Zhang, B., Wang, Z.C.: The analysis of modeling and simulation development direction. J. Syst. Simul. **16**(9), 1901–1904 + 1913 (2004)
2. Xie, W., Nelson, B.L., Barton, R.R.: Statistical uncertainty analysis for stochastic simulation with dependent input models. In: Proceedings of the 2014 Winter Simulation Conference, pp. 674–685. IEEE Press, Savanah (2014)
3. Zeng, Y., Zhang, J.X., van Genderen, J.L., Wang, G.L.: SVM-based multi-textural image classification and its uncertainty analysis. In: 2012 International Conference on Industrial Control and Electronics Engineering, pp. 1316–1319. IEEE Press, Xi'an (2012)
4. Triki, M., Chabchoub, H., Hachicha, W.: A neural network-based simulation metamodel for a process parameters optimization: a case study. In: 2011 4th International Conference on Logistics, pp. 323–328. IEEE Press, Hammamet (2011)
5. Barton, R.R.: Simulation optimization using metamodels. In: Proceedings of the 2009 Winter Simulation Conference, pp. 230–238. IEEE Press, Austin (2009)
6. Ajdari, A., Mahlooji, H.: An adaptive exploration-exploitation algorithm for constructing metamodels in random simulation using a novel sequential experimental design. Commun. Stat. Simul. Comput. **43**(5), 947–968 (2014)
7. Chen, X., Zhou, Q.: Sequential experimental designs for stochastic kriging. In: Proceedings of the 2014 Winter Simulation Conference, pp. 3821–3832. IEEE Press, Savanah (2014)
8. Chen, E.J., Li, M.: Design of experiments for interpolation-based metamodels. Simul. Model. Pract. Theory **44**, 14–25 (2014)
9. Wang, G.G.: Adaptive response surface algorithm using inherited latin hypercube design points. J. Mech. Des. **125**(2), 210–220 (2003)
10. Wei, X.: Research of Global Optimization Algorithm Based on Metamodel. Doctoral Dissertation of Huazhong University of Science and Technology, pp. 70–75 (2012)
11. Liu, Z.Z., Li, W., Yang, M.: Two general extension algorithms of latin hypercube sampling. Math. Probl. Eng. **2015**, 1–9 (2015)
12. Liu, Z.Z., Li, W., Yang, M.: A Generation algorithm of latin hypercube sampling based on original sampling points. In 27th European Modeling and Simulation Symposium, pp. 7–12. Dime University of Genoa Press, Bergeggi (2015)
13. Ding, M., Wang, J.J., Li, S.H.: Probabilistic load flow evaluation with extension latin hypercube sampling. Proc. CSEE. **33**(4), 163–170 (2013)
14. Tong, C.: Refinement strategies for stratified sampling algorithms. Reliab. Eng. Syst. Saf. **91** (10–11), 1257–1265 (2006)

Differential Evolution Improved with Adaptive Control Parameters and Double Mutation Strategies

Jun Liu, Xiaoming Yin, and Xingsheng Gu(✉)

Key Laboratory of Advanced Control and Optimization for Chemical Processes, Ministry of Education, East China University of Science and Technology, Shanghai 200237, China
xsgu@ecust.edu.cn

Abstract. Recently, differential evolution (DE) algorithm has attracted more and more attention as an excellent and effective approach for solving numerical optimization problems. However, it is difficult to set suitable mutation strategies and control parameters. In order to solve this problem, in this paper a dynamic adaptive double-model differential evolution (DADDE) algorithm for global numerical optimization is proposed, and dynamic random search (DRS) strategy is introduced to enhance global search capability of the algorithm. The simulation results of ten benchmark show that the proposed DADDE algorithm is better than several other intelligent optimization algorithms.

Keywords: Differential evolution · Mutation strategies · Adaptive parameters · Dynamic random search

1 Introduction

Differential Evolution (DE) algorithm is a simple and efficient global optimization searching tool, firstly proposed by Storn and Price [1–4] in 1995. It has been widely used in pattern recognition [5], chemical engineering [6], image processing [7], and achieved good results. The reasons why DE has been considered as an attractive optimization method are as follows: (1) Compared with other evolutionary algorithms, DE algorithm is much simple and straightforward. (2) There are less parameters in DE. (3) Its searching is random, parallel and global. Compared with other algorithms, DE is outstanding, but the basic DE algorithm also has the disadvantages just like other intelligent algorithms. The DE algorithm suffers from the contradiction between convergence speed and accuracy, and the problem of premature convergence; additionally, it also suffers from the stagnation problem: the search process may occasionally stop proceeding toward the global optimum even though the population has not converged to a local optimum or any other point; Finally, DE algorithm is sensitive to the choice of the parameters and the same parameter is difficult to adjust to different problems [8].

In recent years, many researchers have carried out the improvement of the basic DE algorithm, which has drawn much attention. Brest et al. [9] presented the jDE algorithm in which the control parameters F and *CR* were encoded into population individuals

L. Zhang et al. (Eds.): AsiaSim 2016/SCS AutumnSim 2016, Part I, CCIS 643, pp. 186–198, 2016.
DOI: 10.1007/978-981-10-2663-8_20

and evolved with the increasing of iterations. Two new arguments were used to adjust control parameters, these arguments are calculated independently. Qin et al. [10] proposed the SaDE algorithm, in which the trial vector generation strategy was chosen from the candidate pool in accordance with the probability obtained from its success rate in generating promising results within the learning period which is a certain number of previous generations. Zhang et al. [11] presented the JADE algorithm, a new mutation strategy and an external archive were used to provide information of progress direction. This strategy is utilized to balance the greediness of the mutation and the diversity of the population. Hamzacebi et al. [12] proposed the dynamic random search (DRS) technique based on basic random search technique, DRS contain two phases: general search and local search. This technique could be applied easily in the process of optimization problem to accelerate convergence rate.

As we know, the effectiveness of basic DE in solving optimization problems mainly depends upon the selected generation (mutation and crossover operations) strategy, and associated control parameters (population size *NP*, mutation parameter *F* and crossover rate *CR*). So when solving optimization problems, the donor vector generation strategy should be determined and suitable values of control parameters needs to be chosen in advance. However, according to the characteristics of the problem and available computation resources, diverse optimization problems require different generation strategies with different control parameter values. This paper proposes a dynamic adaptive double-modle differential evolution (DADDE). In the DADDDE algorithm, the mutation mode combine two basic mutation strategies. To improve the diversity of population and balance the search capability between global and local search, the adaptive mutation parameter and crossover rate are used. In order to promote convergence rate, every iteration process is targeted at current best individual to execute dynamic random search.

The whole paper is generally organized into five parts. In the first part a brief introduction about this study is made. Following that, the second part demonstrates the process of basic differential evolution algorithm. The third part presents a dynamic adaptive double-modle differential evolution (DADDE) algorithm. In the fourth part the experimental study is taken to test the performance of DADDE compared with jDE, SaDE, JADE, PSO as well as the influence of three improvements (double-modle/adaptive parameters/dynamic random search) on DADDE. At last, the fifth part draws the conclusion of this paper.

2 Basic Differential Evolution Algorithm

The DE algorithm involves four basic operations which are called initialization, mutation, crossover and selection respectively. The whole flow chart of DE is shown in Fig. 1.

Step 1. Initialization

$G = 0, 1, 2, \ldots, G_{\max}$ denotes Generation, the ith individual $X_{i,G}$ at Gth generation is represented by:

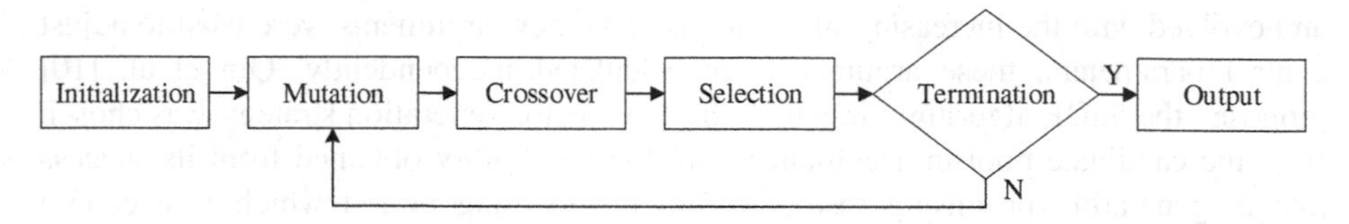

Fig. 1. Flow chart of basic DE

$$X_{i,G} = (x_{i,G}^1, x_{i,G}^2, \ldots, x_{i,G}^D), i = 1, 2, \ldots, NP \quad (1)$$

NP represents the number of population members in DE, *D* denotes dimension. The search space of uniformly and randomly distributed individuals constrained by the prescribed minimum and maximum bounds $[X_{\min}, X_{\max}]$, $X_{\min} = (x_{\min}^1, x_{\min}^2, \ldots, x_{\min}^D)$, $X_{\max} = (x_{\max}^1, x_{\max}^2, \ldots, x_{\max}^D)$. When Generation $G = 0$, the initial population is formed by individuals generate in $[X_{\min}, X_{\max}]$.

$$X_{i,0} = (x_{i,0}^1, x_{i,0}^2, \ldots, x_{i,0}^D), i = 1, 2, \ldots, NP \quad (2)$$

Therefore the jth component of the ith individual should be initialized as $x_{i,0}^j = x_{\min}^j + rand(0,1) \cdot (x_{\max}^j - x_{\min}^j)$, $j = 1, 2, \ldots, D$, $rand[0,1]$ is a uniformly distributed random number within $[0, 1]$.

Step 2. Mutation

Mutation operation contains variant forms. The general process of mutation is expressed by

$$V_{i,G} = X_{r_1,G} + F(X_{r_2,G} - X_{r_3,G}) \quad (3)$$

where i means the ith individual vector of current generation. $r_1, r_2, r_3 \in \{1, 2, \ldots, NP\}$ are three different random integers, besides each one of them should be different from i. $V_{i,G}$ denotes donor vector. The mutation control parameter F is a real and constant factor that controls the amplification of the differential variation.. If $V_{i,G}$ is not within $[X_{\min}, X_{\max}]$, let $V_{i,G} = X_{\min} + rand(0,1) \cdot (X_{\max} - X_{\min})$, $rand[0,1]$ is a uniformly distributed number randomly chosen from $[0, 1]$.

Step 3. Crossover

The operands of crossover are components of the individual. Through this operation, the donor vector $V_{i,G}$ exchanges its components with the target vector $X_{i,G}$ to form the trial vector $U_{i,G} = (u_{i,G}^1, u_{i,G}^2, \ldots, u_{i,G}^D), i = 1, 2, \ldots, NP$

$$u_{i,G}^j = \begin{cases} v_{i,G}^j, & rand_j \le CR \, or \, j = randn_j \\ x_{i,G}^j, & rand_j > CR \text{ and } j \ne randn_j \end{cases}, j = 1, 2, \ldots, D \quad (4)$$

$rand_j$ is a number randomly chosen from $[0, 1]$, $randn_j$ is a randomly chosen index from $\{1, 2, \ldots, D\}$. The crossover control parameter *CR* is a real and constant factor that controls which parameter contributes to which trial vector parameter in the crossover operation, ranging between [0,1].

Step 4. Selection

Selection is based on Greedy policy. The offspring vector is acquired through comparing the fitness value of the trial vector $U_{i,G}$ and target vector $X_{i,G}$ according to

$$X_{i,G+1} = \begin{cases} U_{i,G}, f(U_{i,G}) < f(X_{i,G}) \\ X_{i,G}, f(U_{i,G}) \geq f(X_{i,G}) \end{cases}, \; i = 1, 2, \ldots, NP \quad (5)$$

f is the function of the fitness value. The one which has the better value between $U_{i,G}$ and $X_{i,G}$ should be chosen as the new individual, then add one to generation G. Equation (5) is for dealing with the minimization.

Step 5. Termination

If the population meet the termination conditions or reach the upper limit of generation, Output the optimal solution. Otherwise, go to step 2 till meet the termination conditions.

3 Dynamic Adaptive Double-Model Differential Evolution

This paper proposes a dynamic adaptive double-model differential evolution (DADDE). In DADDE, the mutation mode combine two basic mutation strategies. To improve the diversity of population and balance the search capability between global and local search, the adaptive mutation parameter and crossover rate are used. In order to promote convergence rate, every iteration process is targeted at current best individual to execute dynamic random search. These improvements to basic DE are as the following.

3.1 Double Mutation Strategies

According to the DE algorithm which was firstly proposed by Storn and Price [1–4], there are ten kinds of basic mutation strategies, these strategies are provided in Table 1.

In general, DE/x/y/z denotes different mutation strategies. DE denotes differential evolution, x denotes base vector which contain rand, best, rand-to-best, current-to-best

Table 1. Mutation strategies of DE

Number	Mutation strategies	Number	Mutation strategies
1	DE/best/1/exp	6	DE/best/1/bin
2	DE/rand/1/exp	7	DE/rand/1/bin
3	DE/rand-to-best/1/exp	8	DE/rand-to-best/1/bin
4	DE/best/2/exp	9	DE/best/2/bin
5	DE/rand/2/exp	10	DE/rand/2/bin

and so on. y denotes the number of differential vectors. z denotes crossover strategies which include exponential crossover and binomial crossover.

Each strategies has its own characteristics, but through a large number of studies, Storn and Price found that $DE/rand/1/bin$ and $DE/best/2/bin$ have better performance, also have been applied to the practical industrial process mostly. $DE/rand/1/bin$ is expressed as Eq. (3), $DE/best/2/bin$ is expressed as

$$V_{i,G} = X_{best,G} + F[(X_{r_1,G} - X_{r_2,G}) + (X_{r_3,G} - X_{r_4,G})] \tag{6}$$

$X_{best,G}$ denotes the best individual in current population. In order to make full use of the better global search capability of $DE/rand/1/bin$ and the better convergence ability of $DE/best/2/bin$, Overcome the disadvantages of both strategies as well, Hu [14] combined these two mutations as follows:

$$V_{i,G} = \begin{cases} X_{r_1,G} + F(X_{r_2,G} - X_{r_3,G}), \text{ if } rand \geq \sqrt{\frac{G}{Gm}} \\ X_{best,G} + F[(X_{r_1,G} - X_{r_2,G}) + (X_{r_3,G} - X_{r_4,G})], \text{ otherwise} \end{cases} \tag{7}$$

The threshold value $\varphi = \sqrt{\frac{G}{Gm}}$, is an variable increase with the growth of generation. Here we set a new threshold value:

$$\varphi = \sqrt{\frac{G}{Gm}} \cdot (\varphi_{\max} - \varphi_{\min}) + \varphi_{\min} \tag{8}$$

$[\varphi_{\min}, \varphi_{\max}] = [0.1, 1]$. At the beginning, $DE/rand/1/bin$ will be used much more, as generation increase, algorithm will use $DE/best/2/bin$ more often.

3.2 Adaptive Mutation Parameter and Crossover Rate

Adaptive parameter will achieve a balance between the convergence speed and global search ability. when F have a large value, global optimization ability will be stronger, but convergence rate become slower. A large value of CR will lead to better convergence speed, worse stability and lower success rate of the algorithm, premature convergence become more obvious as well. In order to prevent the occurrence of premature convergence and guarantee fast convergence speed at the same time, taking the follow adaptive mechanism is to assign the parameters.

$$F = F_{\max} - (F_{\max} - F_{\min}) \cdot \sqrt{\frac{G}{Gm}} \tag{9}$$

$$CR = CR_{\min} + (CR_{\max} - CR_{\min}) \cdot \sqrt{\frac{G}{Gm}} \tag{10}$$

In DADDE, $F \in [0.4, 0.9], CR \in [0.6, 0.9]$. With the increase of iteration, F increase and CR decrease, to insure the diversity of population and global search capability at the beginning of the algorithm, to reduce the diversity and promote the algorithm convergence in the later stage of the algorithm.

3.3 Dynamic Random Search

Dynamic random search (DRS) technique is based on searching the solution space randomly to acquire the best value of minimization problem. DRS contain two phases: general search and local search. DRS is simple and easily adaptable for any problems. Because of these two essential advantages, this technique could be applied easily in the process of optimization problem to accelerate convergence speed. Steps of local search phase [12] which is added into basic DE algorithm for soluting continuous minimization problem are as follows (objective function of the problem is described as f(x)) (Fig. 2).

Step 1. Set the initial values: N donotes maximum iteration, E denotes stop criterion, α_k denotes level counter, $k = 0$, epoch = 0, $X_{current} = X_{best}$, $\alpha_k = X_{best}$.
Step 2. Reset the iteration counter, $n = 0$.
Step 3. Generate dX random vector within the range $[-\alpha_k, \alpha_k]$.
Step 4. Update epoch, epoch = epoch + 1.
Step 5. $f_{new} = f(X_{current} + dX)$
if $f_{new} < f_{best}$, then $f_{best} = f_{new}$, $X_{best} = X_{current} + dX$.
Increase iteration number by one, $n = n+1$. Go to step 7.
if $f_{new} < f_{current}$, then $f_{current} = f_{new}$, $X_{current} = X_{current} + dX$.
Increase iteration number by one, $n = n+1$. Go to step 7.
Step 6. $f_{new} = f(X_{current} - dX)$
if $f_{new} < f_{best}$, then $f_{best} = f_{new}$, $X_{best} = X_{current} - dX$.
Increase iteration number by one, $n = n+1$. Go to step 7.
if $f_{new} < f_{current}$, then $f_{current} = f_{new}$, $X_{current} = X_{current} - dX$.
Increase iteration number by one, $n = n+1$. Go to step 7.
Step 7. If iteration counter is less than its maximum value ($n < N$), then go to step 3.
Step 8. $k = k+1$.
Step 9. $\alpha_k = \alpha_{k-1} * 0.5$
Step 10. If stop criterion is reached (epoch = E), then quit. Otherwise, go to step 2.

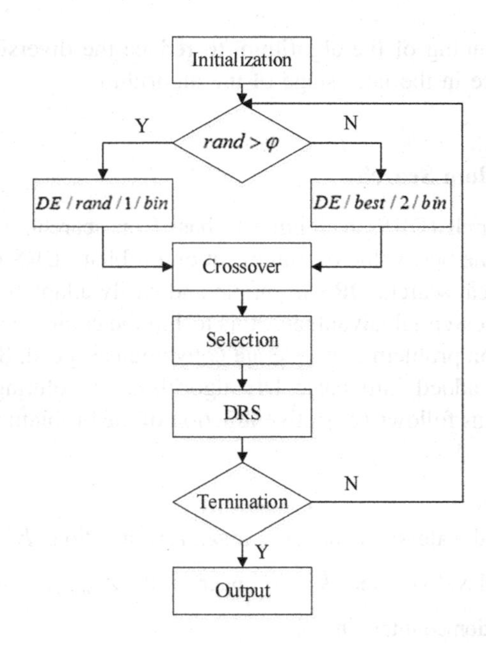

Fig. 2. Flow chart of DADDE

4 Experimental Study

4.1 Benchmark Functions

In this section, 10 global minimization benchmark functions are presented to evaluate the performance of the proposed DADDE algorithm against other intelligent algorithms. These functions (f1–f10) are dimension-wise scalable [15]. Among these benchmark functions, f1–f6 represent unimodal functions, f7–f10 represent multimodal functions. The value of dimension, names, optimum value, and initialization ranges for these benchmark functions are provided in Table 2.

4.2 Experimental Setup

The proposed DADDE algorithm was compared with various outstanding algorithms such as PSO, jDE, JADE and SaDE, to test the performance of DADDE. The experiments were conducted on the suite of 10 test functions listed in Table 4. For all the algorithms, the maximum number of function evaluations was set to 150,000 generations and the population size was set as NP = 100. Other parameters in PSO, jDE, JADE and SaDE, were set based on previous literature [9–11]. Every algorithm ran 30 times on the 10 test functions, the optimal values, the average values and standard deviation of the functions were obtained in 30 runs. The optimal value and the average value can show the quality of the solution obtained from the algorithm, and the standard deviation can be used to explain the stability and robustness of the algorithm.

Table 2. Benchmark functions

Function	Name	Dimension	f (x*)	Initial range
f1	Sphere	30	0	$[-100, 100]^D$
f2	Schwefel 2.22	30	0	$[-10, 10]^D$
f3	Schwefel 1.2	30	0	$[-100, 100]^D$
f4	Schwefel 2.21	30	0	$[-100, 100]^D$
f5	Rosenbrock	30	0	$[-30, 30]^D$
f6	Quartic	30	0	$[-1.28, 1.28]^D$
f7	Schwefel 2.26	30	-12569.5	$[-500, 500]^D$
f8	Rastrigin	30	0	$[-5.12, 5.12]^D$
f9	Ackley	30	0	$[-32, 32]^D$
f10	Griewank	30	0	$[-600, 600]^D$

Before the experiment, in order to illustrate the effectiveness of the repetition of previous algorithm code, a test had been taken. In this test, all the parameters including population size, the maximum number of evaluation, running times were set up as same as the original reference. The results of this test and from the original literature were almost in the same order of magnitude. For example, in literatures [52] parameters of jDE were set as: $\tau_1 = \tau_2 = 0.1$, initialization of F and CR is 0.5, the maximum number of function evaluations is 1500. jDE algorithm ran 50 times on f1, the average values was 1.10E-28 and standard deviation was 1.00E-28 according to the original literature. The results of the code edited in this study showed that the average value was 8.97E-27 and the standard deviation was 4.66E-27. This test proved that the code used in this paper can reflect the performance of previous algorithms, so as to ensure the effectiveness of comparison between DADDE and other algorithms.

4.3 Comparison Between DADDE and Other Algorithms

Table 3 presents the results over 30 independent runs on 10 test functions. Wilcoxon's rank sum test at a 0.05 significance was conducted between DADDE and each of PSO, jDE, JADE and SaDE. Moreover, "+", "-" and "$\approx$" in Table 4 denote that the performance of DADDE is better than, worse than, and similar to that of the corresponding algorithm respectively. Results of comparison based on Wilcoxon's test can be directly observed from Table 4.

It is obviously that the proposed DADDE algorithm performed better than the other compared algorithms. For example, it was better than PSO on all 10 test functions, better than jDE on 7 test function sand similar to it on 2 test functions, better than SaDE on 7 test functions and similar to it on 3 test functions, better than JADE on 6 test functions and similar to it on 3 test functions.

Table 3. Experimental results of 10 benchmark functions

Function	Algorithm	Best	Mean	Std
f1	PSO +	1.37E-012	8.07E-033	3.35E-032
	jDE +	9.24E-067	6.34E-065	2.67E-064
	SaDE +	2.34E-046	4.93E-042	1.17E-043
	JADE ≈	9.37E-065	8.02E-060	2.26E-059
	DADDE	0.00E+000	0.00E+000	0.00E+000
f2	PSO +	1.98E-014	4.12E-013	2.87E-013
	jDE +	9.60E-044	4.57E-043	4.25E-042
	SaDE +	9.38E-021	8.03E-020	6.01E-020
	JADE +	3.95E-035	2.88E-034	3.98E-035
	DADDE	0.00E+000	0.00E+000	0.00E+000
f3	PSO +	1.78E+000	2.86E+000	6.34E+000
	jDE +	3.56E-007	5.21E-007	7.75E-007
	SaDE +	2.45E-003	4.82E-003	7.24E-003
	JADE ≈	1.66E-037	4.33E-037	1.26E-036
	DADDE	4.03E-269	3.63E-250	1.73E-249
f4	PSO +	1.39E+000	2.39E+000	4.32E+000
	jDE +	2.64E-001	1.74E-001	5.62E-001
	SaDE +	4.15E-002	4.77E-002	1.60E-002
	JADE +	5.61E-011	2.26E-011	4.70E-011
	DADDE	1.22E-274	1.56E-252	3.24E-251
f5	PSO +	1.20E+000	2.13E+000	4.17E+000
	jDE +	1.35E-004	7.57E-004	2.23E-004
	SaDE +	4.58E-004	9.66E-004	5.82E-004
	JADE +	3.69E-022	4.90E-021	9.41E-021
	DADDE	0.00E+000	0.00E+000	3.24E+000
f6	PSO +	4.39E-002	5.12E-002	1.71E-002
	jDE ≈	2.81E-003	3.43E-003	2.11E-003
	SaDE ≈	6.40E-003	7.06E-003	3.71E-003
	JADE -	1.93E-003	2.43E-003	1.18E-003
	DADDE	2.64E-003	2.94E-003	1.97E-003
f7	PSO +	1.25E+004	1.20E+004	2.81E+002
	jDE ≈	1.25E+004	1.25E + 004	6.77E+001
	SaDE ≈	1.25E+004	1.25E+004	9.47E+001
	JADE +	1.25E+004	1.22E+004	1.93E+002
	DADDE	1.25E+004	1.25E+004	0.00E+000
f8	PSO +	2.93E-012	1.86E-011	1.08E-011
	jDE +	1.68E-013	2.44E-012	3.83E-012
	SaDE +	1.88E-013	2.78E-012	4.06E-012
	JADE +	3.11E-013	8.98E-0.12	5.12E-012
	DADDE	0.00E+000	0.00E+000	0.00E+000

(*Continued*)

Table 3. (*Continued*)

Function	Algorithm	Best	Mean	Std
f9	PSO +	1.19E-008	2.98E-008	3.88E-008
	jDE -	5.16E-017	6.11E-017	1.25E-017
	SaDE ≈	1.29E-013	3.07E-013	2.41E-013
	JADE ≈	8.64E-015	8.06E-015	6.53E-015
	DADDE	3.28E-015	4.44E-015	2.20E-015
f10	PSO +	1.98E-002	4.12E-002	2.87E-002
	jDE +	1.57E-006	1.97E-006	4.06E-006
	SaDE +	1.55E-005	2.20E-005	1.76E-005
	JADE +	1.75E-006	2.27E-006	4.40E-006
	DADDE	0.00E+000	0.00E+000	0.00E+000

Table 4. Comparison results based on Wilcoxon's rank sum test.

Function	PSO	jDE	SaDE	JADE
DADDE better	10	7	7	6
DADDE worse	0	1	0	1
DADDE equal	0	2	3	3
Success Rate	100 %	90 %	100 %	90 %

4.4 Comparison of the Influences on DADDE with or Without Double-Modle/Adaptive Parameters/Dynamic Random Search

The proposed algorithm is tested to prove that the global search capabilities of DADDE can be enhanced after three improvements (double-modle/adaptive parameters/dynamic random search) are added. For convenience, the algorithm without adaptive parameters and dynamic random search is called DDE, the algorithm without dynamic random search is called ADDE.

In Fig. 3, the convergence graphs show the fitness of function from DE, DDE, ADDE and DADDE on two representative benchmark functions (f4, f9) with $D = 30$, $NP = 100$ and FES = 1500. The convergence speed of DADDE was the best one. Table 4 presents the results after these four algorithms ran 30 times. It can be known that the average values and standard deviation of DADDE were both relatively less than that of others.

According to the evidence provided by Fig. 3 and Table 5, the convergence rate and accuracy of DADDE were better than the other three comparisons, so it came to a conclusion that global search capabilities of DADDE can be enhanced by these presented improvements.

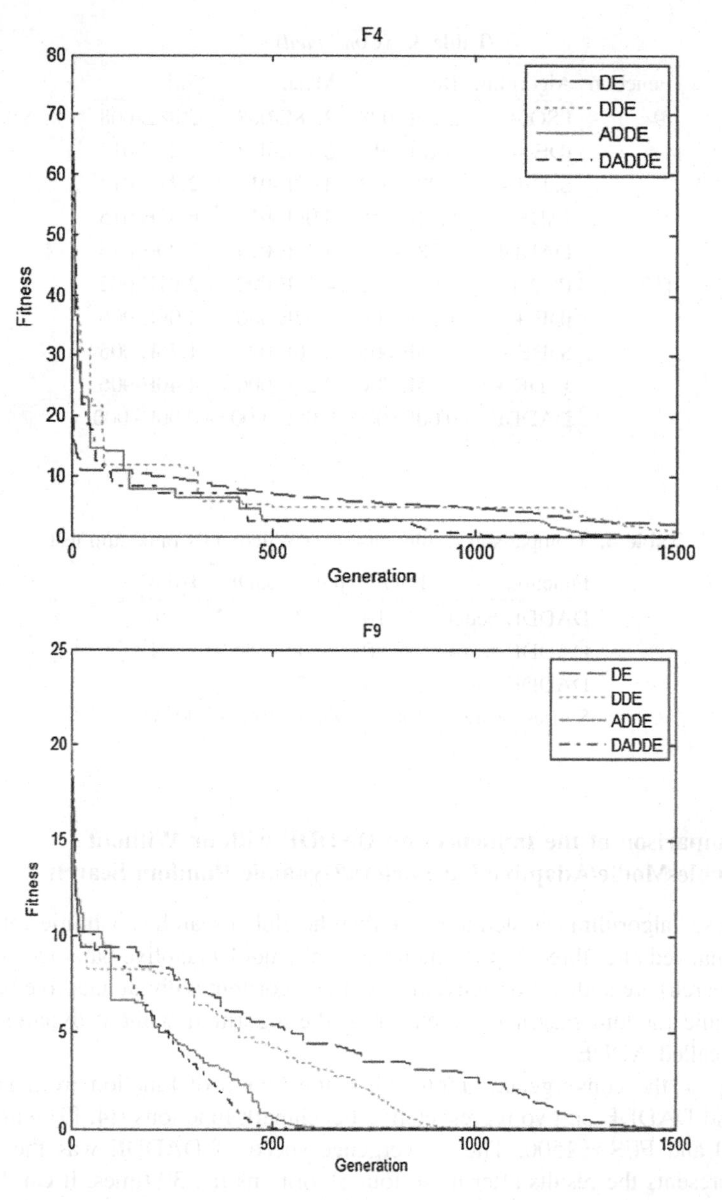

Fig. 3. The convergence graphs for best fitness

This improved algorithm can balance the search capability between global and local search. But by using double mutation strategies and adaptive parameters, good global search capabilities are achieved at the cost of reduction of convergence rate. Although dynamic random search is added to promote convergence rate, on several test functions experimental convergence speed were still influenced, this limitation is more obvious on unimodal functions.

Table 5. Experimental results of DE, DDE, ADDE and DADDE

Function	Algorithm	Best	Mean	Std
f4	DE	4.00E + 00	5.18E + 00	1.39E + 00
	DDE	5.64E-01	8.57E-01	5.17E-01
	ADDE	3.42E-02	4.89E-02	6.92E-02
	DADDE	7.35E-04	6.14E-03	2.08E-03
f9	DE	3.34E-02	4.11E-02	2.87E-02
	DDE	2.67E-10	3.90E-10	4.01E-10
	ADDE	7.93E-13	3.08E-12	5.62E-12
	DADDE	5.18E-15	7.31E-15	4.55E-15

5 Conclusions

As an excellent and efficient search and optimization algorithm, differential evolution (DE) has been widely applied in science and engineering. In the DE algorithm, mutation strategies and control parameters are very significant to the algorithm's performance. However, it is difficult to select a befitting strategy and parameters. Moreover, dynamic random search could be applied easily in the process of optimization problem to accelerate convergence rate. Therefore, a DADDE algorithm is put forward to improve the performance of basic DE.

In this paper, the experimental studies had been executed on ten global numerical optimization functions adopted from previous literature. DADDE was compared with other four advanced optimization algorithms, such as PSO, jDE, SaDE and JADE. The experimental results indicated that the performance of DADDDE was better than the other four algorithms totally. In order to prove that the global search capabilities of basic DE can be enhanced by these three improvements made in DADDE, DADDE was compared with the DE, DDE and ADDE. All of the experimental results showed that the performance of DADDE was more outstanding than other competitors.

Acknowledgements. This work is supported by the National Natural Science Foundation of China (Grant No. 61573144, 61174040), Shanghai Commission of Science and Technology (Grant no. 12JC1403400), and the Fundamental Research Funds for the Central Universities.

References

1. Storn, R., Price, K.V.: Differential evolution: A simple and efficient adaptive scheme for global optimization over continuous spaces, ICSI, USA, Technical Report TR-95–012 (1995)
2. Storn, R., Price, K.V.: Minimizing the real functions of the ICEC 1996 contest by differential evolution. In: Proceedings of the 1996 IEEE International Conference on Evolutionary Computation, pp. 842–844 (1996)
3. Storn, R.: On the usage of differential evolution for function optimization. In: Proceedings of the North American Fuzzy Information Processing Society Conference, pp. 519–523 (1996)

4. Storn, R., Price, K.V.: Differential evolution: A simple and efficient heuristic for global optimization over continuous space. J. Global Optim. **11**(4), 341–359 (1997)
5. Secmen, M., Tasgetiren, M.F.: Ensemble of differential evolution algorithms for electromagnetic target recognition problem. IET Radar Sonar Navig. **7**(7), 780–788 (2013)
6. Sharma, S., Rangaiah, G.P.: An improved multi-objective differential evolution with a termination criterion for optimizing chemical processes. Comput. Chem. Eng. **56**, 155–173 (2013)
7. Zhu, J.X., Wen, X.B., Xu, H.X., Sun, L.Q.: Image sparse decomposition and reconstruction based on differential evolution algorithm. Adv. Inf. Sci. Serv. Sci. **3**(10), 131–137 (2011)
8. Daniela, Z.: Influence of crossover on the behavior of differential evolution algorithms. Appl. Soft Comput. **9**(3), 1126–1138 (2009)
9. Brest, J., Mernik, M.: Population size reduction for the differential evolution algorithm. Appl. Intell. **29**(3), 228–247 (2008)
10. Qin, A.K., Suganthan, P.N.: Self-adaptive differential evolution algorithm for numerical optimization. In: Proceedings of IEEE Congress on Evolutionary Computation (CEC 2005), pp. 1785–1791. IEEE Press, Edinburgh, Scotland (2005)
11. Zhang, J.Q., Sanderson, A.C.: JADE: adaptive differential evolution with optional external archive. IEEE Trans. Evol. Comput. **13**(5), 945–958 (2009)
12. Hamzacebi, C., Kutay, F.: Continuous functions minimization by dynamic random search technique. Appl. Math. Model. **31**(10), 2189–2198 (2007)
13. Hamzacebi, C., Kutay, F.: A heuristic approach for finding the global minimum: adaptive random search technique. Appl. Math. Comput. **173**(2), 1323–1333 (2006)
14. Hu, Z.Q.: The optimization of differential evolution algorithm and its application research, pp. 28–30 (2013). (in Chinese)
15. Yao, X., Liu, Y., Lin, G.M.: Evolutionary programming made faster. IEEE Trans. Evol. Comput. **3**(2), 82–102 (1999)

Collaborative Filtering Recommendation Algorithm Based on Matrix Factorization and User Nearest Neighbors

Zhongjie Wang(✉), Nana Yu, and Jiaxian Wang

Department of Control Science and Engineering, Tongji University,
Shanghai 201804, China
wang_zhongjie@tongji.edu.cn

Abstract. The disadvantage of the traditional CFAbMD algorithm is no consideration of impact of local users' neighbor on item rating. Aiming at this problem, a new CFAbMD algorithm is proposed considering both ALS matrix factorization and user nearest neighbor (CFAbMD-UNN), which integrates the similarity information among users into the matrix factorization of model. Furthermore, the CFAbMD-UNN algorithm was implemented in parallel on Spark. Experiments on Movielens shows that the propsosed CFAbMD-UNN algorithm outperforms the traditional CFAbMD algorithm.

Keywords: Matrix factorization · Collaborative filtering recommendation algorithm · Spark · Algorithm parallelization · User nearest neighbor

1 Introduction

Collaborative filtering algorithm based on matrix factorization (CFAbMD) is a kind of model-based recommendation algorithm. The purpose on model-based collaborative filtering algorithm is to predict and recommend the items that have not been rated by users by training a certain model by mathematical statistics or machine learning methods with existing user preference information. In addition to matrix factorization algorithm, Bayes model and probability related model are also commonly used in model-based recommendation algorithm. This paper mainly focuses on CFAbMD algorithm.

The principle of CFAbMD is to break the user-rating matrix into two or more low-dimensional factor matrices whose product will be used to approximate the original evaluation matrix. Specifically, the prediction matrix is multiplied by factor matrix so as to match the original matrix as much as possible, it is required to make the sum of squared errors between the original matrix and the prediction matrix the smallest [1]. CFAbMD can be translated into a optimization problem.

Currently, two main matrix factorization methods are commonly used, i.e. singular value factorization (SVD) and alternating least squares method (ALS). For SVD-based matrix factorization method, the missing items of the user-item rating matrix R are complemented by weighted averages and a new matrix R' is obtained. Then, the mathematical SVD method is employed to decompose matrix R'. Many improvements

L. Zhang et al. (Eds.): AsiaSim 2016/SCS AutumnSim 2016, Part I, CCIS 643, pp. 199–207, 2016.
DOI: 10.1007/978-981-10-2663-8_21

have been done on SVD methods [2, 3]. ALS method is a new matrix factorization method appeared in the Netflix Prize competition, which was proposed by Pan R, Zhou Y [4] et al. ALS method trains model from a global perspective. For ALS method, the users and items can be expressed by a set of low-dimensional implicit semantic factors which can predict not used item rating. This method not only solves the problem of data sparseness to some extent, but also can be well extended to distributed computation environment. Next, we will give the principle of traditional ALS-based recommendation.

For $m \times n$ matrix R, it is required to find a low-dimensional matrix X to approximate R, i.e.

$$R \approx X = U^T V \tag{1}$$

where, $U \in IR^{l \times m}$, $V \in IR^{l \times n}$, l is the number of implicit semantic factors.

Commonly, $l << r, r \approx \min(m, n)$, the complexity of system reduces from $O(mn)$ to $O((m+n) \times k)$.

According to the above definition, we find the low-dimensional matrix U and matrix V are unknown which need to be estimated. Each column of matrix U and matrix V represents a user feature vector and item feature vector respectively. For estimation purpose, a loss function $L(R, U, V)$ needs to defined firstly.

$$L(R, U, V) = \frac{1}{2} \sum_{i=1}^{m} \sum_{j=1}^{n} I_{ij}^{R} \left(R_{ij} - U_i^T V_j\right)^2 \tag{2}$$

In formula (2), $\left(R_{ij} - U_i^T V_j\right)^2$ is the squared error, I_{ij}^R is a indicator function which is used to judge if user i has rating record for item j. If yes, the value of I_{ij}^R is 1. Otherwise, it is 0.

Because matrix R is sparse, a penalty factor is introduced to formula (2) to prevent over-fitting, and we get,

$$L(R, U, V) = \frac{1}{2} \sum_{i=1}^{m} \sum_{j=1}^{n} I_{ij}^{R} \left(R_{ij} - U_i^T V_j\right)^2 + \frac{\lambda_U}{2} \|U\|_F^2 + \frac{\lambda_V}{2} \|V\|_F^2 \tag{3}$$

$\|U\|_F^2$ and $\|V\|_F^2$ represent the sum of squares of the elements of matrix U and matrix V respectively.

Next, our purpose is to find an efficient way to solve the optimization problem represented by formula (3). According to the principle of least squares method, if the matrix V is known, we can get the derivative of U_i and then matrix U.

$$\frac{\partial L}{\partial U_i} = \sum_{j=1}^{n} I_{ij}^{R} \left((U_i)^T V_j - R_{ij}\right)\left(V_j\right) + \lambda_U U_i \tag{4}$$

Similarly, if the matrix U is known, we can get the derivative of V_j and then matrix V.

$$\frac{\partial L}{\partial V_j} = \sum_{i=1}^{m} I_{ij}^{R}\left((U_i)^T V_j - R_{ij}\right)(U_i)^T + \lambda_V V_j \tag{5}$$

For computation complexity, we suppose $\lambda_U = \lambda_V$.

As discussed above, the nature of ALS-based recommendation method is to update matrix U and matrix V continuously with formula (4) and formula (5). The unused item rating will be predicted by the final value of U and V.

2 Collaborative Filtering Algorithm Based on Matrix Factorization and User Nearest Neighbors

From the above section, we know that the evaluation data of all users are used to train model for CFAbMD recommendation algorithm, whose advantage is relative implementation and good extendibility. The disadvantage of this method is without consideration of impact of local users' neighbor on item rating. For example, the similarity among users may be different before and after matrix factorization.

Aiming at this problem, a new CFAbMD algorithm is proposed based on ALS matrix factorization and user nearest neighbor (CFAbMD-UNN), which integrates the similarity information among users into the matrix factorization of model. The diagram of CFAbMD-UNN algorithm is shown in Fig. 1.

Matrix factorization is actually an optimization problem of the loss function, therefore, a weighting factor is introduced to combine the user's own rating information with its nearest neighbors' rating information, the new loss function $L'(R, U, V)$ is represented by,

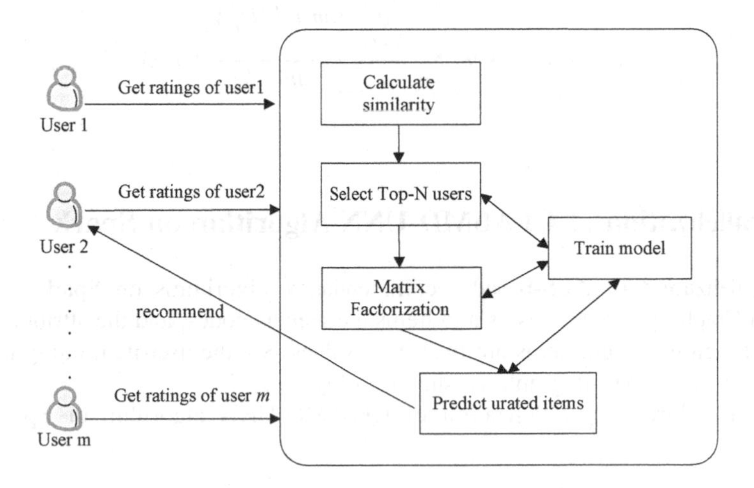

Fig. 1. Diagram of CFAbMD-UNN algorithm

$$L'(R,U,V) = \frac{1}{2}\sum_{i=1}^{m}\sum_{j=1}^{n} I_{ij}^{R}\left(R_{ij} - \left((1-\alpha)U_i^T V_j + \alpha \frac{\sum_{k\in T(i)} sim(i,k)U_k^T V_j}{\sum_{k\in T(i)} sim(i,k)}\right)\right)^2 + \frac{\lambda}{2}\left(\|U_i\|_2^2 + \|V_j\|_2^2\right) \quad (6)$$

where, $T(i)$ is the Top-N users with high similarity to user i, $sim(i,k)$ is Pearson similarity between user i and user k.

Next, the partial derivative of matrix U and matrix V is calculated by formula (6) separately.

$$\begin{aligned}\frac{\partial L'}{\partial U_i} = &(1-\alpha)\sum_{j=1}^{n} I_{ij}^{R} V_j\left(\left((1-\alpha)U_i^T V_j + \alpha\frac{\sum_{k\in T(i)} sim(i,k)U_k^T V_j}{\sum_{k\in T(i)} sim(i,k)}\right) - R_{ij}\right)\\ &+\alpha\sum_{p\in T(k)}\sum_{j=1}^{n}\frac{\sum_{p\in T(k)} sim(p,k)U_k^T V_j}{\sum_{p\in T(k)} sim(p,k)} I_{pj}^{R} V_j\left(\left((1-\alpha)U_p^T V_j\right.\right.\\ &\left.\left.+\alpha\sum_{q\in T(p)}\frac{\sum_{q\in T(p)} sim(p,q)U_q^T V_j}{\sum_{q\in T(p)} sim(p,q)}\right) - R_{pj}\right) + \lambda U_i\end{aligned} \quad (7)$$

$$\begin{aligned}\frac{\partial L'}{\partial V_j} = &\sum_{i=1}^{m} I_{ij}^{R}\left(\left((1-\alpha)U_i^T V_j + \alpha\sum_{k\in T(i)}\frac{\sum_{k\in T(i)} sim(i,k)U_k^T V_j}{\sum_{k\in T(i)} sim(i,k)}\right) - R_{ij}\right)\\ &\times\left((1-\alpha)U_i + \alpha\sum_{k\in T(i)}\frac{\sum_{k\in T(i)} sim(i,k)U_k^T V_j}{\sum_{k\in T(i)} sim(i,k)}\right) + \lambda V_j\end{aligned} \quad (8)$$

3 Parallelization of CFAbMD-UNN Algorithm on Spark

The parallelization of ALS-based recommendation algorithms on Spark is mainly based on Graphx [5], where users and items are seen as nodes, and the attributes of the edges between users and items are the rating values. So, the user-item rating matrix is represented by a bipartite graph, as shown in Fig. 2.

The procedure of parallelization of CFAbMD-UNN algorithm of Spark is as follows.

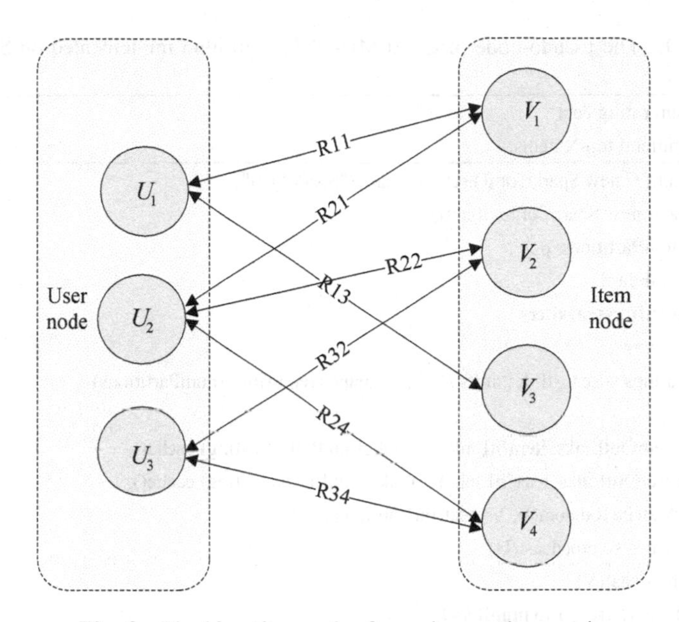

Fig. 2. The bipartite graph of user-item rating matrix

Step 1: Read user-item rating data from HDFS and converting them to RDD form.
Step 2: Set the parameters of matrix factorization model.
Step 3: Initialize matrix V.
Step 4: Fix matrix V, calculate U_i on each node in parallel.
Step 5: Combine the result of each node to obtain matrix U.
Step 6: Fix matrix U, calculate V_j on each node in parallel and obtain matrix V.
Step 7: Judge if the loss function converges or the computing reaches the maximum iteration number. If yes, stop iteration and get the final matrix factorization model. Otherwise, returns to step (4).
Step 8: Use the final optimal model to predict unused items.
Step 9: Choose top-N items with high prediction ratings recommended to users.

The pseudo-code of CFAbMD-UNN algorithm implemented on Spark is shown in Table 1.

In Table 1, Step1 ~ Step2 is the program entry used to initialize the operating environment. Step3 ~ Step6 sets some parameters required for model training. Step7 reads user-item rating matrix information from HDFS and converts them to RDD from for a series of operations. Step8 ~ Step9 creates link information according to bipartite graph. Step10 ~ Step11 initializes and broadcasts vertex data. Step12 mainly executes parallel computing and updates matrix U and matrix V alternately. Step13 ~ Step14 realizes the prediction of unused items. Step15 releases the memory space.

Table 1. The pseudo-code of CFAbMD-UNN algorithm implemented on Spark

```
Input: user-item rating data
Output: recommend top-N items
Step 1: val conf = new SparkConf().setAppName("SparkALS")
Step 2: val sc = new SparkContext(conf)
Step 3: val numPartitions=p
Step 4: val lambda=l
Step 5: val numIters=maxIters
Step 6: val rank=r
Step 7: val ratings = sc.textFile("hdfs://......").map( ).repartition(numPartitions)
.cache()
Step 8: val (itemOutLinks, itemInLinks) = makeLinkRDDs(irating).cache()
Step 9: val (userOutLinks, userInLinks) = makeLinkRDDs(urating).cache()
Step 10: U=Matrix(Random()), V=Matrix(Random())
Step 11: val Ub = sc.broadcast(U)
val Vb = sc.broadcast(V)
Step 12: for (iters from 1 to numIters)
U = updateFeatures(numPartitions,Vb,itemOutLinks, userInLinks)
Ub = sc.broadcast(U)
V = updateFeatures(numPartitions,Ub,userOutLinks, itemInLinks)
Vb = sc.broadcast(V)
end for
Step 13: val predictions = Model(U,V).predict()
Step 14: val recommendations = predictions.collect().sortBy(rating).take(n)
Step 15: sc.stop()
```

4 Experiments

Online public MovieLens [6] is employed to test the proposed algorithm. The dataset includes all users' rating information, the rating ranges from 0 to 5. MovieLens contains data with different sizes, e.g. 100 K, 1 M and 10 M. In this paper, we used the 1 M dataset for recommendation algorithm test. The 1 M dataset includes more than one million rating data that is 6040 users' mark on 3900 movies.

4.1 Performance Indices

As found in most literature, two performance indices are used to measure if a recommendation algorithm is satisfied, i.e. mean absolute error (MAE) and root mean square error (RMSE). These two indices are calculated as follows:

$$MAE = \frac{\sum_{i,j} \left| R_{i,j} - \hat{R}_{i,j} \right|}{N} \tag{9}$$

$$RMSE = \sqrt{\frac{\sum_{i,j} \left(R_{i,j} - \hat{R}_{i,j} \right)^2}{N}} \tag{10}$$

where, $R_{i,j}$ represents the actual rating value of user i for item j, $\hat{R}_{i,j}$ represents the predicted value. N represents the number of all the predicted values.

4.2 Influence of Algorithm Parameters on Recommendation Performances

Two experiments are implemented in this paper. From Sect. 2, it is seen that a weighting factor α is employed to balance the user's own rating and its nearest neighbors' rating for CFAbMD-UNN algorithm, so the first experiment is to investigate the influence of different value of α on the recommendation performances. Besides parameter α, the value of parameter λ, the number of user's neighbors and the maximum iteration number also affect the recommendation performances, so the second experiment is to investigate the impact of these parameters. Furthermore, the traditional ALS-based recommendation algorithm is compared with the proposed CFAbMD-UNN algorithm.

The influence of the parameter α is shown in Fig. 3. For the proposed CFAbMD-UNN algorithm, the value of α determines the recommendation performances. Particularly, when $\alpha = 1$, the predicted rating totally depends on similar neighbors. When $\alpha = 0$, it transforms into the traditional CFAbMD algorithm. From Fig. 3, it shows that the best accuracy of recommendation occurs when $\alpha = 0.4$.

The influence of the value of parameter λ, the number of user's neighbors and the maximum iteration number on recommendation is shown in Table 2.

In Table 2, rank represents the dimension of factor matrix, we chose two values, i.e. 10 and 12. λ represents the regularization constant, which is 0.01 and 10 respectively,

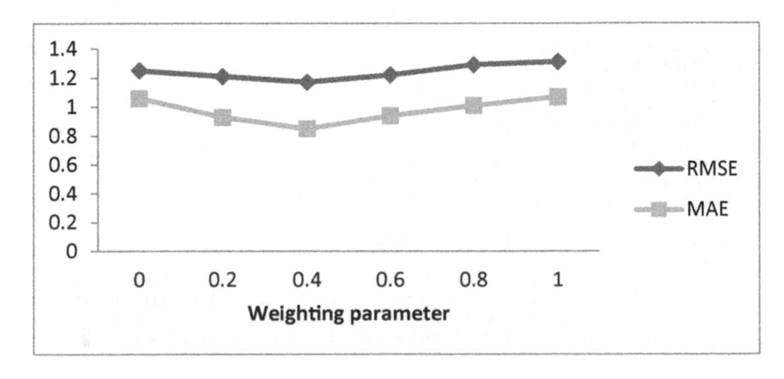

Fig. 3. The influence of the parameter α

Table 2. The influence of model parameters on recommendation performances

	rank	λ	numIters	RMSE	MAE
CFAbMD	10	0.01	20	1.82	1.77
			40	1.46	1.44
		10	20	3.73	3.68
			40	3.61	3.54
	12	0.01	20	1.69	1.62
			40	1.25	1.06
		10	20	3.66	3.59
			40	3.58	3.47
CFAbMD-UNN	10	0.01	20	1.37	1.39
			40	1.29	1.21
		10	20	3.66	3.58
			40	3.54	3.31
	12	0.01	20	1.19	0.93
			40	1.17	0.85
		10	20	3.49	3.42
			40	3.26	3.11

numIters represents the number of iterations, which is 20 and 40 respectively. It showed from Table 2 that the recommendation achieves best performance when $\lambda = 0.01$, rank = 12 and numIters = 40. In addition, it is also clearly seen from Table 2 that the proposed CFAbMD-UNN algorithm outperforms the traditional CFAbMD algorithm.

4.3 Recommendation Result

Without loss of generality, supposed that the user ID is 1, we run CFAbMD-UNN recommendation algorithm. The top 10 movies with higher prediction ratings are selected and recommended to this user, as shown in figure The specific recommendation result is shown in Fig. 4.

```
Movies recommend for you:
 1:Bandits (1997)
 2:Shawshank Redemption, The (1994)
 3:It's a Wonderful Life (1946)
 4:Sixth Sense, The (1999)
 5:Firelight (1997)
 6:Raiders of the Lost Ark (1981)
 7:Before the Rain (Pred dozhdot) (1994)
 8:Life Is Beautiful (La Vita ◆ bella) (1997)
 9:Inherit the Wind (1960)
10:Star Wars: Episode IV - A New Hope (1977)
HERE END
16/03/11 14:42:45 INFO remote.RemoteActorRefProvider$RemotingTermin
16/03/11 14:42:45 INFO remote.RemoteActorRefProvider$RemotingTermin
16/03/11 14:42:45 INFO remote.RemoteActorRefProvider$RemotingTermin
root@SparkMaster:/usr/local/spark/spark-1.2.0-bin-hadoop2.4/bin#
```

Fig. 4. The top 10 movies recommended to user #1

5 Conclusions

The disadvantage of the traditional CFAbMD algorithm is no consideration of impact of local users' neighbor on item rating. Aiming at this problem, a new CFAbMD algorithm is proposed considering both ALS matrix factorization and user nearest neighbor (CFAbMD-UNN), which integrates the similarity information among users into the matrix factorization of model. Furthermore, the CFAbMD-UNN algorithm was implemented in parallel on Spark. Experiments on Movielens shows that the propsosed CFAbMD-UNN algorithm outperforms the traditional CFAbMD algorithm.

References

1. Bing, Liang, Yuzhong, Zhang, Yi, Jin: The research of matrix factorization algorithm in collaborative filtering. Guangdong Commun. Technol. **08**, 76–79 (2013)
2. Van Vleck, E.S.: Continuous matrix factorizations. In: Benner, P., Bollhöfer, M., Kressner, D., et al. (eds.) Numerical Algebra, Matrix Theory, Differential-Algebraic Equations and Control Theory, pp. 299–318. Springer International Publishing, Heidelberg (2015)
3. Benzi, K., Kalofolias, V., Bresson, X., et al.: Song recommendation with non-negative matrix factorization and graph total variation. arXiv preprint, arXiv:1601.01892 (2016)
4. Pan, R., Zhou, Y., Cao, B., et al.: One-class collaborative filtering. In: The Eighth IEEE International Conference on Data Mining, pp. 502–511 (2008)
5. Zhenkun, Tang: Design and Implementation of Machine Learning Platform based on Spark. Xiamen University, Xiamen (2014)
6. http://grouplens.org/datasets/movielens/

Removing Color Cast of Night Image Through Color Constancy Algorithm

Chen Guanghua[1(✉)], Luo Qiyuan[1], and Xian Zhanpeng[2]

[1] Microelectronics R&D Center, Shanghai University, Shanghai 200072 China
chghua@shu.edu.cn, luoqiyuangol2345@163.com
[2] CCDC Drilling and Production Technology Research Institute,
Guanghan, China

Abstract. To solve the color cast of the night image, a color constancy algorithm using depth map to estimate the light source color is proposed. Firstly, the environment light source of night image is simulated by a single light source attenuated in homogeneous medium. Then, the attenuations grey hypothesis is used to provide constrain for estimate light source color. Based on the attenuations grey hypothesis and the simulation of environment light source, the light source color is estimated by the depth map. Experimental results show that the algorithm is effective to solve the color cast of the night image.

Keywords: White balance · Color constancy · Color cast · Night image

1 Introduction

Color can be an important cue for computer vision or image processing related topics, like human-computer interaction, object tracking and object detection. Due to the restrictions of light, the color cast is a general problem for night image. It affects the understanding and judgment for image. Hence, the color cast should be filtered out when the night image is used for the image processing related topics.

There are many successful attempts to solve the color cast of night image. One of them is the Retinex algorithms [1–4]. Based on Retinex theory, the algorithms have excellent ability to solve the color cast of night image. These algorithms are quit robust for night image, but computational expensive. Except the Retinex algorithms, the Dark Channel Prior [5–7] is used to enhance the night image. But it needs the night image meet to the characteristic of fog-degraded image.

In this paper, a color constancy algorithm using depth map to estimate the light source color is proposed. In the algorithm, the environment light source of night image is simulated by a single light source attenuated in homogeneous medium. Based on the single light source, the light source color of night image is estimated by depth map and attenuations grey hypothesis. According to the light source color, the color cast of the image is removed.

L. Zhang et al. (Eds.): AsiaSim 2016/SCS AutumnSim 2016, Part I, CCIS 643, pp. 208–215, 2016.
DOI: 10.1007/978-981-10-2663-8_22

2 Color Constance of Night Image

Color constancy is the ability of human visual system to recognize colors of objects regardless of color of illumination. To stabilize machine color representations, the color constancy algorithm is used in computer vision. Since estimating the light source color of night image is not accurately, the classical algorithms, such as White Pitch [8] and Grey World [9], is failure to remove the color cast of the night image. To estimate light source color of the night image, a night image formation model is proposed. Based on the image formation model, the light source color is estimated by attenuation grey hypothesis and depth map.

2.1 Night Image Formation

For a Lambertian surface, the image values f is dependent on the light source e, the surface reflectance s and the camera sensitivity functions c. The image formation for common images is formulated by the following equation

$$f(x) = \int_{\omega} e(\lambda)s(x,\lambda)c(\lambda)d\lambda \tag{1}$$

where λ is wavelength, ω is the visible spectrum and x is the spatial coordinate in the image. Due to the camera sensitivity is fixed and unknown, the result of estimate the light source color by color constancy algorithms is the light source color captured by the camera. So the light source color in color constancy is formulated by Eq. (2).

$$e' = \begin{pmatrix} e_R \\ e_G \\ e_B \end{pmatrix} = \int_{\omega} e(\lambda)c(\lambda)d\lambda \tag{2}$$

Most of the color constancy algorithm is assume that the scene is illuminated by a single light source. But the scene of night is illuminated by multiple light sources. It makes the light source color of night image is related to the wavelength and spatial coordinate. Due to the position and scope of light source for different image are different, estimating the light source color of the night image is difficult.

In order to reduce the difficulty of estimating the light source color, a night image formation model is proposed. Firstly, the result of the linear or nonlinear superposition of multiple light sources in every pixel location is replaced by the single light source in every pixel location. It makes the multiple light sources of an m*n night image transform to m*n light sources, but one pixel location has only one light source. The mathematical model of the transform process as shown in Eq. (3):

$$e_x(\lambda) = b_1(x)e_1(\lambda) + \ldots + b_n(x)e_n(\lambda) \tag{3}$$

where $b_1(x), \ldots, b_n(x)$ are the light source component parameters of every pixel location, $e_x(\lambda)$ is the single light source of every pixel.

Then, the highest light source color of the m*n light source is assume to be the light source color of the image, other light source in the image is attenuation by the image light source. By this way, the multiple light sources illuminated in night scene have transformed to a single light source. So the light source color of night image is show in Eq. (4).

$$e(x, \lambda) = a(x)e(\lambda) = e_x(\lambda) \tag{4}$$

where $a(x)$ is the attenuation parameters of every pixel location. With the light source color model of night image, the night image formation model can be given by the Eq. (5).

$$f(x) = \int_\omega a(x)e(\lambda)s(x, \lambda)c(\lambda)d\lambda \tag{5}$$

2.2 Attenuations Grey Hypothesis

Through night image formation model, it is easy to known that the task of color constancy is not attainable without further assumptions. Based on this, the attenuations grey hypothesis is used [10]. It assumes that the average of the reflectance with the same attenuation coefficient in a night scene is constant. The mathematical model of attenuations grey hypothesis is

$$\frac{\int a(x)s(x, \lambda)dx}{\int a(x)dx} = k \tag{6}$$

where the constant k is between 0 for no reflectance and 1for total reflectance of the incident light. With the attenuations grey hypothesis, the light source color can be computer from the attenuation average color derivative in the image. The mathematical derivation process is formulated by

$$\begin{aligned} \frac{\int f(x)dx}{\int a(x)dx} &= \frac{1}{\int a(x)dx} \iint_\omega a(x)e(\lambda)s(x, \lambda)c(\lambda)d\lambda dx \\ &= \int_\omega e(\lambda)c(\lambda)\left(\frac{\int a(x)s(x, \lambda)dx}{\int a(x)dx}\right)d\lambda \\ &= k\int_\omega e(\lambda)c(\lambda)d\lambda = ke' \end{aligned} \tag{7}$$

The light source color calculation by the Eq. (7) is inaccurate. In order to accurate estimate the light source color, the Minkowshi frame proposed by Filayson and Trezzi is used [11]. The Minkowshi frame is

$$\left(\frac{\int (f(x))^p dx}{\int dx}\right)^{\frac{1}{p}} = ke' \tag{8}$$

where p is Minkowshi p-norm. When p = 1, Eq. (8) represents the Grey World. When $p = \infty$, Eq. (8) represents the White Pitch. The algorithms used the Minkowshi frame is named Shade of Grey, which is one of the state-of-the-art color constancy methods. When p = 6, the most optimal result is achieved.

To meet the character of the night image, the Minkowshi framework is expanded. The general form to estimate the light source color of the night scenes as follows

$$\left(\frac{\int (f(x))^p dx}{\int a(x) dx}\right)^{\frac{1}{p}} = ke' \tag{9}$$

2.3 The Estimation of Depth Map

According to the Eq. (9), the attenuation message is the key to estimate the light source color. Due to the attenuation is proportional to the depth in the homogeneous medium, the depth map obtain the attenuation message. Therefore, the depth map is used to estimate the light source color of the image.

According to the Beer-Lambert law for a homogeneous, the relation between the scene depth and the transmission is formulated as the Eq. (10).

$$t(x) = e^{-\beta d(x)} \tag{10}$$

where β is the coefficient determined by the property of the medium. If the transmission can be calculated, the depth of the image can be calculated. For estimate the transmission, the Dark Channel Prior proposed by He et al. [12] is used.

The image formation model of Dark Channel Prior is described as

$$I(x) = J(x)t(x) + A(1 - t(x)) \tag{11}$$

where I is the observed light, J is the true reflected light in the scene, $t(x)$ is the transmission and A is the global illuminant.

By taking the minimum operation among three color channels in a local patch, Eq. (11) is transformed to

$$\min_{c\in\{R,G,B\}} \min_{y\in\{\Omega(x)\}} \frac{I^c(y)}{A} = t(x) \min_{c\in\{R,G,B\}} \min_{y\in\{\Omega(x)\}} \frac{J^c(y)}{A} + (1 - t(x)) \tag{12}$$

where $\Omega(x)$ is a local patch centered at x, c is the color channels. According to the Dark Channel Prior, the intensity of J's dark channel is formulated as follow:

$$J^{dark} = \min_{c \in \{R,G,B\}} \min_{y \in \{\Omega(x)\}} J^c(y) = 0 \tag{13}$$

Combine the Eqs. (13) with (12), the transmission is solved by

$$t(x) = 1 - \min_{c \in \{R,G,B\}} \min_{y \in \{\Omega(x)\}} \frac{I^c(y)}{A} \tag{14}$$

Plug the Eqs. (14) in (10), the depth of the image is calculated. In the implementation, the model of depth is modified to Eq. (15).

$$d(x) = \ln\left(\frac{1}{t(x)}\right) = \ln\left(\min_{c \in \{R,G,B\}} \left(\min_{y \in \{\Omega(x)\}} \frac{I^c(y)}{A}\right)^{-1}\right) \tag{15}$$

2.4 Estimate Light Source Color and Color Correction

The depth map calculated by Eq. (15) is the true depth of the night image, but the estimate light source model is based on the simulation of the night image. Therefore, the depth map can't directly use on estimate light source process. But the observed light under two kinds of environment light source is same. Hence, the discrete depth map of two kinds of environment light source is same. Therefore, the discrete depth map can use to the estimate light source color. In order to improve the effect of discrete processing, the depth map is binarized with the Otsu's method [13].

The discrete depth map is included by two parts: the background and the foreground. Because the depth of foreground is low, the light attenuation of the foreground is small. If ignore the light attenuation of the foreground, the environment light source color equal to the light source color of the foreground. Hence, the environment light source color can calculate by the Eq. (9) from the image masking by depth map.

After the matrix $E = diag(e_R^{-1}, e_G^{-1}, e_B^{-1})$ is calculated, the diagonal transform (Eq. (16)) is used for color correction. In the implementation, a diagonal mapping is used to optimizing the output image after correction by the color constancy algorithm, where a perfect white light, i.e.$(1/\sqrt{3}, 1/\sqrt{3}, 1/\sqrt{3})^T$, is used as canonical illuminant [14].

$$J = EI = diag(e_R^{-1}, e_G^{-1}, e_B^{-1})I \tag{16}$$

3 Experimental Results

In this section, the effect of the algorithm is tested by multiple night images, and compared with traditional color constancy algorithms.

Figure 1 illustrates the comparison results. The first column is four typical night image with a significant color cast. The second column is applied by the Grey world

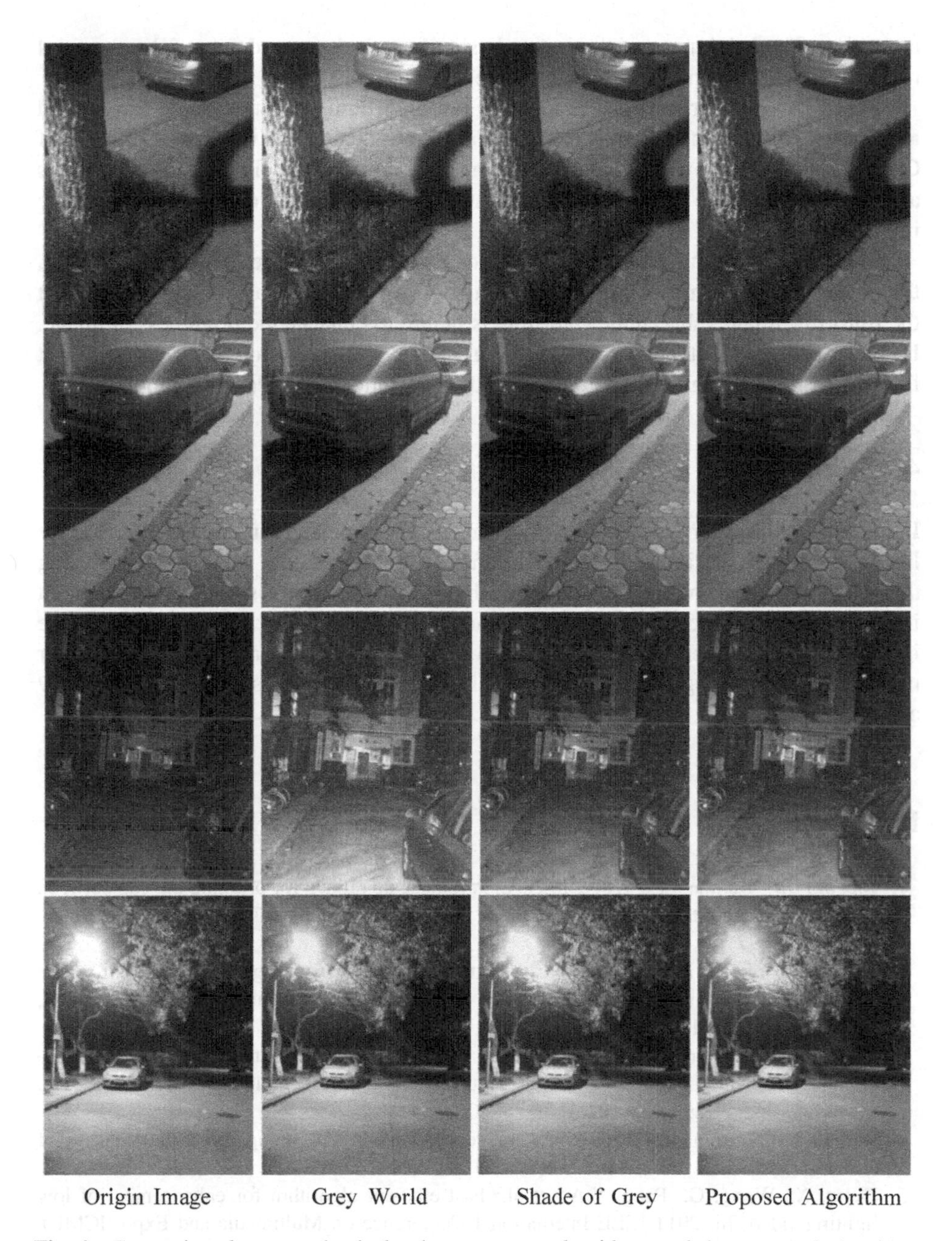

Fig. 1. Comparison between classical color constancy algorithms and the proposed algorithm (Color figure online)

algorithm. The brightness of the image is significantly improved, especially the third row. But the algorithm is not able to solve the color cast.

For a fair comparison, the Shade of Grey algorithms and this paper's proposed algorithms set the same parameters as p = 6 in experiments. The result by the Shade of Grey algorithm is shown in the third column. The result of the first and second row is acceptable. But in the last row, the algorithm is failure to remove the color cast of the image.

The fourth column is the results of proposed algorithm. As the fourth column show, the proposed algorithm has a strong ability to remove the color cast of night image. But the third row images shown the algorithm is failure to enhance the brightness of image. It is due to the light attenuation of the foreground is ignored in proposed algorithm. But for the image the brightness is quite low, the light attenuation can't be ignored.

4 Summary

In this paper, the color constancy of night image is investigated. In order to estimate the light source color of night image, a night image formation model is proposed. By using the depth map and the attenuations grey hypothesis, the light source color of night image is estimate. According to the light source color, the color cast of the night image is removed. The experimental results show that the results of proposed algorithm for night are improved significantly, compared to the results of classical color constancy algorithm.

References

1. Jobson, D.J., Rahman, Z., Woodell, G.A.: A multiscale retinex for bridging the gap between color images and the human observation of scenes. IEEE Trans. Image Process. **6**(7), 965–976 (1997)
2. Wang, W., Li, B., Zheng, J., et al.: A fast multi-scale retinex algorithm for color image enhancement. In: International Conference on Wavelet Analysis and Pattern Recognition, ICWAPR 2008, vol. 1, pp. 80–85 (2008)
3. Rahman, Z., Jobson, D.J., Woodell, G.A.: Investigating the relationship between image enhancement and image compression in the context of the multi-scale retinex. J. Vis. Commun. Image Represent. **22**(3), 237–250 (2011)
4. Reflectance–Illuminance B.: Retinex image processing: improving the visual realism of color images. Int. J. Inf. Technol. **4**(2), 371–377 (2011)
5. Dong, X., Wang, G., Pang, Y.A., et al.: Fast efficient algorithm for enhancement of low lighting video. In: 2011 IEEE International Conference on Multimedia and Expo (ICME), pp. 1–6. IEEE (2011)
6. Zhang, X., Shen, P., Luo, L., et al.: Enhancement and noise reduction of very low light level images. In: 2012 21st International Conference on Pattern Recognition (ICPR), pp. 2034–2037. IEEE (2012)
7. Jiang, X., Yao, H., Zhang, S., et al.: Night video enhancement using improved dark channel prior. In: 2013 20th IEEE International Conference on Image Processing (ICIP), pp. 553–557 IEEE (2013)

8. Land, E.H.: The retinex theory of color vision. Sci. Am **237**, 108–128 (1977)
9. Buchsbaum, G.: A spatial processor model for object colour perception. J. Franklin Inst. **310** (1), 1–26 (1980)
10. Henke, B., Vahl, M., Zhou, Z.: Removing color cast of underwater images through non-constant color constancy hypothesis. In: 2013 8th International Symposium on Image and Signal Processing and Analysis (ISPA), pp. 20–24. IEEE (2013)
11. Finlayson, G.D., Trezzi, E.: Shades of gray and colour constancy. Color Imaging Conf. Soc. Imaging Sci. Technol. **2004**(1), 37–41 (2004)
12. He, K., Sun, J., Tang, X.: Single image haze removal using dark channel prior. IEEE Trans. Pattern Anal. Mach. Intell. **33**(12), 2341–2353 (2011)
13. Otsu, N.: A threshold selection method from gray-level histograms. Automatica **11**(285–296), 23–27 (1975)
14. Gijsenij, A., Gevers, T., Van De Weijer, J.: Computational color constancy: survey and experiments. IEEE Trans. Image Process. **20**(9), 2475–2489 (2011)

Automatic Image Semantic Segmentation by MRF with Transformation-Invariant Shape Priors

Peng Tang(✉) and Weidong Jin

School of Electrical Engineering, Southwest Jiaotong University,
Chengdu 610031, People's Republic of China
tang.peng@home.swjtu.edu.cn

Abstract. Shape priors has greatly enhanced low-level driven image segmentations, however existing graph cut based segmentation methods still restrict to pre-aligned shape priors. The major contribution of this paper is to incorporate transformation-invariant shape priors into the graph cut algorithm for automatic image segmentations. The expectation of shape transformation and image knowledge are encoded into energy functions that is optimized in a MRF maximum likelihood framework using the expectation-maximization. The iteratively updated expectation process improves the segmentation robustness. In turn, the maximum likelihood segmentation is realized integrally by casting the lower-bound of energy function in a graph structure that can be effectively optimized by graph-cuts algorithm in order to achieve a global solution and also increase the accuracy of the probabilities measurement. Finally, experimental results demonstrate the potentials of our method under conditions of noises, clutters, and incomplete occlusions.

1 Introduction

Image segmentation, which usually refers to a process of extracting some meaningful objects from the background, is considered as a fundamental and difficult task in digital image processing and machine vision applications. The challenge of natural image segmentation lies in the practical situations in the presence of noises, clutters, or partial occlusions. Therefore the bottom-up approaches that implement pixel intensity information alone are often insufficient to partition meaningful regions. The essential causation behind the problem is the fact that the joint reconstruction of photometry and geometry from a few images is generally an intrinsically ill-posed problem [6]. Incorporating the image prior information are necessary for fixing the degrees of freedom and resolving ambiguous decisions.

P. Tang—This work was supported by the National Natural Science Foundation of China (61134002) and Fundamental Research Funds for the Central Universities (2682014CX027).

L. Zhang et al. (Eds.): AsiaSim 2016/SCS AutumnSim 2016, Part I, CCIS 643, pp. 216–226, 2016.
DOI: 10.1007/978-981-10-2663-8_23

Various segmentation methods have been proposed under the inspiration of incorporating shape knowledge, which were proved effective and leading to more robust performances. Though the majority of research was carried out under level set framework, it is specially attractive to embed prior information about object shape into graph-cuts based segmentations because of its globally optimizing ability. However, existing graph cut based segmentation methods still restrict to pre-aligned shape priors, while practically objects in natural images may be arbitrarily disposed and are easily perturbed by surrounding environments. To address this problem, in this paper we propose a model for transformation invariant shape prior segmentation. By introducing the expectation of shape transformation, our approach allows affine and perspective geometric transformation of prior shapes, namely, it can handle the general case without knowing the locations, sizes or poses of the desired objects. This amelioration contributes to the major difference of our method from previous work. The lower bound of energy function is designed to be optimized under a graph structure whose network flow can be effectively maximized by graph cut algorithm.

The paper is organized as follows. Section 2 reviews related work. Section 3 describes the details of our algorithm to explain how the transformation-invariant prior shape template can be incorporated into graph based segmentation. Section 4 shows experimental results on various natural images to demonstrate that our approach improves robustness to perturb information. Section 5 draws the conclusion.

2 Previous Work

In this section we briefly review some related researches that is most relevant to our approach, which generally falls into two categories: shape prior aided segmentation, and graph cut base segmentation with priors.

Recent research [2–5] favors prior shape augmented level-set active contour segmentation that biases the curve evolution towards prior guidance. Cremers et al. [4] constructed a variational approach to incorporate a level set based shape difference term into Chan-Vese's segmentation model. While Dambreville [5] successfully use Kernel PCA to introduce shape priors within the GAC framework. Tony Chan [2] improved the approach to a general case that allows translation, scaling and rotation of prior shapes. Then Charpiat [3] proposed to take into account intrinsic shape statistics into the standard active-contour algorithms for segmentation without computing transformation parameters. Deep learning based methods [10,13] also attracted attention most for semantic segmentation for arbitrary pre-learned object type, however due to the pool and unpooling operation, the segmentation boundaries generally lost precise compared to previous methods.

Compared with level sets based method which may trapped in local optimums, the graph cut algorithm, as a robust globally optimal energy minimization method, attracts increasing attention nowadays. Boykov's research [1] made graph cut popular for image segmentation. Inspired by the idea of integral solution to surface evolving PDEs [12], Xu [16] combines active contours with graph cut optimization to iteratively deform the contour. Then Zehiry [7] present a graph cuts based optimization for The Mumford-Shah model. Some researches already began to explored the prior assisted graph cut segmentation. Freedman's solution [8] is to use graph edge-weights which contain information about a level-set function of a template, in addition to the usual boundary and region terms. Malcolm [11] used a shape projection pre-image obtained from kernel principle component analysis to induce an iteratively refined shape prior in a Bayesian manner. The methods mentioned above require user interactive, and is sensitive about initial alignment. While some other researchers interest in generalized priors, Vicente [15] imposed an additional connectivity prior to deal with the shrinking bias of Graph cut segmentation. Slabaugh [14] present a graph cuts-based image segmentation technique that incorporates an elliptical shape prior to restrict the solution space.

3 Our Approach

3.1 Segmentation as Energy Minimization

Specifically, given an observed image $Z = \{z_p \mid p \in \mathcal{P}\}$, where $\mathcal{P}$ is the lattice of corresponding image pixels. The label of each pixel as f_p that is a binary variable is unknown, i.e., $f_p \in \{0, 1\}$ standing for foreground and background respectively. Obviously the segmentation contour C and the labeling sets $\{f_p \mid p \in \mathcal{P}\}$ are mutually equivalent. Namely, with the pixel label being determined, the contour of the segmented object can be represented as $C = \{p \mid f_p = 1, f_q = 0, (p, q) \in \mathcal{N} \subset \mathcal{P}\}$, where $\mathcal{N}$ is the set of neighboring pixels. Both Z and C can be considered as random vectors in feature spaces. To apply the Maximum Likelihood (ML) estimation for f, the log likelihood function of $\Pr(Z \mid C)$ is to be maximized,

$$\tilde{C} = \arg\max_{C} \log \Pr(Z \mid C) \tag{1}$$

Since the object may be arbitrarily disposed in the image without knowing the transformation parameters, the hidden variable θ is introduced to characterize the transformation from prior shape to practical segmentation contour. Then $\Pr(Z \mid C)$ may be expressed as the marginalized probability of transformation parameter θ and can be further decomposed using Bayesian rule.

$$\log \Pr(Z \mid C) = \log \int_{\theta} \Pr(Z, \theta \mid C)\, d\theta = \log \int_{\theta} \Pr(Z \mid \theta, C) \Pr(\theta \mid C)\, d\theta \tag{2}$$

Generally, the image segmentation problem can be properly solved by maximizing the log-likelihood function using Expectation-Maximization (EM) algorithm, which is essentially a lower-bound optimization. If given current segmentation contour $C^{(n)}$, the lower-bound can be obtained using Jensen's inequality [9],

$$\log \Pr(Z \mid C) \geq Q\left(C \mid C^{(n)}\right) \tag{3}$$

where $Q(C \mid C^{(n)})$ is the lower-bound of Eq. 2,

$$Q\left(C \mid C^{(n)}\right) = \int\limits_{\theta} \Pr\left(\theta | Z, C^{(n)}\right) \log\left[\Pr\left(Z | \theta, C\right) \Pr\left(\theta | C\right)\right] d\theta \tag{4}$$

Consequently the next segmentation $C^{(n+1)}$ can be calculated by seeking the parameter that optimizes the lower bound $Q(C \mid C^{(n)})$,

$$C^{(n+1)} = \arg\max_{C} Q\left(C \mid C^{(n)}\right) \tag{5}$$

Note that there is no direct connection between nodes Z and θ in the graphical structure of the specified model, then based on the independence rule, the Eq. 4 can be simplified by considering $\Pr\left(\theta \mid Z, C^{(n)}\right) = \Pr\left(\theta \mid C^{(n)}\right)$ and $\Pr\left(Z \mid \theta, C\right) = \Pr\left(Z \mid C\right)$,

$$\begin{aligned} Q\left(C \mid C^{(n)}\right) &= \int\limits_{\theta} \Pr\left(\theta | C^{(n)}\right) \left[\log \Pr\left(Z | C\right) + \log \Pr\left(\theta | C\right)\right] d\theta \\ &= \log \Pr\left(Z | C\right) + \int\limits_{\theta} \Pr\left(\theta | C^{(n)}\right) \log \Pr\left(\theta | C\right) d\theta \end{aligned} \tag{6}$$

By supposing that image observations Z satisfy the Markovianity assumption, the log-likelihood potential functions would equal to the Markov random fields energy $-\log \Pr\left(Z \mid C\right) = E_{data} + E_{smooth}$ [11]. Similarly the log of conditional probability $-\log \Pr\left(\theta \mid C\right)$ can be considered as Gibbs energy $-\log \Pr\left(\theta \mid C\right) = E_{shape}$. So the Eq. 4 takes the form

$$-Q\left(C | C^{(n)}\right) = E_{data} + E_{smooth} + \langle E_{shape} \rangle_{\Pr(\theta | C^{(n)})} \tag{7}$$

where $\langle \cdot \rangle_{\Pr(\theta | C^{(n)})}$ means the expectation related to the conditional probability $\Pr(\theta | C^{(n)})$. In the following sections, we give a detailed description of minimizing this lower-bound of energy.

3.2 Image Energy Term

Image energy, which is usually considered as a combination of data term and smoothness term, may be formulated over the latent labeling variable f_p of each pixel p under the first-order Markov random field frame work [8]. The data dependent term, also known as region-based term in image segmentation, evaluates the penalty for assigning individual pixels to certain regions. In this paper, the log of the color likelihood $\log \Pr(z_p \mid f_p)$, $f_p \in \{0, 1\}$ is utilized by models such as mixture model of Gaussians (GMM) or histograms in RGB color space.

$$E_{data} = \sum_{p \in \mathcal{P}} R_p\left(f_p\right) = -\sum_{p \in \mathcal{P}} \log \Pr\left(z_p \mid f_p\right) \tag{8}$$

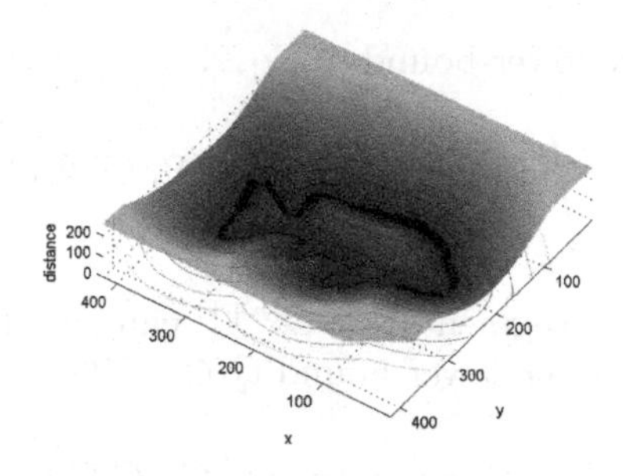

Fig. 1. Given the contour of a fish, the integral distance from C_θ to C_0 equals to the volume indicated by the darken region. The height map is given by a unsigned distance function $\psi_\theta(\cdot)$.

The smoothness or boundary term evaluates the penalty for assigning two neighboring pixels p and q to different regions, i.e. a boundary discontinuity, which is usually defined as exponential of color difference divided by pixel distance.

$$E_{smooth} = \sum_{(p,q)\in\mathcal{N}} B_{p,q}(f_p, f_q) = \sum_{(p,q)\in\mathcal{N}} \frac{\delta(f_p \neq f_q)}{\|p-q\|} \exp\left(-\frac{\|z_p - z_q\|^2}{2\sigma_{pix}^2}\right) \quad (9)$$

where $\|\cdot\|$ is the L_2 norm; $\delta(\cdot)$ is the Dirac-delta function which returns 1 for input zero or returns 0 for otherwise; and σ_{pix} is the predefined bandwidth parameter reflecting pixel color variances.

3.3 Shape Distance Term

The prior shape template C_0 are represented implicitly using silhouette images when no topology constrains are given. In the case of the perspective geometry, the transformed prior shape could be determined given a certain transformation parameter θ, which can be represented as an augmented matrix $\theta = [\theta_{i,j}]_{3\times3} \in \mathbb{R}^{3\times3}$ combined from significant parameters succinctly. Each point on the contour is also represented by an augmented position vector $w_p = (x_p, y_p, 1)^T$, then the transformed shape under parameter θ can be computed by matrix multiplication $C_\theta = \{w_{\theta,p} \mid w_{\theta,p} = \zeta^{-1}\theta^T w_p, p \in C_0\}$, where $w_{\theta,p}$ is the coordinates after transformation and where ζ is the scaling factor that is defined as $\zeta = [\theta_{3,1}, \theta_{3,2}, \theta_{3,3}]\, w_p$. Specially for the affine geometry that can be regarded as simplified cases by the reducing foreshorten effect, free parameters that remains are actually for the translation, rotation, scaling, and shearing, then the θ takes the form of $\theta_{3,1} = 0$, $\theta_{3,2} = 0$, $\theta_{3,3} = 1$, and therefore ζ degrades to $\zeta = 1$.

Defining a distance function $\psi_\theta : \mathbb{R}^2 \to \mathbb{R}$ which defines a point to contour measure that corresponds to Euclidian distance of point p to the nearest transformed-contour C_θ, namely $\psi_\theta(p) = \{\min(\|p, s\|) \mid s \in C_\theta\}$, as show in Fig. 1, the shape energy E_{shape} can be written in the following form.

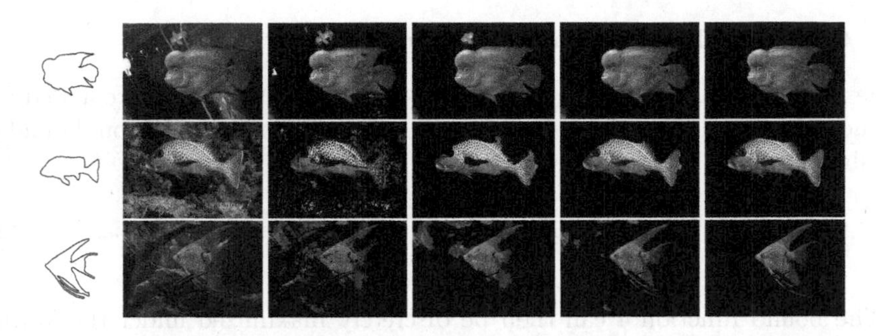

Fig. 2. Segmentation of various fishes in cluttered backgrounds. The first column gives the prior shape templates, the second column is the original image, and the third column is the initial segmentation which merely used imagery information, the fourth, fifth and sixth column are segmentation results of the 2, 5 and 15 iterations respectively.

$$E_{shape} = \sum_{(p,q)\in\mathcal{N}} S_{p,q}^{\theta}(f_p, f_q) = \sum_{(p,q)\in\mathcal{N}} \delta(f_p \neq f_q)\,\psi_\theta\left(\frac{p+q}{2}\right) \tag{10}$$

The Eq. 10 implies that the pixel connections near the shape boundaries are weak and prone to be break in segmentation.

To obtained the expectation of shape energy, the $\Pr\left(\theta|C^{(n)}\right)$ can be calculate using the Gibbs energy of contour deformation of $C^{(n)} \to C_\theta$ based on Markov-Gibbs equivalence. We adopt the distance metric in the shape space proposed by Boykov [12] which measures boundary change in an integral way so as to avoid local differential computations.

$$\Pr\left(\theta \mid C^{(n)}\right) = \frac{1}{\Omega}\exp\left(-\kappa\sum_{p\in\Delta C_\theta}\psi_\theta(p)\right) \tag{11}$$

where κ is a temperature parameter, ΔC_θ is defined as the region between the contours C_θ and $C^{(n)}$, as indicated as dark regions in Fig. 1, and Ω is the normalization constant that makes the probability integrates to one,

$$\Omega = \int_\theta \exp\left(-\kappa\sum_{p\in\Delta C_\theta}\psi_\theta(p)\right)d\theta \tag{12}$$

The the Gibbs energy defined in Eq. 11 collects the weights given to the region of shape difference, so as to integrally represent the contour deformation. Finally, summarizing the previous Eqs. 10, 11 and 12 deduced the third term in Eq. 7:

$$\langle E_{shape}\rangle_{\Pr(\theta|C^{(n)})} = \sum_{(p,q)\in\mathcal{N}}\sum_{\theta}\Pr\left(\theta|C^{(n)}\right)S_{p,q}^{\theta}(f_p, f_q) = \sum_{(p,q)\in\mathcal{N}}\left\langle S_{p,q}^{\theta}(f_p, f_q)\right\rangle_{\Pr(\theta|C^{(n)})} \tag{13}$$

3.4 Graphical Representations of Energy

To be more generally, weighting factors $0 \leq \lambda \leq 1$ and $0 \leq \tau \leq 1$ are added into the the lower-bound function o balance the relative influence of region, boundary and shape term.

$$Q\left(C \mid C^{(n)}\right) = \lambda \sum_{p} R_p + \sum_{p,q \in \mathcal{N}} \left[(1-\tau)\, B_{p,q} + \tau \left\langle S_{p,q} \right\rangle_{\theta \mid C^{(n)}} \right] \tag{14}$$

The bound function 4 can then be discretely maximized under the Markov random fields framework, whose energy equals to the network flow in a corresponding graph $\mathcal{G} = (\mathcal{V}, \mathcal{E})$. The graph node set $\mathcal{P}$ is pixel nodes augmented by two special vertices: the source $\mathcal{S}$ and sink $\mathcal{T}$, which represent object and background respectively, $\mathcal{V} = \mathcal{P} \cup \{\mathcal{S}, \mathcal{T}\}$. The edges set $\mathcal{E} = \mathcal{N} \cup \{(p, \mathcal{S}), (p, \mathcal{T}) \mid p \in \mathcal{P}\}$ consists of all clique pairs of pixels, along with edges between each pixel and the source or sink. Usually 1th or 2nd order neighborhood is chosen. By setting the edge weights $\mathcal{E}$ according to Eq. 14, the graph cut techniques can then be implemented for minimization [1].

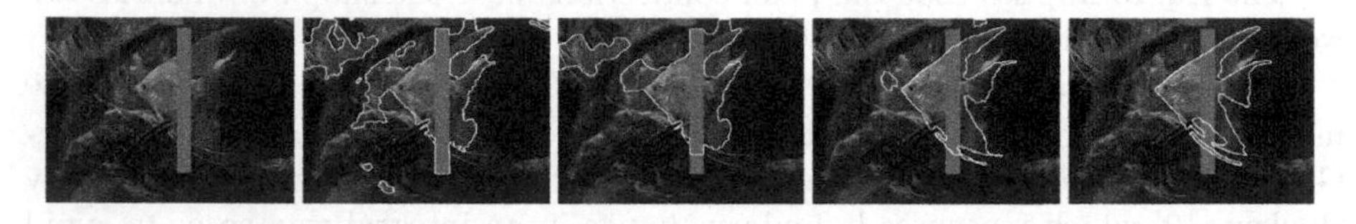

Fig. 3. Segmentation with partial occlusion. The images from left-to-right are original image, the initial segmentation, the segmentation results of the 2, 10, 25 iterations respectively.

3.5 Numerical Implementation

To calculate the expectation of shape energy in Eq. 10, the probability density $\Pr(\theta \mid C^{(n)})$ needs to be acquired despite defined on a high-dimensional space. MCMC techniques are proved to be powerful approaches to solve this integration problems in large dimensional space by approximating original hard combinatorial problems with simple statistical samples. Since generating samples from $\Pr(\theta \mid C^{(n)})$ is computationally costly, it might be preferred to generate candidate samples from an appropriate importance proposal distribution $\Phi(\theta)$. Then we can rewrite the expectation as follows

$$\langle E_{shape} \rangle_{\Pr(\theta \mid C^{(n)})} = \sum_{(p,q) \in \mathcal{N}} \sum_{\theta} \varpi_\theta S^{\theta}_{p,q}(f_p, f_q) \Phi(\theta) = \sum_{(p,q) \in \mathcal{N}} \left\langle \varpi_\theta S^{\theta}_{p,q}(f_p, f_q) \right\rangle_{\Phi(\theta)} \tag{15}$$

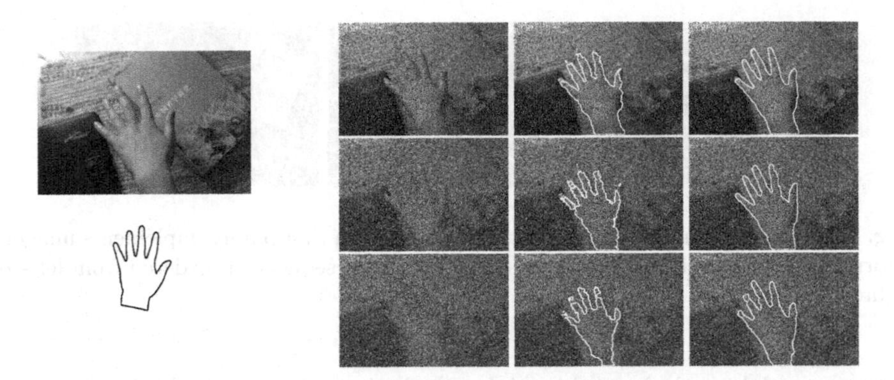

Fig. 4. Segmentation of a hand. The left part gives the original image and the prior shape template. The first, second and third row in right are examples in presence of 30 %, 50 % and 70 % noise respectively. The left column are noisy images; the middle column are segmentation results purely from imagery information; the right column are results of our method after 20 iterations.

where ϖ_θ is known as the importance weight.

$$\varpi_\theta \triangleq \frac{\Pr(\theta \mid C^{(n)})}{\Phi(\theta)} \tag{16}$$

Though the importance distribution may be arbitrarily chosen, its support ought include the support of $\Pr(\theta \mid C^{(n)})$ so as to indicate the sampling attention. A good choice is to utilize previously obtained distributions and initialize uniformly.

$$\Phi(\theta) = \Pr(\theta | C^{(n-1)}) \tag{17}$$

Thus we can represent the probability distribution $\Pr(\theta \mid C^{(n)})$ non-parametrically using N i.i.d samples $\{\theta_i\}_{i=1}^N$ drawn from $\Phi(\theta)$ and their weights $\{\varpi_i\}_{i=1}^N$, which is also called particles. In each iteration of EM process, the particles are evaluated using Eq. 16 to update their weights and compute the shape energy term. Ultimately the Eq. 13 can be approximated as,

$$\langle E_{shape} \rangle_{\Pr(\theta|C^{(n)})} \approx \frac{1}{N} \sum_{(p,q)\in\mathcal{N}} \sum_{i=1}^{N} \varpi_i S_{p,q}^i (f_p, f_q) \tag{18}$$

Consequently sampling importance resampling [9] are applied to the particles according to their importance weights to generate an un-weighted approximation of the probability $\Pr(\theta^{(n)})$ for next iteration. The algorithm is repeated to achieve desired accuracy.

4 Experimental Results and Analysis

To validate the effectiveness and sufficiencies of proposed algorithm, a number of experiments were carried out, including challenging situations such as noises,

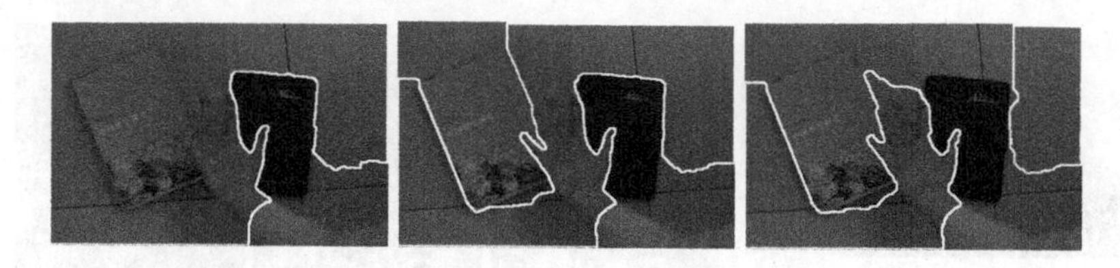

Fig. 5. Our method may fail if the initial segmentation that purely implements imagery information cannot give an apprehensible result. The sequence is ordered from left-to-right.

clutters, weak boundaries and partial occlusions etc. Our method is implemented in C++ with the help of OpenCV 2.4.10, and runs on a PC with Intel Xeon 2630V2 CPU processor and 8GB of RAM. In each experiment, the number of particles is $N = 100$ and the parameters are set as $\tau = 0.4$ and $\lambda = 0.6$ for our method.

Figure 2 demonstrates the effectiveness of the proposed algorithm on real world images of various fishes whose backgrounds are heavily cluttered. It can be seen that the performance of the graph cut segmentation with intensity alone [1] can be considered unsatisfactory. The similarity of foreground and background color distribution, as show in top and bottom rows of Fig. 2, and confused boundaries, as shown in middle row of Fig. 2, lead to the misclassification. Our algorithm outperformed because the shape prior gives extra constraints to avoid misleading contents. Compared with level set based methods [2], the convergence speed of our method is much faster as graph cut is an combinatorial optimization method free of sub-pixel calculation.

Figure 3 verifies the robustness of our algorithm when handling partial occlusion. The method concerning imagery information alone [1] is perceptibly unable to segment the object accurately, because the it is a method based on local pixel statistics. By considering shape regional information, the outperforming of our algorithm is because introducing shape priors complement the missing information and recover a more global solution.

Figure 4 gives a comparison of graph cut segmentation of a hand with and without transformation-invariant shape prior for images corrupted by various amounts of salt and pepper noise. The partition outcome without shape guidance degrades even with moderate amounts of noise because of dramatically missing of visual information. While the shape priors aided segmentation successfully classify the hand from background even with respect to 70 % noise. With the help from shape knowledge, the analysis was performed in a hyper feature space that results in much fine segmentation results even for highly noised images.

The quantitative analysis based on our private object shape oriented datasets are given in Table 1. Compared to the state of art methods, our methods achieved better F-measure and PSNR value, and a closely NRM and MPM value. The result is a proof our methods capability. It should be also pointed out that though the graph cut algorithm guarantees a global optimum of lower bound function in each iteration, the expectation maximization process itself still may trapped

Table 1. Quantitative comparement to the state of art methods.

Method	F-Measure	PSNR	NRM	MPM
GC [12]	85.46 %	16.77	5.29×10^{-2}	1.18×10^{-3}
FCN [10]	91.24 %	14.66	4.31×10^{-2}	0.65×10^{-3}
Ours	93.24 %	18.56	5.17×10^{-2}	1.17×10^{-3}

in local optimum. Inheriting the shortcoming of sensitivity to initial condition from EM algorithm, our method might fail if the imagery energy minimization could not give an moderate meaningful initial segmentation, as shown in Fig. 5.

5 Conclusions

In this work, we introduced transformation invariant prior knowledge as a guidance for graph cut image segmentation under the maximum likelihood framework using the expectation maximization algorithm. The expectation process improve the robustness of maximum likelihood segmentation. While the lower-bound maximization is implemented combinatorially under Markov random fields framework which can be globally optimized by graph cut algorithm for each iteration. As a function of the complexity of the observed image, experimental results demonstrate the effectiveness and robustness of our method. More sophisticated tools that adapts transformation-invariance to the deformable prior shape template is an interesting topic for further research.

References

1. Boykov, Y., Funka-Lea, G.: Graph cuts and efficient n-d image segmentation. IJCV **70**(2), 109–131 (2006)
2. Chan, T., Zhu, W.: Level set based shape prior segmentation. In: Proceedings of the IEEE CVPR, vol. 2, pp. 1164–1170, San Diego, CA (2005)
3. Charpiat, G., Faugeras, O., Keriven, R.: Shape statistics for image segmentation with prior. In: Proceedings of the IEEE CVPR, pp. 1–6, Minneapolis (2007)
4. Cremers, D.: Dynamical statistical shape priors for level set-based tracking. IEEE Trans. PAMI **28**(8), 1262–1273 (2006)
5. Dambreville, S., Rathi, Y., Tannenbaum, A.: Shape-based approach to robust image segmentation using kernel PCA. In: Proceedings of the IEEE CVPR, vol. 1, pp. 977–984. IEEE Press, New York City (2006)
6. Doretto, G., Chiuso, A., Wu, Y.N., Soatto, S.: Dynamic textures. IJCV **51**(2), 91–109 (2003)
7. El-Zehiry, N., Xu, S., Sahoo, P., Elmaghraby, A.: Graph cut optimization for the Mumford-Shah model. In: Proceedings of the 7th IASTED International Conference on Visualization Imaging, and Image Processing, pp. 182–187, Palma de Mallorca, Spain (2007)
8. Freedman, D., Zhang, T.: Interactive graph cut based segmentation with shape priors. In: Proceedings of the IEEE CVPR, vol. 1, pp. 755–761, San Diego, CA (2005)

9. Hadfield, J.D., et al.: MCMC methods for multi-response generalized linear mixed models: the MCMCglmm R package. J. Stat. Softw. **33**(2), 1–22 (2010)
10. Long, J., Shelhamer, E., Darrell, T.: Fully convolutional networks for semantic segmentation. In: Proceedings of the IEEE CVPR, pp. 3431–3440 (2015)
11. Malcolm, J., Rathi, Y., Tannenbaum, A.: Graph cut segmentation with nonlinear shape priors. Proc. IEEE ICIP **4**, 365–368 (2007)
12. Price, B.L., Morse, B., Cohen, S.: Geodesic graph cut for interactive image segmentation. In: 2010 IEEE Conference on Computer Vision and Pattern Recognition (CVPR), pp. 3161–3168. IEEE (2010)
13. Shen, W., Wang, X., Wang, Y., Bai, X., Zhang, Z.: Deepcontour: a deep convolutional feature learned by positive-sharing loss for contour detection. In: Proceedings of the IEEE CVPR, pp. 3982–3991 (2015)
14. Slabaugh, G., Unal, G.: Graph cuts segmentation using an elliptical shape prior. In: Proceedings of IEEE ICIP, pp. 1222–1225 (2005)
15. Vicente, S., Kolmogorov, V., Rother, C.: Graph cut based image segmentation with connectivity priors. In: Proceedings of the IEEE CVPR (2008)
16. Ning, X., Bansal, R., Ahuja, N.: Object segmentation using graph cuts based active contours. Proc. IEEE CVPR **2**, 46–53 (2003)

Adaptive Stacked Denoising Autoencoder for Work Mode Identification of Airborne Active Phased Array Radar

Hui Li[1,2](✉), Weidong Jin[1], Haodong Liu[1], and Kun Zheng[2]

[1] School of Electrical Engineering, Southwest Jiaotong University, Chengdu 610031, China
satlihui@163.com

[2] Science and Technology on Electronic Information Control Laboratory, Chengdu 610036, China

Abstract. This paper proposes a new method to recognize airborne phased array radar (AESA) under different modes, based on multi-level modeling combined with Adaptive Stacked Denoising Autoencoder. In order to analyze the change law of pulses intercepted by intelligence, multi-level modeling is proposed to model the pulses at pulse level, pulse group level and work mode level. Then adaptive stacked denoising auto-encoder is trained to extract amplitude characteristics at the work mode level. Finally Softmax classification is added to the top of deep network to realize work mode recognition of airborne phased array radar. Qualitative experiments show that compared with the original algorithm based on knowledge base, the new method is able to extract essential characteristics of the input, reduce the dependence on prior knowledge, and achieves good performance.

Keywords: Airborne radar · Work mode · Multi-level modeling · Deep learning

1 Introduction

In recent years, with the development of electronic technology, Active Phased array radar has been widely applied in Modern Battlefield [1]. Owing to its good performance in resource management and adaptive update rate, airborne active phased array radar like AESA can track more targets while searching for new ones [2]. What's more, as a multi-function radar, airborne active phased array radar contains a variety of work modes such as track while scan (TWS), track and scan (TAS), multi-target tracking (MTT), single target tracking (STT). Each mode threatens the target at different level, therefore, in order to assess the threat level of the active phased array radar, it is of great significance to identify radar's work mode.

Several relevant work has been done in work mode identification of active phased array radar. With the help of radar knowledge base, Jia [3] constructed feature matrix containing radar parameters such as RF, PW, TOA and PW to reflect the features of different work modes. Visnevski modeled the features of radar under different work modes by using syntactic context-free grammars, then he used the extracted features to match the radar knowledge base [4, 5]. Although those methods realized the work mode identification of radar in different ways. However, they have the same limitations as

L. Zhang et al. (Eds.): AsiaSim 2016/SCS AutumnSim 2016, Part I, CCIS 643, pp. 227–236, 2016.
DOI: 10.1007/978-981-10-2663-8_24

follows: firstly, those methods lack the ability to learn features of the input adaptively, all features are extracted artificially. Secondly, their classification accuracy is strictly restricted by the integrity of knowledge base.

Since suggested in 2006, deep learning has shown a good performance in learning the essential characteristics of the data without supervised training [6, 7]. As a common model in deep learning, denoising auto-encoder yields significantly lower recognition error in many field than auto-encoder, as it can extract and compose robust features from corrupted versions of their inputs [8, 9]. Stacking a plurality of DAE, we get the stack denoising automatic encoder (SDA). However the noise level in SDA is kept fixed during the training thus limited it's performance. To overcome the limitations of Stacked Denoising Autoencoder (SDA), an Adaptive Stacked Denoising Autoencoder (ASDA) was proposed to improve its performance [10].

According to the change law of pulse signal under different modes, we propose multi-level modeling method to describe the emitters at different levels. Then ASDA is introduced to extract the robust and useful features from pulse signal unsupervisedly. Qualitative experiments show that our new method based on multi-level modeling combined with ASDA achieves good performance. Section 2 analysis the change law of pulse signal under different modes and describes the motivation for the proposed method. Sections 3 and 4 give the detailed procedure for multi-level modeling and ASDA. Finally the results are given in Sect. 5.

2 Motivation for Proposed Method

To improve the SNR of Radar Echo, airborne active phased array radar like AESA usually launch one or more groups of coherent pulse signal. Each group contains hundreds of pulses with the same RF, PRI, PW, PA, so it is unwise to analysis such amount of pulses one by one, we only need to get few parameters of the coherent pulse groups such as the starting point, the end time to identify radar's work mode. That is the motivation why we proposed pulse multi-level modeling.

When an active phased array radar is searching or tracking the target, the pulse parameters are essentially random. So it is unable to judge the work mode of radars with parameters of PF, PRI and PW. The way to realize the recognition of work mode by analyzing the regularity of signal's amplitude. Since ASDA has shown strong ability to learn essential characteristics of the input, here we use it to learn useful features of the pulses' amplitude under different work modes.

3 Pulse Multi-level Modeling

3.1 Pulse Level Modeling

Pulse parameters generally include TOA, DOA, RF, PW and PA, other pulse characteristic parameters (such as PRI) are results of analyzing of those parameters [5]. Since the error of DOA is large, so we do not take this into consideration. The ith pulse can be modeled as:

$$Y(i) = [TOA_i, RF_i, PW_i, PA_i, PRI_i]. \quad (1)$$

3.2 Pulse Group Level Modeling

To extract the pulse group's ranking information, we firstly find the starting pulse of the pulse group, then determine the subsequent pulses' confidence belonging to the pulse group, finally, we separate all the pulses so as to realize the information's grade promotion from pulse level to pulse group level. The establishment of pulse group level model includes the following two aspects:

Determination of the Pulse Group's Starting Point. Mainly including:

Step 1. Parameter initialization: set i to be 1.
Step 2. Take the ith pulse ($Y(i)$) as a reference pulse, if the pulse parameters of the next n continuous pulse are the same as the reference pulse (within a certain tolerance range), skip to Step 3, or, set i to be $i + 1$ and repeat Step 2;
Step 3. Set $Y(i)$ as the initial pulse of the pulse group.

Calculation of Pulses' confidence. If there exists dropped pulses or false pulses in the pulse train, to do the confidence calculation by using PRI could be error-prone. Therefore, the following methods are proposed: Starting with the initial pulse of the group, the arrival time of the n continuous pulse can y be expressed as: $y = \{TOA_1, TOA_2, \cdots, TOA_n\}$, x can be expressed as: $x = \{1, 2, \cdots, n\}$.

The fitting curve can be obtained by using the least-square fitting:

$$y = kx + b \quad (2)$$

k: estimated value of the pulse group template's PRI.
b: starting time of the pulse group.

Work out the time-of-arrival interval between the next pulse and the reference pulse, and estimate how many times it is of PRI (denoted by T). Determine whether or not the distance between the point (T, TOA) and the fitting line is within the margin of error. If not, continue to search forward until all the successive m pulse do not belong to the pulse template, and the pulse group parameter extraction is done. If it is, calculate the confidence factor of the pulse's p-th feature belonging to the pulse template, donated by $f(x_p)$.

$$f(x_p) = \begin{cases} \exp(\dfrac{-(x_p - v_{ip} + \Delta v_{ip})^2}{2\sigma_{ip}^2}), & x_p < v_{ip} - \Delta v_{ip} \\ 1, & v_{ip} - \Delta v_{ip} \le x_p \le v_{ip} + \Delta v_{ip} \\ \exp(\dfrac{-(x_p - v_{ip} - \Delta v_{ip})^2}{2\sigma_{ip}^2}), & x_p > v_{ip} + \Delta v_{ip} \end{cases} \quad (3)$$

Where: x_p is the parameter values of the identifying pulse's p feature, v_{ip}, Δv_{ip} and σ_{ip} are respectively the parameter values, parameter deviation and the mean square deviation of the pulse template's pth feature. All the parameters can be set according to the actual data.

After calculating the confidence of each dimension, amalgamate the confidence factor of multiple parameters, we can obtain the total confidence factor based on the joint parameter.

$$\mu = \sum_{p=1}^{N} w_p f(x_p) \tag{4}$$

w_p is the weight of the p-th feature in the recognition.

After the extraction of the pulse group's characteristic parameters, the jth pulse group can be expressed as:

$$CPI_j = [Toastart_j, Toaend_j, RF_j, PW_j, PA_j, PRI_j, Pulsenum_j] \tag{5}$$

Where: $Toastart_j$, $Toaend_j$ and $Pulsenum_j$ are respectively the starting time, ending time and pulse number of the jth pulse group.

3.3 Work Mode Level Modeling

When modeling the work mode of the radar, a plurality of pulse groups in a certain time interval are connected according to the start time, the level of the pulse train's work mode can be expressed as:

$$MODE = [CPI_1, CPI_2, \ldots, CPI_m] \tag{6}$$

According to the analysis of work mode in Sect. 2, to realize the recognition of work mode, we only need to analyze the time regularity of signal's amplitude intercepted by intelligence aircraft. Therefore, the amplitude among the ranking information of the work mode should be sampled, and the sampling frequency is 1024 Hz. After the pulse multi-level modeling, we could convert the sequence of intercepted pulse description words into the change law with time of amplitude of intercepted signal.

4 Adaptive Stacked Denoising Autoencoder

4.1 Stacked Denoising Auto-Encoder

Although traditional autoencoder (AE) can minimize reconstruction error between input and its feature representation, however, we cannot guarantee our autoencoder extract useful features of the input x. To avoid this phenomenon, denoising autoencoder (DAE) was proposed which can extract robust and useful structure of the corrupted input $\tilde{x}$, using a mapping $\tilde{x} = q_D(\tilde{x}|x)$. Then we get the hidden representation y with the traditional autoencoder:

$$y = f_\theta(\tilde{x}) = s(W\tilde{x} + b) \tag{7}$$

In which W is the weight matrix between input and its corresponding hidden representation, b is the offset vector. We can also get reconstructed version of the original input using y:

$$z = g_{\theta'}(y) = s(W'y + b') \tag{8}$$

Unlikely autoencoder, denoising autoencoder trys to reconstruct the uncorrupted input from corrupted one. Thus features learnt by denoising autoencoder is more essential and robust, Fig. 1 describes the structure of DAE. By stacking all trained denoising autoencoders, a deep network called stacked denoising autoencoders (SDA) is created.

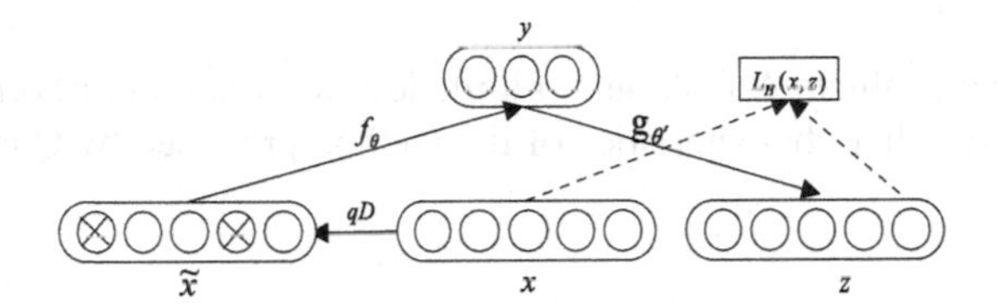

Fig. 1. The structure of DAE

4.2 Adaptive Stacked Denoising Auto-Encoder

When using the Stacked Denoising Autoencoder (SDA), noise level of each layer is kept fixed during the training phase, this actually limit the effect of SDA. Qualities experiment show that optimizing noise level gives better accuracy. To select a suitable noise level, Fig. 2 first depicts the effect of different noise level on search accuracy and auto encoder learning.

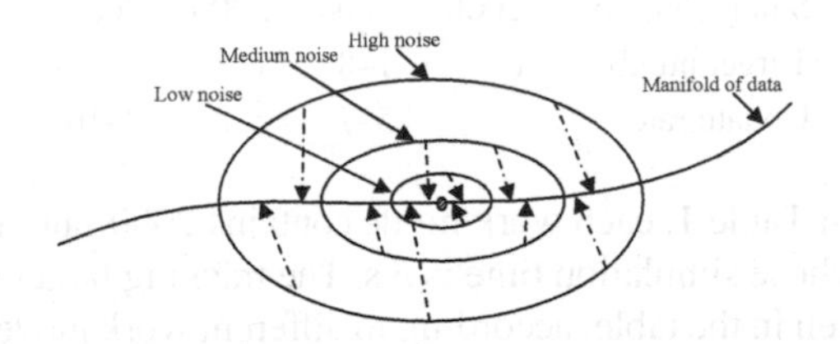

Fig. 2. Effect of noise on search neighborhood and search accuracy. When high noise level is chosen, many values of the input is forced to 0, so the auto encoder is obliged to reconstruct the original data using only few variables. Thus it is forced to learns only general features about the input to minimize the reconstruct error. On the contrary, with low noise, auto encoder can use more input features to reconstruct the clean input, so it is can learns more detail features compared with high noise level [7].

Inspired by the effect of different noise on autoencoder learning, an adaptive noise procedure is proposed in SDA called Adaptive Stacked Denoising auto-encoder (ASDA). During N epochs, average noise level T of ASDA is slowly decreased, from a high noise hyper-parameter A to a low noise hyper-parameter B as given by (9).

$$T(E) = A - (A - B) * \frac{E - 1}{N - 1} \tag{9}$$

We also know that the weight of outgoing connections can reflected its contribution to the activation of hidden neurons, to ensure the autoencoder learn useful and robust features, all the neurons should devote to active hidden neurons equally. So neurons whose outgoing weights is higher than the sum of others should have higher probability to be turned off. The algorithm for ASDA is given by Chandra B [10].

5 Experiment Results and Analysis

In this section, we evaluate ASDA on work mode recognition of airborne phased array radar, and analyze other characteristics of the method proposed by Qualitative experiments.

5.1 Data Source

Due to the particularity of the radar work mode recognition, there is no public data set at present. Therefore, we take confrontation among the aerial mobile platforms as background, uses Matlab simulation software to generate 4000 sample data, assumes that they are produced by airborne multi-function radar in different work modes and intercepted by intelligence aircraft, as shown in Table 1.

Table 1. Data samples of radar

Work mode	TWS	TAS	MTT	STT
Sample number	2000	2000	2000	2000
Target number	0	1–8	1–8	1
Update rate	–	5–7	6–8	7–10

As can be seen in Table 1, each work mode contains 2000 samples, each contains a sequence of PDW whose simulation time is 5 s. The tracking target number and update rate are chosen as seen in the table, according to different work modes. Since the update rate under TWS related to its searching space, so it is hard to give a specific value, but the update rate under TWS is usually very low, such as 0.5 Hz.

5.2 Multi-level Modeling

Scenario 1 is the PDW intercepted by intelligence aircraft, here airborne phased array radar is working in MTT mode while tracking 3 targets as shown in Fig. 3.

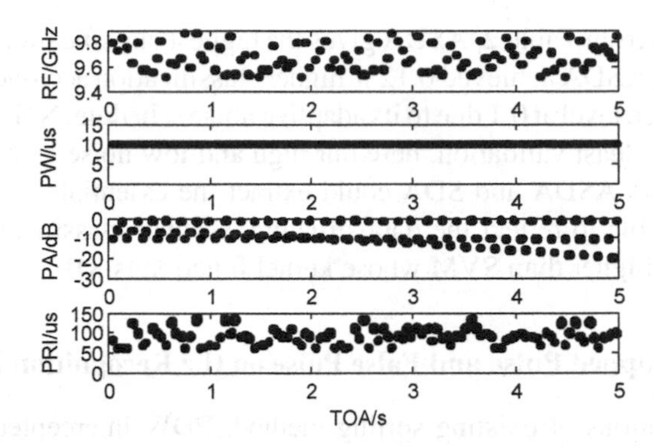

Fig. 3. Time regularity of pulse's amplitude intercepted by intelligence aircraft

According to the multi-level modeling method in Sect. 3, we can model the first pulse received by intelligence aircraft in Fig. 3 as $Y(1) = [38305, 9.8, 10, -9.8, 81.1]$. Similarly, we can model the first pulse group intercepted by intelligence as: $CPI_1 = [38205, 58994, 9.8, 10, -9.9, 81.2]$. In the same way, all the pulse train received can be modeled, $MODE = [CPI_1, CPI_2, \cdots, CPI_{106}]$.

According to the method of pulse multi-level modeling and sampling in Sect. 3, we can convert each sample in Sect. 5.1 to a pulse-amplitude sequence whose sampling frequency is 1024 Hz. Convert signals from the time domain to the frequency domain by FFT, with 4096 sampling points, and take the results as the input of ASDA.

5.3 Training ASDA Network

Using ASDA network to learn useful features from sample data without supervision learning. The first hidden layer has 500 units, the second hidden layer has 50 units, the number of iterations of each layer is 100, learning rate is set to 1, take Sigmoid as the activation function. Stack the 2 trained DAE leads to SDA, add output layer to the top layer of the SDA network, using the Softmax classifier.

5.4 Performance of ADSA Compared with SDA and SAE

To compare the classification results of different methods, select ASDA, SDA and SVM in our experiment. Parameters setting such as the hidden layer units, number of iterations, classifier are in Sect. 5.3. Each sample contains 4096 sampling points. Results of the experiment are shown in Table 2.

Table 2. Classification results of different training models

Method	Classification accuracy (%)
ASDA	96.68
SDA	96.56
SVM	82.55

As can be seen from Table 2, ASDA gives the highest classification accuracy among the three methods, ASDA achieved 0.12 % higher classification accuracy than SDA with optimum fixed noise level at 0.1 due to its adaptive noise schedule. Noise levels of ASDA is chosen based on least validation, here our high and low noise level are respectively 0.25 and 0.05. Also ASDA and SDA could extract the essential characters which are more robust and able to reflect the data structure, so their classification accuracy are 14.13 %, 14.01 % higher than SVM whose kernel function is RBF.

5.5 Effect of Dropped Pulse and False Pulse on the Recognition Result

Due to the Limitations of existing sorting method, PDW intercepted by aircraft will contain a certain proportion of dropped pulses and false pulses inevitably. To study the effect of dropped pulse and false pulse on the recognition results, the concept of RDP (Ratio of Dropped Pulses) and RFP (Ratio of False pulses) is defined:

$$RDP = \frac{n}{N} \times 100\,\% \tag{10}$$

$$RFP = \frac{\varepsilon}{N} \times 100\,\% \tag{11}$$

The number of the pulse train without noise is N, the number of the pulses randomly dropped out and added are expressed as n and ε respectively.

For the sake of analysis, we assume that ratio of dropped pulses is consistent with ratio of false pulses. Results of the experiment are shown in Fig. 4.

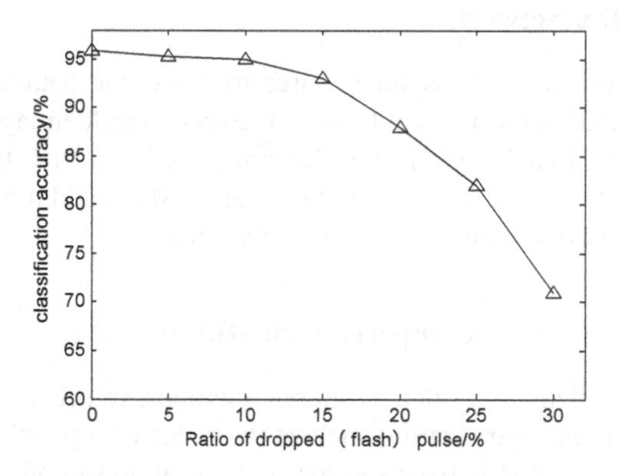

Fig. 4. The effect of dropped pulse (false) pulse

As can be seen from Fig. 4, when dropped pulses (false pulses) ratio is more than 15 %, classification accuracy decreased rapidly. When the ratio is less than or equal to 15 %, the recognition rate remain the same. It is shown that the proposed algorithm is insensitive to dropped pulses and false pulses. Reasons are as follows: (1) after multi-level modeling of the pulses, even if there exists a small amount of dropped pulses and false pulses in the ranking information of the pulse, it would not have any great impact on the ranking information of the pulse, namely the input of SDA is basically unchanged. (2) After learning the input containing noise superimposed, ASDA could extract the essential character of the sample data, and restrains the noise effectively.

5.6 Comparison of ADSA with Different Sample Length

In electronic warfare, we hope to identify work mode of radar with fewer pulses, so as to get initiative of war. Due to the complexity of the radar system, it is difficult to give a precise value of how many pulses are needed. In our experiments, Fewer pulses mean fewer sampling points (sampling frequency is fixed). To study the effect of different sample length, numbers of sampling points in our experiment are changing from 4096 (2^{12}) to 128(2^7), results are shown in Fig. 5.

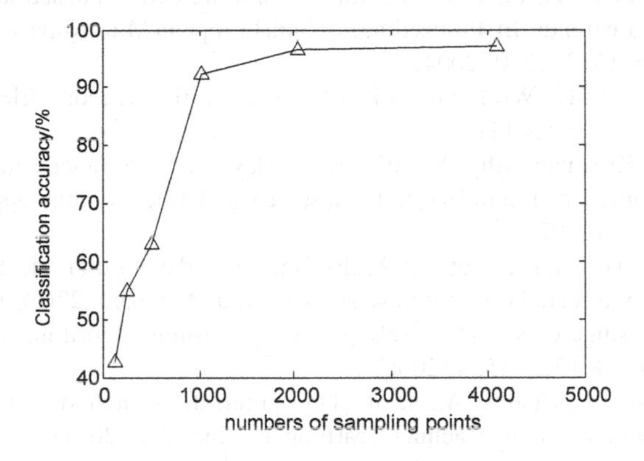

Fig. 5. The effect of different sampling length

As can be seen in Fig. 5, when numbers of sampling points is too few, such as 512, as numbers decrease, classification accuracy also decreased sharply. This indicate that ASDA can not learned essential characteristics with this sample length, more information (pluses) are needed to. However, sampling points is enough, such as more than 1024, classification accuracy increased just slightly, for the reason that ASDA has learned enough useful features with this sample length, more information just help a little. Usually, fewer pluses mean fewer information.

6 Conclusions and Future Work

In this paper, the pulse multi-level modeling method has been proposed to get the expression of intercepted pulses at level of work mode, then we apply ASDA in the learning and identification of airborne active phased array radar under different work modes. ASDA achieves higher classification accuracy than SDA, for it overcomes the limitation of SDA in which noise level is kept fixed. In addition, our method shows insensitivity to dropped pulses and false pulses owing to multi-level modeling and

ASDA. The proposed method can extract the essential characteristics of airborne phased array radar under different modes.

The effects of different hidden layers and its units on the feature learning ability of ASDA are not researched in depth in this article. At present, the selection of those parameters mainly depends on experience, how to select the appropriate network parameters is key for the further work.

References

1. Farina, A., Holbourn, P., Kinghorn, T., Timmoneri, L.: AESA radar-pan-domain multifunction capabilities for future systems. In: 2013 IEEE International Symposium on Phased Array Systems & Technology, Boston, October 2013
2. Hommel, H., Feldle, H.-P.: Current status of airborne active phased array (AESA) radar systems and future trends. In: Proceedings of 34th European Microwave Conference, October 2004, vol. 3, pp. 1517–1520 (2004)
3. Jia, C.-W., Zhou, S.-L.: Work mode identification of airborne radar. Electron. Inf. Warfare Technol. **26**(1), 14–16 (2011)
4. Visnevski, N., Krishnamurthy, V., Wang, A., Haykin, S.: Syntactic modeling and signal processing of multifunction radars: a stochastic context-free grammar approach. Proc. IEEE **95**(5), 1000–1025 (2007)
5. Liu, H.D., Yu, H., Sun, Z., et al.: Multi-function radar emitter identification based on stochastic syntax-directed translation schema. Chin. J. Aeronaut. **27**(6), 1505–1512 (2014)
6. Hinton, G.E., Osindero, S., Whye Teh, Y.: A fast learning algorithm for deep belief nets. Neural Comput. **18**, 1527–1554 (2006)
7. Le, Q.V., Ngiam, J., Coates, A., et al.: On optimization methods for deep learning. In: International Conference on Machine Learning, pp. 265–272 (2011)
8. Vincent, P., Larochelle, H., Lajoie, I., et al.: Stacked denoising auto-encoders: learning useful representations in a deep network with a local denoising criterion. J. Mach. Learn. Res. **11**, 3371–3408 (2010)
9. Vincent, P., Larochelle, H., Bengio, Y., et al.: Extracting and composing robust features with denoising auto-encoders. In: Proceedings of the 25th International Conference on Machine Learning (2008)
10. Chandra, B., Sharma, R.K.: Adaptive noise schedule for denoising autoencoder. In: Loo, C.K., Yap, K.S., Wong, K.W., Teoh, A., Huang, K. (eds.) ICONIP 2014, Part I. LNCS, vol. 8834, pp. 535–542. Springer, Heidelberg (2014)

Simulation Methodology Used in Computer Structure Course

Han Wan, Xiaopeng Gao(✉), and Xiang Long

School of Computer Science and Engineering, Beihang University, Beijing, China
{wanhan,gxp,long}@buaa.edu.cn

Abstract. We describe our reformed Computer Structure course at Beihang University, which won the national teaching achievement award. In this course, we use simulation methodology to help students in understanding the MIPS system. We show how to use MARS to help student grasp the MIPS instruction set and how to use Logisim for the single cycle processor design from sketch. Then we use the ISE to design the pipelined processor, and use FPGA board to evaluate the system design with interruption. The comparisons in terms of excellent rates, pass rates and learning assessments, had shown the blending learning experience with simulation methodology had more rewarding for students.

Keywords: MARS · Logisim · ISE · Simulation methodology · Computer structure course

1 Introduction

Computer Structure is a second-year course offered in School of Computer Science and Engineering at Beihang University. In this course, students need to write a MIPS CPU using Verilog-HDL. The course reform continued in Summer 2013, Fall 2014 and Fall 2015, which had been rewarded by national teaching achievement prize, mainly referenced to the CS61C course at Berkeley [1] and 6.823 computer system architecture course [2] at MIT. We mainly focus on design the pipelined MIPS processor, and using simulation methodology to help students from the module design to the system design.

2 Simulation Methodology Used in the Course

In the Computer Structure Course, students learned the computer structure and assembly language based on MIPS instruction set. The lab need students to implement the MIPS instructions of the Instruction Set Architecture (ISA) using Verilog-HDL. Work could be divided into two parts, one part is to build the 'Datapath' and another part is about the 'Control'. Datapath is the part of the processor which contains the hardware necessary to perform operations required by the processor. And Control is the part of the processor which tells the data path what needs to be done.

We redesigned our course in 2013 according to the two parts work when building the processor. In week 1 and week 2, students need to finish the basic Verilog-HDL

L. Zhang et al. (Eds.): AsiaSim 2016/SCS AutumnSim 2016, Part I, CCIS 643, pp. 237–244, 2016.
DOI: 10.1007/978-981-10-2663-8_25

practices in order to master the language grammars and could evaluate their projects using testbench. They need to know how to code and debug assembly programs in MARS [3] during week3. In the next week, the students using Logisim [4] to help themselves in setting up circuits from sketch. At the end of week 4, they need to finish the design of single cycle CPU which supports the MIPS-Lite1 instructions- {addu, subu, ori, lw, sw, beq, lui}. After that, they need to construct a single cycle CPU using Verilog-HDL support MIPS-Lite2 instructions. Here MIPS-Lite2 instructions just added {addi, addiu, slt, j, jal, jr} into MIPS-Lite1 instructions.

From week 6 to week 7, students learned how to design the multi-cycle CPU to support more than 40 instructions. And in week 8 to week 11, they need to build a MIPS micro-system with serial ports and support interrupts.

2.1 Golden Model for MIPS Simulator- MARS

As shown in Fig. 1, MARS is an IDE for MIPS Assembly Language Programming. Students could compose their assembly language program using the editor, assemble it, and then execute all at once or step by step. 'Text Segment' displays both the source and binary code of the assembly program. A breakpoint could be set using the check box in the leftmost column. At the bottom of MARS, 'Data Segment' shows the program's data storage area. In the Labels window, symbol table information is displayed. On the right-side to the 'Execute' pane displays 'Registers' including general purpose registers, the floating point registers of Coprocessor 1 and the exception

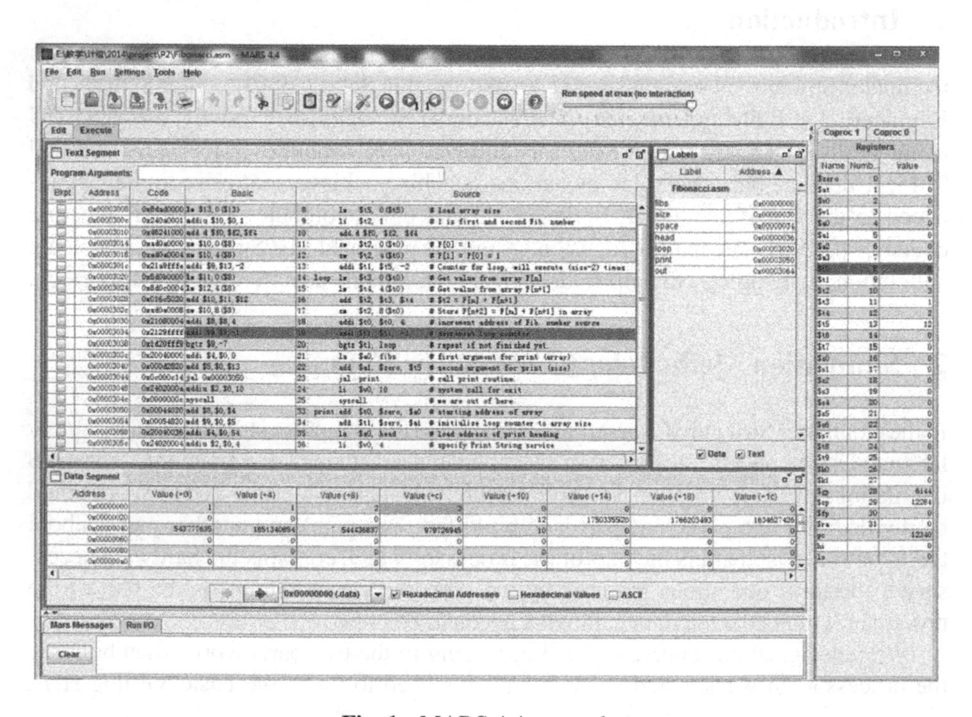

Fig. 1. MARS 4.4 screenshot

registers of Coprocessor0. In the lower portion of the screen is the console window, it shows the messages such as assembly errors and I/O generated by MIPS system calls.

We used MARS as the golden model to evaluate whether the processor that the student built in Logisim or ISE is correct. Using this tool, students can execute the assembly program in single-step to observe all the components' change after one instruction is executed. The same assembly programs ran on each platform, when stepped in we compared the status of registers and memory in MARS with the processor built in Logisim, or the wave generated by the Verilog-HDL model also had been read to compare with the golden model. This aiding tool helped a lot to evaluate the design.

2.2 Graphical Tool for Simulating Logic Circuits - Logisim

Logisim is a graphical tool for designing and simulating digital logic circuits. We use it to facilitate learning the most basic concepts related to logic circuits. With the capacity to build larger circuits from smaller subcircuits, and to draw bundles of wires with a single mouse drag, Logisim can be used to design and simulate entire CPUs from basic logic circuits in sketch.

Figures 2 and 3 shown how to design ALU and IFU in Logisim from simple gates. The IFU model is used for fetch the instruction, and it included PC, IM (instruction memory). IFU could fetch the instructions in sequence or step into a branch.

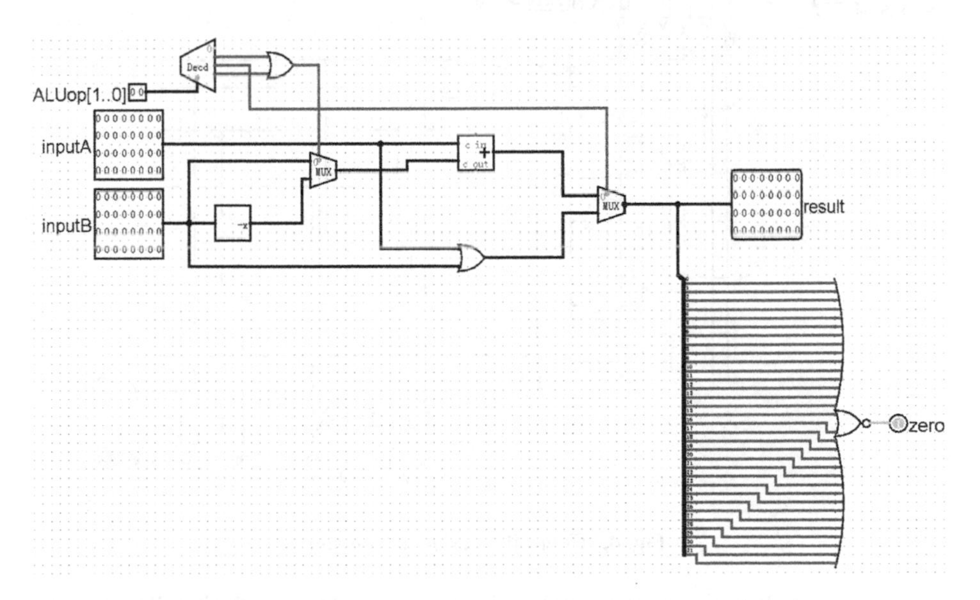

Fig. 2. ALU design in Logisim

When design the controller, as shown in Fig. 4, we used AND logic to generate instruction signals, and used OR logic to generate control signals. Using the similar method, we could construct the GPR file from the basic logic circuits.

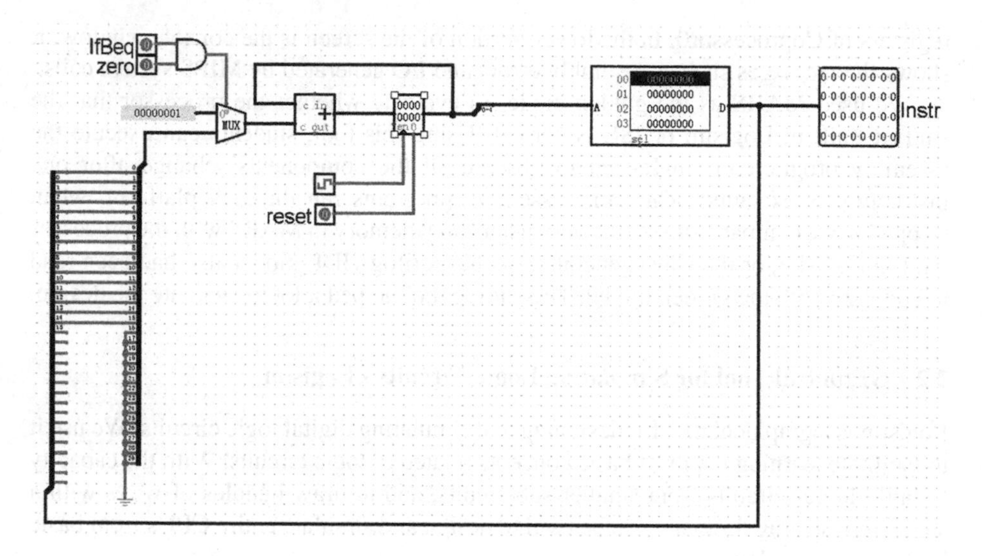

Fig. 3. IFU design in Logisim

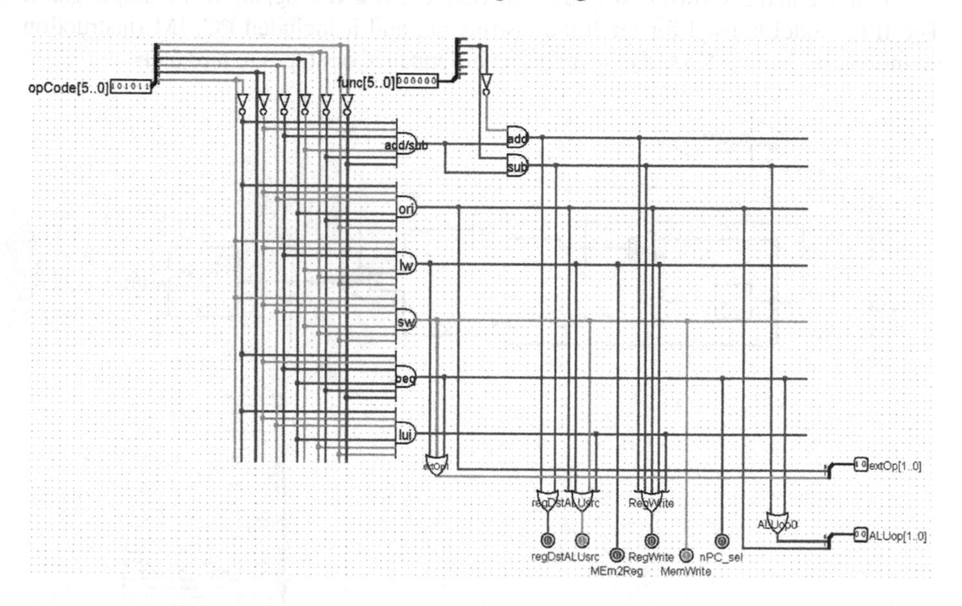

Fig. 4. Controller design in Logisim

As shown in Fig. 5, we can assemble all the component using the bundles of wires. When loading binary code into the instruction memory, students could execute the code step by step to see which signals are on during the execution. Usually, after the executed in each step, we need to compared the status of the whole processor with the golden model MARS.

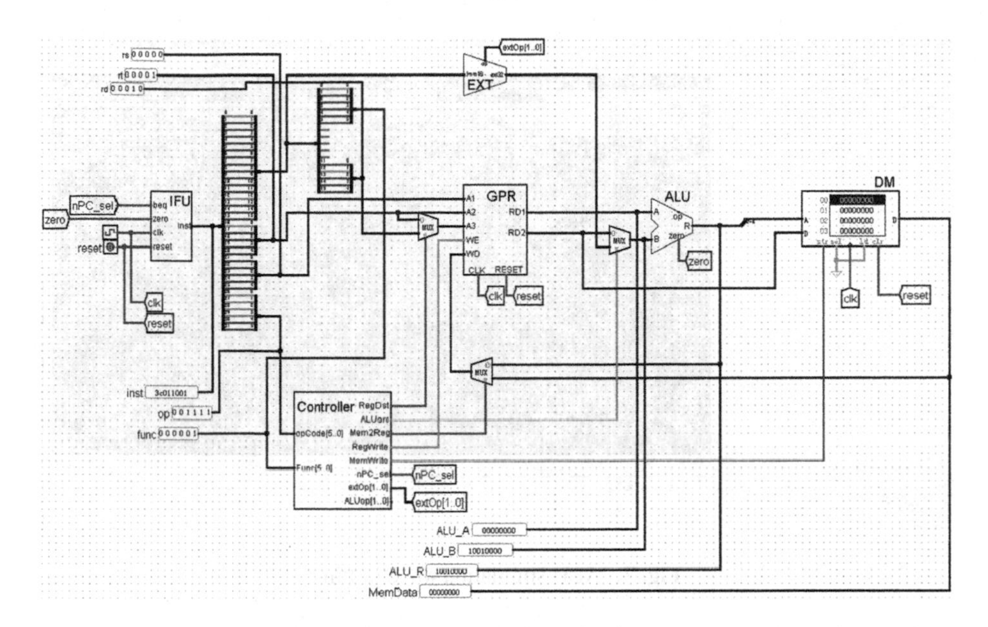

Fig. 5. Single cycle processor in Logisim

2.3 Verilog-HDL Model – ISE

As our object is to help the students in building a system with devices, we suggest the students using ISE to design the Verilog-HDL model. Figure 6 shown how to design ALU using Verilog-HDL.

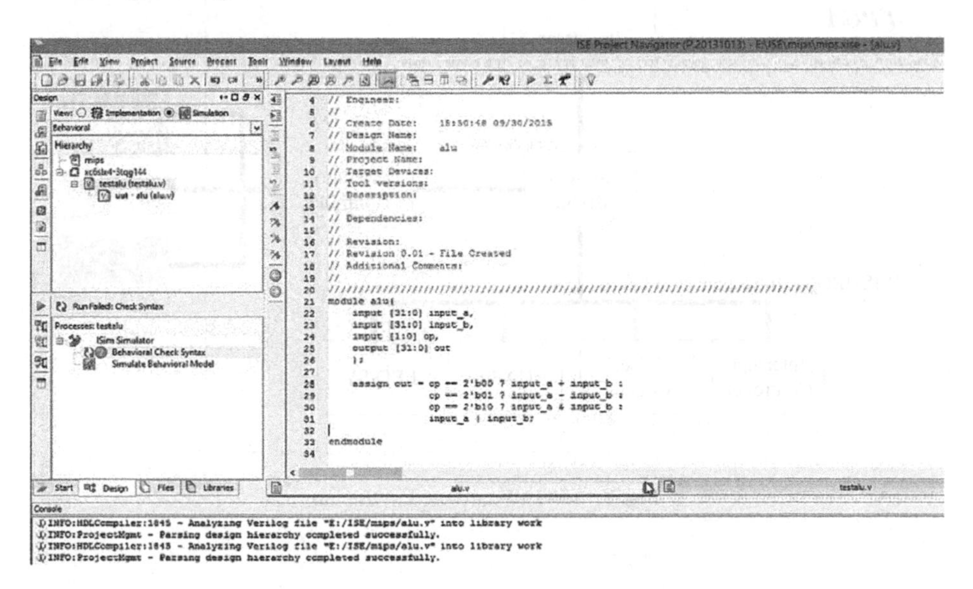

Fig. 6. ALU design using Verilog-HDL in ISE

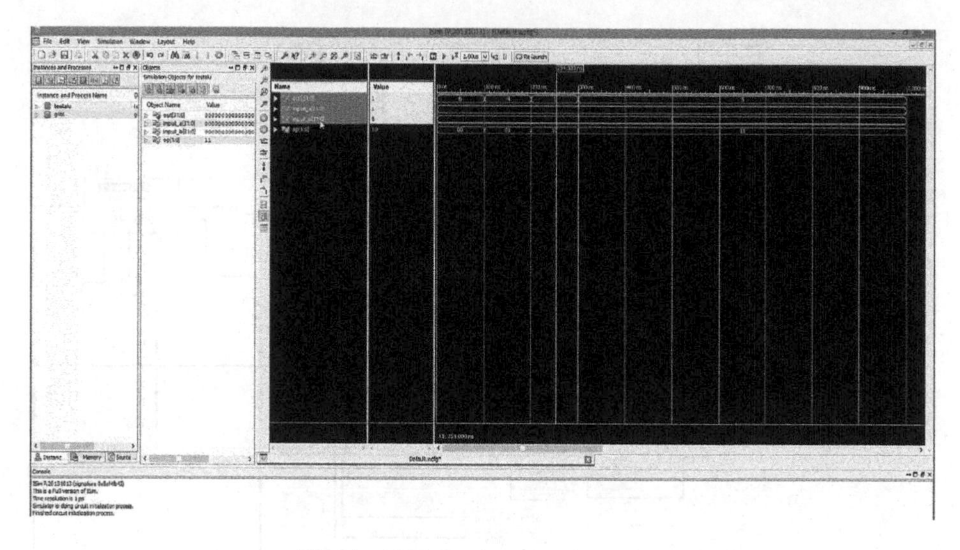

Fig. 7. ALU simulation wave in ISim

For each module, we could do the unit function test by reading the simulation wave, as shown in Fig. 7. Furthermore, the test process also need to do the comparison with the golden model MARS. Students could add the related variables in Verilog-HDL module into the observation list. When the simulation proceeds, the change of the variables' status should be the same with the golden model.

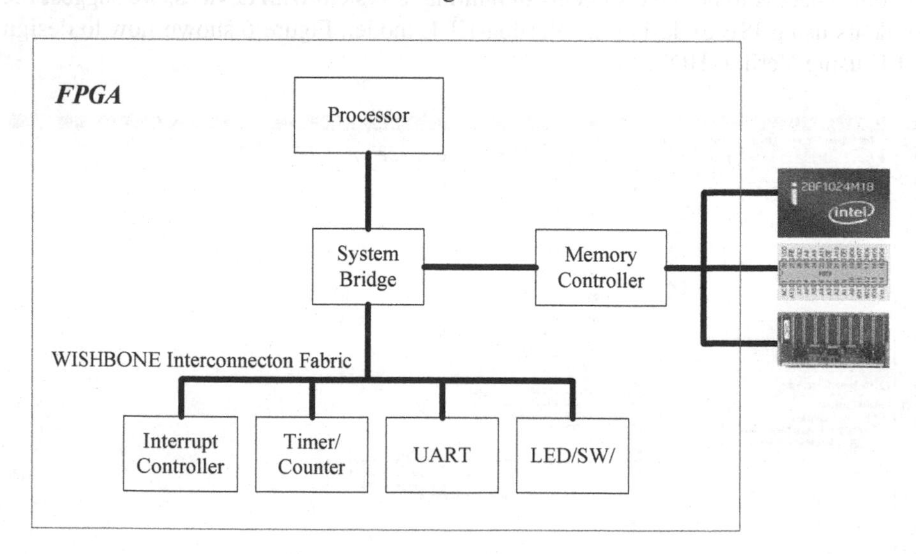

Fig. 8. FPGA board used in the lab

2.4 System Simulation – FPGA Board

When we doing the system design with interruption, the program would run much longer than the design of a simple processor component. It is hard to observe the whole simulation wave. In our course, we design a FPGA board to help in the system design and verification.

As shown in Fig. 8, all the processor components are integrated in this FPGA board, except the external memory, I/O and the network chip. Here external memory refers to FLASH, SRAM and SDRAM, and I/O refers to the keyboards, LED, parallel ports and serial ports. Students could download their design to the FPGA board, and the evaluation process in this method is much easier than observe the simulating wave in ISE.

3 Evaluation and Conclusion

As shown in Table 1, We define our grades according to the completion degree of project.

Table 1. Grade requirements in Summer 2013 and Fall 2014

Grade	Requirements	
	2013	**2014**
D	**Multi-cycle** CPU design using Verilog-HDL, supports the MIPS-Lite3 instructions: {addu, subu, ori, lw, sw, beq, lui, addi, addiu, slt, j, jal, jr, lb, lbu, lh, lhu, sb, sh, slti}	**Pipelined** processor design with full hazard handling, supports MIPS-Lite2 instructions,{addu, subu, ori, lw, sw, beq, lui, j, jal, jr}
C	Multi-cycle CPU design using Verilog-HDL, supports MIPS-C3 instructions: {MIPS-Lite3, SLL, SRL, SRA, SLLV, SRLV, SRAV, AND, OR, XOR, NOR, ORI, XORI, LUI, SLTI, SLTIU, BNE, BLEZ, BGTZ, BLTZ, BGEZ, JALR}	Pipelined processor design support MIPS-C3 instructions,MIPS-C3 instructions: {MIPS-Lite2, lb, lbu, lh, lhu, sb, sh, add, sub, mult, multu, div, divu, sll, srl, sra, sllv, srlv, srav, and, or, xor, nor, addi, addiu, andi, xori, slt, slti, sltiu, sltu, bne, blez, bgtz, bltz, bgez, jalr, mfhi, mflo, mthi, mtlo}
B	MIPS micro-system-V1 including MIPS-processor, UART and timer, supports MIPS-C3 instructions	MIPS micro-system-V1, supports exceptions and interrupts, micro-system including MIPS-processor, bridge and timer. Supports MIPS-C4 instructions: {MIPS-C3, ERET, MFC0, MTC0}
A	Based on MIPS micro-system-V1 with Uart, supports interrupts	Based on MIPS micro-system-V1, adds 8bit-LED segment, 32bit-toggle switch and RS232-communicate-system. Supports MIPS-C4 instructions

Students would get Grade 'D' if they could build a multi-cycle processor in 2013, while in 2014 they need to construct a pipelined processor. Instructor grades the student as 'Excellent' if they could pass the final project and answer questions clearly at the face-to-face stage.

We had 213 students in Summer 2013, 275 students in Fall 2014, and 264 students in Fall 2015. As shown in Fig. 9, our students had a better performance in Fall 2014 than Summer 2013, even it is much harder. The amount of students who are awarded of 'Excellent' in Fall 2014 is nearly 2 times the number in Summer 2013. 14.55 % of the students got 'Grade A' in Fall 2014 compared just 9.39 % in Summer 2013, and 17.05 % in Fall 2015. Students awarded with 'Grade B' from 21.60 % in Summer 2013 to 33.82 % in Fall 2014, and 47.73 % in Fall 2015.

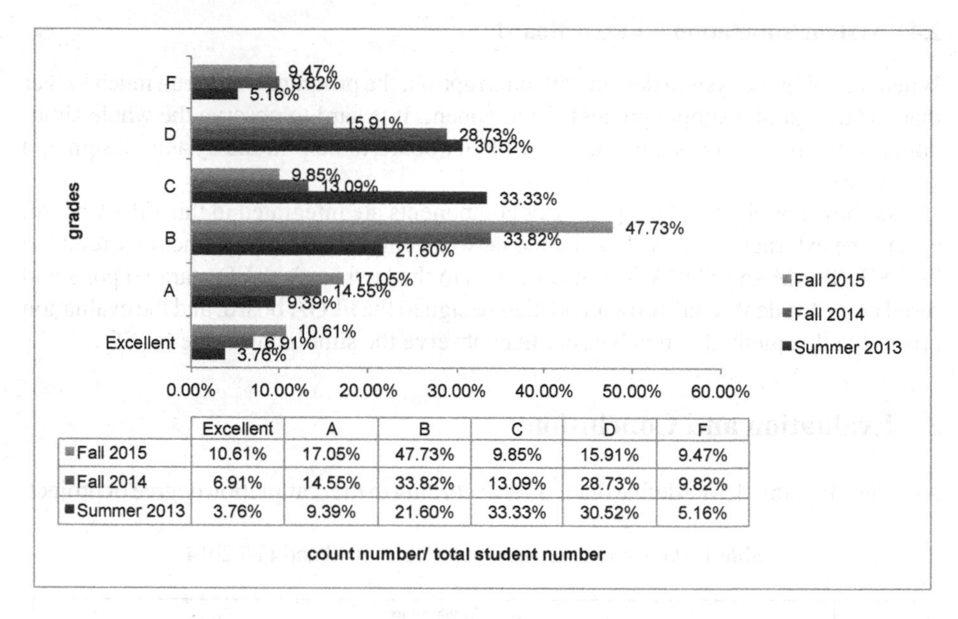

	Excellent	A	B	C	D	F
Fall 2015	10.61%	17.05%	47.73%	9.85%	15.91%	9.47%
Fall 2014	6.91%	14.55%	33.82%	13.09%	28.73%	9.82%
Summer 2013	3.76%	9.39%	21.60%	33.33%	30.52%	5.16%

Fig. 9. Grades distribution compared between Fall 2015, Fall 2014 and Summer 2013

We integrated an automatic testing system and virtual laboratory technique into the open-edX platform in 2015. Student upload their design to the automatic testing system, it will feedback whether they pass through with the error report. This testing system also helped in their self-test at home, resulting in better performance. With the learning-aid tools using simulation methodology, all these course designs empowered the students with the skills, information, and tools that they need to manage their own learning. The comparisons in terms of excellent rates, pass rates and learning assessments, had shown the simulation methodology used in Computer Structure Course had more rewarding for students.

Acknowledgment. Our thanks to the support from Computer Information Specialty Construction Foundation Grant (Beijing, China) - Curriculum design and MOOC development and China Scholarship Council (No. 201406025114).

References

1. Great Ideas in Computer Architecture (Machine Structures). Accessed inst.eecs.berkeley.edu/~cs61c/sp16
2. Computer System Architecture. Accessed csg.csail.mit.edu
3. MARS. http://courses.missouristate.edu/KenVollmar/mars
4. Logisim a graphical tool for designing and simulating logic circuits. Accessed http://www.cburch.com/logisim/

Legendre Collocation Spectral Method for Solving Space Fractional Nonlinear Fisher's Equation

Zeting Liu(✉), Shujuan Lv, and Xiaocui Li

School of Mathematics and Systems Science and LMIB,
Beihang University, Beijing 100191, China
lzt_well@163.com

Abstract. We consider the initial boundary value problem of the space fractional nonlinear Fisher's equations on the general interval (a,b) and the fractional derivative is described in Caputo sense, the boundary conditions are nonhomogeneous. A fully discrete Legendre collocation spectral approximation scheme is structured basing Legendre-Gauss-Lobatto points in space and backward difference in time. We also use the operational matrix of the fractional derivative. Numerical experiments are presented with comparisons between Legendre collocation spectral method and other methods, and the results show that Legendre collocation spectral method is an alternative method for solving Fisher's equation.

Keywords: Space fractional nonlinear Fisher's equations · Legendre collocation spectral method · Caputo derivative · Operational matrix

1 Introduction

Fractional differential equations (FDEs) have been found more realistic in modelling a variety of physical phenomena, engineering process, biological system and financial products, such as anomalous diffusion and non-exponential relaxation patterns [1]. Typically, such scenarios involve long-range temporal cumulative memory effects and/or long-range spatial interactions that can be more accurately described by fractionl-order models [2–4].

Much attention have been gained in FDEs, finding numerical methods to solve FDEs especially for the fractional calculus has been popular in the twenty-first century, such as finite difference/finite element methods [5–8], spectral method or spectal collocation method [9–13], variational iteration method [14–16], spline collocation method [17], and other numerical methods [18–20].

In this paper, we consider space fractional Fisher's equation

$$u_t - D^\alpha u - u(1-u) = g, \qquad x \in [a,b],\ 0 < t \le T, \tag{1}$$

L. Zhang et al. (Eds.): AsiaSim 2016/SCS AutumnSim 2016, Part I, CCIS 643, pp. 245–252, 2016.
DOI: 10.1007/978-981-10-2663-8_26

subject to the initial condition

$$u(x,0) = g_0(x), \quad x \in [a,b], \tag{2}$$

and boundary condition

$$u(a,t) = g_1(t), \;\; u(b,t) = g_2(t), \;\; 0 < t \leq T, \tag{3}$$

where α is a parameter describing the fractional order of the space derivative in the Caputo sense and $1 < \alpha \leq 2$, when $\alpha = 2$, (1) reduces to the classical Fisher's equation. g is known smooth function of x, t.

The Caputo definition of the fractional-order derivative is defined as

$$D^{\alpha} f(x) = \frac{1}{\Gamma(n-\alpha)} \int_a^x \frac{f^{(n)}(t)}{(x-t)^{\alpha+1-n}} \mathrm{d}t, \; n-1 < \alpha \leq n, \; n \in \mathbf{N},$$

where $\alpha > 0$ is the order of the derivative and n is the smallest integer greater than α. The Caputo fractional derivative is considered here because it allows traditional initial and boundary conditions to be included in the formulation of the problem.

Space fractional Fisher's equation has been studied by several researchers using different numerical methods, for example, GDTM and VIM methods [23], radial basis functions method [24] and Von Neumann method [25]. The three papers we mentioned above provide a method for solving the Fisher's equation which the exact solution is unknown, but there are no papers using Legendre collocation method for space fractional Fisher's equation as far as we know, that's our motivation of this paper.

An outline of this paper is as follows. We recall some properties about Legendre polynomials and introduce the shifted Legendre polynomials on a general intervals (a, b) instead of (−1,1) in Sect. 2. In Sect. 3, we build a linear fully discrete Legendre collocation spectral scheme. In Sect. 4, we make a comparison with GDTM and VIM method, the numerical results show that Legendre collocation spectral method is an alternative method for solving space fractional Fisher's equation.

2 Preliminaries

The well-known Legendre polynomials $L_j(z)$ are defined on the interval $[-1,1]$. In order to use Legendre polynomials on the more general interval $[a,b]$, we define the shifted Legendre polynomials by introducing the change of variable $z = \frac{2(x-a)}{b-a} - 1$. Set the shifted Legendre polynomials $L_j(\frac{2(x-a)}{b-a} - 1)$ be denoted by $L_{N,j}$.

As for $L_j(z)$ satisfy the following relation:

$$\int_{-1}^{1} L_j(z)L_k(z)\mathrm{d}z = h_j\delta_{jk}, \quad h_j = \frac{2}{2j+1},$$

where δ_{jk} is the Kronecker fuction. Then for the shifted Legendre polynomials $L_{N,j}$ we have

$$\int_{a}^{b} L_{N,j}(x)L_{N,k}(x)\mathrm{d}z = h_{N,j}\delta_{jk}, \quad h_{N,j} = \frac{b-a}{2}h_j = \frac{b-a}{2j+1}. \tag{4}$$

Now we introduce the Legendre-Gauss-Labatto quadratures in two different intervals $[-1,1]$ and $[a,b]$. Denoting by $x_j(x_{N,j})$ and $w_j(w_{N,j})$, $0 \leq j \leq N$, the nodes and Christoffel numbers of the standard (shifted) Legendre-Gauss-Labatto quadratures on the intervals $[-1,1]$ and $[a,b]$, respectively, then we have the following relations:

$$x_{N,j} = \frac{b-a}{2}(x_j+1)+a, \quad w_{N,j} = \frac{b-a}{2}w_j, \ 0 \leq j \leq N.$$

If P_N denotes the set all the polynomials of degree at most N, then it follows that for any $\phi(x) \in P_{2N-1}$ (cf. [21])

$$\int_{a}^{b} \phi(x)\mathrm{d}x = \frac{b-a}{2}\int_{-1}^{1} \phi(\frac{b-a}{2}(x+1)+a)\mathrm{d}x = \frac{b-a}{2}\sum_{j=0}^{N}\phi(\frac{b-a}{2}(x_j+1)+a)w_j$$
$$= \sum_{j=0}^{N}\phi(x_{N,j})w_{N,j}.$$

We define the discrete inner product and the norm as

$$(u,v)_N = \sum_{j=0}^{N} u(x_{N,j})v(x_{N,j})w_{N,j}, \quad \|u\|_N = (u,u)_N^{\frac{1}{2}}.$$

Thus we have

$$(u,v)_N = (u,v), \quad \forall u \cdot v \in P_{2N-1}.$$

We expand the numerical approximation in terms of shifted Legendre polynomials

$$u_N(x,t) = \sum_{j=0}^{N} \hat{u}_j(t)L_{N,j}(x). \tag{5}$$

Using (4) and the discrete inner product, we have

$$\hat{u}_j(t) = \frac{1}{\gamma_{N,j}}\sum_{i=0}^{N} L_{N,j}(x_{N,i})u_N(x_{N,i},t)w_{N,i}, \quad 0 \leq j \leq N, \tag{6}$$

where $\gamma_{N,j} = h_{N,j}$ for $0 \leq j \leq N-1$ and $\gamma_{N,N} = (L_{N,N}, L_{N,N})_N$. Substituting (6) into (5), we obtain

$$u_N(x,t) = \sum_{i=0}^{N} \Big(\sum_{j=0}^{N} \frac{1}{\gamma_{N,j}} L_{N,j}(x_{N,i}) L_{N,j}(x) w_{N,i} \Big) u_N(x_{N,i},t). \tag{7}$$

The operational matrix of derivative of shifted Legendre polynomials for fractional derivtive in Caputo sense are given by [22]:

$$D^{(\alpha)} = \begin{pmatrix} 0 & 0 & \cdots & 0 \\ \vdots & \vdots & \cdots & \vdots \\ 0 & 0 & \cdots & 0 \\ \sum_{k=\lceil\alpha\rceil}^{\lceil\alpha\rceil} \theta_{\lceil\alpha\rceil,0,k} & \sum_{k=\lceil\alpha\rceil}^{\lceil\alpha\rceil} \theta_{\lceil\alpha\rceil,1,k} & \cdots & \sum_{k=\lceil\alpha\rceil}^{\lceil\alpha\rceil} \theta_{\lceil\alpha\rceil,m,k} \\ \vdots & \vdots & \cdots & \vdots \\ \sum_{k=\lceil\alpha\rceil}^{i} \theta_{i,0,k} & \sum_{k=\lceil\alpha\rceil}^{i} \theta_{i,1,k} & \cdots & \sum_{k=\lceil\alpha\rceil}^{i} \theta_{i,m,k} \\ \vdots & \vdots & \cdots & \vdots \\ \sum_{k=\lceil\alpha\rceil}^{m} \theta_{m,0,k} & \sum_{k=\lceil\alpha\rceil}^{m} \theta_{m,1,k} & \cdots & \sum_{k=\lceil\alpha\rceil}^{m} \theta_{m,m,k} \end{pmatrix}, \tag{8}$$

where $\theta_{i,j,k}$ is given by

$$\theta_{i,j,k} = (2j+1) \sum_{l=0}^{j} \frac{(-1)^{i+j+k+l}(i+k)!(l+j)!}{(b-a)^{\alpha}(i-k)!k!\Gamma(k-\alpha+1)(j-l)!(l!)^2(k+l-\alpha+1)}.$$

Note that ceiling function $\lceil\alpha\rceil$ denotes the smallest integer greater than or equal to α, and in $D^{(\alpha)}$, the first $\lceil\alpha\rceil$ rows, are all zero.

3 Legendre Spectral Collocation Method for Space Fractional Fisher's Equation

Let τ be the step-size in variable t, $t_k = k\tau(k = 0, 1, \cdots, M; M = [T/\tau])$, $u^k = u(x, t_k)$. The fully discrete collocation method for (1) is:

$$\frac{u_N^k(x_n) - u_N^{k-1}(x_n)}{\tau} - D^{\alpha} u_N^k(x_n) - u_N^k(x_n) + u_N^{k-1^2}(x_n) = g^{k-1}(x_n), n = 1, 2, \cdots, N-1.$$

Using (7) and (8), we have

$$\begin{aligned} D^{\alpha} u_N^k(x_{N,n}) &= \sum_{i=0}^{N} \Big(\sum_{j=0}^{N} \tfrac{1}{\gamma_{N,j}} L_{N,j}(x_{N,i}) D^{\alpha} L_{N,j}(x_{N,n}) w_{N,i} \Big) u_N(x_{N,i},t) \\ &= \sum_{i=0}^{N} B_{ni} u_N(x_{N,i},t), \quad n = 0, 1, \cdots, N, \end{aligned}$$

where

$$B_{ni} = \sum_{j=0}^{N} \frac{1}{\gamma_{N,j}} L_{N,j}(x_{N,i}) \Big(\sum_{l=0}^{N} d_{jl} L_{N,l}(x_{N,n}) \Big) w_{N,i}$$
$$= \sum_{j=0}^{N} \sum_{l=0}^{N} \frac{1}{\gamma_{N,j}} L_{N,j}(x_{N,i}) D_{jl}^{(\alpha)} L_{N,l}(x_{N,n}) w_{N,i}.$$

Considering the boundary conditions (3), we assume that

$$b_n^k = B_{n0} g_1^k + B_{nN} g_2^k.$$

Thus we have the following linear algebraic equations:

$$(I + \tau(B(2:N, 2:N) + I))\mathbf{u}^k = \mathbf{u}^{k-1} - \tau({\mathbf{u}^{k-1}}^2 + \mathbf{b}^k + \mathbf{g}^{k-1})$$

where I is the identity matrix,

$$\mathbf{u}^k = [u_N^k(x_{N,1}), u_N^k(x_{N,2}), \cdots, u_N^k(x_{N,N-1})]^T$$

and

$$\mathbf{b}^k = [b_1^k, b_2^k, \cdots, b_{N-1}^k]^T, \quad \mathbf{g}^k = [g^k(x_{N,1}), g^k(x_{N,2}), \cdots, g^k(x_{N,N-1})]^T.$$

4 Numerical Results

In this Section, we present the numerical solution for space fractional Fisher's equation [25] with $\alpha = 1.5$, $[a, b] = [0.0125, 1.0125]$, $g = x^2$, $u(x, 0) = x$ and the boundary conditions:

$$g_1 \approx 0.0125(1+t) + 0.00609375t^2 - 0.082176t^3 - 0.0210541t^4 - 7.16634 \times 10^{-6} t^5,$$

$$g_2 \approx 1.0125(1+t) - 0.518906t^2 - 0.921366t^3 + 0.310529t^4 + 0.0845434t^5.$$

Like most of fractional partial differential equations, the solution of space fractional Fisher's equation is also unknown, therefore we must compare the solution with the known numerical methods such as $GDTM$ and VIM. In all experiments, we set $\tau = 0.1$ and $N = 16$ (Table 1).

From the above comparison, an almost good agreement between shifted Legendre collocation approximation scheme with the other methods is observable. In order to see the results clearly, we also present the Figs. 1 and 2 below.

Table 1. The comparison between present method and other existing methods for different t and x

x	t = 0.1			t = 0.2		
	Present method	GDTM	VIM	Present method	GDTM	VIM
0.012500	0.013727	0.013751	0.013727	0.014553	0.014724	0.014553
0.057060	0.070163	0.062894	0.062841	0.080514	0.068393	0.068023
0.166986	0.202602	0.184016	0.183927	0.234454	0.200657	0.200039
0.326412	0.378975	0.359254	0.359150	0.435632	0.390800	0.390102
0.512500	0.568692	0.563111	0.563047	0.643305	0.609825	0.609529
0.698587	0.753713	0.766216	0.766277	0.835611	0.825954	0.826436
0.858014	0.921463	0.939622	0.939876	1.003833	1.007826	1.010401
0.967940	1.050419	1.058861	1.059305	1.131201	1.132054	1.136316
1.012500	1.107671	1.107121	1.107656	1.187397	1.182081	1.187154
x	t = 0.1			t = 0.2		
	Present method	GDTM	VIM	Present method	GDTM	VIM
0.012500	0.014409	0.014895	0.014409	0.012677	0.013609	0.012676
0.057060	0.083140	0.072461	0.071401	0.073075	0.073726	0.071660
0.166986	0.245219	0.214976	0.213196	0.220030	0.224565	0.221074
0.326412	0.460381	0.417986	0.416090	0.426387	0.437062	0.433661
0.512500	0.684246	0.647999	0.647741	0.655775	0.672032	0.673200
0.698587	0.888877	0.870088	0.874150	0.877498	0.891793	0.904369
0.858014	1.062871	1.053921	1.064463	1.072687	1.067617	1.097053
0.967940	1.191386	1.177179	1.193983	1.219628	1.182069	1.227683
1.012500	1.247392	1.226327	1.246135	1.284323	1.226877	1.280226

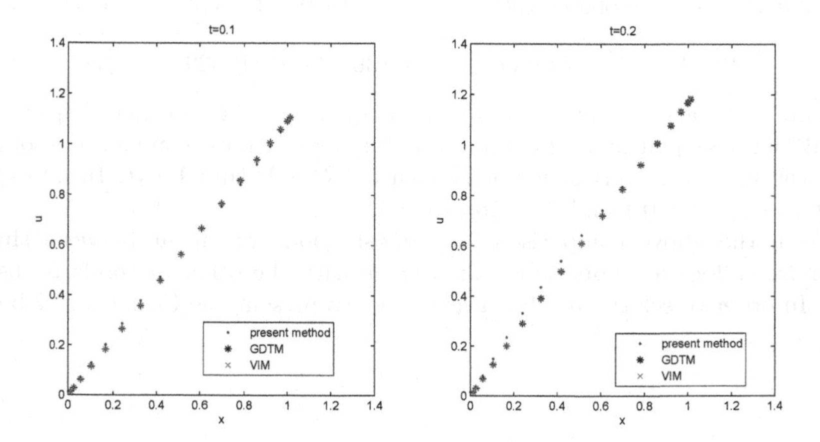

Fig. 1. The comparison between present method and other existing methods for different x at t = 0.1 s and t = 0.2 s, repetively.

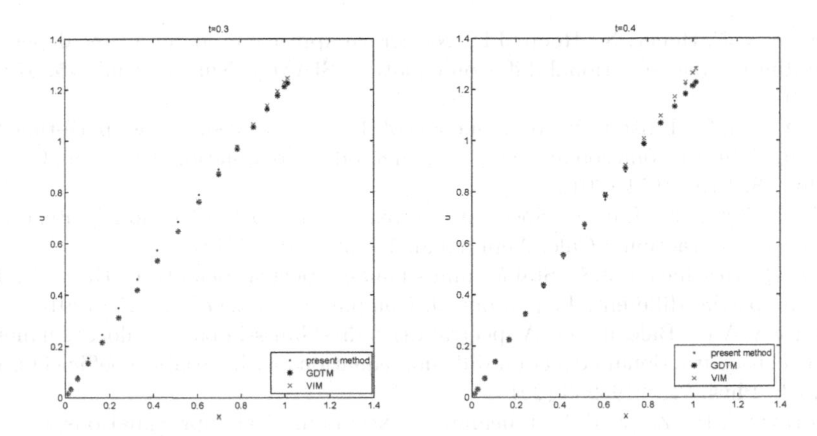

Fig. 2. The comparison between present method and other existing methods for different x at t = 0.3 s and t = 0.4 s, repetively.

5 Conclusion

In this paper, we use shifted Legendre collocation spectral method to solve space fractional Fisher's equation, an efficient numerical scheme is structured basing Legendre-Gauss-Lobatto points in space and backward difference method in timme, the numerical results are given to demonstrate the validity and applicability of the method and they also show that this method is simple and uses a few collocation points. This method can apply to other nonlinear or variable coefficients fractional partial differential equations.

Acknowledgements. This work is supported by the NSF of China (No. 11272024).

References

1. Metzler, R., Klafter, J.: The random walk's guide to anomalous diffusion: a fractional dynamics approach. Phys. Rep. **339**, 1–77 (2000)
2. Kilbas, A.A., Srivastava, H.M., Trujillo, J.J.: Theory and Applications of Frational Differential Equations. Elsevier Science B.V, Amsterdam (2006)
3. Diethelm, K.: The Analysis of Frational Differential Equations. Lecture Notes in Math. Springer, Berlin (2010)
4. Du, Q., Gunzburger, M., Lehoucq, R.B., Zhou, K.: Analysis anf approximation of nonlocal diffusion problems with volume constrains. SIAM Rev. **54**, 667–696 (2012)
5. Meerschaert, M.M., Tadjeran, C.: Finite difference approximations for fractional advection-dispersion flow equations. J. Comput. Appl. Math. **172**, 65–77 (2004)
6. Sun, Z., Wu, X.: A fully discrete difference scheme for a diffusion-wave system. Appl. Numer. Math. **56**, 193–209 (2006)
7. Meerschaert, M.M., Scheffler, H.P., Tadjeran, C.: Finite difference methods for two-dimensional fractional dispersion equation. J. Comput. Phys. **211**, 249–261 (2006)

8. Ervin, V.J., Heuer, N., Roop, J.P.: Numerical approximation of a time dependent, nonlinear, space-fractional diffusion equation. SIAM J. Numer. Anal. **45**, 572–591 (2007)
9. Li, X., Xu, C.: Existence and uniqueness of the weak solution of the space-time fractional diffusion equation and a spectral method approximation. Commun. Comput. Phys. **8**, 1016–1051 (2010)
10. Li, C., Zeng, F., Liu, F.: Spectral approximations to the fractional integral and derivative. Fractional Calc. Appl. Anal. **15**, 383–406 (2012)
11. Xu, Q., Hesthaven, J.S.: Stable multi-domain spectral penalty methods for fractional partial differential equations. J. Comput. Phys. **257**, 241–258 (2014)
12. Bhrawy, A.H., Baleanu, D.: A spectral Legendre-Gauss-Lobatto collocation method for a space-fractional advection diffusion equations with variable coefficients. Rep. Math. Phys. **72**, 219–233 (2013)
13. Bhrawy, A.H., Zaky, M.A., Baleanu, D.: New numerical approximations for space-time fractional Burgers equations via a Legendre spectral-collocation method. Rom. Rep. Phys. **2**, 1–11 (2015)
14. He, J.: A new approach to nonlinear partial differential equations. Commun. Nonlinear Sci. Numer. Simul. **2**, 230–235 (1997)
15. Onur, K., Ayşegül, Ç.: Variational iteration method for a class of nonlinear differential equations. Int. J. Contemp. Math. Sci. **5**, 1819–1826 (2010)
16. Giyas, M., Ergören, H.: Alternative variational iteration method for solving the time-fractional FornbergCWhitham equation. Appl. Math. Model. **39**, 3972–3979 (2015)
17. Pedas, A., Tamme, E.: Numerical solution of non-linear fractional differential equations by spline collocation methods. J. Comput. Appl. Math. **255**, 216–230 (2014)
18. Yi, M., Huang, J.: Wavelet operational matrix method for solving fractional differential equations with variable coefficients. Appl. Math. Comput. **230**, 383–394 (2014)
19. Agheli, B.: Solving fractional partial differential equation by using wavelet operational method. J. Math. Comput. Sci. **7**, 230–240 (2013)
20. Wang, L., Ma, Y., Meng, Z.: Haar wavelet method for solving fractional partial differential equations numerically. Appl. Math. Comput. **227**, 66–76 (2014)
21. Shen, J., Tang, T., Wang, L.: Spectral Methods: Algorithms Analysis and Applications. Springer, Heidelberg (2011)
22. Saadatmandi, A., Dehghan, M.: A new operational matrix for solving fractional-order differential eqautions. Comput. Math. Appl. **59**, 1326–1336 (2010)
23. Momania, S., Odibatb, Z.: A novel method for nonlinear fractional partial differential equations Combination of DTM and generalized Taylor's formula. J. Comput. Appl. Math. **220**, 85–95 (2008)
24. Vanani, S.K., Aminataei, A.: On the numerical solution of the fractional partial differential equations. Math. Comput. Appl. **17**, 140–151 (2012)
25. El-Danaf, T.S., Hadhoud, R.: Computational method for solving space fractional Fishers nonlinear equation. Math. Meth. Appl. Sci. **37**, 657–662 (2014)

Model Engineering for System of Systems

Research on Frequency-Converter Control Strategy Based on VSM Technology

Dong Weijie(✉), Meng Xiaoli, Liu Keyan, Song Xiaohui, Li Yajie, and Ye Xueshun

China Electric Power Research Institute, Beijing 100192, China
dongweijie163@163.com

Abstract. Frequency converter occupies a large proportion in production and daily life, in order to enable it to effectively take part in the process of system frequency regulation, a control strategy based on the virtual synchronous motor technology (VSM) is proposed in this paper. In the inverter part, VSM control strategy is used, using the mechanical inertia and electrical characteristics of the synchronous motor, the power control and frequency control are researched and designed respectively. The frequency converter are simulated under environment of Simulink/Matlab. Simulation results show that the proposed control strategy can make the frequency converter follow the characteristics of VSM, can change the inverter's output voltage and frequency with the change of motor load.

Keywords: Voltage control · Frequency converter · Power frequency control · Frequency adjustment · Virtual synchronous motor (VSM)

1 Introduction

As power Electronics developing rapidly, power electronic devices with flexible control strategy and low dissipation, which could be used for the control of active power, reactive power and power quality as needed, have been used for primary frequency regulation in two forms: distributed generation and power electronic load.

The Synchron-verter is introduced in references [1–3], which described Electromagnetic-mechanical model mathematically, simulated the characteristics of synchronous generator in frequency and excitation regulation, and verified its performance. Renewable power generators have been virtualized as Synchronous Generators with excellent inertial and damping characteristics in researches of Germany and Netherlands [4–6]. The new technology of Virtual Synchronous Generator (VSG) has been used in photovoltaic system in the Europe VSYNC Project [7]. A VSG embodiment with virtual inertial properties and a control strategy of VSG with voltage source has been studied [8]. The influences of the control strategy of Synchronverter on the Quality of Electric Power has been researched [9]. Technologies of VSG has been summarized in the reference [10]. An application strategy about using technologies of VSG has been proposed in micro grids [11]. Researchers about the strategies of voltage regulation and frequency control had focused [12–15]. Meanwhile, the stability of VSG has been studied in recent researches [16–18].

L. Zhang et al. (Eds.): AsiaSim 2016/SCS AutumnSim 2016, Part I, CCIS 643, pp. 255–261, 2016.
DOI: 10.1007/978-981-10-2663-8_27

Although it has these excellent performances, frequency converters have not been used like electric motors in the primary frequency regulation of power system. The technology of virtual synchronous motor (VSM) could be used in the frequency converter if the power stability is meeting problem. In that way, the frequency converter would be used in the primary frequency regulation with the load change. It must be good to the stability of power system.

Based on the analysis above, this paper builds a model of load containing frequency converter based on VSM technology. To participate in the primary frequency regulation, the power output of the model should change as the grid voltage and frequency changes, like external characteristics of synchronous motor. Furthermore, this paper proposes a control strategy of frequency converter based on VSM technology.

1.1 Mathematical Model of Inverter Based on VSM

The basic theory of VSM is to introduce the transient model of the rotor motion equation of the synchronous motor and the electrical equations of the stator into the controller, which make the frequency converter have the operation characteristic of the synchronous motor. In this paper, the classical two order electromechanical transient model is selected.

$$\dot{E}_0 = \dot{V} + \dot{I}R_a + j\dot{I}X_s \tag{1}$$

$$J\frac{\mathrm{d}\Omega}{\mathrm{d}t} = M_T - M_e \tag{2}$$

Among them: $\dot{E}_0$ – electromotive force (EMF) of the stator; $\dot{V}$ – terminal voltage of the stator; $\dot{I}$ – current of the stator; R_a – resistance of the stator; X_s – synchronous reactance; J – rotational inertia; Ω – mechanical angular velocity; M_T – mechanical torque; M_e – electromagnetic torque.

The relationship between electric angle and mechanical angle is $\omega = p\Omega$, Pole pair number is $p = 1$, The synchronous rotating shaft is used as the reference axis, and the formula (2) can be deformed, and the rotor motion equation expressed in the electric angle is obtained:

$$\begin{cases} J\frac{\mathrm{d}\omega}{\mathrm{d}t} = J\frac{\mathrm{d}(\omega - \omega_N)}{\mathrm{d}t} = M_T - M_e = \frac{1}{\omega}(P_T - P_e) \\ \omega = \frac{\mathrm{d}\theta}{\mathrm{d}t} \end{cases} \tag{3}$$

Among them: ω – electric angular velocity; ω_N – Synchronous electric angular velocity; P_T – mechanical power; P_e – electromagnetic power; θ – electric angle.

Unbalanced rotor motion equation represents the torque speed characteristics of the synchronous generator, determines the power output characteristics of the synchronous generator. In order to facilitate in the program to implement this equation, Eq. (3) can be transformed into:

$$\frac{\mathrm{d}(\omega-\omega_N)}{\mathrm{d}t}=\frac{1}{J\omega}(P_T-P_e) \tag{4}$$

$$\omega=\int\frac{1}{J\omega}(P_T-P_e)\mathrm{d}t+\omega_N \tag{5}$$

2 Design of Controller Based on VSM

2.1 Power Frequency Controller

According to the working principle of the synchronous motor, the power frequency controller of the virtual synchronous motor can be introduced. The input-output relationship can be described as:

$$P_\mathrm{T}=K_\mathrm{f}(f_\mathrm{N}-f_\mathrm{T})+P_\mathrm{N} \tag{6}$$

Among them: f_N is the system rated frequency; f_T is the measuring value of system frequency; K_f is the frequency coefficient; P_N is the system rated active power.

2.2 Excitation Controller

The excitation current of the synchronous motor directly determines the voltage and reactive power, so the output voltage of the synchronous motor is related to the internal voltage and the reactive power. The voltage variable of the voltage controller can be composed of two parts:

$$E=E_V+E_Q \tag{7}$$

Internal voltage regulation:

$$E_V=K_V(V_\mathrm{N}-|V|) \tag{8}$$

Internal voltage regulation caused by reactive power:

$$E_Q=-K_QQ_\mathrm{e} \tag{9}$$

Among them: V_N – the rated voltage; $|V|$ – the actual load voltage; K_V – voltage adjustment coefficient; Q_e – load reactive power increment; K_Q – voltage regulation factor caused by reactive power.

According to the above principle, the control principle of the inverter side can be obtained as shown in Fig. 1.

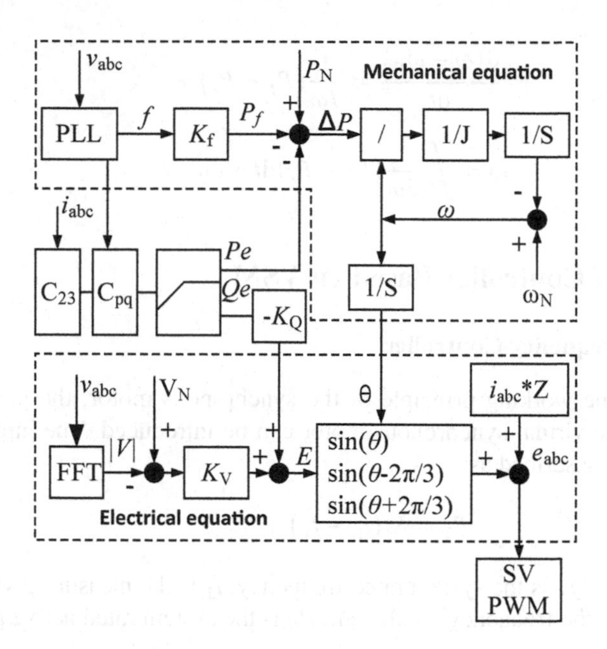

Fig. 1. Inverter control diagram

3 Simulation and Experiment

In order to verify the content of the research, the inverter controller model based on virtual synchronous motor theory is built in matlab/Simulink:

System parameters: line voltage Uabc = 380 V, rated frequency 50 Hz;

Converter parameters: output power rating 16 kW; rectifier side reactance: 1 mH; inverter output impedance is: L = 1 mH, R = 0.02; rated frequency 45 Hz; rated voltage 250 V; KV = 1.5; Kf = 10000; KQ = 0.01.

Inverter Side Control Simulation Based on VSM: Rated active load is 16 kV, when at 0.4 S, the active load increases 2 kW, at the time of 0.8 S, the active load decreases 3 kW. Rated reactive load is 5 kar, at the time of 1.2 S, reactive load increase 2 kVar, at the time of 1.6 S, reactive load decreases 3 kVar. As shown in Fig. 2 is the output power curve of inverter based on VSM, Fig. 3(a) shows the inverter output three-phase

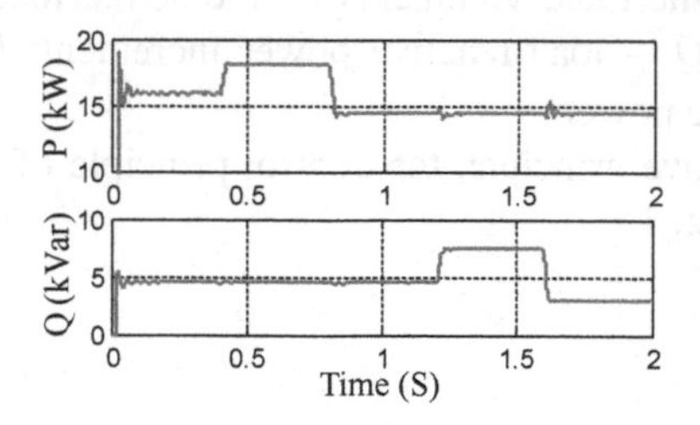

Fig. 2. Output power curve of inverter based on VSM

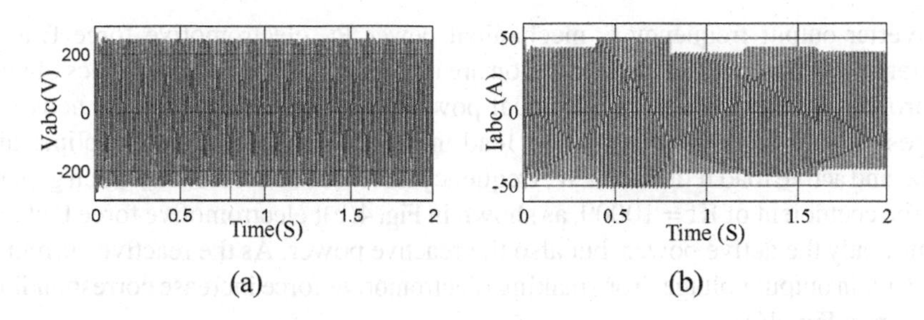

Fig. 3. Voltage and current curve of inverter output based on VSM

AC voltage curve of inverter based on VSM, Fig. 3(b) shows the three-phase current curve of inverter based on VSM. Obviously, the increase of reactive load and active load will increase the effective value of the current, and the output voltage will remain unchanged.

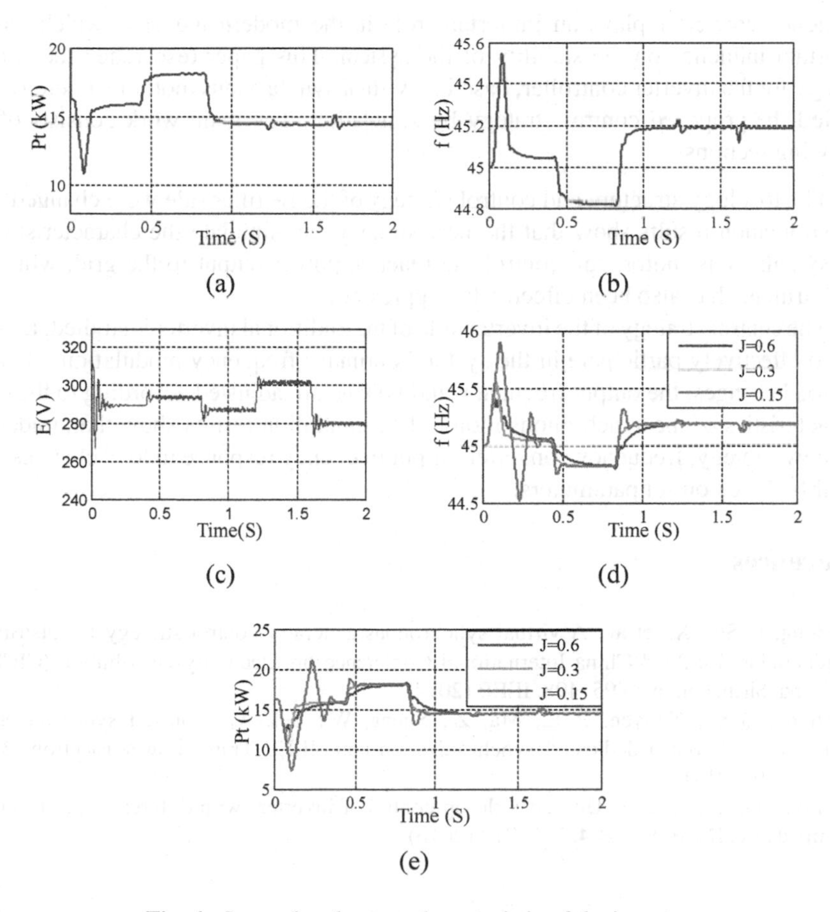

Fig. 4. Internal and output characteristic of the inverter

Inverter output frequency f, mechanical power Pt, electromotive force E are all associated with active load, their variation are the same with the characteristics of virtual synchronous motors. Which: mechanical power Pt can generally track the active load changes, as shown in Fig. 4(a); active load increases 2 kW, frequency declines about 0.2 Hz, and active load reduces 3 kW, frequency increases about 0.3 Hz, which generally meet the coefficient of Kf = 10000, as shown in Fig. 4(b); electromotive force E changes with not only the active power, but also the reactive power. As the reactive current will also result in output voltage drop, making electromotive force increase correspondingly, as shown in Fig. 4(c).

Virtual synchronous motor inertia coefficient J on its running state has a significant effect, for the change of the load, respectively, using J = 0.6, J = 0.3, J = 0.15, output frequency f, mechanical torque Pt changes more and more slowly with J increases. Figures 4(d) and (e).

4 Conclusions and Future Work

Frequency converter plays an important role in the modern industry, which has an important influence on the stability of the system. This paper researched the control strategy for the inverter controller, based on virtual synchronous motor technology, and verified the proposed control strategy by simulation. The main work consists of the following sections:

(1) The topology structure and control strategy of the rectifier side were changed. The simulation results show that the new strategy can simulate the characteristics of synchronous motor, can control the reactive power output to the grid, while the harmonic has also been effectively suppressed;
(2) The control strategy of the inverter side of the traditional inverter is studied. In order to effectively participate in the system's primary frequency modulation, after the load changes, the output frequency and voltage are adjusted according to the characteristics of the synchronous motor. The simulation results show that, under the new strategy, frequency converter output frequency response to load changes flexibly, based on set parameters.

References

1. Meng, J., Shi, X., et al.: A virtual synchronous generator control strategy for distributed generation. In: 2014 China International Conference on Electricity Distribution (CICED), China, Shenzhen, pp. 495–498. IEEE (2014)
2. Zhong, Q.-C., Nguyen, P.-L., Ma, Z., Sheng, W.: Self-synchronized synchronverters: Inverters without a dedicated synchronization unit. IEEE Trans. Power Electron. **29**(2), 617–630 (2014)
3. Zhong, Q.C., Zeng, Y.: Universal droop control of inverters with different types of output impedance. IEEE Access **4**, 702–712 (2016)

4. Alipoor, J., Miura, Y., Ise, T.: Power moment of system stabilization using virtual synchronous generator with alternating inertia. IEEE J. Emerg. Sel. Top. Power. Electron. **3**(2), 451–458 (2015)
5. Lu, L.-Y., Chu, C.-C.: Consensus-based secondary frequency and voltage droop control of virtual synchronous generators for isolated AC Micro-Grids. IEEE J. Emerg. Sel. Top. Circ. Syst. **5**(3), 443–455 (2015)
6. Xiong, L., Zhuo, F., Wang, F., Liu, X., Chen, Y., Zhu, M., Yi, H.: Static synchronous generator model: a new perspective to investigate dynamic characteristics and stability issues of grid-tied PWM inverter. IEEE Trans. Power Electron. **31**(9), 6264–6280 (2016)
7. Liu, J., Miura, Y., Ise, T.: Comparison of dynamic characteristics between virtual synchronous generator and droop control in inverter-based distributed generators. IEEE Trans. Power Electron. **31**(5), 3600–3611 (2016)
8. Kwon, Y.C., Kim, S., Sul, S.K.: Voltage feedback current control scheme for improved transient performance of permanent magnet synchronous machine drives. IEEE Trans. Ind. Electron. **59**(9), 3373–3382 (2012)
9. Guan, M., Pan, W., Zhang, J., Hao, Q., Cheng, J., Zheng, X.: Synchronous generator emulation control strategy for voltage source converter (VSC) stations. IEEE Trans. Power Syst. **30**(6), 3093–3101 (2015)
10. Ashabani, M., Mohamed, Y.A.-R.I.: Novel comprehensive control framework for incorporating VSCs to smart power grids using bidirectional synchronous-VSC. IEEE Trans. Power Syst. **29**(2), 943–957 (2014)
11. Ashabani, M., Mohamed, Y.A.-R.I.: General interface for power management of micro-grids using nonlinear cooperative droop control. IEEE Trans. Power Syst. **28**(3), 2929–2941 (2013)
12. Vandoorn, T.L., Meersman, B., De Kooning, J.D.M., Vandevelde, L.: Directly-coupled synchronous generators with converter behavior in islanded microgrids. IEEE Trans. Power Syst. **27**(3), 1395–1406 (2012)
13. He, J., Li, Y.W., Bosnjak, D., Harris, B.: Investigation and active damping of multiple resonances in a parallel-inverter-based microgrid. IEEE Trans. Power Electron. **28**(1), 234–246 (2013)
14. Van, T.V., Visscher, K., Diaz, J., et al.: Virtual synchronous generator: an element of future grids. In: IEEE Innovative Smart Grid Technologies Conference Europe, Gothenburg, Sweden, pp. 1–7. IEEE (2010)
15. D'Arco, S., Suul, J.A.: Equivalence of virtual synchronous machines and frequency-droops for converter-based MicroGrids. IEEE Trans. Smart Grid **5**(1), 394–395 (2014)
16. Torres L, M.A., Lopes, L.A.C., Morán T, L.A., Espinoza C, J.R.: Self-tuning virtual synchronous machine: a control strategy for energy storage systems to support dynamic frequency control. IEEE Trans. Energy Convers. **29**(4), 833–840 (2014)
17. Zhipeng, L., Wanxing, S., Qingchang, Z., et al.: Virtual synchronous generator and its applications in micro-grid. Proc. CSEE **34**(16), 2951–2963 (2014). (in Chinese)
18. Shintai, T., Miura, Y., Ise, T.: Oscillation damping of a distributed generator using a virtual synchronous generator. IEEE Trans. Power Delivery **29**(2), 668–676 (2014)

Modeling and Analysis of Gyrowheel with Friction and Dynamic Unbalance

Qing Zhao(✉), Yu Yao, Xiaokun Liu, and Hui Zhao

Control and Simulation Center, Harbin Institute of Technology, Harbin 150001, China
majorzq@gmail.com

Abstract. Gyrowheel is an integrated servo device which is applied as both sensor and actuator in micro-spacecraft. In practice, the undesirable mechannical factors generated from manufacturing could effect the accuracy of measurement and actuating, so it is necessary to analyze these undesirable effects on Gyrowheel for diagnosing the kind of mechannical errors even providing a sort of restraining method. In this paper, two common undesirable mechannical factors, the friction of the universal joint cross and the dynamic unbalance of rotor, are described in the Gyrowheel model built by Matlab/SimMechanics. The tilt angles response of the rotor in both time and frequency domains are developed in this paper, which provides simulation foundation and error analysis criterion for Gyrowheel prototype testing.

Keywords: Gyrowheel · Undesirable mechannical factor · Friction · Dynamic unbalance

1 Introduction

Micro-spacecraft is one of advanced research hotspots, which can execute certain special tasks like monitoring and attack. Attitude control system (ACS) is an important component of spacecraft, which is mainly consisted of sensors, controllers and actuators. For micro-spacecrafts, function integration of sensors and actuators can greatly reduce the mass and volume of ACS, while the attitude control function is maintained [1].

Under the guidance of function integration, the concept of Gyrowheel (GW) [2] was proposed in 1999 by Bristol Aerospace Ltd. in Canada. Motived by the structure of dynamically tuned gyroscope (DTG) [3], GW was developed physically. Differing from DTG, GW has to operate in large tilt angles and time-varying rotation speed to provide three-dimensional output torques, the small tilt angle assumption is not suitable for GW system modeling, which requires the full GW system model with large tilt angle assumption. Above all, GW can not only realize the two-dimensional angular rates measurement like DTG, but also provide three-dimensional control torque outputs by adjusting the motor

Q. Zhao—Ph. D. candidate at the School of Astronautics, Harbin Institute of Technology. His current research is control problem of GyroWheel.

L. Zhang et al. (Eds.): AsiaSim 2016/SCS AutumnSim 2016, Part I, CCIS 643, pp. 262–271, 2016.
DOI: 10.1007/978-981-10-2663-8_28

speed and tilting the rotor spin axis like variable-speed double-gimbal control moment gyroscope (VSDGCMG) [4].

Like other precision instrument, undesirable mechanical factors from GW manufacturing could lead to serious drifting, reducing the angular rate sensing and torque outputs capacity. To avoid the shifting of suspension center and reduce price, in our early GW prototype design, the supporting structure is chosen as a rigid universal joint cross without impacting its basic characteristics. When a rigid universal joint cross is applied in GW prototype, it could generate a new problem that can't appear in DTG: the friction of two rotational degrees of freedom. So the friction modeling should be considered [5]. Besides, the mass unbalance of the rotor is inevitable in engineering [6]. The two problems are considered as the major non-ideality factors in early characteristic analysis of GW prototype. Seeking specific signal feature of non-ideality factor can help engineers to distinguish the kind of undesirable mechannical factor and provide corresponding solution, which performs great significance in early GW prototype testing.

This paper is organized as follows: Sect. 2 focuses on the force analysis of each GW component and establishes the equations of three rotating units in GW system by Newton-Euler method. The validity of the forces analysis is verified in Sect. 3, then the friction and mass unbalance modeling are accomplished via Matlab/SimMechanics. Section 4 provides the numerical simulations of different mechannical errors. The conclusion is shown in Sect. 5.

2 Physical Structure and Dynamics of Gyrowheel

The structure of GW prototype is similar to dynamically tuned gyroscope (DTG). It mainly includes base, torquers, motor, universal joint cross, rotor and tilt sensors. According to the structural features of GW prototype, four reference frames can be defined to describe the full motion of GW. The four reference frames are Case-Referenced frame $\mathcal{F}_0$:O-$x_c y_c z_c$, Motor-Referenced frame $\mathcal{F}_1$:O-$x_m y_m z_m$, Gimbal-Referenced frame $\mathcal{F}_2$:O-$x_g y_g z_g$, and Rotor-Reference frame $\mathcal{F}_3$:O-$x_r y_r z_r$, respectively.

The position relationship of the four reference frames can be described as: θ_z is the rotation angle of the motor shaft; θ_x, θ_y represent the two rotation angles of the universal joint cross. The above three rotation angles $(\theta_x, \theta_y, \theta_z)$ can represent three degrees of freedom of GW prototype. In order to obtain the constraining forces of the universal joint cross, the Newton-Euler approach [6] is adopted to derive the GW full dynamic equations. Thus, the force analysis of each component of GW is given by Figs. 1, 2 and 3, respectively.

In Fig. 1, the frame $Ox_r y_r z_r$ is the body frame of rotor. Constraining forces F_X, F_Z acting on the rotor result from the connection between the rotor and universal joint cross, which act along Ox_r, Oz_r axes of rotor body frame, obviously they are the source of the friction. $K_y\theta_y + C_y\dot{\theta}_y$ represents the sum of stiffness torque and damping torque caused by the universal joint cross. $(T_x^{'}, T_y^{'}, T_z^{'})$ are the projection of the external control torques $(T_{cx}, T_{cy}, T_{cz})$from

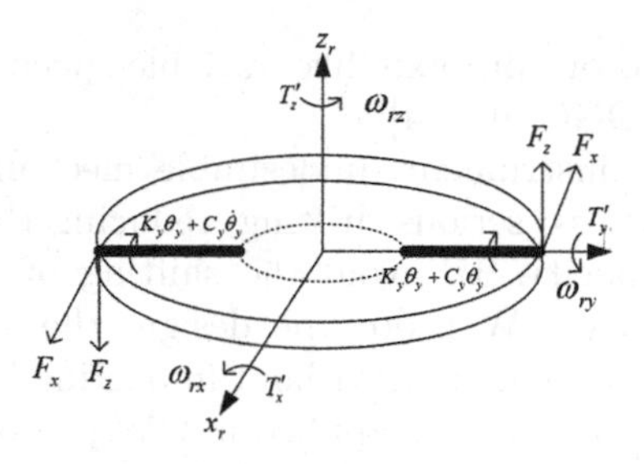

Fig. 1. Force analysis of rotor

case-referenced frame to rotor-referenced frame. M_{rx}, M_{ry}, M_{rz} are the resultant external torques in the rotor-reference frame.

From Fig. 1, the Newton-Euler equations of rotor can be written as:

$$\begin{cases} I_{rx}\dot{\omega}_{rx} - (I_{ry} - I_{rz})\omega_{ry}\omega_{rz} = M_{rx} \\ I_{ry}\dot{\omega}_{ry} - (I_{rz} - I_{rx})\omega_{rx}\omega_{rz} = M_{ry} \\ I_{rz}\dot{\omega}_{rz} - (I_{rx} - I_{ry})\omega_{ry}\omega_{rx} = M_{rz} \end{cases} \tag{1}$$

Where $M_{rx} = 2F_zR_r + T'_x$, $M_{ry} = -2(K_y\theta_y + C_y\dot{\theta}_y) + T'_y$,$M_{rz} = 2F_xR_r + T'_z$, I_{rx}, I_{ry}, I_{rz} are moments of inertia along three principle axes of rotor body frame, respectively. R_r represents the radius of the rotor. K_y, C_y are torsional stiffness and damping coefficient of the universal joint cross, respectively.

The frame $Ox_gy_gz_g$ in Fig. 2 is the body frame of gimbal. $K_x\theta_x + C_x\dot{\theta}_x$ represents the sum of stiffness torque and damping torque caused by the universal joint cross. Constraining forces $F_x^{'}, F_z^{'}$ acting on the gimbal result from the connection between the rotor and gimbal, which act along Ox_g, Oz_g axes of gimbal body frame. Constraining forces $G_y^{'}, G_z^{'}$ acting on the gimbal result from the connection between the gimbal and motor, which act along Oy_g, Oz_g axes of gimbal body frame. And the relationship between F_x, F_z and $F_x^{'}, F_z^{'}$ can be derived as Eq. (2) by the coordinate transformation between gimbal body frame and rotor body frame.

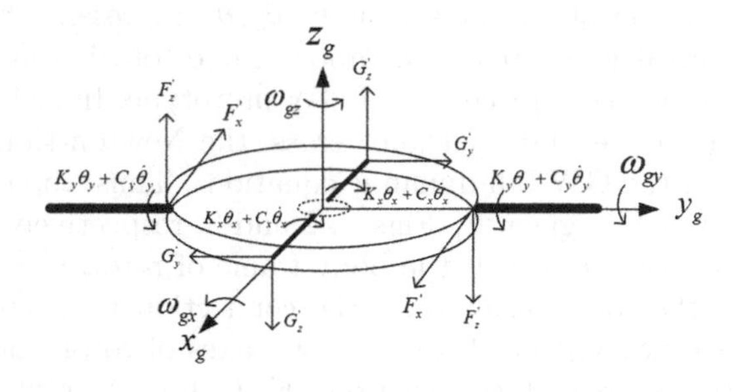

Fig. 2. Force analysis of gimbal

$$
\begin{aligned}
2F_x^{'}R_g &= 2F_zR_r\cos\theta_y + 2F_xR_r\sin\theta_y \\
2F_z^{'}R_g &= -2F_zR_r\sin\theta_y + 2F_xR_r\cos\theta_y
\end{aligned} \tag{2}
$$

Where R_g represents the radius of the gimbal.

From Fig. 2, the Newton-Euler equations of gimbal can be written as:

$$
\begin{cases}
I_{gx}\dot{\omega}_{gx} - (I_{gy} - I_{gz})\omega_{gy}\omega_{gz} = M_{gx} \\
I_{gy}\dot{\omega}_{gy} - (I_{gz} - I_{gx})\omega_{gx}\omega_{gz} = M_{gy} \\
I_{gz}\dot{\omega}_{gz} - (I_{gx} - I_{gy})\omega_{gy}\omega_{gx} = M_{gz}
\end{cases} \tag{3}
$$

where $M_{gx} = -2F'_zR_g - 2(K_x\theta_x + C_x\dot{\theta}_x)$,$M_{gy} = -2G'_zR_g + 2(K_y\theta_y + C_y\dot{\theta}_y)$, $M_{gz} = -2F'_xR_g - 2G'_yR_g$. I_{gx}, I_{gy}, I_{gz} are moments of inertia along three principle axes of gimbal body frame, respectively. K_x, C_x are torsional stiffness and damping coefficient of universal joint cross, respectively.

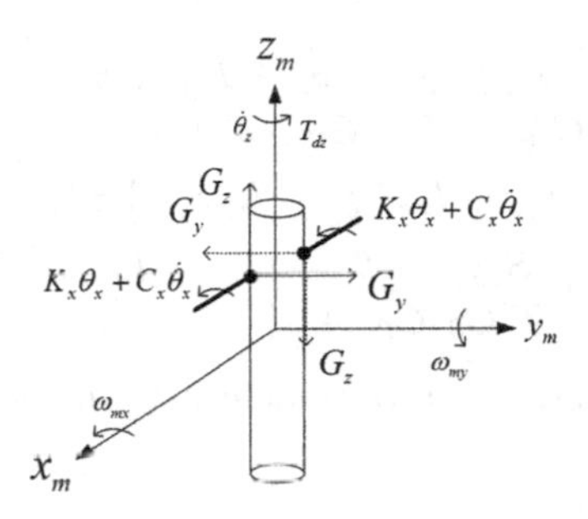

Fig. 3. Force analysis of motor

The frame $Ox_my_mz_m$ in Fig. 3 is the body frame of motor. $\dot{\theta}_z$ is the angular velocities about its z axis, ω_{mx} and ω_{my} assumed as zero are the angular velocities about the axis Ox_m and Oy_m. Constraining forces G_y, G_z acting on the motor result from the connection between the gimbal and motor, which act along Oy_m and Oz_m axes of motor body frame. T_{dz} is the sum of driving torque and friction torque acting on the motor driving axis. And the relationship between G_y, G_z and $G_y^{'}, G_z^{'}$ can be derived as Eq. (4) by the coordinate transformation between gimbal body frame and Motor body frame.

$$
\begin{aligned}
2G_ZR_m &= 2G_Z^{'}R_g\cos\theta_x - 2G_Y^{'}R_g\sin\theta_x \\
2G_YR_m &= 2G_Z^{'}R_g\sin\theta_x + 2G_Y^{'}R_g\cos\theta_x
\end{aligned} \tag{4}
$$

where R_m is the radius of the motor shaft. Similarly, the Newton-Euler equation of motor can be written as:

$$
\begin{cases}
I_{mx}\dot{\omega}_{mx} - (I_{my} - I_{mz})\omega_{my}\omega_{mz} = M_{mx} \\
I_{my}\dot{\omega}_{my} - (I_{mz} - I_{mx})\omega_{mx}\omega_{mz} = M_{my} \\
I_{mz}\dot{\omega}_{mz} - (I_{mx} - I_{my})\omega_{my}\omega_{mx} = M_{mz}
\end{cases} \tag{5}
$$

Where $M_{mx} = 0, M_{my} = 0, M_{mz} = I_{mz}\dot{\omega}_{mz}$.

Combining kinematic equations and their differentiation operators, as well as the relationship between two sets of constraining forces (2)(4), the full dynamic equations of the two axes of universal joint cross and the motor shaft (1)(3)(5) can be derived as follows:

$$\begin{aligned}&\left(I_{gx}+I_{rx}C_{\theta_y}^2+I_{rz}S_{\theta_y}^2\right)\ddot{\theta}_x+2C_x\dot{\theta}_x+2K_x\theta_x=\\&T_x'C_{\theta_y}+T_z'S_{\theta_y}-\left(I_{rz}-I_{rx}\right)S_{2\theta_y}\cdot\dot{\theta}_x\dot{\theta}_y-\\&\tfrac{1}{2}\left(I_{rz}-I_{rx}\right)C_{\theta_x}S_{2\theta_y}\ddot{\theta}_z\\&\left[\left(I_{rz}-I_{rx}\right)C_{2\theta_y}-I_{ry}\right]S_{\theta_x}\cdot\dot{\theta}_y\dot{\theta}_z-\\&\tfrac{1}{2}(I_{gz}-I_{gy}-I_{ry}+I_{rx}S_{\theta_y}^2+I_{rz}C_{\theta_y}^2)S_{2\theta_y}\dot{\theta}_z^2\end{aligned}\tag{6}$$

$$\begin{aligned}&I_{ry}\ddot{\theta}_y+2C_y\dot{\theta}_y+2K_y\theta_y=T_y'-I_{ry}S_{\theta_x}\cdot\ddot{\theta}_z+\\&\tfrac{1}{2}\left(I_{rz}-I_{rx}\right)S_{2\theta_y}\cdot\dot{\theta}_x^2-\tfrac{1}{2}\left(I_{rz}-I_{rx}\right)C_{\theta_x}^2S_{2\theta_y}\cdot\dot{\theta}_z^2-\\&\left[\left(I_{rx}-I_{rz}\right)C_{2\theta_y}+I_{ry}\right]C_{\theta_x}\cdot\dot{\theta}_x\dot{\theta}_z\end{aligned}\tag{7}$$

$$\begin{aligned}&I_z\ddot{\theta}_z+\left(I_{rz}-I_{rx}\right)C_{\theta_x}S_{\theta_y}\ddot{\theta}_x+I_{ry}S_{\theta_x}\ddot{\theta}_y+\\&\left[\left(I_{rz}-I_{rx}\right)C_{2\theta_y}+I_{ry}\right]C_{\theta_x}\cdot\dot{\theta}_x\dot{\theta}_y+\\&\left(I_{gy}+I_{ry}-I_{gz}-I_{rz}C_{\theta_y}^2-I_{rx}S_{\theta_y}^2\right)S_{2\theta_x}\cdot\dot{\theta}_x\dot{\theta}_z+\\&\left(I_{rx}-I_{rz}\right)C_{\theta_x}^2S_{2\theta_y}\cdot\dot{\theta}_y\dot{\theta}_z+\left(I_{rx}-I_{rz}\right)S_{\theta_x}S_{\theta_y}S_{\theta_y}\dot{\theta}_x^2=\\&-T_x'C_{\theta_x}S_{\theta_y}+T_z'C_{\theta_x}C_{\theta_y}+T_{dz}\end{aligned}\tag{8}$$

For simplification, C_{θ_i} and S_{θ_i} represent $\cos\theta_i$ and $\sin\theta_i, i=x,y,z$, respectively. And

$$I_z=I_{mz}+\left(I_{gy}+I_{ry}\right)S_{\theta_x}^2+\left(I_{gz}+I_{rx}S_{\theta_y}^2+I_{rz}C_{\theta_y}^2\right)C_{\theta_x}^2$$

Considering that the angles of universal joint cross θ_x, θ_y are immeasurable, so the measuring function is realized by sensing the rotor tilt angles ϕ_x, ϕ_y in case-reference frame, and the relationship between the two sets of angles is as follows:

$$\begin{aligned}\phi_x&=arc\tan\frac{S_{\theta_x}C_{\theta_y}C_{\theta_z}-S_{\theta_y}S_{\theta_z}}{C_{\theta_x}C_{\theta_y}}\\\phi_y&=\arcsin(S_{\theta_x}C_{\theta_y}S_{\theta_z}+S_{\theta_y}C_{\theta_z})\end{aligned}\tag{9}$$

and the relationship between the control torques (T_{cx}, T_{cy}, T_{cz}) from the torquers and the torques (T_x', T_y', T_z') can be shown:

$$\left[T'_x\;T'_y\;T'_z\right]^T=A_{cr}\left[T_{cx}\;T_{cy}\;T_{cz}\right]^T\tag{10}$$

where A_{cr} is the orientation cosine matrix from rotor frame to case frame.

3 Description of Friction and Dynamic Unbalance

3.1 Validate the Correctness of Forces Analysis

As stated before, ideally the constraining forces F_X, F_Z do not work, but in practice the friction coefficient of the universal joint cross is not zero. Beides,

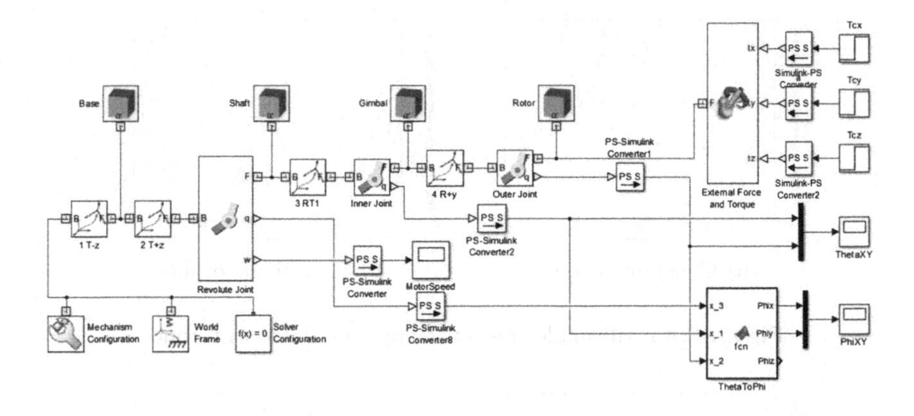

Fig. 4. Simulation diagram of GW based on SimMechanics

the inevitable dynamic unbalance of the rotor can lead to extra high-frequency oscillation when the rotor is rotating in high speed. When the two undesirable mechanical factors act on the GW together, mathematical derivation like (6)(7)(8) will be very difficulty, so the modeling of friction and dynamic unbalance is accomplished via Matlab/SimMechanics Toolbox as Fig. 4:

The design parameters are applied in numerical simulation. The moments of inertia of rotor, gimbal and motor are shown as Eq. (11), and the motor rotates in an initial velocity of 3600 rpm (376.9911 rad/s).

$$\begin{aligned} I_r &= diag\,[1062, 1062, 1779]\; kg \cdot mm^2 \\ I_g &= diag\,[1.611, 1.611, 2.39]\; kg \cdot mm^2 \\ I_m &= diag\,[2000, 2000, 5.12]\; kg \cdot mm^2 \end{aligned} \tag{11}$$

Considering the universal joint cross is rigid, the damping and stiffness are assumed as $K_x = K_y = 0, C_x = C_y = 0$.

The two-dimensional control torques T_{cx}, T_{cy} from torques along radial axis directions are given by constant control torques ($T_{cx} = 0.0039Nm, T_{cy} = 0Nm$) and sinusoidal torques ($T_{cx} = 0.0039\sin(0.2\pi \cdot t)Nm, T_{cy} = 0Nm$), respectively. The open-loop response curves are shown as Fig. 5(a), (b), and the corresponding error curves of two models are obtained as Fig. 6(a), (b).

From the error curves in Fig. 6, the order of magnitude of absolute error in the open-loop response between the Newton-Euler model and SimMechanics model is not more than 10^{-8}, which can be viewed as miscalculation and ignored. Therefore, the validity of the forces analysis can be guaranteed.

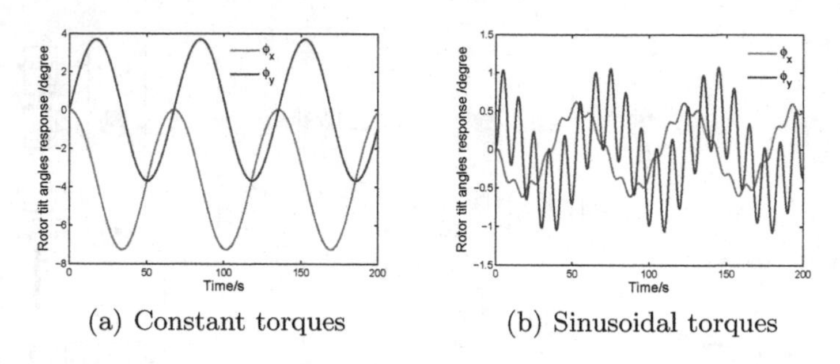

(a) Constant torques (b) Sinusoidal torques

Fig. 5. Rotor tilt angles response applying different torques

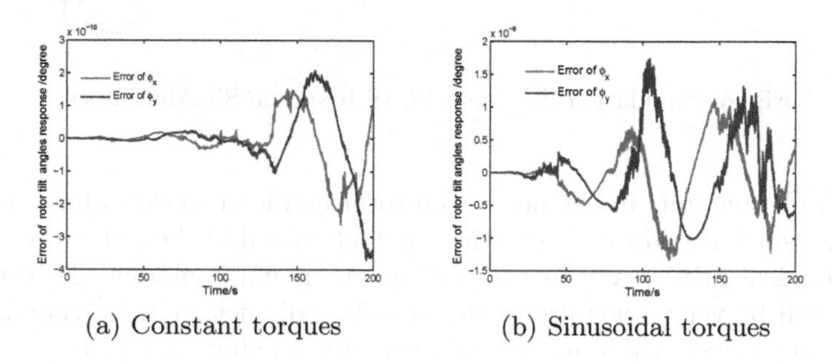

(a) Constant torques (b) Sinusoidal torques

Fig. 6. Error of rotor tilt angles between two models

3.2 Modeling of Dynamic Unbalance and Friction

In this paper, the dynamic unbalance is described by products of inertia, namely the non-diagonal elements shown in the following inertia tensor matrix.

$$I = \begin{bmatrix} I_{rxx} & -I_{rxy} & -I_{rxz} \\ -I_{ryx} & I_{ryy} & -I_{ryz} \\ -I_{rzx} & -I_{rzy} & I_{rzz} \end{bmatrix}$$

Taking the rotor for example, when the products of inertia are not zero, the angular momentums of each axis are as follows:

$$\begin{aligned} H_{rx} &= I_{rxx}\omega_{rx} - I_{rxy}\omega_{ry} - I_{rxz}\omega_{rz} \\ H_{ry} &= -I_{ryx}\omega_{rx} + I_{ryy}\omega_{ry} - I_{ryz}\omega_{rz} \\ H_{rz} &= -I_{rzx}\omega_{rx} - I_{rzy}\omega_{ry} + I_{rzz}\omega_{rz} \end{aligned} \tag{12}$$

Where $I_{rxy} = I_{ryx}, I_{rxz} = I_{rzx}, I_{ryz} = I_{rzy}$ are the products of inertia, $I_{rxx}, I_{ryy}, I_{rzz}$ are the moments of inertia of three principal axes. Similar to Eq. (1), the Newton-Euler equations of rotor considering the dynamic unbalance can be written as:

$$\begin{aligned} \dot{H}_{rx} + \omega_{ry}H_{rz} - \omega_{rz}H_{ry} &= T'_x + 2F_zR_r = M_{rx} \\ \dot{H}_{ry} + \omega_{rz}H_{rx} - \omega_{rx}H_{rz} &= T'_y = M_{ry} \\ \dot{H}_{rz} + \omega_{rx}H_{ry} - \omega_{ry}H_{rx} &= T'_z + 2F_xR_r = M_{rz} \end{aligned} \tag{13}$$

From Eq. (13), the constraining forces F_X, F_Z can be expressed as:

$$F_z = \frac{M_{rx} - T'_x}{2R_r}, F_x = \frac{M_{rz} - T'_z}{2R_r}$$

Utilizing the sensing property of revolute joint in SimMechanics, the position $(\theta_x, \theta_y, \theta_z)$, the angular velocity $(\dot{\theta}_x, \dot{\theta}_y, \dot{\theta}_z)$ and the angular acceleration $(\ddot{\theta}_x, \ddot{\theta}_y, \ddot{\theta}_z)$ of generalized coordinates can be obtained directly. From (12)(13), the resultant external torques M_{rx}, M_{ry}, M_{rz} of the rotor-reference frame also can be calculated. The torques (T'_x, T'_y, T'_z) are from the case-frame control torques (T_{cx}, T_{cy}, T_{cz}) as Eq. (10).

The equal constraining force acting on the rotor is $F_{eq} = \sqrt{F_x{}^2 + F_z{}^2}$, then the sliding friction torque on the second degree of freedom of the universal joint cross is as follows:

$$T_{fy} = -\mu F_{eq} R_j \text{sign}(\dot{\theta}_y) \tag{14}$$

Where μ is the friction coefficient, R_j represents the radius of the rigid rod represented by the second degree of freedom of the universal joint cross. The friction on the first degree of freedom of the universal joint cross T_{fx} can be calculated in the similar idea. The two modeled frictions T_{fx}, T_{fy} are applied to act on the "Inner Joint" and "Outer Joint" in Fig. 4 respectively.

4 Simulation of Dynamic Unbalance and Friction

In this section, the open-loop response of tilt angles with constant torques acting are studied. The moments of inertia of rotor, gimbal and motor are shown as Eq. (11), $K_x = K_y = 0, C_x = C_y = 0$. The motor rotates in an initial velocity of 3600 rpm (376.9911 rad/s). The control torques from case-reference frame are $T_{cx} = 0.0039Nm, T_{cy} = 0Nm, T_{cz} = 0Nm$. Thus the tilt angles response and their FFT analysis are shown Figs. 7 and 8:

In time domain, Fig. 7 describes the tilt angles response motivated by constant torques in ideal and two undesirable states. From Fig. 7(a) and (b), we can see that the dynamic unbalance hardly effects the time-domain response of tilt angles; While comparing the Fig. 7(b) and (c), the time-domain response of tilt angles are changed obviously duo to the friction: the two-dimensional tilt angles

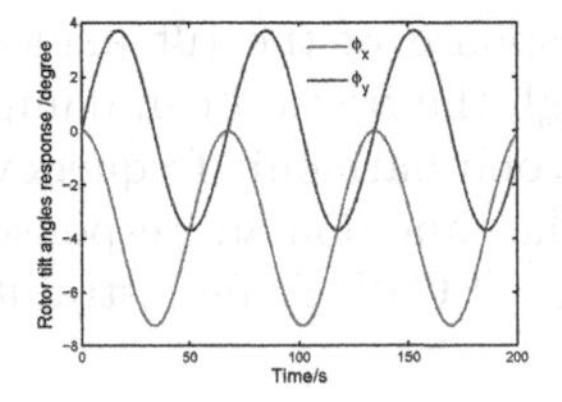

(a) Tilt angles without non-ideality factor

(b) Tilt angles with dynamic unbalance

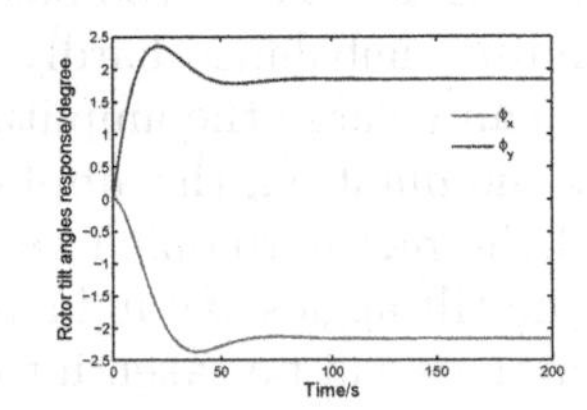

(c) Tilt angles with dynamic unbalance and friction

Fig. 7. Rotor tilt angles response with different situation

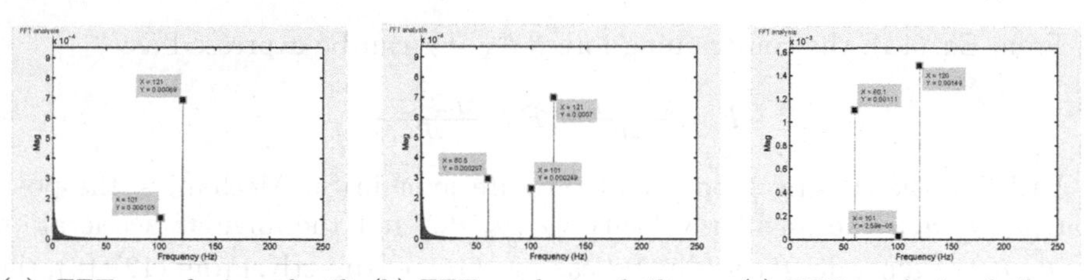

(a) FFT analysis of tilt angles without non-ideality factor (b) FFT analysis of tilt angles with dynanmic unbalance (c) FFT analysis of tilt angles with dynanmic unbalance and friction

Fig. 8. FFT of rotor tilt angles response

response converge to certain constant values instead of the oscillations periodic motion. Actually, the friction functions as a "quivalent damping".

The frequency-domain response is more complex. Firstly, without undesirable factor, because the rotor and motor shaft are connected via the specific universal joint cross, the spinning axis of rotor diverging from motor shaft could generate the second harmonic frequency (121 Hz) shown in Fig. 8(a). Like DTG, the frequency component 101 Hz near the second harmonic frequency is the nutation frequency. These are the essential and inevitable components. From Fig. 8(b), the dynamic unbalance introduces another frequency component: the first harmonic frequency (60.5 Hz), which does not effects the second harmonic frequency but enhances the amplitude of the nutation. With the friction process in Fig. 8(c), no extra frequency component appears, but the switching effect of sliding friction greatly enhances the amplitude of the second harmonic frequency and the first harmonic frequency, meanwhile the nutation is almost damped out because of the "quivalent damping".

5 Conclusion

This paper firstly accomplishes the forces analysis of each components of GW, and accordingly the Newton-Euler model of GW is derived. Then, the validity of the forces analysis is guaranteed by another GW model built by Matlab/SimMechanics Toolbox. From the simulation, we can conclude that the dynamic unbalance hardly effects the time-domain response of the tilt angles but can enlarge the amplitude of the nutation. Although the friction can damp out the nutation, the amplitude amplification of the second harmonic frequency and the first harmonic frequency, especially changing the time-domain response of the tilt angles can influence the sensing and actuating of GW. Some restraint strategies will be taken into account in later research.

Acknowledgments. This work is supported by National Nature Science Foundation under Grant 61427809, China Postdoctoral Scientific Research Foundation 2015M571415 and Heilongjiang Postdoctoral Foundation under Grant LBH-Z14088.

References

1. Richie, D.J., Lappas, V.J., Prassinos, G.: A practical small satellite variable-speed control moment gyroscope for combined energy storage and attitude control. Acta Astronaut. **65**(11), 1745–1764 (2009)
2. Tyc, G., Whitehead, W., Pradhan, S., Staley, D., Ower, C., Cain, J., Wiktowy, M.: GyroWheel^{TM}-an innovative new actuator/sensor for 3-axis spacecraft attitude control. In: 13th Annual AIAA/USU Conference on Small Satellites, 199, no. 1 (1999)
3. Cain, J.S.: Stability analysis of a dyanmically tuned gyroscope. J. Guidance Control Dyn. **29**(4), 965–969 (2004)
4. Stevenson, D., Schaub, H.: Nonlinear control analysis of a double-gimbal variable-speed control moment gyroscope. J. Guidance Control Dyn. **35**(3), 787–793 (2012)
5. Luo, X.: The frictional contact analysis of joints in multibody system. Dalian University of Technology, China (2011)
6. Feng, X.Y.: Dynamic balancing for low inertia power systems. In: IEEE Power and Energy Society General Meeting, pp.1–5 (2013)

Simulation for Harmonic Analysis of an Integrated Power System

De-jia Zhou[1(✉)], Ru-quan Mao[2], Ya-ping Zhuang[1], and Shan-ming Wang[3]

[1] Navy Academe of Armament, Beijing 100161, China
largeappletree@163.com
[2] Representative Office of Naval Warship Design and Research, Shanghai 200011, China
[3] Department of Electrical Engineering and Applied Electronic Technology, Tsinghua University, Beijing 100084, China

Abstract. Modeling and Simulation is an effective way to predict the behaviors of Shipboard Integrated Power System (IPS). This paper presents the methods applying simulink blockset to building the models of twelve-phase synchronous machine and twelve-phase voltage-fed inverter, whereby the hybrid simulation method using SimPowerSystem blocks and Simulink models for the harmonic analysis of the IPS simulation is proposed. The results of the harmonic analysis of the system which is a system of the AC-DC-AC driving twelve-phase synchronous motor show that the convenient eleventh and thirteenth LC filters can improve deeply the Total Harmonic Distortion (THD) of line current in the AC source of system, and with the loads increased, the THD of the line voltage of the AC source is increased, on the contrary, the THD of the current of AC source is decreased.

Keywords: Simulation · Harmonic analysis · Integrated power system

1 Introduction

Shipboard integrated power system (IPS) integrates power generation, power services distribution, power electronics conversion, electric propulsion, auxiliary electric devices, power management. On the initial phase of research, proceeding to the computer simulation is an effective way to optimize the characteristics of the system and reduce the risk of research. The first important tasks are extensive modeling, and then to build different kinds of simulation models according to the variety and complexity of the system.

In this paper, twelve-phase synchronous machine and twelve-phase voltage-fed inverter are built by using Matlab-Simulink blocks. Then the hybrid simulation method using SimPowerSystem blocks and Simulink models is proposed. The method is applied to the harmonic analysis of an integrated power system. The results of the harmonic analysis of the system simulation which is a six phase AC-DC-AC source driving multi-phase synchronous motor show that the convenient eleventh and thirteenth LC filters can improve deeply the Total Harmonic Distortion of current in the AC source of system.

L. Zhang et al. (Eds.): AsiaSim 2016/SCS AutumnSim 2016, Part I, CCIS 643, pp. 272–280, 2016.
DOI: 10.1007/978-981-10-2663-8_29

2 Twelve-Phase Synchronous Machine Model

There are several ways to build the models of twelve-phase synchronous machine with four Y-connected three-phase symmetrical windings displaced in turn by 15^0 [1]. This paper presents the method applying the flux-linkage as state variables to build the twelve-phase synchronous motor model, which is convenient to proceed the device-level computer simulation and the system-level computer simulation. This method is also convenient to simulate the effects of saturation in the direct axis of a synchronous machine or in both axes of a round rotor machine [2, 3]. We can write the per unit mathematical model of the twelve-phase synchronous machine using the flux linkages per second as state variables in the d-q-0 Rotor Reference Frame.

The stator flux linkages per second integral equations

$$\begin{cases} \psi_{qns} = \dfrac{\omega_b}{p}[v_{qns} - \dfrac{\omega_r}{\omega_b}\psi_{dns} + \dfrac{r_s}{X_{ls}}(\psi_{mq} - \psi_{qns})] & n = \overline{1,4} \\ \psi_{dns} = \dfrac{\omega_b}{p}[v_{dns} + \dfrac{\omega_r}{\omega_b}\psi_{qns} + \dfrac{r_s}{X_{ls}}(\psi_{md} - \psi_{dns})] & n = \overline{1,4} \\ \psi_{0ns} = \dfrac{\omega_b}{p}\left(v_{0ns} - \dfrac{r_s}{X_{ls}}\psi_{0ns}\right) \quad n = \overline{1,4} \end{cases} \tag{1}$$

where ω_b denotes the base electrical angular velocity, ω_r denotes the actual rotor electrical angular velocity, ψ denotes the flux linkages per second, r_s denotes the stator resistor, p denotes the differential operator.

The rotor damper wind flux linkages per second

$$\begin{cases} \psi'_{kq1} = \dfrac{\omega_b}{p}[v'_{kq1} + \dfrac{r_{kq1}}{X_{lkq1}}(\psi_{mq} - \psi'_{kq1})] \\ \psi'_{kq2} = \dfrac{\omega_b}{p}[v'_{kq2} + \dfrac{r'_{kq2}}{X'_{lkq2}}(\psi_{mq} - \psi'_{kq2})] \\ \psi'_{kd} = \dfrac{\omega_b}{p}[v'_{kd} + \dfrac{r'_{kd}}{X'_{lkd}}(\psi_{md} - \psi'_{kd})] \end{cases} \tag{2}$$

The rotor exciter wind flux linkage per second

$$\begin{cases} \psi'_{fd} = \dfrac{\omega_b}{p}[\dfrac{r'_{fd}}{X_{md}}e'_{xfd} + \dfrac{r'_{fd}}{X'_{lfd}}(\psi_{md} - \psi'_{fd})] \\ e'_{xfd} = v'_{fd}\dfrac{X_{md}}{r'_{fd}} \end{cases} \tag{3}$$

During steady state rated speed operation, one per unit e'_{xfd} produces one per unit open-circuit terminal voltage [2].

The stator currents

$$\begin{cases} i_{qns} = \frac{1}{X_{ls}}(\psi_{qns} - \psi_{mq}) & n = \overline{1,4} \\ i_{dns} = \frac{1}{X_{ls}}(\psi_{dns} - \psi_{mq}) & n = \overline{1,4} \\ i_{0ns} = \frac{1}{X_{ls}}\psi_{0ns} \quad n = \overline{1,4} \end{cases} \quad (4)$$

The rotor currents

$$\begin{cases} i_{kq1} = \frac{1}{X'_{lkq1}}(\psi'_{kq1} - \psi_{mq}) \\ i_{kq2} = \frac{1}{X'_{lkq2}}(\psi'_{kq2} - \psi_{mq}) \\ i'_{kd} = \frac{1}{X'_{lfd}}(\psi'_{kd} - \psi_{md}) \\ i'_{fd} = \frac{1}{X'_{lfd}}(\psi'_{fd} - \psi_{md}) \end{cases} \quad (5)$$

where ψ_{md} and ψ_{mq} which are useful when representing saturation are defin

$$\begin{cases} \psi_{md} = X_{md}(\sum_{n=1}^{4} i_{dns} + i'_{fd} + i'_{kd}) \\ \psi_{mq} = X_{mq}(\sum_{n=1}^{4} i_{qns} + i'_{kq1} + i'_{kq2}) \end{cases} \quad (6)$$

apply (4) and (5) into (6)

$$\begin{cases} \psi_{md} = X_{ad}(\sum_{n=1}^{4} \frac{\psi_{dns}}{X_{ls}} + \frac{\psi'_{fd}}{X'_{lfd}} + \frac{\psi'_{kd}}{X'_{lkd}}) \\ \psi_{mq} = X_{aq}(\sum_{n=1}^{4} \frac{\psi_{qns}}{X_{ls}} + \frac{\psi'_{kq1}}{X'_{lkq1}} + \frac{\psi'_{kq2}}{X'_{lkq2}}) \\ \mathrm{X}_{ad} = (\frac{1}{X_{md}} + \frac{4}{X_{ls}} + \frac{1}{X'_{lfd}} + \frac{1}{X'_{lkd}})^{-1} \\ \mathrm{X}_{aq} = (\frac{1}{X_{mq}} + \frac{4}{X_{ls}} + \frac{1}{X'_{lkq1}} + \frac{1}{X'_{lkq2}})^{-1} \end{cases} \quad (7)$$

therefore the saturation of the d-q magnetic flux linkage can be simulated according to the reference [2].

The electromagnetic torque and rotor speed

$$\mathrm{T}_e = \frac{1}{4}\sum_{n=1}^{4}(i_{qn}\psi_{dn} - i_{dn}\psi_{qn}) \tag{8}$$

$$\omega_r = \frac{\omega_b}{2Hp}(T_\mathrm{e} - T_L) \tag{9}$$

$$H = \left(\frac{1}{2}\right)\left(\frac{2}{\mathrm{P}}\right)^2 \frac{J\omega_b^2}{\mathrm{p}_b} \tag{10}$$

where J is often the combined inertia of the rotor and H is inertia constant of the system in seconds.

For the twelve-phase synchronous machine, this involves referring the stator voltage variables to the common d-q reference frame of the rotor with (11), then transforming the resultant stator d-q current variables to the twelve-phase stator current variables with (12).

$$\mathrm{K_s} = diag(\mathrm{k_{s1}},\ \mathrm{k_{s2}},\ \mathrm{k_{s3}},\ \mathrm{k_{s4}} \tag{11}$$

$$\mathrm{K_s^{-1}} = diag(\mathrm{k_{s1}^{-1}},\ \mathrm{k_{s2}^{-1}},\ \mathrm{k_{s3}^{-1}},\ \mathrm{k_{s4}^{-1}} \tag{12}$$

$$\mathrm{k_{sn}} = \frac{2}{3}\begin{bmatrix} \cos(\theta_r - \theta_n) & \cos\left(\theta_r - \frac{2\pi}{3} - \theta_n\right) & \cos\left(\theta_r + \frac{2\pi}{3} - \theta_n\right) \\ \sin(\theta_r - \theta_n) & \sin\left(\theta_r - \frac{2\pi}{3} - \theta_n\right) & \sin\left(\theta_r + \frac{2\pi}{3} - \theta_n\right) \\ \frac{1}{2} & \frac{1}{2} & \frac{1}{2} \end{bmatrix}$$

$$\mathrm{k_{sn}^{-1}} = \begin{bmatrix} \cos(\theta_r - \theta_n) & \sin(\theta_r - \theta_n) & 1 \\ \cos(\theta_r - \frac{2\pi}{3} - \theta_n) & \sin(\theta_r - \frac{2\pi}{3} - \theta_n) & 1 \\ \cos(\theta_r + \frac{2\pi}{3} - \theta_n) & \sin(\theta_r + \frac{2\pi}{3} - \theta_n) & 1 \end{bmatrix}$$

$$\theta_n = (n-1)\frac{\pi}{12} \qquad n = \overline{1,4}$$

where θ_r is the electrical angular displacement of the rotor.

Block diagrams showing the computer simulation of a Twelve-phase synchronous machine in the rotor reference frame are shown in Fig. 1

3 Twelve-Phase Inverter Model

This paper applies the switch method to simulate the function of an ideal twelve-phase inverter [4]. Each leg of the inverter is represented by a "switch" which has three input terminals and one output terminal. The output of a switch ($V_{aok,}$ V_{bok}, or V_{cok}, $k = \overline{1,4}$) is connected to the upper input terminal (+0.5 V_d) if the PWM control signal(middle

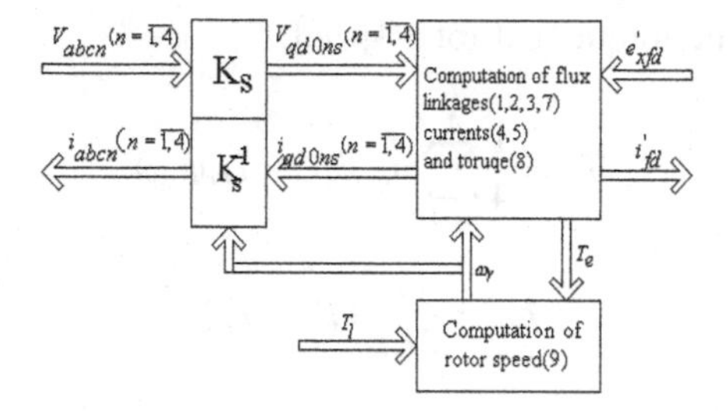

Fig. 1. Block diagram of the simulation of a twelve-phase synchronous machine in the rotor reference frame

input) is positive. Otherwise, the output is connected to the lower input terminal (−0.5 V_d), The output voltages of the switches thus oscillates between +0.5V_d and −0.5V_d, which is characteristic of a pole of an inverter. The model of the twelve-phase PWM control signals is made from the crossovers of the modulated sine signals and the triangle carried signals. The output twelve-phase voltages are constructed by the following equations:

$$\begin{cases} V_{ak} = \frac{2}{3}V_{aok} - \frac{1}{3}V_{bok} - \frac{1}{3}V_{cok} & k = \overline{1,4} \\ V_{bk} = \frac{2}{3}V_{bok} - \frac{1}{3}V_{aok} - \frac{1}{3}V_{cok} & k = \overline{1,4} \\ V_{ck} = \frac{2}{3}V_{cok} - \frac{1}{3}V_{aok} - \frac{1}{3}V_{bok} & k = \overline{1,4} \end{cases} \tag{13}$$

4 Harmonic Analysis of System

Harmonic analysis in the paper is based on the integrated power system which consists of three-phase Sources, 11th filter, 13th filter, three-phase three windings transformer, twelve-phase voltage-fed inverter, twelve-phase synchronous motor and load. This kind of simulation is called the hybrid system simulation applied SimPowerSystem blocks and Simulink models in this paper. The method is the use of voltage measurement block to measure the direct voltage of rectified power source side, then the simulink singal of DV is applied to the twelve-phase inverter models, next the twelve-phase PWM voltage signals of the twelve-phase inverter is linked to the twelve-phase synchronous motor, then the twelve-phase current of motor is acquired through the computation of the twelve-phase synchronous motor model. At the same time, using the PWM control signals to identify the power electronics' state of switch on/off, the DC is acquired from the sum of the currents of the upper power electronics of the twelve-phase voltage-fed inverter, then the DC signals is provided to the controlled current source which is series connection at the side of rectified power source. This kind of system simulation solves the question of interlink between the SimPowerSystem blocks and the Simulink models, which improve the efficiency of system simulation and is convenient to observe the dynamic changes of some important state variables. Figure 2 shows the harmonic analysis model of simple IPS simulation block diagram. Figure 3 shows the power subsystem model which consist of the three-phase sources, filters, transformer, rectified system.

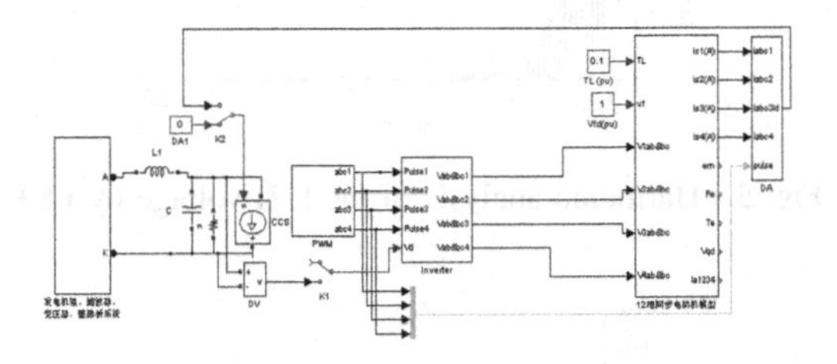

Fig. 2. Harmonic analysis model of the simple integrated power system

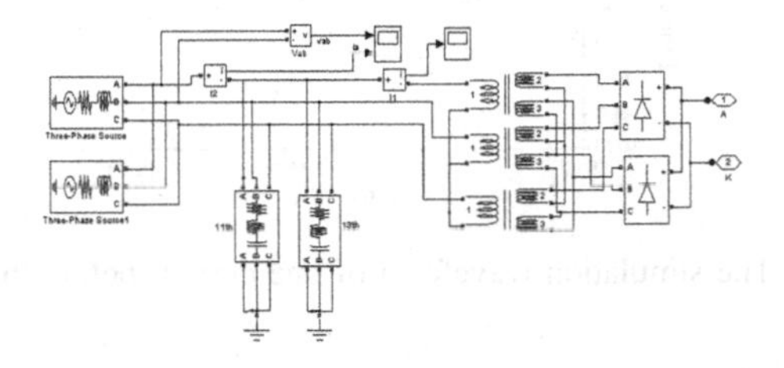

Fig. 3. Subsystem consists of three-phase sources, filters, transformer, rectified system

Three-phase source parameters: phase to phase rms voltage 6.6 kV, frequency 50 Hz, $R_s = 0.8929\ \Omega$, $L_{sl} = 0.18$ mH. The eleventh filter parameters: $L = 20.87$ mH, $F = 4.012\mu$F, $R = 0.7214\ \Omega$.

The thirteenth filter parameters: $L = 14.95$ mH, $F = 4.012\ \mu$F, $R = 0.6104\ \Omega$.

The twelve-phase synchronous motor parameters: nomal power 25 MVA, L-L rms voltage 3.3 kV, frequency 50 Hz, The inertia constant H 0.6 s, pairs of poles 6.

The twelve-phase voltage-fed inverter parameters: carrier frequency 540 Hz, frequency of output voltage 18 Hz, modulation index 1.

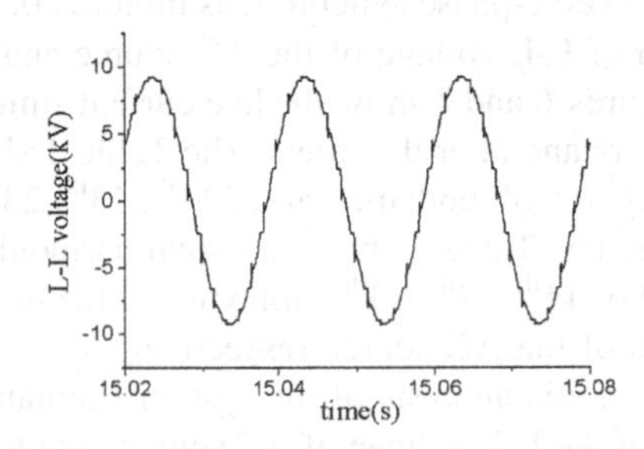

Fig. 4. The simulation waveform of L-L voltage of the AC source

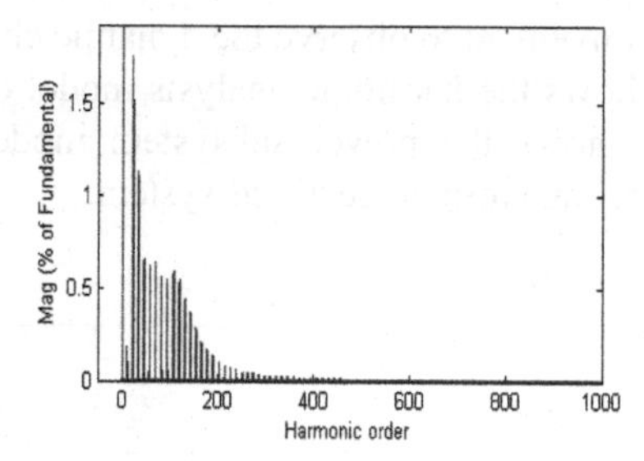

Fig. 5. Harmonic analysis of the L-L voltage by FFT

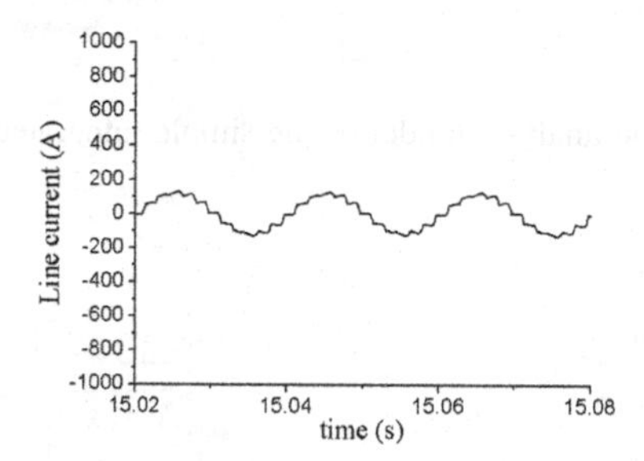

Fig. 6. The simulation waveform of line current before the filters

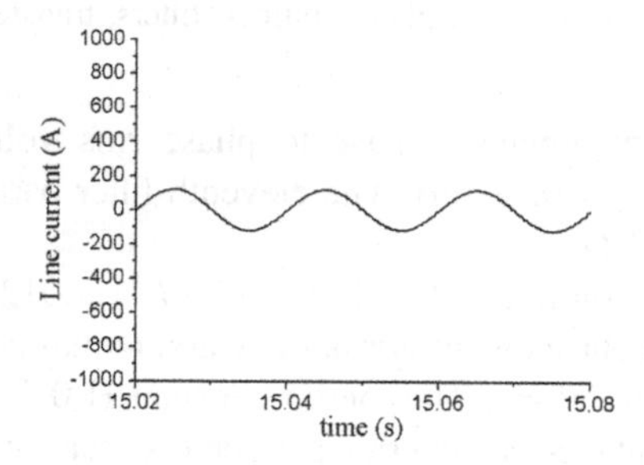

Fig. 7. The simulation waveform of line current after the filters

When the load of the twelve-phase synchronous motor is 0.1pu, Figs. 4 and 5 show the simulation waveform of L-L voltage of the AC source and its results of harmonic analysis respectively. Figures 6 and 7 show the line current simulation waveform of the AC source before the filters and after the filters. The Table 1 shows the total harmonic distortion (THD), the Mag. (% of fundamental) of 11th, 13th, 23th harmonics of the L-L voltage of the AC source. The Table 2 shows the total harmonic distortion (THD), the Mag. (% of fundamental) of 11th, 13th, 23th harmonics of the line current of the forth(F) and back(B) of the filters of the AC source respectively.

The results of the harmonic analysis of the system simulation show that the THD and the main harmonics of the L-L voltage of AC source are increasing gradually when

Table 1. The THD and main harmonics of AC L-L voltage

TL(pu)	THD	11th	13th	23th
0.1	3.31 %	0.18 %	0.09 %	1.75 %
0.2	4.79 %	0.31 %	0.18 %	2.71 %
0.3	5.98 %	0.45 %	0.28 %	3.37 %
0.5	7.67 %	0.75 %	0.47 %	4.25 %

Table 2. The THD and main harmonics of AC current at the forth and back of the filter

TL (pu)	THD		11th		13th		23th	
	F	B	F	B	F	B	F	B
0.1	11.87 %	1.76 %	9.78 %	0.27 %	5.46 %	0.12 %	3.01 %	1.30 %
0.2	10.75 %	1.37 %	8.7 %	0.23 %	5.52 %	0.11 %	2.32 %	1.0 %
0.3	10.07 %	1.11 %	8.12 %	0.21 %	5.43 %	0.11 %	1.85 %	0.80 %
0.5	9.14 %	0.75 %	7.38 %	0.19 %	5.15 %	0.10 %	1.22 %	0.53 %

the loads of motor are increasing, while the THD and the main harmonics of the line currents of AC source are decreasing gradually when the loads of motor are increasing, the simple LC filters can improve apparently the THD of the AC currents. This system simulation can predict and optimize the characteristics of the IPS by modeling and simulating the shipboard integrated power system.

5 Conclusion

A harmonic analysis method based on simulation of shipboard integrated power system is presented through building the models of twelve-phase synchronous machine, twelve-phase voltage-fed inverter, etc. The results of the harmonic analysis of the system by FFT show that the THD of the L-L voltage of AC source are increasing gradually and the THD of the line currents of AC source are decreasing as the loads of motor are being increased, the simple LC filters can improve deeply the THD of the AC currents. The results of the system simulation show that proceeding to the computer simulation is an effective way to optimize the characteristics of the integrated power system on the initial phase of research.

References

1. Ma, W.: Research on a twelve-phase generator-rectifier system, Ph.D. dissertation, Beijing: Tsinghua University (1995). [in Chinese]
2. Krause, P.C.: Analysis of Electric Machinery. McGraw-Hill Book Company, New York (1986)

3. Krause, P.C., Wasynczuk, O., Sudhoff, S.D.: Analysis of Electric Machinery and Drive Systems. IEEE Press, New York (2002)
4. Bose, B.K.: Modern Power Electronics and AC Drives. China Machine Press, Beijing (2003)
5. Mohan, N., Robbins, W.P., Undeland, T.M., et al.: Simulation of power electronic and motion control systems-an overview. Proc. IEEE **82**(8), 1287–1302 (1994)
6. Buckley, J.: Future trends in commercial and military shipboard power systems. In: Power Engineering Society Summer Meeting, pp. 340–342. IEEE (2002)
7. Clayton, D.H.,Sudhoff, S.D.,Grater, G.F.: Electric ship drive and power system. In: Power Modulator Symposium, pp. 85–88. IEEE CNF (2000)
8. Methven, P.: Modeling of a Full Electric Propulsion System Using Matlab-Simulink & Power System Blockset, Master's thesis. London: Mechanical Engineering University College London (1998)
9. Ma, W., et al.: Experimental study of a diode-bridge-loaded twelve-phase synchronous generator system for ship propulsion. In: Proceedings of IMECE 1994, Shanghai, China, vol. 10 (1994)
10. Schiferl, R.F., Ong, C.M.: Six phase synchronous machine with AC and DC stator connections, part i: equivalent circuit representation and steady-state analysis. IEEE Trans. Power Appar. Syst. **PAS-102**(8), 2685–2693 (1983)
11. Zhou, D., Wang, S., Chai, J.: Research on simulation of an integrated electric propulsion system of ship using matlab-simulink. J. Tsinghua Univ. Sci. Technol., Beijing (2006)
12. Math Works Inc. Simulink Users's Guide Version 5.1 (2003)

Atmospheric Environment Five Dimensional Representation Model

Liren Xu(✉), Jun Cai, Runqiang Chen, Kun Li, Haiyang Sun, and Xingtao Su

Beijing Institute of Applied Meteorology, Beijing 100029, China
xuliren2016@sina.com

Abstract. Modern simulation applications need physically consistent atmospheric environment representation. The consistency, standardized and effective atmospheric environment data representation are critical for simulation applications, it is the basis of realizing interoperability and reusability of simulation. In this paper, considering the characteristics of atmospheric environment simulation data and application requirements of simulation, atmospheric environment five dimensional representation model is designed, five dimension rectangular grid form of atmospheric environment simulation results are expressed, to regulate the level of resolution, vertical stratification, time step and characteristic parameters, can reflect truly the characteristics of temporal and spatial variations of the actual atmospheric environment. Atmospheric environment simulation data is stored and managed effectively through five dimensional representation model, atmospheric environment simulation model base is generated. The reusability of the simulation model is improved.

Keywords: Atmospheric environment five dimensional representation model · Rectangle grid · Temporal and spatial variation

1 Introduction

Many countries in the world attaches great importance to the authoritative representation of the natural environment [1]. To meet the consistency and interoperability requirements of synthetic natural environment simulation model, U.S. Department of defense Modeling and Simulation Office (DMSO) announced the "integrated natural environment programme (INE) in 2000, concentrate on providing the integrated authoritative representation in terrain, ocean, atmosphere and space environment. In the modern simulation application, it is needed to deeply understand the natural environment, to extract the representation of physical consistency natural environment and to establish the authoritative and reliable environmental data model [2–4]. The credibility of the atmospheric environment simulation depends on the validity of the representation of atmospheric environment. How to describe the atmospheric environment effectively is an important problem in the simulation of atmospheric environment [5].

Around the needs of modern modeling and simulation technology for atmospheric environment simulation model, the atmospheric environment five dimension representation model is designed, the model library of atmospheric environment simulation based

L. Zhang et al. (Eds.): AsiaSim 2016/SCS AutumnSim 2016, Part I, CCIS 643, pp. 281–286, 2016.
DOI: 10.1007/978-981-10-2663-8_30

on the way of representation is established. The physical consistency between internal models of atmospheric environment and the interoperability between external models are improved, so as to improve the simulation efficiency.

2 The Characteristic of Atmospheric Environment Simulation Data

The atmosphere is a complex fluid motion, varies dynamically with time and space. The basic factors of controlling atmospheric motion includes both the external factors, such as solar radiation and the periodic and nonperiodic vibration of energetic particles, the earth's surface friction, the distribution of sea and land, the influence of topography, and the internal factors, such as compression, continuity, flow and atmospheric horizontal scale and vertical scale distribution characteristics of the atmosphere itself. The interaction of atmosphere internal and external different scales systems, dynamic and thermal forcing of underlying surface will result the dynamic changes of atmospheric environment. Dynamic property is one of the important attributes of the atmospheric environment. Atmospheric motion varies from microscopic scale to large scale movement caused by adverse weather. It needs to consider the influence of different scale to reflect accurately the structural characteristics of the atmospheric environment and its variation comprehensive results. Multiscale is one of the important attributes of the atmospheric environment. Atmospheric environment is very complicated, is used to describe the characteristic quantity of atmospheric physical properties including wind, temperature, pressure, humidity, and the cloud, rain, fog, rain. Atmospheric environment has many variables and parameters. The datas to describe the movement state of atmospheric environment have the features of multi parameter. Through a variety of instruments and equipment to detect atmospheric elements, is the most direct means to understand the physical properties of the atmosphere. Modern atmospheric observation and detection methods are various, integration of space, atmosphere and earth as a whole, thus causing sources attribute data of atmospheric environment. Atmospheric environmental data is correlated with time and space position, is a data field that it varies dynamically with time, have characteristic of the big data. Therefore, it is very necessary to build different scales resolution model according to the needs of different levels of simulation application and provide users for authority and reliable data of atmospheric environment.

3 Atmospheric Environment Five Dimensional Representation

Atmospheric environment simulation has different characteristics and forms of representation according different simulation level and objectives. In practical application, it is necessary to completely describe the atmospheric environment that research data polymorphism and design corresponding data representation model. The simulation results are normalized, are stored and exchanged in a standard common format for data storage. The integrity and polymorphic data representation of integrated atmosphere environment simulation data are achieved the overall [6, 7]. It is very necessary to accurately describe the evolution of atmospheric environment for improving the consistency and reusability of the simulation model and data. Taking into account the application objectives and characteristics of atmospheric environmental data field, atmospheric environment simulation results are expressed by the five dimensional rectangular grid form, atmospheric environment five dimensional representation model (AEFDRM) is established, as shown in Fig. 1. The data of each grid point is composed of 3 spatial dimensions, 1 time dimension and 1 physical variables, namely F (*x*, *y*, *z*, *t*, *V*,), *x* represents longitude, *y* represents latitude, *z* represents height, *t* represents time, and *V* represents physical variables. The space dimensions include 2 horizontal spatial dimension and one vertical position dimension, defined 2-dimensional horizontal spatial location of data (such as longitude and latitude) and the height position of the elements, and a time dimension defined time of data; a physical variable dimension defined the name and unit of element, the model is dynamic, can truly reflect the variable characteristics of actual atmospheric environment.

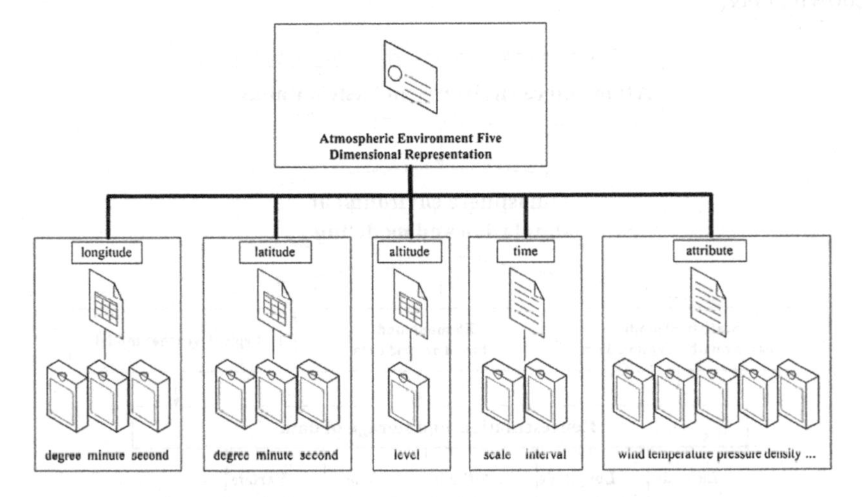

Fig. 1. Atmospheric environment five dimensional representation

4 Atmospheric Environment Simulation Model Database

4.1 Simulation Model Library Design

Kinds of Atmospheric environmental data are rich, including a variety of conventional and unconventional observational data, reanalysis data, numerical forecast products, historical climate data. Such information is usually stored at different locations, their structures are not identical. As a result, the atmospheric environment simulation database has the obvious characteristics of heterogeneous and distributed demand. According to the characteristics of atmospheric environmental data, such as, multi-source, big data access and interactive features in the distributed simulation platform [8–10], multi hierarchy, multi application interface of atmospheric environment simulation model base are constructed by distributed heterogeneous database technology. It can avoid many questions of the centralized development caused by the way of reconcetrtion and overhead data communication and improve the utilization efficiency of big data storage space. The efficient management and quick transform of data are realized. It can enhance the expansibility and interoperability of database in the distributed environment. According to the characteristics of the various elements of the atmospheric environment, the elements are divided into basic grid information (unit, precision, etc.), grid index information (longitude and latitude, the station point, etc.), linear abstract information (contour), plane abstract information (rain, wind). Datas are stored and managed by the classification from the data type, intermediate results and simulation results. The distribution storage management and rapid search of atmospheric environment simulation database are achieved by solving the database structure design, database classification storage, data representation and exchange, memory data scheduling, multi user access to database, multi rate query, management and services of database. The atmospheric environment simulation model base is generated, the process of information flow as shown in Fig. 2.

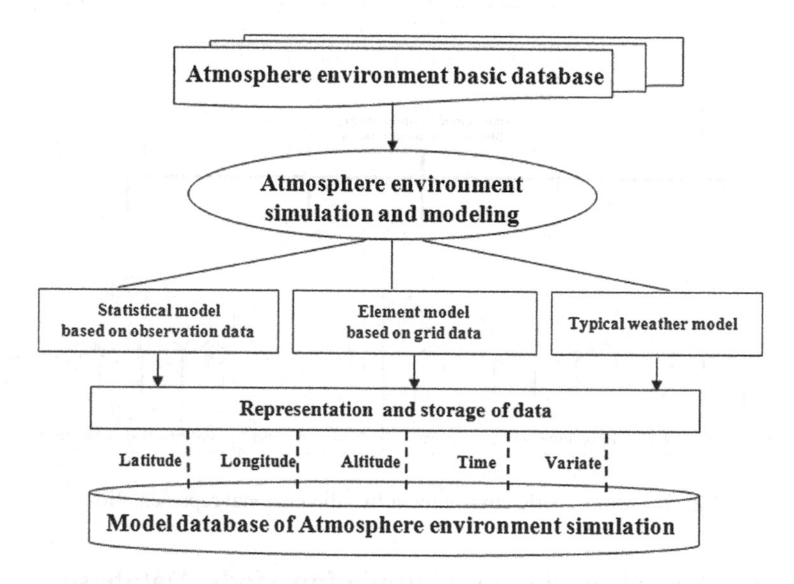

Fig. 2. The process of atmospheric environment simulation model database

4.2 Simulation Model Representation

The environmental data representation model, application program interface (API) and data transmission format are the key technologies to solve the representation and storage of atmospheric environment simulation data. In order to facilitate the data storage, the based storage mode of atmospheric environment data is generally divided into the database table and file. The object oriented API atmospheric environment data model is designed according to the characteristics of atmospheric observational data from station point that the elements are relatively fixed and are summarized by the unified code. For the grid point data, with the spatial location and time attributes, the amount of information is very large, is stored by the file format that the meteorological industry commonly used Grib format. The useful data format of simulation operation is generated by mapping, association, organization and storage of simulation data. The environmental data is exchanged between the atmospheric environment simulation and its various applications through the unified and effective standard to promote internal coordination, mutual adaptation and reuse. The information flow process of the atmospheric environment five dimensional representation model is shown in Fig. 3.

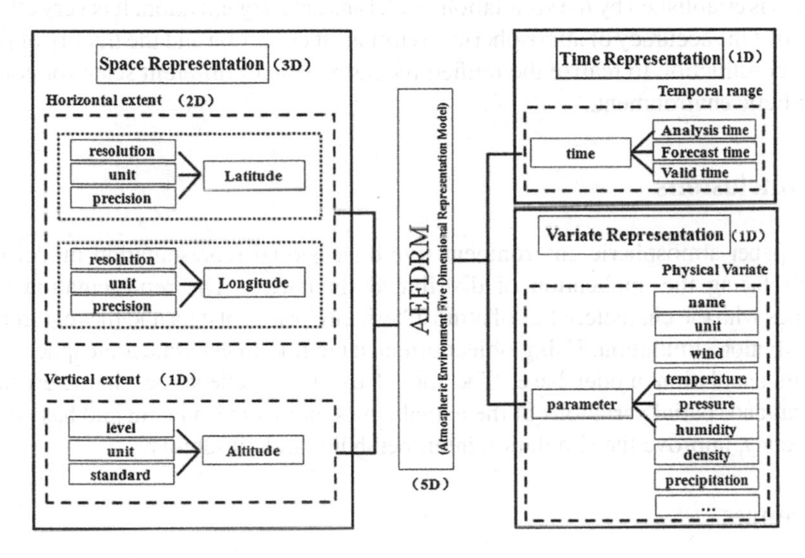

Fig. 3. The information flow process of atmospheric environment five dimensional representation model

4.3 Simulation Model Data Organization

The atmospheric environment simulation datas for observational data from station point and grid data from numerical model are organized and analyzed by the atmospheric

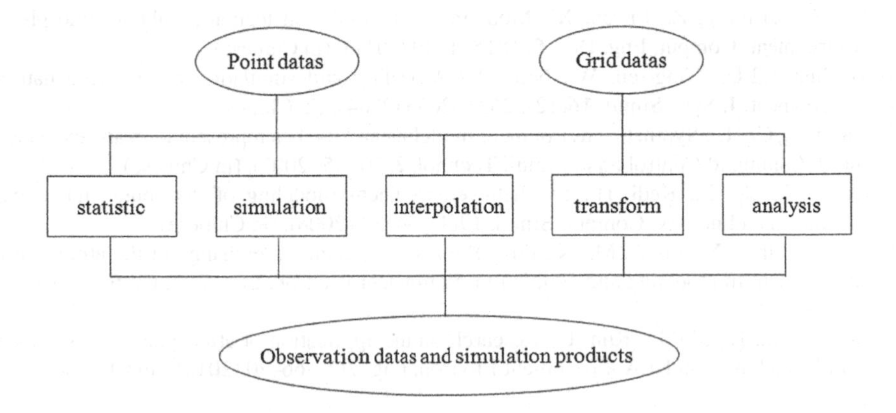

Fig. 4. The organizational structure of simulation model

environment five dimensional data structure (longitude, latitude, altitude, time and atmospheric parameters). The point data and grid data are formed by using statistic, simulation, interpolation, transform and analysis method, as shown in Fig. 4. The grid data are stored in the 5-dimenion data column. The data model is classified to store in a database. The multi-resolution data model that can express the macroscopic topology characteristics and microscopic statistical properties of the atmospheric environmental elements is established by the simulation model and data organization. It is very effective to improve the accuracy of atmospheric environment cognition and the fidelity of panoramic reconstruction to realize the unified reconstruction of different scale for complex atmospheric environment.

5 Conclusions

In this paper atmospheric environment five dimensional representation model is put forward facing the application of distributed simulation. The representation model combines with the characteristics of atmospheric environment data and the requirements of distribution simulation. Using object oriented method to generate atmospheric environment simulation model base. The model can truly reflect the characteristics of temporal and spatial variations of the actual atmospheric environment and has physical consistency, improve the simulation interoperability and reusability.

References

1. Department of Defense. Under Secretary of Defense for Acquisition and Technology. Modeling and simulation (M&S) master plan, October 1995
2. Li, B., Chai, X., Zhu, W., et al.: Some focusing points in development of modelling and simulation technology. J. Syst. Simul. **16**(9), 1871–1878 (2004)
3. Kedi, H., Baohong, L., Jian, H.: A survey of military simulation technologies. J. Syst. Simul. **16**(9), 1887–1895 (2004). (in Chinese)
4. Xing-ren, W.: Research and discussion on technologies of modeling and simulation. J. Syst. Simul. **16**(9), 1896–1897 (2004). (in Chinese)
5. Jun, C., Li-ming, Z., Li-ren, X.: Modeling and simulation tecnology about atmospheric environment. Comput. Eng. Des. **5**, 1815–1819 (2011). (in Chinese)
6. Weihua, L.I.U., Xing-ren, W., Ning, L.: Modeling and simulation of synthetic natural environment. J. Syst. Simul. **16**(12), 2631–2635 (2004). (in Chinese)
7. Gang, G., Ge, L.: Synthetic environment modeling and its data representation and exchange. Intell. Command Control Syst. Simul. Technol. **2**, 50–55 (2001). (in Chinese)
8. Gang, G., Ge, L., Kedi, H.: Synthetic environment modeling of distributed interactive simulation technology. Comput. Simul. **19**(1), 34–37 (2008). (in Chinese)
9. Jun, C., Liren, X., Liang, M., Kun, L.: Representation and interchange of the atmospheric environment in modeling and simulation. Equipment Environ. Eng. **7**(2), 61–63 (2010). (in Chinese)
10. Jun, C., Xu, L., Ma, L., Kun, L.: Research on the application of atmospheric environment simulation based on HLA. Equipment Environ. Eng. **7**(3), 66–70 (2010). (in Chinese)

Research on Control and Management Technology of Joint Distributed Simulation Experiment Platform

Xibao Wang(✉), Ge Li(✉), Peng Wang(✉), and Xiaodong Zhu(✉)

College of Information System and Management, National University of Defense Technology, Changsha, China
xbwang1990@126.com, {geli,wangpeng_nudt,zhuxiaodong}@nudt.edu.cn

Abstract. At present, simulation experiment complexity is increasing dramatically due to the weapon system of system becoming more and more complex. Single machine simulation experiment has been unable to meet the project needs. As the development of computer and network technology, Advanced Distributed Simulation (ADS) has been widely used in high-tech and complex weapon systems' experiment, argumentation and evaluation, which overcomes disadvantages of the single machine simulation. However, a large-scale integrated simulation experiment for weapon systems' argumentation and design is a system engineering, which leads to explosive increase in simulation resources. As a result, the functional structure becomes more and more diverse, the interactive relationship becomes more and more complex and the operation control becomes more and more difficult. In order to be faster, more accurate and more convenient to complete the simulation experiment and evaluation, there is an urgent need to design and develop a macro control and management system for large-scale comprehensive simulation experiment to support its full life cycle control and management. In this paper, distributed simulation experiment control and management technology is studied under the background of the Joint Distributed Simulation Experiment Platform (JDSEP) project. This paper proposes and expounds the architecture of JDSEP, the framework of the macro management and control system and the simulation resources management tool respectively in accordance with the order from the whole to local, which provides a conceptual framework and theoretical guidance for the follow-up realization and implementation.

Keywords: Advanced Distributed Simulation (ADS) · System of system (SoS) · Joint Distributed Simulation Experiment Platform (JDSEP) · Management and control (M&C) · Simulation resources management

1 Introduction

Distributed simulation is a very important technique for emulating large-scale complex systems using distributed system and distributed computing. Distributed simulation interconnects simulation models and equipment distributed in different geographical locations according to coherent structure, standard, protocol and database to form an integrated simulation experiment environment, which is unified in space and time, consistent in logic. Under the comprehensive simulation experiment environment,

L. Zhang et al. (Eds.): AsiaSim 2016/SCS AutumnSim 2016, Part I, CCIS 643, pp. 287–295, 2016.
DOI: 10.1007/978-981-10-2663-8_31

complex simulation calculation is assigned to a number of computer nodes and is processed parallel. The final result is the combination of every node's calculation results. Figure 1 shows a typical distributed simulation system structure [1, 2].

Nowadays, with the enlargement of weapon system of system's scale, the simulation resources becomes more and more, the interactive relationship becomes more and more complex, the operation control becomes more and more difficult in distributed simulation experiment, which gives rise to difficult management in simulation experiment. The traditional manual management mode can't meet the requirements of comprehensive distributed simulation experiment. How to build an integrated simulation experiment environment which includes numerous independent, decentralized, incompatible subsystems so as to realize macro management and control over the simulation platform, to improve the automation degree of experiment process and to lower the difficulty of the application of distributed simulation technology is a system engineering.

Management and control (M&C) technology are important issues for constructing heterogeneous simulation platform. Recently, support for distributed simulation experiment management in large-scale network environments remains in its early stages. Although, a number of existing solutions and tools address the management needs of a single type of simulation experiment environment, yet few solutions and tools provide a unified framework which is adaptable enough to be used for other simulation platform [3]. The DSEMS (Distributed Simulation Experiment Management System) proposed in [4–8] discussed various aspects about experiment management and control, like experiment planning technique, simulation procedure control, daemon design and implementation, etc. Although DSEMS is limited to HLA, all these researches play a guiding role to extend management techniques to generalized distributed simulation.

Generally, simulation experiment management means a sequence of procedures required for conducting an experiment, in order to achieve particular purposes effectively. These procedures include designing, deploying, controlling, monitoring, analyzing and working out conclusion [9]. Figure 2 shows the typical experiment process of distributed simulation. For complex simulation experimental platforms running on resources that are spread across the wide-area, distributed experiment management is a time-consuming and error-prone process. After the initial deployment of the software, the applications need mechanisms for detecting and recovering from inevitable failures and problems endemic to distributed environments. To achieve availability and reliability, applications must be carefully monitored and controlled to ensure continued operation and sustained performance. Operators in charge of deploying and managing these distributed simulation applications facing a daunting list of challenges: discovering and acquiring appropriate simulation resources and appropriately configuring the resources (and re-configuring them if operating conditions change) [3].

In this paper, we will study the control and management (M&C) framework under the background of JDSEP. The remainder of this paper discusses the architecture of JDSEP, which consists of application service layer, simulation running support layer, simulation proxy layer and simulation physical entity layer. All the four layers' composition and function are demonstrated respectively. Afterwards, this paper illustrates the framework of the macro management and control module and simulation resources management tool respectively, which both are important parts of the simulation platform.

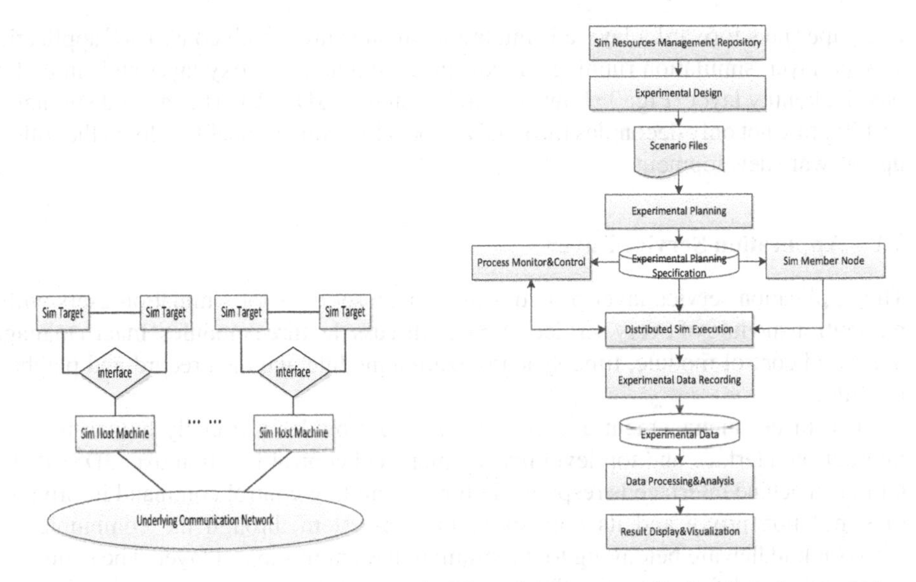

Fig. 1. Typical structure of distributed simulation system

Fig. 2. Process of distributed simulation experiment

2 Architecture of JDSEP

JDSEP is a typical distributed simulation system which consists of simulation equipment and software located in different places and accomplishes demonstration, analysis and evaluation of weapon systems through interconnection of hardware and collaborative control of software [10]. In order to make JDSEP's function more perfect, structure more clear, module more general, development more convenient and extension more flexible,

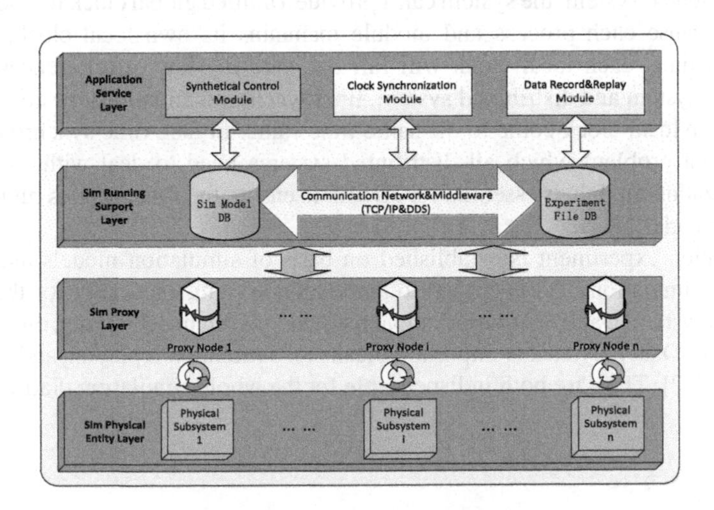

Fig. 3. Architecture of JDSEP

this paper puts forward a layered simulation architecture which consists of application service layer, simulation running support layer, simulation proxy layer and simulation physical entity layer (Fig. 3 shows the architecture of JDSEP). The layered simulation architecture not only decouples the platform but also reduces the difficulty in the follow-up software development.

2.1 Application Service Layer

The application service layer provides three main services for simulation users with a realization module of every service. We will discuss the three modules: macro management and control module, time synchronization module and data record and playback module.

The macro management and control module provides a friendly human-machine interaction interface and top level management and control function over JDSEP. The human-machine interface is responsible for transmitting control command information to simulation proxy and its corresponding sub-system through the communication network middleware belonging to the simulation running support layer. The simulation users only need focus on simulation experiment itself because system services and underlying data logic are both transparent to users. For example, simulation users can accomplish experiment design and planning, and then assign it to specified simulation equipment. Also, the users can transmit control command, such as start, pause, continue and stop, to simulation proxy node and control the physical simulation equipment indirectly through the proxy. The real time dynamic status information coming from terminal simulation equipment can also be returned back to the macro control and management module interface. All running status of every proxy and sub-system is under monitoring of simulation users. The macro management and control module adopts the object-oriented design, which realizes the full life cycle control and management for distributed simulation experiment.

In distributed system, the system can't provide a unified global clock for independent module because each process and module maintains its own local clock. With the passage of time, each local clock will fall out step. In view of differences between centralized system and distributed system, time synchronization must be conducted for making each local clock come to the same time value. In fact, time synchronization is an important problem which all distributed systems need to deal with, so the time synchronization module is essential for JDSEP to ensure the synchronous running of all simulation nodes [11].

Simulation experiment is established on basis of simulation models and data, so apparently simulation data is crucial to simulation system, especially for the military simulation system. Data record is principal method for system debugging, online display and analysis. Data playback is important means for simulation replaying and simulation evaluation [12]. They are both indispensable for the whole simulation platform.

2.2 Simulation Running Support Layer

Interconnection network and middleware, which lies between application service layer and simulation proxy layer, is the core layer of JDSEP and key bridge for resources interaction and information transmission. As the simulation experiment is established on simulation models and data, so both simulation model warehouse and experiment data warehouse are important for JDSEP, the former provides management of resources, we will discuss later in Sect. (4), the later provides data support for data record and playback.

2.3 Simulation Proxy Layer

A proxy is a simulation system that is connected to two different infrastructure solutions. It comprises the common elements—entities and events—that are shared between the two solutions and uses the interface provided by the infrastructure for simulation systems [13]. In this paper, simulation proxy in simulation proxy layer is the key to realize the seamless integration between simulation physical entity layer and simulation platform. All kinds of simulation resources in physical entity layer can't integrate directly with simulation platform due to differences in hardware and software. In addition, the simulation resources can't interact with each other due to the protocol and hardware differences, so we need simulation proxy which accomplishes protocol conversion to realize information transmission and interaction.

3 Framework of Macro Management and Control System

The macro management and control module is the center to realize the whole course management and control for JDSEP, is the key to guarantee effective operation for the simulation experiment process and is also the interactive window between simulation platform and simulation users. The integrated management and control module is divided into three parts according to simulation experiment sequence (Fig. 4 shows the framework of macro control module): simulation resources management, experiment design and planning before the simulation; simulation experiment process control and

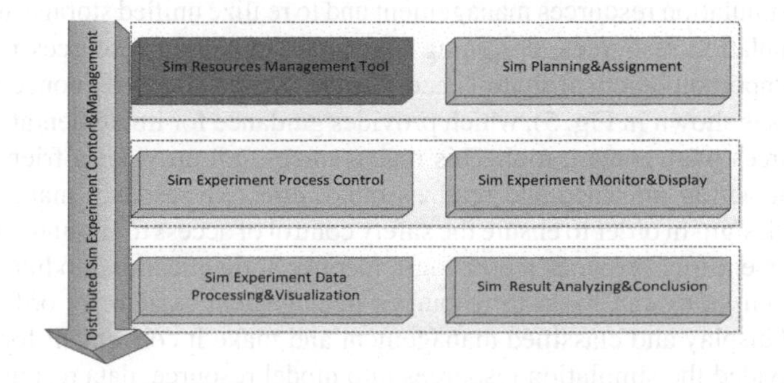

Fig. 4. Framework of the macro control module

online dynamic status monitoring and displaying within the simulation; simulation experiment data processing, analysis and visualization after the simulation.

The experiment scheme design is to determine the participated simulation resources and logging data list, which is prepared for initializing the simulation. The experiment planning and assignment takes the scheme files and logging data lists as input, and then it determines software and hardware resources, computer node and its composition, at last it distributes scenarios to every terminal simulation host machine and finishes simulation initialization work.

Experiment process control means that simulation users can start, pause, continue and stop every terminal simulation node at all times. Simulation experiment monitor deals with runtime information and dynamic status from subsystem models and operating environment. Subsystem models' real-time data help users get to know which step the system is running to. Operating environment information generally contains the computing nodes' name, position, resource usage, performance evaluation, etc. They directly reflect computing and network resources' consumption, which play important roles in checking out bugs when unexpected errors come out [9].

Experiment data analysis and visualization refers to data format conversion and statistical analysis after finishing the simulation experiment. There are many methods to visualize the processing results, such as two-dimensional table, curve and three-dimensional situation display, etc. Finally, the domain experts evaluate the simulation system and experiment according to the visualization results.

4 Simulation Resources Management Tool (SRMT)

The system analysis, experiment evaluation and simulation application in large-scale integrated simulation platform are all established around all kinds of simulation resources, so the simulation resources management is a crucial work. The simulation resources management refers to storage and management of simulation models and experiment data, which is basis of simulation experiment design, is precondition of simulation experiment management and control and is important component of macro management and control module (as is shown in Fig. 4). There are some kinds of problems needed to be solved in simulation resources management work, such as distribution, diversity, reusability and security of simulation resources. In order to improve the effectiveness of simulation resources management and to realize unified storage and management of simulation resources, designing a general simulation resources management tool has an important practical significance. This paper puts forward a conceptual design of SRMT (as is shown in Fig. 5), which provides guidance for implementation of simulation resources management tool. This management tool provides a friendly human-machine interaction interface and realizes rapid, effective resource management and experiment design. In order to ensure the safety control of access to simulation resources, this management tool provides a user login identity authentication module, only those who get permissions can login to resources management system. In order to realize hierarchical display and classified management and make it convenient for simulation users, we divided the simulation resources into model resource, data resource, mission resource and node resource (as is shown in Fig. 5). The model resource refers to simulation model developed for specific purpose by simulation modeling experts. The mission resource is the instance of integrated simulation models that is organized to achieve a specific simulation process. Data resource includes parameters, scenario and simulation results related to the simulation experiment task. Node resource means all elements such as software and hardware, even people involved in the simulation experiment [14]. The resource management and display module realizes hierarchical display and classified management which enables simulation users to locate specific simulation resources quickly. Also, simulation users can edit, modify and save the simulation resources stored in the warehouse. The scenario generation and edit module helps simulation users acquire specific resources quickly, design experiment scheme effectively and generate specific format experiment file or modify and edit existed experiment files. The last but not least, simulation resources repository includes all kinds of simulation resources used by the simulation platform and guarantees that the SRMT could be operated effectively.

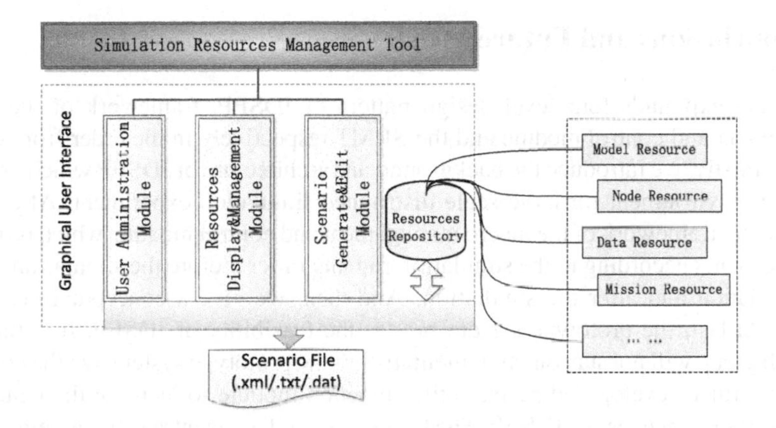

Fig. 5. Conceptual design of SRMT

5 Validation

All mentioned above is preliminary exploration of our research group in constructing JDSEP which is a system engineering needing multi-sectoral coordination. Being limited to experiment conditions, we principally study the conceptual design about the architecture of JDSEP. Although JDSEP is difficult to be constructed, our research group has still carried out a simple prototype system which includes a missile mathematic model and its corresponding simulation proxy (as is shown in Fig. 6). The prototype system proves that the macro management and control system of JDSEP can not only realizes real-time management and control of the whole platform, but also meets the requirement of real-time data transmission, which verifies the correctness and validity of conceptual design of JDSEP and lays a solid foundation for our future research work.

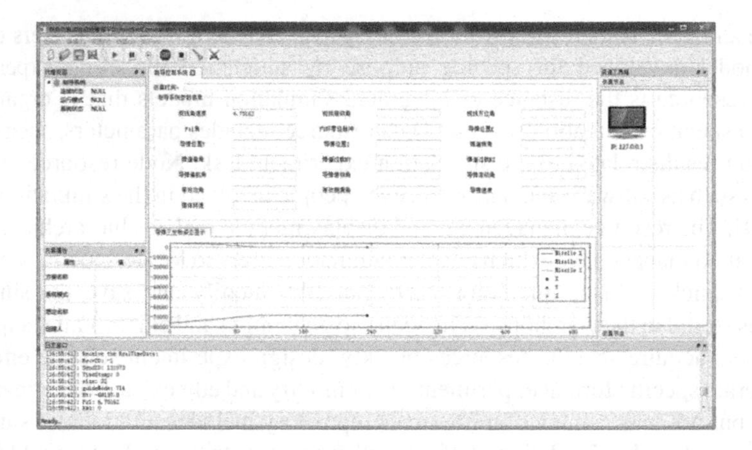

Fig. 6. Screenshot of prototype system

6 Conclusions and Future Work

This paper expounds four level design pattern of JDSEP, framework of the macro management and control module and the SRMT respectively in the order from overall to local. Firstly, we introduce the background and architecture of JDSEP which provides a support environment for large-scale distributed simulation experiment. Afterwards, we illustrate framework of the macro management and control module, which is divided into three parts according to the simulation running order: before the simulation, within the simulation and after the simulation. And then, we give a conceptual design for SRMT. At last, the prototype system proves the feasibility of JDSEP. In future, our research group will not stay on implementation of the prototype system. On the contrary, we will further develop and perfect other function module to increase the generality, scalability and openness of JDSEP. The future work will concentrate on implementation of SRMT and data record and playback module based on DDS.

Acknowledgments. We appreciate the support from National Natural Science Foundation of China (No. 61374185).

References

1. Liu, F.: Design and implementation of scenario system in distributed interactive system. Beijing University of Posts and Telecommunications Master's Degree thesis (2007)
2. Jiao, S.-H.: Research on distributed simulation technology. Ch. High Tech Enterp. **12**(3), 28–30 (2015)
3. Albrecht, J., Braud, R., Dao, D., et al.: Remote control: distributed application configuration, management, and visualization with plush. In: 21th Large Installation System Administration Conference, pp. 185–203 (2007)
4. Peng, C.-G., et al.: Formalization of distributed simulation experiment plan. J. Syst. Simul. **23**(5), 917–949 (2011)

5. Liu, J., et al.: Design and implementation of daemon in distributed simulation experiment management system. J. Syst. Simul. **20**(24), 6636–6638 (2008)
6. Liu, X.-C., et al.: Design of the simulation procedure controller in distributed simulation experiment management system. J. Syst. Simul. **20**(24), 6646–6649 (2008)
7. Zhang, K., et al.: Design and implementation of distributed simulation experiment management system. J. Syst. Simul. **20**(24), 6627–6630 (2008)
8. Duan, W., et al.: Research of experiment planning technique in distributed management system. J. Syst. Simul. **20**(24), 6631–6635 (2008)
9. Xu, X., Li, G.: A management and control infrastructure for integrated real-time simulation environment. In: 17th International Symposium on Distributed Simulation and Real Time Applications, pp. 197–204 (2013)
10. Zhang, P.: Research on the key technology of the management of distributed simulation experiment. National University of Defense Technology Master's Degree thesis (2007)
11. Yong-Jun, X., Liu, Y., Wang, F.: The Key Technology of Internet of Things. Publishing House of Electronics Industry, Beijing (2012)
12. Yang, Z.: Design of a distributed data record and replay model. Electron. Technol. Softw. Eng. **15**(2), 208–209 (2010)
13. Tolk, A.: Engineering Principals of Combat Modeling and Distributed Simulation. Wiley, New York (2012)
14. Zhang, Y.-P., et al.: Research on resource management in simulation integrated environment. J. Syst. Simul. **8**(10), 1606–1609 (2011)

Capture Dynamics Modeling and Simulation of the Space Flexible Manipulator

Simiao Yu, Zhiyong Qu(✉), Shutao Zheng, and Junwei Han

Institute of Electrohydraulic Servo Simulation and Test System,
Harbin Institute of Technology, Harbin 150001, China
quzyhit@163.com

Abstract. The ground simulation based on the dynamics of the flexible manipulator capture is an important method for researching the docking characteristics. This paper proposed a capture dynamics modeling method, in which the space flexible manipulator was equivalent to a six dimensional spring-damper system. Utilizing the mechanical characteristics of the six dimensional spring-damping system to simulate the flexibility of the space manipulator, and the capture dynamics model was established by applying of the Newton-Euler method. This proposed modeling method considered the flexibility of the manipulator and avoided the complex modeling method of the flexible manipulator with large amount of calculation. The relative motion results between the capture mechanism and the captured mechanism and the stress results of the equivalent spring-damping system were obtained by numerical solution of the capture dynamics model. Then a simulation model was accomplished in the ADAMS software with the same parameters used in the theoretical model to verify the effectiveness and accuracy of the capture dynamics model. The proposed capture dynamics model provided a theoretical basis for the ground simulation of the space flexible manipulator capture.

Keywords: Space flexible manipulator · A six dimensional spring-damping system · Capture dynamics · Numerical solution · Ground simulation

1 Introduction

The space manipulator with dexterity and multifunction is the predominant method for On-Orbit Capture [1]. The end-effector which locates at the terminal of the space manipulator captures the interface which locates at the passive spacecraft to realize the operation of the passive spacecraft [2–6]. In the process of the capture, the end-effector's capture devices will collide multiple times with the passive spacecraft's capture interface [7, 8]. Under the effect of the collision force, passive spacecraft, active spacecraft, end-effector and manipulator will produce complex motions. Passive spacecraft may break away from the end-effector's capture space and even collide with the end-effector, which can cause the capture failed or capture devices damaged. Therefore, in order to ensure the capture successful, it is necessary to simulate the space manipulator capturing process on the ground to confirm key issues include initial capture conditions. And to simulate the process of the capture is the process to describe

L. Zhang et al. (Eds.): AsiaSim 2016/SCS AutumnSim 2016, Part I, CCIS 643, pp. 296–307, 2016.
DOI: 10.1007/978-981-10-2663-8_32

the capture dynamics of the space manipulator. Thus we need to establish the capture dynamics model. Utilizing the capture dynamics model, the relative movement parameters between the mechanisms are solved under the action of the collision force, and then the movement of the mechanisms is reproduced based on the solved motion parameters to complete the capture process. Therefore, capture dynamics is a key factor which affects the success of the On-Orbit Capture.

At present, the rigidity docking and the dynamics modeling of the manipulator have been studied in domestic and abroad [9–14] (Docking mechanisms and the spacecraft are regarded as rigid bodies). However, there are few literatures about the modeling and analysis of the spacecraft capture dynamics based on flexible manipulator. The modeling of flexible manipulator capture and docking has the following characteristics: (1) More mechanisms are involved in the docking; (2) In addition to the dynamics of the rigid body, the modeling of the flexible manipulator is complex. (3) The dynamic characteristics of the mechanisms are influenced by each other, rigid and flexible dynamic models are coupled. As a result, the capture and docking dynamics model of manipulator is more complicated.

This paper studies the actual capture conditions with the following characteristics: the manipulator joints are locked in the process of capture in order to reduce the adverse effect of residual vibration at the terminal of the manipulator. It means that the manipulator has no movement except flexible deformation after positioning the end-effector to meet the location of the capture. We can measure or analyze the stiffness and damping when the two installation positions on manipulator generate a small range of relative motion along the six degrees of freedom. For this feature, this paper avoids the complex modeling method of the flexible manipulator; the space flexible manipulator is equivalent to six dimensional spring-damping system, utilizing the mechanical characteristics of the six dimensional spring-damping system to simulate the flexibility of the space manipulator. Then the capture dynamics model is established and the dynamic characteristics of each mechanism is obtained, which provides a basis for the simulation experiment.

2 Assumptions and Coordinate Systems Definition

Active spacecraft, passive spacecraft and end-effector are regarded as rigid body in the paper. The flexible manipulator is equivalent to a six dimensional spring-damping system, with which the manipulator and the end-effector are connected. The flexible deformation of the spring-damping system is utilized to simulate the flexible deformation of the manipulator. The effects of the spacecraft's gravity, centroid vibration and liquid tank in the capture process are not considered. Four coordinate systems for establishing the mathematical models are shown in Fig. 1.

$O_S XYZ$–Inertial coordinate system. At the moment of the passive spacecraft and the end-effector first contact, the origin of the coordinate OS is coincident with the active spacecraft's centroid, and the directions of the coordinate axes are consistent with the directions of the spacecraft's inertial principal axes.

$O_1X_1Y_1Z_1$–Body-fixed coordinate system of the End-effector. The coordinate origin locates at the centroid of the end-effector.

$O_2X_2Y_2Z_2$–Body-fixed coordinate system of the passive spacecraft. The coordinate origin locates at the centroid of the passive spacecraft.

$O_3X_3Y_3Z_3$–Body-fixed coordinate system of the Active spacecraft. The coordinate origin locates at the comprehensive centroid of the active spacecraft and the manipulator.

$O_4X_4Y_4Z_4$–The stiffness damping coordinate system. Coordinate origin locates at the installation position of the manipulator.

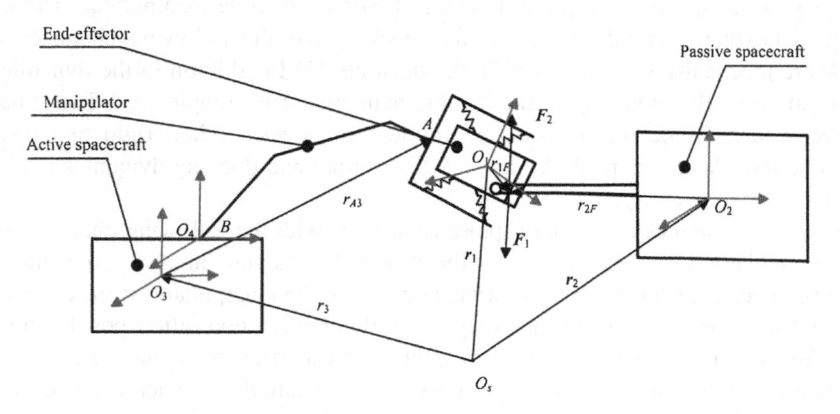

Fig. 1. Introduction of the mechanisms in the capture process.

The relative rotation of the active spacecraft, the passive spacecraft and the end-effector can be decomposed into three times rotation around the body-fixed coordinate axis according to a certain sequence. It also called Euler angle. The Euler angles rotating order is defined that rotate around Z axis γ angular, and then rotate around Y axis β angular, rotate around X axis α angular at last. Then, the direction cosine matrix of the body-fixed coordinate system relative to the static coordinate system is:

$$R = \begin{bmatrix} \cos\beta\cos\gamma & -\cos\alpha\sin\gamma + \sin\alpha\sin\beta\cos\gamma & \sin\alpha\sin\gamma + \cos\alpha\sin\beta\cos\gamma \\ \cos\beta\sin\gamma & \cos\alpha\cos\gamma + \sin\alpha\sin\beta\sin\gamma & -\sin\alpha\cos\gamma + \cos\alpha\sin\beta\sin\gamma \\ -\sin\beta & \sin\alpha\cos\beta & \cos\alpha\cos\beta \end{bmatrix} \quad (1)$$

3 Dynamics Modeling of the Capture Process

3.1 Dynamics Modeling of the Active Spacecraft and the End-Effector

If there is no other outside force when colliding, the collision force impacting on the end-effector is $\boldsymbol{F}_1$, the force and torque of the spring-damping system impacting on the end-effector are $\boldsymbol{F}_h$ and $\boldsymbol{M}_h$ respectively. Then according to the Newton equation, the accelerations of the end-effector and the active spacecraft in the inertial coordinate system are written as:

$$\ddot{\boldsymbol{r}}_3 = \frac{\boldsymbol{F}_h}{m_1} \tag{2}$$

$$\ddot{\boldsymbol{r}}_3 = \frac{\boldsymbol{F}_h + \boldsymbol{F}_1}{m_1} \tag{3}$$

Where m_3 represents the total mass of the active spacecraft and the manipulator, m_1 represents the mass of the end-effector, $\boldsymbol{r}_3$ represents the position vector of the active spacecraft's centroid relative to the inertial coordinate system, $\boldsymbol{r}_1$ represents the position vector of the end-effector's centroid relative to the inertial coordinate system.

Therefore, acceleration vector of O_1 relative to O_3 in inertial system is:

$$\boldsymbol{a}_{13} = \ddot{\boldsymbol{r}}_1 - \ddot{\boldsymbol{r}}_3 = \frac{\boldsymbol{F}_h + \boldsymbol{F}_1}{m_1} - \frac{\boldsymbol{F}_h}{m_3} \tag{4}$$

Relative acceleration between two mechanisms in the body-fixed coordinate system can be written as the following form:

$$\dot{\boldsymbol{V}}_{13} = \boldsymbol{a}_{13} - 2\omega_3 \times \boldsymbol{V}_{13} - \dot{\omega}_3 \times \boldsymbol{r}_{13} - \omega_3 \times (\omega_3 \times \boldsymbol{r}_{13}) \tag{5}$$

Where $\boldsymbol{V}_{13}$ represents the velocity of the end-effector relative to the active spacecraft in O_3 coordinate system, ω_3 represents the angular velocity of the active spacecraft.

Therefore the relative velocity vector and the relative displacement vector between two mechanisms in O_3 coordinate system can be written as:

$$\boldsymbol{V}_{13} = \int \dot{\boldsymbol{V}}_{13} \cdot dt + \boldsymbol{V}_{13}(0) \tag{6}$$

$$\boldsymbol{S}_{13} = \int \boldsymbol{V}_{13} \cdot dt + \boldsymbol{S}_{13}(0) \tag{7}$$

Where $\boldsymbol{V}_{13}$ (0) and $\boldsymbol{S}_{13}$ (0) are the initial velocity and initial displacement respectively when collide.

The above equations are the relative translation model of the active spacecraft and the end-effector. Based on the Euler equation, concrete expressions of the relative rotation model between two mechanisms are as follows:

$$\boldsymbol{J}_3 \cdot \varepsilon_3 + \omega_3 \times (\boldsymbol{J}_3 \cdot \omega_3) = \boldsymbol{r}_{A3} \times \boldsymbol{F}_h + \boldsymbol{M}_h \tag{8}$$

$$\boldsymbol{J}_1 \cdot \varepsilon_1 + \omega_1 \times (\boldsymbol{J}_1 \cdot \omega_1) = \boldsymbol{r}_{1F} \times \boldsymbol{F}_1 - \boldsymbol{r}_{A1} \times \boldsymbol{F}_h - \boldsymbol{M}_h \tag{9}$$

Where ε_3 and ε_1 represent the angular acceleration of active spacecraft and the angular acceleration of end-effector respectively, $\boldsymbol{r}_{1F}$ represents the position vector of the collision contact point to the end-effector's centroid, $\boldsymbol{r}_{A3}$ and $\boldsymbol{r}_{A1}$ represent the vectors of point A to the active spacecraft's centroid and point A to the end-effector's centroid respectively, $\boldsymbol{J}_3$ and $\boldsymbol{J}_1$ represent the inertia tensors of the active spacecraft and the end-effector respectively.

Through Eqs. (8) and (9) we can obtain ω_3 and ω_1, then angular velocity vector of the end-effector relative to the active spacecraft is:

$$\omega_{13} = \omega_1 - \boldsymbol{R}_{13}^{-1} \cdot \omega_3 \tag{10}$$

Euler-angle change rate of the end-effector relative to the active spacecraft is:

$$\begin{bmatrix} \dot{\alpha}_{13} \\ \dot{\beta}_{13} \\ \dot{\gamma}_{13} \end{bmatrix} = \boldsymbol{E}_{13}^{-1} \cdot \omega_{13} \tag{11}$$

$$\boldsymbol{E}_{13} = \begin{bmatrix} 1 & 0 & -\sin\beta_{13} \\ 0 & \cos\alpha_{13} & \cos\beta_{13}\sin\alpha_{13} \\ 0 & -\sin\alpha_{13} & \cos\beta_{13}\cos\alpha_{13} \end{bmatrix} \tag{12}$$

Integration of Eqs. (11) and (12) we can obtain the Euler-angle of the end-effector relative to the active spacecraft $\boldsymbol{\Phi}_{13} = [\alpha_{13}\ \beta_{13}\ \gamma_{13}]'$.

In conclusion, the relative position parameters of the end-effector relative to the active spacecraft could be solved.

$\boldsymbol{F}_1$, $\boldsymbol{r}_{1F}$ and $\boldsymbol{M}_h$ are unknown parameters in the above models. While during the capture simulation experiment, collision force and torque can be measured by six-dimensional force sensors which installed on each mechanism. Therefore, when applying the capture dynamics models, $\boldsymbol{F}_1$ and $\boldsymbol{r}_{1F} \times \boldsymbol{F}_1$ can be regarded as known parameters. The spring force $\boldsymbol{F}_h$ and the spring torque $\boldsymbol{M}_h$ can be obtained through the following process.

3.2 Force and Torque Modeling of the Six Dimensional Spring-Damping System

As shown in Fig. 2, the positions of the manipulator installed on the end-effector and the active spacecraft are described with point A and point B respectively. The initial vector of the relative position is $\boldsymbol{r}_{AB}(0)$. After the collision, coordinate systems located at point A and point B will generate relative translation and rotation. Combining the stiffness and damping parameters, the spring force and torque models of the spring-damping system can be established.

Hypothesis, the Euler-angle of the O_4 coordinate system relative to the O_3 coordinate system is $\boldsymbol{\Phi}_{h3} = [\alpha_{h3}\ \beta_{h3}\ \gamma_{h3}]'$, then the Euler-angle $\boldsymbol{\Phi}_{h1} = [\alpha_{h1}\ \beta_{h1}\ \gamma_{h1}]'$ of the O_4 coordinate system relative to the O_1 coordinate system can be solved according to the coordinate of vector $\boldsymbol{r}_{AB}(0)$ in two coordinate systems.

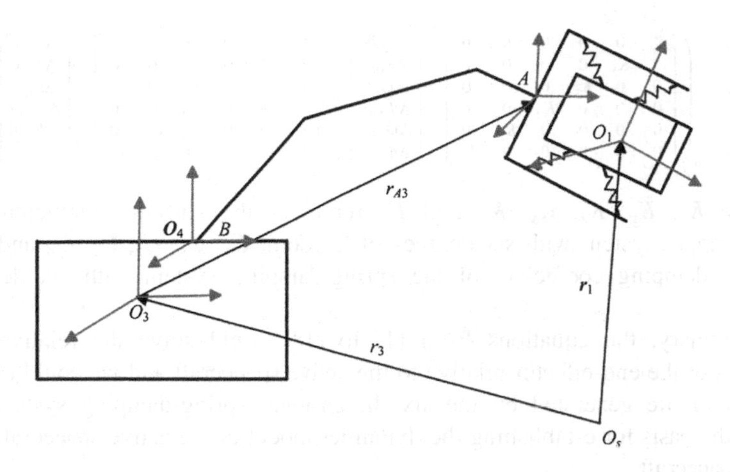

Fig. 2. Definition of the spring-damping system's coordinate system.

Velocity vector of point A relative to O_3 in the inertial system is:

$$\boldsymbol{v}_{A3} = \int \boldsymbol{a}_{13} \cdot dt + \boldsymbol{\omega}_1 \cdot \boldsymbol{r}_{1h} \tag{13}$$

Velocity vector of point A relative to O_3 in the O_3 coordinate system is:

$$\boldsymbol{V}_{A3} = \boldsymbol{R}_3^{-1} \cdot (\boldsymbol{v}_{A3} - \omega_3 \cdot \boldsymbol{r}_{A3}) \tag{14}$$

Then relative position vector of point A relative to point B in the O_4 coordinate system is:

$$\boldsymbol{r}_{AB} = \boldsymbol{R}_{h3}^{-1} \cdot \left(\int \boldsymbol{V}_{A3} \cdot dt - \boldsymbol{r}_{3h}\right) \tag{15}$$

Variation of relative position in the O_4 coordinate system is:

$$\Delta\boldsymbol{r}_{AB} = \boldsymbol{r}_{AB} - \boldsymbol{r}_{AB}(0) \tag{16}$$

The relative rotation angle of coordinate systems located at the point A and point B is:

$$\Delta\boldsymbol{\Phi}_{AB} = \int (\boldsymbol{R}_{13} \cdot \boldsymbol{R}_{h1} \cdot \omega_1 - \boldsymbol{R}_{h3}^{-1} \cdot \omega_3) \cdot dt \tag{17}$$

Where $\boldsymbol{R}_{1h}$ represents the coordinate transformation matrix of the O_1 coordinate system relative to the O_4 coordinate system, and $\boldsymbol{R}_{h3}$ represents the coordinate transformation matrix of the O_4 coordinate system relative to the O_3 coordinate system.

The force and torque generated by the six dimensional spring-damping system can be obtained through the following equation:

$$\begin{bmatrix} F_h \\ M_h \end{bmatrix} = R_{h3} \cdot \left(\begin{bmatrix} K_x & 0 & 0 & 0 & 0 & 0 \\ 0 & K_y & 0 & 0 & 0 & 0 \\ 0 & 0 & K_z & 0 & 0 & 0 \\ 0 & 0 & 0 & K_\alpha & 0 & 0 \\ 0 & 0 & 0 & 0 & K_\beta & 0 \\ 0 & 0 & 0 & 0 & 0 & K_\varphi \end{bmatrix} \cdot \begin{bmatrix} \Delta r_{AB}x \\ \Delta r_{AB}y \\ \Delta r_{AB}z \\ \Delta \Phi_{AB}\alpha \\ \Delta \Phi_{AB}\beta \\ \Delta \Phi_{AB}\gamma \end{bmatrix} + \begin{bmatrix} C_x & 0 & 0 & 0 & 0 & 0 \\ 0 & C_y & 0 & 0 & 0 & 0 \\ 0 & 0 & C_z & 0 & 0 & 0 \\ 0 & 0 & 0 & C_\alpha & 0 & 0 \\ 0 & 0 & 0 & 0 & C_\beta & 0 \\ 0 & 0 & 0 & 0 & 0 & C_\varphi \end{bmatrix} \cdot \begin{bmatrix} \Delta \dot{r}_{AB}x \\ \Delta \dot{r}_{AB}y \\ \Delta \dot{r}_{AB}z \\ \Delta \dot{\Phi}_{AB}\alpha \\ \Delta \dot{\Phi}_{AB}\beta \\ \Delta \dot{\Phi}_{AB}\gamma \end{bmatrix} \right) \tag{18}$$

Where K_x, K_y, K_z, K_α, K_β and K_γ represent the stiffness coefficient of the spring-damping system with six degrees of freedom. C_x, C_y, C_z, C_α, C_β and C_γ represent the damping coefficient of the spring-damping system with six degrees of freedom.

In summary, the equations from (1) to (18) could solve the relative motion parameters of the end-effector relative to the active spacecraft and we could obtain the force and torque generated by the six dimensional spring-damping system, which provides the basis for establishing the dynamics model of the active spacecraft and the passive spacecraft.

3.3 Kinematics Modeling of the Passive Spacecraft Relative to the Active Spacecraft

The force impacting on the passive spacecraft is F_2 when colliding; based on the Newton equation, accelerations of the active spacecraft and the passive spacecraft in the inertial coordinate system are written as:

$$\ddot{r}_3 = \frac{F_h}{m_3} \tag{19}$$

$$\ddot{r}_2 = \frac{F_2}{m_2} \tag{20}$$

Where represents the total mass of the passive spacecraft and the manipulator, r_2 represents the position vector of the passive spacecraft's centroid relative to the inertial coordinate system.

Therefore, acceleration vector of the O_2 relative to the O_3 in the inertial system is:

$$a_{23} = \ddot{r}_2 - \ddot{r}_3 = \frac{F_2}{m_2} - \frac{F_h}{m_3} \tag{21}$$

Relative acceleration between the two mechanisms in the body-fixed coordinate system can be written as the following form:

$$\dot{V}_{23} = a_{23} - 2\omega_3 \times V_{23} - \dot{\omega}_3 \times r_{23} - \omega_3 \times (\omega_3 \times r_{23}) \tag{22}$$

Where V_{23} represents the velocity of the passive spacecraft relative to the active spacecraft in the O_3 coordinate system.

Therefore, the relative velocity vector and relative displacement vector between the two mechanisms in the O_3 coordinate system represent written as:

$$V_{23} = \int \dot{V}_{23} \cdot dt + V_{23}(0) \tag{23}$$

$$S_{23} = \int V_{23} \cdot dt + S_{23}(0) \tag{24}$$

Based on the Euler equation, concrete expression of the rotation modeling of the passive spacecraft is as follows:

$$J_2 \cdot \varepsilon_2 + \omega_2 \times (J_2 \cdot \omega_2) = r_{2F} \times F_2 \tag{25}$$

Where ε_2 represents the angular acceleration of the passive spacecraft, r_{2F} represents the position vector of the collision contact point to the passive spacecraft's centroid, J_2 represents the inertia tensor of the passive spacecraft.

Through Eqs. (8) to (25), we can obtain ω_3 and ω_2. Angular velocity vector of the passive spacecraft relative to the active spacecraft is:

$$\omega_{23} = \omega_2 - R_{23}^{-1} \cdot \omega_3 \tag{26}$$

Euler-angle change rate of the passive spacecraft relative to the active spacecraft is:

$$\begin{bmatrix} \dot{\alpha}_{23} \\ \dot{\beta}_{23} \\ \dot{\gamma}_{23} \end{bmatrix} = E_{23}^{-1} \cdot \omega_{23} \tag{27}$$

$$E_{23} = \begin{bmatrix} 1 & 0 & -\sin\beta_{23} \\ 0 & \cos\alpha_{23} & \cos\beta_{23}\sin\alpha_{23} \\ 0 & -\sin\alpha_{23} & \cos\beta_{23}\cos\alpha_{23} \end{bmatrix} \tag{28}$$

Integration of Eqs. (27) and (28) we can obtain the Euler-angle of the passive spacecraft relative to the active spacecraft $\Phi_{23} = [\alpha_{23}\ \beta_{23}\ \gamma_{23}]'$.

Combining F_h, M_h and Eqs. (19) to (28), we could solve the relative motion parameters S_{23} and Φ_{23}. In the experiment of capture simulation, usually the movement between two experiment mechanisms is reproduced according to the parameters S_{23} and Φ_{23}.

4 Numerical Calculation of the Capture Dynamics and Results Comparison

The above proposed capture dynamics model is solved by numerical calculation, in order to verify the correctness and accuracy of the capture dynamics model, a simulation model is established in ADAMS software. In the simulation model, the force and torque results of the six dimensional spring-damping system and the relative motion parameters between the passive active spacecraft and the active spacecraft are solved by ADAMS, the established passive spacecraft, active spacecraft, end-effector and the six dimensional spring-damping system use the same parameters value used in the above context. In additional, the main parameters are as follows: total mass of the active spacecraft and manipulator is 6000 kg, mass of the passive spacecraft is 1000 kg, and mass of the end-effector is 60 kg.

The collision force and torque are assumed known parameters, specific value and other parameters are listed in Table 1. The results comparisons of the two methods are shown from Figs. 3, 4, 5 and 6, in which force results of the six dimensional spring-damping system, torque results of the six dimensional spring-damping system, relative displacement of the passive spacecraft relative to the active spacecraft, and relative Euler-angle of the passive spacecraft relative to the active spacecraft are shown. In additional, red curves are the results of the numerical solution and the blue ones are the ADAMS simulation results.

Through the above results we can see that the results of the numerical solution are almost coincident with the results of ADAMS simulation, which embodies the consistency of the two methods and verifies the correctness of the capture dynamics model.

Table 1. Main parameters of the numerical calculation

Parameters/Axis	X	Y	Z
Total inertia tensor of the active spacecraft and the manipulator (kg·m2)	60000	60000	55000
Inertia tensor of the passive spacecraft (kg·m2)	1000	1100	1200
Inertia tensor of the end-effector (kg·m2)	100	110	120
The Euler-angle of O4 coordinate system relative to O3 coordinate system	0	0	0
Initial displacement of the end-effector relative to the active spacecraft (m)	3.18	3.59	3.45
Initial Euler-angle of the end-effector relative to the active spacecraft (°)	30	30	30
Initial displacement of passive spacecraft relative to the active spacecraft (m)	4.5	4.5	4.5
Initial Euler-angle of the passive spacecraft relative to the active spacecraft (°)	0	0	0
Translation stiffness coefficient of the spring-damping system (N/m)	10000	10000	10000
Rotation stiffness coefficient of the spring-damping system (N/rad)	10000	10000	10000
Translation damping coefficient of the spring-damping system (N/(m/s))	0.01	0.01	0.01
Rotation damping coefficient of the spring-damping system (N/(rad/s))	0.01	0.01	0.01
Collision force on the end-effector (N)	1000	1100	1200
Collision force on the passive spacecraft (N)	-1000	-1100	-1200

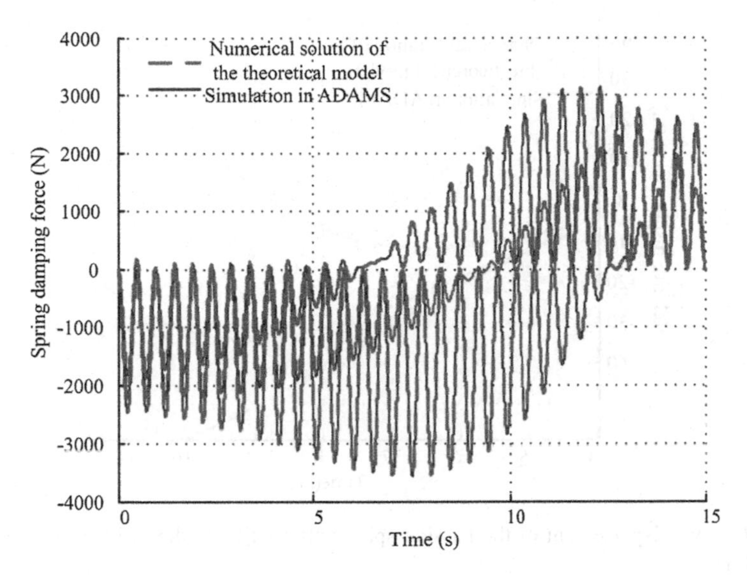

Fig. 3. Force results of the six dimensional spring-damping system. (Color figure online)

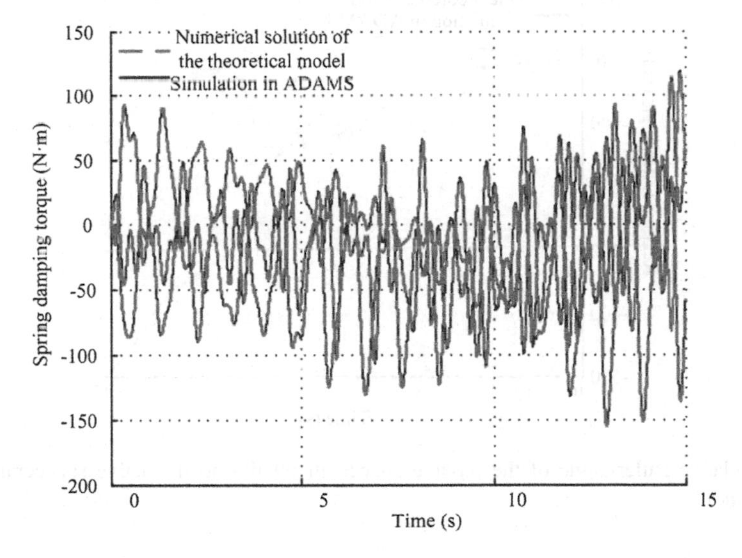

Fig. 4. Torque results of the six dimensional spring-damping system. (Color figure online)

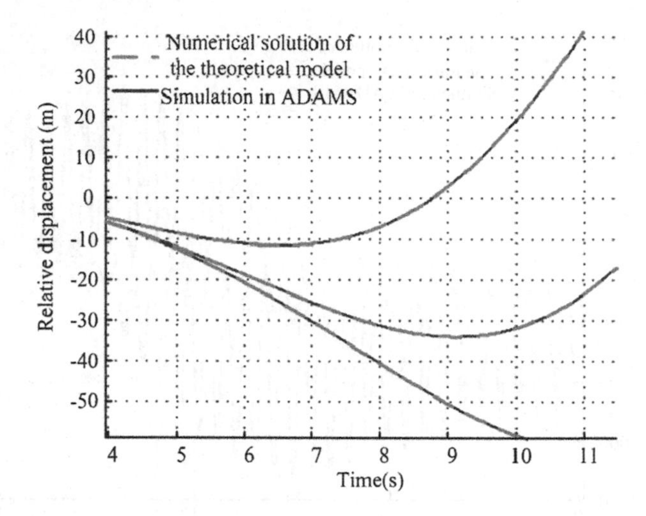

Fig. 5. Relative displacement of the passive spacecraft relative to the active spacecraft. (Color figure online)

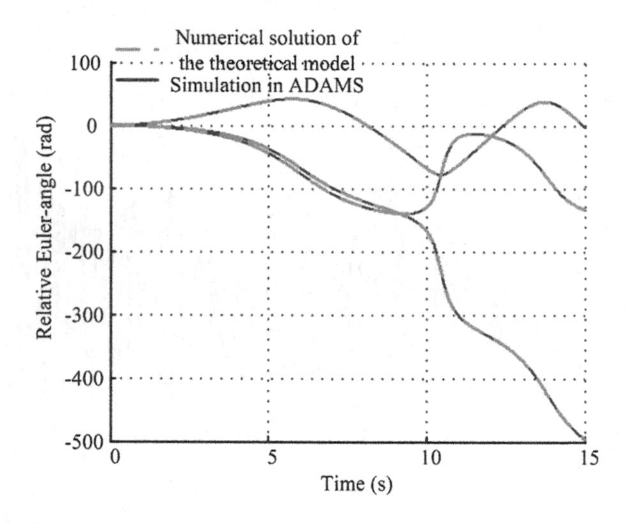

Fig. 6. Relative Euler-angle of the passive spacecraft relative to the active spacecraft. (Color figure online)

5 Conclusion

A capture dynamics model of the space flexible manipulator is established in this paper, in which the flexibility of the manipulator is considered and the complex modeling method of the flexible manipulator with large amount of calculation is avoided. In this paper the manipulator is equivalent to a six dimensional spring-damping system, and the dynamics model is established by applying of the Newton-Euler method. Then corresponding results are obtained by numerical solution. The effectiveness and accuracy of the dynamics model is verified by comparing with the ADAMS simulation model. This paper provides a theory basis for the ground capture simulation.

Acknowledgements. This work is supported by the project of China "Test platform development of the end-effector's comprehensive properties" and the National Natural Science Foundation of China (No. 51475116).

References

1. Feng, F.: Research on space large misalignment tolerance end-effector and its soft capture strategy. Ph.D. thesis, Harbin: Harbin Institute of Technology, Harbin (2013) (in Chinese)
2. Feng, F., Liu, Y.W., Liu, H., Cai, H.G.: Design schemes and comparison research of the end-effector of large space manipulator. Chin. J. Mech. Eng. **25**, 674–687 (2012)
3. Liu, H., Tan, Y.S., Liu, Y.W., Jie, D.Y., Gao, K., Cai, H.G.: Development of Chinese large-scale space end-effector. J. Cent. S. Univ. Technol. (Engl. Ed.) **18**, 600–609 (2011)
4. Feng, F., Liu, Y.W., Liu, H., Cai, H.G.: Development of space end-effector with capabilities of misalignment tolerance and soft capture based on tendon-sheath transmission system. J. Cent. S. Univ. Technol. (Engl. Ed.) **20**, 3015–3030 (2013)
5. Quitner, E., Vandersluis, R., Rakhsha, J.: System and concept design of the SSRMS latching end effector. In: Proceedings of the 3rd European Space Mechanisms and Tribology Symposium, Madrid, Spain (1987)
6. Kumar, R., Hayes, R.: System requirements and design features of space station remote manipulator system mechanisms. In: 25th Aerospace Mechanisms Symposium, California, United States. NASA Conference Publication (1991)
7. Shi, K.Y.: Path planning and impact modeling of space manipulator for target capturing. Master thesis, Harbin: Harbin Institute of Technology, Harbin (2008) (in Chinese)
8. Spong, M.W.: Modeling and control of elastic joint robots. J. Dyn. Syst. Meas. Contr. **109**, 310–319 (1987)
9. Spong, M.W., Khorasani, K., Kokotovic, P.V.: An integral manifold approach to the feedback control of flexible joint robots. IEEE J. Rob. Autom. **3**, 291–300 (1987)
10. Yue, S.G., Yu, Y.Q., Bai, S.X.: Flexible rotor beam element for the manipulators with joint and link flexibility. Mech. Mach. Theory **32**, 209–219 (1997)
11. Zhang, X., Yu, Y.Q.: A new spatial rotor beam element for modeling spatial manipulators with joint and link flexibility. Mech. Mach. Theory **35**, 403–421 (2000)
12. Guan, Y.Z.: Study on dynamics and Simulation of spacecraft docking process. Ph.D. thesis, Harbin: Harbin Institute of Technology, Harbin (2008) (in Chinese)
13. Pan, D., Zhao, Y.: Dynamic modeling and analysis of space manipulator considering the flexible of joint and link. Adv. Mater. Res. **823**, 270–275 (2013)
14. Chen, K.P., Fu, L.C.: Nonlinear adaptive motion control for a manipulator with flexible joints. In: IEEE International Conference on Robotics and Automation, Scottsdale, AZ (1989)

Simulation Model for Container Logistics System of Waterway Transportation

Deng Xiaoyun(✉)

Waterborne Transport Research Institute, MOT, Beijing 100088, People's Republic of China
dengxy@wti.ac.cn

Abstract. This paper summarizes and analyzes the development and application of simulation technique as well as the technology and method for the establishment of simulation model of complex system, illustrates the study on simulation model of port & terminal operation system, transportation, logistics system and the like at home and abroad, and proposes the composition of simulation model for container logistics system of waterway transportation. The model includes corresponding base modules, entities, subsystems, a simulation model for the operation system of container terminal and a simulation model for container logistics system of waterway transportation.

Keywords: Waterway transportation · Container logistics system · Simulation modeling

1 Introduction

Since the birth of digital simulation machine and professional simulation software, the system simulation technology technique has achieved resource sharing for information and simulation, interoperability and reusability of simulation system. The different corresponding modeling approaches are applied to Discrete-Event system Simulation, Continuous-Event system Simulation, Combined Discrete continuous-Event system Simulation and other different events: event oriented, procedure oriented and object oriented ways are mainly applied to Discrete-Event system Simulation, linear/nonlinear, constant/time variant, lumped parameter/distribution parameter, determination/random and the like are mainly applied to Continuous-Event system Simulation, and for the Combined Discrete continuous-Event system Simulation, the above two modeling approaches should be considered.

2 Research Status on the Simulation of Transportation System

2.1 Study on Simulation of Port and Terminal Operation System

The relevant studies on the simulation of traffic and transportation system at abroad have been implemented, and there were more relevant contents, especially for the aspect of the operation system modeling for container terminal and other ports. Veeke and Ottjes

L. Zhang et al. (Eds.): AsiaSim 2016/SCS AutumnSim 2016, Part I, CCIS 643, pp. 308–315, 2016.
DOI: 10.1007/978-981-10-2663-8_33

[1] set up computer simulation model to provide decision support for the further operating direction of wharf while expanding the Port of Rotterdam. Ha, and Park [2] applied simulation software to establish a real-time 3D visual port simulation model, including various loading and unloading equipment in ports to obtain different running conditions of ports under different states via changing equipment parameters, so as to timely reflect the operating state of wharf. Martagan and Eksioglu [3] set up port simulation model under emergency logistics conditions to obtain the operating state of supply chain under different routes. Mosca [4] studied the layout of wharf in front and rear parts of storage yard via modeling to verify and solve planning, design and other problems of wharf. Demirci [5] applied AweSim emulational language to set up a simulation model of harbour capacity specific to Trabzon port, and to analyze the choke point of development of harbour capacity. Shabavek and Yeung [6] established a simulation model specific to kwai chung wharf to predict its operating conditions (Fig. 1).

Relevant domestic researches are more focused on port terminal operation system, especially on the aspects of modeling and simulation of container terminal and port terminal operation system. Such as, Wang and Jiang [7] applied bi-level programming model to make decision for the choices of inland distribution center and transport network of regional port logistics system, and to propose the dual coordination algorithm solution for such model. Cai [8] studied and applied the simulation and optimization techniques of seaport container logistics system mainly from the aspects of Petri network modeling, berth allocation, wharf front leading layout and the like, and applied eM-Plant software to set up simulation model to verify the validity and rapidness of simulation method. Li [9] applied the theory of Discrete-Event system Simulation to set up the queuing network model of container terminal logistics system, and applied simulation software Arena for achieving modeling. With the iron ore import port logistics system of a certain port in southern part of China as a research object, Li and Zhao [10] set up Discrete-Event dynamic system model (DEDS model) based on Petri network, and established a simulation model for iron ore import port logistics system (Fig. 2).

2.2 Study on Logistics System Simulation of Waterway Transportation

Based on the analysis for the current situation of container transportation in Yangtze river basin, inclusive of Yangtze River waterway, layout of port, container volume, route operator, ship type and the like, Zhou [11] set up the port berths system model via mathematical analysis modeling, and applied Queuing Theory for solution, finally, Wuhan port is set as an example, through considering the mutual benefits of ship and port comprehensively, the optimal modeling scale was obtained. With each port of Yangtze River as a starting point, and Port of Shanghai (Yangshan Port and Waigaoqiao Port Area) as terminal point, container transportation system plan was designed to obtain more superior scheme via comparing necessary freight rate and to carry out sensitivity analysis.

With container transport network as a research object, and through calculating the 3 performance indicators of time, cost and service quality for each possible route, Shi [12] set up a specific transportation scheme to carry out dynamic simulation via Extend system software, analyze and observe the influence and function of each transportation element in container transportation organization via sensitivity analysis, so as to obtain optimal and comparable route, and such simulation could achieve the adjustment in the transportation speed, service quality and other parameters (Fig. 3).

Shang, Qin and Cheng [13] implemented the simulation and optimization studies on ship form and system for coal export transportation. The optimization procedures of the ship form were divided into two levels rationally: firstly, the simulation and optimization method of stochastic discrete-time system was applied to optimize the load capacity and navigational speed of ships, and then, based on the technical property requirements of ships, its principal dimension was decided (Fig. 4).

3 Composition of Simulation Model

Waterway transportation system covers port, ships, channel, related road, railway, cargo and the like with relatively complex system composition. The model applies the modeling route of module and entity first, and then system procedure to build container generation module, train and truck collecting and distributing ports module, starting transshipment port operating module, channel operating module, weather and sea conditions generation module, data statistic analysis module, and other basic module, and then, according to actual simulation demands, it is available to respectively build simulation model for container port and wharf operating system, the simulation model for waterway container logistics system of whole basin.

The container waterway transportation hinderland of Yangtze river generally contains Shanghai. etc. 9 provinces and cities, 35 medium and large cities along the river. The container logistics system mainly contains of 25 container ports, totally 59 special berths, divided into port of loading and transshipment. The Yangtze River waterway is about 2800 km, divided into upstream, midstream and downstream. The container ship liner has more than 100 lines, separate into domestic feeder, near-sea shipping line and domestic trade routes. The container capacity container develops into 200TEU from 48TEU (Fig. 5).

3.1 Base Module and Entity Composition of Model

(1) Local Container Generator Modular – LCGM

Sub-module: Local container generator modular, Container generating operation modular; Entity: local container generator.

(2) Ship Generator Modular – SGM:

Sub-module: Ship generator modular; Entity: Ships, ships queue.

(3) Ship Loading & Unloading Modular – SLUM

Sub-module: Ship transportation modular

(4) Train Generator Modular – TaGM:

Sub-module: Train generator modular; Entity: Trains, Trains queue.

(5) Train Loading & Unloading Modular – TaLUM:

Sub-module: Train transportation modular

(6) Truck Generator Modular – TcGM:

Sub-module: Truck generator modular; Entity: Trucks, Trucks queue.

(7) Truck Loading & Unloading Modular – TcLUM:

Sub-module: Truck loading & unloading modular

(8) Starting Port Generator Modular –SPGM

Sub-module: Starting port generator modular, Ship generator modular, Starting port running modular; Entity: Starting port, Container, Ships, Ships queue (Fig. 6).

(9) Transshipment Port Generator Modular –TPGM

Sub-module: Transshipment port generator modular, Transshipment port running modular; Entity: Transshipment port, Container, Ships, Ships queue.

(10) Terminal Manager Modular –TMM

Sub-module: Terminal manager modular, Anchorage operation modular, Berth operation modular, Loading bridge operation module, Trailer operation modular, Rubber-tyred gantry crane operation modular, Gate operation modular, Queue operation modular

Entity: Anchorage, Berths, Loading bridges, Trailers, Rubber, Doors, Doors queue

(11) Yard Operation Modular –YOM

Sub-module: Yard management modular, Operation modular of container section

Entity: Storage yard, Container section, Display of yard container storage volume

(12) Channel Operation Modular –ChaOM

Sub-module: Channel modular, Route operation modular, Ship transportation modular; Entity: Route, Ship queue.

(13) Weather and Sea State Modular –WeSSM

Sub-module: Weather and sea state modular; Entity: Weather and sea state.

(14) Data Analysis Modular – DaAM

Sub-module: Data input, Data conversion module, Data statistics sub-module, Data output

Entity: Data input, Data statistics, Output statement.

3.2 Composition of Model Operation Subsystem

The handling technology of container terminal can be divided into the following several parts: (1) ship loading and unloading, container is from ships ⟺ storage yard; (2) train loading and unloading, container is from train ⟺ storage yard; (3) truck collecting, distributing and pickup, truck ⟺ storage yard. The flow chart for each part is as follows:

(1) Flow chart of ship loading & unloading system

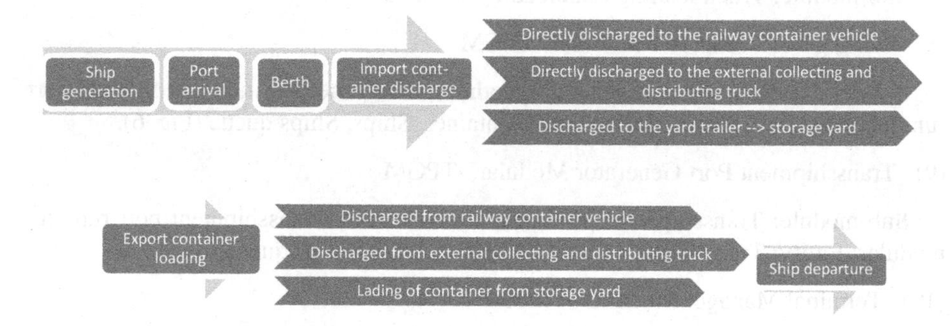

Fig. 1. Flow chart of ship loading & unloading system

(2) Flow chart of train collecting and distributing port subsystem

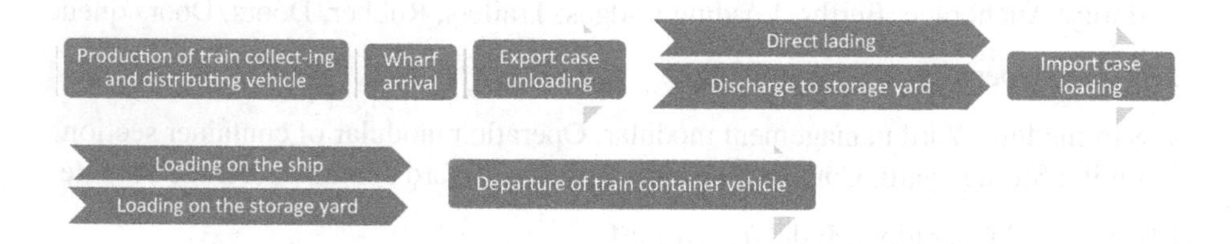

Fig. 2. Flow chart of train collecting and distributing port subsystem

(3) Flow chart of truck collecting and distributing port subsystem

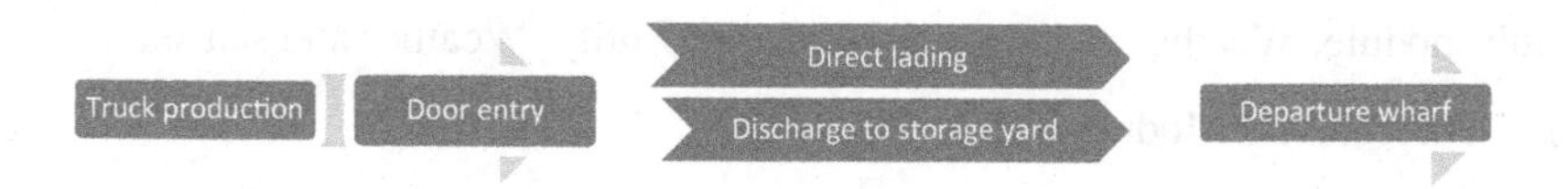

Fig. 3. Flow chart of truck collecting port subsystem

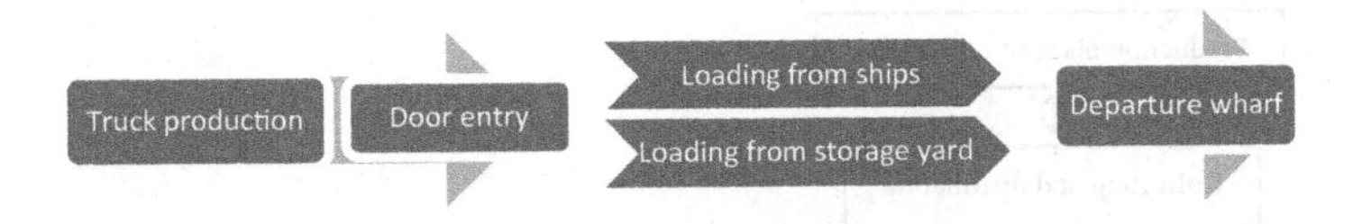

Fig. 4. Flow chart of truck distributing port subsystem

3.3 Simulation Model for Operation System of Container Port and Terminal

Combined with the above related base modules, entity, subsystem and other combination, based on the system flow of container ports and terminals operating system, build the simulation model for operation system of container port and terminal as shown in the figure below:

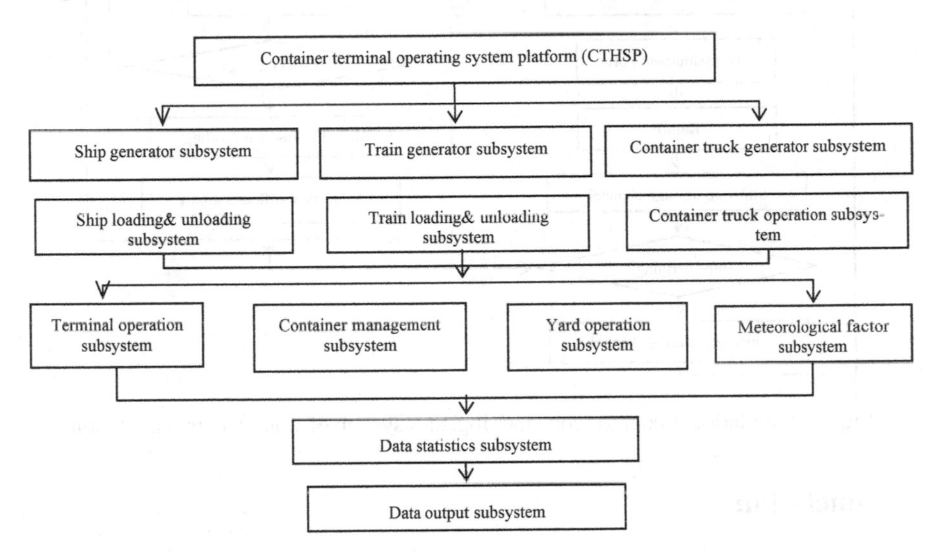

Fig. 5. Flow chart of simulation model for container ports and terminals

3.4 Simulation Model for Container Logistics System of Waterway Transportation

Combined with the actual operation process of container logistics system of Yangtze River waterway transportation, collecting the operating data related to actual system to complete mathematics and model description for each module, operating parameters of entity and other contents, for container logistics system of waterway transportation was developed. The flow of driving model operation is mainly as follows: the container transportation from starting port to port of call, transshipment and back tracking, and the main flow of model is as shown in the figure below:

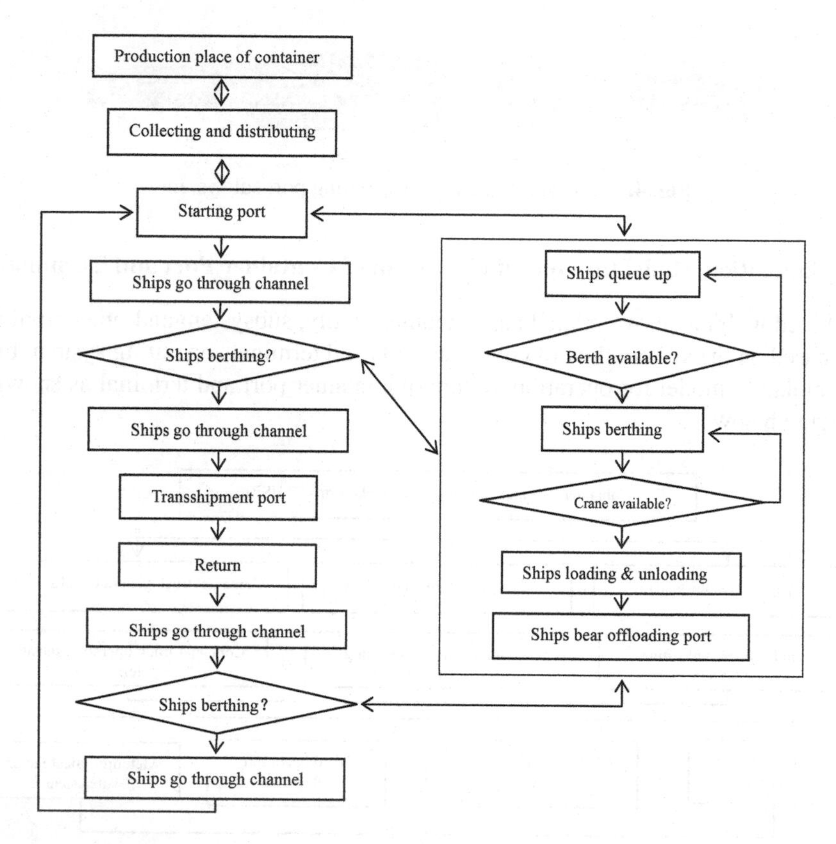

Fig. 6. Simulation model for container logistics system of waterway transportation

4 Conclusion

Through the analysis and study on the actual logistics system of the existing container terminal, the operating data related to actual system is collected to complete mathematics and model description for each module, operating parameters setting of entity and other contents, and to build corresponding system simulation model on a simulation platform, so as to verify the reliability of the model and carry out relevant experimental study. The flexibility, portability, repeatability and the like of object-oriented modeling and modular modeling provide conditions for building multiple simulation models in a platform.

In this paper, only two sets of simulation model composition are proposed: namely, one is the simulation model for container port and terminal operating system, and another one is the simulation model of container logistics system for waterway transportation. The simulation model of container port and terminal operation system can be used for carrying out the analysis on the aspects of handling system efficiency, equipment capacity, technological process, yard capacity of ports and terminals to improve the efficiency and benefits of single port and terminal. And the simulation model of container logistics system for waterway transportation can be used for verifying and analyzing the volume of container in production place, completion of port handling capacity, the conditions of ports and ships operating parameters, the rationality of system other operating parameter as well, furthermore, it can be used for analyzing the internal capacity, efficiency and cost of system, carbon emission index, studying the influences of the changes existing in the volume of container in production place, and the changes in the internal capacity, efficiency and cost on the system, so as to provide quantitative analysis tools for implementing corresponding studies on container terminals & ports, and logistics system.

References

1. Veeke, H.P.M., Ottjes, J.A.: a generie simulation model for system of container terminal. Model. Simul. **16**(4), 184–191 (2002)
2. Ha, B.-H., Park, E.-J., Hopkinson, K.M., et al.: Proceedings of the 2007 Winter Simulation Conference, Washington D.C, 3007. Washington University of Washington Press (2007)
3. Martagan, T.G., Eksioglu, B., Giovanini, R., et al.: Proceedings of the 2009 Winter Simulation Conference, Baltimore Maryland, 2008. Baltimore: University of Maryland Press (2009)
4. Mosca, R., Giribone, P., Bruzzone, A.G.: Simulation of dock management and planning in a port terminal. Int. J. Model. Simul. **20**(2), 153–157 (2000)
5. Demirci, E.: Simulation modeling and analysis of a port investment. Simulation **79**(2), 94–105 (2003). (S0037-5497)
6. Shabavek, A.A., Yeung, W.W.: A simulation model for the Kwai Chung container terminals in Hong Kong. Euro. J. Oper. Res. **140**, 1–10 (2002)
7. Wang, C.-X., Jiang, L.-K.: Bi-level programming based optimization on regional port Inland transportation network. J. Ind. Eng. Manage. **22**(4), 67–71 (2008)
8. Cai, Y.: Simulation & optimization researched and applied in port container logistics system, Wuhan University of Technology (2005)
9. Li, W.: Optimization of logistics system for container terminal with simulation approach, Dalian University of Technology (2006)
10. Yongzhuang, L., Qiuguo, Z.: Simulation model development of imported iron ore terminal based on witness. Shipp. Manage. **10**, 24–26 (2011)
11. Zhou, K.: Research and simulation on container transportation system of the yangtze river, Wuhan University of Technology (2015)
12. Shi, Y.: Dynamic simulation on container transport system. J. Shanghai Marit. Univ. **29**(2), 72–77 (2008)
13. Tang, X., et al.: Simulation–optimization of ship types for Chinese exportation of coal through modeling of transport systems. J. Shanghai Jiaotong Univ. **5**, 22–28 (1994)

An Ontology Based Domain-Specific Composable Modeling Method for Complex Simulation Systems

Xiaobo Li[1,2(✉)], Tianjun Liao[3], Weiping Wang[1], Zhe Shu[1], Ning Zhu[1], and Yonglin Lei[1]

[1] College of Information Systems and Management, National University of Defense Technology, Changsha, China
lixiaobo@nudt.edu.cn
[2] Department of Mathematics and Computer Science, University of Antwerp, Antwerp, Belgium
[3] State Key Laboratory of Complex System Simulation, Beijing Institute of System Engineering, Beijing, China

Abstract. Simulation modeling for complex systems should be both domain-specific to reflect domain characteristics of different subsystems and composable to integrate different domain models. Current research fails to provide a unified method to meet the two requirements simultaneously. In this work, an ontology-based domain-specific composable modeling method is proposed to solve this problem. This method employs layered ontologies including an upper ontology and a series of subdomain ontologies to formally represent the knowledge of the complex simulation system; and uses the ontology knowledge to design DSMLs for each subdomain. The case study on combat systems effectiveness simulation shows that domain models designed with different DSMLs can be technically and semantically composed since they have an explicit interaction framework and a common semantic foundation.

Keywords: Domain specific modeling · Composable modeling · Ontological metamodeling · Domain specific modeling language · Effectiveness simulation

1 Introduction

In the last decades, Modeling and Simulation (M&S) has played an irreplaceable role in complex systems research since M&S can significantly reduce development time and cost of complex systems. However, Complex systems usually have heterogeneous subsystems involving different subject domains. When interacting with the environment and other systems, the complicated structure of complex systems can generate non-linear or even emergent behavior. Thus, different subsystems and subject domains have different structural and behavioral characteristics, which need to be modeled with correspondingly appropriate methods. Moreover, these models of different subsystems and subject domains should be composed into a single simulation application to enable integrative simulation experimentation.

Simulation modeling for complex systems should be both domain-specific to reflect domain characteristics of different subsystems and composable to integrate different

L. Zhang et al. (Eds.): AsiaSim 2016/SCS AutumnSim 2016, Part I, CCIS 643, pp. 316–324, 2016.
DOI: 10.1007/978-981-10-2663-8_34

domain models. These two requirements are difficult to satisfy at the same time since domain particularity and composability are seemingly contradictory. Using the same method to model different systems naturally support domain composition while loses domain particularity, meanwhile the usage of different methods will enable appropriate domain modeling but hamper domain composition.

On the one hand, the M&S community has launched research on unified modeling methods to enable composable modeling, which can be roughly divided into four groups, namely unified formalisms, model specification, model framework and simulation protocol. On the other hand, domain-specific modeling (DSM) in software engineering field has been introduced into M&S community to model the domain characteristics appropriately [1]. However, these two aspects are seldom combined together to provide a unified method which is both domain-specific and composable.

To cope with these two "contradictory" requirements, we had proposed a model-framework based domain specific composable modeling (DSCM) method in previous work [2, 3]. This method combines the efforts of the two aforementioned aspects (the unified model framework and DSM), but the domain-specific modeling language (DSML) composition in this method lacks a formal semantic foundation. Thus in this work, we propose an ontology-based method to provide layered ontologies as a semantic foundation for domain specific composable modeling.

The rest of the paper is organized as follows. Section 2 presents the proposed method. Section 3 selects combat systems modeling for effectiveness simulation as the case study, and Sect. 4 proposes future work.

2 An Ontology Based DSCM Method

In this section we firstly discuss the essential problem of our method - the knowledge-language duality of DSML; Secondly, the domain specific composable modeling process is proposed; thirdly, ontological metamodels-based design of DSML is presented as the key technology of the method.

2.1 The Knowledge-Language Duality of DSML

Unlike general purpose languages which mainly have linguistic characteristics, the DSML holds the characteristics of the knowledge-language duality (similar to the wave-particle duality of the matters in Physics): on the one hand, DSML technically is a modeling language, thus it possesses linguistic characteristics, e.g., the linguistic instantiation attribute in four-layered metamodeling hierarchy proposed by Object Management Group; On the other hand, the elements of the DSML come from domain concepts which are familiar to domain modelers, so DSML have logical relationship of domain knowledge. Thus, DSML design should not only conform to formal syntax rules, but also stick to the logic relationship based on the domain knowledge to exhibit appropriate semantics.

So the essential problem of DSCM is to design a series of DSMLs which own the knowledge-language duality. Then these DSMLs not only describe their own subject domains, but also can be composed based on a common knowledge foundation.

2.2 Domain-Specific Composable Modeling Process

The DSCM for complex simulation systems should consider the following aspects: (1) M&S activity for complex systems is an taxing endeavor which requires joint efforts of different roles (e.g., domain experts, M&S experts, and software engineers), thus this method should provide a comprehensive framework which enable participation and cooperation of these roles. (2) The DSCM for complex simulation systems is not the same as DSCM in software engineering, so the modeling process should introduce M&S research fruits and knowledge to improve the DSCM process in software engineering. (3) The proposed method should support semantic composition of different domain models.

To meet these three aspects, a DSCM modeling framework is proposed as illustrated in Fig. 1. This method comprises the following steps: (1) Ontological metamodel-based DSML design via incorporation of layered ontologies and M&S formalisms; (2) Meta-model-based generation of domain specific modeling environment (DSME); (3) DSML-based domain modeling; (4) ontology-based model verification and formalism-based model analysis; (5) Code generation-based model implementation; (6) model frame-work-based model integration.

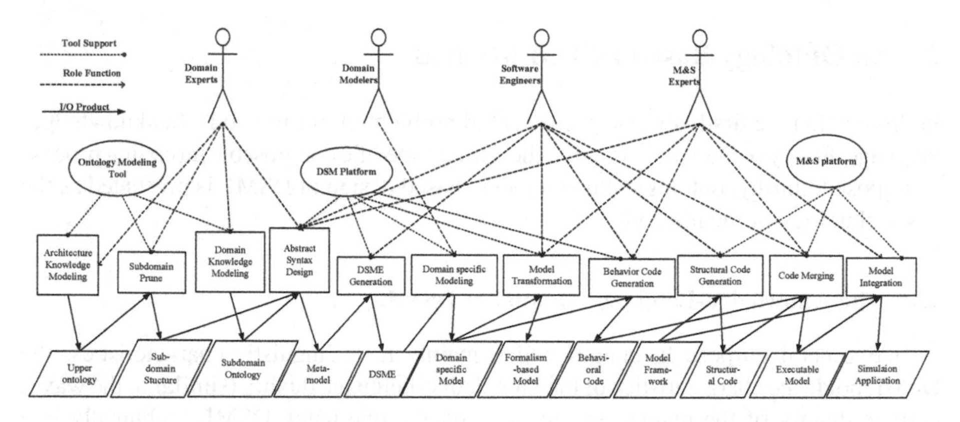

Fig. 1. The ontology-based domain-specific composable modeling process

This method needs effective cooperation of domain experts, software engineers (language engineers are incorporated into software engineers) and M&S experts to provide domain modelers with a DSCM infrastructure (including DSML and DSME). (1) Domain experts mainly construct two kinds of ontologies to provide knowledge for DSML design and model framework development: an upper ontology which specifies the knowledge of the complex systems and how its subsystems connect and interact with one another, and subdomain ontologies which describe the knowledge in each domain.

(2) The tasks of software engineers include software implementation of modeling infrastructure and simulation model. The concrete efforts of software engineers comprise: DSML design and DSME generation together with M&S experts, code generator construction, and model integrator development. (3) M&S experts take charge of the whole modeling process and coordinate the joint efforts of three roles. They design the DSML with the help of software engineers, conduct model verification and analysis, and guide the model implementation and integration.

2.3 The key technology: Ontological metamodel-based design of DSML

Section 2.1 had pointed out the essential problem of DSCM, so the key technology of the method is ontological metamodel-based design of DSML which provide the foundation for both domain-specific modeling and composable modeling. This paper concentrates on metamodeling the DSML, and the details of other aspects (such as DSME generation, code generation, model framework-based model integration) of the whole process can be found in our previous work [2–4].

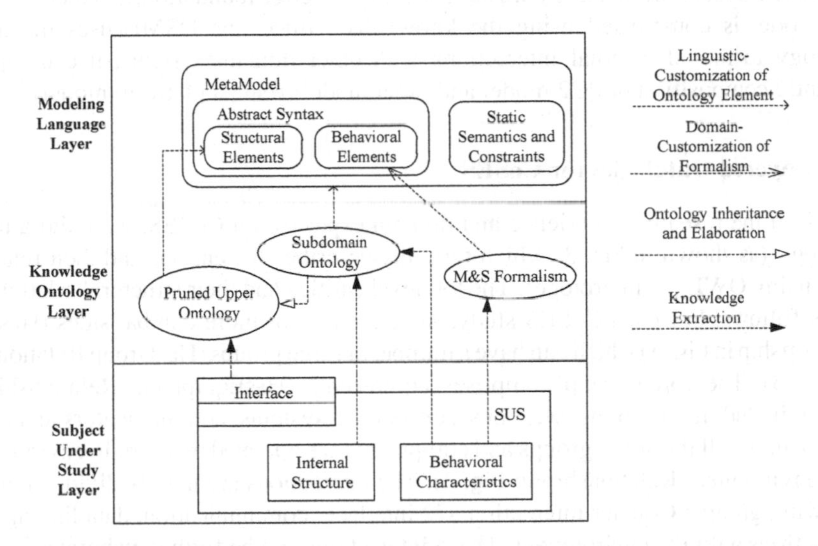

Fig. 2. A layered Ontologies-based metamodels design of DSML

The layered ontology-based metamodeling approach of the DSML is presented in Fig. 2, which includes the following steps. (1) Upper ontology prune. This step extracts subdomain-relevant structural information to figure out the boundary and external interfaces of the subdomain. (2) Knowledge refinement of subdomain ontology. This step inspects all the concepts and its relationship of the subdomain ontology and chooses the ones relevant to the problem, especially the knowledge of internal structure and behavioral patterns of the subdomain. (3) Structural aspect design. This step extracts the structural concepts and relationship from the subdomain ontology and the external interfaces from the pruned upper ontology to design the structural aspect of the DSML. (4) Behavioral aspect design. This step choose one or more M&S formalism as the backbone of the behavioral aspect based on the behavioral patterns recognizes in the second step, and use domain concepts to make the chosen formalisms domain-specific. (5) Abstract syntax design. This step uses meta-metamodel to design the metamodel of the DSML abstract syntax based on the combination of the structural aspect and behavioral aspect. (6) Static semantics design. This step uses constraint language (e.g., object constraint language) to define the static semantics and constraints based on the knowledge of the subdomain ontology.

3 Case Study on Combat Systems Effectiveness Simulation

Combat systems effectiveness simulation (CoSES) is a typical example of M&S research on complex systems, and is selected as the case study in this work. CoSES usually comprise multiple subsystems (e.g., combat platforms carry sensors, weapons and communication devices) from different domains.

In this case study, layered ontologies including a upper ontology and a platform C2 system (PC2 for short) ontology are built as the knowledge foundation, and then a DSML metamodel is constructed using the knowledge. Since this DSML uses the upper ontology to model external interactions with other domain systems, it can support semantic composition of PC2 model and other models (e.g., a platform model).

3.1 Layered Ontologies for CoSES

Based on the research experience and domain expertise on CoSES, we build a upper ontology (as shown in Fig. 3) which formally describes the entities and their relationships using OWL [5] in Protégé[1]. The top level entities and their structural relationship are as follows. For each CoSES study, there are two or more combat sides (HasSide Relationship in Fig. 3) which can have a number of force groups (HasGroup Relationship in Fig. 3). The force group comprises equipments (HasEquipment Relationship in Fig. 3), including platforms, weapons, sensors, C2 systems, communicators and countermeasures. All the sides, groups and equipments are operated in a certain environment (HasEnvironment Relationship in Fig. 3). The interactions are mainly divided into the following groups: Counter interaction, C2 interface, communication, data linking, and interactions with the environment. These interactions can be further elaborated.

The PC2 is a pivot component for CoSES, since it commands and controls all other kinds of equipment and interacts with its superior system. As shown in Fig. 4, a domain ontology for PC2 is built based on the inheritance and elaboration of the upper ontology, i.e., PC2 is a type of C2 system. PC2 have the same structural and behavioral attribute as the C2 system of the upper ontology. Moreover, PC2 describes the entities and relationship in detail, e.g., PC2 uses operators and values to calculate whether certain conditions listed in the condition space are satisfied. The relationships of these entities include order relationships, decision relationships, condition relationships, phase relationships,

[1] http://protege.stanford.edu/ .

and task relationships. These relationships can be further elaborated as shown in the right part of Fig. 4.

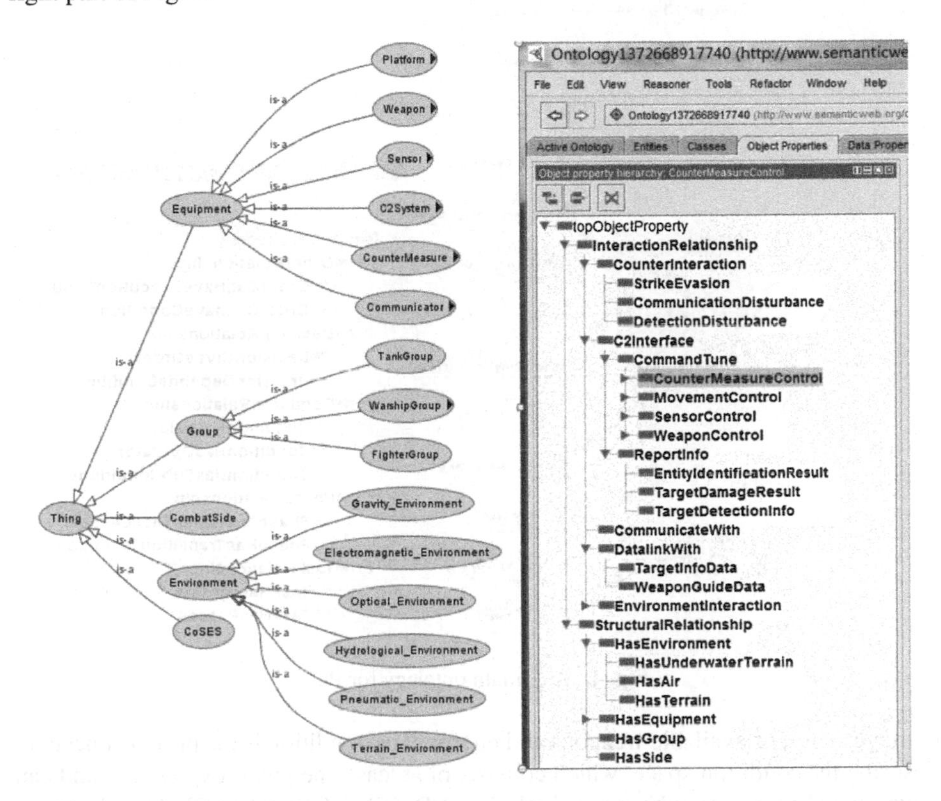

Fig. 3. An upper ontology for CoSES

3.2 Ontological Metamodel-Based Design of PC2 DSML

We use GME platform [6] to design a PC2 DSML metamodel as shown in Fig. 5 based on the method presented in Fig. 2. The core concepts for decision modeling are task, phase, condition, and tactic action. The Task is a tactical objective the platform attempts to achieve by a sequence of tactic actions based on a series of platform phases. A Task should have at least two actions: one initial action and one end action (for conciseness we attribute these two fake actions to tactic actions). Tasks can contain sub-tasks and are connected by TaskSequence. The action is an instantaneous decision order, which is triggered by two kinds of situations: the first is an action sequence (ActionSequence), namely by finishing the former action which it connects to; the second is when the value of a decision condition is evaluated to be true, which has a link whose destination is the action. The action has an enumerated attribute ActionType to specify the type of the action. A Phase is a typical state of the platform and the transition is activated when the PhaseTransCon is evaluated to be true. The Phase has an enumerable attribute called PhaseType and typical phase type is usually specified according to its movement modes,

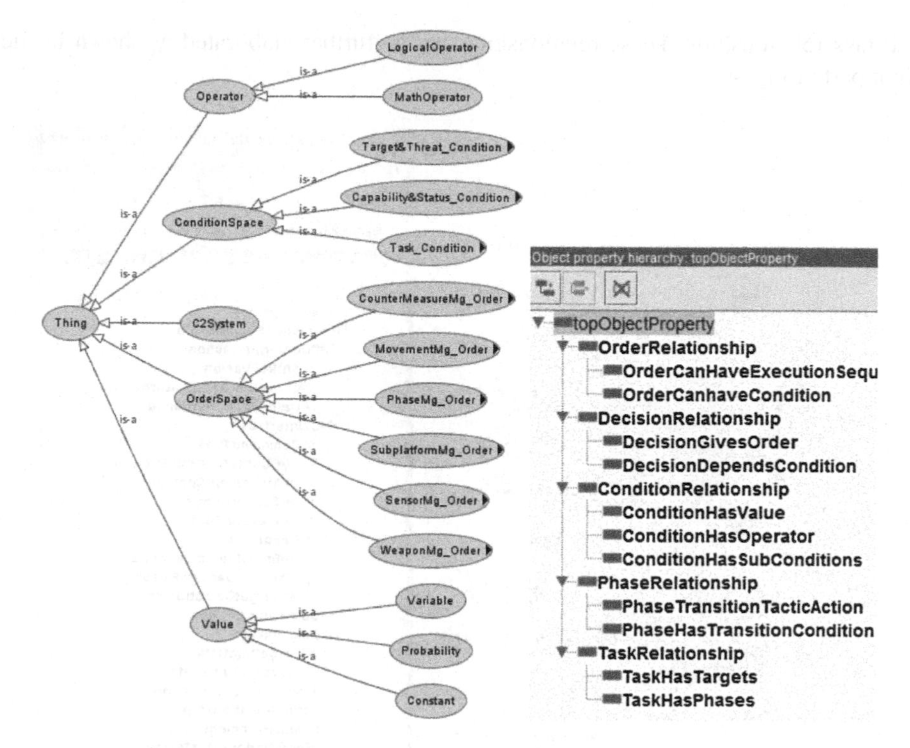

Fig. 4. A domain ontology for PC2

damage status, or available weapons and energy. The condition is the primal concept to describe the condition space, which consists of at least one guard expression, and can have logical operators (whose type include AND, OR, XOR and NOT). Guard expressions are connected by LogicalOperators to calculate a Boolean value for the condition. For length limitation we don't list the concrete types of Phase, EventTrigger, Variable, LogicalOperator and MathOperator of the metamodel.

The layered ontologies and M&S formalism play important roles in the metamodel design. (1) This metamodel uses the upper ontology to design the external interface elements of the DSML. These interfaces are from two kinds of the upper ontology: the first kind is command tunes of C2Interfaces which are represented as CountermeasureCtrl, MovementCtrl, SensorCtrl and WeaponCtrl of the metamodel; the second kind is ReportInfo of the C2Interfaces, which is represented as EventTrigger in the metamodel. (2) This metamodel mainly uses the entities and relationships of the domain ontology as the essential modeling elements, e.g., the order space, condition space, operators and values. (3) This metamodel uses state diagram as the main behavioral pattern since the platform is usually at typical states which have different tactical strategy. For example, the combat process of the fighter plane comprises takeoff state, cruise state, engagement state and return state, and in each state the condition space and the order space of plane C2 have corresponding characteristics.

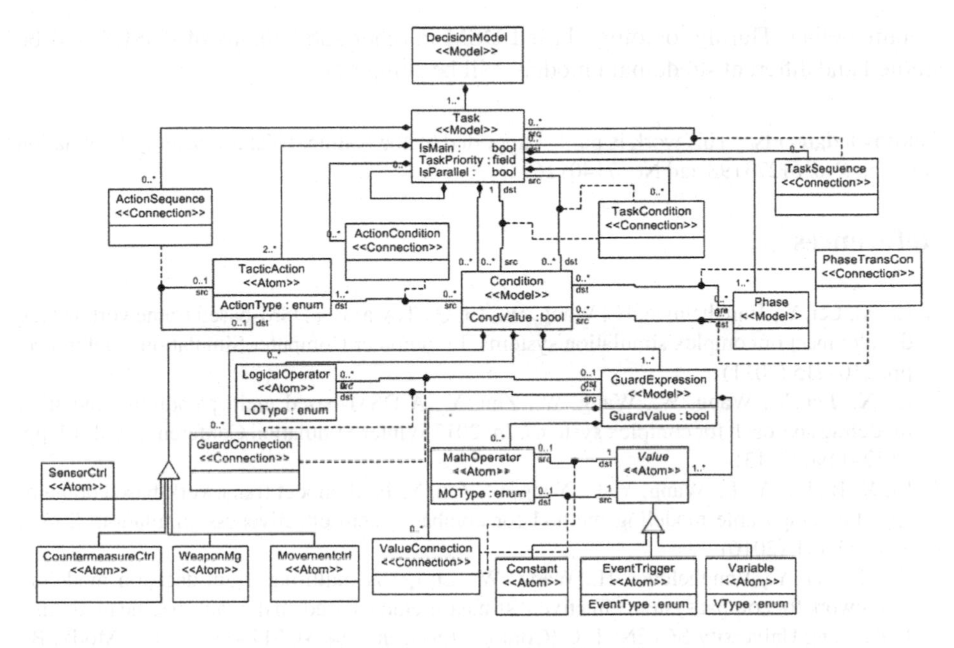

Fig. 5. A domain ontology for PC2

3.3 Discussions

The GME platform provides the function of DSME generation from the metamodel. We can generate a similar DSME to the one present in Fig. 5 of [4] from the aforementioned metamodel. The DSME is friendly to the domain modelers since the modeling elements represented by domain-specific icons are familiar to them.

Although we only discuss one subdomain DSML in the case study, other subdomain DSML design have similar processes. The layered ontologies lay a sound foundation for semantic composition of different domain models. As shown in Sect. 3.2, the upper ontology specifies the structural and behavioral interfaces of subdomains, and subdomains use this specification and subdomain ontologies to design their DSMLs. So different subdomain models achieve semantic compositions through a common knowledge-foundation. Moreover, the upper ontology can be transformed to the model framework. As we had studied the model framework-based model composition in our previous work [3], the upper ontology-based model framework will further facilitate the code merging for model implementation as discussed in Fig. 1.

4 Future Work

The future work is as follows. Firstly, ontology-based formal reasoning techniques will be used to enable model verification and analysis. Secondly, a plug-in of GME will be developed to automatically read XML-based ontology file of protégé to support DSML metamodeling. Thirdly, ontology-based DSM in other subdomains of CoSES will be studied and different subdomain models will be composed.

Acknowledgments. This work is partly supported by the National Natural Science Foundation of China (No. 61273198 and No. 71401167).

References

1. Li, X., Lei, Y., Vangheluwe, H., Wang, W., Li, Q.: Towards a DSM-based framework for the development of complex simulation systems. In: Summer Computer Simulation Conference, pp. 210–215 (2011)
2. Li, X., Lei, Y., Wang, W., Wang, W., Zhu, Y.: A DSM-based multi-paradigm simulation modeling approach for complex systems. In: 2013 Winter Simulation Conference, vol. 12, pp. 1179–1190 (2013)
3. Li, X.-B., Lei, Y.-L., Wang, Y.-P., Yang, F., Zhu, Y.-F.: A model framework-based domain-specific composable modeling method for combat system effectiveness simulation. Softw. Syst. Model. (2016)
4. Li, X., Lei, Y., Vangheluwe, H., Wang, W., Li, Q.: A multi-paradigm decision modeling framework for combat system effectiveness measurement based on domain specific modeling. J. Zhejiang University-SCIENCE C (Comput. Electron.), 14(5), 311–331 (2013). Motik, B., Patel-Schneider, PF., Horrocks, I.: OWL 2 Web Ontology Language: Structural Specification and Functional-Style Syntax. W3C (2012)
5. Vanderbilt University. GME manual and user guide – generic modeling environment 10. Nahsville, TN: Vanderbilt University (2010)

Automatic Evaluation System of Anchoring Operation in Navigation Simulator

Xiao-bin Jiang(✉), Hong-xiang Ren, and Jing-jing Liu

Navigation College, Dalian Maritime University, Dalian 116026, Liaoning, China
dmu_jxb@163.com

Abstract. In order to make the evaluation on crew anchoring operation more efficient, objective and scientific. An automatic evaluation system of anchoring operation is established in the navigation simulator. The relevant anchoring operation evaluation indices, their weights and standard values are obtained through the expert evaluation method. An automatic evaluation model of anchoring operation is established by fuzzy comprehensive evaluation method. The object-oriented Visual C++ language is used to develop an automatic evaluation system of anchoring operation. The evaluation system has many function modules to set questions, answer the questions and evaluate them, and manage data. The system was tested in V_Dragon 3000 navigation simulator developed independently by Dalian Maritime University. The test result shows that the evaluation result of the system is the same with the trainer evaluation result. The system can do objective and accurate automatic evaluation the crew anchoring operation and meet the automatic evaluation requirement.

Keywords: Navigation simulator · Anchoring operation · Automatic evaluation system · Evaluation index

1 Introduction

At present, the crew theory exam has already nationwide unified by computer. However, the operation evaluation exam is still in charge of MSA. And operation evaluation exam has many issues. Navigation simulator has been used in the maritime education and training. The research of automated evaluation system based on navigation simulator has practical significance. Some scholars at home and abroad have studied in this respect. For example the HARRO [1] has designed the collision avoidance automatic evaluation system according to the collision regulate; Shanghai Maritime University has made the theoretical analysis by using fuzzy comprehensive evaluation method about exam and evaluation system in navigation simulator [2]; Tao Jun [3] from Dalian maritime university evaluated the ship inward and outward port through the delphi method; Fang Xiwang

This work is supported by the national 863 task under Grant 2015AA010504 and Ministry of Communications applied basic research project under Grant 2015329225240.

L. Zhang et al. (Eds.): AsiaSim 2016/SCS AutumnSim 2016, Part I, CCIS 643, pp. 325–335, 2016.
DOI: 10.1007/978-981-10-2663-8_35

[4] used fuzzy comprehensive evaluation method to establish the berthing and unberthing evaluation model; Wang Delong [5] has building the automatic evaluation system in ship operation simulator preliminary. There is not a system study of automatic evaluation about anchoring control in navigation simulator in China. Research and development of anchoring operation automatic evaluation system, not only can promote the crew anchoring manipulation level but also can reduce the workload of evaluator. The system was based on V_Dragon 3000 navigation simulator developed independently by Dalian maritime university. This paper has researched the evaluation methods, evaluation model for anchoring operation. The automatic evaluation system includes setting exam, answering and evaluating the exam, data management.

2 Establish Mathematic Evaluation Models

Operating automatic evaluation system needs to acquire the state of ship and crew's operation data timely. While submit the test, the system would calculate the final score. Evaluation model is the kernel of the automatic evaluation system. Establish a scientific and reasonable evaluation model is the key to guarantee the accuracy of the evaluation results [6]. Evaluation model is set up mainly including the selection of evaluation methods, the establishment of evaluation index, the determine membership function of evaluation indexes, the calculation of evaluation index weights and evaluation results four aspects.

2.1 Evaluation Methods

There are many methods that can be used in evaluate currently, such as: fuzzy comprehensive evaluation method, system engineering analysis evaluation method, probabilistic risk evaluation method, risk classification method, safety index method, etc. [7]. Anchoring operation results are influenced by the external environment, ship condition and manipulate skills, so anchoring operation of evaluate is very complicated [8]. In order to ensure the evaluation accuracy, in this paper, the evaluation model has used expert evaluation method and membership function evaluation method. Firstly determining the anchoring operation evaluation index system, according to different evaluation indexes to establish the corresponding membership functions, getting the membership value of each evaluation index, combining weight value received by expert evaluation method and analytic hierarchy process (AHP), Finally crew evaluation result is calculated.

2.2 Evaluation Index

Anchoring operation can be divided into single anchor and double anchors manipulate, two anchors can be further divided into eight anchor, ordinary mooring and parallel anchor. For ships, the most common way of anchoring is single anchor, so this paper analyzes the single anchor. In the process of anchoring operation main factors to consider are as follows[9]: (1) route into the anchorage, anchorage selection; (2) position, speed, posture control; (3) choose anchored method according to water depth and ship condition; (4) chain length control; (5) judge the anchor grasp to bottom, etc. Through the analysis of the various data and expert questionnaire, determine the evaluation index of the single anchoring operation, as shown in Fig. 1.

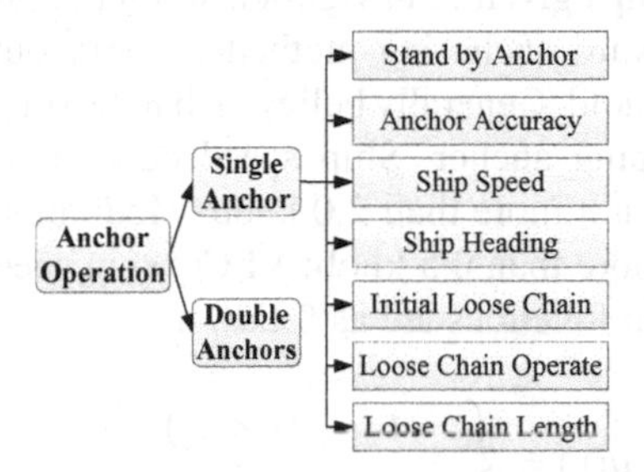

Fig. 1. Evaluation Index for Maneuver of Single Anchoring

2.3 Membership Function

In order to improve the evaluation accuracy, automatic evaluation system makes the influencing factors quantitative. Get the standard value of influence factors and establish the evaluation index of membership functions by relevant theory and sailing practice. Some factors are hard to quantify. We can only carry on the qualitative analysis to set the corresponding evaluation result to 0 or 1. When meet the result of the qualitative analysis, the membership degree value is 1, otherwise value is 0. Then we will analyze the membership function of evaluation indexes, such as the accuracy of anchor position, ship speed while anchoring, ship heading during anchoring, the laying out length of chain, etc.

2.3.1 Accuracy of Anchor Position

Dropping anchor to stop the ship in the designated berth is an important test of crew's operation level. The accuracy of anchor position is the distance between the position of anchor at ship bow and the anchor position designated. While the anchor distance nearer the designated anchor position, the crew's anchor operation level is higher. According to the operation experience, we take the length of ship width as the maximum error precision. Membership functions are as follows:

$$\mu(d) = \begin{cases} 1 & (d < d_s) \\ e^{\frac{-(d-d_s)^2}{50}} & (d \geq d_s) \end{cases} \tag{1}$$

Where: d_s is standard value of anchor accuracy.

2.3.2 Ship Speed When Anchoring

Single anchoring operation has forward and backward anchoring two kinds of anchoring methods. Forward anchoring method only applies in small ships or Warcraft. In order to ensure the grip the bottom of the sea, merchant ships use backward anchoring method generally. Many of the ships given in navigation simulator are merchant ships. So this article is aimed at backward anchoring method to carry out the research. Dropping Anchor time is difficult to hold. Generally believed that the ship is slightly back to ground is the best time to dropping anchor. Ship speed depends on the size of the ship's displacement. Small ship not more than 2.0 knob; Medium-sized ship no more than 1 knob; Large ship is not more than 0.5 knob; VLCC ship speed when dropping anchor even smaller. Membership functions are as follows:

$$\mu(v) = \begin{cases} 1 & (v < v_s) \\ e^{-(v-v_s)^2} & (v \geq v_s) \end{cases} \quad (2)$$

Where v_s is standard value of ship speed.

2.3.3 Ship Heading During Anchoring

When ship drops anchor the angle between ship bow direction and the combine direction of the wind and the current has a direct impact about the safety of anchoring operation. In order to ensure the safety when dropping anchor, Angle between ship bow direction and the combine direction of the wind and the current as small as possible, commonly should not be more than 15° and avoid to dropping anchor while the horizontal wind and cross current. This article sets 15° as the standard angle between ship bow direction and the combine direction of the wind and the current. Membership functions are as follows:

$$\mu(\alpha) = \begin{cases} 1 & (\alpha < 15°) \\ e^{\frac{-(\alpha-15)^2}{50}} & (\alpha \geq 15°) \end{cases} \quad (3)$$

Where α is ship heading while anchoring.

2.3.4 Laying Out Length of Chain

The premise condition of Safe anchorage is to ensure sufficient anchoring force. For the mooring ship, in order to against the external force we need to veer away certain chain at the end of the anchoring operation [10]. To ensure the safety of anchoring the total length of the chain required is [11]:

$$l_s = s + l' = \sqrt{h_0 \cdot (h_0 + \frac{2 \times T_0}{W_c})} + \frac{T_0 - \lambda_a W_a}{\lambda_c W_c} \quad (4)$$

Where l_s is loose chain length; s is catenary chain length; l' is ground cable length; T_0 is Horizontal force.

From (4) we know that calculate the horizontal force is quite complicated. Therefore, the chain length often used the following empirical formula:

$$l_s = \begin{cases} 3h + 90\,m & (v < 20\,m/s) \\ 4h + 145\,m & (v \geq 20\,m/s) \end{cases} \tag{5}$$

Where h is water depth; v is wind speed.

The membership functions of final loose chain length are as follows:

$$\mu(l) = e^{-100(l/l_s - 1)^2} \tag{6}$$

l is final loose chain length; l_s is standard values of eventually chain length.

2.4 Evaluation Index Standard Value and Weight

This paper uses the analytic hierarchy process (AHP) to determine weights of evaluation indexes. According to expert advice and navigation practice, Use 1–9 scaling method to determine the relative important degree about evaluation indexes, constructing judgment matrix. Through the judgment matrix calculate the maximum characteristic root and the corresponding eigenvectors. Normalize the judgment matrix. $W = (\omega_1, \omega_2, \ldots \omega_n)$. Finally use the weighted average method to calculate the result of the anchoring operation. The final evaluation result can be represented as:

$$S = \sum_{i=1}^{7} \mu_i \omega_i \tag{7}$$

Where μ_i is membership value, ω_i is weight of evaluation index. The system will give default standard value and weight as a reference. In order to improve flexibility the expert can change the value while set the exam. The Original value is shown in Table 1.

3 Realize of System

The system is based on Dalian Maritime University developed navigation simulator. Use the Visual C++ language to develop the anchoring operation automatic evaluation system. The evaluation has many function modules to set questions, answer the questions and evaluate them and manage the data. Dalian Maritime University navigation simulator is composed of a coach station (edit exam) and many own ship station (answer exam). The coach station is set exam module, it can edit and save the exam. Own ship station in answer and evaluate module. The coach station start the emulator program, and initialize the exam environment, the own ship station receive the exam and let the crew manipulate it. After complete exam the system will calculate the score according to the crew operation data, at the same time store the crew operation data and the related

Table 1. Original standard values and weights

MageshEvaluate index	Standard value	Weight	Data need to support
Stand by anchor	h + D-d-2 < L<h + D + 1, (h < 25 m, △ < 80000t) h + D-d-10 m < L<h + D-d, (h < 25 m, △ >=80000t) h + D-d-10 m < L<h + D-d, (25 <=h < 50 m) L = h + D-d + -1 m, (h >=50 m)	20	L is anchoring chain length while stand by anchor, D is ship depth, d is ship draft, h is water depth, △ is displacement.
Anchor accuracy	$d_s = B$	20	d_s is distance between ship bow position and anchor position while anchoring. B is ship bread.
Ship speed	v_s < 2kn, (△ < 10000t) v_s < 1kn, (10000 <= △ < 80000t) v_s < 0.5kn, (80000 <= △)	10	v_s is ship speed while anchoring, △ is displacement.
Ship heading	15°	10	angle between Airflow direction and ship bow direction.
Initial loose chain Length	L = 2 h + −2 m, (h < 25 m) L = h+10 ~ 20 m, (25 <=h < 50 m) L=h+5 ~ 10 m, (h>=50 m)	10	L is Loose chain length, h is water depth.
Loose chain operate	Walk out when the chain tight, then braked, tight again and then walk out and stopped, and so on.	10	Walk out when the chain tight, then braked, tight again and then walk out and stopped, and so on.
Loose chain length	$l_s = 3\,h + 90$; V_w < 20 m/s $l_s = 4\,h + 145$; V_w >=20 m/s	20	l_s is final loose chain length, V_w is wind speed, is water depth at anchorage.

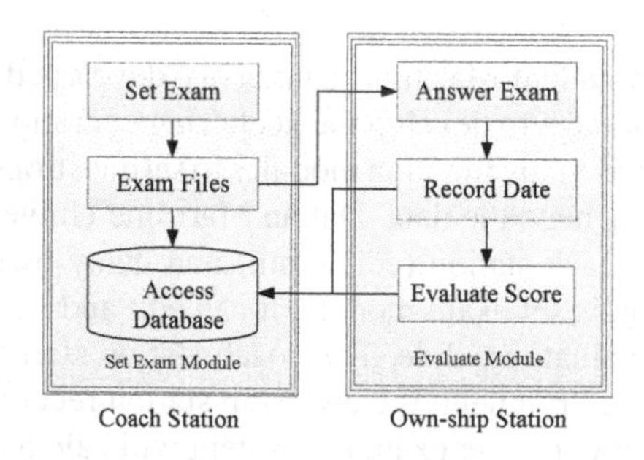

Fig. 2. Evaluation system architecture diagram

information through database management module. The overall architecture of the anchoring operation automatic evaluation system is shown in Fig. 2.

3.1 Set Exam

When we set the exam through the coach station in navigation simulator, firstly we need to set navigation condition information, then set evaluation exam. That is to say, we need to select chart, initial own ship and target ship and set the wind, current environment, etc. Then the system will according to the practice of setting the default evaluation indexes, as well as the standard value and weight of each evaluation index and the membership degree parameters and relative membership degree curve. Coaches can according the experience and the actual situation to increase or delete the evaluation index, change the standard valuc and weight value, adjust the value of membership degree parameters, etc. adjust values to the reasonable standard. The evaluation index set interface is shown in Fig. 3. The coach station can save the exam set into file, sent the file to own ship program.

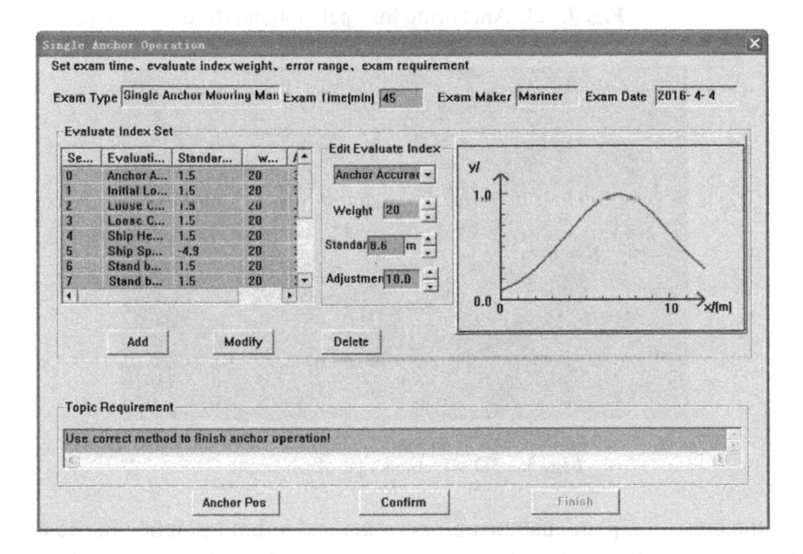

Fig. 3. Evaluation index set interface

3.2 Answer and Evaluate

While own ship program received the exam, crew operate the simulator and answer the exam in own ship. In order to increase the sense of reality about anchoring operation, this paper based on the original two-dimensional anchoring operation interface (as shown in Fig. 4), use of Unity 3D engine developed three dimensional anchor operation scenes (as shown in Fig. 5). In 3D scene, the crew can use the mouse to operation the windlass. The control process is as like as real vessel. The original 2D control interface and the development of new 3D can linkage. Crew can choose 2D interface or 3D scene in Anchoring operation.

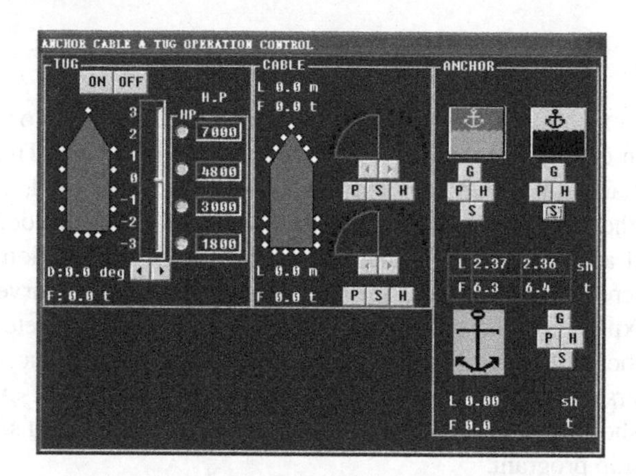

Fig. 4. 2D Anchoring manipulation interface

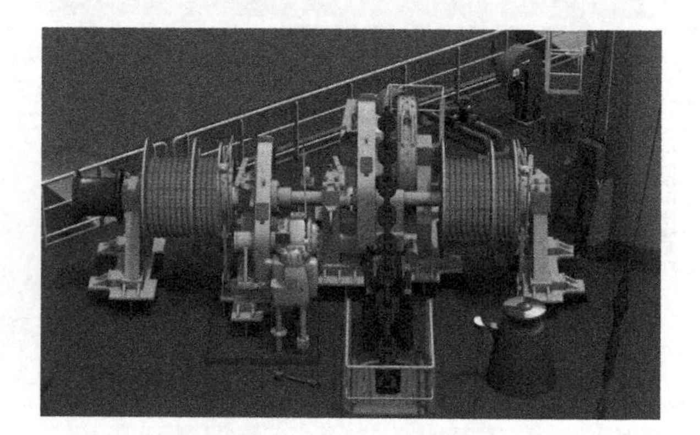

Fig. 5. 3D windlass operation scene

After the crew complete anchoring operation and submit practice in the own ship, evaluation system will based on the operation data and through the evaluation model to calculate the score of each evaluation index and then get total evaluation score. The assess process is shown in Fig. 6. Figure 7 record a crew's single anchoring operation result used by automatic evaluation system. In the interface shows the individual score of each evaluation index and the total evaluation score.

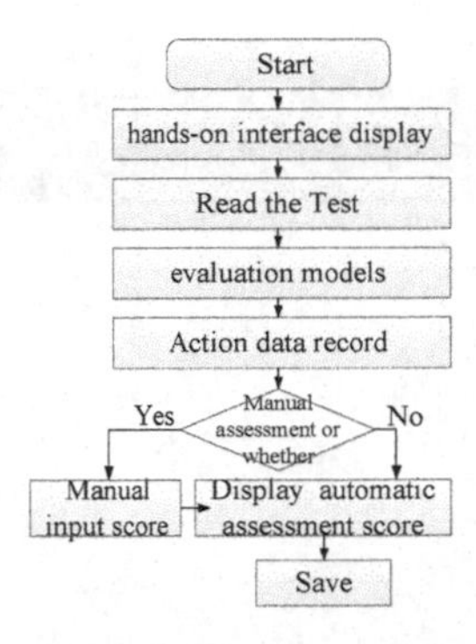

Fig. 6. Evaluation process

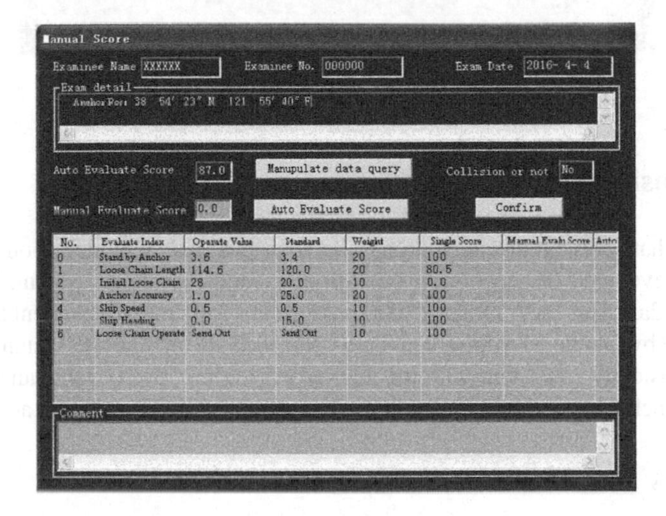

Fig. 7. Evaluation score

While automatic evaluation system given the automatic evaluation results. At the same time, coaches can choose artificial judgment, so as to realize compare between the automatic evaluation and artificial. This ratio is very useful at the beginning of the evaluation system development. Through a large number of compare, can analyze the insufficient of automatic evaluation model and improved it. So that can make the automatic evaluation more reasonability and flexibility.

3.3 Database Administration

In order to real-time record the crew manipulation data and save the exam scores. This article uses the Microsoft Access database to store related information. The access database use ADO technique. Figure 8 is anchor operation data records by a crew.

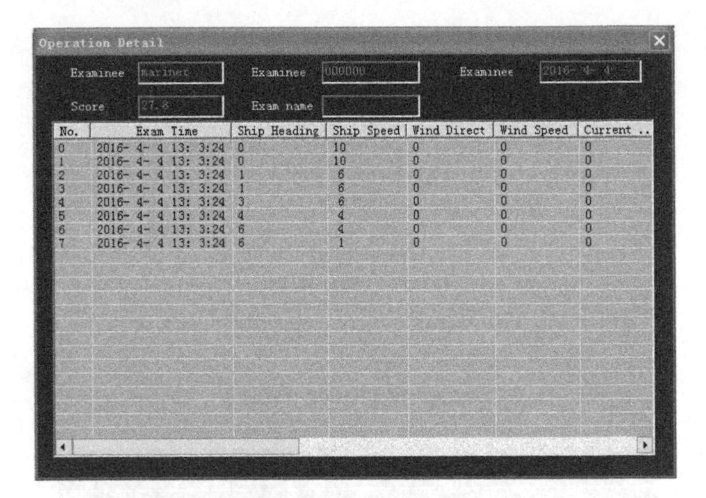

Fig. 8. Display of operation detail

4 Conclusion

This article have researched anchoring operation evaluation model about navigation simulator. Developed the anchoring operation automatic evaluate system. The system goes by abundant tests in V_Dragon 3000 navigation simulator independent research and development by Dalian Maritime University. Practice shows that the system evaluation results are basically consistent with the manual evaluation. The system can evaluate the crew about anchoring operation for automatic evaluation objectively and accurately.

References

1. Harro, G.: Simulator training and the internet. In: CAORF/JSACC Conference 2000, pp. 1–8 (2000)
2. Zhou, Z.-C.: Ship Handling Safety Comprehensive Evaluation in Narrow Channel. Shanghai Maritime University, Shanghai (2005)
3. Tao, J., Yin, Y., Lian, J.: Research on evaluation of ship entering port in navigation simulator. Ship Electron. Eng. **31**(2), 119–122 (2011)
4. Fang, X.-W., Ren, H.-X.: Mooring handling evaluation model based on handling simulator. J. Dalian Marit. Univ. **39**(1), 31–34 (2013)
5. Wang, D.-L., Ren, H.-X., Zhao, Y.-L., et al.: The automatic evaluation system about ship entering and leaving port handling. J. Dalian Marit. Univ. **42**(2), 27–30 (2014)
6. Yang, Y.-F.: The design and development of the automatic evaluation system on china coast guard vessel simulator. In: Proceedings of 4th International Conference on Computer Science and Education, pp. 1231–1234 (2009)
7. Liu, J.-P.: Collision Risk Evaluation Method Based on Fuzzy Pattern Recognition. Dalian Maritime University, Dalian (2011)
8. Jin-biao, C.H.E.N., Guang-yu, W.U., Shi-jun, Y.I.N.G.: Evalutation of large-vessel handling simulation based on synthetic grey-fuzzy method. J. Shanghai Marit. Univ. **32**(4), 1–5 (2008)

9. Gu, Q.-M.: Harbor Engineering Design Manual: First Volume. China Communications Press, Beijing (2001)
10. Wu, J.-L., Wu, B.-G., Liu, D.-G., et al.: Ship security evaluation system under the condition of high wind in Tianjin port anchoring. J. Dalian Marit. Univ. **39**(1), 49–52 (2013)
11. Hong, B.-G.: Ship Handling. Dalian Maritime University Press, Dalian (2008)

Research on Modeling of Complex System Integrated Development Platform

Rong An(✉) and Zhiming Song

Systems Engineering Research Institute, CSSC, Beijing 100036, China
anr2001@sina.com

Abstract. The main characteristics and deficiency of complex large system integration development at present are analyzed. The framework model of development platform for complex large system is built based on the system engineering V model and the Hall model. This model takes the integrated designing as the main body, the R&D process as the main line, the knowledge engineering and quality management as the important auxiliary. The main parts of the framework model are studied and described. The application shows that this model is effective to guide the construction of development platform, and the R&D ability of enterprise is rapidly and comprehensively improved.

Keywords: Complex system · Integrated development · Platform · System engineering · R&D process · Knowledge engineering · Quality management

1 Introduction

With the rapid development of world science and technology, and the integration of information technology and industrialization, many domestic high-tech enterprise are carrying out informationization and digitalization construction in recent years, such as digital design, product data management and so on. And the efficiency and quality of R&D have been significantly improved [1, 2].

However, the technical foundation of our country is weak, and reverse design has been the main development mode of most enterprise over the years. Compared with international advanced level, domestic enterprises still have obvious deficiency as the following shown: advanced, standard and detailed research process is absent; advanced R&D tools have been underutilized; the knowledge has not been effectively precipitated, managed and applied; multidisciplinary collaborative and optimizing ability is insufficient; integration of development and management is not enough, and so on. The R&D ability of enterprise involve multiple factors such as organization, rules, criterion, manpower, technology, platform and so on, and the platform is the foundation and key of R&D capability construction, because it is the physical carrier of the whole ability system and the main environment of the R&D activities.

L. Zhang et al. (Eds.): AsiaSim 2016/SCS AutumnSim 2016, Part I, CCIS 643, pp. 336–346, 2016.
DOI: 10.1007/978-981-10-2663-8_36

2 The Analysis of Comprehensive Integrated Development of Complex System

The typical process of comprehensive integration design and development is shown in Fig. 1. In the project demonstration phase, the top level design and demonstration for product should be carried out based on the users' requirements (especially the potential demands) and the developer's R&D abilities, and the target image of the product is described, the necessity of product and the realizability of technology are demonstrated. In the scheme design phase, the overall architecture, main functions, key performance, working process of the product are designed, and the functions and performance indexes are distributed to the low levels. In the engineering development phase, according to the overall scheme, each subsystem is designed in detail, and the prototype of each part of the product is made, and eventually they are integrated into a complete system. In the accreditation phase, the real tests of the product are carried out in the real working environment, and the flaws are found and corrected, till the product meet the practical requirements of users, the product design state is cured down.

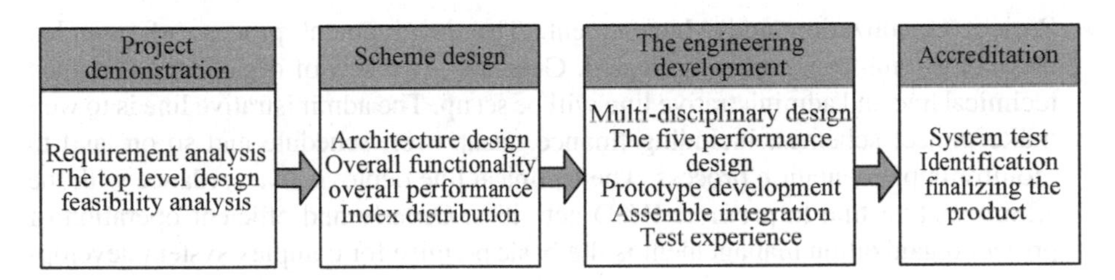

Fig. 1. The process of complex system product integration development

In the above process the development activities generally experience three big stages: "whole - branches – whole", as shown in Fig. 2. The overall design is carried out in the scheme design phase. Usually the general design unit organize all the subsystem design units to complete the overall design cooperatively. In this stage, the digital simulation method is mainly used to verify the rationality of the design. After confirming the solution, the project convert into the engineering development phase. Each unit who is responsible for some subsystem carry out the design and development in parallel, meanwhile, a lot of collaborative work need to do between the related subsystems. The general design unit need to especially make well organization and coordination work, supervise and ensure the realization of the overall design requirements. In this phase, design work is gradually carried out. Among the subsystems, and between the subsystems and the overall system, a large number of iterative modification may need to be done. Every specialty has appropriate digital design and simulation tools. On the one hand, these tools can assist efficiently completing the professional design and development, on the other hand, based on the integration of different tools, the coordination simulation tests of multidisciplinary digital prototype can be carried out to promote the comprehensive optimization, and the efficiency and quality of the development can be improved greatly. After finishing the prototype of each subsystem, the project convert into the overall system integration phase. From part to whole, the assembling and integration for a full system is gradually completed, and the integration test need to be carried out to ensure the overall product meet the design requirements and can be reliable running.

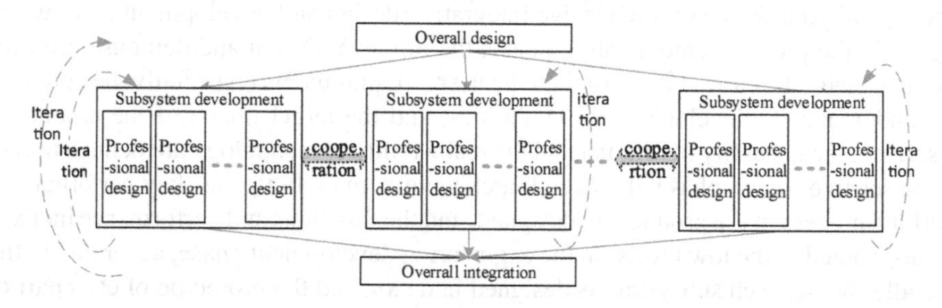

Fig. 2. The breakdown and integration of system development

Based on the R&D practice for many years, we consider that the core and key of integration development of complex systems include the following aspects:

- Project Organization and Management. The development process of complex product is long-term and complicated. Generally, two sets of organizations named technical line and administrative line will be set up. The administrative line is to well make project schemes, including finance, manpower, schedule and so on, and to monitor implementation process. The technical line deploys in accordance with the administrative line to promote R&D activities. Orderly and efficient operation of project organization management is the basic premise for complex system development.
- Development Process. The R&D process is the lifeline of the high-tech enterprise. Whether the process is suitable determines the efficiency of scientific research, product function and quality, etc. And the management strategies such as organization and rules should also be set up according to the R&D process. System engineering theory reveals the principle that the complex system development should follow the regular pattern of top-down design and bottom-up integration. Different enterprises should customize the more elaborate, suitable and feasible research process based on their own business, what's more, with the progress of science and technology, the process should be constantly adjusted and the R&D capabilities will be gradually improved.
- Requirements Management. Requirements are the origin of products. Generally the requirements of complex system can't be gained in one step. First the user demands should be captured as far as possible at the early stage of development, and then, more deeply work need to do to gradually excavate the potential product requirements during the whole development process, or even to correct the impossible or unnecessary demands which are proposed before. For the complex system, the scale is large, the development period is long, the developers and units are numerous, how to effectively manage and monitor the requirements has always been very difficult.
- Development Environment. Development of advanced and complex product must rely on the advanced R&D environment. With the rapid development of digital

technology, almost all of the modern industrial fields have mature digital design tools. So each subsystem of complex product can choose appropriate tools to carry out the design. Meanwhile, the public supporting environment should be built for the common means of different profession, such as public data storage and management, cloud services, and so on.

- Multi-specialties Cooperation. Complex product usually involves multiple disciplines and specialties. Multidisciplinary fusion and multi-objective optimization are the typical characteristics and difficulties of the complex large system development. In the US and Europe, the developer mainly use advanced design tools and integrate the tools to carried out digital design, especially the simulation test and verification are used throughout the entire development cycle to do iterative optimization, and the optimal solution can be effectively seek.
- Quality Management. Over the years, the quality control mean of most domestic enterprises is mainly to inspect and control turning points of different phase. But during the development phase, the designers often can not actively carry out quality design and quality inspection, so the quality management and the development process are seriously apart. As a result, the product's hidden troubles are more, the product's robustness is not strong, most of the design defects are exposed in the late stage of development, and a large number of rework lead to increased cost and time delay.
- Knowledge Engineering. The development of complex systems, especially need to reuse many kinds of knowledge such as the past experience, data, model and so on. At present, the data and knowledge are dramatically increasing, and playing the more and more important role for R&D. Implementing knowledge management and knowledge engineering, effectively precipitating, management and using knowledge, have become the key development direction for high-tech enterprises, meanwhile, they have also become the important symbol of advanced degree.

To construct the R&D platform of the enterprise, the above key contents should be comprehensively researched and solved. Through fully integration and coordination of these contents, the advanced comprehensive ability of R&D can be formed.

3 The Modeling Theory of R&D Platform

3.1 The V Model of System Engineering

The V model theory of system engineering reveals the basic process and regularity of "top-down design and bottom-up integration" [3], as shown in Fig. 3.

In the left side of the V model, the system development may start with the requirement development stage so it is named the forward engineering, or may start with the middle or behind stage so it is named the reverse engineering. Defining the different development starting point as the different design capability level can reflect the level of innovation and development ability of the enterprise [4]. To construct the advanced R&D platform, the enterprise should firstly follow the principle of V model, take the forward design pattern as the goal, and set up the R&D process, platform and management rules which are adapted with the actual condition of the enterprise.

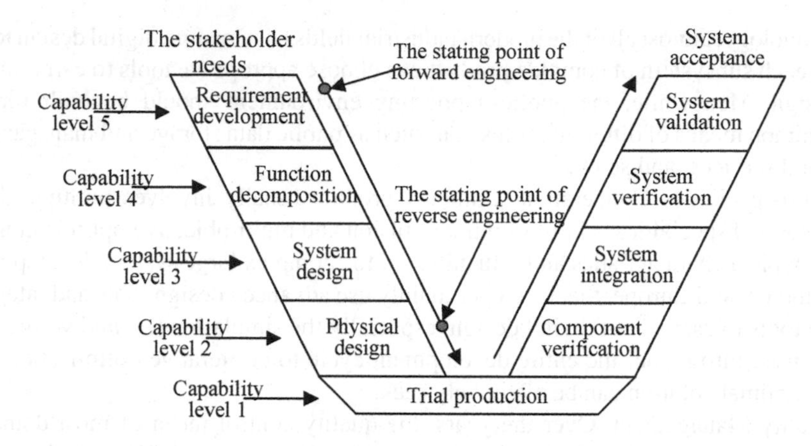

Fig. 3. The V model of system engineering

3.2 Hall Model

The Hall model is one of the important system engineering methodology which guide the development of complex product [5], as shown in Fig. 4, it focus on system development from three dimensions.

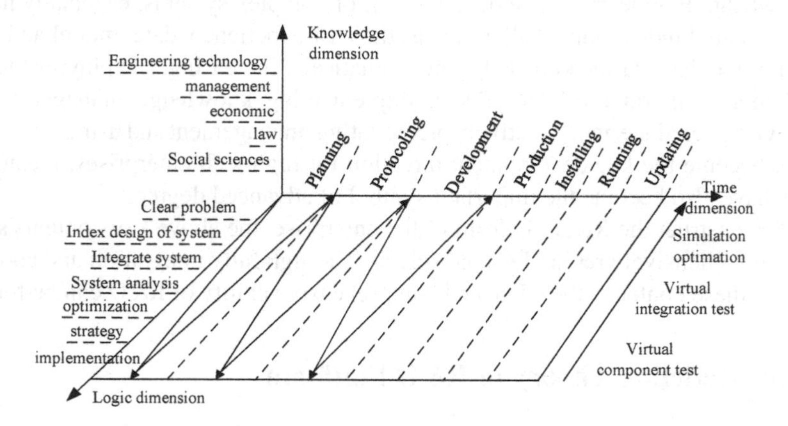

Fig. 4. Hall model

Time dimension describes the whole process of system development which is from project starting to product delivery and maintenance phase. Each work of phase rank with one after another on time and depend on each other. As time goes by, the system development across every phase, the product is more and more complete and mature. It generally includes the project demonstration, scheme design, engineering development, production, installation, deployment, running, and maintaining.

Logic dimension describes the logic of thinking, decision and implementation for each work task. In every stage of time dimension we should follow certain logic and finish stage task in order. The logic dimension generally includes clearing problems, analyzing problems, preliminary plan, detailed design and implementation. With the development and mature of digital simulation technology, simulation based design and verification are widely used to the development process of complex product. In the different stages of development, the modeling and simulation technology is used to develop the corresponding simulation prototype, and then simulation test is carried out to verify the design. In this case, corresponding to the planning, drafting and development stage of time dimension, after the implementation in the above logic dimension, still need continue to carry out virtual parts test, virtual integration test and design verification based on simulation, thus in the corresponding phase of time dimension, form the small "V" process, as shown in Fig. 4.

Knowledge dimension describes many knowledge and skills such as technology, engineering, management, economy, law, social science, art and so on. They should be comprehensively applied in all stages and each step of product development. At the same time, the new knowledge are also refined and precipitated, and the R&D ability are improving along with the product development. The modern enterprises should constantly improve their own research condition, especially carry out the knowledge management or knowledge engineering, and effectively manage and apply knowledge.

4 Modeling the R&D Platform

4.1 The Framework Model of R&D Platform

Based on the principle of system engineering and according to the analysis of above R&D business characteristics, the R&D platform framework model for high-tech enterprise is built as shown in Fig. 5.

This model includes development management environment, integrated development environment, knowledge management system, quality management system, business resources environment and the bottom hardware. Inside it, the integrated development environment is the main body, and most of the tools for all profession and whole development cycle are integrated into the environment. So the different professional tools are connected and integrated and it provides advanced means for business collaboration. The development and management process is the main line of the platform, especially the development process is more important and the management process is set according to it. Through the development management environment the explicit process of development and management are maintained. Furthermore, the requirements management system is set up in this environment, and surrounding the process, the product requirements is monitored and managed. The knowledge engineering system and quality management system are important auxiliary of the platform. They provide the IT means to precipitate, manage and apply knowledge and implement the fine quality monitoring during the whole project cycle. The business resources environment is the foundation of the platform, it provides the resources such as data, models, rules and so on to support the development.

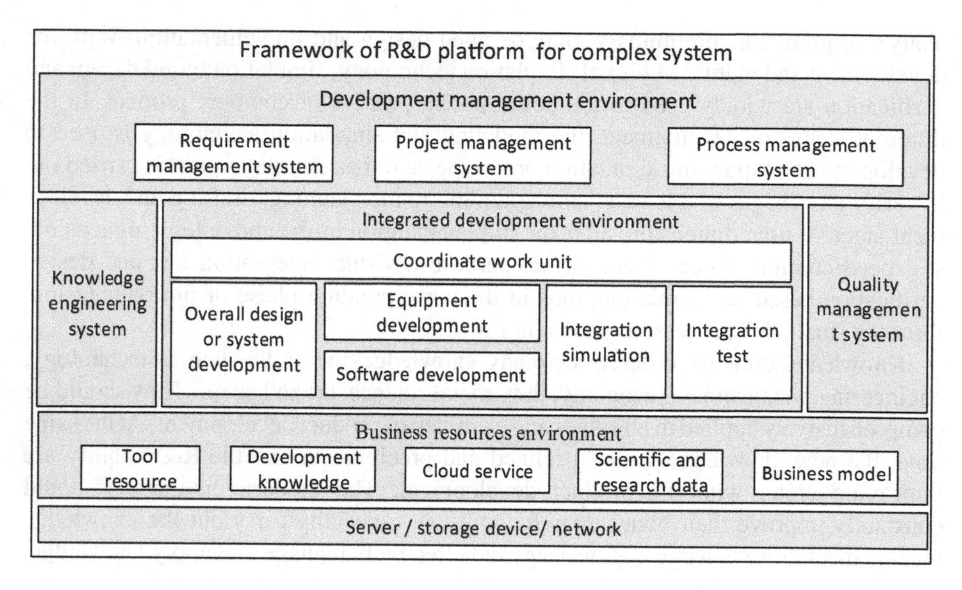

Fig. 5. The framework of R&D platform for complex system

4.2 The Models of Main Component

- Modeling the R&D Process. Based on the management process of WBS and the technical process of V model, the R&D process of high-tech enterprise is set up. The development activities of whole project cycle is decomposed according to WBS measure, and the decomposing is from coarse to fine till reaching the minimum work package. The task, tools, resource requirements, design constraints, input and output of each work package are defined. All the work packages are connected according to the input and output, and the primary R&D process is built. Then the related knowledge, tools and quality control measures are linked to the process, and the complete and advanced development process is obtained. The modeling process is as shown in Fig. 6.

  Among above, the decomposition of R&D activities are the foundation and key. For the complex large system of special area, there must be some basic and common R&D rules to follow. These rules should be summarized and cured as the top R&D activities of the enterprise, and all projects will abide. Based on the top activities, the specific decomposition are sequentially carried out according to the characteristics of different kind of the product. Generally the minimum work package can be the scale that need one person to complete in about one week.

  To ensure the implementation of R&D process, the corresponding management system is needed to construct in the platform. The main functions of the system include the management of basic R&D process, project planning, process visualization, and process monitoring, etc.
- Modeling the Integrated Development Environment. The design activities are the core and main body of the R&D platform. The development of complex large system must be the collaboration of amount persons, tools and many professions. Therefore,

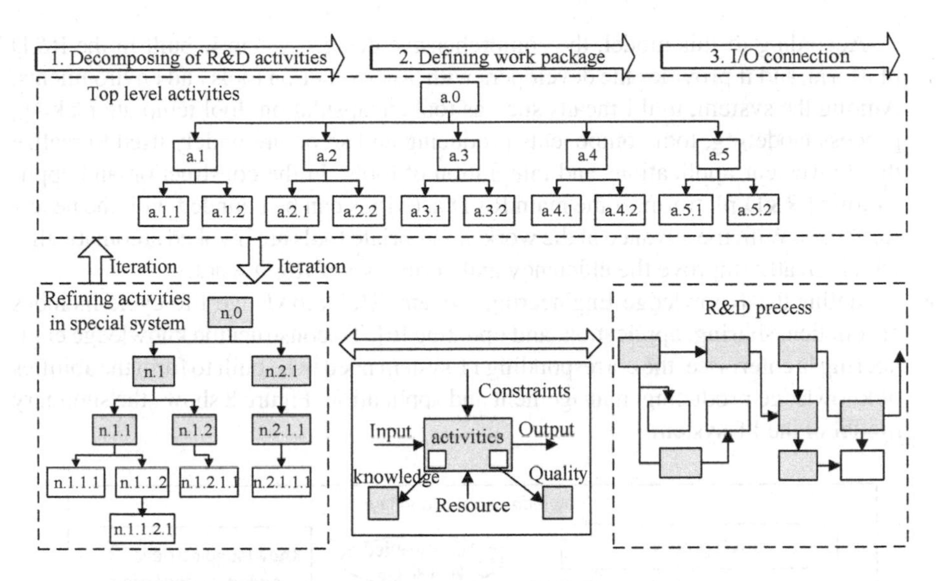

Fig. 6. Procedure of Modeling R&D process

the platform construction need to focus on the comprehensive design, integration and global optimization. Following the V model and orienting the whole R&D cycle, the suitable tools need to be selected and integrated into the development environment, such as the top-level demonstration and design tools, requirements management tools, quality management tools, professional digital design tools, auxiliary tools in integration testing phase and so on. The key is to solve the integration of tools which highly couple with each other. The model is shown in Fig. 7.

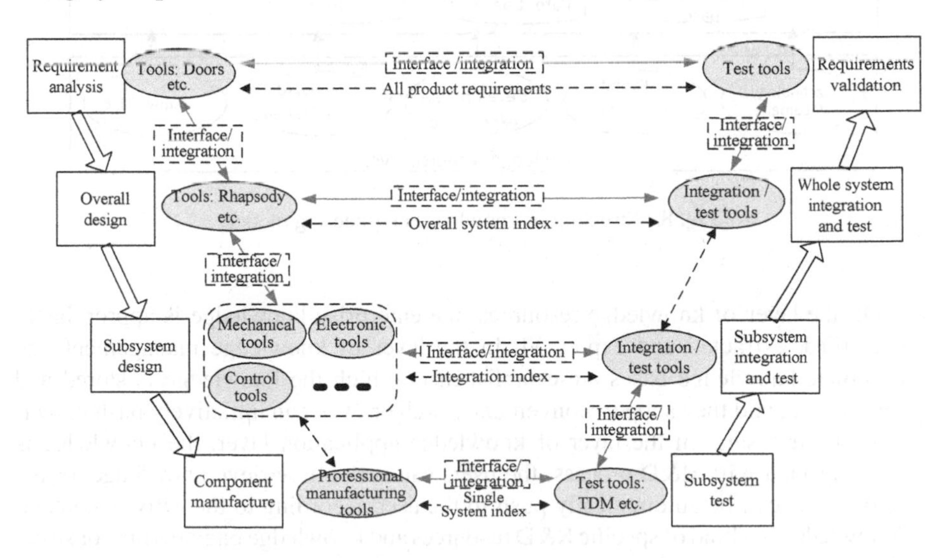

Fig. 7. V model based comprehensive design

According to this model, the comprehensive design system is built in the R&D platform, and it provides the developers with task execution tools and environments. Among the system, multi-means such as tool encapsulation, tool template making, process modeling, tool components producing and so on are widely used to realize the convenient applications and integration of tools. In the construction and application of R&D platform, some main R&D activities can be bounded with the necessary tools. With the advance of the work, appropriate tools are invoked automatically, which greatly improve the efficiency and normative of R&D work.

- Modeling the Knowledge Engineering System. The knowledge life cycle includes production, sharing, application, and updating [6]. To construct the knowledge engineering in enterprise, the corresponding IT system need to be built to form the abilities of knowledge producing, management and application. Figure 8 shows the summary model of the IT system.

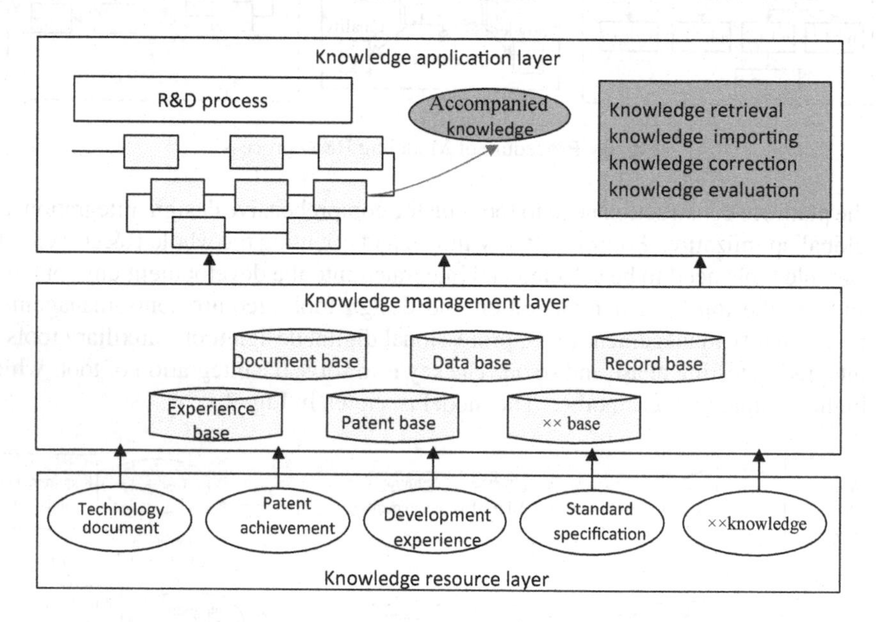

Fig. 8. Structure of knowledge engineering model

In the layer of knowledge resources, the enterprise knowledge is appropriately classified, extracted and expressed. In the layer of knowledge management, the complete knowledge bases are established in which the knowledge is stored and maintained, and they support convenient search or even can initiatively push knowledge to the users. In the layer of knowledge application layer, the knowledge is accompanied with R&D process, the users can actively retrieve knowledge, or the knowledge can be automatically push to the user according to the activity content. Knowledge is a kind of specific R&D resources and knowledge engineering construction has its own peculiar regularity. The special knowledge management system is needed to build in the R&D platform, which can both run separately, or be tightly coupled with the R&D platform and interacted with other function systems.

- Modeling the Quality Management System. The modern high-tech enterprise should focus on the construction of fine quality management means which is digital, visual and facing the whole process of R&D. The complete quality management model are as shown in Fig. 9. In this model, the main contents includes quality planning, quality prevention, process quality control and process quality monitoring. They take the R&D activities, R&D process and project management process as the center, follow the whole product development process. Among the above, quality planning is the forerunner, and it's the necessary inputs and constraints of R&D activities. Quality prevention is incorporated into the R&D process, based on quality information the quality trends is forecasted and much problems are prevented. Process quality monitoring implement the control of the phase conversion and the process quality control implement the detail inspection and control for the R&D sub-procedure. All above quality management business connect with each other, and the product quality is iteratively optimized and effectively guaranteed.

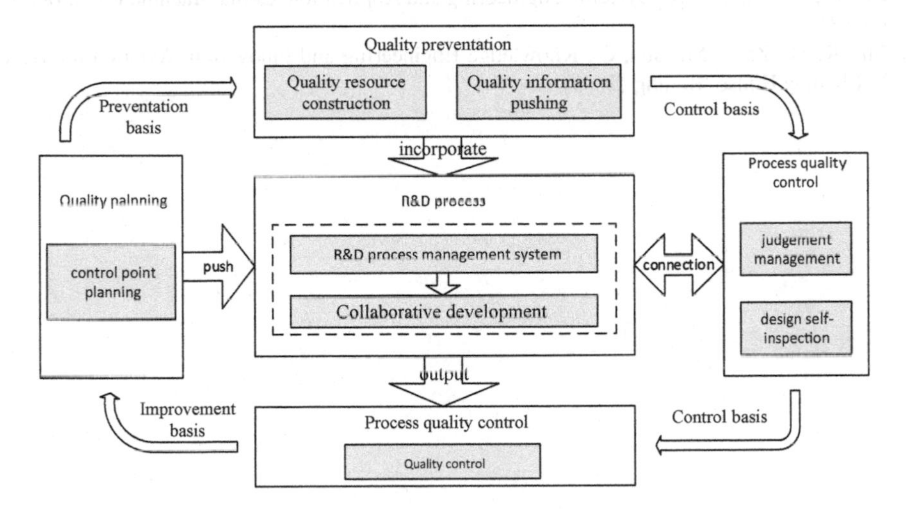

Fig. 9. Model of quality management

5 Conclusions and Future Work

According to the basic principle of system engineering, we explore the construction of R&D platform for many years. New theory and methods are concluded through practice, meanwhile the construction of platform are guided by the theories. At present, we have preliminarily built the R&D platform framework, which contains R&D process management system, integrated development environment, knowledge management system, quality management system and the resources environment. Taking the existing product as test case and carrying out the development in the platform, the result shows that the platform and the theories of this paper are both correct and effective. The construction of R&D platform has no end and will be a progressive process. We will gradually improve the platform by its flexible structure along with the progress of technology and the change of our businesses. The proposed methods can provide useful reference for the R&D capabilities construction of other enterprises.

References

1. Cui, D.L., et al.: The role of enterprise application integration technology in the optimization design of complex products. Digi. Mil. Ind. **14**(8), 61–64 (2008)
2. Huang, N., et al.: The current situation and trend of development of military product virtual design technology. Digi. Mil. Ind. **43**(1), 26–29 (2011)
3. Estefan, J.A.: Survey of model-based systems engineering methodologies. In: International Council on Systems Engineering (INCOSE), Seattle (2008)
4. Tian, F., et al.: The implementation plan of fine and high efficiency development. Beijing (2015)
5. Li, H.-B., Zhang, C.-X.: Systems Engineering and Application. China Machine Press, Beijing (2013)
6. Shi, R.-M., Zhao, M., Sun, C.: Knowledge Engineering and Innovation. Aviation Industrial Publishing House, Beijing (2009)

Dynamic Slot Partition Algorithm of Contention-Avoid Positioning of UWB Label Based on Markov Model

Li Li(✉), Fa-zhong Li, and Zhi Kun Liu

College of Electronic Engineering, Naval University of Engineering, Wuhan, China
bingxuehantian@126.com

Abstract. Multiple mobile UWB labels' positioning without conflict in a intensive environment is a problem, we put forward a method that takes the labels number as the only limited units in the envelope area with conflict-free collision conditions for time slot length optimization, it is concluded the optimal capacity is estimated under the transition probability of markov and constraint functions. In order to keep balance between sampling data frequency of labels' effective positioning and increasing the utilization rate of time slot in each time frame as far as possible, we will construct dynamic time slot that is based on the algorithmic label numbers. Flight experiments were carried out to verify the result. We take a rectangle envelope as a multiple base station area for an example. Data processing and analysis are proved to optimize the positioning rate of each UWB label and to reduce the formation of large sparse time slot and empty slots, which is compared to a primary model of the fixed time slot in the fixed time frame.

Keywords: UWB · Multiple labels · Markov model · Optimized time slot division

1 Introduction

Position of multiple labels in the intensive environment has a problem, namely how to position these labels of high frequency signal without conflict of disturbance each other. Because multiple UWB label in the dense environment can produce mutual interference signal in the air during transmission, accurate detection and positioning are very difficulty. Therefore we must establish the function of the time slot division and a positioning management entity which can divide a limited time into many small time-slot on the basis of rule, such as fixed, dynamic, appointment, competition etc. The purpose is that the reasonable time slots will be made to enable UWB signals orderly and to use time slot utilization efficient, at the same time which will meet the requirements of label positioning' data sampling rate, in order to improve the positioning' accuracy.

Recently, a lot of research about anti-collision algorithm of radio frequency (RFID) is based on the uncertainty algorithm of ALOHA and a deterministic binary tree algorithm, literature [2] adopted some random TDMA time slots that were based on ALOHA methods, which had improved the low efficiency of traditional ALOHA. ALOHA methods can divide the time into multiple synchronization time slot, which reduces the collision by half. However, its sole shortcoming is which confines to identify the static

L. Zhang et al. (Eds.): AsiaSim 2016/SCS AutumnSim 2016, Part I, CCIS 643, pp. 347–355, 2016.
DOI: 10.1007/978-981-10-2663-8_37

label information. Literature [3, 4] proposes a method that is in accordance with the algorithm of label' number to divide the time into some static slots. Literature [5] proposes a method of the enhanced dynamic EDFSA, which can groups each time slot that is suitable for a large number of labels in the RF field, the rate of the label recognition has reached 34.6 %–36.8 %. These results also show that the information transmission time is totally random, if the scope of the label number is greater than time slot number, the probability of collision will increase obviously, signal' channel utilization and system throughput will be markedly reduced.

UWB is also a carrier of wireless transmission, which is also the new RFID technology. The paper is to solve a sampled data problem of many moving UWB labels in a UWB signal positioning system, so unrelated data acquisition of the different labels is to fit their own trajectory. First he UWB tag structure is described, according to the working principle of structure, we put forward a method that can solve the time slot length of the enable label in a common positioning envelope area. It takes a limited regional capacity of labels as the adjustable variables in the case of meeting a conflict-free collision condition, then gets every optimizatal estimated time slot value based on Markov probable model that is experiential or experimental evidence. The purpose is to balance effective positioning of each label sampling rate and use the time slot division algorithm to estimate the label number dynamically.

2 Structure Models of the UWB Label System

First, UWB positioning system is introduced and adopted, which uses a transmitted pulse, many positioning base station will receive the pulse at the same time. Signal process is shown in Fig. 1, the label is composed of communication link, control circuit, pulse circuit. Communication link is responsible to receive the synchronous signal from the ground control station, which is triggered by the control center in each time slot, the control center can control to launch the ID order command; control circuit controls the synchronous start, the decoding ID and the matching calculation ID signal pulse, the

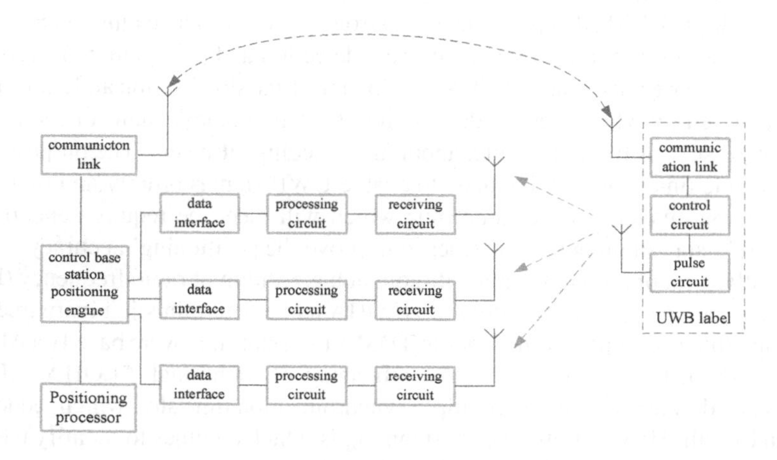

Fig. 1. The flow chart of UWB positioning signal

pulse is generated by the pulse circuit, then gets through the UWB antennas into the surrounding space. The positioning base-station includes the receiving circuit, the processing circuit and the data interface. The receiving circuit amplifies the UWB narrow pulse signal from receiving antenna, the processing circuit will enlarge the pulse peak time relationship into a digital signal, then enter the positioning algorithm processing engine by data interface circuit. The control base-station positioning engine is responsible for synchronizing signal generation, managing label positioning slot division and distributing and controling the positioning trigger.

The label can launche the UWB pulse sequence signal, which includes the ID Identification, the positioning pulse of arriving time detection. The structure of UWB pulse sequence frame is shown in Fig. 2.

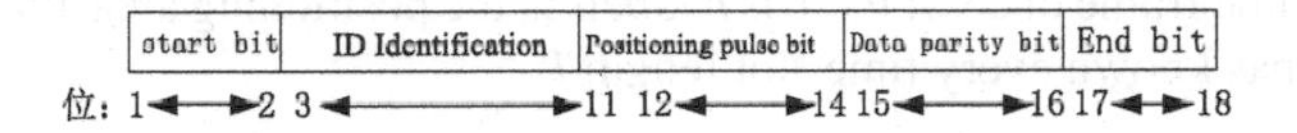

Fig. 2. The UWB pulse sequence frame

3 Dynamic Time Slot of UWB Label Positioning

3.1 Optimization Settings of Dynamic Time Slot Length

To reduce the conflict probability, UWB signals need to be set a asynchronous transfer mode, namely when label signal transmits data, it is be within the prescribed time slot. Label communication link as synchronous signal control in every time frame sends the label startup command, when a silent mobile label in the positioning area receives the orders, its positioning pulse returns ID information in the specific time slot. However many labels will appear at the positioning area, the number is unknown. This is the focus of our study.

The study takes estimated label numbers as the only variable value, in order to meet the time slot allocation situation effectively, according to balancing data sampling rate of each label, then increases the utilization rate of time slot as far as possible, From the above knowable, It is necessary for us to establish the long time slot division algorithm. In order to simplify the model, we have following basic assumptions:

- Each UWB label entry and exit the positioning area evenly;
- Time of entering and exiting the positioning area is random.

First, each label slots is mainly done roughly the following content, as shown in Fig. 3:

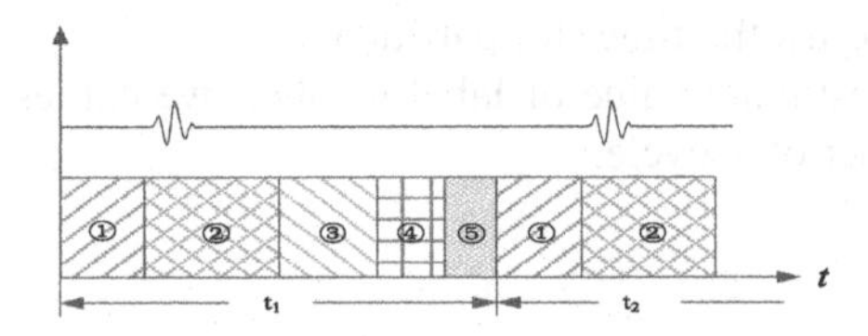

Fig. 3. Time slot form

1. UWB pulse sequence signal startup time T_{in};
2. UWB pulse generating and transmission time T_{out};
3. UWB pulse receiving time T_{loc};
4. UWB pulse processing time T_{do};
5. Protection interval T_{pro}.

T_{loc} and T_{do} are set constants according to positioning system, $T_{out} = \mathbf{R}/C + \delta\,\mathbf{R}$ is distance vector between control stations to each UWB label, δ is time measurement error, T_{pro} can be used as an empty slot, Consideration should be given to the relationship between unknown label number m and every time frame T.

If time frame is T, $T = \{T_1, T_2, \cdots, T_m\}$, $m \le n$ it is a fix, communication link will synchronize time frame once. If there is n labels in the positioning area, this is total label number. We has known every time slot length T_j.

$$T_j = T_{in} + T_{out} + T_{loc} + T_{do} + T_{prot} \qquad j \le m \tag{1}$$

$$T = \sum_{j=1}^{m} T_j + \Delta\delta \tag{2}$$

δ is a noise, that obeys the normal distribution.

According to ISO/IEC18000-6C collision requirement, there is three response types in a time slot. $(C_0\ C_1\ C_k)$, that is the empty slot, no collision time slot and a collision time slot.

When there are many the labels, label response event in the time slot can approximate to poisson distribution. Probability of response is $P_x = \frac{\lambda^x}{x!}e^{-\lambda}$ x is no collision slot type, we know if x is equal to 1, the type shows label response. In this case, the utilization rate of slot will be the biggest, at this time. $P_1 = P_0 = 0.37$ Protect time $\sum T_{pro}$ is equal to setting a suitable empty slot to ensure the signal without conflict. In order not to make time slot too sparse highly, which leads to the sampling period longly. We must standardize the utilization rate of time slot and the uniform data sampling. So

$$\begin{cases} \max f(m) = P_n^m * T_j \qquad f(m) \sim U(1, T) \\ s.t.\ T_{pro}/T = [T - \sum_{1}^{m} (T_{in} + T_{out} + T_{loc} + T_{do})_i]/T \le 0.37 \end{cases} \tag{3}$$

we need to estimate label number m at the end of each frame in the positioning area, used to dynamically adjust the time slot partition.

Because $\hat{m}_i$ show estimate value of label number, we can establish Markov chain according to the number of T cycle.

$$\begin{array}{c} \\ a_1 \\ a_2 \\ \vdots \\ a_i \\ \vdots \end{array}\begin{array}{c} a_1 \; a_2 \; \cdots \; a_j \; \cdots \\ \begin{bmatrix} p_{11} & p_{12} & \cdots & p_{1j} & \cdots \\ p_{21} & p_{22} & \cdots & p_{2j} & \cdots \\ \vdots & \vdots & & \vdots & \\ p_{i1} & p_{i2} & \cdots & p_{ij} & \cdots \\ \vdots & \vdots & & \vdots & \end{bmatrix} \end{array} = \mathbf{P} \tag{4}$$

After several tests, the value is corrected constantly.

3.2 Work Flow of the Algorithm in this Positioning System

The control base-station first determines the original length. By the formulas 1, 2 and 3, we will estimate the UWB tag number of the first frame time slot, time slots are divided, and assigned to estimate the number of each unknown UWB label, the station base starts the positioning, the actual ID label information and ID order return back the control process computer according to the time slot, statistics utilization rate of statistical time slot. Compare corresponding probability of markov chains, repeat the above steps, until the time frame to complete. According to markov chain transfer probability, we will choose the number of labels, repeat the above process. As shown in Fig. 4.

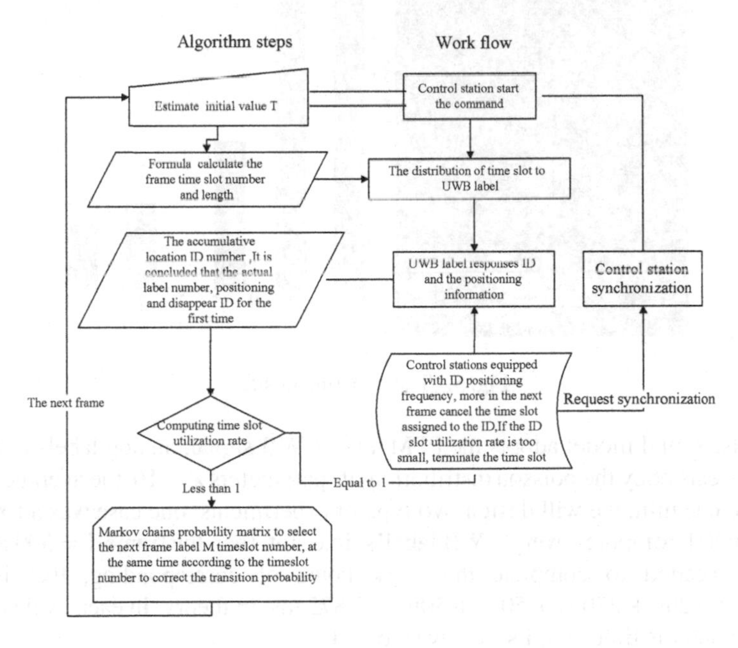

Fig. 4. Work flow

4 Experiment, Simulation and Discussion

Flight experiments were carried out to verify the effectivity of the time slot division. We take a rectangle envelope as a multiple base station location area, for example, as shown in Fig. 5. We take with UWB label craft, the UWB label has a injection of ID Numbers, according to the statistics, which entries and exits by obeying poisson distribution, parameters for arrival time interval is on average, and the initial transition probability matrix of markov chain is established.

$$\begin{array}{c} \\ 1 \\ 2 \\ \vdots \\ j \\ 50 \end{array}\begin{array}{c} \begin{array}{cccccc} 1 & 2 & \cdots & j & 50 & \end{array} \\ \begin{bmatrix} 0.2674 & 0.1498 & \cdots & p_{1j} & \cdots \\ 0.1498 & 0.3856 & \cdots & p_{2j} & \cdots \\ \vdots & \vdots & & \vdots & \\ p_{i1} & p_{i2} & \cdots & p_{ij} & \cdots \\ 0.0001 & \vdots & & \vdots & 0.2687 \end{bmatrix} \end{array} = \mathbf{P}$$

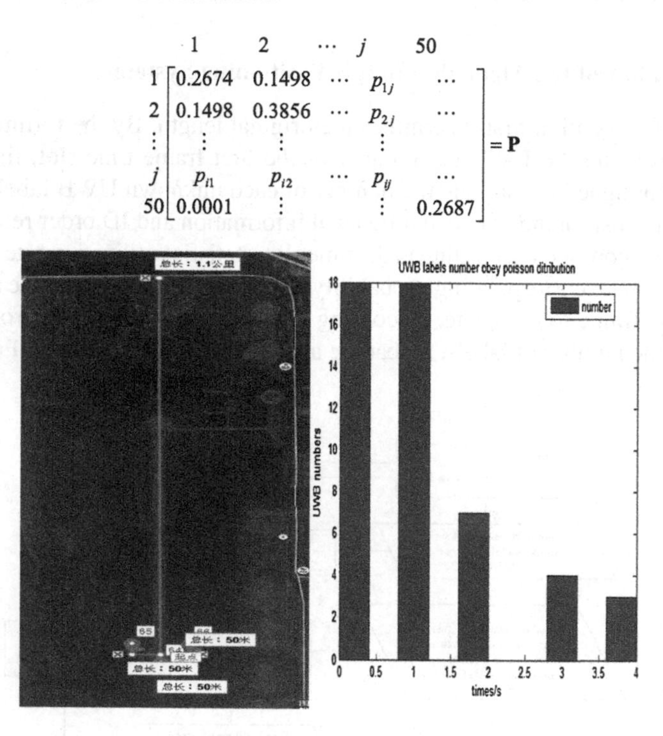

Fig. 5. The experiment site

UWB pulse signal model adopts the PPM TH - UWB signal, analog labels in locating regional events obey the poisson distribution, its parameters $\lambda = 10$, the average interval is equal to one min. we will design two type of experiments, one case was a fixed time slot, formula 1 computes every UWB label's time slot, then the frame T = 500 ms, each time slot needed to complete the work hours of corresponding, that is about $t_i = 2.5\text{ ms} + 2\text{us} + 270\text{us} + 50\text{us} + 50\text{us} = 2.872\text{ ms}$, in theory, in each cycle could be divided in 500 ms time slot, its total was to 174.

In order to simplify our model, We still have following basic assumptions:

1. Each UWB label entered and exited the positioning area evenly, it takes a minute to exist in the positioning area;
2. The moving UWB label were appearing according to poisson distribution.

We compare the fixed time slot allocation algorithm and the algorithm proposed in this study. According to the control base station finally obtains the accumulative total of each UWB label sampling, after our analysis, The rationality of the time slot division avoids UWB goal conflict, and can also meet the requirements to maximize the utilization ratio of time slot frequency at the times (Table 1).

Table 1. Fix time slot partition (Time frame/150 ms)

t_i(m) positioning	UWB number	Time slot utilization
0~0.5	18	43 %
0.8~1.2	18	45 %
1.6~2	7	55 %
2.7~3.2	4	66 %
3.6~4	3	68 %

Another kind experiment is the method of slot length partition algorithm based on dynamic UWB label quantity. According to the dynamic slot division model algorithm is proposed in this study in Fig. 4, because the situation of the simplified model, the trend of the UWB label number into the positioning area is increasing by and by. Basically, setting the time slot by the target number in the localization process is target number, as long as the UWB signal detection, normal label can be located. So idle time slot is very little, the unit of time frame cycle will shrink, positioning frequency higher than fixed time slot, the reasonable allocation of time slot size can also avoid the conflict of signals (Table 2).

Table 2. Dynamic time slot partition

t_i(m) positioning	UWB number	Time slot utilization
0~1	18~36	68 %
1~2	9~15	78 %
2~3	4	83 %
3~4	4~6	87 %

Figure 6 shows two case positioning results of every UWB label. We can observe that there are more positioning number distribution when we use dynamic slot length partition algorithm. Each label is located more than two times at least.

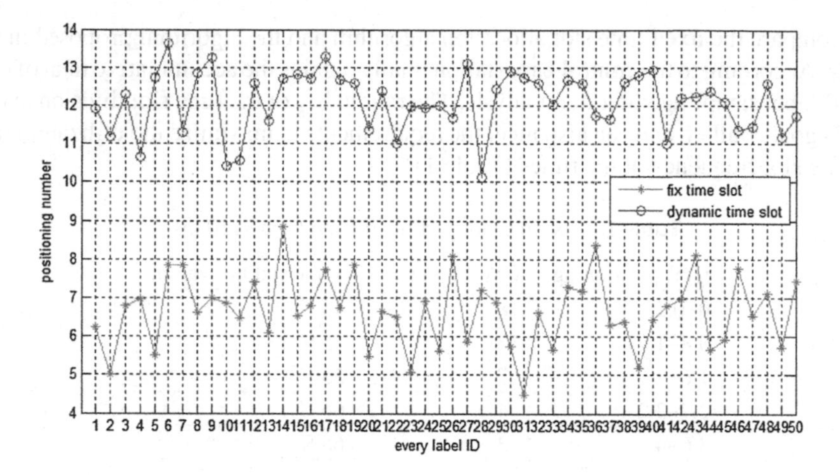

Fig. 6. Two case positioning results of every UWB label

5 Conclusions and Future Work

In the study of the multiple mobile UWB label positioning without conflict, positioning envelope region capacity about label number is limited, so adjusts only time slot dynamic partition, and resolves the conflicts without collision. Its premise condition is the time slot length optimization. It is concluded that markov chain transition probability can be established when the optimal frame estimates every time. So as to meet the mobile label positioning data sampling rate and the demand of the time slot utilization rate, thus rich and coherent datas will improve the positioning accuracy of every moving label.

By theoretical analysis the poisson flow events under the markov transition probability, we did an experiment out the field. And got some measure of each time slot time and frame number and positioning of frequency, the relationship between the rationality of the time slot division to avoid conflict, the test confirmed this algorithm has better applicability.

References

1. Bao, L., Garcia-Luna-Aceves, J.J.: A new approach to channel access scheduling for ad hoc networks. In: Proceedings of the 7th Annual International Conference on Mobile Computing and Networking [S. l], pp. 210–221. ACM Press (2001)
2. Floerkemeier, C., Wille, M.: Comparison of transmission schemes for framed aloha based RFID Protocols. In: IEEE Proceedings of the International Symposium on Applications and the Internet Workshops, pp. 23–27 (2006)
3. Cha, J.R., Kim, J.H.: Novel anti-collision algorithms for fast object identification in RFID system. In: Proceedings of the 11th International Conference on Parallel and Distributed systems, Washington D.C., USA. IEEE Computer Society (2005)
4. EPC Global. EPCTM Radio-frequency Identity Protocals Class-1 Generation-2 UHF RFID Protocal for Communications at 860 MHz-960 MHz (Version 1.0.9) 2009-01

5. Yang, P.I., Chang-jiang, L.I.U.: Anti-collision algorithm for dynamic distribution slotted ALOHA. Comput. Eng. **35**(7), 270–274 (2009)
6. Fei, W., Wu, Z.: Grouping of dynamic frame-slotted Aloah algorithm. Comput. Syst. Appl. **22**(2), 77–80 (2013)
7. Gao-feng, C.A.O., Jian-jun, L.U., Xiao-lu, W.A.N.G.: Dynamic frame slotted Aloha algorithm and anti-collision in positioning system. J. Xi'an Inst. Posts Telecommun. **16**(5), 23–25 (2011)
8. Liu, W., Zhao, X.: Setting time slot length based on number of nodes in wireless LAN. Comput. Eng. Appl. **50**(13), 114–117 (2014)

A Model Framework for Supporting Online Construction of Low-Fidelity Kinematic Models

Dong Meng(✉), Yi Yao(✉), and Teng-fei Hu

College of Information System and Management,
National University of Defense Technology, Changsha, Hunan, China
donemen@yeah.net, {ypyao,tfhu}@nudt.edu.cn

Abstract. Replacing the high-fidelity model with a low-fidelity model can be considered as an availability solution to improve the simulation performance. However, the exciting studies could not cope with the diversity in the type of kinematic objects perfectly. To resolve this problem, we proposed a flexible model framework which can be used to construct the low-fidelity models for the kinematic objects by using the trajectory information received online. The framework could support the low-fidelity model construction for each different kinematic model in the system during simulation experiment execution time, and provides the foundation of a workable solution to further improve the computing and communication performance of kinematic models.

Keywords: Kinematic model · Low-fidelity model · Model framework · Dynamic mapping function

1 Introduction

In the analytic simulation, especially the military simulation, kinematic object is the most important simulation object [1]. With the increasing demand of the simulation accuracy, the step time of simulation system tends to become smaller than before. Sometimes it could reach second level or even millisecond level, that implies that it needs 3,600,000 times model computation to describe an hour of motion state of a kinematic model; with this fact, there will be a large number of data to be transferred. Especially when the scale of kinematic entity increases rapidly, the performance of simulation system will cannot be guaranteed. Therefore, in the large-scale simulation system, the computing of kinematic model which is a computation and communication intensive process can be an important limiting factor for guaranteeing simulation performance.

To relieve the contradiction between accuracy and efficiency of simulation system, the researcher put forward a solution that replacing the high-fidelity model with a low-fidelity model (e.g., Dead Reckoning algorithm, Metamodel-based Optimization). The core idea is to reduce the computing and communication cost by executing a simplified approximate mathematical model which should still maintain the validity of simulation. The implementation of the solution has two main problem need to be addressed to resolve the above-mentioned problem: (1) replacing different kinematic models in simulation system with the same low-fidelity model will result in the final optimization

L. Zhang et al. (Eds.): AsiaSim 2016/SCS AutumnSim 2016, Part I, CCIS 643, pp. 356–363, 2016.
DOI: 10.1007/978-981-10-2663-8_38

performance varies with the type of kinematic objects; (2) developing corresponding low-fidelity model for each kinematic model in the simulation system respectively is generally troublesome. In another word, the exciting solution could not cope with the diversity in the type of kinematic objects perfectly. This article proposed a flexible model framework to support the online construction of the low-fidelity model for kinematic objects. The proposed framework provides the foundation for a workable solution to further optimize the computing and communication performance of simulation system.

2 Related Works

Several investigations have been reported on reducing computation and communication overheads by employing the methods that replacing the high-fidelity model with a low-fidelity model. This section mainly analyses the work with some of the close investigations related to kinematic models.

Dead reckoning (DR) algorithm is the most widely employed mechanism to reduce traffic of kinematic model in the Distributed Interactive Simulation. The DR algorithm, in other words, will maintain two parallel models (a high-fidelity model and a low-fidelity model) for a particular entity during the runtime of the simulation system. The original model is the high-fidelity and project the original outputs to describe the state of a particular simulation object. The low-fidelity model, which is referred to as a dead reckoning model (DRM) in DR algorithm, often is a simple mathematical model (or a mathematical equation) and is used to estimate the motional state of the remote kinematic entities with their last known information. The most wildly used DRM include first order and second order. The previous often used to describe a smooth trajectory; the last one is more suitable when there are a lot of sudden changes in the movement direction [2]. There has been a lot of research related to improving the accuracy of such low-fidelity model as DRM for specific simulation scenario. It is clear that enhancing the prediction ability of DRM, such as exploiting and utilizing the data feature of the specific kinematic entity, could improve the performance of DR algorithm in the complex case. Zhang et al. provide a novel information model of dead reckoning [3]. In the paper [4], Kharitonov proposed a motion-aware adaptive dead reckoning algorithm which divides the whole complex trajectory into four different simple paths. Wei Shi et al. [5], Youfu Chen et al. [6], and Yanyavi et al. [7] states that traditional DRM predicts object position by assuming that each simulation object moves with fixed way or make little changes to its direction and velocity and otherwise its performance may degrade in some conditions). And these studies incorporate other factors (e.g., user play patterns [5], human behavior [6] and players' interests [7]) into the DRM used for traditional DR algorithm. A major drawback of the existing research is that only using pure first order or second order kinematic models to construct low-fidelity model. Even though some works take other related factors into account, these kinematic models depended on Newton's law cannot satisfy the needs of a variety of kinematic object.

Simulation metamodeling is another way to reducing the computation cost of simulation system relies on the execution of a low-fidelity model. As simulation models become more and more complex and time-consuming, the execution costs of these models become intolerable. Metamodeling technology aims at replacing the execution of the high-fidelity (the original time-consuming model) with a corresponding low-fidelity (a simplified mathematical model). Under the metamodeling technology, the most commonly used methods to build a low-fidelity model include: spline models, regression models, neural networks, Kriging models and response surfaces and so on. Among these metamodeling methods, parametric polynomial response surface approximation is the most popular technique used for kinematic object modeling. Although this method provides a good estimate for the state of the simple kinematic object, an important restriction, however, is its lack of flexibility to achieve a global fit.

3 The Model Framework for Building Low-Fidelity Model of Kinematic Objects

Trajectory information is the main component of kinematic objects state, and there is always a linear or nonlinear trend in the trajectory. The trajectory is usually constituted by a combination of simple movement (e.g., constant motion, variable acceleration motion, rectilinear motion, parabolic motion), and can be described with various equation sets. In this paper, we describe the trajectory with a function (or piecewise function) of time (namely mapping trajectory to time). The function is named as Dynamic Mapping Function (DAMF) and each subsection in the piecewise function called DAMF item. The DAMF are used to describe each simple movement processes.

3.1 A Uniform Pattern Used to Construct Low-Fidelity Kinematic Model

To cope with the variety of kinematic model, a uniform model framework will be useful to construct corresponding low-fidelity model. Therefore we design a model framework depended on the above-mentioned idea. The proposed model framework is composed of five data interfaces and several capability functions. The data interfaces are responsible for receiving and projecting the related data, such as setting parameter, input and output data. The capability function is used to implement the function of model and is mainly composed of DAMFs. The framework can be described by a typical Low-fidelity Kinematic Model (LKM):

$$\mathrm{LKM} = \langle T, I, \mathrm{O}, M, Q, N, E, \Delta t, \ \Omega, \Psi, \mathrm{V}, \mathrm{C}, \Gamma, \Phi \rangle$$

Where: T denotes the simulation time; I denotes the set of input data; O denotes the set of output data; M denotes the functions set in the model; Q denotes the set of all possible states that each function can be in; N denotes the set of DAMF item the model may contain; E denotes the set of event corresponded to the functions set; event in the LKM includes DAMF construction, DAMF realization, DAMF verification, DAMF execution and the cancel of LKM;

$\Delta \mathrm{t}$ denotes the minimal time the model has stayed in a state;

$\Omega = \{(\mathrm{t}, \mathrm{i}) | \mathrm{t} \in \mathrm{T}, \mathrm{i} \in \mathrm{I}\}$ denotes the input sequence at the simulation time t;

$\Psi = \{(\mathrm{t}', \mathrm{o}) | \mathrm{t}' \in \mathrm{T}, \mathrm{o} \in \mathrm{O}\}$ denotes the output sequence at the simulation time t′;

$V = \{e, invoke(m, c) | e \in E, m \in M, c \in C\}$ denotes the event handling sequence, each event in the LKM correspond to different function;

$C = \{c_e : Q \rightarrow \{0, 1\} | \forall e \in E\}$ denotes the condition of each event handling operation, namely is the performing condition of the corresponding function;

$\Gamma = \{f(t, y') | f \in N, t \in T, y' \in \Psi\}$ denotes the computing functions in the DAMF item;

$\Phi = \left\{f | f_s, f_g, f_i, f_p, f_o\right\}$ denotes the data interfaces set, where:

f_s = setparameter(S), which is the parameter setting interface. Before schedule the mathematical model, it is needed that set the state of each function correctly (e.g., the coefficients setting of each DAMF item); the external variable S will provide the required parameters.

f_g = getparameter(S′), which represents the parameter getting interface. S′ represents the parameter that can be used to record the information of the current model.

f_i = input(t, x_i), which represents the input interface, and is responsible for providing input data $x \in \Omega$ for the execution of each capability function.

f_p = process(t′), which represents the interface that responsible for calling and implementing the capability function through schedule the event handling sequence V.

f_o = output(t′, y_i), which represents the output interface, the system get the outputs $y \in \Psi$ of the model through this interface after the every execution.

3.2 Execution Flow of a Low-Fidelity Kinematic Model

Figure 1 represents the inner execution flow of a Low-fidelity Kinematic Model introduced in the previous, which is described in the following:

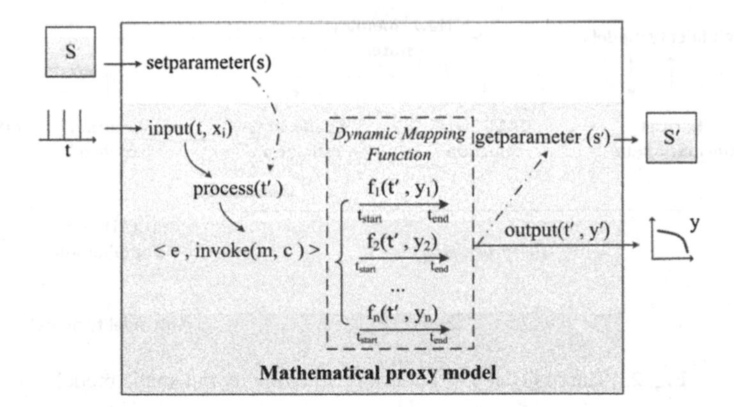

Fig. 1. Execution flow of a Low-fidelity Kinematic Model

(1) Firstly, if a parameters variable S is given, system could reconstruct the low-fidelity kinematic model, by calling the parameters setting interface setparameter(S), to realize the function in the model (e.g., the coefficients setting of each DAMF item);
(2) Selecting appropriate DAMF and estimating the related coefficient based on the kinematic state o original model is another way to construct a low-fidelity kinematic

model. The history kinematic state (x_i) and the corresponding timestamp (t) will be delivered to the corresponding function through the input interface as long as the related input data is ready;

(3) The interface: process (t′) is the core of the low-fidelity kinematic model. It is responsible for invoking different capability functions to implements some important operations. Figure 1 represents the procedure for handing DAMF computing event. Each DAMF item has a start time (t_{start}) and end time (t_{end}) described its period of validity. The DAMF will choose the appropriate item to perform computing according to whether the parameters t′ at the period or not;

(4) Calling output interface output(t′, y_i) to project the results;

(5) Get the parameters of the low-fidelity kinematic model (e.g., the coefficients setting of each DAMF item) through invoking the interface: getparameter(S′), and an external variable S′ is used to store the parameters. Steps (1) and (5) will be used to reconstruct the determined model and only be called when necessary.

4 The Basic Step of Building a Low-Fidelity Kinematic Model

Figure 2 represents the basic steps of building a low-fidelity kinematic model based on our model framework. The kinematic data received from the original model (high-fidelity model) through the input data interface is mostly used as a set of training data. Once the training data is sufficient, the framework will start to select the appropriate DAMF and estimate the related coefficients. After the building procedure finished, it outputs a low-fidelity model constructed by an appropriate DAMF.

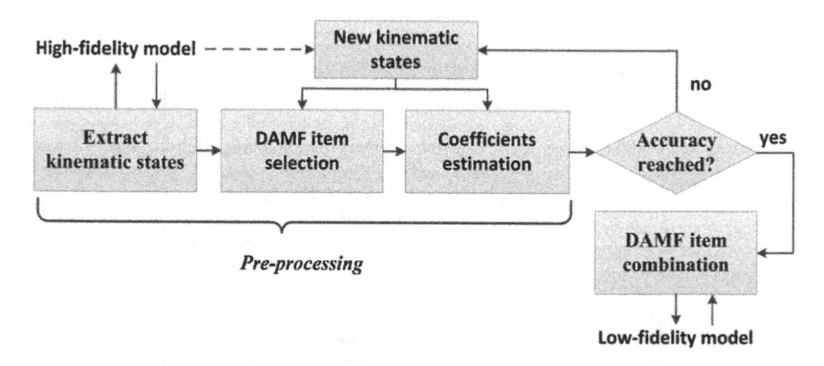

Fig. 2. The basic step of building a low-fidelity kinematic model

(1) The first step is to extract kinematic states from the outputs of the high-fidelity model. This step aims to draw out the entity position, velocity, and orientation from the history entity state and to combine them with the corresponding timestamp into N samples for using as the training set. The training set is a critical part of fitting a suitable low-fidelity model as it must appropriately describe the trajectory of the original kinematic model.

(2) In order to select appropriate DAMFs which construct the core of the low-fidelity model, we pre-defined a collection of basic function item to describe frequently-used motion. Some of the coefficients of each DAMF item are predefined according to the type of kinematic object; however, the remaining coefficients will be determined in a "trial-and-error" approach. Whether the DAMF is appropriate will depend on the accuracy criterion described in the next step.
(3) The final step is evaluating the accuracy of the selected DAMF according to several predefined measures. This step will also help to adjust the size of the training set to suitable and select the most appropriate DAMF item. The accuracy criterion, which is measured by the Root Mean Square Error (RMSE) and Max Absolute Error (MAE), indicates the average and the max deviation of the high-fidelity model outputs (y_i) from the low-fidelity model outputs $(\hat{y}_i)$ respectively.

$$RMSE = \sqrt{\sum_{i=1}^{n} (y_i - \hat{y}_i)^2 \Big/ \sum_{i=1}^{n} y_i^2} \tag{1}$$

$$MAE = \frac{\max|y_i - \hat{y}_i|}{\sqrt{\frac{1}{n} \sum_{i=1}^{n} (y_i - \bar{y}_i)^2}} \tag{2}$$

Where: n denotes the number of validation point, $\bar{y}$ denotes the average value of y_i at validation point.

In this paper, we employ "leave-k-out cross validation strategy" [8] to evaluate the accuracy using the above-mentioned accuracy criterion. In this type of cross-validation, K samples will be chosen from the training set which includes N samples and used to test; the N-K samples will be used to train the DAMF item. This procedure will be repeated C_N^K times and the total and average errors are calculated for each DAMF item. If the desired accuracy has not yet been reached, the building process will return the step (2) and wait for a few simulation step-time to collect more entity state and extend the size of the training set.

5 Experiment and Evaluation

The experiments are implemented on a high-performance computing node which has two 2.93 GHZ Inter (R) Xeon(R) X5670 processors (6 cores), 24 GBRAM memory and 150 GB disk. The experiments conducted were aimed at evaluating the accuracy of low-fidelity model which constructed based on proposed framework using above-mentioned metric: RMSE and MAE. The experiments also implemented with traditional first-order and second-order DR algorithm (DRM_{first} and DRM_{second} respectively). The two different simulation scenarios are described as follow:

In the first scenario (see Fig. 3), the simulation object with constant angular velocity moves in a curvilinear path, and the trajectory is a closed circle. We predefined a basic circular equation as the candidate DAMF item used to construct the DAMF in the low-fidelity kinematic model. This scenario aims to present the ability of the proposed framework to approximate a simple trajectory. As expected, the trained mathematical model behaves as intended. Compared to the first-order and second-order DR algorithm, the mathematical model shows much better accuracy. This is due to its ability to describe the behavior of the original kinematic model.

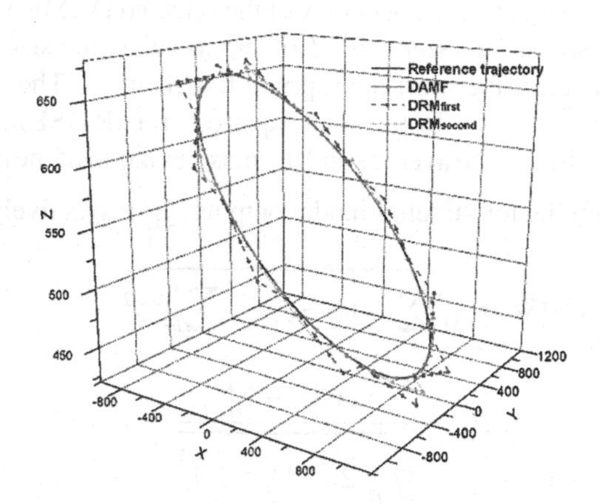

Fig. 3. Scenario 1: circular motion

The second scenario (see Fig. 4) describes a complex trajectory which is composed of several different movement. In the current scenario implementation, we predefined constant motion equation, uniformly accelerated motion equation, variable acceleration motion equation, and curvilinear motion equation as candidate DAMF items used to construct the DAMF in the low-fidelity kinematic model. The testing aimed to evaluate the ability of the proposed model framework to approximate the kinematic model with complex trajectory. Figure 4 demonstrate that the constructed mathematical model provides more accurate results compared to DRM.

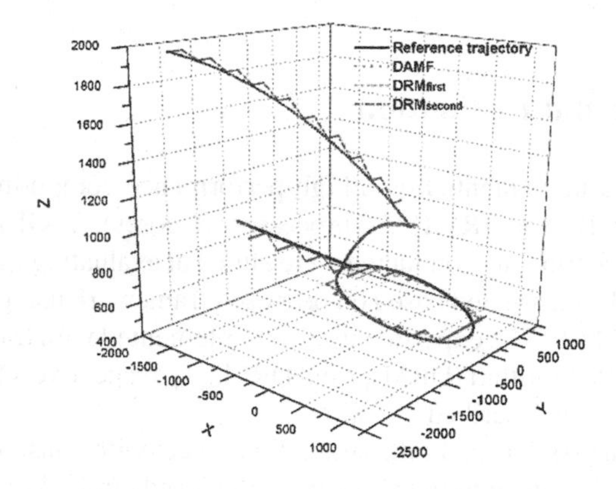

Fig. 4. Scenario 2: complex motion

6 Conclusions and Future Work

Replacing the high-fidelity model with a low-fidelity model is an available method to reduce the computation and communication overhead of kinematic model. This study proposed a model framework to develop a low-fidelity model for each different kinematic model in the simulation system. As the core of the model framework, the Dynamic Mapping Function (DAMF) is constructed by several basic motion equation items which are used to describe the motion pattern in the whole trajectory. The DAMF item should be pre-provided by the user, and the coefficients of each item would be determined through training by received trajectory information. The multiple replication characters of simulation experiment will provide enough data for the training. Due to the simpleness of DAMF item pre-provided by the user, it is hard to construct a good approximation for the kinematic objects with much more complex trajectory. For future work, we plan to improve the construction methods of DAMF by using machine learning algorithm.

Acknowledgments. This work was supported in part by the research Project of State Key Laboratory of High-Performance computing of National University of Defense Technology (No. 201303-05).

References

1. Yun-xiao, L., Man-hao, Ma., Wei-wei, Y.: Combat Model and Simulation, pp. 221–230. National University of Defense Technology Press, Changsha (2006)
2. Singhal, S.K., Cheriton, D.R.: Exploiting position history for efficient remote rendering in networked virtual reality. Presence: Teleoperators Virtual Environ. **4**(2), 169–193 (1995)
3. Zhang, X., Ward, T.E., Mcloone, S.: Towards an information model of consistency maintenance in distributed interactive applications. Int. J. Comput. Games Technol. **4**, 1–10 (2008)
4. Kharitonov, V.Y.: Motion-aware adaptive dead reckoning algorithm for collaborative virtual environments. In: Proceedings of 11th ACM SIGGRAPH International Conference on Virtual-Reality Continuum and Its Applications in Industry, Singapore, pp. 255–261. ACM (2012)
5. Shi, W., Corriveau, J.-P., Agar, J.: Dead reckoning using play patterns in a simple 2D multiplayer online game. Int. J. Comput. Games Technol. **2014**, 18 (2014)
6. Chen, Y., Liu, E.S.: A path-assisted dead reckoning algorithm for distributed virtual environment. In: 2015 IEEE/ACM 19th International Symposium on Distributed Simulation and Real Time Applications, pp. 108–111 (2015)
7. Yahyavi, A., Huguenin, K., Kemme, B.: AntReckoning: dead reckoning using interest modeling by pheromones. In: The International ACM SIGCOMM Workshop on Network and System Support for Games (2011)
8. Meckesheimer, M., Booker, A.J., Barton, R.R., et al.: Computationally inexpensive metamodel assessment strategies. AIAA J. **40**(10), 2053–2060 (2002)

High Performance Computing and Simulation

Parallel Coevolution of Quantum-Behaved Particle Swarm Optimization for High-Dimensional Problems

Na Tian[1(✉)], Yan Wang[2], and Zhicheng Ji[2]

[1] Institute of Educational Informatization, Jiangnan University, Wuxi 214122, China
tianna@jiangnan.edu.cn

[2] Institute of Electrical Automation, Jiangnan University, Wuxi 214122, China

Abstract. Quantum-behaved particle swarm optimization (QPSO) has successfully been applied to unimodal and multimodal optimization problems. However, with the emergence and popularity of big data and deep machine learning, QPSO encounters limitations with high dimensional problems. In this paper, a parallel coevolution framework of QPSO (PC_QPSO) is designed, in which an improved differential grouping method is used to decompose the high dimensional problems into several sub-problems. These sub-problems are optimized independently with occasional communication. Each sub-population is evaluated with context vector, which is constituted by the global best solutions in each sub-problem. The numerical experimental results show that PC_QPSO with differential grouping strategy is able to improve the solution quality without breaking the relationship between interacted variables.

Keywords: High-dimensional · Quantum-behaved particle swarm optimization · Parallel coevolution · Domain decomposition · Differential grouping strategy

1 Introduction

With the emergence and popularity of big data and deep machine learning, swarm intelligence is encountered with limitations for its scalability to high dimensional problems [1]. As we all know, performance of the stochastic optimization algorithms (including particle swarm optimization (PSO), genetic algorithms (GA)) deteriorates as the dimensionality of the search space increases. In the near past years, several approaches were proposed to deal with high dimensional optimization problems, aiming to obtain satisfied solution without requiring too much computational cost. Cheng et al. [2] proposed a competitive PSO, in which the loser had to learn from its opponent, while the winner went to next generation without updating. In this way, 50 % of the computational cost was reduced in each generation, but it is the number of decision variables that determine the complexity of the optimization problems. Therefore, a natural approach to deal with high-dimensional optimization problems is

L. Zhang et al. (Eds.): AsiaSim 2016/SCS AutumnSim 2016, Part I, CCIS 643, pp. 367–376, 2016.
DOI: 10.1007/978-981-10-2663-8_39

to adopt a divide-and-conquer strategy. Clearly, the effectiveness of such approach depends heavily on the adopted decomposition strategies. Especially for non-separable problems, the interdependencies among different variables could not be captured well enough.

In [3], Potter et al. firstly suggested that the search space should be partitioned into several smaller vectors, and found that the decomposition lead to a significant improvement in performance over the classic GA, but the interdependence between variables were not taken into consideration. An attempt to apply Potter's CC model to PSO is made in [4], where two cooperative models, CPSO-S_k and CPSO-H_k were developed. Yang et al. [5] proposed a new decomposition method based on random grouping and adaptive weighting to deal with non-separable problems. Omidvar reveals that it is even more beneficial to apply random grouping more frequently [6], and proposed a delta grouping strategy for non-separable functions [7]. The recent work in [8] proposed a new PSO cooperative coevolution (CC) framework with ring topology (lbest), a new strategy to update personal best and global best vector, and dynamically changing group size, which shows competitive performance and scales up to higher dimension of 2000. A differential grouping method to discover the hidden interaction structure of decision variables was presented in [9], but the performance is sensitive to the value of threshed to distinguish interaction between variables.

Diversity maintaining is of great importance for population-based algorithms to converge to the global optimum [10]. It is much more difficult to measure diversity in parallel coevolution framework, and a new diversity measure method defined as 'average distance around the swarm center' for PC_QPSO was proposed in [11].

QPSO, proposed by Sun in 2004 [12], has been proven to perform better than PSO both in exploration and exploitation abilities [13, 14]. However, improved variants of QPSO were just tested on low dimensional problems (10, 20 or 30). The scalability to high dimensions have not been validated. Based on previous work, this paper gives a parallel coevolution framework on QPSO (PC_QPSO) to solve large scale optimization problems.

The rest of the paper is organized as follows. Section 2 simply introduced the classic PSO and QPSO. The details of the PC_QPSO are described in Sect. 3. Section 4 presents the experimental settings, results and analysis. Finally Sect. 5 gives the conclusion.

2 Quantum-Behaved Particle Swarm Optimization

A minimization problem is assumed in this paper:

$$\min f(x),\ x \in \Omega \tag{1}$$

where $\Omega \subset R$ is the search space, x is a vector with dimensional D.

PSO is a well-known population-based optimization technique originally proposed by Kennedy and Eberhart in 1995 [16]. A PSO system simulates the knowledge evolvement of a social organism, in which particles representing candidate solutions of an optimization problem. The position of each particle is evaluated according to the objective function (Eq. (1)). Particles share their personal experience, which are used to adjust the particles' flying velocities, and their subsequent positions. It has already been shown that PSO has promising performance in various areas [17].

In a PSO system with M particles in the D-dimensional space, the position and velocity vector of particle i at the tth iteration are represented as $X_i(t) = (X_{i1}(t), X_{i2}(t), \cdots, X_{iD}(t))$ and $V_i(t) = (V_{i1}(t), V_{i2}(t), \cdots, V_{iD}(t))$. Each particle moves according to the following equations:

$$V_i(t+1) = \omega V_i(t) + c_1 r_1 (P_i(t) - X_i(t)) + c_2 r_2 (P_g(t) - X_i(t)) \tag{2}$$

$$X_i(t+1) = X_i(t) + V_i(t+1) \tag{3}$$

where $i = 1, 2, \cdots, M, j = 1, 2, \cdots, D$, c_1 and c_2 are acceleration coefficients. r_1 and r_2 are random numbers uniformly distributed in (0,1). ω is called inertia weight to control the balance between exploration and exploitation. Vector $P_i = (P_{i1}, P_{i2}, \cdots, P_{iD})$ is the previous best position of particle i, and vector $P_g = (P_{g1}, P_{g2}, \cdots, P_{gD})$ is the position of the best particle g, which is obtained by:

$$g = \arg\min_i f(P_i) \tag{4}$$

However, it has been proven that PSO is not guaranteed to be global convergent [18]. Trajectory analysis in [19] demonstrated the fact that the convergence of PSO may be achieved if each particle converges to its local attractor, $p_i = (p_{i1}, p_{i2}, \cdots p_{iD})$ defined as:

$$p_i(t) = \varphi P_i(t) + (1 - \varphi) P_g(t) \tag{5}$$

where $\varphi \in (0, 1)$. It can be seen that p_i is a stochastic attractor of particle i that lies in a hyper-rectangle with P_i and P_g being two ends of its diagonal and moves following P_i and P_g.

Different from classical physics, the velocity of a particle is meaningless in quantum world. Therefore in QPSO system, position is the only state to depict the particles, which moves according to the following equation [12]:

$$X_i(t+1) = p_i(t) \pm \alpha |mbest(t) - X_i(t)| \ln(1/u) \tag{6}$$

where u is a random number uniformly distributed in (0,1); $mbest(t)$ called mean best position, is defined as mean of personal best positions of all the particles:

$$mbest(t) = \left(\frac{1}{M}\sum_{i=1}^{M} P_{i1}(t), \frac{1}{M}\sum_{i=1}^{M} P_{i2}(t), \ldots, \frac{1}{M}\sum_{i=1}^{M} P_{iD}(t)\right) \quad (7)$$

The parameter α in Eq. (6) is named as Contraction-Expansion (CE) coefficient, which can be adjusted to control the convergence rate. The most commonly used method to control α is linearly decreasing from $\alpha_{\max}$ to $\alpha_{\min}$:

$$\alpha = (\alpha_{\max} - \alpha_{\min})(t_{\max} - t)/t_{\max} + \alpha_{\min} \quad (8)$$

where t is the current iteration number, $t_{\max}$ is the predefined maximum number of iterations,$\alpha_{\max}$ and $\alpha_{\min}$ are the upper bound and lower bound values of α.

3 Parallel Coevolution (PC) Framework

3.1 Variable Interaction

A function is called separable if the global optimum can be found by optimizing one dimension at a time regardless of the values in other dimensions, otherwise, it is non-separable.

The idea of using parallel coevolution framework on higher dimensional problems has attracted much attention and has been incorporated into several algorithms, including GA [3], PSO [4]. However, a major difficulty in applying CC is the choice of a good decomposition strategy, because interdependence between variables may greatly affect the performance of the algorithm and the knowledge about the structure of a given problem is often insufficient. Therefore, it is desirable to find out the hidden correlation structure of decision variables.

3.2 Interaction Learning Algorithms

Variables interaction learning algorithms were generally classified into four categories: random, perturbation, interaction adaptation, and model building.

The random grouping method [5] randomly permutes the order of decision variables in every cycle to increase the probability of placing two interacting variables in the same subcomponent. This method is easy to use, but it is required to specify the number and the size of each subcomponent.

The perturbation methods detect the interactions between decision variables by monitoring the changes of the objective function. These methods rely on various heuristics to identify interacting variables. Differential grouping method is a typical perturbation technique [9].

In this paper, an improved differential grouping method with adaptive interaction detection parameter is proposed. The differential grouping method was derived from the definition of partially additively separable functions, which represents many real-world problems. The pseudocode of differential grouping is shown in Algorithm DG. The algorithm checks the pairwise relationship between one variable and the other variable. If an interaction is detected, the two variables are added into the same subcomponent. The process is repeated until all the variables are checked. The variable is considered to be separable if no interaction with other variables is detected.

Note in Algorithm DG that vector x is initialized randomly in $[lbound, ubound]$, while it is initialized to the lower bound of the search space in [9]. Vector y is set to the same value as x except for the i th variable and Δ_1 is calculated. $y(i)$ is taken as a random value in $[lbound, ubound]$ rather than the upper bound. Then, the j th element of x and y is changed to be a random value $r(r \in [lbound, ubound])$, and Δ_2 is calculated. The i th and j th decision variables are defined to be interacted if the value of $|\Delta_1 - \Delta_2|$ is greater than a threshold value ε, which is an important parameter to control the algorithm performance and depends on the size of the objective space.

3.3 Parallel Coevolution Framework

In PC framework, the search space is decomposed into K smaller components by Algorithm DG (defined in Sect. 3.2) and each of them is assigned to a subpopulation. These subpopulations are evolved separately with the only cooperation during fitness evaluation.

However, evaluation of the i th subcomponent cannot be computed directly because it is only a part of the given problem. A context vector is able to provide a suitable context in which a subcomponent can be evaluated. The simplest scheme is to take the global best particles from each of the K subpopulations and concatenate them to form a D-dimensional vector (Eq. (9)).

$$contex\_vector \equiv \left(P_g^1, P_g^2, \ldots, P_g^{k-1}, P_g^k, P_g^{k+1}, \ldots, P_g^K\right) \tag{9}$$

in which, P_g^k represents position of the global best particle in the k th subpopulation. To calculate the fitness of particles in swarm k, the other $K - 1$ components in the context vector are kept unchanged, while the k th component of the context vector is replaced in turn by each particle in swarm k. The concatenation of the k th subcomponent with context vector is defined as:

$$b(X_i^k) \equiv \left(P_g^1, P_g^2, \ldots, P_g^{k-1}, X_i^k, P_g^{k+1}, \ldots, P_g^K\right) \tag{10}$$

```
Algorithm IDG: allgroups ← grouping(f, lbound, ubound, D)

seps ← {}
allgroups ← {}
flag = zeros(1,D)
for i = 1 : D && flag(i) == 0
   group ← {i}
   flag(i) = 1
   for j = i+1 : D && flag(j) == 0
      x ← (ubound + lbound) × rand(1,D) − lbound
      y ← x
      y(i) ← (ubound + lbound) × rand() − lbound
      Δ1 = f(x) − f(y)
      x(j) ← r    // r is a random number in (lbound, ubound)
      y(j) ← r
      Δ2 = f(x) − f(y)
      if |Δ1 − Δ2| > ε then
         group ← group ∪ j
         flag(j) = 1
      endif
   endfor
   if length(group) = 1 then
      seps ← seps ∪ group
   else
      allgroups ← allgroups ∪ group
   endif
endfor
allgroups ← allgroups ∪ seps
```

This idea is to evaluate how well X_i^k cooperates with the best individuals from the other swarms. Therefore, the parallel framework of PC_QPSO is given as follows (Algorithm PC_QPSO):

```
Algorithm PC_QPSO
Master: allgroups ← grouping(f, lbound, ubound, D);
        Initialize X;
        Distribute the kth sub-population (X^k, k ∈ [1,2,...,K]) to the kth slave;
        Initialize the context vector with all global best particles in each sub-swarm;
        Broadcast context_vector to all the slaves;
Slave:
    while (the predefined maximal number of fitness evaluations is not reached):
        for each particle i ∈ [1,...,swarmSize]:
            if f(b(X_i^k)) < f(b(P_i^k)) then
                P_i^k ← X_i^k;
                if f(b(X_i^k)) < f(b(P_g^k)) then
                    P_g^k ← X_i^k;
                endif
            endif
            Update context_vector and broadcast it in the community;
            Update position of particle i in swarm k by equation (6);
        endfor
        Update α by equation (8);
    endwhile
Output context_vector
```

4 Experimental Studies

4.1 Experimental Setup

Six benchmark functions (as listed in Table 1) proposed in CEC2008 special session on large-scale optimization [15] are used in this section to test PC_QPSO and compare with other algorithms, in which f_1, f_2, and f_4 are separable functions, f_3, f_5, and f_6 are non-separable functions.

Experiments are conducted on the above 6 functions for 100 and 500 dimensions. For each test function, the average results of 25 independent runs were recorded. For each run, the maximal number of fitness evaluations (Max_FES) is set to 5000* D. The population size for each sub_swarm is set to 30.

Experiments are implemented on a server with an Intel Xeon CPU E7-4809 (4 processors) and 128 GB RAM. The algorithm is written in Fortran on Intel Visual Fortran with MPICH2.

Table 1. Benchmark functions for large scale global optimization

Function	Definition	Domain
f_1	$f_1(X) = \sum_{i=1}^{D} x_i^2$	$[-100, 100]^D$
f_2	$f_2(X) = \max\{\lvert x_i \rvert, 1 \leq i \leq D\}$	$[-100, 100]^D$
f_3	$f_3(X) = \sum_{i=1}^{D-1} \left(100(x_i^2 - x_{i+1})^2 + (x_i - 1)^2\right)$	$[-100, 100]^D$
f_4	$f_4(X) = \sum_{i=1}^{D} (x_i^2 - 10\cos(2\pi x_i) + 10)$	$[-5, 5]^D$
f_5	$f_5(X) = \sum_{i=1}^{D} \frac{x_i^2}{4000} - \prod_{i=1}^{D} \cos\left(\frac{x_i}{\sqrt{i}}\right) + 1$	$[-600, 600]^D$
f_6	$f_6(X) = -20\exp\left(-0.2\sqrt{\frac{1}{D}\sum_{i=1}^{D} x_i^2}\right) - \exp\left(\frac{1}{D}\sum_{i=1}^{D}\cos(2\pi x_i)\right) + 20 + e$	$[-32, 32]^D$

If the function is completely separable, the size of each group is taken as 20. If it is non-separable, the variables interacted with each other are grouped together. However, if the topology of variables looks like a ring (e.g. f_3 in Fig. 1a), we need to cut some connections and divide them into several groups (the size of each group has 20 variables). The most complicated function is that variables are connected with each other (e.g. f_5 and f_6 in Fig. 1b). In this case, we prefer to adopt random decomposition method.

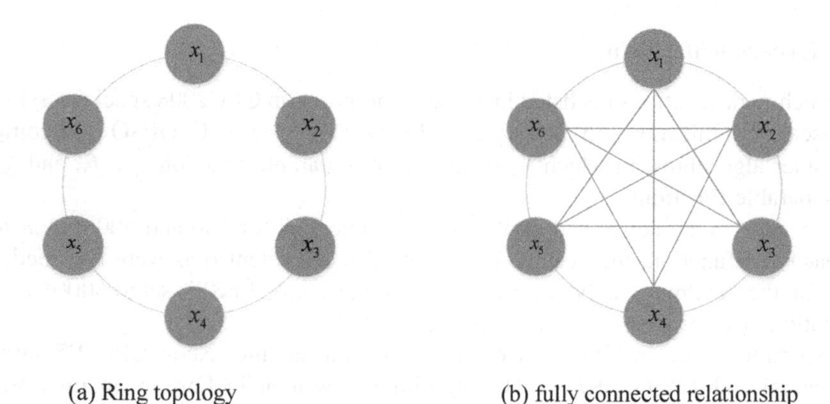

(a) Ring topology (b) fully connected relationship

Fig. 1. Relationship between variables

Table 2. Performance comparison in terms of solution accuracy

	Mean best fitness standard deviation					
	100-D			500-D		
	CSO	QPSO	PC_QPSO	CSO	QPSO	PC_QPSO
f_1	9.02E-15 (5.53E-15)	7.73E-14 (3.23E-14)	**9.11E-29 (1.10E-28)**	2.25E-14 (6.10E-15)	3.00E-13 (7.96E-14)	**6.75E-23 (3.90E-24)**
f_2	2.31E+01 (1.39E+01)	3.35E+01 (7.83E+00)	**6.08E+00 (5.38E+00)**	2.60E+01 (1.74E+01)	5.79E+01 (4.21E+01)	**2.12E+01 (2.4E+00)**
f_3	4.31E+00 (5.53E+01)	4.23E+02 (8.65E+02)	**3.90E+02 (1.26E+01)**	5.74E+02 (1.67E+02)	7.24E+02 (1.54E+02)	**2.93E+02 (3.59E+01)**
f_5	2.78E+02 (3.43E+01)	**3.98E-02 (1.99E-01)**	5.60E+01 (7.48E+00)	2.18E+03 (1.51E+02)	**3.98E-02 (1.99E-01)**	3.19E+02 (2.16E+01)
f_4	2.96E-04 (1.48E-03)	3.45E-03 (4.88E-03)	**0 (0)**	7.88E-04 (2.82E-03)	1.18E-03 (4.61E-03)	**2.22E-16 (0.00E+00)**
f_6	2.12E+01 (4.02E-01)	1.44E-13 (3.06E-14)	**1.20E-14 (1.52E-15)**	2.15E+01 (3.10E-03)	5.34E-13 (8.61E-14)	**4.13E-13 (1.10E-14)**

4.2 Results and Analysis

To verify the performance of PC_QPSO for high dimensional optimization, comparison with the sequential QPSO and one of the state-of-the-art algorithms (CSO [2]) is given in Table 2. The same criteria proposed in [15] are adopted here.

It can be seen from Table 2 that PC_QPSO outperforms the other two algorithms except in function f_4, which is a completely nonseparable function. PC_QPSO is effective and efficient in optimizing separable functions and nonseparable functions with simple topology. The problem space is divided into several subspaces which are optimized by independent processors with occasional communication about the context vector. However, connections between variables in complicated nonseparable functions are completely destroyed, and therefore the parallel performance is not so good as that with sequential framework.

5 Conclusions

In this paper, a parallel coevolution QPSO was proposed, in which an improved differential grouping method is used to divide the search space into several sub-spaces and optimize them separately. A context vector is maintained in the community to help evaluate the particles in each sub-swarm. The numerical experimental results show that PC_QPSO has comparative or even better performance than other algorithms.

Acknowledgment. This work is supported by National Hi-tech Research and Development Program of China (2014AA041505), National Science Foundation of China (61572238), the Provincial Outstanding Youth Foundation of Jiangsu Province (BK20160001).

References

1. Zhou, Z.-H., Chawla, N.V., Jin, Y., Williams, G.J.: Big data opportunities and challenges: discussions from data analytics perspectives. IEEE Comput. Intell. Mag. **9**(4), 62–74 (2014)
2. Cheng, R., Jin, Y.: A competitive swarm optimizer for large scale optimization. IEEE Trans. Cybern. **45**(2), 191–204 (2015)
3. Potter, M.A., De Jong, K.A.: A cooperative coevolutionary approach to function optimization. In: Davidor, Y., Schwefel, H.-P., Männer, R. (eds.). LNCS, vol. 866, pp. 249–257Springer, Heidelberg (1994). doi:10.1007/3-540-58484-6_269
4. van den Bergh, F., Engelbrecht, A.P.: A cooperative approach to particle swarm optimization. IEEE Trans. Evol. Comput. **8**(3), 225–239 (2004)
5. Yang, Z., Tang, K., Yao, X.: Large scale evolutionary optimization using cooperative coevolution. Inf. Sci. **178**(15), 2986–2999 (2008)
6. Omidvar, M.: Cooperative co-evolution for large scale optimization through more frequent random grouping. In: 2010 IEEE CEC, pp. 1754–1761. IEEE Xplore (2010)
7. Omidvar, M.N., Li, X.D., Yao, X.: Cooperative co-evolution with delta grouping for large scale non-separable function optimization. In: 2010 IEEE Congress on Evolutionary Computation, pp. 1–8. IEEE Xplore (2010)
8. Li, X.D., Yao, X.: Cooperatively coevolving particle swarms for large scale optimization. IEEE Trans. Evol. Comput. **16**(2), 210–214 (2012)
9. Omidvar, M.N., Li, X.D., Mei, Y., Yao, X.: Cooperative co-evolution with differential grouping for large scale optimization. IEEE Trans. Evol. Comput. **18**(3), 378–393 (2014)
10. Olorunda, O., Engelbrecht, A.: Measuring exploration/exploitation in particle swarms using swarm diversity. In: Proceedings of IEEE Congress on Evolutionary Computation, pp. 1128–1134 (2008)
11. Ismail, A., Engelbrecht, A.P.: Measuring diversity in the cooperative particle swarm optimizer. In: Dorigo, M., Birattari, M., Blum, C., Christensen, A.L., Engelbrecht, A.P., Groß, R., Stützle, T. (eds.) ANTS 2012. LNCS, vol. 7461, pp. 97–108. Springer, Heidelberg (2012). doi:10.1007/978-3-642-32650-9_9
12. Sun, J., Feng, B., Xu, W.B.: Particle swarm optimization with particles having quantum behavior. In: IEEE Congress Evolutionary Computation, vol. 70(3), pp. 1571–1580. IEEE Xplore (2004)
13. Sun, J.: Quantum-behaved particle swarm optimization: analysis of individual particle behavior and parameter selection. Evol. Comput. **20**(3), 349–393 (2012)
14. Sun, J.: Convergence analysis and improvements of quantum-behaved particle swarm optimization. Inf. Sci. **193**, 81–103 (2012)
15. Tang, K., Yao, X., Suganthan, P.: Benchmark functions for the CEC 2008 special session and competition on large scale global optimization. Nature Inspired Computation and Applications Laboratory, USTC, China (2007). http://nical.ustc.edu.cn/cec08ss.php
16. Kennedy, J., Eberhart, R.C.: Particle swarm optimization. In: IEEE International Conference on Neural Networks, Perth, Australia (1995)
17. Eberhart, R.C., Shi, Y.: Comparison between genetic algorithms and particle swarm optimization. In: Porto, V.W., Saravanan, N., Waagen, D., Eiben, A.E. (eds.) EP 1998. LNCS, vol. 1447, pp. 611–616. Springer, Heidelberg (1998). doi:10.1007/BFb0040812
18. F. Van den Bergh, An analysis of particle swarm optimizers, Ph.D. dissertation. University of Pretoria, South Africa (2001)
19. Clerc, M., Kennedy, J.: The particle swarm: explosion, stability, and convergence in a multi-dimensional complex space. IEEE Trans. Evol. Comput. **6**, 58–73 (2002)

Equipment Residual Useful Life Prediction Oriented Parallel Simulation Framework

Chenglong Ge[1(✉)], Yuanchang Zhu[1], Yanqiang Di[1], and Zhihua Dong[2]

[1] Mechanical Engineering College, Shijiazhuang, Hebei 050003, China
08gechenglong@163.com

[2] Baicheng Ordnance Test Center of China, Baicheng, Jilin 137001, China

Abstract. Equipment residual useful life (RUL) prediction is the main contents of Condition Based Maintenance (CBM) research and the reasonableness of CBM decision is determined by RUL prediction accuracy. Due to the equipment state are complicated with uncertainty, predicting RUL has become a research difficulty according to the equipment state. Simulation provides an effective way to solve the RUL prediction problem. The concept and technology framework of equipment residual useful life prediction oriented parallel simulation are proposed based on parallel system theory in this paper and the concept, characteristics, capacity demands and functional compositions of parallel simulation are introduced. The essential technologies of equipment RUL prediction oriented parallel simulation are discussed which include awareness of equipment state, construction of equipment state space model and evolution of equipment state space model, thus providing references for building equipment RUL prediction oriented parallel simulation system.

Keywords: Parallel simulation · Model evolution · Residual useful life · Condition based maintenance · State awareness · State space model · Data assimilation

1 Introduction

With the development of state monitoring technology, fault prediction technology and maintenance decision technology, Condition Based Maintenance (CBM) has widely used in the field of equipment maintenance and support and has become a hot issue in this research field [1]. Based on the traditional condition monitoring and fault diagnosis technology, CBM can obtain equipment state information by means of embedded sensors, external test equipment and portable measuring devices and accurately monitor the actual state of the equipment, and accordingly decide to replace or repair the equipment. CBM can also improve the equipment availability with the premise of ensuring reliability by predicting residual useful life (RUL) and contribute to realize equipment precision support, reducing the costs of maintenance support. Currently, theoretical study of CBM focuses on state feature extraction, RUL prediction and CBM decision-making, and RUL prediction which is an important basis of implementing

L. Zhang et al. (Eds.): AsiaSim 2016/SCS AutumnSim 2016, Part I, CCIS 643, pp. 377–386, 2016.
DOI: 10.1007/978-981-10-2663-8_40

CBM has become a research emphasis. The reasonableness of CBM decision is determined by RUL prediction accuracy.

RUL prediction refers to predict residual useful life from the present time to functional fault time based on the equipment operational status and relevant history state data. RUL prediction methods [2] mainly include mathematical statistics based prediction, data driven based prediction, model based prediction and similarity based prediction. The complexity of weapon equipment determines the equipment state with characteristics of time-varying, uncertainty and big information quantity. Thus, it is difficult to predict RUL according to the state and make a correct CBM decision. Simulation provides an effective way to solve the RUL prediction problem. Aiming at improving RUL prediction accuracy, the simulation technology is applied in real weapon equipment by real-time state awareness and model evolution. Then the online RUL prediction will be realized and the more accurate equipment state and maintenance recommendation will be supplied to maintenance personnel. The above simulation application technology is called equipment RUL prediction oriented parallel simulation technology in this paper.

In China, the concept of parallel system based on ACP (Artificial societies, Computational experiments, Parallel execution) was originally proposed by Professor Feiyue Wang [3] in 2004. Parallel system refers to establish an artificial system which operates parallel to the physical system by utilizing complex system modeling theory and execute computational experiments in the artificial system and then the analysis, control and prediction for physical system are realized ultimately by parallel execution, evolutional approximation and feedback control between physical system and artificial system. Parallel system theory combines artificial society with computational experiments and parallel execution, aiming to solve the control and management issues of complex system, such as socio-economic system. The theory and methods of dynamic data driven simulation for real-time combat decision support which can improve effectiveness, accuracy and adaptability of command decision by injecting real-time battlefield situation into simulation system dynamically were presented by Yun Zhou in 2010. In 2012, Professor Feiyue Wang proposed the concept of parallel military system and applied parallel system theory in military field. To solve emergency management issue, National University of Defense Technology successfully developed KD-ACP [4] platform and this platform has implied in the research of "A-H1N1 influenza event", public opinion evolution on haze. On the basis of parallel system theory, the domestic scholars have proposed concepts of parallel control, parallel test and social computing which have further expanded the application fields of parallel system theory.

In abroad, in the early 1980 s, Frederica Darema [5] gave rise to the idea of DDDAS (Dynamic Data Driven Application Systems) and as a result, the US National Science Foundation (NSF) formally established the DDDAS concept in 2000. Then many DDDAS projects, funded by NSF, began to be performed. In 2007, the US Department of Defense Advanced Research Projects Agency (DARPA) presented "deep green" program [6] which aimed at embedding simulation into command control system and real-time supporting military operations in order to improve commander's decision-making speed and quality. The program's basic process is that relevant information is obtained from the battlefield in real-time by simulation system and the battlefield situation is updated by the way of dynamic data driven and then the simulation is performed based on the latest situation data. In 2010, DDDAS seminar was held by NSF and the US Air Force Office of Scientific Research (AFOSR) and DDDAS is regarded as an infosymbiotics system [7]. The concept of symbiotic simulation [8] was originally defined by Richard Fujimoto at the International Conference on Modeling and Simulation in 2002. Compared with DDDAS paradigm, the mainly purpose of symbiotic simulation is that emphasizing the effects simulation system bring to physical system. Symbiotic simulation system is a discrete event simulation system with the commensalism mechanism between simulation system and physical system. The simulation system benefits from real-time measurement about the physical system which is provided by corresponding sensors. The physical system, on the other side, may benefit from the effects of decisions which are made by what-if analysis (WIA) of simulation system. Although the "parallel" word does not appear in DDDAS and symbiotic simulation, the intension of DDDAS and symbiotic simulation is in accordance with parallel system. The above theories are the paradigms which consist of simulation system and physical system and emphasize on predicting, analyzing and controlling the physical system by utilizing simulation system to guide or optimize the physical system.

The domestic and abroad scholars have different understanding on the concept of parallel simulation. In recent years, the domestic simulation experts also put forward some ideas on parallel simulation, such as Professor Xiaofeng Hu presented the concept of semi-reality embedded parallel simulation in 2013 and Professor Changjian Bi proposed the concept of embedded simulation based on parallel system in 2015. These studies build theoretical foundation for this paper. Domestic research on parallel system for military field is still in beginning stage and there is no research applying the concept of parallel in RUL prediction. In this paper, aiming at improving the accuracy of RUL prediction, an equipment RUL prediction oriented parallel simulation framework is proposed based on parallel system theory.

2 Concept and Characteristics

2.1 Concept

Equipment RUL prediction oriented parallel simulation refers to construct simulation system which operates parallel with physical system and the latest equipment state information is obtained by simulation system and as a result, equipment state space model(SSM) is updated which is called model evolution. And then based on fast simulation method, equipment RUL can be predicted according to historical state and the current state, so the equipment maintenance personnel can master the health status of equipment which can be considered as data basis for CBM decision-making. Equipment RUL prediction oriented parallel simulation method is shown in Fig. 1. Parallel simulation system can support equipment RUL prediction through the following steps:

- Awareness of equipment state. Parallel simulation system continuously obtains equipment real-time state which is regarded as driven data of equipment SSM evolution and RUL prediction.

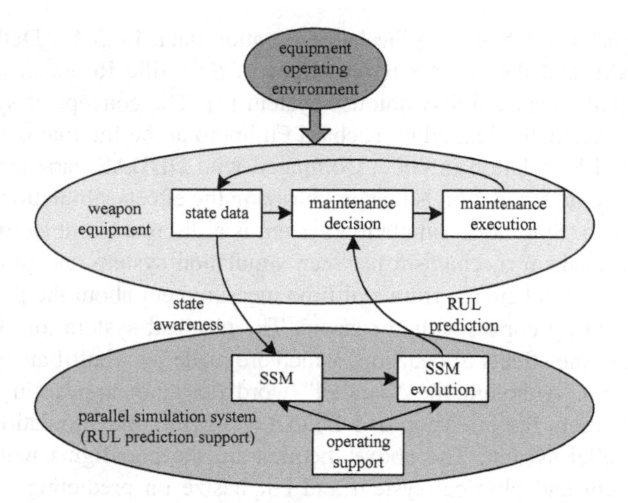

Fig. 1. Diagram of equipment RUL prediction oriented parallel simulation

- SSM Construction. According to the characteristics of equipment state data, the appropriate equipment state space model is selected, including SSM of linear dynamic system and SSM of nonlinear dynamic system.
- SSM evolution. According to real-time dynamic state data of the equipment, the current SSM is updated to approximate the true state of the equipment.
- Equipment RUL prediction. Based on parallel simulation operating technology, such as fast simulation, the equipment RUL is predicted by utilizing SSM and equipment benefits from the feedback results to support maintenance decision-making and improve equipment support efficiency.

2.2 Characteristics

Compared with ordinary simulation technology, parallel simulation has the following characteristics in structures and operation mechanism:

- Symbiotic structure. Weapon equipment and simulation system are connected through a specific interface devices to form a symbiotic structure, and there is interaction and response between weapon equipment and simulation system.
- Data driven. Parallel simulation system needs to execute data assimilation based on the sensed equipment state data, enabling the equipment SSM evolution to improve RUL prediction accuracy.
- Model evolution dynamically. The model of general simulation system belong to model of one-time construction, but the model of parallel simulation belong to the evolutionary model, including dynamic data driven model selection and model evolution. In other word, the equipment SSM is selected dynamically according to the equipment real state and then SSM is updated dynamically to predict equipment RUL.

- Efficient operation. Parallel simulation system and weapon equipment operate simultaneously from beginning to end and the running speed of parallel simulation system is generally faster than the weapon equipment.

3 Capacity Demands and Functional Compositions

3.1 Capacity Demands

To support equipment RUL prediction, combining the characteristics of parallel simulation, parallel simulation system has the following capacity demands:

- Receiving and processing equipment state information in real-time. As a parallel execution system with the equipment, the parallel simulation system receives state data continuously from equipment. Thereby, parallel simulation system needs to have the ability of receiving and processing equipment state information in real-time.
- SSM evolution. As the model basis of RUL prediction, SSM should be selected to fit the characteristics of current equipment state. Then parallel simulation system should update equipment SSM to improve RUL prediction accuracy according to the latest equipment state. Accordingly, parallel simulation system needs to have the ability of equipment SSM evolution dynamically.
- Interoperability between parallel simulation system and weapon equipment. On one hand, parallel simulation system should not only receive and process equipment state information continuously from equipment, but also construct and update equipment SSM and then predict residual useful life according to the latest observational state. On the other hand, maintenance personnel receive feedback results from parallel simulation system to make appropriate maintenance decision. Therefore, parallel simulation system needs to have the ability of interoperability with weapon equipment.
- Fast and efficient operation. Parallel simulation system needs to fast select and update equipment SSM according to the equipment state and then predict equipment RUL. Due to the complexity of weapon equipment and uncertainty of equipment state, the parallel simulation system should have the capability of fast and efficient operation.

3.2 Functional Compositions

In Fig. 2, parallel simulation system consists of equipment state awareness, SSM construction, SSM evolution, RUL prediction and efficient simulation engine. Parallel simulation system receives and processes equipment state through state awareness function which is regard as the data driven basis of SSM construction and evolution. Selecting SSM dynamically is the model basis of RUL prediction. The function of SSM evolution can update SSM output through data assimilation to improve predict accuracy. The function of RUL prediction can effectively predict the residual useful life of

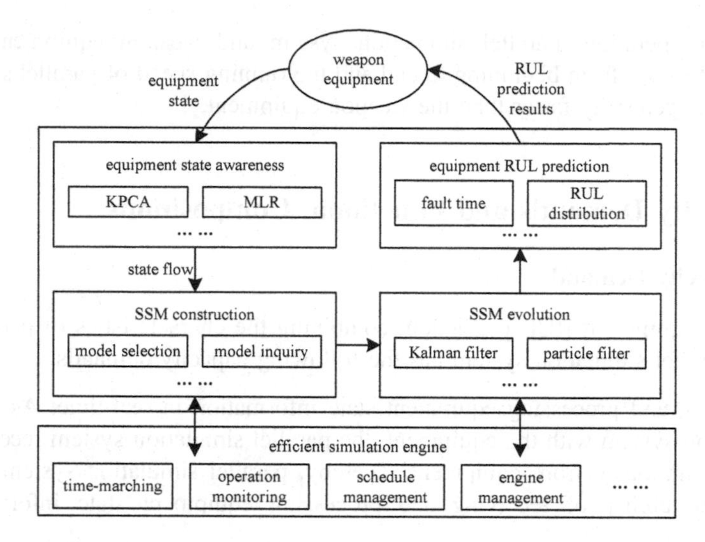

Fig. 2. Functional compositions of parallel simulation system

the equipment to support maintenance decision. The efficient simulation engine can provide other functions with the services of time-marching, operation monitoring, schedule management and engine management, etc.

4 Key Technologies

The main technology of equipment RUL prediction oriented parallel simulation can be classified as modeling technology, system operation technology and simulation application technology and this paper focuses on modeling techniques. Modeling of parallel simulation is a dynamic data driven modeling process, so awareness of equipment state is the first concern which is regarded as the source of data driven. Next, it is need to select and update equipment state space model according to the changes of equipment state. To sum up, it is need to research three issues, including awareness of equipment state, constriction of equipment SSM and evolution of equipment SSM, which is named ACE (Awareness-Construction-Evolution) issue in this paper.

4.1 Awareness of Equipment State Based on KPCA and MLR

Awareness technology in parallel simulation refers to sense the state changes of equipment to support SSM construction, evolution and RUL prediction. The obtained state through state monitoring general include vibration, temperature, voltage, current and pressure with the characteristics of large data amount, high data dimension and strong nonlinear. If all the collected state is used to RUL prediction, it will result in a sharp increase in the amount of calculation, so the first issue state awareness to solve is data dimension reduction. Data dimension reduction refers to generate new low-dimensional state information without losing the original information as much as possible, and the generated low-dimensional state components are independent with each other. Principal Component Analysis (PCA) is a commonly used method of feature extraction, but PCA considers only second order statistics information of original state without using higher-order information. Therefore, Scholokopf [9] proposed Kernel Principal Component Analysis (KPCA) method which can extract non-linear dada feature from high-dimensional feature space.

After obtaining the low-dimensional state feature, it is required to achieve appropriate state feature which is convenient for RUL prediction through further data processing. Multi-linear Regression (MLR) might be adopted to achieve an equipment health index (*HI*) in system level by synthetically utilizing the above state feature. The health index is as follows,

$$y = b_0 + B^T X = b_0 + \sum_{i=1}^{N} b_i x_i \tag{1}$$

Where $X = (x_1, x_2, \cdots, x_N)$ is the state vector through KPCA, y is the health index in system level and $(b_0, B) = (b_0, b_1, \cdots, b_N)$ are MLR model parameters. To determine this $N+1$ parameters, it is need to train MLR model based on historical data which can be obtained from the equipment state of no fault and entirely fault. Awareness of equipment state based on KPCA and MLR is shown in Fig. 3.

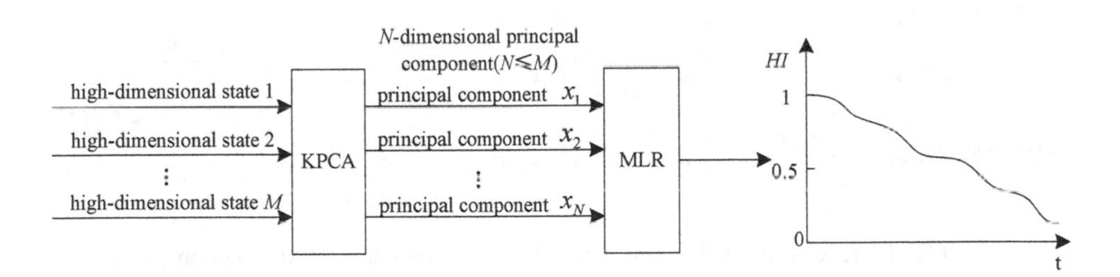

Fig. 3. Diagram of equipment state awareness based on KPCA and MLR

4.2 Construction of Equipment SSM

To execute RUL prediction based on parallel simulation, the model which reflects the change of equipment state is established firstly, i.e., state space model. SSM is a model that fully describes the behavior of dynamic system in time domain, including state equation and observation equation. The state equation reflects conversion relationship of equipment state between neighboring time and observation equation reflects the relationship between observations and equipment state. SSM can be expressed as follows,

$$\begin{cases} x_t = f(x_{t-1}, u_t, \theta_t, w_t) \\ y_t = h(x_t, u_t, \theta_t, v_t) \end{cases} \tag{2}$$

Where $x \in \mathbf{R}^n$ is the state variable, $u \in \mathbf{R}^p$ is the input variable, $y \in \mathbf{R}^m$ is observed variable, $\theta \in \mathbf{R}^q$ is the model parameter, $w \in \mathbf{R}^n$ is the process noise, $v \in \mathbf{R}^m$ is measurement noise. $w \in \mathbf{R}^n$ and $v \in \mathbf{R}^m$ are independent with each other.

The constructed SSM need to adapt to the current state of equipment and it mainly refers to select appropriate model between linear SSM and nonlinear SSM. SSM selection can be seen as special pattern recognition that SSM recognizes the feature of equipment state. The neural network has a strong capability of pattern recognition, this paper presents a KPCA and BP neural network based equipment SSM selection technique which is shown in Fig. 4. At first, the weight matrix $\boldsymbol{W}_{ji}$ between input layer and hidden layer and the weight matrix $\boldsymbol{T}_{lj}$ between hidden layer and output layer are determined based on the training results of BP neural network according to historical data. Then the N-dimensional principal components x_j are achieved by KPCA and $x_j^{'}$ is obtained through normalization and regarded as the input of BP neural network. Next, the state space model o_l which is appropriate with the current equipment state is determined through pattern reorganization.

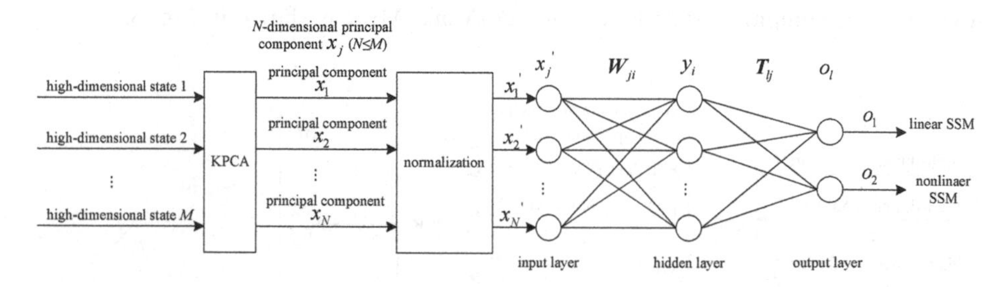

Fig. 4. KPCA and BP neural network based equipment SSM selection

4.3 Data Assimilation Algorithm Based SSM Evolution

As a data driven simulation method, the essential technology of parallel simulation to improve RUL prediction accuracy is the data assimilation (DA) which is performed between the latest state data and SSM output and then the evolution of state space model is realized by DA process. The most commonly used data assimilation methods include Kalman filter (KF) and particle filter (PF). Kalman filter [10] can be obtained the state optimal estimation under the circumstances of error varies linearly and obey Gaussian distribution. Prediction and updating are the two steps in KF to realize SSM evolution. Prediction refers to forecast the state at k+1 time according to the state at current time k. Updating refers to update the state at k+1 time according to the state observed at k+1 time and then obtain state optimal estimation at k+1 time. The basic equations of KF are as follows,

$$X^f_{k+1} = M_{k,k+1} X^a_k \tag{3}$$

$$X^a_{k+1} = X^f_{k+1} + K_{k+1}(Y^o_{k+1} - H_{k+1} X^f_{k+1}) \tag{4}$$

$$K_{k+1} = (H_{k+1} P_{k+1})^T [H_{k+1}(H_{k+1} P^f_{k+1})^T + R_{k+1}]^{-1} \tag{5}$$

Where X^f_{k+1} is the state predictive value at time k+1, X^a_k is the equipment state analysis value at time k, $M_{k,k+1}$ is the relation of state linear change from time k to time k+1, K_{k+1} is the gain matrix at k+1 time, Y^o_{k+1} is the state observation value at time k +1, H_{k+1} is the observation operator at k+1 time, P_{k+1} is the error covariance matrix of state analysis value at time k+1, P^f_{k+1} is the error covariance matrix of state predictive value at time k+1 and R_{k+1} is covariance matrix of observation noise at time k+1.

Particle filter [11], also known as Sequence Monte Carlo method (SSC), is an effective method to solve state optimal Bayesian estimation of nonlinear dynamic system. The core idea of PF is to use a set of random samples and their corresponding weights to approximate the posterior probability density function, a process known as sequential importance sampling (SIS) and the random samples are called particles. Providing that N samples with weights $\{X^a_{i,k}, w_{i,k}\}(i = 1, 2, \cdots, N; k = 1, 2, \cdots, T)$ can be obtained independently from the equipment state posterior probability distribution and $w_{i,k}$ is the weight of each particle, N is the number of particles and T is the assimilation time. When N is large enough, the state posterior probability can be obtained approximately by Eq. (6):

$$p(X^a_k | Y_{1:k}) \approx \sum_{i=1}^{N} w_{i,k} \delta(X^a_k - X^a_{i,k}) \tag{6}$$

Where $\delta(\cdot)$ is Dirac function, $w_{i,k} \propto \frac{p(X^a_{i,k}|Y_{1:k})}{q(X^a_{i,k}|Y_{1:k})}, \sum_{i=1}^{N} w_{i,k} = 1, q(X^a_{i,k}|Y_{1:k})$ is the importance probability density function. Particle filter can obtain optimal Bayesian estimation through two steps, also including prediction and updating. Prediction refers to obtaining prior probability at time k+1 of state prediction value $p(X^f_{k+1}|Y_{1:k})$ according to the posterior probability at time k of state analysis value $p(X^a_k|Y_{1:k})$ and updating refers to obtain the posterior probability at time k+1 of state prediction value $p(X^a_{k+1}|Y_{1:k+1})$ based on $p(X^f_{k+1}|Y_{1:k})$. The essential step of PF is to obtain $X^a_{i,k}$ and $w_{i,k}$ through SIS. However, the particle degradation issue exists in particle filter and resample is a common and efficient solution.

5 Conclusions and Future Work

Aiming at improving RUL prediction accuracy, the equipment RUL prediction oriented parallel simulation framework is proposed based on parallel system theory. The concept, characteristics and functional requirements of parallel simulation are discussed.

And the key technologies of parallel simulation is emphatically introduced, including awareness of equipment state, constriction of equipment state space model and evolution of equipment state space model. The proposed equipment RUL prediction oriented parallel simulation framework will be verified with specific weapon equipment in future research.

References

1. Compare, M., Martini, F., Zio, E.: Genetic algorithms for condition-based maintenance optimization under uncertainty. Eur. J. Oper. Res. **244**, 611–623 (2015)
2. Mehta, P., Werner, A., Mears, L.: Condition based maintenance systems integration and intelligence using Bayesian classification and sensor fusion. J. Intell. Manuf. **26**, 331–346 (2015)
3. Fei-yue, W.A.N.G.: Parallel system methods for management and control of complex systems. Control Decis. **19**(5), 485–489 (2004). (in Chinese)
4. Chen, B.: KD-ACP: A software framework for social computing in emergency management. Math. Probl. Eng. **21**(3), 35–38 (2014)
5. Darema, F.: Dynamic data driven application systems. NSF Workshop Report (2000)
6. Surdu, J.R., Kittka, K.: The deep green concept. In: Spring Multiconference 2008, Military Modeling and Simulation Symposium (MMS), pp. 103–107. DARPA, Ottawa (2008)
7. Darema, F., Douglas, C., Patra, A.: InfoSymbiotics/DDDAS: the power of dynamic data driven applications systems. NSF Workshop Report (2010)
8. Fujimoto, R., Lunceford, D., Page, E., Uhrmacher, A.M.: Grand challenges for modeling and simulation. Dagstuhl Rep. **8**, 49–52 (2002)
9. Scholkopf, B., Smola, A., Muller, K.R.: Nonlinear component analysis as a kernel eigenvalue problem. Neural Comput. **10**(1), 1299–1319 (1998)
10. Reichle, R.H., Walker, J.P., Koster, R.D., et al.: Extended versus ensemble Kalman filtering for land data assimilation. J. Hydrometeorol. **3**(6), 728–740 (2002)
11. Vrugt, J.A., ter Braak, C.J.F., Disks, C.G.H., et al.: Hydrologic data assimilation using particle Markov chain Monte Carlo simulation: theory, concepts and application. Adv. Water Resour. **51**, 457–478 (2013)

Research on Parallel Large-Scale Terrain Modeling for Visualization

Luhao Xiao(✉) and Guanghong Gong

School of Automation Science and Electrical Engineering, Beihang University, Beijing, China
shawmoso@163.com

Abstract. One of challenges in large-scale terrain visualization is to rapidly build numerous 3D terrain models with crucial geomorphic features and adequate simplicity. This paper proposes a solution involving a terrain pyramid modeling method based on parallel programming that gives a boost to modeling speed of DEM/texture pyramid, and an effective approach to generate meshes from DEM by combining the VIP algorithm with regular square grids. In the pyramid modeling method, different input data are loaded by multiple processes simultaneously into a shared memory so that the parent process is capable of performing a parallel aggregation algorithm in GPU subsequently. Moreover, a speedup strategy is adopted to reduce running time of the VIP algorithm by limiting its input to centers of regular grids partitioning the input DEM. Experimental results successfully validate the two methods presented in the paper.

Keywords: Terrain modeling · Parallel computation · TIN construction

1 Introduction

Efficient terrain modeling technique has important implications for large-scale terrain visualization. Due to limitations in storage space and computation capability of computer, 3D terrain models have to keep both small size and crucial geomorphic features. Moreover, the LOD (Level of Details) technique widely employed in large-scale terrain visualization partitions the scene into multiple 3D models with different levels of details, which are usually organized in a terrain pyramid, a hierarchical structure for spatial data management. As the amount of levels increases, there is an approximate exponential growth in quantity of 3D models in a pyramid, leading to a long modeling time.

An ever-increasing amount of researches focus on multicore-CPU, GPU and computer-cluster for the intention of boosting terrain modeling. CPU/GPU solutions apply to a single host or multi-hosts, while cluster solutions rely on many computers to speed up processing. Tesfa et al. developed a geospatial processing approach depending on MPI, which can run in a cluster [1]. Kerr proposed two methods for geographic data manipulation using Hadoop and MPI respectively [2]. Huang et al. [3] and Qin et al. [4] severally conducted researches on geospatial parallel processing framework.

Computer-cluster solutions may be cost-prohibitive in spite of their high performance. By contrast, GPU, a lower-cost specialized processor designed for computer

L. Zhang et al. (Eds.): AsiaSim 2016/SCS AutumnSim 2016, Part I, CCIS 643, pp. 387–397, 2016.
DOI: 10.1007/978-981-10-2663-8_41

graphics are also efficient at parallel computation. Qin et al. exploited GPU to parallelize two algorithms commonly used in geographic analysis [5], while Zhang et al. built a geospatial parallel framework, CudaGIS [6]. Further, Scott et al. utilized multi-GPUs in a computer to get better performance in geospatial processing [7].

Digital Elevation Model (DEM), consisting mainly of grid points storing elevation values, has been popular in numerous applications including terrain modeling due to its convenience in creation, geographic analysis and mesh generation. Nevertheless, there is redundancy in Regular Square Grid (RSG), the 3D model directly built from DEM, such as flat regions with no need for many points and triangles in visualization. For this reason, Triangulated Irregular Network (TIN), a relatively efficient 3D model, is a better choice for terrain modeling.

Methods to form TIN from DEM are categorized into four groups, namely, skeleton, feature, refinement, and decimation methods. The skeleton method extracts feature points and lines taken as input for triangulation. It is simple and effective but not suitable for large-scale modeling on account of long running time. Refinement and decimation methods iteratively assess point's significance from a global perspective, thus forming high-quality meshes. However, they both tend to generate long and thin triangles. The feature method has advantages including rapidity and simplicity, as it estimates significance according to each point's neighbors at only one traversal, such as the VIP (Very Important Points) algorithm [8]. However, meshes derived from the method are usually of poor quality as it is centered merely on local spatial features.

This paper presents a fast, cost-effective parallel 3D terrain modeling solution aiming at large-scale terrain visualization in a single host, involving an efficient pyramid modeling approach utilizing multiprocessing and GPU to boost the modeling procedure, and an improved VIP algorithm combined with the idea of building RSGs, to create high-quality TINs without need of traversing all points in DEM. These two methods are experimentally verified.

2 Overview

A terrain pyramid comprises a certain number of terrain models, where models of same resolution are grouped into one layer, i.e., one level of pyramid. As the level enhances, both the resolution and the quantity of models it contains increase correspondingly, and its position is closer to the bottom of pyramid. In essence, terrain pyramid modeling is a domain decomposition strategy. The pyramid is generally represented in a quadtree, whose height means the number of pyramid layers, as seen in Fig. 1. There are three pyramids required to be built in the modeling procedure, including DEM, texture, and mesh pyramid. All blocks in a DEM or texture pyramid have the same dimensions. After completion of creating a DEM pyramid, it is taken as the basis of a 3D terrain model pyramid, also called a terrain mesh pyramid, where high-level models have larger size and lower resolution.

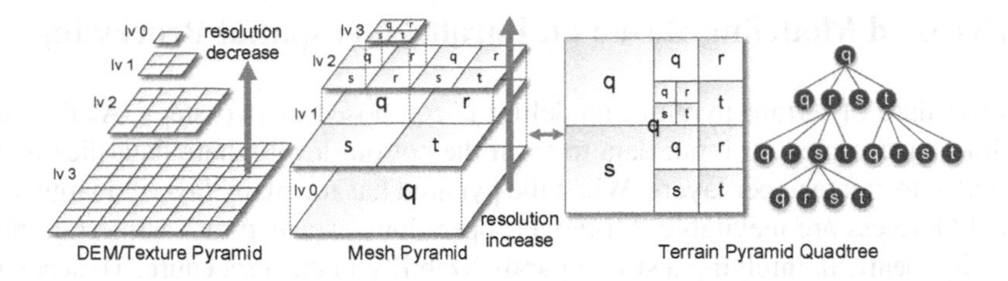

Fig. 1. Terrain pyramid

To avoid cracks between terrain blocks, adjacent data files need to overlap each other in boundary points. Additionally, early graphics hardware does not support NPOT (Non-Power-Of-Two) textures so that it is usually of necessity to resample images in the texture pyramid to POT (Power-Of-Two) textures. The resampled size of each terrain block in a pyramid is

$$sizeOfBlock = 2^k, k \in \left\{ k \in N^+ | 2^k \le \frac{sizeOfSource}{2^{level}} \le 2^{k+1} \right\} \tag{1}$$

where *level* denotes the number of pyramid's layers, *sizeOfSource* is the size of source data. Thus, the dimension of source data file after resampling is

$$sizeOfResampleSource = 2^{level} \times sizeOfBlock - \left(2^{level} - 1\right) \tag{2}$$

Figure 2 shows the entire procedure of 3D terrain modeling. A DEM pyramid and a texture pyramid are produced from corresponding input data. After completion of DEM pyramid modeling, the mesh generation algorithm turns every DEM into a triangulated mesh. Pyramid modeling utilizes multiprocessing and GPU for handling geospatial data in parallel, and an improved VIP algorithm is employed in mesh pyramid modeling to reduce running time. Triangulation in this procedure relies on a fast Delaunay triangulation algorithm using GPU implemented by Rong et al. [9].

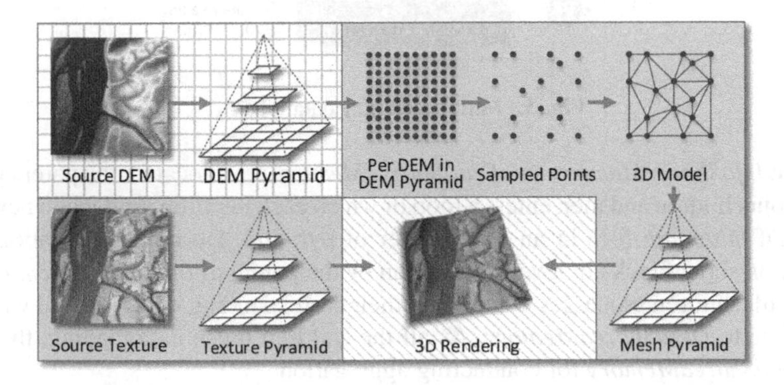

Fig. 2. Procedure of terrain modeling

3 Pyramid Modeling Based on Parallel Geospatial Processing

The procedure of terrain pyramid modeling is composed of two steps. At first, data partition is performed on input data to form the bottom level where data files is then aggregated to create upper layers. When the pyramid has too many layers, a large quantity of I/O access are inevitable. Moreover, operations executed on each terrain block are totally identical, implying a strong parallelizability in this procedure. To accelerate pyramid construction, a parallel scheme exploiting four processes to load input data to a shared memory for the purpose of being shared with the parent process is implemented. All the data in the shared memory is subsequently transmitted to GPU for a parallel aggregation algorithm, and upper levels are obtained consequently.

When producing upper layers of pyramid, level *k* provides level *k-1* with source data in a manner that four adjacent data files constituting a *2*2* grid in level *k* are aggregated to one file in level *k-1*. In detail, a point's elevation or a pixel's RGB in level *k-1* is a mean of values of four neighboring points in a *2*2* grid in level *k*. A serial algorithm can only read four files in sequence, resulting in the waste of running time. Thus, a multiprocessing data loading scheme is designed for acceleration as illustrated in Fig. 3. Firstly, two shared memories of different sizes, namely, *InfoSharedMemory* for storing information about terrain blocks and *DataSharedMemory* for storing block data, are allocated by the parent process. *InfoSharedMemory* is restricted in space as an area for the parent transferring information including file paths, offsets and sizes of regions of interest, etc. to its children. Each child reads information from its corresponding fixed position in *InfoSharedMemory*. By contrast, the larger *DataSharedMemory* is split into four areas for storing different block's data.

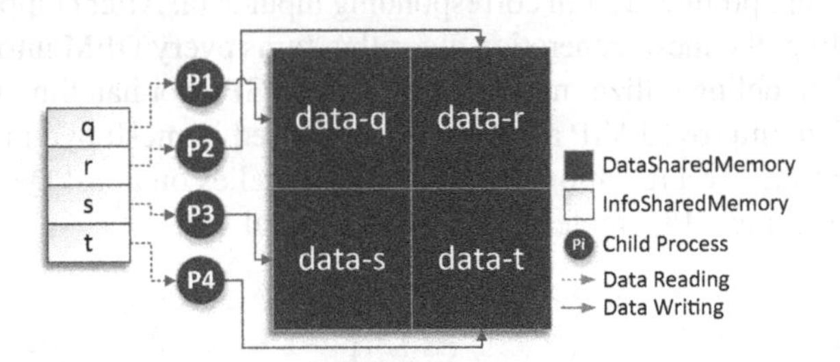

Fig. 3. Multiprocessing data loading

When *InfoSharedMemory* and *DataSharedMemory* are allocated, the parent process creates four children and then enters a loop of which each iteration produces a new block (a new DEM/texture file) in an upper layer of pyramid. During one iteration, basic information about blocks in level *k* is written by the parent to *InfoSharedMemory*, thus shared with children processes which load their corresponding data files and writes the loaded data to *DataSharedMemory*. As all the children finish data loading, the parent visits *DataSharedMemory* for conducting aggregation.

The aggregation algorithm can be parallelized by CUDA (Compute Unified Device Architecture), a powerful parallel computing platform using GPU. In CUDA, data is processed by a large amount of threads. Processors and memories in a GPU are regarded as in a device side, while other hardware such as CPU and memory in a computer is taken as in a host side. Data in host provide no access to threads in device until it is totally copied from host memory to device memory, also called Global Memory. Similarly, the parent process is unable to directly visit data in device, so the output of aggregation needs to be transferred to host memory. Therefore, the influence of transmission between host and device should be considered when a parallel algorithm in GPU is applied.

Thread is the basic processing unit in CUDA, and lots of threads constitute a group called a thread grid. A grid consists of a plurality of thread blocks, each of which is of same threads, as illustrated in Fig. 4. Obviously, the grid and geospatial raster data have similar structure. Every thread corresponds to one or more pixels in a raster file. As *DataSharedMemory* is filled by children processes, the data it contains is copied by the parent to device memory, and threads in a grid are launched to perform the aggregation algorithm. Given that a warp comprising 32 threads is the basic scheduling unit in GPU from the point of view on hardware, the total number of threads is usually set up to an integral multiple of 32 for a higher performance.

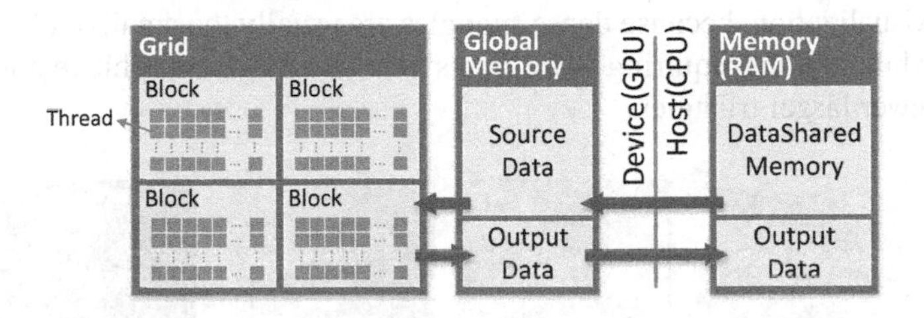

Fig. 4. Data transmission between CPU and GPU

Suppose that *sizeOfBlock*sizeOfBlock* is the size of terrain block in level *k*, and the output's size as well as the amount of threads in GPU is also *sizeOfBlock*sizeOfBlock*. In detail, the thread in *rowIdx*-th row, *colIdx*-th column in the grid acquires values from (*2*rowIdx, 2*colIdx*), (*2*rowIdx, 2*colIdx + 1*), (*2*rowIdx + 1, 2*colIdx + 1*) and (*2*rowIdx + 1, 2*colIdx*) in global memory, computes their average value and store it in the output area. After completion of all threads' calculations, the output is transmitted to host memory, and written by the parent to disk finally. Experimental results in Sect. 5.1 implies that the aggregation algorithm running in GPU overcomes a serial one in CPU when the size of source data is large.

4 An Efficient Approach to Generate Terrain Meshes

The terrain mesh modeling procedure is divided into two steps: DEM simplification for extracting a set of points, and triangulation for reconstructing a mesh from the point set. In this paper, an improved approach based on the VIP algorithm is presented, which enhances both efficiency and mesh quality. In the VIP algorithm, all the points in DEM are traversed for estimating significance, the basis of the subsequent sorting for extracting relatively important points on accordance with a predefined sampling rate. The importance of a point depends on elevation of itself and its 8-neighborhood:

$$significance_P = \frac{d_{P-l_{NW-SE}} + d_{P-l_{N-S}} + d_{P-l_{W-E}} + d_{P-l_{NE-SW}}}{4} \tag{3}$$

where $d_{P\text{-}l}$ denotes distance between point P and line l. Though the method traverses all points in only one iteration that leads to a $\Theta(n)$ running time, it still has to do lots of calculations when handling a large raster file.

Furthermore, meshes derived from the VIP algorithm usually have dense triangles in rugged or richly detailed areas, because it merely focuses on local features of DEM. Figure 5 (Left) shows that there may be some detail-rich regions in a mesh. Although these regions may account for a small area, many points in them are easily chosen to the output on account of high significance. When more points in these areas are selected, there are less of the remaining areas in the output. Consequently, in the generated mesh, facets in some regions look markedly larger and sparser than the others, resulting from their lower density of points. The case of uneven triangles distribution has a negative impact on visualization, because dense triangles are usually too small to observe in 3D rendering while regions requiring more facets to reflect its geomorphic feature are only drawn by fewer larger triangles.

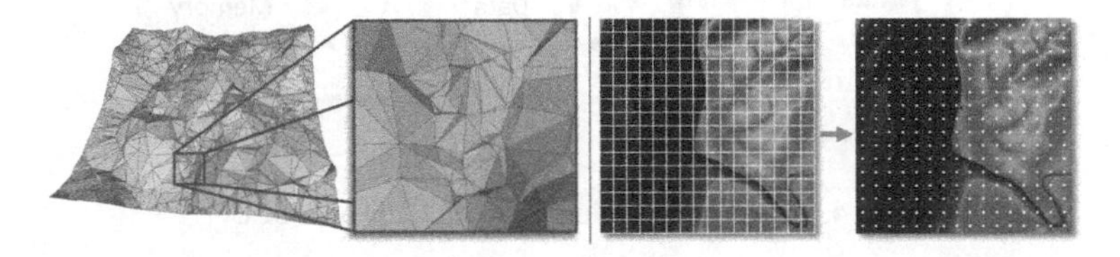

Fig. 5. (Left) Dense triangles in terrain mesh as a result of VIP algorithm; (Right) DEM partition by a regular square grid for reduction of sampling points

Compared with TIN, i.e., the mesh derived from DEM simplification, a RSG of same points has a perfect uniform distribution, in spite of the loss of many geomorphic details. In the RSG modeling approach, points are selected at a fixed sampling interval in two perpendicular horizontal directions. In other words, this approach assesses points from a global perspective. In order to take global feature into consideration for avoiding TIN's shortcomings, the core idea of RSG is introduced into the VIP algorithm. As seen in Fig. 5 (Right), a DEM is partitioned by a regular grid at an interval *sampleInterval*. The significance estimation is only performed on the centers of square cells for restricting candidate points to a limited point set. As a result, the running time are remarkably decreased. Given that *sampleRate* is the sampling rate, and *sizeOfBlock**sizeOfBlock* the size of DEM, *sampleInterval* should satisfy the following condition:

$$\left(\frac{sizeOfBlock}{sampleInterval}\right)^2 > (sizeOfBlock - 2)^2 \times sampleRate \tag{4}$$

where the left term means the amount of cells as well as the potential output points, and the right one represents the required number of output points. Since the VIP algorithm computes significance in each point's 8-neighborhood, boundary points of DEM do not participate in calculation. If n denotes the size of DEM, the running time of this new method is $\Theta(n/sampleInterval^2)$ which is less than the VIP's $\Theta(n)$ time.

The value of *sampleInterval* affects visual effect. On the one hand, the modified method is tantamount to the VIP algorithm when $sampleInterval = 1$. On the other hand, when both sides of inequality (5) balance, *sampleInterval* equals:

$$sampleInterval = \frac{sizeOfBlock}{\sqrt{(sizeOfBlock - 2)^2 \times sampleRate}} = sI_{\max} \tag{5}$$

Thus, the output points are distributed evenly over the horizontal plane, leading to a RSG instead of TIN, which strays from the original intention of the VIP algorithm. Only when *sampleInterval* lies between 1 and sI_{max} does the improved method keep more geomorphic details in the case of decreasing computations. Experimental results shows that the new method has a good visual effect as the sampling interval is assigned:

$$sample\ Interval = \frac{1}{k \times sI_{\max}}, k \in \left\{k \in N^{+} | k \geq 2\right\} \tag{6}$$

where k represents a positive integer greater than or equal to 2. Since adjacent blocks overlap on boundaries, all the boundary points of DEM is sampled at a fixed interval. Finally, as simplification is accomplished, a GPU-based Delaunay triangulation algorithm turns the output points into a triangulated mesh. All the terrain meshes in the mesh pyramid are applied to 3D rendering.

5 Experiments and Results

To validate the two methods presented above, several experiments are conducted using DEM in GeoTiff format and texture files in JPEG2000 format from the PASDA (Pennsylvania Spatial Data Access) project. The computer for experiments has an Intel E8500 3.16 GHz CPU with 2 cores, 2 GB RAM, and a GeForce GTX 560 GPU. Geospatial processing relies on GDAL. Terrain meshes are in Ogre (Object-Oriented Graphics Rendering Engine) Mesh format (.mesh).

5.1 Parallel Pyramid Modeling

Table 1 shows experimental results of two pyramid modeling approaches for input of varying size, including both a serial and parallel approach, i.e., the multiprocessing data loading method proposed above. Both of them perform a serial aggregation algorithm running in CPU. *LOD* represents the number of the pyramid's levels and *Size* the size of the input DEM. As can be seen from Table 1, the parallel method is nearly 4 times the speed of the serial one, thus greatly saving time. Besides, as *Size* or *LOD* increases, the parallel method can achieve a higher speedup.

Table 1. Experimental results of pyramid modeling

Size	LOD	Serial/s	Parallel/s	Speedup
2048^2	2	0.545	0.524	1.0401
	3	1.485	1.267	1.1721
	4	16.075	4.299	3.7392
	5	161.258	42.954	3.7542
3072^2	2	0.689	0.573	1.2024
	3	1.504	1.268	1.1861
	4	18.140	5.502	3.2970
	5	202.026	53.855	3.7513
4096^2	2	3.885	1.199	3.2402
	3	5.537	1.842	3.0060
	4	21.609	6.490	3.3296
	5	206.351	53.331	3.8693
6144^2	2	3.693	1.209	3.0546
	3	4.430	1.856	2.3869
	4	21.758	6.070	3.5845
	5	209.181	55.739	3.7529
8192^2	2	11.940	3.673	3.2507
	3	14.372	4.531	3.1719
	4	23.751	6.233	3.8105
	5	202.416	53.267	3.7998

Comparison of the aggregation algorithms is listed in Table 2, where $Size_{tex}$ denotes the size of the source texture and $Size_{DEM}$ the size of the source DEM. From the table it can be seen that only when handling a relatively large data does the parallel aggregation algorithm achieve a better performance than the serial one, on account of the host-device data transmission. Therefore, whether a serial method or a parallel method should be chosen depends on the size of the data.

Table 2. Experimental results of aggregation algorithms

$Size_{tex}$	Serial/s	Parallel/s	Speedup	$Size_{DEM}$	Serial/s	Parallel/s	Speedup
1024^2	0.031	0.202	0.1535	1024^2	0.015	0.208	0.0721
2048^2	0.140	0.234	0.5983	2048^2	0.032	0.213	0.1502
4096^2	0.546	0.422	1.2938	4096^2	0.093	0.224	0.4152
6144^2	1.232	0.577	2.1352	6144^2	0.218	0.201	1.0846
8192^2	2.184	0.718	3.0418	8192^2	0.453	0.230	1.9696

5.2 Terrain Mesh Modeling

The experimental results of the VIP algorithm and the improved algorithm are recorded in Table 3, both of which process a 1562-by-1562 pixels DEM. The term *Interval* means the sampling interval, which specifically stands for the original VIP algorithm if *Interval = 1*. Because of the uniqueness of Delaunay triangulation, the structure of TIN is completely decided by the simplified point set of DEM, and metrics for 3D visual quality assessment, such as *RMSE* (Root-Mean-Square Error), *AME* (Average Mean Error) and *Hd* (Hausdorf Distance), are available for analyzing a DEM simplification algorithm. *RMSE* is commonly applied to assess the modeling accuracy of TIN, which compares elevation errors between TIN and DEM. *RMSE* is computed as follows:

$$RMSE = \sqrt{\frac{\sum_i \left(h_{TINi} - h_{DEMi}\right)^2}{n}} \tag{7}$$

h_{TINi} and h_{DEMi} represent elevation in the same horizontal position of TIN and DEM respectively. Another frequently-used metric is Hausdorf distance defined as follows:

$$Hd\left(P_{TIN}, P_{DEM}\right) = \max\left(H_{TIN}\left(P_{TIN}, P_{DEM}\right), H_{DEM}\left(P_{DEM}, P_{TIN}\right)\right) \tag{8}$$

$$H_A\left(P_A, P_B\right) = \max_{v_i^A \in P_A}\left(e\left(v_i^A, P_B\right)\right) = \max_{v_i^A \in P_A}\left(\min_{v_i^B \in P_B}\left(d\left(v_i^A, v_i^B\right)\right)\right) \tag{9}$$

with d the Euclidean distance between v_i^A and v_i^B, the i-th vertices of point set A and of point set B. Hd describes the maximum error between TIN and DEM.

Table 3. Comparison between the VIP algorithm and the improved algorithm (Sampling rate 0.0020)

Interval	Time/s	RMSE	AME	Hd
1	1.217	4.52918	2.78986	45.6528
3	0.158	2.74570	1.78615	22.8101
5	0.055	2.63621	1.67776	26.6292
7	0.032	2.61987	1.66414	26.8348
9	0.016	2.50892	1.63938	20.9950
11	0.016	2.32119	1.49952	20.2866
13	0.009	2.50212	1.37354	21.2610

In comparison with the original VIP algorithm, the improved method costs much less running time because of the significant reduction of calculation times. Besides, all the mesh quality metrics of the improved method are lower than the original one, which illustrates that the mesh derived from the new method are closer to its source DEM. Furthermore, as seen in Table 4, experimental results of various sampling rate shows that the improved method is faster and the meshes it generates is better.

Table 4. Experimental results in different sampling rate

Rate	Interval	Time/s	RMSE	AME	Hd
0.0015	1	1.185	4.98268	3.20123	46.3375
	3	0.145	3.27190	2.11134	27.2100
	5	0.061	3.05287	1.94305	27.3835
	7	0.030	3.04829	1.92613	26.8348
0.0010	1	1.201	6.39912	4.13416	46.3375
	3	0.140	4.28388	2.71340	35.5582
	5	0.060	3.82492	2.46991	31.2305
	7	0.019	3.62882	2.30405	28.5381
0.0005	1	1.233	11.3579	6.89887	75.8685
	3	0.141	6.51108	4.12163	53.5112
	5	0.063	5.98843	3.65049	49.1298
	7	0.032	5.48157	3.41902	37.6161

6 Conclusion

This paper proposes a solution to large-scale terrain modeling involving a pyramid modeling method based on parallel computation and, an improved VIP algorithm to generate terrain meshes efficiently. In the pyramid modeling method, a multiprocessing data loading scheme and a parallel aggregation algorithm running in GPU are applied, both of which boost the pyramid modeling procedure markedly. In addition, the improved VIP algorithm takes advantage of the core idea of RSG creation to greatly reduce running time. Meanwhile, meshes derived from the improved algorithm's output have higher quality than those generated from the original one. The feasibilities of the methods mentioned above are all verified by experimental results.

References

1. Tesfa, T.K., Tarboton, D.G., Watson, D.W., et al.: Extraction of hydrological proximity measures from DEMs using parallel processing. Environ. Model. Softw. **26**(12), 1696–1709 (2011)
2. Kerr, N.T.: Alternative approaches to parallel GIS processing. Dissertation, Arizona State University (2009)
3. Huang, F., Liu, D., Li, X., et al.: Preliminary study of a cluster-based open-source parallel GIS based on the GRASS GIS. Int. J. Digit. Earth **4**(5), 402–420 (2011)
4. Qin, C.Z., Zhan, L.J., Zhu, A.: How to apply the geospatial data abstraction library (GDAL) properly to parallel geospatial raster I/O? Trans. GIS **18**(6), 950–957 (2014)
5. Qin, C.Z., Zhan, L.: Parallelizing flow-accumulation calculations on graphics processing units—From iterative DEM preprocessing algorithm to recursive multiple-flow-direction algorithm. Comput. Geosci. UK **43**, 7–16 (2012)

6. Zhang, J., You, S.: CudaGIS: report on the design and realization of a massive data parallel GIS on GPUs. In: Proceedings of the Third ACM SIGSPATIAL International Workshop on GeoStreaming, Redondo Beach, CA, 7–9 November 2012, pp. 101–108. ACM, New York (2012)
7. Scott, G.J., Backus, K., Anderson, D.T.: A multilevel parallel and scalable single-host GPU cluster framework for large-scale geospatial data processing. In: Geoscience and Remote Sensing Symposium (IGARSS), Québec, Canada. IEEE, New York: 2475–2478 (2014)
8. Chen, Z.T., Guevara, J.A.: Systematic selection of very important points (VIP) from digital terrain model for constructing triangular irregular networks. In: Proceedings of the Auto-Carto Conference (1987)
9. Rong, G., Tan, T.S., Cao, T.T.: Computing two-dimensional delaunay triangulation using graphics hardware. In: Proceedings of the 2008 Symposium on Interactive 3D Graphics and Games, pp. 89–97. ACM, New York (2008)

High Performance of RSA Simulation System Based on Modified Montgomery Algorithm

Jingjing Liu[1], Guanghua Chen[1](✉), Zhanpeng Xiao[2], Shiwei Ma[1], Wanquan Liu[3], and Weimin Zeng[1]

[1] School of Mechatronical Engineering and Automation, Shanghai University, Shanghai, China
{liu.jingjing,chghua,masw}@shu.edu.cn, wmzeng@gmail.com

[2] CCDC Drilling and Production Technology Research Institute, Chengdu, China
48364873@qq.com

[3] Department of Computing, Curtin University, Perth, WA, Australia
w.liu@curtin.edu.au

Abstract. In order to eliminate the effect of the factor R^{-1} and decrease the number of iteration of modular exponentiation algorithm, a high performance scalable of Right-to-Left scan public-key cipher RSA simulation system is proposed. An advanced high radix Montgomery modular multiplication algorithm is presented to calculate by using an adder and a shift register, and the complexity of the circuit is minimized. The computation kernel of the device is two 32 bits multipliers with pipelining architecture, and it operates concurrently. The result of the hardware implementation shows that the improved RSA coprocessor is synthesized by CSMC 0.18 um library, the area optimization design of 42 k gates with 213 ms/RSA are obtained to complete a 1024 bits encryption at 10 MHz. Compared with previous works, the proposed architecture can achieve better performance for the chip area and speed.

Keywords: Modular exponentiation algorithm · Right-to-Left scan · RSA simulation system · Montgomery modular multiplication

1 Introduction

Recent years have witnessed a growing interest in search for data security. The problem of finding a encrypt algorithm to a appropriate system structure is a popular topic. For one of the basic sub-systems of Wireless Sensor Network, due to its property of shorter key and inexpensive computing resources, the public-key cryptosystem RSA (Rivest, Shamir, Adleman) [1] is a suitable choice for data encryption implementation. However, the conventional modular multiplication of RSA is slower and the cryptographic coprocessor can only be realized at very large scale. Therefore, the study of high performance RSA algorithm and its VLSI (Very Large Scale Integration) design for the WSNs application is much necessary.

L. Zhang et al. (Eds.): AsiaSim 2016/SCS AutumnSim 2016, Part I, CCIS 643, pp. 398–408, 2016.
DOI: 10.1007/978-981-10-2663-8_42

The Modular exponentiation which is the core of RSA [2] has obtains high performance by the modular multiplication operation. So various Montgomery algorithm modifications and hardware designs were proposed in [3–11]. In order to achieve higher efficiency, the suitable radix technique was adopt to reduce the required clock cycle number in literature [3,5]. Moreover, shifting 2bits of multiplicand for the quotient determination was avoided in literature [4]. All of this has achieved a higher performance of modular multiplication. However, the input operands and intermediate results are supposed to be in no redundant binary form or redundant representation in the next branch process, so all the methods are sustained the over large residue, which increases the hardware and cycle time complexity. Although this problem is settled in literature [8,9], the cycle times of iteration are doubled. Moreover, in literature [10,11], the Montgomery modular multiplication algorithm is realized by systolic array structure, but the VLSI area of structure is too large for the application in relatively smaller WSNs.

From the above discussion, there are two common approaches to alleviate this difficulty. One is to increase the speed of modular multiplication, the other is to decrease the area of the circuit, in this paper, we are interested in both of the condition for the modular multiplication problem, and proposed an modified algorithm to reduce the area of circuit but also decrease the clock cycles which is suitable for the application of WSNs devices based on the combining the Montgomery modular exponentiation scheme, which is quite fast and stable.

The remainder of this paper is organized as follows. Section 2 overview the theoretical work. Section 3 prove the Novel Montgomery algorithm, after pre and post processing, the multiplication operation is reduced, and the output will fall in the right range. In (Sect. 4), the corresponding hardware is designed according to the new algorithm of MMRSA. (Seciton 5), some numerical experiments are conducted and compared to show the efficiency of the proposed algorithm. Finally ,this paper concluded in Sect. 6.

2 Theoretical Overview

2.1 The RSA Public-Key Cryptosystem

The RSA was proposed by R.L. Rivest et al. in 1978 [1], it is the more successful and useful public-key cryptosystem in the theoretical and practical applications. Based on Number theory, its security is difficult to impose the large integer factorization as prime factor [3]. The algorithm is as follows: (1) Two large prime numbers P and Q have been obtained by random number generator. (2) The modulus N and Euler Totient Function $\varphi(N)$ are calculated by expression $P \times Q$ and $(P-1) \times (Q-1)$. (3) The greatest common divisor of e and $\varphi(N)$ equals to 1 should be selected. (4) The integer d which is the multiplicative inverse of e modulus $\varphi(N)$ is computed by $d \times e \equiv 1 \bmod \varphi(N)$. (5) The positive integers (e, N) and (d, N) are the public key and private key. (6) The message M is encrypted by $C = M^e \bmod N$, on the contrary, the cipher text C is decrypted by $M = C^d \bmod N$.

However, the encryption (decryption) process of RSA is essentially a kind of modular exponentiation operation, which is be identified as a series of modular multiplications by the application of exponentiation heuristics. It is very difficult to direct modular exponentiation when the operand $M, e, C, dandN$ are more than 1024 bits, and it is concerned to disintegrate to the basic modular multiplication operation (Table 1).

2.2 Montgomery Modular Multiplication Algorithm

The Montgomery modular multiplication(MM) algorithm was first proposed by P.L. Montgomery in 1985 [2], which is the most crucial operation in RSA algorithm. Given two n bits operands U and V and a n bits positive number N(modular), $0 < U, V < N$, so MM algorithm can be described as follows,

$$T = U \cdot V \cdot R^{-1} \bmod N \tag{1}$$

where $2^{k-1} \leq N < 2^k$ and $R = 2^k$, so $\gcd(N, R) = 1$, $R \cdot R^{-1} - N \cdot N' = 1$, it can be seen that R^{-1} and N' are calculated by the Euclidean extension algorithm. So we can obtain the Eq. (1) by a multiplication combined k bits right shift operation. The pseudo-code is as follows:

Table 1. Montgomery algorithm.

Input:	$U, V < N$, N: odd number and n bit
Output:	$T = MonPro(U, V) = U \cdot V \cdot R^{-1} \bmod N$
1. $G = U \cdot B$	
2. $M = G \cdot N' \bmod R$	
3. $T = (G + M \cdot N)/R$	
4. if $T \geq N$, then return $T - N$, else return T	

However, It also have some disadvantages: (1) The first step is to compute the $U \cdot V$, which is more than n bits numbers, so the $2n$ bits of the intermediate results will be produced, and a lot of space will be wasted. (2) In step4, T is the final calculations, $0 < T < 2N$, and T is the result of the right shift n times, so the result algorithm may be greater than N, then it must be added a judgment in the loop to avoid it. (3) The result of Montgomery is not exactly $U \cdot V \bmod N$, but is $U \cdot V \cdot R^{-1} \bmod N$. The extra factor of R^{-1} is better to be eliminated which is affect the modular exponentiation processing. To address these problems, a modified Montgomery algorithm is proposed by chen [12], which have a simpler modular reduction step and smaller range of output result. However, the step of iteration is increased from n to $2n$.

3 Modified Modular Exponentiation Algorithm

3.1 Modified Montgomery Algorithm (MMRSA)

As reviewed in Sect. 2, in order to eliminate the extra subtraction operation, and maintain the step of iteration as in the original Montgomery algorithm, a modified high radix MMRSA algorithm is proposed. The inputs block of operand U and N are extended for $(n+1)$ bits, from the Eq. (2), is described as follows:

$$R \cdot R^{-1} - N \cdot N' = 1 \bmod r^n \tag{2}$$

For simplification, the following notation is well defined:

$$N' \bmod r = (-N)_r^{-1} = (r - N[0])_r^{-1} \tag{3}$$

In the proposed algorithm, n bits input data is divided into r blocks ($n = t{\cdot}r$), in order to use the normal $r \cdot r$ bits multiplier, choose $W = 2^w$, We note that it does not need the complete value of N', so minimum w bits can be used to replace N' ,

$$N'[0] = -N[0]^{-1} \bmod 2^w \tag{4}$$

So the MMRSA modular multiplication is obvious that (Table 2):

Table 2. Modified Montgomery algorithm (MMRSA)

Input:	$U, V < 2N$, U,V,N:n+1 bits, N: odd number and n bit
Output:	$P = U \times V \times \beta^{-n} \bmod N$

Part 1: Computing intermediate results coexist in $P[i]$
1. $p[0] = 0$ (p *is* $n/2$ *bits*)
2. $m_0 = N[w, 0]$, $a =\sim (m_0^{-1}\%2^w) + 1, q = (a \times u_0)\%2^w$
3. for $i = 0$ to t-1
   3.1 $p_0(t) = p[t]\%2^w$
   3.2 $q_t = [q \times v_t + a \times p_0(t)]\%2^w$
   3.3 $p[t+1] = (U \times v_t + p[t] + q_t \times N)/2^w$
Part 2: Adjust the volume to $[0, n]$
4. if $q_0 = 0$, return $(P[t-1] \cdots P[0])$, else return $(P[2t-1] \cdots P[t])$

In addition, the main contributions of this algorithm include: (1) Simplifying the process. The introduction of q is used to ensure that p is a divisible result. The operand V shift to the left for 1 bit, and $v_0 = 0$, so the value of $q[i]$ is only related to the $P[t]$, because $P[0] = 0$, so $q_0 = 0$. (2) Reduce addition operation. The length of large numbers U, V and N are changed to w bits computing operation at each cycle, such as words multiplication and words addition, so it is suitable for the hardware implementation. It also employs the least significant bit of the intermediate result N_0 to execute addition, and executes a shift down operation to replace a shift up on each iteration. (3) The original algorithm needs three times large numbers multiplication, but in the MMRSA algorithm, N' is pre-computed, so it is decomposed into $2t^2 + t$ words multiplication. (4) Eliminate subtraction operation. If $q_0 = 0$, and then it can prove that $P < N$.

Compared with the original algorithm, the execution time is shortened, for the inversion algorithms in large numbers to participate in the iteration are w bits. Fixed with same input bits, this method takes double computing time than the other multiplication algorithm, which is efficient in computing modular inverse. So it is very much suitable to design the hardware for the basic arithmetic operations.

3.2 Modified Modular Exponentiation Algorithm

On account of the extra factor R^{-1} , the improved Montgomery algorithm cannot be directly employed to modular exponentiation. Another Montgomery modular multiplication is performed by a constant of value R^2 mod N. Under this model framework, some processing steps are added to address these problems. (1) To limit the range of the output data, one extra bit of U and V for precision consideration is added. It will increase the iteration from n to $n+2$ steps, meanwhile, the extra factor will be $2^{-(n+2)}$. The extra factor is not removed completely. So pre-process M_0 from $M_0 = MMA(M, C, N)$, then the undesired factor will be removed. (2) After the last operation of modular multiplication, R is post-processed by taking $R = MMA(R, 1)$ to remove the R^{-1}. It can be observed that if the input operand is 1, the $C[n+1, \cdots 2]$ will be zero, so the output result of post-process will be less than the modulus N. Therefore, it does not only get rid of the redundant factor $2^{(n+2)}$, but also put the result fall in the correct range after post processing. Table 3 describes the modified algorithm (MMERSA) for modular exponentiation.

Table 3. Modified modular exponentiation (MMERSA) algorithm

Input:	$const\_c$ is (2n + 1)bits, c, M_0 , $R[n]$ are n bits
Output:	$R[n]$

1. $const\_c[n*2] = 1, c = const\_c\%n$
   $M_0 = MMRSA(M, C, N)$, $e\_lengh = scan\_lengh(e)$, $R[0] = M_0$
2. Loop
   2.1. if (int $i = 0$; $i < e\_lengh - 1$; $i++$)
     2.1.1 $R[i+1] = MMRSA(R[i], R[i], n)$
     2.1.2 if $(e\_lengh - i - 2) == 1)$
       $R[i+1] = MMRSA(R[i+1], M_0, n)$
3. $R[e\_lengh - 1] = MMRSA(R[e\_lengh - 1], 1, n)$
4. return $R[e\_lengh - 1]$

It is also worth pointing out that the MMERSA algorithm adopt the same cycles as Montgomerys algorithm [10–13] when employed to modular exponentiation, but achieve less time with the shorter critical path. With the equal probability of RSA modular exponentiation, the number of modular multiplication is $(2n+2)$ or $(1.5n+2)$ as it for the different conditions(worst condition or average condition). Under the worst condition condition, the modified algorithm consume $(2n+2) \cdot n$ clock cycles, which is shorter than that in $(2n+2) \cdot 2n$ cycles [5] to complete a modular exponentiation. Since clock cycle is equal to that in literature [5], the new proposed algorithm obtain less time and higher performance to complete RSA operations.

4 Hardware Design and Realization

4.1 The Structure of Modular Multiplier

Apparently, according to the MMRSA algorithm, the modulo multiplication combined with the line structure features is designed directly. if $w = 32$ bits, there is no correlation between $u[i]v[j]$ and $q[i]n[j]$, so in a clock cycle, two parallel 32 bits multiplier of the core structure completes two multiplication operations. Based on the MMRSA algorithm, some registers are abandoning in the calculation. When added a register, the data path analog multiplier is three stage pipeline structures, enhancing the degree of parallelism. FIFO saves some of the intermediate results to speed up the running time. The input value of Selector MUX is controlled by the e_i, which is scanned from right to left to complete the RSA modular exponentiation operation. Based on MMRSA algorithm, if $k = 1024$ bits and $w = 32$ bits, then $t = k/w = 32$. As $u[i]v[j]$ and $q[i]n[j]$ of the two by two parallel multiplier 32 in parallel, the execution time amount to t^2 clock cycle. In addition, there is only one data correlation between the two product terms. For the three-stage pipeline structure, the second process should wait three clock cycles. Two operations require $3t$ for each clock cycle. Similarly, the adjustment also require t clock cycles for carrying out t times addition. Practically, it has been done by $2t^2 + 4t$ clock cycles. Finally, The exponentiation shows that it requires one MMRSA modular multiplication algorithm when $e_i = 0$, and requires two MMRSA modular multiplication algorithm when $e_i = 1$. And in the average condition, it will be 1.5 times modular multiplication. Considered the worst condition, if all the $e_i = 1$, then the number of clock cycles become $2h(t^2 + 4t)$. Based on 10 MHz clock, when $h = 1024$, the average execution cputime is shown as follows:

$$1.5 \times 1024 \times (t^2 + 4t)/(10 \times 10^6) = 177\,ms \tag{5}$$

It can be seen that the 32 bits multiplier is the largest consumption in the hardware design, it is also the data path architecture of the critical, which is the maximum delay of the combinational logic. Moreover its reasonable design, the RSA Cipher Coprocessor satisfies the limit of the area and CPUtime of circuit.

4.2 The Data Path of Modular Multiplier

Once the hardware design of MMERSA is received, the clock cycles rate can be represented by the modular multiplication, so the data path architecture of modular multiplier should be in the specified area to reduce the clock cycles rate of multiplication as much as possible (Fig. 1).

Before the Modular multiplication, A, B and N are input into the register REG_U, REG_V, REG_N, which are denote to reset. To reprogram the multiplier operation, Encoder sequential multiplier of two from the least significant bit to the most significant bit is processed in each loop, and the multiplicand must be completed the two shift operation in each iteration, data shift to the leftshift one bit at a time, when two shift operation is completed then the $DFAS\_1$ is used to shift the data. After the completion of the two shift operation, then the $DFAS\_1$ is apply to do the subtract operation, the $DFAS\_2$ is mainly obtianed to complete part of accumulative operation and the part of product symbol reduction operations. REG_U, REG_V, REG_2V, REG_N, REG_R are all 1024 bits, in practice, the operation CPUtime and the data processing is inversely proportional to the length of W, the greater value of W, the faster of operation, but

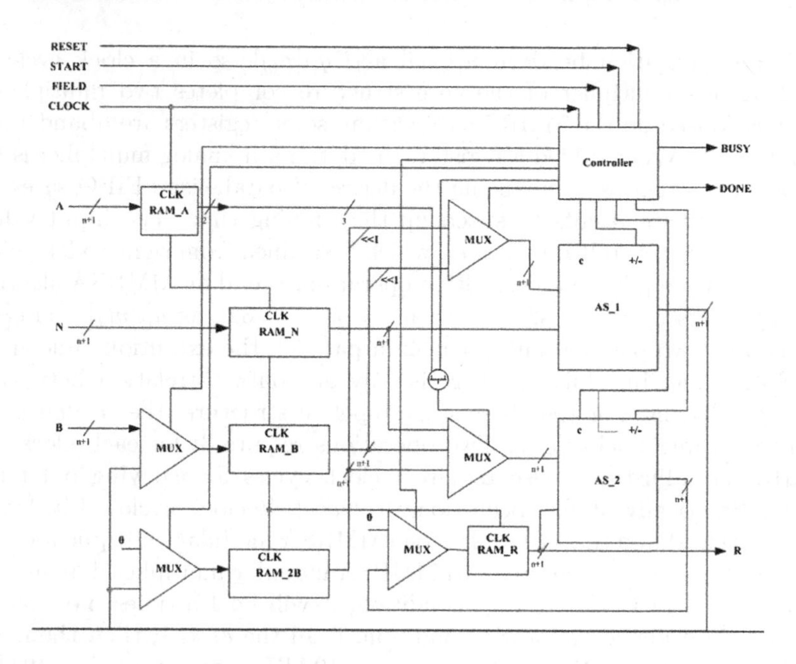

Fig. 1. Data path of modular multiplier

the corresponding area of the chip will be larger, in this paper, for the limit of CPUtime and area of the chip, denote the W = 32 in this unit.

4.3 The Architecture of RSA

After the hardware design and data path architecture of the modular multiplier are completed, one method of scanning modular exponentiation, in other words, the Right-to-Left scan method of exponentiation for RSA core is performed. It can be seen that all of RSA operation are based on Montgomery multiplication, therefore, the reduction and pre-computation of Montgomery are very important before processing. However, for the consecutive Montgomery algorithm, these operations can be executed in one step to reduce the overhead time.

Figure 2 shows a block diagram of our RSA core, which consists of five components: API interface unit, RSA core unit, Control unit, Data unit and RAM unit. API interface module is primarily responsible for RSA coprocessor data communication with the master MCU. Control unit coordinates the work of various units chronological. Data unit stores data temporarily. RAM unit is expandable, the advantage in this design up gradation is to increase a simple RAM unit and modify the RAM Controller module, our task is to facilitate the subsequent expansion of the circuit, which greatly improves the flexibility and reliability of the design.

It shows that the RSA core which performs state transition control and generates the control signals for the data path core, has a three-level hierarchical

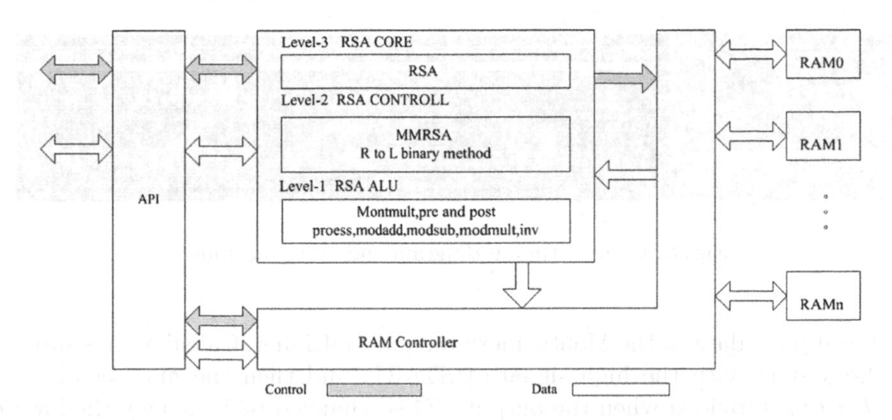

Fig. 2. RSA coprocessor architecture

structure. In Level-1, the pre-processing and post-processing functions for Montgomery multiplication are supported. Level-2 carry out a modular exponentiation by RL binary method. Levels-3 disposes the multiple iteration of RSA core operations. Control-Data processing are also provided in this hierarchy. Due to the high flexibility of functional extensions, Our architecture has a clearly separated control structure and thus it is very easy to design and modify.

5 Simulation Results

Depending on the users requirements, the approach of modular exponentiation algorithms are selected. Using the CSMC library, the RSA coprocessor is exhaustively generated and synthesized. So the users can easily choose the best radix of the improvement algorithm by evaluating the features of RSA core.

5.1 Simulation Results of RSA Core Module

To begin with the testing of encryption/decryption operation, based on the MMRSA algorithm, a set of RSA parameters has been selected. Then the parameters have been embedded into the RSA core module. The simulation results of the Encryption and Decryption being processed with a Modelsim.

In Fig. 3, the state diagram machine controller is archived, which is responsible for controlling the signals of all the modules. It can be observed from the block, the control signal are responsible for processing and control the external data into the input registers, EN represents RSA enable control signal, NWR represents the write control signal of the righter, NRD represents the read control signal of the register. The input and output signals are divided into several 32 bits blocks because registers can only supports 32 bits in one single block. According to the value of the ADDR, input 32 bits data into registers needs 6 times at each cycle, when it is the high level.

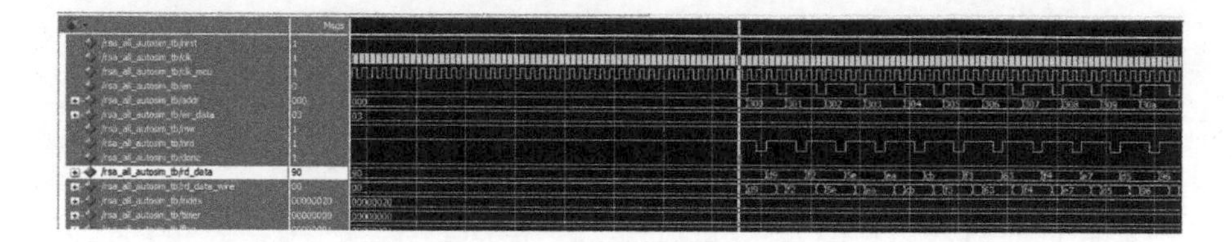

Fig. 3. Control timing diagram and state machine

Let input a data to the Montgomery module multiplier, Calculation is started in the system with the high signal of START, and then the first set of data *DATA_O* is provided when the output DONE changed to 1, namely the lowest 32 bits of 1024 bits data is output in Fig. 4, compared with original data of SystemC model, it is concluded that the encryption process works successfully. It can be shown that the result of proposed RSA algorithm is same to the original one, and is benefit for preparing to design the following circuit.

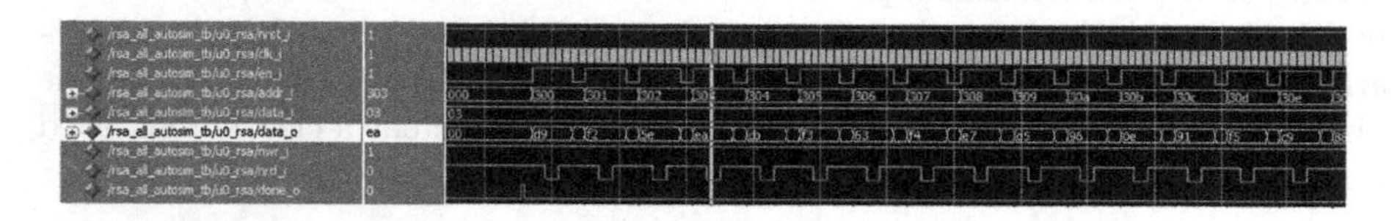

Fig. 4. The simulation results of the multiplier

From Fig. 5, compared with SystemC model, it is concluded that the encryption process works successfully. It shows that the modified RSA algorithm is correct, and is prepared for the following circuit design.

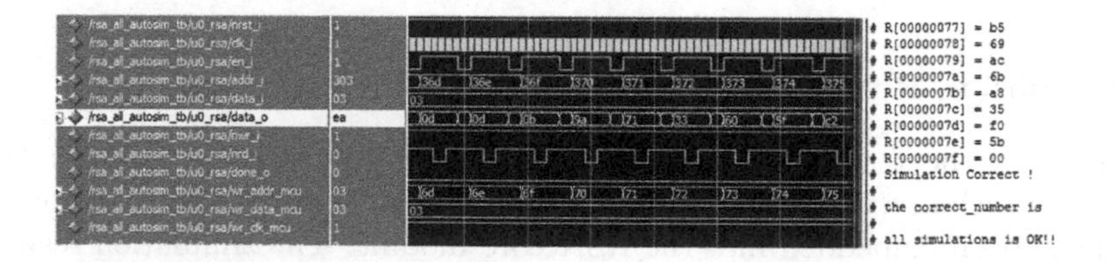

Fig. 5. The encryption results of Modular multiplication

5.2 Performance Comparison

After functional simulation, comprehensive optimization process is designed with Synopsys' DC (Design Compiler) and CSMC 0.18 library tool. The main objective is to complete a comprehensive RLT code into gate-level netlist conversion, as well as design area and timing optimization. The prime aim is to speed up the computing time of RSA coprocessor. Merits of performance resources and

Table 4. RSA performance comparison

Reference design	Clock	Length(bits)	Speed	Area (Gate)
literature [14]	-	1024	930 ms	37860
Siemens [15]	5 MHz	1024	880 ms	55000
Literature [9]	471 MHz	1024	7.27 ms	11437
literature [16]	10 MHz	1024	330 ms	26168.5
MMRSA	10 MHz	1024	213 ms	42043.5

speed are considered while designing an IC chip. The improved RSA coprocessor is synthesized by CSMC 0.18 library, and the total logic resources is 26k gates, Simulation results shows that it takes an average of 330 ms to complete a 1024 bits Encryption. Simulation proves the correctness and consistency of decryption. Results comparison is mentioned in the table below.

The purpose of ASIC experiments is to compare proposed algorithm to Zeng's [16], which is smallest area of 26 k gates with 330 ms/RSA, For MMRSA, the performance is better than literature [14–16] with the same length of key, it can be seen that the literature [9] has the faster speed and smaller area, but expend so much clock cycles. The carry-save method that [14–16] used has difficulties in extending radix to higher length because single processing unit will be too large to be optimized for current EDA tools. As Table 4 shows that our architecture has the similar scale as [14]. After comprehensive comparison, it is concluded that RSA coprocessor has certain advantages in terms of speed and size. Therefore, the performance of this design is better than others.

6 Conclusion

In this paper, based on modified Montgomery algorithm, a new framework of RSA simulation system is proposed, which provides the field high radix duel modular multiplication, avoids the final adjustment of residue and reduces the iteration time. Moreover, in addition to the approach from the modified algorithm to the hardware circuit, the 1024 bits RSA core with RL scan method are applied to shorten the clock cycles from $(2n+2) \cdot 2n$ to $(2n+2) \cdot n$ is designed. The hardware implementation shows that improvement of RSA core with 42 k gates@213 ms/RSA in a 0.18 um CSMC standard cell library is obtained by the length of 1024bits. Practically, this simulation system can be shown is effective under appropriate conditions of data path architectures. Other than this design, users are able to freely choose the best design to fit their applications from these combinations and also select other technique.

In future, some of the best RSA simulation systems will be implemented in ASICs and evaluated in terms of tamper resistance as well as circuit performance, such as using CRT to decryption and the generation of big prime numbers. Meanwhile, more work on other public-key cryptographic algorithms, such as elliptic curve cryptography, will be conducted.

Acknowledgments. This work was financially supported by the Shanghai Science and Technology Foundation (13510500400) and the Shanghai Educational Commission Foundation (12ZZ083).

References

1. Rivest, R.L., Shamir, A., Adleman, L.: A method for obtaining digital signatures and public-key cryptosystems. Commun. ACM **21**(2), 120–126 (1978)
2. Montgomery, P.L.: Modular multiplication without trial division. Math. Comput. **44**, 519–521 (1985)
3. Aragona, R., Gozzini, F., Sala, M.: A real life project in cryptography: assessment of RSA keys. In: Baldi, M., Tomasin, S. (eds.) Physical and Data-Link Security Techniques for Future Communication Systems. LNEE, vol. 358, pp. 197–203. Springer, Heidelberg (2016). doi:10.1007/978-3-319-23609-4_13
4. Kiss, A., Kramer, J., Rauzy, P., et al.: Algorithmic countermeasures against fault attacks and power analysis for RSA-CRT. In: Constructive Side-Channel Analysis and Secure Design (COSADE 2016) (2016)
5. Sun, C.C., Lin, B.S., Jan, G.E., et al.: VLSI design of an RSA encryption/decryption chip using systolic array based architecture. Int. J. Electron. **103**, 1–12 (2016)
6. Wang, Y., Maskell, D.L., Leiwo, J.: A unified architecture for a public key cryptographic coprocessor. J. Syst. Archit. **54**, 1004–1016 (2008)
7. Gueron, S., Krasnov, V.: Speed records for multi-prime RSA using AVX2 architectures. In: Latifi, S. (ed.) Information Technology: New Generations. AISC, vol. 448, pp. 237–245. Springer, New York (2016)
8. Miyamoto, A., Homma, N., Aoki, T., Satoh, A.: Systematic design of RSA processors based on high-radix montgomery multipliers. IEEE Trans. Very Large Scale Integr. (VLSI) Syst. **19**(7), I136–1146 (2011)
9. Zhao, T., Ran, Q., Yuan, L., et al.: Information verification cryptosystem using one-time keys based on double random phase encoding and public-key cryptography[J]. Optics Lasers Eng. **83**, 48–58 (2016)
10. Koc, C.K., Acar, T., Kaliski Jr., B.S.: Analyzing and comparing montgomery multiplication algorithms. IEEE Micro. Chip Syst. Softw. Appl. **16**, 26–33 (1996)
11. Asbullah, M.A., Ariffin, M.R.K.: New attacks on RSA with modulus N= p2q using continued fractions. J. Phys. Conf. Ser. **622**(1), 012019 (2015). IOP Publishing
12. Bautista, J.N., Alvarado-Nava, O., Prez, F.M.: Co-procesador matemtico de aritmtica entera basado en un FPGA (2012)
13. Perin, G., Mesquita, D.G., Martins, J.B.: Montgomery modular multiplication on reconfigurable hardware: systolic versus multiplexed implementation. Int. J. Reconfigurable Comput. **2011** (2011). Article No. 6
14. Huang, M., Gaj, K., Kwon, S., El-Ghazawi, T.: An optimized hardware architecture for the montgomery multiplication algorithm. In: Cramer, R. (ed.) PKC 2008. LNCS, vol. 4939, pp. 214–228. Springer, Heidelberg (2008). doi:10.1007/978-3-540-78440-1_13
15. Handschuh, H., Paillier, P.: Smart card crypto-coprocessors for public-key cryptography. In: Quisquater, J.-J., Schneier, B. (eds.) CARDIS 1998. LNCS, vol. 1820, pp. 372–379. Springer, Heidelberg (2000). doi:10.1007/10721064_35
16. Zeng, W., et al.: RSA cryptography coprocessor based on modified montgomery algorithm. Microelectron. Comput, **2015**(08), 115–119, 124 (2016)

Warship Reusable Component Model Development Approach for Parallel and Distributed Simulation

Haibo Ma(✉), Yiping Yao, and Wenjie Tang

College of Information System and Management,
National University of Defense Technology, Changsha, China
mahaibo168@126.com, {ypyao,tangwenjie}@nudt.edu.cn

Abstract. Model reuse is a key issue to be resolved in parallel and distributed simulation when developing military simulation applications at present. However, component model built by different domain experts usually have diversiform interfaces, couple tightly and bind with simulation platforms and specific applications closely. As a result, they are difficult to be reused across different simulation platforms as well as applications. In addition, traditional model reuse ways lack consideration about reusability efficiency of similar reusable models. As for developing warship models in practical application, there also lack pragmatic method to describe its simulation space from conception space. To address the problem, this paper first proposed the parameterization-configurable framework for reusable component model that supports similar models once developed but multiple reused adapting to varied function requirement. Based on this framework, then our reusable model development approach for warship model is elaborated, which contains three phases: (1) design the warship configurable function set based on capacity demand; (2) use CMPA (Capacity, Mission, Process, Action) description method to map the function set from conception model to simulation model; (3) implement and encapsulate the model with the reusable simulation model development specification. The approach provides a pragmatic technical means for developing warship component reusable models in complex military simulation application, which helps improving efficiency of development and could be referenced for other similar models.

Keywords: Reuse · Parameterization-configurable framework · Warship simulation modeling · CMPA

1 Introduction

With the rapid development of simulation platforms and applications during the last decades, in particular for parallel and distributed simulation, one of the most important challenges is how to respond quickly to new application requirements while reducing the development costs [1, 2]. Building application from existing simulation models rather than from scratch is considered as a promising approach to improve the development efficiency, as well as to minimize engineering efforts and resource costs [3, 4]. Reuse-oriented models are developed to be reused across simulation platforms with little or even no modification. At the same time, the reuse of component models together with

L. Zhang et al. (Eds.): AsiaSim 2016/SCS AutumnSim 2016, Part I, CCIS 643, pp. 409–418, 2016.
DOI: 10.1007/978-981-10-2663-8_43

visual programming technology makes it possible to drag and drop existing component models to assemble the simulation application, thus significantly reducing development time [5]. In addition, model reuse not only improves productivity but also has a positive impact on the quality of software products because of the obvious fact that a simulation application will work properly if it has already worked before [6].

Motivated by the advantages of model reuse, diverse reusable model development approaches have been developed. (1) Based on specific modeling language that designs special simulation function module as primitive and control module as simulator, different models created with the same modeling language can be reused for the corresponding simulator. However, most of simulation modeling languages are usually related to domain knowledge, so that there is congenitally deficiency for them to create models to be reused across multi-domain platforms, such as continue system simulation language ACSL [7], discrete event system simulation language GPSS [8], and multi-field physical simulation language MODELICA [9]. (2) Some models are based on simulation environment which provides runtime supporting platform for model running. However the reusability of the models is also limited. Taking HLA [10] for instance, each federate provides some interfaces which compiles with the HLA interface specification, and federates developed by different developers can communicate with each other via the runtime infrastructure using these interfaces. But these federates are hard to use in other simulation platforms, such as SUPE (Simulation Utilities for Parallel Environment) [11] and POSE [12], because these platforms cannot "identify" any HLA service interfaces. (3) Using a modeling specification which defines uniform internal structure, behavior constraint, and external interfaces for model. But most existing modeling specifications do not emphasize that model development should be independent with other simulation platforms.

For example, ESA proposed SMP (Simulation Model Portability Standards) [13], yet it does not support well to reuse the models on other runtime platforms, because the execution of a SMP model depends on services provide by the SMP simulation platform. Fortunately, one of our team's previous research achievements, a reusable simulation model development specification (RUM Specification) [14, 15] was presented to avoid the above problems and realize development for reusable models without binding with simulation platforms. It takes service-oriented technique into account, and seven standard operational interfaces are defined to satisfy scheduling demand of simulation model for Parallel and Discrete Event Simulation (PDES) [16]. However, even a suitable specification is still not easy enough to develop a specific reusable component model. Especially in military simulation fields, applications usually contain a large number of different models such as warship, plane and submarine component. Developing these models usually involves combined knowledge of both very specific domain and parallel and discrete simulation, but the models are usually are developed by domain experts who are not simulation experts. When developing a special model, taking warship for example, requires interactive cooperation work of warship domain experts, military operational experts and PDES program experts, which mains development the warship reusable model is much more complex. Even worse, there also lacks a pragmatic method to describe warship simulation program space from conception space. In addition, traditional model reuse ways mostly focus on model reuse transforming across different platforms while lack consideration about reusability efficiency of similar reusable models. For example, similar warships have to be remodeled and coded repeatedly if demanding multiple type warship models, which will definitely lead to huge program and test work by multiple fields experts as well as high risk complex VV&A work according to military simulation model confidence. Therefore, based on demand pain points from our experience of developing several practical large-scope military analysis simulation application systems in recent two years, we point out that it is shortsighted to achieve one model reuse only considering transforming across different platforms, but should also think highly of promote reuse efficiency of similar models. Because we do not often necessarily need to reuse our warship model from SUPE platform to other simulation platforms like POSE, but we do need to reuse the X-warship model to get likely a Y-warship model in different military simulation applications in SUPE platform.

In this paper, motivated to solve the above mentioned issues, we first discussed insufficiencies existed in the practical applications, and analyzed demand for developing reusable warship simulation models for military PDES applications. Next we proposed the parameterization-configurable framework for reusable component model that supports similar warship models once developed and multiple reused adapting to varied function requirement. Based on this framework, then our reusable model development approach for warship model is elaborated, which contains three phases: (1) design the warship configurable function set based on capacity demand; (2) use CMPA (Capacity, Mission, Process, Action) approach to map the function set from conception model to simulation model; (3) implement and encapsulate the model with RUM Specification. By the approach, developers can avoid reprogram for developing similar warship simulation models and practically improve efficiency of their reusability. Our final goal is to use pragmatic method to describe warship conception space to its simulation space and fleetly develop reusable models achieving flexible both cross-platform and cross-application reuse in parallel and distributed simulation. Section 2 discusses insufficiencies existed in development of reusable model, and introduces the parameterization-configurable framework for model reuse. The following subsection presents our reusable component model development approach for general naval vessels. Section 3 demonstrates implementation and application of the naval vessels model using the approach. Finally, our conclusion will be made with an indication of the future work.

2 Reusable Component Model Development Approach

2.1 Insufficiency in Current Reusable Model

Reusable component model refers to an independent replaceable part of a simulation system that can be independently developed and delivered as a unit and reused in different platforms and applications [17]. Such component models can be selected from a model resource library, thus reducing both model developing time and costs when compared with a new development [18]. Component-based software development is associated with a shift from object-oriented coding to system building by plugging together components. Figure 1 shows the simulation application development process based on traditional way of model reuse. Component models are selected from a model resource library to assemble applications running on the corresponding simulation platform.

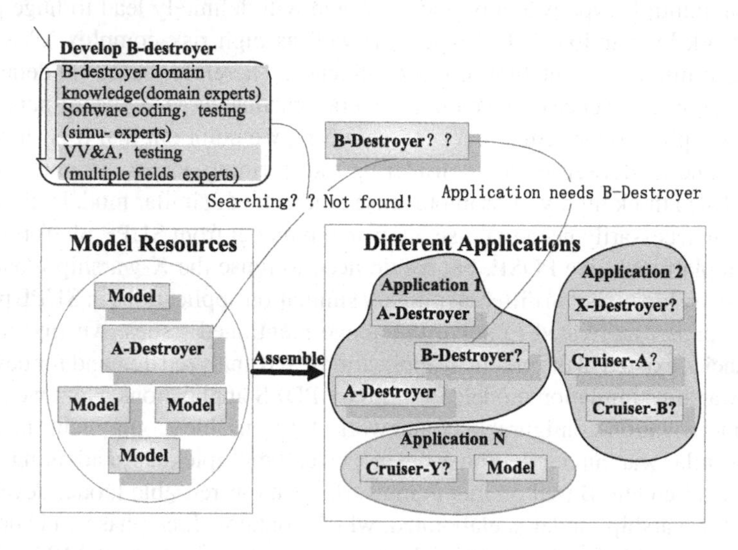

Fig. 1. Insufficiency of traditional model reuse

However, there are deficiencies existed in this way. Taking A-Destroyer for instance, it is developed as the model software with specific functions for specific application1 in the resource library. If there appears another application requires exactly A-Type destroyer, there is no doubt that the model is reused. But what if the application1 further increasingly needs B-Destroyer and application 2 demands for X-Destroyer, Cruiser-A as well as Cruiser-Y?

In practical projects usually the model developers have to recoding and retesting for each specific type naval vessel models. The minimum cost is to modify A-Destroyer code file to get the other new models. However as we know, that modifying the domain model involves complex program work for domain knowledge and huge VV&A test work. As a result, we have to repeat modeling and coding work for the warships, although these models have obviously very common and similar function modules such as route planning algorithm and target detection algorithm that has a huge potential for reuse. Consequently, there should be an approach designed to organize these general function modules for the similar warship simulation model supporting configurable generating specific models through the prototype warship model software, so as to facilitate efficiency for model reuse. Thus, the parameterization-configurable framework for reusable component model is proposed to achieve this goal.

2.2 Reusable Component Model Parameterization-Configurable Framework

The framework mainly contains three parts: a visual configuration interface; intrinsic configurable performance architecture based on capability requirements; the simulation model software encapsulated with RUM Specification. The configurable performance architecture is designed based on capability requirements according to the warship common functions, while the domain experts and simulation developers cooperate on implementing the prototype model software encapsulated with RUM Specification. User, usually the military simulation application developer, configures different performance parameters for the specific warship simulation model through the visual interface to generate executable model software with automatic generation of performance and interface documentation that usually written by developers manually inefficiently. The parameterization-configurable framework provides high efficiency for the warship model reuse, which dramatically decrease time of developing simulation applications supporting models once developed but multiple reused adapting to varied function requirement. As Fig. 2 shows the parameterization-configurable framework, there is a visual configuration interface outside the prototype simulation model software that includes three aspects: the basic information attributes set; the performance indicators set; the capability set. The surface combatant warship prototype model software can be easily and quickly configured to generate many specific similar warship models with specific combat capacity such as A-Destroyer, X-Destroyer as well as Y-Cruiser. Compared to Figs. 1 and 3 indicates that the parameterization-configurable framework efficiently solves the remodeling insufficiency in reusable component model-based simulation applications development.

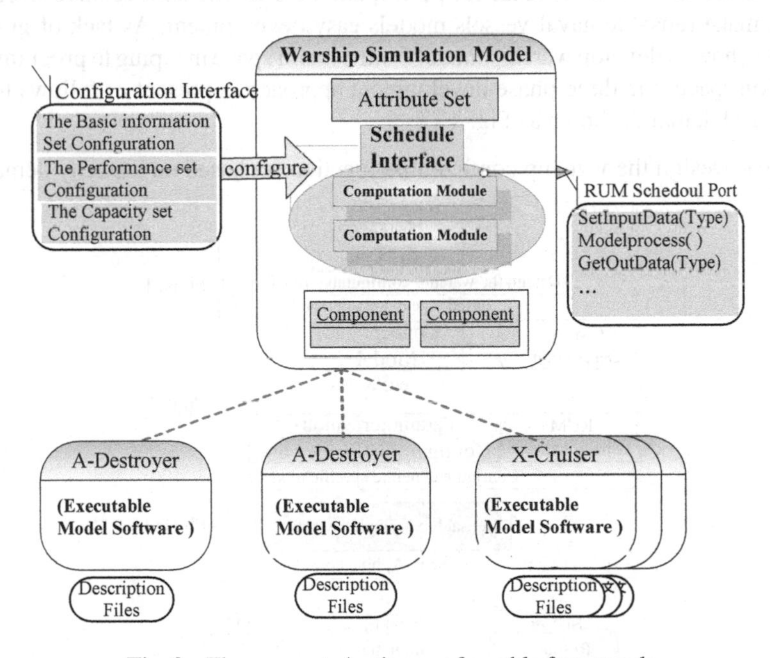

Fig. 2. The parameterization-configurable framework

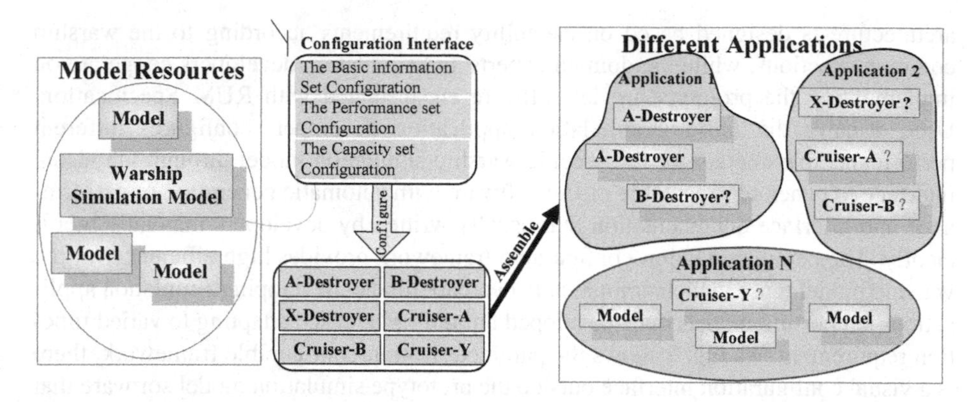

Fig. 3. The parameterization-configurable reusable model for development process in parallel and distributed simulation

2.3 Three-Phase Development Approach

As mentioned in above sections, the parameterization-configurable framework helps solve insufficiency in model reuse for PDES, but there is still some relative work to do so as to make reusable naval vessels models easy development. As lack of guideline describing how to develop warship model from domain space mapping to programmable simulation space, the three-phase development approach is present as follows to meet the practical demand, shown as Fig. 4.

- Phase1: Design the warship configurable function set based on capacity demand.

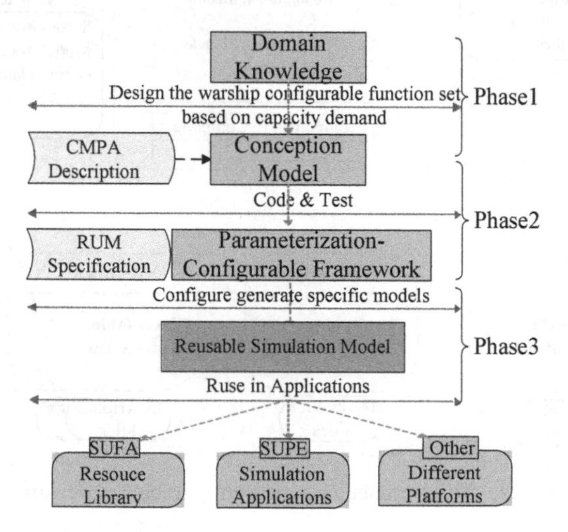

Fig. 4. The three-phase development approach

The configurable performance architecture is designed based on capability requirements according to the warship functions includes three aspects:

(1) The basic attribute set, is key information about the warship such as identity information id, name, and physical size; (2) the performance indicators set, is the parameter set for the warship's performance index standard and extremes. For example cruising speed and maneuver radius; (3) the capability set, is the parameterization description of general operational function of naval ships, such as route planning, target detection, missile strike and artillery strike. These configurable set should be defined as global variables that support configuring by the visual interface.

- Phase2: Use CMPA (Capacity, Mission, Process, Action) description method to map the function set from conception model to simulation model.

Capacity: the abstract representation of the potential ability of completing the specific mission and strategic objectives; Mission: the description of the operational mission and operational objectives of the equipment; Process: the task of the implementation of the mission with a certain relationship between the operation of the action set; Action: is the atomic elements of the process, which is the basic operational behavior cannot be divided or not necessary. As shown in Fig. 5, a warship model is analyzed by its mission, the mission is draw as combat process, and the process is decomposed into actions. Each action will be mapping to a capacity index for configuration.

- Phase3: Implement and encapsulate the model with RUM Specification.

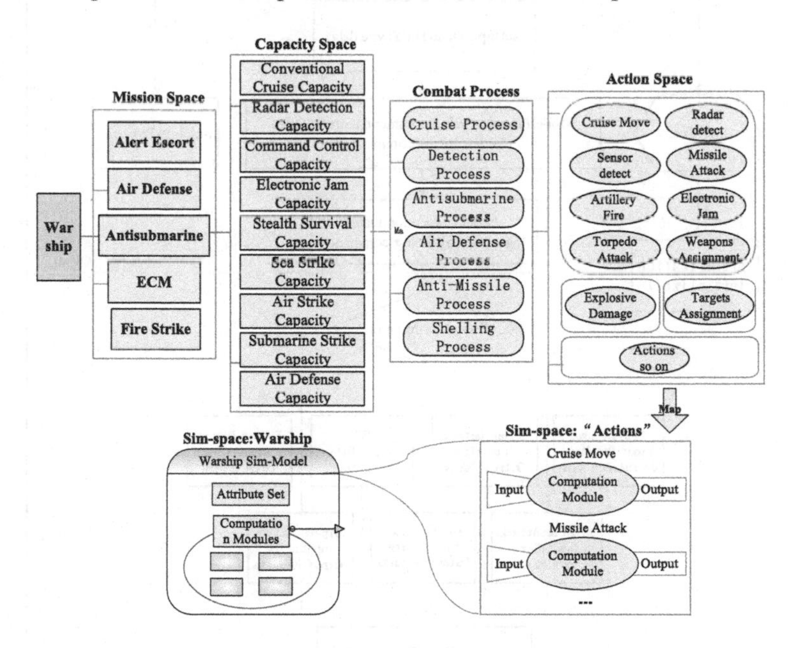

Fig. 5. The CMPA description method

RUM Specification guides the implementation of platform independent and loose-coupling scheduling between models, which is introduced in the published paper [15].

3 Implementation and Application of Naval Vessels Model Using the Development Approach

According to the naval vessel simulation model requirement in military application project of SUPE platform, we designed and implemented the basic software framework and its parameterize configuration tool using our reusable component model development approach, to support generate different type naval vessels simulation model meeting various requirement of performance, which is show as Figs. 6 and 7. Generally,

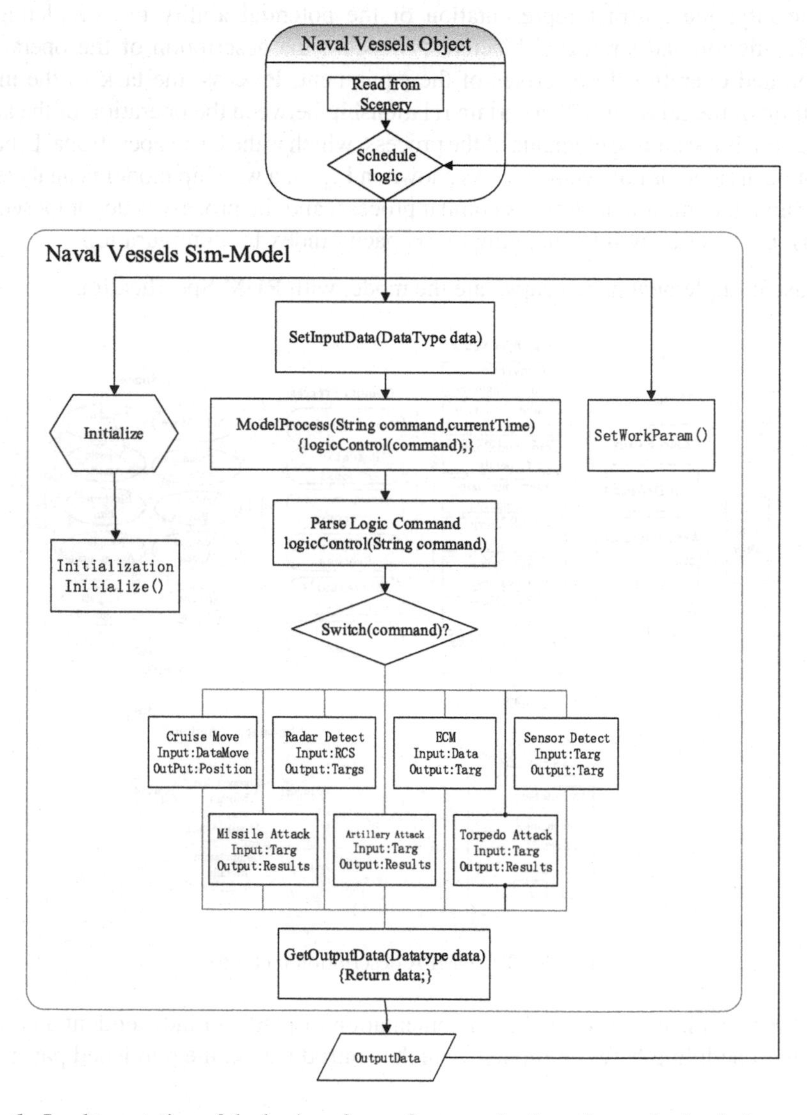

Fig. 6. Implementation of the basic software framework of naval vessels simulation model

our approach reduced development cycle from one month to about one day compared with the previous ways when develop a new naval vessel simulation model.

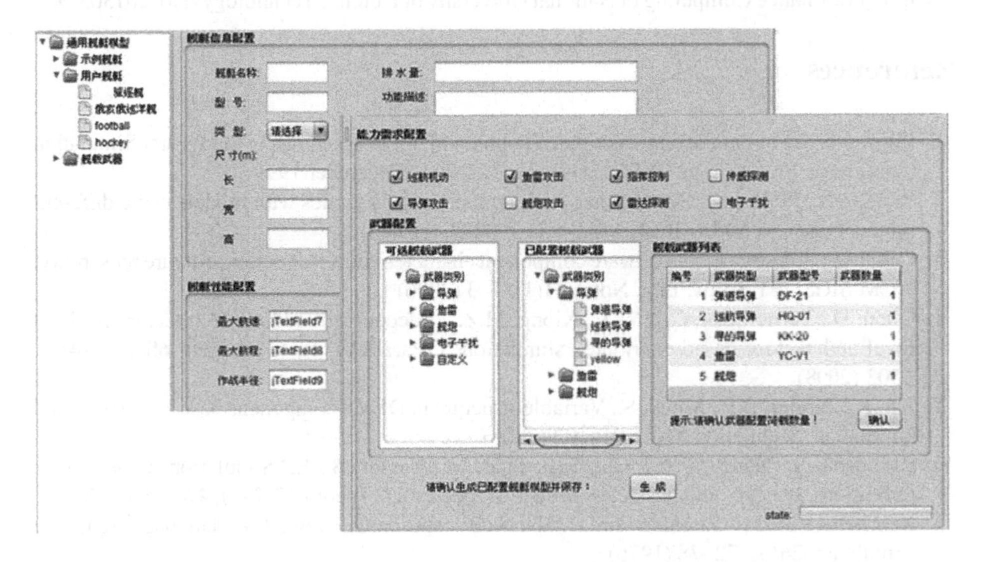

Fig. 7. Parameterize configuration tool

4 Conclusions and Future Work

Model reusability is very important for reusable component model-based simulation application of parallel and distributed simulation, not only for minimizing engineering efforts and resource costs, but also for improving the reliability. Current model development methods face several obstacles hindering model reuse across simulation platforms and applications, such as bind together with simulation platforms, traditional model reuse ways lack consideration about reusability efficiency of similar reusable models and lacking pragmatic method to describe programmable simulation space from conception space. To solve these problems, with the main contribution in this paper, we firstly proposed the parameterization-configurable framework for reusable component model that supports similar models once development, multiple times using adapting to varied function requirement and firstly proposed CMPA description method for practical demand for developing warship reusable model in PDES military simulation. Based on this framework, then our three-phase reusable model development approach for warship model is elaborated. The approach provides an important technical means for the model reuse in the complex military simulation fields, and helps facilitate model reuse efficiency, which has been successfully applied in warship model project. As for our future work, we plan to study and implement more general naval vessels simulation reusable models for PDES applications to fulfill the requirements of different clients.

Acknowledgments. We appreciate the support from Research Fund for Doctoral Program of High Education of China (No. 20124307110017) and Research Project of State Key Laboratory of High Performance Computing of National University of Defense Technology (No. 201303-05).

References

1. Fujimoto, R.M.: Parallel and distributed simulation. In: Proceedings of the Winter Simulation Conference Proceedings (WSC 1999), pp. 122–131, December 1999
2. Sandor, R., Fodor, N.: Simulation of soil temperature dynamics with models using different concepts. Sci. World J. **2012**, Article ID 590287, 8 p (2012).
3. Gill, N.B.: Importance of software component characterization for better software reusability. ACM SIGSOFT Softw. Eng. Notes **31**(1), 1–3 (2006)
4. Chen, D., Turner, S.J., Cai, W.T., Xiong, M.Z.: A decoupled federate architecture for high level architecture-based distributed simulation. J. Parallel Distrib. Comput. **68**(11), 1487–1503 (2008)
5. Hu, X., Zeigler, B.P., Mittal, S.: Variable structure in DEVS component-based modeling and simulation. Simulation **81**(2), 91–102 (2005)
6. Robinson, S., Nance, R.E., Paul, R.J., Pidd, M., Taylor, S.J.E.: Simulation model reuse: definitions, benefits and obstacles. Simul. Model. Pract. Theory **12**(7–8), 479–494 (2004)
7. Mitchell, E.E.L., Gauthier, J.S.: Advanced continuous simulation language (ACSL). Simulation **26**(3), 72–78 (1976)
8. Cox, S.W.: GPSS world: a brief preview. In: Proceedings of the Winter Simulation Conference, pp. 59–61, December 1991
9. Mattsson, S.E., Elmqvist, H.: Physical system modeling with Modelica. Control Eng. Pract. **6**(4), 501–510 (1998)
10. SISC, IEEE standard for modeling and simulation high level architecture (HLA) framework and rules (2000)
11. Yao, Y.P., Zhang, Y.X.: Solution for analytic simulation based on parallel processing. J. Syst. Simul. **20**(24), 6617–6621 (2008)
12. Wilmarth, T.L., Kale, L.V.: POSE: getting over grain size in parallel discrete event simulation. In: Proceedings of the International Conference on Parallel Processing (ICPP 2004), pp. 12–19, August 2004.
13. Koo, C., Lee, H., Cheon, Y.: SMI compatible simulation scheduler design for reuse of model complying with SMP standard. J. Astron. Space Sci. **27**(4), 407–412 (2010)
14. Zhu, F., Yao, Y.P., Chen, H.L.: Reusable component model development approach for parallel and distributed simulation. Sci. World J., March 2014
15. Zhu, F., Yao, Y.P., Tang, W.J., Chen, D.: A high performance framework for modeling and simulation of large-scale complex systems. Future Gener. Comput. Syst. **2015**(51), 132–141 (2015)
16. Zeigler, B.P.: DEVS today: advances in discrete event based information technology. In: Proceedings of the 11th IEEE/ACM International Symposium on Modeling, Analysis and Simulation of Computer Telecommunications Systems (MAS-COTS 2003), pp. 148–161 (2003)
17. Ulgen, O.M., Thomasma, T., Otto, N.: Reusable models: making your models more user-friendly. In: Proceedings of the Winter Simulation Conference Proceedings, pp. 148–151, December 1991
18. Gossler, G., Sifakis, J.: Composition for component-based modeling. Sci. Comput. Program. **55**(1–3), 161–183 (2005)

Research of Resource Selection Algorithm of Parallel Simulation System for Command Decisions Support Driven by Real-Time Intelligence

Lin Jianning[1(✉)], Jiang Jing[2], Sun Liyang[1], and Mao Shaojie[1]

[1] Science and Technology on Information System Engineering Laboratory, CETC 28th, Nanjing, China
oliver_ljn@126.com

[2] Nanjing University Posts and Telecommunications, Nanjing, China

Abstract. At present, operational decision to the commanders rely mainly on human judgment. C4ISR system can hardly assist commanders to predict situation as well as formulate and evaluate operational plans because they are lack of effective tools and methods. Parallel simulation provide an effective to solve the above problems. However, the uncertain and incomplete battlefield intelligence in the 'battlefield fog' bring great disturbance to construct parallel simulation system. So it's an urgent problem to be solved to select the most suitable battlefield entity model based on real-time battlefield intelligence in order to increase models reliability and fidelity. In this paper we propose a parallel simulation system resource selection algorithm (PSSRSA). This algorithm adopts an improved particle swarm optimum (PSO). It also has dynamic inertia weight and an alternative method of mutation. The PSSRSA can overcome traditional PSO shortcomings that may easily fall into local optima or have slow convergence rate. Through the experiment we test the algorithm performance. The results indicate the PSSRSA that is feasible and effective in parallel simulation system resource selection.

Keywords: Parallel simulation system · Simulation resource selection · Particle swarm algorithm · Dynamic inertia weight · Particle mutation

1 Introduction

With the continuous development of information technology, the accelerating pace of warfare, the expanding scopes of operations, as well as the improvement of awareness methods and abilities, commanders are confronted with massive complicated battlefield information. Therefore, one of the key problems that the C4ISR systems need to solve is how to help commanders predict the trend of battlefield more timely and exactly, analyze and optimize the operational plan, control the force action reasonably so that they can obtain superiorities in information, decision and action. Presently, the operational decision mainly rely on the judgment of the commander and the C4ISR systems is lack of effective tools and methods to assist the commander to predict the situation,

L. Zhang et al. (Eds.): AsiaSim 2016/SCS AutumnSim 2016, Part I, CCIS 643, pp. 419–430, 2016.
DOI: 10.1007/978-981-10-2663-8_44

and work out and evaluate the operational plan [1]. The parallel simulation for command decision provides an effective method for this problem. Based on the modeling and simulation technology, it constructs a virtual battlefield corresponding to the realistic one, continually receiving the real-time battlefield intelligence. By simulating the super real-time battlefield running, it can analyze possible operational intentions of the adversary and predict the future trend of the battlefield. It can also feed this information back to the commander and thus providing support for the commander's final decision.

The parallel simulation method for the decision support constructs simulation systems that run in parallel with C4ISR systems. By interconnecting and exchanging information with C4ISR systems, simulation systems constantly obtain latest battlefield information from C4ISR systems, establish simulation models of battlefield entities, constantly make judgments about the possible operational intentions and behavior of enemy targets through super-real-time simulation of the models, generate the predictions of battlefield situations for the next moment and give feedback on such results to C4ISR systems. In this way, simulation systems assist commanders in developing battle plans and make deduction and assessment of the expected effects of the battle plans, providing support for C4ISR systems' prediction of situations and assessment of decision schemes and enabling commanders to "see through" the future and respond timely.

Parallel simulation systems have changed the non-dominant position of previous simulation systems from being negative to positive, from being static to dynamic, from being offline to online, and finally from being subordinate to of equal status, making simulation the constituent part of the core competency of C4ISR systems. The conceptual schematic of the parallel simulation method for the decision support of C4ISR systems is shown in Fig. 1.

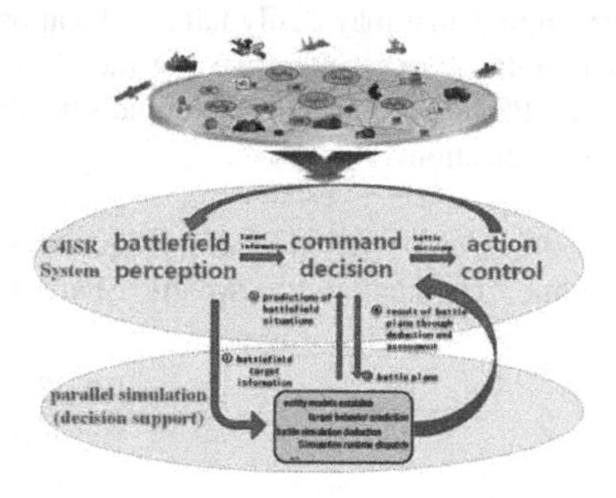

Fig. 1. The conceptual schematic of parallel simulation for the command decision support

The concept of parallel simulation comes from Prof. Wang's parallel system [2] and ACP theory [3], which are already used in several areas such as urban traffic [4] and internet public opinion spread [5], and developed to the concepts of CC5.0 [6], knowledge automation [7], etc. Prof. Qiu uses the parallel concept on the contingency management of social emergency [8–11] and proposes the concept of parallel military system [12]. Prof. Fujimoto [13] proposes a simulation paradigm called Symbiotic Simulation, which is similar to the parallel simulation in nature. The applications of

Symbiotic Simulation include disaster emergency prediction [14], real-time traffic optimization [15], ecological system analysis [16], financial decision management [17], cloud computing task scheduling [18], industrial manufacturing [19], etc. In these areas, parallel simulation system is mainly used for solving the process uncertainty problem of the running real system, but the simulation model itself is relatively fixed and specific.

In the area of military operational command decision, Parallel simulation utilizes complex system modelling and simulation theory to construct simulation systems that run in parallel with C4ISR systems and provides decision support for C4ISR systems through the parallel execution, evolving approximation, and feedback control of parallel simulation systems and C4ISR systems using computational experiments. Compared with general simulation of decision support, the most noteable characteristic of parallel simulation is dynamic evolution. A general simulation system focuses on one-off construction and cannot correct the approximation of the simulation system to the real system in the running process. However, a parallel simulation system focuses more on enabling the simulation system to approximate to the real system through parallel execution and dynamic evolution. Therefore, a parallel simulation system is in essence characterized by dynamic evolution.

Since the operational process is a rivalry game of both sides, uncertain and incomplete battlefield intelligence (and even the misleading information) in the "Battlefield Fog" will bring huge interference to the construction of parallel simulation system model for the command decision. Thus, an imperative problem to be solved is to select the most appropriate battlefield entity model in order to make it with high credibility and fidelity based on the real-time battlefield intelligence.

At present, research on modeling of military area is mainly focused on aspects of experiment, training, etc. It lacks of the model of directly applying on the command decision [20], and is mostly based on static models [22], thus lacking of the dynamic evolvement feature of the model. The Deep Green plan [23] proposed by the US army is a typical application of parallel simulation technology in the command decision area. However, we cannot see any public report about this modeling technology because of the importance of the operational models. Prof. Hu [24] proposes a concept of "half-real" embedded parallel simulation, which provides theoretical support for the modeling problem of parallel simulation system. Based on the research of Parallel/Symbiotic simulation, Prof. Zhou [25] chooses operational simulation driven by dynamic data as the research background. It is focused on the operating mechanism of simulation systems as well as related supporting technologies rather than the research of simulation models. According to the ubiquitous uncertainty of resource availability in execution environment of military mission planning, Zhang [26] proposes a forecast managing algorithm of military mission planning. It effectively solves the problem of uncertainty of resource availability in military mission planning. However, the selected operational resources do not have the ability of dynamic changing according to the real-time intelligence.

Specific to the uncertain battlefield intelligence, a resource selection technology of parallel simulation system for the command decision support is discussed in this paper. The battlefield intelligence data is transformed into requirements of performance parameters for the simulation models. Moreover, a resource selection algorithm of parallel simulation system is proposed based on the improved particle swarm optimization. The experiment result shows that this algorithm has a relatively good convergence and selection accuracy.

2 Resource Selection Model of Parallel Simulation System

2.1 Problem Description and Analysis

The parallel simulation system for command decision support is able to select model (simulation resources) dynamically based on the inputting real-time battlefield intelligence. Firstly, we give the description of the resource selection problem of parallel simulation system. Assuming that the battlefield intelligence includes m battlefield entities, and each entity Ni is corresponding to the simulation model library ML_i, which contains N_i modle options (SM_1,…, SM_{ni}). That is ML_i = (SM_1,…, SM_{ni}). The specific selection process is shown in Fig. 2.

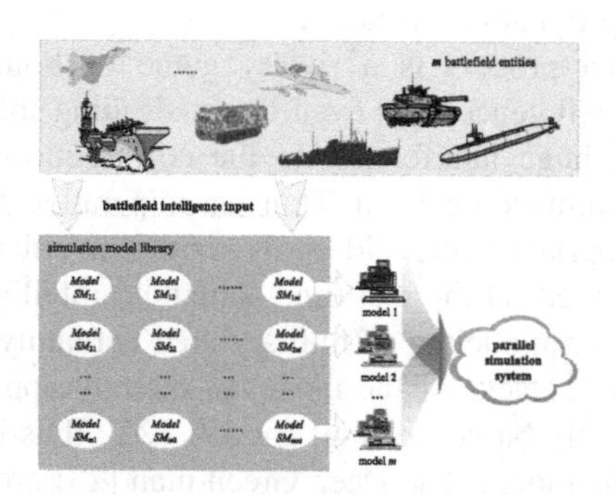

Fig. 2. Resources selection process of parallel simulation system

2.2 Building the Resources Selection Model

In this section, *pss* is used to express the parallel simulation system. Assuming that the number of types of resources which participate in the construction of *pss* is E, and the $l(l = 1, 2, \cdots E)$ the simulation resource set $X^{(l)}$ includes M_l simulation resources $\{ x_1^{(l)}, x_2^{(l)}, \cdots, x_{M_l}^{(l)} \}$ which can be used. In this paper, we use X to refer a simulation resource set unless we point out a specific kind of simulation resources, and we use x to refer one participating resource unless we point out a specific simulation resource. Each simulation resource x can be expressed by D $(D = 1, 2, \cdots)$ indices, $x = [x_1, x_2, \cdots, x_D]^T$.

In the construction process of parallel simulation system, five kind of resources Qos parameters are selected as indices (D = 5) to evaluate every available resource x, which are denoted by the resource payoff *P(x)*, resource running time *T(x)*, resource transfer latency *L(x)*, resource reputation level *Rep(x)* and resource reliability *R(x)*, respectively.

Resource Payoff ***P*(*x*)**: denotes the cost paid by the developer of simulation system to call and execute the simulation resources. Here, the price of resources is given by resource provider.

Running Time ***T*(*x*)**: denotes the time period between sending request of simulation resource call and obtaining the result. It includes two parts, one is the time of resource itself used to deal with user's request, denoted by T_{pro}, and the other is the responding time of the server, denoted by T_{res}. Thus, the simulation resource running time can be expressed as $T = T_{pro} + T_{res}$. Considering a simulation system resource x, we use historical data of running time to calculate $T(x)$: $T(x) = \sum_{a=1}^{n} T_a(x)/n$, where $T_a(x)$ denotes the running time of resource x at the ath time and n denotes the total times of running.

Network Latency ***L*(*x*)**: is quite small and can be ignored comparing to the calculation time of server in distributed systems in *LAN* environment. However, in net-centric simulation environment, because of the large amount of simulation resources, the heavy information traffic in networks and the dynamically changing network states, network latency becomes a parameter not to be ignored in selecting simulation system resources. In this paper, we use the end to end time difference of system resources to calculate the network latency.

Reliability ***R*(*x*):** denotes the probability of successfully calling and executing simulation resources. Traditionally, reliability is related to not only system's hardware and software, but also the network connection conditions. Here, the reliability of simulation system resource x is decided by resource running time T(x) and resource price $P(x)$:

$$R(x) = e^{-(T(x) + P(x))} \tag{1}$$

Reputation Level ***Rep(x)***: denotes the user evaluation and satisfaction of system resources. We use users' feedback statistics to calculate this index. $Rep_a(x)$ denotes the user a's evaluation of system resource x, it is related to the reliability $R_a(x)$ and network latency $L_a(x)$:

$$Rep_a(x) = R_a(x)/L_a(x) \tag{2}$$

When building simulation systems, it is important to select some simulation resources which can meet users' requirements from different types of simulation resource sets. In this paper, the objectives of selecting resources to build *pss* are minimum payoff, shortest time and minimum network latency. At the same time, we expect to meet the minimum threshold requirements of the community's reputation level and reliability, which are denoted by Rep_O and R_O, respectively. Thus, the general model of simulation system resource selection can be expressed as,

$$\begin{cases} \min\limits_{\mathbf{x}^{(l)} \in \mathbf{X}^{(l)}, l=1,2,\cdots,E} & (P_{pss}(x^{(1)}, x^{(2)}, \cdots x^{(E)}), T_{pss}(x^{(1)}, x^{(2)}, \cdots x^{(E)}), L_{pss}(x^{(1)}, x^{(2)}, \cdots x^{(E)})) \\ s.t. & R_{pss}(x^{(1)}, x^{(2)}, \cdots x^{(E)}) \geq R_O, \quad Rep_{pss}(x^{(1)}, x^{(2)}, \cdots x^{(E)}) \geq Rep_O \end{cases} \tag{3}$$

where P_{pss}, T_{pss}, L_{pss}, R_{pss} and Rep_{pss} denote the parallel simulation system *pss*'s resource payoff function, resource running time function, resource network latency function, resource reliability function and resource reputation level function, respectively.

Formula (3) is a multi-objective optimization problem. The objective function is also called fitness function. Different test functions can be selected as objective function according to different application requirements. Its value of function is also called fitness function value or fitness value for short.

In this paper, it is assumed that each specific resource's QoS information would be static when running the algorithm. The resource selection model designed in this section should be able to extend or reduce based on different application requirements of simulation system resource selection. This model can also be extended to arbitrary number of objective functions and constraint conditions.

3 Parallel Simulation System Resource Selection Algorithm (PSSRSA)

We use Particle Swarm Optimization (PSO) algorithm as the basic resource selection algorithm of parallel simulation system. The basic PSO algorithm has the local optimum problem which is called "premature". In literature [27], two reasons caused this problem in basic PSO are concluded: lacking of inertia weight parameter and no considering of the influence of population diversity to the algorithm. Therefore, before we use PSO algorithm on resource selection, we have to solve two problems below: one is how to dynamically adjust the inertia weight to meet the searching requirement on different stages; the other is how to ensure population diversity to avoid local optimization. The Parallel Simulation System Resource Selection Algorithm (PSSRSA) proposed in this paper will use PSO as the basic algorithm and extend it with inertia weight and diversity parameters. In Sect. 3.1, we propose an inertia weight dynamic adjustment strategy. And in Sect. 3.2, we propose a self-adaptive variation disturbance method to increase population diversity and avoid local optimization effect.

3.1 Inertia Weight Dynamic Adjustment Strategy

PSSRSA considers the dynamic adjustments of inertia weight comprehensively by the number of iterations and the diversity of the current particle swarm. While enhancing the local exploitation ability, the risk of concentrate all particles to a certain local point is reduced, thereby ensuring a certain level of global searching ability of the swarm. The population diversity $d(t)$ is obtained with the measuring method proposed in literature [28].

Inertia weight is dynamically adjusted according to formula (4).

$$w(t) = w_{\max} + e^{-d(t)} * \left(1 - e^{(Iter - Iter_{\max})} \cdot \frac{Iter}{Iter_{\max}}\right) * (w_{\max} - w_{\min}) \tag{4}$$

Where $Iter_{\max}$ and $Iter_{\min}$ are respectively the maximum and minimum numbers of iterations, *Iter* is the current number of iterations, $w_{\min}$ is the initial weight, $w_{\max}$ is the final weight, and *d(t)* is the population diversity at time point *t*.

It can be seen from formula (4) that when t is small and w is large, the particle swarm inclines to global searching, and the increase of t and gradual decrease of w could accelerate the particle swarm's local searching. This adjustment strategy enables self-adaptive adjustment of the optimizing speed of PSSRSA, improves the rate of convergence, and prevents the algorithm from being trapped in local optimization and premature.

3.2 Self-adaptive Variation Disturbance Method

In addition to preventing local convergence through the adjustment of inertia weight, a great number of studies performed variation to the population. In literature [29], the variance of the fitness degrees of the particle swarm is used as the global optimization variation condition, and a self-adaptive variant particle swarm optimization algorithm was proposed. In literature [30], the evolution stagnant steps *S* is used as triggering condition to perform random disturbance simultaneously on the individual extremum x_p and the global extremum x_g. This algorithm adjusts the individual and global extremums to make all particles move to new locations. It makes all particles migrate and re-gather, and the new searching paths and domains increase the possibility of finding more optimal solutions.

An optional random disturbing method is employed in PSSRSA in case the following two situations occur to the particle swarm at the same time.

1. The variance of the fitness values of the particle swarm convergent to 0, which means the population might be trapped in one or more optimal points. The variance of fitness values is defined as below:

$$\sigma^2 = \sum_{i=1}^{n} \left(\frac{f_i - \bar{f}}{f}\right)^2 \tag{5}$$

where f_i is the fitness value of particle i, $\bar{f}$ is the average fitness value of the swarm, and f is defined as below:

$$f = \begin{cases} \max|f_i - \bar{f}|, & \text{if} \max|f_i - \bar{f}| > 1, \\ 1, & \text{else.} \end{cases}$$

2. The number of global optimal value stagnant steps is greater than the triggering condition *S*, which means the population might be trapped in local optimal point.

The extremum interrupting strategy is as below:

$$x'_{\mathrm{p}} = \begin{cases} \Delta(s, UB - x_{\mathrm{p}}) + x_{\mathrm{p}}, & \text{if } \mathit{flip} = 0, \\ \Delta(s, x_{\mathrm{p}} - LB) + x_{\mathrm{p}}, & \text{if } \mathit{flip} = 1. \end{cases}$$
$$x'_{\mathrm{g}} = \begin{cases} \Delta(s, UB - x_{\mathrm{g}}) + x_{\mathrm{g}}, & \text{if } \mathit{flip} = 0, \\ \Delta(s, x_{\mathrm{g}} - LB) + x_{\mathrm{g}}, & \text{if } \mathit{flip} = 1. \end{cases} \quad (6)$$

where *filp* is a random event that returns 0 or 1, UB indicates the upper bound of variables x_{g} and x_{p}, while LB indicates the lower bound of them. Function Δ is defined as below:

$$\Delta(s, x) = x(1 - r^{(1 - \frac{s}{\max\_t})b}). \quad (7)$$

Where r is a random numeral in the range of [0, 1], *max_t* is the maximum number of iterations, and s is the current number of iterations. Parameter b determines the independence degree of the interruption, and in this article, it's given the value of 2.

4 Verification of Resource Selection Algorithm

In this work, we use Rastrigin function as the testing function. Rastrigin function is a non-convex simple objective function used as a performance test problem for optimization algorithms. It is a typical example of non-linear multimodal function with a lot of local minima. Finding the minimum of this function is a fairly difficult problem due to its large search space and large number of local minima. The resource selection problem also has the objectives of minimum payoff, shortest running time and minimum network latency of the parallel simulation system. The indices of the system built by the optimum resources have the accordance with Rastrigin function's minimum. Therefore, using Rastrigin function as the testing function is very suitable for the background of the parallel simulation system resource selection application. Moreover, due to large number of types of simulation resources and large number of resources when building parallel simulation system, using simple objective testing function will be helpful in decreasing the number of calculations for system resource selection and increasing the selecting speed. In summary, we use Rastrigin function as the target function for resource selection.

In this work, we use resource running time T, resource payoff P and resource transfer network latency L in the resource selection model (formula (3)) as three parameters in Rastrigin function. Therefore, we transform three optimization objectives (T, P, L) in the multi-objective optimization model into the simple objective optimum selection problem of the testing function. At the same time, we also use resource reputation *Rep* and resource reliability R as two constraint conditions. To normalize the calculation result, we set parameter in each dimension (x_d) of every resource x between range [0, 1]. Without loss of generality, we consider one type of available simulation resource sets. In the range of resources, 5000 points are randomly generated to represent optional resources of parallel simulation system.

After the generation of optional resources, we set the iteration times of resource selection process being 1000, 2000 and 3000, respectively. And in each iteration process, we set the corresponding particle swarm size being from 100 to 1000, 200 to 2000 and 400 to 4000, respectively, to test the searching performance of PSSRSA algorithm under different circumstances. In addition, we compare the testing result with those of basic PSO algorithm, DWPSO algorithm [31] and AMPSO algorithm [32]. Here we use the average value of 10 times as the final experiment result. Both DWPSO and AMPSO algorithms are optimization algorithms based on PSO. DWPSO uses an inertia weight dynamic adjustment strategy, while AMPSO is an optimization algorithm with extremum disturbance. Both of them are used to avoid local optimization result. In this work, we set the parameters of PSSRSA as follows: $w_{initial} = 0.9$, $w_{final} = 0.5$, $c_1 = c_2 = 1.4$.

Table 1 records the numbers of convergence of four algorithms under experiments with different times of iterations. From Table 1 we can find that generally the number of convergence of PSSRSA is less than other algorithms'. In fact, sometimes other

Table 1. Numbers of convergences of each algorithm under three different iteration times

iteration times	N / algorithm	100	200	300	400	500	600	700	800	900	1000
1000	PSO	516	500	368	381	354	358	294	267	312	300
	DWPSO	529	503	382	385	436	355	401	320	279	382
	AMPSO	522	389	422	352	368	352	286	346	270	307
	PSSRSA	454	364	389	360	367	348	266	260	287	254
	N / algorithm	200	400	600	800	1000	1200	1400	1600	1800	2000
2000	PSO	418	389	427	344	305	283	267	264	267	257
	DWPSO	440	451	457	354	284	350	294	337	299	287
	AMPSO	453	459	396	319	284	362	264	333	260	269
	PSSRSA	400	428	354	338	283	297	298	285	270	253
	N / algorithm	400	800	1200	1600	2000	2400	2800	3200	3600	4000
3000	PSO	319	316	260	269	292	257	273	256	253	253
	DWPSO	356	337	254	260	275	254	257	301	253	265
	AMPSO	351	262	308	265	258	254	303	263	273	253
	PSSRSA	338	286	292	254	254	260	258	254	256	254

optimization algorithms have the problem of not finding the optimum result in the simulation experiments. Table 1 shows that due to the smaller swarm size under the experiment with 1000 times iterations, all algorithms need more number of convergences. However, comparing to the others, PSSRSA shows a relatively much better searching performance with at least tens of convergence numbers dropped. With the swarm size increasing, the performance of each algorithm becomes stable. Especially when the particle swarm size increases to 4000, the numbers of convergences of each algorithm become nearly identical. However, PSSRSA still has about ten times of convergence advantage.

Figure 3 shows the experiment results in form of line chart. From it we can find that the number of convergence of PSSRSA is less than the others under every iteration process, thus proving that PSSRSA has a faster convergence speed. Moreover, when the swarm size is larger than 700, the number of convergence of PSSRSA is almost the same, which means PSSRSA has a more stable convergence process.

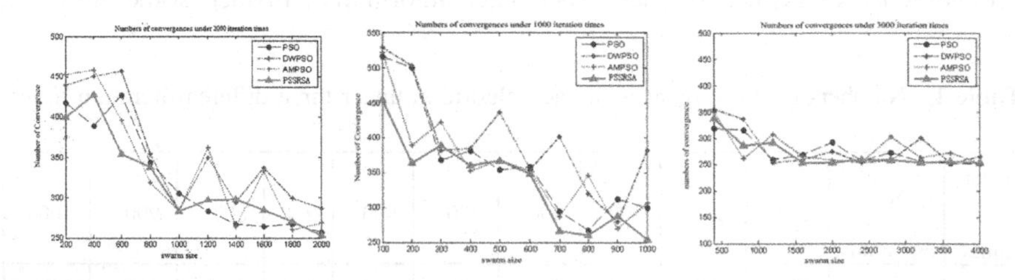

Fig. 3. Numbers of convergences of each algorithm under three different iteration times

5 Conclusions

The main contribution of this paper is the proposed parallel simulation system resource selection algorithm (PSSRSA). Firstly, we build the resource selection model of parallel simulation system and select five resource QoS parameters. Secondly, we transform the resource selection problem of building parallel simulation system into the global optimization problem based on QoS with some constraint conditions. Then we propose the PSSRSA algorithm, which improves the method with inertia weight parameter and variation disturbance. Lastly, we verify PSSRSA algorithm through simulation experiments. Simulation result shows that PSSRSA algorithm is faster and better than other optimization algorithms based on PSO. It has not only good convergence speed but also high precision searching result. Moreover, PSSRSA has a good performance under large population diversity and large iteration times, which makes it suitable for building large-scale simulation system.

References

1. Zaijinag, T., Xue Qin, X., Haohua, Y.S.: Reserch on embeded combat simulation system for assistant decision making. Comput. Simul. **31**(4), 14–16 (2014)
2. Feiyue, W.: Parallel system methods for management and control of complex systems. Control Decis. **19**(5), 485–489 (2004)
3. Feiyue, W., Derong, L., Gang, X., Changjian, C., Dongbin, Z.: Parallel control theory of complex systems and application. Complex Syst. Complexity Sci. **3**, 1–12 (2012)
4. Xiaoming, L., Zhengxi, L.: Parallel systems for urban passenger transport hub. Acta Automatica Sinica **40**(12), 2756–2765 (2014)
5. Fang, Z., Rui, W.: Test method for network opinion based on parallel system. Command Inform. Syst. Technol. **4**(3), 1–7 (2013)
6. Feiyue, W.: CC 5.0: Intelligent command and control systems in the parallel age. J. Command Control **1**(1), 107–120 (2015)
7. Feiyue, W.: Software-defined systems and knowledge automation: a parallel paradigm shift from newton to merton. Acta Automatica Sinica **41**(1), 1–8 (2015)
8. Feiyue, W., Xiaogang, Q., Dajun, Z., Zhidong, C., Zongchen, F.: A computational experimental platform for emergency response based on parallel systems. Complex Syst. Complexity Sci. **7**(4), 1–10 (2010)
9. Rongqing, M., Xiaogang, Q., Laobing, Z., Zongchen, F., Peng, Z., Zhichao, S.: Parallel emergency management oriented computation experimental frame. Syst. Eng. Theory Pract. **35**(10), 2459–2466 (2015)
10. Peng, Z., Bin, C., Rongqing, M., Laobing, Z., Xiaogang, Q.: Model development and management in the computational experiment oriented to emergency management. J. Nat. Univ. Defense Technol. **37**(3), 173–178 (2015)
11. Zhichao, S., Yuanzheng, G., Hongqiu, D., Xiaogang, Q.: The research on agent-based simulation oriented to emergency management. Commun. Comput. Inform. Sci. **461**, 256–267 (2014)
12. Xiaogang, Q., Peng, Z.: Knowledge engineering in simulation of parallel military system. J. Syst. Simul. **27**(8), 1665–1670 (2015)
13. Fujimoto, R., Lunceford, D., Page, E., Uhrmacher, A.M.: Summary of the parallel/distributed simulation working group. In: Fujimoto, R., Lunceford, D., Page, E., Uhrmacher, A.M. (eds.) Grand Challenges for Modeling and Simulation, Dagstuhl Report, August 2002, pp. 49–5 (2002)
14. Brun, C., Cortés, A., Margalef, T.: Coupled dynamic data-driven framework for forest fire spread prediction. In: First International Conference of Dynamic Data-Driven Environmental Systems Science. Cambridge, MA, USA (2014)
15. Sunderrajan, A., Cai, W., Aydt, H., et al.: Map stream: Initializing what-if analyses for real-time symbiotic traffic simulations. In: Proceedings of the 2014 Winter Simulation Conference (2014)
16. Gang, W., Xiao, F., Chu, K.H.: Symbiosis analysis on industrial ecological system. Chinese J. Chem. Eng. **22**(6), 690–698 (2014)
17. Xu, Z., Zhao, N.: Information fusion for intuitionistic fuzzy decision making - an overview. Inform. Fusion **28**, 10–23 (2016)
18. Abdullahi, M., Ngadi, M.A., Abdulhamidb, H.M.: Symbiotic organism search optimization based task scheduling in cloud computing environment. Future Gener. Comput. Syst. **56**, 640–650 (2016)
19. Meng, X., Zhang, L., Wang, M.: Symbiotic simulation of assembly quality control in large gas turbine manufacturing. In: 13th International Conference on Systems Simulation (2013)

20. Mccune, R., Purta, R., Dobski, M., et al.: Investigations of DDDAS for command and control of UAV swarms with agent-based modeling. In: Proceedings of the 2013 Winter Simulation Conference (2013)
21. Biller, B., Corlu, C., Akcay, A., et al.: A simulation-based support tool for data-driven decision making operational testing for dependence modeling. In: Proceedings of the 2014 Winter Simulation Conference (2014)
22. Xinzhong, W.: Multi-agent based modeling of warship combat command and control system. Appl. Mech. Mater. **246–247**, 898–902 (2013)
23. DARPA: Deep Green. Initial Broad Agency Announcement (BAA 07-56) (2007)
24. Xiaofeng, H., Xiaoyuan, H., Xulin, X.: The challenge and consideration about M & S in big data time. Sci. China Press **44**(5), 676–692 (2014)
25. Yun, Z.: Research on the theory and methods of dynamic data driven simulation for realtime combat decision support. National University of Defense Technology, Changsha (2010)
26. Yingxin, Z., Chao, C., Zhong, L., Jianmai, S.: Method for modeling and solving military mission planning with uncertain resource availability. J. Nat. Univ. Defense Technol. **35**(3), 30–35 (2015)
27. Engelbrecht, A.P.: Fundamentals of Computational Swarm Intelligence. Tsinghua University Press, Beijing (2009)
28. Riget, J., Vesterstorem, J.S.: A diversity-guided particle swarm optimizer-the ARPSO, Technical report 2002-02. Department of Computer Science, University of Aarhus, Denmark, pp. 345–350 (2002)
29. Zhensu, L., Zhirong, H.: Paticle swarm optimization with adaptive mutation. Acta Electronica Sinica **32**(3), 416–420 (2004). (in Chinese)
30. Wang, H., Zhishu, L.: A simpler and more effective particle swarm optimization algorithm. J. Softw. **18**(4), 861–868 (2007). (in Chinese)
31. Atanassov, K.: Intuitionistic fuzzy sets. Fuzzy Sets Syst. **20**(1), 87–96 (1986)
32. Hwang, L.C., Yoon, K.: Multiple Criteria Decision Making. Lecture Notes in Economics and Mathematical Systems. Springer, Heidelberg (1981)

The High Performance Computing for 3D Dynamic Holographic Simulation Based on Multi-GPU Cluster

Zhang Yingxi[1(✉)], Lin Tingyu[2,3], and Guo Liqin[2,3]

[1] Beijing Simulation Center, Beijing 100854, China
zhang360896270@sina.com
[2] Beijing Complex Product Advanced Manufacturing Engineering Research Center, Beijing Simulation Center, Beijing 100854, China
[3] State Key Laboratory of Intelligent Manufacturing System Technology, Beijing Institute of Electronic System Engineering, Beijing 100854, China

Abstract. Two different methods for high performance calculation cluster are proposed to optimize holographic algorithms of computer generated holography (CGH). We completed the numerical simulations and finish the experience. Results show that we can reconstruct a satisfied object by using our holography. Moreover, the computation process of CGH for three-dimensional (3D) dynamic holographic display has been sped up by programming with these methods. Not only can it optimize file loading process but also inline calculation process. The CGH of gigabyte data is generated finally. Besides, the first method can effectively reduce time costs of loading and writing files on CPU. It is believed the proposed method can support the huge data processing for 3D dynamic holographic simulation and virtual reality in near future.

Keywords: High performance computation · 3D holographic simulation · Virtual reality

1 Introduction

With the increase of people's growing material and cultural demands, the improvement of display technology has never stopped. Holographic simulation is one of the most promising technologies. Achievements have been made in different aspects with the development of holography. Elimination of a zero-order beam [1, 2], handling of occlusion issue [3], increasing of viewing angle [4] and so on, all of them has made great contributions to the three-dimensional (3D) holographic simulation. However, holographic calculation process cost a lot of time, which is still a hard problem for holographic simulation. It keeps us far away from real-time holographic simulation for 3Dobjects.

This work was supported by the national 863 program (2015AA042101).

L. Zhang et al. (Eds.): AsiaSim 2016/SCS AutumnSim 2016, Part I, CCIS 643, pp. 431–441, 2016.
DOI: 10.1007/978-981-10-2663-8_45

Many different methods have been proposed to solve this problem. During the past few decades, integral photography has been used in a capture and reconstruction system which can reconstruct a 3D live scene generated by fast Fourier transform (FFT) at 12 frames per second [5]. The ray-tracing approach [6] is a basic computer generated hologram (CGH) computation method. 3D objects are discretized into huge amounts of object points and every point is considered as a point light source. In this way, a hologram can be calculated by the sum interference fringes of each point. We can reconstruct quite high-quality 3D objects by this algorithm with consuming so much time. In order to optimize it, some of the calculation steps can be transferred to the offline process, which can reduce computational work inline. It leads to the presence of look-up table (LUT) method [7]. It is a table saved in computer that stores the pre-calculating results. LUT algorithm can use it to trade space for time, which can optimize the hologram generation speed of coherent ray trace (CRT). Because of the rise of this thought, some new methods have been proposed. Split look-up table (S-LUT) algorithm [8] splits the LUTs into horizontal and vertical vectors by using the Fresnel approximation, but its offline tables are very huge. It will grow fast with the increasing of hologram size. Furthermore, compressed look-up table (C-LUT) [9] splits the z modulation factor using Fraunhofer diffraction to compress the offline table. C-LUT is a fast and memory reduced method and suitable to calculate large size hologram with limited store space, but the reconstructed object from C-LUT algorithm cannot reach expected quality. All methods mentioned above are used to accelerate the generation of a real-time hologram.

2 The Method to Generate a Hologram

2.1 Common Optimization Methods

There are other optimized methods that take a good use of the characteristics of programming languages or high performance hardware devices. In recent years, mixed programming has been proposed. it can accelerate the generation speed of CGH to some extent [10]. Although combining the advantages of different programming languages is a good idea, people are concern more about high performance computing hardware now [11, 12]. Definitely, advanced computing hardware contributes a lot to the high speed calculation, so it can also be used in holographic simulation. Graphic processing unit (GPU), as the special chip for big data processing, has been designed properly for holographic simulation. Its parallel architecture is far away more effective than central processing unit (CPU) and it has a superb performance in the processing of floating type data [13]. This special mechanism can be good for the holographic simulation job to generate the large-pixel-count hologram [14]. Nowadays, GPU is used generally to improve the computation speed of algorithm with independent data. With the improvement of high performance calculating ability, the size of hologram is also increasing. Most recently, a hologram with 9 k $\times$ 9 k size can be generated using FFT-based method [15]. Those methods can be accelerated but the coding process is complex and data communication speed is not good enough for realizing dynamic 3D holographic simulation.

2.2 The Theroy of Holographic Simulation

In this paper, we use two effective methods based on the attributes of the high performance computing device, GPU and CPU, to accelerate the computation algorithm of a CGH. In addition, we use dynamic parallelism [16–18] and file memory mapping techniques [19] based on the characteristics of the high performance computing devices which can implement two different LUT methods by programming in C/C ++. The size of hologram can be calculated has reached 1 gigabyte with these methods. Currently, the whole computation job can be completed in about 120 s and the reconstructed 3D image quality is good, which can be easily recognized by the human's eyes. Multiple GPUs are put into use as high performance computing hardware facilities and one CPU is responsible for the logical controlling. We also use the Compute Unified Device Architecture (CUDA) as a programming platform. This platform is promoted by NVIDIA. Besides, the loading speed of offline tables is improved on CPU by using the file mapping technique.

In order to increase the speed of CRT method, LUT method stores whole offline computation results so that computing devices have to move tables into computer's memory when the algorithm try to generate a hologram inline. S-LUT algorithm using Fresnel approximation has decreased the inline computation load without the sacrifice of the quality of reconstructed image. It splits the horizontal light modulation factor

$$H\left(x_p^{'} - x_j, z_j\right) = e^{-ik\sqrt{\left(x_p^{'}-x_j\right)^2 + \left(d-z_j\right)^2}} \tag{1}$$

and vertical light modulation factor

$$V\left(y_q^{'} - y_j, z_j\right) = e^{-ik\sqrt{\left(y_q^{'}-y_j\right)^2 + \left(d-z_j\right)^2}}. \tag{2}$$

Both of these factors are computed offline and stored in hard disk. The inline process of S-LUT is also departed into two steps:

$$H_s\left(x_p^{'}\right) = \sum\nolimits_{j=0}^{p_n} a_j * H(x_p^{'} - x_j, z_j), \tag{3}$$

$$I\left(x_p^{'}, y_q^{'}\right) = V\left(y_q^{'} - y_j, z_j\right) \times H_s\left(x_p^{'}\right). \tag{4}$$

According to the equation above, $\left(x_p^{'}, y_q^{'}\right)$ represents the point location on hologram plane. (x, y, z) is the object point coordinate and z_j is the coordinate of every slice of the object. d is the distance between the object plane and the hologram.

The consumption of storage space grows fast with the increasing of hologram size by using S-LUT algorithm. It is a fast and useful algorithm to generate a hologram in proper size. When we want to compute a huge size hologram, the offline tables even cannot be stored in video memory at one time. C-LUT can solve this problem effectively. It takes an advantage of Fraunhofer diffraction to achieve the further approximation compared with S-LUT. It defines the z light modulation factor based on this.

$$L\left(z',z_{j_z}\right)=e^{-ik\frac{(x_p'^2+y_q'^2)}{2d}}. \tag{5}$$

Because of it, there are some changes of H and V factor,

$$H\left(x_p',x_j\right)=e^{-ik\frac{x_p'x_j}{d}}, \tag{6}$$

$$V\left(y_q',y_j\right)=e^{-ik\frac{y_q'y_j}{d}}. \tag{7}$$

C-LUT can cut down the offline storage to one slice so that make it possible to generate a much larger hologram with less memory. It also costs much less time to load the off-line files. The same as S-LUT, its inline process also has two steps:

$$H_s\left(x_p'\right)=\sum\nolimits_{j=0}^{p_n}a_j*H\left(x_p',x_j\right), \tag{8}$$

$$I\left(x_p',y_q'\right)=\sum\nolimits_{j_z=0}^{n_z-1}\{V\left(y_q',y_j\right)\times H_s\left(x_p'\right)\}*L(z',z_{j_z}), \tag{9}$$

where n_z represents the number of slices on z-axis.

3 The Method to Optimize Hologram Computation Process

3.1 The Dynamic Parallelism Technology

For the high performance computing cluster of multi-GPU, CUDA is a general parallel computing architecture which can implement the complex computation job with proper time consumption. It is so appropriate to support the highly parallel structure of LUT algorithm. The newest version of CUDA provides a characteristic called dynamic parallelism which can accommodate the size of blocks and threads in terms of the computation complexity. This new property makes the nested programming much simpler than before and can accelerate the LUT method to some extent. It has been used extensively in many other fields. This technique allows GPU to make a judgment of the results of the computation directly without transferring the data back to CPU. Based on this new characteristic, it can reduce the time spent on the data communication between GPU and CPU. Computing process with this mechanism is shown in Fig. 1.

In our method, we allocate the blocks and threads as the Fig. 1 shown above and realize S-LUT and C-LUT algorithm in this way. It divides the whole hologram into pieces and adjusts the calculation work to the current computing resources optionally. The advantages of dynamic parallelism are that this method can reduce the complexity of nested program and covert it to be more controllable. We can change the size of each sub-hologram nearly without modifying the code. In order to take advantage of

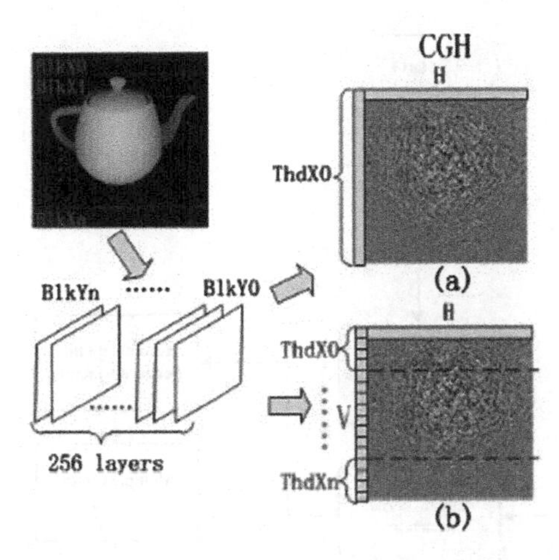

Fig. 1. Computation Diagram of hologram based on dynamic parallelism.

dynamic parallelism mechanism of CUDA, we consider the light intensity information of each object point as a 1 × 1 matrix and multiply it with its H vector of modulation factor. Therefore, the accumulation of H light modulation factor in the same row of the object can be computed as a kind of matrix manipulation. With the change of accumulation, we can use the dynamic parallelism to split the H factor into many segments and then sum up each part together concurrently. It does finish a job to accelerate accumulation procedure. The inline process flowchart is shown in Fig. 2. File mapping and dynamic parallelism technique play the role as host and device respectively. Device is responsible for the implementation of S-LUT and C-LUT. The complex data we process consists of two single-precision data format.

For the computation of hologram with the size larger than 16384 * 16384 based on S-LUT algorithm, offline tables are much too large for the limited video memory on multi-GPU cluster that the offline tables have to be loaded for many times. This kind of data manipulation wastes some extra resources, which can be avoided by increasing video memory. The results are shown in Fig. 3.

In Ref. [9], the author generated a hologram computed by about 10 k object points at 1027 * 768 resolutions, which spent 500 ms. With these methods, it can generate a hologram with the same object points and the size of 1920 * 1080 in approximately 250 ms. The granularity level of blocks and threads also affect the speed of calculation in our experiment. We divide the part of hologram computed in a GPU into smaller sub-holograms, which means making the parallel computation have a finer level of granularity. It can reduce the processing time consumption to some extent.

3.2 The File Memory Mapping Technology

As we have mentioned above, the LUT Algorithm trades the storage spaces for the inline run time overhead, so we have to save the whole offline tables in memory before start computing inline. It costs us huge amounts of time when we use the file stream

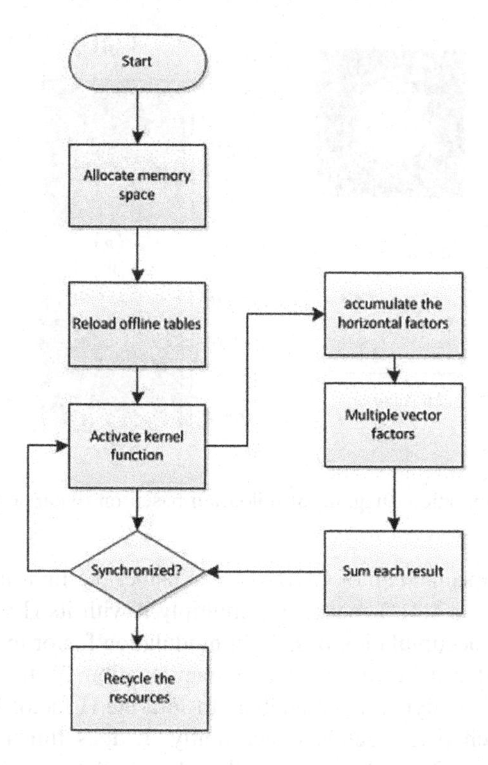

Fig. 2. Inline process flowchart.

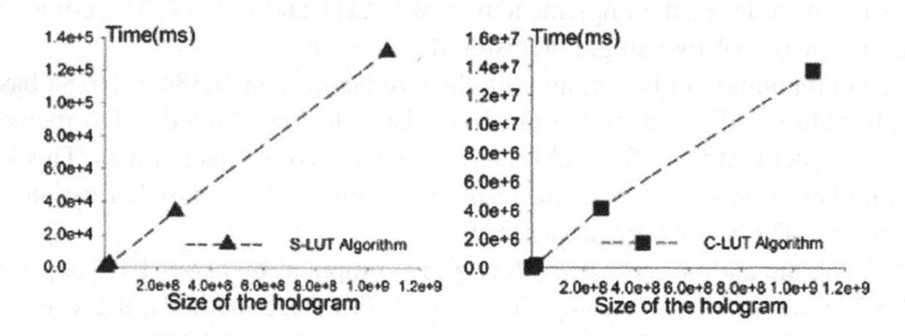

Fig. 3. Time consumption of S-LUT and C-LUT algorithms.

functions to load the offline tables of a large hologram. Both of the file inputting and outputting are very time-consuming. Memory mapping file technique is under the control of operation system, which is a memory management method in CPU. Operation system grants the permission to application so that it can access to the files in disk through a memory pointer. In other words, this technique build the connection between the whole or part of the offline tables in hard-drive and the fixed area of the virtual address space of the process. In this way, we can avoid both the file stream I/O operation and file buffer, and access a file directly. It is especially efficient to complete the loading job for processing some huge size files. We describe the process of writing and reading offline tables as a graphic example in Fig. 4.

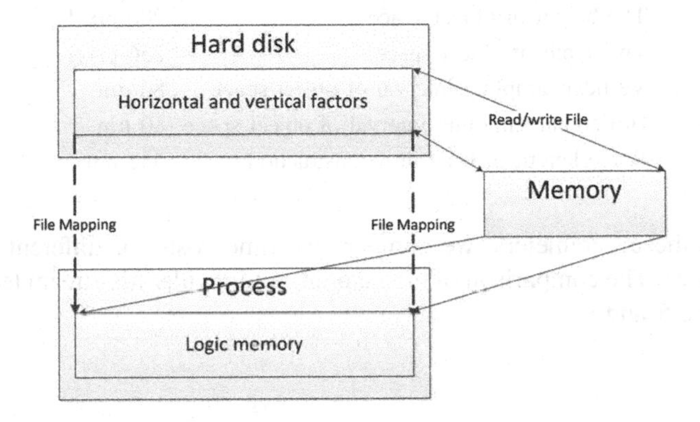

Fig. 4. Illustration of file mapping technology

As it shows in Fig. 4, firstly, we build a mapping between the logic memory and hard disk before we try to input or output the light modulation factor H and V offline tables in the disk. The virtual logic address represented by the file pointer is one-to-one mapping for the physical address now. Secondly, because there is no related data in logic memory, the operation system will trigger a page fault interrupt to call for the offline holographic data, when the program want to get the data of offline table files. Thirdly, these data are loaded into memory and then obtained by the process. This file reading and writing mechanism avoids the regular buffer copies, so we can retrieve the data at one time rather than twice process the offline table data in this way, which means it can support the multi-process programming suitably.

Our experiments are accomplished by a computer with specifications as Table 1. Our program is running on a cluster consisted of CPUs and GPUs. Parameters we used are listed in Table 2.

Table 1. Specifications of PC

Item	Model	Details
CPU	Intel Xeon E5-2670	8 cores 2.6 GHz
GPU	Tesla K20Xm	2 GB memory each one
Memory	DDR3	666.5 MHz, 192 GB
OS	Windows 7	64 bit with SP1
IDE	Visual Studio 2010	32 bit
GPU API	NVIDIA	CUDA v5.5

Table 2. Parameters of CGH computation

Item	Value
The width of object space	200 pixel
The height of object space	200 pixel
The depth of object space	256 pixel
Vertical sampling interval of object space	80 μm
Horizontal sampling interval of object space	80 μm
Wave length of laser in reconstruction	532 nm

Based on these parameters, we compare the time costs for different offline table processing cases. The comparison of file mapping and regular file stream techniques are shown in Figs. 5 and 6.

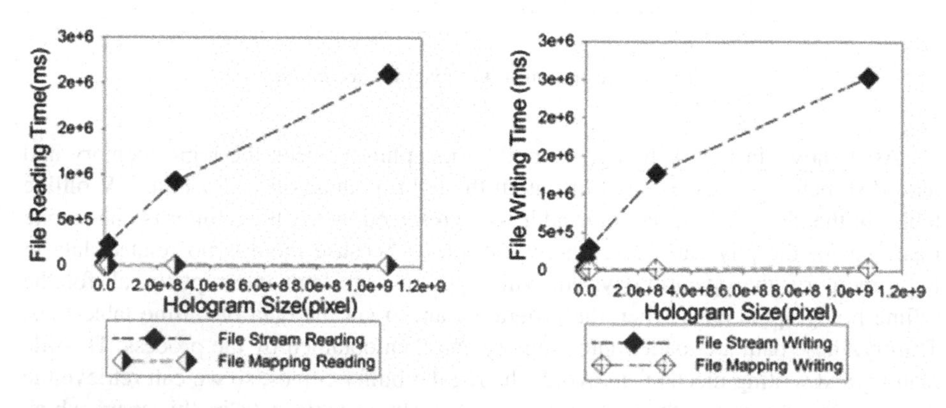

Fig. 5. The cost time comparison of reading file process and writing file on S-LUT Algorithm.

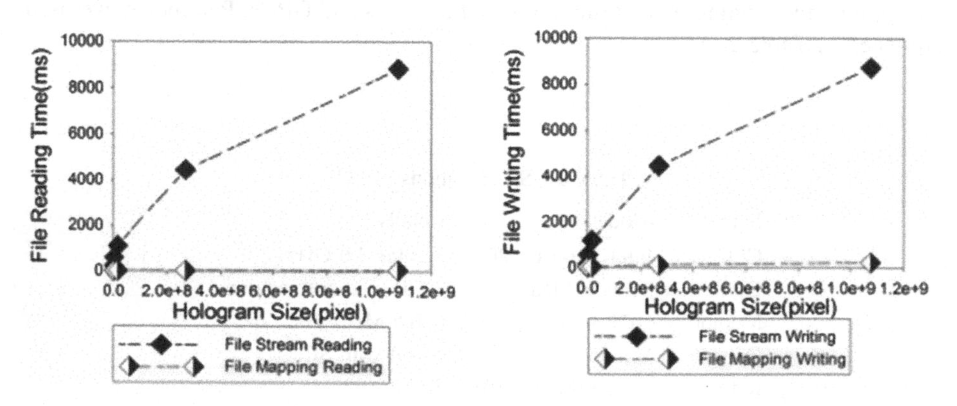

Fig. 6. The cost time comparison of reading file process and writing file on C-LUT Algorithm

Moreover, it shows that file mapping technique can reduce the time costs when we read or write data of offline tables from disk to the memory. We can compare the relationship of hologram size and file loading time consumption through those figures. File mapping technique can keep relatively gentle with the increasing of the size of hologram and slow time expenditure. For different cases, the file processing time consumptions of S-LUT are 40 ~ 250 times than C-LUT because of the different size of processing data size. The average time of writing offline holographic data for file stream method on S-LUT case is about 14 min, which is nearly 56 times than file mapping method. For the reading case of S-LUT, cost time of file stream is 11 min in average. In the method, the average cost time of file mapping is less than 4 s.

3.3 Our Experiments

We realize the numerical and experimental reconstructions of holographic simulation. The CGHs with 1920 * 1080 resolution are also generated by different algorithms. The simulations and experiments are shown in Fig. 7.

Fig. 7. Origin 3D scene and reconstructed 3D objects with different focuses.

Our program is flexible for different sizes by the way, which is able to generate huge size CGH with less quality loss. The method can generate 1 gigabyte hologram with more than 10^7 object points in a suitable time. It costs about 120 s. We also use the occlusion processing method in our generation process, which can speed up the calculation. The calculation precision and speed are in good agreement with the theoretical predictions. Furthermore, dynamic parallelism technique reduces the code complexity, which shorts the length of code and makes the program much easy to be understood.

4 Conclusion

In conclusion, we proposed two methods to speed up the generation process of CGH by high performance cluster based on multi-GPU and CPU. Dynamic parallelism is benefit for a simpler programming and easier management of thread granularity than regular programming method. Besides, it can also reduce the inline time consumption of both two holographic simulation algorithms. File mapping technique saves more than 100 times of handling data than file I/O stream method in average. The method can compute huge data up to 10^{16} totally now, which is a useful reference to implement the real-time 3D holographic simulation and virtual reality in the future. Recently, part of the information of huge size hologram can be used to reconstruct the object with a higher quality by a new encoding method [20, 21]. It is meaningful to generate such a huge hologram. Besides, these methods could also be applied to the big data processing for various applications, such as 3D real-time simulation, cloud computation and soon.

References

1. Hao, Q.-Y., Mao-Bin, H., Cheng, X.-Q., Song, W.-G., Jiang, R., Qing-Song, W.: Pedestrian flow in a lattice gas model with parallel update. Phys. Rev. E **82**(2), 2365–2376 (2010)
2. Zhang, H., Xie, J., Liu, J., et al.: Elimination of a zero-order beam induced by a pixelated spatial light modulator for holographic projection. Appl. Opt. **48**(30), 5834–5841 (2009)
3. Zhang, H., Tan, Q., Jin, G.: Holographic display system of a three-dimensional image with distortion-free magnification and zero-order elimination. Opt. Eng. **51**, 075801 (2012)
4. Zhang, H., Collings, N., Chen, J., et al.: Full parallax three-dimensional display with occlusion effect using computer generated hologram. Opt. Eng. **50**(7), 074003-1–074003-5 (2011)
5. Jia, J., Wang, Y., Liu, J. et al.: 3D holographic display with enlarged image using a concave reflecting mirror. In: Proceedings of SPIE, vol 8557: 85570B_1–5 (2012)
6. Ichihashi, Y., Oi, R., Senoh, T., Yamamoto, K., Kurita, T.: Real-time capture and reconstruction systemwith multiple GPUs for a 3D live scene by ageneration from 4 K IP images to 8 K holograms. Opt. Express **20**(19), 21645–24655 (2012)
7. Stein, A.D., Wang Jr., Z., Leigh, J.S.: Computer-generated holograms: a simplified ray-tracing approach. Comput. Phys. **6**, 389 (1992)
8. Lucente, M.: Interactive computation of holograms using a look-up table. J. Electr. Imag. **2**, 28–34 (1993)
9. Pan, Y., Xu, X., Solanki, S., et al.: Fast CGH computation using S-LUT on GPU. Opt. Express **17**(21), 18543–18555 (2009)
10. Jia, J., Wang, Y., Liu, J., Li, X., et al.: Reducing the memory usage for effective computer-generated hologram calculation using compressed look-up table in full-color holographic display. Appl. Opt. **52**(7), 1404–1412 (2013)
11. Zhang, Y., Wang, P., Chen, H., et al.: Computer-generated-hologram-accelerated computing method based on mixed programming. Chin. Opt. Lett. **12**(3), 030902-1–030902-4 (2014)
12. Jia, J., Wang, Y., Liu, J., et al.: Progress of dynamic 3D display of the computer-generated hologram. Laser & Optoelectronics Progress **49**(5), 050002 (2012)
13. Shimobaba, T., Ito, T., Masuda, N., et al.: Fast calculation of computer-generated-hologram on AMD HD5000 series GPU and OpenCL. Opt. Express **18**(10), 9955–9960 (2010)
14. Ahrenberg, L., Benzie, P., Magnor, M., et al.: Computer generated holography using parallel commodity graphics hardware. Opt. Express **14**(17), 7636–7641 (2006)
15. Pan, Y., Xu, X., Liang, X.: Fast distributed large-pixel-count hologram computation using a GPU cluster. Appl. Opt. **52**(26), 6562–6571 (2013)
16. Jackin, B.J., Miyata, H., Ohkawa, T., et al.: Distributed calculation method for large pixel-number holograms by decomposition of object and hologram planes. Opt. Letters **39** (24), 6867–6870 (2014)

17. Merrill, D., Grimshaw, A.: High performance and scalable radix sorting: a case study of implementing dynamic parallelism for GPU computing. Parallel Process Lett. **21**(2), 245–272 (2011)
18. Dong, J., Wang, F., Yuan, B.: Accelerating BIRCH for clustering large scale streaming data using CUDA dynamic parallelism. In: Yin, H., Tang, K., Gao, Y., Klawonn, F., Lee, M., Weise, T., Li, B., Yao, X. (eds.) IDEAL 2013. LNCS, vol. 8206, pp. 409–416. Springer, Heidelberg (2013)
19. Wang, J., Yalamanchili, S.: Characterization and analysis of dynamic parallelism in unstructured GPU applications. In: Proceedings of the 2014 IEEE International Symposium on Work-load Characterization (2014)
20. Sun, Z.: Application of File Mapping in the Real-time Historical Database of DCS. Comput. Knowl. Technol. **9**(19), 4363–4366 (2013)
21. Zheng, G., Muhlenbernd, H., Kenney, M., Li, G., Zentgraf, T., Zhang, S.: Metasurface holograms reaching 80 % efficiency. Nat. Nanotechnol. **10**, 308–312 (2015)

User Attributes Clustering-Based Collaborative Filtering Recommendation Algorithm and Its Parallelization on Spark

Zhongjie Wang[(✉)], Nana Yu, and Jiaxian Wang

Department of Control Science and Engineering, Tongji University, Shanghai 201804, China
wang_zhongjie@tongji.edu.cn

Abstract. Personalized recommendation system is an important means for people to get interested information and product quickly. This traditional user-based collaborative filtering algorithm cost too much computation on similarity calculation. In order to solve this problem, a new collaborative filtering recommendation algorithm based on K-Means clustering of user's attributes is proposed. In this algorithm, the longitude and latitude of users' are first clustered, and then the similarity of users' are calculated within each cluster. Finally, parallelization of this proposed algorithm on Spark is implemented. Experiments show that the user attributes-based collaborative filtering has satisfied performance.

Keywords: Collaborative filtering recommendation · User attribute · Clustering · Spark · Parallelization

1 Introduction

With the rapid growth of E-commerce, the amount and kinds of products also increase rapidly. Customers will cost a lot of time to find certain product they are interested in. In this case, customer loss may happen due to too much browsing on irrelevant information and production. The purpose of personalized recommendation system is to recommend particular information and products to customers according to their historical data, e.g. interest, shopping history etc.

User-based Collaborative filtering (CF) recommendation algorithm is based on the target user's history ratings by calculating the similarity among users to find the users with high similarity (namely N-nearest neighbors). Then, the recommendation system will predict the ratings about target users of the unused items based on the N-nearest neighbors' rating records. The specific principle is shown in Fig. 1.

If user1 is interested in item A and C, user2 is interested in item B, user3 is interested in item A, C and D, then from these historical evaluation information, we find user1 and user3 have similar evaluation, and user3 also has evaluation on item D, then we can predict that user1 may also be interested in item D. Therefore, the item D will be recommended to user1.

L. Zhang et al. (Eds.): AsiaSim 2016/SCS AutumnSim 2016, Part I, CCIS 643, pp. 442–451, 2016.
DOI: 10.1007/978-981-10-2663-8_46

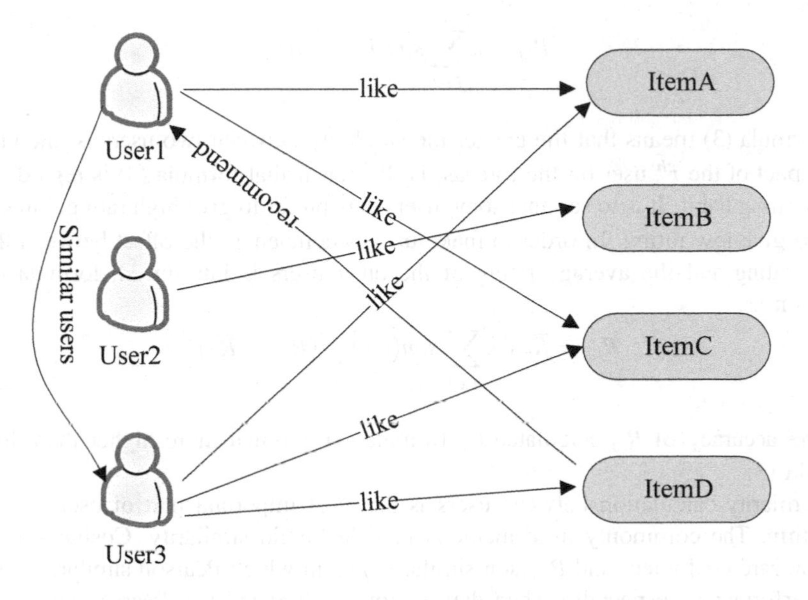

Fig. 1. User-based collaborative filtering recommendation

Supposed m users' ratings on n items is a matrix model,

$$R = \begin{pmatrix} R_{11} & R_{12} & R_{13} & \cdots & R_{1n} \\ R_{21} & R_{22} & R_{23} & \cdots & R_{2n} \\ R_{31} & R_{32} & R_{33} & \cdots & R_{3n} \\ \vdots & \vdots & \vdots & & \vdots \\ R_{m1} & R_{m2} & R_{m2} & \cdots & R_{mn} \end{pmatrix} \quad (1)$$

where, if a user has no rating on some item, then its default value is 0. Typically, the prediction formula of user i for item j is represented by,

$$R_{i,j} = \underset{i' \in I}{aggr}\, R_{i',j} \quad (2)$$

In formula (2), I indicates a user group, these users own high similarity to user i and they all have the ratings on item j. $\boldsymbol{aggr}(\cdot)$ is the prediction function of $R_{i,j}$. Three methods are usually used to calculate $R_{i,j}$. The easiest way employs the average value of all the users' rating in set I to predict $R_{i,j}$, i.e. $R_{i,j} = \sum_{i' \in I} R_{i',j} \Big/ N$. However, the mostly used way is to employ weighted average approach to calculate $R_{i,j}$. For example,

$$R_{i,j} = k\sum_{i' \in I} sim(i, i') \times R_{i',j} \tag{3}$$

Formula (3) means that the greater the similarity between two users is, the greater the impact of the ith user on the forecast is. It is clear that formula (3) is regardless of user's rating habit. It is to say that some users may prefer to give high rating, but others tend to give low rating. In order to make up this deficiency, the offset between the ith user's rating and the average rating of the other users is introduced, formula (3) is rewritten as,

$$R_{i,j} = \overline{R_i} + k\sum_{i' \in I} sim(i, i') \times (R_{i',j} - \overline{R_{i'}}) \tag{4}$$

The accuracy of $R_{i,j}$ calculated by formula (4) is much more higher than that by formula (3).

Similarity calculation between users is the most important part of user-based CF algorithm. The commonly used methods include Euclid similarity, Cosine similarity and, Jaccard coefficient and Pearson similarity [1], in which Pearson similarity has the best performance, especially when data is not standardized [2]. Pearson similarity is calculated as followed,

$$sim(x, y) = \frac{\sum_{i \in I_{xy}} (R_{x,i} - \bar{R_x})(R_{y,i} - \bar{R_y})}{\sqrt{\sum_{i \in I_{xy}} (R_{x,i} - \bar{R_x})^2}\sqrt{\sum_{i \in I_{xy}} (R_{y,i} - \bar{R_y})^2}} \tag{5}$$

After calculating similarity between users, the next step is to select the top N users as the nearest neighbors. It is much more important to select the value of N. Too small N may result in inaccurate recommendation. However, too large N will increase the computational complexity. According to Pearson similarity, the value of N can be selected by,

$$T(x) = \{y | y \in Top - N(x), sim(x, y) > 0,\ x \neq y\} \tag{6}$$

$Top - N(x)$ is the nearest neighbors set of user x.

Finally, the rating of user x for items can be predicted by,

$$P(x, s) = \bar{R_x} + \frac{\sum_{y \in Top - N(x)} sim(x, y)(R_{y,s} - \bar{R_y})}{\sum_{y \in Top - N(x)} sim(x, y)} \tag{7}$$

2 Collaborative Filtering Recommendation Algorithm Based on User's Attributes

In practical application, the number of users is huge. If we calculate all the similarities between different users, computational complexity will increase greatly without doubt. Aiming this problem, we proposed a new collaborative filtering recommendation algorithm based on K-Means clustering of user's attributes.

2.1 Users' Attributes

In order to reduce computation complexity of the similarities between users, it is necessary to narrow the similarity calculation range. Our idea is to use users' own attribute information for this purpose. This is because that multiple attributes can well reflect a user's unique characteristic. Furthermore, for most of current recommendation systems, if new users appear, they are required to register first, the register information often contains the gender, age, height, address, occupation, and so on.

For example, in the online shopping, female users are always interested in cosmetics and women dress, while male users are interested in shaver and man dress. Therefore, the attribute information of users determines their needs and preference to some degree. This paper argues that similar attributes users have similar habits and interests. Thus, according to the attribute information of users, users may be classified into different clusters, each user cluster's preferences are basically the same, but different cluster has different preferences. If so, the similarity can be calculated in small clusters.

As for user attributes-based collaborative filtering recommendation, some research has been done. In literature [3], similarity is calculated first based on user's attributes and then clustering is carried out. This method involves similarity relationship between any two users, so it is difficult to determine the cluster center. In literature [4], different weight was set for each attribute and a comprehensive similarity is obtained finally, based on which the clustering is carried out. This method needs many experiments to determine the selected weight value. However, in this paper, clustering is be done directly based on the attribute values.

Supposed that there are m users, each user has q attributes, the users' attribute matrix can be expressed by,

$$Attr = \begin{pmatrix} Attr_{11} & Attr_{12} & \cdots & Attr_{1q} \\ Attr_{21} & Attr_{22} & \cdots & Attr_{2q} \\ \vdots & \vdots & & \vdots \\ Attr_{m1} & Attr_{m2} & \cdots & Attr_{mq} \end{pmatrix} \quad (8)$$

2.2 K-Means Clustering

K-means method is a typical clustering algorithm based on partition, which has been widely used in many fields [5, 6]. Supposed that there are M objects, the idea of

K-means clustering algorithm is to classify this M objects into K clusters, with similar objects in the same cluster, but the similarity in different clusters is very low. K-Means algorithm employs spatial distance among objects to measure the similarity. The smaller the distance is, the more similar the two objects is.

In this paper, longitude and latitude of a user is used to classify the users. Let $X = \{x_1, x_2, \cdots, x_m\}$ represent m users, x_i is a 2-D vector representing the longitude and latitude information of the ith user. The procedure of K-Means clustering algorithm is as follows.

(1) Set the number of clusters K, $K \leq m$, choose K objects as the initial centers of cluster $c_1, c_2, \cdots, c_K$.
(2) Calculate the distance between the ith cluster center and all the other objects, $d = (x_i - c_j)^2$.
(3) According to the minimum distance principle, put objects into some cluster. $C_i := \arg\min |x_i - c_j|^2$.
(4) Calculate the average of all the objects in each cluster as the new cluster centers.
(5) Determine whether the cluster center is converged or the maximum iteration number has reached. If not, the process returns to step (2). If yes, output the cluster results.

With the above steps, all the users will be divided into K different clusters. Each cluster has similar attributes. Next, recommendations can be given within the same cluster according to the historical ratings.

This improved user-based CF takes into account the user's own attributes. It can not only reduce the calculation complexity, but also solve the cold start problem of new user.

3 Parallelization of Collaborative Filtering Algorithm Based on Users' Attribute

The parallelization of collaborative filtering algorithm based on users' attribute is implemented on Spark, which includes two parts. One is to parallelize user attribute clustering; the other is to parallelization of Pearson similarity calculation.

3.1 Parallelization of User Attribute Clustering

Parallelization of K-Means algorithm on Spark is to divide a large clustering task into many sub-clustering tasks on data nodes to execute computation simultaneously. First, local clustering on the sub-dataset of each node, and then merge all the clustering result on each data node to constitute the global clustering result. The procedure of this part is shown in Fig. 2. The pseudo-code of K-Means clustering on Spark is shown in Table 1.

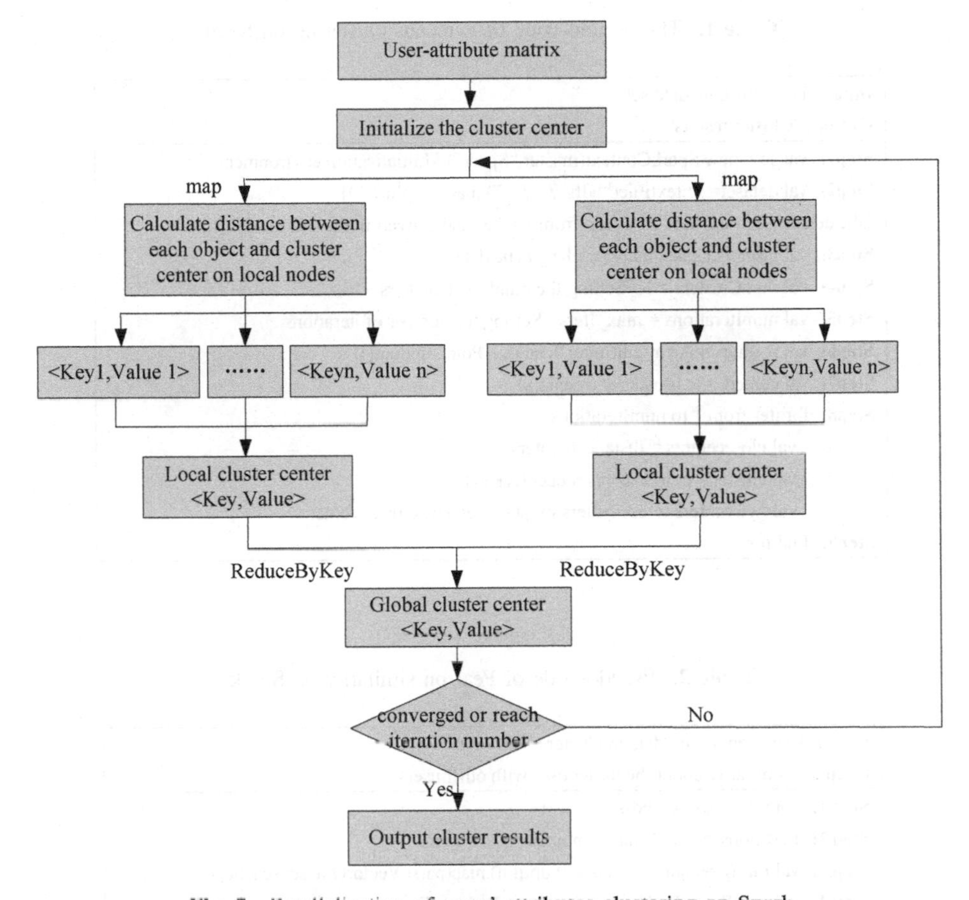

Fig. 2. Parallelization of users' attributes clustering on Spark

3.2 Parallelization of Pearson Similarity

Read rating data from HDFS, and convert it to RDD form. Without loss of generality, supposed that the target user for recommendation is in cluster 1. The pseudo-code of Pearson similarity on Spark is shown in Table 2.

During the parallelization of user attribute clustering and Pearson similarity, the data always exists in the form of RDD. We can choose to use map, groupByKey, filter API to operate RDD. Because RDD is stored in Spark memory, it only needs to read data from HDFS for one time. Therefore, it reduces the times of reading disk, which differs from Hadoop and MapReduce.

Table 1. The pseudo-code of K-means clustering on Spark

Input: User-attribute data set **Output:** Cluster results

Step1: val sc = new SparkContext(master,"Spark") //Initialization environment
Step2: val dataset= sc.textFile("hdfs://…/…").map.(_.split(" "))
//the default user-attribute data read from HDFS, and convert to the //form of RDD
Step3: val points=dataset.map().cache()//The data cache
Step4: val numClusters = K//Setting the number of clusters
Step5: val numIterations = max_Iters //Setting the number of iterations
Step6: val rcenters = Array.fill(numClusters) {Point.random()}
Step7: val centers =sc.broadcast (rcenters)
Step8: for iter from 1 to numIterations
val closecenters = distance(centers)
val clusters=points.map().recuceByKey()
val newcenters=closecenters.map() //Get new cluster center
Step9: End for

Table 2. Pseudo-code of Pearson similarity on Spark

Input: User-item rating data in cluster1 **Output:** Similarity about the target user with other users
Step 1: data=sc.textFile("hdfs://……") **Step 2:** Partitions = n//Setting the number of partitions **Step 3:** val rating = data.parallelize(0 until n).map(parseVectorOnUser).cache() **Step 4:** val numRatersPerUser=rating.groupBy(userID).map() **Step 5:** val ratingsWithSize=rating.groupBy(userID).join(numRatersPerUser) .flatMap() **Step 6:** val ratings= ratingsWithSize.keyBy(itemID) **Step 7:** val ratingParirs = ratingsWithSize.keyBy(itemID).join(ratings).filter() **Step 8:** val vectorCalcs= ratingParirs.map().groupByKey() **Step 9:** val similarity = scala.math.sqrt(sum()) **Step 10:** val topn = similarity.sortBy()

4 Experiments

Online public MovieLens [7] is employed to test the proposed algorithm. The dataset includes all users' rating information, the rating ranges from 0 to 5. MovieLens contains data with different sizes, e.g. 100 K, 1 M and 10 M. In this paper, we used the 1 M dataset for recommendation algorithm test. The 1 M dataset includes more than one million rating data that is 6040 users' mark on 3900 movies.

4.1 Performance Indices

As found in most literature, two performance indices are used to measure if a recommendation algorithm is satisfied, i.e. mean absolute error (MAE) and root mean square error (RMSE). These two indices are calculated as follows

$$MAE = \frac{\sum_{i,j} |R_{i,j} - \hat{R}_{i,j}|}{N} \tag{9}$$

$$RMSE = \sqrt{\frac{\sum_{i,j} (R_{i,j} - \hat{R}_{i,j})^2}{N}} \tag{10}$$

where, $R_{i,j}$ represents the actual rating value of user i for item j, $\hat{R}_{i,j}$ represents the predicted value. N represents the number of all the predicted values.

4.2 Influence of Algorithm Parameters on Recommendation Performances

The experiments in this part include two groups. One is to investigate the influence of cluster number K on performance indices, as shown in Fig. 3. The other is to investigate the influence of the target user's nearest neighbors number on performance indices, which is compared with the traditional user-based CF algorithm, as shown in Fig. 4.

In this paper, similarity is calculated after K Means clustering, so the clustering number K plays a crucial role in the whole process of recommendation. Bad clustering will affect the accuracy of similarity calculation seriously.

From Fig. 3, it can be seen that the accuracy of performance indices are similar when K less than 10, while the performance indices will get worse if K greater than 10. The reason is that when the clustering number is small, users with similar preference

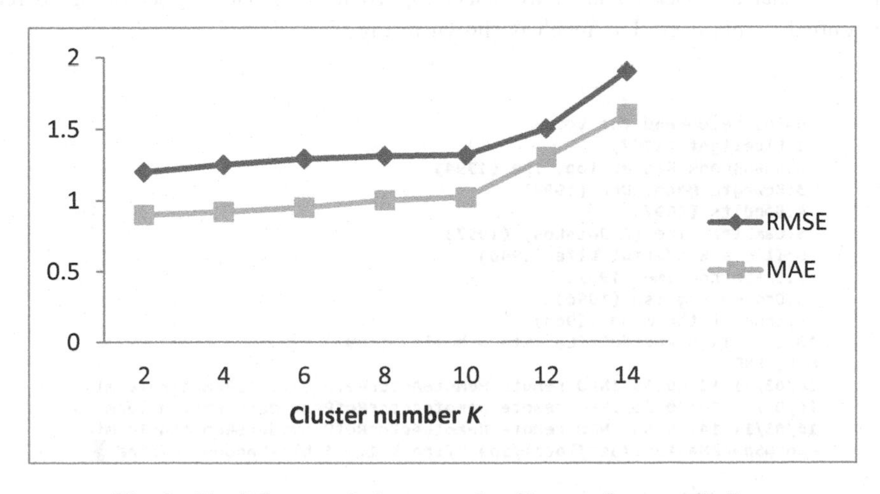

Fig. 3. The influence of cluster number K on performance indices

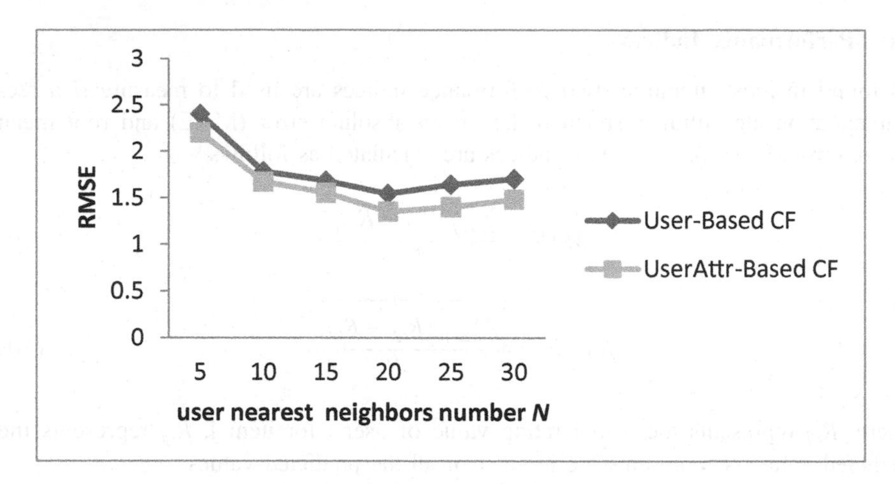

Fig. 4. Influence of user nearest neighbors number N on recommendation results

are divided into a cluster easily. But, if clustering number is large, users with higher similarity are more likely to be divided in different clusters, which will affect the choice of the nearest neighbors. However, if the clustering number is too small, the range of searching similar users will be very large and the calculation complexity will be bigger. Therefore, the best value of clustering number K is 10 in the experiments.

From Fig. 4, it showed that the improved CF algorithm outperforms the traditional user-Based CF. When N equals to 20, the RMSE of these two algorithms achieve the minimum. When N is small, not all the users with high similarity are taken into account, which will make the forecast inaccurate. However, large N will introduce dissimilar users into the algorithm, which may reduce the accuracy of prediction.

4.3 Recommendation Results

Supposed that the user ID is 1, we select top 10 movies with higher rating to recommended to this user. The result is shown in Fig. 5.

```
Movies recommend for you:
 1:Firelight (1997)
 2:Shawshank Redemption, The (1994)
 3:Bewegte Mann, Der (1994)
 4:Bandits (1997)
 5:Gambler, The (A J◆t◆kos) (1997)
 6:It's a Wonderful Life (1946)
 7:Smashing Time (1967)
 8:Broken English (1996)
 9:Inherit the Wind (1960)
10:Life Is Beautiful (La Vita ◆ bella) (1997)
HERE END
16/03/11 14:40:55 INFO remote.RemoteActorRefProvider$RemotingTermina
16/03/11 14:40:55 INFO remote.RemoteActorRefProvider$RemotingTermina
16/03/11 14:40:55 INFO remote.RemoteActorRefProvider$RemotingTermina
root@SparkMaster:/usr/local/spark/spark-1.2.0-bin-hadoop2.4/bin# █
```

Fig. 5. The top 10 movies recommended to #1 user

5 Conclusions

This paper investigated the user-based collaborative filtering recommendation algorithm. A new collaborative filtering recommendation algorithm based on K-Means clustering of user's attributes is proposed. In this algorithm, the longitude and latitude of users' are first clustered, and then the similarity of users' are calculated within each cluster. Finally, parallelization of this proposed algorithm on Spark is implemented. Experiments on Movielens show that the user attributes-based collaborative filtering algorithm outperforms the traditional used-based commendation algorithm.

References

1. Xiang, Z.: The research and implementation of parallel personalization recommendation algorithm for large-scale user behavior data. Beijing Jiaotong University (2012)
2. Ma, H., King, I., Lyu, M.R.: Effective missing data prediction for collaborative filtering. In: Proceedings of the 30th International ACM SIGIR Conference on Research and Development in Information Retrieval (SIGIR 2007), pp. 39–46 (2007)
3. Kui, H.: Research on collaborative recommendation system based on user clustering. Southwest Jiaotong University (2011)
4. Ba, Q., Li, X., Bai, Z.: Clustering collaborative filtering recommendation system based on SVD algorithm. In: Proceedings of the 4th IEEE International Conference on Software Engineering and Service Science (ICSESS), pp 963–967 (2013)
5. Tao, Z., Huiling, L.: The research progress of clustering algorithm in data mining. Comput. Eng. Appl. **48**(12), 100–111 (2012)
6. Bollmann, S., Hölzl, A., Heene, M., et al.: Evaluation of a new k-means approach for exploratory clustering of items (2015)
7. http://grouplens.org/datasets/movielens/

Simulation of Ground Clutter Based on GPU and RTX

Jun Xu[1], Duzheng Qing[1,3(✉)], Jing Ma[1,2], Han Zhang[1], and Zheng Mei[1]

[1] Science and Technology on Special System Simulation Laboratory,
Beijing Simulation Center, Beijing 100854, China
xujun711@sina.com, qing_dz@163.com, 13301067916@189.cn,
601550855@qq.com, xia_mei2000@163.com

[2] State Key Laboratory of Intelligent Manufacturing System Technology,
Beijing Institute of Electronic System Engineering, Beijing 100854, China

[3] Beijing Complex Product Advanced Manufacturing Engineering Research Center,
Beijing Simulation Center, Beijing 100854, China

Abstract. Clutter computation becomes a bottleneck of radar simulation. To solve this problem, a parallel simulation method for clutter computation is introduced based on GPU platform. Blocks in GPU compute the clutter of each scattering unit in parallel, and threads in each block parallel compute the clutter of each differential unit in scattering unit. Combined with the RTX real-time operating system, the system based on RTX and CUDA cooperative work is designed, which had been applied in hardware-in-the-loop simulation. The experimental result shows that the introduced method achieves a significant speedup of clutter computation in a relevant missile test of hardware-in-the-loop simulation, while ensuring the accuracy of the calculation.

Keywords: Clutter computation · GPU · RTX · Parallel computation

1 Introduction

Using the electromagnetic scattering characteristic to find and identify the target is the normal principle of radar operation process. Target exists or hides in the complex environment with interference, while the interference of electromagnetic scattering on radar target signal is called radar clutter. At present, there are three typical methods to establish the radar clutter model [7]: (1) The model which describes the probability density function of the backscattering coefficient; (2) Using the experimental data to regress the relationship between the backscattering coefficient and the radar equipment parameters, such as frequency, polarization, pitch angle and environmental parameters; (3) The theoretical model which describes the principle of clutter scattering unit. In general, the fluctuation statistical characteristics and spectral characteristics of clutter are more important, and the model which describes the probability density function of the backscattering coefficient is normally used to simulate the clutter.

To simulate radar clutter, there are three typical methods [7]: (1) Monte Carlo simulation of radar clutter. This method is based on statistical models according to theoretical method and measured data, such as the amplitude probability distribution model. The basic principle is non-memory nonlinear transformation or Spherically Invariant

L. Zhang et al. (Eds.): AsiaSim 2016/SCS AutumnSim 2016, Part I, CCIS 643, pp. 452–459, 2016.
DOI: 10.1007/978-981-10-2663-8_47

Random Process. (2) Based on the theoretical model of electromagnetic scattering, the computer numerical simulation method with various environmental and radar operating parameters; (3) Considering the specific radar environment and radar parameters, the clutter simulation method based on the radar equation. The method is applied to radar function simulation and radar signal simulator.

Clutter is an integral part of complex environment simulation. In each step of simulation process, within the range of radiation, radar needs to receive the information of entities having reflective properties to calculate the clutter, such as target locations. Because of the large range of radiation, a large number of ground grids are involved in the clutter computation. When the operational entities of the battlefield (such as radars, missiles, aircrafts and so on) increase, the calculation of clutter in the simulation system will be surged. With technology improvement, the radar detection resolution has significantly increased. However, the current clutter modeling and simulation method could not fit for the requirement of parameter accuracy and computing efficiency. The time consuming of clutter computation becomes a bottleneck of simulation system. To solve this problem, this paper discusses how to reduce the time consuming of clutter computation.

2 Parallel Computation of Clutter

With high computing density, GPU is widely used to solve problems that can be expressed as data parallel computing. The method of clutter simulation divides the ground to independent units, which are intensive and parallel data. In order to solve the problem of clutter computing in radar simulation, the high-efficiency computer of CPU/GPU hybrid structure is utilized to improve performance, including reducing system communication, optimizing data storage and parallel computing.

In the actual simulation of clutter, the ground is divided to grids according to the resolution. The smaller of distance between grids, the higher accuracy of the computing result, while leading to the longer computing time consuming. Reflected from a point target echo, the clutter can be expressed as the following equation:

$$s_n(t) = A\exp\left\{j\pi k_r\left(t - \frac{2R}{c}\right)^2 + \varphi_0\right\}\exp\left\{-j\pi\frac{4R}{\lambda}\right\}\exp\left\{j\pi f_d\frac{4R}{c}\right\} \quad (1)$$

Where the first exponential term represents the delay transmission signal, the second exponential term represents the phase shift of propagation, and the third term represents the phase related to Doppler frequency. A is the amplitude of the echo signal, and R is the distance between the radar and the target.

Because of the limited resolution of radar, the total echo of radar can be regarded as the coherent combination of a large number of resolution units. The computation equation is as follows:

$$S_n(t) = \sum_i A_i \exp\left\{ j\pi k_r \left(t - \frac{2R_i}{c}\right)^2 + \varphi_0 \right\} \exp\left\{ -j\pi \frac{4R_i}{\lambda} \right\} \exp\left\{ j\pi f_{di} \frac{4R_i}{c} \right\} \quad (2)$$

Where the subscript i indicates the unit number, and the echo signal of each scattering unit is as Eq. (1) shows. The echo signal power of the scattering unit can be computed by the radar equation.

In order to divide the ground to scattering unit, the antenna gain, Doppler shift, distance, angle of incidence, and clutter reflectivity of each unit are approximately constants. Assuming the clutter is uniform, which means the backscatter signals from different scattering units are statistically independent, and there is no coherence in the space. Under this assumption, the computation of the clutter signal is simplified to the coherent superposition of the echo signal in each scattering unit, and the echo signal of each unit can be calculated in parallel. The ground is divided to scattering unit based on the distance ring, as shown in Fig. 1 below.

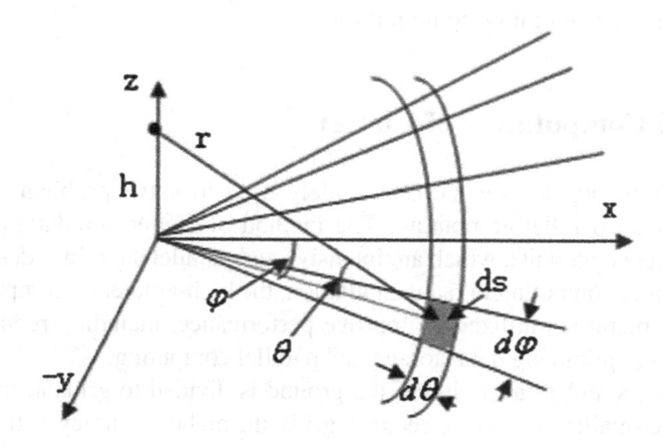

Fig. 1. Scattering unit division

In the CUDA architecture of GPU, the parallel process will be organized on two levels: the blocks in GPU and the threads in block, via shared memory and barrier synchronization. Thus the clutter of the same distance ring scattering unit corresponds to the block parallel computing, and the clutter of each differential unit in scattering unit corresponds to the thread parallel computing. The method of calculating process is shown below (Fig. 2).

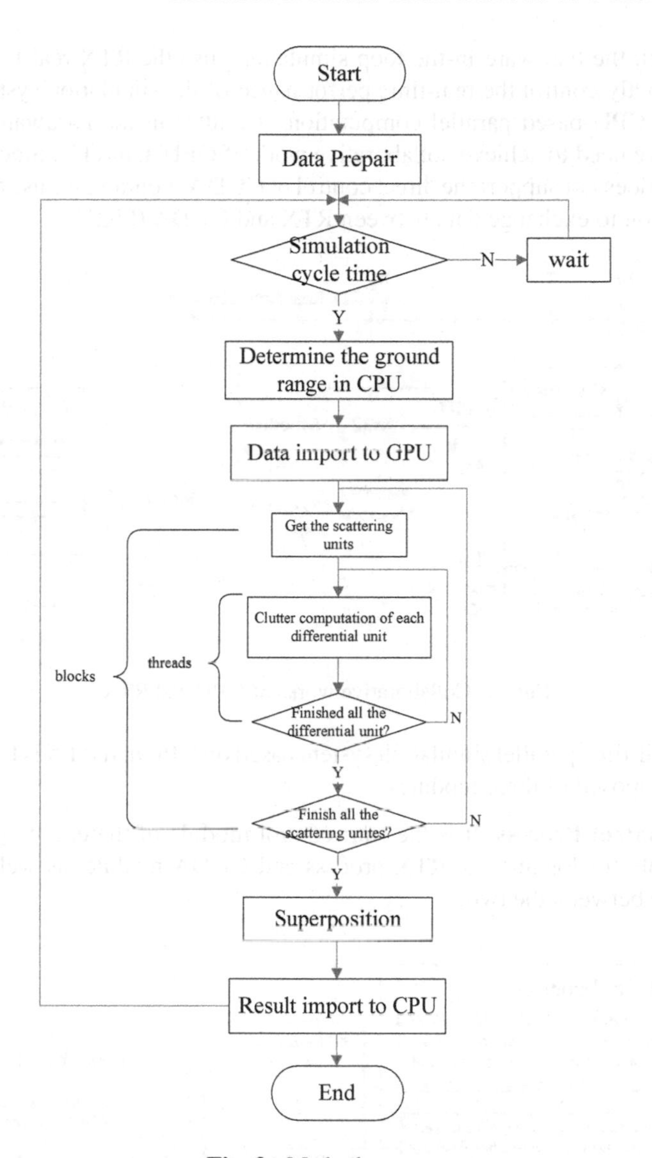

Fig. 2. Method process

3 Real-Time Simulation Based on GPU and RTX

In order to solve the requirements for real-time tasks, Interval Zero released the RTX real-time operating system. RTX-based applications can make use of the interface in Windows operating system, and Windows third-party development programming resources. These applications have excellent real-time scheduling. Therefore, RTX is widely used in military aerospace, fire control, ship, public transportation, medical, industrial automation and other fields.

At present, the hardware-in-the-loop simulations use the RTX real-time operating system to strictly control the real-time performance of the simulation system. In order to apply the GPU-based parallel computation of clutter in the hardware-in-the-loop simulation, we need to achieve collaborative work of GPU and RTX. Since the current RTX system does not support the direct control of CUDA program, we use the Windows communication to exchange data between RTX and CUDA (Fig. 3).

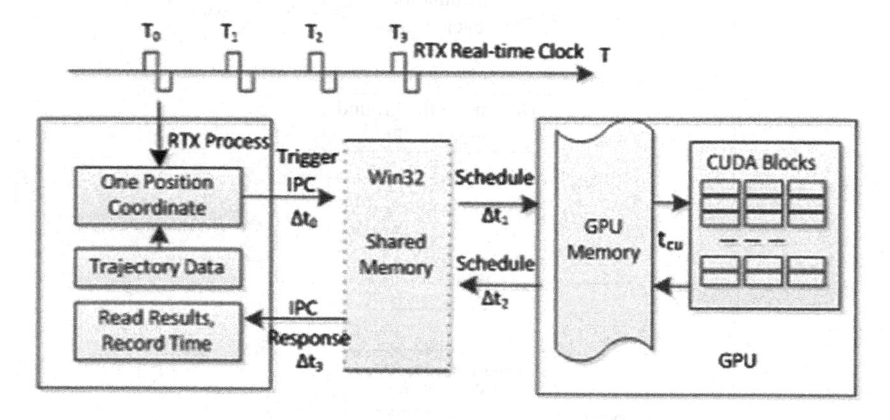

Fig. 3. Collaborative works of GPU and RTX

Thus a real-time parallel simulation system based on GPU and RTX is formed, which is mainly composed of three modules:

1. **Main Control Process**. It is the start control module of the entire system, and is responsible for loading the RTX process and CUDA module, as well as the data exchange between the two;

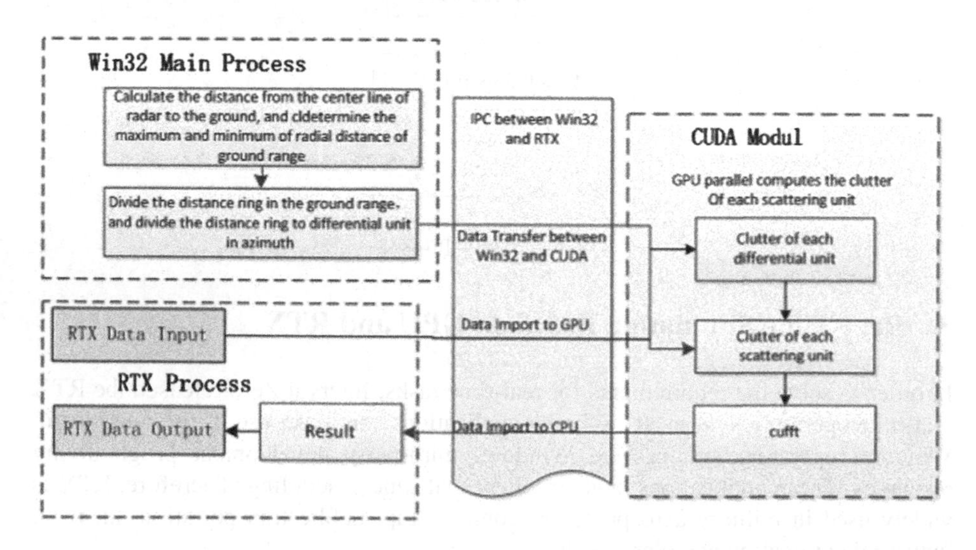

Fig. 4. Architecture of real-time parallel simulation system

2. **RTX Process**. It provides accurate control of the simulation process. In real time, the data of external equipment is transferred to the main control process, and the result of the calculation is transferred back;
3. **CUDA Module**. It is responsible for the parallel calculation of clutter, and the results will be returned to the shared memory of Windows (Fig. 4).

4 Experiment Results

We design software to compare the performance of GPU-Based method and CPU-Based method. The contrast tests are operated on the high performance computer with NVIDIA GeForce Titan. With a target position (7122.0, 0, 25.0) and speed (−300.0, 0, 0), missile position (7103.73, −0.434, 29.33) and speed (1245.59, 1.99, −108.17), RCS value 2.0 as input, comparison of the calculated results of GPU-Based and CPU-Based proves that the calculation result is reasonable after transplanting from CPU code to CUDA code (Fig. 5).

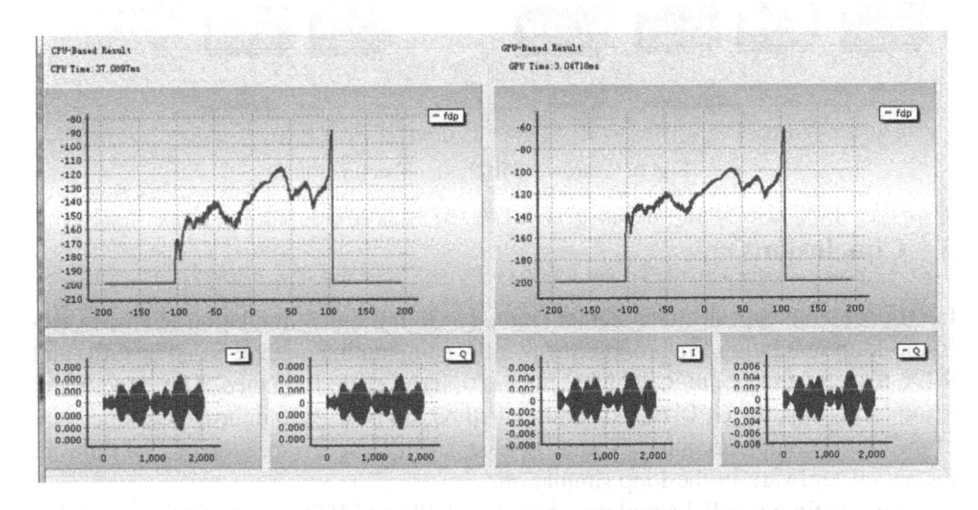

Fig. 5. Results of GPU-based method and CPU-based method

Through the analysis with multiple test (see Table 1), it comes to conclusion that when the clutter is computed with high accuracy (resolution 0.1°), GPU-Based computing speedup of 43.0 times, and when clutter is computed with low accuracy (resolution 1.0°), the GPU-Based computing speedup of 12.3 times with smaller computation.

Table 1. Time consuming of CPU-based method and GPU-based method

	Resolution	CPU-Based	CPU-Based	Speedup
1	1.00°	0.037 s	0.003 s	12.3
2	0.50°	0.146 s	0.005 s	29.2
3	0.25°	0.552 s	0.013 s	42.5
4	0.10°	2.921 s	0.068 s	43.0

Combined with the RTX real-time operation system, we developed a software system to apply the method to a relevant missile test of hardware-in-the-loop simulation. The development environment is Microsoft visual Studio 2010, RTX 7.0 and CUDA 6.5. The equipments of hardware-in-the-loop simulation are shown in Fig. 6. The high performance computer and the hardware-in-the-loop simulation system are connected by the optical fiber communication network.

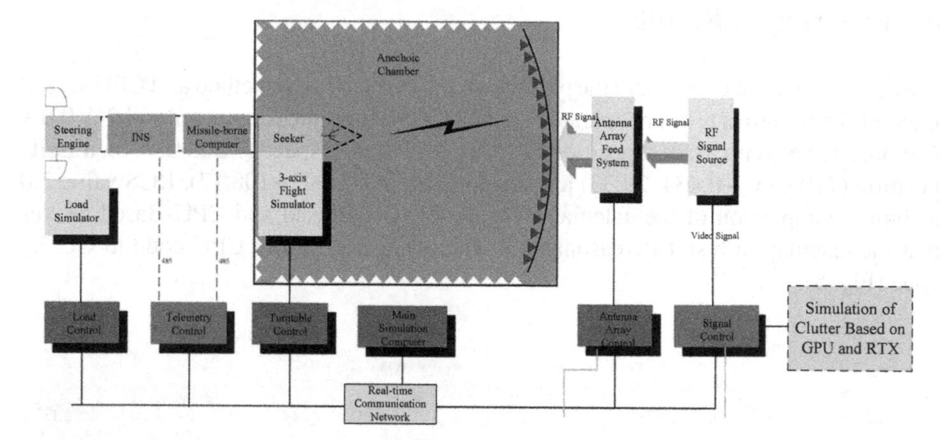

Fig. 6. Hardware-in-the-loop simulation

5 Conclusions

For the low efficiency of clutter computational in digital signal simulation and hardware-in-the-loop simulation, we propose the parallel computation method based on GPU and RTX to computing clutter, which achieves improved performance. The experiment results show that the GPU-Based parallel method can be used to improve the efficiency of the clutter computation by 10 times at least, and it can get a speedup of 29.4 times in the actual hardware-in-the-loop simulation.

The real-time parallel simulation based on GPU and RTX can be further extended to the field of weapon equipment demonstration, weapon system simulation, training simulation and so on, to achieve better real-time performance and scale expansion of the simulation system.

References

1. NVIDIA CUDA Compute Unified Device Architecture: Programming guide 2.0
2. Greco, M.S., Gini, F.: statictical analysis of high-resolution SAR ground clutter data. IEEE Trans. Geosci. Remote Sens. **3**(45), 1–14 (2007)
3. Xia, Y., Li, K., Li, X.: Accelerating geospatial analysis on GPUs using CUDA. J. Zhejiang Univ. Sci. C (Comput. Electron) **12**(2), 990–999 (2011)
4. Wang, Z.-G., Luo, Z.-T., Li, J., Sun, Y.: Clutter modeling of airborne MIMO radar based on CUDA. Fire Control Radar Technol. **12**(40), 35–39 (2011)

5. Hao, L., Zhang, Y.S., Li, Z., Xu, J.: Clutter modeling and characteristic analysis for airbborne MIMO radar. Electron. Opt. Control **2**(22), 46–50 (2015)
6. Yuan, B.-Z., Wang, L.-B., et al.: Modeling and analysis of clutter for space-air based biostatic radar. J. Signal Process. **5**(31), 611–620 (2015)
7. Zhang, J.: Computer Simulation of Radar Clutter. XiDian University (2013)
8. Shnidman, D.A.: Radar detection in clutter. IEEE Trans. Aerosp. Electron. Syst. **3**(41), 1056–1067 (2005)

M&S for Smart City

Modeling and Simulation of UHVDC Transmission Project Under Hierarchical Connection Mode to AC Grid

Jingbo Zhao[1], Zhenkai Zhou[2], Rong Fu[2(✉)], Ming Ni[3], and Jiankun Liu[1]

[1] State Grid Jiangsu Electric Power Research Institute, Nanjing 211103, Jiangsu Province, China
[2] College of Automation, Nanjing University of Posts and Telecommunications, Nanjing 210023, Jiangsu Province, China
furong@njupt.edu.cn
[3] NARI Technology Co. Ltd., Nanjing 211106, Jiangsu Province, China

Abstract. An ultra HVDC hierarchical connection mode was proposed by scholars in China to address the technical problems in multi-infeed HVDC system from the aspect of grid structure, but the control of UHVDC system with this kind of connection mode is not clear and needs to be further studied. In this paper, the control strategy of the system is discussed and designed. On this base, accurate models of AC system, converter transformer, AC/DC filter, converter, smoothing reactor and transmission line are built up in PSCAD/EMTDC software according to practical parameters based on Ximeng-Taizhou UHVDC transmission project which will use the new connection mode. The conclusion is that the control strategy designed for the AC-DC system in this paper is effective and simulation results of the model are in agreement with the actual operation characteristics. So the model can be used as a tool for further study.

Keywords: Hierarchical connection mode · UHVDC · DC control system · PSCAD/EMTDC

1 Introduction

Transient simulation of UHVDC transmission system plays an important role in power system research, planning, design and operation. In order to better reflect the interaction between AC and DC system, the time domain simulation method is adopted in the present study [1–4]. When the electromechanical transient simulation is carried out, the quasi steady state model is used to describe the converter. As a consequence, DC system is too simple to accurately represent the recovery progress after system fault, and even erroneous conclusions would be drawn. Therefore, it is necessary to describe the DC circuit and DC control system effectively and accurately in the simulation model when considering the fault of DC circuit and recovery characteristics of converter.

PSCAD/EMTDC software package is a kind of off-line power system electromagnetic transient simulation program, and the main function is to carry out the power

L. Zhang et al. (Eds.): AsiaSim 2016/SCS AutumnSim 2016, Part I, CCIS 643, pp. 463–474, 2016.
DOI: 10.1007/978-981-10-2663-8_48

system time domain and frequency domain simulation. The main function of EMTDC, a core program of PSCAD/EMTDC simulation, is electric power system transient analysis, which has developed into a kind of multi-functional tool that can be applied in the research of AC and DC power system. It also can complete the simulation of power electronic and nonlinear control. Beyond that, PSCAD/EMTDC software package has the accurate model of the DC components, convenient data input interface and powerful data analysis function, which has been widely used in the design of HVDC and FACTS controllers, power system harmonic analysis and the simulation calculation in the field of power electronics.

2 A New Connection Mode to AC Grid for UHVDC

With the development and widespread use of ultra high-voltage alternate current (UHVAC) and ultra high-voltage direct current (UHVDC) transmission technology in China, the multi-infeed HVDC system in load center of China will be the prominent problem in the development of China power grid. Because of the increasing capacity of DC transmission power and the intensive landing points of which are very rare in the world, the existing DC connection mode to AC grid will not be conducive to power flow evacuation and would bring a series of voltage support problems to receiving end power grid. For these reasons, LIU Zhenya and other scholars put forward a novel UHVDC hierarchical connection mode to address these technical problems in multi-infeed HVDC system from the aspect of grid structure, and also discuss the advantages of the connection mode in improving the voltage support ability of the receiving end power grid, and in leading power flow to be in a reasonable distribution between the 1000 kV layer and 500 kV layer [5]. This paper, taking ± 800 kV Ximeng-Taizhou UHVDC transmission project as background, designs a control strategy for hierarchical connection mode and builds its simulation model in software firstly. And then, start-up characteristic of the AC-DC system and its transient response under fault are simulated to validate the accuracy of the model. At last, some conclusions are got.

New construction planning of ± 800 kV Ximeng-Taizhou UHVDC transmission project will use hierarchical connection mode. In the project, DC power of 10000 MW will be evenly divided into two parts (each part is 5000 MW) by upper inverter valve and lower inverter valve in the inverter side, and then the power of two parts would be fed respectively into 1000 kV AC grid and 500 kV AC power grid through bipolar DC lines. The difference between UHVDC with traditional connection mode to AC grid and UHVDC with the hierarchical connection mode to AC grid lies in the inverter side of UHVDC system. The biggest feature is that two tandem inverter valves of inverter station are connected respectively to two different converter buses with different voltage levels.

The simplified model of UHVDC hierarchical connection mode is shown in Fig. 1. The AC system is equivalent to constant impedance and constant electromotive force using Thevenin's theorem. In Fig. 1, $E_i\angle\xi$ is equivalent electromotive force of AC system; $Z_i\angle\theta_i$ is equivalent impedance of AC system; $Z_{ij}\angle\theta_{ij}$ is coupling impedance of 500 kV layer and 1000 kV layer; $U_i\angle\delta_i$ is voltage of converter bus; B_{ci} is equivalent

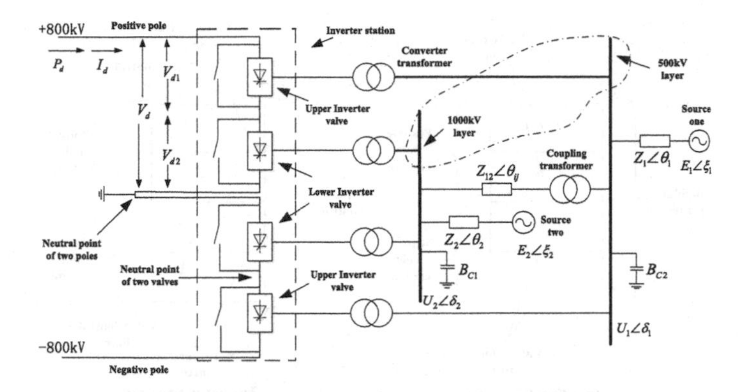

Fig. 1. Simplified model of UHVDC under hierarchical connection mode

admittance of AC filters and reactive compensation capacitors; $V_{\mathrm{d}i}$ is DC voltage of two ends on the inverter valve; P_{d} is DC transmission power and I_{d} is current of DC line; i, j = *1, 2,* and i$\neq$ j among variables mentioned above.

3 Control System Design for the New Connection Mode

3.1 Structure and Characteristics of the UHVDC Control System

Although the whole structures of DC control system of UHVDC under hierarchical connection mode is basically the same as that of traditional two-terminal UHVDC. There are some differences between the structures of the control system in inverter station, because the UHVDC system with new connection mode needs to be coordinated with two AC systems of different voltage levels [6]. The whole control system should have the following characteristics:

1. Upper rectifier value and lower rectifier value of the sending end are in a shared rectifier station and connected to the same 500 kV AC system, which is identical to common UHVDC system. So the control system of rectifier station can take the same structure and configuration as the common UHVDC system in the control layer of bipolar, pole and valve group.
2. Inverter side of the UHVDC under the new connection mode is still a structure of series-wound double 12 pulsation for each pole, therefore, structure and device configuration of different control layers in inverter side still can refer to the design of traditional UHVDC. So the general control system frame is divided into three layers shown in Fig. 2, which are bipolar control, pole control and valve control. On this account, both rectifier and inverter stations are respectively configured with a set of bipolar control device for one station, configured with two layer control devices for one pole and configured with four sets of independent valve control devices. Devices of different control layer, bipolar, pole and valve, can communicate each other through high speed control buses.

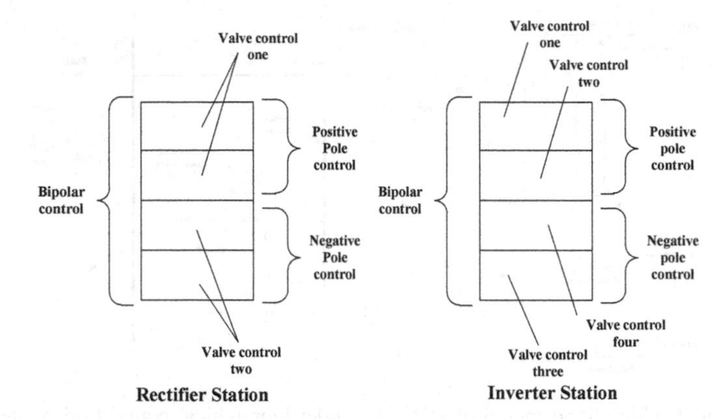

Fig. 2. Block structure of control system for rectifier and inverter station under hierarchical connection mode

3. Control strategy of inverter station under the new mode is roughly the same as that of common UHVDC system. The difference lies in that 500 kV layer control system and 1000 kV layer control system of the bipolar should respectively response to signals of voltage, frequency, tap of converter transformer, emergency control and co-ordination between AC and DC system and these signals should be coped with according to different system parameters and operating station. At the same time, 500 kV layer control system and 1000 kV layer control system need to be united and harmonized to accommodate control and operation of whole DC system. So it can be arrived that valve one and valve three generate trigger signals based on the information of 500 kV AC system and valve two and valve four generate trigger signals based on the information of 1000 kV AC system.

3.2 Design of the UHVDC Control System

Volt-Ampere Characteristic of UHVDC under Hierarchical Connection Mode. UHVDC under the hierarchical connection mode can be regarded as a series of three terminals DC transmission system. For one pole, two converter valves in the rectifier side can be seen as a rectifier station and two converter valves in the inverter side can be equivalent to two independent inverter stations. The characteristic of the system is that DC current through the converter stations and lines is the same, so it is advisable to use constant current operating mode. In order to ensure the UHVDC system has stable operating point, a converter station (rectifier station is chosen as normal) is selected to be responsible for maintaining DC current constant, and other converter stations are adjusted as the definite trigger or to keep extinction angle steady. This method of adjustment is relatively simple and total reactive power consumption of all converters is the lowest.

Figure 3 is the volt-ampere characteristic of normal operation of the UHVDC under the new connection mode. The Rectifier station is in constant current (CC) control mode and upper inverter valve and lower inverter valve of the inverter station are both in constant extinction angle (CEA) control mode. V_{dr}, the DC voltage of the rectifier station, is:

$$V_{dr} = V_{d1} + V_{d2} + \Delta V \tag{1}$$

Where ΔV is line total voltage drop.

When the rectifier station get into state of constant trigger angle due to voltage drop of converter bus in the sending end AC system or voltage rise of converter bus in the receiving end AC system, one of inverter valve (a inverter valve is preferred if AC system it connected to is relatively strong) will shoulder the responsibility of keeping DC current constant. But the DC current of operating should be reduced by ΔI_d. The value of ΔI_d can be the same as that of common UHVDC system, and there is no particularly stringent requirement about it. If the voltage is further decreased or further increased and the inverter valve chosen to control DC current reaches the limit of regulation, the role of holding current as set will be transmitted to the other inverter valve while the operating current should have a cut of another ΔI_d.

Apart from converter station adjusting DC current, other stations are able to realize the function of accommodation of active power by changing DC voltage of two ends

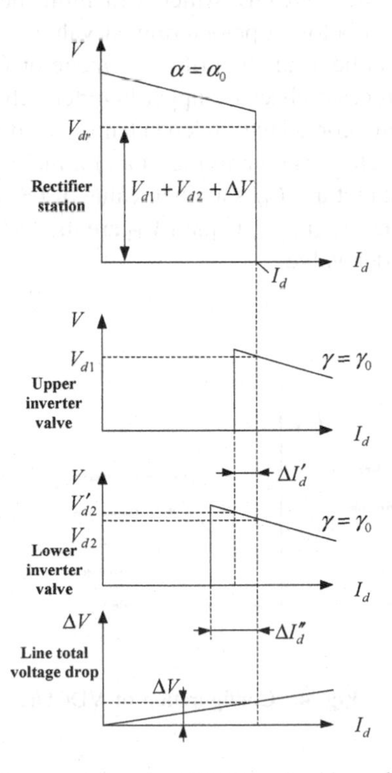

Fig. 3. Volt-Ampere characteristic of UHVDC under hierarchical connection mode

on station. When these stations operates at the set of trigger angle or the fixed extinction angle, the position of tap of converter transformer can be changed to regular the DC voltage. But the adjustment range is not wide and the speed is low. If wanted a large-scale adjustment range or rapid adjustment speed, these stations can be changed to operate in constant voltage (CV) mode, and the adjustment of power can be realized by changing the voltage setting value. In addition, operating current should be reduced for power loss of DC transmission lines when stations are all under light load state.

VDCOL (Voltage Dependent Current Order Limiter). It is impossible to maintain the rated DC current or rated power under low voltage condition. The reasons are as follows:

1. When voltage drop of a converter station is more than 30 %, reactive power demand of converter station which is far away from it will increase, which may have a negative effect on AC system these converter connected to. It is reason that the trigger angle of converters of the far end must be higher to control the DC current, thus casing the increase of consumption of reactive power. To make matters worse, the reduction of system voltage also significantly reduces the reactive power provided by filters and capacitors as most of the reactive power absorbed by the converter is given by compensation equipment mentioned above.
2. Inverter will face the risk of commutation failure and voltage instability when the voltage is reduced. Issues related to the operation of low voltage condition can be prevented by introducing VDCOL, which will limit the maximum allowable DC current if the voltage is below a predetermined value.
3. The VDCOL curve can be a function of AC voltage or DC voltage. It is needed to equip two VDCOL processes because upper inverter valve and lower inverter valve of inverter station are connected independently to different AC systems. The Configuration of VDCOL is shown in Fig. 4 and it includes two limit links and two minimum links. In the picture, I_{d0} is a given value of DC current; I_{ord} is value of the current instruction after judgment; $V_{\mathrm{d1}}$and V_{d2} are the DC voltages of upper inverter valve and lower inverter valve.

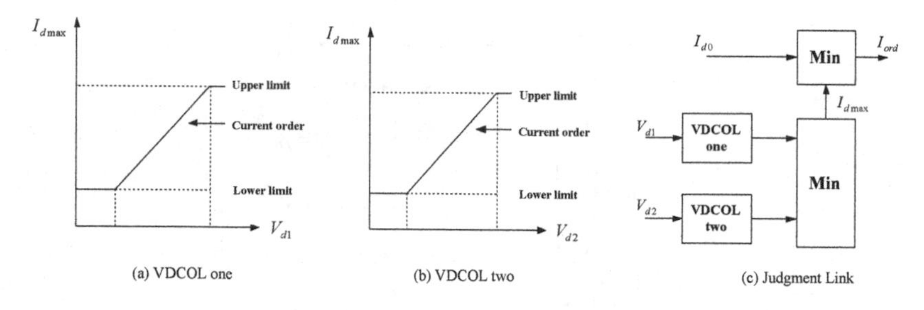

Fig. 4. Configuration of VDCOL

3.3 Basic Structure of DC Control System

In summary, the realization of UHVDC system control scheme is shown in Fig. 5. The input signals are DC voltages and extinction angles of upper and lower inverter valves, current of DC line and a given value of DC current; the output signals are trigger angle to rectifier station and advance firing angle to each inverter valve. *PI* control policy is used for the UHVDC system, and these functions can be achieved that are constant current (CC) control and constant firing angle (CFA) control for rectifier station and constant current (CC) control, constant firing angle (CFA) control and constant extinction angle (CEA) control for inverter station.

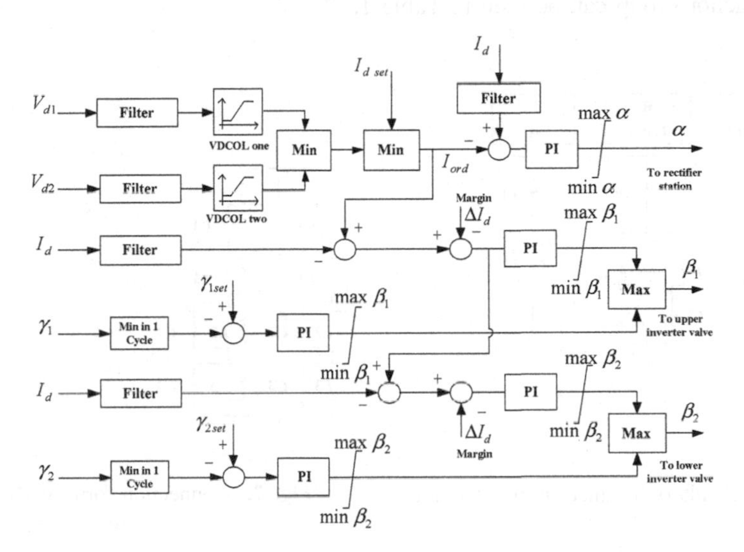

Fig. 5. The basic structure of DC control system

4 Configuration and Parameters

4.1 Configuration of Filters

AC Filters. Harmonic analysis and its suppression are one of the important technical problems in UHVDC transmission system. Due to the nonlinear characteristics of converter, harmonic voltage and harmonic current that appear in AC system and DC system will affect and harm the system itself and consumer equipment. Filter equipment are required in order to restrain harmonic, meanwhile, these equipment can provide reactive power needed by converter. The compensation capacity of reactive power is determined as follows:

1. Under the rated converter bus voltage and rated DC power, total reactive power AC filters and shunt capacitor group deliver is exactly balanced by that converter consumes.

2. The rated capacity of a single filter or capacitor group is determined by voltage step test. The voltage step caused by switching the single equipment should not be more than 5 % of rated voltage of converter bus.

Because of upper inverter valve and lower inverter valve of inverter station connecting to 500 kV converter bus and 1000 kV converter bus separately, AC filter equipment need to be respectively configured according to different voltage level. The connecting diagram of AC filters installed in inverter side is shown in Fig. 6. There are doubled turned filters removing the 12th and 24th characteristic harmonics and single tuned filters removing 3th characteristic harmonics. The specific parameters of these filters and capacitor group can be seen in Table 1.

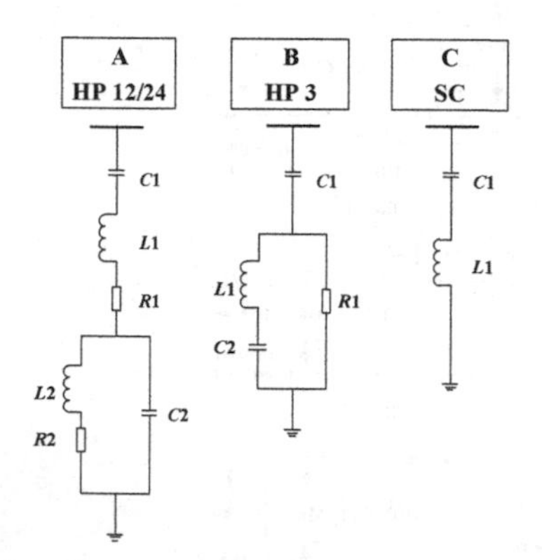

Fig. 6. AC filters installed in inverter side

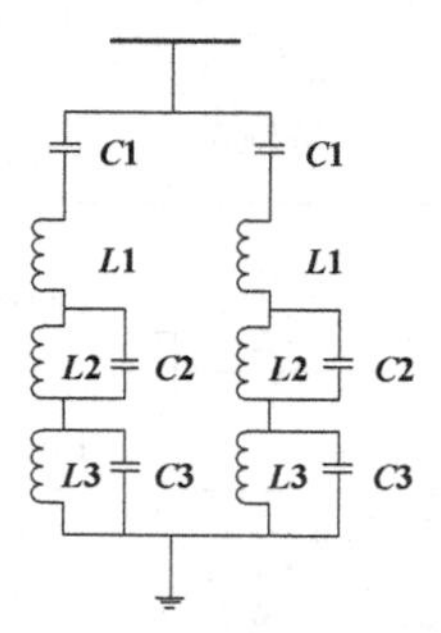

Fig. 7. Connection form of DC filter

DC Filters. In the DC side of the converter, the harmonic current is generated by the harmonic voltage. The amplitude of the harmonic current is determined by the delay angle, the extinction angle, the overlap angle and the impedance of the DC line. In the model, it is equipped with two sets of three tuned DC filters for per pole, and the filter of rectifier side is the same as that of inverter side. The connection form is shown in Fig. 7, of which parameters are that $C1 = 2.0\ \mu F$, $L1 = 11.773\ mH$, $C2 = 3.415\ \mu F$, $L2 = 10.266\ mH$, $C3 = 11.773\ \mu F$, and $L3 = 4.77\ mH$.

Smoothing Reactor. The value of inductance of smoothing reactor is determined by the following factors:

1. When inverter commutation failure occurs, peak value of DC current flowing through converter valve and the current rise rate are limited to a specified limit.
2. In the worst case, discharge current that flows through valve arrester is restricted under a specified limit.
3. Ensure stability of UHVDC transmission system.
4. Avoid resonance of DC line at fundamental frequency and second harmonic frequency.

Table 1. Parameters of AC filters in inverter side

Items	HP 12/24 (525 kV)	HP 3 (525 kV)	SC (525 kV)	HP 12/24 (1050 kV)	SC (1050 kV)
$C1/\mu F$	2.872	2.8841	2.4721	1.005	0.909
$L1/mH$	9.571	439.14	1.49	34.995	2
$C2/\mu F$	8.378	23.0728	–	2.011	–
$L2/mH$	5.375	–	–	17.499	–
$R1/\Omega$	300	1103.7	–	1500	–
$R2/\Omega$	1	–	–	1	–
Tuning frequency/Hz	600/1200	150	–	600/1200	–
Rated $Q/Mvar$	245	245	210	350	315
Number of sets	8	1	5	6	4

After considering criteria above, it is equipped with two sets of dry smoothing reactor of 75mH in pole-bus and neutral-bus in rectifier side and inverter side respectively for per pole.

4.2 Converter Valve

Valve group of rectifier side and inverter side of one pole consists of two series units of twelve-pulse bridge-type converter, which can be seen in Fig. 8. Each converter withstands one-half of rated DC voltage. The voltage distribution between thyristors is not uniform due to the different characteristic of the semiconductor components. So it is necessary to install a pressure equalization device to limit the degree of uniformity. In addition, because of the existence of the stray capacitance of the valve and the inductance of the circuit, oscillation caused by commutation needs to be refrained by setting damping device.

4.3 Converter Transformer

In simulation, converter transformers of inverters adopt three-phase double winding structure with connection of Y0/Y and Y0/Δ. Rated capacity of each transformer is 1500 MVA, leakage reactance is 0.18 p.u., rated voltages of AC side are 525 kV for upper inverter valve and 1050 kV for lower inverter valve, and rated voltage of DC side is 169 kV. The tap control of transformer connected to different converter buses is independent so as to regulate DC voltage of inverter valves independently.

4.4 DC Line

In the design of mechanical structure, there is no significant different between the DC overhead transmission line and the AC overhead line. In the electric field, there are

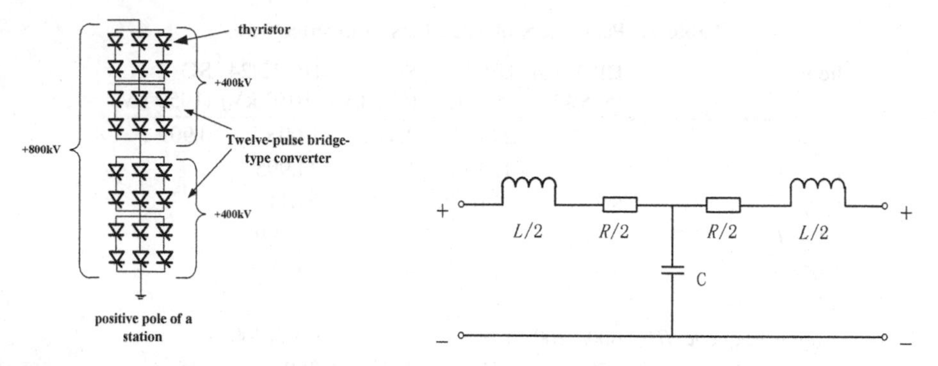

Fig. 8. Composition of converter valve group

Fig. 9. Model of DC line

some similarities between them. When high frequency response is not important, the DC line can be equivalent to circuit of type of T, as shown in Fig. 9. *R*, resistor of DC line, is 10.15 Ω. *L*, inductance of DC line, is 2200 *m*H. *C*, capacitance to earth, is 40 μF.

5 Simulation

5.1 Simulation of Start-up

In this paper, a simplified model of UHVDC under hierarchical connection mode to 500 kV/1000 kV grids as shown in Fig. 1 is built in PSCAD/EMTDC software. Rated operating DC voltage of the system is ± 800 kV and rated operating DC current is 6.25 kA. Steady-state voltage of sending end AC system is 525 kV, and short-circuit current is 44 kA. Steady-state voltages of receiving end AC system are respectively 1050 kA for 1000 kV AC grid with short-circuit current of 42 kA and 525 kV for 500 kV AC grid with short-circuit current of 48 kA.

Under the accordance with the structure and control strategy of the system mentioned above, the DC voltage soon reaches the rated value and the DC current also reaches the given value rapidly. Voltage of the neutral point between upper inverter valve and lower inverter valve is fluctuating in a reasonable range with the average value is about 400 kV. Power transmitted by the DC line is 5000 MW for one pole eventually. Related simulation curves are shown in Fig. 10.

5.2 Simulation of Transient Response of the UHVDC Under AC System Fault

The converter bus of 500 kV layer is arranged on the three-phase grounding fault, and the transition resistance is 20 Ω. The AC Fault occurs at 1 s, and its duration is 0.2 s. Figure 11-(a) is curve of DC voltage and Fig. 11-(b) are curves of DC current and its order value. It can be seen from the pictures that the DC current increases instantly and

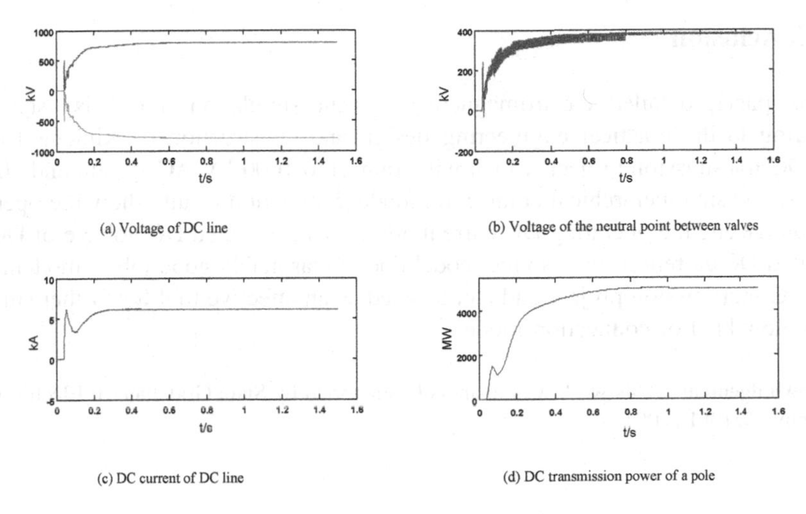

Fig. 10. Start-up characteristic of the UHVDC

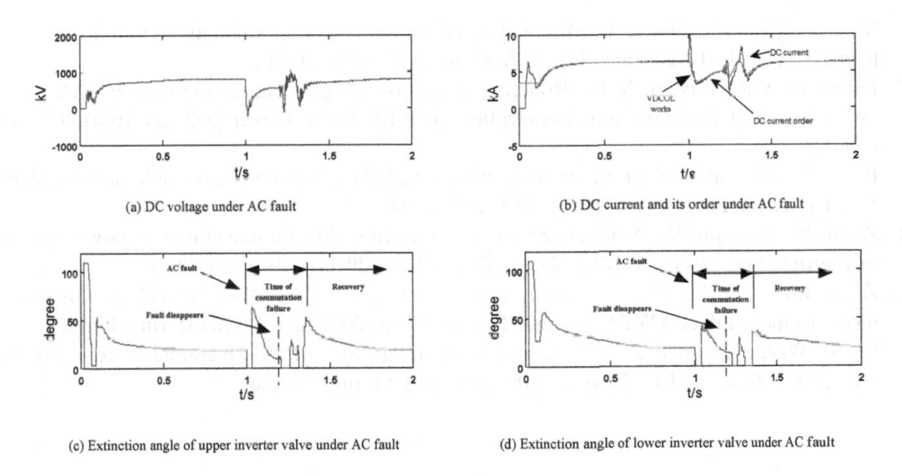

Fig. 11. Response of the UHVDC under AC fault

the DC voltage drops heavily. VDCOL link will be triggered which leads to a decrease of the current order value given by rectifier station. Figure 11-(c) and (d) are extinction angles of upper inverter valve and lower inverter valve. It can be seen that failure of single layer AC system will cause two valves get into the state of commutation failure simultaneously, but they can quickly recover from it with the help of DC control system when AC fault disappears.

6 Conclusion

In this paper, detailed electromagnetic transient simulation model is established according to the practical engineering design and construction of Ximeng-Taizhou UHVDC transmission project, which will connect to 1000 kV AC system and 500 kV AC system using hierarchical connection mode. Simulation results show the operating DC voltage and the operating DC current are the same as rated DC voltage of DC line and rated DC current of line, so the model does a reasonably good job of modeling the UHVDC transmission project and can be used as an effective tool for further studying on the new kind of connection mode.

Acknowledgement. This work was financially supported by State Grid Jiangsu Electric Power Company (5210EF14001P).

References

1. Mahseredjin, J., Lefebvre, S., Mukhedkar, D.: Power converter simulation module connected to the EMTP. J. IEEE Trans. Power Syst. **6**(1), 501–510 (1996)
2. Dinavahi, V.R., Iravani, M.R., Bonert, R.: Real-time digital simulation of power electronic apparatus interfaced with digital controllers. J. IEEE Trans. Power Delivery **16**(4), 775–781 (2001)
3. Pekarek, S.D.: An efficient multirate simulation technique for power electronic-based systems. J. IEEE Trans. Power Syst. **19**(1), 339–409 (2004)
4. Zhou, Y., Ajjarapu, V.: A novel approach to trace time-domain trajectories of power systems in multiple time scales. J. IEEE Trans. Power Syst. **20**(1), 149–155 (2005)
5. Zhenya, Z., Qin, X., Zhao, L.: Study on the application of UHVDC hierarchical connection mode to multi-infeed HVDC system. J. Proc. CSEE **33**(10), 1–7 (2013). (in Chinese)
6. Li, S., Wang, X., Zhang, W.: Control system design for UHVDC hierarchical connection to AC grid. J. Proc. CSEE. **35**(10), 2409–2416 (2015). (in Chinese)

Modeling and Simulation of Rainfall Impacts on Urban Traffic Flow: A Case Study in Beijing

Yuhan Jia, Jianping Wu, and Yiman Du(✉)

Department of Civil Engineering, Tsinghua University, Beijing 10084, China
yhjiathu@126.com, jianpingwu@tsinghua.edu.cn,
ymducp@gmail.com

Abstract. Recently many studies have emphasized the negative influence of inclement weather on microscopic and macroscopic traffic flow characteristics, including road capacity and operating speed. Although many conclusions have been drawn, only a few researches have investigated simulation-oriented rainfall influences on urban traffic systems. Simulation of rainfall scenario requires detailed theoretical study and statistical calibration, from both demand side and supply side, where related study is limited. This paper proposes a systematic study process to realize the simulation of rainfall scenario, based on a case area in Beijing, China. Firstly, rainfall impacts on urban traffic flow from both demand side and supply side are investigated by using traffic detector data and weather data. Then results are utilized to build a rainfall-integrated module in the microscopic simulation software of FLOWSIM. Results show that with rainfall module, FLOWSIM can describe the rainfall impacts on urban traffic systems with higher accuracy than without rainfall consideration. The methodology can be useful as references for similar studies and future applications; and the calibrated rainfall-integrated simulator can facilitate to improve traffic evaluation, operation, and management. Both data analysis and simulation tests conclude that rainfall has negative impact on urban traffic flow.

Keywords: Rainfall impact · Urban traffic system · Traffic simulation

1 Introduction

Without a comprehensive understanding of adverse weather influence on urban traffic system, traffic operation authorities cannot implement related policies to improve traffic efficiency and safety. Among adverse weather, rainfall is a prime factor. Over the past years, many studies have concluded that rainfall weather has negative influence on traffic flow characteristics such as capacity and operating speed.

It has been concluded that wet pavement and low visibility affects operating speed significantly on rural highways under heavy rain condition (Lamm et al. 1990). Ibrahim and Hall (1994) also studied the reductions of capacity and operating speed on freeways during rainfall weather. A research of various weather influences on German autobahns has been carried out (Brilon and Ponzlet 1996). Reductions about 9.5 km/h for speed and 350 vehicles per hour for capacity on two-lane sections, and 12 km/h for

L. Zhang et al. (Eds.): AsiaSim 2016/SCS AutumnSim 2016, Part I, CCIS 643, pp. 475–484, 2016.
DOI: 10.1007/978-981-10-2663-8_49

speed and 500 vehicles per hour for capacity on three-lane sections were estimated under rainfall condition. Furthermore, other adverse weather conditions, like fog and sonw, were studied, in which similar results were found (Liang et al. 1998; Kyte et al. 2001). With the original studies, traffic researchers have paid more attention to rainfall impacts, particular to that on road capacity, free-flow speed, operating speed and travel demand (Transportation Research Board 2000).

Although previous papers concluded that rainfall could affect traffic flow characteristics, limited studies have focused on the quantitative impacts intensities due to the limitation of access to high resolution data. With the availability of high resolution data, many recent studies could investigate the rainfall impacts on systems by dividing the intensity into different categories to carry out data analysis and model development. A paper analyzed quantitative rainfall influence on road capacity and traffic speed on freeway (Smith et al. 2004). It is found that heavy rain decreases capacity greater than that recommended by the HCM2000, while operating speed reductions are smaller during light rain. The influence of rain, temperature, winds, snow, and visibility on demand, flow and road safety was investigated (Maze et al. 2006). It was revealed that the research results are significantly influenced by traffic data collecting sensors. Chung et al. (2006) paid effort to study the Tokyo Metropolitan Expressway at various levels of intensity, and found that in light rain, capacity reductions are from 4–7 %, but the figure rises to 14 % during heavy rain. They also observed free-flow speed reductions about 4.5 % and 8.2 % in light and heavy rain, respectively. Similar results were found in a recent research (Asamer and Reinthaler 2010), which utilized a product limit method to calculate the capacity and speed loss during rainfall conditions considering the probability characteristics of traffic flow and found similar results. In addition, many scientists have analyzed weather impact based on local data (Agbolosu-Amison et al. 2004; Camacho et al. 2010; Lam et al. 2013). It is noticeable that weather impact is significantly different, which is caused by distinctions among regional driving behavior and traffic facility conditions. Additionally, traffic demand can also be affected. Researchers examined the rain influence on the Tokyo expressways and concluded that traffic demand is less sensitive to weather on weekdays than on weekends (Chung et al. 2005). In Melbourne, scientists investigated the relation of adverse weather with flow volume and found decreases of traffic volume about 1.35 % in winter and 2.11 % in spring (Keay and Simmonds 2005).

However, study on statistical rainfall effects on urban traffic system is still limited, especially for urban traffic systems, which are more challenging because urban links have lower operating speeds, more distractions and congestions. Furthermore, explicit speed-flow-rainfall models should be developed by using high resolution data to estimate the rainfall influence under various intensities other than categories. To solve this question, a latest study (Lam et al. 2013) focused on the development and calibration of generalized rainfall-impact model for traffic management and prediction, showed good application results. In addition, there is an increasing focus on deploying traffic simulation system to describe the weather impacts. The simulation analysis of different rainfall conditions on urban traffic system is essential for traffic planners and managers to improve related operations and managements. Colyar et al. (2003) investigated how weather affects traffic system, and assessed the sensitivity traffic parameters in simulator. This paper developed references for applying the simulator of

CORSIM to simulate the adverse weather in traffic system. Lieu and Lin (2004) introduced CORSIM to evaluate the benefits of signal retiming in adverse weather. It is concluded that can help mitigate congestion by signal retiming in adverse weather for arterial and also network. The study also indicated that in bad weather potential operational benefits of retiming signals can be realized only when traffic flows are moderately high, other than low or oversaturated. Other papers (Perrin et al. 2001; Al-Kaisy and Freedman 2006; Agbolosu-Amison et al. 2005) examined the development of signal retiming during rainfall weather and investigated the potential benefits of implementing weather-responsive signal control. To improve estimation and prediction accuracy, Hou et al. (2013) developed a systematic procedure for the entire calibration process for the successful application of weather-sensitive simulation system of TrEPS. Valid results show that with weather integration, simulation system is capable of reflecting the weather effects on traffic.

Based on previous studies, existing shortcomings can be summarized. Although most papers estimated the rainfall impacts on highways and freeways, inclement weather also has a strong influence on urban traffic system, which needs more attention. Because of regional characteristics ranging from traffic demand, driving behaviors to facility conditions, rainfall impacts could be significantly different. Therefore, studies should be implemented based on local data to benefit traffic authorities. But there has been limited work in China. In addition, more investigations are required to realize the rainfall scenario in simulator for traffic operation and management applications. A systematic procedure for model development, calibration and validation should be studied as a demonstration for further researches.

This paper proposes the entire study process based on a case area in Beijing to investigate the modeling and simulation of quantitative rainfall impact on urban traffic system, considering both demand side and supply side. The first objective is to develop a systematic procedure for model development and calibration during rainfall weather to evaluate traffic flow characteristics. The second objective is to integrate the model into the microscopic traffic simulation system FLOWSIM to build a rainfall scenario and then use the rainfall-integrated simulator for operation and management. The principal contribution is the successful simulation for urban traffic system with rainfall consideration by the simulator FLOWSIM. The methodology and results provide guidelines and references for similar studies focusing on rainfall impacts on traffic system and rainfall-integrated simulation.

The following section describes the data collection and processing. The third part presents modeling procedures to quantify the rainfall impacts. Then, the integration and experiment of rainfall module in FLOWSIM are proposed in part four. The last section gives the summary.

2 Survey Site and Data Collection

In this paper, the survey site is a 1.7-kilometer long arterial between Deshengmenqiao and Madianqiao in the downtown Beijing. The section is without signalized intersection and thus represents general condition in urban area in Beijing.

High-resolution traffic and rainfall historical data are essential in this research. On the study section, traffic flow rate, mean speed and occupancy are recorded in 2-min aggregation interval using loop detectors and archived by the Beijing Traffic Management Bureau (BTMB). Furthermore, hourly rainfall data of the center urban area is collected by weather station from the National Meteorological Center (NMC) in the unit of millimeter per hour. The research period in this paper is from June to September 2014, and both traffic data and rainfall intensity data are used from database for the corresponding time. Figure 1 shows the study area.

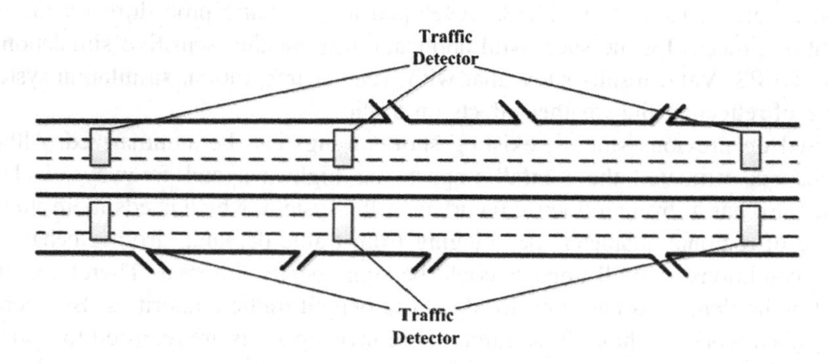

Fig. 1. Diagram of study section.

It is noticed that the original intervals of traffic data and rainfall data are different, which necessitates data processing. Previous study (Smith and Ulmer 2003) showed that traffic data with an aggregation of 10-min. can still accurately capture traffic flow characteristics. So a 10-min. time interval is assumed in this research to process traffic detector data, using weighted average method by flow rate, given as

$$\begin{cases} Flow_{10\,\text{min}} = \sum Flow_{2\,\text{min}} \\ Speed_{10\,\text{min}} = \sum \left(Flow_{2\,\text{min}} \times Speed_{2\,\text{min}}\right) / Flow_{10\,\text{min}} \end{cases}. \tag{1}$$

For rainfall intensity, hourly data is assumed to be constant for 10-min. sub-interval. Other methods to process the rainfall intensity data will be introduced in future research. Based on research (Angel et al. 2014), we introduce the typical rainfall intensity classification by the American Meteorological Society (AMS). Furthermore, data during festival (e.g., Dragon Boat Festival, 2nd June, 2014) and night (24:00 to 6:00) are removed to avoid distraction.

3 Rainfall Impact Modeling

3.1 Impacts on Demand Side

The rainfall impact on traffic demand can be described by the Origin-Destination (OD) matrix under different rainfall condition. To acquire demand data, traffic volume on study section is utilized to estimate OD matrix during weekday morning peak hours for various rainfall scenarios. Based on this rainfall category, the data collection time are the morning peak hours for 2nd July, 2nd September and 30th July, under small rainfall, moderate and heavy rainfall, respectively. For each weather, OD is calculated based on the flow count using TransCAD.

3.2 Impacts on Supply Side

To build the rainfall-integrated scenario in FLOWSIM, other weather related parameters should be analyzed including road capacity and free-flow speed. The reductions of these parameters are decided mainly by rainfall intensity. This goal could be achieved by the calibration of traffic supply model under different rainfall scenarios using all rainfall data during the study summer. Then the model could be applied for FLOWSIM to simulate the influence under user defined rainfall condition.

To decide the form of model function, we chose several modified Greenshields models and examine the fitting results by nonlinear regression for each rainfall condition. The better one is selected from reference (Hou et al. 2013), described as

$$q = uk_j[1 - (\frac{u - u_0}{u_f - u_0})^\alpha] \ , \tag{2}$$

where q is road capacity, u is speed, u_0 and u_f are the minimum speed and free-flow speed, k is density, k_j is the congestion density, and α is the parameter to be calibrated.

This model could represent both the congestion state and free flow state of the traffic situation in case study area, thus it is selected to do the calibration of principal parameters. For calibration, the algorithm of Simultaneous Perturbation Stochastic Approximation (SPSA) could be utilized for the calibration using integrated traffic and weather data under clear weather, light rain, moderate rain and heavy rain. SPSA was developed by Spall (1992) to improve the computational time of typical Stochastic Approximation (SA) algorithm, using constant number of perturbations for the gradient estimation. This algorithm and its improved form (Lu et al. 2015) have been used in the calibration of traffic simulator and the performance has been testified.

The objective function could be mathematically presented as:

$$\min z(\boldsymbol{\theta}) = \sum_{j=1}^{D} (\widehat{q}_j - q_j)^2 \tag{3}$$

Subject to:

$$\widehat{q}_j = u_j k_j [1 - (\frac{u_j - u_0}{u_f - u_0})^\alpha] \tag{4}$$

where $\widehat{q}_j$ is the estimated value of capacity, q_j is observed capacity, $\boldsymbol{\theta}$ is the vector of parameters to be calibrated, D is the size of data, u_j is observed speed.

The iterative form of SPSA is:

$$\hat{\theta}_{k+1} = \hat{\theta}_k - a_k \widehat{g}_k(\hat{\theta}_k) \tag{5}$$

where $\hat{\theta}_k$ is the estimation of parameters in the k th iteration, $\widehat{g}_k(\hat{\theta}_k)$ is the estimated gradient at $\hat{\theta}_k$, a_k is the step size, which is usually calculated as:

$$a_k = \frac{a}{(A+k+a)^{\alpha}} \tag{6}$$

where a, α and A are preset parameters.

The SPSA could efficiently estimate the gradient by simultaneously perturbing all the parameters to be calibrated. The function is

$$\widehat{g}_{ki}(\hat{\theta}_k) = \frac{z(\hat{\theta}_k + c_k\Delta_k) - z(\hat{\theta}_k - c_k\Delta_k)}{2c_k\Delta_{ki}} \tag{7}$$

where $\widehat{g}_{ki}(\hat{\theta}_k)$ is the ith element in the gradient vector, Δ_k is random perturbation vector, Δ_{ki} is the i th element in Δ_k, c_k is perturbation amplitude calculated as

$$c_k = \frac{c}{(k+1)^{\gamma}} \tag{8}$$

where c and γ are preset parameters.

The calibrated curves of supply model are shown in Fig. 2. From calibration results, it is observed that parameter u_0, k_j, and α are weather insensitive, while u_f is significantly influenced by rainfall weather.

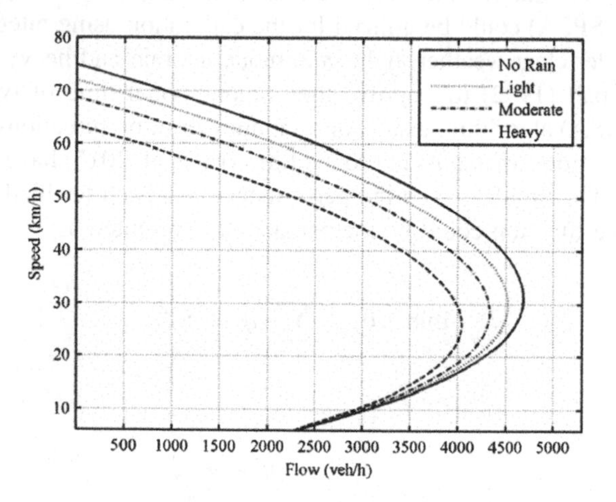

Fig. 2. Calibrated speed-flow functions.

4 Rainfall Scenario Simulation

The microscopic traffic simulation software FLOWSIM is chosen as the simulation system for this study. FLOWSIM is developed in University of Southampton based on fuzzy logic model (Wu et al. 2000). It has been used for traffic management and evaluation in UK and China and shows good performances (Wu et al. 2003; Du et al. 2015). Especially, FLOWSIM is well calibrated using field data from big cities in China, making it more suitable for simulation purpose in this study. For the development of rainfall scenario in FLOWSIM, the calibrated models for different rainfall category are integrated into the simulator. Based on user defined date and rainfall information, FLOWSIM is capable to automatically adjust the supply parameters by calculating the reductions of road capacity and free-flow speed. Then together with user input travel demand data and road geometric information, FLOWSIM could implement rainfall-integrated traffic simulation.

To test the rainfall scenario in FLOWSIM, three days are selected for simulation, which are 2nd July, 2nd September and 30th July, for small rainfall, moderate and heavy rainfall, respectively. Road geometry, travel demand and rainfall data are input into FLOWSIM. Then simulation tests are implemented with and without rainfall-integrated module for corresponding rainfall hours of the three days, each for 10 times using different simulation seeds to obtain average results. Simulated traffic data including flow count and average speed are generated in 10-min. interval to make a comparison with field data. To evaluate the effectiveness of the proposed model, we use two performance indexes, expressed in Eqs. (9) and (10).

$$\mathrm{MRE} = \frac{1}{N}\sum_{i=1}^{N}\frac{|x_i - y_i|}{x_i} \tag{9}$$

$$\mathrm{RMSE} = \sqrt{\frac{1}{N}\sum_{i=1}^{N}(x_i - y_i)^2} \tag{10}$$

where x_i is the observed data, y_i is the simulated data, and N is the sample size.

Simulation results are shown in Table 1. The lower values of MRE and RMSE with rainfall module mean that the discrepancies between simulated and observed data are smaller than without considering rainfall influence. Simulation results indicate that with the rainfall-integrated module in FLOWSIM, the simulator has the ability to reflect urban traffic flow under rainfall condition with higher accuracy. It is also observed that with higher rainfall severity, the performances of simulator without rainfall consideration are more unrealistic, which indicates the meaningfulness of deploying rainfall-integrated module.

Table 1. Performance comparison of MRE and RMSE with/without rainfall module.

Rainfall category		Light	Moderate	Heavy
Without Rainfall	MRE_{speed}	0.14	0.23	0.27
Module	MRE_{flow}	0.28	0.33	0.42
With Rainfall	MRE_{speed}	0.08	0.11	0.19
Module	MRE_{flow}	0.06	0.07	0.27
Without Rainfall	$RMSE_{speed}$	8.91	9.15	10.40
Module	$RMSE_{flow}$	126.36	174.44	192.83
With Rainfall	$RMSE_{speed}$	5.38	5.84	6.24
Module	$RMSE_{flow}$	40.24	45.53	57.35

5 Summary and Conclusions

This paper does a in depth study on rainfall impacts on urban traffic system in Beijing by using local traffic data and weather data. The calibrated model is utilized to develop a rainfall-integrated module in the simulator FLOWSIM. The improved simulation model can reflect realistic traffic system under inclement weather conditions than without considering weather effects. Both statistical and simulation results show that rainfall has a negative impact on urban traffic flow parameters, including road capacity and free-flow speed. The principal contribution is the successful simulation for urban traffic system with rainfall consideration by the simulator FLOWSIM. The methodology and results can be utilized as references for similar studies and future applications, and the calibrated rainfall-integrated simulator can facilitate to improve traffic evaluation, operation and management. More detailed data is needed to improve model accuracy and more scenarios should be considered in further studies.

Acknowledgement. This study is funded by China Scholarship Council, and also by China Postdoctoral Science Foundation (2013M540102).

References

Agbolosu-Amison, S.J., Sadek, A.W., ElDessouki, W.: Inclement weather and traffic flow at signalized intersections: case study from northern New England. Transp. Res. Rec. **1867**, 163–171 (2004)

Agbolosu-Amison, S.J., Sadek, A.W., Henry, B.: Factors affecting benefits of implementing special signal timing plans for inclement weather conditions. Transp. Res. Rec. **1925**, 146–155 (2005)

Al-Kaisy, A., Freedman, Z.: Weather-responsive signal timing: practical guidelines. Transp. Res. Rec. **1978**, 49–60 (2006)

Angel, M.L., Sando, T., Chimba, D., Kwigizile, V.: Effects of rain on traffic operations on Florida freeways. In: Proceedings of the 93th Transportation Research Board Annual Meeting. Transportation Research Board, Washington D.C. (2014)

Asamer, J., Reinthaler, M.: Estimation of road capacity and free flow speed for urban roads under adverse weather conditions. In: Proceedings of the 13th International IEEE Annual Conference on Intelligent Transportation Systems. IEEE, Madeira Island (2010)

Brilon, W., Ponzlet, M.: Variability of speed-flow relationships on german autobahns. Transp. Res. Rec. **1555**, 91–98 (1996)

Camacho, F.J., García, A., Belda, E.: Analysis of impact of adverse weather on freeway free-flow speed in Spain. Transp. Res. Rec. **2168**, 150–159 (2010)

Chung, E., Ohtani, O., Warita, H., Kuwahara, M., Morita, H.: Effect of rain on travel demand and traffic accident. In: Proceedings of the 8th International IEEE Annual Conference on Intelligent Transportation Systems. IEEE, Vienna (2005)

Chung, E., Ohtani, O., Warita, H., Kuwahara, M., Morita, H.: Does weather affect highway capacity. In: Proceedings of the 5th International Symposium on Highway Capacity and Quality of Service. Transportation Research Board, Yakoma (2006)

Colyar, J., Zhang, L., Halkias, J.: Identifying and assessing key weather-related parameters and their impact on traffic operations using simulation. In: 2003 Institute of Transportation Engineering Annual Meeting. Institute of Transportation Engineers, Washington, D.C. (2003)

Du, Y., Wu, J., Qi, G., Jia, Y.: Simulation studyof bicycle multi-phase crossing at intersections. ICE Transp. **168**(5), 457–465 (2015)

Hou, T., Mahmassani, H.S., Alfelor, R.M., Kim, J., Saberi, M.: Calibration of traffic flow models under adverse weather and application in mesoscopic network simulation. Transp. Res. Rec. **2391**, 92–104 (2013)

Ibrahim, A.T., Hall, F.L.: Effects of adverse weather conditions on speed-flow-occupancy relationships. Transp. Res. Rec. **1457**, 184–191 (1994)

Keay, K., Simmonds, I.: The association of rainfall and other weather variables with road traffic volume in Melbourne, Australia. Accid. Anal. Prev. **37**(1), 109–124 (2005)

Kyte, M., Khatib, Z., Shannon, P., Kitchener, F.: Effects of weather on free-flow speed. Transp. Res. Rec. **1776**, 60–68 (2001)

Lam, W.H.K., Tam, M.L., Cao, X., Li, X.: Modeling the effects of rainfall intensity on traffic speed, flow, and density relationships for urban roads. J. Transp. Eng. **139**(7), 758–770 (2013)

Lamm, R., Choueiri, E.M., Mailaender, T.: Comparison of operating speeds on dry and wet pavements of two-lane rural highways. Transp. Res. Rec. **1280**, 199–207 (1990)

Liang, W.L., Kyte, M., Kitchener, F., Shannon, P.: The effect of environmental factors on driver speed: a case study. Transp. Res. Rec. **1635**, 155–161 (1998)

Lieu, H.C., Lin, S.M.: Benefit assessment of implementing weather-specific signal timing plans by using CORSIM. Transp. Res. Rec. **1867**, 202–209 (2004)

Lu, L., Xu, Y., Antoniou, C., Ben-Akiva, M.: An enhanced SPSA algorithm for the calibration of Dynamic Traffic Assignment models. Transp. Res. Part C **51**, 149–166 (2015)

Maze, T.H., Agarwai, M., Burchett, G.: Whether weather matters to travel demand, traffic safety, and traffic operations and flow. Transp. Res. Rec. **1948**, 170–176 (2006)

Perrin, H.J., Martin, P.T., Hansen, B.G.: Modifying signal timing during inclement weather. Transp. Res. Rec. **1748**, 66–71 (2001)

Smith, B.L., Byrne, K.G., Copperman, R.B., Hennessy, S.M., Goodall, N.J.: An investigation into the impact of rainfall of freeway traffic flow. In: Proceedings of the 83th Transportation Research Board Annual Meeting. Transportation Research Board, Washington D.C. (2004)

Smith, B.L., Ulmer, J.M.: Freeway traffic flow rate measurement: investigation into impact of measurement time interval. J. Transp. Eng. **129**(3), 223–229 (2003)

Spall, J.C.: Multivariate stochastic approximation using a simultaneous perturbation gradient approximation. IEEE Trans. Autom. Control **37**(3), 332–341 (1992)

Transportation Research Board: Highway capacity manual 2000. Transportation Research Board, National Research Council, Washington, DC (2000)

Wu, J., Brackstone, M., McDonald, M.: Fuzzy sets and systems for a motorway microscopic simulation model. Fuzzy Sets Syst. **116**, 65–76 (2000)

Wu, J., Brackstone, M., McDonald, M.: The validation of a microscopic simulation model: a methodological case study. Transp. Res. Part C **11**(6), 463–479 (2003)

Research on Coupling Simulation Model of Metro Train Operation and Traction Power System

Huang Chengzhou[1(✉)], Li Yuezong[2], Zhang Jiahua[2], Xu Jianjun[2], Zhu Jinling[1], Zeng Li[2], and Jiang Jin[3]

[1] Chengdu Yunda Technology Co., Ltd., Chengdu 611731, China
chengzhouhuang@foxmail.com,
huangzhoukevin@163.com
[2] Southwest Jiaotong University, Chengdu 610031, China
[3] Locomotive Depot of Chengdu Railway Bureau, Chengdu 610081, China
jiangjin207@126.com

Abstract. The coupling relation between the Metro Traction Power Supply System (MTSPS) and the Metro Train Traction Drive System (MTTDS) was rarely considered in the existing Metro Traction Power Supply Simulation System (MTSPSS), so the system could not describe the train-network real-time electrical coupling phenomenon of multi-train operation on the actual line of the metro site accurately and effectively. Therefore, in this paper, the trains model are added into the MTSPS to build a train-network simulation model of the MTSPS, combining the traction characteristic of the MTTDS and the relation of train-network, then this paper analyses the influence of the trains on the Traction Power Supply Network (TPSN) and the TPSN on the trains performance, and discusses what effect the multi-train operation and the different departure intervals have on the whole traction network voltage fluctuation. The experimental results indicates that the train-network coupling model built in this paper can describe the coupling relation between the trains and the traction network in the actual system of metro more accurately, which has some certain guidance functions on the capacity design of the MTSPS and the schedule of the timetable.

Keywords: Metro traction power system · Coupling relation · Power flow values · Network voltage

1 Introduction

At present, the MTSPS mostly adopts DC 750 V or DC 1500 V bilateral power supply mode in china, for this power supply mode, many domestic and foreign scholars did large-scale deep researches on the DC side modeling methods and power flow calculation methods of the MTSPS, most of them took the loop current [1, 2] and the node voltage [3–7] as the models of the MTSPS, the loop current model can be only used in the simple system composed of the catenary, the rail and the return-line, which is used to calculate the voltage and the current of the catenary and rail, and the longitudinal distribution along the catenary; the node voltage model is widely applied to the traction

L. Zhang et al. (Eds.): AsiaSim 2016/SCS AutumnSim 2016, Part I, CCIS 643, pp. 485–496, 2016.
DOI: 10.1007/978-981-10-2663-8_50

network with arbitrary topology structure, which is also suitable for the traction network under the other power supply distribution systems. The literature [8] regarded the train as the load of consumption power to raise Study of unified AC/DC power flow in DC traction power supply system, Based on the multi-conductor transmission line model, the literature [9] built a general mathematical model that could be applicable to the TPSN with different structure and power supply distribution mode, then it raised a power flow values calculation method for the train-network coupling of the high speed train, however, it did not give the actual traction force when the train worked at the under-voltage operating mode. The literature [10] pointed out that the train-network united simulation was the method that set the output of the traction calculation as the input of the MTSPS, but it neglected the relation of the repeated coupling between the train and the network. The literature [11] was inconsiderate of the effects of the train-network real-time coupling, getting the not very accurate simulation calculation result by separating the train and the network to do research and analysis.

There are many deficiencies in the existing MTSPSS, for example, the equivalent model of the train is not accurate and the coupling relation of the train-network is not fully considerate. Therefore, this paper embeds the train model into the traction power supply network to build a coupling model of the train-network, then studies the mutual coupling relation between the metro train and the traction network and points out the influence of the relation on the TPSN voltage and the traction drive performance, aiming to describe the train operation state more accurately, this paper can help to adjust the train scheduling reasonably and effectively, aiming at reducing the network voltage fluctuation effects on the traction drive performance.

2 The Modeling of MTSPS

2.1 The Model Building

The MTSPS rectifies the AC 35 kV and reduces it to DC 1500 V or DC 750 V from the mid-voltage substation output voltage, supplying to the train traction, the battery charging and the other DC power supplies as well as the train lighting, the air conditioners, the air compressors and the other AC supplies, the DC 1500 V is mainly for the catenary supply mode and the DC 750 V is mainly for the third track. This paper assumes that the AC side power supply system has sufficient capacity and stable voltage without considering the under-voltage or the voltage instability of the mid-voltage side, focusing on the model building of the DC power supply system, involving the traction substation, the DC feeder line, the TPSN, the train and the return-line, etc. Figure 1. is the diagram of the metro bilateral MTSPS based on the substation unit.

Assuming that the feeder line, the traction substation, the rail and the other electrical elements are uniform material and can be equivalent to uniform resistance, the calculation of the power flow in the MTSPS is mainly related to the number of trains, the position of the trains, the power of the trains and the DC side voltage of the MTSPS. So, in a computation cycle, the traction substation is regarded as the voltage source in series with resistance, the train is taken as a constant power source model and

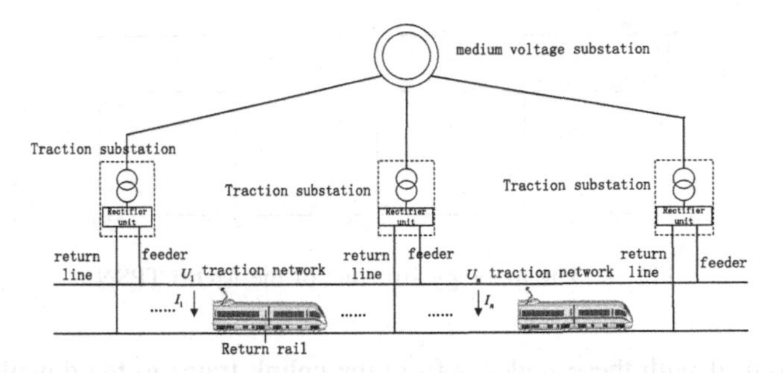

Fig. 1. The metro bilateral power supply system

the distribution line which is always in the energy consumption of the active and reactive load, is equivalent to the π circuit to calculate. Figure 2 is the physical equivalent model of Fig. 1.

In Fig. 2, P_{uj} is the power of the train absorption / feedback, U_{uj} is the network voltage of the point where the train take the current, I_{uj} is the current the train takes, r_{iuc} is the equivalent TPSN resistance of the section i, U_{iu} is the outlet voltage of the traction substation i, the DC traction substation can be equivalent to the voltage source V_{si} in series with the resistance R_{eqi}; according to the theory of uniform transmission line, the rail can be equivalent to the type π model, r_{ri} is the equivalent rail resistance of the section i, g_i is the rail leakage resistance of the section i.

2.2 The Model Solving

The each node admittance value of the TPSN is calculated, then the corresponding admittance matrix is created according to the physical model of the MTSPS and its power element attribute parameter in Fig. 2. The specific implementation steps and methods are as follows:

Step1: Scan the topology of the traction power supply network, and get the locations of each train online.

Step2: Sort the locations of the substations and the trains, the number sequence of the network nodes is: the feed nodes of the substations, the return nodes of the substations, the current-getting nodes of the trains, the return-line nodes of the trains.

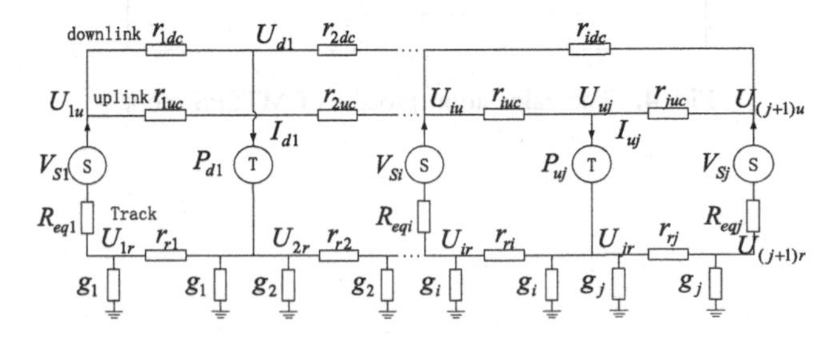

Fig. 2. The physical model of the metro traction power supply network

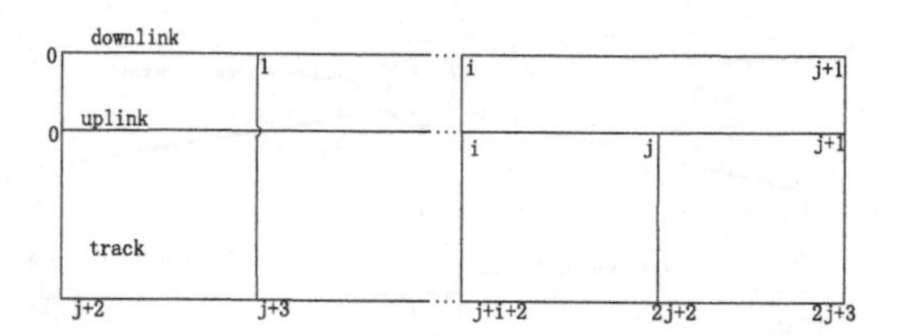

Fig. 3. The topology structure of the Metro TPSN

The order to deal with these nodes is from the uplink trains to the downlink trains as shown in Fig. 3.

Step3: According to the physical model of MTSPS in Fig. 2 and the topology structure of the Metro TPSN in Fig. 3. the current of each node is calculated: the current of the substation feed node is $I_j = \sum_{i=1}^{n} Y_{j,i} U_{iu}$, the current of the substation return-line node is $-I_j = \sum_{i=1}^{n} Y_{j,i} U_{iu}$. Because the train is equivalent to the constant power source in Fig. 2, for the current-getting node and the return-line node, their power balance equations can be listed, where the power of the current-getting node is $-P_{uj} = U_{uj} \sum_{i=1}^{n} Y_{j,i} U_{iu}$, and the return node's is $P_{uj} = U_{uj} \sum_{i=1}^{n} Y_{j,i} U_{iu}$.

The node admittance matrix and the injection current of the TPSN can be generated by the branch addition method, and the specific program flow chart is shown in Fig. 4.

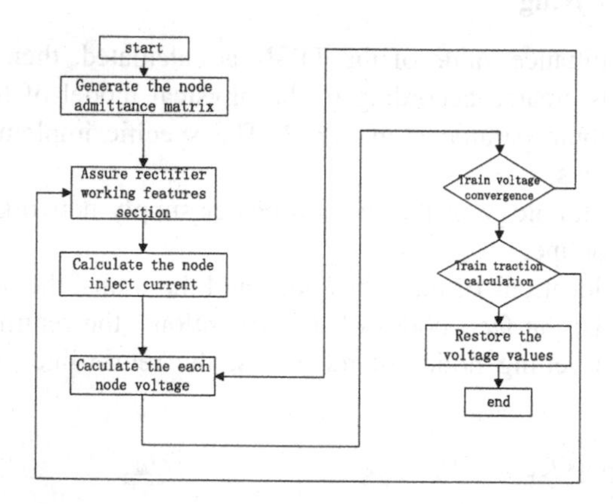

Fig. 4. The calculation process of MTSPS mode

3 The Model of Metro Train Operation

3.1 The Traction Calculation

In this paper, the model of the train traction calculation is multi-particle model, which considers the traction force, the combined braking force, the basic resistance and the additional resistance of the train at the same time, the mass of the train generally takes AW2 load. The model of the metro train traction calculation is as follows:

$$\begin{cases} \dfrac{dt}{ds} = \dfrac{1}{v} \\ v\dfrac{dv}{ds} = \dfrac{u_t F_t(v) - u_b B_b(v)}{Mg} - \omega_0(v) - \omega_j(x) \end{cases} \tag{1}$$

in the Eq. (1), v-the running speed of the train, unit *m/s*; t-the running of the train, unit second (s); s-the running distance of the train unit *km*; $F_t(v)$-the maximum traction force at the speed v, unit *N*; u_b-breaking level; $\omega_j(x)$-the operation unit basic resistance, unit *N/kN*; M-the train mass, unit ton (t); where, $u_t \in [0, 1]$, $u_b \in [0, 1]$.

3.2 The Influence of the Network Voltage on the Performance of the Train

The MTTDS generally works in a specific range of network voltage, and has a maximum current limit, if the train operates at different network voltage, its traction braking performance will be affected to some degree, as shown in Fig. 5.

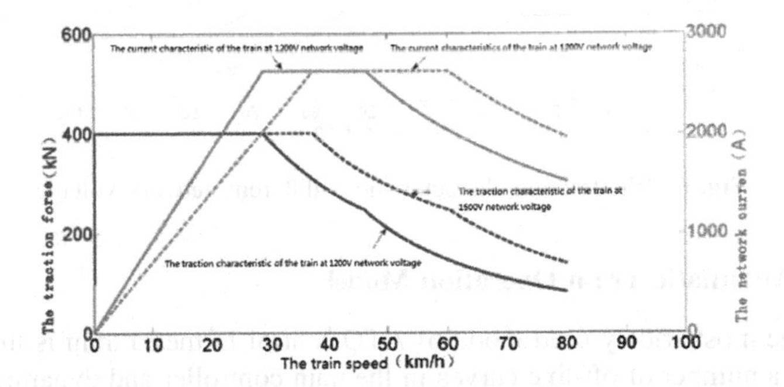

Fig. 5. The influence of the network Voltage on the MTTDS

Figure 5 shows the variation of traction force and network current with train running speed when the network voltage is changing, when the train network side voltage is low, in order to maintain the train operation with the constant traction force, the network side current is rising fast, and its limit value reaches in advance, at this time, the traction motor reaches the constant power operation in advance, and the power is lower than that at the normal network voltage.

If the train traction motor works in the constant torque area, then there is an equation at the uniform speed v:

$$U_u \times I_u \times t \times \mu = F_t(v) \times v \times t \tag{2}$$

Assuming that the energy conversion efficiency is the same, (there is an energy conservation relationship between the 1400 V and the 1500 V network voltage.), the relation can be represented as the following equation:

$$U_{1400} \times I_{1400} = U_{1500} \times I_{1500} \tag{3}$$

That is: $\frac{I_{1400}}{I_{1500}} = \frac{1500}{1400}$. The equation shows that both the constant-torque and the constant-power-area contract U_{1400}/U_{1500} at the 1400 V network voltage.

At this time, the acceleration of the train at a lower speed can be guaranteed, but the linear acceleration area is relatively short, so the average acceleration of the train is slightly lower than that at the rated network voltage. Similarly, the constant power point of the traction characteristic will be extended to a certain proportion at the higher network voltage. Figure 6 shows that the traction characteristic of different voltage at the rated load level:

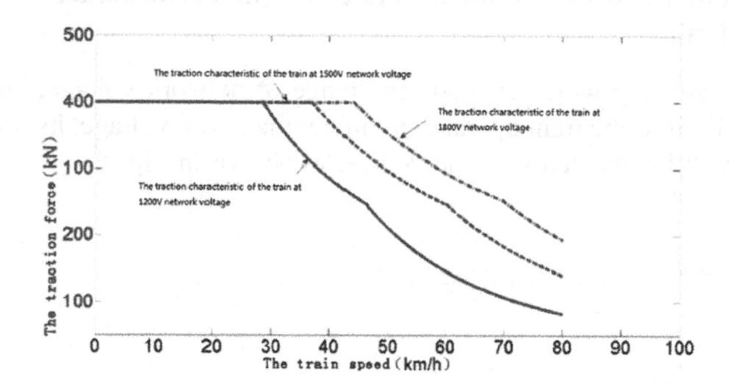

Fig. 6. The traction characteristic at different network voltage

3.3 The Automatic Train Operation Model

Currently the most widely used mode of ATO control in metro train is the mode that first presets a number of off-line curves in the train controller and dynamically adjusts the train tracking off-line curve operation according to the time, the train off-line operation optimization curve is a calculated optimized curve, which is in accordance with a specific mathematical model of the train and external constraints, this curve contains all information about the operation point of the whole line. This curve can be solidified in the train control system, the corresponding control command can be generated by referring to the operating point information to control the train operation. This paper takes this method to simulate the real train operation state as far as possibly, and the method presents multiple off-line optimal curves (generated according to the different operation time requirements and so on) in the ATO, then automatically calculates the optimal curves of next operation interval according to the time, this method chooses the different optimal curve as a reference to control the train operation when there are external interferences (such as delay, etc.). The generation of the off-line curve takes into account the safety, comfort and parking accuracy of the train and so on. The metro train operation curves are shown in Fig. 7.

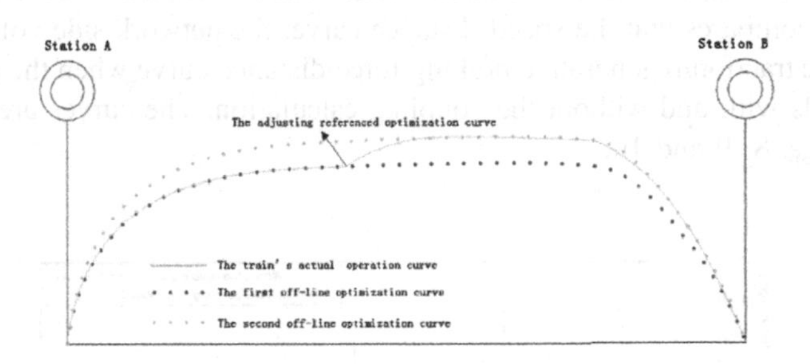

Fig. 7. The train controlling principle of the ATO

4 The Calculation and Analysis of the Train-Network Coupling

Based on the model of MTSPS and the train operation control built above, this paper chooses ShenZhen Metro as an example to carry out the simulation calculation. The conditions of the simulation are as follows:

Train Parameters:

1. Grouping: four moving and four dragging
2. AW2 load: 342.6t
3. Maximum speed: 80 *km/h*
4. Basic operation resistance: $F_r = 9.19 + 0.001334v^2(kN)$
5. The traction characteristics:

$$F = 400\ (kN)\ \text{Speed Range}\ [0, 37]\ (km/h)$$
$$F = 14800/V\ (kN)\ \text{Speed Range}\ [37, 60]\ (km/h)$$
$$F = -892800/V^2\ (kN)\ \text{Speed Range}\ [60, 85]\ (km/h)$$

6. The regenerative braking characteristics:

$$F = 0\ (kN)\ \text{Speed Range}\ [0, 6]\ (km/h)$$
$$F = -432/V\ (kN)\ \text{Speed Range}\ [6, 55]\ (9km/h)$$
$$F = -23100/V^2\ (kN)\ \text{Speed Range}\ [55, 85]\ (km/h)$$

Line data: There are 13 stations with a total length of about 15 km on No. 1 Line of ShenZhen Metro, including the containing of ramps, curves, stations, and so on.

4.1 The Coupling Calculation of the Train-Network

Since the operation data among the train stations is so large, it intercepts that the data of three operation ranges (LuoHu Station-Grand Theater Station) for comparison. It respectively compares that the speed-distance curve, the network side voltage-distance curve and the traction/regenerative braking force-distance curve when the train is in the three intervals with and without the coupling calculation. The curves are respectively shown in Figs. 8, 9 and 10.

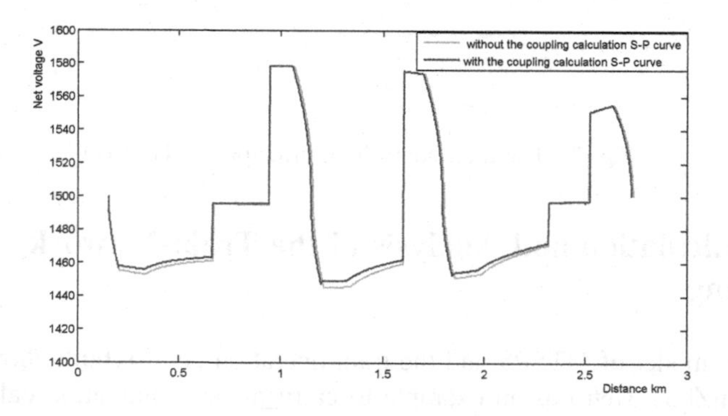

Fig. 8. The network side voltage-distance curve

Figure 8 shows the variation of network voltage with train running distance when the coupling calculation method is used or not, the fluctuation range of the train-network voltage is smaller than that of not using the method, The reason is that with considering the coupling calculation, the network side voltage affects the performance of the traction motor power. In the regenerative braking condition, assuming that the network voltage level is always in the allowable range of the traction substation, the network voltage increases slightly, but in the traction condition, the decrease of the network voltage leads to the train traction characteristic moving forward, the motor power going down, thus it reduces the reductions of the network voltage.

Figure 9 shows that the variation of speed with train running distance when the coupling calculation method is used or not, the network voltage is lower than the rated voltage of the MTTDS and the constant power point of the traction characteristic will change, so at the high speed, the traction force is lower than that at the rated network voltage at the same speed, and the maximum operation speed of the train is also lower than that at the normal network voltage.

Figure 10 shows the variation of traction/regenerative braking force with train running distance when the coupling calculation method is used or not, that after using

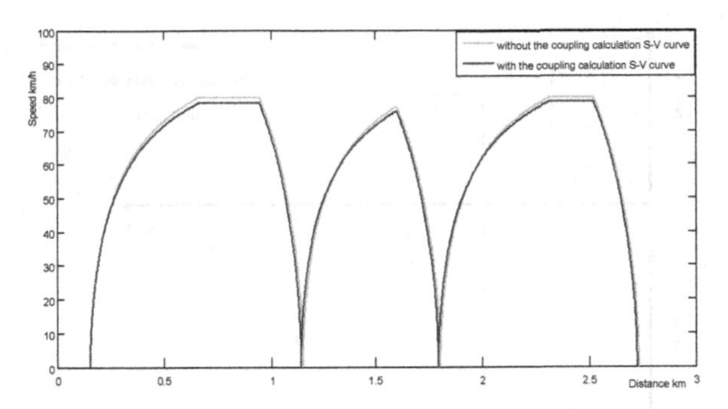

Fig. 9. The speed-distance curve

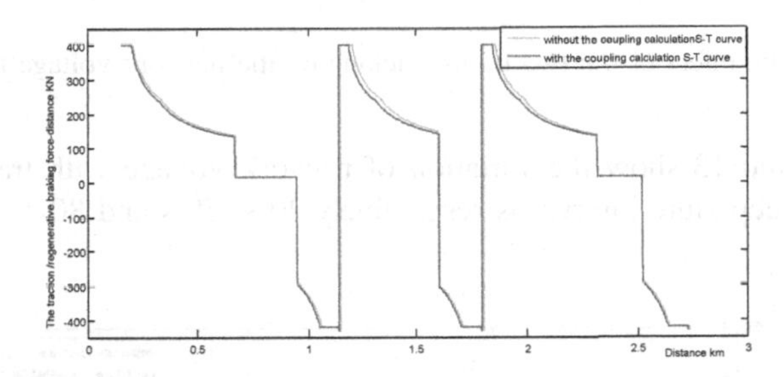

Fig. 10. The traction/regenerative braking force-distance curve

the coupling calculation method, also the train traction force affected by the reduction of the network voltage, it is lower than that at the normal network voltage when the train works in the traction operation condition and the situation is basically the same when the train is in the regenerative braking condition.

4.2 The Effect of Different Departure Intervals on the Voltage Fluctuation of the Train Network

Assuming that there are two trains in the tracking operation on the line at the same time T, when both trains running under the operation condition shown in the area A, they two are in the traction operation and get the current from the network at the same time, so the network voltage drops fast. When in the area B, the latter train consumes energy by traction acceleration and the former feeds back the electric energy to the network by regenerative braking, the two operation condition mutually suppress the sharp fluctuation of the network voltage, even offset the effect of the network voltage fluctuation, so is it in the area C. When in the area D, both trains are in the condition of regenerative braking, causing a sharp rise in the network voltage. In the above analysis, there is a possibility that the two trains can be kept operating in the area B or area C by adjusting the departure interval, which can suppress the network voltage fluctuation of the whole TPSN in some way. The results of the experiment are shown in Fig. 11.

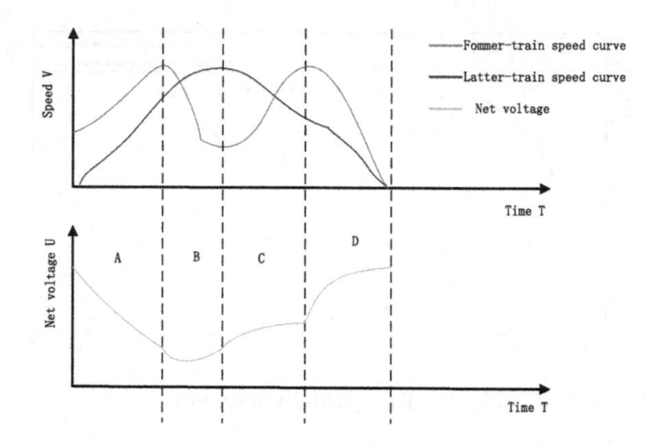

Fig. 11. The effect of the two trains tracking on the network voltage fluctuation

Figures 12 and 13 show the variation of network voltage with train running distance when the departure interval is respectively 20 s, 50 s and 80 s.

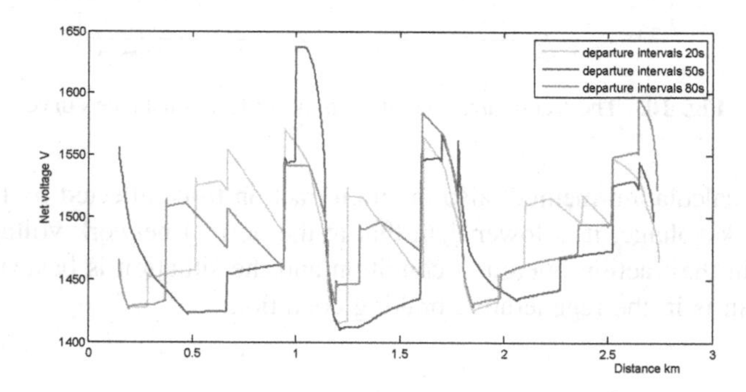

Fig. 12. The network voltage fluctuation of the former train under the different departure intervals

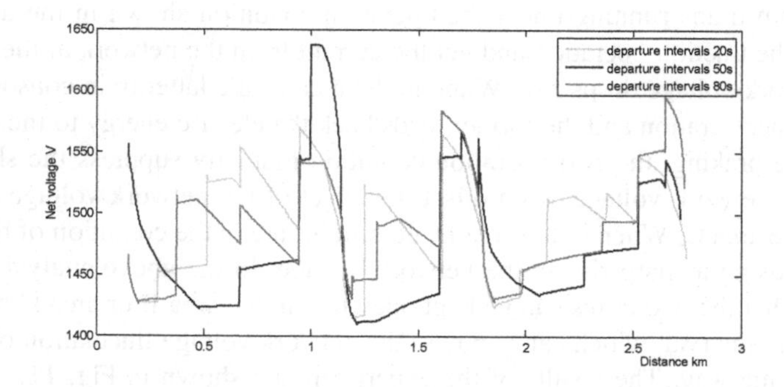

Fig. 13. The network voltage fluctuation of the latter train under the different departure intervals

Figure 12 shows that the network voltage fluctuation is larger when the interval is 50 s, the reason is that the operation time is about 50 s between the two stations, when the latter train departs after 50 s the former operated, the two trains just differ an interval, that means the two trains are in full traction or breaking to stop at the same time, as shown in the area A and B in Fig. 11, at this time, the network voltage fluctuation is strong. When the departure interval is about 20 s or 80 s, the former train is in the middle of the range, namely, the traction is turning into the parking breaking, at the same time, the latter train is in full traction condition as shown in area B or C in Fig. 11, at this time, the network voltage of the two trains suppresses with each other, so the fluctuation is small.

Figure 13 shows that the network voltage fluctuation of the latter train is similar to the former's, when the interval is about 50 s, the network voltage fluctuation is the largest, while the interval is 20 s and 80 s, owing to that the energy cancels with each other, the fluctuation is smaller. So it can be concluded that the reasonable time of the table layout can make full use of the multiple trains energy transformation trend to offset or even inhibit the voltage fluctuation, thereby increasing the safety redundancy of the MTSPS, and maintaining the stable operation of the train.

5 Summary

This paper firstly gives a comprehensive analysis on the coupling relation between the metro train and the MTSPS as well as the calculation principle and model of the power flow in the MTSPS, then it explains the interaction relation between the network voltage and the MTTDS. Finally, it discusses the influence of different departure intervals on the network voltage fluctuation. This paper gives the following conclusions by comparing the experiment results: (1) the train operation curve is affected when the traction force of the train is limited due to the fluctuation of the network voltage. So the effect of network voltage on the train operation should be considerate in the research of the train-energy-saving controlling strategy when the substation capacity is too small, the train power is too large or in the multi-train operation condition. (2) When the wheel traction force of the train is limited due to the fluctuation of the network voltage, if considering the coupling of the train-network, the network voltage getting from the power flow calculation is higher than that without considering the coupling, this result reflects the distribution of the network voltage with the coupling of the train-network. (3) In the multi-train operation condition, the reasonable departure time interval can effectively suppress the network voltage fluctuation, which makes the train traction and braking having good performance. (4) The model built in this paper is correct and reasonable and the algorithm has good convergence, so the model can be used as a basis for further research on the multi-train control platform.

References

1. Shi, F., Yu, S.: To found and to find the solution for mathematical method of metro traction power system. J. Beijing Union Univ. **2**, 60–62 (2003)
2. Goodman, C.J., Siu, L.K.: DC railway power network solutions by diakoptics. In: Proceedings of the 94 ASME/IEEE Joint Railroad Conference, pp. 103–110 (1994)
3. Cai, Y., Irving, M.R., Case, S.H.: Modelling and numerical solution of multibranched DC rail traction power systems. IEE Proc. Electr. Power Appl. **142**(5), 323–328 (1995)
4. Hu, H., Wang, J., He, Z., et al.: Study on power flow algorithm for metro traction supply system. J. China Railway Soc. **34**(11), 22–28 (2012)
5. Liu, H., Ho, T., Yuan, Z., et al.: Simulation of DC traction power for mass transit railway. J. Syst. Simul. **16**(9), 1944–1947 (2004)
6. Xuejun, L.I.U., Songwei, Y.U., Xue, L.I.U.: Model and algorithm for traction power system simulation of urban railline. J. Comput. Simul. **21**(12), 213–218 (2004)
7. Hu, H., He, Z., Wang, J.: AC/DC power flow calculation method for metro system considering harmonic power. Proc. CSEE **32**(34), 112–119 (2012)
8. Wei, L.I.U., Qunzhan, L.I., Minwu, C.H.E.N.: Study of unified AC/DC power flow in DC traction power supply system. Power Syst. Prot. Control **38**(8), 128–133 (2010)
9. Chen, H., Geng, G., Jiang, Q.: Power flow algorithm for traction power supply system of electric railway based on locomotive and network coupling. Autom. Electric Power Syst. **36** (3), 76–80 (2012)
10. Wang, Y., Wu, : Modelling of DC traction substations in the train operation simulation. Electr. Railway **4**, 4–7 (2005)
11. Wang, N., Wei, X.: Equilibrium current analysis and calculation of axial double split 12-pulse traction rectifier transformer. Transformer **37**(3), 1–6 (2000)

Outlier Detection and Correction During the Process of Groundwater Lever Monitoring Base on Pauta Criterion with Self-learning and Smooth Processing

Limin Li[1(✉)], Zongzhou Wen[1], and Zhongsheng Wang[2]

[1] College of Electronics and Information, Xi' an Polytechnic University, Xi'an 710048, China
liliminxiaomi@mail.nwpu.edu.cn

[2] School of Aeronautics, Northwestern Polytechnical University, Xi'an 710072, China

Abstract. Underground water level monitoring is vital for human sustainable development, accurate understanding of underground water level is vital for government decision-making. But usually data collected by the ground water level monitoring device contains a large number of outliers which diverge from the normal data, and it will affect the actual judgment. In this paper, on the basis of a large number of field data analysis, outliers monitoring methodology was proposed based on self-learning Pauta criterion, and outliers correction method was proposed based on smoothing processing. Pauta criterion can detect outliers under the condition of the confidence probability of 99.7 %, for the abnormal values points detected, through the data statistics before, using mean of several values before and after to obtain the revised data. Experimental results show that outliers of underground water during the process of level monitoring can be effectively detected, and ideal curve was gained through revising.

Keywords: Groundwater lever monitoring · Pauta criterion · Self-learning · Smooth processing

1 Introduction

In recent years, groundwater's over-pumping lead to recovery of water lever was slow, water levels have continued decline trend, which makes the limited water resources shortage, more accurate and effective intelligent water-level monitoring can not only improve the accuracy of the traditional artificial water level monitoring, it can also preserve historical data orderly, so that water level change law and tendency in the future can be analyzed [1, 2].

At present, there are all kinds of water level monitoring equipment, More commonly used include pressure type and float type, but generally there is a serious problem, which is that in the data collecting process, data set collected contained a lot of outliers, the outlier is too big or too small compared to the normal data, which do not tally with the actual situation, the cause of outliers can be listed as follows: (1) the random disturbance; (2) acquisition device are influenced by environmental deviation is bigger [3, 4]. Aiming at this problem, the current method used by researchers and designers is to use all the data in front of the mean to describe the abnormal value.

L. Zhang et al. (Eds.): AsiaSim 2016/SCS AutumnSim 2016, Part I, CCIS 643, pp. 497–503, 2016.
DOI: 10.1007/978-981-10-2663-8_51

The method mentioned above can improve the outliers to some extent, but robustness is not high, the reason is that gap between data in a period of time and other data over a period of time is bigger, so it is essential to correct previous statistical law by method. In this paper, outliers detecting method was proposed based on self-learning Pauta criterion [5], meanwhile we use smoothing processing [6, 7] method for correction of outliers.

2 Principle of Pauta Criterion with Self Learning and Smooth Processing

2.1 Principle of Pauta Criterion with Self Learning

Pauta criterion was proposed for outlier detecting of sample data, the basic thoughts of Pauta criterion used to judge of gross error is given the confidence probability of 99. 7 % for the standard, with three times the standard deviation of column limit as the basis, any more than the error of the line, just judge it does not belong to the category of random error, but a gross error. Measurement contains gross error called outliers, under the circumstances, this value is not desirable, it should be removed from the measured data.

Assume sample data set during a period of time, the process of detecting outlier by Pauta criterion can be listed as follows:

Algorithm of Pauta criterion:
1. Calculate mean $\overline{X}$ of $X_i (i = 1,2,3,\ldots,n)$; 2. Calculate standard deviation σ based on $\overline{X}$ and X_i, $\sigma = \sqrt{\sum_{i=1}^{n} (X_i - \overline{X})/(n-1)}$; 3. When judging $X_{i+1}, X_{i+2}, \ldots$, only judging whether $\lvert X_{i+1} - \overline{X} \rvert > 3\sigma$, if it is so, it shows that X_{i+1} is a outlier, on the contrary, reserving X_{i+1}.

Amplitude of groundwater lever changed with time according to some factors, such as the temperature and season, so if only using collected data over a period of time to determine whether all collected data are outliers is less accurate, thus it is possible to add self learning algorithm into Pauta criterion. Figure 1 shows the process of outliers detection based on Pauta criterion with self learning.

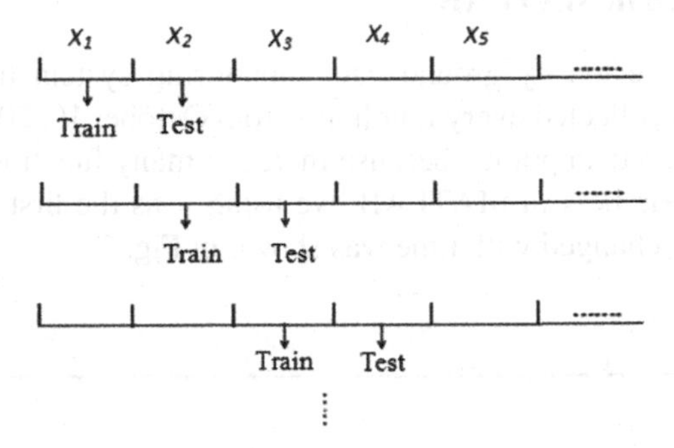

Fig. 1. Outliers detection based on Pauta criterion with self learning

It follows equations as follows.

Algorithm of Pauta criterion with self learning:
1. Calculate mean $\overline{X}$ of $X_i(i=1,2,3,\ldots,n)$;
2. Calculate standard deviation σ based on $\overline{X}$ and X_i, $\sigma=\sqrt{\sum_{i=1}^{n}(X_i-\overline{X})/(n-1)}$;
3. When judging $X_{i+1}, X_{i+2}, \ldots\ldots$, only judging whether $\lvert X_{i+1}-\overline{X}\rvert > 3\sigma$, if it is so, it shows that X_{i+1} is a outlier, on the contrary, reserving X_{i+1}.
4. $X_i = X_{i+1}$, if $i<n$, go to step 1; else end.

2.2 Principle of Smooth Processing

When outliers detected by Pauta criterion with self learning algorithm, it is essential to correct it by smoothing process, which can obey the equation as follows.

Set $x_i(i = 1, 2, \ldots, n1)$ as elements of X_i, when x_{i+1} was detected as outlier, using Eq. 2-1 to correct it.

$$x_{i+1} = \frac{x_{i-5} + x_{i-3} + x_{i-1} + x_{i+2}}{4} \tag{2-1}$$

When x_{i+1} was detected as normal one, using Eq. 2-2 to represent it.

$$x_{i+1} = x_{i+1} \tag{2-2}$$

3 Test Process and Result

3.1 Test Algorithm in MATLAB

Source data was collected by groundwater monitoring system from a site in Inner Mongolia. Data was collected every four hours from October 10, 2015 to December 22, 2015, so there are 438 data points, because there are many functions which have been tested by many researchers in MATLAB, we using it as the first tool for testing our algorithm, the curve changed with time was shown in Fig. 2.

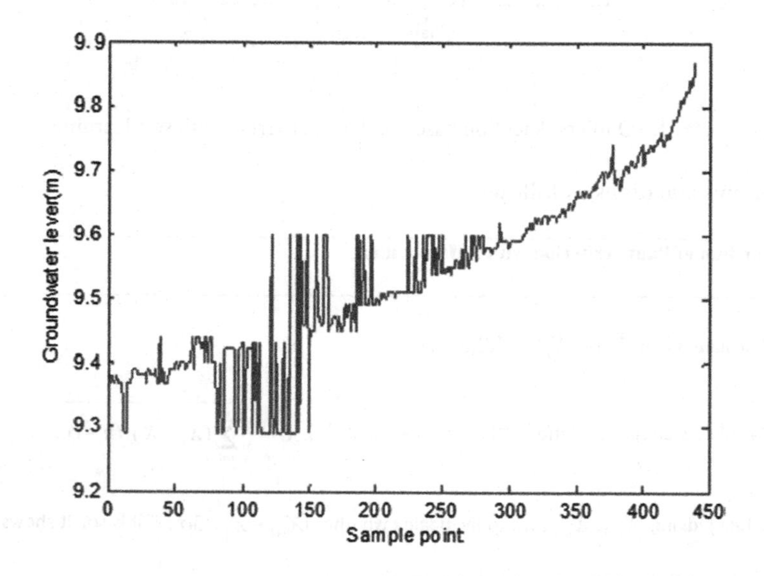

Fig. 2. Source data collected from a site in Inner Mongolia

From Fig. 2 we can see that the trend of groundwater is rising with time, but there are a lot of abnormal sample data, for example sample data from sample point 80 to 300, how to smooth this abnormal sample data is our target.

In this paper, we using Pauta criteria with self learning algorithm and smooth processing as the solving strategies. In order to show the outstanding performance of this algorithm, we test this algorithm and algorithm without self learning.

The test result are shown in Figs. 3 and 4.

After performing detection algorithm using Pauta criteria with self learning and smooth algorithm on source data, we can see from Fig. 4 that the curve is smoother than before, which show that algorithm using Pauta criteria with self learning is effective.

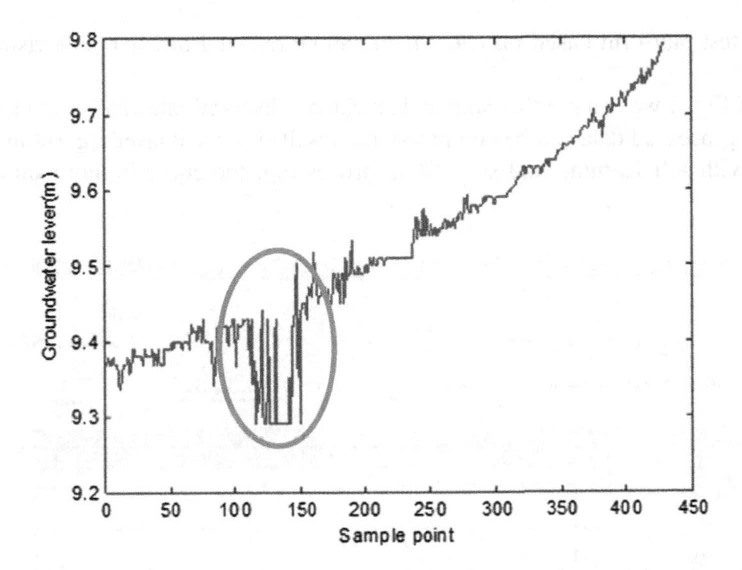

Fig. 3. Curve obtained by Pauta criteria and smooth processing

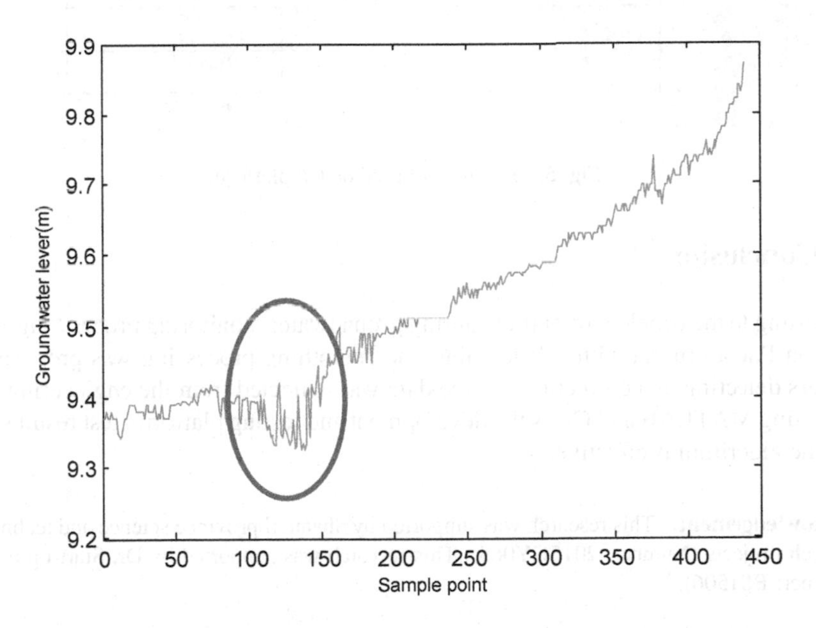

Fig. 4. Curve obtained by Pauta criteria with self learning and smooth processing

3.2 Test Algorithm in C#

In order to test the effectiveness of algorithm proposed in this paper conveniently, and the most important thing is that in order to transplant algorithm to hardware, it is essential to build test platform based on C#, which can be realized in Microsoft visual studio 2010.

From Fig. 5 we can see that source data can be observed intuitively, and the source data and processed data can be compared, the result show that after algorithm of Pauta criteria with self learning and smoothing processing, the curve is more smooth than before.

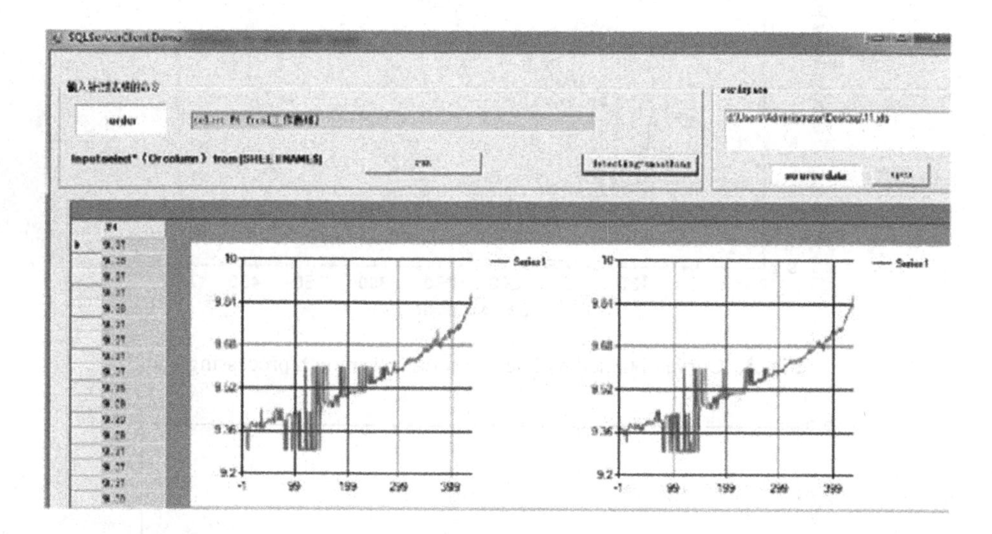

Fig. 5. Test result based on C# platform

4 Conclusion

According to the problem of outliers during groundwater monitoring process, algorithm base on Pauta criteria with self learning and smoothing processing was proposed for outliers detecting and correcting, source data was collected from the engineering practice, using MATLAB and C# as the development and testing platform, test result shows that the algorithm is effective.

Acknowledgement. This research was supported by Shaan xi province science and technology research projects (Number: 2015GY065); This research was supported by Dr. Start-up funding (Number: BS1506).

References

1. Liu, L., Fang, J., Zhao, Z., et al.: Design of groundwater level remote monitoring terminal in irrigation district. Agric. Mechanization Res. **6**, 97–100 (2015)
2. Deng, H., Yang, J.: Case study of groundwater dynamic monitoring technology. Value Eng. **29**, 103–105 (2015)

3. Wang, H., Qiu, G., Xiong, Y.: Research on the way of detecting abnormal altitude data in survey under water. Sichuan Province Surv. Mapp. **27**(1), 36–38
4. Liu, Y.: Exploration on application of groundwater level automatic observation system. Shanxi Hydrotechnics **1**, 88–89 (2011)
5. Liang, Y., Long, C., Xin, Z., et al.: Weak link determination of anti-shock performance of shipboard equipments based on pauta criterion. Chinese J. Ship Res. **2**(5), 10–14 (2007)
6. Sun, M.: Smooth processing methods of vibration signal based on MATLAB. Electr. Measur. Technol. **30**(6), 55–57 (2007)
7. Song, X., Wu, Y., Ma, Y., et al.: Military simulation big data: background, state of the art, and challenges. Math. Probl. Eng. **1**, 1–20 (2015)

A Variable-Volume Earthwork Scheduling Algorithm and Its Visualization

Ting Liao[1], Liping Zheng[2(✉)], Chang Lu[1], and Benzhu Xu[1]

[1] School of Computer and Information, Hefei University of Technology, Hefei 230009, China
{1535512613,84919733}@qq.com

[2] School of Software, Hefei University of Technology, Hefei 230009, China
zhenglp@hfut.edu.cn

Abstract. Earthwork balancing and scheduling is very important for high-filled loess project in civil engineering, and an optimal scheme needs to be considered to transport earthwork from the digging areas to filling ones with the least cost. In this paper, two parameters, loose coefficient and compaction degree, are introduced to capture the characteristics of high-filled loess, and a new scheduling algorithm is presented based on linear programming method. GIS based visualization and analysis are performed to vividly demonstrate the algorithm process. Finally, the proposed algorithm is applied in a real civil engineering project, and experimental results show that it can find out an optimal solution to reduce the cost of earthmoving and speed up the construction progress.

Keywords: Earthwork scheduling · Loose coefficient · Compaction degree · Visualization

1 Introduction

Earthworks are a fundamental part of heavy construction engineering and involve the moving and processing of the soil surface of earth [1]. Dynamic scheduling of earthwork is closely related to the process of the whole project and investment budget. The primary value of models is heuristic, which show the difference between reality and prediction [2]. A good earthwork scheduling scheme can not only reduce costs, but also shorten the construction period. Therefore, selecting a good scheduling algorithm based on original landscape of the construction site needs to be taken seriously, and two properties of soil, loose coefficient and compaction degree should also be taken into consideration, which can effectively save construction costs and shorten construction period.

Earthwork scheduling problem, first proposed by Hieheoek and Kantorovic, is essentially a transportation problem of operations research. Dynamic programming model, multi-objective decision optimization model, large system theory model and linear programming model [3] are commonly used in earthwork scheduling research.

Fund project: Project supported by the National Key Technology R&D Program (Grant No. 2013BAJ06B00).

L. Zhang et al. (Eds.): AsiaSim 2016/SCS AutumnSim 2016, Part I, CCIS 643, pp. 504–513, 2016.
DOI: 10.1007/978-981-10-2663-8_52

Now, linear programming has become a major algorithm of various optimization problems to determine the optimal solution of multivariable linear function under the linear constraint condition. Stark and Nicholls [4] first proposed the idea that using linear programming method to optimize earthwork design. Mayer and Stark [5] developed the linear program model with the objective of minimizing hauling cost over constraints that balance earth quantities. Moreb [6] combined the road slope in road engineering with earthwork scheduling and set up a linear programming model which took road slope as decision variables to reduce the total cost. Linear programming is very suitable for earthwork scheduling problem with its simplification, rapidity and accuracy.

Optimal transportation problem was first proposed by the famous French mathematician Gaspard Monge, he proposed that moving some kind of mass distribution to another as efficiently as possible and using average distance of transport to express the efficiency criteria. Cohen and Guibas [7] presented a monotonically convergent iteration which can be applied to a large class of EMD (Earth Mover's Distance) under transformation problems, although the iteration may converge to only a locally optimal transformation. Rubner [8] proved that EMD had a better performance than the other distances in content-based image retrieval. Shiang-Tai Liu [9] developed a procedure to derive the fuzzy objective value of the fuzzy transportation problem based on the extension principle in that the cost coefficients and the supply and demand quantities are fuzzy numbers. Xia [10] modified the initial transport path as much as possible by using both local and global minimization algorithms and provided numerical simulation of optimal transport paths. Fitschen et al. [11] extended the framework to color image processing and showed how the transportation problem for RGB color images can be tackled by prescribing periodic boundary conditions in the color dimension.

Various dynamic scheduling schemes of earthwork has been proposed under the condition that soil is not expandable and compressible. Two characteristics of soil, the volume in suppliers (digging areas) gets larger with the increasement of loose coefficient and the volume in demanders (filling areas) gets smaller due to the influence of compaction degree, are rarely considered. Therefore, loose coefficient and compaction degree needs to be introduced to optimize the scheduling model.

2 Earthwork Scheduling Model

2.1 Loose Coefficient and Compaction Degree of Soil

Loose coefficient is very important for earthwork productivity, site planning and earthwork scheduling in civil engineering. The volume of soil in natural state will expand after been excavated and can't restore its original volume although been compacted later. Initial loose coefficient is an important parameter for calculating excavator productivity, the number of earthmoving vehicles and abandoned pit volume, it can be expressed in $K_S = V_2/V_1$. Final loose coefficient is an important parameter for calculating site leveling elevation and volume of excavation, and it can be expressed by the formula $K_S' = V_3/V_1$. The compaction degree of soil is one of the key indicators in construction quality inspection of subgrade and pavement. Soil will have a better performance with higher compaction degree, and we can use the formula $T = V_3/V_2$ to express.

V_1 represents the volume of soil under natural conditions, V_2 indicates the loose volume of soil after excavation, V_3 refers to the volume of soil after compaction. In this paper, the initial and final loose coefficients are derived from the reference [12].

2.2 Mathematical Model

Selecting an optimal path to transport earthwork can be summed up as a problem to minimize the cost of earthwork scheduling. The total cost is composed of three parts, excavation cost, transportation cost and compaction cost. In order to minimize the total engineering cost, loose coefficient and compaction degree of soil are both introduced into the research, and a new earthwork scheduling model is established. The objective function is as follows:

$$MinZ = \sum_{i=1}^{m}\sum_{j=1}^{n}[\alpha * (c_{ij}x_{ij}k_i) + \beta * (A_i x_{ij}) + \gamma * (B_j x_{ij}/t_j)] \tag{1}$$

s.t.

$$\sum_{j=1}^{n} x_{ij}k_i \le s_i, i = 1, 2, \ldots, m \tag{2}$$

$$\sum_{i=1}^{m} (x_{ij}/t_j) \le d_j, j = 1, 2, \ldots, n \tag{3}$$

$$1 \le k_i \le 2 \tag{4}$$

$$0 \le t_j \le 1 \tag{5}$$

$$0 \le \alpha \le 1, 0 \le \beta \le 1, 0 \le \gamma \le 1 \tag{6}$$

$$c_{ij} \ge 0, A_i \ge 0, B_j \ge 0 \tag{7}$$

where, Z is the total cost, $c_{ij}x_{ij}k_i$ is transportation cost, $A_{ij}x_{ij}$ is excavation cost, $B_j x_{ij}/t_j$ is compaction cost, α, β and γ, respectively, refers to the proportion of each cost in the total cost, c_{ij} refers to price matrix of per unit volume of earthwork transportation, x_{ij} refers to the earthwork from the i digging area to the j filling area, k_i refers to loose coefficient of the i digging area, A_i represents excavation cost of per unit volume, B_j represents compaction cost of per unit volume, t_j indicates compaction degree of the j filling area.

3 Solving Ideas

3.1 Mathematical Model Description of Earthwork Scheduling

Problem description: the best scheduling scheme of transporting variable-volume earthwork from digging areas to filling areas.

Features:

(1) multiple digging areas and multiple filling areas;
(2) volume of soil to be dug in each digging area is different, and so is the volume of soil to be filled in each filling area;
(3) the freight costs of each digging - filling area are different;
(4) actual volume of earthwork involved in transportation and the volume of earthwork after final settlement will change because of the impact of loose coefficient and compaction degree of soil.

Goal: we want to introduce loose coefficient and compaction degree of soil into linear programming model as constraint conditions and organize dynamic scheduling of earthwork reasonably under the premise of satisfying the requirements of each digging - filling area, so as to achieve minimum transportation cost and speed up the construction progress (Fig. 1).

Supposing that there are m digging areas $W_1, W_2, \ldots, W_m$ ($m \geq 0$), the theoretical amount of excavation correspondingly is $s_1, s_2, \ldots, s_m$ ($s_i \geq 0$, $i = 1, 2, \ldots, m$); n filling areas $T_1, T_2, \ldots, T_n$ ($n \geq 0$), the theoretical amount of filling correspondingly is $d_1, d_2, \ldots, d_n$ ($d_j \geq 0$); loose coefficient is k_i ($i = 1, 2, \ldots, m$); compaction degree is $t_1, t_2, \ldots, t_j$ ($j = 1, 2, \ldots, n$). Transportation cost can be expressed as the formula (8):

$$Z' = \sum_{i=1}^{m} \sum_{j=1}^{n} c_{ij} x_{ij} k_i \tag{8}$$

where, Z' represents earthwork transportation cost.

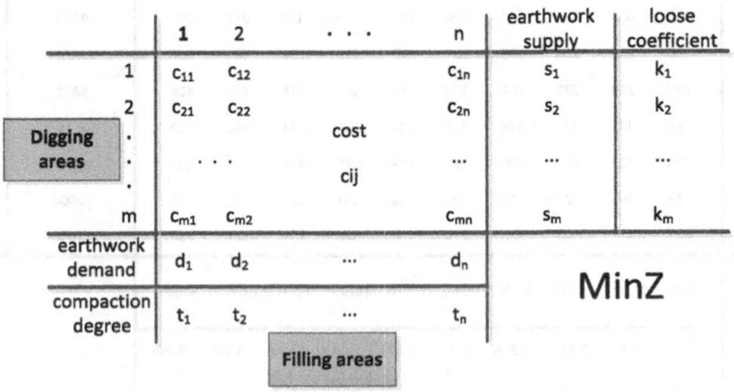

Digging areas	1	2	...	n	earthwork supply	loose coefficient
1	c_{11}	c_{12}		c_{1n}	s_1	k_1
2	c_{21}	c_{22}	cost	c_{2n}	s_2	k_2
.		...		...	...	...
.			cij			
m	c_{m1}	c_{m2}		c_{mn}	s_m	k_m
earthwork demand	d_1	d_2	...	d_n	MinZ	
compaction degree	t_1	t_2	...	t_n		

Filling areas

Fig. 1. Sketch map of earthwork scheduling problem

3.2 Earthwork Calculation of Digging - Filling Areas

Triangular prism method has been used in this paper to calculate earthwork volume. We firstly calculate filling (digging) earthwork volume of each triangular prism based on the given terrain surface and designed surface, and then get all filling (digging) earthwork volume of triangular prism within the region.

4 Experimental Results and Visualization

4.1 Analysis of Experimental Results

The experimental data in this paper come from a piece of construction area in high-filled loess project. The following figure contains a lot of data including digging volume of each piece of digging area, filling volume of each piece of filling area, the freight costs of each path and loose coefficient and compaction degree of soil in each experimental area (Fig. 2).

Without considering loose coefficient and compaction degree, the transportation cost of classic earthwork algorithm is 1.79297×10^7 yuan. However, the actual transportation cost is much more than the theoretical calculation values because the volume of soil under the nature state will expand after excavation, and different soil has different expansion extent. If loose coefficient and compaction degree are both introduced into the model, actual transportation cost will be bigger, and so is the excavation cost. Scheduling scheme and the total cost under such condition are as follows:

The above data show that current scheduling scheme is not optimal for not considering the swelling characteristic of soil. Therefore, we firstly calculates the theoretical digging volume under the natural state, and then the actual digging earthwork

digging areas \ filling areas (freight yuan/ m^3)	0	1	2	5	6	7	12	13	18	19	earthwork supply (m^3)	loose coefficient
3	389	258	128	401	276	162	237	200	300	330	13050	1.35
4	527	396	266	536	408	284	332	242	330	300	5993	1.27
8	401	276	162	389	258	128	162	100	200	242	12105	1.375
9	536	408	284	527	396	256	284	170	242	200	4136	1.29
10	200	239	328	100	164	279	261	389	401	536	9874	1.25
11	239	200	238	164	100	164	130	258	276	408	3331	1.29
14	563	443	332	536	408	284	266	138	170	100	2041	1.475
15	300	327	397	200	239	328	279	401	389	527	21245	1.375
16	327	300	327	239	200	238	164	276	258	396	10000	1.21
17	397	327	300	328	238	200	100	162	128	266	11000	1.125
earthwork demand (m^3)	31109	15800	3240	9300	9500	10170	10700	8600	11054	4000		
compaction degree	0.835	0.83	0.84	0.835	0.83	0.835	0.85	0.84	0.86	0.905		

Fig. 2. Sample data of experimental areas

volume can be reduced because the volume of soil will swell to the theoretical value under the impact of loose coefficient. Improved scheduling scheme is as follows:

4.2 Visualized Analysis

In order to simulate the rugged and complex terrain vividly, we use C ++ programming language to develop system with the help of GIS which has strong spatial information processing functions. We build 3D digital model DEM for the whole construction site and use Triangulated Irregular Network (TIN) model to display the terrain. TIN can be used to approximate terrain surface through a series of non-crossing, non-overlapping triangles, and express complex terrain at different levels of resolution. Delaunay triangulation is best in fitting terrain, and often adopted to generate TIN. Split-merge algorithm, triangulation growth algorithm and point-by-point insertion algorithm are common generation algorithms of D_triangulation, and each method has its own strengths. Split-merge algorithm is choosed in this paper, the flow chart of this algorithm is as follows:

The terrain data include number, east coordinate Y(m), north coordinates X(m) and elevation H(m). These scattered points are used to construct the surface of the terrain though D_ triangulation method. Then we use the geomorphic layered method to add ribbon bar, and different elevation thus can be displayed by different color. Finally, vegetation models are added to make the terrain more vivid.

Construction process of high-filled loess project is actually a process of transporting earthwork from high mountains to ravines for urban construction. It is very important for construction managers to understand the change of the terrain and digging-filling thickness. In order to optimize dynamic scheduling of earthwork and simulate the process more vivid, we divide the construction area into $m \times n$ $(m, n = 1, 2, \ldots \infty)$

freight (yuan/m^3) / filling areas / digging areas	0	1	2	5	6	7	12	13	18	19	theoretical value of earthwork supply (m^3)	loose coefficient	actual value of earthwork supply (m^3)
3	0	7987	3857	0	0	5773	0	0	0	0	13050	1.35	17617
4	0	4627	0	0	0	0	0	0	2984	0	5993	1.27	7611
8	0	0	0	0	0	6406	0	10238	0	0	12105	1.375	16644
9	0	0	0	0	0	0	0	0	3926	1409	4136	1.29	5335
10	0	0	0	11137	1205	0	0	0	0	0	9874	1.25	12342
11	0	0	0	0	4296	0	0	0	0	0	3331	1.29	4296
14	0	0	0	0	0	0	0	0	0	3010	2041	1.475	3010
15	29211	0	0	0	0	0	0	0	0	0	21245	1.375	29211
16	0	0	0	0	5944	0	213	0	5943	0	10000	1.21	12100
17	0	0	0	0	0	0	12375	0	0	0	11000	1.125	12375
theoretical value of earthwork demand(m^3)	31109	15800	3240	9300	9500	10170	10700	8600	11054	4000	excavation cost:	1.20541×10^5(yuan)	
compaction degree	0.835	0.83	0.84	0.835	0.83	0.835	0.85	0.84	0.86	0.905	transportation cost:	2.4182×10^7(yuan)	
											compaction cost:	1.08006×10^5(yuan)	
actual value of earthwork demand(m^3)	37256	19036	3857	11137	11445	12179	12588	10238	12853	4419	total cost:	2.44105×10^7(yuan)	

Fig. 3. The actual scheduling scheme and cost after considering the loose coefficient and compaction degree

parts. The value of m and n in this paper are both 10. There are 10 digging areas and 10 filling areas.

After using improved linear programming earthwork scheduling algorithm, the actual situation of the earthwork scheduling is shown in the Figs. 3, 4, 5, 6 and 7 below:

digging areas \ filling areas (freight yuan/m^3)	0	1	2	5	6	7	12	13	18	19	theoretical value of earthwork supply (m^3)	loose coefficient	actual value of earthwork supply (m^3)
3	0	0	3857	0	0	9193	0	0	0	0	9666.7	1.35	13050
4	0	0	0	0	0	821	0	0	5172	0	4718.9	1.27	5993
8	0	0	0	0	0	1867	0	10238	0	0	8803.6	1.375	12105
9	0	0	0	0	0	0	0	0	1758	2378	3206.2	1.29	4136
10	0	0	0	9874	0	0	0	0	0	0	7899.2	1.25	9874
11	0	0	0	0	3331	0	0	0	0	0	2582.2	1.29	3331
14	0	0	0	0	0	0	0	0	0	2041	1383.7	1.475	2041
15	19982	0	0	1263	0	0	0	0	0	0	15450.9	1.375	21245
16	0	0	0	0	8114	298	1588	0	0	0	8264.5	1.21	10000
17	0	0	0	0	0	0	11000	0	0	0	9777.8	1.125	11000
theoretical value of earthwork demand(m^3)	31109	15800	3240	9300	9500	10170	10700	8600	11054	4000	excavation cost:	7.17537×10^4 (yuan)	
compaction degree	0.835	0.83	0.84	0.835	0.83	0.835	0.85	0.84	0.86	0.905	transportation cost:	1.69127×10^7 (yuan)	
											compaction cost:	1.08006×10^5 (yuan)	
actual value of earthwork demand(m^3)	37256	19036	3857	11137	11445	12179	12588	10238	12853	4419	total cost:	1.70924×10^7 (yuan)	

Fig. 4. Improved scheduling scheme and costs

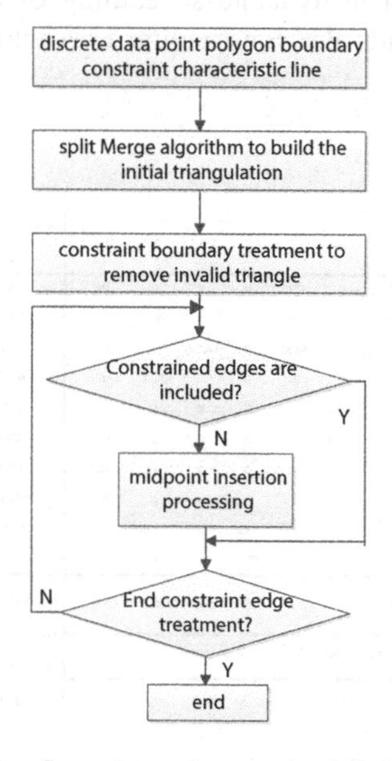

Fig. 5. Construction flow chart of constrained Delaunay triangulation

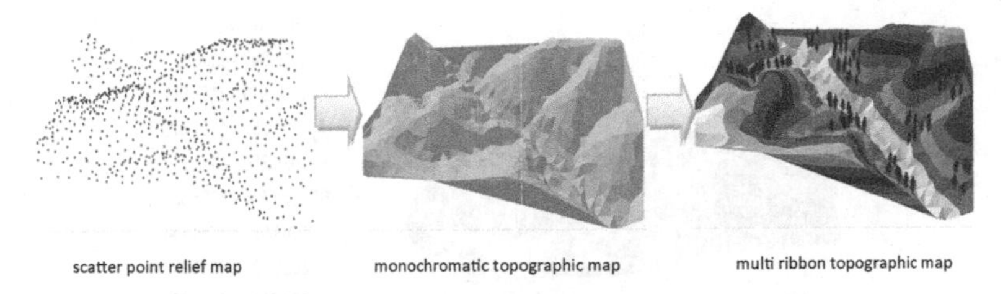

Fig. 6. Generation and rendering process of terrain map

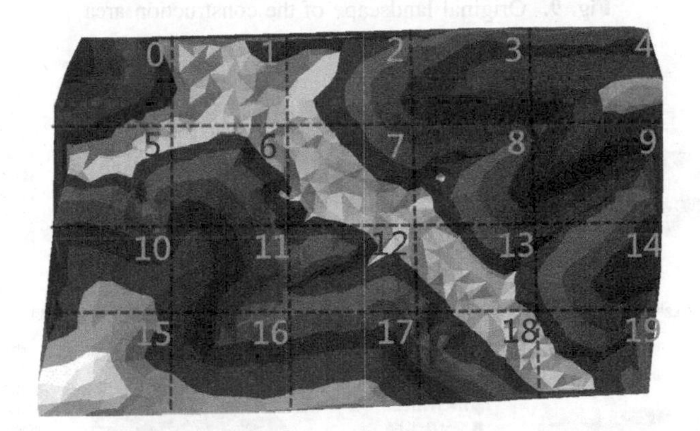

Fig. 7. Division of construction area

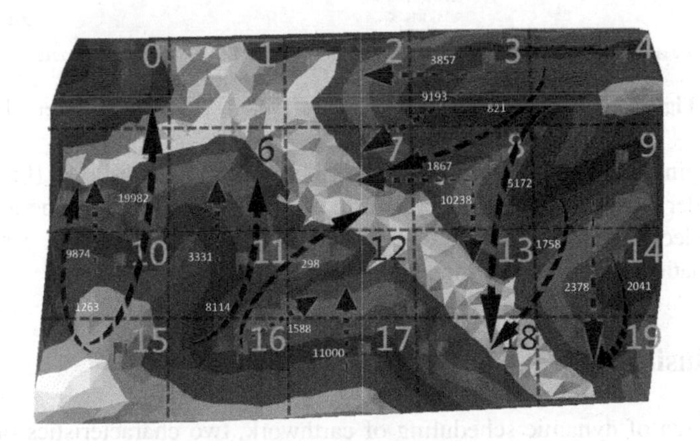

Fig. 8. Earthwork scheduling route

In the diagram, the arrows point to the directions of earthwork scheduling, the numbers beside the arrows are earthwork volume of the transportation route, its unit is m^3. The corresponding partitions of earthwork scheduling are: 3 -> 2, 7, 4 -> 7, 18, 8 -> 7, 13, 9 -> 18, 19, 10 -> 5, 11 -> 6, 14 -> 19, 15 -> 5, 10, 16 -> 6, 7, 12, 17 -> 12 (Fig. 8).

Fig. 9. Original landscape of the construction area

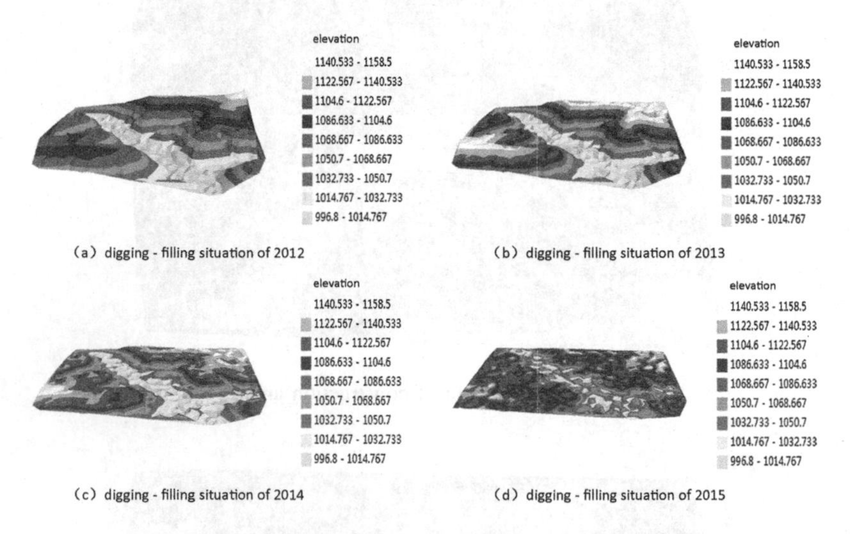

Fig. 10. Digging-filling visualization of different construction periods

The original landscape map of the construction area is as follows (Fig. 9):

We render a digging-filling effect picture of the terrain in different periods based on the data collected by builders and equipment in different construction periods to provide information support for future construction (Fig. 10).

5 Conclusion

In the research of dynamic scheduling of earthwork, two characteristics of soil, loose coefficient and compaction degree are both introduced into the linear programming model to minimize costs, and a better scheduling scheme is presented to make the allocation more reasonable. Visualization and analysis are performed to simulate the process of reclamation and dynamic scheduling of earthwork. Experimental results and visualization show that the improved algorithm have a better performance than old ones, and can effectively save construction cost, shorten construction period and guarantee the smooth completion of the earthwork scheduling project.

References

1. Fu, J: Logistics of earthmoving operations: simulation and optimization. Traffic Logistics (2013)
2. Oreskes, N., Shrader-Frechette, K., Belitz, K.: Verification, validation, and confirmation of numerical models in the Earth sciences. Science **263**(5147), 641–646 (1994)
3. Xiaowei, L., Dawei, L., Shaoyang, J., et al.: Dynamic allocation system simulation of earth-rock based on linear programming. Yellow River **35**(3), 120–123 (2013)
4. Stark, R.M., Nicholls, R.L.: Mathematical Foundations for Design: Civil Engineering Systems. McGraw-Hill, New York (1971). J. Technology and Engineering
5. Mayer, R., Stark, R.: Earthmoving logistics. J. Constr. Div. **107**(2), 297–312 (1981)
6. Moreb, A.A.: Linear programming model for finding optimal roadway grades that minimize earthwork cost. Eur. J. Oper. **93**(1), 148–154 (1996)
7. Cohen, S., Guibas, L.: The earth mover's distance under transformation sets. In: The Proceedings of the Seventh IEEE International Conference on Computer Vision, 1999, vol. 2, pp. 1076–1083. IEEE (1999)
8. Rubner, Y., Tomasi, C., Guibas, L.J.: The earth mover's distance as a metric for image retrieval. Int. J. Comput. Vision **40**(2), 99–121 (2000)
9. Liu, S.T., Kao, C.: Solving fuzzy transportation problems based on extension principle. Eur. J. Oper. Res. **153**(3), 661–674 (2004)
10. Xia, Q.: Numerical simulation of optimal transport paths. In: Second International Conference on Computer Modeling & Simulation-volume. IEEE Computer Society, pp. 521–525 (2008)
11. Fitschen. J.H., Laus, F., Steidl, G.: Dynamic optimal transport with mixed boundary condition for color image processing. In: 2015 International Conference on Sampling Theory and Applications (SampTA). IEEE (2015)
12. Zhengrong, J., Guoliang, Z.: Concise Construction Manual, Fourth edn. China Architecture & Building Press, Beijing (2005)

The Power Flow Simulation and Calculation Method for Metro Power Supply System Based on the Train-Network Coupling

Chengzhou Huang[1](✉), Jiahua Zhang[2], Yuezong Li[2], Li Zeng[2], Jianjun Xu[2], and Jinling Zhu[1]

[1] Chengdu Yunda Technology Co., Ltd., Chengdu 611731, China
chengzhouhuang@foxmail.com
[2] Southwest Jiaotong University, Chengdu 610031, China
zhangjiahua2006@foxmail.com

Abstract. Based on the analysis of the equivalent models of the traction transformer and the train in the existing metro power supply system (MPSS), this paper embeds the coupling relation between the metro traction power supply system (MTPSS) and the train operation into the model and combines with the corresponding range of the output current, the voltage and the resistance of the 6 section type equivalent external characteristic curve of the 12-pulse rectifier unit to research and design the AC/DC power flow calculation method for the MPSS, this paper analyzes the operation efficiency and the power flow calculation error of the method. The result shows that this method can effectively improve the accuracy of the power flow value calculation and has the advantages of the fast calculation speed and the good real-time performance, besides the model can describe coupling relations between the train and traction network more accurately.

Keywords: Metro · Traction power supply system · Power flow calculation · Rectifier unit

1 Introduction

With the rapid development of the city rail transportation industry and the social economy, the people have higher requirements for the transportation's comfort, rapidity, safety and punctuality, so it has important theoretical and practical significance to design the secure and punctual metro operation. Chinese MPSS mostly adopts the DC750 V or DC1500 V bilateral power supply mode [1], for this mode, the domestic and foreign scholars have made a lot of researches on the modeling method of the DC side of MTPSS and the related power flow calculation methods, the most significant results are the current loop model [2] and the node voltage model [3]. The loop current model is only suitable for the simple system consisting of the catenary, the rail and the return line, which is used to calculate the voltage and current of the catenary and the rail and the longitudinal distribution of the catenary; the node voltage model is widely applied to the catenary with arbitrary topology structure, which is also suitable for the catenary under the other power supply modes, it is widely used but

L. Zhang et al. (Eds.): AsiaSim 2016/SCS AutumnSim 2016, Part I, CCIS 643, pp. 514–525, 2016.
DOI: 10.1007/978-981-10-2663-8_53

rarely involves the modeling and the power flow calculation of the high-voltage and mid-voltage systems [4–7]. The literature [8] got the train location and the power distribution information by the Train Diagram based on the model of 12-pulse rectifier unit, which could calculate the power flow in the MPSS, but it always took the power flow value in the rated area of rectifier unit as the benchmark, so it would lead some errors in the calculation results. The literature [9] embedded the AC side into the DC side in the MPSS, which regarded the DC side power convergence as the index, so it was not easy to extract and distinguish the power flow value of the AC side.

In this paper, the DC traction substation is equivalent to the controlled voltage source with the resistance, and the train is equivalent to the power source model. According to the train operation information from the Traffic Dispatching System, this paper takes the voltage and current ranges of the 12-pulse rectifier unit 6 section type characteristic curve to calculate the DC side power flow value, then it delivers the value to the AC side for iterative calculation, finally it feeds the power flow value calculated by the AC side to the DC side to do cross iterative calculation. The theoretical and experimental analyses show that the method can effectively improve the calculating speed of the power flow value, and has the advantages of the fast computing speed, the good real-time performance, at the same time, the model can more accurately describe the coupling relations between the metro train and the traction network.

2 The Modeling of the MPSS

2.1 The Structure of the MPSS

The MPSS is the power source of urban rail transit operation, which is mainly responsible for the electrical energy transmission, transformation and supplies, it supplies the electric train and provides the power lighting electricity for the subway station, the interval, the depot, the control center and other buildings. According to the different functions of the system, the MPSS is divided into: the external power supply, the main substation or switch substation, the traction substation, and the power substation. The MPSS mainly consists of three parts, the high-voltage power supply system, the MTPSS and the power lighting power supply system. As shown in Fig. 1.

Where the external power source is the direct power source of the main substation or the switch substation, which is the ultimate power supplier of the whole power supply system, it is mainly the power plant; the high-voltage power supply system change the AC110 kV imported from the main substation or the switch substation into AC35 kV by the step-down transformer, then supplies it to the traction power supply system and the power lighting power supply system; the MTPSS rectifies and reduces the AC35 kV to the DC1500 V or DC750 V, supplying to the train traction, the battery charging and the other DC power supply as well as the train lighting, the air conditioners, the air compressors and the other AC supplies, where the DC1500 V is mainly used for the catenary power supply mode, and the DC750 V is mainly applied for the contact rail power supply mode. The power lighting system transforms the AC35 kV into AC400 V to supply for the stations as well as the lighting, the air conditioners, the elevators, the blower fans and the other power sources between stations, besides, it also

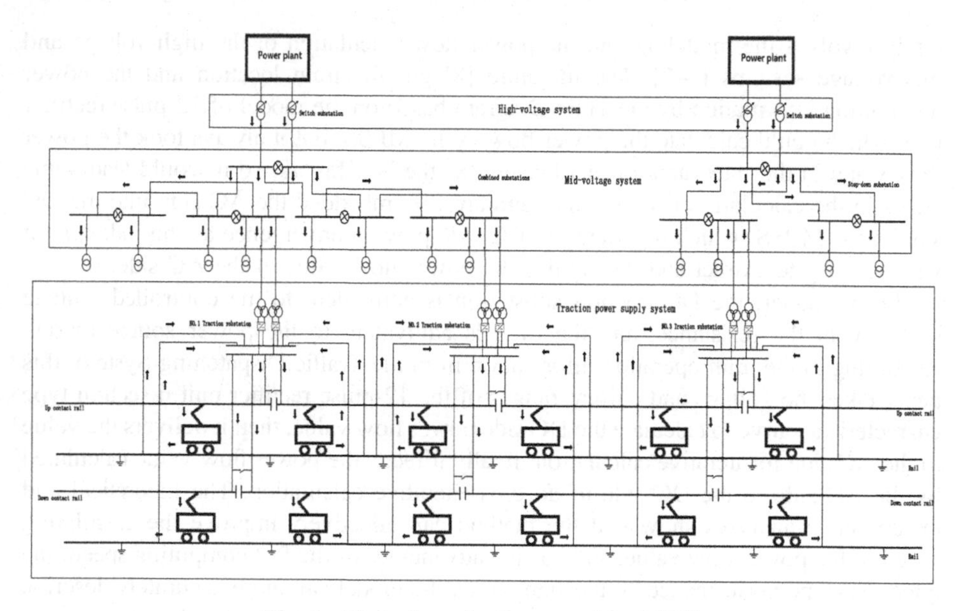

Fig. 1. The schematic diagram of the MPSS

provides the communication, the signal, the automation and the other equipment power supply with electricity.

2.2 The Power Components Modeling

The MTPSS belonging to the DC power supply part mainly includes the traction substations, the trains, the transmission lines, the catenaries, and the running rails, etc., and the high-voltage power supply system and the power lighting power supply system belonging to the AC power supply side mainly include the main substations, the substations, the transmission lines and the power loads.

2.2.1 The DC Power Supply Side

The power components of the MTPSS is equivalent with the network model of the catenary-rail-ground, which ignores the effect of the drainage network on the power flow calculation. The following are the equivalent models for the traction substation, the train, the rail, the running rail and ground in the DC power supply side.

(1) The traction substation

The traction substation modeling is mainly the modeling of the rectifier unit, the 24-pulse rectifier unit is equivalent to two 12-pulse rectifier unit in parallel, because the 24-pulse rectifier unit's circuit structure and its output characteristics are complex, but they are similar to the 12-pulse rectifier unit's. The 12-pulse rectifier unit external characteristic curve is the curve that the output voltage of the DC side changes with the load current I_d. The rectifier unit can be divided into five different operation areas

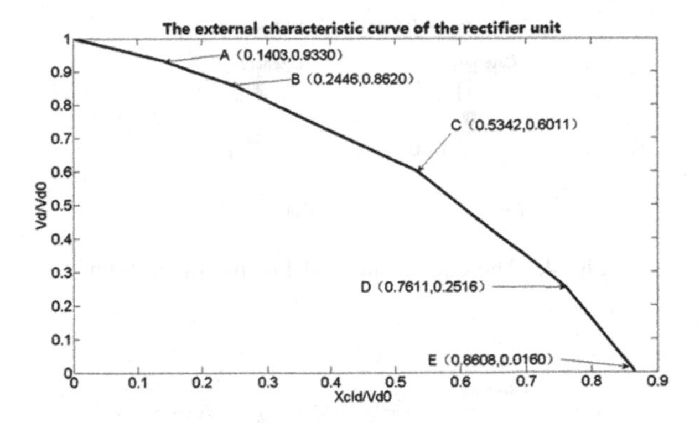

Fig. 2. The equivalent external characteristic curve of the rectifier unit

according to its number of the conductive diodes and the change range of the load current. When the $k \in (0, 0.4226)$, the external characteristic curve of the rectifier unit can be equivalent to six sections as shown in Fig. 2.

According to Thevenin theorem and the rectifier unit equivalent external characteristic curve, the traction substation is equivalent to the controlled voltage source with the resistance in series model as shown in Fig. 3.

(2) The metro train

The train is equivalent to the power source model as shown in Fig. 4, compared with the current source model, the power source model is closer to the reality system and considers the current-getting influence of the adjacent trains. It can also calculate out the current the train gets and the network voltage of the catenary at any time.

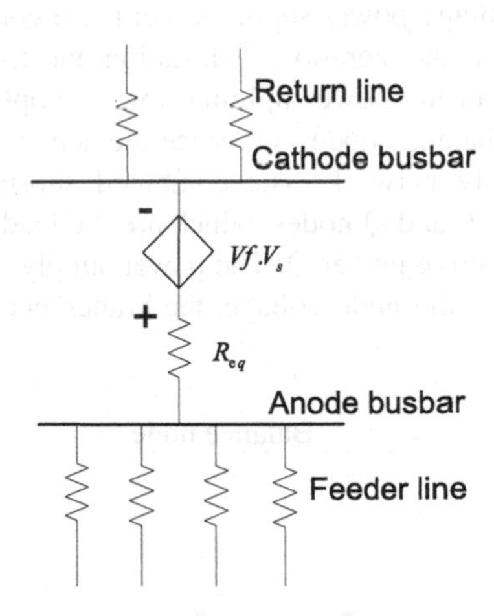

Fig. 3. The equivalent model of traction substation

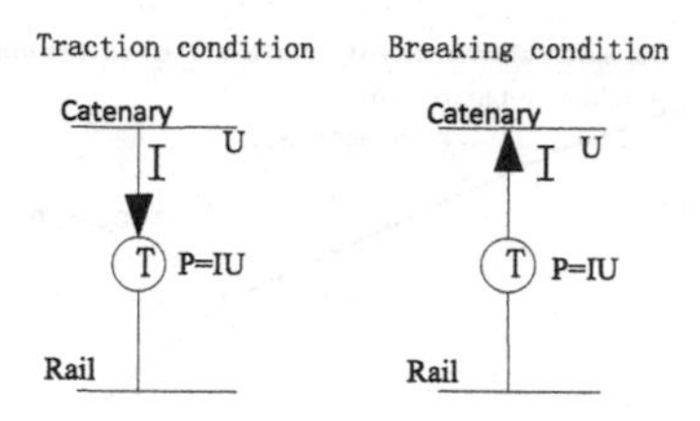

Fig. 4. The equivalent model of the metro train

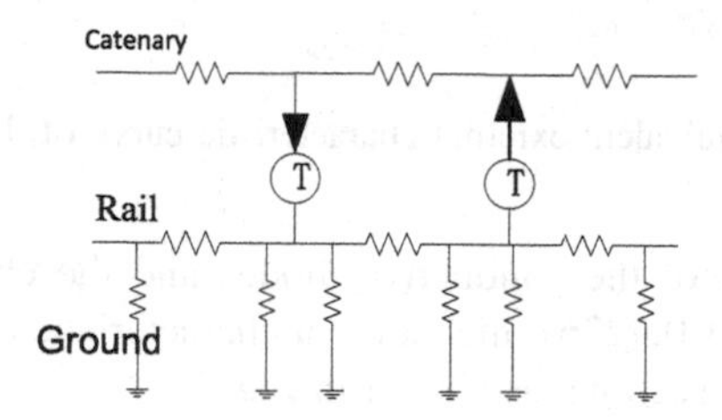

Fig. 5. The equivalent model of DC side power supply distribution

(3) The catenary, the rail and the ground

The three layer model is used to replace the up and down catenaries and the rails with different values of the resistance. The model is equivalent to the π circuit with considering the leakage resistance of the rail to the ground as shown in Fig. 5.

2.2.2 The AC Power Supply Side

The AC power supply side modeling focuses on the equivalent models of the main substations in the high-voltage power supply system, the combined substations in the traction network, as well as the step-down substation and its corresponding transmission line and power load in the power lighting power supply system. The main substation is regarded as the balance node to balance the active and reactive power of the whole metro power supply network. The combined substation and the step-down substation are taken as the P and Q nodes, which are the load that always consume the active power P and the reactive power Q. The power supply circuit is equivalent to the π circuit model to calculate the node voltage, the branch current, the load current, the

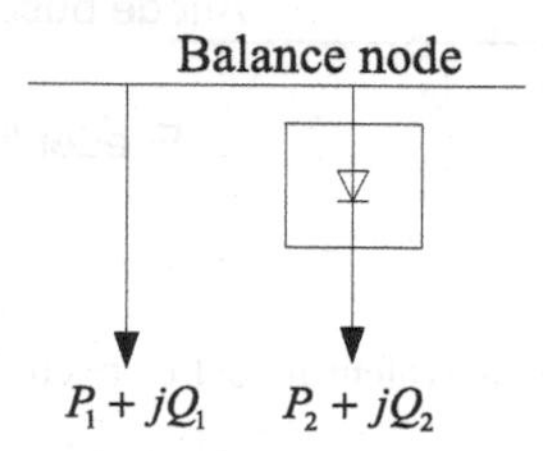

Fig. 6. The equivalent model of the substation

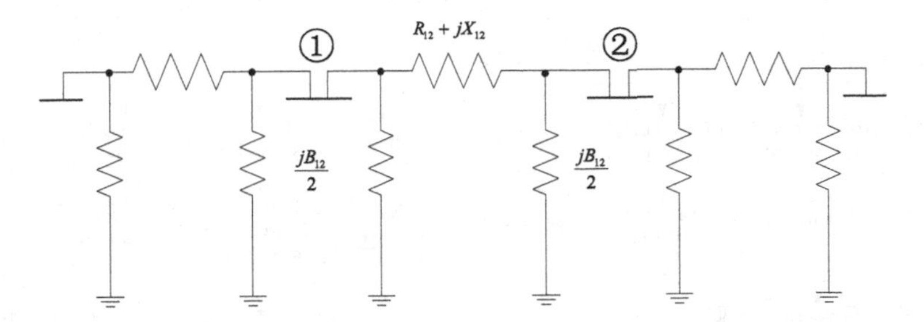

Fig. 7. The equivalent model of the AC side power supply distribution

load power and so on. The equivalent model of the substation and the power supply circuit are shown in Figs. 6 and 7.

3 The Power Flow Calculation

3.1 The Framework Design of the Power Flow Calculation

According to the electric components model and their attribute parameters of the MTPSS, combined with the basic line data and the train operation information, this paper builds the AC and DC side power supply models, then calculate the related AC/DC power value based on the initial value of the rectifier unit and the AC side power flow value iteration. The framework of the power flow calculation is shown in Fig. 8.

3.2 The Power Flow Calculation of the DC Traction Bow Net

This paper builds the DC side traction power supply model shown in Fig. 9, according to the locations and numbers of the traction substations, the length of the power supply lines as well as the location and the received power the of the train getting from the Traffic Dispatching System at the moment. The detailed calculation steps and implementation methods are as follows:

Step1: Respectively number the traction substations nodes, the trains nodes, the catenaries nodes, and the rails nodes in sequence;
Step2: Create the node admittance matrix Y according to the power components attribute parameter and the information of the train operation (the location and the received power), and set the $flag = 0$;
Step3: Judge whether the flag is 0, if $flag = 0$, solve the linear equals according to the related power value and node voltage equation $U = Y^{-1}I$ of the rectifier unit operation area;
Step4: Judge whether the solved load current I_n (n = 1,2,...... is the node number) is in the load current range $I_i \in (I_{\min}, I_{\max})$ of the rectifier unit operation area, if all the current I_n (n = 1,2,......) of the rectifier unit is in the range, it is unnecessary to adjust the rectifier unit operation area, otherwise the rectifier unit operation area

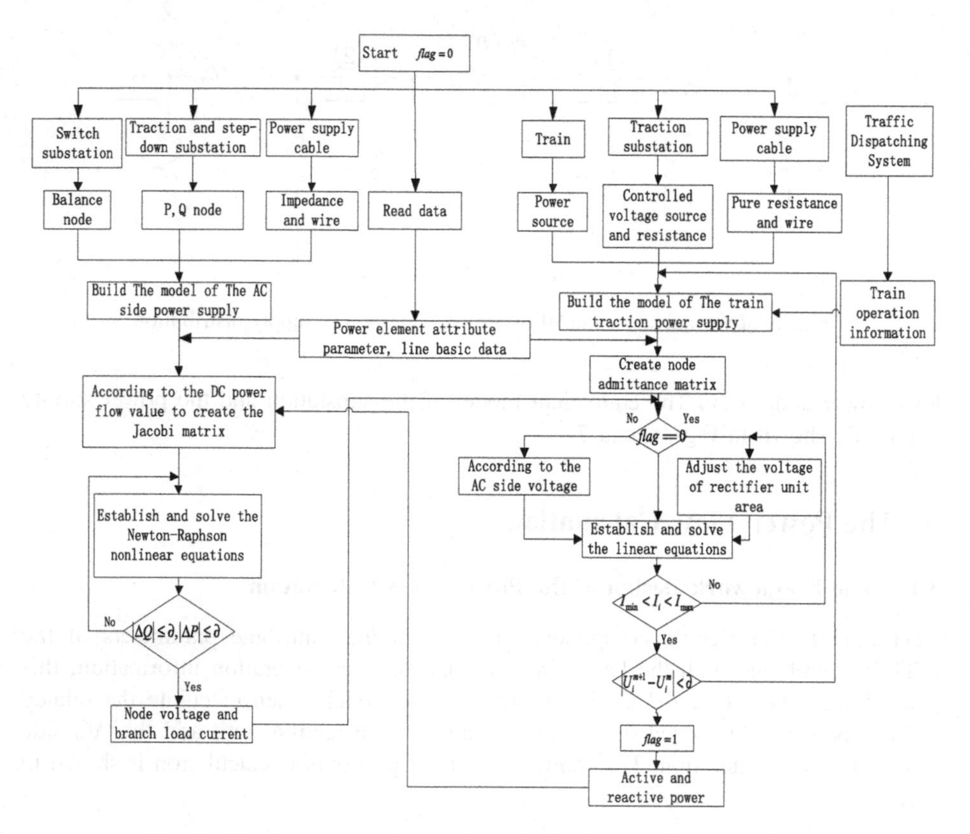

Fig. 8. The framework design of the AC/DC power flow calculation

should be adjusted, if $I_n < I_{\min}$, which means the load current is less than the minimum current of the operation area, set the rectifier unit operation area to the previous one, else set to the latter one.

Step5: Judge whether the node voltage of each train meets the convergence precision $\left|U_i^{m+1} - U_i^m\right| < \partial$, if it does not, modify the attribute parameters of train power source model and return to the **Step2** until the voltage is convergent, where the U_i^m is the traction network voltage after m iterations when the No.i train is at the current location.

Step6: If $flag = 1$, which means the train node voltage of the DC side is convergent, it needs to establish the node voltage equation $U = Y^{-1}I$ according to the AC side power flow value.

Step7: Judge whether the node voltage of each train meets the convergence precision $\left|U_i^{m+1} - U_i^m\right| < \partial$, if it does not, modify the attribute parameters of train power source model and return to the Step2 until the voltage is convergent.

Step8: The system is convergent, then solve the active and reactive power consumed by the DC side.

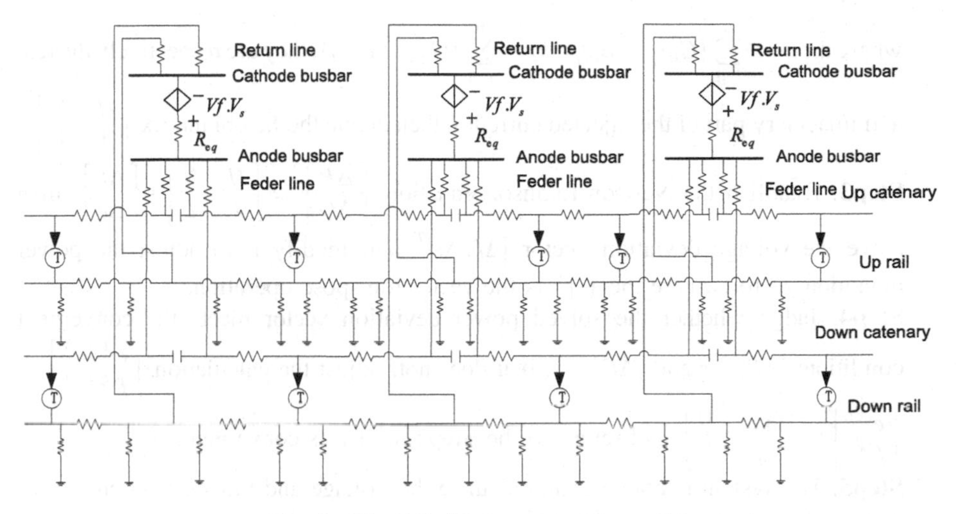

Fig. 9. The DC side power supply model

3.3 The Power Flow Calculation of the AC Traction Bow Net

According to the main substations, the combined substations and the step-down substations and its corresponding power supply distributions equivalent models, also combined with the attribute parameters of the equivalent model and line basic data, this paper builds the DC side power supply model as shown in Fig. 10. The specific steps and implementation methods are as follows:

Step1: Respectively number the main substations nodes, the combined substations nodes and the step-down substations nodes in sequence, then solve the admittance of each node $Y_{ij} = G_{ij} + jB_{ij}$ according to the parameters of the power components, and preset the initial value of the each node voltage as e_0, f_0 (i = 1,2,……,n, n is the number of the nodes), for the balance node (the main substation): $e_0 = 1.1, f_0 = 0$, for the PQ node (the combined substation and the step-down substation): $e_0 = 1$, $f_0 = 0$.

Step2: Calculate the power deviation vector according to the initial value of each node voltage: $\Delta P_i = P_{is} - e_i \sum_{j=1}^{n} (G_{ij}e_j - B_{ij}f_j) - f_i \sum_{j=1}^{n} (G_{ij}f_j + B_{ij}e_j)$, where P_{is} is the injected active power of the PQ node i, j (i, j = 1,2,…,n) are the row and column in the matrix; $\Delta Q_i = Q_{is} - f_i \sum_{j=1}^{n} (G_{ij}e_j - B_{ij}f_j) + e_i \sum_{j=1}^{n} (G_{ij}f_j + B_{ij}e_j)$, where the Q_{is} is the injected active power of the PQ node i, then calculate the Jacobi matrix elements according to the voltage of each node and its corresponding admittance value, if $i \neq j$, $H_{ij} = \frac{\partial \Delta P_i}{\partial \Delta \delta_j} = -G_{ij}f_i + B_{ij}e_i, N_{ij} = -G_{ij}e_i + B_{ij}f_i, J_{ij} = -G_{ij}e_i + B_{ij}f_i = -N_{ij}$, $L_{ij} = -G_{ij}f_i + B_{ij}e_i = H_{ij}$, $L_{ij} = -G_{ij}f_i + B_{ij}e_i = H_{ij}$, if $i = j$, $H_{ii} = -b_i + B_{ii}e_i - G_{ii}f_i, N_{ii} = -a_i - G_{ii}e_i - B_{ii}f_i$, $J_{ii} = -a_i + G_{ii}e_i + B_{ii}f_i, L_{ii} = b_i + B_{ii}e_i - G_{ii}f_i$, where the $a_i = \sum_{j=1}^{n} \left(G_{ij}e_j - B_{ij}f_j\right), b_i = \sum_{j=1}^{n} \left(G_{ij}f_j + B_{ij}e_j\right)$, they are respectively the real and imaginary part of the injected current I_i then create the Jacobi matrix $\begin{bmatrix} H & N \\ J & L \end{bmatrix}$.

Step3: Establish the Newton-Raphson equation $\begin{bmatrix} \Delta P \\ \Delta Q \end{bmatrix} = \begin{bmatrix} H & N \\ J & L \end{bmatrix} \cdot \begin{bmatrix} \Delta f \\ \Delta e \end{bmatrix}$, then solve the voltage deviation vector $[\Delta f, \Delta e]^T$ and modify it to adjust the power deviation vector, where the $\{\cdot\}^T$ is the vector transpose operation.

Step4: Judge whether the solved power deviation vector meets the convergent condition: $|\Delta P| \le \varepsilon$ and $|\Delta Q| \le \varepsilon$, if it does not, adjust the calculation $\begin{bmatrix} e^{(k+1)} \\ f^{(k+1)} \end{bmatrix} = \begin{bmatrix} e^{(k)} \\ f^{(k)} \end{bmatrix} - \begin{bmatrix} \Delta e^{(k+1)} \\ \Delta f^{(k+1)} \end{bmatrix}$ and return to the **Step2** until it is convergent.

Step5: The system is convergent, calculate the voltage and branch load current of each node as well as its active and reactive power.

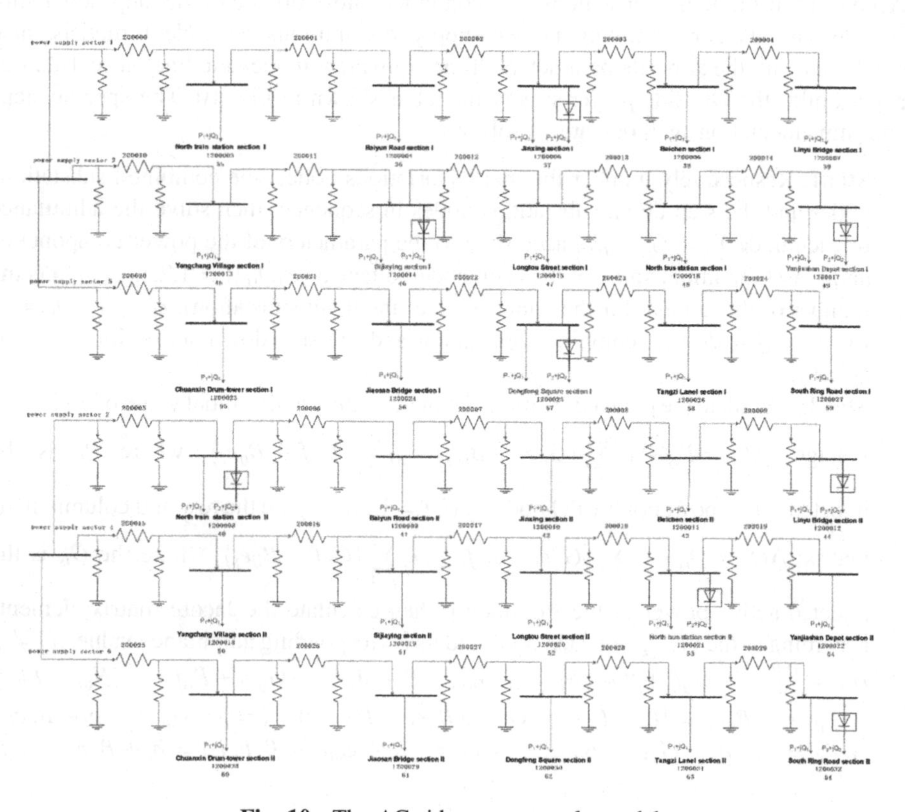

Fig. 10. The AC side power supply model

4 The Analysis on the Simulation Example

In order to evaluate the performance of the method in this paper, a large number of experimental analyses on the power supply system power flow value calculation model before and after the improvement were conducted, then the operating efficiency and calculation error of the power flow was respectively calculated with different models and different number of stations.

4.1 The Analysis on the Operating Efficiency

Define the time efficiency ratio $\varphi = \frac{T_{\Delta}}{T_{\max}}$, where the $T_{\max}$ is the maximum cycle of the power flow calculation in the power supply system, the T_{Δ} is the real-time cycle for the power flow calculation and the φ is smaller, the operating efficiency is higher.

Because the power flow of the MTPSS is real-time displaying and dynamically calculated, the power dispatcher will control the power components according to the power flow value to make the train operation safe and on time, which requires high-performance of real-time. This paper took the 42 stations data to test the operational efficiency of the power supply model before and after the improvement, the results are shown in Fig. 11.

The Fig. 11 shows the variation of PQ nodes with the time efficiency when the power components equivalent model is changing. When the number of stations is less than 9 (n < 9), the calculation error is in the allowable range, the operational efficiency of the two models is almost the same, and the real-time performance is high. However, with the increase of the number of stations, the operational efficiency of the power supply calculation model before improved is gradually deteriorated. The improved power supply calculation model is more suitable when the number of stations is more than 9 (n > 9).

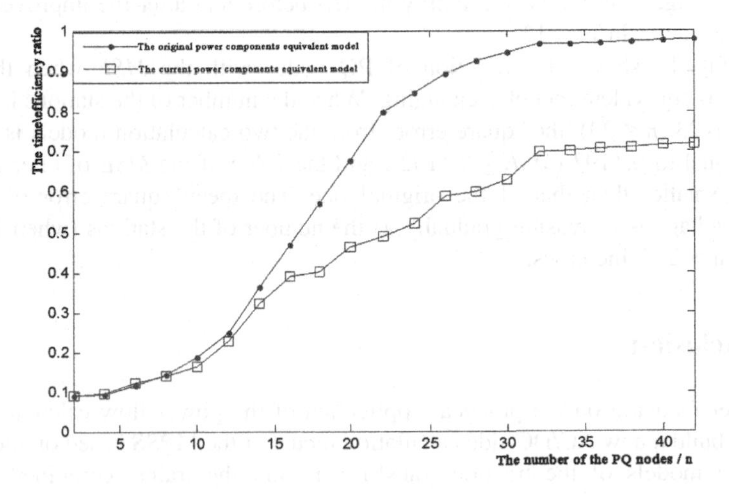

Fig. 11. The efficiency comparison of the power supply system models

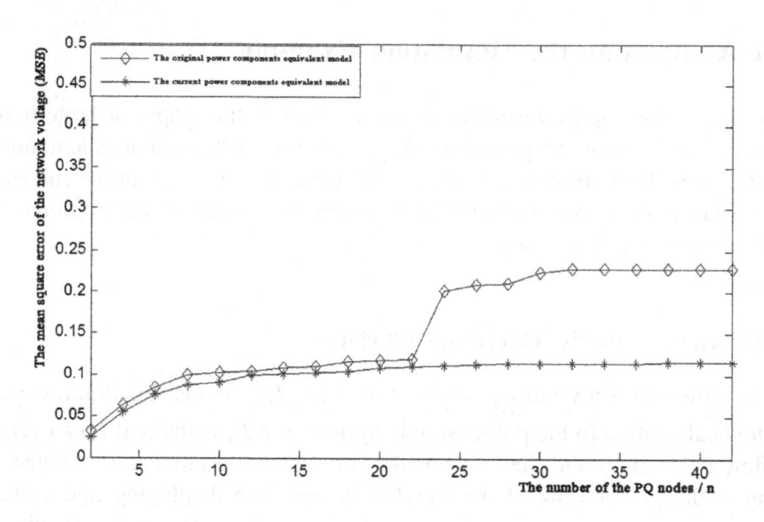

Fig. 12. The train network voltage comparison of the power supply system models

4.2 The Analysis on the Error of the Power Flow Value

Defy the mean square error $MSE = \sqrt{\frac{1}{N}\sum_{i=1}^{N}(U(i) - \hat{U}(i))^2}$, where the $U(i)$ is the actual train network voltage, $\hat{U}(i)$ is the calculated voltage of the train network according to the built model, the N is the network voltage sequence length. When the value of MSE is smaller, it indicates that the calculation of the train network voltage is more accurate. The power flow value is the important message for the metro power dispatcher to control the electric components, and its accuracy of the calculation directly affects the safety of the train operation. So it is crucial to build the metro power supply model with small calculation error. This paper took the 42 stations data to calculate the train network voltage with the power supply models before and after the improvement, the results are shown in Fig. 12.

The Fig. 12 shows the variation of PQ nodes with the MSE when the power components equivalent model is changing. When the number of the stations is less than or equal to 23 ($n \leq 23$), the square errors from the two calculation models is both less than or equal to 0.1192 ($MSE \leq 0.1192$), and the value of the MSE of after improved model is smaller than that of the original one. The mean square error of the train network voltage is increasing gradually as the number of the stations (when it is more than 23 (n > 23)) increases.

5 Conclusion

This paper focusing on the practical application of the power flow calculation in the MPSS to build a new AC/DC side calculation model of the MPSS based on the existing equivalent models of the traction transformers and the trains, combined with the coupling relation between the MTPSS and train operation and also took advantage of the voltage and current ranges of the 12-pulse rectifier unit 6 section type characteristic curve of the traction substation. Then this paper researched and designed AC/DC power flow calculation method for the MPSS and finally analyzed and discussed the calculation error of the operation efficiency and the power flow value with this method. The simulation experiment shows that this method can effectively improve the calculation accuracy of the power flow value, with fast calculation speed and great convergence, besides, the model can more accurately describe the coupling relations between the metro train and the traction network.

References

1. Shi, F., Yu, S.: To found and to find the solution for mathematical method of metro traction power system. J. Beijing Union Univ. **2**, 60–62 (2003)
2. Goodman, C.J., Siu, L.K.: DC railway power network solutions by diakoptics. In: Proceedings of 94 ASME/IEEE Joint Railroad Conference, pp. 103–110 (1994)
3. Cai, Y., Irving, M.R., Case, S.H.: Modelling and numerical solution of multibranched DC rail traction power systems. IEE Proc. Electric Power Appl. **142**(5), 323–328 (1995)
4. Hu, H., Wang, J., He, Z., et al.: Study on power flow algorithm for metro traction supply system. J. China Railway Soc. **34**(11), 22–28 (2012)
5. Liu, H., Ho, T., Yuan, Z., et al.: Simulation of dc traction power for mass transit railway. J. Syst. Simul. **16**(9), 1944–1947 (2004)
6. Liu, X., Yu, S., Liu, X.: Model and algorithm for traction power system simulation of urban railline. J. Comput. Simul. **21**(12), 213–218 (2004)
7. Hu, H., He, Z., Wang, J.: AC/DC power flow calculation method for metro system considering harmonic power. Proc. CSEE **32**(34), 112–119 (2012)
8. Liu, W., Li, Q., Chen, M.: Study of unified AC/DC power flow in DC traction power supply system. Power Syst. Protection Control **38**(8), 128–133 (2010)
9. Chen, H., Geng, G., Jiang, Q.: Power flow algorithm for traction power supply system of electric railway based on locomotive and network coupling. Autom. Electric Power Syst. **36** (3), 76–80 (2012)

Fault Diagnosis for the Pitch System of Wind Turbines Using the Observer-Based Multi-innovation Stochastic Gradient Algorithm

Dinghui Wu(✉), Wen Liu(✉), Yanjie Zhai, and Yanxia Shen

Key Laboratory of Advanced Process Control for Light Industry of Ministry of Education, Jiangnan University, Wuxi 214122, Jiangsu, China
wdh123@jiangnan.edu.cn, 1198892429@qq.com

Abstract. Based on the characteristic that pitch system faults of wind turbines will lead to the change of system parameters, the observer-based multi-innovation stochastic gradient algorithm as a fault diagnosis method is proposed in this paper. The multi-innovation identification algorithm can improve the parameter estimation accuracy by extending the innovation length. According to the observer canonical state space system model, the algorithm that combines the multi-innovation stochastic gradient algorithm with the state observer can obtain the interactive estimation between system states and system parameters. Firstly, the pitch system model is transformed into an identification model by converting into a canonical state space model. Then, the algorithm proposed is adopted to estimate system states and system parameters. The fault diagnosis problem is transformed into a parameter estimation issue. At the end, pitch system faults could be diagnosed through the variation of system parameters. The simulation results show that the proposed method is able to diagnose the pitch system faults effectively.

Keywords: Wind turbine · Pitch system · Fault diagnosis · Multi-innovation identification · State estimation · Parameter estimation

1 Introduction

Wind energy is the fastest growing and the most competitive renewable source [1]. With the increase of demand for wind power, wind farms have been developed rapidly. However, restricted by geographical conditions, wind farms are most likely to be built in the desert or off-shore where the wind resource is rich but the natural environmental conditions are severe [2]. Affected by their surroudings, wind turbines malfunction easily and can't get timely maintenance. The fault poses a threat to the safe operation of wind turbines, affects the wind power system stability, and even results in system downtime. Fault tolerant control methods are often adopted to maintain normal operation for wind turbines. So the fault diagnosis is the premise and necessary condition [3].

For wind power systems, fault diagnosis methods based on the model have attracted more and more attention by researchers in recent years. In [4, 5], the observer

L. Zhang et al. (Eds.): AsiaSim 2016/SCS AutumnSim 2016, Part I, CCIS 643, pp. 526–538, 2016.
DOI: 10.1007/978-981-10-2663-8_54

and filter are designed respectively to generate redundant information for diagnosing the blade root bending moment sensor faults and blade pitch actuator faults based on the dynamical model of the wind turbine system. The adaptive parameter estimation algorithm, which is based on the dynamic model of the pitch system, is used to detect the fault of hydraulic pressure leakage in the pitch system [6]. In [7], an unknown input observer is adopted to detect the rotor and generator speed sensor faults. Generator sensor and pitch sensor faults in wind turbines can be diagnosed by a model based fault detection and diagnosis scheme developed using fuzzy modeling and identification methods [8]. In [9], the interval observer approach is applied to address the problem of fault diagnosis in sensors and actuators of wind turbines.

The pitch system is an important component of wind turbines. When wind speed is higher than the rated value and lower than the cut out value, wind turbines modulate the power captured by the rotor through adjusting the pitch angle, so that the wind power system can keep a constant power output [10]. When the pitch system is under the faulty condition, the pitch system dynamic response speed is restricted by the fault, so it makes the system output power unstable. Therefore, an accurate fault diagnosis is necessary for wind turbine pitch systems.

In this paper, a fault diagnosis method based on the observer-based multi-innovation stochastic gradient algorithm (O-MISG) is utilized to diagnose the pitch system faults. In the system identification method, the system's input and output data are used to estimate parameters [11]. When the pitch system fails, the system states and system parameters change accordingly. The system states and system parameters in the state space model of the pitch system become unknown; thus they have the product of nonlinear relationship. So the identification problem becomes a complicated issue. In accordance with the observer canonical state space systems model of the pitch system, the identification model can be achieved. After that, the method which combines the multi-innovation stochastic gradient algorithm with the state observer is adopted to accomplish the interactive estimation between the system states and the parameters [12]. Finally, the estimated values are compared with theoretical values to detect faults and identify the fault type.

The rest of this paper is organized as follows. Section 2 describes the model of wind turbines and faults in pitch systems. In Sect. 3, the pitch system model is transformed into the observer canonical state space systems model applying to the parameter identification. Section 3 introduces the O-MISG algorithm and presents the structure of the fault diagnosis system. Section 4 verifies the effectiveness of the O-MISG algorithm with a simulation. Finally, a conclusion is given in Sect. 5.

2 Wind Turbine Model

Wind turbines will translate the wind power captured by the rotor into mechanical power via the rotation of blades. And then the aerodynamic torque achieved by the aerodynamic subsystem will be passed to the generator to produce electricity through the drive train subsystem. The wind turbine system includes the aerodynamic subsystem, the pitch subsystem, the drive train subsystem and the power subsystem. The mutual connection relation between each subsystem is shown in Fig. 1.

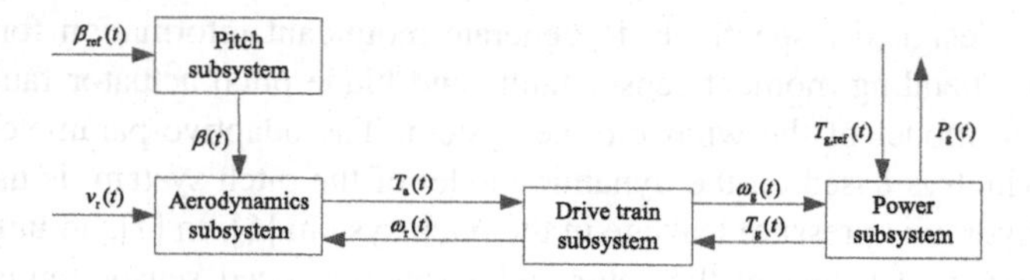

Fig. 1. Relationship between subsystems of the wind turbine system model

2.1 Aerodynamic Subsystem Model

Wind turbines convert wind energy into the rotor side through the blades and the wind power captured by the rotor is dependent on the wind velocity, the air density, the blade swept area and the power coefficient. The tip-speed ratio $\lambda(t)$ is the ratio of the blade tip circumferential velocity and wind speed and it represent the running state of the rotor when the wind speed changes. The tip-speed ratio is defined as

$$\lambda(t) = \frac{2\pi Rn}{v_{\mathrm{r}}(t)} = \frac{\omega_{\mathrm{r}}(t)R}{v_{\mathrm{r}}(t)} \tag{1}$$

where R is the radius of the blade, $\omega_{\mathrm{r}}(t)$ is the rotor speed, $v_{\mathrm{r}}(t)$ the wind speed.

The aerodynamic torque $T_{\mathrm{a}}(t)$ applied to the rotor can be expressed as

$$T_{\mathrm{a}}(t) = \frac{1}{2\omega_{\mathrm{r}}(t)}\rho\pi R^2 v_{\mathrm{r}}^3 C_{\mathrm{p}}(\lambda(t), \beta(t)) \tag{2}$$

where ρ is the air density, $C_{\mathrm{p}}(\lambda(t), \beta(t))$ is the power coefficient depending on the tip speed ratio $\lambda(t)$ and the pitch angle $\beta(t)$.

2.2 Drive Train Subsystem Model

The drive train subsystem mainly includes the turbine rotors, low-speed shaft, gear box and high-speed shaft. The rotor captures the kinetic energy in the wind to makes the low-speed shaft rotation. Consequently, a corresponding mechanical torque is generated. Then the low-speed shaft is connected to the high-speed shaft via a gearbox, the rotational speed of the rotor is improved to a higher speed required by the generator, the mechanical torque will be transferred to the high-speed shaft and then accessed by the generator. The drive train subsystem model is

$$J_{\mathrm{r}}\dot{\omega}_{\mathrm{r}}(t) = T_{\mathrm{a}}(t) + \frac{B_{\mathrm{dt}}}{N_{\mathrm{g}}}\omega_{\mathrm{g}}(t) - K_{\mathrm{dt}}\theta_{\Delta}(t) - (B_{\mathrm{dt}} + B_{\mathrm{r}})\omega_{\mathrm{r}}(t) \tag{3}$$

$$J_{\mathrm{g}}\dot{\omega}_{\mathrm{g}}(t) = \frac{K_{\mathrm{dt}}}{N_{\mathrm{g}}}\theta_{\Delta}(t) + \frac{B_{\mathrm{dt}}}{N_{\mathrm{g}}}\omega_{\mathrm{r}}(t) - (\frac{B_{\mathrm{dt}}}{N_{\mathrm{g}}^2} + B_{\mathrm{g}})\omega_{\mathrm{g}}(t) - T_{\mathrm{g}}(t) \tag{4}$$

$$\dot{\theta}_{\Delta}(t) = \omega_{r}(t) - \frac{1}{N_{g}}\omega_{g}(t) \tag{5}$$

where $\theta_{\Delta}(t)$ is the torsion angle, J_r is the moment of inertia of the low-speed shaft, J_g is the moment of inertia of the high-speed shaft, B_{dt} is the torsion damping coefficient, N_g is the gear ratio, K_{dt} is the torsion stiffness, B_r is the viscous friction of the low-speed shaft, B_g is the viscous friction of the high-speed shaft.

2.3 Power Subsystem Model

Power subsystem consists of the generator and converter. Electrical energy is produced by the generator and accesses the grid through the converter. The generator torque $T_g(t)$ is controlled by the reference to the generator torque $T_{g,ref}(t)$. The converter is modeled as

$$\dot{T}_{g}(t) = -\frac{1}{\tau_{g}}T_{g}(t) + \frac{1}{\tau_{g}}T_{g,ref}(t) \tag{6}$$

where τ_g is the time constant.

The electric power produced by the generator is described as

$$P_{g}(t) = \eta_{g}\omega_{g}(t)T_{g}(t) \tag{7}$$

where η_g is the efficiency of the generator.

2.4 Pitch Subsystem Model Including Fault Model

The pitch system is composed of three selfsame pitch actuators. The pitch actuator controls the blade pitch angle by rotating the blade. The pitch actuator can be modeled as a transfer function between the blade pitch angle $\beta(t)$ and the reference to the blade pitch angle $\beta_{ref}(t)$. $\beta(t)$ is the output of the pitch system and $\beta_{ref}(t)$ is the set value which is given by the wind turbine controller. The pitch actuator is modeled as a second order transfer function

$$\frac{\beta(s)}{\beta_{ref}(s)} = \frac{\omega_{n}^{2}}{s^{2} + 2\zeta\omega_{n}s + \omega_{n}^{2}} \tag{8}$$

where ω_n and ζ are the natural frequency and the damping coefficient of the pitch actuator model.

The pitch actuator dynamic model is

$$\ddot{\beta}(t) = -2\zeta\omega_{n}\dot{\beta}(t) - \omega_{n}^{2}\beta(t) + \omega_{n}^{2}\beta_{ref}(t) \tag{9}$$

The considered faults of the pitch system in this paper are high air content in the hydraulic oil, hydraulic leakage and pump wear. Faults make the pitch system dynamic characteristics worse by changing the actuator natural frequency and damping coefficient. Under the influence of the fault, the natural frequency and the damping coefficient change from the nominal value $\omega_{n,0}$ and ζ_0 to three kinds of fault parameter values, which are $\omega_{n,ha}$, ζ_{ha}, $\omega_{n,hl}$, ζ_{hl}, $\omega_{n,pw}$ and ζ_{pw}. Parameters for the faulty pitch actuator are shown in Table 1.

Table 1. Fault parameters' value

Fault type	Parameters' value	
No fault	$\omega_{n,0} = 11.11$ rad/s	$\zeta_0 = 0.6$
High air content in the hydraulic oil	$\omega_{n,ha} = 5.73$ rad/s	$\zeta_{ha} = 0.45$
Hydraulic leakage	$\omega_{n,hl} = 3.42$ rad/s	$\zeta_{hl} = 0.9$
Pump wear	$\omega_{n,pw} = 7.27$ rad/s	$\zeta_{pw} = 0.75$

The dynamic model of the pitch actuator with faults is

$$\ddot{\beta}(t) = -2\zeta(t)\omega_n(t)\dot{\beta}(t) - \omega_n^2(t)\beta(t) + \omega_n^2(t)\beta_{ref}(t) \tag{10}$$

where $\omega_n(t)$ and $\zeta(t)$ have different values under different faults. The specific expression is

$$\omega_n(t) = (1 - \eta_{ha}(t))\omega_{n,0} + \eta_{ha}(t)\omega_{n,ha} \tag{11}$$

$$\zeta(t) = (1 - \eta_{ha}(t))\zeta_0 + \eta_{ha}(t)\zeta_{ha} \tag{12}$$

$$\omega_n(t) = (1 - \eta_{hl}(t))\omega_{n,0} + \eta_{hl}(t)\omega_{n,hl} \tag{13}$$

$$\zeta(t) = (1 - \eta_{hl}(t))\zeta_0 + \eta_{hl}(t)\zeta_{hl} \tag{14}$$

$$\omega_n(t) = (1 - \eta_{pw}(t))\omega_{n,0} + \eta_{pw}(t)\omega_{n,pw} \tag{15}$$

$$\zeta(t) = (1 - \eta_{pw}(t))\zeta_0 + \eta_{pw}(t)\zeta_{pw} \tag{16}$$

where $\eta_{ha}(t)$, $\eta_{hl}(t)$ and $\eta_{pw}(t)$ are the indicators of high air content in the hydraulic oil, the hydraulic leakage and the pump wear, and $0 \le \eta_{ha}(t) \le 1$, $0 \le \eta_{hl}(t) \le 1$, $0 \le \eta_{pw}(t) \le 1$. Obviously, when the value of the indicator is equal to zero, it means that there is no fault in the pitch system. On the other hand, when the value of the indicator equals one, the failure happens entirely. For high air content in the hydraulic oil, $\eta_{ha}(t) = 0$ and $\eta_{ha}(t) = 1$ represent that the air content are 7 % and 15 % in the hydraulic oil. With regard to the hydraulic leakage, the pressure for $\eta_{hl}(t) = 1$ corresponds to 50 % of the nominal pressure. Pump wear is irreversible without replacing the pump. The fault described by $\eta_{pw}(t) = 1$ corresponds to a pressure level of 75 %.

3 Description of the Fault Diagnosis Method

3.1 Identification Model of the Pitch System

For the dynamic model of the pitch actuator with faults in Eq. (10), $\left[\dot{\beta}(t) \quad \beta(t)\right]^{\mathrm{T}}$ is chosen as the state variables. $y(t) = \beta(t)$ is chosen as the output. Considering the running noise $v(t)$. So the continuous state space equation is

$$\begin{bmatrix} \ddot{\beta}(t) \\ \dot{\beta}(t) \end{bmatrix} = \begin{bmatrix} -2\zeta(t)\omega_{\mathrm{n}}(t) & -\omega_{\mathrm{n}}^2(t) \\ 1 & 0 \end{bmatrix} \begin{bmatrix} \dot{\beta}(t) \\ \beta(t) \end{bmatrix} + \begin{bmatrix} \omega_{\mathrm{n}}^2(t) \\ 0 \end{bmatrix} \beta_{\mathrm{ref}}(t) \tag{17}$$

$$y(t) = \begin{bmatrix} 0 & 1 \end{bmatrix} \begin{bmatrix} \dot{\beta}(t) \\ \beta(t) \end{bmatrix} + v(t) \tag{18}$$

Considering the sampling period as T_0, the discrete model from Eqs. (17) and (18) is

$$\begin{bmatrix} \dot{\beta}(k+1) \\ \beta(k+1) \end{bmatrix} = \bar{\boldsymbol{A}}(k) \begin{bmatrix} \dot{\beta}(k) \\ \beta(k) \end{bmatrix} + \bar{\boldsymbol{B}}(k)\beta_{\mathrm{ref}}(k) \tag{19}$$

$$y(k) = \bar{\boldsymbol{C}} \begin{bmatrix} \dot{\beta}(k) \\ \beta(k) \end{bmatrix} + v(k) \tag{20}$$

where $\bar{\boldsymbol{A}}(k) = \begin{bmatrix} 1 - 2\zeta(k)\omega_{\mathrm{n}}(k)T_0 & -\omega_{\mathrm{n}}^2(k)T_0 \\ T_0 & 1 \end{bmatrix}$, $\bar{\boldsymbol{B}}(k) = \begin{bmatrix} \omega_{\mathrm{n}}^2(k)T_0 \\ 0 \end{bmatrix}$, and $\bar{\boldsymbol{C}} = \begin{bmatrix} 0 & 1 \end{bmatrix}$.

The system observability matrix is $\boldsymbol{Q_o} = \begin{bmatrix} \bar{\boldsymbol{C}} \\ \bar{\boldsymbol{C}}\bar{A} \end{bmatrix} = \begin{bmatrix} 1 & 0 \\ T_0 & 1 \end{bmatrix}$, $\operatorname{rank} \boldsymbol{Q_o} = 2$, the observability matrix is full rank, so the system can be observed.

Define $\tilde{\boldsymbol{x}}(k) = \boldsymbol{Q}\left[\dot{\beta}(k) \quad \beta(k)\right]^{\mathrm{T}}$, have

$$\tilde{\boldsymbol{x}}(k+1) = \tilde{\boldsymbol{A}}(k)\tilde{\boldsymbol{x}}(k) + \tilde{\boldsymbol{B}}(k)\beta_{\mathrm{ref}}(k) \tag{21}$$

$$y(k) = \tilde{\boldsymbol{C}}\tilde{x}(k) + v(k) \tag{22}$$

Where

$$\tilde{\boldsymbol{A}}(k) = \boldsymbol{Q}(k)\bar{\boldsymbol{A}}(k)\boldsymbol{Q}^{-1}(k) = \begin{bmatrix} 0 & -(1 - 2\zeta(k)\omega_{\mathrm{n}}(k)T_0 + \omega_{\mathrm{n}}^2(k)T_0^2) \\ 1 & -(2\zeta(k)\omega_{\mathrm{n}}(k)T_0 - 2) \end{bmatrix}$$

$$\tilde{\boldsymbol{B}}(k) = \boldsymbol{Q}(k)\bar{\boldsymbol{B}}(k) = \begin{bmatrix} \omega_{\mathrm{n}}^2(k)T_0^2 \\ 0 \end{bmatrix}, \tilde{\boldsymbol{C}} = \bar{\boldsymbol{C}}\boldsymbol{Q}^{-1}(k) = \begin{bmatrix} 0 & 1 \end{bmatrix},$$

$$\boldsymbol{Q}(k) = \begin{bmatrix} 1 & 2\zeta(k)\omega_{\mathrm{n}}(k)T_0 - 2 \\ 0 & 1 \end{bmatrix}.$$

$\mathbf{x}(k) = [x_1(k),\ \ x_2(k)]^{\mathrm{T}},\ x_1(k) = \beta(k),\ x_2(k) = \dot{\beta}(k) + (2\zeta(k)\omega_{\mathrm{n}}(k)T_0 - 2)\beta(k)$ are defidend as the new state variables, defined input as $u(k) = \beta_{\mathrm{ref}}(k)$, output as $y(k)$, the observer canonical state space system of the pitch actuator in wind turbines is

$$\mathbf{x}(k+1) = \boldsymbol{A}(k)\boldsymbol{x}(k) + \boldsymbol{B}(k)u(k) \tag{23}$$

$$y(k) = \boldsymbol{C}\boldsymbol{x}(k) + v(k) \tag{24}$$

where $\boldsymbol{A}(k) = \begin{bmatrix} -a_1(k) & 1 \\ -a_2(k) & 0 \end{bmatrix}$, $\boldsymbol{B}(k) = \begin{bmatrix} 0 \\ b_2(k) \end{bmatrix}$, and $\boldsymbol{C} = [1\ \ 0]$. And in $\boldsymbol{A}(k)$ and $\boldsymbol{B}(k)$, have

$$a_1(k) = 2\zeta(k)\omega_{\mathrm{n}}(k)T_0 - 2 \tag{25}$$

$$a_2(k) = 1 - 2\zeta(k)\omega_{\mathrm{n}}(k)T_0 + \omega_{\mathrm{n}}^2(k)T_0^2 \tag{26}$$

$$b_2(k) = \omega_{\mathrm{n}}^2(k)T_0^2 \tag{27}$$

Form Eqs. (23) to (24), have

$$x_1(k+1) = -a_1(k)x_1(k) + x_2(k) + b_1(k)u(k) \tag{28}$$

$$x_2(k+1) = -a_2(k)x_1(k) + b_2(k)u(k) \tag{29}$$

$$y(k) = x_1(k) + v(k) \tag{30}$$

Referring to the method in [13], have

$$x_1(k) = -\sum_{i=1}^{2} a_i(k)x_1(k-i) + b_2(k)u(k-2) \tag{31}$$

Define the parameter vector $\boldsymbol{\theta}(k)$ and the information vector $\boldsymbol{\varphi}(k)$ as

$$\boldsymbol{\theta}(k) = [a_1(k), a_2(k), b_2(k)]^{\mathrm{T}},\ \ \boldsymbol{\varphi}(k) = [-x_1(k-1), -x_1(k-2), u(k-2)]^{\mathrm{T}}$$

The identification model of the system in Eqs. (23) and (24) is

$$y(k) = x_1(k) + v(k) = \boldsymbol{\varphi}^{\mathrm{T}}(k)\boldsymbol{\theta}(k) + v(k) \tag{32}$$

3.2 The Observer-Based Multi-innovation Stochastic Gradient Algorithm

Based on the identification model in Eq. (32), the stochastic gradient identification algorithm is

$$\hat{\boldsymbol{\theta}}(k) = \hat{\boldsymbol{\theta}}(k-1) + \frac{\boldsymbol{\varphi}(k)}{r(k)} e(k) \tag{33}$$

$$e(k) = y(k) - \boldsymbol{\varphi}^{\mathrm{T}}(k)\hat{\boldsymbol{\theta}}(k-1) \tag{34}$$

$$r(k) = r(k-1) + \|\boldsymbol{\varphi}(k)\|^2, r(0) = 1 \tag{35}$$

where $\hat{\boldsymbol{\theta}}(k)$ is the estimate of $\boldsymbol{\theta}(k)$, $e(k)$ is the innovation. The state variables $x_1(k-i)$ of the information vector $\boldsymbol{\varphi}(k)$ are replaced by their estimated states $\hat{x}_1(k-i)$, the estimate of $\boldsymbol{\varphi}(k)$ is

$$\hat{\varphi}(k) = [-\hat{x}_1(k-1), -\hat{x}_1(k-2), u(k-2)]^{\mathrm{T}}.$$

Define the stacked output vector $\boldsymbol{Y}(p,k)$ and the information matrix $\hat{\boldsymbol{\Phi}}(p,k)$ as

$$\boldsymbol{Y}(p,k) = [y(k), y(k-1), \cdots, y(k-p+1)]^{\mathrm{T}},$$
$$\hat{\boldsymbol{\Phi}}(p,k) = [\hat{\varphi}(k), \hat{\varphi}(k-1), \cdots, \hat{\varphi}(k-p+1)].$$

In the stochastic gradient identification algorithm, $e(k)$ in Eq. (33) is the single innovation. By introducing the innovation length p, the innovation vector $\boldsymbol{E}(p,k)$ can be obtained as

$$\boldsymbol{E}(p,k) = \begin{bmatrix} y(k) - \hat{\boldsymbol{\varphi}}^{\mathrm{T}}(k)\hat{\boldsymbol{\theta}}(k-1) \\ y(k-1) - \hat{\boldsymbol{\varphi}}^{\mathrm{T}}(k-1)\hat{\boldsymbol{\theta}}(k-1) \\ \vdots \\ y(k-p+1) - \hat{\boldsymbol{\varphi}}^{\mathrm{T}}(k-p+1)\hat{\boldsymbol{\theta}}(k-1) \end{bmatrix}$$
$$= \boldsymbol{Y}(p,k) - \hat{\boldsymbol{\Phi}}^{\mathrm{T}}(p,k)\hat{\boldsymbol{\theta}}(k-1)$$

The states of the observer take the place of the states $x_1(k-i)$ in the information vector, and the observer's states are calculated by utilizing the previous parameter estimates; so the O-MISG algorithm is obtained as [14]

$$\hat{\boldsymbol{\theta}}(k) = \hat{\boldsymbol{\theta}}(k-1) + \frac{\hat{\boldsymbol{\Phi}}(p,k)}{r(k)} \boldsymbol{E}(p,k) \tag{36}$$

$$\boldsymbol{E}(p,k) = \boldsymbol{Y}(p,k) - \hat{\boldsymbol{\Phi}}^{\mathrm{T}}(p,k)\hat{\boldsymbol{\theta}}(k-1) \tag{37}$$

$$r(k) = r(k-1) + \left\|\hat{\boldsymbol{\Phi}}(p,k)\right\|^2, r(0) = 1 \tag{38}$$

$$\boldsymbol{Y}(p,k) = [y(k), y(k-1), \cdots, y(k-p+1)]^{\mathrm{T}} \tag{39}$$

$$\hat{\boldsymbol{\Phi}}(p,k) = [\hat{\varphi}(k), \hat{\varphi}(k-1), \cdots, \hat{\varphi}(k-p+1)] \tag{40}$$

$$\hat{\varphi}(k) = [-\hat{x}_1(k-1), -\hat{x}_1(k-2), u(k-2)]^{\mathrm{T}} \tag{41}$$

$$\hat{\boldsymbol{x}}(k+1) = \hat{\boldsymbol{A}}(k)\hat{\boldsymbol{x}}(k) + \hat{\boldsymbol{B}}(k)u(k) \tag{42}$$

$$\hat{\boldsymbol{A}}(k) = \begin{bmatrix} -\hat{a}_1(k) & 1 \\ -\hat{a}_2(k) & 0 \end{bmatrix} \tag{43}$$

$$\hat{\boldsymbol{B}}(k) = \left[0, \hat{b}_2(k)\right]^{\mathrm{T}} \tag{44}$$

$$\hat{\theta}(k) = \left[\hat{a}_1(k), \hat{a}_2(k), \hat{b}_2(k)\right]^{\mathrm{T}} \tag{45}$$

3.3 Structure of the Fault Diagnosis Method

Based on the observer canonical state space system of the pitch actuator, the input for the fault diagnosis method proposed is the reference to the blade pitch angle $\beta_{\mathrm{ref}}(t)$ and the output is blade pitch angle $\beta(t)$. When the pitch actuator fails, the natural frequency ω_{n} and the damping coefficient ζ change. Form Eqs. (25) to (27), a_1, a_2 and b_2 will change accordingly. Therefore, a_1, a_2 and b_2 can be estimated by the O-MISG algorithm. And the occurrence and type of the pitch system faults can be judged through the parameter variation. The structure of the fault diagnosis method is illustrated in Fig. 2.

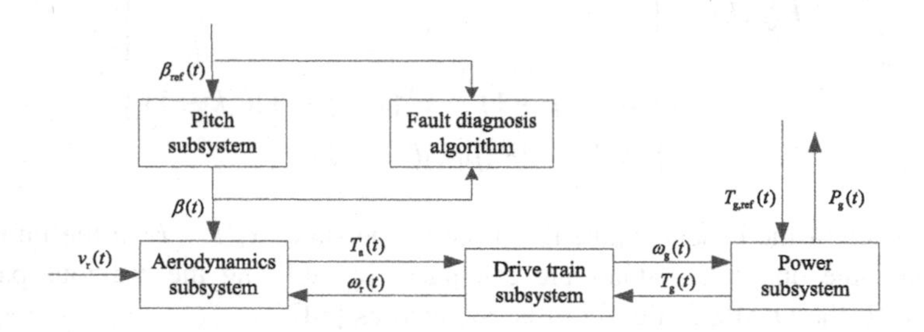

Fig. 2. Structure of the fault diagnosis method

4 Simulation and Analysis

The simulation is based on the 4.8 MW wind turbine benchmark model which is described in detail in Sect. 2 [15], the fault diagnosis system shown in Fig. 2, and the O-MISG algorithm described in Sect. 3.2. Wind turbine simulation parameters are shown in Table 2.

Form (11)–(16), under the faults which are high air content in the hydraulic oil, hydraulic leakage and pump wear, the expressions of the natural frequency $\omega_{\mathrm{n}}(t)$ and the damping coefficient $\zeta(t)$ possess the same structure. Therefore, in the simulation,

Table 2. The simulation parameters of wind turbines

Parameters	Value	Parameters	Value
R	57.5 m	ρ	1.225 kg/m^3
J_r	55×10^6 kg·m^2	J_g	390 kg·m^2
B_r	27.8 kNm/rad·s^{-1}	B_g	3.034 Nm/rad·s^{-1}
B_{dt}	945 kNm/rad·s^{-1}	K_{dt}	2.7 GNm/rad
N_g	95	η_g	0.92

Table 3. Parameter values of a_1, a_2 and b_2

Parameters	No fault	High air content in the hydraulic oil
a_1	−1.86668	−1.94843
a_2	0.87902	0.95171
b_2	0.01234	0.00328

the fault of high air content in the hydraulic oil is chosen to validate the proposed fault diagnosis method only. When the fault of high air content in the hydraulic oil occurs, the natural frequency $\omega_n(t)$ is reduced to 5.73 rad/s from the nominal value 11.11 rad/s. And the damping coefficient $\zeta(t)$ is decreased to 0.45 from nominal value 0.6. The parameter variations result in worse dynamic characteristics for the pitch system. a_1, a_2 and b_2 will alter in line with the changes of the natural frequency and the damping coefficient. The sampling period T_0 is 0.01 s. a_1, a_2 and b_2 with no fault and high air content in the hydraulic oil are shown in Table 3.

In simulation, the fault is supposed to happen between 100 s and 200 s, the fault indicators signal are

$$\eta_{ha}(t) = \begin{cases} 0, 0 < t \le 100\,\text{s},\ 200\,\text{s} < t \le 250\,\text{s} \\ 1, 100\,\text{s} < t \le 200\,\text{s} \end{cases} \tag{46}$$

The parameter estimation results are shown in Figs. 3, 4 and 5. When the wind turbine is in normal operation in from 0 s to 100 s, the natural frequency $\omega_n(t)$ and the damping coefficient $\zeta(t)$ are the normal value 11.11 rad/s and 0.6. So a_1, a_2 and b_2 are −1.86668, 0.87902 and 0.01234 respectively. When the fault of high air content in the hydraulic oil comes up in 100 s, the natural frequency $\omega_n(t)$ and the damping coefficient $\zeta(t)$ are changed to 5.73 rad/s and 0.45. a_1, a_2 and b_2 turn into −1.94843, 0.95171 and 0.00328 respectively. If the fault disappears after 200 s, the parameter value will become the nominal value. So it is apparent that the changes in a_1, a_2 and b_2 are able to indicate the fault in the pitch system.

Because the changes in a_1, a_2 and b_2 are caused by the variations of $\omega_n(t)$ and $\zeta(t)$. In order to prove the reliability of the diagnosis result, the estimated values of $\omega_n(t)$ and $\zeta(t)$ obtained from Eqs. (25) to (27) are shown in Figs. 6 and 7. From the simulation results we can draw a conclusion that the O-MISG algorithm can achieve the fault diagnosis of the pitch system by estimating a_1, a_2 and b_2.

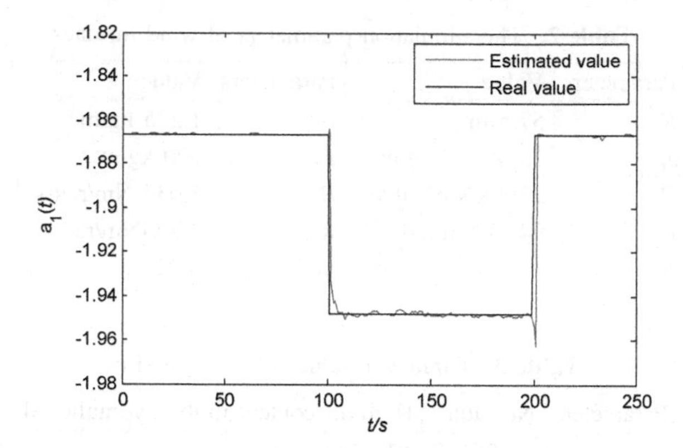

Fig. 3. Parameter value of a_1

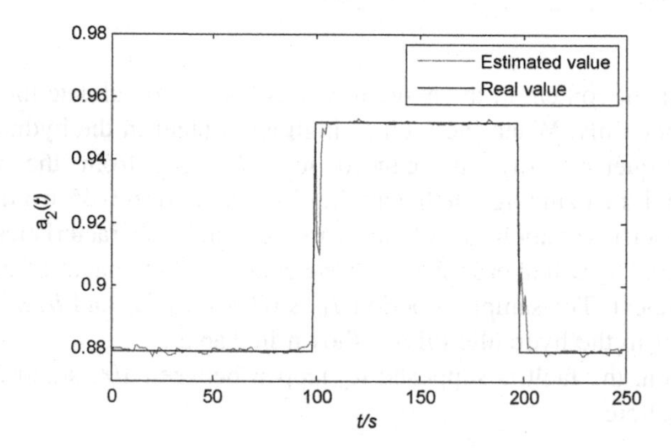

Fig. 4. Parameter value of a_2

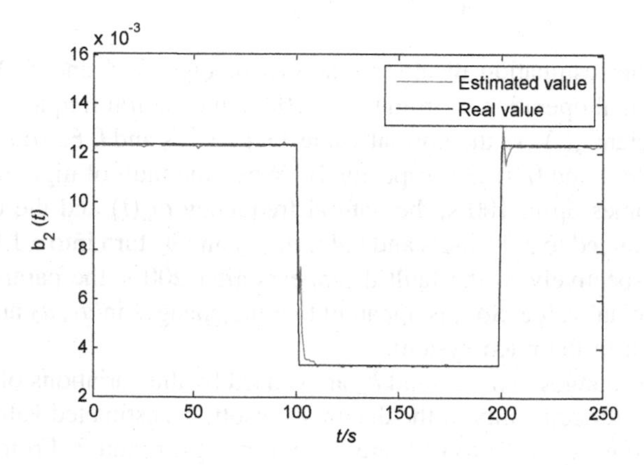

Fig. 5. Parameter value of b_2

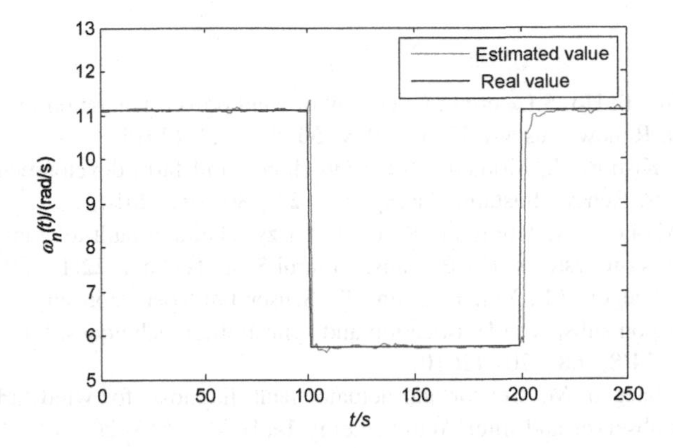

Fig. 6. Parameter value of $\omega_{\mathrm{n}}(t)$

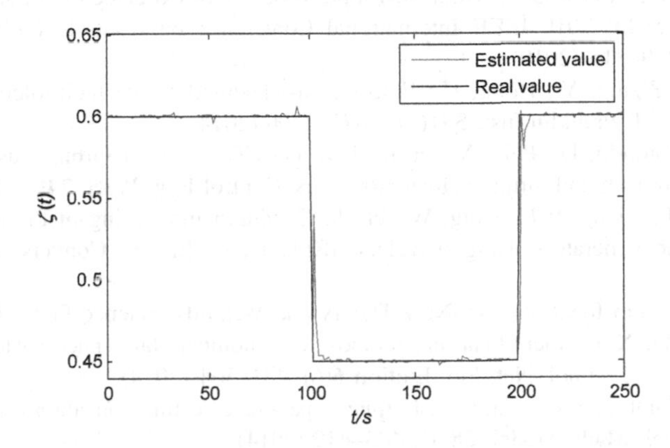

Fig. 7. Parameter value of $\zeta(t)$

5 Conclusion

Faults in the pitch system of wind turbines will slow down their dynamic response and give rise to changes in system parameters simultaneously. According to the characteristics of the pitch system faults, the system identification method is applied to fault diagnosis of the pitch system, which transmits the problem into a system identification issue. The O-MISG algorithm which can achieve the interactive estimation between the system states and the parameters is adopted to diagnose the pitch system faults in light of the identification model transformed from the observer canonical state space system of the pitch actuator. And then on the basis of the change of estimated parameters, the pitch system faults can be diagnosed effectively. Simulation results verify the feasibility and effectiveness of the O-MISG algorithm based fault diagnosis method.

References

1. Feng, Y., Lin, H., Ho, S.L., et al.: Overview of wind power generation in China: status and development. Renew. Sustain. Energy Rev. **50**, 847–858 (2015)
2. Perveen, R., Kishor, N., Mohanty, S.R.: Off-shore wind farm development: present status and challenges. Renew. Sustain. Energy Rev. **29**, 780–792 (2014)
3. Kamal, E., Aitouche, A., Ghorbani, R., et al.: Fuzzy scheduler fault-tolerant control for wind energy conversion systems. IEEE Trans. Control Syst. Technol. **22**(1), 119–131 (2014)
4. Wei, X., Verhaegen, M., Van Engelen, T.: Sensor fault detection and isolation for wind turbines based on subspace identification and kalman filter techniques. Int. J. Adapt. Control Sig. Process. **24**(8), 687–707 (2010)
5. Wei, X., Verhaegen, M.: Sensor and actuator fault diagnosis for wind turbine systems by using robust observer and filter. Wind Energy **14**(4), 491–516 (2011)
6. Wu, X., Li, Y., Li, F., et al.: Adaptive estimation-based leakage detection for a wind turbine hydraulic pitching system. IEEE/ASME Trans. Mechatron. **17**(5), 907–914 (2012)
7. Odgaard, P.F., Stoustrup, J.: Unknown input observer based detection of sensor faults in a wind turbine. In: 2010 IEEE International Conference on Control Applications (CCA). IEEE, pp. 310–315 (2010)
8. Badihi, H., Zhang, Y., Hong, H.: Fuzzy gain-scheduled active fault-tolerant control of a wind turbine. J. Franklin Inst. **351**(7), 3677–3706 (2014)
9. Blesa, J., Rotondo, D., Puig, V., et al.: FDI and FTC of wind turbines using the interval observer approach and virtual actuators/sensors. Control Eng. Pract. **24**(3), 138–155 (2014)
10. Watson, S.J., Xiang, B.J., Yang, W., et al.: Condition monitoring of the power output of wind turbine generators using wavelets. IEEE Trans. Energy Convers. **25**(3), 715–721 (2010)
11. Ding, F.: System Identification–New Theory and Methods. Science Press, Beijing (2013)
12. Ding, F., Ma, X.Y.: Identification methods for canonical state space systems. J. Nanjing Univ. Inf. Sci. Technol. Nat. Sci. Edition **6**(6), 481–504 (2014)
13. Ding, F.: Combined state and least squares parameter estimation algorithms for dynamic systems. Appl. Math. Model. **38**(1), 403–412 (2014)
14. Ma, X.Y., Ding, F.: Gradient-based parameter identification algorithms for observer canonical state space systems using state estimates. Circ. Syst. Sig. Process. **34**(5), 1697–1709 (2015)
15. Sloth, C., Esbensen, T., Stoustrup, J.: Robust and fault-tolerant linear parameter-varying control of wind turbines. Mechatronics **21**(4), 645–659 (2011)

Radio Channel of Through-the-Earth Communication Fitted for the Subway Condition

Zeng Jiajia and Su Zhong(✉)

Beijing Key Laboratory of High Dynamic Navigation Technology, Beijing Information Science and Technology University, Beijing 100101, China
Sylvia_spring@126.com, sz@bistu.edu.cn

Abstract. The purpose of this paper is to select the optimal operating frequency for wireless through-the-earth communication fitted for the subway condition. Based on theory of the electromagnetic plane wave and Fresnel formulas, propagation channel model for wireless through-the-earth communication fitted for the subway condition is established, and the propagation attenuation, interface reflection and transmission characteristics of electromagnetic wave penetrating media are analyzed. Then, the relationship between the amplitude ratio of electric field and frequency is discussed when signals transfer in the wet soil, the concrete and the dry soil respectively. The simulative calculation results show that the optimal operating frequency for wireless through-the-earth communication fitted for the subway condition should be lower than 10 kHz.

Keywords: Through-the-earth communication · Subway condition · Radio channel

1 Introduction

Because the influence of communication signal is vulnerable to transmission medium blocking and multipath propagation factors, it is particularly important to study the radio channel of through-the-earth communication fitted for the subway condition even warehouses, supermarkets, libraries, the airport hall, exhibition hall, underground parking, subway and other complex environment [1]. Almost all of the wireless through-the-earth communication systems are used in the mine, but it is seldom used in the subway environment. In this paper, propagation channel model for wireless through-the-earth communication fitted for the subway condition is established and analyzed, and eventually, the optimal operating frequency for wireless through-the-earth communication fitted for the subway condition is selected, providing a prerequisite for the next step of research and development of underground wireless

This work is supported by The National Natural Science Foundation of China (Grant No. 61261160497), Beijing Municipal Commission of Education (Grant No. TJSHG201310772025) and Beijing Science and Technology Project (Grant No. Z131100005313009).

L. Zhang et al. (Eds.): AsiaSim 2016/SCS AutumnSim 2016, Part I, CCIS 643, pp. 539–545, 2016.
DOI: 10.1007/978-981-10-2663-8_55

communication system. The results has a certain reference value for the similar urban complex environment in the wireless communication.

2 Simulation Models

2.1 Electromagnetic Characteristics of Lossy Medium

Parameters of dielectric and electrical properties refer to ε which means permittivity, μ meaning permeability and σ which means electrical conductivity. In general, ε_r means the relative dielectric constant of the transmission medium and $\varepsilon_r = \varepsilon/\varepsilon_0$. When the channel is ideal transmission medium, the energy storage and discharge in a cycle is equal without energy loss, meanwhile, both ε and μ are real numbers. However, the actual medium is a loss medium, and it is divided into conductive loss media, polarization loss medium and magnetic loss medium, or both [2]. Common media are usually non- magnetic media with $\mu \approx \mu_0 = 4\pi \times 10^{-7} H/m$, where μ_0 means permeability of free space, and $\mu_r = \mu/\mu_0 \approx 1$ [2]. Considering polarization loss medium and a conductive dielectric loss medium, and now the dielectric constant is expressed in a complex number,

$$\tilde{\varepsilon} = \varepsilon' - j\varepsilon'' \tag{1}$$

When the media is conductive loss one,

$$\varepsilon' = \varepsilon \tag{2}$$

$$\varepsilon'' = \sigma/\omega \tag{3}$$

Where σ means the conductive properties of the medium. When $\sigma = 0$, the media is ideal medium; and when $\sigma = \infty$, the media is ideal conductor; and the media is conductive medium as σ is value between 0 and ∞.

2.2 Transmission Channel Modeling and Analysis

The three layer plane layered propagation channel model is the most basic one of through-the-earth communication fitting for the subway condition. For convenience's sake, the channel is considered as an ideal homogeneous medium for isotropic media in this paper, and the ground and underground space can be idealized as free space, and the interface between different media is abstracted as a smooth surface, and we only consider simplex radio communication from underground to ground. The channel model used in this paper is shown in Fig. 1.

The stratum media is ideal homogeneous medium and its thickness is h, where $h = h_2 - h_1$, and its refractive index is n_2. The ground $(y > h_2)$ and underground $(0 < y < h_1)$ can be idealized as free space, which refractive index is n_1. Thus, a wireless channel of through-the-earth communication fitted for the Subway condition is constructed.

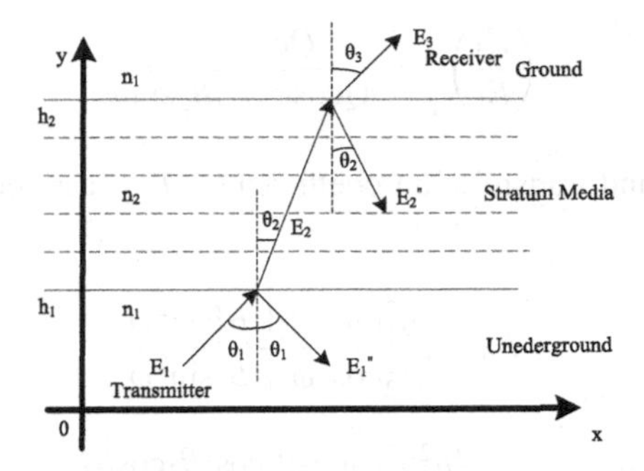

Fig. 1. Simplified wireless channel model of through-the-earth communication fitted for the Subway condition

Only simplex communication is considered in this study, that is, when the electromagnetic wave enters the plane of $y = h_1$ with the angle of θ_1, the reflection can lead to partial power loss; and another part enters the stratum media with the angle of θ_2, the electromagnetic wave is reflected and transmitted through many times in the stratum media ($h_1 < y < h_2$), resulting in a larger interference signal, and then entering the ground space to form a transmission wave.

As shown in the above figure, E_1 is incident wave and E_1' is reflected wave when the electromagnetic wave enters stratum media, and E_2 is incident wave, E_2' is reflected wave and E_3 is transmitted wave when the electromagnetic wave enters the ground space. It can be obtained by Snell's law [3],

$$\mathrm{E}_i = e_x E_i e^{j(k_i x - \omega t)} \tag{4}$$

$$\mathrm{E}_i' = e_x E_i e^{j(k_i' x - \omega t)} \tag{5}$$

Where e_x is the positive unit vector of x axis, and $k_i = n_i\omega/c$. When the electromagnetic wave penetrates through the different media, the reflection and refraction phenomena occurs. The uniform plane wave can be took into account, and supposing that the medium interface is smooth. Reflection and refraction waves are also vertically polarized wave because of the continuity of electromagnetic wave at the interface when the incident wave is the vertical polarized wave. And reflection and refraction waves are parallel polarized wave when the incident wave is the parallel polarized wave [4].

It can be seen from Eqs. (4) and (5): if the incident wave is the vertical polarized wave, the amplitude of electric field strength of reflected wave and incident wave when electromagnetic wave penetrates through from underground to stratum media, and the amplitude of electric field strength of transmitted wave and incident wave when electromagnetic wave penetrates through from stratum media to ground are as follows:

$$\left(\frac{E_1'}{E_1}\right)_\perp = \frac{A_1\cos\varphi - iB_1\sin\varphi}{A_2\cos\varphi - iB_2\sin\varphi} \tag{6}$$

$$\left(\frac{E_3}{E_1}\right)_\perp = \frac{Qe^{jk_3 h\cos\theta_3}}{A_2\cos\varphi - iB_2\sin\varphi} \tag{7}$$

Reflection $(R_\perp)$ and transmission coefficients $(T_\perp)$ can be seen from Eqs. (6) and (7),

$$R_\perp = \frac{A_1^2\cos^2\varphi + B_1^2\sin^2\varphi}{A_2^2\cos^2\varphi + B_2^2\sin^2\varphi} \tag{8}$$

$$T_\perp = \frac{4n_1^2 n_2^2 n_3 \cos\theta_1 \cos^2\theta_2 \cos\theta_3}{A_2^2\cos^2\varphi + B_2^2\sin^2\varphi} \tag{9}$$

If the incident wave is parallel polarized wave, its corresponding reflection $R_{//}$ and transmission coefficients $T_{//}$ are as follows:

$$\mathrm{R}_{//} = \frac{C_1^2\cos^2\varphi + D_1^2\sin^2\varphi}{C_2^2\cos^2\varphi + D_2^2\sin^2\varphi} \tag{10}$$

$$\mathrm{T}_{//} = \frac{4n_1^2 n_2^2 n_3 \cos\theta_1 \cos^2\theta_2 \cos\theta_3}{C_2^2\cos^2\varphi + D_2^2\sin^2\varphi} \tag{11}$$

It can be seen from Eqs. (8) to (11): If $\theta_1 = 0, R_\perp = R_{//}, T_\perp = T_{//}$; if $\theta_1 \to 0$, the transmission coefficient basically remains unchanged; if $\theta_1 \geq \mathrm{C}$ (C is certain a constant), the transmission coefficient attenuates rapidly; if total transmission phenomenon occurs, the transmission coefficient is proportional to the refractive index of the medium and the oscillation changes with the increase of the transmission depth.

3 Simulation and Discussion

According to the analysis of the 2.1 and 2.2 section, the main effects of electromagnetic wave propagation in the medium include: Permittivity, permeability and electrical conductivity [5, 6]. The radio channel of through-the-earth communication fitting for the Subway condition can be considered as a good conductor, so $\tilde{\varepsilon} \approx j\varepsilon''$, and $\mu \approx \mu_0 = 4\pi \times 10^{-7} H/m.$ It can be seen from Eqs. (4) and (5): When the electromagnetic wave pass through in the medium, its electric field intensity or magnetic field intensity presents exponential decay. Taking the strength of electric field as an example, the amplitude of electromagnetic wave after penetrating through a certain distance in the subway condition can be expressed as:

$$\mathrm{E} = E_0 e^{-\beta d} \tag{12}$$

Where E means the amplitude of the electric field intensity at the receiving point, and E_0 is the amplitude of the electric field intensity at the source, and d is distance from source to receiver, and β is attenuation constant [7] and satisfies Eq. (13):

$$\beta = \omega\sqrt{\frac{u\varepsilon}{2}[\sqrt{1+(\varepsilon''/\varepsilon')^2}-1]} \tag{13}$$

After the transmission medium is determined, its electromagnetic parameters are also determined. If the electrical conductivity is known, the intensity of the electric field is determined by the frequency. To describe the attenuation rules, the amplitude ratio of electric field κ is defined as $\kappa = \mathrm{E}/E_0 = e^{-\beta d}$. It can be seen that Fig. 2(a), (b) and (c) describe the relationship between κ and frequency when signals penetrate through the wet soil, the concrete and the dry soil respectively. The corresponding electromagnetic parameters of wet soil are: $\varepsilon_r = 20$, $\sigma = 0.01s/m$; the electromagnetic parameters of concrete are: $\varepsilon_r = 6.5$, $\sigma = 0.001s/m$; the electromagnetic parameters of dry soil: $\varepsilon_r = 2$, $\sigma = 0.0001s/m$ [8, 9].

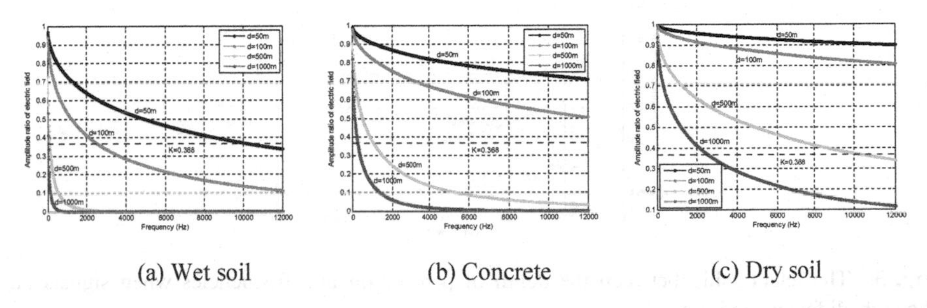

(a) Wet soil (b) Concrete (c) Dry soil

Fig. 2. The relationship between amplitude ratio of electric field and frequencies when signals penetrate through different medium

By comparing Fig. 2(a), (b) and (c), we can see the fact that $\kappa_{wet\,soil}$ is less than $\kappa_{concrete}$, and $\kappa_{concrete}$ is less than $\kappa_{dry\,soil}$ when the transmission distance and the communication frequency are constant. It shows that the attenuation after electromagnetic wave signal passing through wet soil is the largest and the attenuation after passing through dry soil is the minimal. It can be separately analyzed from these three figures: In the same medium, the amplitude ratio of electric field κ decreases with the increase of frequency. It means the attenuation of electromagnetic wave signal is increased with the increase of frequency. At the same frequency, the amplitude ratio of electric field κ decreases with the increase of the propagation distance. It means that the more the propagation distance, the greater the attenuation of the electromagnetic wave signal.

It is generally accepted that it has a higher transmitting rate when the amplitude ratio of electric field κ is higher than 36.8 %. Now suppose the depth of communication in urban subway environment is 50 m, and it can be seen from Fig. 2(a): If $\kappa \geq 36.8\%$ and the depth of communication reaching 500 meters are to be meet, the operating frequency should be no more than 10 kHz when signals penetrate through the wet soil. It can be seen from Fig. 2(b): In the case of ensuring higher transmission rate, the depth of communication can reach 100 meters if the frequency is 10 kHz when signals penetrate through the concrete. Figure 2(c) shows that In the case of ensuring higher transmission rate, the depth of communication can reach 500 meters if the frequency is 10 kHz when signals penetrate through the dry soil. According to Fig. 2 (a), (b) and (c), if κ is more than 36.8 % and the depth of communication reaching 50 meters are to be meet, the operating frequency should be no more than 10 kHz when signals penetrate through these three media mentioned above.

Below is researched from the angle of penetration depth, its simulation result is displayed as Fig. 3, it describes the relationship between the depth of penetration and frequencies when signals pass through the wet soil, the concrete and the dry soil respectively. It is obvious that the operating frequency should be no more than 10 kHz under the premise of reaching 50 meters and achieving a better transmission rate in these three media.

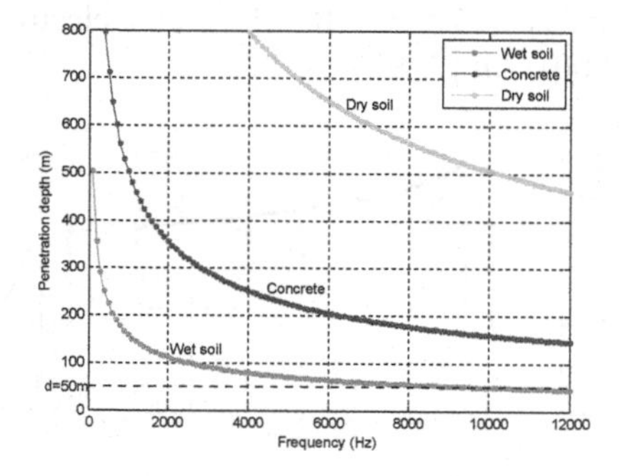

Fig. 3. The relationship between the depth of penetration and frequencies when signals pass through different medium

In summary, the selection of the optimum frequency band for wireless through-the-earth communication fitted for the subway condition is considered from two aspects of attenuation and penetration depth respectively, and the operating frequency should be less than 10 kHz if electromagnetic signals have certain penetration ability for wireless through-the-earth communication fitted for the subway condition.

4 Conclusion and Future Work

In this paper, propagation channel model for wireless through-the-earth communication in the subway is established, and the propagation attenuation, interface reflection and transmission characteristics of electromagnetic wave penetrating media are analyzed. The relationship between the amplitude ratio of electric field and frequency is discussed when signals transfer in the wet soil, the concrete and the dry soil respectively. The simulative calculation results show that the optimal operating frequency for wireless through-the-earth communication in the subway should be lower than 10 kHz. In the following study, wireless communication system will be built for through-the-earth communication fitted for the subway condition.

References

1. Hao, J.-J., Wang, F.-Y.: Multipath characteristics of through-the-earth stratified medium channel of elastic wave signal communication. J. China Coal Soc. **37**(4), 695–699 (2012)
2. Guo, Y.-J., Wu, K., Zhao, Y., et al.: Research of fast acquisition method for low bit rate spread spectrum signal of mine through-the-earth communication. Ind. Mine Autom. (6): 32–35 (2013). [3]
3. Zheng, P., Liu, L.-H., Wei, Y.-K.: HT_cSQUID low frequency receiver and through-wall receiving experiments. Acta Phys. Sin. **19**, 055 (2014)
4. Jia, Y., Li, F., Tao, J., et al.: Transmission characteristics of very low frequency electromagnetic wave of mine-seam wireless through-the-earth communication system. Ind. Mine Autom. **41**(9), 31–33 (2015)
5. Yan, L., Waynert, J., Sunderman, C., et al.: Statistical analysis and modeling of VLF/ELF noise in coal mines for through-the-earth wireless communications. In: Industry Applications Society Annual Meeting, 2014 IEEE, pp. 1–5. IEEE (2014)
6. Li, Y.-B., Xiang, X., Ling, L.-W.: Miniaturized design and testing of antenna for through-the-earth communication system. Ind. Mine Autom. (7), 18–22 (2013)
7. Yan, L., Waynert, J., Sunderman, C.: Earth conductivity estimation from through-the-earth measurements of 94 coal mines using different electromagnetic models. Appl. Comput. Electromagnet. Soc. J. **29**(10), 755–762 (2014)
8. Hong, Y.K., Bae, S.: Through-the-earth (TTE) communication systems and methods: U.S. Patent 8,886,117. November 11 2014
9. Tao, J., Zhang, Y.: Study on the effect of frequency on conductivity of underground strata in coal mine through-the-earth wireless communication. Sens. Transducers **178**(9), 111 (2014)

Research on Low-Cost MSINS/GPS Vehicle Integrated Navigation Error Correction

Shu-Ping Liu(✉) and Qing Li

Beijing Key Laboratory of High Dynamic Navigation Technology,
Beijing Information Science and Technology University, Beijing 100101, China
1525462984@qq.com, liqing@bistu.edu.cn

Abstract. For Low-cost MSINS/GPS vehicle integrated navigation system, a real-time error correction algorithm is proposed in the paper, aiming at the problem that MSINS cannot meet the accuracy of the problem for a long time when GPS reduces location precision or even invalid. In the proposed algorithm, vehicle constraint information is introduced according to the incomplete constraint method of the carrier motion characteristics. The velocity errors are set to be observed quantity and is used to correct position errors. To verify the method, a simulation of the estimation of misalignment angles and position error is de-signed. And the results prove that this method can largely improve the accuracy of misalignment angles and position and ensure the continuity of vehicle navigation information.

Keywords: Vehicle integrated navigation · MIMU · GPS · Error correction

1 Introduction

Vehicle navigation and locating system is an important part of intelligent transportation system. (ITS). It can provide a safe efficient and comfortable transportation service for people, improve traffic efficiency, reduce the accident and save energy and reduce pollution. So it has gradually become an indispensable auxiliary tool in people's life [1].

At present, most of vehicle navigation systems are based on GPS. However, positioning systems using GPS alone can temporary loss the satellite connection and signal error under the shelter of buildings, tunnels or overpass. They cannot provide continuous and accurate position data. The inertial navigation system is a fully independent navigation system and has several advantages: such as good concealment, anti-interference, not influenced by geographical environment and meteorological conditions. The traditional INS is, nevertheless, restricted in the application of vehicle navigation due to expensive price and large volume. With the development of Micro Electrical-Mechanical System (MEMS), micro inertial sensors are beginning to appear and widely used. Because of the advantages of small in volume, light in weight, low in cost, low in power and easy mounting, MSINS is more and more popular in the field of

This work is supported by The National Natural Science Foundation of China (Grant No.61471046).

L. Zhang et al. (Eds.): AsiaSim 2016/SCS AutumnSim 2016, Part I, CCIS 643, pp. 546–554, 2016.
DOI: 10.1007/978-981-10-2663-8_56

vehicle navigation. The combination of MSINS and GPS can combine strong points to each other and can make navigation precision and dependability better, which has become a hot spot in the vehicle navigation [2–4].

Due to the limitation of the manufacturing technology of MEMS gyroscope, MEMS gyroscope random drift is relatively large, generally ranging from $10°/h$ to $1000°/h$ [5]. Some MEM accelerometer zero bias stability can reach below 1 mg. Consequently, the combination of low precision MIMU and GPS cannot work alone to provide to meet the navigation accuracy continuously. According to this problem, the car body constraint conditions is designed as state variables to correct position and attitude error, improving the location precision of vehicle.

2 Simulation Model

Some of the symbols in the paper are as follows:

n — Navigation coordinate system
p— Platform coordinate system
b — Body coordinate system
ϕ — Attitude angle errors
v — Velocity
∇ — Position, including L, λ, H
L — Latitude
λ — Longitude
H — Height
R — Earth radius
Ω — Angular rate of earth rotation
ω — Angular velocity
{ — Specific force
ε — Gyro drift
$\mathbf{\nabla}$ — Acceleration bias

2.1 Error Correction Principle

2.1.1 Algorithm Frame

The proposed algorithm mainly includes three parts: the strap-down inertial navigation solution, the velocity restriction of vehicle, the design of Kalman filter. The algorithm working principle is shown in Fig. 1.

When GPS fails, based on the characteristics of the vehicle, the vehicle horizontal and vertical velocity errors are set as the observed quantity, and Kalman filter is utilized to compute positioning errors and to make compensation in real time.

2.1.2 Vehicle Velocity Restriction

The body frame is defined as following in the Fig. 2.

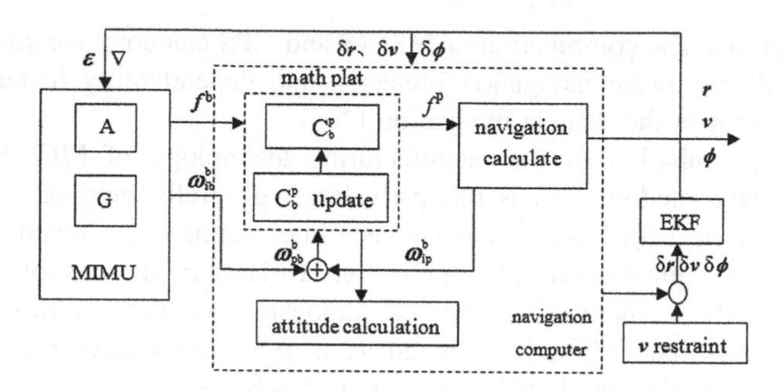

Fig. 1. Algorithm frame

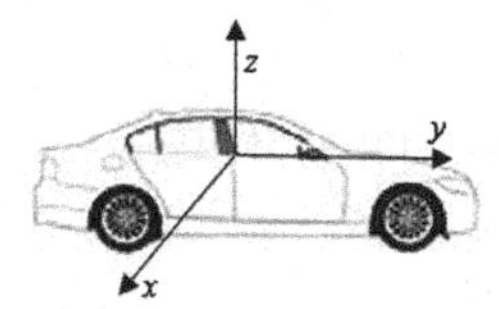

Fig. 2. The body frame

The velocity conversion formula from navigation frame to body frame:

$$v^b = C_n^b v^n \tag{1}$$

Where

$$C_n^b = \begin{bmatrix} c_{11} & c_{12} & c_{13} \\ c_{21} & c_{22} & c_{23} \\ c_{31} & c_{32} & c_{33} \end{bmatrix}$$
$$= \begin{bmatrix} \sin\psi\sin\theta\sin\gamma + \cos\psi\cos\gamma & \cos\psi\sin\theta\sin\gamma - \sin\psi\cos\gamma & -\cos\theta\sin\gamma \\ \sin\psi\cos\theta & \cos\psi\cos\theta & \sin\theta \\ -\sin\psi\sin\theta\cos\gamma + \cos\psi\sin\gamma & -\cos\psi\sin\theta\cos\gamma - \sin\psi\sin\gamma & \cos\theta\cos\gamma \end{bmatrix}$$

where ψ is to indicate the head angle, θ is to indicate the pitch angle and γ is to indicate the roll angle.

The differential equation of (1) is

$$\delta v^b = C_n^b \delta v^n + \delta C_n^b v^n \tag{2}$$

Where δC_n^b is caused by the deviation of math platform (p) to ideal navigation system (n). Assuming that platform misalignment angle is $\phi = [\phi_E, \phi_N, \phi_U]^T$, we have

$$C_n^b = C_n^p C_p^b = (I - [\boldsymbol{\phi}\times])C_p^b \tag{3}$$

Where

$$[\boldsymbol{\phi}\times] = \begin{bmatrix} 0 & -\phi_U & \phi_N \\ \phi_U & 0 & -\phi_E \\ -\phi_N & \phi_E & 0 \end{bmatrix} \tag{4}$$

We substitute Eqs. (3) and (4) into Eq. (2).

$$\delta \boldsymbol{v}^b = C_n^b \delta \boldsymbol{v}^n - [\boldsymbol{\phi}\times]\boldsymbol{v}^b = C_n^b \delta \boldsymbol{v}^n - \left[\boldsymbol{v}^b\times\right]\boldsymbol{\phi} \tag{5}$$

That is

$$\delta \boldsymbol{v}^b = C_n^b \begin{bmatrix} \delta v_E \\ \delta v_N \\ \delta v_U \end{bmatrix} + \begin{bmatrix} 0 & v_z^b & -v_y^b \\ -v_z^b & 0 & v_x^b \\ v_y^b & -v_x^b & 0 \end{bmatrix} \begin{bmatrix} \phi_E \\ \phi_N \\ \phi_U \end{bmatrix} \tag{6}$$

Assuming that vehicle runs smoothly without sideslip and jolt, the velocity theoretical values of vehicle in the horizontal and vertical directions are zero. Namely,

$$v_x^b = 0, v_z^b = 0 \tag{7}$$

In the view of Eq. (6), we have

$$\delta \boldsymbol{v}^b = C_n^b \begin{bmatrix} \delta v_E \\ \delta v_N \\ \delta v_U \end{bmatrix} + \begin{bmatrix} 0 & 0 & -v_y^b \\ 0 & 0 & 0 \\ v_y^b & 0 & 0 \end{bmatrix} \begin{bmatrix} \phi_E \\ \phi_N \\ \phi_U \end{bmatrix} \tag{8}$$

2.2 SINS Error Equation

The SINS error equation is the foundation of constructing system error model. The navigation system (n coordinate system) is defined as the local lever North-East-Down frame. SINS error equation is based on n coordinate system. Referred to [6], the equations of misalignments $\boldsymbol{\phi}$ are

$$\begin{aligned} &\phi_E = (\Omega \mathrm{sin} L + v_E \mathrm{tan} L/R)\phi_N - (\Omega \mathrm{cos} L + v_E/R)\phi_U - \delta v_N/R + \varepsilon_E \\ &\phi_N = -(\Omega \mathrm{sin} L + v_E \mathrm{tan} L/R)\phi_E - \phi_U v_E/R + \delta v_E/R - \Omega \mathrm{sin} L \delta L + \varepsilon_N \\ &\phi_U = -(\Omega \mathrm{cos} L + v_E/R)\phi_E + \phi_U v_N/R + \delta v_E \mathrm{tan} L/R + \left(\Omega \mathrm{cos} L + v_E \mathrm{sec}^2 L/R\right)\delta L + \varepsilon_U \end{aligned} \tag{9}$$

The velocity error equation is representative with $\delta \boldsymbol{v}$:

$$\begin{aligned} \delta v_E =& -f_U\phi_E - f_N\phi_U + (v_N \tan L/R - v_U/R)\delta v_E + (2\Omega \sin L + v_E \tan L/R)\delta v_N \\ & - (2\Omega \cos L + v_E/R)\delta v_U + \nabla_E \\ \delta v_N =& f_U\phi_E - f_E\phi_U - (2\Omega \sin L + v_E \tan L/R)\delta v_E - \delta v_N v_E/R - \delta v_U v_U/R + \nabla_N \\ \delta v_U =& f_N\phi_E - f_E\phi_U - (2\Omega \cos L + v_E/R)\delta v_E + 2\delta v_N v_E/R + \nabla_U \end{aligned} \quad (10)$$

The position error equation is representative with δr:

$$\begin{aligned} \delta L &= \delta v_N/R \\ \delta \lambda &= \delta v_E \sec L/R \\ \delta H &= \delta v_U \end{aligned} \quad (11)$$

Where

$$\begin{bmatrix} \varepsilon_E \\ \varepsilon_N \\ \varepsilon_U \end{bmatrix} = C_b^n \begin{bmatrix} \varepsilon_x^b \\ \varepsilon_y^b \\ \varepsilon_z^b \end{bmatrix}, \begin{bmatrix} \nabla_E \\ \nabla_N \\ \nabla_U \end{bmatrix} = C_b^n \begin{bmatrix} \nabla_x^b \\ \nabla_y^b \\ \nabla_z^b \end{bmatrix}, \begin{bmatrix} f_E \\ f_N \\ f_U \end{bmatrix} = C_b^n \begin{bmatrix} f_x^b \\ f_y^b \\ f_z^b \end{bmatrix} \quad (12)$$

2.3 The Design of Kalman Filter

2.3.1 State Equation

The misalignment angles, position errors, the gyro drifts and accelerometer zero bias are selected as state variables.

$$X = \left[\phi_E, \phi_N, \phi_U, \delta v_E, \delta v_N, \delta v_U, \delta L, \delta \lambda, \delta H, \varepsilon_x^b, \varepsilon_y^b, \varepsilon_z^b, \nabla_x^b, \nabla_y^b, \nabla_z^b\right] \quad (13)$$

The models of gyro and accelerometer are

$$\dot{\boldsymbol{\varepsilon}} = 0, \ \boldsymbol{\varepsilon} = \boldsymbol{\varepsilon}_c + \boldsymbol{w}_\varepsilon \quad (14)$$

And

$$\dot{\boldsymbol{\nabla}} = 0, \boldsymbol{\nabla} = \boldsymbol{\nabla}_c + \boldsymbol{w}_{\boldsymbol{\nabla}} \quad (15)$$

Where ε_c and ∇_c are constant drift, w_ε and w_∇ are white noises. Their means are zero and their variance is Q.

According to the error equation in the 2.2 section, the equation of state of Kalman filter is obtained:

$$\dot{X}(t) = F(t)X(t) + \Gamma(t)W(t) \quad (16)$$

$W(t)$, system state noise, is:

$$W(t) = \left[w_{\varepsilon}^{T}, w_{\nabla}^{T}\right]^{T} = \left[w_{\varepsilon x}, w_{\varepsilon y}, w_{\varepsilon z}, w_{\nabla x}, w_{\nabla y}, w_{\nabla z}\right]^{T} \quad (17)$$

The state matrix $F(t)$ is

$$F(t) = \begin{bmatrix} F_{11} & F_{12} & F_{13} & F_{14} & 0_{3\times3} \\ F_{21} & F_{22} & 0_{3\times3} & 0_{3\times3} & F_{25} \\ 0_{3\times3} & F_{32} & F_{33} & 0_{3\times3} & 0_{3\times3} \\ 0_{6\times3} & 0_{6\times3} & 0_{6\times3} & 0_{6\times3} & 0_{6\times3} \end{bmatrix} \quad (18)$$

in which the following definitions apply:

$$F_{11} = \begin{bmatrix} 0 & \left(\Omega+\dot{\lambda}\right)\sin L & -\left(\Omega+\dot{\lambda}\right)\cos L \\ -\left(\Omega+\dot{\lambda}\right)\sin L & 0 & -\dot{L} \\ \left(\Omega+\dot{\lambda}\right)\sin L & \dot{L} & 0 \end{bmatrix}, F_{12} = \begin{bmatrix} 0 & -1/R & 0 \\ 1/R & 0 & 0 \\ \tan L/R & 0 & 0 \end{bmatrix}$$

$$F_{13} = \begin{bmatrix} 0 & 0 & 0 \\ -\Omega\sin L & 0 & 0 \\ \Omega\sin L + \dot{\lambda}\big/\cos L & 0 & 0 \end{bmatrix}, F_{14} = -C_b^n, F_{21} = C_b^n \begin{bmatrix} 0 & -f_z^b & f_y^b \\ f_z^b & 0 & -f_x^b \\ -f_y^b & -f_x^b & 0 \end{bmatrix}$$

$$F_{22} = \begin{bmatrix} \dot{\lambda}\sin L - \dot{L} & \left(2\Omega+\dot{\lambda}\right)\sin L & -\left(2\Omega+\dot{\lambda}\right)\cos L \\ -\left(2\Omega+\dot{\lambda}\right)\sin L & -\dot{L} & -\dot{L} \\ \left(2\Omega+\dot{\lambda}\right)\sin L & 2\dot{L} & 0 \end{bmatrix}, F_{25} = C_b^n$$

$$F_{32} = \begin{bmatrix} 0 & 1/R & 0 \\ \sec L/R & 0 & 0 \\ 0 & 0 & 1 \end{bmatrix}, F_{33} = \begin{bmatrix} 0 & 0 & 0 \\ \dot{\lambda}\tan L & 0 & 0 \\ 0 & 0 & 0 \end{bmatrix}.$$

The state noise input matrix $\Gamma(t)$ is

$$\Gamma(t) = \begin{bmatrix} C_b^n & 0_{3\times3} \\ 0_{3\times3} & C_b^n \\ 0_{9\times3} & 0_{9\times3} \end{bmatrix} \quad (19)$$

2.3.2 Measurement Equation

According to the algorithm description in the section of 2.1, we select the horizontal and vertical velocity errors as the measurements.

$$Z = \left[\delta v_x^b, \delta v_z^b\right]^T \tag{20}$$

In view of Eq. (8), we obtain

$$Z(t) = H(t)X(t) + V(t) \tag{21}$$

The measurement matrix $H(t)$ is

$$H(t) = \begin{bmatrix} 0 & 0 & -v_y^b & c_{11} & c_{12} & c_{13} & 0 & 0 & 0 & 0 & 0 & 0 & 0 & 0 & 0 \\ v_y^b & 0 & 0 & c_{31} & c_{32} & c_{33} & 0 & 0 & 0 & 0 & 0 & 0 & 0 & 0 & 0 \end{bmatrix} \tag{22}$$

Actually, the sideslip and jolt phenomenon is inevitable in the movement of the vehicle. Therefore, the measurement noises $V(t) = [v_{v_x}, v_{v_z}]^T$ are considered. Their means are zero and their variance is $R = \begin{bmatrix} \sigma_{v_x}^2 & 0 \\ 0 & \sigma_{v_z}^2 \end{bmatrix}$, respectively.

3 Simulation and Analysis

To verify the algorithm with practicability and effectiveness, the simulation on initial navigation error equation is made and the characteristic of error estimation before and after the addition of vehicle constraint condition is analyzed.

The simulation conditions are as follows:

Initial latitude is 40° and initial longitude is 116°;
Initial misalignments $\phi_x = 0.1°$, $\phi_y = 0.1°$, $\phi_z = 0.3°$;
The constant gyro drifts $\varepsilon_x = 0.1°/h$, $\varepsilon_y = 0.1°/h$, $\varepsilon_z = 0.1°/h$;
The random gyro noises $w_{\varepsilon_x} = 0.1°/h, w_{\varepsilon_y} = 0.1°/h, w_{\varepsilon_z} = 0.1°/h$;
The accelerator bias $\nabla_x = 0.1\,mg$, $\nabla_y = 0.1\,mg$, $\nabla_z = 0.1\,mg$;

The accelerator noises $w_{\nabla_x} = 0.1\,mg$, $w_{\nabla_y} = 0.1\,mg$, $w_{\nabla_z} = 0.1\,mg$.

We compare the performances between the methods without and with the constraint conditions. The estimations of attitude and position error with and without the constraint conditions are shown in the Figs. 3 and 4, respectively.

According to Fig. 3, the attitude and position errors of pure INS composed of low precision MIMU rapidly diverge. During two hours of simulation time, the three attitude angle errors reached 1500 arc seconds, 1900 arc seconds and 3000 arc seconds respectively; North position error is up to 6×10^4 m and the east is 5×10^4 m. By an amplification, we can see the North position error is 100 m and the east is 200 m in 100 s. And usually, the positioning accuracy is at least within 50 m to predict a block

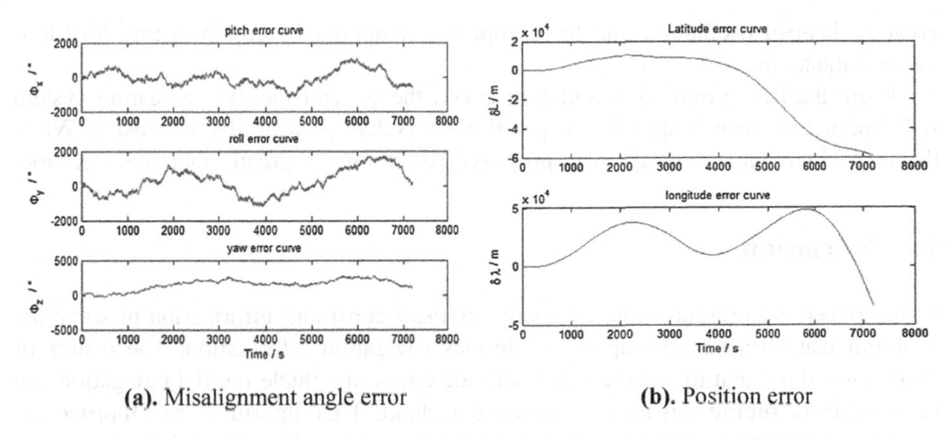

(a). Misalignment angle error (b). Position error

Fig. 3. The characteristic of error without the constraint conditions

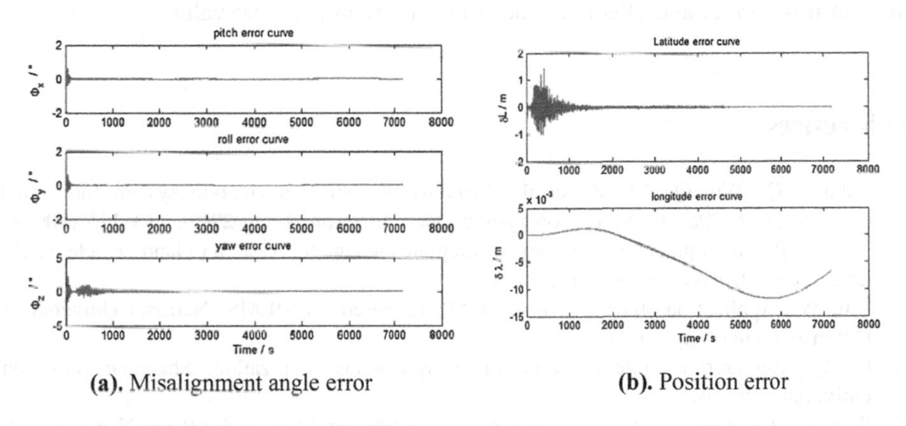

(a). Misalignment angle error (b). Position error

Fig. 4. The characteristic of error with the constraint conditions

or a road traffic conditions. So it is difficult for the INS to demand for the precision of vehicle navigation.

As shown in Fig. 4, the simulation errors of proposed algorithm are reduced by three orders of magnitude and converge very fast within two hours. Of those, longitude

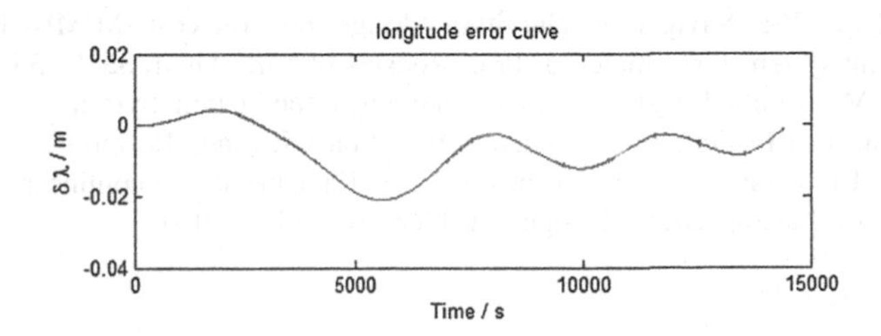

Fig. 5. Longitude error in simulation time of 4 h

error is damped oscillation and to asymptotically approach zero from Fig. 5 of four hours simulation.

From the two groups of simulation curve, the general inertial navigation system will lead to the carrier's attitude and position errors diverge with time increasing. While the inertial navigation system with proposed algorithm can greatly increase precision.

4 Conclusion

In the paper, we present a method using auxiliary constraint information to solve the problem that GPS cannot supply continuous navigation information. The results of simulation show that the position and attitude errors of vehicle inertial navigation can be effectively suppressed by the proposed method. This algorithm can improve the accuracy of position error estimation, and the accuracy and rapidity of the horizontal misalignment angle estimation are very high. The simulation results show that the algorithm is correct and effective, and it has a certain practical value.

References

1. Shang, Q., Wu, Q., Xu, Z., et al.: Actuality of vehicle navigation system and vehicle experiment of GPS/DR navigation system. Mod. Electron. Tech. **29**(9), 113–115 (2006)
2. Xia, Q.: Research on key technology of integrated navigation system in land vehicle. Harbin Engineering University, Harbin (2010)
3. Liu, W.: Application study of low-cost MIMU based on MEMS. National University of Defense Technology (2004)
4. Li, Q.: Research on integrated GPS/INS system and realization. Shanghai Jiao Tong University (2010)
5. Wan, D., Jiancheng, F.: Initial alignment of INS. Southeast University Press, Nanjing (1998)
6. Su, Z.: Inertial technology. National Defence Industry Press (2010)
7. Yuan, G., Liang, H., et al.: Design of integrated navigation algorithm based on low-cost vehicular navigator. J. Chin. Inert. Technol. **19**(1), 69–74 (2011)
8. Qin, Y.: Kalman filter and integrated navigation principle. Northwestern Polytechnic University Press (1998)
9. Wu, J.W., Tsang, K.M., Nie, L.J.: Estimation of the INS's error. J. Chin. Inert. Technol. **30** (20), 4509–4518 (2002)
10. Ben, Y., Sun, F., Gao, W., et al.: Study of zero velocity update for inertial navigation. J. Syst. Simul. **20**(17), 4639–4642 (2008)
11. Liu, J., Lyu, Y.: Navigation algorithm design on low-cost MIMU/GPS integrated measurement system for vehicles. J. Proj. Rockets Missiles Guid. **35**(4), 35–38 (2015)
12. Rogers, R.M.: Applied Mathematics in Integrated Navigation Systems, 2nd edn, p. 78. Reston American Institute of Aeronautics & Astronautics Inc., Reston (2007)
13. Julier, S.J., Uhlmann, J.K.: New extension of the Kalman filter to nonlinear systems. Signal Process. Sens. Fusion Target Recogn. VI **3068**, 182–193 (2010)

The Research of Capability Simulation Module on Modern Railway Logistics Center

Xuchao Chen(✉) and Shiwei He

School of Traffic and Transportation, Beijing Jiaotong University, Beijing, China
{15114208, shwhe}@bjtu.edu.cn

Abstract. Logistics industry has grown rapidly in China. The amount of logistics industry has doubled in last 6 years. Along with the logistic reengineering process of railway corporations, railway logistics centers play an important role in railway freight network. Simulation is an effective method on study of logistics capability. In this paper, operation processes of logistic center were analyzed. A simulation model of railway logistics center was built with the theory of discrete event dynamics systems and Petri-net. Train route scheduling simulation was created to improve the accuracy of simulation. A simulation tool named SIMRLC was developed using C# based on this module. The effectiveness of this module has been verified by case study of the Qianchang railway logistics center in Xiamen.

Keywords: Simulation · Capability · Railway logistics center · Discrete event dynamics system · Petri-net

1 Introduction

Modern railway logistics centers are going to become important components in Chinese railway freight network with the rapid development of logistics industry. The amount of logistics industry has doubled in last 6 years (from 96.6 trillion RMB in 2009 to 220 trillion RMB in 2015). There are some differences between Chinese railway logistics centers and Western railway logistics centers. Railway logistics centers in Europe and America mainly deal with container cargo and express cargo businesses. However, Chinese railway logistics centers contain more types of cargo operations, such as bulk cargo (e.g. coal and ore), special cargo, container cargo, etc., which makes the system more complicated.

Railway logistics center is a kind of discrete event dynamic system (DEDS), which means the state of system only get changed at discrete points in time as a result of stochastic events. This kind of system is difficult to use mathematical equation to describe. However, discrete event simulation is an effective method on study of DEDS. It provides a structured approach to determine optimal input parameter values where optimal result is measured by a function of output variables associated with a simulation model. There are many good literatures in this field. Andrea E. Rizzoli [1] built a simulation model of the flow of intermodal terminal units (ITUs) among and within inland intermodal terminals using MODSIMIII as development tool. During the simulation, various statistics are gathered to assess the performance of the terminal

L. Zhang et al. (Eds.): AsiaSim 2016/SCS AutumnSim 2016, Part I, CCIS 643, pp. 555–567, 2016.
DOI: 10.1007/978-981-10-2663-8_57

equipment. Sönke [2] gave an approach for generating scenarios of sea port container terminals which can support solving optimization problems in container terminal. Swisher et al. [3] presented a brief survey of the literature on discrete-event simulation optimization since 1988. Zhou et al. [4] proposed an approach to model and analyze production logistics system with eM-Plant. The application of simulating technology in logistics distribution, facility layout and supply chain management refers to Wu et al. [5], Huang et al. [6] and Griffis et al. [7]. Q He [8] used eM-plant simulation platform to establish the layout model of the unloading lines. Marinov M [9] provided a yard simulation modelling methodology for analyzing and evaluating flat-shunted yard operations using SIMUL8. Fugihara M K [10] gave a way of simulation technology which can generate several benefits in distribution centers projects. Vidalakis C et al. [11] presented a logistical analysis of construction supply chains by assessing the impact of varying demand on the performance of builders 'merchants' logistics. Chen K et al. [12] gave a method to construct logistics simulation system by using agent and swarm platform. Hou S [13] developed a simulation model with Flexsim software and tested it with different scenarios.

Logistics capability is an important ability logistics firms to deliver the value and services to the customers. The method of measuring logistics capability has been a vital problem. Swartz S M et al. [14] gave a method of assessing the capability in airfield. Zhang L et al. [15] presented a logistics system model based on TPN (Timed Petri Net) and achieved it with Arena. Li H [16] developed an evaluation index system of logistics capability by a combination of the key performance indicator (KPI) method and the performance prism method. Wang M et al. [17] examined the relationship between logistics capability and supply chain uncertainty and risk basing on the factor analysis. Shang K C et al. [18] examined the relationships among logistics capabilities, performance, and financial performance based on a survey of 1200 manufacturing firms in Taiwan using structural equation modelling.

Previous findings have shown that the simulation method is very heartening and widely used in measuring capability of logistics system. This paper is organized as follows: after the introductory considerations and literature analysis, Sect. 2 presents the operation process analysis of railway logistics center. Section 3 contains a simulation module of railway logistics center using the theory of discrete event dynamics systems and Petri-net, based on this module, a simulation tool named SIMRLC was programed. And a case study using SIMRLC is presented in Sect. 4.The final Sect. 5 presents the concluding remarks and directions for future research.

2 Operation Process Analysis

Railway logistics center is a very complex discrete event system which contains large scale of events and elements. A layout of typical railway logistics center is shown in Fig. 1a. Operation process analysis aims at providing a clear logical network of all logistics elements and is the basis of building simulation module. Operation process in different freight yards has strong connection and certain similarities. Considering the similarities among all freight yards and in order to avoid redundancy, an operation process analysis of container cargo yard is given in the following.

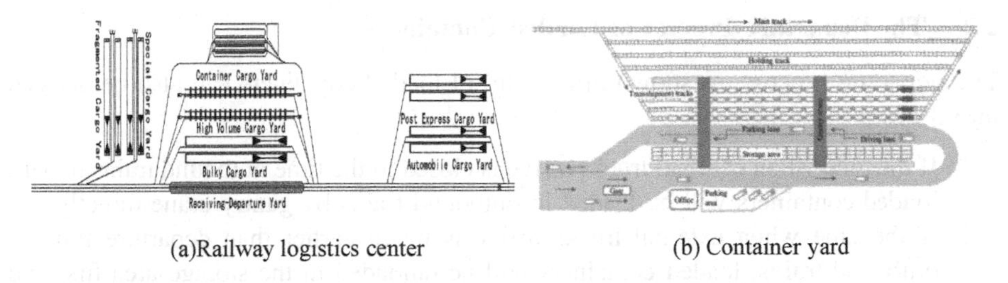

(a)Railway logistics center (b) Container yard

Fig. 1. Layout of railway logistics center and container yard

A typical container cargo yard (as shown in Fig. 1b) consists of tracks, containers, storage area, etc. Containers are the key elements of container yard system. According to the types of containers, operation process can be divided into 4 parts: the arrival process of loaded containers, the departure process of loaded containers, the process of transfer containers, and the process of empty containers.

2.1 The Arrival Process of Loaded Containers

The arrival process of loaded containers (as shown in Fig. 2a) can be divided into 3 cases.

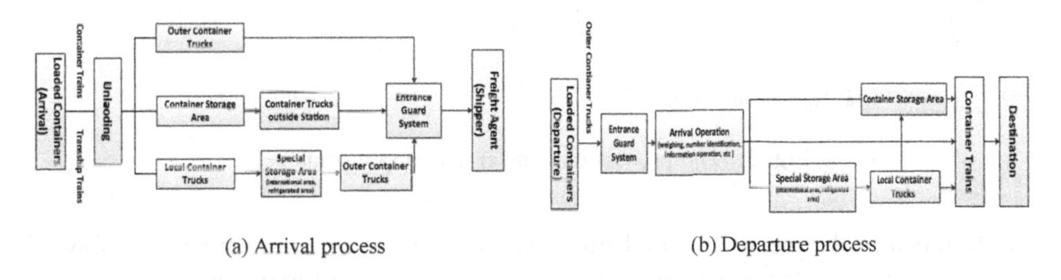

(a) Arrival process (b) Departure process

Fig. 2. The operation process of loaded containers

i. If the time when external trucks arrive is close to the time when inbound trains arrive, containers will be transferred from trains to trucks by gantry cranes directly.
ii. If container train arrives much earlier than external trucks, loaded containers will be unloaded in the arrival storage area first, and then be loaded in external trucks when they arrive.
iii. Some special containers (e.g. refrigerated containers) will be moved to auxiliary storage area first by internal trucks for relevant operations or inspection and then be picked up by external trucks.

2.2 The Departure Process of Loaded Containers

The departure process (as shown in Fig. 2b) of loaded containers can also be divided into 3 cases.

i. If the time when external trucks arrive is closed to the time outbound trains depart, loaded containers will be loaded in outbound trains by gantry crane directly.
ii. If the time when external trucks arrive is much earlier than departure time of outbound trains, loaded containers will be unloaded in the storage area first and then be loaded in the outbound trains.
iii. Special containers will be unloaded in auxiliary storage area first. After certain operations, they will be delivered to container storage area by internal trucks and then be loaded in outbound trains.

2.3 The Process of Transfer Containers

The process of transfer containers (as shown in Fig. 3a) can be divided into 2 cases.

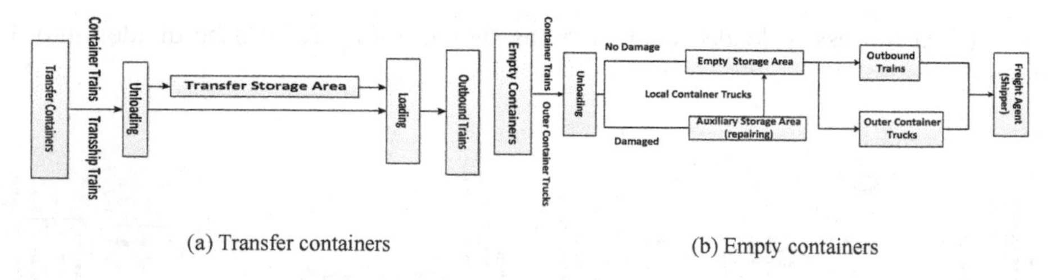

(a) Transfer containers

(b) Empty containers

Fig. 3. The process of transfer and empty containers

i. If the arrival time of inbound trains is close to the departure time of outbound trains, the transfer containers will be loaded in outbound trains directly.
ii. If the arrival time of inbound trains is much earlier than departure time of outbound trains, transfer containers will be loaded in transfer storage area first, and then be loaded in outbound trains.

2.4 The Process of Empty Containers

The process of empty containers (as shown in Fig. 3b) can be divided into 2 cases.

i. If the empty container is not damaged, it will be delivered to empty containers storage area.
ii. If the empty container is damaged, it will be unloaded in the auxiliary storage area to get repaired, and then be delivered to empty containers storage area.

3 Simulation Module of Railway Logistics Center Basing on Petri Net

Petri net is a kind of module using graphic elements as representation. Petri net can be effective method to describe the processes of entities in complex system. Based on the operation process analysis, the simulation module is divided into 3 parts: the Petri net module of train arrival and departure process, truck arrival and departure process, and the loading and unloading process.

3.1 Petri Net Module of Train Arrival and Departure Process

Petri net module of train arrival and departure process is proposed in which places represent the states of trains, train lines and train route scheduling system.

For each train, 8 places (P0-P7 as shown in Table 1) are added to the net, indicating the different states of trains after finishing a series of transitions. For each line, 2 places are added, indicating the line is occupied or is idle. Train route scheduling system is created to realize the simulation of train route selection, which is the key factor to ensure simulation quality. The detail of train route selection will be introduced in Sect. 3.4. Graphically, the Petri net module is presented in Fig. 4. All places and transitions are shown in Table 1.

3.2 Petri Net Module of Truck Arrival and Departure Process

In the Petri net module of truck arrival and departure process (as shown in Fig. 4), places represent the states of trucks, handling machineries or truck channels. For each handling machinery and truck channel, 2 places are added. All definitions of places and transitions are presented in Table 2.

3.3 Petri Net Module of Loading and Unloading Process in Container Cargo Yard

In the Petri net module of loading and unloading process (as shown in Fig. 4), places represent the states of trains, containers and gantry cranes. Trains are divided into 2 categories, the empty trains and the loaded trains. The definitions of all places and transitions are shown in Table 3.

3.4 Train Routes Scheduling Simulation

There are 2 types of relationships between train routes: the conflicting routes and the parallel routes. As shown in Fig. 5a, train route R1 (the gold line) has a common track (marked by the red circle) with train route R2 (the blue line), which means if one train takes up R1 then R2 was locked too for there is no possibility that two trains occupy the

Table 1. Showing the places and transitions of Petri-net module of train arrival and departure process

Places			
P0	Train that arrives at logistics center	P-A	Receiving tracks that are occupied
P1	Train that is assigned to arriving line	P-A′	Receiving tracks that are idle
P2	Train that enters arriving line	P-L	Loading-unloading lines that are occupied
P3	Train that is assigned to loading-unloading line	P-L′	Loading-unloading lines that are idle
P4	Train that enters loading-unloading line	P-D	Departure tracks that are occupied
P5	Train that finishes loading or unloading task	P-D′	Departure tracks that are idle
P6	Train that is assigned to departure line	P-TR	Train routes scheduling system
P7	Train that enters the departure line		
Transitions			
T0	Trains arrive at logistics center basing on certain distribution	T11/12	Trains get loaded or unloaded
T1	Trains are assigned to arriving lines	T5	Trains are assigned to departure lines
T2	Trains enter arriving lines	T6	Trains enter departure lines
T3	Trains are assigned to loading-unloading lines	T7	Trains leave railway logistics center
T4	Trains enter loading-unloading lines		

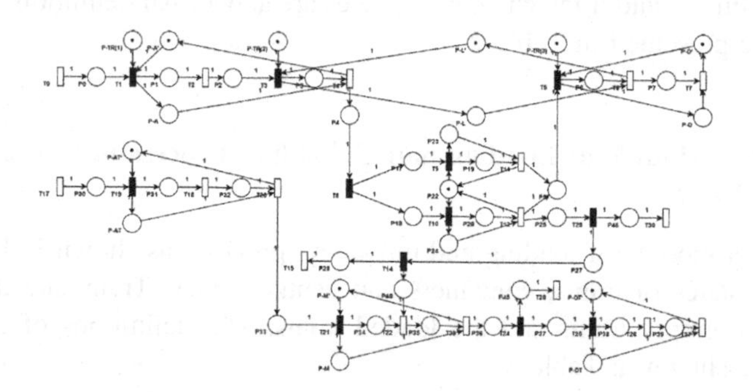

Fig. 4. The Petri net module of container cargo yard

common track at the same time. Contrary to the conflicting train routes, there is no space conflicts among parallel routes, as shown in Fig. 5b.

Based on the analysis of train routes, a train route scheduling simulation method was designed in which train routes are regarded as a kind of resource. The process of train route scheduling simulation is shown in Table 4.

Table 2. Definations of places and transitions in Petri-net module of truck arrival and departure process

Places			
P30	Arrival truck that arrives at railway logistics center	P38	Loaded truck that has been assigned to checking channel
P31	Truck that enters the arrival checking channel	P39	Loaded truck that finishes the checking task
P32	Truck that finishes the checking	P-A	Arrival checking channels that are occupied
P33	Truck that enters the freight yard	P-A'	Arrival checking channels that are idle
P34	Truck that has been assigned to a certain truck space	P-M	Truck spaces that are occupied
P35	Truck that finishes the loading or unloading task	P-M'	Truck spaces that are idle
P36	Departure truck that arrives at railway logistics center	P-D	Departure checking channels that are occupied
P45	Empty truck	P-D'	Departure checking channels that are idle
P37	Loaded truck		
Transitions			
T17	Trucks arrive at logistics center basing on certain distribution	T23	Trucks leave the freight yard
T19	Trucks are assigned to arrival checking channels	T24	Trucks are classified according to loading condition
T18	Trucks get checked for entering railway logistics center	T28	Empty trucks railway logistics center
T20	Trucks enter the freight yard	T25	Loaded trucks are assigned to departure checking channel
T21	Trucks are assigned to a certain truck space	T26	Trucks get checked for leaving railway logistics center
T22	Trucks get loaded or unloaded	T27	Loaded trucks leave railway logistics center

4 Case Study: Simulation of Qianchang Railway Logistics Center

Based on the simulation module, a simulation tool named SIMRLC was programed using C#. The interface of SIMRLC is shown in Fig. 6a. Based on SIMRLC, a case study of Qianchang railway logistics center is presented in this chapter.

Qianchang railway logistics center locates in Xiamen, the southeast of Fujian Province, and is one of the most important railway freight hubs in China. There are 6 arrival-departure lines and 7 types of freight yards in the Qianchang railway logistics center. The layout of Qianchang railway logistics center edited by SIMRLC software is

Table 3. Definations of places and transitions in Petri net module of loading and unloading process

Places			
P4	Train that arrives at container cargo yard	P28	Container that is picked up by local trucks
P18	Loaded trains	P17	Empty trains
P20	Loaded Train that has been assigned to certain crane	P19	Empty Train that has been assigned to certain crane
P25	Container that has been unloaded	P5	Empty Train that finishes the loading task
P46	Container that is unloaded to storage area	P-M1	Gantry crane that is occupied
P27	Container that is unloaded on trucks	P-M2	Gantry crane that is occupied
P48	Container that is picked up by outer trucks	P-M′	Gantry crane that is idle
Transitions			
T4	Trains arrive at container cargo yard	T29	Containers are classified according to unloading target
T8	Trains are classified to loaded and empty trains	T30	Containers are piled up in storage area
T9	Empty trains are assigned to gantry cranes	T14	Container are classified according to types of trucks
T11	Empty trains get loaded	T22	Containers are picked up by external trucks
T10	Loaded trains are assigned to gantry cranes	T15	Containers are picked up by local trucks
T12	Loaded trains get unloaded		

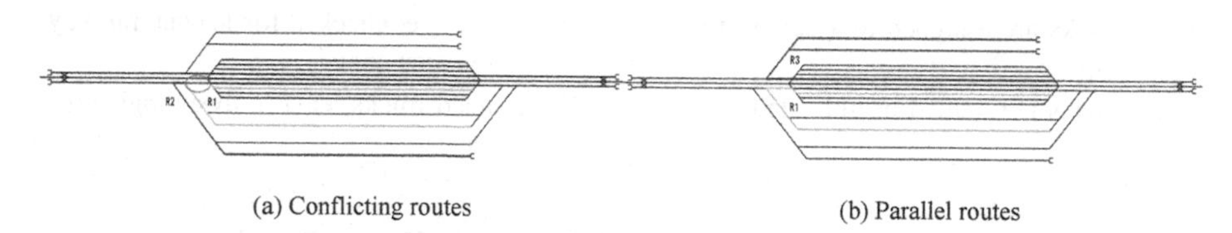

(a) Conflicting routes (b) Parallel routes

Fig. 5. The typical sample of conflicting routes and parallel routes (Color figure online)

presented in Fig. 7. All parameters used in simulation are derived from the feasibility study report of Qianchang railway logistics center.

The simulation time was set to 30 days, after inputting the data into SIMRLC, and running it with 20 replications the following information was obtained. The interface during simulation process is shown in Fig. 6b. Table 5 illustrates the simulation results of freight volumes in railway logistics center. The total freight volume in 30 days is 1.06 million tons, and the freight volume of fragmented yard is the largest which has reached 26 % of the total volume. The blue line representing the freight volume by

Table 4. Showing the process of train route scheduling simulation method

While a train(t) is prepared to use train route(r) **do**
1.Build up the conflicting train route list of r named **Lr**
2.Determine the state of **Lr**
  if every train route(r') in **Lr** is idle then **Lr** is idle
  else the state of **Lr** is occupied
3.**If** the state of **Lr** is idle **do**
  t monopolizes **r** and **r** get occupied
 else
  t is added into the waiting train list named **Lt**
4.Update the state of **Lr** when some trains release train routes and check **Lt**
  if Lt≠null **do** go back step 2
  else end

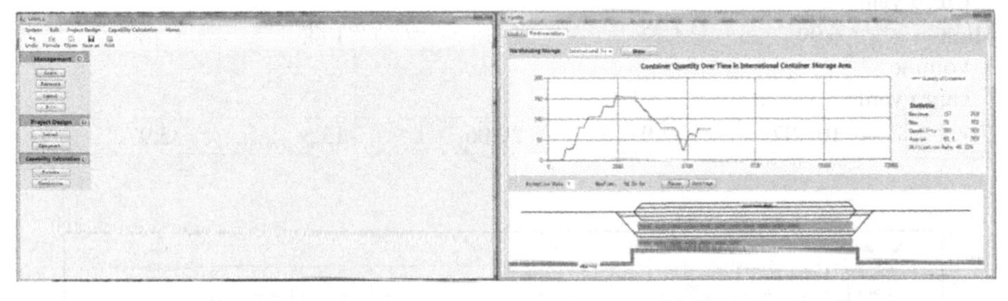

(a) Initial interface (b) Operation interface

Fig. 6. The interface of SIMRLC

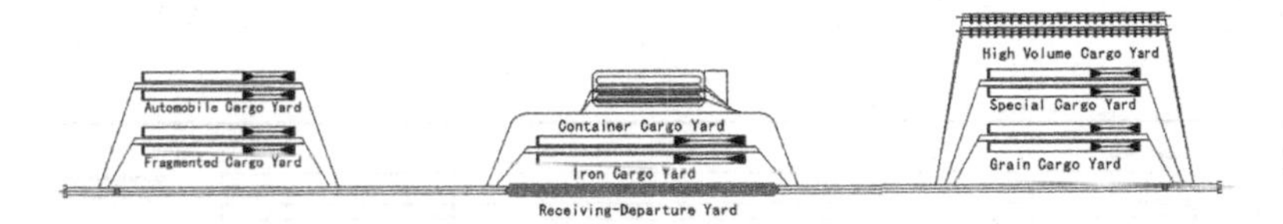

Fig. 7. The layout of Qianchang railway logistics center

trains dose not overlap the red line representing the freight volume by trucks, which means that the arrival and departure freight volumes are not balanced (as shown in Figs. 8 and 9).

There are 534 trains arrives at center during 30 days. The loading time varies in different freight yards, ranging from 2 h to 7.9 h, and the average loading time is 4 h (as shown in Table 6). Average waiting time for loading is 1.4 h, which means there is a common queuing phenomenon for lack of idle handling machineries. The total number of external trucks is 16770, and nearly 1/3 of trucks are headed to automobile cargo yard. This is caused by the large number of automobile cars carried by trains. The

Table 5. Showing the simulation results of freight volume ($10^4 \times$ tons)

Yard type	Freight volume (Fv)	Fv carried by arrival trains	Fv carried by departure trains	Fv carried by arrival trucks	Fv carried by departure trucks
Container yard	10321 (TEU)	6213 (TEU)	4108 (TEU)	1153 (TEU)	1796 (TEU)
Iron cargo yard	13.94	12.35	1.59	0.64	8.05
Grain cargo yard	13.36	13.36	0	0	5.89
Automobile cargo yard	11056 (Cars)	6224 (Cars)	4832 (Cars)	4000 (Cars)	3896 (Cars)
Special cargo yard	8.81	5.5	3.31	3.25	2.6
Fragmented cargo yard	22.9	18	4.9	3.02	11.49
High volume cargo yard	6.99	4.23	2.76	1.68	1.26
Total	106.97	77.91	29.06	13.5	35.97

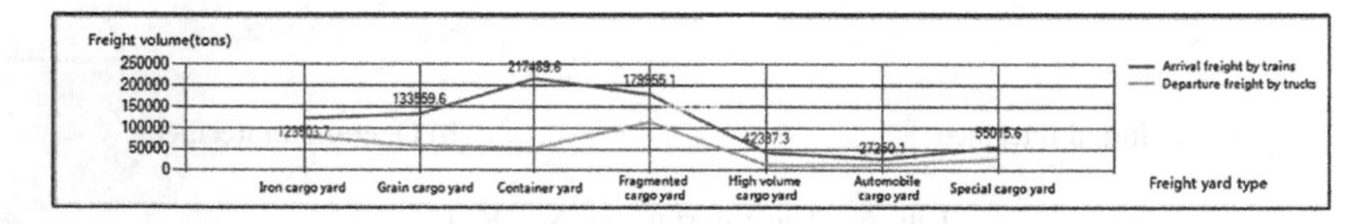

Fig. 8. Freight volume relationship between arrival trains and departure trucks (Color figure online)

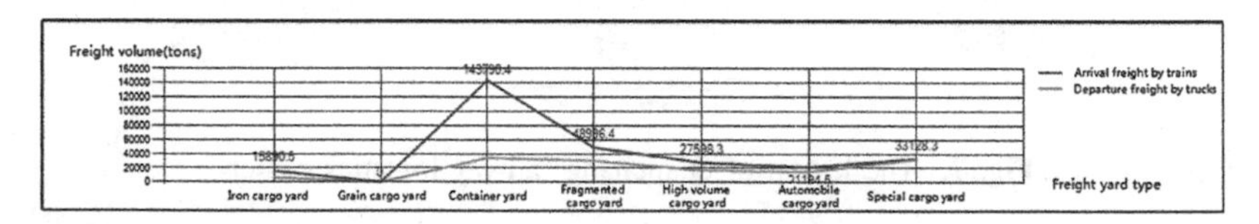

Fig. 9. Freight volume relationship between departure trains and arrival trucks (Color figure online)

average staying time of each truck is 35.7 min, including the loading time which is 18.3 min and the waiting time for loading which is 5.3 min (as shown in Table 7).

The simulation results of the fixed equipment in railway logistics center is presented in Table 8. There are some abnormal figures in this table, the utilization rate of storage area in grain and special cargo yard has exceeded 100 %, which means the storage capacity cannot meet the storage requirement. This is caused by the unbalance of the freight volume between departure and arrival cargo. Handling machineries in

Table 6. Showing the simulation results of trains in each freight yard

Train type	Train number	Average loading time (h)	Average waiting time for loading (h)	Average staying time (h)
Container trains	129	2	1.4	3.5
Iron cargo trains	79	4.4	0.9	5.5
Grain cargo trains	77	4.4	1.4	5.9
Automobile cargo trains	28	7.9	2.2	10.2
Special cargo trains	50	4.4	1.6	6.2
Fragmented cargo trains	131	4.4	1.2	5.7
High volume cargo trains	40	4.4	1.7	6.2
Total	534	4	1.4	6.4

Table 7. Showing the simulation results of external trucks in each freight yard

Truck type	Truck number	Average loading time (min)	Average waiting time for loading (min)	Average staying time (min)
Container trucks	2946	22.1	0.2	22.5
Iron cargo trucks	1990	22.2	0.2	22.5
Grain cargo trucks	2949	6	6.6	12.8
Automobile cargo trucks	4923	22.1	13.9	36.2
Special cargo trucks	997	22.1	0.2	22.5
Fragmented cargo trucks	987	6	0.2	6.3
High volume cargo trucks	1978	22.2	0.2	22.5
Total	16770	18.3	5.3	35.7

fragmented cargo yard is the busiest among all yards, of which the average working time is 8.14 h per day and the utilization rate has reached 50.9 %.

In general, Qianchang railway logistics center is able to meet the requirement of large scale of cargo operations, but the freight volumes of departure cargo and arrival cargo is unbalanced. The freight volume carried by trains is much higher than that of trucks. This indicates that the capability of trucks is not enough compared with the capability of trains. And because of the imbalance, some cargo piles up in storage area and exceeds the capacity limit. This phenomenon should be avoided in practice and can be solved by further simulation analysis. The simulation result of the Qianchang

Table 8. Showing the simulation results of fixed equipment in each yard

Yard type	Utilization rate of railway lines	Utilization rate of storage area	Average working time of machinery	Utilization rate of machinery	Volume of work
Container cargo yard	29.96 %	76.45 %	5.35	33.44 %	10321 (TEU)
Iron cargo yard	29.05 %	72.02 %	4.94	30.89 %	22.63
Grain cargo yard	20.32 %	299.15 %	3.31	20.70 %	19.24
Automobile cargo yard	35.87 %	15.93 %	2.59	16.19 %	11056 (Cars)
Special cargo yard	20.83 %	200.24 %	3.16	19.76 %	14.66
Fragmented cargo yard	33.36 %	151.85 %	8.14	50.90 %	37.41
High volume cargo yard	16.66 %	89.42 %	2.29	14.30 %	9.94

railway logistics center is reasonable in logic and is able to prove the validity of the simulation module.

5 Conclusion and Future Work

Based on the characteristics of railway logistics centers in China, the operation processes of railway logistics center were analyzed. With the theory of discrete event dynamics, a simulation module of railway logistics center based on Petri net was developed. To improve the accuracy of simulation module, train route scheduling simulation method was created. And a simulation tool named SIMRLC was programed based on this module using C#.

Based on SIMRLC software, a case study of Qianchang railway logistics center was given. The simulation results showed that there is an imbalance of the arrival and departure cargo. The freight volume of arrival cargo is 19.6 % more than the volume of departure cargo, which indicates there are some problems in the storage systems. The capability of picking up cargo needs to be enhanced by increasing check channels or by improving the operation efficiency of handling machineries. With the case study of Qianchang railway logistics center, the validity of simulation module has been proved.

Optimization of the logistics system of railway logistics center by using simulation method could be valuable future research direction. It would also be beneficial to search for the balanced point of arrival and departure capability of railway logistics center using simulation method.

References

1. Rizzoli, A.E., Fornara, N., Gambardella, L.M.: A simulation tool for combined rail/road transport in intermodal terminals. Math. Comput. Simul. **59**(1–3), 57–71 (1999)
2. Hartmann, S.: Generating scenarios for simulation and optimization of container terminal logistics. In: Günther, H.-O., Kim, K.H. (eds.) Container Terminals and Automated Transport Systems, pp. 101–122. Springer, Heidelberg (2005)
3. Swisher, J.R., Hyden, P.D., Jacobson, S.H., Schruben, L.W.: A survey of simulation optimization techniques and procedures. Proc. Simul. Conf. **1**, 197–200 (2000)
4. Zhou, X.J., Xu, X.B., Zhu, W.: Simulation and optimization in production logistics based on eM-plant platform. CCTA **2010**(4), 486–493 (2010)
5. Wu, X., Chen, L., Zhang, L.: Logistics distribution business process simulation and optimization based on petri nets. In: Proceedings of International Conference on Pervasive Computing and Applications, pp. 126–128 (2011)
6. Huang, D.M., Zhang, G.J., Shi, S.X.: Research on simulation and optimization of facility layout in flexible manufacturing workshop. Appl. Mech. Mater **108**, 24–29 (2012)
7. Griffis, S.E., Bell, J.E., Closs, D.J.: Metaheuristics in logistics and supply chain management. Bus. Logist. **33**(2), 90–106 (2012)
8. He, Q.: Layout of unloading lines at railway logistics centers based on computer simulation. Logist. Technol. (2013)
9. Marinov, M., Viegas, J.: A simulation modelling methodology for evaluating flat-shunted yard operations. Simul. Model. Pract. Theory **17**, 1106–1129 (2009)
10. Fugihara, M.K., D'Audenhove, A., Karassawa, N.T.: Randomless as a critical point: simulation fitting better planning of distribution centers. In: 2007 Winter Simulation Conference, pp. 2371–2371. IEEE (2007)
11. Vidalakis, C.: Logistics simulation modelling across construction supply chains. Constr. Innov. **11**(2), 212–228 (2011)
12. Chen, K., Gao, G.: Using agent and swarm platform to construct logistics simulation system. J. Convergence Inf. Technol. **8**(5), 454–463 (2013)
13. Hou, S.: Distribution center logistics optimization based on simulation. Res. J. Appl. Sci. Eng. Technol. **5**(21), 5107–5111 (2013)
14. Swartz, S.M., Mingee, G.: Using the airfield simulation tool for airfield capacity-capability assessment. Air Force J. Logist. Fall **28**(3), 38 (2004)
15. Zhang, L., Yan, T., Chi, X.: Research on simulation and optimization of logistics element capability in distribution center based on TPN. In: International Conference on Transportation, Mechanical, and Electrical Engineering, pp. 248–252. IEEE (2011)
16. Li, H., Zhang, B., Yang, N.: Evaluation and optimization on logistics capability of the postal agricultural logistics system. In: 2014 International Conference on. Management Science and Engineering (ICMSE), pp. 621–627. IEEE (2014)
17. Wang, M.: Evaluating logistics capability for mitigation of supply chain uncertainty and risk in the Australian courier firms. Asia Pac. J. Mark. Logist. **27**(3), 486–498 (2015)
18. Shang, K.C., Marlow, P.B.: Logistics capability and performance in Taiwan's major manufacturing firms. Transp. Res. Part E Logist. Transp. Rev. **41**(3), 217–234 (2005)

A Feature Extraction Method Based on Stacked Auto-Encoder for Telecom Churn Prediction

Ruiqi Li, Peng Wang, and Zonghai Chen(✉)

Department of Automation, University of Science and Technology of China, Hefei, China
lirq@mail.ustc.edu.cn, {pwang,chenzh}@ustc.edu.cn

Abstract. Customer churn prediction is a key problem to customer relationship management systems of telecom operators. Efficient feature extraction method is crucial to telecom customer churn prediction. In this paper, stacked auto-encoder is introduced as a nonlinear feature extraction method, and a new hybrid feature extraction framework is proposed based on stacked auto-encoder and Fisher's ratio analysis. The proposed method is evaluated on datasets provided by Orange, and experimental results verify that it is authentically able to enhance the performance of prediction models both on AUC and computing efficiency.

Keywords: Churn prediction · Feature extraction · Stacked auto-encoder

1 Introduction

Telecommunication industry depends heavily on customer base to maintain stable profits. Service providers nearly have no choice but paying more attention to retain customers. Therefore, an efficient customer relationship management system, especially a churner prediction model, is badly needed by telecommunication industry.

Many factors influence the accuracy of churn prediction models. In general, a prediction model performs better if the original dataset contains more characteristic variables, which are also called features. However, too many characteristic variables usually bring about some other troubles e.g. over-fitting, or frequently require too large memory etc. In consequence, rebuilding characteristic variables in data preprocessing stage plays a significant role in the whole modeling process, which is named as feature extraction professionally.

Several data mining technologies have been applied in churner prediction successfully, including artificial neural networks [1] (ANNs), decision trees [2], Bayesian networks [3], logistic regression [4], Ada-Boosting [5], random forest [4], proportional hazard model [6] and SVMs. What's more, abundant research achievements have been provided recently. Utku Yabas et al. [7] built an ensemble classifier consisting of a group of well performing meta-classifiers, demonstrating that the performance of churn prediction can be significantly improved. Bashar Al-Shboul et al. [8] investigated the application of a churn prediction approach by combining Fast Fuzzy C-Means (FFCM) and Genetic Programming (GP) for predicting possible churners, and proved promising capability in the field. However, studies that focus on feature extraction methods are relatively less. E.g. Yin Wu et al. [9] proposed a framework which was adaptable to

L. Zhang et al. (Eds.): AsiaSim 2016/SCS AutumnSim 2016, Part I, CCIS 643, pp. 568–576, 2016.
DOI: 10.1007/978-981-10-2663-8_58

different data types and carried experiments out on a structured module to demonstrate the validity of the two-phase feature selection method. Wei-Chao Lin et al. [10] concluded that feature selection and data reduction in data preprocessing could produce better datasets to structure an optimal model, while the cost of training was observably decreased.

Considering all the views above, we attempt to introduce the stacked auto-encoder (SAE), based on the deep learning theory, as a nonlinear feature extraction method for churn prediction, which is inspired by its successful application in computer vision. Furthermore, we propose another feature extraction framework named Hybrid Stacked Auto-Encoder (HSAE), which combines the SAE with Fisher's ratio analysis. The proposed framework aims to extract intrinsic features of an original dataset and improve the performance of the telecom churn prediction model both on AUC and computing efficiency.

We organize this paper into three main sections. In Sect. 2, we introduce two conventional feature extraction methods and the proposed method sequentially. In Sect. 3, experiments and tabulated results that demonstrate our contributions are exhibited. The paper is concluded in the final section in order to direct future studies.

2 Feature Extraction Methods and Criterions

In general, feature extraction methods are recognized as two types. One is to select the most effective part of features from the original high-dimensional features directly. The generated dataset is a subset of the original dataset practically. Suppose that the original dataset X contains N features, and a new datasets Y contains n features, then the expression is:

$$\begin{gathered} X:\{x_1, x_2, \cdots, x_N\} \rightarrow Y:\{y_1, y_2, \cdots, y_n\} \\ y_i \in N, i = 1, 2, \cdots, n; n < N \end{gathered} \tag{1}$$

The other one is to project the original features from high-dimensional space to low-dimensional space. The generated dataset is a map of original dataset. Suppose that the original dataset X contains N features, and a new dataset Y contains M features, then the expression is:

$$\begin{gathered} X:\{x_1, x_2, \cdots, x_N\} \rightarrow Y:\{y_1, y_2, \cdots, y_M\} \\ (y_1, y_2, \cdots, y_M) = f(x_1, x_2, \cdots, x_N) \end{gathered} \tag{2}$$

Among various feature extraction methods, Fisher's ratio analysis is a representative method belongs to the first type, and principal component analysis (PCA) is a representative method belongs to the second type. What's more, the introduced SAE belongs to the second type as well and the proposed hybrid framework aims to combine both advantages of the two types.

2.1 Fisher's Ratio Analysis

Fisher's ratio analysis [11], which is also called Fisher linear discriminant, is an efficient approach for feature extraction in statistical pattern recognition. Suppose that there exist two types of label points in a k-dimension data space, and each dimension denotes a feature component. For a certain feature, once the square of the difference between means of each class is bigger and the sum of variances of each class is smaller, then the feature has better discriminability. Formally, it can be formulated as follow:

$$J(F_k) = \frac{(\mu_1 - \mu_2)^2}{\sigma_1^2 + \sigma_2^2}, \tag{3}$$

in which μ_i, σ_i^2 $(i = 1, 2)$ are respectively the mean and variance of the ith class.

The above idea is to estimate Fisher's ratio for every feature in the original dataset, and select the ones with top scores in feature selection phase.

2.2 Principal Component Analysis

PCA [12] is a linear feature extraction method, which performs by transforming the data into a low-dimensional linear subspace. Mathematically, a workflow for the PCA includes following steps.

- Step 1: Figure out the sample mean of the original dataset $\chi = \frac{1}{o} \sum_{i=1}^{o} x_i$
- Step 2: Compute the covariance matrix $C = \frac{1}{o} \sum_{i=1}^{o} (x_i - \chi) \cdot (x_i - \chi)^T$
- Step 3: Calculate the eigenvalues $\lambda_1, \cdots, \lambda_l$ with the corresponding eigenvector $h_1, \cdots, h_l$ of the matrix C, and arrange the eigenvalues in descending order.
- Step 4: Record the transformation matrix as $H^T = [h_1, h_2, \cdots, h_l]^T$, and the projected matrix is $S = [s_1, s_2, \cdots, s_o]^T = XH^T$.

Only the first several eigenvectors ranked in descending order of the eigenvalues are used, so that the number of selected principal components is decreased, and features are extracted simultaneously.

2.3 Stacked Auto-Encoder

To avoid the potential (nonlinear) information loss caused by Fisher's ratio analysis and PCA, we introduce SAE [13] as a new technique to be applied in telecom churn prediction field, which can be treated as a nonlinear feature extraction method based on the deep learning theory.

Generally, SAE is a feedforward neural network with an odd number of hidden layers, which is shown schematically in Fig. 1. The whole neural network is designed to minimize the mean squared error between the output and the input layer. Conceptually, it is trained to recreate the input and to compress the original data in the hidden layer, while preserve as much intrinsic features as possible. When data point x_i is used as input, the new representation y_i, which is usually projected to a space of lower dimensionality, can be acquired by extracting node values in the middle hidden layer. Mathematically, details for pre-training the SAE module are described as follows.

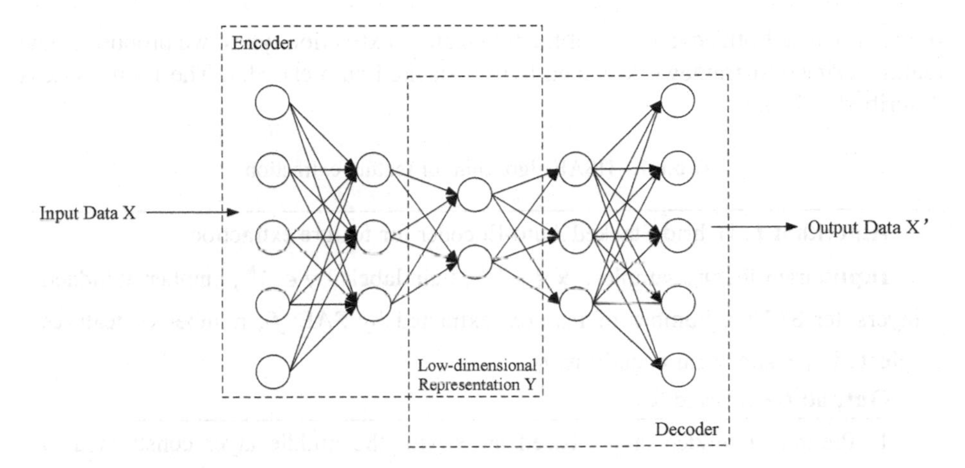

Fig. 1. Schematic structure of a SAE

SAE [14] is a deep network constituted with autoencoding neural networks in each layer. In the single-layer case, corresponding to an input vector $x \in \mathbb{R}^n$, the activation of each neuron, $h_i, i = 1, \cdots, m$ is computed by

$$h(x) = f(W_1 x + b_1), \tag{4}$$

where $h(x) \in \mathbb{R}^m$ is the pattern of neuron activations, $W_1 \in \mathbb{R}^{m \times n}$ is the weight matrix, $b_1 \in \mathbb{R}^m$ is the bias vector, and sigmoid activation function is generally used to allow the auto-encoder learning a nonlinear mapping between the low-dimensional and high-dimensional data representation. Output of the network is formulated by

$$\hat{x} = f(W_2 h(x) + b_2), \tag{5}$$

where $\hat{x} \in \mathbb{R}^n$ is the pattern of output values, $W_2 \in \mathbb{R}^{n \times m}$ is a weight matrix, and $b_2 \in \mathbb{R}^n$ is a bias vector. Once a set of p input vectors $x^{(i)}, i = 1, \cdots, p$ is given, the weight matrices W_1 and W_2 are calculated by back-propagation and gradient descent methods to minimize the reconstruction error

$$e(\mathbf{x}) = \sum_{i=1}^{p} ||x^{(i)} - \hat{x}^{(i)}||^2. \tag{6}$$

In the multi-layer case, we train up the network layers in a greedy layer-wise approach successively. The first layer receives training samples with original features as input. After its reconstruction error achieves acceptable levels, a second layer is added, then a third layer, etc. Furthermore, fine-tuning can be executed once we obtain the train labels $\mathbf{y} \in \mathbb{R}$ for supervised learning.

2.4 Hybrid Stacked Auto-Encoder

In order to take both advantages of the two feature extraction types, we propose a new feature extraction framework named hybrid stacked auto-encoder. The framework is described in Table 1.

Table 1. HSAE algorithm for feature extraction

Algorithm 1. Hybrid Stacked Auto-Encoder for feature extraction **Input:** train feature samples: $\mathbf{x} \in \mathbb{R}^{D \times N}$, train labels: $\mathbf{y} \in \mathbb{R}^{N}$, number of hidden layers for SAE: *l*, number of features extracted by SAE: f_1, number of features selected by Fisher's ratio analysis: f_2. **Output:** f_2 extracted features.
1. Pre-train *l* hidden layers based on **x** with the middle layer constrained to contain f_1 neurons; 2. fine-tune the deep network according to labels **y** with back-propagation and gradient descent methods; 3. extract the f_1 node values in the middle hidden layer and reconstruct them in a new dataset named as *T-temp*; 4. Compute Fisher's ratio F_i of *i*th feature in the *T-temp*; 5. Rearrange features according to F_i by descending and select the first f_2 features as output.

2.5 Classification and Criterions

Criterions can hardly be carried out directly on the extracted features. It is common to set a criterion function to combine feature extraction methods with subsequent classification algorithms.

The classifier employed in the experiment is Logistic Regression. Mathematically, it can be formulated as a task of finding a minimizer of a convex function

$$f(\mathbf{w}) = \frac{\lambda}{2}||\mathbf{w}||_2^2 + \frac{1}{n}\sum\nolimits_{i=1}^{n} \log(1 + \mathrm{e}^{-y\mathbf{w}^T\mathbf{x}}), \tag{7}$$

the vectors $x_i \in \mathbb{R}^d$ are the training data examples, and $y_i \in \mathbb{R}$ are their corresponding labels. The fixed parameter $\lambda \geq 0$ for L2-regularization defines the trade-off between the two goals of minimizing the loss and the model complexity.

For telecom churn prediction, the algorithm outputs a binary logistic regression model eventually. Given a new data point, denoted by x, the model makes prediction by applying the logistic (sigmoid) function

$$f(\mathbf{w}^T\mathbf{x}) = \frac{1}{1 + e^{-\mathbf{w}^T\mathbf{x}}}, \tag{8}$$

and outputs a probability value for each class. Therefore, there is a prediction threshold, e.g. t, which determines what the predicted class will be. If $f(\mathbf{w}^T\mathbf{x}) > t$, the outcome is positive, or negative otherwise.

Tuning the prediction threshold will change the precision and recall of the model. So we use the receiver operating characteristics [15] (ROC) graph as the criterion. The area under the ROC curve, abbreviated as AUC, has an important property in statistics: the AUC of a classifier equals to the probability that the classifier ranks a randomly chosen positive instance higher than a randomly chosen negative instance. As a result, we regard the classifier with higher AUC as the better choice, and the embedded feature extraction method as the better choice as well.

3 Experiments and Discussions

The raw dataset for our experiments is gathered from KDD website based on marketing databases from the French telecom company Orange. The standard desktop computing platform is equipped with dual core 3.20 GHz processor and a RAM of 8 Gb. The experiment is conducted with Scala based on Spark machine learning library and Matlab toolbox for dimensionality reduction.

3.1 Dataset and Initial Preprocessing

The raw dataset has 50,000 examples with 230 original features, including 190 numeric features and 40 categorical features. It's impossible to use domain expertise because the data were encrypted and feature names were hidden [7]. Variables are polluted by large numbers of missing values. Worse still, most of the variables are in different dynamic ranges. Therefore, initial preprocessing and feature extraction play crucial roles.

The initial preprocessing includes handing of missing values, discretization of the numeric features, aggregating of the categorical values, encoding prepared variables and removal of redundant features. First, we remove the features with more than 95 % missing values. Then, missing values in numeric features are replaced with the mean, while add additional features coding for the presence of each missing value correspondingly. Missing values in categorical features are tagged as "missing", which are treated as new values. After that, numeric features are discretized into 6 new categorical features equably, which will be encoded together with other categorical features through one-hot encoders. If a categorical feature has more than 10 distinct values, then we keep the 9 most frequent categories and group the rest in a category called "Others". After removing the original numeric features and other redundant features, we finally obtain 496 features with binary value "0" or "1" simply.

Furthermore, if we regard each feature as a pixel, which is a basic conception in computer vision field, then every data sample can be treated as a 31*16 grayscale image, which is shown in Fig. 2. We denominate the image as “customer's information-portrayal” tentatively. The 50,000 examples with 496 features are then used as the material for feature extraction stage.

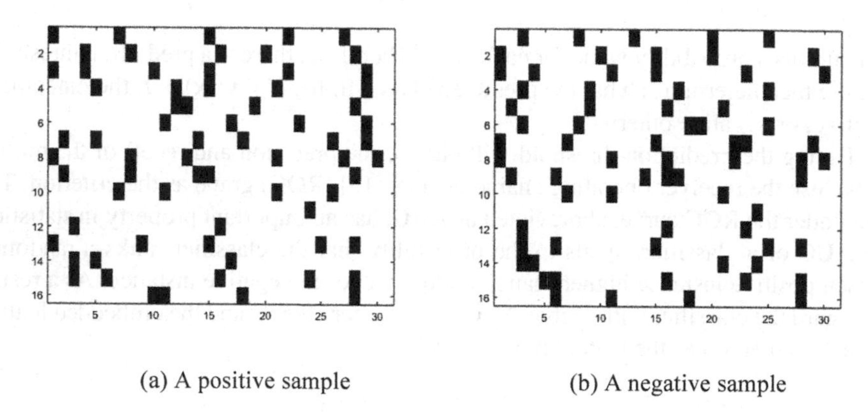

(a) A positive sample (b) A negative sample

Fig. 2. Customer's information-portrayals

3.2 Feature Extraction

A series of experiments are designed to compare conventional feature extraction methods with the new proposed method. They are principally divided into 4 groups as follows:

- Group 1: Extract features with PCA
- Group 2: Extract features with Fisher's ratio
- Group 3: Extract features with SAE
- Group 4: Extract features with HSAE

50, 40, 30 and 20 features are extracted respectively for classification in each group. In details, the SAEs in group 3 and group 4 are designed with 7 layers without the output and input layer. To be highlighted, the first hidden layer is designed to be expanded to compensate for the representational capacity of sigmoid functions used in each layer, on the fact that neuron activations which transformed through the sigmoid function can't represent as much information and variance as real-valued data.

3.3 Results and Discussions

There still exists another two steps before classification. One is over-sampling. Copy the whole positive instances 13 times as the simplest over-sampling approach. The ratio of the positive and negative instances then equals to 1:1 approximately. The other step is data partition for cross-validation. The dataset is split into 2 subsets and the ratio of the training and testing sets equals to 7:3.

The AUC values of each experimental group are arranged and tabulated as follows.

From Table 2 we conclude that a single SAE performs better than PCA, and it is approximately the same as Fisher's ratio analysis. Moreover, the average runtime of SAE is about 2 h while the average runtime of Fisher's ratio analysis is over 7 h. Furthermore, the proposed method in group 4 is verified to be better both in AUC and computing efficiency, which shortens the average runtime by 3.5 h comparing to group 2.

Table 2. AUC of each experimental group

	50 Features	40 Features	30 Features	20 Features
PCA	0.6871	0.6839	0.6696	0.6656
Fisher's Ratio	0.6972	0.6914	0.6914	0.6848
SAE	0.6964	0.6937	0.6909	0.6893
HSAE	0.6989	0.6942	0.6925	0.6903

4 Conclusion and Future Works

In this paper, we introduce SAE to extract features in telecom churn prediction, which is compared with two types of conventional feature extraction methods. A new HSAE framework to accomplish the same task is also proposed. The experimental results demonstrate the efficiency of the proposed method.

As the new conception of "customer's information-portrayal" is proposed above, we will attempt to employ other deep learning algorithms, such as deep belief networks, convolutional neural networks etc., to deal with the telecom churn prediction problems, or even employ these algorithms to deal with other binary classification problems in the future.

References

1. Tsai, C.F., Lu, Y.H.: Customer churn prediction by hybrid neural networks. J. Expert Syst. Appl. **36**, 12547–12553 (2009)
2. Qi, J., Zhang, L., Liu, Y., et al.: ADTreesLogit model for customer churn prediction. J. Ann. Oper. Res. **168**, 247–265 (2009)
3. Kisioglu, P., Topcu, Y.I.: Applying bayesian belief network approach to customer churn analysis: a case study on the telecom industry of Turkey. J. Expert Syst. Appl. **38**, 7151–7157 (2011)
4. Burez, J., Van den Poel, D.: CRM at a pay-TV company: using analytical models to reduce customer attrition by targeted marketing for subscription services. J. Expert Syst. with Appl. **32**, 277–288 (2007)
5. Glady, N., Baesens, B., Croux, C.: Modeling churn using customer lifetime value. J. Eur. J. Oper. Res. **197**, 402–411 (2009)
6. Van den Poel, D., Lariviere, B.: Customer attrition analysis for financial services using proportional hazard models. J. Eur. J. Oper. Res. **157**, 196–217 (2004)

7. Yabas, U., Cankaya, H.C.: Churn prediction in subscriber management for mobile and wireless communications services. In: 2013 IEEE Globecom Workshops, pp. 991–995. IEEE Press, New York (2013)
8. Al-Shboul, B., Faris, H., Ghatasheh, N.: Initializing genetic programming using fuzzy clustering and its application in churn prediction in the telecom industry. J. Malays. J. Comput. Sci. **28**, 213–220 (2015)
9. Wu, Y., Qi, J., Wang C.: The study on feature selection in customer churn prediction modeling. In: 2009 IEEE Systems, Man and Cybernetics, pp. 3205–3210. IEEE Press, New York (2009)
10. Lin, W.C., Tsai, C.F., Ke, S.W.: Dimensionality and data reduction in telecom churn prediction. J. Kybernetes **43**, 737–749 (2014)
11. Wang, S., Li, D., Song, X., et al.: A feature selection method based on improved fisher's discriminant ratio for text sentiment classification. J. Expert Syst. Appl. **38**, 8696–8702 (2011)
12. Zhang, M., Li, G., Gong, J., et al.: Predicting configuration performance of modular product family using principal component analysis and support vector machine. J. J. Cent. South Univ. **21**, 2701–2711 (2014)
13. Van der MLJP PEO, van den HH J.: Dimensionality reduction: A comparative review. In: Tilburg, Netherlands: Tilburg Centre for Creative Computing, Tilburg University, Technical report. 2009-005(2009)
14. Goodfellow, I., Lee, H., Le, Q.V., et al.: Measuring invariances in deep networks. In: Advances in neural information processing systems, pp. 646–654 (2009)
15. Fawcett, T.: An introduction to ROC analysis. J. Pattern Recogn. Lett. **27**, 861–874 (2006)

Adaptive Fuzzy Control Algorithm for an Integrated Navigation of SINS and the Odometer

Pengpeng Liu(✉), Zhili Zhang, Zhaofa Zhou, He Chen, and Jianguo Xu

Xi'an High-Tech Research Institute, Xi'an, 710025, China
siyuefool@126.com

Abstract. Accuracy is one of the most important requirements for land vehicle navigation. Since the accuracy of SINS degrades rapidly with time while that of odometer degrades with distance, a SINS/OD integrated navigation system based on Kalman filter is adopted to improve positioning precision by making full use of the advantages of both methods. The measurement result of the odometer is greatly influenced by the road condition, and sometimes the output value is even wrong. Therefore, a novel adaptive fuzzy control algorithm is put forward to improve the robustness and accuracy of the navigation system. The in-out subjection factor functions are set up based on the innovation information of the filter and the velocity ratio between the values measured by SINS and the odometer; the velocity gain of the odometer can be adaptively changed based on the selected fuzzy control rules. Simulation results show that the proposed algorithm can increase the navigation precision by adaptively correcting the measurement error of the odometer.

Keywords: SINS · Odometer · Integrated navigation system · Adaptive fuzzy control algorithm

1 Introduction

Odometer [1] is always used to measure the vehicle's velocity and distance, but it cannot be used alone. Based on the orientation and position acquired by the SINS, odometer can be used to set up the dead reckoning system. The SINS and the odometer don't receive signals from the environment or transmit signals to the environment, so the SINS/OD integrated navigation system [2] has the advantages of high accuracy, good independence and strong anti-interference ability, showing good engineering application outlook in the military vehicle positioning and orientation areas. For example, without GPS data, the France SIGMA-30 navigation system based on the integration of SINS and odometer has the accuracy of 5 m + 0.1 % mileage (Fig. 1).

SINS and odometer [3] are both installed in the vehicle. As is known to all, the vehicle's back wheels are generally the driving wheels, and the front wheels are driven wheels. The back wheels are prone to skid or slide which may cause big errors of the odometer, so the odometer is installed on the axes of the front wheels.

The accuracy of the odometer is one of the most important factors that influence the accuracy of the SINS/OD integrated navigation system. The odometer's performance is

L. Zhang et al. (Eds.): AsiaSim 2016/SCS AutumnSim 2016, Part I, CCIS 643, pp. 577–584, 2016.
DOI: 10.1007/978-981-10-2663-8_59

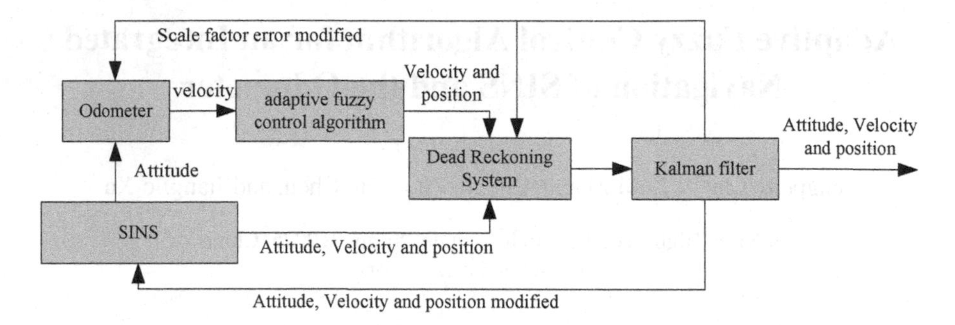

Fig. 1. SINS/OD integration navigation system

greatly affected by the road conditions and sometimes it may even output wrong data due to harsh working environments. To improve the robustness of the integrated navigation system, the failure types of odometer are analyzed, and a novel adaptive fuzzy control algorithm [4, 5] is proposed based on the system's working state and the innovation of Kalman filter. In the proposed algorithm, the velocity gain of the odometer is adaptively modified by the fuzzy controller to keep the mean of the filter innovation zero, the variance matrix of the observation noise is calculated using the modified innovation, and the gain of the Kalman filter is adjusted to accelerate the filtering process and to decrease the navigation deviation.

2 The Fault Handling of the Odometer

The outputs of the odometer sometimes may be wrong because of the bad road conditions or the vehicle's abnormal working states. The failure types include skid, slide and sideslip. The skid occurs when the ground's friction is not big enough to support the vehicle's preceding driving, in which case the wheels will be idling, resulting in the distance measured by the odometer longer than the actual one that the vehicle moves. The slide, contrary to the skid, occurs when the vehicle is braked or decelerated urgently, making the distance measured by the odometer shorter than the vehicle's actual moving distance. When the vehicle runs normally, it does not have the transverse velocity. Sideslip occurs when the vehicle produces a transverse velocity due to the slippery road.

The measurement data must be eliminated or modified when the vehicle's odometer is at fault. The most regular method is the biggest threshold method, namely when velocity measurement difference between the odometer and the SINS is bigger than a given threshold, the odometer's measurement is supposed not useful and will be eliminated. Since the value measured by the SINS is considered to be accurate, the vehicle's position and orientation is calculated using the SINS outputs alone. When the odometer becomes normal, the integration system starts to work again.

The threshold mentioned above must be set properly. If it is too big, the fault signals will be omitted, and the position error will increase gradually; if it is too small, the SINS/OD system will use the SINS navigation mode solely in a long time, making the odometer output not fully used and the navigation errors increase greatly with time. Besides, the deviations of the system observation values are related to the vehicle's velocity, that's to say the deviations in the high speed are often bigger than that in the low speed, so the threshold should also varies with the speed. Furthermore, if the vehicle both skids and slides, the distance difference measured by the odometer and the SINS may be not big enough to exceed the threshold, and the Kalman filter [6–9] is used to estimate the errors; if the vehicle runs in that road condition for a long time, it will cause a big error in the Kalman filter due to bad observation values.

To solve these problems, an adaptive fuzzy control algorithm is adopted to eliminate the odometer's faults and keep the observation value small.

3 Design of the Adaptive Fuzzy Controller

Fuzzy control is a theory set in the fuzzy class based on the language rule and fuzzy logic. Fuzzy logic imitates human's thinking modes to express and analyze uncertain and inaccurate information. Different from classical logic, fuzzy logic does not have definite boundary between true and false. Instead, the change from true to false is a gradual process, which is described with the subjection factor function. The subjection factor function is often described in functions, among which the most popular ones are the trigonometric function and the exponential function. The analytic expression of the exponential function is given as

$$\mu_A(x) = e^{\frac{(x - x_0)^2}{2\sigma^2}} \tag{1}$$

Where x_0 is the central value of the subjection factor function, and σ^2 is the variance. The fuzzy controller of the system is mainly set up based on the following rules.

(1) Skid and slid in a short time: The velocity values measured by the odometer and SINS are different evidently. So the biggest threshold method can be used, when the difference between the values of the two groups reach some value, the odometer is supposed to break down and the navigation is done based on the output of the SINS. The time in this condition will not be long, when the odometer becomes normal, the integrated navigation can be used again.
(2) Sideslip: The sideslip is related with the vehicle's yaw. When the yaw changes greatly, the transverse velocity becomes biased, the sideslip is supposed to occur; and the odometer breaks down, the system will choose the SINS to navigate.
(3) Running and sliding: In this situation, the velocity values measured by the odometer and SINS are different, but are not large, so the fault cannot be eliminated by setting threshold method. If the fuzzy rules are designed only by the innovation, the fault cannot be diagnosed when it is very small, but will affect the state x_k, and make the state x_k follow the fault; so the innovation values will be decreased, and the effect of the fault diagnose will be worse. So the adaptive fuzzy control algorithm is proposed based on system's working state and the innovation of Kalman filter. This paper mainly focuses on this kind of vehicle fault to eliminate and modify the velocity error.

According to the definition, the innovation of the integrated navigation filter is given by

$$\boldsymbol{r}_k = \boldsymbol{Z}_k - \boldsymbol{H}_k\hat{\boldsymbol{X}}_{k/k-1} = \tilde{\boldsymbol{v}}_{SINS} - \alpha_1 \cdot \tilde{\boldsymbol{v}}_{OD} - \boldsymbol{H}_k\hat{\boldsymbol{X}}_{k/k-1} \tag{2}$$

The innovation represents the difference between the observation values and the one-step prediction values, when the system works normally, 95 % of the innovation sequence will stay within the 2σ range of the mean zero. When the odometer skids or slides, the innovation will evidently exceed this area. So the adaptive fuzzy control algorithm is adopted to eliminate the odometer's faults and keep the innovation near mean zero.

In the adaptive fuzzy control algorithm [10], firstly a fuzzy controller (as shown in Fig. 2) is sets up, then the input value and output value are determined; thirdly the subjection factor function is set up. The fuzzy rules used by the fuzzy controller are determined by the prior information. According to the compound rules for fuzzy relation, fuzzy logic consequences can deal with several fuzzy rules working in relevant modes simultaneously, and produce fuzzy subclasses for corresponding input values. The process of solving the fuzzy logic is to transform the output fuzzy subclass to the unfussy digital value. According to the rules, the in-out values are determined to restrain the noises' interference and the filter's volatilization.

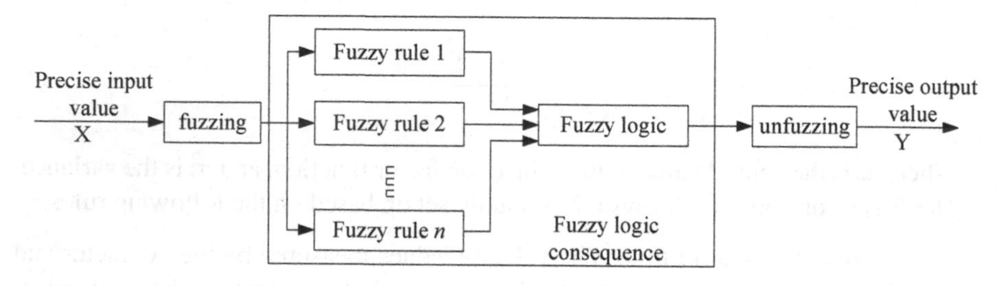

Fig. 2. The fuzzy controller

The state estimation equation is given by

$$\hat{\boldsymbol{X}}_k = \hat{\boldsymbol{X}}_{k/k-1} + \boldsymbol{K}_k\boldsymbol{r}_k \tag{3}$$

Where r_k is the innovation, Z_k is the measurement vector, $\boldsymbol{H}_k$ is the measurement matrix that relates the measurements with the states when there is no noise, $\tilde{\boldsymbol{v}}_{SINS}$ is the velocity value measured by the SINS, and $\tilde{\boldsymbol{v}}_{OD}$ is the velocity value measured by the odometer. α_1 is the odometer velocity gain adjusting factor, and if $\alpha_1 = 1$, the odometer works normally. Matching factor dm_1 is given by

$$dm_1 = \tilde{\boldsymbol{v}}_{SINS}/\tilde{\boldsymbol{v}}_{OD} \tag{4}$$

There are three fuzzy input quantities including the matching factor dm_1, the yaw variation H and the average value of the innovation r, the fuzzy output is the odometer velocity gain adjusting factor α_1. According to the analysis, dm_1 has five fuzzy aggregations, T is much small, S is small, Z is normal, B is big, L is much big, and the subjection factor function is shown in Fig. 3; H has three fuzzy aggregations: S is small, M is middle, B is big, and the subjection factor function is shown in Fig. 4; the average value of the innovation r has three fuzzy aggregations: S is small, M is middle, B is big, and the subjection factor function is shown in Fig. 5; the odometer velocity gain adjusting factor α_1 has five fuzzy aggregations, T is much small, S is small, Z is normal, B is big, L is much big, and the subjection factor function is shown in Fig. 6.

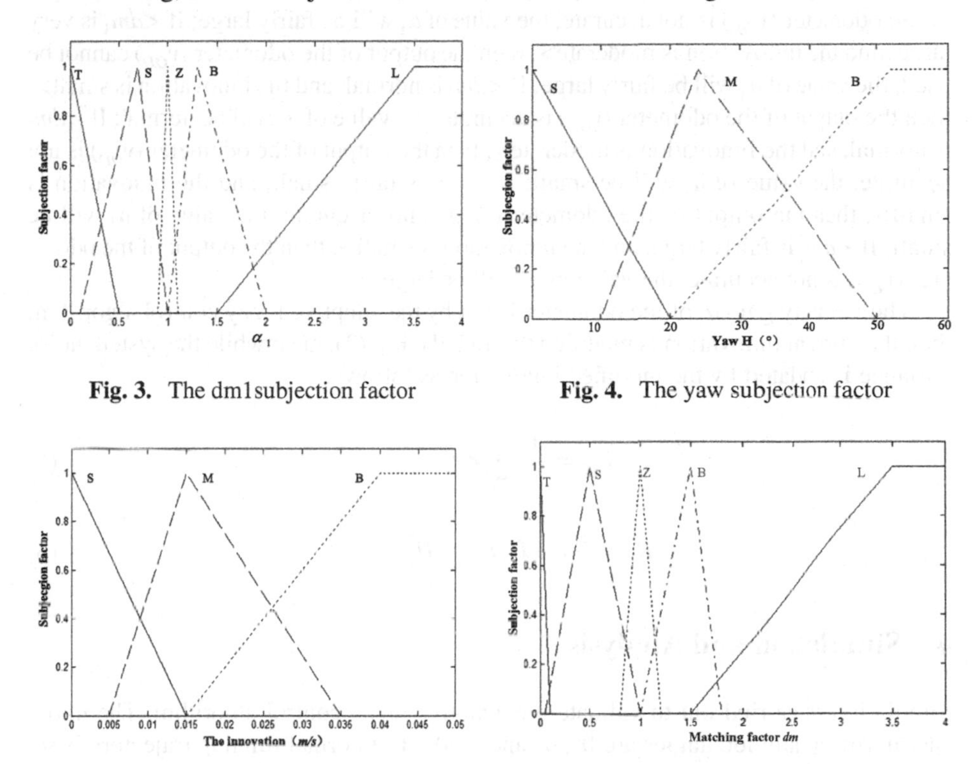

Fig. 3. The dm1subjection factor

Fig. 4. The yaw subjection factor

Fig. 5. The innovation mean subjection factor

Fig. 6. The output factor α_1 subjection factor

When the velocity ratio of SINS and the odometer reaches extremum bias, if the innovation is small, the vehicle runs slowly, and the innovation can be decreased by adjusting the output of the odometer. While the innovation is big, the vehicle runs quickly, then the velocity of the odometer is supposed to be equal to the velocity of SINS, the navigation uses the single SINS like the biggest threshold method. When the system state and the innovation are in other conditions, the odometer gain will be modified according to the measurement of the system state and the innovation, then the innovation is modified to keep it close to the average zero all the time; meanwhile the system measurement noise variance will be updated by the modified innovation; so the convergence of the filter is guaranteed, and the system state will not be biased greatly. In this way, the shortcoming of the biggest threshold is overcome, and the navigation accuracy is improved.

The rules of the fuzzy control are as follows. If <dm_1 is fairly large and the yaw variable quantity ΔH is large>, then the vehicle sideslips, the odometer cannot be used; If <dm_1 is very small, and the innovation is very small>, then the output of the odometer (v_{OD}) is not accurate, the value of α_1 will be small; If <dm_1 is very small, and the innovation is moderate>, then the output of the odometer (v_{OD}) cannot be used, the value of α_1 will be very small; If <dm_1 is very large, and the innovation is small>, then the output of the odometer (v_{OD}) is not accurate, the value of α_1 will be fairly large; If <dm_1 is very large, and the innovation is moderate>, then the output of the odometer (v_{OD}) cannot be used, the value of α_1 will be fairly large; If <dm_1 is normal, and the innovation is small>, then the output of the odometer (v_{OD}) is accurate, the value of α_1 will be normal; If <dm_1 is normal, and the innovation is moderate>, then the output of the odometer (v_{OD}) is not accurate, the value of α_1 will be small; If <dm_1 is fairly small, and the innovation is small>, then the output of the odometer (v_{OD}) is not accurate, the value of α_1 will be small; If <dm_1 is fairly large, and the innovation is small>, then the output of the odometer (v_{OD}) is not accurate, the value of α_1 will be large.

The velocity gain α_1 of the odometer is got by the adaptive fuzzy control algorithm, then the current innovation is modified through the Eq. (2), meanwhile the system noise variance is updated by the modified innovation as follows.

$$\hat{C}_{rk} = \frac{1}{N} \sum_{j=j_0}^{k} \boldsymbol{r}_j \boldsymbol{r}_j^{\mathrm{T}} \tag{5}$$

$$\boldsymbol{R}_k = \hat{\boldsymbol{C}}_{rk} - \boldsymbol{H}_k \boldsymbol{P}_{k/k-1} \boldsymbol{H}_k^{\mathrm{T}} \tag{6}$$

4 Simulation and Analysis

Simulation is carried out to validate the adaptive fuzzy control algorithm. The initial east-north-up attitude angles are 0°, 0° and −90°. The normal running trajectory is set as follows: firstly the vehicle runs east for 500 s, then it turns left to the north and runs for 700 s, thirdly it turns right for 45° to the northeast and runs for 700 s, after that it turns right for 90° to the southeast and runs for 1000 s, finally it turns left for 45° to the east and runs for 700 s; the total time is one hour. The initial velocity is 0 m/s, and after the initial alignment, the vehicle accelerates for 10 s at the acceleration of 2 m/s^2, then the vehicle runs at the speed of 20 m/s^2. The radius of the vehicle's turning is 10 m; the vehicle will slow down before the turning at the acceleration of −2 m/s^2 for 8 s, after the turning, the vehicle will accelerate to the speed of 20 m/s^2. The skid fault is set on 600 s in the running, and the fault lasts for 3 s; then the slid fault is set on 1600 s in the running, and the fault also lasts for 3 s; between the time of 2000 s and 2100 s, the vehicle is set in the state of running and skidding in a slippery upgrade road, and the velocity measured by the odometer is 1–1.3 times the actual velocity. The results of the simulation are shown in the Figs. 7 and 8.

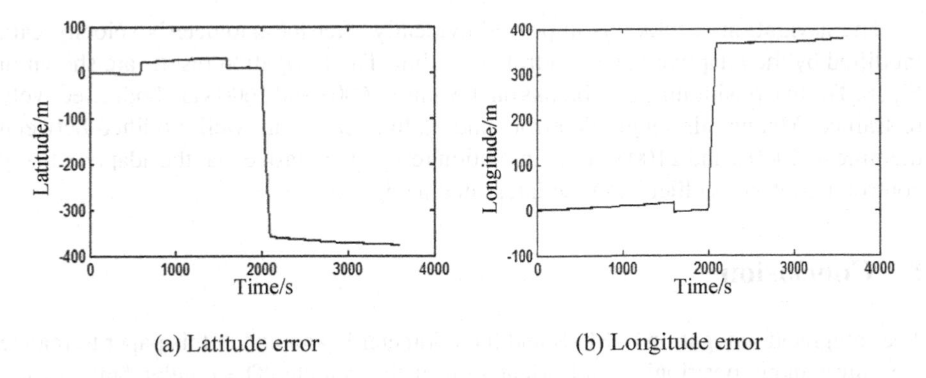

(a) Latitude error (b) Longitude error

Fig. 7. The navigation error when the odometer's faults are not modified

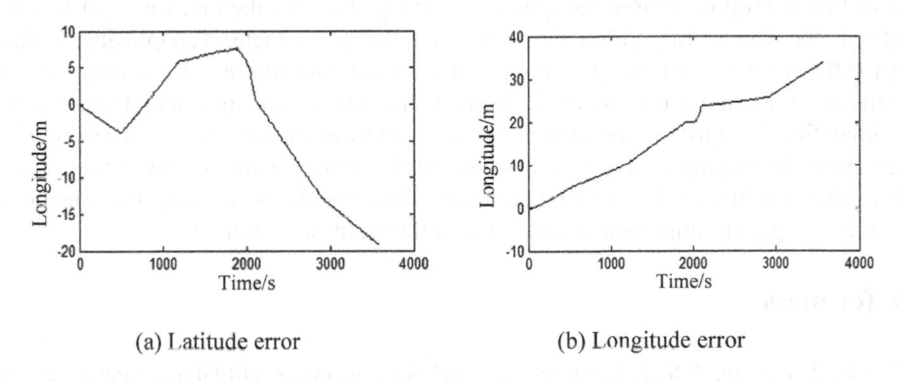

(a) Latitude error (b) Longitude error

Fig. 8. The navigation error with the faults modified by the adaptive fuzzy algorithm

According to the analysis of the simulation results, it can be concluded that the latitude of the vehicle's position on 600 s was large biased without the modifying of the adaptive fuzzy algorithm shown in Fig. 7, increasing about 20 m, whereas the latitude is small biased. This was because the velocity measured by the odometer was much larger than the velocity measured by SINS, the integrated navigation used the velocity measured by the odometer to modify the velocity of SINS, and so the reckoning velocity of SINS was larger than the vehicle's actual velocity. And during this time the vehicle was running north straightly, so the latitude was affected evidently by the velocity bias of the odometer, and the latitude error was big; whereas the longitude bias was mainly up to the yaw misalignment, so its error was not changed. On the fault time of 1600 s, the vehicle was running northeast, then the longitude error and the latitude error were all affected by the velocity biases caused by the odometer, the positioning errors both all little changed. But the navigation results were little affected because the times of the two faults were both short. During the time of 2000 s and 2100 s, the vehicle was running southeast; the velocity measured by the odometer was larger than the vehicle's actual velocity. And the integrated navigation used the velocity measured by the odometer to modify the velocity of SINS, so the velocity error of SINS was becoming larger gradually, the longitude error and the latitude error was becoming larger gradually.

The navigation accuracy is improved evidently after the odometer's velocity gain modified by the adaptive fuzzy control algorithm. The navigation results are shown in Fig. 8. The two positioning bias breaks on the time of 600 s and 1600 s are both effectively restrained. Meanwhile longitude errors and latitude errors are well modified between the time of 2000 s and 2100 s. The simulation results well prove that the adaptive fuzzy control algorithm is efficient in the integrated navigation.

5 Conclusion

The integrated navigation of SINS and the odometer is adopted in this paper to realize the autonomous positioning and orientation of the vehicle. The regular faults of the odometer when the vehicle is in motion are analyzed. Then one adaptive fuzzy control algorithm is proposed based on system's working state and the innovation of Kalman filter. In the proposed algorithm, the velocity gain of the odometer is adaptively modified by the fuzzy controller to keep the mean of the filter innovation zero, the variance matrix of the observation noise is calculated using the modified innovation, and the gain of the Kalman filter is adjusted to accelerate the filtering process and to decrease the navigation deviation. The regular faults are set in the simulation tests, and the adaptive fuzzy control algorithm is validated. The simulation results show that the positioning and orientation accuracy is greatly improved compared with the traditional method.

References

1. Cho, S.Y., Choi, W.S.: Robust positioning technique in low-cost DR/GPS for land navigation. IEEE Trans. Instrum. Meas. **55**(4), 1132–1142 (2006)
2. Georgy, J., Noureldin, A., Korenberg, M.J., et al.: Modeling the stochastic drift of a MEMS-based gyroscope in Gyro/Odometer/GPS integrated navigation. Trans. Intell. Transp. Syst. **11**(4), 856–872 (2010)
3. Yan, G., Qin, Y., Ma, J.: Research on INS/OD integrated navigation system algorithm. Comput. Meas. Control **14**(8), 1085–1087 (2006)
4. Miu, L., Li, C., Guo, Z., et al.: Independently integrated navigation system of SINS and distance-transfer-unit for land vehicles. J. Beijing Inst. Technol. **24**(9), 808–811 (2004)
5. Basil, H.: Adaptive Kalman filter tuning in integration of low-cost MEMS-INS/GPS. In: Guidance, Navigation and Control Conference and Exhibit, vol. 8, pp. 1–11 (2004)
6. Wei, G., Li, J., Zhou, G., et al.: Adaptive Kalman filtering with recursive noise estimator for integrated SINS/DVL systems. J. Navig. **68**, 142–161 (2015)
7. Gao, S., Song, F., Jiang, W.: Robust adaptive model predictive filtering algorithm and application to integrated navigation. J. Chin. Inertial Technol. **19**(6), 701–705 (2011)
8. Wang, W., Xiang, Z., Wang, G.: Fiber optic gyroscope SINS/GNSS tight integrated navigation based on adaptive Kalman filter. Infrared Laser Eng. **42**(3), 686–691 (2013)
9. Xue, L., Gao, S., Hu, G.: Adaptive Sage-Husa particle filtering and its application in integrated navigation. J. Chin. Inertial Technol. **21**(1), 84–88 (2013)
10. Wang, Q., Xu, X., Zhang, T., et al.: Application of fuzzy adaptive filter to integrated navigation system of underwater vehicle. J. Chin. Inertial Technol. **16**(3), 320–325 (2008)

Parallel Computing Education Through Simulation

Han Wan[1], Xiaoyan Luo[2(✉)], Xiaopeng Gao[1], and Xiang Long[1]

[1] School of Computer Science and Engineering, Beihang University, Beijing, China
{wanhan, gxp, long}@buaa.edu.cn

[2] School of Astronautics, Beihang University, Beijing, China
luoxy@buaa.edu.cn

Abstract. With the advent of parallel computing, CS departments must face the question of how to integrate the parallel computing knowledge into the curricula. In this paper, we introduced our practice in the parallel computing education which used simulation methodology. In our course, students learned the basics of GPU architectures, parallel computing along with optimization techniques to tuning the performance. Furthermore, we elaborated the work which combined simulation-based architecture research and parallel computing – a cache simulator based on GPU. In this part, the common architecture research methodology with tool, such as simulation methodology and Pin tool were introduced. This study case has shown as an effective supplement to our teaching philosophy: balance design based on quantitative characterization.

Keywords: Parallel computing education · Architecture and organization course · Curriculum design · Practice

1 Introduction

The rapid advances in parallel system have led to an increased demand for trained professionals with parallel computing skills to solve challenging scientific problems. CS Curriculum 2013 [1] has shifted parallel computing from elective status into the core.

Computer Architecture and Organization (AR) course usually includes the contents as follows: basic principles of computer design, performance evaluation, trends and new enabling technologies [2]. Introducing parallelism concepts into the curriculum using GPU became an effective method.

1.1 Course Orientation and Improvement

University of Illinois [3] opened the summer school -"accelerators for science and engineering applications: GPUs and multicores". This summer school helped the participants to understand algorithm styles that are suitable for accelerators. Furthermore, the most important architectural performance considerations to developing applications were elaborated.

L. Zhang et al. (Eds.): AsiaSim 2016/SCS AutumnSim 2016, Part I, CCIS 643, pp. 585–591, 2016.
DOI: 10.1007/978-981-10-2663-8_60

Stanford University [4] considered the modern application of large-scale computing problems, the main course used CUDA parallel programming environment based on NVIDIA processors for the programming and optimization.

CS525 GPU Programming [5] described how to use GPUs for graphics processing and general parallel computation through a series of lectures and projects.

University of Wisconsin, Madison [6] opened "ME964: High-Performance Computing for Applications in Engineering". This course introduced the GPU computing with CUDA, and presented case studies such as parallel prefix scan and reduction. It also elaborated parallel computing via OpenMP and MPI.

Caltech [7] introduced CUDA programming model and syntax together with the GPU architecture, parallel algorithms, CUDA libraries and applications of GPU computing.

Parallel knowledge had been introduced based on the CUDA environment by many other universities [8, 9]. In this paper, we outline the changes made to the Computer Architecture course at Beihang University. The main portion of the course expansion focused on general purpose computing on graphic processing unit (GPU) using CUDA C [10]. In Spring 2014, we referenced Illinois ECE 408 [11, 12], and combined with our own experience and teaching philosophy. Through examples and projects, students learned the basics of GPU architectures, along with optimization the execution of their programs using the GPU's global and shared memories, and they gained the familiarity with thread synchronization and experience in using atomic operations.

To inject the parallel computing into architecture research, we elaborated the course with a parallel cache simulator [13], which was speeded up using CUDA C. This work introduced how to do the architecture research, using simulator together with Pin tool [14], in order to characterize cache performance. Furthermore, we analyzed how to utilize the computation ability of GPU to parallel the simulation of multi-level cache in coarse and fine granularities.

Our practices shown that the necessary structural knowledge helped students in understanding the basic parallel GPU system composition, in conjunction with the simulation methodology helped students to further explore the course topics.

1.2 Simulation Methodology in Computer Architecture Research

In AR course, it is important for student to learn how to do the architecture research, as well as learn how to evaluate the system performance under the benchmark. The simulation methodology usually has been used to do the architecture research, especially used in the evaluation of different architecture designs.

We focused on the Cache design, and first introduced the traditional trace-driven simulation [15]. After discussed the parallelism in the Cache simulation, we shown how to mapping the parallel simulation onto GPU. Then analyzed trace-driven simulation's backward compared to the binary instrumentation tool Pin.

Our course practices indicated that participants could understand the most important architectural performance considerations to developing GPGPU applications, as well as do the architecture research using simulation methodology.

2 Architecture Simulation Based on GPU

In our AR course, how to use detailed memory characteristics of workload in evaluating Cache system is elaborated. We introduced how to parallel Cache simulation on GPU, including decompose the task, implement parallelism using CUDA and the performance tuning.

On the other hand, due to expansion of the design space, the length of cache traces may run to hundreds of millions of references in traditional trace-driven simulation. We illustrated Pin [16] as the trace generator to characterize memory system behavior of application during the running time.

2.1 Analysis the Parallelism in Cache Simulation

The Cache simulation process is shown in Fig. 1: first fetch the memory reference from the trace file, and then compute the set number, tag information, block number and block offset according to the Cache configuration. Finally, update the set status and metrics after search in the corresponding set under certain replacement policy.

For trace belongs to different Cache sets, they are independent in the following process. In addition to set-parallelism, searching process in each Cache set can also work in parallel.

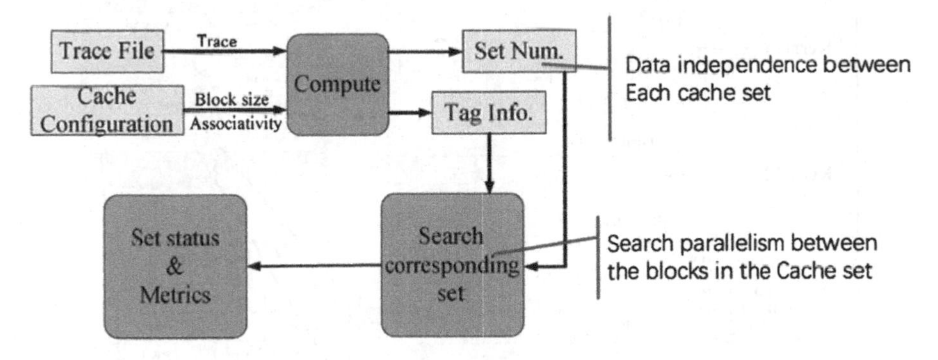

Fig. 1. Parallelism analysis in Cache simulation

2.2 Mapping the Cache Simulation into GPU Architecture

As shown in Fig. 2, memories on GPU vary greatly, according to the size and access speed requirement, the memory model mapping in Cache simulation is as follows: the trace data stored in the global memory due to the size requirement; the Cache set information that should be accessed frequently stored in shared memory.

Figure 3 shows how to parallel single-level Cache simulation on GPU. Since different Cache set simulation process are independent, their work mapped to different thread blocks. In the same thread block, each thread can be responsible for simulate different cache configurations in parallel.

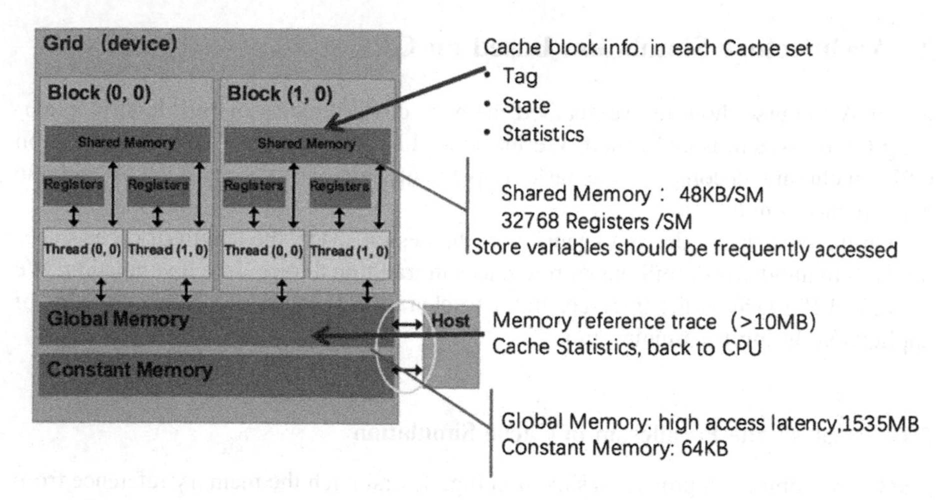

Fig. 2. Data storage in Cache simulator based on GTX480

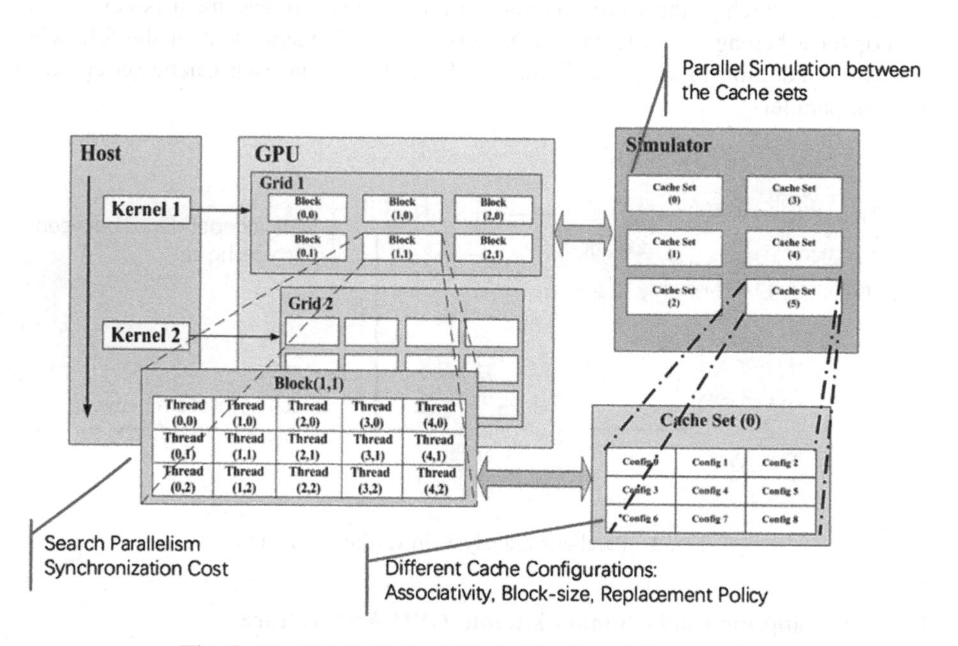

Fig. 3. Parallel single-level Cache simulator based on GPU

The simulation process of two-level Cache can be divided into two parts: do the L1 Cache simulation in the first kernel and generate the memory references for L2 Cache access, and then the second kernel finish the L2 level simulation.

2.3 Using Pin-Tool in the Architecture Research

The memory traces may occupy several gigabytes of disk space, and may vary from different compilers. In the course, we introduced Pin as the functional model that provides the Cache simulator with memory traces [17].

Here the client process fills the shared memory with traces produced by the Pin-tool, and then sends the readable signal to the simulation server process when the buffer is full. Then the trace-producer is blocked, and waiting for the writeable signal from the trace-consumer. It will fill the other buffer with traces and go on circularly until the application that running on the Pin is finished.

2.4 More on the Simulation Work

To improve the simulator's performance, the process of trace generates and consume processes can be executed in pipeline. This parallelism focuses on the task.

On the other hand, the simulation can use another timing partitioning parallel algorithm as mentioned in [18]. This work delighted that sometimes we need other directions to look at the problem: maybe we need to change a lot, but it deserved to do the improvement. We also helped the students to analysis the parallelism in the multi-core Cache simulation as described in [13].

3 Assessment and Conclusions

The great principles of computing in [19] can be grouped into seven categories: computation, communication, coordination, recollection, automation, evaluation and design. For our parallel computing topic, we determined the principles that must be brought out in our course:

- The basic architecture of GPU - the parallel computing systems are built from processing core, with the memory hierarchy to store the information (computation, recollection).
- The communication in the GPU - how thread exchange information and coordination between CPU and GPU (communication).
- Predict the performance of the system based on the hardware resources' usage (evaluation).
- Decompose systems into sequential and parallel parts (design).

From the teaching practices, we found the following teaching philosophy do help students' comprehension.

3.1 Historical Perspective to Study the Evolution

In the AR course, we first elaborated the architecture about CPU and GPU's evolution. When we introduced the GPU architecture, students need to know the control logic and memory model differences between CPU and GPU. This helped them in understanding the reason about the huge gap in the throughput of peak floating computation between CPU and GPU.

The introduction about the GPU's evolution from fixed function graphics pipeline was also necessary. When they can understand the graphics processor inheritance, the advantages and disadvantages of the current major computing model can be understood, especially help them to comprehend the modern GPU design philosophy – "massive parallel threads, a relatively small cache, and increased memory bandwidth". This also helped to grasp the future GPU development trend.

3.2 Balance Design Based on Quantitative Characterization

The influence of different resources allocation on the performance are introduced using quantitative characterization.

For example, the increase usage of the register for each thread may results in performance cliff, that decreases number of thread block parallel execution. When tuning the performance of Matrix multiplication, each thread can compute two elements in the result matrix instead of just compute one element. This programming improvement may decrease the access number to the global memory and increase the independent instructions in the prefetching ploy. But on the other hand, this improvement may use more registers and shared memory, which may all lead to performance cliff.

In the Cache simulator case study, students also need to do balance design from the system-investigated view using quantitative characterization.

3.3 Students' Feedback

We done the course survey at the end of the Spring 2014' and Spring 2015. The first part questions related to the course structure, nearly 77% students clearly recognized the structure and found it helpful to approach the subject.

The second part questions focus on the lab sections. Most students gave positive feedback about the practical work done in the lab sessions. They like the lab difficulty from the easier to the more advanced. And they announced that the hands-on programming based on the skeleton programs is welcomed. The lab sessions can help most students to learn and understand the content presented in class.

The third part questions are about the architecture research session. Most students denoted that this session helped them lots in knowing the common architecture research methodology with tool, such as simulation methodology and Pin tool.

The overall valuation of the course turned out positive, but the flood of information still overwhelmed less than 20% students. Based on our students' assignments, labs and comments, we thought that our injection of parallel computing into AR with simulation methodology was successful.

Acknowledgments. This work is funded by China Scholarship Council (No. 201406025114) and the National High Technology Research and Development Program (2007AA01Z183).

References

1. The Joint Task Force on Computing Curricula Association For Computing Machinery (ACM). IEEE Computer Society, Computer science curricula 2013, 20 December 2013. DOI: 10.1145/2534860
2. Hennessy, J.L., Patterson, D.A.: Computer Architecture: A Quantitative Approach, 5th edn. Morgan Kaufmann, Burlington (2011). ISBN 978-0-12-383872-8
3. Programming Massively Parallel Processors [EB/OL]. http://www.greatlakesconsortium.org/events/GPUMulticore/agenda.html
4. Methods in Numerical Analysis [EB/OL]. http://www.stanfordcourses.com/CME342
5. GPU Programming [EB/OL]. http://www.evl.uic.edu/aej/525/
6. High-Performance Computing for Applications in Engineering [EB/OL]. http://sbel.wisc.edu/Courses/ME964/
7. CS 179, GPU Programming [EB/OL]. http://courses.cms.caltech.edu/cs101gpu/
8. Engineering Tool IV - Introduction to GPU Programming [EB/OL]. http://www.cse-lab.ethz.ch/index.php/teaching/42-teaching/classes/576-etvgpufall2013
9. CUDA University Courses [EB/OL]. http://www.nvidia.cn/object/cuda_university_courses_cn_old.html
10. Nvidia CUDA Zone [EB/OL]. https://developer.nvidia.com/cuda-zone
11. Applied Parallel Programming [EB/OL]. http://courses.engr.illinois.edu/ece408/
12. Kirk, D.B., Hwu, W.-M.W.: Programming Massively Parallel Processors: A Hands-On Approach. Morgan Kaufmann Publishers, Burlington (2010). ISBN 0-123-81472-3
13. Wan, H., Long, X., Gao, X.P., Li, Y.: GPU accelerating for rapid multi-core cache simulation. In: 25th IEEE International Parallel & Distributed Processing Symposium, IPDPS2011, Anchorage, AL, United states, pp. 1387–1396. IEEE Computer Society (2011)
14. Pin - A Dynamic Binary Instrumentation Tool (EB/OL). https://software.intel.com/en-us/articles/pintool
15. Uhlig, R.A., Mudge, T.N.: Trace-driven memory simulation: a survey. ACM Comput. Surv. **29**, 128–170 (1997)
16. Reddi, V., Settle, A.M., Connors, D.A. Cohn, R.S.: Pin: a binary instrumentation tool for computer architecture research and education. In: Proceedings of the Workshop on Computer Architecture Education, June 2004
17. Han, W., Gao, X., Long, X., Wang, Z.: Using GPU to accelerate a pin-based multi-level Cache simulator. In: Spring Simulation Multiconference 2010, SpringSim 2010
18. Kiesling, T.: Using approximation with time-parallel simulation. Simulation. **81**(4), 255–266 (2005)
19. Denning, P.J.: Great principles of computing. Commun. ACM **46**(11), 15–20 (2003)

Adaptive Energy-Efficient Data Acquisition Algorithm in Wireless Sensor and Actuator Network

Wang Yan(✉), Gao Yun, and Ji Zhicheng

Engineering Research Center of Internet of Things Technology Applications
Ministry of Education, Jiangnan University, Wuxi 214122, China
wangyan88@jiangnan.edu.cn

Abstract. Funnel effect will cause the network energy cavity and the imbalance of node load in wireless sensor and actuator network. To improve this situation, an adaptive data acquisition algorithm of mobile nodes is presented in this paper. Firstly, dynamically changing residing position of the collection node is one effective way to balance the energy in the network. Here, we use Artificial Bee Colony (ABC) algorithm to find the best residing positions of collection nodes according to the energy consumption. The mobile collection nodes will then move to their corresponding best positions dynamically with assigned directions. Then, an adaptive transmission strategy based on SINK proxy mechanism and dynamic data acquisition rate is studied to balance the load during the collection nodes moving. Experiments show that the proposed algorithm can improve the situation of energy cavity for data acquisition in WSAN. Transmission reliability and network resource utilization at the MAC layer are also improved.

Keywords: Wireless sensor and actor network · Energy cavity · Mobile node · Collection rate

1 Introduction

Wireless sensor and actor network is widely used in the fields of environmental monitoring, smart home, military surveillance, and so on. The process of monitoring data collection is more flexibility and extensibility due to the mobility of actuator nodes. Besides, more sufficient energy of actuator nodes makes it possible to become cluster heads for data transmission and avoid energy consumption for changing cluster head frequently. However, since the sensor nodes are static, the closer the distance between actuator nodes and sensor nodes, the more tasks of data forwarding for sensor nodes. It leads to faster energy consumption of nodes and early death because of the energy cavity [1]. So, prolonging the lifecycle of WSAN and improving the network resource utilization in the MAC layer become very important. Recently, some WSAN dynamic data acquisition algorithms [2–4] have been put forward for the purpose of energy consumption balance and network lifecycle extension.

A dynamic load balancing data acquisition algorithm based on ACO is proposed in literature [2]. It takes node load information as stimulating factor to adaptively adjust

L. Zhang et al. (Eds.): AsiaSim 2016/SCS AutumnSim 2016, Part I, CCIS 643, pp. 592–602, 2016.
DOI: 10.1007/978-981-10-2663-8_61

the direction of data transmission and balance load of nodes. However, the method ignores the energy cavity problem near the actuator node area caused by the fixed position of actuators. A mobile sink proxy mechanism and network quality evaluation strategy is studied in literature [3]. The moving path of sink depends on the network quality. But, the exact location of sink nodes and data transmission of nodes during the node moving are not taken into consider. The sink node location update strategy proposed in literature [4] aims to solve the imbalance between energy consumption of network and transmission delay.

In this paper, an adaptive energy-efficient data acquisition approach based on Artificial Bee Colony (ABC) algorithm is proposed to improve energy cavity and imbalance. First, the WSAN model and funnel effect are described. Second, based on the model, a moving strategy of actuator node is put forward based on ABC algorithm. It decides whether the actuator nodes should change their data acquisition residing positions, also gives the best residing positions and moving directions. Third, an adaptive strategy of node data acquisition frequency is presented to balance the node load during the data acquisition process with the proxy mechanism. Finally, some numerical examples are given to show the effectiveness of the proposed algorithm.

2 Network Model

2.1 Partition in the Cluster

Here, the actuator node is seen as a cluster head and the sensor nodes as the slave nodes, as shown in Fig. 1. This circular cluster with the actuator node as center of radius R_{cluster} is divided into n annular regions. Sensor nodes are distributed in different annular regions. Define the closest annular region to the center as zone 1, nearly is zone 2 and so on. At the beginning of cluster partition, The actuator node sends data with the communication distance R, $2R$, $3R$, ... $\lceil \frac{R_{\text{cluster}}}{R} \rceil R$, respectively. Then, each sensor will take the minimum data it receives as its zone number.

In order to describe the connection between network nodes, node degree index is introduced. For one node, it's degree index is the number of it's neighbor nodes with communication distance less than R. We define the node degree index as k_j. Furthermore, clustering coefficient c_j [6] is introduced to describe the compactness and link condition between the node j and its neighbor nodes. Clustering coefficient c_j can be defined as the following formula.

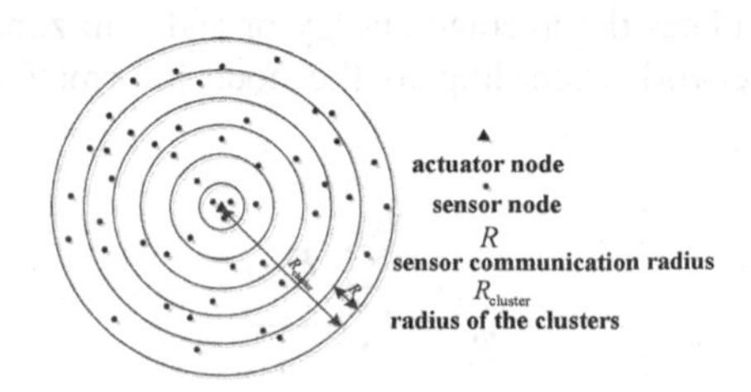

Fig. 1. N area evenly divided within clusters

$$c_j = \frac{2e_j}{k_j(k_j - 1)} \tag{1}$$

Where, e_j is the number of the neighbor nodes which can form triangle with node j.

2.2 Funneling Effect

In WSAN, funnel effect [7] is an inherent characteristic during the data collection process. Energy of the nodes in low areas will consume much faster than that of nodes in high areas. For the whole network, the problems of energy cavity, congestion, and node life exhausting appear since the imbalance of energy consumption. To improve these problems in WSAN, the actuator node as the collector node should adjust their residing positions and transmission rate adaptively according to the network situation.

3 ABC Algorithm Based Moving Strategy of Actuator Node

3.1 Mechanism of Bee Colony

In natural, bees will extend outward when they reproduce too many. After Yukon worm stage, the population of bees sharply rises and nest will become very crowded. Therefore, worker bees will foster a new batch of queen bees and periodically scout in all directions to find new nests. Worker bees will fly back to the old nest and declare others about the finding of new nest by the way of dancing. Different dancing activity levels reflect different qualities of the new nests. Sometimes, the worker bees will find several new nests at the same time. The other bees will play as supporters and propagandist of the new nests they like. Consequently, the nests with good condition will get increasing supporters and those received less support are excluded gradually. If the supporters' number of a new nest reaches the quorum, all the bees will fly to their new home.

3.2 Moving Decision Based on Bee Colony Mechanism

Similar in WSAN, the average rest energy of nodes in zone 1 is used to decide whether to move based on the mechanism of bee colony. The analogy between bee colony and WSAN network is in the following figure (Table 1).

Actuator node calculates the average energy of nodes in zone 1 and rest energy of nodes in the whole network according to the node information carried by the data packet.

$$E_A = \frac{\sum_{i=1}^{N_{h_m=1}} E_{resi}}{N_{h_m=1}} \tag{2}$$

Table 1. Analogy between bee colony and WSAN network

Bee colony	WSAN network
Nesting	Actuator node resident location
Bee	Sensor node
Beehive	Actuator node
Activity degree of bee dancing	Rest energy of nodes
Quorum of supporters	Threshold of actuator mobility

In this formula, $N_{h_m=1}$ is the nodes of zone 1.

$$E_w = \frac{\sum_{i=1}^{n} E_{resi}}{n} \tag{3}$$

Where, n is the total number of sensor nodes in the cluster. Actuator node will decide whether to move every period T, Current state of the actuator node is indicated by X. $X = 1$, actuator is performing tasks; $X = 0$, actuator is idle. In order to avoid the situation that actuator node cannot change motion state when performing tasks, the moving strategy rules are designed as follows.

(a) When a period begins, detect the state of actuator X at this time firstly. If X = 1, then skip the actuator moving operations; Otherwise proceed to next step.
(b) Compare E_A and E_w. If E_A smaller than E_w, actuator node will move; Otherwise not move.
(c) When the actuator node decides to move, the next problem is to determine the move position.

3.3 Best Residing Position and Moving Direction

In this section, we presented a moving algorithm to decide the best residing position and moving direction for the moving actuator. The actuator node and its corresponding degree nodes are seen as a node unit. Influencing factor B_j is used to determine the moving direction of the actuator node, which consists of three parts: the average rest energy of node unit $E_{j-\text{cluster}}$, the concentration coefficient of node unit c_j, the number of source nodes in the node unit f_j.

A node unit with more source nodes has greater probability to be the hot pot monitoring area in one period. If the actuator node moves to this unit, the real-time performance and energy consumption will be improved since the less transmission distance. Therefore, the influencing factor of moving direction for actuator node can be expressed as follows:

$$B_j = \alpha c_j + \beta f_j + \theta E_{j-\text{cluster}} \tag{4}$$

Where, α, β, θ are weight coefficients, and $\alpha + \beta + \theta = 1$. After one moving period, the actuator node will calculate influencing factor of every unit in its cluster. Then, it selects the unit with the largest influencing factor as the moving target area.

After the node unit A is selected as the target region, the final position should be determined to satisfy the condition that all the nodes in the unit are included in the zone 1 of actuator node. Also, the total transmission power of sensor nodes should be minimized.

As shown in Fig. 2, A is the target node and B, C, D, E are its neighbor nodes. According to TWORAYGROUND model [9], the transmitted power of a sensor node can be written as:

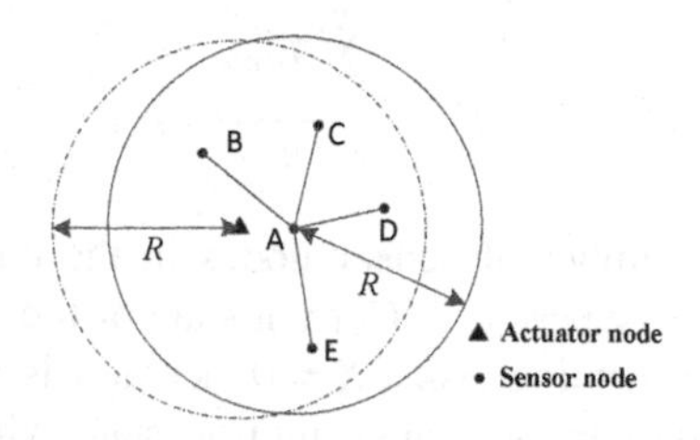

Fig. 2. Residing place of actuator node

$$P_t = \frac{P_r \cdot d^4 \cdot L}{G_t \cdot G_r \cdot h_t^2 \cdot h_r^2} \tag{5}$$

Where, P_r is the threshold of receiving power, d is transmission distance, L is antenna length, h_t is transmitted antenna height, h_r is receiving antenna height; G_r is receiving antenna gain. P_r, L, h_t, h_r, G_r are constant. So, final transmitted power of a sensor node is related to the distance between sensor node and actuator node. Take the total transmission power of all the sensor nodes in zone 1 of actuator node P_{all} as the objective function.

The object of the moving strategy is to find (x_a, y_a), which minimizes the following performance index:

$$P_{all} = \sum_{i=1}^{n_j+1} p_i = \sum_{i=0}^{n_j+1} \frac{P_r \cdot d_{a-s_i}^4 \cdot L}{G_t \cdot G_r \cdot h_t^2 \cdot h_r^2} \tag{6}$$

where,$d_{a-s_i} = \sqrt{(x_a - x_{s_i})^2 + (y_a - y_{s_i})^2}$ is the Euclidean distance between actuator node and sensor node s_i after movement.

Constraint condition:

$$\max\{d_{a-s_i}\} \leq R$$

Where, $1 \leq i \leq n_j + 1$. Considering ABC algorithm has strong robustness, it is used to find the optimal position of actuator node in this paper.

The steps of using ABC algorithm to find the best position of the actuator node can be described as the follows.

(1) Generating *SN* feasible solution as the initial source position $(X_i, Y_i)(i = 1, 2, \ldots, SN)$. The worker bees and scout bees are assumed to be the same number of *SN*.
(2) Calculating the fitness function for each source position

$$f(x, y) = \frac{1}{P_{all}},$$

where, $(x, y) = (X_i, Y_i)$.
(3) Computing the new solution $\left(X_i^{'}, Y_i^{'}\right)$ according to the following iteration formulas:

$$\begin{cases} X_i^{'} = X_i + \phi_i(X_i - X_k) \\ Y_i^{'} = Y_i + \phi_i(Y_i - Y_k) \end{cases}$$

Where, $(k = 1, 2, \cdots, SN, k \neq i)$, ϕ_i is a random number in the interval $[0, 1]$. Then, comparing the new solution $\left(X_i^{'}, Y_i^{'}\right)$ with the original solution (X_i, Y_i), the better one will be chosen by greedy strategy. Each scout bee chooses the source according to the probability p_i,

$$p_i = \frac{f(X_i, Y_i)}{\sum_{i=1}^{SN} f(X_i, Y_i)} \tag{7}$$

(4) For the chosen source position, scout bees search the new feasible solutions by the formula (7). After all the worker bees and scout bees finished the solution searching, the source position will be given up if its fitness had not improved during the expected steps. Also, the worker bees will change their roles to be scout bees and continue to search the new solution by the following formulas. Then, turn to step 2.

$$\begin{cases} X_{id} - X^{\min} + r\left(X^{\max} - X^{\min}\right) \\ Y_{id} - Y^{\min} + r\left(Y^{\max} - Y^{\min}\right) \end{cases} \tag{8}$$

Where, r is a random number in the interval of [0, 1], $X^{\min}$, $X^{\max}$, $Y^{\min}$, $Y^{\max}$, are the upper and lower bounds of x, y.

4 Adaptive Strategy of Data Acquisition Frequency

In order to ensure the data transmission continuity of sensor nodes during the actuator node moving, it is necessary to select a proxy node from the nodes in zone 1 as the temporary terminal.

The actuator node will choose the node with great residual energy and free queue as the proxy node. The proxy node probability selection formula is as follows:

$$W(i) = \lambda_e \frac{e_i}{E_i} - \lambda_q \frac{q_i}{Q_i} \tag{9}$$

Where, e_i is the residual energy of senor node i, E_i is the initial energy of node i, q_i is occupied queue length, Q_i is the total queue length, λ_e and λ_q are weight parameters of energy and queue length, respectively. $\lambda_e + \lambda_q = 1$. When the proxy node is selected by the actuator node, it will send a notification signal to the sensor nodes in cluster with transmitting distance $\left\lceil \frac{R_{\text{cluster}}}{R} \right\rceil R$. This signal includes the proxy node ID, moving target position, and moving time t_m. The moving time is determined by

$$t_m = \frac{\sqrt{(x_{a_0} - x_a)^2 + (y_{a_0} - y_a)^2}}{v}$$

Where, (x_{a_0}, y_{a_0}) is the initial position of actuator node, v is moving speed of the actuator node.

The receiving data rate of the proxy node can be calculated by the following formula.

$$M_{i\_receive} = \frac{Q_i - q_i}{t_m} \tag{10}$$

To reduce the energy consumption and data queue length of the proxy node during data reception, an adaptive strategy of data acquisition frequency is proposed as the follows.

(1) The proxy node detects the current data transmission state of sub-layer neighbor nodes. If some nodes are transmitting data, then the proxy node will send a data transmitting speed control signal to each neighbor nodes in sub-layer. When these nodes receive speed control signal, they adjust their transmitting speed by the following formula (9) and go to step (2).

$$M_{\text{i}-1\_\text{send}} = \frac{M_{i\_receive}}{n_i} \tag{11}$$

Where, n_s is the number of neighbor nodes in sub-layer which are transmitting data. If there is none node which is transmitting data, then the proxy node will be in waiting for reception state and go to step (4).

(2) The nodes in second layer detect the data transmission state of its sub-layer neighbor nodes sequentially. If there is data transmission node, then send data rate control signal. Data sending rate of the sub-layer neighbor nodes of the second layer is related to free queue length of the second layer's nodes, number of sub-layer neighbor nodes that transmitting data currently and self-rate for transmitting data. Namely,

$$[(Q_{i-1} - q_{i-1}) - (n_{i-1} \times M_{i-1-1\_send} - M_{i-1\_\mathrm{send}}) \times T] = 0$$

So,

$$M_{i-1-1\_send} = \frac{\frac{Q_{i-1} - q_{i-1}}{T} + M_{i-1\_\mathrm{send}}}{n_{i-1}} \tag{12}$$

Where, T is the sampling period of sensor node. By this analogy, data transmitting rate of the last layer could be calculated.

(3) If a node's parent node do not distribute data transmitting rate quota to it, and its sub-layer neighbor nodes need to send monitoring data to it in period T, then the data transmitting rate it feed back to its sub-layer neighbor node is:

$$M_{i-k-1\_send} = \frac{Q_{i-k} - q_{i-k}}{n_{i-k}(T - T_1)} \tag{13}$$

Where, T_l is the time that this node keeps wait state of data reception in T.

(4) After a period T, agent node will allot transmitting rate quota layer by layer.

(5) After time t_m, namely after actuator node move to target location, take actuator node as cluster head and perform the annular partition operation.

5 Case Study

Suppose a 100 m × 100 m square monitoring area with 100 random deployed sensor nodes and an actuator node. Sensor nodes are used to detect emergency. Actuator node is responsible for collecting monitoring data and performing special feedback action according to the event. Experimental parameters are shown in the following table.

Table 2 simulation results are shown in Fig. 3, where rhombus solid point means sensor node and triangle means actuator node. In Fig. 3, the initial locations of actuator nodes are random. At this time, node 20, node 10, node 33 and node 72 were chosen as the inner nodes of actuator node. Source node collects event information, and sends it to actuator node through relay node. Figure 4 shows the trajectory of actuator node in a certain time. Take the second location of actuator node as an example, it moved to the node unit area which includes node 62, node 85, node 14 and node 57. Location selection is related to average rest energy of node unit, frequency that nodes in node unit being resource node and number of nodes in node unit. Node unit is selected by actuator node as location section combined with these three factors. Then, the final location is determined according to optimal selection algorithm based on ABC. This

Table 2. Experimental Parameters

Parameter name	Value
Communication radius of node	5 m
α	0.3
β	0.1
θ	0.6
Detect period of node energy	10 min
μ	0.4
ω	0.6
Sampling period of nodes	30 s

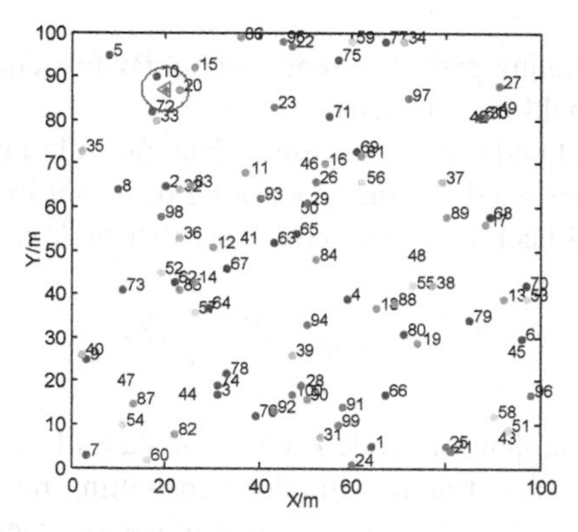

Fig. 3. Initial position of network nodes

method keeps actuator moving to the optimal location to ensure the whole energy balance of nodes.

In order to analysis proposed algorithm more comprehensively, SLM algorithm [8] and LDG-MS algorithm [9] are compared to this method. In Fig. 5, death rate of nodes in the algorithm proposed in this paper is significantly slower than other two algorithms, which demonstrates this algorithm has good effect on the improvement of node energy consumption balance. In this method, location of actuator is decided by average rest energy periodically. Therefore, rest energy of nodes in network is balanced and lifetime is also prolonged. In SLM algorithm, SLM node is defined to find actuator node and send information to sensors when they transmit monitoring data package. It causes excessive energy consumption of SLM node and its neighbor nodes, and also reduces the life of the network. In LDG-MS algorithm, outer nodes find the location of actuator node indirectly according to data transmission behavior of inner nodes. This method also consumes extra energy for detection, and add information transmission load of nodes. Besides, as shown in Fig. 6, resource utilization of MAC layer in the proposed algorithm is significantly higher than other two algorithms when actuator node is moving. Algorithm proposed in this paper adjust the data transmission rate of nodes in each layer adaptively according to load of transmission nodes and data

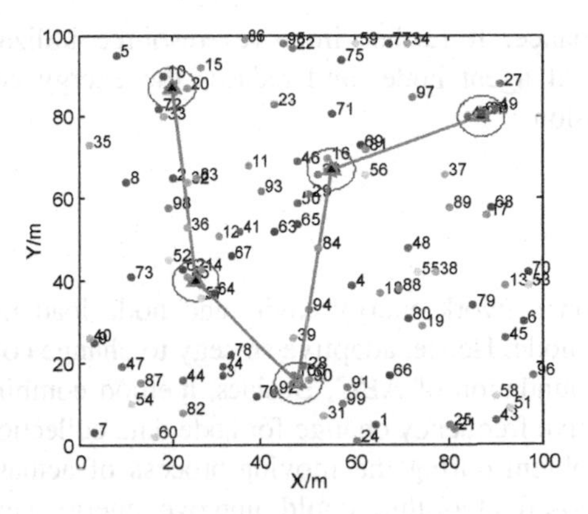

Fig. 4. The trajectory of actuator node

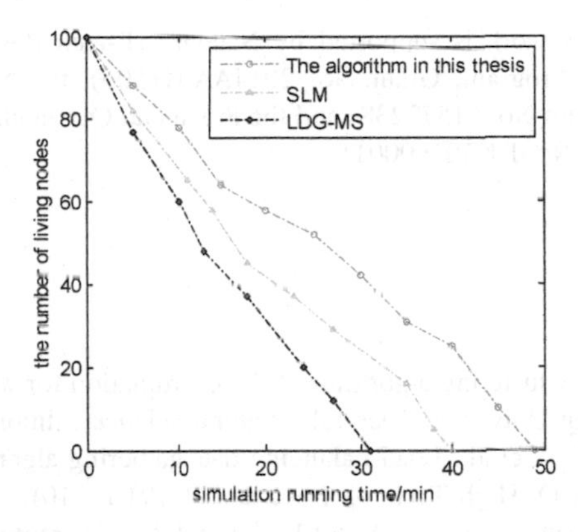

Fig. 5. The variation of survival number of nodes in each algorithm

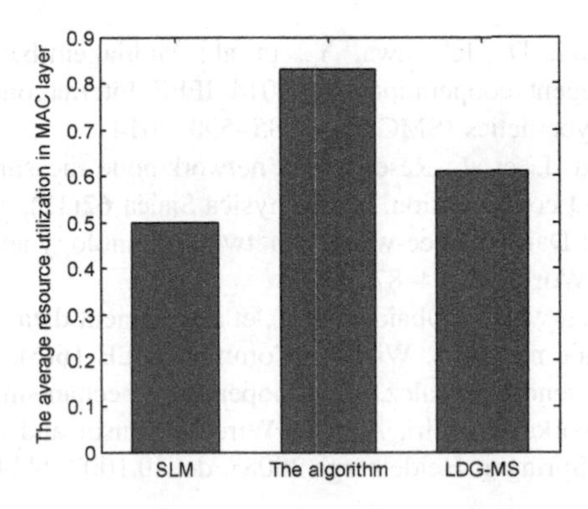

Fig. 6. Resource utilization of MAC layer in each algorithm

transmission performance. It further improves resource utilization of MAC layer, avoids data overrun of agent node, and reduces the energy consumption of nodes redundancy transmission.

6 Conclusion

This paper focuses on network energy cavity and node load imbalance during data collection of actuator node. Hence, adaptive strategy to change collection node location is presented on the foundation of ABC. Besides, method combined with SINK agent mechanism and adaptive frequency change for node data collection is used to solve the data transmission problem during the moving process of actuator node. Experiment shows that the proposed algorithm could improve energy cavity on the basis of real-time data transmission, enhance reliability of node data transmission and resource utilization of MAC layer. It also improves the comprehensive performance of network.

Acknowledgement. This work is supported by National Hi-tech Research and Development Program of China (863 Program, Grant No. 2014AA041505), the National Natural Science Foundation of China (Grant No. 61572238) and the Provincial Outstanding Youth Foundation of Jiangsu Province (Grant No. BK20160001).

References

1. Yi, J., Li, T., Shi, W.: Clustering algorithm of SA coordination for wireless sensors and actor networks. J. Huazhong Univ. Sci. Technol. (Natural Science Edition) **39**, 89–93 (2011)
2. Tang, Y., Shi, W., Yi, J., et al.: Load-balancing data gathering algorithm for wireless sensor networks based on ACO. High Technol. Lett. **8**, 784–791 (2010)
3. Zheng, S., Che, H., Fan, Y., et al.: Agent-based mobile sink routing algorithm in wireless sensor networks. J. Electr. Measur. Instrum. **02**, 127–134 (2013)
4. Chen, Y., Wang, Z., Zhao, Z., et al.: Online model-driven data acquisition for wireless sensor networks. In: Wireless Communications and Networking Conference (WCNC), 2015 IEEE, pp. 1572–1577 (2015)
5. Takano, R., Yamazaki, D., Ichikawa, Y., et al.: Multiagent-based ABC algorithm for autonomous rescue agent cooperation. In: 2014 IEEE International Conference on IEEE Systems, Man and Cybernetics (SMC), pp. 585–590 (2014)
6. Ren, Z., Shao, F., Liu, J., et al.: Research on network node measurement method based on importance degree and concentration. Acta Physica Sinica **62**(12), 128901 (2013)
7. Zhang, G., Zhang, Z.: Dance of bee-wireless network technology and applications of zigbee. Electron. Eng. Prod. World **03**, 84–87 (2006)
8. Dhurandher, S.K., Khairwal, S., Obaidat, M.S., et al.: Efficient data acquisition in underwater wireless sensor Ad Hoc networks. Wireless Commun. IEEE **16**(6), 70–78 (2009)
9. Ruiz-Ibarra, E., Villasenor-Gonzalez, L.: Cooperation mechanism taxonomy for wireless sensor and actor networks. In: Miri, A. (ed.) Wireless Sensor and Actor Networks II. IFIP, vol. 264, pp. 62–73. Springer, Heidelberg (2008). doi:10.1007/978-0-387-09441-0_6

Solving Flexible Job Shop Scheduling Problem Using a Discrete Particle Swarm Optimization with Iterated Local Search

Song Huang(✉), Na Tian, Yan Wang, and Zhicheng Ji

Engineering Research Center of Internet of Things Technology Applications
Ministry of Education, Jiangnan University, Wuxi, China
huangson2@163.com.cn

Abstract. Considering tri-objective flexible job shop scheduling problem (FJSP), multi-objective-based discrete particle swarm optimizer (MOPSO) integrating iterated local search is presented to search the optimal scheduling. First of all, three discrete operators are embedded in MOPSO to produce new particles with a probability. Then global-best set and self-best sets are defined to obtain global-best position and self-best positions. Thirdly, iterated local search integrating two neighborhoods is introduced to search the neighborhoods of the global-best set. Evaluated on Kacem instances, MOPSO show its validity for solving FJSP.

Keywords: Multi-objective problem · Discrete particle swarm optimization · Iterated local search · Flexible job shop scheduling

1 Introduction

FJSP is a well-known scheduling problem in workshop manufacture field, which should determine processing machines and sequence of operations. Particle Swarm Optimizer (PSO) [1], Taboo Search (TS) [2] and Genetic Algorithm(GA) [3, 4], firefly algorithm (FA) [5], which are proved to be more efficient methods to solve NP-hard problem, are presented to address the FJSP. Shao et al. developed a combinative algorithm, which used a global search process of discrete particle swarm optimizer (DPSO) and a local search process of Simulated Annealing, and then a hybrid of crowding distance and Pareto ranking is incorporated into the proposed algorithm [1]. However, it's also hard for these algorithms to solve FJSP completely.

In our paper, MOPSO is proposed to solve FJSP with three objectives. Special discrete operators (f_1,f_2,f_3) are embedded in position update formula to guide the population. Then, self-best sets and one global-best set are defined to determine the self-best position and the global-best position, and non-dominated set update strategy is developed to renew the self-best sets and global-best set. To enhance the exploitation, iterated local search is implemented on the global-best set for a further search.

L. Zhang et al. (Eds.): AsiaSim 2016/SCS AutumnSim 2016, Part I, CCIS 643, pp. 603–612, 2016.
DOI: 10.1007/978-981-10-2663-8_62

2 The FJSP Model

2.1 Problem Description

Consider a n jobs $\times$ m machines system. We denote job set and machine set as $J = \{J_i | i = 1, 2, \ldots, n\}$ and $M = \{M_k | k = 1, 2, \ldots, m\}$, respectively. Job J_i has n_i operations, which is denoted as $O_i = \{O_{ij} | j = 1, 2, \ldots, n_i\}$ and each operation can be assigned to partial or all machines, which is denoted as M_s. FJSP is classified as two types, partial flexibility $(M_s \in M)$ and total flexibility $(M_s = M)$. The decision variable is denoted as χ_{ijk} and its process time is denoted as p_{ijk}. Three general objectives are given to optimize: (1) The makespan C_M; (2) The total workload W_T; (3) The maximal workload W_M.

$$C_M = \max_{1 \leq k \leq m} \{C_k\}$$

$$W_T = \sum_{i=1}^{n} \sum_{j=1}^{n_i} \sum_{k=1}^{m} p_{ijk} \chi_{ijk}$$

$$W_M = \max_{1 \leq k \leq m} \sum_{i=1}^{n} \sum_{j=1}^{n_i} p_{ijk} \chi_{ijk}$$

2.2 Encoding and Decoding

For FJSP, operation-based representation is introduced to encode operation sequence vector, and machine assignment vector is encoded by machine numbers with the ascending order of job number. For example, the vector [2 1 3 2 3 1] in Fig. 1(a) represents the order of operations $[O_{21}, O_{11}, O_{31}, O_{22}, O_{32}, O_{12}]$, and the vector [3 1 2 1 2 3] in Fig. 1(b) represents the machine assignment (O_{11}, M_3), (O_{12}, M_2), (O_{21}, M_1), (O_{22}, M_2), (O_{31}, M_1), (O_{32}, M_3). Decoding the representation to a semi-active schedule will lead a rise in makespan. Therefore, a left-shift function [6] is adopted to decode the representation of the FJSP.

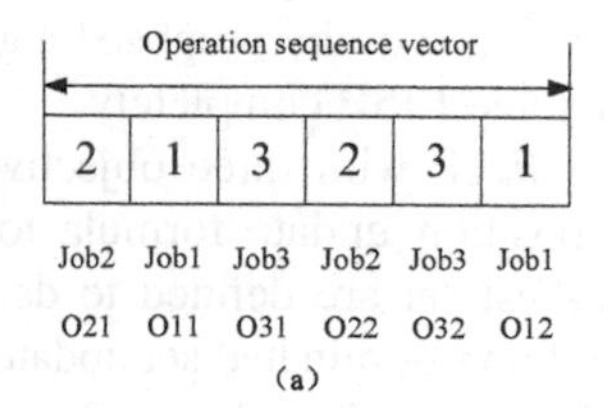

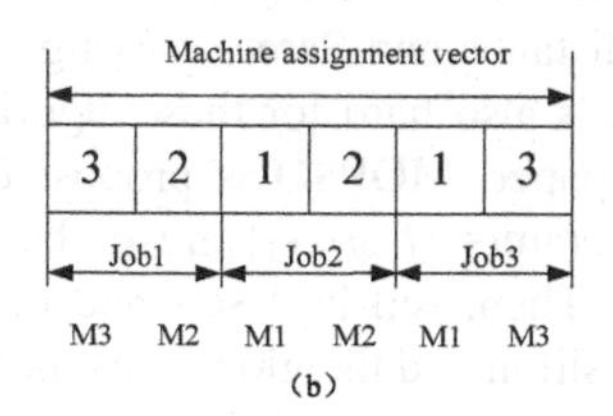

Fig. 1. Two-vector representation

3 The MOPSO for FJSP

3.1 Initialization

In this paper, operation sequence vector is initialized randomly. The assignment rules (AL) are valid dispatching rules for machine assignment vector [7]. To acquire high-quality assignment, three AL rules, which are proposed by Kacem et al. [7]., are used to dispatch the initial machines. 60 % of machine assignment vector are produced randomly, 20 % are produced by GPT, and 20 % are produced by LPT.

3.2 Theory of PSO

Particle swarm optimizer is a bio-inspired approach, which is developed by Kennedy and Eberhart [8], and attracts much attention for solving NP-hard problems due to its simplicity and efficiency. It has N particles and each particle has three attributes: velocity, position and self-best position. The population has a global-best position. Suppose the four attributes of particle i are denoted as $\boldsymbol{v}_i$, $\boldsymbol{x}_i$, $\boldsymbol{p}_i$ and $\boldsymbol{g}_{best}$, then the velocity $\boldsymbol{v}_i^{t+1}$ and position $\boldsymbol{x}_i^{t+1}$ can be calculated according to the followings:

$$\boldsymbol{v}_i^{t+1} = \omega \boldsymbol{v}_i^t + c_1 r_1 (\boldsymbol{p}_i^t - \boldsymbol{x}_i^t) + c_2 r_2 (\boldsymbol{g}_{best}^t - \boldsymbol{x}_i^t) \quad (1)$$

$$\boldsymbol{x}_i^{t+1} = \boldsymbol{x}_i^t + \boldsymbol{v}_i^{t+1} \quad (2)$$

where c_1, c_2 are two coefficients. ω is inertia weight. Two random number, r_1 and r_2, are in the range of (0, 1). t is present iteration.

3.3 The Detail of MOPSO

In our proposed algorithm, special discrete operators are embedded in PSO and the position $\boldsymbol{x}_i^{t+1}$ of MOPSO can be manipulated according to the followings:

$$\boldsymbol{x}_i^{t+1} = \omega \otimes f_1(\boldsymbol{x}_i^t) + c_1 \otimes f_2(\boldsymbol{x}_i^t, \boldsymbol{p}_i^t) + c_2 \otimes f_2(\boldsymbol{x}_i^t, \boldsymbol{g}_{best}^t) \quad (3)$$

where $\otimes$ is defined as probability operation, which means that the following operator will carry on with the corresponding probability. + means that the following operator will be implemented. ω, c_1 and c_2 are the probabilities. In detail, c_2 equals to $1 - c_1$ in our algorithm. f_1 and f_2 are two discrete operators. The details of these operators are introduced in Sect. 3.4.

3.4 The Discrete Operators

f_1 is applied to keeping the current particles unchanged and f_2 is to cross these particles with global-best position and self-best positions. f_3 is applied to the particle for exploring more other area. Two parents are PA_1 and PA_2; and two children are C_1 and

C_2. Two phases of f_2 is implemented and the phases are operation sequence phase and machine assignment phase. The first phase of f_2 works as follows:

Step 1. The length of machine assignment vector is l, and then randomly produce a vector R including l elements of integer 0 and 1.

Step 2. Find these places with the number '1' in R, and then copy the elements of PA_1 and PA_2 in the same places to C_1 and C_2, respectively.

Step 3. Remove the same operations of PA_2 that are included in C_1 and of PA_1 that are included in C_2, and then copy the rest elements of PA_2 and PA_1 to C_1 and C_2 in the same order, respectively.

The second phase of f_2 is multipoint preservative crossover (MPX) [9] and it works as follows:

Step 1. Find machine assignment vectors of PA_1 and PA_2.

Step 2. Use the same vector R, and find the locations equaling to 1 in R. And then exchange the machine of these locations in PA_1 and PA_2.

Step 3. Copy the rest machine in PA_1 and PA_2 to C_1 and C_2. Two phases of f_2 work as Fig. 2(a–b).

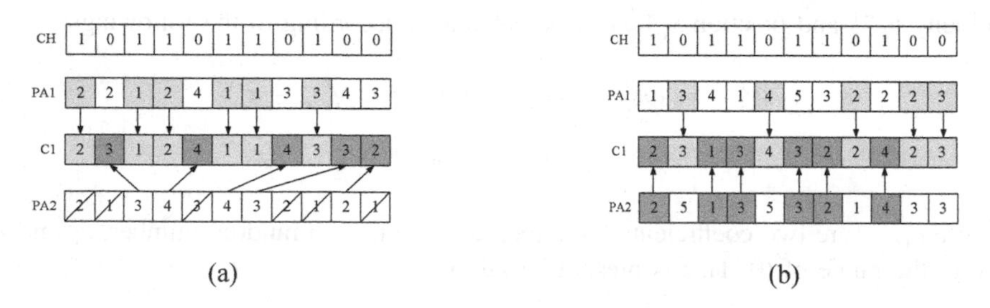

Fig. 2. Detail of f_2

The discrete operator f_3: Earliest completion machine (ECM) is more effective dispatching approach to reduce the makespan [10]. Therefore, with the probability c_3, we use the ECM rule to reduce the makespan. The ECM rule (f_3) proceeds as follows: According to the order in operation sequence vector, calculate completion time of each operation for all machines, and then selected the machine with minimal completion time for each operation.

3.5 Iterated Local Search (ILS)

ILS has strong exploiting ability and it can significantly improve the performance of algorithm [11]. Consequently, ILS is applied to exploit the neighborhoods of the global-best set. The procedure of ILS is illustrated in Algorithm 1.

Algorithm 1. Iterated Local Search

01: For every particle s in global-best set
02: $s' \leftarrow$ LocalSearch(s);
03: While ($r \le R_{max}$)
04: $s'' \leftarrow$ Produce a neighborhood $k\#$ of s'.
05: $s''' \leftarrow$ LocalSearch(s'').
06: If $s''' \succ s'$
$s' \leftarrow s'''$; $r \leftarrow 1$;
Else
$r \leftarrow r+1$.
End
07: End
08: $s \leftarrow s'$;
09: End

Where $s''' \succ s'$ represents s''' dominate s'. R_{max} is neighborhood type number and R_{max} equals to 2. In Algorithm 1, the neighborhoods are required to be defined and local search needs to implement. Unchanging critical paths cannot reduce the makespan. Therefore, two neighborhoods on critical operations and public critical block are defined as follows:

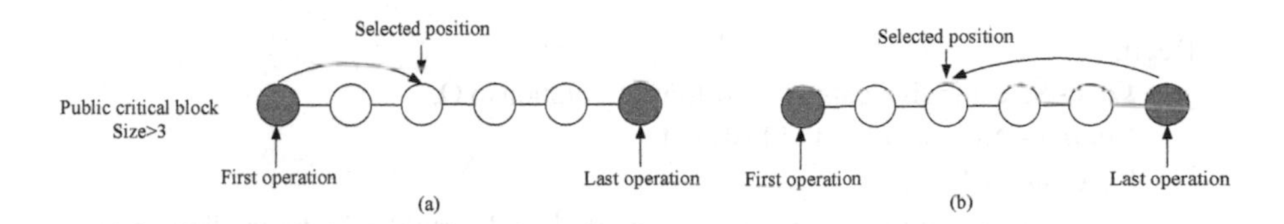

Fig. 3. Neighborhood 2#

Neighborhood 1#: Randomly choose a public critical operation O_{ij} of s with multi-optional machines and then randomly select another particle s' in global-best set. Find the assigned machine M'_k on the operation O_{ij} of s', then assign the machine M'_k to the operation O_{ij} of s.

Neighborhood 2#: Randomly select a public critical block π with more than three operations, and then select an random operation O_i^{π} different from the first operation or the last operation in π. And then insert the first operation or the last operation of the block π into a random selected position in π. Neighborhood 2# is illustrated in Fig. 3.

After the neighborhoods are defined, local search is implemented in Algorithm 2.

Algorithm 2. LocalSearch

01:For $k = 1$ to N_S

02: $s'' \leftarrow$ Produce a neighborhood $k\#$ of s'.

03: If $s'' \succ s'$

$s' = s''$.

End

04:End

Where N_S is the neighborhoods number and N_S equals to 10.

3.6 Global-Best Position and Self-best Positions

In this paper, each particle has a self-best set and the population has one global-best set. The limited size of each self-best set is N_p, and the limited size of global-best set is N_a. To restore the non-dominated solutions obtained by particle i, the self-best set Ω_i^{t+1} is selected from the last self-best set Ω_i^t and particle i by non-dominated set update strategy. To restore the non-dominated solutions obtained by the population, the global-best set Ω_a^{t+1} is selected from the last global-best set Ω_a^t and the non-dominated solutions Ω_x^t of the current population by non-dominated set update strategy. Here N_p=5, and N_a=15. Suppose the limited size of the set Ω is N'. The non-dominated set update strategy of Ω is as follows:

Begin

$\Omega_1 \leftarrow$ Select individuals with different solution in Ω.

Count $\leftarrow$ Number of individuals in Ω_1.

If $Count > N'$

Generates three random weights in $[0\ 1]$, and sort them in descending order.

Assign $\omega_1, \omega_2, \omega_3$ by these weights.

Calculate $\boldsymbol{F}$ for each individuals in Ω_1: $\boldsymbol{F} = \omega_1 f_1 + \omega_2 f_2 + \omega_3 f_3$.

Sort individuals in Ω_1 by $\boldsymbol{F}$ in ascending order.

$\Omega \leftarrow$ Select N_a individuals in Ω_1 with lower rank.

End

End

After updating self-best sets and global-best set, randomly select one position from its self-best set as its self-best position and randomly select one position from the global-best set as the global-best position. Base on the description, we give the MOPSO flowchart as shown in Fig. 4.

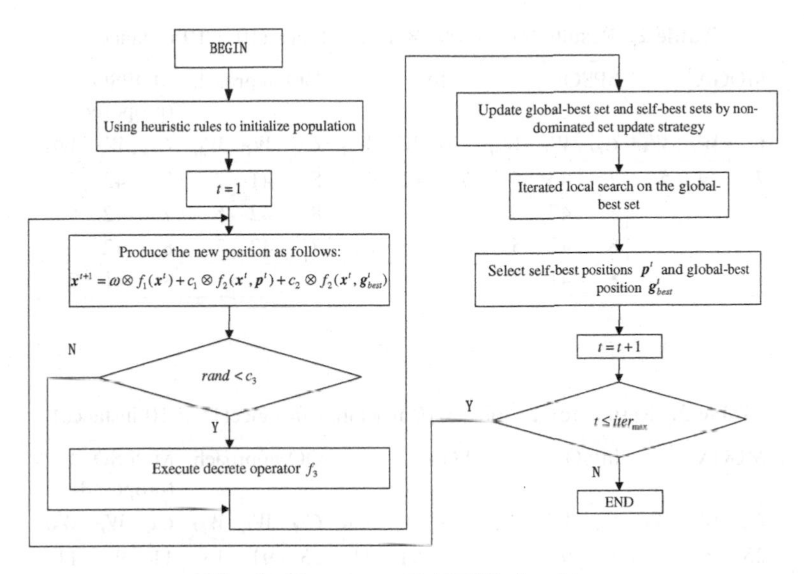

Fig. 4. Flowchart of MOPSO algorithm

4 Experiments and Results

Kacem instances [12] are considered to evaluate the performance of MOPSO. MOPSO is implemented on Lenovo PC with 4G RAM and 2.4G CPU. The software is Matlab 2011a. In order to obtain reliable results, each instance is tested ten times independently. The parameters are fixed experimentally: N=100, $iter_{\max}$=300, ω=0.98, c_1=0.6, c_2=0.4, c_3=0.02. The compared algorithms are MOGA [13], hPSO [14], hGA [15], OO approach [16] and their results are from the literature [16].

Tables 1, 2 and 3 lists the obtained solutions by five compared algorithms for 8 × 8 instance, 10 × 10 instance, 15 × 10 instance. For 15 × 10 instance, the best Gantt chart obtained by MOPSO is illustrated in Fig. 5. For 8 × 8 instance and 10 × 10 instance, MOPSO obtains more non-dominated solutions than that obtained by MOGA, hGA and OO approach, and obtains the same solutions as hPSO. For 15 × 10 instance, the solutions obtained by MOPSO dominates some solutions obtained by MOGA, hPSO and OO approach and obtains more non-dominated solutions than that obtained by

Table 1. Results for 8 jobs × 8 machines (8 × 8 instance)

MOGA			hPSO			hGA			OO approach			MOPSO (proposed)		
C_M	W_T	W_M	C_M	W_T	W_M	C_M	W_T	W_M	C_M	W_T	W_M	C_M	W_T	W_M
16	75	13	14	77	12	15	75	12	16	73	13	14	77	12
			15	75	12				15	75	12	15	75	12
			16	77	11							16	77	11
			16	73	13							16	73	13

Table 2. Results for 10 jobs × 10 machines (10 × 10 instance)

MOGA			hPSO			hGA			OO approach			MOPSO (proposed)		
C_M	W_T	W_M	C_M	W_T	W_M	C_M	W_T	W_M	C_M	W_T	W_M	C_M	W_T	W_M
7	44	5	7	43	5	7	43	5	8	41	7	7	43	5
			7	42	6				8	42	5	7	42	6
			8	42	5				7	43	7	8	42	5
			8	41	7							8	41	7

Table 3. Results for 15 jobs × 10 machines instance(15 × 10 instance)

MOGA			hPSO			hGA			OO approach			MOPSO (proposed)		
C_M	W_T	W_M	C_M	W_T	W_M	C_M	W_T	W_M	C_M	W_T	W_M	C_M	W_T	W_M
23	99	11	11	91	11	11	91	11	13	91	13	11	91	11
			12	93	10				14	91	12	11	93	10
			11	95	10									

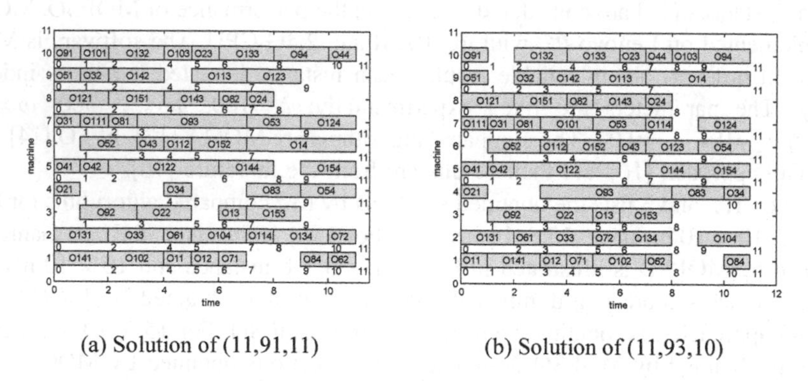

(a) Solution of (11,91,11)

(b) Solution of (11,93,10)

Fig. 5. Gantt chart of 15 jobs 10 machines

hGA. The comparisons show that the performance of MOPSO is superior to the other four algorithms.

5 Conclusions and Future Work

Multi-objective FJSP is hard to solve and we developed a discrete PSO with iterated local search to strengthen exploitation ability for solving FJSP. Discrete operators are used in MOPSO to deal with discrete variables, then the self-best sets and global-best set are defined to restore non-dominated solutions. ILS integrating two neighborhoods is applied to improve the local search capability of the proposed MOSPO. The results implemented on Matlab show the improved performance of MOPSO for FJSP. The future work will concentrate attention upon more robust algorithm for addressing real job shop problems.

Acknowledgement. This work is supported by the National High-tech Research and Development Projects of China (Project No: 2014AA041505), by the National Natural Science Foundation of China (Project No: 61572238), by the Provincial Outstanding Youth Foundation of Jiangsu Province (BK20160001).

References

1. Shao, X., Liu, W., Liu, Q., et al.: Hybrid discrete particle swarm optimization for multi-objective flexible job-shop scheduling problem. Int. J. Adv. Manufact. Technol. **67**(9–12), 2885–2901 (2013)
2. Jia, S., Hu, Z.H.: Path-relinking Tabu search for the multi-objective flexible job shop scheduling problem. Comput. Oper. Res. **47**(9), 11–26 (2014)
3. Li, Y., Chen, Y.: An improved genetic algorithm of bi-level coding for flexible job shop scheduling problems. J. Netw. **9**(7), 1783–1789 (2014)
4. Song, L.B., Xue-Jun, X.U., Sun, Y.M.: A hybrid genetic algorithm for flexible job shop scheduling problem. J. Manage. Sci. China **890**(11), 1179–1184 (2010)
5. Nouiri, M., Bekrar, A., Jemai, A., et al.: An effective and distributed particle swarm optimization algorithm for flexible job-shop scheduling problem. J. Intell. Manufact. 1–13 (2015)
6. Li, J., Pan, Q., Liang, Y.C.: An effective hybrid tabu search algorithm for multi-objective flexible job-shop scheduling problems. Comput. Ind. Eng. **59**(4), 647–662 (2010)
7. Kacem, I., Hammadi, S., Borne, P.: Approach by localization and multiobjective evolutionary optimization for flexible job-shop scheduling problems. IEEE Trans. Syst. Man Cybern. Part C Appl. Rev. **32**(1), 1–13 (2002)
8. Kenndy, J., Eberhart, R.C.: Particle swarm optimization. In: Proceedings of IEEE International Conference on Neural Networks, vol. 4, pp. 1942–1948 (1995)
9. Zhang, C.Y., Rao, Y.Q., Li, P.G., Shao, X.Y.: Bilevel genetic algorithm for the flexible job-shop scheduling problem. Chin. J. Mech. Eng. **43**(4), 119–124 (2007)
10. Lin, J.: A hybrid biogeography-based optimization for the fuzzy flexible job-shop scheduling problem. Know. Based Syst. **78**(C), 59–74 (2015)
11. Lourenço, H.R, Martin, O.C., Stützle, T.: Iterated local search: framework and applications. In: Handbook of Metaheuristics, pp. 363–397. Springer, Heidelberg (2010)
12. Kacem, I., Hammadi, S., Borne, P.: Pareto-optimality approach for flexible job-shop scheduling problems: hybridization of evolutionary algorithms and fuzzy logic. Math. Comput. Simul. **60**(3), 245–276 (2002)
13. Saad, I., Hammadi, S., Benrejeb, M., et al.: Choquet integral for criteria aggregation in the flexible job-shop scheduling problems. Math. Comput. Simul. **76**(5), 447–462 (2008)
14. Shao, X., Liu, W., Liu, Q., et al.: Hybrid discrete particle swarm optimization for multi-objective flexible job-shop scheduling problem. Int. J. Adv. Manufact. Technol. **67**(9–12), 2885–2901 (2013)

15. Gao, J., Gen, M., Sun, L., et al.: A hybrid of genetic algorithm and bottleneck shifting for multiobjective flexible job shop scheduling problems. Comput. Ind. Eng. **53**(1), 149–162 (2007)
16. Kaplanoğlu, V.: An object-oriented approach for multi-objective flexible job-shop scheduling problem. Expert Syst. Appl. **45**(C), 71–84 (2016)

Series Capacitors Configuration in Distribution Network Considering Power Loss and Voltage Quality

Zhi Gong[1,2](✉), Weiwei Xu[1](✉), Xiaoming Huang[1](✉), and Dong Liu[3](✉)

[1] State Grid Zhejiang Electric Power Research Institute, Hangzhou, Zhejiang, China
gongzhi1994@163.com, vvvvei@126.com, 13605717725@139.com

[2] Electric Engineering College, Zhejiang University, Hangzhou, Zhejiang, China

[3] Shanghai Jiao Tong University, Shanghai, China
dongliu@sjtu.edu.cn

Abstract. Series capacitors are usually used in transmission networks to improve voltage quality. Practice has proved that distribution-fixed series capacitors (D-FSC) also play an important role in improving voltage quality and reducing power loss. How D-FSC impacts the voltage profile and power loss in a radical circuit with distributed loads is discussed. The method to determine the configuration of D-FSC considering power loss and voltage deviation through Matlab-based load flow calculation and GA optimization is discussed at the end of the paper.

Keywords: D-FSC · Voltage quality · Power loss · Radical distribution network

1 Introduction

Voltage is an important index of power quality, and power loss has a great impact on network economy. It is proved that the irrationality of reactive configuration usually causes low voltage along radical distribution network. Constant power loads draw more current under low voltage condition, which increases the power loss. In some cases where the distribution line is long and power facilities are relatively aged, the power loss is usually relatively high and under voltage occurs at the end of the network [1]. High voltage deviation sometimes can be dangerous, especially for voltage-sensitive loads, causing damage proportional to the square of the voltage deviation [2].

Series capacitors are generally installed in transmission networks. It enhances power system stability and transmission capacity [3, 4]. Practice has proved that it is also effective in distribution networks [2, 5–8]. Distribution-fixed series capacitors (D-FSC) reduce the inductive reactance, raise voltage and have advantages such as self-adaption and real-time response comparing with shunt capacitors. Therefore, D-FSC is an important facility to improve voltage quality and reduce power loss.

L. Zhang et al. (Eds.): AsiaSim 2016/SCS AutumnSim 2016, Part I, CCIS 643, pp. 613–621, 2016.
DOI: 10.1007/978-981-10-2663-8_63

Nowadays, D-FSC is widely researched around the world. Paper [5, 6] analyze and model the D-FSC in detail and discuss the theory, application, advantages and disadvantages compared with other compensation facilities. Paper [5] points out the rough location of D-FSC, but the exact location is not discussed. GA and other optimization methods are used in paper [2, 7] to minimize the power loss or voltage deviation, but the way to minimize both of them and provide specific capacitor location needs more study. Former studies usually only focus on distribution network with single lump load at the end of the circuit, and the distributed loads are not considered [8, 9]. Paper [10] discusses the optimal location of series capacitors in high-voltage transmission networks. Whether its conclusion applicable in distribution network remains to be studied. Therefore, how the exact location and capacitive reactance of D-FSC in one radical distribution network impacts power loss and voltage profile requires more research, and the method minimizing both power loss and voltage deviation should be discussed, which can reduce damage to load and improve network economy.

This paper puts forward a method to determine the location and capacitive reactance of D-FSC in one radical network using Matlab-based load flow calculation and GA optimization algorithm. The goal of the method is to install capacitors of appropriate capacitive reactance at the proper location, minimizing the power loss and voltage deviation. GA algorithm is widely used in optimization problems, for example paper [7, 8, 11], but this algorithm hasn't been used in this problem. This paper applies GA algorithm to solve a multi-objective optimization problem. How the exact location and capacitive reactance of D-FSC in one radical distribution network impacts power loss and voltage profile is also studied in this paper.

2 Calculation Method

2.1 Power Flow Calculation and GA Algorithm

Apply Backward/Forward Sweep Power Flow Algorithms in Matlab. This algorithm is useful in radical networks and has good convergence property.

The power flow calculation is separated into two parts. The first program imports the load and network structure information into the workspace, and the second program calculates the power flow along the network and exports voltages of each node and the total power loss. When analyzing a network with series capacitors, change the first program to update the network structure, and then execute power flow calculation. This paper focuses on the location and capacitive reactance of D-FSC, so the first program has 2 inputs: (1) the length from the load upstream to the capacitor (km); (2) the capacitive reactance of capacitors (ohm).

To apply GA algorithm, gatool in Matlab is used. GA algorithm searches for the global minimum of the fitness function and avoids local minimums, which makes this algorithm a good way to solve optimization problems. Specify the fitness function and nonlinear constraints in gatool, and the solver will give results. Notice that gatool doesn't need a starting point for iteration, thus the optimization results may be slightly different when the calculation is carried out for several times repeatedly.

2.2 Optimization Problem

The total power loss ΔP is calculated by power flow program. Therefore, the power flow calculation is integrated into the objective function. The power flow program outputs ΔP to workspace, and then the objective function invokes ΔP.

In order to quantify the voltage deviation, we define [2]:

$$\emptyset = \sum\nolimits_{i=1}^{m} (\frac{U_i - U_N}{U_N})^2$$

Where: m is the amount of loads in the radical distribution network; U_i is the voltage of the i-th load (kV); U_N is the rated voltage of the network (kV). Smaller $\emptyset$ means smaller voltage deviation.

It is obvious that ΔP and $\emptyset$ are in different order of magnitude and have different dimensions, so it is necessary to normalize them before analysis. Normalization method is shown as follows.

$$\tilde{f} = \frac{f - f_{min}}{f_{max} - f_{min}}$$

Where: f is the function before normalization; $\tilde{f}$ is the function after normalization; f_{max} and f_{min} are the maximum and minimum of the original function. This optimization problem has 2 objectives, so consider integrating them with weight factor ω after normalization. The objective function is shown as follows [11].

$$\min F(x_1, x_{2,}) = \omega * \tilde{f}_1 + (1 - \omega) * \tilde{f}_2$$

Where: ω is the weight factor ranging from 0 to 1.

The objective function is calculated under constraints (including but not confined to):

$$0 \le l \le l_{max}$$
$$0 \le X_c$$
$$abs(U - U_N) \le U_N * 7\%$$

Other constraints can be included if necessary.

3 Voltage Profile and Power Loss After Applying D-FSC

To illustrate clearly how D-FSC configuration influences voltage profile and power loss along a distribution network, we analyze the 2 parameters separately before conclusion.

Firstly, fix the location of capacitors and change the capacitive reactance, and the voltage along the circuit is shown as follow.

In Fig. 1, vertical lines indicate the locations of loads. Curve A shows the voltage before applying D-FSC. Capacitive reactance (X_c) of curve B, C and D are 6 O, 8 O and 10 O respectively (assuming no over-compensation).

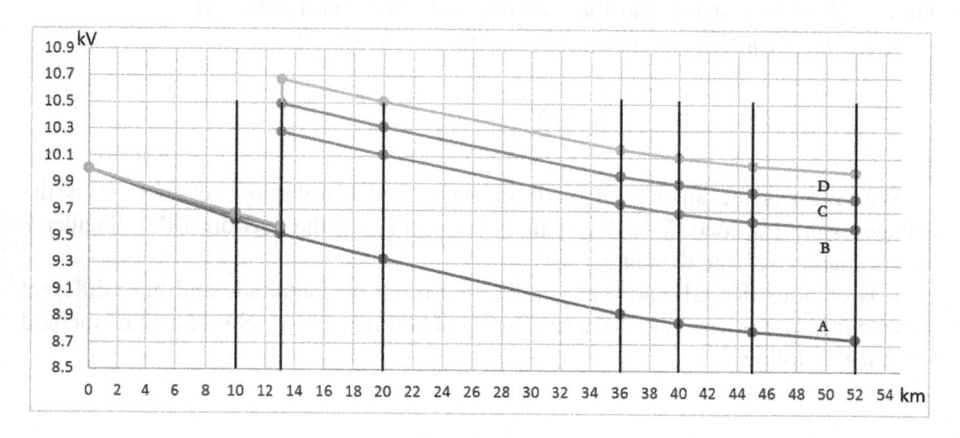

Fig. 1. Voltage profile after applying D-FSC

As is shown in Fig. 1, the circuit experiences a voltage boost at the location of D-FSC. With the increase of X_c, the voltage boost becomes stronger. Notice that voltage of nodes upstream the capacitors also rises. This is because loads downstream draw less current from the network and thus reduces the power loss. Therefore, it is obvious that with the increase of X_c, all load nodes voltage will rise, and the power loss will decrease.

Then we fix X_c and change the location of capacitors. This situation is trickier and requires more discussion. The voltage profile is shown as follow.

In Fig. 2, vertical lines indicate the location of loads. Curve A shows the voltage profile before applying D-FSC. Curve B, C and D fix X_c as 15.6 O (assuming no over-compensation) and install D-FSC at different locations. In case C, the capacitors are installed upstream the load at 20 km.

If we move the capacitors between 2 neighbor nodes, i.e. C and D, then all voltages of nodes will not change. Therefore, the current drown by loads stays constant, and power loss also stays constant.

If we move the capacitors across nodes, i.e. B and D, the situation will be different. In case B, only 4 loads are downstream the D-FSC, so the current via capacitors is relatively smaller. Therefore, the voltage boost is also smaller, causing all node voltages lower than case D and power loss higher than case D. In order to get the same voltage as case D, we have to increase X_c in case B, which may not be economy.

Above all, capacitors should be installed upstream the node from which voltage is lower than limit. Then calculate power loss separately when capacitors are put between different load nodes. For example, node 4 is under voltage originally, so the capacitors can be put between node 1 and 2, node 2 and 3, node 3 and 4. For each case, in order to minimize the power loss, capacitors should be installed at the downstream node, and

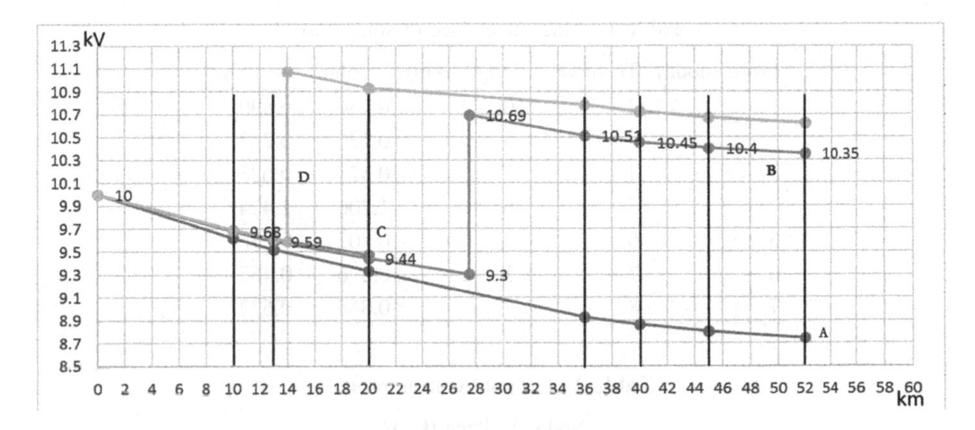

Fig. 2. Voltage profile after applying D-FSC

adjust the X_c until the voltage of this node reaches limit. This configuration ensures minimum power loss. Finally, compare the power loss of each case and find the minimum power loss.

Notice that capacitor configuration calculated to minimize power loss may cause relatively high voltage deviation from rated value. This is the reason why this paper introduces voltage deviation as a consideration in capacitor configuration.

4 Study Case

We consider a radical distribution network with several distributed load. The network is shown as Fig. 3.

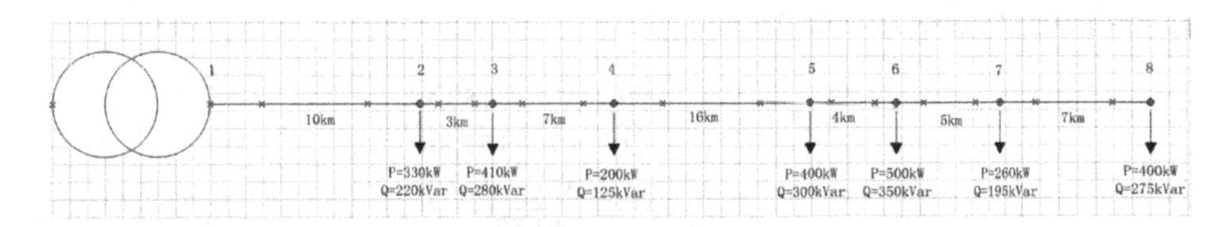

Fig. 3. Study case

The rated voltage is 10 kV. All lines are overhead wire, and capacitance of lines are ignored. Load P and Q are shown in Fig. 3, and we assume all loads are constant P loads. Line impedance are shown in Table 1.

All node voltages may deviate from rated value at most 7 %.

Run power flow calculation on Matlab, and the voltage profile before applying D-FSC is shown in Table 2. The total power loss is 207.45 kW.

It can be seen in Table 2 that from node 5 the voltage is below the lower limit, and capacitors should be installed before node 5.

Table 1. Line impedance of study case

From (node)	To (node)	Length (km)	R (ohm)	X (ohm)
1	2	10	0.754	0.890
2	3	3	0.226	0.267
3	4	7	0.528	0.623
4	5	16	1.206	1.424
5	6	4	0.302	0.356
6	7	5	0.496	0.465
7	8	7	0.868	0.672

Table 2. Original voltage profile

Node	Voltage (kV)
1	10.000
2	9.619
3	9.519
4	9.326
5	8.932
6	8.859
7	8.796
8	8.735

Since the voltage of node 4 is quite close to the lower limit, we put the capacitor between node 3 and node 4. Determine the objective function first to apply GA algorithm. Because series capacitors increase every node's voltage, the maximum ΔP is the original power loss (i.e. Without capacitors, 207.45 kW). Then put the capacitor right before node 4, adjust capacitive reactance and run power flow until the voltage of node 4 reaches upper limit, and now ΔP reaches its minimum 157.88 kW. Therefore, the normalized expression of ΔP is:

$$\Delta P(\widetilde{l, X_c}) = \frac{\Delta P(l, X_c) - 157.88}{207.45 - 157.88} = \frac{\Delta P(l, X_c) - 157.88}{49.57}$$

The maximum and minimum of Φ is calculated by GA algorithm. The objective function is Φ, and constraints are illustrated in Sect. 2.2. The results are as follows:

$$\emptyset_{min} = 0.009030592, \ \emptyset_{max} = 0.071675551$$

Therefore, the normalized expression of Φ is:

$$\emptyset(\widetilde{l, X_c}) = \frac{\emptyset(l, X_c) - 0.009030592}{0.062644959}$$

The objective function is as follows:

$$\min F(l, X_c, \omega) = \omega * \frac{\Delta P(l, X_c) - 157.88}{49.57} + (1 - \omega) * \frac{\emptyset(l, X_c) - 0.009030592}{0.062644959}$$

The constraints are:

$$0 \leq l \leq 7;$$

$$0 \leq X_c;$$

$$abs(U - U_N) \leq 0.7$$

Weight factor ω represents the emphasis on power loss and voltage deviation. Now we change ω from 0 to 1 with step 0.1, run GA algorithm, and results are as follows (Table 3).

Table 3. GA optimization results

Case	ω	$1 - \omega$	L (km)	X_c (ohm)
1	0	1.0	1.82	8.12
2	0.1	0.9	3.14	8.58
3	0.2	0.8	4.98	9.18
4	0.3	0.7	7	9.96
5	0.4	0.6	7	10.85
6	0.5	0.5	7	12.31
7	0.6	0.4	7	13.06
8	0.7	0.3	7	13.06
9	0.8	0.2	7	13.06
10	0.9	0.1	7	13.06
11	1.0	0	7	13.06

According to the study case, L should be between 0 km and 7 km, and all node voltages should not be lower than 9.3 kV nor higher than 10.7 kV. Because of these constraints, case 7 ~ 11 have the same optimization result.

It can be implied that the more attention paid to power loss (i.e. higher ω), the optimization results become closer to the conclusion stated in Sect. 3. Especially in case 11, when we completely ignore the voltage deviation, the optimization result shows that we should put the capacitor before node 4, and the X_c renders that voltage of node 4 reaches upper limit, which is exactly what has been discussed in Sect. 3.

On the other hand, the more attention we pay to voltage profile (i.e. lower ω), the capacitor should be installed closer to node 3, and X_c is also smaller, which guarantees smaller Φ.

As is analyzed above, the configuration that minimize Φ and the configuration that minimize ΔP are opposite. In order to determine the final configuration, we need to specify ω first according to realities, economy and so on. Then run the GA algorithm and get results.

5 Conclusion and Future Work

This paper analyzes how the location and capacitive reactance of D-FSC in a radical distribution network influence the voltage profile and power loss. A new method considering minimization of voltage deviation and power loss using Matlab power flow and GA algorithm is presented. This paper studied how D-FSC influence both line loss and voltage deviation in distributed load network, which lacks research previously. The presented method normalizes power loss and voltage deviation, integrates them with weight factor ω, and then solve the optimization problem by GA algorithm. The results of the study case correspond with former studies and provide a reference for practical projects.

There are still a few questions need further discussion.

- Voltage constraints. In this paper, one of the nonlinear constraints is that all node voltages should not deviate from rated value at most 7 %. In reality, there can be some loads which require more accurate voltage, and different nodes may have different voltage requirements. If so, these requirements should be specified in nonlinear constraints, and other nodes with low requirement of voltage may not be included in the constraints to improve the convergence of the algorithm.
- Complex load model. This paper assumes that all loads are constant power loads. In fact, some constant Z loads are integrated with constant power loads. Furthermore, P and Q of some loads are function of frequency and node voltage. Considering the periodic load change during a day or a year, the load model can be more complex. For purpose of more accurate and comprehensive calculation, these complex load models can be integrated into Matlab power flow procedure.
- Weight factor ω. As is illustrated in Sect. 4, ω has a great impact on the final result of optimization. Therefore the way to determine ω needs more studied. ω should be related to the property of loads, the structure of network, the operation of the power grid and so on. For example, if all loads are civil and have no voltage-sensitive loads, ω can be relatively higher. If there are some loads which require less voltage deviation, we should evaluate ω in a proper way before optimization.
- Percent of compensation k. k is defined as follows:

$$k = \frac{X_c}{X_E} * 100\,\%$$

Where: X_E is the total inductive reactance from the source to the location of capacitors. The value of k ranges from 0 to1. So it is a constraint for X_c. Notice that external grid feeding the distribution network can be equivalent to a power source and a reactive resistance. The reactive resistance is included in X_E, but its value is usually unknown. In order to avoid over-compensation, it is advised to determine X_E first.

References

1. Xiao-liang, D.A.I.: Application of reactive compensation technology for distribution network. Power Syst. Technol. **23**(6), 1–7 (1999). (in Chinese)
2. Bucatariu, I., Coroiu, F.: Optimal location of series capacitor in radial distribution networks with distributed load. IEEE 978-1-4244-8782-0/11/$26.00 ©2011
3. Del Rosso, A.D., Cañizares, C.A., Doña, V.M.: A study of TCSC controller design for power system stability improvement. IEEE Trans. Power Syst. **18**(4), 1487–1496 (2003)
4. Xian-zhang, L.E.I.: Series compensation for a long distance AC transmission system. Power Syst. Technol. **22**(11), 35–38 (1998)
5. Miske, S.A.: Considerations for the application of series capacitors to radial power distribution circuits. IEEE Trans. Power Delivery **16**(2), 306–318 (2001)
6. Zhuo, G., Jiang, D., Liang, Y., Lian, X., Liang, C.: A research of D-FSC for improving voltage quality in distribution networks. Power Syst. Protect. Control **41**(8), 61–67 (2013). (in Chinese)
7. Das, S., Das, D.: Series capacitor compensation for radial distribution networks. In: 2011 IEEE PES Innovative Smart Grid Technologies – India (2011)
8. Zhang, L., Ai, S., Gao, F., Zhou, X., Huang, Y.: Comprehensive energy savings evaluation of the fixed series capacitor compensation in distribution network. Power Syst. Technol. **40**, 276–282 (2016)
9. Zhao, W., Wang, D.: Application analysis of series reactive power compensation in distribution network. Low Voltage Apparatus **5**, 37–44 (2010). (in Chinese)
10. Tai-jun, L.I.: Research on selecting the location of series compensation. Electric Power **42** (9), 42–47 (2009). (in Chinese)
11. Wei, L., Zhao, B., Wu, H., Zhang, X.: Optimal allocation model of energy storage system in virtual power plant environment with a high penetration of distributed photovoltaic generation. Autom. Electr. Power Syst. **39**(23), 66–74 (2015). (in Chinese)

Collaborative Planning Capacities in Distribution Centers

Mauricio Becerra Fernández[1(✉)], Elsa Cristina González La Rotta[1(✉)], Milton Mauricio Herrera Ramírez[2(✉)], and Olga Rosana Romero Quiroga[3(✉)]

[1] Engineering Faculty, Catholic University of Colombia, Bogotá, Colombia
{mbecerra,ecgonzalez}@ucatolica.edu.co,
mauriciobecerrafernandez@gmail.com
[2] Engineering of Markets, Pilot University of Colombia, Bogotá, Colombia
milton-herrera@upc.edu.co
[3] Suppla S.A., Technical Management, Bogotá, Colombia
olga.romero@suppla.com, olgarosana@gmail.com

Abstract. Horizontal collaboration allows the competitors in the market to cooperate in logistics processes. This research proposes the development of a dynamic model for resource planning of a logistics operator in distribution centers processes, in which strategies of collaboration and non-collaboration are contrasted considering performance measures of demand growth and the use of resources. The model is developed using system dynamics approach, considering representative information of a logistics operator in the Colombian market as a case of study. Results indicate that horizontal collaborative planning affects the demand's growth and the level of resources used for the logistics operator, improving system performance and impacting positively the competitiveness of the companies involved.

Keywords: Horizontal collaboration · Logistics capacities · Distribution center · System dynamics

1 Introduction

The national government in Colombia has defined logistics as one of the key factors in achieving the goal of being one of the three most competitive countries in Latin America by 2032 [1]. This goal was defined under the National System for Competitiveness and Innovation, based on achieving an export economy of goods and services with high benefits and innovation.

However, according to the World Economic Forum and the Global Competitiveness Report (2014–2015) [2]. Colombia is ranked 66 in the world, surpassed in Latin America by Chile, Panama, Costa Rica, Brazil, Mexico and Peru, ranked 33, 48, 51, 57, 61, 65 respectively, exhibiting that one of the most backward factors is the inadequate infrastructure and logistics networks. Also, the Logistic Performance Index LPI developed by the World Bank [3], places the country in 97th out of 160 countries evaluated, showing deficiencies in logistics competences, which can be reflected in the behavior of logistics costs, which in Colombia reached 18 % of the total cost [4], exceeding all

L. Zhang et al. (Eds.): AsiaSim 2016/SCS AutumnSim 2016, Part I, CCIS 643, pp. 622–632, 2016.
DOI: 10.1007/978-981-10-2663-8_64

regions, including the overall average for Latin America. Even in winter, logistics costs in Colombia can reach up to 22 %.

According to Guasch [5], distribution of logistics costs in Latin America and the Caribbean focuses on storage processes and inventory management (reaching 38 %), making distribution centers strategic nodes to encourage strategies towards more efficient logistics.

Additionally, after evaluating the implementation of collaborative processes in distribution centers, mainly in logistics operators (85 %), there is evidence that load generators are still delimiting requirements to their own needs under models of exclusivity, this being a common practice at the time of outsource logistics operation storage and inventory management [6].

This reveals the need to develop strategies to increase productivity and competitiveness for more efficient logistics operations, with responsibility for logistics operators, providing solutions which integrate the diverse needs of companies that have the ability to be agglomerated and form close collaborative processes to improve their performance. Hence, regarding the importance of the implementation of the collaborative capacities model in distribution centers, specifically for logistics operators in the Colombian context, it's important to take into account the complexity in managing supply chains, the allocation capacity against fluctuations in demand, the uncertainty in the availability of resources, and the generation of satisfactory financial results for all stakeholders, being necessary to address the problem from a dynamic perspective.

Within the system dynamics models for capacity planning, there are [7–10]. Some are applied in manufacturing [11, 12]. In the field of telecommunications are [13–20]. In the case of project planning are [21, 22]. In public, medical, recruitment, and financial services it highlights [23–28].

According to the literature review, collaborative logistics subject has been addressed as the vertical integration of the various links of the supply chain, developing strategies such as demand planning or synergies along the logistics network, but not with a collaborative perspective among companies within the same sector. Horizontal integration could generate synergy due to the similarity of characteristics and homogeneity of target markets. This could lead companies to be integrated through a key player as it's the logistics operator, specialist in the efficiencies generation, with plenty opportunity to collaborative planning capacities resulting from sectorial integration, which can impact its efficiency, obtaining better financial results and business's growth, reflecting the motivation generated in the market and whose benefits can be shared to customers, depending on the quality of processes and competitive logistics costs.

The development of the model, seeks to test the dynamic hypothesis, which considers that in order for a logistics operator to plan collaboratively the resources from the aggregate demand of its customers in distribution centers, logistics performance measures are improved, increasing demand and resource use.

2 Simulation Model

The implemented methodology begins with the formulation of the research problem, so that it can establish the hypothesis under study and then design model to represent adequately the system, identifying the necessary elements for its operationalization and subsequent measurement (see Fig. 1).

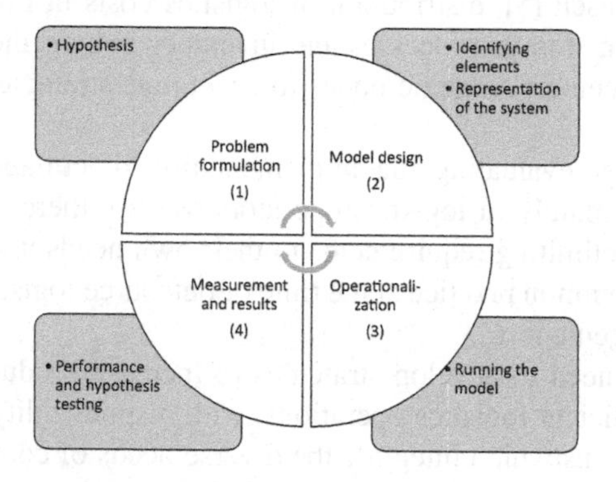

Fig. 1. Methodology

The model developed in this research was conducted using simulation software iThink, supported by other software such as SPSS, Microsoft Excel and StatFit, with information provided by a Colombian logistics operator.

2.1 Causal Loops Diagram (CLD)

Relationships between the model variables can be seen through the causal loop diagram, which represents the ratio of demand behavior associated with capacity and its effect on financial behavior, as shown in the Fig. 2.

The dynamic behavior of the system and its effects are analyzed through the feedback loops as discussed below.

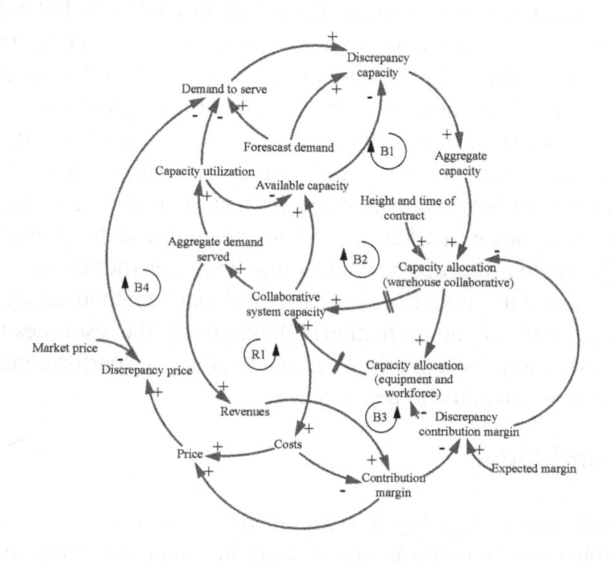

Fig. 2. Causal diagram loop

Effect on Demand and System Capacity. The demand for logistics positions in the distribution center is affected by the ability of collaborative system, determined by the allocation of resources, space, labor and equipment mobilization, that from an aggregate demand planning, allows a better use of resources. The feedback connection to demand is evident on the balancing loop B1, acting as a target to meet and the balancing loop B2 seeks stabilization in the use of available resources, generating an oscillatory effect on the demand due to the delay in the allocation of resources.

Financial Effect. Served and aggregate demand, and the capacity allocated to address it, generates effects at the cost level. Price and total income received influences the gross margin of the logistics operation. The effects are reflected in the loops described below.

- Cost. The collaborative system capacity depends on the availability of monetary resources, i.e. it affects the allocation of resources for policy compliance profitability of the operation. This allocation of resources, generates operating costs which in turn affects the gross margin. The feedback connection is evident in the balancing loop B3, seeking the stabilization of the logistics cost by the effect of oscillation.
- Price. The result of the logistics operation, generates a price storage position in the distribution center, which when contrasted with the market price, calculates a discrepancy that encourages positive or negative demand, affecting costs by resource allocation and income earned, focusing on gross margin. The feedback connection is evident in the balancing loop B4, seeking the stabilization of price and logistics oscillation effect.
- Income. Aggregate served demand, can be affected by an income effect of executed sales, affecting the gross margin, which in order to meet expected margin policies enables the allocation of resources to demand attention. A positive feedback loop is evident in R1, seeking growth but exhibiting oscillations effects for the delay in the capacity allocation.

2.2 Capacities Model

The model focuses on behavioral analysis of capabilities for the provision of logistics services in distribution centers, so that growth must be determined following the financial policies and techniques [29].

Aggregate Demand for the Logistics Positions (D_{ilk}). Defined as the amount of logistical positions projected in the month *i* according to the height *l* and lease time *k*.

Required Capacity of Logistics Positions (Cn_{ilk}). Defined as the amount of logistics positions required depending on the discrepancy in demand to serve and existing capacity in the system, in the month *i* according to the height *l*, and lease time *k*.

Installed Capacity of Logistics Positions (CI_{ilk}). Defined as the total number of logistical positions usable in the available space in the month *i* according to the height *l* and lease time *k*.

Capacity Utilization of Logistics Positions (CU_{ilk}). Total logistics positions used in accordance with the demand to meet and the system's capacity in the month *i* according to the height *l* and lease time *k*.

Equipment Required Capacity (CE_{ilk}). Defined as the amount of mobilization equipment in the month *i* according to the height *l* and lease time *k*.

Equipment Installed Capacity (CIE_{ilk}). Defined as the number of logistics positions to deal with mobilization equipment allocated in the month *i* according to the height *l* and lease time *k*.

Equipment Capacity Utilization (CUE_{ilk}). Equivalence between the positions used and equipment allocated according to demand to meet and the system's capacity in the month *i* according to the height *l* and lease time *k*.

Necessary Workforce Capacity (CF_{ilk}). Defined as the necessary labor force in the month *i* according to the height *l* and lease time *k*.

Installed Capacity by the Workforce (CIF_{ji}). Defined as the number of logistics positions to meet according to the available labor force *j* in the month *i*.

Capacity Utilization Equipment (CUF_{ilk}). Logistics positions used equivalent to the workforce allocated according to demand to meet and the system's capacity in the month *i* according to the height *l* and lease time *k*.

System Capacity (CS_{ilk}). Number of logistics positions able to serve in the month *i* according to the height *l* and lease time *k*.

$$CS_{ilk} = Min\{CIE_{ilk};CIF_{ilk};CI_{ilk}\} \tag{1}$$

Discrepancy Capacity (DS_{ilk}). Defined as the difference between the capacity of the system (CS_{ilk}) and the logistics positions aggregated demand (D_{ilk}).

Discrepancy Margin (DSF_i). Defined as the difference between the achieved margin and expected margin in the month *i*.

Price Discrepancy (DSP_i). Defined as the difference between the price for logistics position offered for the company and the market price for logistics position in the month *i*.

Idle Capacity (CO_{ilk}). Defined as the difference of installed capacity minus used capacity.

$$Co_{ilk} = CI_{ilk} - CU_{ilk} \tag{2}$$

Capacity Allocation. Allocation of the volumetric space capacity, equipment and labor are subject to the discrepancy of the desired range versus the achieved margin.

- Assigning volumetric capacity. This must comply with a maximum allowable discrepancy of the expected margin and a constant need for the last 6 months, greater than or equal to 3500 m^2 for warehouse between 8 and 12 meters height and 2500 m^2 for warehouse 16 meters height.

$$\text{Warehouse 8–12 m: } DSF_{ilk} < 0,5 \wedge \frac{\sum_{i=1}^{6} DS_{ilk}}{6} \geq 3500 \tag{3}$$

$$\text{Warehouse 16 m: } DSF_{ilk} < 0,5 \wedge \frac{\sum_{i=1}^{6} DS_{ilk}}{6} \geq 2500 \tag{4}$$

Capacity Allocation in Equipment and Workforce. This must meet a maximum permitted discrepancy less than the expected margin.

$$DSF_{ilk} < 0,5 \tag{5}$$

2.3 System Dynamics Model

Sectors Definition. The logistics distribution center requires various components, which are structured to provide the service and are represented through the sectors that characterize the system.

- Demand and volumetric capacity of the system. Generates demand to be served and logistics positions capacity.
- Equipment mobilization. Resource which is assigned as part of the total system capacity.
- Workforce (employees). Resource which is assigned as part of the total system capacity.
- Financial performance. Associated with the behavior of costs by the allocation of resources, income and price offered to the market, which determines the viability and business continuity.

The stock and flow diagram for the system dynamics model is shown in the Fig. 3.

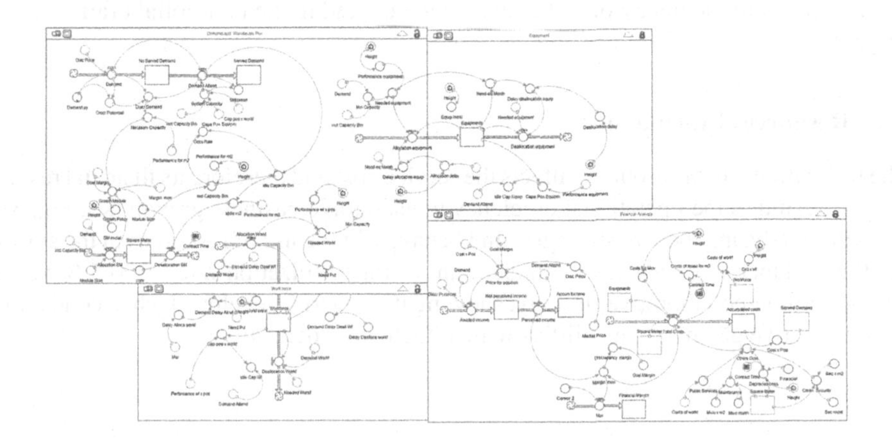

Fig. 3. Stock and flow diagram

3 Simulation and Discussion

After modeling the system, the following results by contrasting the collaborative strategy versus non-collaborative were obtained

- Strategy 1. Non-collaborative model based on the performance of capacity planning independently by each customer.
- Strategy 2. Collaborative model based on the performance of resource planning, through the planning aggregate demand.

The best result is 12 meters height for the warehouse with the lease time in 120 months.

3.1 Demand Behavior

The expected demand is the result of the involvement of the projections by the behavior of the system (see Fig. 4).

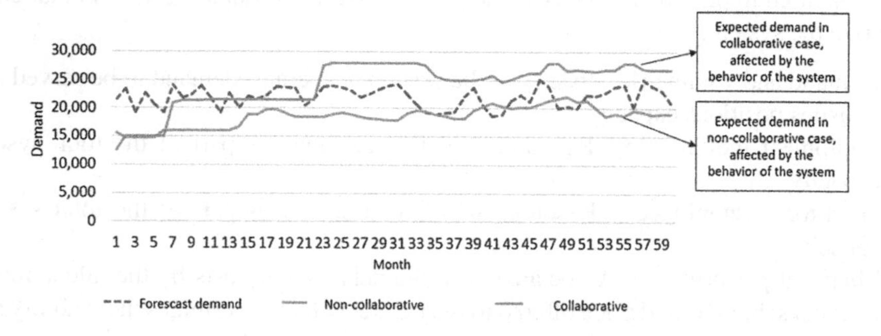

Fig. 4. Contrast estimated demand (collaborative and non-collaborative)

Demand in the collaborative scenario is increased regarding to the initial projection, contrary to the behavior of the expected demand in the non-collaborative initial projection.

3.2 Resources Utilization

The utilization rate of resources affects the service cost and therefore its financial results, i.e. it determines the operational efficiency to encourage business growth (see Fig. 5).

After analyzing the two strategies and behavior in the use of resources in the system for the collaborative case it is obtained, an average utilization rate of 90.5 % versus 84.5 % for non-collaborative strategy, showing the synergy developed when conducting a collaborative planning capabilities with a fluctuating demand.

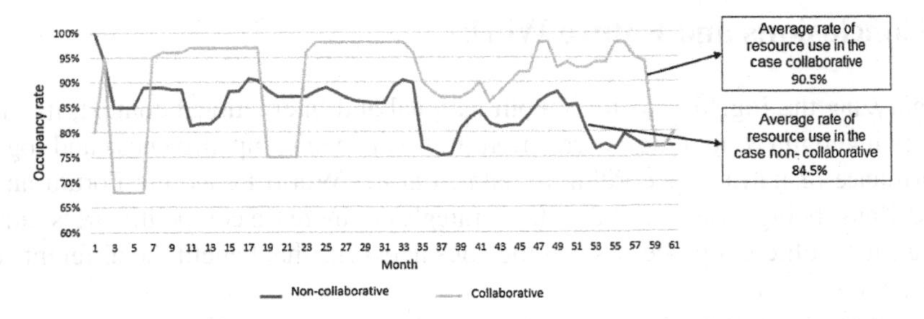

Fig. 5. Resources utilization

3.3 Hypothesis Testing

Planning Model (Collaborative and Non-collaborative) and Affectation on Served Demand.

- H_0: The planning model (collaborative or non-collaborative) does not influence the served demand.
- H_1: The planning model (collaborative or non-collaborative) influences the served demand.
- With a significance level α 0.05

$$F \sim F_{0.05;2;116} = 3.07 < F_c = 3294 \tag{6}$$

- Decision: Reject the null hypothesis.
- Conclusions: There is not enough evidence to affirm that the model used for resource planning (either collaborative or non-collaborative) does not influence the resulting in served demand for logistics operation in the distribution center.

Planning Model (Collaborative and Non-collaborative) and Affectation on Resources Utilization.

- H_0: The planning model (collaborative or non-collaborative) does not influence the resources utilization.
- H_1: The planning model (collaborative or non-collaborative) influences the resources utilization.
- With a significance level α 0.05

$$F \sim F_{0.05;2;116} = 3.07 < F_c = 9091 \tag{7}$$

- Decision: Reject the null hypothesis.
- Conclusions: There is not enough evidence to affirm that the model used for resource planning (either collaborative or non-collaborative) does not influence the resulting in resources utilization for logistics operation in the distribution center.

4 Conclusions and Future Works

By analyzing the logistics sector at both national and international context, its importance is highlighted, to a high correlation (0.9) between competitiveness and logistics performance of nations, according to data from the World Economic Forum and the World Bank, being essential to develop strategies to increase competitiveness indexes, through more efficient processes and logistics networks that benefit the different actors in the supply chain.

It is there that where alliances and cooperation processes, take greater importance, the effect of the potential benefits to generate synergies between them, which for this case study is denoted in distribution centers as infrastructure generating value for customers and consumers.

Despite this, generating collaborative processes is an arduous task requiring to meet several conditions for synchronization and simultaneous coordination of requirements, such as, product characteristics, target markets, information, real intention of cooperation between companies, but above all, it's required to have a central actor with the integrated ability to manage the diverse needs of supply chains, as the logistics operator.

In addressing this situation from the perspective of system dynamics, it is possible to analyze the causal links between elements of the system and its feedback, identifying the effect of typical situations in real systems, but not always considered in decision-making, as delays in the allocation of resources or failure of corporate policies that affect business performance.

In this research, through the development and use of a system dynamics model, it is possible to plan capacities in distribution centers, considering the variability of the demand for a logistics operator, to a system that depends on environmental conditions, such as availability of resources, market prices or development of infrastructure of distribution centers with different heights and times of contract, among other things, that being modeled by planning strategies resources collaboratively and not collaborative, facilitates decision making, and also allows to develop performance measures resulting from the simulation which seek to increase the competitiveness of logistics networks, conditioning its growth and facilitating the evaluation of strategies to achieve the objectives of stakeholders.

Future research suggests that an extended model should be developed in order to consider other relevant variables when designing and selecting distribution centers, such as the height of the warehouse, which not only defines the availability of volumetric space, but also defines the investment and equipment needed to operate, variables directly affecting the definition of processes and logistics performance. It is also important to expand the performance measures involved, so one can determine the impact of horizontal collaboration on logistics costs by the interested parties in the development of the processes analyzed.

References

1. National Planning Department of Colombia: Conpes 3439, National Competitiveness System. http://www.colombiacompetitiva.gov.co/sncei/Documents/Conpes-3439-de-2006.pdf
2. Sala-i-Martín, X., Schwab, K.: The global competitiveness report 2014–2015. Technical report, Word Economic Forum (2014)
3. The World Bank, Logistic Performance Index. http://data.worldbank.org/indicator/LP.LPI.OVRL.XQ
4. Capgemini Consulting Group: 2012 third-party logistics study the state of logistics outsourcing. http://www.3plstudy.com/media/downloads/2012/2012_3PL_Study.pdf
5. Guasch, J.L.: Logistics as a driver of competitiveness in Latin America and the Caribbean. Technical report, Inter-American Development Bank (2011)
6. Romero, O.R.: Exclusive operations in distribution centers. Technical report, Suppla S.A. (2014)
7. Senge, P.M., Rogelio, O.: Developing a theory of service quality/service capacity interaction. In: The 11th International Conference of the System Dynamics Society. System Dynamics Society, Cancun (1993)
8. Edward, A.J.: Managing software implementers in the information services industry: an example of the impact of market growth on knowledge worker productivity and quality. In: The 16th International Conference of the System Dynamics Society. System Dynamics Society, Québec (1998)
9. Anderson, E.G., Morrice, D., Lundeen, G.: The physics of capacity and backlog management in service and custom manufacturing supply chains. Syst. Dyn. Rev. **21**(3), 217–247 (2005)
10. Becerra, M., Romero O.R., Herrera, M.M., Trujillo, J.: Modeling the demand for logistics storage services through system dynamic. In: IX Latin American Congress of System Dynamics and II Brazilian Congress of System Dynamics. Latin American Charter of System Dynamics Society, Brasilia (2011)
11. Georgantzas, N.C.: Perceptual dynamics of "good" and "poor" service quality. In: The 11th International Conference of the System Dynamics Society. System Dynamics Society, Cancun (1993)
12. Homer, J.: Macro- and micro-modeling of field service dynamics. In: The 16th International Conference of the System Dynamics Society. System Dynamics Society, Québec (1998)
13. Barnes, J., Burton, F., Hawker, I., Lyons, M.H.: Scenario modelling of demand for future telecommunications services. In: The 12th International Conference of the System Dynamics Society. System Dynamics Society, Stirling (1994)
14. Lynch, T., Skelton, S., Lyons, M.H.: Strategic analysis of global telecoms services provision. In: The 12th International Conference of the System Dynamics Society. System Dynamics Society, Stirling (1994)
15. Barrón, A., Martinez S., López, J.M.: A simulation model for telecommunications services partially substituting. In: The 14th International Conference of the System Dynamics Society. System Dynamics Society, Cambridge (1996)
16. Mojtahedzadeh, M., Andersen, D.: Assessing the system-wide impacts of automated voice customer service technologies. In: The 14th International Conference of the System Dynamics Society. System Dynamics Society, Cambridge (1996)
17. Matthews, A., Osborne, J.: Development of a management flight simulator to enable the strategic planning and targeting of telecommunications networks resources and services to the most profitable customers. In: The 17th International Conference of the System Dynamics Society. System Dynamics Society, Wellington (1999)

18. Rowland, C.J.: The role of change agents in an IT services corporation: a systems approach to developing a strategy for improvement. In: The 17th International Conference of the System Dynamics Society. System Dynamics Society, Wellington (1999)
19. Osborne, J.: Dynamic Modelling to assist in the understanding of consumer take-up and the diffusion of new telecommunications services. In: The 17th International Conference of the System Dynamics Society. System Dynamics Society, Wellington (1999)
20. Jackson, F.: Systems thinking for the next millennium: the future of the IT services industry. In: The 17th International Conference of the System Dynamics Society. System Dynamics Society, Wellington (1999)
21. Honggang, X., Mashayekhi, A., Saeed, K.: Effectiveness of infrastructure service delivery through earmarking: the case of highway construction in China. Syst. Dyn. Rev. **14**(2–3), 221–255 (1998)
22. Kunc, M.: Achieving a balanced organizational structure in professional services firms: some lessons from a modeling project. Syst. Dyn. Rev. **24**(2), 119–143 (2008)
23. Barton, J.: The management of urban water services - a study in long-term institutional dynamics. In: The 12th International Conference of the System Dynamics Society. System Dynamics Society, Stirling (1994)
24. Morgan, T., Ammentorp, B.: Human service systems: a theoretical perspective. In: The 13th International Conference of the System Dynamics Society. System Dynamics Society, Tokyo (1995)
25. Wolstenholme, E.F.: A patient flow perspective of U.K. health services: exploring the case for new "intermediate care" initiatives. Syst. Dyn. Rev. **15**(3), 253–271 (1999)
26. Ackere, A., Smith, P.: Towards a macro model of National Health service waiting lists. Syst. Dyn. Rev. **15**(3), 225–252 (1999)
27. Calvo, B.N.: Is the contraction of demand an excuse for the laissez-faire human resource practices at professional service companies? Syst. Dyn. Rev. **27**(3), 294–312 (2011)
28. Becerra, M. Orjuela, J.A., Romero, O.R., Herrera M.M.: Model for calculating operational capacities in service providers using system dynamics. In: The 31th International Conference of the System Dynamics Society. System Dynamics Society, Cambridge (2013)
29. Romero, O.R., Becerra M., González, E.C., Rueda F.J.: Planning of capacities of a logistic operator in distribution centers. In: Latin American Congress and Colombian Meeting of System Dynamics. Latin American Charter of System Dynamics Society, Cartagena (2015)

Micro-Evolution Algorithms for Solving the Dynamic Location Problem of Customized Bus Stops

Shiwei He(✉) and Rui Song

School of Traffic and Transportation, Beijing Jiaotong University, Beijing, China
{shwhe, rsong}@bjtu.edu.cn

Abstract. Customized bus is one of the new public transit services by applying GPS, Internet+ and other new technologies which involves in the bus stops location and bus routing problem. In the Customized Bus Stops Location Problem (CBSLP), passengers specify transportation requests with their origins, destinations, and desired pickup or delivery times through internet in real time. The Customized bus operator or transit company will determine dynamically the bus stops from their candidate stops to best accommodate the demand and try to minimize the walking distance of passengers from their homes (or offices) to the bus pickup stops. This paper addresses the dynamic location problem of customized bus stops with maximum walking distance constraints. The micro-evolution algorithm (MEA) is designed based on gene structure evolution method for the solution of the problem. The traditional Primal-Dual Mapping Operator is improved by MEA to capture the changed environment information. Simulation tests show that the MEA performs better than conventional GA both in quality and efficiency in dynamic environment. Thus, an improving tool for better decision of customized bus system is provided.

Keywords: Intelligent and optimization algorithms · Micro-evolution algorithm · Customized bus · Dynamic location problem

1 Introduction

Currently, public transportation system is undergoing innovation to provide more flexible bus service by applying GPS, Internet+ and other new technologies such as wireless communication network, etc. [1]. Customized bus (or called feasible bus, variable bus, adaptive bus) is one of the public transit services which can provide shared-ride door-to-door service with flexible or customized bus stops, routes and schedules [2, 3]. Customized bus is intended to provide intermediate service between conventional buses and taxis in terms of both operating cost and level of service. In a customized bus service, passengers specify transportation requests with their origins,

Supported by National Basic Research Program of China (No. 2012CB725403), National Natural Science Foundation of China (No. 61374202).

L. Zhang et al. (Eds.): AsiaSim 2016/SCS AutumnSim 2016, Part I, CCIS 643, pp. 633–642, 2016.
DOI: 10.1007/978-981-10-2663-8_65

destinations, and desired pickup or delivery times through internet. The customized bus operator or transit company will determine the bus stops from their candidate stops and a set of routes and schedules to best accommodate the demand dynamically. Usually, customized bus service problem involves in bus stops location problem and bus routing problem [3, 4]. Since better accessibility to public transportation has become an important objective for many transit systems across the world, the Customized Bus Stops Location Problem (CBSLP) has been addressed in the paper to minimize the walking distance of passengers from their homes (or offices) to the bus pickup stops when the routes and schedules are provided for customized bus.

Usually, location of bus stops is determined according to the passengers request and physical street or parking conditions. The transit company will find some potential stops which satisfy the physical conditions to park the bus in advance. Then, the actually stops will determined according to the actual demands of passengers.

In CBSLP, two types of service requests are considered: advance requests and real-time requests. The advance requests usually refer to those received at least one day before the service is provided, so that bus stops can be planned before the start of the service. Real-time requests are those asking for same-day service either as soon as possible or at specified times. If all the requests are advance requests (and assuming all other factors, such as traffic conditions, are predictable), then the determination of the stops is a static p-median Location Problem; otherwise, the problem becomes a dynamic problem, in which the stops must be determined in real-time. The Dynamic Location problem of customized bus will be considered in the paper.

The p-Median problem is a central facilities location problem by selecting p facilities from a network of n point for minimizing a weighted distance objective function. Generally, the weight could be considered as the served demands. The complexity of p-Median problem is NP-hard [5]. Traditionally, the static p-Median problem could be solved with heuristic or branch-bound methods [6–8]. However, the solution is satisfied neither in quality nor in efficiency with the scale of the problem boosted. In recent years, with the developing of intelligent computing technologies such as genetic algorithm, tabu search, ant colony and other methods [9–11], more and more applications of intelligent methods have been found for the solution of location problem [12, 13].

While for dynamic optimization problems (DOPs), the goal of intelligent methods is no longer to find a satisfactory solution to a fixed problem, but to track the trajectory of moving optima in the search space [10, 14]. This poses great challenges to traditional intelligent methods because they cannot track the changing optimal solutions well once converged. For solving the problem, several approaches have been developed into traditional intelligent methods to address DOPs [15]. These approaches can roughly be grouped into four categories: diversity schemes increasing the population diversity after a change is detected [16], or maintaining the population diversity during the run [17, 18], memory schemes [14, 19], multipopulation and speciation schemes [20], and adaptive schemes [21].

The micro-evolution algorithm (MEA) is a stochastic search method based on the mechanics of natural and biological evolution, which is always subject to dynamic environments, and hence possess potential properties to adapt in dynamic environments by using the gene structure evolution strategy and primal-dual mapping operator to trace the changing environment information. It is different from the traditional intelligent approaches and has been shown to be very useful in solving a variety of combination optimal problems [22]. MEA will be used for the solution of Dynamic Location Problem of Customized Bus Stops.

The remainder of the paper is organized in following sections. Section 2 describes the model. Section 3 presents the solution algorithm. Section 4 describes a real-world deployment of MEA on benchmark problems. Finally, Sect. 5 draws conclusions and recommends further implementations.

2 Problem Formulation

Notations: $M = \{1, 2, \cdots, m\}$, M is the bus stop set; $N = \{1, 2, \cdots, n\}$, N is the demand set; d_{ij} represents the shortest distance from demand point i to the nearest bus stop point j; w_i denotes the demand from demand point i; p represents the number of bus stops needs to be established; s denotes the maximum distance between bus stop point and its served demand point; M_i represents the bus stop set within the permitted maximum distance s to demand point i, $\forall i \in N, M_i \subseteq M$.

Variables: x_{ij} = 1 if demand point i is served by bus stop point j, 0 otherwise.

The p-median problem can be stated mathematically as:

$$\min Z = \sum_{i \in N} \sum_{j \in M_i} w_i d_{ij} x_{ij} \tag{1}$$

$$\sum_{j \in M_i} x_{ij} = 1 \quad \forall i \in N \tag{2}$$

$$x_{jj} \geq x_{ij} \quad \forall i \in N, i \neq j, \forall j \in M_i \tag{3}$$

$$\sum_{j \in M} x_{jj} = p \tag{4}$$

$$x_{ij} \geq 0 \quad \forall i \in N, \forall j \in M \tag{5}$$

$$x_{jj} = \{0, 1\} \quad \forall j \in M \tag{6}$$

Where, objective (1) minimize the average weighted distance from bus stop point to the demand point. Constraint (2) ensures that every demand point is served by one bus stop point within the permitted maximum distance. Constraint (3) ensures that each demand point is only assigned to the bus stop points within the p-median set. Constraint (4) ensures the number of bus stops is p.

3 Micro-Evolution Algorithm

Micro-evolution Algorithm (MEA) is some like the conventional Genetic Algorithm (GA). The major difference of two algorithms lies in two aspects: first, MEA is designed based on gene structure evolution and the GA is on gene bit evolution. Second, the traditional Primal-Dual Mapping Operator is improved by MEA with the consideration of changed environment information. The general procedure of MEA is shown as follows:

```
Procedure general MEA
Begin
  Parameterize(pop_size,pc,pm)
  t:=0;
  initializePopulation(P(0));
  evaluatePopulation(P(0));
  repeat
     p'(t):=selectForRecombination(P(t));
     p″(t):= Structure-based crossover(p'(t));
     mutation(p″(t));
     evaluatePopulation(P″(t));
     P(t+1):=selectForSurvial(P(t)+P″(t));
     If ( circumstance is changed )
     {
      D(t+1):=selectForDualEvolution(P(t+1));
      for each chromosome x in D(t+1) do
        executeRevisedPDMoperation(x);
      endfor
     }
t:=t+1;
until a termination condition is met;
end
```

3.1 Encoding Scheme (Representation)

As the traditional binary representation is not well suited for p-Median problem, a direct encoding method with structure information is adopted where the location facilities are represented as chromosomes:

$S = \{s_1, \dot{s}_2, s_3, \dot{s}_4, \cdots, s_p\}$

s_i denotes the ith facility point, $s_i \in N$.

$\dot{s}_k$ denotes the kth facility point which belongs to the dominance set, $\dot{s}_k \in N'$ and N' is the dominance set where the facility points are evaluated to be fitter than others in the changed environment. Usually, the same genes in the top 5–10 % chromosomes will be saved in the dominance set.

3.2 Fitness Evaluation

Let Z_{best} denote the average weighted distance traveled from demand points to facility sites of the best chromosome, Z_k denote the average weighted distance traveled from demand points to facility sites of the kth chromosome, λ is a constant. When the distance between a demand point and a facility site exceeds the maximum distance limit s, a large number M will be added to the objective function, The fitness ε_k for kth chromosome is calculated as follows:

$$\varepsilon_k = \lambda Z_k / Z_{best} \tag{7}$$

3.3 Dominance Gene Structure

For a chromosome $S = \{s_1, \dot{s}_2, s_3, \dot{s}_4, \cdots, s_p\}$, let $\dot{s}_k$ denotes the kth facility point which belongs to the dominance set N', we call the set $S' = \{\dot{s}_2, \dot{s}_4, \cdots, \dot{s}_k, \cdots\}$, where $\dot{s}_k \in N'$ and $S' \subset S$, a dominance gene structure of chromosome S. In the structure-based crossover operation of MEM, the dominance gene structure will be preserved in the evolution procedure.

3.4 Micro-Evolution Operators

3.4.1 Selection Strategy

We give more reproductive chances to the populations that are the most fit. The K highest-rated chromosomes will be preserved to next generation.

3.4.2 Structure-Based Crossover Operator

(1) Two parents are selected randomly from the population. For example, the two parents are: $P_1 : 1\ \dot{2}\ 5\ 6\ \dot{7}\ 9 \quad P_2 : 3\ \dot{4}\ \dot{7}\ 8\ 9\ 10$

(2) The same segments from two parents are copied into the front of $P_1(P_2)$. The rest genes (separated by '|') are chosen randomly and the crossover sub-segments (marked by '—') are gotten as: $C_1' : \dot{7}\ 9 \mid 1\ \underline{\dot{2}\ 5}\ 6 \quad C_2' : \dot{7}\ 9 \mid 3\ \underline{\dot{4}\ 8}\ 10$

(3) If the sub-segments (marked by '—') have genes in dominance set, the genes in dominance set will be accepted with a low probability. Mostly they will be re-chosen or directly treated to make sure the dominance structure will not be destroyed in the crossover operation.

First: $C_1' : \dot{7}\ 9 \mid 1\ \underline{\dot{2}\ 5}\ 6 \quad C_2' : \dot{7}\ 9 \mid 3\ \underline{\dot{4}\ 8}\ 10$

If not accepted, re-choose the crossover sub-segments $C_1' : \dot{7}\ 9 \mid 1\ \dot{2}\ \underline{5\ 6} \quad C_2' : \dot{7}\ 9 \mid 3\ \dot{4}\ \underline{8\ 10}$

Or release the gene in dominance set directly

$$C_1' : \dot{7}\,9 \mid 1\,\dot{2}\,\underline{5}\,6 \quad C_2' : \dot{7}\,9 \mid 3\,\dot{4}\,\underline{8}\,10$$

(4) Exchange the crossover sub-segments of two parents to get two offspring corresponding to above three cases: $C_1'' : \dot{7}\,9 \mid 1\,\underline{\dot{4}\,8}\,6$ $C_2'' : \dot{7}\,9 \mid 3\,\underline{\dot{2}\,5}\,10$ or $C_1' : \dot{7}\,9 \mid 1\,\dot{2}\,\underline{8\,10}$ $C_2' : \dot{7}\,9 \mid 3\,\dot{4}\,\underline{5\,6}$

$$\text{or}\, C_1' : \dot{7}\,9 \mid 1\,\dot{2}\,\underline{8}\,6 \quad C_2' : \dot{7}\,9 \mid 3\,\dot{4}\,\underline{5}\,10$$

(5) After adjusting the sequence, the final offspring corresponding to above three cases are: $C_1 : 1\,\dot{4}\,6\,\dot{7}\,8\,9$ $C_2 : \dot{2}\,3\,5\,\dot{7}\,9\,10$ or $C_1' : 1\,\dot{2}\,\dot{7}\,8\,9\,10$ $C_2' : 3\,\dot{4}\,5\,6\,\dot{7}\,9$ or $C_1' : 1\,\dot{2}\,6\,\dot{7}\,8\,9$ $C_2' : 3\,\dot{4}\,5\,\dot{7}\,9\,10$

3.4.3 Revised Primal-Dual Mapping (PDM) Operator

Primal-Dual Mapping (PDM) Operator is revised to trace the change of environment on the structure of chromosome. Inspired by the complementary mechanism in nature, a chromosome could be recorded with primal-dual method. A chromosome recorded explicitly in the population is called a primal chromosome in PDM Operator. The chromosome that has maximum distance to a primal chromosome in a distance space is called its dual chromosome. In traditional binary-encoded space, the Hamming distance (the number of locations where the corresponding bits of two chromosomes differ) is usually used as the definition of distance. Given a primal chromosome $x = (x_1, x_2, \cdots, x_p) \in I = \{0, 1\}^p$ of fixed length p, its dual or its implement $x' = dual(x) = (x_1', x_2', \cdots, x_p') \in I = \{0, 1\}^p$, where dual(.) is the primal-dual mapping function and $x_i' = 1 - x_i$. In the dynamic location problem, a primal chromosome could be represents as $S = \{s_1, \dot{s}_2, s_3, \dot{s}_4, \cdots, s_p\}$, its dual or its implement $S' = dual(S) = \{s_1', \dot{s}_2', s_3', \dot{s}_4', \cdots, s_p'\}$, where dual(.) is the primal-dual mapping function and $s_i' = f(s_i)$ with the maximum weighted distance to node s_i when the demand of passengers is changed. For example, when the demand is changed, the new primal-dual mapping function $s_i' = f(s_i)$ is as follows,

$$\begin{array}{ll} \textit{The primal}\ \text{gene}: & 1\,2\,3\,4\,5\,6\,7\,8\,9 \\ \textit{The primal}-\textit{dual mapping}: & \downarrow\downarrow\downarrow\downarrow\downarrow\downarrow\downarrow\downarrow\downarrow \\ \textit{The dual}\ \text{gene}: & 8\,7\,5\,9\,3\,8\,6\,7\,1 \end{array}$$

An example of applying primal-dual mapping operator to a 6-bit string chromosome is shown as follows:

$$\begin{array}{ll} \textit{The primal chromosome}: & 1\,4\,6\,7\,8\,9 \\ \textit{The primal}-\textit{dual mapping}: & \downarrow\downarrow\downarrow\downarrow\downarrow \\ \textit{The dual chromosome}: & 8\,9\,8\,6\,7\,1 \end{array}$$

If there are same genes, such as "8" in above dual chromosome, a random selection method is used to find a different gene "3" to replace "8" as follows:

$$\begin{array}{ll} \textit{The primal chromosome}: & 1\,4\,6\,7\,8\,9 \\ \textit{The primal}-\textit{dual mapping}: & \downarrow\downarrow\downarrow\downarrow\downarrow \\ \textit{The dual chromosome}: & 8\,9\,3\,6\,7\,1 \end{array}$$

With above definition, a set of low fitness primal chromosomes are selected to evaluate their duals for the next generation each time when the environment is changed (here, the environment could be the demands of the stops). For every candidate, it is replaced with the dual if the dual is evaluated to be fitter; otherwise it is survived into the next generation.

3.4.4 Mutation Operator

The mutation operator adopts a single node exchanging method. First, the going out index s_i in the solution $S = \{s_1, s_2, \cdots, s_p\}$ is selected randomly. Then, an index j in node set N is also selected randomly. If $j \notin S$ and $j \neq s_i$, exchange two nodes. The operation will avoid the indices already in the solution. For example:

$$O_2: \; 4 \;\; 2 \;\; 7\,5 \;\; 6$$

After randomly selecting the mutation point No. 3 that is 7, we select another mutation point $j = 9$ in $N = \{123456789\}$. The final chromosome is muted into

$$O_2: 4\,2\,9\,5\,6$$

3.4.5 Termination-Condition

Predefined maximum number of generation or time limit is reached.

4 Simulation Experiments

In this section, we provide simulation tests to illustrate the solution procedure of micro-evolution algorithm (MEA) as previously outlined. The parameters as weight of 150 nodes and distances between each pair of nodes are shown in the paper [12]. The number of bus stops to be opened, p, was set to 20, 40, 60, 80, and 100 whereas the maximum distance parameter, s, was set to 200 m, 300 m, and 400 m. When the pop size is 300, crossover rate is 0.85, and the mutation rate is 0.05, it needs no more than 10 s when generation is 2000 on ThinkPad T400/2.8 GHz. The tests show that MEA performs more efficiently than the conventional GA for the static location problem. Some comparison tests results are shown in Table 1.

Since for dynamic optimization problems a single, time-invariant optimal solution does not exist, the goal is not only to find the extremum but also to track their progression through the space as closely as possible. We design the test experiment of MEA and conventional GA on the periodically shifting CBSLP. The maximum allowable generation is set to 5000 and the fitness landscape is shifted every 500 generations in first 3000 generations. That is, there are 6 change periods for MEA and conventional GA. The demand of each potential bus stop is randomly generated and

Table 1. Some comparison tests results

Facility num. *p*	Distance *s*	Optimal results	The Optimal rates at generation 2000 (± 10 s time diversity)	
			MEA (20 times)	Conventional-GA (20 times)
100	200	122094	90 %	60 %
	300	122094	95 %	70 %
	400	122094	95 %	65 %
80	200	355618	90 %	75 %
	300	355618	95 %	80 %
	400	355618	90 %	80 %
60	200	771652	95 %	75 %
	300	771652	100 %	80 %
	400	771652	95 %	70 %
40	200	1696328[a]	90 %	75 %
	300	1604999	90 %	70 %
	400	1604999	95 %	80 %
20	250	524499	90 %	75 %
	300	4318959	95 %	70 %
	400	4072860	95 %	65 %

[a]Optimal solution for this instance is 1,692,948

accumulated from the node weight set in [12] at each change period. After 3000 generations, the demand of each potential bus stop will back to the former weight of nodes in [12] to compare the final optimal results of two solutions. Figure 1 shows the results of MEA and conventional GA on the CBSLP in dynamic environments where the number of bus stops to be opened, p, was set to 100 whereas the maximum distance parameter, s, was set to 400 m.

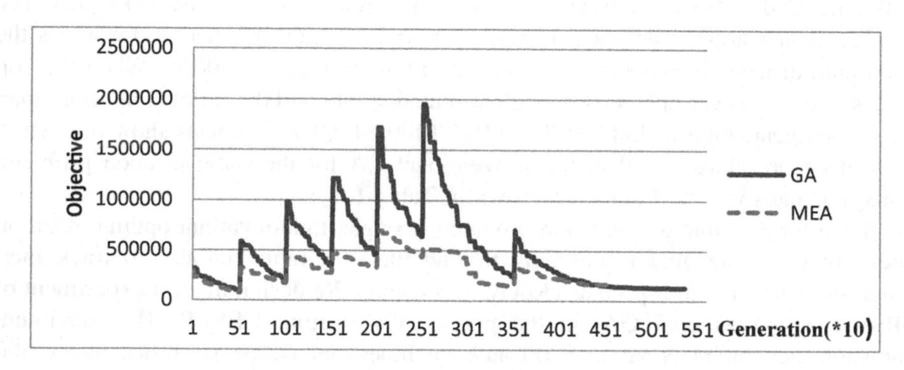

Fig. 1. Evolution curves in dynamic environments

From Fig. 1, MEA outperforms the conventional GA in all periods. For MEA, its performance curve shown with dot line is lower than GA's with solid line which means the PDM operator of MEA can keep sufficient diversity in the population and make the individuals to jump quickly to the new optimum point or nearby when the environment changes. Also, see the generations from 3500 to 5500, MEA is more efficient to find the final optimal result than GA. The performance curve of conventional GA gains almost no improvement even if a re-initialization method is used that more than 50 % individuals in the population is generated again randomly after a change occurs. And conventional GA behaves much less efficiently than the MEA due to the dominance structure destroy in crossover and mutation operations.

More experimental results show that MEA has stronger robustness and adaptability than conventional GA in the dynamic environments. The PDM and dominance gene structure preserving scheme used in MEA are found useful to improve the operations adaptability under dynamic environments. Due to the page limitations of the proceedings, the other detailed results for the 150-nodes data set are available from the first author.

5 Conclusions

This paper addresses the dynamic location problem of customized bus stops with maximum distance constraints. The micro-evolution algorithm (MEA) is designed based on gene structure evolution method for the solution of the problem. The traditional Primal-Dual Mapping Operator is improved by MEA to capture the changed environment information. Experimental results with the 150-nodes location benchmark data set show that MEA has stronger robustness and adaptability than conventional GA in the dynamic environments. Thus, an improving aided tool for better decision of customized bus system has been provided.

There are several future works relevant to this paper. It is a straightforward work to analyze the gene structure preserving mechanism of MEM and examine their performance in dynamic environments. The methods to identify the key or dominant genes to prevent early convergence of the algorithm need to be further explored. We believe that the well-designed gene structure preserving scheme could improve the performance of MEM. To hybridize the proposed MEM with other approaches developed into MEM, such as the memory and multi-population schemes, will be another interesting future work. In the paper, only a set of low fitness primal chromosomes are selected to evaluate their duals for the next generation each time when the environment is changed. It is valuable to further investigate how much the number of PDM operations in the generation affects the performance of MEM. Finally, MEM should be compared with more dynamic optimal methods, which is left as a future research.

References

1. Song, R.: Unban Transit System. Beijing Jiaotong University Publishing Company, Beijing (2014)
2. Kim, M.E., Schonfeld, P.: Maximizing net benefits for conventional and flexible bus services. Transp. Res. Part A **80**, 116–133 (2015)
3. Cordeau, J.F., Laporte, G.: The dial-a-ride problem: models and algorithms. Ann. Oper. Res. **153**(1), 29–46 (2007)
4. Markovic', N., Nair, R., Schonfeld, P., Miller-Hooks, E., Mohebbi, M.: Optimizing dial-a-ride services in Maryland: benefits of computerized routing and scheduling. Transp. Res. Part C **55**, 156–165 (2015)
5. Moon, D., Chaudhry, S.S.: An analysis of network location problems with distance constraints. Manage. Sci. **30**, 290–307 (1984)
6. Mirchandani, P.B., Francis, R.L.: Discrete Location Theory. Wiley, New York (1990)
7. Teitz, M.B., Bart, P.: Heuristic methods for estimating the generalized vertex median of a weighted graph. Oper. Res. **16**, 955–961 (1968)
8. Choi, C., Chaudhry, S.S.: The p-median problem with maximum distance constraints: a direct approach. Location Sci. **1**(3), 235–243 (1993)
9. Eberhart, R., Simpson, P., Dobbins, R.: Computational Intelligence PC Tools. Academic Press, Boston (1996)
10. Branke, J.: Evolutionary Optimization in Dynamic Environments. Kluwer, Norwell (2002)
11. He, S., Chaudhry, S.S., Lei, Z., Baohua, W.: Stochastic vendor selection problem: chance-constrained model and genetic algorithms. Ann. Oper. Res. **168**(4), 169–179 (2009)
12. Chaudhry, S.S., He, S., Chaudhry, P.E.: Solving a class of facility location problems using genetic algorithms. Expert Syst. **20**(2), 86–91 (2003)
13. Farahani, R.Z., Asgari, N., Heidari, N., Hosseininia, M., Goh, M.: Covering problems in facility location: a review. Comput. Ind. Eng. **62**, 368–407 (2012)
14. Yang, S., Yao, X.: Population-based incremental learning with associative memory for dynamic environments. IEEE Trans. Evol. Comput. **12**(5), 542–561 (2008)
15. Jin, Y., Branke, J.: Evolutionary optimization in uncertain environments—a survey. IEEE Trans. Evol. Comput. **9**(3), 303–317 (2005)
16. Vavak, F., Fogarty, C., Jukes, K.: Adaptive combustion balancing in multiple burner boilers using a genetic algorithm with variable range of local search. In: 7th International Conference on Genetic Algorithms, pp. 719–726 (1996)
17. Grefenstette, J.J.: Genetic algorithms for changing environments. In: Proceedings of the 2nd International Conference on Parallel Problem Solving From Nature, pp. 137–144 (1992)
18. Yang, S.: Genetic algorithms with memory- and elitism-based immigrants in dynamic environments. Evol. Comput. **16**(3), 385–416 (2008)
19. Yang, S.: Associative memory scheme for genetic algorithms in dynamic environments. In: Rothlauf, F., Branke, J., Cagnoni, S., Costa, E., Cotta, C., Drechsler, R., Lutton, E., Machado, P., Moore, J.H., Romero, J., Smith, G.D., Squillero, G., Takagi, H. (eds.) EvoWorkshops 2006. LNCS, vol. 3907, pp. 788–799. Springer, Heidelberg (2006)
20. Parrott, D., Li, X.: Locating and tracking multiple dynamic optima by a particle swarm model using speciation. IEEE Trans. Evol. Comput. **10**(4), 440–458 (2006)
21. Morrison, R.W., De Jong, K.A.: Triggered hypermutation revisited. In: Proceedings of IEEE Congress on Evolutionary Computation, pp. 1025–1032 (2000)
22. Liu, X., He, S., Cheng, S., Chao, L.: Multi-agent evolutionary algorithm of VRP problem with time window. J. Traffic Transp. Eng. **14**(3), 105–110 (2014)

R&D on an Embedded System of the Material Management for Internet of Things

Shengxi Wu, Youwei Si, Jie Chen, and Xingsheng Gu(✉)

Key Laboratory of Advanced Control and Optimization for Chemical Processes, Ministry of Education, East China University of Science and Technology, No.130 of Meilong Road, Shanghai 200237, China
{wushengxi,xsgu}@ecust.edu.cn, scott.si@hotmail.com, 692717249@qq.com

Abstract. A highly efficient design project on embedded system for Internet of Things (IOT) is presented for materials margin management system. As the key instruments of IOT, the acquisition and transmission of weight system data is based on embedded STC15W201S. RS485 bus and Ethernet are used to link microcontroller and PC which make a complete materials margin for real-time dynamic management system. Communication between host computer and instruments and software of host computer are provided to implement of weighting system. As the key technologies, communication between PC and Ethernet, weighting calibration and data filtering are discussed. Test results show that this embedded system can satisfy the design purpose to materials management for Internet of Things.

Keywords: Internet of things · Material management · Weighting system · Calibration · First-order filter

1 Introduction

There are more and more requirements on material management for factories, laboratories and family life with the development of Internet of Things (IOT). It provides convenience for the users query in real time, accurate information to support distribution for suppliers or future of intelligent logistics.

Figure 1 is the function block diagram of material margin management system based on IOT. It mainly includes three parts: user, material suppliers and material users (factory, community and laboratory shown in Fig. 1). The material users can upload data to the server with material margin management system. Aimed at material management system based IOT, weighting system is designed and implemented with STC15W201S and mini X86 host.

Network control system is used by local intelligent sensor, data acquisition and processing and remote host monitoring at the same time exchange information with users through Internet. Figure 2 is structure diagram of the weighing system.

MCS-51 single chip sends data uploaded by HX711 to upper computer according to the coding command sent by upper computer.

L. Zhang et al. (Eds.): AsiaSim 2016/SCS AutumnSim 2016, Part I, CCIS 643, pp. 643–651, 2016.
DOI: 10.1007/978-981-10-2663-8_66

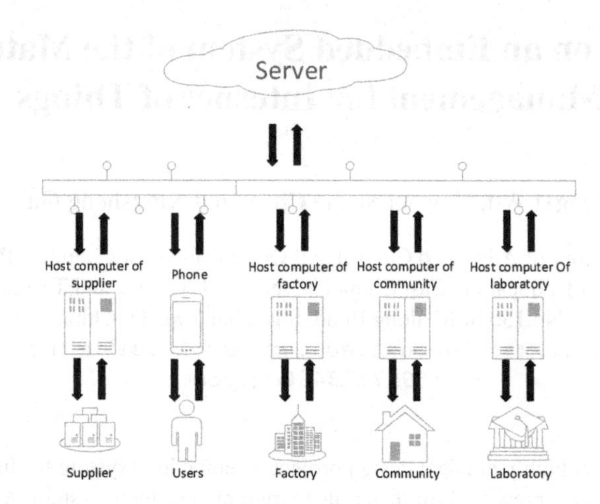

Fig. 1. Function block diagram of material margin management system

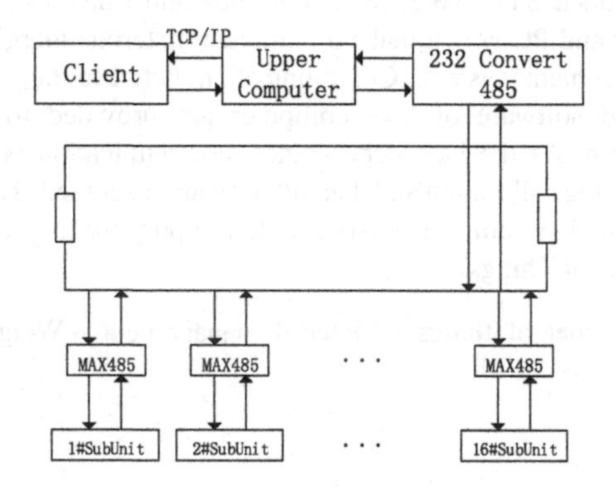

Fig. 2. Structure block diagram of the weighing system

2 Design of Hardware Circuit

2.1 Hardware Design and Implementation of the Weighing Module

Weighting sensor uses a resistive strain gauge load cell. The main parts consist of several resistance strain gauges, elastomers and detection circuit. Elastomer deforms under external force, so that strain gauges which are pasted the surface of the resistance also accompanied deformed after the deformation resistance strain gauge. A/D converter is used electronic scales dedicated chip HX711, which is a 24 A/D converter chip designed for high-precision electronic scales. Compared with the same type of other chip, it integrates the peripheral circuits including power supply, and on-chip clock oscillator [2].

DIP (dual inline-pin package) switch is designed to operate a control address switch which can be portable and convenient in hardware. When there is an extension failure, the corresponding DIP switch will be adjusted. It's not necessary to change the source code to achieve the replacement extension. However, the address switch can control up to 16 extensions. If more than 16 extensions, it can only be extended by cascading approach, increasing the PC code complexity.

General method is as follows:

In Fig. 3, each of the devices only need to read four pin of address switch, and it can set the address of the extension. Since the extensions are strung together, only one variable is set to read the low 4 bits of P1 port in the program to achieve the extensions address setting.

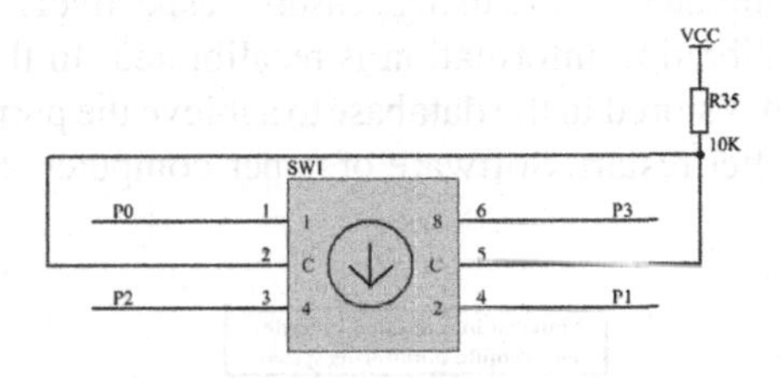

Fig. 3. A circuit diagram of DIP switch

In the serial communication program, host sends three bytes of information based on Table 1 to a selected extension. Every extension compares address information extracted from the bus with its own address information. Only matching extension sends information in accordance with Table 2 to the upper compute. Due to HX711 A/D converter collect 24-bit data, it is necessary to extract only the high 16-bit data according to precision. One conversion data is split into transmission in two times. In Table 2, every two bytes of data combined with measurement is one time conversion data after the third byte. Every Transmission is consists of ten continuous data in order to filter the data to improve the accuracy of measurement data.

Table 1. Communication format of PC to extension

Byte	Value	Function
1	0 × 5F	Start flag
2	0 × XX	Address
3	0 × AF	End flag

Table 2. Communication format of extension to PC

Byte	Value	Function
1	0 × 5F	Star flag
2	0 × XX	Address
3–22	0 × YY	Measure data
23	0 × AF	End flag

Tables 1 and 2, respectively, includes the communication format between PC and extension.

Similarly, after receiving the data, the host computer will first determine whether the received correctly or not according to the data communication format, then the data will be handled respectively.

2.2 Software Structure and Functional Design

Due to different materials, it's necessary to use different sensors, and every lower machine needs to be calibrated before using sensors, respectively. To prevent the restart after power off, the calibration information is recalibrated. In the present system, the calibration information is stored in the database to achieve the purpose that software can be used immediately after restart. Software of upper computer structure of function is shown in Fig. 4.

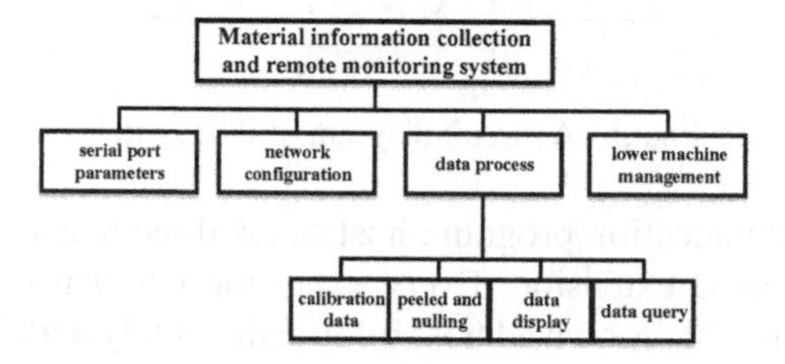

Fig. 4. Software of upper computer structure of function

The host PC as primary monitor collects information from every lower computer, such as margin, temperature, humidity, etc. It will display the collected data after certain transformation and filtering. PC can also send collected information to the client in a certain format by the network. So the client can obtain real-time information to collect up the status of each extension, and then take the next step.

Figure 5 is a system software interface. Its main functions are:

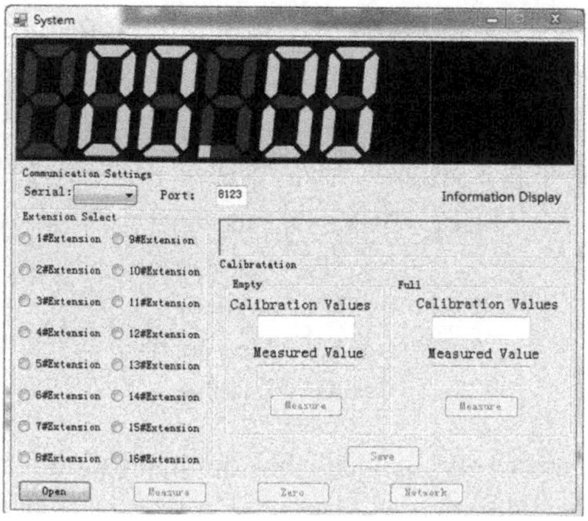

Fig. 5. Software interface

1. Communication setting area: It includes the selection of the serial and setting of the port. Serial choice is to solve the limitation that hardware DIP switch only controls up to 16 extensions. And the extension number can be further expanded by selecting a COM port.
2. Information display frame: This frame displays the host working status, extension status, and the operation of the error message.
3. Extension Select Area: Clicking the one extension is able to display the corresponding extension status, the calibration information and the collection data.
4. Calibration Area: The calibration value is set by the user, and the measured value is the data transmitted by extension in the case of no-load and full-load.
5. Function buttons: Measurement Button can work only after the calibration of the extension is complete. Zero drift occurs when the extension worked, so it's necessary to manually adjust to zero which makes the results more accurate.
6. Network: When user opens the transmission network, system will send data to the client according to a certain format by all COM. At the same time PC server can also receive commands from the client, and the command determines the next action. PC uses asynchronous communication and multithreaded method and Fig. 6 is the host network asynchronous communication flowchart. The main threads created in running system are the main thread including the connection threaded, the data transmission thread, and the data reception thread.

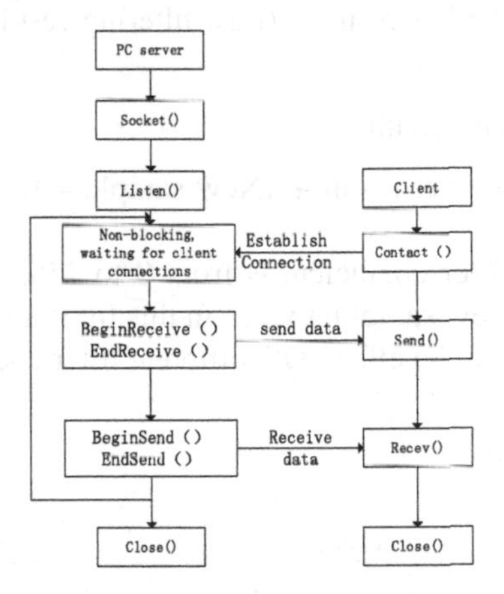

Fig. 6. Host network asynchronous communication flowchart

2.3 Data filtering

Figure 7 is an unprocessed data waveform.

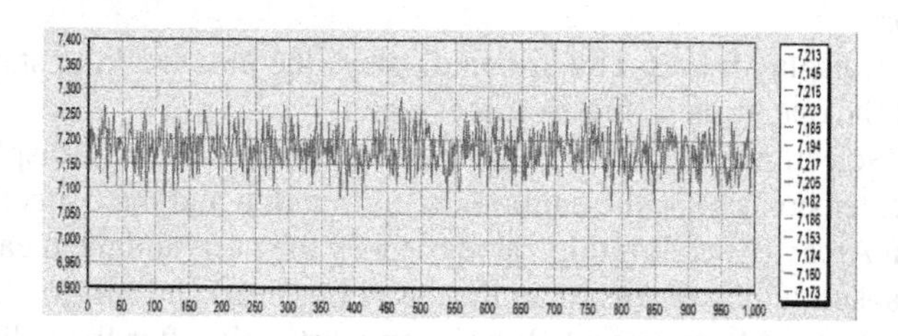

Fig. 7. An unprocessed data waveform.

First-order low-pass filtering algorithm formula is as Eq. (1),

$$Y(n) = \alpha X(n)\,(1 - \alpha)Y(n - 1) \tag{1}$$

Where, α is the filter coefficient. X(n) is the present value of samples. Y (n–1) is the previous filter output value. Y(n) is the present filter output value.

- New sample < Last filter result:

Filtering result = Last filter result – (Last filtering result – New sample) × filter coefficient ÷ 256

- New sample > Last Filter result

Filtering result = Last filter result + (New sample – Last filtering result) × filter coefficient ÷ 256

Where, the range of filter coefficient is from 0 to 255. And the coefficient value determines weight of the new sampling value in this filtering result.

Figures 8 and 9 represent he effect with different filter coefficients.

- Filter Coefficient = 30
- Filter Coefficient = 200

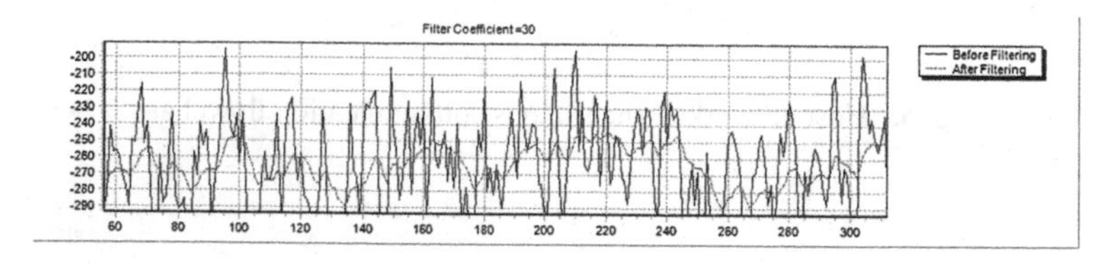

Fig. 8. The waveform of filter coefficient equal to 30

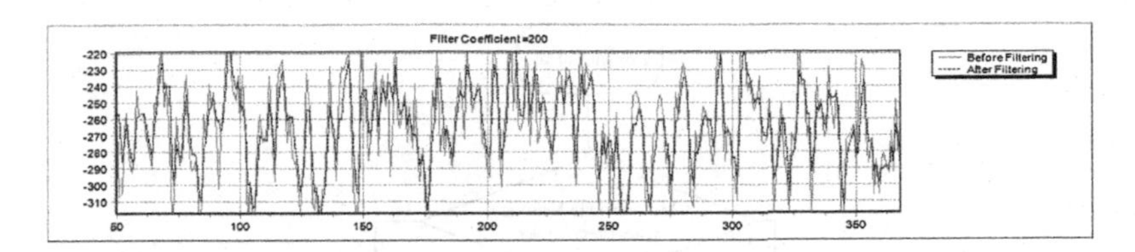

Fig. 9. The waveform of filter coefficient equal to 200

From Figs. 8 and 9, the filter coefficient is smaller, and the filter result is more stable.

- Filter Coefficient = 30

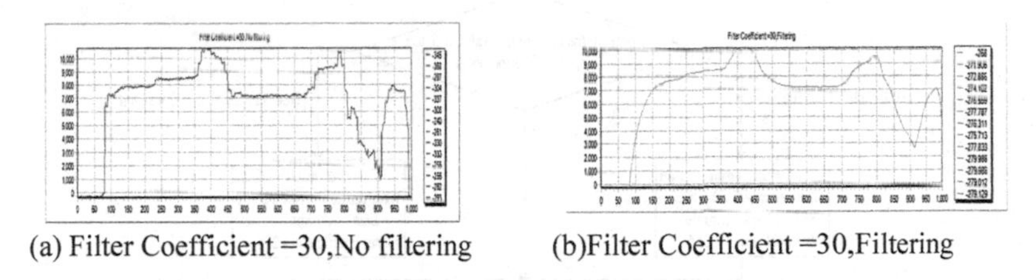

(a) Filter Coefficient =30,No filtering (b)Filter Coefficient =30,Filtering

Fig. 10. The waveform of filter coefficient equal to 30

- Filter Coefficient = 200

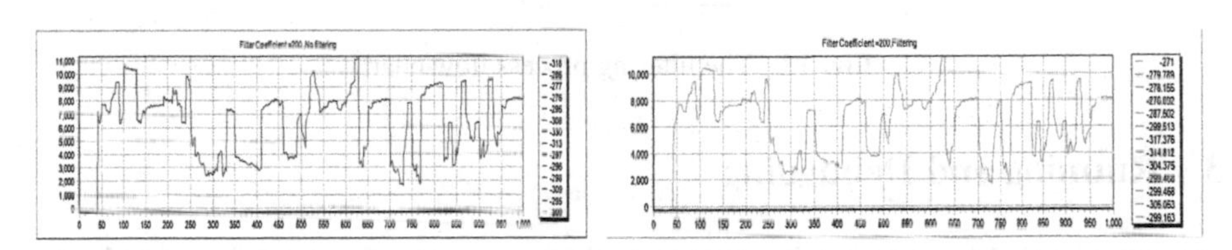

(a) Filter Coefficient =200, No filtering (b) Filter Coefficient =200, Filtering

Fig. 11. The waveform of filter coefficient equal to 200

From Figs. 10 and 11, the smaller filter coefficient is, more insensitive but more accurate the system is. And the bigger filter coefficient is, the more sensitive but less accurate system is.

In summary, Fig. 12 is the filtering process flow chart.

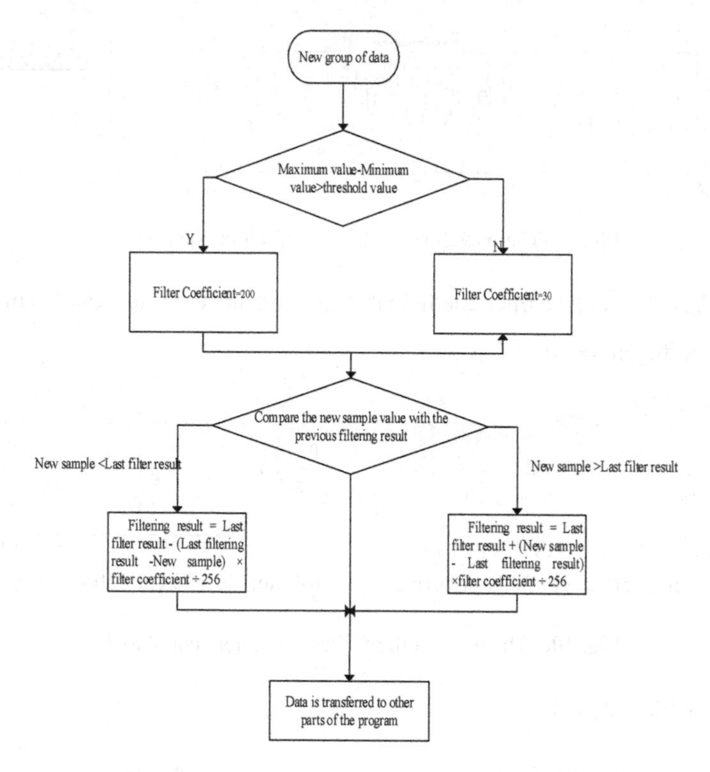

Fig. 12. The filtering process flow chart

3 Running and Debugging

Figures 13 and 14, respectively, represents the three parts of system designed by this paper. In order to facilitate the debugging, there is a program running to log running state of PC software. There is no obvious problem during the long-running process. And the software stays stable, which achieves the purpose of practical application.

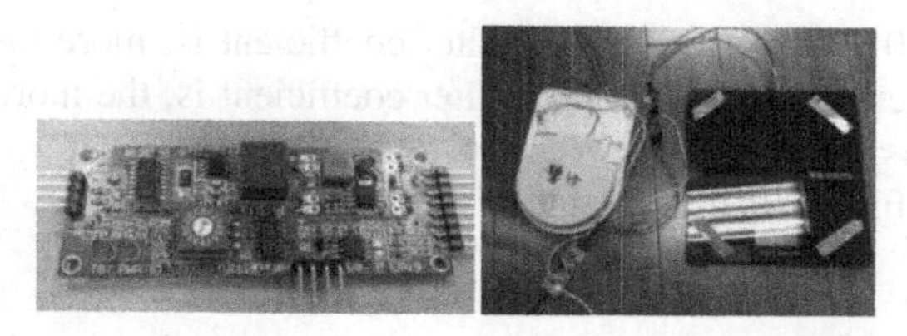

(a)Physical model of MCU (b)MCU and weighing module connection diagram

Fig. 13. Physical map

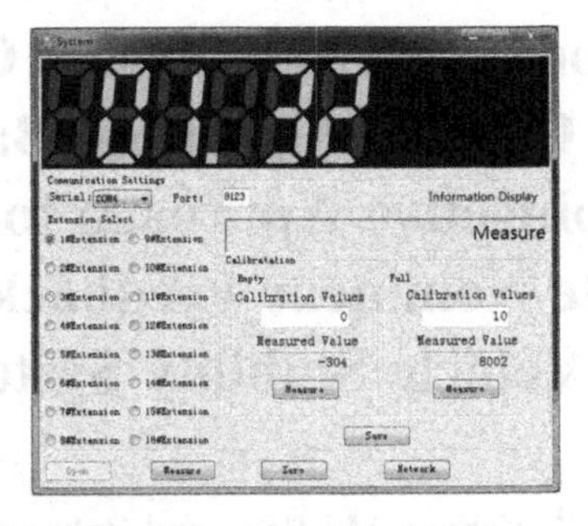

Fig. 14. The software running diagram

4 Conclusions and Future Work

The system can be applied to any occasions about material margin management. It contains the lower computer based on MCS-STC8051 and connects with upper computer by RS485 and Ethernet which can achieve the purpose that users can know the margin in any time. At the same time, the upper computer analyses data to make management of materials more effective. This paper focuses on the lower computer hardware selection and design, upper and lower computer communication protocols, and PC software design ideas. Finally, the weighting system designed by the paper has used in certain material margin management based on IOT to realize the automatic material management in a pharmaceutical laboratory.

Acknowledgements. This work was supported by the National Natural Science Foundation of China (61573144) and the Shanghai Leading Academic Discipline Project (B504).

References

1. Ma, C.: Embedded MCU and PC composite applications. China Comput. Commun. **9**, 17–18 (2015)
2. Wang, X.-W.: Automatic meter digital electronic scales designed based on HX711. Silicon Valley **5**, 68 (2015)
3. Wang, X.-W., Wang, G.-H., Wang, Y.-J.: Digital filtering technology apply on weighing sensor. Shandong Ind. Technol. 15, 256–257 (2015)
4. Ao, Y.-H., He, J.: AVR Based Embedded Fire Automatic Detection and Suppression System for Wind Turbine. Mach. Tool Hydraulics **43**(2), 132–134 (2015)
5. Mi, S.-T., Wang, T., Zhang, R.: Coal storage aspects of AT89C51 embedded management system. Coal Technol. **32**(2), 240–242 (2013)
6. Zhang, W.-T., Ma, W.-H., Wang, Z.-S.: Wireless ad hoc networks routing algorithm of electronic scale for automatic quality supervision. Microcontroller Embed. Syst. **1**, 16–19 (2016)
7. Zhang, L., Jiang, G., Zhi-Feng, X.: Research on localization system for mobile robot based on ATmega16 and PC. Microcontroller Embed. Syst. **12**, 11–13 (2010)
8. Albahari, J., Albahari, B.: C# 5.0 in a Nutshell, vol. 5. O'Reilly Media, USA (2012)

A Comparison of Particle Swarm Optimization and Genetic Algorithm Based on Multi-objective Approach for Optimal Composite Nonlinear Feedback Control of Vehicle Stability System

Liyana Ramli(✉), Yahaya Md Sam, and Zaharuddin Mohamed

Faculty of Electrical Engineering,
Universiti Teknologi Malaysia, Johor Bahru, Johor, Malaysia
liyana208@gmail.com, {yahaya, zahar}@fke.utm.my

Abstract. This paper proposes an intelligent tuning methods of linear and nonlinear parameters for composite nonlinear feedback (CNF) control using multi objective particle swarm optimization (MOPSO) and multi objective genetic algorithm (MOGA). The main advantage of the methods lies in its efficient fitness/objective evaluation approach of the algorithms such that it can be computed rapidly to obtain an optimal CNF with good system response. In order to yield an efficient technique for fitness evaluation, it is achieved by utilizing a multi objective approach, thus avoiding the use of single objective approach to evaluate the fitness. MATLAB simulations are used to test the effectiveness of the proposed techniques. Nonlinear vehicle model is constructed to validate the controller performance. The model is also simplified to a linear model for designing the CNF. The superiority of the proposed methods over the manual tuning method are improved with 98 percent reduction in error.

1 Introduction

Vehicle stability system is crucial to be control precisely especially in a severe cornering maneuver to avoid oversteer or understeer situations. Hence, active front steering system (AFS) has been widely investigated by many researchers for vehicle yaw rate tracking control to achieve a good system response. The implementation of composite nonlinear feedback (CNF) controller for active front steering system (AFS) is significant owing to its benefit mainly in improving the transient performance. In CNF, the optimal tuning parameters namely linear feedback gain F and nonlinear gain parameters ($\boldsymbol{\gamma}$ and γ) are desirable to obtain a good system response.

The CNF controller was formerly designed by [1]. Linear feedback gain can be designed by ensuring the closed loop system has a small damping ratio in order to achieve a fast output response. From the previous works, the techniques that have been applied are pole placement [2], H_2 and H_∞ [3], LQR method [4] and many more. In the CNF nonlinear part, the designer is required to tune the nonlinear gain parameters. As in [5], they selected the nonlinear gain parameters by using the classical root locus

L. Zhang et al. (Eds.): AsiaSim 2016/SCS AutumnSim 2016, Part I, CCIS 643, pp. 652–662, 2016.
DOI: 10.1007/978-981-10-2663-8_67

theory. According to [6], the value of γ can be fixed by setting the steady state system with a desired damping ratio that has been initially chosen. The other implementation to optimize the CNF parameters is by using Hooke Jeeves method for controlling the speed of DC motor [6].

Despite of the other tuning methods addressed in the previous works, there appear to be an absence in utilizing an artificial intelligent technique to optimize the parameters. It is a powerful method to save the computational time and ease the complexity in designing the CNF controller. Thus, this paper proposes multi-objective particle swarm optimization (MOPSO) and multi-objective genetic algorithm (MOGA) for CNF controller tuning parameters to achieve the desired transient and steady state performance of yaw rate response. Multi-objective approach seems to be a suitable method to be applied in the optimization algorithm, because each of these criteria can be computed together as a multi-objective function rather than just consider a single objective function. It has an ability to perform the trade-off between each of the fitness functions to produce the optimal performance of the system.

2 Vehicle Modeling

The nonlinear vehicle model is constructed with 7 DOFs as below

- Translation of longitudinal direction (vehicle speed).
- Translation of lateral direction (vehicle lateral speed).
- Yaw motion about the z-axis (vehicle yaw rate).
- Rotational of the 1st wheel to 4th wheel (wheel angular velocity).

It is assumed that the vehicle has low center of gravity with stiff suspension. Figure 1 illustrate the structures of 7 DOF nonlinear vehicle model, 2 DOF linear vehicle model and wheel rotation motion. The equations for vehicle speed at center of gravity, sideslip angle and yaw rate dynamics [7, 8] are shown respectively as

$$\dot{v} = \frac{1}{mv}[(F_{x1} + F_{x2})\cos(\beta - \delta) + (F_{x3} + F_{x4})\cos(\beta) + (F_{y1} + F_{y2})\sin(\beta - \delta) + (F_{y3} + F_{y4})\sin(\beta)] \quad (1)$$

$$\dot{\beta} = \frac{1}{mv}[-(F_{x1} + F_{x2})\sin(\beta - \delta) - (F_{x3} + F_{x4})\sin(\beta) + (F_{y1} + F_{y2})\cos(\delta - \beta) + (F_{y3} + F_{y4})\cos(\beta)] - \dot{\psi} \quad (2)$$

$$\ddot{\psi} = \frac{1}{I_z}[F_{x1}\left(l_f \sin\delta - \frac{T}{2}\cos\delta\right) + F_{x2}\left(l_f \sin\delta - \frac{T}{2}\cos\delta\right) + \frac{T}{2}(F_{x4} - F_{x3}) + F_{y1}\left(\frac{T}{2}\sin\delta - l_f\cos\delta\right) + F_{y2}\left(l_f\cos\delta - \frac{T}{2}\sin\delta\right) - l_r(F_{y3} + F_{y4})] \quad (3)$$

The lateral tire forces F_{yi} and nonlinear longitudinal tire forces F_{xi} are derived based on Pacejka tire model [9]. The formulation of tire side slip angles α [7] are given as

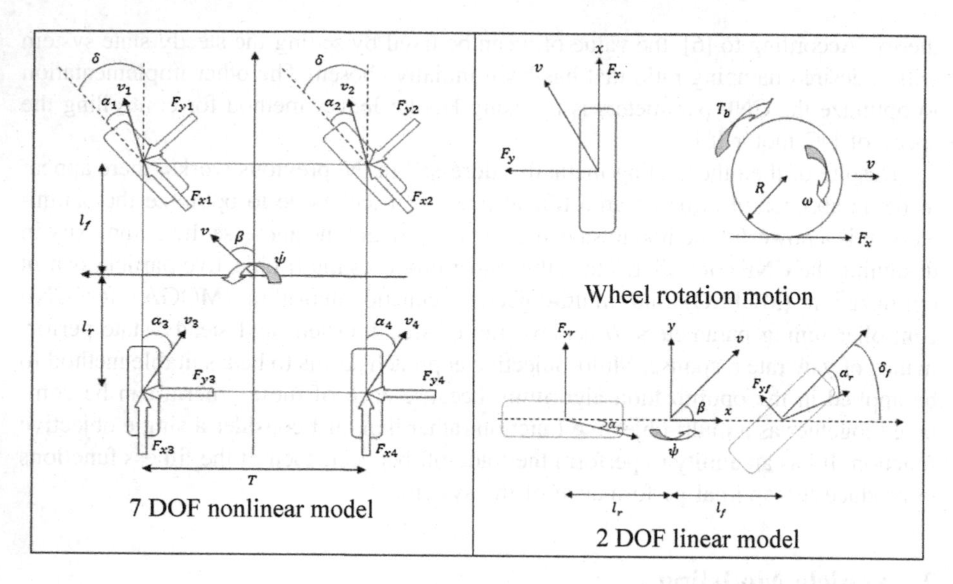

Fig. 1. Structure of vehicle models

$$\alpha_1 = \alpha_2 = \delta - \beta - \frac{l_f \dot{\psi}}{v} \text{ and } \alpha_3 = \alpha_4 = -\beta + \frac{l_r \dot{\psi}}{v} \tag{4}$$

The tire longitudinal slip λ_i during braking condition can be derived as

$$\lambda_i = \frac{v_i - R\omega_i}{v_i} \tag{5}$$

Along with the presence of moment of inertia of the wheel I_w, the wheel angular velocity ω can be calculated as

$$I_w \dot{\omega} = T_{drive_i} - T_{Br_i} - RF_{xi} \tag{6}$$

Moreover, the vehicle trajectory can be obtained [10] as

$$X = \int \left(v_x \cos \dot{\psi} - v_y \sin \dot{\psi} \right) dt \tag{7}$$

$$Y = \int \left(v_x \sin \dot{\psi} + v_y \cos \dot{\psi} \right) dt \tag{8}$$

In 2 DOF linear vehicle model [11], the state variables are vehicle body side slip angle β and yaw rate $\dot{\psi}$ with v as a constant parameter. The control input for the system is steer angle δ. The state space equation is shown as

$$\begin{bmatrix} \dot{\beta} \\ \ddot{\psi} \end{bmatrix} = \begin{bmatrix} -\frac{C_{yf}+C_{yr}}{mv} & \frac{-l_f C_{yf}+l_r C_{yr}}{mv^2} - 1 \\ -\frac{l_f C_{yf}-l_r C_{yr}}{I_z} & -\frac{l_f^2 C_{yf}+l_r^2 C_{yr}}{I_z v} \end{bmatrix} \begin{bmatrix} \beta \\ \dot{\psi} \end{bmatrix} + \begin{bmatrix} \frac{1}{mv} C_{yf} \\ \frac{1}{I_z} l_f C_{yf} \end{bmatrix} \delta + \begin{bmatrix} 0 \\ \frac{1}{I_z} \end{bmatrix} w \tag{9}$$

with an output of the system is given by

$$\dot{\psi} = \begin{bmatrix} 0 & 1 \end{bmatrix} \begin{bmatrix} \beta \\ \dot{\psi} \end{bmatrix} \tag{10}$$

where disturbance vector is $w = M_z$. The cornering stiffness at front and rear are $C_{yf} = C_{y1} + C_{y2}$ and $C_{yr} = C_{y3} + C_{y4}$ respectively. The desired side slip angle and desired yaw rate are determined based on [12]. The desired yaw rate equation is given as

$$\dot{\psi}_d = \frac{v}{(l_f + l_r) + k_{us} v^2} \delta_{fd} \tag{11}$$

where k_{us} is under steer parameter which is given by

$$k_{us} = m(l_r C_r - l_f C_f)/(l_r + l_f) C_f C_r \tag{12}$$

3 Controller Design

CNF involves the composition between two laws, that are linear and nonlinear feedback laws. Figure 2 shows system model control, where δ_f is a front wheel angle, δ_{fd} is a steer input of front wheel demanded by the driver and δ_c is a corrective steer angle by the CNF controller. The relationship of these angles is given as

$$\delta_f = \delta_{fd} + \delta_c \tag{13}$$

Consider a second order linear system as

$$\dot{x} = Ax(t) + Bsat(u(t)), x(0) = x_0, y = Cx(t) \tag{14}$$

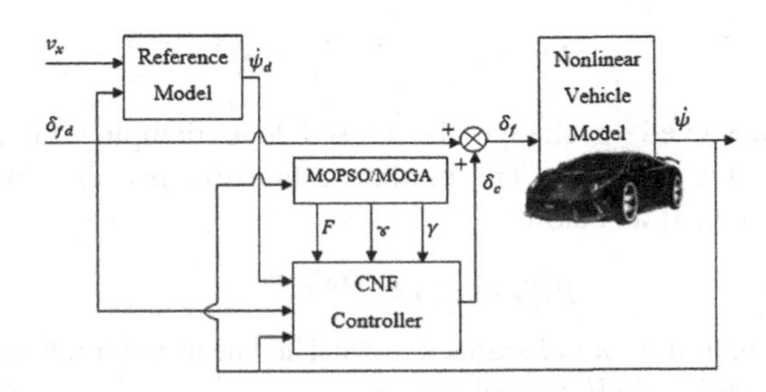

Fig. 2. System model control

where $x \in \Re^n$, $u \in \Re$ and $y \in \Re$ are the state variables, control input and controlled output vector respectively. A, B and C are the appropriate dimensional constant system matrices, and sat: $\Re \rightarrow \Re$ represents actuator saturation which can be expressed by,

$$sat(u) = sgn(u)min\{u_{max}, |u|\} \tag{15}$$

where u_{max} indicates saturation level for actuator input. The pair (A, B) is controllable. Below are the steps taken for designing the control strategy of CNF controller by using state feedback method [5].

Step 1 (Linear feedback law design): The linear feedback law is given as

$$u_L = Fx + Gr \tag{16}$$

$$\dot{x} = (A + BF)x + BGr \tag{17}$$

where r is step command input which is the signal of reference to be tracked by output y and $F = [f_1 f_2]$ is selected such that $A + BF$ is asymptotically stable and closed loop system has a low damping ratio. Since the objective is to achieve $y = r$, scalar G can be obtained as

$$G = -[C(A + BF)^{-1}B]^{-1} \tag{18}$$

The presence of G ensures the output y to track the constant reference signal r. When the output y tracks r, then the state variable x becomes new steady state value x_e.

$$x_e = G_e r, G_e = -(A + BF)^{-1}BG \tag{19}$$

The value of $W > 0$ must be a positive definite matrix. Matrix P can be obtained such that $A + BF$ is asymptotically stable and can be obtained based on Lyapunov equation.

$$(A + BF)^T P + (A + BF)P = -W \tag{20}$$

Step 2 (Nonlinear feedback law design): The nonlinear control law is designed to increase the damping ratio, so that the overshoot can be reduced or eliminated. The nonlinear feedback law is given by

$$u_N = \rho(y, r)B^T P(x - x_e) \tag{21}$$

This law is designed to change the closed loop damping ratio, as the output approaches the target reference. The nonlinear function $\rho(r, y)$ is a function of the tracking error $y - r$ [13] as below

$$\rho(r, y) = \gamma e^{-\gamma\gamma_0 |y - r|} \tag{22}$$

Step 3: Combination of both feedback laws: The linear and nonlinear feedback laws are combined to yield a CNF control law as

$$u = \delta_f = u_L + u_N = Fx + Gr + \rho(r, y)B^T P(x - x_e) \tag{23}$$

4 Design of Multi-objective PSO and GA Algorithms

A multi-objective approach for MOPSO is based on weighted sum approach [11, 14] for the fitness evaluation. Three criteria assigned for fitness function are over-shoot (OS), settling-time (TS) and steady-state-error (SSE) to solve the minimization problem. The fitness of ith particle is given as

$$Fitness_{ij} = w_{SSE}(SSE)_{ij} + w_{OS}(OS)_{ij} + w_{Ts}(TS)_{ij} \tag{24}$$

Table 1 shows the weight value assigned for each of the fitness given in Eq. (24)

Table 1. Weight value for fitness evaluation

	Weight value assigned for	Weight value	Priority
w_{OS}	OS	0.7	Highest
w_{TS}	TS	0.2	Medium
w_{SSE}	SSE	0.1	Lowest

The control variables are Υ and γ as in Eq. (22) and $F = [f_1 f_2]$ as in Eq. (16) indicate the position vector of ith particle in the multi-dimensional search space at time step t. The velocity of ith particle is given as

$$v_{ij}^{t+1} = \omega_I v_{ij}^t + c_1 r_{1j}^t \left[P_{best,i}^t - x_{ij}^t\right] + c_2 r_{2j}^t [G_{best} - x_{ij}^t] \tag{25}$$

By considering a minimization problem, all the particles are evaluated based on *Fitness* value. The personal best position $P_{best,i}$ to solve a minimization problem at $t+1$ is defined as

$$P_{best,i}^{t+1} = \begin{cases} P_{best,i}^t, & Fitness(x_i^{t+1}) > Fitness(x_i^t) \\ x_i^{t+1}, & Fitness(x_i^{t+1}) \le Fitness(x_i^t) \end{cases} \tag{26}$$

Furthermore, to calculate the global best position G_{best} at time step t is given as

$$G_{best} = \min\left\{P_{best,i}^t\right\} \tag{27}$$

Every particle position is updated by the velocity until it finally reach one of the stopping criterion such as the difference value between the maximum and minimum of fitness is approximately equal to 0.00001 or the algorithm has reached the maximum iteration defined by user. In MOGA, the fitness evaluation assigned for the multi-objective strategy is using a similar technique as in Eq. (24). The fitness value

$Fitness_{ij}$ for each of the chromosome in the current population is calculated which indicates the quality and chance of the chromosome to be selected for the next generation. The probability of fitness is obtained as

$$P_{ij} = \frac{Fitness_{ij}}{\sum_{i=1}^{N} Fitness_{ij}} \tag{28}$$

Roulette Wheel method is then computed in selection process to find the optimal fitness. The cumulative probability value is given as

$$C_i = P_i + C_{i-1} \tag{29}$$

The process including crossover and mutation are repetitive until the stopping criterion is met and the optimal value is achieved.

5 Result and Discussion

The results are obtained through the simulation work by using Matlab software. The J-turn maneuver as in Fig. 3 is tested with the external disturbance which representing a side wind as in Fig. 4.

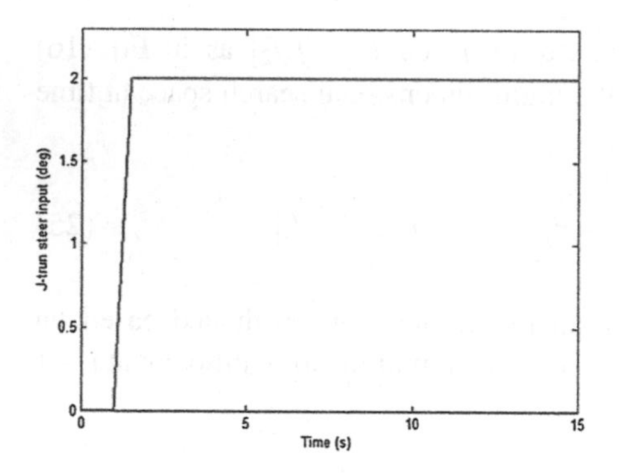

Fig. 3. J-turn maneuvre

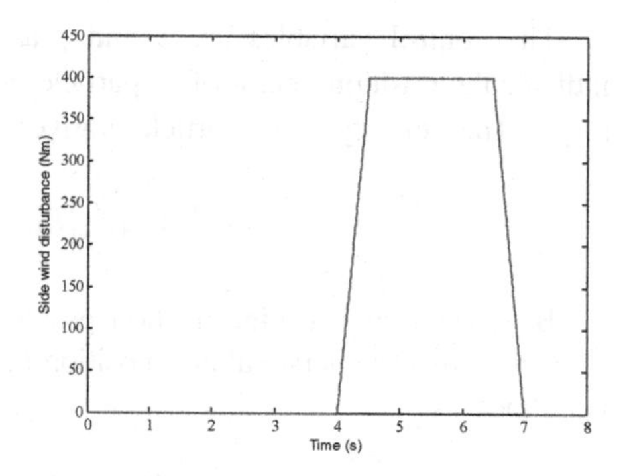

Fig. 4. Wind disturbance

For the simulation, the 2-degree driver steer input of front wheel δ_{fd} is used. The steering ratio of hand wheel steer angle to the front wheel steer input is 20:1 [15]. The vehicle is set with a constant velocity, 100 km/h. Table 2 shows all the vehicle parameters for the simulation as below

The 2 DOF single track vehicle model for front steering system is obtained as

$$\dot{x} = \begin{bmatrix} -3.9026 & -0.9839 \\ 6.9689 & -3.8942 \end{bmatrix} x + \begin{bmatrix} 2.2343 \\ 35.9250 \end{bmatrix} sat(u), y = [0\ 1]x \tag{30}$$

Table 2. Vehicle parameters

Vehicle parameter	Value
Mass, m	1704.7 kg
Moment inertia, I_z	3048.1 kgm^2
Distance from the center of gravity (CG) to the front axis, l_f	1.035 m
Distance from CG to the rear axis, l_r	1.655 m
Front tire cornering, C_{yf}	105.8 kN
Cornering stiffness (rear tire), C_{yr}	79 kN
Track, T	1.540 m
Moment of inertia, I_w	0.99 kgm^2
Tire radius, R	0.313 m
Road adhesion coefficient, μ	1
Steering wheel ratio, n_s	20
Gravity constant, g	9.8 ms^{-2}

The yaw reference in Eq. (11) is determined as

$$\dot{\psi}_d = 7.0654\delta_{fd} \tag{31}$$

The parameters initialization that has been set for MOPSO are number of particles in a swarm ($N - 20$), maximum iteration $t_{\max} = 150$, acceleration coefficients (c_1 and c_2) = 1.4, maximum weight value $\omega_{I_{max}} = 0.9$ and minimum weight value $\omega_{I_{min}} = 0.4$. In MOGA, the parameters are number of chromosomes $N = 20$, maximum number of iteration = 150, crossover rate $cr = 0.7$ and mutation rate $mr = 0.2$. The manual tuning method involves ITAE criterion to solve the minimization problem [6] that can be determined as

$$\min \int_0^\infty [t|e|dt] \tag{32}$$

e indicates the closed loop tracking error. Figure 5 illustrates the yaw rate by using MOPSO, MOGA and manual tuning method with 2-degree steer input of J-turn maneuver. Figure 6 illustrates the side slip angle responses for all the techniques used. It can be visualized that the responses are stable and do not exceed the limitation. Figure 7 illustrates the trajectory of the vehicle on the road for 2-degree steer input. The vehicle trajectory of CNF by MOPSO and MOGA are still capable to follow the reference path and remain on the track with minimal error. The vehicle path movement by CNF (manual tuning) has shown slight deviation from the desired track, meanwhile the vehicle trajectory without controller shows that the vehicle has fully deviated from the desired. This situation is called understeer movement that could lead to an accident.

Table 3 tabulates the mean squared error (MSE). MSE is the average of the squares of errors indicates the difference of the actual and desired yaw rate response. MOPSO achieved better results for both steer inputs which are slightly smaller value of MSE than MOGA and followed by the manual tuning method. The result by using the

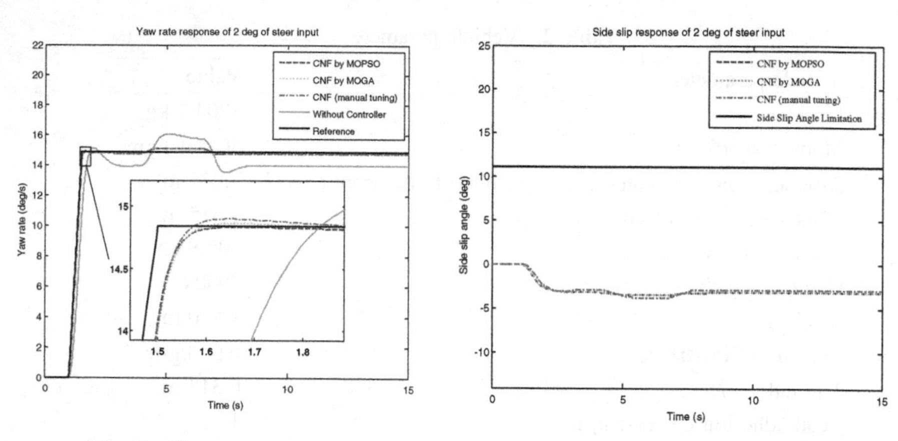

Fig. 5. Yaw rate responses

Fig. 6. Side slip angles

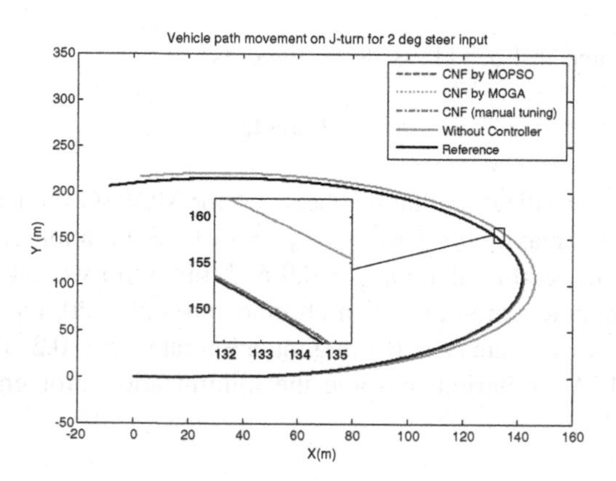

Fig. 7. Vehicle trajectory

manual tuning method has achieved a good performance in transient and steady state responses. However, the result can be improved more because it is proven that an optimal result can be produced by using MOPSO and MOGA. Manual tuning method requires prediction of certain parameters to finally achieve the minimal value of ITAE. If the ITAE value has recorded unsatisfactory result, the process must be repeated again and longer time required to achieve an optimal response which is not practical.

Table 3. Mean squared error

Method	MOPSO	MOGA	Manual tuning
MSE	0.0357	0.0437	0.0449

6 Conclusion

As a conclusion, the combination of linear and nonlinear control law may produce a good CNF controller especially when it is optimized by MOPSO and MOGA methods. Thus, the weakness of manual tuning method can be overcome by using these algorithms which are more suitable and effective due to its intelligent features. Overall, MOPSO has shown better result compared to MOGA but both algorithms have ability in minimizing the objective function with a small tracking error produced. Thus, the vehicle can move safely without any dangerous accident such as skidding, spinning, over steering and under steering conditions.

References

1. Lin, Z., Pachter, M., Banda, S.: Toward improvement of tracking performance nonlinear feedback for linear systems. Int. J. Control **70**, 1–11 (1998)
2. Ma, D., Cao, Y., Fan, D.: Design and implementation of an electro-optical tracking servo system via composite nonlinear control approach. In: Intelligent Computation Technology and Automation (ICICTA), pp. 1139–1142 (2010)
3. Chen, B.M., Weiyao, L.: On improving transient performance in tracking control for a class of nonlinear discrete-time systems with input saturation. IEEE Trans. Autom. Control **52**, 1307–1313 (2007)
4. Yingjie, H., Chen, B.M., Chao, W.: Composite nonlinear control with state and measurement feedback for general multivariable systems with input saturation. In: IEEE Conference on Decision and Control, pp. 4469–4474 (2003)
5. Chen, B.M., Lee, T.H., Kemao, P., Venkataramanan, V.: Composite nonlinear feedback control for linear systems with input saturation: theory and an application. IEEE Trans. Autom. Control **48**, 427–439 (2003)
6. Weiyao, L., Thum, C.K., Chen, B.M.: A hard-disk-drive servo system design using composite nonlinear-feedback control with optimal nonlinear gain tuning methods. IEEE Trans. Ind. Electr. **57**, 1735–1745 (2010)
7. Kiencke, U., Nielsen, L.: Automotive Control Systems for Engine, Driveline and Vehicle. Springer, Heidelberg (2010)
8. Başlamişli, S.Ç., Köse, İ.E., Anlaç, G.: Handling stability improvement through robust active front steering and active differential control. Veh. Syst. Dyn. **49**, 657–683 (2010)
9. Pacejka, H.B.: Tyre and Vehicle Dynamics. Butterworth-Heinemann, Oxford (2002)
10. Jazar, R.N.: Vehicle Dynamics: Theory and Application. Springer, New York (2008)
11. Ramli, L., Sam, Y.M., Mohamed, Z., Khairi Aripin, M., Fahezal Ismail, M.: Composite nonlinear feedback control with multi-objective particle swarm optimization for active front steering system. Jurnal Teknologi **72**, 13–20 (2015). Scopus
12. Mirzaei, M.: A new strategy for minimum usage of external yaw moment in vehicle dynamic control system. Transp. Res. Part C: Emerg. Technol. **18**, 213–224 (2010)
13. Weiyao, L., Chen, B.M.: On selection of nonlinear gain in composite nonlinear feedback control for a class of linear systems. In: IEEE Conference on Decision and Control, pp. 1198–1203 (2007)

14. Ismail, F.S.: Self organizing genetic algorithm for multi-objective optimization problems. Universiti Teknologi Malaysia (2011)
15. He, J.: Integrated vehicle dynamics control using active steering, driveline and braking. University of Leeds (United Kingdom), Ann Arbor (2005)

Feature Recognition Based on Fuzzy Neural Network for Clone Car

Yanjuan Hu[1,2(✉)], Luquan Ren[1], Hongwei Zhao[1], and Yao Wang[3]

[1] College of Biological and Agricultural Engineering, Jilin University, Changchun, China
yanjuan_hu@126.com, {lqren,hwzhao}@jlu.edu.cn

[2] Mechatronic Engineering, Changchun University of Technology, Changchun, China

[3] College of Mechanical Engineering, Beihua University, Jilin City, China
wangyao7731@126.com

Abstract. In order to solve the problem of the same type, the same color, the same number of the clone car identification problem, the time credibility and traffic unobstructed degree are the evaluation factors, the membership function of the input vectors was constructed by using the typical function method, and the clone car suspected degree were divided into not suspicious, slight suspicious, suspicious,very suspicious, extreme suspicious of 5 grades. A neural network with 4 layers of nodes is established, which is the input layer, the fuzzy layer, the fuzzy inference layer and the output layer. The simulation results show that the actual output of the network is basically in line with the output of the network forecast, which can meet the requirements of the system.

Keywords: Fuzzy neural network · Feature recognition · Time credibility · Traffic unobstructed degree

1 Introduction

The same type, the same color, the same number of clone car identification is a key and difficult clone car recognition technology. This clone car cannot be recognized by image processing and pattern recognition technology. Assuming that the same type, the same color, the same number vehicles appear in A and B places at the moment T_1, T_2 respectively. In this paper, according to the city speed limit, the shortest travel time passed through the two places A, B is calculated. By comparing the actual running time and T_{min}, whether the vehicle is suspected is determined.

Fuzzy system [1–3] for knowledge extraction is more convenient, it can deal with some of the problems of thinking reasoning, for some incomplete, inaccurate information, can be dealt with based on experience and knowledge; it is good for the use of expert knowledge, and the sample requirement is low, suitable for fuzzy or qualitative knowledge. But the fuzzy system is lack of self-learning and self-adaptation ability, it cannot be based on the input and output characteristics of the system to adaptively update the fuzzy membership function parameters, moreover, the fuzzy system has many defects, such as manual intervention, slow reasoning and low precision.

L. Zhang et al. (Eds.): AsiaSim 2016/SCS AutumnSim 2016, Part I, CCIS 643, pp. 663–671, 2016.
DOI: 10.1007/978-981-10-2663-8_68

The artificial neural network [4–6] is composed of many small processing units, and the function of each processing unit is simple. However, a large number of processing units jointly acting and parallel computing can quickly get the desired results. And the fault tolerance of neural network is very strong, the local neuron damage, which will not cause a great impact on the overall situation. Neural network has strong learning ability, manual intervention is less and the precision is higher, but it is not suitable for the expression of knowledge based on rules. Therefore, in the network training, the neural network cannot better use the existing experience knowledge, and network training time is long, and easy to fall into the local optimal solution.

Fuzzy neural network (FNN) [7–10] is the product of the combination of fuzzy theory and neural network. Fuzzy neural network combines the two organically, brings together the advantages of neural network and fuzzy theory. It can solve some problems that cannot be solved by conventional information processing, but also can solve the problem of consciousness category or sample information incomplete.

This paper uses FNN technology to determine suspicious degree of vehicle clone plate, this kind of evaluation information does not need to be expressed accurately, but it is in the form of membership degree. The system will ultimately determine the vehicle belonging to which warning level. The vehicles belonging to different levels are managed at different grades, and the vehicle of high level is included in the black list database, self-identification and early warning of the clone car can be implemented.

2 Determine the Input and Output of Network

2.1 Problem Description

Two basis of identifying the same type, the same color, the same number clone car are time credibility ξ and traffic unobstructed degree Ψ, among them, the smaller the time credibility is, the more likely it is to clone car. Under the condition of same time credibility, when the traffic is more crowded and the traffic flow is smaller, the possibility for the clone car is more.

Time credibility ξ is quantitative factor, and traffic unobstructed degree Ψ is qualitative factors. These two points are used as the input variables of the network.

The output of the network is the suspicious degree υ of clone car, and the greater the suspected degree is, the bigger the possibility of the car deck is.

This article will take Changchun city as an example, through the analysis of the traffic flow on the main road in urban areas, to analyze and establish the fuzzy neural network model.

2.2 Evaluation Factor

Time Credibility. The degree of credibility of vehicle in the monitoring time period from the A to the B, can be obtained by the Eq. 1.

$$\xi = \frac{T - T_{\min}}{T_{\min}} \quad (1)$$

Where, $T = |T_2 - T_1|$, $T_{\min}$ represents the shortest time obtained by the Eq. 2:

$$T_{\min} = \frac{S_{\min}}{V} \quad (2)$$

Where, $S_{\min}$ represents the shortest distance between A and B, which can be obtained by the shortest path algorithm. V is the maximum speed limit of the city.

By sample calculation, when $\xi > 1$, the possible of clone car can be eliminated; when $\xi < -0.5$, the car can be determined is the clone car. So the discourse domain of ξ is [−0.5, 1], Fuzzy set is divided into ξ = {low, slight low, middle, slight high, high}.

Traffic Unobstructed Degree. The traffic unobstructed degree describes the unobstructed degree where the road that the vehicle is on at the monitoring time. When the traffic is heavy, in the same time period, the distance that car can travel is shorter. In other words, the two cars pass the same road section at the same time, and in the traffic jam the possibility that the running vehicle is clone car is greater. The traffic unobstructed degree considered here is a qualitative factor, which should be quantified according to the expert scoring method. The fuzzy set of quantitative criteria can be divided into Ψ = {very poor, poor, common, slight good, good} to mark, and score is as an input variable.

Because the domain scope of the input variables ξ and Ψ of network is not uniform, first, the domain should be converted, and be linearly converted to the [0, 1] range, then

Table 1. ξ and Ψ data table

The *i*th group \ Evaluation indicator	ξ	Ψ
1	0.9725	0.4500
2	0.6908	0.7500
3	0.8252	0.3500
4	0.8447	0.4500
5	0.8022	0.6500
6	0.2743	0.1500
7	0.4554	0.2500
8	0.8348	0.5500
9	0.6369	0.7500
10	0.9125	0.7500

fuzzy computing is implemented. The Table 1 is ξ and Ψ data obtained by calculating the data of 10 groups monitored actually.

2.3 The Establishment of the Fuzzy Membership Function

The fuzzy method is used to calculate the membership degree of influencing factors as the input of neural network, the membership function of fuzzy set is established firstly. For the same fuzzy concept, different people will form different fuzzy membership function. However, as long as they can reflect the fuzzy concept, in solving practical problems they are the same. The determination method of fuzzy membership function mainly has fuzzy statistical method, the example method, the expert experience method and the two element contrast method.

Different membership function curves have different influence on the control characteristics. Fuzzy subset with a sharp shape in the membership function curves, its resolution is higher, and the control sensitivity is higher. On the contrary, the membership function curve is relatively flat, its control characteristic is relatively gentle, and the stability is good. Therefore, it is need to choose a more suitable membership function curve according to the actual problem. In this paper, the membership functions of the input vectors are constructed by using the typical function method. After a lot of data analysis and experimental verification, the membership function is determined as the Gauss type membership function. Gauss distribution function is shown in Fig. 1.

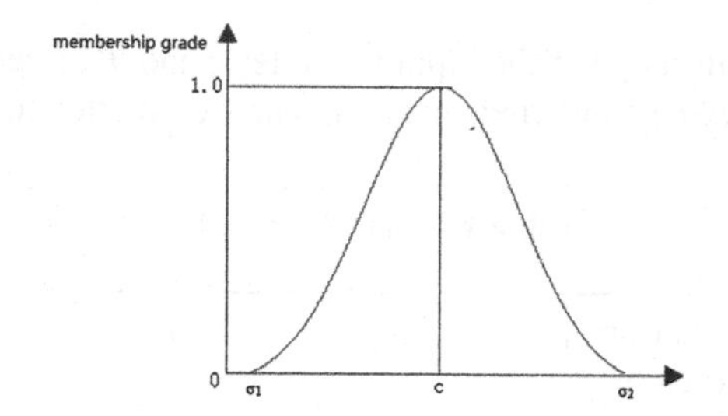

Fig. 1. Gauss type membership function curve

In Fig. 1, c represents the center, and $\sigma 1$, $\sigma 2$ indicate the width of the left and right sides respectively.

For time credibility ξ, fuzzy set is divided into ξ = {low, slight low, middle, slight high, high}, Gauss membership function distribution center c = {0, 0.2, 0.4, 0.6, 1}. Through the analysis of a large number of monitoring data, according to the principle "the vast majority of vehicles running on the road are vehicles that are legally licensed", the regional of the low and slight low credibility is divided more detailed, so this type of regional resolution is relatively high. The time reliability of the membership function is shown in Fig. 2.

In Fig. 2, the red curve represents the membership function curve of the lowξ, orange, yellow, blue and green are in turn slight low ξ, middle ξ, slight high ξ, high ξ. See from

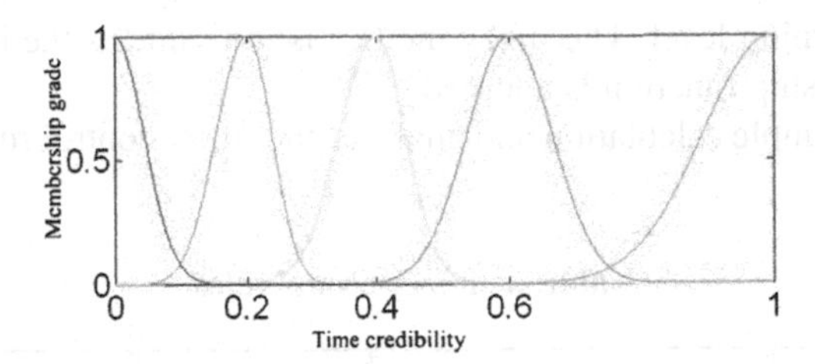

Fig. 2. The membership function curve of time reliability ξ (Color figure online)

the graph, the red, orange and yellow area classifications are fine, and the resolution is higher.

For traffic unobstructed degree Ψ, the fuzzy set can be divided into Ψ = {very bad, bad, common, slight good, good}, and Gauss membership function distribution center $c = \{0, 0.25, 0.45, 0.75, 1\}$. Membership function curve of Ψ is shown in Fig. 3.

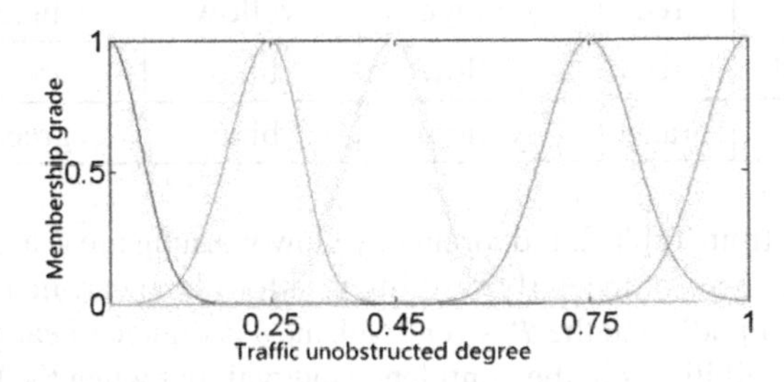

Fig. 3. The membership function curve of traffic unobstructed degree Ψ (Color figure online)

In Fig. 3, the red, orange, yellow, blue and green curves respectively correspond to Ψ "very poor", "poor", "general", "slight good" and "good" situations.

Because the data collected by the data acquisition equipment is clear, it cannot be used as the input of the fuzzy neural network. Therefore, the data in Table 1 can be calculated the corresponding degree of membership of each distribution center by the established fuzzy membership function,and the membership degree is used as the input of the fuzzy neural network.

3 The Establishment of Fuzzy Control Rules

The fuzzy neural network output in this paper describes the suspicious degree of the vehicle whether is the clone car, which is referred to as clone car suspicious degreeυ, its domain is [0, 1], and the fuzzy set is divided into υ = {not suspicious, slight suspicious, suspicious, very suspicious, extreme suspicious}. In order to facilitate the description, the fuzzy set is in turn defined as υ = {green, blue, yellow, orange, red}, which respectively represent early warning level of different degrees. Firstly, the network is used to solve a precise value of υ, then it will be blurred, finally, the car is determined to belong to which early warning level. The fuzzy method is the same as the input variable, and the Gauss membership function is adopted.

Based on the sample calculation and analysis, the fuzzy control rules are established as Table 2.

Table 2. Fuzzy control rules

υ / Ψ \ ξ	low	Slight low	Middle	Slight high	high
Very poor	red	red	orange	yellow	blue
poor	red	orange	yellow	blue	green
common	red	orange	yellow	blue	green
Slight good	red	yellow	blue	green	green
good	orange	yellow	blue	green	green

As can be seen from Table 2, red, orange, yellow warning areas are relatively small, and this part is the focus of the early warning area for clone car. In Table 2, under the situation of the ξ is middle and the Ψ is very bad, the υ is orange of early warning, which reflects the time credibility is in the confidence interval, but when the traffic situation is very poor, the suspicious degree is higher. However, under the situation of the ξ is slight low and the Ψ is good, the υ is yellow of early warning, which illustrates in the case of low credibility, but the traffic if very good, the vehicle also cannot be determined is the clone car. The situation described in the table fully reflects that the clone car is determined by the two factors of time credibility ξ and traffic unobstructed degree Ψ.

4 Structure Model of Network

In this paper, the structure of fuzzy neural network is four layers neural network, where, the input layer, fuzzy layer, fuzzy inference layer and output layer node number are respectively 2, 10, 25 and 1. The structure of fuzzy neural network is shown in Fig. 4.

5 Analysis of Model Simulation Results

1000 groups of data are randomly selected as the network simulation data. The first 550 groups of data are selected as the training sample data, and the input vector is input into the network, the expert value is the expected output of the network. The back 450 groups of data are as the test data, and the test data is input into the network that has studied. The simulation result is shown in Fig. 5.

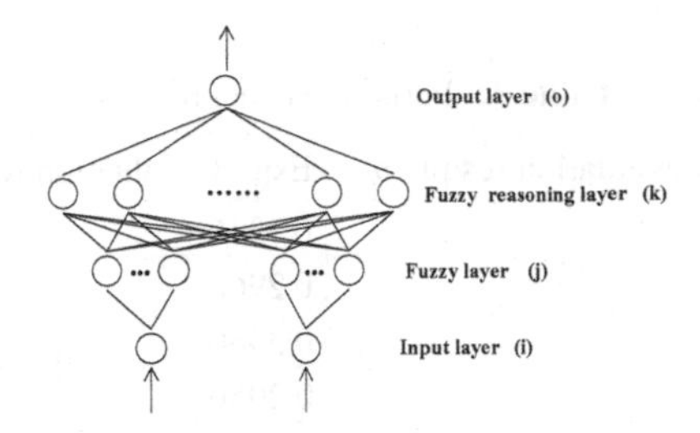

Fig. 4. Four layers schematic diagram of the structure of neural network

As shown in Fig. 5, the black line shows the predicted output of the network, the red line shows the actual output of the network. In the 450 groups of experimental data, clone car suspicious degree most concentrate in the following 0.5, and Only a few is more than 0.6, which shows that the vehicle sample is basically a legitimate vehicle, and the proportion for clone car is very small, so the selected samples are in line with the actual traffic conditions. The actual output of the network is basically in line with the network forecast output. The error curve is shown in Fig. 6, and error is kept between −0.02 and +0.02, which will not affect determination of the system for the early warning level. Some test results are shown in Table 3.

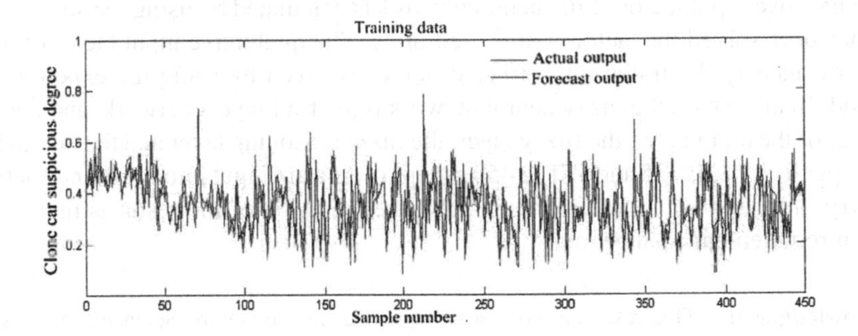

Fig. 5. Simulation results

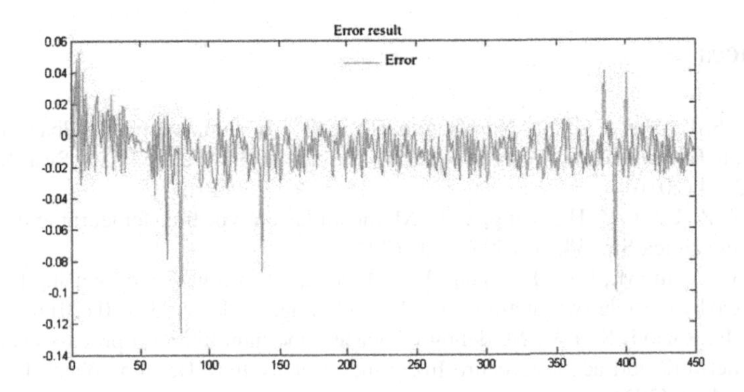

Fig. 6. Experimental error

Table 3. Parts of the test results

ξ	Ψ	Network evaluation results υ	Expert evaluation results υ_{expect}	Error
0.9725	0.43	0.1439	0.1346	0.0093
0.6908	0.74	0.2816	0.2968	−0.0152
0.7012	0.39	0.2706	0.3980	−0.1274
0.8447	0.42	0.2118	0.2056	0.0062
0.8022	0.68	0.2174	0.2147	0.0027
0.2743	0.12	0.7892	0.7874	0.0018
0.4554	0.28	0.5913	0.5834	0.0079
0.8348	0.55	0.1736	0.1755	−0.0019
0.6369	0.73	0.3487	0.3510	−0.0023
0.9125	0.49	0.1754	0.1811	−0.0057

6 Conclusions

The same type, the same color, the same number clone cars cannot be identified by image processing method, so a method based on fuzzy neural network is proposed in this paper. A quantitative input factor of the neural network is calculated by using the shortest path that has been solved,the factor is time credibility. The qualitative input factor of neural network, namely the traffic unobstructed degree is given by using the expert scoring method. In this paper, the fuzzy neural network is the four layers network, and the layer number of the input layer, the fuzzy layer, the fuzzy reasoning layer and the output layer are respectively 2, 10, 25 and 1. The 450 groups of data are input into the trained network to carry out the simulation experiment, and the precision of the result is high, so the system requirements can be met.

Acknowledgment. This research work was supported by the Nature Science Foundation of China, and the project name is "Research on the theory and method of manufacturability evaluation in cloud manufacturing environment", no. 51405030; the Youth Science Foundation of Jilin Province, no. 20160520069JH.

References

1. Huang, S.-J., Yang, G.-H.: Non-fragile H-infinity dynamic output feedback control for uncertain Takagi-Sugeno fuzzy systems with time-varying delay. Int. J. Syst. Sci. **47**(12), 2954–2964 (2016)
2. Jiang, Y.-Z., Deng, Z.-H., Wang, S.-T.: Mamdani-larsen type transfer learning fuzzy system. Acta Automatica Sin. **38**(9), 1393–1409 (2012)
3. Wang, G., Wan, M., Liu, H., Zhang, W.: Modeling of milling force by using fuzzy system optimized by particle swarm algorithm. J. Mech. Eng. **47**(13), 123–130 (2011)
4. Salehi, F., Razavi, S.M.A.: Modeling of waste brine nanofiltration process using artificial neural network and adaptive neuro-fuzzy inference system. Desalin. Water Treat. **57**(31), 14369–14378 (2016)

5. Xiaoyu, G., Yujun, S., Yifu, W., Jingyuan, L.: Improved artificial neural network for determination of plant leaf area. Trans. Chin. Soc. Agric. Mach. **44**(2), 200–204 (2013)
6. Shi, L., Deng, Q., Lu, L., Liu, W.: Prediction of PM10 mass concentrations based on BP artificial neural network. J. Cent. S. Univ. (Science and Technology) **43**(5), 1969–1974 (2012)
7. Zhang, D., Li, H., Liu, X., Zhang, W.: A integrated predication method of wavelet-fuzzy neural network for nonlinear time series. Chin. J. Manag. Sci. **21**, 647–651 (2013). Special issue
8. Ma, X., Liu, G., Zhou, W., Feng, J.: Apple recognition based on fuzzy neural network and quantum genetic algorithm. Trans. Chin. Soc. Agric. Mach. **44**(12), 227–251 (2013)
9. Chen, X., Li, D., Bai, Y., Xu, Z.: Application of type-II fuzzy neural network to adaptive double axis motion control system. Opt. Precis. Eng. **19**(7), 1643–1650 (2011)
10. Xia, W., Shen, L.: A network selection algorithm based on fuzzy neural network for heterogeneous networks. J. Southeast Univ. (Nat. Sci. Ed.) **40**(4), 663–669 (2010)

Configuration Optimization and Surface Accuracy Investigation of Solid Surface Deployable Reflector

Qifeng Cui[1,2,3], Ming Li[2(✉)], Zhilong Peng[2], and Haijun Luo[2]

[1] The State Key Laboratory of Mechanical Transmissions, Chongqing University, Chongqing 400044, China
[2] Aerospace System Engineering Shanghai, Shanghai 201109, China
liming.ases@gmail.com
[3] Shanghai Key Laboratory of Spacecraft Mechanism, Shanghai 201109, China

Abstract. As the most important payload of communication satellites, scout satellites, relay satellites and remote sensing satellites, the solid surface deployable parabolic reflector has a high surface accuracy, a high stiffness but a heavy weight and a low folding ratio. The configure optimization and surface accuracy investigation become the perquisite of the engineering design due to the ascending requirement of the operating frequency and folding ratio. This paper dedicates on the coupling multi-parameter configuration optimization and the stochastic procedure based surface accuracy investigation of a solid surface deployable parabolic reflector. It can be concluded that the folding ratio of the optimized reflector attains to 0.296; the repeating error plays the most important role in surface accuracy and the exist of the machining error leads to a more unify surface accuracy. This investigation may lead to an intensive comprehension on the solid surface deployable reflectors.

Keywords: Solid surface · Deployable reflector · Configuration · Surface accuracy · Monte Carlo simulation

1 Introduction

The purpose of a reflector is to confine most of the electromagnetic energy over a distributed aperture into a focal plane for communication or energy transfer [1]. The earliest use can be traced to the 2nd Punic Wars in the thrid century BC, Archimedes used parabolic reflectors to focus the Sun's heat to burn attacking Roman ships at the siege of Syracuse [1]. The concept of using a parabolic reflector to focus electromagnetic energy was first described in the 10th century by Ibn Sahl, an Arabian physicist [2] and the first application of parabolic reflectors in non optical frequencies was the reflector used in the demonstration experiment of Maxwell's electromagnetic wave by Hertz in 1888 [1].

As the most important payload of communication satellites, scout satellites, relay satellites and remote sensing satellites, the parabolic reflectors should have a larger caliber, a higher surface accuracy and a lighter weight in order to fulfill a more effective communication. However, due to the restriction of launching capability, the parabolic

L. Zhang et al. (Eds.): AsiaSim 2016/SCS AutumnSim 2016, Part I, CCIS 643, pp. 672–684, 2016.
DOI: 10.1007/978-981-10-2663-8_69

reflector should be deployable and a deployable mechanism should be installed on the reflector. Therefore, the deployable reflector can be restricted during the launching and deployed then locked after orbit injecting. The deployable reflectors can be categorized into rigid assemblies, cable-strut assemblies, tensegrity structures and inflatable systems [3]. One of the most important index of the parabolic reflectors is the gain, which indicates the extent of concentration. The relationship among the actual gain G, the theoretical gain G_0 and the surface accuracy error δ can be expressed as Eq. (1),

$$\frac{G}{G_0} = e^{-\frac{4\pi\delta}{\lambda}} \tag{1}$$

Herein, λ stands for the wavelength and the surface accuracy error is represented by root-mean-square (RMS). Generally, the surface accuracy error should locates between $\lambda/30 \sim \lambda/50$. It can be clarify that the more the communication efficiency, the shorter the wavelength will be, and as a result, a higher surface accuracy should be obtained. The solid surface deployable parabolic reflector is preferred because of the high surface accuracy.

However, the deployment of the solid surface reflector is driven by the elastic energy stored in the hinges, the repeating error, coupling with the machining error determines the surface accuracy error. This paper dedicates on the coupling multi-variable configuration optimization and the stochastic investigation on the surface accuracy, for purpose of a thorough comprehension on the behavior of solid surface deployable reflector.

2 State of the Art

Most of the solid surface schemes are prototypes [3]. The very first scheme was proposed by Thompson-Ramo-Wooldridge, which is named by Sunflower. As illustrated in Fig. 1, Sunflower is constituted by 19 petals. The revolute joints are adopted for the deployment and folding. Sunflower has a high surface accuracy and a simple mechanism, but a low folding ratio and a high weight.

Figure 2 illustrates the modified Sunflower designed by Toshiba/NASDA. In this scheme, the joints between the petals are more complicated than Sunflower in order to

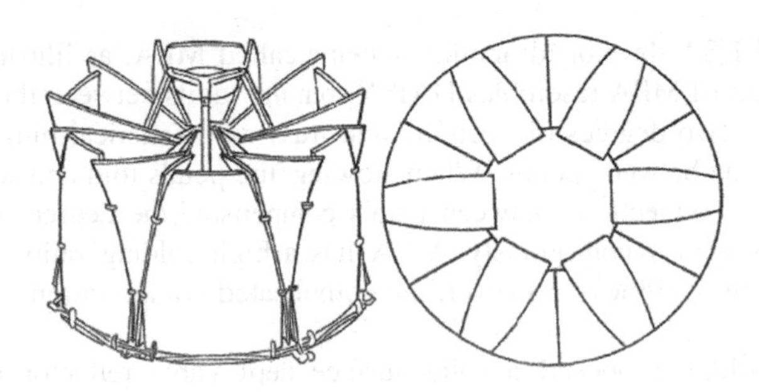

Fig. 1. Sunflower [3]

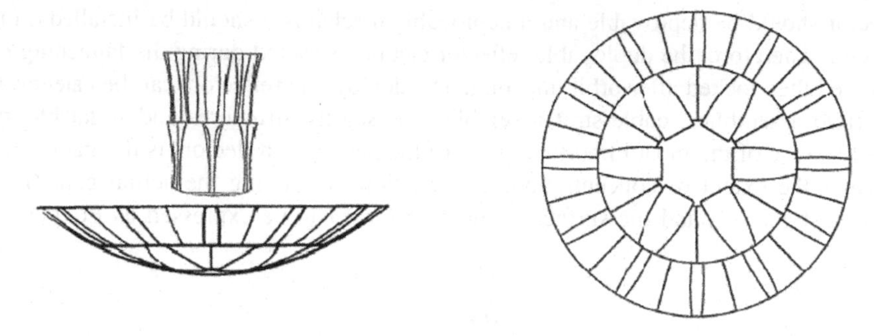

Fig. 2. Modified sunflower [3]

achieve a better folding ratio. However, the modified Sunflower had not improved the disadvantages of Sunflower essentially.

DAISY, short for Deployable Antenna Integral System, was designed by Dornier and European Space Agency (ESA), is illustrated in Fig. 3. DAISY is a Cassegrain antenna, constituted by 25 petals. The petals are connected to the central disc with radiating distributed revolute joints and supported by cross braces. DAISY has a high surface accuracy and a high stiffness because of the cross braces, in the other hand, it is also weighted heavily.

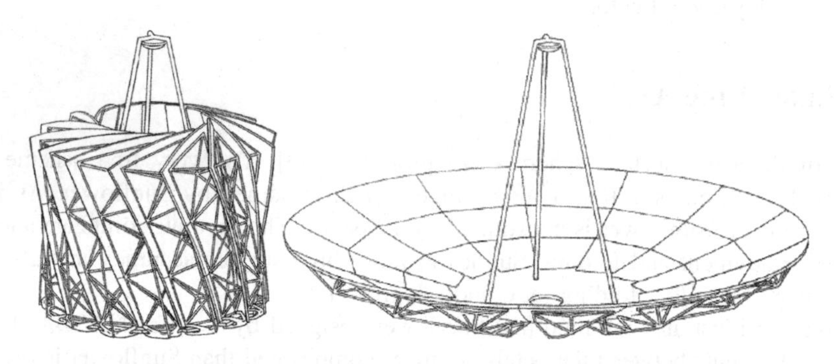

Fig. 3. DAISY [3]

Dornier and ESA developed another scheme called MEA, as illustrated in Fig. 4. The configuration of MEA resembles DAISY, but the joints between the petals and the central disc have two degrees of freedom, and truss with spherical hinges are adopted for the connections between petals. When stowing, the petals fold and twist around the central disc. The connections between petals compensate the degree of freedom and keep the deployment synchronously. MEA has a high folding ratio, a high surface accuracy and a high stiffness, however, the complicated configuration induces a heavy weight.

DSL, Cambridge proposed a solid surface deployable reflector named SSDA, which is illustrated in Fig. 5. The petals of SSDA are divided into several subpanels

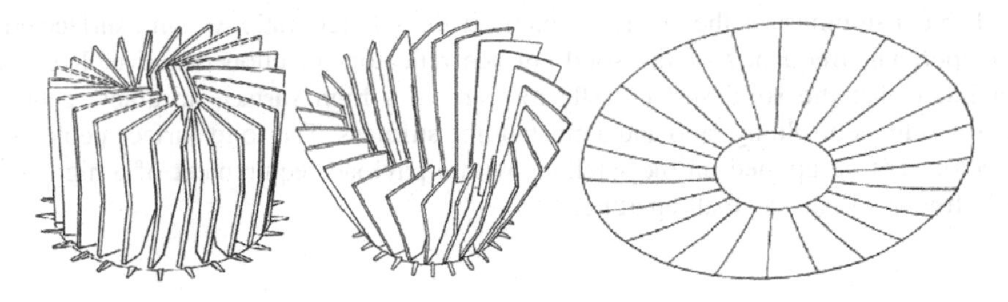

Fig. 4. MEA [3]

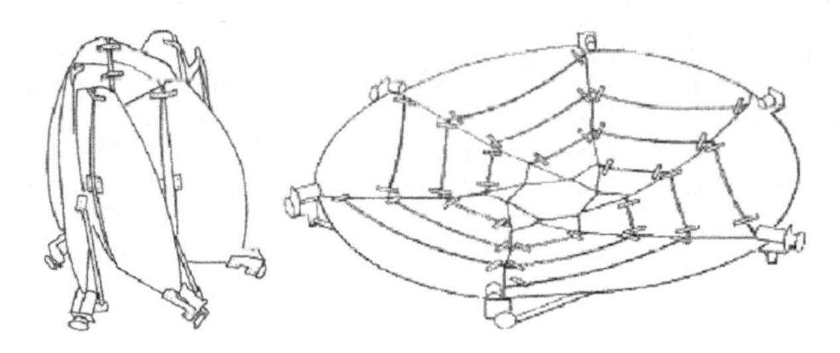

Fig. 5. SSDA [3]

connected by revolute joints. SSDA has a high folding ratio but the amounts of hinges deduces the reliability of deployment.

RadioAstron, which is designed by Russian NPO Lavochkin, was carried by Spektr-R satellite and launched by Zenit-3M in 18th July, 2011. RadioAstron is constituted by 27 petals and the diameter attains to 10 m, which is the largest in-orbit solid surface deployable reflector. The surface accuracy attains to 0.5 mm due to the existence of the braces. In Fig. 6, the deployed and stowed RadioAstron are illustrated [4, 5].

(a) (b)

Fig. 6. RadioAstron (a) deployed, (b) stowed [6]

Table 1 summarizes the diameter, diameter ratio, height ratio, weight, surface error and operating frequency of the solid surface reflectors mentioned above. It can be concluded that the solid surface reflectors are of a high surface accuracy, a heavy weight, a limited folding ratio and a outstanding stiffness. The solid surface deployable reflectors can be applied on the satellites with a payload requirement of a high operating frequency and a small aperture.

Table 1. Comparision of solid surface reflector schemes [4, 5, 7]

Scheme	State	Diameter/m	Diameter ratio	Height ratio	Weight/kg	Surface error/mm	Operating frequency/Hz
Sunflower	Prototype	4.90	0.44	0.37	31	0.051	60
Modified sunflower	Prototype	15.00	0.29	0.44	–	–	–
DAISY	Prototype	8.00	0.36	0.51	–	0.008	3000
MEA	Prototype	4.70	0.36	0.51	94	0.200	30
SSDA	Prototype	1.50	0.37	0.54	–	–	–
RadioAstron	In orbit	10.00	0.36	0.76	1340	0.500	25.112

3 Modeling

3.1 Configuration

In this research, a solid surface model resembling RadioAstron is established as illustrated in Fig. 7. The equation of the reflector surface can be expressed as Eq. (2),

$$z = \frac{1}{4f}\left(x^2 + y^2\right) \tag{2}$$

Where z is the operating direction of the reflector, f stands for the focal distance. Figure 8 shows the projection of the reflector to $x - y$ plane and the key variables are also annotated. Herein, r_1 is the radius of the inner circle or the central disc, r_2 is the radius of the outer circle, i.e. the boundary of the reflector. The petal is highlighted in Fig. 8, which is divided by the wrap angle θ, separated from the central disc, and

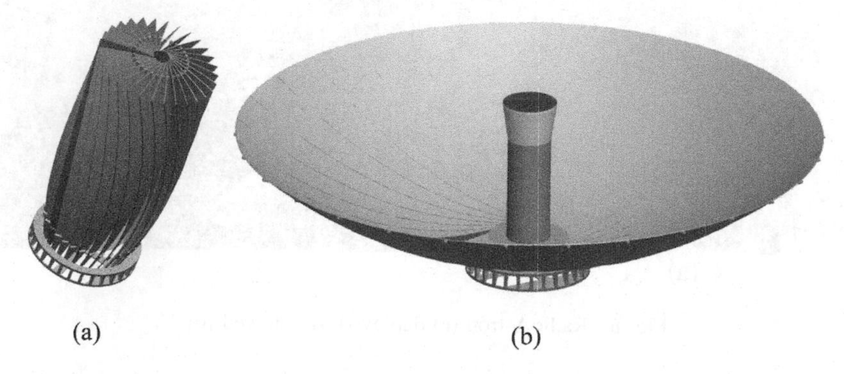

Fig. 7. (a) stowed and (b) deployed solid surface reflector

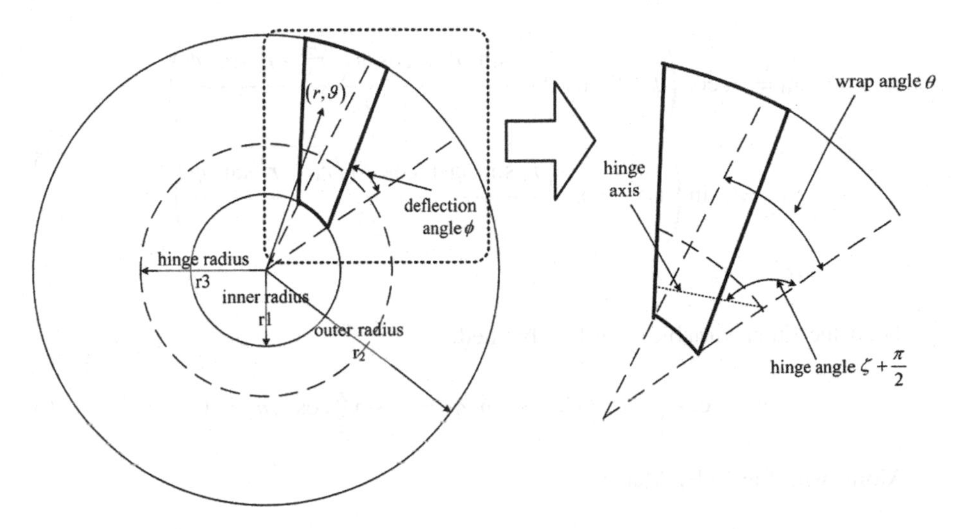

Fig. 8. Variables of deployable reflector

deflected by angle ϕ. The revolute joints are installed around the hinge circle with a radius r_3, and the angle between the axis of the hinge and the starting edge of the petal is defined as the hinge angle $\zeta + \pi/2$. The stowing and deployment of the reflector is implemented by the revolution of the petals around the hinges. Therefore, a certain point on the reflector can be expressed as Eq. (3) using polar coordinate,

$$
\begin{aligned}
x &= r\cos\vartheta \\
y &= r\sin\vartheta \\
z &= ar^2
\end{aligned}
\tag{3}
$$

Assume that the kth petal has a starting angle $k\theta$ and a destination angle $(k+1)\theta$ in the reflector coordinate and a certain point on this petal has a angular coordinate of ψ in this petal coordinate. As a result, the point on this petal can be expressed in the reflector coordinate,

$$
\begin{aligned}
\vartheta &= k\theta + \psi + \beta \\
\beta &= \cos^{-1}\frac{r_1\sin^2\phi + \cos\phi\sqrt{r^2 - r_1^2\sin^2\phi}}{r}
\end{aligned}
\tag{4}
$$

Suppose the folding angle of the hinges between the stowed and deployed state is χ, and a rigid body assumption is adopted, therefore the revolution of the petals can be represented by Euler theory. Taking the kth petal into account, a certain point on it can be expressed in Cartesian coordinate,

$$
\begin{aligned}
x_0 &= r_3 \cos\left(k\theta + \cos^{-1}\frac{r_1 \sin^2\phi + \cos\phi\sqrt{r_3^2 - r_1^2\sin^2\phi}}{r_3^2}\right)\\
y_0 &= r_3 \sin\left(k\theta + \cos^{-1}\frac{r_1 \sin^2\phi + \cos\phi\sqrt{r_3^2 - r_1^2\sin^2\phi}}{r_3^2}\right)\\
z_0 &= ar_3^2
\end{aligned}
\tag{5}
$$

Then the Euler variables can be obtained,

$$
q_0 = \cos\frac{\chi}{2}, q_1 = \sin\frac{\chi}{2}\sin\delta, q_2 = -\sin\frac{\chi}{2}\cos\zeta, q_3 = 0 \tag{6}
$$

Along with the Euler Matrix,

$$
\mathbf{A} = \begin{pmatrix} 2(q_0^2 + q_1^2) - 1 & 2(q_1q_2 + q_0q_3) & 2(q_1q_3 - q_0q_2) \\ 2(q_1q_2 - q_0q_3) & 2(q_0^2 + q_2^2) - 1 & 2(q_2q_3 + q_0q_1) \\ 2(q_1q_3 + q_0q_2) & 2(q_2q_3 - q_0q_1) & 2(q_0^2 + q_3^2) - 1 \end{pmatrix} \tag{7}
$$

Finally, a certain point after the revolution of χ can be expressed as,

$$
\begin{pmatrix} x' \\ y' \\ z' \end{pmatrix} = \mathbf{A}\begin{pmatrix} x - x_0 \\ y - y_0 \\ z - z_0 \end{pmatrix} + \begin{pmatrix} x_0 \\ y_0 \\ z_0 \end{pmatrix} \tag{8}
$$

3.2 Surface Accuracy

The surface accuracy of the solid surface reflector can be evaluated by surface error, which is coupled by the machining error of the petals Δ_m and the repeating error of the hinges Δ_χ. The machining error is the deviation between the theoretical shape and the actual shape induced by the manufacturing. Generally, the machining error yields to normal distribution,

$$
\Delta_m \sim \mathrm{N}(0, \varepsilon) \tag{9}
$$

Where ε stands for the standard deviation of the normal distribution, i.e. the root-mean-square (RMS).

The repeating error is a random angle in the repeating error interval $[-\alpha, \alpha]$ for one time deployment. Wu et al. [8] studied locking angle of several hinges and pointed out the locking angle yields to normal distribution statistically. Therefore, the repeating error can be treated as a normal condition with mean 0, standard deviation $\alpha/3$,

$$\Delta_{\chi} \sim N\left(0, \frac{\alpha}{3}\right) \tag{10}$$

Suppose a certain point on the reflector has a Cartesian coordinate (x, y, z) and the actual position perturbed by the machining error and the repeating error is (x', y', z'). The surface error Δ of this point can be expressed as,

$$\Delta = \sqrt{(x' - x)^2 + (y' - y)^2 + (z' - z)^2} \tag{11}$$

Therefore the surface accuracy can be represented by the RMS of the surface error,

$$RMS = \sqrt{\frac{1}{N}\sum \Delta^2}$$

Where N stands for the sampling number.

4 Configuration Optimization

During the design procedure of the solid surface reflector, the configuration parameters should be optimized considering the volume envelop as the optimization target. In Table 2, the determinate parameters are listed. The number of petals $2\pi/\theta$, folding angle χ and the hinge angle $\zeta + \pi/2$ are to be optimized.

Table 2. Parameters of solid surface reflector

Parameters	Inner radius/mm	Outer radius/mm	Hinge radius/mm	Focal distance/mm	Deflection angle/rad
Values	$r_1 = 175$	$r_2 = 1000$	$r_3 = 220$	$f = 600$	$\phi = \pi/10$

4.1 Number of Petals

Without losing generality, suppose the folding angle $\chi = 78°$ and the hinge angle $\zeta = 9.7°$, the number of petals should be optimized firstly. Figure 9 illustrates the relationship between the volume envelop and the number of petals. It can be concluded from Fig. 9 that the volume envelop declines rapidly and the derivative of the volume envelop ascends steadily as the number of petals ascends when the number of petals is under 30. When the number of petals surpasses 30, the volume envelop has a decelerated descending and the derivative of the volume envelop tends to be 0.

It can be summarized that when the number of petals is less than 30, the volume envelop is sensitive to the variation of the number of petals and the ascending of the number of petals leads to a evidently descending of the volume envelop. Considering the number of petals should not be too low or too high because of the involved difficulty of mechanical design and the weight of hinges respectively, the optimized number of petal should be 30, i.e. the wrap angle should be $\theta = \pi/12$.

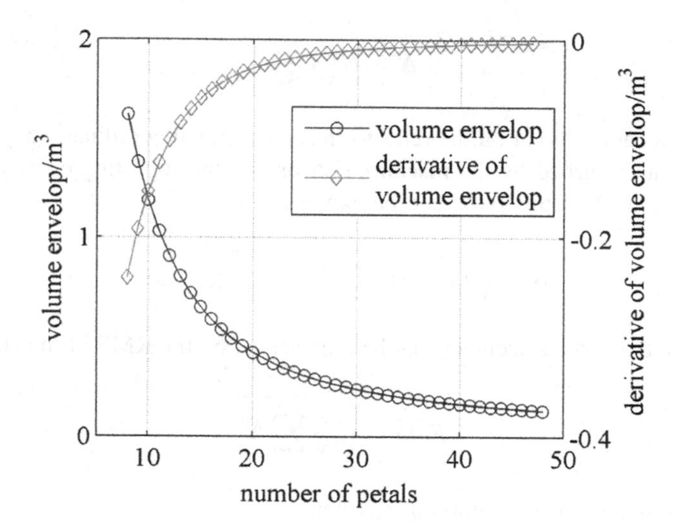

Fig. 9. Relationship between the volume envelop and the number of petals

4.2 Angle of Deployment

Figure 10 illustrates the relationship between the volume envelop, the folding angle and the hinge angle. It is evident that the volume envelop reaches its minimum with a high folding angle and a low hinge angle. Considering that the petals should not interfere with each other, the optimized folding angle should be $\chi = 78°$ and the optimized hinge angle should be $\zeta = 9.7°$.

Therefore, the deployed, 26° folded, 52° folded and the stowed optimized solid surface reflector are illustrated in Fig. 11. It can be concluded that this scheme has a steady deployment with no interferes. The stowed height is 862.68 mm and the stowed radius reaches 296.14 mm. The folding ratio becomes to be 0.296 as a optimization result.

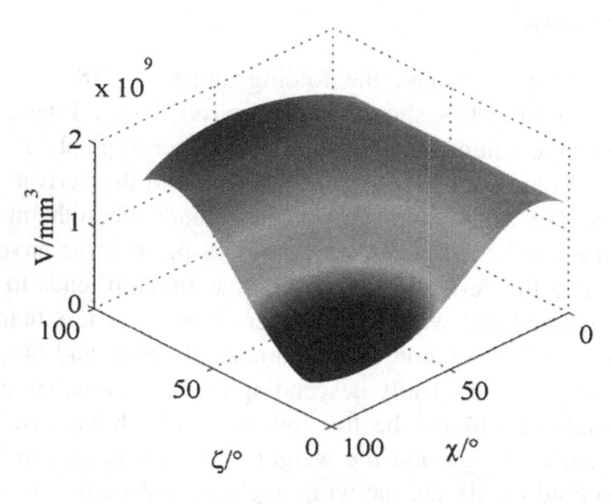

Fig. 10. Relationship between the volume envelop, the folding angle and the hinge angle

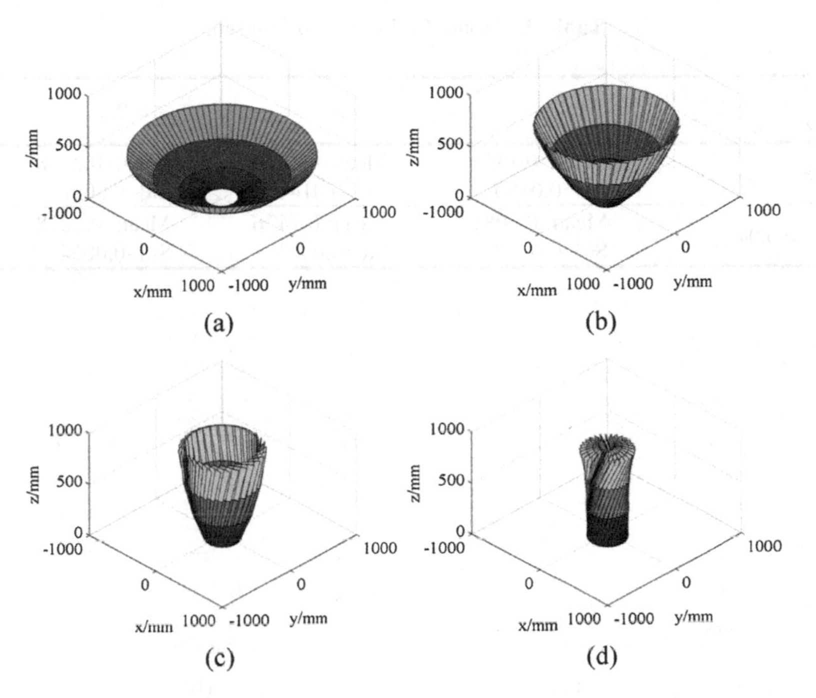

Fig. 11. (a) deployed, (b) folding 26°, (c) folding 52°, (d) stowed

5 Surface Accuracy Investigation

From the surface accuracy model it can be summarized that the machining error of a certain point on the reflector yields to normal distribution and the machining error of the points do not consist with each other. For one deployment, the repeating error of a certain hinge yields to normal distribution, and the repeating error of the hinges do not consist with each other. Therefore, the surface accuracy error is a stochastic procedure in time and space. Monte Carlo simulation should be implemented for a statistical analysis.

Monte Carlo method was proposed by Satislaw Ulam when he was studying nuclear weapon at Los Alamos National Laboratory in 1940s, which was name by Nicholas Metropolis after the Monte Carlo Casino. The very first code of Monte Carlo simulation was programmed by John von Neumann on ENIAC. In 1949, the article on Monte Carlo method by Metropolic and Ulam [9] was published.

One of the typical application of Monte Carlo simulation is to obtain a great number of samples from one stochastic variable, and implementing statistical investigation on the system responses. In the area of aerospace engineering, Wu et al. [8] established a statistical model of SAR considering repeating errors of hinges. The deviation of flatness and pointing accuracy are estimated. Mobrem [10] applied Monte Carlo analysis on estimating the RMS of the surface error for a large deployable antenna due to manufacturing imperfection and pointed out that each individual case of

Table 3. Monte Carlo simulation results

ε / mm \ α / mm	$\varepsilon = 0.0$	$\varepsilon = 0.1$	$\varepsilon = 0.2$
$\alpha = 0.05^{\circ}$	Mean=0.1352 Std=0.0180	Mean=0.1686 Std=0.0140	Mean=0.2418 Std=0.0098
$\alpha = 0.04^{\circ}$	Mean=0.1081 Std=0.0140	Mean=0.1476 Std=0.0103	Mean=0.2278 Std=0.0064

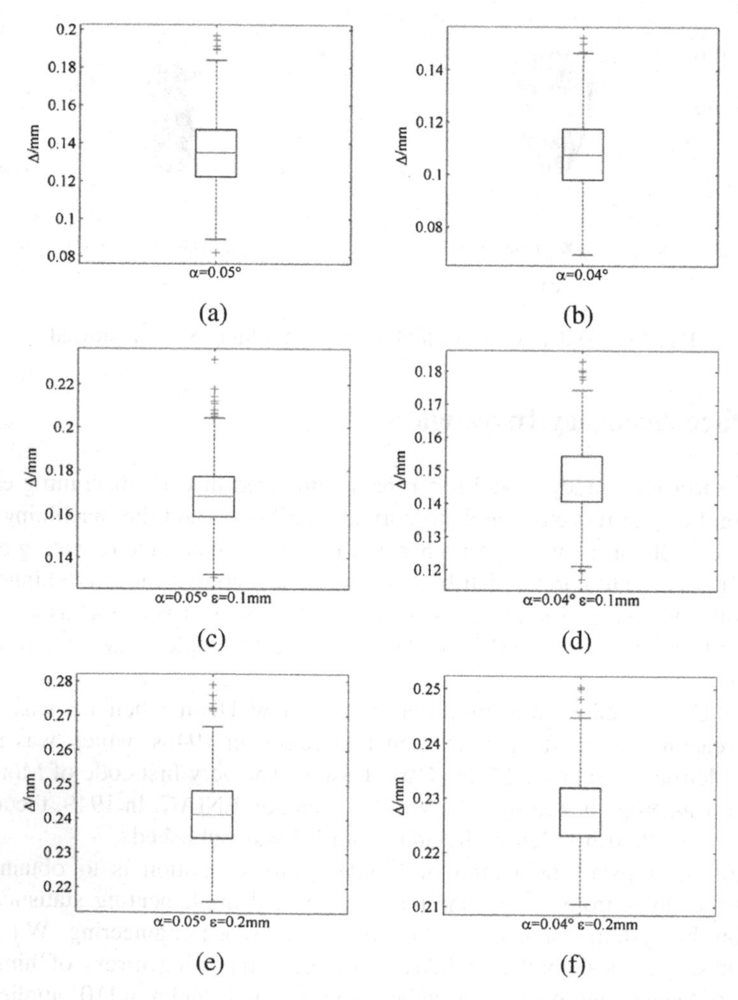

Fig. 12. Box plots (a) repeating error $\alpha = 0.05°$, (b) repeating error $\alpha = 0.04°$, (c) repeating error $\alpha = 0.05°$ and machining error $\varepsilon = 0.1$, (d) repeating error $\alpha = 0.04°$ and machining error $\varepsilon = 0.1$, (e) repeating error $\alpha = 0.05°$ and machining error $\varepsilon = 0.2$, (f) repeating error $\alpha = 0.04°$ and machining error $\varepsilon = 0.2$

the Monte Carlo analysis represents a real case. However, in the retrieval articles, there is no research on the surface accuracy of solid surface reflectors.

Monte Carlo simulation should be implemented on the surface accuracy of the solid surface reflector. The number of samples on space is 10000 points per petal and 1000 times deployment should be carried out. Therefore, 1000 surface accuracy errors are obtained after Monte Carlo simulation, which should be investigated statistically. 6 simulations should be implemented,

1. Repeating error $\alpha = 0.05°$, no machining error;
2. Repeating error $\alpha = 0.04°$, no machining error;
3. Repeating error $\alpha = 0.05°$, machining error $\varepsilon = 0.1$;
4. Repeating error $\alpha = 0.04°$, machining error $\varepsilon = 0.1$;
5. Repeating error $\alpha = 0.05°$, machining error $\varepsilon = 0.2$;
6. Repeating error $\alpha = 0.04°$, machining error $\varepsilon = 0.2$.

The statistical results are listed in Table 3 and the box plots are illustrated in Fig. 12. It can be summarized that the control of repeating error leads to a descending surface accuracy error mean value; the ascending machining error leads to a descending surface accuracy error standard deviation. Therefore, it can be concluded that the repeating error plays the most important role in surface accuracy and the exist of the machining error leads to a more unify surface accuracy.

6 Conclusion

1. A configuration model of solid surface deployable parabolic reflector is established. A machining error model and a repeating error model are established based on normal distribution respectively;
2. The folding ratio attains to be 0.296 after the configuration optimization about number of petals, folding angle and hinge angle;
3. It can be concluded from Monte Carlo simulation that the repeating error plays the most important role in surface accuracy and the exist of the machining error leads to a more unify surface accuracy.

Acknowledgement. The authors are grateful for the supports received from the open program from the state key laboratory of mechanical transmissions, Chongqing University (SKLMT-KFKT-201404).

References

1. Rahmat-Samii, Y., Densmore, A.: A history of reflector antenna development: past, present and future. In: 2009 SBMO/IEEE MTT-S International Microwave and Optoelectronics Conference, Belem, Brazil (2009)
2. Murphey, T.W.: Historical perspectives on the development of deployable reflectors. In: 50th AIAA/ASME/ASCE/AHS/ASC Structures, Structural Dynamics, and Materials Conference, Palm Springs, California, US (2009)

3. Kiper, G., Soylemez, E.: Deployable space structures. In: 4th International Conference on Recent Advances in Space Technologies (2009)
4. Kovalev, Y.Y., Kardashev, N.S., Kellermann, K.I., Edwards, P.G., Team, T.R.: The RadioAstron Space VLBI Project. In: 31th URSI General Assembly and Scientific Symposium (2014)
5. Popov, M.: Status and main parameters of space VLBI mission RadioAstron. In: 30th URSI General Assembly and Scientific Symposium (2011)
6. http://www.asc.rssi.ru/radioastron/
7. Liu, R., Tian, D., Deng, Z.: Research actuality and prospect of structure for space deployable antenna. J. Mach. Des. **27**(9), 1–10 (2010). (in Chinese)
8. Wu, J., Wang, C., Wang, H.: Accuracy analysis of satellite antenna plate deployment based on Monte Carlo method. Spacecraft Recovery Remote Sens. **34**(6), 89–94 (2013). (in Chinese)
9. Metropolis, N., Ulam, S.: The Monte Carlo method. J. Am. Stat. Assoc. **44**(27), 335–341 (1949)
10. Mobrem, M.: Methods of analyzing surface accuracy of large antenna structures due to manufacturing tolerances. In: 44th AIAA/ASME/ASCE/AHS Structures, Structural Dynamics, and Materials Conference, Norfolk, Virginia, US (2003)

Modeling and Application on System Influence to Lean Practice Based on Relationship Network

Yongjian Liang[1], Siqing Shan[2], Lihong Qiao[1(✉)], and Guangxun Yang[1]

[1] School of Mechanical Engineering and Automation, Beihang University, Beijing, China
{liangyongjian, lhqiao}@buaa.edu.cn, yangguangxun@263.net

[2] School of Economics and Management, Beihang University, Beijing, China
shansiqing@buaa.edu.cn

Abstract. Lean practices support each other by different weight values, forming a relationship network, which are a directed-weighted lean practices relationship network (referred to as DWLPRN) and a network system. This network system influences the implementation of lean practice. In this study, a system influence model was developed to reveal the framework and degree of network system influence to lean practice. This model need to structure DWLPRN, search on the maximum-weight lean practice tree and calculate relationship difficulty degree. And, the structured approach was created to conduct the system influence model. Practical use was shown in the actual DWLPRN obtained from a manufacturing cell. It provides reliability and effectiveness of this system influence model, which helps the lean production reform.

Keywords: Directed-weighted lean practices relationship network · System influence model · Maximum-weight lean practice tree · Relationship difficulty degree

1 Introduction

With the development of lean production, some new lean concepts have been developed, such as lean principles and lean practices. There are 5 basic principles of lean thinking [1], and 14 principles of Toyota Production System (TPS) which are presented [2]. The 22 lean practices are classified as four "bundles" [3].

A central idea of lean production is to "banish waste and create wealth" by the implementation of lean practices [4]. However, there can be no certainty that the

Research is supported by the National Natural Science Foundation of China (No. 71332003), the National High-Tech. R&D Program of China (No. 2015AA042101), and the key program of the Engineering Research Center of Complex Product Advanced Manufacturing System, Ministry of Education.

L. Zhang et al. (Eds.): AsiaSim 2016/SCS AutumnSim 2016, Part I, CCIS 643, pp. 685–693, 2016.
DOI: 10.1007/978-981-10-2663-8_70

utilization of lean practices ensure attaining the objective of lean production [5]. In fact, there is a lack of study on the contextual factors' relationship of lean practices. Many manufacturers have successfully applied lean practices [6–9]. And others too had difficulty in replicating others' success [10–12]. One chief reason may be that many manufacturers have only applied isolated lean practices [13–15]. Good theory must know both what is it and how to do [16]. So, it is a natural progression to research the lean practices relationship in establishing the lean theory. Few researches have analyzed the lean practices in a relationship difficulty review based on the quantitative approaches.

This paper tries to establish system influence model for revealing the framework and degree of network system influence to lean practice. This model can structure the directed-weighted lean practices relationship network, maximum-weight lean practice tree and compute the relationship difficulty degree (RDD) of lean practice. Based on the system influence model, lean production manager can analyze lean practice and make a strategic decision to select the lean practices to implement in lean reform.

2 System Influence Model to Lean Practice

The system influence model to lean practice based on relationship network has three parts, such as input information, process, and result. In the first part, the input information includes lean practices, directed support relationships of lean practices, and weighted values of relationships. These three data compose the essential components. In the second part, based on the input information, the model can build a directed-weighted lean practices relationship network (referred to as DWLPRN). In this network, the maximum-weight lean practice tree of lean practice can be structured. Then, the lean practice RDD can be calculated. In the 3rd part, the model output the result of the system influence. The maximum-weight lean practice tree of lean practice is the framework of system influence to lean practice. The lean practice RDD is the degree of

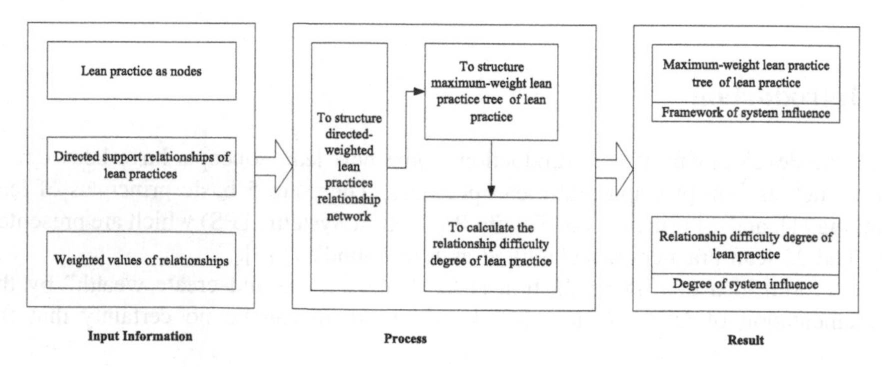

Fig. 1. The system influence model to lean practice based on relationship network

system influence to lean practice. The system influence model is described in Fig. 1.

2.1 The Input Information

In this section, an example is shown. There is input information of a simple DWLPRN. In the example, there are nine lean practices, such as lean practice 1 (referred to as LP_1), lean practice 2 (LP_2), …, lean practice 9 (LP_9).

The relationship of two lean practices is that lean practice 1 (LP_1) supports (influences, enhances, strengthens, reinforces, upholds, intensifies, helps) lean practice 2 (LP_2), which is the directed support relationships.

There are some difficulties in lean practice implementation, which include external and internal difficulties. The former is controlled by the constraints of the relationships which support this lean practice. The weight of relationship has been taken here as the external difficulty. The weight value of relationship from LP_1 to LP_2 is denoted by W_{12}. The directed support relationships and weighted values in this example are listed in Table 1. The later is the independent element to be implemented within it.

Table 1. The directed support relationships and weighted values of relationships

No.	Supporting	Supported	Wight value	No.	Supporting	Supported	Wight value
1	LP_2	LP_1	W_{21}	7	LP_1	LP_3	W_{13}
2	LP_3	LP_1	W_{31}	8	LP_2	LP_3	W_{23}
3	LP_4	LP_1	W_{41}	9	LP_4	LP_3	W_{43}
4	LP_5	LP_1	W_{51}	10	LP_3	LP_4	W_{34}
5	LP_6	LP_2	W_{62}	11	LP_7	LP_4	W_{74}
6	LP_9	LP_2	W_{92}	12	LP_8	LP_4	W_{84}
				13	LP_9	LP_6	W_{96}

On the other hand, in the real application of the system influence model, the lean practices, relationships and weight values are based on literature reviews and/or practical experiences of lean expert.

2.2 The Directed-Weighted Lean Practices Relationship Network

The directed-weighted lean practices relationship network (DWLPRN) includes many lean practices, directed support relationships of lean practices, and weighted values of relationships. The lean practice is the vertex in DWLPRN. The directed support relationships are the directed lines, which from the supporting lean practices to the supported lean practices. The weighted value of relationships is signed on the directed line. These essential components structure a directed-weighted lean practices relationship network. Based on the data in Table 1, a DWLPRN is shown in Fig. 2a.

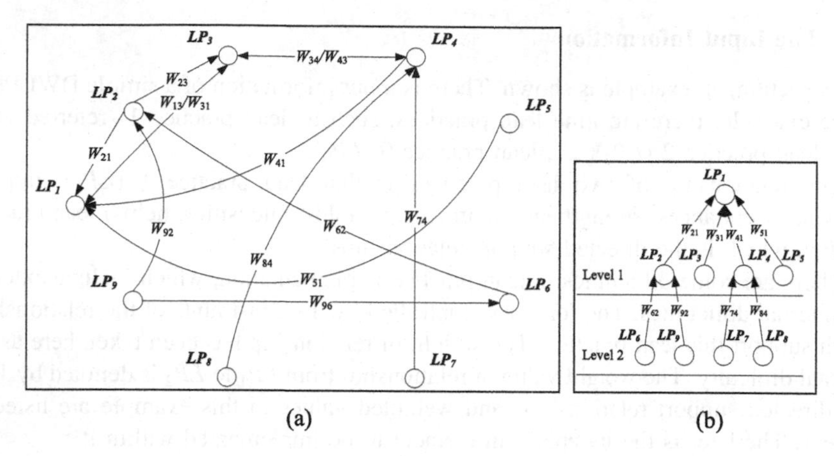

Fig. 2. DWLPRN from Table 1 and lean practice trees of LP_1

2.3 The Maximum-Weight Lean Practice Tree

The lean practice tree (LP-tree) is a supported relationships network. A root vertex is directed by others, and every vertex except the root has one parent [17]. The maximum-weight lean practice tree (MWLP-tree) is one of the LP-trees of root vertex, and this LP-tree has the maximum weighted summation based on certain conditions.

The LP_1 is assumed as the root vertex. There are many directed trees of vertex LP_1. In Fig. 2b, a lean practice tree of LP_1 is shown. The root vertex has several generation children vertices in the directed tree. The weight values of directed edges stay in different generations and these weight values do not have the similar influence upon the root vertex. It is noted that the weight value of the first generation child vertices completely influences the root vertex. The second generation child vertices support the root vertex indirectly. This influence the root vertex up to some degree and the influence ratio (R) of the weight value is more than 0 and less than 1. In the third generation child vertices, the influence ratio of the weight value is R^2. Similarly, in the kth generation child vertices, the influence ratio of the weight value is R^{k-1}.

In Fig. 2a, the weight value W_{ij} is assumed in $[a, b]$ ($a > 0, b > 0$). In this paper, the range of R is limited less than $\frac{a}{b}$, only the MWLP-tree of lean practice should be the shortest tree, which has the shortest length of all directed tree of vertex LP_1 (Fig. 2b).

2.4 The Relationship Difficulty Degree of Lean Practice

The relationship difficulty degree (RDD) of lean practice in the DWLPRN is the product sum of weights and influence ratio in the MWLP-tree of root vertex. The RDD can be calculated as the Eq. (1):

$$\mathrm{RDD}_{LP_j} = \begin{cases} 0 & LP_j \text{ has no child vertices} \\ \sum_{i \in G_1} W_{ij}, & LP_j \text{ has 1 generation child vertices} \\ \sum_{i \in G_1} W_{ij} + \sum_{k=2}^{K} R^{k-1} \left(\sum_{\substack{i \in G_k \\ j \in G_{k-1}}} maxW_{ij} \right), & LP_j \text{ has more than 2 generation child vertices} \end{cases} \quad (1)$$

Where:

i, j: the index of lean practice;

k: the kth generation child lean practices of LP_j in maximum-weight tree,

K: the maximum generation number of LP_j;

G_k: the collection of the kth generation child vertices of the LP_j,

Obviously, the maximum-weight tree may not be unique. However, the G_k and the value of RDD_{LP_j} are unique solution.

Then, a structured approach is designed to search on the MWLP-tree and calculate the RDD of the root lean practice (or vertex) as follows:

Step 1. Select the LP_j as the root lean practice (or vertex) in the DWLPRN.

Step 2. To search all the lean practices to direct LP_j in sequence, defined as the 1st generation child of the LP_j, and denoted by G_1 as the collection of them.

Step 3. Just search the vertices which are unvisited yet in the below steps.

Step 4. To search the adjacent lean practices supporting the vertices in G_1, called the 2nd generation child vertices of the LP_j, and denoted by G_2.

Step 5. Return to Step 4 until all vertices are searched, and gain the G_3, …, G_k.

Step 6. Select the weight value that belongs to the RDD of LP_j. If a vertex in G_k supports two or more vertices in G_{k-1}, there will be two or more weight values. The maximum weight value is exclusively selected to calculate the RDD of LP_j.

Step 7. Summate the weight values of the relationships between G_k and G_{k-1} and denote it as SW_k.

Step 8. Structure MWLP-tree of root vertex (LP_j) and compute the RDD of LP_j by the sum of SW_k in different influence ratios $(R^0, R^1, R^2, \ldots, R^{k-1})$.

Step 9. If one of the vertices in DWLPRN is not to be selected, we should go to Step 1 to compute the RDD of other lean practice.

2.5 The Result of System Influence Model

The result of system influence model is the maximum-weight lean practice trees and RDD values of all lean practices.

3 Application and Discussion

The system influence model was applied in this section. The input information come from a lean practices relationship model in manufacturing cell [18]. The lean practices used and their abbreviations were given in Table 2.

Table 2. The lean practice abbreviation

No.	Lean practice	Abbreviation
1	Standardized work	STW
2	Continuous improvement	CI
3	Teamwork and leadership	TWL
4	Visibility and information exchange	VIS
5	Visual management of production control	VPC
6	Visual management of quality control	VQC
7	Workers' autonomy	WAU
8	Organisation by the dominant flow	ODF
9	Layout size and shape	LSS
10	One-piece-flow	ONE
11	Multi-functionality and cross-training	MCT
12	Pull production	PULL
13	Quick setups	QST
14	Total productive maintenance	TPM
15	Smoothed production	SPR
16	Workplace housekeeping	WHK

The directed support relationships were analyzed on the lean practices relationship model in manufacturing cell [18]. The weighted values of relationships of these lean practices had been summarized based on the lean experts' practical experiences. The weight values were obtained by surveys using a five-point Likert scale. The format of this scale would be like this: 0 - no support; 1 - weak support; 2 - moderate support; 3 - strong support; 4 - strongest support. Based on the Pareto principle, the minimum weight value should be 0.8. So, the weight value W_{ij} fell within the normal range of 0.8–4. In this paper, the influence ratio (R) has been selected as 0.2 based on the Pareto principle. The result was listed in Table 3.

Based on the data in Tables 2 and 3, a directed-weighted lean practices relationship network (DWLPRN) was shown in Fig. 3a. The DWLPRN has 16 lean practices, 47 directed relationships and 47 weight values of relationships.

Then, the structured approach was used to search on the MWLP-tree and calculate the RDD. The result of system influence model is shown in Fig. 3b. Figure 3b is the maximum-weight lean practice trees of PULL. These RDD values of all lean practices were listed in Table 4.

The ODF had no child generation lean practices. So, The ODF did not own the maximum-weight lean practice tree. Then, the framework of system influence to ODF did not exist. At the same time, the RDD of ODF equaled zero and was the minimum value in all lean practices. Therefore, the degree of system influence to ODF is minimal in all lean practices. That meant that the implementation of ODF was less influenced by the DWLPRN. When other conditions were same for several lean practices, the ODF should been selected firstly to implement.

Table 3. The directed support relationships and weighted values of relationships

No.	Supporting	Supported	Wight value	No.	Supporting	Supported	Wight value
1	STW	CI	3.33	24	VPC	PULL	3.1
2	TWL	CI	2.95	25	VQC	PULL	1.3
3	VIS	CI	2.05	26	CI	QST	2.8
4	VPC	CI	2.58	27	ONE	SPR	3.85
5	VQC	CI	3.7	28	PULL	SPR	3.78
6	WAU	CI	2.58	29	QST	SPR	3.7
7	ODF	LSS	2.15	30	TPM	SPR	2.73
8	ONE	LSS	1.15	31	CI	STW	1.53
9	STW	MCT	1.15	32	WHK	STW	1.9
10	TWL	MCT	1.23	33	STW	TPM	2.28
11	LSS	ONE	2.13	34	TWL	TPM	2.8
12	ODF	ONE	1.08	35	WHK	TPM	3.18
13	PULL	ONE	2.88	36	MCT	TWL	3.93
14	QST	ONE	2.95	37	VPC	TWL	1.98
15	STW	ONE	1.23	38	WAU	TWL	3.55
16	TPM	ONE	2.13	39	LSS	VIS	1.23
17	LSS	PULL	1.53	40	VIS	VPC	3.93
18	ODF	PULL	2.05	41	VIS	VQC	3.85
19	ONE	PULL	3.93	42	MCT	WAU	3.1
20	QST	PULL	3.1	43	STW	WAU	1.83
21	SPR	PULL	3.85	44	VIS	WAU	1.9
22	STW	PULL	2.13	45	CI	WHK	1.38
23	TPM	PULL	1.23	46	STW	WHK	3.33
				47	TPM	WHK	3.55

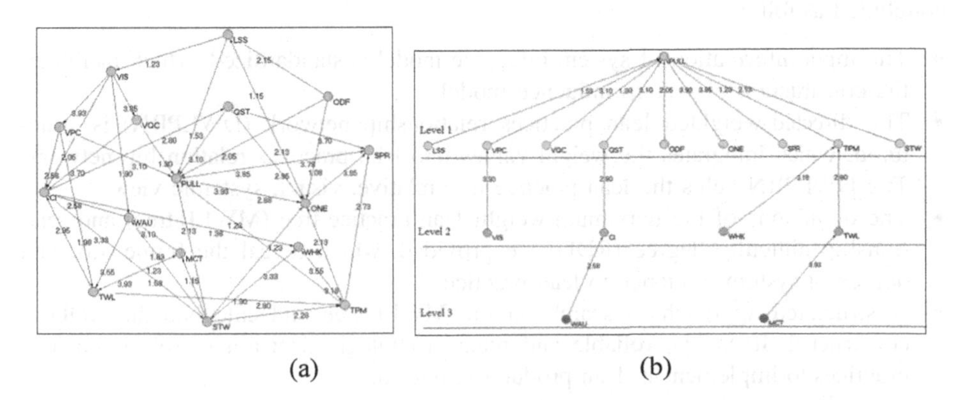

(a) (b)

Fig. 3. DWLPRN and MWLP-Tree of PULL

Table 4. The RDD values of all lean practices

No.	Lean practice	RDD	No.	Lean practice	RDD
1	STW	7.15	9	LSS	5.91
2	CI	18.93	10	ONE	16.26
3	TWL	10.89	11	MCT	4.63
4	VIS	2.41	12	PULL	25.06
5	VPC	4.4	13	QST	6.58
6	VQC	4.33	14	TPM	10.78
7	WAU	8.59	15	SPR	18.44
8	ODF	0	16	WHK	11.27

Similarly, the degree order of system influence to lean practice from smallest to largest was {ODF, VIS, VQC, VPC, MCT, LSS, QST, STW, WAU, TPM, TWL, WHK, ONE, SPR, CI, PULL}. The RDD of PULL in Table 4 was 25.06, which was the largest value. The system influence to PULL was huge. The ideal implement of PULL would be hard to do. So, the reformers of lean production should have firm conviction and enough persistence to apply these lean practices in lean reform.

It was shown that the system influence model to lean practice based on lean practices relationship network was a very reliable model to analyze lean practice and make a strategic decision to select the lean practices to implement in lean production reform. For it was easily used on computer, the system influence model might offer satisfactory solutions.

4 Conclusions and Future Work

Unlike prior researches on the lean production, this paper built a system influence model to lean practice based on lean practices relationship network to explore the system influence to lean practice. The system influence model includes three parts, such as input information, process and result. The main contribution of this study can be concluded as follows:

- The input information of system influence model is standardized, which facilitates the construction of system influence model.
- The directed-weighted lean practices relationship network (DWLPRN) is structured, which integrates the weight values into lean practices relationship network. The DWLPRN helps the lean practice in a relative, visual, systemic view.
- The definitions of the maximum-weight lean practice tree (MWLP-tree) and relationship difficulty degree (RDD) are provided, which reveal the framework and degree of system influence to lean practice.
- A structured approach to search on the MWLP-tree and calculate the RDD is constructed. It can be reliable and make a strategic decision to select the lean practices to implement in lean production reform.

The future work should be focused on the following directions:

- Analyzing the scalability of this system influence model in a larger DWLPRN, which includes more lean practices, relationships, and weighted values.
- Studying the different influence ratio (*R*) of the weight value to the MWLP-tree.
- Expanding the theory of system influence model to lean practice based on lean practices relationship network to different relationship research fields.

References

1. Womack, J.P., Jones, D.T.: Lean Thinking: Banish Waste and Create Wealth in Your Corporation. Simon & Schuster, Sydney (1996)
2. Liker, J.K.: The Toyota Way: 14 Management Principles from the World's Greatest Manufacturer, 1st edn. McGraw-Hill, New York (2004)
3. Shah, R., Ward, P.T.: Defining and developing measures of lean production. J. Oper. Manage. **25**(4), 785–805 (2007)
4. Browning, T.R., Heath, R.D.: Reconceptualizing the effects of lean on production costs with Evidence from the F-22 program. J. Oper. Manage. **27**, 23–44 (2009)
5. Spear, S., Bowen, H.K.: Decoding the DNA of the Toyota production system. Harvard Bus. Rev. **9**, 97–106 (1999)
6. Lasa, I.S., Castro, R., Laburu, C.O.: Extent of the use of lean concepts proposed for a value stream mapping application. Prod. Plann. Control **20**(1), 82–98 (2009)
7. Pool, A., Wijngaardn, J., Zee, D.: Lean planning in the semi-process industry, a case study. Int. J. Prod. Econ. **131**, 194–203 (2011)
8. Garza-Reyes, J.A., Oraifige, I., Soriano-Meier, H., et al.: The development of a lean park homes production process using process flow and simulation methods. J. Manufact. Technol. Manage. **23**(2), 178–197 (2012)
9. Belekoukias, I., Garza-Reyes, J.A., Kumar, V.: The impact of lean methods and tools on the operational performance of manufacturing organisations. Int. J. Prod. Res. **52**(18), 5346–5366 (2014)
10. Safayeni, F., Purdy, L.: A behavioral case study of just-in-time implementation. J. Oper. Manage. **10**(2), 213–228 (1991)
11. Mehri, D.: The darker side of lean: an Insider's perspective on the realities of the Toyota production system. Acad. Manage. Perspect. **20**(2), 21–42 (2006)
12. Chen, H., Lindeke, R.R.: Lean automated manufacturing: avoiding the pitfalls to embrace the opportunities. Assembly Autom. **30**(2), 117–123 (2010)
13. Holweg, M., Pil, F.: Successful build-to-order strategies start with the customer. Sloan Manage. Rev. **43**(1), 74–83 (2001)
14. Shirouzu, N., Moffett, S.: As Toyota closes in on gm, quality concerns also grow. Wall Street J. A1, 4 August 2004
15. Spear, S., Bowen, H.K.: Decoding the DNA of the Toyota production system. Harvard Bus. Rev. **9**, 97–106 (1999)
16. Handfield, R.B., Melnyk, S.A.: The scientific theory-building process: a primer using the case of TQM. J. Oper. Manage. **16**(4), 321–339 (1998)
17. Mei, J., Ren, W., Ma, G.: Distributed containment control for lagrangian networks with parametric uncertainties under a directed graph. Automatica **48**, 653–659 (2012)
18. Saurin, T.A., Marodin, G.A., Ribeiro, J.L.D.: A framework for assessing the use of lean production practices in manufacturing cells. Int. J. Prod. Res. **49**(11), 3211–3230 (2011)

Web-Based Marine Engineering English Intelligent Training System Design

Ning Zhang[1,2(✉)], Zhenzhen Dong[1], Zhipeng Shen[1], Chen Guo[1], and Weihua Luo[2]

[1] College of Information Science and Technology, Dalian Maritime University, Dalian, Liaoning, China
jenny@dlmu.edu.cn

[2] School of Foreign Languages, Dalian Maritime University, Dalian, Liaoning, China

Abstract. In order to simulate the special language practicing environment of marine engineering English, a marine auxiliary boiler simulation system is designed to represent the real ship system environment. Differing from traditional simulation systems, the simulation system designed in this research not only can carry out simulation exercise, but also test learners' marine engineering English proficiency and technical skills. Moreover, web technology is adopted, so that operation time and locations are no longer constrained, therefore, the flexibility of learners' independent learning is significantly enhanced.

Keywords: Marine auxiliary boiler · Active server pages · Examination system · Marine engineering english

1 Introduction

The boom of world trade makes it necessary for marine transport industries to recruit more and more qualified sailors. In order to enhance navigation and marine engineering majors' professional qualifications, both device operation skills and marine engineering English proficiency need to be trained. To minimize training cost, software simulators have certain advantages, including low investment, high security, and easy maintenance. Therefore, software simulators are welcome among various marine universities [1]. However, traditional software simulators are mainly operated offline, and most of them cannot help enhance learners' marine engineering English proficiency.

Based on the above mentioned problems, traditional software simulators [2] and web technology is combined in this research. With marine auxiliary boiler as the research object, a web-based marine auxiliary boiler intelligent examination system is developed to test learners' operation skills, unexpected events reactions, and marine engineering English proficiency. This is a pilot study for web technology application in simulation research field.

2 System Overall Design

The aim of the system design is to train students skillful enough to operate based on their theoretical knowledge about marine auxiliary boiler [3]. Therefore, it is a must for

L. Zhang et al. (Eds.): AsiaSim 2016/SCS AutumnSim 2016, Part I, CCIS 643, pp. 694–701, 2016.
DOI: 10.1007/978-981-10-2663-8_71

the system to simulate all the exercises to test students' skills. In order to record students and teachers' information, "log in" and "register" functions are designed in the system. The overall framework of the system is showed in Fig. 1.

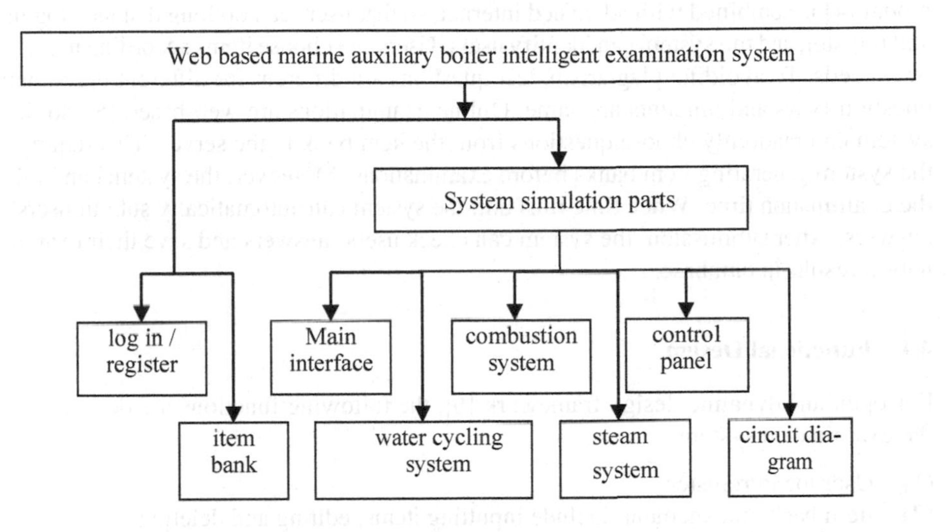

Fig. 1. System framework

The system consists of three parts, that is, log in/register, item bank, and simulations. There are two kinds of modes in the simulation part. One is practicing mode, the other is examination mode.

3 System Development Program

With the help of convenient internet network, web technology and ASP active web pages development technology are adopted to design a set of web based marine auxiliary boiler training simulation system. B/S model is applied, which usually consists of three levels, that is, browser + web, server + database server. Microsoft IIS web server is applied. Due to the limited data storage of the system, light database Access is selected. With default VB script as the back-end programming language, general purpose Javascript language is adopted for customer end. Firefox browser is used as customer end testing tool because of more standardization.

Customer end is realized by Fireworks, Dreamweaver, and Firefox. Fireworks is used for image processing. Dreamweaver is chosen as the main system development tool. Back end is made by Dreamweaver, IIS server, Access database, and IE browser. The whole system uses ASP active web pages development technology, therefore, only binding Microsoft IIS server can be used as the server. IE browser is the only tool can debug ASP, so it is used as back end web pages debugging tool.

4 Examination System Design

In order to realize safe, stable, and reliable operations, the traditional LAN examination modal [4] is combined with advanced internet, so that users can do long distance log in and register, and the system can identify users. Users can choose items according to their own needs. To avoiding plagiarism, test questions are different for different users, but question types and amounts are same. Online examinations are web-based [5], so the system can randomly choose questions from the item bank in the server. This requires the system generating item banks before examinations. Moreover, the system can limit the examination time. When time runs out, the system can automatically submit users' answers. After submission, the system can check users' answers and save their examination results in database.

4.1 Functional Design

For open and dynamic design framework [6], the following functions are designed in the examination system:

(1). User log in/register
(2). Item bank management: include inputting items, editing and deleting.
(3). Automatic items generation: randomly choosing a set of items from item banks for examinations.
(4). Online examination [7]: can control the whole examination process, including time and permissions. Students can only answer questions in fixed time, once time runs out, the system can automatically submit.
(5). Automatic checking: the system can mark students' examination results, and save the results in database.
(6). Results checking: different users have different permissions. Students can query their examination results, and teachers can query all the students' examination results.
(7). Multi-tasking: massive online operation is realized in the system design, with user-friendly interface designed iteratively based on heuristic evaluations [8], both safety and stability are validated.

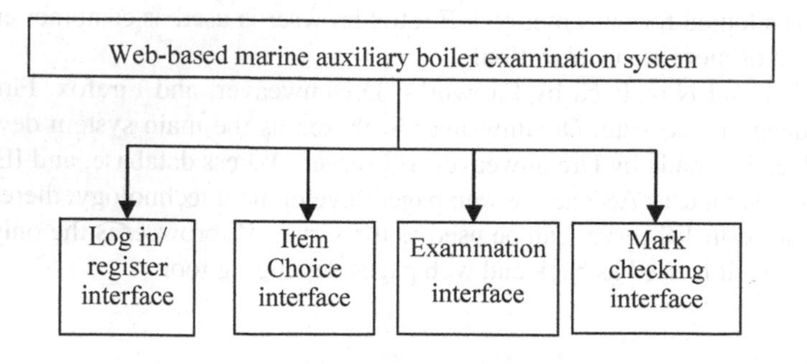

Fig. 2. Examination system framework

Based on the analysis mentioned above, the examination system framework is illustrated in Fig. 2.

4.2 Database Design

Based on the analysis on examination process, system database saves the following information:

(1). Learners' information: identification number, user name, password, Email, address, telephone.
(2). Teachers' information: identification number, user name, password.
(3). Item bank information: item numbers, item specifications, correct answers and explanations.
(4). Results information: test paper identification number, candidate number, item completion rate, mark for each item, overall results.

System database flow is showed in Fig. 3. As it is required for information storage, exam database has to be built in Access, and then four tables were generated according to information categories.

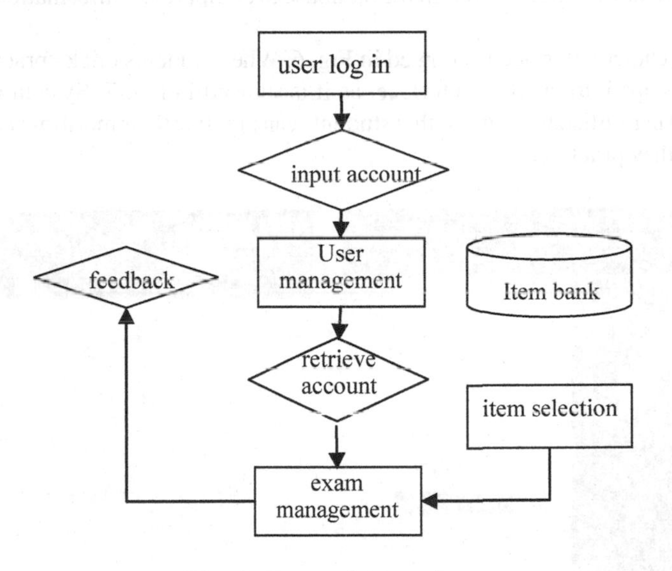

Fig. 3. System database flow

4.3 Module Design

The majority users of the system are students and teachers. Register and log in interface are showed in Figs. 4 and 5. Textbox will turn red if users input incorrect information.

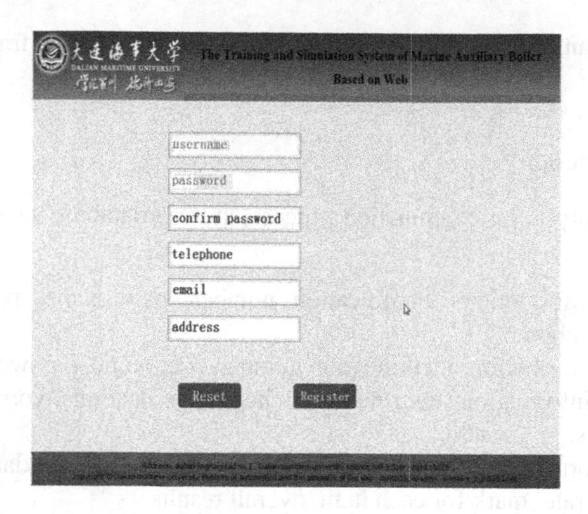

Fig. 4. Register interface

Reguest.com is applied to extract information. When users click "register" button, correct information will be saved in the database to compare the information when users log in.

Module choice interface is showed in Fig. 6. When students click "practice" button, the system skips into practice interface, as it is showed in Fig. 7. System interface are all designed in English version, so that students can practice their maritime English terms every time they practice.

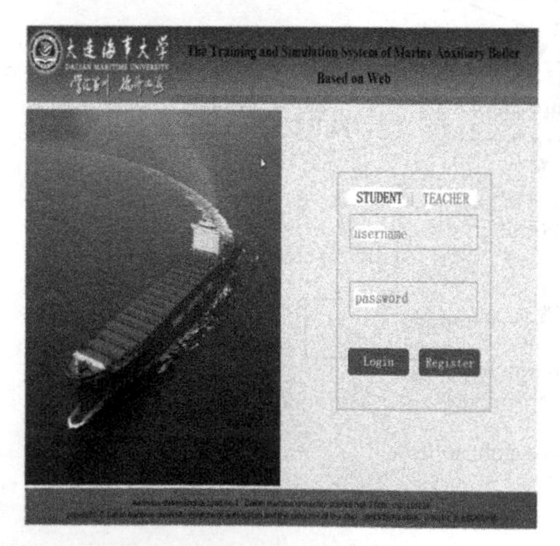

Fig. 5. Log in interface

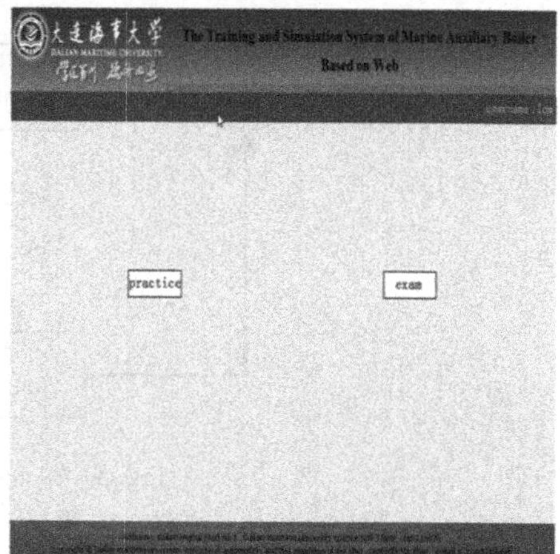

Fig. 6. Module choice interface

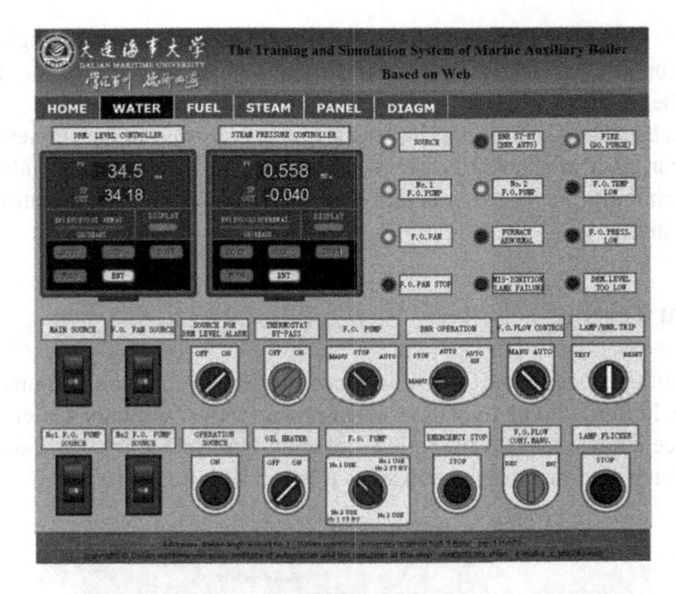

Fig. 7. Control panel interface

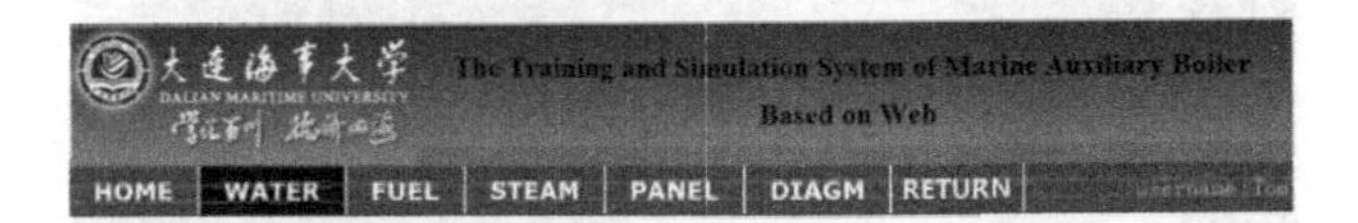

Fig. 8. Teachers' practice interface

大连海事大学
DALIAN MARITIME UNIVERSITY
The Training and Simulation System of Marine Auxiliary Boiler
Based on Web
RETURN

user	score1	score2	score3	score4	score5	score6	score7	score8	score9	score10	total
[illegible]	13	30	10	30	0	0	0	0	0	0	83
[illegible]	40	30	40	30	0	0	0	0	0	0	140
[illegible]	40	30	30	20	0	0	0	0	0	0	120
[illegible]	40	20	20	10	0	0	0	0	0	0	90
[illegible]	230	30	20	10	0	0	0	0	0	0	290
[illegible]	330	440	220	40	0	0	0	0	0	0	1030
[illegible]	230	320	320	320	0	0	0	0	0	0	1190
[illegible]	20	20	30	20	0	0	0	0	0	0	90
[illegible]	0	0	0	0	0	0	0	0	0	0	0
[illegible]	0	0	0	0	0	0	0	0	0	0	0
[illegible]	0	0	0	0	0	0	0	0	0	0	0
[illegible]	0	0	0	0	0	0	0	0	0	0	0
[illegible]	0	0	0	0	0	0	0	0	0	0	0
[illegible]	0	0	0	0	0	0	0	0	0	0	0
[illegible]	0	0	0	0	0	0	0	0	0	0	0
[illegible]	0	0	0	0	0	0	0	0	0	0	0
[illegible]	0	0	0	0	0	0	0	0	0	0	0
[illegible]	0	0	0	0	0	0	0	0	0	0	0
[illegible]	0	0	0	0	0	0	0	0	0	0	0
[illegible]	0	0	0	0	0	0	0	0	0	0	0

Fig. 9. Marks query interface

The whole system is voice-assisted to enhance students' maritime English listening comprehension skills, clicking any button triggers voice to vocalize the name of the button and the interface content.

After teachers successfully log in, user name are showed in the rightest part of the navigation bar, as it is showed in Fig. 8. Teachers can query all the students' marks, including their daily practice marks and the mid-term and final examination marks, as it is showed in Fig. 9.

5 System Testing

In system testing process, we choose the most important function, manual ignition as the example. In item choice interface, users choose item "auxiliary boiler combustion time sequence control system operation—manual ignition", click "examination", and the system enters examination interface, as it is showed in Fig. 10.

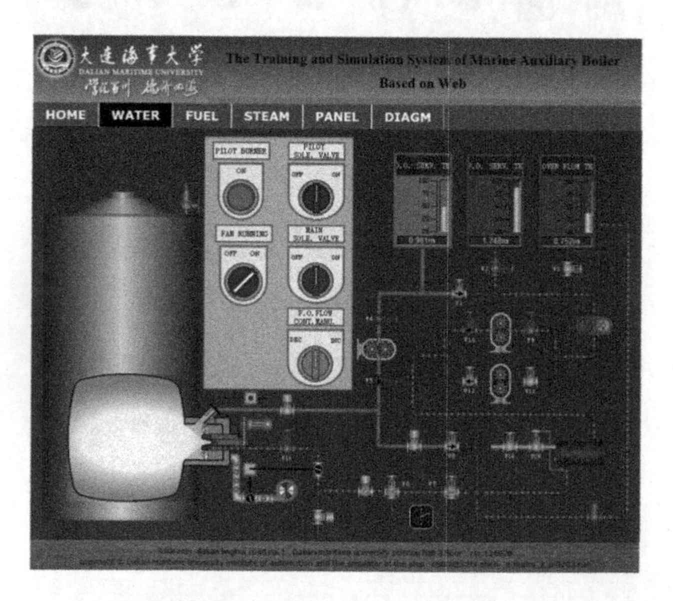

Fig. 10. Heavy oil combustion

50 students were recruited to participate in testing the function and the usability of the developed system. Most of the students are generally satisfied with the web-based system, comparing with the traditional software version. Some students expect that there could be multi-model interactions with the system, like voice interaction, gesture interaction, and most expected, 3D interface to simulate the real ship environment.

System usability [9] still needs to be improved. The current system interface is not friendly enough touchscreen users. Icons and font size need to be enlarged for better user experience of touchscreen interactions.

In system practice module, the explanations of every English word on each interface need to be displayed when clicked, so that students do not have to check up in dictionary.

Words' explanations are also in English, and words' pronunciations are provided to enhance students' communication skills.

83 % of the students believe their maritime English can be improved if they frequently practice through the system; the rest of the students prefer Chinese version of the system interface, especially for examinations.

6 Conclusions and Future Work

Traditional software simulator and web technology are combined in this research. With marine auxiliary boiler as the research object, a set of English versioned marine auxiliary boiler intelligent examination system was developed. The developed system can not only realize the simulation operations of the traditional marine auxiliary boiler, but also test learners' operation skills and their specialized English. However, the developed system still needs improved for touchscreen interactions. How to design system interface for touchscreen users, especially for small-sized touchscreen devices like cellphones, is a big challenge for system developers and future research.

Acknowledgement. This research is supported by the Fundamental Research Funds (No. 3132016086, No. 3132016311) for the Central Universities in China, and teaching reform project (No. 2014Y28) of Dalian Maritime University, China.

References

1. Shen, Z., Wang, Y.: Research on the operational training system for ship marine auxiliary boiler. Adv. Comput. Sci. Environ. Ecoinformatics Edu. **217**, 459–464 (2011)
2. Liu, H., Wan, L., Xu, Y.: Research on simulation of marine auxiliary boiler system. Mech. Electr. Eng. Technol. **44**(7), 89–91 (2015)
3. Yan, J., Ye, W.: The design and realization of marine engineering English examination and training system. Marit. Edu. Res. **1**, 92–94 (2010)
4. Song, X., Zhang, N., Ma, Q.: Research on the simulation of auxiliary boiler system on ships. Adv. Mater. Res. **594–597**, 2099–2105 (2012)
5. Smierzchalski, R.: Simulation system for marine engine control room. In: 11th Biennial Baltic Electronics Conference, Tallinn, Estonia (2008)
6. Shen, Z., Yang, Y., Guo, C.: Research on hardware-in-loop simulation system for Ship motion control [J]. J. Syst. Simul. **12**, 2838–2841 (2010)
7. Di, M.: Performance evaluation based marine autopilot controller design. Shanghai Jiaotong University (2008)
8. Shneiderman, B., Plaisant, C.: Designing the User Interface: Strategies for Effective Human-Computer Interaction. Publishing House of Electronics Industry, Beijing (2006)
9. Alan, D., Janet, F., Gregory, D.A., et al.: Human Computer Interaction. Publishing House of Electronics Industry, Beijing (2007)

Author Index

Printed in the United States
by Baker & Taylor Publisher Services

Printed in the United States
by Baker & Taylor Publisher Services